A People & A Nation

A People & A Nation

A History of The United States

BRIEF NINTH EDITION

MARY BETH NORTON
Cornell University

CAROL SHERIFF
College of William and Mary

DAVID W. BLIGHT
Yale University

HOWARD P. CHUDACOFF
Brown University

FREDRIK LOGEVALL
Cornell University

BETH BAILEY
Temple University

DEBRA MICHALS
Merrimack College

WADSWORTH
CENGAGE Learning

Australia • Brazil • Japan • Korea • Mexico • Singapore • Spain • United Kingdom • United States

WADSWORTH
CENGAGE Learning

A People and A Nation, Brief Ninth Edition

Mary Beth Norton, Carol Sheriff, David W. Blight, Howard P. Chudacoff, Fredrik Logevall, Beth Bailey, Debra Michals

Senior Publisher: Suzanne Jeans

Senior Sponsoring Editor: Ann West

Development Editor: Julia Giannotti

Assistant Editor: Megan Chrisman

Senior Marketing Manager: Katherine Bates

Marketing Coordinator: Lorreen Pelletier

Marketing Communications Manager: Caitlin Green

Senior Content Project Manager: Jane Lee

Senior Art Director: Cate Rickard Barr

Senior Print Buyer: Judy Inouye

Senior Rights Acquisition Specialist: Katie Huha

Production Service: Elm Street Publishing Services

Text Designer: Cia Boynton

Senior Photo Manager: Jennifer Meyer Dare

Cover Image: Henri, Robert (1865–1929). *The Laundress*, c. 1916 (oil on canvas). Credit: Phoenix Art Museum, Arizona, USA/Gift of Mr. and Mrs. Norman Hirschl/ The Bridgeman Art Library

Compositor: Integra Software Services Pvt. Ltd.

For product information and technology assistance, contact us at **Cengage Learning Customer & Sales Support, 1-800-354-9706**

For permission to use material from this text or product, submit all requests online at **www.cengage.com/permissions**. Further permissions questions can be emailed to **permissionrequest@cengage.com**.

Library of Congress Control Number: 2010934558

Student Edition:

ISBN-13: 978-0-495-91619-2

ISBN-10: 0-495-91619-6

Wadsworth
20 Channel Center Street
Boston, MA 02210
USA

Cengage Learning is a leading provider of customized learning solutions with office locations around the globe, including Singapore, the United Kingdom, Australia, Mexico, Brazil and Japan. Locate your local office at **international.cengage.com/region**

Cengage Learning products are represented in Canada by Nelson Education, Ltd.

For your course and learning solutions, visit **www.cengage.com**.

Purchase any of our products at your local college store or at our preferred online store **www.cengagebrain.com**.

Printed in Canada
2 3 4 5 15 14 13 12

Brief Contents

Maps *xiii*

Figures *xiv*

Tables *xiv*

Preface *xv*

1 Three Old Worlds Create a New, 1492–1600 *1*

2 Europeans Colonize North America, 1600–1650 *28*

3 North America in the Atlantic World, 1650–1720 *55*

4 American Society Transformed, 1720–1770 *79*

5 Severing the Bonds of Empire, 1754–1774 *106*

6 A Revolution, Indeed, 1774-1783 *131*

7 Forging a National Republic, 1776-1789 *156*

8 The Early Republic: Conflicts at Home and Abroad, 1789-1800 *182*

9 Defining the Nation, 1801-1823 *204*

10 The Rise of the South, 1815–1860 *230*

11 The Restless North, 1815–1860 *260*

12 Reform and Politics, 1824–1845 *287*

13 The Contested West, 1815–1860 *314*

14 Slavery and America's Future: The Road to War, 1845–1861 *342*

15 Transforming Fire: The Civil War, 1861–1865 *369*

16 Reconstruction: An Unfinished Revolution, 1865–1877 *404*

17 The Development of the West, 1865–1900 *432*

18 The Machine Age, 1877–1920 *458*

19 The Vitality and Turmoil of Urban Life, 1877–1920 *486*

20 Gilded Age Politics, 1877–1900 *514*

21 The Progressive Era, 1895–1920 *540*

22 The Quest for Empire, 1865–1914 *568*

23 Americans in the Great War, 1914–1920 *593*

24 The New Era, 1920–1929 *620*

25 The Great Depression and the New Deal, 1929–1941 *649*

26 The United States in a Troubled World, 1920–1941 *678*

27 The Second World War at Home and Abroad, 1941–1945 *702*

28 The Cold War and American Globalism, 1945–1961 *727*

29 America at Midcentury, 1945–1960 *755*

30 The Tumultuous Sixties, 1960–1968 *786*

31 Continuing Divisions and New Limits, 1969–1980 *815*

32 Conservatism Revived, 1980–1992 *846*

33 Into the Global Millennium, America Since 1992 *875*

Appendix *A-1*

Index *I-1*

Contents

Maps   *xiii*
Figures   *xiv*
Tables   *xiv*
Preface   *xv*

1   Three Old Worlds Create a New, 1492–1600   *1*

American Societies   *2*

VISUALIZING THE PAST: **City of the Sun**   *5*

North America in 1492   *6*
African Societies   *9*
European Societies   *11*
Early European Explorations   *13*
Voyages of Columbus, Cabot, and Their Successors   *14*
Spanish Exploration and Conquest   *17*
The Columbian Exchange   *19*

LINKS TO THE WORLD: **Maize**   *21*

Europeans in North America   *22*

LEGACY FOR A PEOPLE AND A NATION: **Kennewick Man/ Ancient One**   *24*

Summary   *24*

2   Europeans Colonize North America, 1600–1650   *28*

Spanish, French, and Dutch North America   *30*

VISUALIZING THE PAST : **Acoma Pueblo**   *31*

The Caribbean   *34*
English Interest in Colonization   *36*
The Founding of Virginia   *38*
Life in the Chesapeake   *40*
The Founding of New England   *43*

LINKS TO THE WORLD: **Turkeys**   *46*

Life in New England   *49*

LEGACY FOR A PEOPLE AND A NATION: **Blue Laws**   *51*

Summary   *52*

3   North America in the Atlantic World, 1650–1720   *55*

The Growth of Anglo-American Settlements   *56*
A Decade of Imperial Crises: The 1670s   *62*
The Atlantic Trading System   *64*

LINKS TO THE WORLD: **Exotic Beverages**   *67*

Slavery in North America and the Caribbean   *68*
Imperial Reorganization and the Witchcraft Crisis   *72*

VISUALIZING THE PAST: **Debating the Witchcraft Trials**   *75*

LEGACY FOR A PEOPLE AND A NATION: **Americans of African Descent**   *76*

Summary   *76*

4   American Society Transformed, 1720–1770   *79*

Geographic Expansion and Ethnic Diversity   *80*

VISUALIZING THE PAST: **Slaves' Symbolic Resistance**   *85*

Economic Growth and Development in British America   *88*
Colonial Cultures   *90*

LINKS TO THE WORLD: **Smallpox Inoculation**   *92*

Colonial Families   *95*
Politics: Stability and Crisis in British America   *99*
A Crisis in Anglo-American Religion   *100*

LEGACY FOR A PEOPLE AND A NATION: **"Self-Made Men"**   *103*

Summary   *103*

5 Severing the Bonds of Empire, 1754–1774   106

Renewed Warfare Among Europeans and Indians   107

LINKS TO THE WORLD: The First Worldwide War   112

1763: A Turning Point   113

The Stamp Act Crisis   116

Resistance to the Townshend Acts   119

VISUALIZING THE PAST: The Revolutionary Symbolism of Female Spinners   121

Confrontations in Boston   123

Tea and Turmoil   125

LEGACY FOR A PEOPLE AND A NATION: Women's Political Activism   127

Summary   128

6 A Revolution, Indeed, 1774–1783   131

Government by Congress and Committee   132

Contest in the Backcountry   135

VISUALIZING THE PAST: Frontier Refugees   136

Choosing Sides   137

LINKS TO THE WORLD: New Nations   139

War and Independence   140

The Struggle in the North   144

Life in the Army and on the Home Front   147

Victory in the South   149

LEGACY FOR A PEOPLE AND A NATION: Revolutionary Origins   152

Summary   153

7 Forging a National Republic, 1776–1789   156

Creating a Virtuous Republic   157

VISUALIZING THE PAST: Depicting Virtue   159

LINKS TO THE WORLD: Writing and Stationery Supplies   161

The First Emancipation and the Growth of Racism   163

Designing Republican Governments   166

Trials of the Confederation   169

Order and Disorder in the West   171

From Crisis to the Constitution   172

Opposition and Ratification   176

LEGACY FOR A PEOPLE AND A NATION: The Township and Range System   179

Summary   179

8 The Early Republic: Conflicts at Home and Abroad, 1789–1800   182

Building a Workable Government   183

Domestic Policy Under Washington and Hamilton   185

The French Revolution and the Development of Partisan Politics   188

Partisan Politics and Relations with Great Britain   190

John Adams and Political Dissent   193

VISUALIZING THE PAST: Newspapers of the Early Republic   195

The West in the New Nation   196

"Revolutions" at the End of the Century   198

LINKS TO THE WORLD: Haitian Refugees   200

LEGACY FOR A PEOPLE AND A NATION: Dissent During Wartime   201

Summary   201

9 Defining the Nation, 1801–1823   204

Political Visions   205

National Expansion Westward   209

The Nation in the Orbit of Europe   213

The War of 1812   216

VISUALIZING THE PAST: Selling War   218

The Nationalist Program   220

Sectionalism Exposed   223

LINKS TO THE WORLD: Industrial Piracy   225

LEGACY FOR A PEOPLE AND A NATION: States' Rights and Nullification   227

Summary   227

10   The Rise of the South, 1815–1860 *230*

The "Distinctive" South *231*

Southern Expansion, Indian Resistance and Removal *235*

LINKS TO THE WORLD: The Amistad Case *236*

Social Pyramid in the Old South *241*

The Planters' World *245*

Slave Life and Labor *249*

Slave Culture and Resistance *251*

VISUALIZING THE PAST: Imaging Nat Turner's Rebellion *256*

Summary *256*

LEGACY FOR A PEOPLE AND A NATION: Reparations for Slavery *257*

 11   The Restless North, 1815–1860 *260*

Or Is It the North That Was Distinctive? *261*

The Transportation Revolution *264*

LINKS TO THE WORLD: Internal Improvements *268*

Factories and Industrialization *269*

Consumption and Commercialization *271*

VISUALIZING THE PAST: Images of Boom and Bust *272*

Families in Flux *274*

The Growth of Cities *276*

LEGACY FOR A PEOPLE AND A NATION: P.T. Barnum's Publicity Stunts *283*

Summary *284*

 12   Reform and Politics, 1824–1845 *287*

From Revival to Reform *289*

VISUALIZING THE PAST: Engaging Children *292*

Utopian Experiments *294*

Abolitionism *296*

LINKS TO THE WORLD: The International Antislavery Movement *297*

Women's Rights *300*

Jacksonianism and Party Politics *301*

Federalism at Issue: The Nullification and Bank Controversies *303*

The Whig Challenge and the Second Party System *307*

LEGACY FOR A PEOPLE AND A NATION: Moral Reformers' Abstinence Campaigns *310*

Summary *311*

 13   The Contested West, 1815–1860 *314*

The West in the American Imagination *315*

Expansion and Resistance in the Trans-Appalachian West *318*

The Federal Government and Westward Expansion *322*

LINKS TO THE WORLD: Gold in California *325*

The Southwestern Borderlands *327*

VISUALIZING THE PAST: Paintings and Cultural Impressions *329*

Cultural Frontiers in the Far West *332*

The Politics of Territorial Expansion *336*

Summary *338*

LEGACY FOR A PEOPLE AND A NATION: Descendants of Early Latino Settlers *339*

 14   Slavery and America's Future: The Road to War, 1845–1861 *342*

The War with Mexico and Its Consequences *344*

VISUALIZING THE PAST: The Mexican War in Popular Imagination *346*

1850: Compromise or Armistice? *349*

Slavery Expansion and Collapse of the Party System *353*

LINKS TO THE WORLD: William Walker and Filibustering *356*

Slavery and the Nation's Future *359*

Disunion *361*

LEGACY FOR A PEOPLE AND A NATION: Terrorist or Freedom Fighter? *365*

Summary *366*

15 **Transforming Fire: The Civil War, 1861–1865**   *369*

America Goes to War, 1861–1862   *371*

War Transforms the South   *376*

Wartime Northern Economy and Society   *379*

The Advent of Emancipation   *383*

The Soldiers' War   *387*

VISUALIZING THE PAST: Black Soldiers in the Civil War   *389*

1863: The Tide of Battle Turns   *390*

Disunity: South, North, and West   *391*

1864–1865: The Final Test of Wills   *395*

LINKS TO THE WORLD: The Civil War in Britain   *397*

LEGACY FOR A PEOPLE AND A NATION: Abraham Lincoln's "Second Inaugural Address"   *400*

Summary   *401*

 16 **Reconstruction: An Unfinished Revolution, 1865–1877**   *404*

Wartime Reconstruction   *406*

The Meanings of Freedom   *408*

VISUALIZING THE PAST: Sharecropping: Enslaved to Debt   *411*

Johnson's Reconstruction Plan   *412*

The Congressional Reconstruction Plan   *414*

Politics and Reconstruction in the South   *419*

Retreat from Reconstruction   *423*

LINKS TO THE WORLD: The "Back to Africa" Movement   *426*

LEGACY FOR A PEOPLE AND A NATION: The Lost Cause   *429*

Summary   *429*

 17 **The Development of the West, 1865–1900**   *432*

The Economic Activities of Native Peoples   *434*

The Transformation of Native Cultures   *435*

VISUALIZING THE PAST: Attempts to Make Indians Look and Act Like "Americans"   *439*

Life on the Natural Resource Frontier   *440*

Irrigation and Transportation   *445*

LINKS TO THE WORLD: The Australian Frontier   *447*

Farming the Plains   *448*

The Ranching Frontier   *452*

LEGACY FOR A PEOPLE AND A NATION: National Parks   *455*

Summary   *455*

 18 **The Machine Age, 1877–1920**   *458*

Technology and the Triumph of Industrialization   *459*

LINKS TO THE WORLD: The Atlantic Cable   *462*

Mechanization and the Changing Status of Labor   *465*

VISUALIZING THE PAST: Impact of the 1913 Triangle Shirtwaist Fire   *469*

Labor Violence and the Union Movement   *470*

Standards of Living   *474*

The Corporate Consolidation Movement   *478*

The Gospel of Wealth and Its Critics   *481*

LEGACY FOR A PEOPLE AND A NATION: Technology of Recorded Sound   *483*

Summary   *483*

 19 **The Vitality and Turmoil of Urban Life, 1877–1920**   *486*

Growth of the Modern City   *487*

Urban Neighborhoods   *493*

Living Conditions in the Inner City   *496*

Managing the City   *498*

VISUALIZING THE PAST: Street Cleaning and Urban Reform   *500*

Family Life   *502*

The New Leisure and Mass Culture   *505*

LINKS TO THE WORLD: Japanese Baseball   *507*

LEGACY FOR A PEOPLE AND A NATION: Children and Mass-Produced Toys   *511*

Summary   *511*

20 Gilded Age Politics, 1877–1900   514

The Nature of Party Politics   515

Issues of Legislation   517

Tentative Presidents   519

VISUALIZING THE PAST: The Spectacle of Gilded Age Politics   521

Discrimination, Disfranchisement, and Responses   522

Agrarian Unrest and Populism   526

LINKS TO THE WORLD: Russian Populism   530

The Depression and Protests of the 1890s   531

The Silver Crusade and the Election of 1896   534

Summary   536

LEGACY FOR A PEOPLE AND A NATION: Interpreting a Fairy Tale   537

21 The Progressive Era, 1895–1920   540

The Varied Progressive Impulse   542

LINKS TO THE WORLD: Foreign Universities and Study Abroad   546

Government and Legislative Reform   547

New Ideas in Social Institutions   549

Challenges to Racial and Sexual Discrimination   552

VISUALIZING THE PAST: Heavyweight Boxing Champion Jack Johnson as Race Hero   554

Theodore Roosevelt and Revival of the Presidency   557

Woodrow Wilson and Extension of Progressive Reform   562

LEGACY FOR A PEOPLE AND A NATION: Margaret Sanger, Planned Parenthood, and the Birth-Control Controversy   564

Summary   564

22 The Quest for Empire, 1865–1914   568

Imperial Dreams   570

VISUALIZING THE PAST: Messages in Advertising   572

LINKS TO THE WORLD: National Geographic   574

Ambitions and Strategies   576

Crises in the 1890s: Hawai'i, Venezuela, and Cuba   577

The Spanish-American War and the Debate over Empire   580

Asian Encounters: War in the Philippines, Diplomacy in China   582

TR's World   584

LEGACY FOR A PEOPLE AND A NATION: Guantánamo Bay   589

Summary   590

23 Americans in the Great War, 1914–1920   593

Precarious Neutrality   595

The Decision for War   597

Winning the War   599

LINKS TO THE WORLD: The Influenza Pandemic of 1918   604

Mobilizing the Home Front   605

VISUALIZING THE PAST: Eating to Win   607

Civil Liberties Under Challenge   609

Red Scare, Red Summer   611

The Defeat of Peace   613

LEGACY FOR A PEOPLE AND A NATION: Freedom of Speech and the ACLU   616

Summary   617

24 The New Era, 1920–1929   620

Big Business Triumphant   621

Politics and Government   623

A Consumer Society   625

Cities, Migrants, and Suburbs   627

New Rhythms of Everyday Life   629

LINKS TO THE WORLD: Pan American Airways   630

VISUALIZING THE PAST: Expansion of Suburbs in the 1920s   631

Lines of Defense   635

The Age of Play   638

Cultural Currents   640

The Election of 1928 and End of the New Era   642

LEGACY FOR A PEOPLE AND A NATION: Intercollegiate
Athletics   *644*

Summary   *645*

25 The Great Depression and the New Deal, 1929–1941   *649*

Hoover and Hard Times, 1929–1933   *651*

Franklin D. Roosevelt and the Launching
of the New Deal   *656*

Political Pressure and the Second New Deal   *661*

Labor   *665*

VISUALIZING THE PAST: The Women's Emergency Brigade and
the General Motors Sit-Down Strike   *666*

Federal Power and the Nationalization
of Culture   *667*

LINKS TO THE WORLD: The 1936 Olympic Games   *670*

The Limits of the New Deal   *671*

LEGACY FOR A PEOPLE AND A NATION: Social Security   *675*

Summary   *675*

26 The United States in a Troubled World, 1920–1941   *678*

Searching for Peace and Order in the 1920s   *680*

The World Economy, Cultural Expansion, and Great
Depression   *682*

U.S. Dominance in Latin America   *685*

The Course to War in Europe   *687*

VISUALIZING THE PAST: German *Blitzkrieg* in Poland   *690*

Japan, China, and a New Order in Asia   *691*

U.S. Entry into World War II   *693*

LINKS TO THE WORLD: Radio News   *695*

LEGACY FOR A PEOPLE AND A NATION: Presidential Deception
of the Public   *698*

Summary   *699*

27 The Second World War at Home and Abroad, 1941–1945   *702*

The United States at War   *703*

The Production Front and American Workers   *707*

Life on the Home Front   *709*

VISUALIZING THE PAST: Portraying the Enemy   *711*

The Limits of American Ideals   *713*

LINKS TO THE WORLD: Tokyo Rose   *714*

Life in the Military   *717*

Winning the War   *718*

LEGACY FOR A PEOPLE AND A NATION: Nuclear
Proliferation   *723*

Summary   *723*

28 The Cold War and American Globalism, 1945–1961   *727*

From Allies to Adversaries   *729*

VISUALIZING THE PAST: Stalin: Ally to Adversary   *731*

Containment in Action   *735*

The Cold War in Asia   *738*

The Korean War   *739*

Unrelenting Cold War   *742*

LINKS TO THE WORLD: The People-to-People
Campaign   *744*

The Struggle for the Third World   *746*

LEGACY FOR A PEOPLE AND A NATION: The National
Security State   *751*

Summary   *752*

29 America at Midcentury, 1945–1960   *755*

Shaping Postwar America   *757*

Domestic Politics in the Cold War Era   *761*

Cold War Fears and Anticommunism   *764*

The Struggle for Civil Rights   *766*

Creating a Middle-Class Nation   *770*

Men, Women, and Youth at Midcentury   *773*

VISUALIZING THE PAST: Moving to Levittown   *774*

LINKS TO THE WORLD: Barbie   *777*

The Limits of the Middle-Class Nation   *778*

LEGACY FOR A PEOPLE AND A NATION: The Pledge of
Allegiance   *782*

Summary   *782*

30 The Tumultuous Sixties, 1960–1968 *786*

Kennedy and the Cold War   *788*
Marching for Freedom   *792*
Liberalism and the Great Society   *794*

VISUALIZING THE PAST: **"Project C" and National Opinion**   *795*

Johnson and Vietnam   *799*
A Nation Divided   *804*

LINKS TO THE WORLD: **The British Invasion**   *808*

1968   *809*

LEGACY FOR A PEOPLE AND A NATION: **The Immigration Act of 1965**   *811*

Summary   *812*

31 Continuing Divisions and New Limits, 1969–1980 *815*

The New Politics of Identity   *817*
The Women's Movement and Gay Liberation   *820*
The End in Vietnam   *823*

VISUALIZING THE PAST: **The Image of War**   *826*

Nixon, Kissinger, and the World   *827*

LINKS TO THE WORLD: **OPEC and the 1973 Oil Embargo**   *829*

Presidential Politics and the Crisis of Leadership   *830*
Economic Crisis   *834*
An Era of Cultural Transformation   *837*
Renewed Cold War and Middle East Crisis   *839*

LEGACY FOR A PEOPLE AND A NATION: **The All-Volunteer Force**   *842*

Summary   *843*

32 Conservatism Revived, 1980–1992 *846*

Reagan and the Conservative Resurgence   *848*
Reaganomics   *851*
Reagan and the World   *856*
American Society in the 1980s   *860*

VISUALIZING THE PAST: **Combating the Spread of AIDS**   *863*

The End of the Cold War and Global Disorder   *865*

LINKS TO THE WORLD: **CNN**   *870*

LEGACY FOR A PEOPLE AND A NATION: **The Americans with Disabilities Act**   *871*

Summary   *872*

33 Into the Global Millennium, America Since 1992 *875*

Social Strains and New Political Directions   *877*
Globalization and Prosperity   *884*
9/11 and the War in Iraq   *887*
Domestic Politics in Post 9/11 America   *892*
Americans in the First Decade of the New Millennium   *896*

LINKS TO THE WORLD: **The "Swine Flu" Pandemic**   *901*

LEGACY FOR A PEOPLE AND A NATION: **The Internet**   *903*

Summary   *903*

VISUALIZING THE PAST: **Arizona's Immigration Law**   *904*

Appendix   *A-1*

Index   *I-1*

Features

Maps

MAP 1.1 Native Cultures of North America   7

MAP 1.2 European Explorations in America   15

MAP 1.3 Major Items in the Columbian Exchange   20

MAP 2.1 European Settlements and Indian Tribes in Eastern North America, 1650   33

MAP 3.1 The Anglo-American Colonies in the Early Eighteenth Century   58

MAP 3.2 Atlantic Trade Routes   66

MAP 4.1 Louisiana, ca. 1720   82

MAP 4.2 Major Origins and Destinations of Africans Enslaved in the Americas   84

MAP 5.1 European Settlements and Indians, 1754   110

MAP 6.1 The War in the North, 1775–1778   145

MAP 6.2 The War in the South   150

MAP 7.1 African American Population, 1790: Proportion of Total Population   165

MAP 7.2 Western Land Claims and Cessions, 1782–1802   168

MAP 9.1 Louisiana Purchase   211

MAP 9.2 Missouri Compromise and the State of the Union, 1820   226

MAP 10.1 Removal of Native Americans from the South, 1820–1840   240

MAP 11.1 Major Roads, Canals, and Railroads, 1850   267

MAP 11.2 Major American Cities in 1820 and 1860   277

MAP 12.1 Presidential Election, 1824   302

MAP 12.2 Presidential Election, 1828   303

MAP 13.1 Westward Expansion, 1800–1860   317

MAP 13.2 Settlement in the Old Southwest and Old Northwest, 1820 and 1840   319

MAP 13.3 Western Indians and Routes of Exploration   323

MAP 13.4 Mexico's Far North   328

MAP 13.5 The California Gold Rush   335

MAP 14.1 The Kansas-Nebraska Act and Slavery Expansion, 1854   350

MAP 14.2 The Divided Nation—Slave and Free Areas, 1861   363

MAP 15.1 Battle of Gettysburg   390

MAP 15.2 Sherman's March to the Sea   398

MAP 16.1 The Reconstruction   416

MAP 16.2 Presidential Election of 1876 and the Compromise of 1877   428

MAP 17.1 The Development and Natural Resources of the West   441

MAP 17.2 The United States, 1876–1912   444

MAP 17.3 Agricultural Regions of the United States, 1890   450

MAP 18.1 Industrial Production, 1919   461

MAP 19.1 Urbanization, 1880 and 1920   490

MAP 20.1 Presidential Election, 1896   536

MAP 21.1 Woman Suffrage Before 1920   557

MAP 22.1 Imperialism in Asia: Turn of the Century   584

MAP 22.2 U.S. Hegemony in the Caribbean and Latin America   585

MAP 23.1 American Troops at the Western Front, 1918   603

MAP 25.1 The Tennessee Valley Authority   669

MAP 26.1 Japanese Expansion Before Pearl Harbor   692

MAP 26.2 The German Advance   694

MAP 27.1 The Allies on the Offensive in Europe, 1942–1945   706

MAP 27.2 The Pacific War   720

MAP 28.1 Divided Europe   736

MAP 28.2 The Rise of the Third World: Newly Independent Nations Since 1943   747

MAP 29.1 Rise of the Sunbelt, 1950–1960   771

MAP 30.1 Southeast Asia and the Vietnam War   801

MAP 31.1 The Continued Shift to the Sunbelt in the 1970s and 1980s   836

MAP 32.1 The United States in the Caribbean and Central America   858

MAP 32.2 The End of the Cold War in Europe   867

MAP 33.1 The Middle East   891

MAP 33.2 Mapping the United States's Diversity   897

Figures

FIGURE 2.1 Population of Virginia, 1625   *42*

FIGURE 4.1 Regional Trading Patterns   *90*

FIGURE 7.1 Depreciation of Continental Currency, 1777–1780   *170*

FIGURE 11.1 Major Sources of Immigration to the United States, 1831–1860   *279*

FIGURE 14.1 Voting Returns of Counties with Few Slaveholders, Eight Southern States, 1860 and 1861   *364*

FIGURE 15.1 Comparative Resources, Union and Confederate States, 1861   *373*

FIGURE 18.1 Distribution of Occupational Categories Among Employed Men and Women, 1880–1920   *467*

FIGURE 18.2 Children in the Labor Force, 1880–1930   *468*

FIGURE 20.1 Consumer Prices and Farm Product Prices, 1865–1913   *527*

FIGURE 22.1 The Rise of U.S. Economic Power in the World   *573*

FIGURE 23.1 The Federal Budget, 1914–1920   *605*

FIGURE 24.1 Changing Dimensions of Paid Female Labor, 1910–1930   *633*

FIGURE 24.2 Sources of Immigration, 1907 and 1927   *637*

FIGURE 25.1 The Economy Before and After the New Deal, 1929–1941   *660*

FIGURE 25.2 Distribution of Total Family Income Among the American People, 1929–1944 (percentage)   *664*

FIGURE 26.1 The United States in the World Economy   *683*

FIGURE 29.1 Birth Rate, 1945–1964   *759*

FIGURE 29.2 Marital Distribution of the Female Labor Force, 1944–1970   *775*

FIGURE 30.1 Poverty in America for Whites, African Americans, and All Races, 1959–1974   *799*

FIGURE 32.1 America's Rising National Debt, 1974–1989   *853*

FIGURE 32.2 While the Rich Got Richer in the 1980s, the Poor Got Poorer   *856*

FIGURE 32.3 Poverty in the America by Race, 1974–1990   *862*

FIGURE 33.1 The Growth of the U.S. Hispanic Population   *898*

FIGURE 33.2 The Changing American Family   *899*

Tables

TABLE 2.1 The Founding of Permanent European Colonies in North America, 1565–1640   *32*

TABLE 2.2 Tudor and Stuart Monarchs of England, 1509–1649   *37*

TABLE 3.1 Restored Stuart Monarchs of England, 1660–1714   *57*

TABLE 3.2 The Founding of English Colonies in North America, 1664–1681   *59*

TABLE 4.1 Who Moved to America from England and Scotland in the Early 1770s, and Why?   *87*

TABLE 5.1 The Colonial Wars, 1689–1763   *109*

TABLE 5.2 British Ministries and Their American Policies   *120*

TABLE 7.1 Ratification of the Constitution by State Conventions   *178*

TABLE 12.1 United States Presidents, 1824–1845   *310*

TABLE 14.1 New Political Parties   *349*

TABLE 14.2 The Vote on the Kansas-Nebraska Act   *354*

TABLE 14.3 Presidential Vote in 1860 (by State)   *362*

TABLE 16.1 Plans for Reconstruction Compared   *417*

TABLE 17.1 Summary: Government Land Policy   *452*

TABLE 18.1 American Living Standards, 1890–1910   *475*

TABLE 24.1 Consumerism in the 1920s   *626*

TABLE 25.1 New Deal Achievements   *659*

TABLE 29.1 Geographic Distribution of the U.S. Population, 1930–1970 (in percentages)   *760*

TABLE 30.1 Great Society Achievements, 1964–1966   *798*

TABLE 33.1 U.S. Military Personnel on Active Duty in Foreign Countries, 2009   *902*

Preface

In this ninth edition, *A People and A Nation, Brief,* has undergone significant revisions, while still retaining the narrative strength and focus that have made it so popular with students and teachers alike. Like other teachers and students, we are always re-creating our past, restructuring our memory, and rediscovering the personalities and events that have influenced us, injured us, and bedeviled us. This book represents our continuing rediscovery of America's history—its diverse people and the nation they created and have nurtured. As this book demonstrates, there are many different Americans and many different memories. We have sought to present as many of them as possible—in triumph and tragedy, in division and unity.

About *A People and A Nation, Brief*

A People and A Nation, first published in 1982, was the first major textbook in the United States to fully integrate social and political history. From the outset, the authors have been determined to tell the story of *all* the people of the United States. This book's hallmark has been its melding of social and political history—its movement beyond history's common focus on public figures and events to examine the daily life of America's people. All editions of the book have stressed the interaction of public policy and personal experience, the relationship between domestic concerns and foreign affairs, the various manifestations of popular culture, and the multiple origins of America and Americans. We have consistently built our narrative on a firm foundation in primary sources—on both well-known and obscure letters, diaries, public documents, oral histories, and artifacts of material culture. We have long challenged readers to think about the meaning of American history, not just to memorize facts. Both students and instructors have repeatedly told us how much they appreciate and enjoy our approach to the past.

This brief ninth edition, as with earlier brief editions, aims to preserve the integrity of the complete work—along with its unique approach—while condensing it. This edition reflects the scholarship, readability, and comprehensiveness of the full-length version. It also maintains the integration of social, cultural, political, economic, and foreign relations history that has been a hallmark of *A People and A Nation*.

Dr. Debra Michals has worked with us again, ensuring that the changes in content and organization incorporated in the full-length ninth edition were retained in the condensation. The authors attained reductions by paring down details rather than deleting entire sections. The brief ninth edition thus contains fewer statistics, fewer quotations, and fewer examples than the unabridged edition. The brief edition also includes more pedagogy than the unabridged edition: each main heading has a marginal question to give students a preview of the key topics covered. These questions are answered at the end of the chapter in the "Summary." Throughout the chapters, students get assistance from key terms that are boldfaced in the text and defined in the margins.

Themes in This Book

Several themes and questions stand out in our continuing effort to integrate political, social, and cultural history. We study the many ways Americans have defined themselves—gender, race, class, region, ethnicity, religion, sexual orientation—and the many subjects that have reflected their multidimensional experiences. We highlight the remarkably diverse everyday lives of the American people—in cities and on farms and ranches, in factories and in corporate headquarters, in neighborhoods and in legislatures, in love relationships and in hate groups, in recreation and in work, in the classroom and in military uniform, in secret national security conferences and in public foreign relations debates, in church and in voluntary associations, in polluted environments and in conservation areas. We pay particular attention to lifestyles, diet and dress, family life and structure, labor conditions, gender roles, migration and mobility, childbearing, and child rearing. We explore how Americans have entertained and informed themselves by discussing their music, sports, theater, print media, film, radio, television, graphic arts, and literature, in both "high" culture and popular culture. We study how technology has influenced Americans' lives, such as through the internal combustion engine and the computer.

Americans' personal lives have always interacted with the public realm of politics and government. To understand how Americans have sought to protect their different ways of life and to work out solutions to thorny problems, we emphasize their expectations of governments at the local, state, and federal levels; governments' role in providing answers; the lobbying of interest groups; the campaigns and outcomes of elections; and the hierarchy of power in any period. Because the United States has long been a major participant in world affairs, we explore America's participation in wars, interventions in other nations, empire-building, immigration patterns, images of foreign peoples, cross-national cultural ties, and international economic trends.

What's New in This Edition

This edition builds on its predecessors in continuing to enhance the global perspective on American history that has characterized the book since its first edition. From the "Atlantic world" context of European colonies in North and South America to the discussion of international terrorism, the authors have incorporated the most recent globally oriented scholarship throughout the volume. As in the eighth edition, we have worked to strengthen our treatment of the diversity of America's people by examining differences within the broad ethnic categories commonly employed and by paying attention to immigration, cultural and intellectual infusions from around the world, and America's growing religious diversity. We have also stressed the incorporation of different peoples into the United States through territorial acquisition as well as through immigration. At the same time, we have integrated the discussion of such diversity into our narrative so as not to artificially isolate any group from the mainstream. We have continued the practice of placing three probing questions at the end of each chapter's introduction to guide students' reading of the pages that follow.

Primary Sources

We believe students need lots of opportunities to engage in historical thinking around primary sources, and we have provided more opportunities for this type of work in the ninth edition. The new "Visualizing the Past" feature described below helps students engage with visual sources with guided captions and questions. In addition, the authors have identified for each chapter a set of primary sources that would add useful context for students; these are noted (with a feather icon) in the margins of the text. Students will be able to access each of these sources through links on the student CourseMate website. Instructors who want a fully integrated online primary source reader to use in conjunction with *A People and A Nation* will find it available as an "Editor's Choice" option inside the new CourseReader for U.S. History (described in the supplements section).

As always, the authors reexamined every sentence, interpretation, map, chart, illustration, and caption, refining the narrative, presenting new examples, and bringing to the text the latest findings of scholars in many areas of history, anthropology, sociology, and political science. Some chapter-opening vignettes are new to this edition. The maps have been completely redesigned and revised in this edition to be more dynamic, engaging, and relevant.

"Legacies," "Links to the World," and "Visualizing the Past"

Each chapter contains two brief feature essays: "Legacies for A People and A Nation" and "Links to the World." "Legacies" appears toward the end of each chapter and offers compelling and timely answers to students who question the relevance of historical study by exploring the historical roots of contemporary topics. New subjects of "Legacies" includes P.T. Barnum's publicity stunts, abstinence campaigns by moral reformers, Lincoln's second inaugural address, national parks, and mass-produced toys for children. Numerous other "Legacies" have been updated.

"Links to the World" examines both inward and outward ties between America (and Americans) and the rest of the world. "Links" appears at appropriate places in each chapter to explore specific topics at considerable length. Tightly constructed essays detail the often little-known connections between developments here and abroad. The topics range broadly over economic, political, social, technological, medical, and cultural history, vividly demonstrating that the geographical region that is now the United States has never lived in isolation from other peoples and countries. New to this edition are "Links" on turkeys, writing and stationery supplies, internal improvements, filibustering, the "back to Africa" movement, study abroad programs, Tokyo Rose, and swine flu. Each "Link" highlights global interconnections with unusual and lively examples that will both intrigue and inform students.

A brand new feature in this edition—"Visualizing the Past"—aims to give students the chance to examine primary source material and engage in critical thinking about them. For each chapter, the authors have selected one or two visual sources (including cartoons, photographic images, artwork, and magazine covers) that tell a story about the era with captions that help students understand how the careful examination of primary source content can reveal deeper insights into the period under discussion. We have chosen to focus on visual sources for this feature because these are often the hardest for instructors to find and prepare good pedagogy around—and because we have always given visual material a strong role in the text. An example from Chapter 25 includes a photograph of the women's "emergency brigade" demonstration during the 1937 sit-down strike by automobile workers in Flint, Michigan. The caption describes the scene and then asks questions that guide students in a deeper analysis of the image—and of its historical significance.

Section-by-Section Changes in This Edition

Mary Beth Norton, who had primary responsibility for Chapters 1 through 8 and served as coordinating author, augmented the treatment of early European explorations of the Americas (including the publicist Richard Hakluyt) and now explores the use of the calumet (the so-called peace pipe) by Indian nations and Europeans alike. She expanded the discussion of religious diversity in England and its colonies and the religious impulse for colonization and revised the section on the middle passage to give more attention to the experience of enslaved captives on shipboard. To clarify chronology, she moved some material on the French and Spanish colonies in North America from Chapter 3 to Chapter 4 and in the latter greatly increased coverage of the residents of the west in the eighteenth century—Native Americans, Spaniards, and French people alike. A new opening vignette is featured in Chapter 4 about Marie-Joseph Angélique, a slave convicted of starting a fire that destroyed the merchant quarter of Montreal. New scholarship on the Seven Years' War, the American Revolution, and the Constitutional Convention has been incorporated into Chapters 5 through 7. A table now conveniently summarizes state conventions' ratification votes. More information on women's political roles and aims has been added in conjunction with a considerably expanded treatment of partisanship in the early republic.

 Carol Sheriff, responsible for Chapters 9 and 11 through 13, enhanced coverage of the nationalistic culture of the early republic and early New Orleans and revised the discussion of the War of 1812 and Aaron Burr. She has added discussions of the penny press, Henry David Thoreau, science and engineering, women's activities, and penitentiaries. The treatment of politics in general has been reworked, with special attention to political violence, and a new chart detailing the era's presidents has been included. Chapter 13 now contains considerably more information on the southwestern borderlands, includes more quotations from residents of the American West, and deals with anti-expansionism and the abuse of Indians in Catholic missions.

 David W. Blight, who had primary responsibility for Chapter 10 and Chapters 14 through 16, has enhanced the discussion of the economic causes of secession and the Civil War and the economic history of the war itself, drawing on extensive new scholarship. Chapter 10 features a new chapter-opening vignette on the 1827 slave auction held at Monticello and Jefferson and Sally Hemings. He now considers the Union soldiers' ideology and has added material on the effects of the cultural impact of the large numbers of war dead in both North and South. Chapters 15 and 16 both include new treatments of judicial topics, and the latter also discusses scalawags and carpetbaggers at greater length than before.

Howard P. Chudacoff, responsible for Chapters 17 through 21 and Chapter 24, has extensively revised and updated the treatment of technological change in the late nineteenth century and of women's suffrage. He has added discussions of Native peoples in the Southwest, western folk heroes, government and water rights, labor violence in the West, female entertainers (and opposition to them from moralists like Anthony Comstock), Woodrow Wilson's racism, Marcus Garvey, and the Great Migration of African Americans to the North in the twenties. The new Chapter 20 opening vignette features the life of Frances Willard, the president of the Women's Christian Temperance Union. He has also consolidated the analysis of settlement houses in Chapter 21 to avoid repetition.

Fredrik Logevall, with primary responsibility for Chapters 22, 23, 26, and 28, updated the discussions of late nineteenth-century American imperialism and the origins of the Cold War and added new material on nurses and African American soldiers in WWI.

Beth Bailey, primarily responsible for Chapters 25, 27, and 29, incorporated new scholarship on popular culture, the institutional history of the New Deal, the ecological crisis of the thirties, the internment of Japanese citizens and Japanese Americans during WWII, the liberation of Europe, the GI Bill, and the return of veterans in the postwar period. She enhanced the discussion of wartime propaganda and censorship. The new Chapter 29 opening vignette on downwinders ties more closely to the cold war coverage through the chapter. Parts of Chapter 29 underwent extensive revision and reorganization as well.

Bailey and Logevall shared responsibility for Chapters 30 through 33. These chapters now include expanded consideration of the struggle for civil rights and social justice in the north and the opposition to that struggle in the form of protests against school busing. Chapter 31 has a new section on the freedom and responsibilities of youth and enhanced discussions of popular culture, women in the military, and religious cults. New material has been added on foreign policy and changes in American living patterns. As is always the case, Chapter 33, which covers the recent past, underwent thorough revision and reorganization. It covers the second term of George W. Bush, the election of Barack Obama, the Great Recession, and the Iraq and Afghanistan wars.

Teaching and Learning Aids

The supplements listed here accompany the ninth edition of *A People and A Nation*. They have been created with the diverse needs of today's students and instructors in mind.

For the Instructor

Aplia. Aplia™ is an online learning solution that helps students take responsibility for their learning by engaging them with course material, honing their critical thinking skills, and preparing them for class. Created by an instructor for other instructors, Aplia prompts history students to read carefully and think critically. For every chapter, text-specific exercises ask students to consider individual details that support larger historical concepts and draw conclusions rather than reciting historical facts. Every chapter includes at least one set of questions based on a map from the text. The assignments also give students experience reading and interpreting primary source documents, images, and other media. The automatically graded assignments include detailed, immediate explanations that ensure students put forth effort on a regular basis. Gradebook analytics help instructors monitor and address student performance on an individual or group basis. For more information, visit www.aplia.com/cengage.

Instructor Companion Site. Instructors will find here all the tools they need to teach a rich and successful U.S. History Survey course. The protected teaching materials include the *Instructor's Resource Manual* written by George C. Warren of Central Piedmont Community College, a set of customizable Microsoft® PowerPoint® lecture slides created by Barney Rickman of Valdosta State University, and a set of customizable Microsoft® PowerPoint® slides including all the images (photos, art, maps) from the text. The companion website also provides instructors with access to HistoryFinder and to the Wadsworth American History Resource Center (see descriptions below). Go to www.Cengage.com/history to access this site.

PowerLecture CD-ROM with ExamView® and JoinIn®. This dual-platform, all-in-one multimedia resource includes the *Instructor's Resource Manual*; Test Bank in Word® and PDF formats; customizable Microsoft® PowerPoint® slides of both lecture outlines and images from the text; and *JoinIn®* PowerPoint® slides with clicker content. Also included is ExamView®, an easy-to-use assessment and tutorial system that allows instructors to create, deliver, and customize tests in minutes. The test items, written by George C. Warren of Central Piedmont Community College, include multiple-choice, identification, geography, and essay questions.

HistoryFinder. This searchable online database allows instructors to quickly and easily search and download selections from among thousands of assets, including art, photographs, maps, primary sources, and audio/video clips. Each asset downloads directly into a Microsoft® PowerPoint® slide, allowing instructors to easily create exciting PowerPoint presentations for their classrooms.

eInstructor's Resource Manual. Written by George C. Warren of Central Piedmont Community College, this manual contains for each chapter a set of learning objectives, a comprehensive chapter outline, ideas for classroom activities, discussion questions, suggested paper topics, and a lecture supplement. It is available on the instructor's companion website and in the PowerLecture CD-Rom.

WebTutor™ on Blackboard® and WebCT®. With WebTutor's text-specific, pre-formatted content and total flexibility, instructors can easily create and manage their own custom course website. WebTutor's course management tool gives instructors the ability to provide virtual office hours, post syllabi, set up threaded discussions, track student progress with the quizzing material, and much more. For students, WebTutor offers real-time access to a full array of study tools, including audio chapter summaries, practice quizzes, glossary flashcards, and weblinks.

CourseMate. Cengage Learning's CourseMate brings course concepts to life with interactive learning, study, and exam preparation tools that support the printed textbook. Watch student comprehension soar as your class works with the printed textbook and the *A People and A Nation* CourseMate site, with interactive teaching and learning tools, and EngagementTracker, a first-of-its-kind tool that monitors student engagement in the course. Learn more at www.cengagebrain.com.

Student Resources

CourseMate. For students, CourseMate provides an online source of interactive learning, study, and exam preparation outside the classroom. Students will find outlines and objectives, focus questions, flashcards, quizzes, primary source links (including those noted in the text and marked with the feather icon), and video clips. CourseMate also includes an integrated *A People and A Nation* **eBook**. Students taking quizzes will be linked directly to relevant sections in the ebook for additional information. The ebook is fully searchable and students can even take notes and save them for later review. In addition, the ebook links to rich media assets such as video and MP3 chapter summaries, primary source documents with critical thinking questions, and interactive (zoomable) maps. Students can use the ebook as their primary text or as a companion multimedia support. It is available at www.cengagebrain.com.

Wadsworth American History Resource Center. Wadsworth's American History Resource Center gives your students access to a "virtual reader" with hundreds of primary sources, including speeches, letters, legal documents and transcripts, poems, maps, simulations, timelines, and additional images that bring history to life, along with interactive assignable exercises. A map feature, including Google Earth™ coordinates and exercises, will aid in student comprehension of geography and use of maps. Students can compare the traditional textbook map with an aerial view of the location today. It's an ideal resource for study, review, and research. In addition to this map feature, the resource center also provides blank maps for student review and testing. Ask your sales representative for more information on how to bundle access to the HRC with your text.

cengagebrain.com. Save your students time and money. Direct them to www .cengagebrain.com for choice in formats and savings and a better chance to succeed in class. Students have the freedom to purchase à la carte exactly what they need—when they need it. There, students can purchase a downloadable ebook or electronic access to the American History Resource Center, the premium study tools and interactive ebook in the *A People and A Nation* CourseMate, or eAudio modules from *The History Handbook*. Students can save 50 percent on the electronic textbook and can pay as little as $1.99 for an individual eChapter.

Reader Program. Cengage Learning publishes a number of readers, some containing exclusively primary sources, others a combination of primary and secondary sources, and many designed to guide students through the process of historical inquiry. Visit Cengage.com to browse the catalog of history offerings or ask your sales representative to recommend a reader that would work well for your specific needs.

Custom Options

Nobody knows your students like you, so why not give them a text tailored to their needs? Cengage Learning offers custom solutions for your course—whether it's making a small modification to *A People and A Nation* to match your syllabus or combining multiple sources to create something truly unique. You can pick and choose chapters, include your own material, and add supplementary map exercises along with the Rand McNally Atlas (including questions developed around the maps in the atlas) to create a text that fits the way you teach. Ensure that your students get the most out of their textbook dollar by giving them exactly what they need. Contact your Cengage Learning representative to explore custom solutions for your course.

Rand McNally Atlas of American History, 2e. This comprehensive atlas features more than 80 maps, with new content covering global perspectives, including events in the Middle East from 1945 to 2005, as well as population trends in the United States and around the world. Additional maps document voyages of discovery; the settling of the colonies; major U.S. military engagements, including the American Revolution and World Wars I and II; and sources of immigrations, ethnic populations, and patterns of economic change.

CourseReader. Cengage Learning's new CourseReader lets instructors create a customized electronic reader in minutes. Instructors can choose exactly what their students will be assigned by searching or browsing the extensive CourseReader database. Sources include hundreds of historical documents, images, and media, plus literary essays that can add interest and insight to a primary source assignment. Or instructors can start with the "Editor's Choice" collection created for *A People and A Nation* and then update it to suit their particular needs. Each source comes with all the pedagogical tools needed to provide a full learning experience—including headnotes and objective and essay questions, descriptive headnotes that put the reading into context, and both critical-thinking and multiple-choice questions designed to reinforce key points. Contact your local Cengage Learning sales representative for more information and packaging options.

Acknowledgments

The authors would like to thank the following persons for their assistance with the preparation of this edition: Philip Daileader, David Farber, Danyel Logevall, Jon Parmenter, Anna Daileader Sheriff, Benjamin Daileader Sheriff, and Selene Sheriff.

At each stage of this revision, a sizable panel of historian reviewers read drafts of our chapters. Their suggestions, corrections, and pleas helped guide us through this momentous revision. We could not include all of their recommendations, but the book is better for our having heeded most of their advice. We heartily thank:

Sara Alpern, Texas A&M University
Friederike Baer, Temple University
Troy Bickham, Texas A&M University
Robert Bionaz, Chicago State University
Victoria Bynum, Texas State University, San Marcos

Mario Fenyo, Bowie State University
Walter Hixson, University of Akron
Allison McNeese, Mount Mercy College
Steve O'Brien, Bridgewater State College
Paul O'Hara, Xavier University
John Putman, San Diego State University
Thomas Roy, University of Oklahoma
Manfred Silva, El Paso Community College
Michael Vollbach, Oakland Community College

The authors thank the helpful Cengage people who designed, edited, produced, and nourished this book. Many thanks to Ann West, senior sponsoring editor; Julia Giannotti, senior development editor; Jane Lee, content product manager; Debbie Meyer, project editor; Pembroke Herbert, photo researcher; and Charlotte Miller, art editor.

M. B. N.
C. S.
D. B.
H. C.
F. L.
B. B.

About the Authors

Mary Beth Norton

Born in Ann Arbor, Michigan, Mary Beth Norton received her B.A. from the University of Michigan (1964) and her Ph.D. from Harvard University (1969). She is the Mary Donlon Alger Professor of American History at Cornell University. Her dissertation won the Allan Nevins Prize. She has written *The British-Americans* (1972); *Liberty's Daughters* (1980, 1996); *Founding Mothers & Fathers* (1996), which was one of three finalists for the 1997 Pulitzer Prize in History; and *In the Devil's Snare* (2002), which was one of five finalists for the 2003 *LA Times* Book Prize in History and which won the English-Speaking Union's Ambassador Book Award in American Studies for 2003. She has co-edited three volumes on American women's history. She was also general editor of the *American Historical Association's Guide to Historical Literature* (1995). Her articles have appeared in such journals as the *American Historical Review, William and Mary Quarterly,* and *Journal of Women's History.* Mary Beth has served as president of the Berkshire Conference of Women Historians, as vice president for research of the American Historical Association, and as a presidential appointee to the National Council on the Humanities. She has appeared on Book TV, the History and Discovery Channels, PBS, and NBC and as a commentator on Early American history; and she lectures frequently to high school teachers through the Teaching American History program. She has received four honorary degrees and in 1999 was elected a fellow of the American Academy of Arts and Sciences. She has held fellowships from the National Endowment for the Humanities; the Guggenheim, Rockefeller, and Starr Foundations; and the Henry E. Huntington Library. In 2005–2006, she was the Pitt Professor of American History and Institutions at the University of Cambridge and Newnham College.

Carol Sheriff

Born in Washington, D.C., and raised in Bethesda, Maryland, Carol Sheriff received her B.A. from Wesleyan University (1985) and her Ph.D. from Yale University (1993). Since 1993, she has taught history at the College of William and Mary, where she has won the Thomas Jefferson Teaching Award, the Alumni Teaching Fellowship Award, and the University Professorship for Teaching Excellence. Her publications include *The Artificial River: The Erie Canal and the Paradox of Progress* (1996), which won the Dixon Ryan Fox Award from the New York State Historical Association and the Award for Excellence in Research from the New York State Archives, and *A People at War: Civilians and Soldiers in America's Civil War, 1854–1877* (with Scott Reynolds Nelson, 2007). Carol has written sections of a teaching manual for the New York State history curriculum, given presentations at Teaching American History grant projects, consulted on an exhibit for the Rochester Museum and Science Center, and appeared in the History Channel's *Modern Marvels* show on the Erie Canal, and she is engaged in several public-history projects marking the sesquicentennial of the Civil War. At William and Mary, she teaches the

U.S. history survey as well as upper-level classes on the Early Republic, the Civil War Era, and the American West. Most recently, Carol has been named Class of 2013 term distinguished professor in recognition of her teaching, scholarship, and service.

David W. Blight

Born in Flint, Michigan, David W. Blight received his B.A. from Michigan State University (1971) and his Ph.D. from the University of Wisconsin (1985). He is now Class of 1954 Professor of American History and director of the Gilder Lehrman Center for the Study of Slavery, Resistance, and Abolition at Yale University. For the first seven years of his career, David was a public high school teacher in Flint. He has written *Frederick Douglass's Civil War* (1989) and *Race and Reunion: The Civil War in American Memory, 1863–1915* (2001), which received eight awards, including the Bancroft Prize, the Frederick Douglass Prize, and the Abraham Lincoln Prize, as well as four prizes awarded by the Organization of American Historians. His most recent book is *A Slave No More: The Emancipation of John Washington and Wallace Turnage* (2007), which won three prizes. He has edited or co-edited six other books, including editions of W. E. B. DuBois, *The Souls of Black Folk* and *Narrative of the Life of Frederick Douglass.* David's essays have appeared in the *Journal of American History, Civil War History,* and Gabor Boritt, ed., *Why the Civil War Came* (1996), among others. In 1992–1993, he was senior Fulbright Professor in American Studies at the University of Munich, Germany; in 2006–2007, he held a fellowship at the Dorothy and Lewis B. Cullman Center, New York Public Library. A consultant to several documentary films, David appeared in the 1998 PBS series, *Africans in America.* He has served on the Council of the American Historical Association and teaches summer seminars for secondary school teachers as well as for park rangers and historians of the National Park Service.

Howard P. Chudacoff

Howard P. Chudacoff, the George L. Littlefield Professor of American History and Professor of Urban Studies at Brown University, was born in Omaha, Nebraska. He earned his A.B. (1965) and Ph.D. (1969) from the University of Chicago. He has written *Mobile Americans* (1972), *How Old Are You?* (1989), *The Age of the Bachelor* (1999), *The Evolution of American Urban Society* (with Judith Smith, 2004), and *Children at Play: An American History* (2007). He has also co-edited with Peter Baldwin *Major Problems in American Urban History* (2004). His articles have appeared in such journals as the *Journal of Family History, Reviews in American History,* and *Journal of American History.* At Brown University, Howard has co-chaired the American Civilization Program and chaired the Department of History, and serves as Brown's faculty representative to the NCAA. He has also served on the board of directors of the Urban History Association. The National Endowment for the Humanities, Ford Foundation, and Rockefeller Foundation have given him awards to advance his scholarship.

Fredrik Logevall

A native of Stockholm, Sweden, Fredrik Logevall is the John S. Knight Professor of International Studies and Professor of History at Cornell University, where he serves as director of the Mario Einaudi Center for International Studies. He received his B.A. from Simon Fraser University (1986) and his Ph.D. from Yale University (1993). His most recent book is *America's Cold War: The Politics of Insecurity* (with Campbell Craig, 2009). His other publications include *Choosing War* (1999), which won three prizes, including the Warren F. Kuehl Book Prize from the Society for Historians of American Foreign Relations (SHAFR); *The Origins of the Vietnam War* (2001); *Terrorism and 9/11: A Reader* (2002); as co-editor, *Encyclopedia of American Foreign Policy* (2002); and, as co-editor, *The First Vietnam War: Colonial Conflict and Cold War Crisis* (2007). Fred is a past recipient of the Stuart L. Bernath article, book, and lecture prizes from SHAFR and is a member of the SHAFR Council, the Cornell University Press faculty board, and the editorial advisory board of the Presidential Recordings Project at the Miller Center of Public Affairs at the University of Virginia. In 2006–2007, he was Leverhulme Visiting Professor at the University of Nottingham and Mellon Senior Fellow at the University of Cambridge.

Beth Bailey

Born in Atlanta, Georgia, Beth Bailey received her B.A. from Northwestern University (1979) and her Ph.D. from the University of Chicago (1986). She is now a professor of history at Temple University. Her research and teaching fields include war and society and the U.S. military, American cultural history (nineteenth and twentieth centuries), popular culture, and gender and sexuality. She is the author, most recently, of *America's Army: Making the All-Volunteer Force* (2009). Her other publications include *From Front Porch to Back Seat: Courtship in 20th Century America* (1988), *The First Strange Place: The Alchemy of Race and Sex in WWII Hawaii* (with David Farber, 1992), *Sex in the Heartland* (1999), and *The Columbia Companion to America in the 1960s* (with David Farber, 2001). She is co-editor of *A History of Our Time* (with William Chafe and Harvard Sitkoff, 7th ed., 2007). Beth has served as a consultant and/ or on-screen expert for numerous television documentaries developed for PBS and the History Channel. She has received grants or fellowships from the American Council of Learned Societies, the National Endowment for the Humanities, and the Woodrow Wilson International Center for Scholars; and she was named the Ann Whitney Olin scholar at Barnard College, Columbia University, where she was the director of the American Studies Program, and Regents Lecturer at the University of New Mexico. She has been a visiting scholar at Saitama University, Japan; at Trinity College at the University of Melbourne; and a senior Fulbright lecturer in Indonesia. She teaches courses on sexuality and gender and war and American culture.

Three Old Worlds Create a New

1

1492–1600

F ive years later, Alvar Nuñez Cabeza de Vaca still recalled the amazement he had encountered. "I reached four Christians on horseback who registered great surprise at seeing me so strangely dressed and in the company of Indians. They...neither spoke to me nor dared to ask anything."

Cabeza de Vaca and three other men, one an enslaved North African named Estevan, had just walked across North America. They, along with about six hundred others, had left Spain in June 1527 on an ill-fated expedition. After exploring the west coast of Florida, eighty men, including Cabeza de Vaca, were shipwrecked in late 1528 on the coast of modern Texas (probably near Galveston), at a place they named Isla de Malhado, or Island of Misfortune. Most of the survivors—alternately abused, aided, or enslaved by different Indian nations—gradually died. Cabeza de Vaca reached the mainland, where he survived as a traveling trader, exchanging seashells for hides and flint.

In January 1533, he stumbled on the other three. The Spaniards and Estevan plotted to leave but were unable to until September 1534. They walked south, then turned inland and headed north, exploring the upper reaches of the Rio Grande. They continued west, almost reaching the Pacific before turning south once more, guided from village to village by Indians. Vaca described the diets, living arrangements, and customs of many of the villages they saw, thus providing modern historians and anthropologists with an invaluable record of native cultures as they met Europeans.

For thousands of years before 1492, human societies in the Americas had developed in isolation from the rest of the world. That ended in the Christian fifteenth century, as Europeans sought treasure and trade, peoples from different cultures came into regular contact for the first time and were profoundly changed. Their interactions over the next 350 years involved cruelty and kindness, greed and deception, trade and theft, sickness and enslavement. The history of the colonies that would become the United States must be seen in this broad context of European exploration and exploitation.

Chapter Outline

American Societies
Ancient America | Mesoamerican Civilizations | Pueblos and Mississippians | Aztecs

VISUALIZING THE PAST *City of the Sun*

North America in 1492
Gendered Division of Labor | Social Organization | War and Politics | Religion

African Societies
West Africa (Guinea) | Complementary Gender Roles | Slavery in Guinea

European Societies
Gender, Work, Politics, and Religion | Effects of Plague and Warfare | Political and Technological Change | Motives for Exploration

Early European Explorations
Sailing the Mediterranean Atlantic | Islands of the Mediterranean Atlantic | Portuguese Trading Posts in Africa | Lessons of Early Colonization

Voyages of Columbus, Cabot, and Their Successors
Columbus's Voyage | Columbus's Observations | Norse and Other Northern Voyagers | John Cabot's Explorations

Spanish Exploration and Conquest
Cortés and Other Explorers | Capture of Tenochtitlán | Spanish Colonization | Gold, Silver, and Spain's Decline

The Columbian Exchange
Smallpox and Other Diseases | Sugar, Horses, and Tobacco

LINKS TO THE WORLD *Maize*

1

Europeans in North America
Trade Among Indians and Europeans | *Contest Between Spain and England* | *Roanoke* | *Harriot's* Briefe and True Report

LEGACY FOR A PEOPLE AND A NATION
Kennewick Man/Ancient One

SUMMARY

Link to Cabeza de Vaca's original narrative in English.

The continents that European sailors reached in the late fifteenth century had their own histories, which the intruders largely ignored. The residents of the Americas were the world's most skillful plant breeders; they developed vegetable crops more nutritious and productive than in Europe, Asia, or Africa and invented systems of writing and mathematics. As in Europe, their societies rose and fell as leaders succeeded or failed. But the arrival of Europeans immeasurably altered the Americans' struggles with one another.

After 1400, European nations tried to acquire valuable colonies and trading posts worldwide. Initially interested in Asia and Africa, Europeans eventually focused mostly on the Americas. Even as Europeans slowly achieved dominance, their fates were shaped by Americans and Africans. In the Americas of the fifteenth and sixteenth centuries, three old worlds came together to produce a new.

As you read this chapter, keep the following questions in mind:

* **What were the key characteristics of the three worlds that met in the Americas?**

* **What impact did their encounter have on each of them?**

* **What were the crucial initial developments in that encounter?**

American Societies

What led to the development of major North American civilizations in the centuries before Europeans arrived?

Human beings originated on the continent of Africa, where human-like remains about 3 million years old have been found in what is now Ethiopia. Over many millennia, the growing population dispersed to other continents. Because the climate was far colder than it is now, much of the earth's water was concentrated in huge rivers of ice called glaciers. Sea levels were lower, and land masses covered a larger proportion of the earth's surface. Scholars long believed that the earliest inhabitants of the Americas crossed a land bridge known as Beringia (at the site of the Bering Strait) approximately 12,000–14,000 years ago. Yet new archaeological discoveries suggest that parts of the Americas may have been settled much earlier, possibly in three successive waves beginning roughly 30,000 years ago. When, about 12,500 years ago, the climate warmed and sea levels rose, Americans were separated from the connected continents of Asia, Africa, and Europe.

Paleo-Indians: The earliest peoples of the Americas.

Ancient America

The first Americans are called **Paleo-Indians**. Nomadic hunters of game and gatherers of wild plants, they spread throughout North and South America, probably as bands of extended families. By about 11,500 years ago, the Paleo-Indians were making fine stone projectile points, which they attached to wooden spears and used to kill bison (buffalo), woolly mammoths, and other large mammals. But as the Ice Age ended and the human population increased, all the large American mammals except the bison disappeared.

Chronology

12,000–10,000 B.C.E.	Paleo-Indians migrate from Asia to North America across the Beringia land bridge	1494	Treaty of Tordesillas divides land claims between Spain and Portugal in Africa, India, and South America
7000 B.C.E.	Cultivation of food crops begins in America	1496	Last Canary Island falls to Spain
ca. 2000 B.C.E.	Olmec civilization appears	1497	Cabot reaches North America
ca. 300–600 C.E.	Height of influence of Teotihuacán	1513	Ponce de León explores Florida
ca. 600–900 C.E.	Classic Mayan civilization	1518–30	Smallpox epidemic devastates Indian population of West Indies and Central and South America
1000 C.E.	Ancient Pueblos build settlements in modern states of Arizona and New Mexico	1519	Cortés invades Mexico
1001	Norse establish settlement in "Vinland"	1521	Aztec Empire falls to Spaniards
1050–1250	Height of influence of Cahokia	1524	Verrazzano sails along Atlantic coast of United States
	Prevalence of Mississippian culture in modern midwestern and southeastern United States	1534–35	Cartier explores St. Lawrence River
14th century	Aztec rise to power	1534–36	Vaca, Estevan, and two companions walk across North America
1450s–80s	Portuguese explore and colonize islands in the Mediterranean Atlantic	1539–42	Soto explores southeastern United States
		1540–42	Coronado explores southwestern United States
1477	Marco Polo's *Travels* describes China	1587–90	Raleigh's Roanoke colony vanishes
1492	Columbus reaches Bahamas	1588	Harriot publishes *A Briefe and True Report of the New Found Land of Virginia*

Consequently, by approximately nine thousand years ago, the residents of what is now central Mexico began to cultivate food crops, especially maize (corn), squash, beans, avocados, and peppers. In the Andes Mountains of South America, people started to grow potatoes. As knowledge of agricultural techniques improved, vegetables proved a more reliable source of food than hunting and gathering. Most Americans started to adopt a more sedentary lifestyle that enabled them to tend fields regularly. Some established permanent settlements; others moved several times a year among fixed sites. They cleared forests through controlled burning, which created cultivable lands, by killing trees and fertilizing the soil with ashes and opened meadows to deer and other wildlife. Although they traded such items as shells, flint, salt, and copper, no society ever became dependent on another group.

Wherever agriculture dominated, complex civilizations flourished. With steady supplies of grains and vegetables, societies could broaden their focus from subsistence to trade, accumulating wealth, producing ornamental objects, and creating elaborate rituals and ceremonies. In North America, the successful cultivation of nutritious crops seems to have led to the growth and development of all the major civilizations: first the large city-states of Mesoamerica (modern Mexico and Guatemala) and then the urban clusters known collectively as the Mississippian culture (in the present-day United States). Each reached its peak influence after achieving success in agriculture. Each later collapsed after reaching the limits of its food supply.

Mesoamerican Civilizations

Scholars know little about the first major Mesoamerican civilization, the Olmecs, who about four thousand years ago lived in cities near the Gulf of Mexico. The Mayas and Teotihuacán, which developed approximately two thousand years later, are better recorded. Teotihuacán, founded in the Valley of Mexico about 300 B.C.E. (Before the Common Era), became one of the largest urban areas in the world, housing 100,000 people in the fifth century C.E. (Common Era). Teotihuacán's commercial network extended hundreds of miles, and Pilgrims traveled long distances to visit Teotihuacan's impressive pyramids and the great temple of Quetzalcoatl—the feathered serpent, primary god of central Mexico.

On the Yucatan Peninsula, in today's eastern Mexico, the Mayas built urban centers containing tall pyramids and temples, studied astronomy, and created an elaborate writing system. Their city-states engaged in near-constant warfare with one another—combined with inadequate food supplies, this caused the collapse of the most powerful cities by 900 C.E., thus ending the era of Mayan civilization.

Pueblos and Mississippians

Ancient native societies in what is now the United States learned to grow maize, squash, and beans from Mesoamericans. The Hohokam, Mogollon, and ancient Pueblo peoples of the modern states of Arizona and New Mexico subsisted by combining hunting and gathering with agriculture in an arid region of unpredictable rainfall. Hohokam villagers constructed extensive irrigation systems, but relocated when water supplies failed. Between 900 and 1150 C.E., Chaco Canyon, at the juncture of perhaps four hundred miles of roads, served as a major trading and processing center for turquoise. Yet the aridity caused the Chacoans to migrate to other sites.

Almost simultaneously, the unrelated Mississippian culture flourished in what is now the midwestern and southeastern United States. Relying largely on maize, squash, nuts, pumpkins, and venison, the Mississippians lived in hierarchically organized settlements. Their largest urban center was the **City of the Sun** (now called Cahokia), near modern St. Louis. Located on rich farmland near the confluence of the Illinois, Missouri, and Mississippi Rivers, Cahokia, like Teotihuacán and Chaco Canyon, served as a focal point for religion and trade. At its peak (in the eleventh and twelfth centuries C.E.), the City of the Sun covered more than 5 square miles and had a population of about twenty thousand—small by Mesoamerican standards but larger than London.

City of the Sun (Cahokia): Area located near modern St. Louis, Missouri, where about twenty thousand people inhabited a metropolitan area.

The sun-worshipping Cahokians developed an accurate calendar. The city's main pyramid (one of 120 of varying sizes), today called Monks Mound, remains the largest earthwork in the Americas. Yet following 1250 C.E., the city was abandoned. Archaeologists believe that climate change and the degradation of the environment, caused by overpopulation and the destruction of nearby forests, contributed to its collapse. Afterwards, warfare increased as large-scale population movements destabilized the region.

Aztecs

Far to the South, the Aztecs (also called Mexicas) migrated into the Valley of Mexico during the twelfth century. Their chronicles record that their primary deity, Huitzilopochtli—a war god represented by an eagle—directed them to establish their capital on an island where they saw an eagle eating a serpent. That island city became Tenochtitlán, the center of a

City of the Sun

Today the remains of the City of the Sun (Cahokia) are preserved in a state park in southern Illinois. The mounds are now either largely gone or greatly reduced in size, but archaeologists have been able to visualize the site. Few of their finds were more important than the two shown here: the woodhenge and the Birger figurine. Archaeologists discovered the post holes where the woodhenge once stood, showing how the sun-worshipping Cahokians monitored the sun's annual movements through shadows cast by poles they erected in a precise formation. The red clay Birger figurine, found near Cahokia, depicts a woman with a vine winding around her body sitting on a cat-faced serpent (symbol of the earth) and holding a hoe. Why would the woodhenge have been important for Cahokia's farmers? What is the significance of the squash vine and the other attributes of the Birger figurine?

Cahokia Mounds Historic Site

An artist's conception of the construction of Cahokia's woodhenge. Monks mound is in the background.

Courtesy of the Illinois State Archaeological Survey, University of Illinois

Front view of the Birger figurine.

Courtesy of the Illinois State Archaeological Survey, University of Illinois

Back view of the Birger figurine.

stratified society composed of hereditary classes of warriors, merchants, priests, common folk, and slaves.

The Aztecs conquered their neighbors, forcing them to pay tribute in textiles, gold, foodstuffs, and human sacrifices to Huitzilopochtli. They also engaged in ritual combat for further sacrificial victims to the war god. In the Aztec year Ten Rabbit (1502), at the coronation of Motecuhzoma II (the Spaniards mispronounced his name as Montezuma), thousands were sacrificed by having their hearts torn from their bodies.

North America in 1492

Over the centuries, the Americans who lived north of Mexico adapted their once similar ways of life to different climates and terrains, thus creating the diverse culture areas (ways of subsistence) that the Europeans encountered (see Map 1.1). Scholars often refer to such culture areas by language group (such as Algonquian or Iroquoian). Bands that lived in environments not suited to agriculture followed a nomadic lifestyle typified by the Paiutes and Shoshones, who inhabited the Great Basin (now Nevada and Utah). Because finding sufficient food was difficult, such hunter-gatherer bands were small, usually composed of one or more related families. The men hunted small animals, and women gathered seeds and berries.

In more favorable environments, larger groups, like the Chinooks of present-day Washington and Oregon, combined agriculture with gathering, hunting, and fishing. Residents of the interior (for example, the Arikaras of the Missouri River valley) hunted large animals while also cultivating maize, squash, and beans.

Trade routes linked distant peoples. For instance, hoe and spade blades manufactured from stone mined in modern southern Illinois have been found as far northeast as Lake Erie and as far west as the Plains. Commercial and other interactions among disparate groups speaking different languages were aided by the universal symbol of friendship—the calumet, a feathered tobacco pipe offered to strangers at initial encounters.

Gendered Division of Labor

Societies that relied on hunting large animals, such as deer and buffalo, assigned that task to men, allotting food preparation and clothing production to women. Before acquiring horses from the Spaniards, women carried the family's belongings whenever the band relocated. This sexual division of labor was universal among hunting peoples. Agricultural societies assigned work in divergent ways. The Pueblo defined agricultural labor as men's work. In the east, peoples speaking Algonquian, Iroquoian, and Muskogean languages allocated most agricultural chores to women, although men cleared the land. In all farming societies, women gathered wild foods and prepared food for consumption or storage, whereas men hunted.

Almost universally, women cared for young children, while older youths learned adult skills from their same-sex parent. Children had a lot of freedom. Young people commonly chose their own marital partners, and in most societies couples could easily divorce. Infants and toddlers were nursed until age two or older, and taboos prevented couples from having sexual intercourse during that period.

MAP 1.1

Native Cultures of North America

The Natives of the North American continent effectively used the resources of the regions in which they lived. As this map shows, coastal groups relied on fishing, residents of fertile areas engaged in agriculture, and other peoples employed hunting (often combined with gathering) as a primary mode of subsistence.
Source: Copyright © Cengage Learning

Social Organization   Southwestern and eastern agricultural peoples similarly lived in villages, sometimes with a thousand or more inhabitants. The Pueblos resided in multistory buildings constructed on terraces along the sides of cliffs or other easily defended sites. Northern Iroquois villages (in modern New York State) were composed of large, rectangular, bark-covered structures, or long houses; the name Haudenosaunee, which the Iroquois called themselves, means "People of the Long House." In the present-day southeastern United States, Muskogeans and southern Algonquians lived in large thatch houses. Most of the eastern villages were surrounded by wooden palisades and ditches to fend off attackers.

7

Collection of Mary Beth Norton

Jacques Le Moyne, an artist accompanying the French settlement in Florida in the 1560s (see page 30), produced some of the first European images of North American peoples. His depiction of native agricultural practices shows the gendered division of labor: men breaking up the ground with fishbone hoes before women drop seeds into the holes. But Le Moyne's version of the scene cannot be accepted uncritically: unable to abandon a European view of proper farming methods, he erroneously drew plowed furrows in the soil.

In all the agricultural societies, each dwelling housed an extended family defined matrilineally (through a female line of descent). Mothers, their married daughters, and their daughters' husbands and children all lived together. Matrilineal descent did not imply matriarchy, or the wielding of power by women, but denoted kinship and linked extended families into clans. The nomadic bands of the Prairies and Great Plains were most often related patrilineally (through the male line).

War and Politics

Long before Europeans arrived, residents fought one another for control of the best hunting and fishing territories, the most fertile agricultural lands, or the sources of essential items, such as salt (for preserving meat) and flint (for making knives and arrowheads). Bands of Americans protected by wooden armor engaged in face-to-face combat, since the clubs and throwing spears they used were effective only in close proximity. They began to shoot arrows from behind trees only when they confronted European guns. War captives were sometimes enslaved, but slavery was never an important labor source in pre-Columbian America.

Political structures varied considerably. Among Pueblos, the village council, composed of ten to thirty men, was the highest political authority; no government structure connected the villages. The Iroquois had an elaborate hierarchy incorporating villages into nations and nations into a confederation. A council comprising representatives from each nation made crucial decisions of war and peace. Women more often assumed leadership roles among agricultural peoples than among nomadic hunters. Female sachems (rulers) led Algonquian villages in what is now Massachusetts, but women never became heads of hunting bands. Iroquois women did not become chiefs, yet older women chose village chiefs and could both start wars (by calling for the capture of prisoners to replace dead relatives) and stop them (by refusing to supply warriors with foodstuffs).

Religion

All the American peoples were polytheistic, worshiping a multitude of gods. The major deities of agricultural peoples like the Pueblos and Muskogeans were associated with cultivation, and festivals centered on planting and harvest. The most important gods of hunters like those living on the Great Plains were associated with animals. Women held the most prominent positions in those agricultural societies where they were also the chief food producers; in hunting societies, men took the lead in religious and political affairs.

A variety of cultures, comprising more than 10 million people speaking over one thousand languages, inhabited America north of Mexico when Europeans arrived. The hierarchical kingdoms of Mesoamerica bore little resemblance to the nomadic hunting societies of the Great Plains or to the agriculturalists of the Northeast or Southwest. They did not consider themselves one people, nor did they consider uniting to repel the European invaders.

African Societies

Fifteenth-century Africa similarly housed a variety of cultures. In the north, along the Mediterranean Sea, lived the Berbers, who were Muslims, or followers of the Islamic religion. On the east coast of Africa, Muslim city-states engaged in extensive trade with India, the Moluccas (part of modern Indonesia), and China. Sustained contact and intermarriage among Arabs and Africans created the Swahili language and culture. Through the East African city-states passed the Spice Route, water-borne commerce between the eastern Mediterranean and East Asia; other trade traversed the Silk Road, the long land route across Central Asia.

South of the Mediterranean coast in the African interior lie the great Saharan and Libyan Deserts. The introduction of the camel in the fifth century C.E. made long-distance travel possible, and as Islam expanded after the ninth century, commerce controlled by Muslim merchants helped spread religious and cultural ideas. Below the deserts, the continent is divided between tropical rain forests (along the coasts) and grassy plains (in the interior). South of the Gulf of Guinea, the grassy landscape came to be dominated by Bantu-speaking peoples, who left their homeland in modern Nigeria about two thousand years ago.

> What were the chief characteristics of West African societies in the fifteenth century?

West Africa (Guinea)

West Africa was a land of tropical forests and savanna grasslands where fishing, cattle herding, and agriculture supported the inhabitants for ten thousand years before Europeans arrived in the fifteenth century. The northern region of West Africa, or Upper Guinea, was heavily influenced by Mediterranean Islamic culture. Trade via camel caravans between Upper Guinea and the Muslim Mediterranean was sub-Saharan Africa's major connection to Europe and West Asia. Africans sold ivory, gold, and slaves to northern merchants to obtain salt, dates, silk, and cotton cloth.

Upper Guinea runs northeast-southwest from Cape Verde to Cape Palmas. The people of its northernmost region—the so-called Rice Coast (present-day Gambia, Senegal, and Guinea)—fished and cultivated rice in coastal swamplands. The Grain Coast, to the south, was thinly populated and with only one good harbor (modern Freetown, Sierra Leone), not easily accessible from the sea. Its people farmed and raised livestock.

In Lower Guinea, south and east of Cape Palmas, most Africans were farmers who practiced traditional religions, rather than Islam. Like the agricultural Americans, they believed spirits inhabited particular places, and they developed rituals to ensure good harvests. Individual villages composed of kin groups were linked into hierarchical kingdoms, creating the decentralized political and social authority that existed when Europeans arrived.

Complementary Gender Roles

As in the Americas, West African societies assigned different tasks to men and women. The sexes generally shared agricultural duties. Men also hunted, managed livestock, and fished. Women were responsible for childcare, food preparation, manufacture, and trade. They managed local and regional networks through which families, villages, and small kingdoms exchanged goods.

Lower Guinea had similar social systems organized according to what anthropologists have called the dual-sex principle. Each sex handled its own affairs: male political and religious leaders governed men; females ruled women. Many West African societies practiced polygyny (one man's having several wives, each of whom lived separately with her children). Thus, few adults lived permanently in marital households, but the dual-sex system ensured that they were monitored by their own sex.

Throughout Guinea, religious beliefs stressed complementary male and female roles. Both women and men served as heads of the cults and secret societies that directed village spiritual life. Young women were initiated into the Sandé cult, young men into Poro. Although West African women rarely held formal power over men, female religious leaders governed women within the Sandé cult, enforcing conformity to behavioral norms.

Slavery in Guinea

West African law recognized individual and communal land ownership, but men seeking wealth needed labor—wives, children, or slaves—who could work the land. West Africans enslaved for life were vital to the economy. Africans could be enslaved for committing crimes, but usually slaves were enemy captives or people who enslaved themselves or their children to pay debts. An African slave owner had a right to the products of slaves' labor, although slave status did not always descend to the next generation. Some slaves were held as chattel; others could engage in trade, retaining a portion of their profits; and still others achieved prominent political or military positions. All, however, could be traded at any time.

Agricultural peoples, West African men and women enjoyed a relatively egalitarian relationship and worked communally in family groups or with members of their sex. Carried as captives to the Americas, they became essential laborers for European colonists.

European Societies

What were the motives behind fifteenth- and sixteenth-century European explorations?

In the fifteenth century, Europeans, too, were agricultural peoples. In the hierarchical European societies, a few families wielded autocratic power over the majority. English society was organized as a series of interlocking hierarchies; that is, each person (except those at the top or bottom) was superior to some, inferior to others. Although Europeans were not subjected to perpetual slavery, Christian doctrine permitted the enslavement of "heathens" (non-Christians). Some Europeans, too, were held as serfs, which tied them to the land or to specific owners. In short, Europe's kingdoms resembled those of Africa or Mesoamerica but differed from the more egalitarian societies in America north of Mexico.

Gender, Work, Politics, and Religion

Most Europeans, like Africans and Americans, lived in small villages. European farmers, called peasants, owned or leased separate landholdings but worked the fields communally. Because fields had to lie fallow (unplanted) every second or third year to regain fertility, a family could only ensure its food supply if all villagers shared the work and the crops. Men did the fieldwork; women helped at planting and harvesting. In some regions, men concentrated on herding livestock. Women's duties consisted of childcare and household tasks, including preserving food, milking cows, and caring for poultry. If a husband was a city artisan or storekeeper, his wife might assist him in business. Because Europeans kept domesticated animals (pigs, goats, sheep, and cattle) for meat, hunting had little economic importance.

Men dominated European society. A few women—notably Queen Elizabeth I of England—achieved power by birthright, but most were excluded from political authority. They also held inferior social, religious, and economic positions, yet wielded power over children and servants.

Christianity was the dominant European religion. In the West, authority rested in the Catholic Church, based in Rome. Although Europeans were nominally Catholic, many adhered to local belief systems that the church deemed heretical. Still, Europe's Christian nations from the twelfth century on publicly united to drive nonbelievers (especially Muslims) from their domains and from the holy city of Jerusalem, triggering wars known as the Crusades. Nevertheless, in the fifteenth century, Muslims dominated the commerce and geography of the Mediterranean, especially after they conquered Constantinople (capital of the Christian Byzantine empire) in 1453. Few would have predicted that Christian Europeans would ever pose a challenge.

Effects of Plague and Warfare

When the fifteenth century began, European nations were recovering from the devastating Black Death epidemic, which traders seem to have brought from China in 1346. The disease recurred with severity in the 1360s and 1370s. The best estimate is that one-third of Europeans died. A precipitous economic decline followed—as did severe social, political, and religious disruption.

As plague ravaged the population, England and France waged the Hundred Years' War (1337–1453), initiated because English monarchs claimed the French throne. The war interrupted overland trade routes connecting England and Antwerp (in modern Belgium) to Venice, a Christian trading center, and thence to India and China. Needing a new way to their northern trading partners, eastern Mediterranean merchants forged a maritime route to Antwerp. Using a triangular, or lateen, sail (rather than square rigging) improved a ship's maneuverability, enabling vessels to sail from the Mediterranean and north around the European coast.

Political and Technological Change

After the Hundred Years' War, European monarchs consolidated their political power and raised revenues by taxing an already hard-pressed peasantry. The military struggle inspired new pride in national identity over former regional and dynastic loyalties. In England, Henry VII in 1485 founded the Tudor dynasty and united a previously divided land. In France, Charles VII's successors unified the kingdom. Most successful were Ferdinand of Aragón and Isabella of Castile; in 1492, they defeated the Muslims, who had lived in Spain and Portugal for centuries, thereafter establishing a strongly Catholic Spain by expelling Jews and Muslims.

movable type: Type in which each character is cast on a separate piece of metal.

printing press: A machine that transfers lettering or images by contact with various forms of inked surface onto paper or similar material fed into it in various ways.

The fifteenth century also brought technological change to Europe. **Movable type** and the **printing press**, invented in Germany in the 1450s, made information more accessible, including books about fabled lands across the seas. The most important books were Ptolemy's *Geography,* a description of the known world written in ancient times, first published in 1475; and Marco Polo's *Travels,* published in 1477. The *Travels* recounted a Venetian merchant's adventures in thirteenth-century China and described that nation as bordered on the east by an ocean. That book led Europeans to believe they could reach China by sea rather than via the Silk Road or the Spice Route. If it existed, a transoceanic route would allow northern Europeans to circumvent the Muslim and Venetian merchants who controlled their access to Asian goods.

Motives for Exploration

In the fifteenth and sixteenth centuries, European countries craved easy access to African and Asian goods—silk, dyes, perfumes, jewels, sugar, gold, and especially spices, which were desirable for seasoning food and as possible medicines. The allure of cinnamon or cloves stemmed from their rarity, extraordinary cost, and mysterious origins. They passed through so many hands en route to London or Seville that no European knew exactly where they came from. Acquiring products directly would improve a nation's income and its standing relative to other countries, thus providing a powerful incentive for exploration.

Spreading Christianity around the world supplemented the economic motive. Fifteenth-century Europeans saw no conflict between materialistic and spiritual goals. Explorers and colonizers—especially Roman Catholics—sought to convert "heathen" peoples and also hoped to increase their nation's wealth via direct trade with Africa, China, India, and the Moluccas.

Early European Explorations

What sailing innovation ultimately facilitated the widespread exploration of the Atlantic and Pacific?

To establish that trade, European mariners first had to explore the oceans. Seafarers needed not just maneuverable vessels and navigational aids but also knowledge of the sea, its currents, and winds. Wind would power their ships. But where would Atlantic breezes carry their square-rigged ships, which needed the wind directly behind the vessel?

Sailing the Mediterranean Atlantic

The answers would be found in the Mediterranean Atlantic, the expanse of ocean located south and west of Spain and bounded by the Azores (on the west) and the Canaries (on the south), with the Madeiras in their midst. Europeans reached all three sets of islands during the fourteenth century. Sailing to the Canaries from Europe was easy because strong Northeast trade winds blew southward along the Iberian and African coastlines. The voyage took about a week.

The Iberian sailor returning home, however, faced winds that blew directly at him. Rowing and tacking back and forth against the wind were tedious and ineffectual. Instead of waiting for the wind to change, mariners developed the new technique of sailing "around the wind"—literally sailing as directly against the wind as possible without changing course. In the Mediterranean Atlantic, a mariner would head northwest into the open ocean, until—weeks later—he reached the winds that would carry him home, the so-called Westerlies. This solution became the key to successful exploration of the Atlantic and the Pacific Oceans. Faced with a contrary wind, a sailor could simply sail around it until he found a wind to carry him on his way.

Islands of the Mediterranean Atlantic

During the fifteenth century, Iberian seamen regularly visited the three island groups. The uninhabited Azores were soon settled by Portuguese migrants who raised wheat for sale in Europe and sold livestock to passing sailors. By the 1450s, Portuguese colonists who settled the uninhabited Madeiras were employing slaves (probably Jews and Muslims brought from Iberia) to grow sugar for export. By the 1470s, Madeira had developed a colonial **plantation** economy. For the first time in history, a region was settled explicitly to cultivate a valuable crop—sugar—for sale elsewhere. Because the work was so backbreaking, only a supply of enslaved laborers (who could not quit) could ensure the system's success.

plantation: A large-scale agricultural enterprise growing commercial crops and usually employing coerced or slave labor.

The Canaries had indigenous residents—the Guanche people, who traded animal skins and dyes with Europeans. After 1402 the French, Portuguese, and Spanish sporadically attacked the islands. The Guanches resisted but were weakened by European diseases. The seven islands fell to Europeans, who carried off Guanches as slaves to the Madeiras or Iberia. Spain conquered the last island in 1496 and devoted it to sugar plantations.

Portuguese Trading Posts in Africa

Other Europeans saw the Mediterranean Atlantic islands as steppingstones to Africa. In 1415, Portugal seized control of Ceuta, a Muslim city in North Africa. Prince Henry the Navigator, son of King John I of Portugal, dispatched ships southward along the

African coast, attempting to discover an oceanic route to Asia. Not until after his death did Bartholomew Dias round the southern tip of Africa (1488) and Vasco da Gama finally reach India (1498), where at Malabar he located the richest source of peppercorns in the world.

Although West African states resisted European penetration of the interior, they let Portugal establish trading posts along their coasts. The African kingdoms charged traders rent and levied duties on imports. The Portuguese gained, too, profiting from transporting African gold, ivory, and slaves to Europe. By bargaining with African masters to purchase slaves and carrying those bondspeople to Iberia, the Portuguese introduced black slavery into Europe.

Lessons of Early Colonization

Portugal's success grew after it colonized São Tomé, located in the Gulf of Guinea, in the 1480s. With Madeira at its sugar-producing capacity, São Tomé proved an ideal new locale, and plantation agriculture there expanded rapidly. Planters imported slaves to work in the cane fields, creating the first economy based primarily on the bondage of black Africans.

By the 1490s, Europeans had learned three key colonization lessons in the Mediterranean Atlantic. First, they learned how to transplant crops and livestock to exotic locations. Second, they discovered that native peoples could be conquered (like the Guanches) or exploited (like the Africans). Third, they developed a model of plantation slavery and a system for supplying many such workers. The stage was set for a pivotal moment in world history.

Voyages of Columbus, Cabot, and Their Successors

Christopher Columbus understood the lessons of the Mediterranean Atlantic. Born in 1451 in the Italian city-state of Genoa, this self-educated son of a wool merchant was by the 1490s an experienced sailor and mapmaker. Drawn to Portugal and its islands, he voyaged to the Portuguese outpost on the Gold Coast, where he became obsessed with gold and witnessed the economic potential of the slave trade.

What three themes in Columbus's log about his explorations would come to mark much of the future settlement of Europeans in the Americas?

Like all accomplished seafarers, Columbus knew the world was round. But he thought that China lay only three thousand miles from the southern European coast. Thus, he argued, it would be easier to reach Asia by sailing west. Experts scoffed, accurately predicting that the two continents lay twelve thousand miles apart. When Columbus in 1484 asked the Portuguese rulers to back his plan, they rejected what appeared to be a crazy scheme.

Christopher Columbus: Italian explorer who claimed the island of San Salvador in the Bahamas for the king and queen of Spain.

Columbus's Voyage

Ferdinand and Isabella of Spain, jealous of Portugal's successes in Africa, agreed to finance Columbus's risky voyage. They hoped profits would finance a new expedition to conquer Muslim-held Jerusalem. On August 3, 1492, in command of three ships—the *Pinta,* the *Niña,* and the *Santa Maria*—Columbus set sail from the Spanish port of Palos.

On October 12, the vessels found land approximately where Columbus thought Cipangu (Japan) was located (see Map 1.2). He and his men landed on an island in

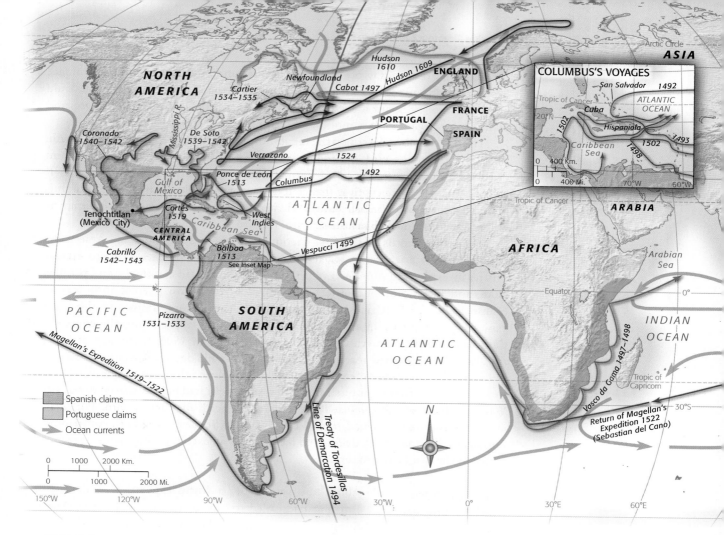

MAP 1.2

European Explorations in America

In the century following Columbus's voyages, European adventurers explored the coasts and parts of the interior of North and South America.

Source: Copyright © Cengage Learning

the Bahamas, which its inhabitants called Guanahaní but he renamed San Salvador. Later, he explored the islands now known as Cuba and Hispaniola, which their residents, the Taíno people, called Colba and Bohío. Because he thought he had reached the East Indies (the Spice Islands), Columbus referred to the inhabitants as "Indians." The Taínos thought the Europeans had come from the sky, and crowds gathered to meet and exchange gifts with Columbus.

Link to the logbook of Columbus's first voyage.

Columbus's Observations

Three themes predominate Columbus's log. First, he insistently asked the Taínos where he could find gold, pearls, and spices. They replied (via signs) that such products were on other islands or on the mainland. He came to mistrust such answers, noting, "They will tell me anything I want to hear."

Second, Columbus wrote about the strange and beautiful plants and animals. His interest was not only aesthetic. "There are many plants and trees here that could be worth a lot in Spain for use as dyes, spices, and medicines," he observed and planned to carry home "a sample of everything I can" for experts to examine.

Third, Columbus described the inhabitants, seizing some to take back to Spain. The Taínos were, he said, handsome, gentle, and friendly, though they told him of the fierce Caniba (today called Caribs) who lived on other islands, raided their villages, and ate some captives (hence today's word *cannibal*). Although Columbus distrusted the Caribs, he believed the Taínos to be likely converts to Catholicism as well as "good and skilled servants."

Link to Columbus's letter to Ferdinand and Isabella announcing his discoveries.

Thus, the records of the first encounter between Europeans and Americans revealed significant themes for centuries to come. Europeans wanted to extract profits by exploiting American resources, including plants, animals, and peoples alike, and like Columbus others later divided the native peoples into "good" (Taínos) and "bad" (Caribs). Columbus made three more voyages to the west, exploring most of the major Caribbean islands and sailing along the coasts of Central and South America. Until the day he died in 1506 at the age of fifty-five, he believed he had reached Asia. Even before his death, others knew better. Because the Florentine Amerigo Vespucci, who explored the South American coast in 1499, was the first to publish that a new continent had been discovered, Martin Waldseemüller in 1507 labeled the land "America." By then, Spain, Portugal, and Pope Alexander VI had signed the Treaty of Tordesillas (1494), confirming Portugal's dominance in Africa—and later Brazil—in exchange for Spanish preeminence in the rest of the Americas.

Norse: Also known as Vikings, they were a warrior culture from Scandinavia.

Norse and Other Northern Voyagers

About the year 1001, a **Norse** expedition under Leif Ericsson had sailed to North America across the Davis Strait, which separated their Greenland villages from Baffin Island (located northeast of Hudson Bay; see Map 1.1) by just 200 nautical miles, settling at a site they named **"Vinland."** Attacks by residents forced them out after a few years. In the 1960s, archaeologists determined that the Norse had established an outpost at what is now L'Anse aux Meadows, Newfoundland, but Vinland itself was probably farther south.

Vinland: The site of the first known attempt at European settlement in the Americas.

Some historians argue that during the fifteenth century Basque whalers and fishermen (from modern northern France and Spain) located rich fishing grounds off Newfoundland but kept the information secret. Fifteenth-century seafarers voyaged regularly between the European continent, England, Ireland, and Iceland. The mariners who explored the region that would become the United States and Canada built on their knowledge.

John Cabot's Explorations

The European generally credited with "discovering" North America is Zuan Cabboto, known today as **John Cabot**. More precisely, Cabot brought to Europe the first formal knowledge of the northern continental coastline and claimed the land for England. Like Columbus, Cabot was a master mariner from the Italian city-state of Genoa; the two men probably knew each other. Calculating that England—which traded with Asia only through intermediaries—would be eager to sponsor exploratory voyages, he gained financial backing from King Henry VII. He sailed from

John Cabot: Italian explorer who established English claims to the New World

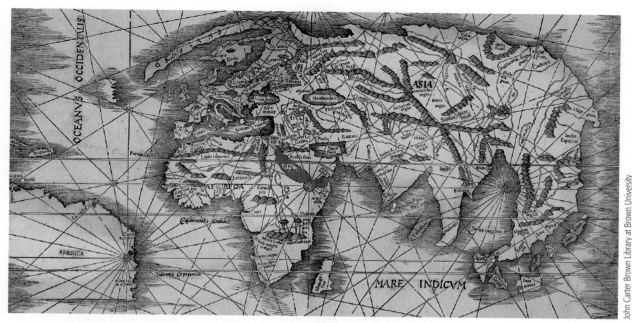

In 1507, German mapmaker Martin Waldseemüller was the first person to designate the newly discovered southern continent as "America." He named the continent after Amerigo Vespucci, the Italian explorer who realized he had reached a "new world" rather than islands off the coast of Asia.

Bristol in late May 1497, reaching North America a month later. After exploring the coast of modern Newfoundland, Cabot rode the Westerlies back to England, arriving in fifteen days.

The voyages of Columbus, Cabot, and their successors linked the Eastern and Western Hemispheres. The Portuguese explorer Pedro Álvares Cabral reached Brazil in 1500; John Cabot's son Sebastian arrived in North America in 1507; France financed Giovanni da Verrazzano in 1524 and Jacques Cartier in 1534; and in 1609 and 1610, Henry Hudson explored the North American coast for the Dutch West India Company (see Map 1.2). All were searching for the legendary, nonexistent "Northwest Passage" through the Americas, an easy route to the riches of Asia. But, foreshadowing the future, Verrazzano observed that "the [American] countryside is, in fact, full of promise and deserves to be developed for itself."

Spanish Exploration and Conquest

What model of colonization did Spain establish that other nations would later attempt to follow?

Only Spain began colonization immediately. On his second voyage in 1493, Columbus brought to Hispaniola seventeen ships loaded with twelve hundred men, seeds, plants, livestock, chickens, and dogs—along with microbes, rats, and weeds. The settlement named Isabela (in the modern Dominican Republic) and its successors became the staging area for the Spanish invasion of America.

Cortés and Other Explorers

At first, Spanish explorers fanned out around the Caribbean basin. In 1513, Juan Ponce de León reached Florida, and Vasco Núñez de Balboa crossed the Isthmus

conquistadors: Spanish conquerors or adventurers in the Americas.

of Panama to the Pacific Ocean, followed by Pánfilo de Narváez and others who traced the coast of the Gulf of Mexico. In the 1530s and 1540s, **conquistadors** explored other regions claimed by Spain: Francisco Vásquez de Coronado journeyed through the southwestern portion of what is now the United States while Hernán de Soto explored the Southeast. Francisco Pizarro, who ventured into western South America, acquired the world's richest silver mines by conquering the Incas. But the most important conquistador was Hernán Cortés, who in 1521 seized the Aztec Empire.

Cortés landed a force on the Mexican mainland in 1519 to search for rumored wealthy cities. Local Mayas presented him with young enslaved women. One of them, Malinche (whom the Spaniards baptized as a Christian and renamed Doña Marina), became Cortés's translator, bore Cortés a son, Martín—one of the first *mestizos,* or mixed-blood children—and eventually married one of his officers.

Capture of Tenochtitlán

Traveling toward the Aztec capital, Cortés, with Malinche's help, recruited peoples whom the Aztecs had long subjugated. The Spaniards' strange beasts (horses, livestock) and noisy weapons (guns, cannon) awed their new allies. Yet the Spaniards, too, were awed. Years later, Bernal Díaz del Castillo recalled his first sight of Tenochtitlán: "We were amazed…on account of the great towers and cues [temples] and buildings rising from the water, and all built of masonry." Spaniards also brought smallpox to Tenochtitlán. The disease peaked in 1520, fatally weakening Tenochtitlán's defenders. Largely as a consequence, Tenochtitlán surrendered in 1521, and the Spaniards built Mexico City on its site. Cortes and his men seized a treasure of gold and silver. Thus, the Spanish monarchs controlled the richest, most extensive empire Europe had known since ancient Rome.

Spanish Colonization

Spain established the model of colonization based on three major elements that other countries would later imitate. First, the Crown sought tight control over the colonies, imposing a hierarchical government that allowed little autonomy to American jurisdictions. That included carefully vetting and limiting prospective emigrants and insisting that the colonies import all manufactured goods from Spain. Roman Catholic priests attempted to ensure colonists' conformity with orthodox religious views.

Second, men constituted most of the first colonists. Although some Spanish women later immigrated to America, the men took primarily Indian—and, later, African—women as wives or concubines, a development often encouraged by colonial administrators. They thereby began the racially mixed population that characterizes much of Latin America today.

Third, the colonies' wealth was based on the exploitation of the native population and slaves from Africa. Spaniards took over the autocratic rule once assumed by native leaders, who exacted labor and tribute from their subjects. Cortés established the ***encomienda* system**, which granted Indian villages to conquistadors in return for services, thus legalizing slavery in all but name.

encomienda **system:** Grants by the Spanish which awarded Indian labor to wealthy colonists.

In 1542, after criticism from colonial priest Bartolomé de las Casas, the monarch formulated new laws forbidding the conquerors from enslaving Indians yet allowing them to collect money and goods from tributary villages. That, combined with the declining Indian population, led the *encomenderos* to import Africans as their controlled labor force. They employed Indians and Africans primarily in gold and silver mines; on sugar plantations; and on horse, cattle, and sheep ranches. African slavery was more common on the larger Caribbean islands than on the mainland.

Many demoralized residents of Mesoamerica accepted the Christian religion brought to New Spain by Franciscan and Dominican friars—men who had joined religious orders bound by vows of poverty and celibacy. Spaniards leveled cities, constructing cathedrals and monasteries on the former sites of Aztec, Incan, and Mayan temples. Indians were exposed to European customs and religious rituals designed to assimilate Catholic and pagan beliefs. Friars juxtaposed the cult of the Virgin Mary with that of the corn goddess, and Indians melded aspects of their worldview with Christianity in a process called *syncretism*. Thousands of Indians embraced Catholicism, partly because it was the religion of their new rulers.

Gold, Silver, and Spain's Decline

The New World's gold and silver, initially a boon, ultimately brought about the decline of Spain as a major power. China gobbled up about half of the total output of New World silver mines. In the 1570s, the Spanish dispatched silver-laden galleons annually from Acapulco (on Mexico's west coast) to trade at their new settlement at Manila, in the Philippines, which netted them easy access to luxury Chinese goods, such as silk and Asian spices.

Such unprecedented wealth led to rapid inflation, which caused Spanish products to be overpriced in international markets and imported goods to become cheaper in Spain. The Spanish textile-manufacturing industry collapsed, as did many other businesses. The seemingly endless income from American colonies emboldened Spanish monarchs to spend lavishly on wars against the Dutch and the English. Late sixteenth- and early seventeenth-century monarchs repudiated the state debt, wreaking havoc on the nation's finances. When the South American gold and silver mines faltered in the mid-seventeenth century, Spain's economy crumbled, ending its international importance.

The Columbian Exchange

A mutual transfer of diseases, plants, and animals (called the **Columbian Exchange** by historian Alfred Crosby; see Map 1.3) resulted from the fifteenth and sixteenth century European voyages and from Spanish colonization. Many large mammals, such as cattle and horses, were native to the connected continents of Europe, Asia, and Africa, but not the Americas. The Americas' vegetable crops—particularly maize, beans, squash, cassava, and potatoes—were more nutritious and produced higher yields than those of Europe and Africa. In time, native peoples learned to raise and consume European livestock, and Europeans and Africans planted and ate American crops. The diets of all three peoples were enriched, helping the world's population to double over the next three hundred years. About three-fifths of all crops cultivated worldwide today were first grown in the Americas.

> What were the results of contact between native populations and European settlers and explorers?

Columbian Exchange: The widespread exchange of animals, plants, germs, and peoples between Europe, Africa, and the Americas.

Smallpox and Other Diseases

Diseases carried from Europe and Africa, though, devastated the Americas. Indians fell victim to microbes that had long infested other continents, killing hundreds of thousands of Europeans but leaving survivors with some immunity. When Columbus landed on Hispaniola in 1492, approximately half a million people resided there. Fifty years later, there were fewer than two thousand native inhabitants.

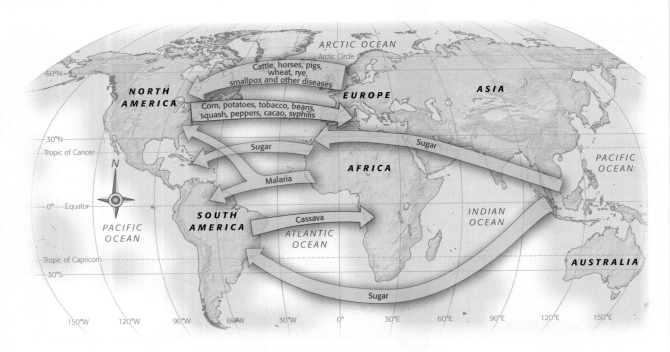

MAP 1.3
Major Items in the Columbian Exchange

As European adventurers traversed the world in the fifteenth and sixteenth centuries, they initiated the "Columbian Exchange" of plants, animals, and diseases. These events changed the lives of the peoples of the world forever, bringing new foods and new pestilence to both sides of the Atlantic.

Source: Copyright © Cengage Learning

Although measles, typhus, influenza, malaria, and other illnesses severely afflicted the native peoples, the greatest killer was smallpox. Historians estimate that over time, alien microorganisms could have reduced the precontact American population by as much as 90 percent. The epidemics recurred at twenty- to thirty-year intervals, appearing in tandem or in quick succession. Large numbers of deaths further strained native societies, rendering them more vulnerable to droughts, crop failures, or other challenges. A great epidemic, probably viral hepatitis, swept through coastal villages north of Cape Cod from 1616 to 1618, wiping out up to 90 percent of the inhabitants. Because of this dramatic depopulation, a few years later English colonists established settlements virtually unopposed.

The Americans, though, probably gave the Europeans syphilis, a virulent venereal disease. The first recorded European case occurred in Barcelona, Spain, in 1493, after Columbus's return from the Caribbean. Although less likely than smallpox to be fatal, syphilis was debilitating. Carried by soldiers, sailors, and prostitutes, it spread through Europe and Asia, reaching China by 1505.

Sugar, Horses, and Tobacco

The exchange of three commodities significantly altered Europe and the Americas. The European demand for sugar—a luxury foodstuff—led Columbus to take Canary Island sugar canes to Hispaniola in 1493. By the 1520s, Greater Antilles plantations worked by African slaves regularly shipped sugar to Spain. Half a century later,

Links to the World

Maize

Maize, to Mesoamericans, was a gift from Quetzalcoatl, the plumed serpent god. Cherokees told of an old woman whose blood produced the prized stalks after her grandson buried her body in a field. For the Abenakis, the crop began when a beautiful maiden ordered a youth to drag her by the hair through a burned-over field. The long hair turned into silk, the flower on corn stalks. Both tales' symbolic association of corn and women supports archaeologists' recent suggestion that—in eastern North America at least—female plant breeders were responsible for substantial improvements in the productivity of maize.

Sacred to the Indians who grew it, maize was a major dietary staple. They dried the kernels; ground into meal, maize was cooked as a mush or baked as flat cakes, the forerunners of modern tortillas. Although European invaders initially disdained maize, they soon learned it could be cultivated under many conditions—from sea level to twelve thousand feet, in abundant rainfall or in dry land. So Europeans, too, came to rely on corn, growing it in their American settlements and their homelands.

Maize cultivation spread to Asia and Africa. Today, China is second only to the United States in corn production, and corn is more widely grown in Africa than any other crop. Still, the United States produces 45 percent of the world's corn, and it is the nation's single largest crop.

More than half of American corn is consumed by livestock. Much of the rest is processed into syrup as a sweetener or into ethanol, a gasoline additive that reduces pollution and dependence on fossil fuels. Of the ten thousand products in a modern American grocery store, about one-fourth rely on corn. Today, this crop provides one-fifth of all the calories consumed by the earth's peoples. The gift of Quetzalcoatl has linked the globe.

The LuEsther T. Mertz Library, NYBG/Art Resource, NY

The earliest known European drawing of maize, the American plant that was to have such an extraordinary impact on the entire world.

Portugal's Brazil colony (founded 1532) produced sugar for the European market on a larger scale, and after 1640, sugar cultivation became the crucial component of English and French colonization in the Caribbean.

Through trade and theft, horses—which Columbus brought to America in 1493—spread among the peoples of the Great Plains by 1750. Lakotas, Comanches, and Crows, among others, used horses for transportation and hunting, calculated their wealth in number of horses owned, and waged war on horseback. After acquiring horses, their mode of subsistence shifted from hunting combined with gathering and agriculture, to almost entirely hunting buffalo.

In America, Europeans encountered tobacco, which at first they believed was medicinal. Smoking and chewing the "Indian weed" became a European fad after it was planted in Turkey in the sixteenth century. Despite the efforts of King James I of England, who in 1604 pronounced smoking "hatefull to the Nose, harmfull to the brain, [and] dangerous to the Lungs," tobacco's popularity climbed.

Europeans in North America

What were the reasons behind the failure of England's, Portugal's, and France's initial attempts at colonization?

Europeans were initially more interested in exploiting North America's natural resources than in establishing colonies. John Cabot reported that fish were plentiful near Newfoundland, so the French, Spanish, Basques, and Portuguese rushed to take advantage of abundant codfish. In the early 1570s, the English joined the Newfoundland fishery, selling salt cod to the Spanish in exchange for valuable Asian goods. The English became dominant in the region, which by century's end was the focal point of valuable European commerce.

Trade Among Indians and Europeans

Fishermen quickly realized they could increase profits by exchanging cloth and metal goods, such as pots and knives, for native trappers' beaver pelts, used to make fashionable hats in Europe. Initially, Europeans traded from ships along the coast, but later male adventurers set up outposts on the mainland.

Indians similarly desired European goods that could make their lives easier and establish their tribal superiority. Some bands concentrated completely on trapping for the European market and abandoned their traditional economies and became partially dependent on others for food. The intensive peltry trade also had serious ecological consequences. In some regions, beavers were wiped out. The disappearance of their dams led to soil erosion, which later increased when European settlers cleared forests for farmland.

Contest Between Spain and England

The English watched enviously as Spain was enriched by its American possessions. In the mid-sixteenth century, English "sea dogs" like John Hawkins and Sir Francis Drake raided Spanish treasure fleets from the Caribbean, helping to foment a war that in 1588 culminated in the defeat of the Spanish Armada off the English coast. English leaders started to consider planting colonies in the Western Hemisphere, thereby gaining better access to trade goods while preventing Spain from dominating the Americas.

Encouraging the queen and her courtiers in that aim was Richard Hakluyt, a clergyman who was fascinated by tales of exploratory voyages. He published English translations of numerous accounts of discoveries, insisting on England's preeminent claim to North America. In *Divers Voyages* (1582) and especially *Principall Navigations* (1589), he promoted the benefits of English colonization.

The first English colonial planners hoped to reproduce Spanish successes by dispatching to America men who would exploit the native peoples for their nation's benefit. A group that included Sir Walter Raleigh promoted a scheme to establish outposts for trade with the Indians and as bases for attacks on New Spain. Pleased, Queen Elizabeth I authorized Raleigh to colonize North America.

Roanoke

After two preliminary expeditions, in 1587 Raleigh sent 117 colonists to the territory he named Virginia, after Elizabeth, the "Virgin Queen." They established a settlement on Roanoke Island, in what is now North Carolina, but in 1590 a resupply ship found the colonists had vanished, leaving only the word *Croatoan* (the name of a nearby island) carved on a tree. Recent tree-ring studies have shown that the North Carolina coast experienced a severe drought between 1587 and 1589 that may have led colonists to abandon Roanoke.

Thus, England's first attempt to plant a permanent settlement on the North American coast failed, as had Portugal in Cape Breton Island (early 1520s), Spain in modern Georgia (mid-1520s), and France in South Carolina and northern Florida (1560s). All three enterprises collapsed because of the hostility of neighboring peoples and colonists' inability to be self-sustaining in foodstuffs.

Harriot's *Briefe and True Report*

Such failures are explained in Thomas Harriot's *A Briefe and True Report of the New Found Land of Virginia*, published in 1588. Harriot, a noted scientist sailing with the second voyage to Roanoke, revealed that, although the explorers depended on nearby villagers for food, they antagonized them by killing some of them for what Harriot admitted were unjustifiable reasons.

Harriot advised later colonizers to treat native peoples more humanely. But his book's description of America's economic potential illustrated why that advice would rarely be followed. Harriot stressed three points: the availability of familiar

A watercolor by John White, an artist with Raleigh's second preliminary expedition (and who later was governor of the ill-fated 1587 colony). He identified his subjects as the wife and daughter of the chief of Pomeioc, a village near Roanoke. Note the woman's elaborate tattoos and the fact that the daughter carries an Elizabethan doll, obviously given to her by one of the Englishmen.

Kennewick Man/ Ancient One

On July 28, 1996, Will Thomas, a college student wading in the Columbia River near Kennewick, Washington, felt a skull underfoot. Shocked, Thomas initially believed he had found a recent murder victim. Soon the skull was determined to be about 9200 years old. During the next decade, the skeleton dubbed "Kennewick Man" (by the press) or "Ancient One" (by local Indian tribes) was featured on television news and in magazines.

The oldest nearly complete skeleton found in the United States, the remains became the subject of a major federal court case. The issue was the interpretation of the Native American Graves Protection and Repatriation Act (NAGPRA), adopted by Congress in 1990 to prevent the desecration of Indian gravesites and to provide for the return of bones and sacred objects to native peoples. It defined the term *Native American* as "of, or relating to, a tribe, people, or culture that is indigenous to the United States." Led by the Umatillas, area tribes prepared to reclaim and rebury the remains. But eight anthropologists filed suit in federal court, contending that bones of such antiquity were unlikely to be linked to modern tribes and requesting access to them for scientific study.

Although the U.S. government supported the tribes' claims, in late August 2002 a federal judge ruled in favor of the anthropologists, a decision upheld on appeal two years later. He declared that the Interior Department had erred in concluding that all pre-1492 remains found in the United States should automatically be considered Native American. The Umatillas protested, contending that he clearly contradicted Congress's intent in enacting NAGPRA. In June 2006, Umatilla leaders visited the bones at a Seattle museum to honor and pray for them.

The debate over the skeleton reveals one facet of the continuing legacy of the often-contentious relationship between the nation's indigenous inhabitants and later immigrants.

Link to Harriot's text, illustrated by John White.

European commodities such as grapes, iron, copper, and fur-bearing animals; the potential profitability of exotic American products, such as maize and tobacco; and the relative ease of manipulating the native population. Harriot's *Briefe and True Report* depicted a bountiful land full of profitable opportunities. The people there would, he thought, "in a short time be brought to civilitie" through conversion to Christianity, admiration for European superiority, or conquest—if they did not die from disease. But European dominance of North America was never fully achieved as Harriot and others intended.

Summary

Initial contact among Europeans, Africans, and Americans that ended near the close of the sixteenth century, began approximately 250 years earlier when Portuguese sailors explored the Mediterranean Atlantic and the West African coast. Those seamen established commercial ties that brought African slaves first to Iberia and then to the islands Europeans conquered and settled. The Mediterranean Atlantic and its island sugar plantations nurtured the mariners. Except for the Spanish, early explorers regarded the Americas primarily as a barrier keeping them from an oceanic route to the riches of China and the Moluccas. European fishermen were the first to realize that the northern coasts had valuable products of fish and furs.

The Aztecs experienced hunger after Cortés's invasion, and their great temples were destroyed as Spaniards used their stones (and Indian laborers) to construct cathedrals. The conquerors employed, first Americans and later enslaved Africans to till the fields, mine the precious metals, and herd the livestock that generated immense profits.

The initial impact of Europeans on the Americas proved devastating in just decades. Europeans' diseases killed millions, and their livestock, along with other imported animals and plants, irrevocably modified the American environment. Europe, too, was changed: American foodstuffs like corn and potatoes improved nutrition, and American gold and silver first enriched, then ruined, the Spanish economy.

By the end of the sixteenth century, fewer people resided in North America than had lived there before Columbus's arrival. The Indians, Africans, and Europeans there inhabited a new world that combined foods, religions, economies, ways of life, and political systems that had developed separately for millennia. Understandably, conflict permeated that process.

Chapter Review

American Societies

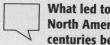

What led to the development of major North American civilizations in the centuries before Europeans arrived?

Agricultural success facilitated the rise of North American civilizations in the era before Europeans arrived. After the Ice Age ended and the prevalence of large mammals decreased, many native peoples in what is now central Mexico about 9000 years ago shifted from hunting to cultivating food crops for survival, including maize (corn), squash, beans, avocados, and peppers. As agricultural methods improved, vegetables became a reliable and nutritious food source, and native people established more permanent settlements. Early Americans began developing trade, accumulating wealth, creating elaborate cultural ceremonies and rituals, and building urban centers. But food supply was so keenly linked to a civilization's success that the first large city-states of Mesoamerica and Mississippian culture ultimately collapsed when food sources became scarce.

North America in 1492

What were the gender dimensions of labor in native cultures?

Like Europeans, Native American societies assigned various tasks and responsibilities to members along gender lines. Native societies that were predominantly hunting assigned women to making food and clothing and carrying the family's possessions whenever they moved. Agricultural peoples had different patterns of the gendered division of labor; some, like the Pueblos, defined farming as men's work, while others, like the Algonquian, Iroquoian, and Muskogean, gave women most agricultural chores, and men hunted and cleared the land. Women just about everywhere raised children, gathered wild foods, and prepared all of what people ate. Agricultural families were defined matrilineally, through the female line of descent, and women assumed more leadership roles than in nomadic hunter peoples. They rarely became chiefs, but older women chose chiefs and could start or stop wars.

African Societies

What were the chief characteristics of West African societies in the fifteenth century?

People in West Africa made their living fishing, cattle herding, or farming, depending on where they lived. Those in Upper Guinea fished and grew rice; those in Lower Guinea farmed. Upper Guinea was also the region's trade link to Europe and Asia. Islamic culture influenced life in Upper Guinea, while people in the lower region practiced more traditional religions. Like other cultures around the world, West Africans designated tasks according to gender, although their roles were seen as complementary. Both sexes farmed; men hunted and managed livestock and fished, while women cared for children, prepared the food, and managed trade networks. In Lower Guinea, male political and religious leaders ruled men, while women ruled women. Polygyny was common throughout West Africa. So was slavery. In West Africa, a person could be enslaved for committing a crime, to repay debts, or as an enemy's captive, but slave status did not automatically transfer to the next generation, and some slaves could engage in trade and keep some of the profits or rise to important military or political positions.

European Societies

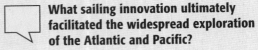

What were the motives behind fifteenth- and sixteenth-century European explorations?

The driving force behind early European explorations was the quest for a transoceanic trade route—the Northwest Passage—that would provide direct access to desirable African and Asian goods such as silks, dyes, jewels, sugar, gold, and spices. If such a route existed, it would allow northern Europeans to bypass the Muslim and Venetian merchants who served as middle men for these items. Rulers also believed that the more they controlled access to these much-desired products, the better their nation's standing would be relative to other countries. Another, secondary motivation was to spread Christianity and convert those they considered to be heathen peoples.

Early European Explorations

What sailing innovation ultimately facilitated the widespread exploration of the Atlantic and Pacific?

The new technique of "sailing around the wind" made travel faster and less arduous for explorers, which ultimately made them increasingly inclined to take on such expeditions. While sailors would travel with the wind in one direction, returning home had previously meant rowing against the wind or waiting for the wind to change on their journeys home, so return trips were difficult and took weeks longer. But sailing around the wind sped up the journey; when mariners met with a difficult wind, they would now literally sail around it until they could find a wind that would easily and quickly carry them on their way. Consequently, more and more mariners set out to explore the Atlantic and Pacific.

Voyages of Columbus, Cabot, and Their Successors

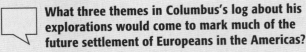

What three themes in Columbus's log about his explorations would come to mark much of the future settlement of Europeans in the Americas?

First, Columbus's log notes his quest for gold and other riches and his mixed attitudes toward the native peoples he encountered. Second, he wrote that the region's resources (plants, animals, and people) could be exploited to generate profits for his host country of Spain. In particular, he described the vast potential value of the dyes, spices, and medicines that could be made from plants found in the Americas. Third, Columbus wrote that the inhabitants could be easily converted to Catholicism and remade into servants. His and other explorers' discoveries inspired further exploration by European nations, though for most, colonization would lag for generations.

Spanish Exploration and Conquest

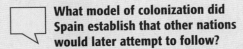

What model of colonization did Spain establish that other nations would later attempt to follow?

Spain developed a model of colonization in the Americas based on three key concepts. First, Spain's monarchy maintained firm control over its colonies with virtually no autonomy granted to American colonies. Second, men made up the majority of early colonists, taking first Indian, and later African, women as wives or concubines. Third, the development of the colonies and the exploitation of their resources was based on exploiting native people and African slaves as labor.

The Columbian Exchange

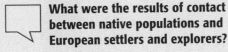

What were the results of contact between native populations and European settlers and explorers?

Native Americans and Europeans exchanged diseases, plants, and animals when they came into contact in North and South America in the fifteenth and sixteenth centuries. Native American vegetable crops were more nutritious than those in Europe and Africa, while Europeans brought livestock that helped enrich Indians' diets, too. The Spanish also brought horses to their American territories, which aided the shift in native society of the Great Plains from hunting combined with some farming and gathering, to almost exclusively hunting buffalo as their main form of subsistence. Europeans brought many diseases from typhus to malaria to hepatitis, all of which devastated tribal populations, but none as much as smallpox. Europeans, meanwhile, acquired syphilis from Native Americans, which was debilitating, but not usually fatal.

Europeans in North America

 What were the reasons behind the failure of England's, Portugal's, and France's initial attempts at colonization?

In a nutshell, all three failed because colonists were unable to be self-sustaining and at the same time, did little to diminish hostilities between them and native peoples. In fact, while many colonists relied on Indians for food, they also antagonized them by, as one British scientist wrote, unjustly killing some. Ironically, the solution this scientist, Thomas Harriot, proposed was on the one hand to treat native people with greater humanity, but on the other hand, to take advantage of the fact that they are easily manipulated toward whatever ends Europeans sought.

Suggestions for Further Reading

David Abulafia, *The Discovery of Mankind: Atlantic Encounters in the Age of Columbus* (2008)

Alfred W. Crosby, *The Columbian Exchange: Biological and Cultural Consequences of 1492* (1972)

John H. Elliott, *Empires of the Atlantic World: Britain and Spain in America, 1492–1830* (2006)

Alvin Josephy, Jr., ed., *America in 1492* (1992)

Peter C. Mancall, *Hakluyt's Promise: An Elizabethan's Obsession for an English America* (2007)

Charles C. Mann, 1491: *New Revelations of the Americas Before Columbus* (2005)

D. W. Meinig, *Atlantic America, 1492–1800* (1986)

Samuel Eliot Morison, *The European Discovery of America: The Southern Voyages*, A.D. 1492–1616 (1974); *The Northern Voyages*, A.D. 1500–1600 (1971)

John K. Thornton, *Africa and Africans in the Making of the Atlantic World, 1400–1680* (1992)

Europeans Colonize North America

1600–1650

2

Chapter Outline

Spanish, French, and Dutch North America
New Mexico | Quebec and Montreal | Jesuit Missions in New France | New Netherland

VISUALIZING THE PAST *Acoma Pueblo*

The Caribbean
Warfare and Hurricanes | Sugar Cultivation

English Interest in Colonization
Social and Economic Change | English Reformation | Puritans, Separatists, and Presbyterians | Stuart Monarchs

The Founding of Virginia
Jamestown and Tsenacommacah | Algonquian and English Cultural Differences | Tobacco Cultivation | Indian Assaults | End of Virginia Company

Life in the Chesapeake
Demand for Laborers | Conditions of Servitude | Standard of Living | Chesapeake Families | Chesapeake Politics

The Founding of New England
Contrasting Regional Demographic Patterns | Contrasting Regional Religious Patterns | Separatists | Pilgrims and Pokanokets | Massachusetts Bay Company | Governor John Winthrop | Covenant Ideal | New England Towns | Pequot War and Its Aftermath | Missionary Activities

LINKS TO THE WORLD *Turkeys*

Life in New England
New England Families | Impact of Religion | Roger Williams | Anne Hutchinson

LEGACY FOR A PEOPLE AND A NATION *Blue Laws*

SUMMARY

Captain William Rudyerd seemed like the sort of man Puritan colonists in the Americas would prize, so when his older brother urged the planners of the new settlement to appoint him muster master general, they agreed. Rudyerd followed the dissenting English faith, and as a soldier, he vigorously trained the settlers to defend themselves from attack. He also vigorously defended his status, wreaking havoc in the fragile community. He beat to death a servant suffering from scurvy (whom he mistook as lazy) and quarreled with settlers, whom he believed failed to show him the respect due to a gentleman of noble birth.

One of Rudyerd's antagonists was the Reverend Lewis Morgan, with whom the captain argued about religious books and church services. The disagreements escalated into insults. "Your foul mouthed answer deserves rather sharp retribution than any equal respect from a gentleman," the captain once haughtily told the clergyman.

Similar conflicts occurred throughout the Anglo-American settlements, as gentlemen accustomed to unquestioning deference learned that in the colonies, their social standing could be challenged. But Rudyerd and Morgan's disputes were especially dangerous because they lived on Providence Island, an isolated Puritan outpost off the coast of modern Nicaragua.

Providence Island, founded by Puritans in 1630—the same year as Massachusetts Bay—sought to establish an English beachhead in the tropics as an entrée to colonizing Central America. Yet its perilous location amid Spanish settlements, its failure to establish a local economy, and, ultimately, its desperate attempts to stay afloat financially by serving as a base for English privateers caused its downfall. That decision angered the Spaniards, who attacked in 1635 and 1640. In May 1641, a Spanish fleet of seven ships carrying two thousand soldiers and sailors captured the island. The survivors scattered to other Caribbean settlements, to English mainland colonies, or back to England.

Spain no longer predominated in the Americas. By the 1640s, France, the Netherlands, and England had colonies in

North America. Like Spanish outposts, French and Dutch colonies were settled largely by European men who interacted with indigenous peoples, using their labor or seeking to convert them to Christianity. As with conquistadors, French and Dutch merchants (on the mainland) and planters (in the Caribbean) hoped to make a quick profit and return home. The English were also interested in profiting from North America, but along different lines.

Unlike other Europeans, most English settlers came to stay. In the area that became New England, they arrived in family groups and re-created the European agricultural economy and family life to an extent impossible in colonies where single men predominated. English colonies in the Chesapeake and Caribbean islands were based on large-scale agricultural production, relying on servants and slaves for labor.

Setters prospered only after adapting to the environment, something the Providence Islanders never achieved. The first permanent English colonies survived because Indians helped them learn to grow such unfamiliar American crops as maize and squash. They also developed trading relationships with native peoples and other European colonies. Needing field laborers, they first used English indentured servants, then African slaves. Thus, the early history of what became the United States and the English Caribbean is best understood as a series of complex interactions among European, African, and American peoples and environments.

As you read this chapter, keep the following questions in mind:

* **Why did different groups of Europeans choose to migrate to the Americas?**

* **How did different native peoples react to their presence?**

* **In what ways did the English colonies in the Chesapeake and New England differ, and in what ways were they alike?**

Chronology

1558	Elizabeth I becomes queen
1565	Founding of St. Augustine (Florida), oldest permanent European settlement in present-day United States
1598	Oñate conquers Pueblos in New Mexico for Spain
1603	James I becomes king
1607	Jamestown founded, first permanent English settlement in North America
1608	Quebec founded by the French
1610	Founding of Santa Fe, New Mexico
1614	Fort Orange (Albany) founded by the Dutch
1619	Virginia House of Burgesses established, first representative assembly in the English colonies
1620	Plymouth colony founded, first permanent English settlement in New England
1622	Powhatan Confederacy attacks Virginia

1624	Dutch settle on Manhattan Island (New Amsterdam) English colonize St. Kitts, first island in Lesser Antilles settled by Europeans James I revokes Virginia Company's charter
1625	Charles I becomes king
1630	Massachusetts Bay colony founded
1634	Maryland founded
1636	Williams expelled from Massachusetts Bay, founds Providence, Rhode Island Connecticut founded
1637	Pequot War in New England
1638	Hutchinson expelled from Massachusetts Bay, goes to Rhode Island
1642	Montreal founded by the French
1646	Treaty ends hostilities between Virginia and Powhatan Confederacy

Spanish, French, and Dutch North America

How did the Jesuits' treatment of Native Americans differ from that of explorers and other settlers?

Spaniards established the first permanent European settlement within the modern United States, but others had tried previously. Twice in the 1560s, Huguenots (French Protestants) escaping persecution planted colonies on the south Atlantic coast. A passing ship rescued the starving survivors of the first, located in present-day South Carolina. The second, near modern Jacksonville, Florida, was destroyed in 1565 by a Spanish expedition commanded by Pedro Menéndez de Avilés, who sought Spanish domination of the strategically important region. Menéndez set up a small fortified outpost named St. Augustine—now the oldest continuously inhabited European settlement in the United States.

The local Guale and Timucua nations initially allied themselves with the powerful newcomers and welcomed Franciscan friars. The relationship ruptured quickly as natives resisted Spanish authority. Still, the Franciscans offered the Indians spiritual solace for the diseases and troubles besetting them after the Europeans' invasion. Eventually, they gained numerous converts across Florida and the islands along the Atlantic coast.

New Mexico

In 1598, roughly thirty years after the founding of St. Augustine, Juan de Oñate, a Mexican-born adventurer whose wife descended from Cortés and Moctezuma, led about five hundred soldiers and settlers to New Mexico seeking riches. The Pueblo peoples greeted them cordially. But when the Spaniards used torture, murder, and rape to extort food and clothing from the villagers, the residents of Acoma killed several soldiers, including Oñate's nephew. The invaders responded ferociously, killing more than eight hundred people and capturing the remainder. All the captives above age twelve were enslaved for twenty years, and men older than twenty-five had one foot amputated. Horrified, other Pueblo villages surrendered.

Oñate's bloody victory proved illusory. New Mexico held little wealth and was too far from the Pacific coast to help protect Spanish sea-lanes. Many Spaniards returned to Mexico, and officials considered abandoning the isolated colony, which lay 800 miles north of the nearest Spanish settlement. Instead, they maintained a small military outpost and a few Christian missions, with the capital at Santa Fe (founded 1610) (see Map 4.1). As in southern regions, Spanish leaders were granted *encomiendas* guaranteeing them control over Pueblo villagers' labor. But in the absence of mines or fertile agricultural lands, such grants yielded small profit.

Quebec and Montreal

On the Atlantic coast, the French focused on the area that Jacques Cartier had explored in the 1530s. They tried to establish permanent bases along the Canadian coast but failed until 1605, when they founded Port Royal. In 1608, Samuel de Champlain set up a trading post at an interior site that he renamed Quebec (the Iroquois called it Stadacona). It was the most defensible spot in the St. Lawrence River valley and controlled access to the continent's heartland. In 1642, the French established a second post, Montreal, at the falls of the St. Lawrence.

Prior to these settlements, fishermen were the major transporters of North American beaver pelts to France, but the new posts quickly took over (see Table 2.1). Only a few Europeans resided in New France; most were men; some married Indian women. The colony's leaders gave land grants along the river to wealthy seigneurs (nobles), who imported tenants to work their farms. A few Frenchmen brought their

Acoma Pueblo

Today, as in the late sixteenth century when it was besieged and eventually captured by the Spanish conquistador Juan de Oñate, the Acoma Pueblo sits high atop an isolated mesa. Long before the Spaniards arrived in modern New Mexico, the location was selected because it was easily defensible; some structures that date back to the eleventh century are still standing in the middle of the village. Building on a mesa 365 feet high was safer than living on the plains below, but it caused other problems—most notably, with the water supply. To this day there is no source of water in the village. Acoma's residents had to carry water up a steep set of stairs cut into the mesa's side (today there is an almost equally steep road). The women of Acoma were and are accomplished potters. Some pots, like the one shown here, were designed with a low center of gravity. How would that design help women to reach the top of the mesa with much needed water? How would they carry such pots?

© Kevin Fleming/CORBIS

Acoma Pueblo today. The village is now used primarily for ritual purposes; few people reside there permanently because all water must be trucked in.

Field Museum of Natural History FMNH Neg # A109998c

A pot designed for carrying water to the top of the mesa.

TABLE 2.1   The Founding of Permanent European Colonies in North America, 1565–1640

Colony	Founder(s)	Date	Basis of Economy
Florida	Pedro Menéndez de Avilés	1565	Farming
New Mexico	Juan de Oñate	1598	Livestock
Virginia	Virginia Co.	1607	Tobacco
New France	France	1608	Fur trading
New Netherland	Dutch West India Co.	1614	Fur trading
Plymouth	Separatists	1620	Farming, fishing
Maine	Sir Ferdinando Gorges	1622	Fishing
St. Kitts, Barbados, et al.	European immigrants	1624	Sugar
Massachusetts Bay	Massachusetts Bay Co.	1630	Farming, fishing, fur trading
Maryland	Cecilius Calvert	1634	Tobacco
Rhode Island	Roger Williams	1636	Farming
Connecticut	Thomas Hooker	1636	Farming, fur trading
New Haven	Massachusetts migrants	1638	Farming
New Hampshire	Massachusetts migrants	1638	Farming, fishing

wives and took up agriculture; still, twenty-five years after Quebec's founding, there were just sixty-four resident families, along with traders and soldiers. Northern New France never grew much beyond the river valley between Quebec and Montreal (see Map 2.1). Thus, it differed from New Spain, characterized by scattered cities and direct supervision of Indian laborers.

Jesuit Missions in New France

French missionaries of the Society of Jesus (Jesuits), a Roman Catholic order dedicated to converting nonbelievers to Christianity, first arrived in Quebec in 1625. The Jesuits, whom the Indians called Black Robes, tried to persuade indigenous peoples to live near French settlements and adopt European agricultural methods. Failing that, they tried to introduce Catholicism without insisting that Indians fundamentally alter their traditions. The Black Robes learned Indian languages and traveled to remote regions, where they lived among hundreds of potential converts.

Link to excerpts about Indian and Jesuit relations.

Jesuits sought to gain the confidence of influential men and to undermine the authority of village shamans, the traditional religious leaders. Immune to smallpox (having survived it already), they explained epidemics as God's punishment for sin. It helped that shamans' traditional remedies proved ineffective against the new pestilence. Jesuits predicted eclipses and amazed the villagers by communicating with each other over long distances through marks on paper (letters). The Indians' desire to harness the power of literacy made them receptive to the missionaries' spiritual message.

Over time, the Jesuits gained thousands of converts. Catholicism offered women the inspiring role model of the Virgin Mary, personified in Montreal and Quebec by communities of nuns who taught and ministered to Indian women and children. Many converts altered native customs allowing premarital sexual relationships

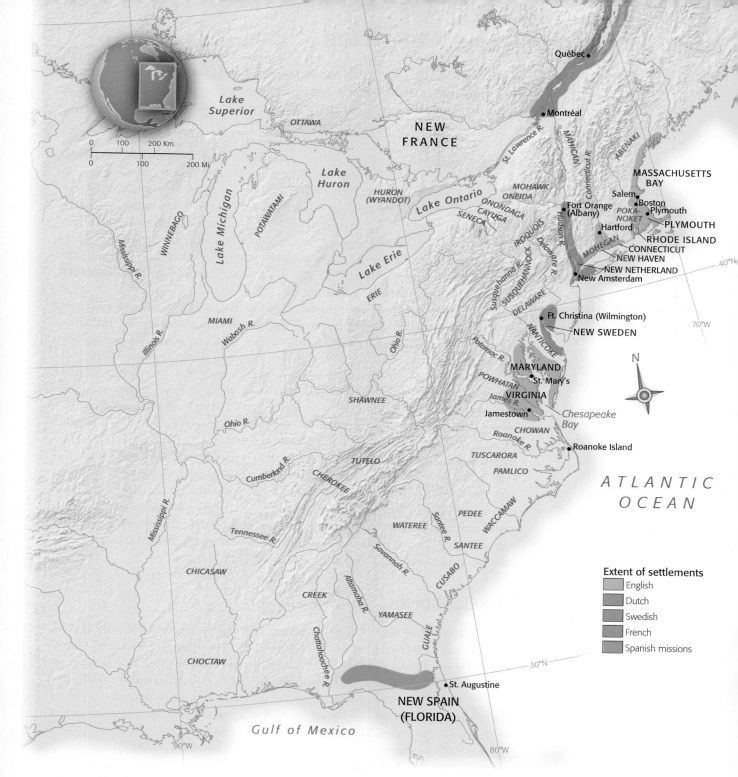

MAP 2.1

European Settlements and Indian Tribes in Eastern North America, 1650

The few European settlements established in the East before 1650 were widely scattered, hugging the shores of the Atlantic Ocean and the banks of its major rivers. By contrast, America's native inhabitants controlled the vast interior expanse of the continent, and Spaniards had begun to move into the West.

Source: Copyright © Cengage Learning

and easy divorce because Catholic doctrine prohibited both. Yet they resisted strict European child-rearing methods. Jesuits recognized that aspects of native culture could be compatible with Christianity. Their conversion efforts were further aided by their lack of interest in labor tribute or land.

New Netherland

Jesuit missionaries faced little competition from other Europeans, but not so for French fur traders. In 1614, five years after Henry Hudson explored the river that now bears his name, his sponsor, the Dutch West India Company, established an outpost (Fort Orange) at present-day Albany, New York. The Dutch sought beaver pelts, and their presence so close to Quebec threatened French regional domination. The Netherlands, at the time the world's dominant commercial power, sought trade rather than colonization. Thus, **New Netherland** remained small. The colony's southern anchor was **New Amsterdam**, founded in 1624 on Manhattan Island.

New Netherland: Dutch colony in America.

New Amsterdam: Dutch colony that would become New York.

New Netherland was a small outpost of the Dutch West India Company's vast commercial empire extending to Africa, Brazil, the Caribbean, and modern-day Indonesia. Autocratic directors-general ruled the colony. Few migrants arrived despite an offer in 1629 of large land grants, or patroonships, to anyone bringing fifty settlers to the province. (Only one such tract—Rensselaerswyck, near Albany—was ever developed.) As late as the mid-1660s, New Netherland had only about five thousand inhabitants. Some were Swedes and Finns in the former colony of New Sweden (founded in 1638 on the Delaware River; see Map 2.1), which the Dutch seized in 1655.

Indian allies of New France and New Netherland clashed partly because of fur-trade rivalries. In the 1640s, the Iroquois, who traded chiefly with the Dutch and lived in modern upstate New York, warred with the Hurons, who traded primarily with the French and lived in present-day Ontario. The Iroquois wanted to become the major peltry supplier to Europeans and protect their hunting territories. With guns from the Dutch, they virtually exterminated the Hurons, whose population was already decimated by a smallpox epidemic. The Iroquois thus established themselves as a major force in the region.

The Caribbean

In the first half of the seventeenth century, the Spanish concentrated on colonizating the Greater Antilles—Cuba, Hispaniola, Jamaica, and Puerto Rico. They ignored smaller islands, partly because of resistance by their Carib inhabitants, partly because the mainland offered greater wealth for less effort. But the tiny islands attracted other European powers as bases from which to attack Spanish vessels loaded with American gold and silver and as sources of valuable tropical products such as dyes and fruits.

What made the Caribbean islands initially desirable for colonization?

Warfare and Hurricanes

England was the first northern European nation to establish a permanent foothold in the smaller Caribbean islands (the Lesser Antilles), settling on St. Christopher (St. Kitts) in 1624, then other islands, such as Barbados (1627) and Providence (1630). France colonized Guadeloupe and Martinique by defeating the Caribs, whereas the Dutch easily gained control of St. Eustatius (strategically located near St. Christopher). Along with indigenous inhabitants, Europeans worried about conflicts with Spaniards and each other. Like Providence Island, many colonies changed hands during the seventeenth century. For example, the English drove the Spanish out of Jamaica in 1655, and the French soon assumed half of Hispaniola, creating St. Domingue (modern Haiti).

Great windstorms called *hurakán* by the Taíno (hurricanes in English) also posed a threat. Almost annually in late summer, one or two islands suffered significant hurricane damage. Survivors expressed awe at the destructive storms, which repeatedly forced them to rebuild and replant.

Sugar Cultivation

Sugar was the primary reason Europeans wanted these imperiled islands. Europeans loved sugar with its sweet taste and quick energy boost. Sugar entered Europe at approximately the same time as coffee and tea—the stimulating, addictive, and bitter Asian drinks improved by sweetening.

After experimenting with tobacco, cotton, and indigo, English residents of Barbados discovered in the 1640s that the island's soil and climate were ideal for sugar cane. At the time, sugar came primarily from the Madeiras, the Canaries, São Tomé, and Brazil. Barbadians initially copied the Brazilians' machinery and small-scale production methods, which used servants and slaves. By the mid-1650s, substantial planters increased the size of their landholdings, built sugar mills, and purchased more laborers—first English and Irish servants, then African slaves.

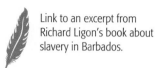

Link to an excerpt from Richard Ligon's book about slavery in Barbados.

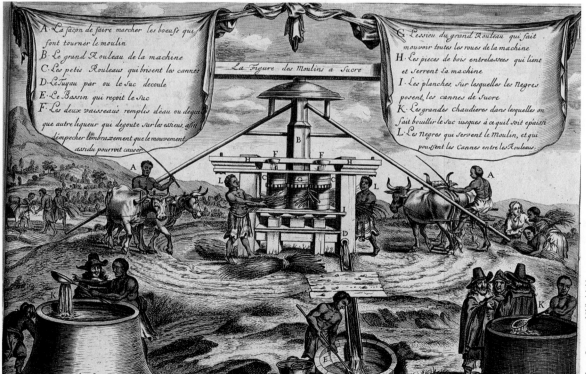

In the 1660s, a French book illustrated the various phases of sugar processing for curious European readers. Teams of oxen (A) turned the mill, the rollers of which crushed the canes (C), producing the sap (D), which was collected in a vat (E), then boiled down into molasses (K). African slaves, with minimal supervision by a few Europeans (foreground), managed all phases of the process.

Sugar remained the most valuable American commodity for more than a century. In the 1700s, sugar grown by slaves in British Jamaica and French St. Domingue dominated the world market. Yet the future economic importance of the Europeans' American colonies lay on the mainland.

English Interest in Colonization

After Raleigh's Roanoke colony failed, two decades passed before the English attempted to settle North America again. When they tried in 1606, they were successful using a model unlike those of other European powers. England sent large numbers of men and women to establish agriculturally based colonies on the mainland. Two major developments prompted approximately 200,000 English people to move to North America in the seventeenth century.

What two developments prompted England to consider North American colonization in the early seventeenth century?

Social and Economic Change

The first was dramatic social and economic change. In the 150 years after 1530, largely due to importation of nutritious American crops, England's population doubled. More people competed for food, clothing, and other goods; this led to inflation. Wages also fell as the number of workers increased. Some English people—especially those with sizable landholdings that could produce food and clothing fibers for the growing population—substantially profited. Others, particularly landless laborers and those with small landholdings, fell into poverty. When landowners raised rents, seized lands that peasants had long used in common (enclosure), or combined small holdings into large units, they forced tenants out. Consequently, the population of the cities swelled. London more than tripled in size to 375,000 by 1650.

Homeless people filled the streets. Fearing overcrowding, officials concluded that colonies established in North America could siphon off England's "surplus population." Similarly, many English people hoped they could improve their circumstances by migrating to a land-rich, apparently empty continent and its islands. Emigration proved attractive to younger sons of gentlemen as William Rudyerd, who were excluded from inheriting land by wealthy families' practice of primogeniture, which reserved all real estate for the eldest son.

English Reformation

The sixteenth century also witnessed a religious transformation that eventually led many English dissenters to leave. In 1533, Henry VIII, wanting a male heir and infatuated with Anne Boleyn, asked the pope to annul his twenty-year marriage to Spanish-born queen Catherine of Aragón, despite the birth of a daughter. When the pope refused, Henry founded the Church of England and—with Parliament's concurrence—proclaimed himself its head. Initially, the reformed Church of England differed little from Catholicism. Under Henry's daughter Elizabeth I (child of his later marriage to Anne Boleyn), though, new currents of religious belief dramatically affected the established church, so termed because it had the official imprimatur of the government and was supported by tax revenues.

These currents constituted the **Protestant Reformation**, led by Martin Luther, a German monk, and **John Calvin**, a French cleric and lawyer. Challenging the Catholic doctrine that priests were intermediaries between laypeople and God, Luther and Calvin insisted that people could interpret the Bible for themselves. Both rejected Catholic rituals and the elaborate church hierarchy. They also asserted that the key to

Protestant Reformation: Split of reformers from Roman Catholic church; triggered by Martin Luther.

John Calvin: Early Protestant theologian who believed in "predestination."

salvation was faith in God, rather than the Catholic combination of faith and good works. Calvin went further, stressing the need for total submission to God's will.

Puritans, Separatists, and Presbyterians

Elizabeth I tolerated diverse forms of Christianity as long as she was acknowledged as head of the Church of England. During her long reign (1558–1603), Calvin's ideas gained influence in England, Wales, and especially Scotland. (In Ireland, also part of her realm, Catholicism remained dominant.) The Scottish church eventually adopted Presbyterianism, which eliminated bishops and placed religious authority in clerics and laymen called presbyteries. By the late sixteenth century, though, many Calvinists—including those who came to be called Puritans, because they wanted to purify the church, or Separatists, because they wanted to leave it—believed that English and Scottish reformers had not gone far enough. Henry had simplified the church hierarchy and the Scots had altered it; they wanted to abolish it. Henry and the Scots had subordinated the church to the state; they wanted a church free from political interference. The established churches of England and Scotland, like similar entities throughout Europe, continued to nominally encompass all residents of the realm. Calvinists in England and Scotland wanted to confine church membership to the "saved"—those they believed God had selected for salvation before birth.

Paradoxically, a key article of their faith insisted that people could not know if they were "saved" because mortals could not comprehend or affect their predestination to heaven or hell. Thus, pious Calvinists daily confronted serious dilemmas: If one was predestined and could not alter one's fate, why attend church or do good works? Calvinists admitted that their judgments as to eligibility for church membership only approximated God's unknowable decisions. And they reasoned that God gave the elect the ability to accept salvation and lead a good life. Therefore, piety and good works could indicate one as saved.

Stuart Monarchs

Elizabeth I's Stuart successors—her cousin James I (1603–1625) and his son Charles I (1625–1649)—exhibited less tolerance for Calvinists. As Scots, they also had little respect for the representative government that developed in England under the Tudors and (see Table 2.2). The wealthy landowners in Parliament had grown accustomed to having considerable influence on government policies. But James I publicly declared the divine right of kings, the notion that a monarch's power came from God and that his subjects had a duty to obey him.

TABLE 2.2   Tudor and Stuart Monarchs of England, 1509–1649

Monarch	Reign	Relation to Predecessor
Henry VIII	1509–1547	Son
Edward VI	1547–1553	Son
Mary I	1553–1558	Half-sister
Elizabeth I	1558–1603	Half-sister
James I	1603–1625	Cousin
Charles I	1625–1649	Son

Both James I and Charles I wanted to enforce religious conformity. Because Calvinists—and remaining Catholics in England and Scotland—challenged many important precepts of the established churches, the Stuart monarchs authorized the removal of dissenting clergymen. In the 1620s and 1630s, some Puritans, Separatists, Presbyterians, and Catholics decided to move to America, where they hoped to practice their beliefs freely. Some fled to avoid arrest and imprisonment.

The Founding of Virginia

How did English cultural traditions clash with those of Native Americans in Virginia?

joint-stock companies: Business corporations that amassed capital through sales of stock to investors.

Jamestown: First successful English colony, established in 1607.

The impetus for England's first permanent colony in the Western Hemisphere was religious and economic. The newly militant English Protestants wanted to combat "popery" at home and in the Americas. Accordingly, in 1606 a group of merchants and wealthy gentry, some of them aligned with religious reformers, obtained a royal charter for the Virginia Company as a **joint-stock company**. Such forerunners of modern corporations pooled the resources of many small investors through stock sales. Yet colonies required ongoing capital investments. The lack of immediate returns thus generated tension between stockholders and colonists. Although Virginia Company investors anticipated great profits, neither the Maine nor **Jamestown** settlement earned much.

Jamestown and Tsenacommacah

In 1607, the Virginia Company dispatched 104 men and boys to a region near Chesapeake Bay called Tsenacommacah by its native inhabitants. In May, they established a settlement called Jamestown on a swampy peninsula in a river. Ill-equipped for survival, the colonists fell victim to dissension and disease. The gentlemen and soldiers at Jamestown expected to rely on local Indians for food and tribute, but they refused. Moreover, the settlers arrived in the midst of a severe drought (now known to be the worst for 1,700 years), which persisted until 1612.

The weroance (chief) of Tsenacommacah, Powhatan, had inherited rule over six Algonquian villages and later controlled twenty-five others (see Map 2.1). In late 1607 negotiations with colonial leader Captain **John Smith**, the weroance tentatively agreed to an alliance with the Englishmen. In exchange for foodstuffs, Powhatan wanted guns, hatchets, and swords, which would give him a technological advantage over his people's enemies.

John Smith: Colonial leader of Jamestown who established order, good relations with Indians.

Link to John Rolfe's letter explaining why he wants to marry Pocahontas.

The fragile relationship soon foundered on mutual mistrust. The weroance relocated his primary village in early 1609 to a place the newcomers could not access easily. Without Powhatan's assistance, the settlement experienced a "starving time" (winter 1609–1610). Many died and at least one colonist resorted to cannibalism. In spring 1610, the survivors left on a newly arrived ship but en route encountered a new governor, more settlers, and supplies, so they returned to Jamestown. To gain the upper hand with Indians, settlers in 1613 kidnapped Powhatan's daughter, Pocahontas. In captivity, she converted to Christianity and married colonist John Rolfe. He had fallen in love, but she probably married him for diplomatic reasons; their union initiated peace between the English and Powhatans. Funded by the Virginia Company, she and Rolfe sailed to England to promote the colony. She died at Gravesend in 1616, leaving an infant son who returned to Virginia as a young adult.

Algonquian and English Cultural Differences In Tsenacommacah and elsewhere on the North American coast, English settlers and local Algonquians focused on their cultural differences, although both groups held deep religious beliefs, subsisted primarily through agriculture, accepted social and political hierarchy, and observed well-defined gender roles. English men regarded Indian men as lazy because they did not cultivate crops and spent their time hunting (a sport, not work, in English eyes). Indian men thought English men effeminate because they did the "woman's work" of cultivation.

Among Algonquians like the Powhatans, political power and social status did not necessarily pass through the male line, instead flowing through sisters' sons. English gentlemen inherited their position from their father. English political and military leaders ruled autocratically, whereas Algonquian leaders (even Powhatan) had limited authority over their people. Accustomed to the powerful kings, the English overestimated the chief's ability to make treaties that would bind their people.

Furthermore, Algonquian and English concepts of property differed. Most Algonquian villages held their land communally. Land could not be bought or sold absolutely, although certain rights to use it (for example, for hunting or fishing) could be transferred. Once, English villagers, too, had used land in common, but in the previous century had become accustomed to individual farms. The English also refused to accept Indians' claims to traditional hunting territories, insisting that only cultivated land could be owned or occupied. Ownership of such "unclaimed" property, the English believed, lay with the English monarchy, in whose name **John Cabot** had claimed North America in 1497.

The English believed in the superiority of their civilization. Although they often anticipated living peacefully alongside indigenous peoples, they expected native peoples to adopt English customs and convert to Christianity. They showed little respect for the Indians when English interests were at stake, as was demonstrated in Virginia once the settlers found a salable commodity.

John Cabot: Italian explorer who established English claims to North America.

Tobacco Cultivation

That commodity was tobacco. In 1611, John Rolfe planted seeds of a variety from the Spanish Caribbean, which was superior to the strain Indians grew. Nine years later, Virginians exported 40,000 pounds of cured leaves, and by the late 1620s shipments jumped to 1.5 million pounds. The great tobacco boom had begun, fueled by high prices and profits. The price later fell sharply and fluctuated annually depending on supply and international competition.

Tobacco cultivation made Virginia prosper and altered life for everyone. It required abundant land, because a field could produce only three satisfactory crops before it had to lie fallow for several years to regain its fertility. Thus, applicants asked the Virginia Company for land grants on both sides of the James River. Virginians established farms far from apart along the riverbanks—which was convenient for tobacco cultivation but dangerous for defense.

Indian Assaults

Opechancanough, Powhatan's brother and successor, watched the English colonists' expansion and attempts to convert natives to Christianity. Recognizing the danger, he attacked along the James River on March 22, 1622. By day's end, 347 colonists (about one-quarter) lay dead. Only a warning from two Christian converts saved Jamestown from destruction.

Reinforced by shipments of men and arms from England, the settlers repeatedly attacked Opechancanough's villages. A peace treaty was signed in 1632, but in April 1644 the elderly Opechancanough assaulted the invaders one last time; then, in 1646, survivors formally subordinated themselves to England.

End of Virginia Company

The 1622 assault killed the Virginia Company, which remained unprofitable due to internal corruption and the heavy cost of settlement. Before its demise, the company developed two precedent-setting policies. First, to attract settlers, in 1617 it established the "headright" system, giving each arrival who paid his or her own way a land grant of 50 acres; those who financed the passage of others received similar headrights. To English farmers who owned little or no land, the headright system offered a powerful incentive to move to Virginia. To wealthy gentry, it promised the possibility of vast agricultural enterprises. Two years later, the company authorized landowning men of major Virginia settlements to elect representatives to an assembly called the **House of Burgesses**. Just as they had at home, English landholders expected to elect members of Parliament and control local governments.

House of Burgesses: First elected representative legislature in North America that first met in 1619.

When James I revoked the charter in 1624, transforming Virginia into a royal colony, he continued the company's headright policy but abolished the assembly. Virginians protested, and by 1629 the House of Burgesses was functioning again. Two decades after the first permanent English settlement in North America, the colonists successfully insisted on governing themselves. Thus, England's American possessions differed from the autocratic rule in the Spanish, Dutch, and French colonies.

Life in the Chesapeake

What were the myths and realities of indentured servitude in the Chesapeake?

By the 1630s, tobacco was the chief source of revenue in Virginia and in the second English Chesapeake colony: Maryland. Given by Charles I to George Calvert, first Lord Baltimore, as a personal possession (proprietorship), it was settled in 1634. (Virginia and Maryland border Chesapeake Bay—see Map 2.1—and are referred to collectively as "the Chesapeake.") The Calvert family intended the colony as a haven for persecuted fellow Catholics. Cecilius Calvert, second Lord Baltimore, became the first colonizer to offer freedom of religion to all Christian settlers codified in Maryland's Act of Religious Toleration (1649).

Except for religion, the two Chesapeake colonies were similar. Tobacco planters spread out along riverbanks because rivers offered dependable transportation and established isolated farms instead of towns. Each farm or group of farms had its own wharf, where oceangoing vessels could load or discharge cargo.

Demand for Laborers

Planting, cultivation, harvesting, and curing tobacco were repetitious, time-consuming, and labor-intensive tasks. Successful Chesapeake farms required workers, but with their populations reduced by war and disease, Indians could not supply such needs. Nor were enslaved Africans available: traders could more easily and profitably sell slaves to Caribbean sugar planters. By 1650, only three hundred blacks lived in Virginia.

Chesapeake tobacco farmers thus looked primarily to England for labor. Because of the headright system, a tobacco farmer could obtain land and labor by importing Enlish workers. He could use his profits to pay for the passage of more workers and thereby gain more land. Success could even bring him into the region's new planter gentry.

Male laborers and a few women immigrated to America as **indentured servants**— that is, in return for their passage they contracted to work from four to seven years. Indentured servants accounted for 75 to 85 percent of the approximately 130,000 English immigrants to Virginia and Maryland during the seventeenth century. The rest were young couples with one or two children.

Roughly three-quarters of servants were males ages fifteen to twenty-four; only one in five or six was female. Most young men came from farming or laboring families, often from regions experiencing severe social disruption. Some had moved several times within England before relocating to America. Typically, they came from the middling ranks—what contemporaries called the "common sort."

indentured servants: Young men and women, usually unemployed and poor, who were given free passage to America, plus basic needs such as food, shelter, and clothing, in exchange for labor, usually for four to seven years.

Conditions of Servitude

Servants who fulfilled their indenture earned "freedom dues" of clothes, tools, livestock, corn, tobacco, and sometimes land. From a distance at least, America seemed to offer chances for advancement unavailable in England. Yet servants typically worked six days a week, ten to fourteen hours a day, in sweltering climates. Masters could discipline or sell them, and they faced severe penalties for running away. Laws required masters to supply servants with sufficient food, clothing, and shelter and prohibited beating them excessively. Cruelly treated servants could seek court assistance, sometimes winning verdicts directing their transfer to more humane masters or release from indenture.

All Chesapeake residents first had to survive "seasoning," a bout with disease (probably malaria) that usually occurred during their first Chesapeake summer. They often endured recurrences of malaria, along with dysentery, typhoid fever, and other illnesses. About 40 percent of male servants did not survive to become freedmen. Even men of twenty-two who weathered seasoning could expect to live only another twenty years.

For those who survived, though, opportunities were real. Until the late seventeenth century, former servants often became independent farmers ("freeholders"). But in the 1670s, tobacco prices entered a fifty-year period of stagnation and decline, while land grew scarce and expensive. In 1681, Maryland dropped its requirement that servants receive land with their freedom dues, forcing many freed servants to live as wage laborers or tenant farmers. By 1700, the Chesapeake was no longer a land of opportunity.

Standard of Living

Life in the early Chesapeake was hard. Farmers (and sometimes their wives) toiled in the fields alongside servants. Because hogs needed little tending, Chesapeake households subsisted mainly on pork and corn, a filling diet but not sufficiently nutritious. Families supplemented with fish, shellfish, wildfowl, and vegetables they grew such as lettuce and peas. The difficulty of preserving food for winter consumption magnified the health problems caused by epidemic disease.

Few households had more than farm implements, bedding, and basic cooking and eating utensils. Chairs, tables, candles, and knives and forks were luxury items. The ramshackle houses commonly had just one or two rooms. Colonists devoted their income to their farms, purchasing livestock and laborers instead of improving their standard of living. Rather than making clothing or tools, families imported them from England.

Chesapeake Families   The predominance of males (see Figure 2.1), the incidence of servitude, and the high mortality rates produced unusual patterns of family life. Female servants could not marry while indentured because masters feared pregnancies would deprive them of workers. Many male ex-servants could not marry at all because of the scarcity of women. In contrast, nearly every free Chesapeake woman married, and widows usually remarried within months of a husband's death. Because of high infant mortality and marriages delayed by servitude or broken by death, Chesapeake women commonly reared only one to three healthy children, where English women had at least five.

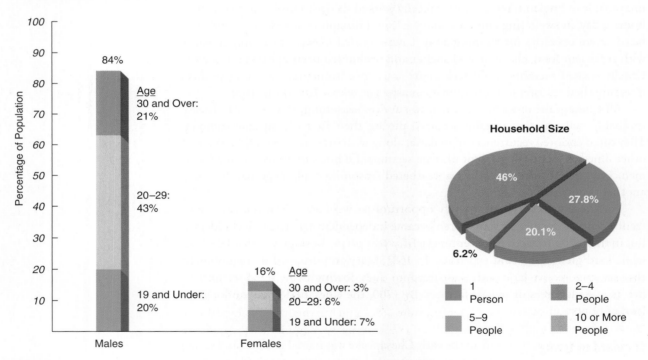

Age and Sex Composition

Household Size

FIGURE 2.1
Population of Virginia, 1625

The only detailed census taken in the English mainland North American colonies during the seventeenth century was prepared in Virginia in 1625. It listed a total of 1,218 people, constituting 309 "households" and living in 278 dwellings—so some houses contained more than one family. The chart shows, on the left, the proportionate age and gender distribution of the 765 individuals for whom full information was recorded, and, on the right, the percentage variation in the sizes of the 309 households. The approximately 42 percent of the residents of the colony who were servants were concentrated in 30 percent of the households. Nearly 70 percent of the households had no servants at all.

Source of data: Robert S. Wells, *The Population of the British Colonies in America Before 1776*. © 1975 Princeton University Press, 2003 renewed PUP. Reprinted by permission of Princeton University Press.

Thus, Chesapeake families were few, small, and short-lived. In one Virginia county, more than three-quarters of the children had lost at least one parent by age twenty-one. Children were put to work as soon as possible on the farms of parents, stepparents, or guardians. Their schooling, if any, was haphazard; whether Chesapeake-born children learned to read or write depended on whether their parents were literate and taught them.

Chesapeake Politics   Throughout the seventeenth century, immigrants composed a majority of the Chesapeake population. Most members of Virginia's House of Burgesses and Maryland's House of Delegates (established in 1635) were immigrants; they also dominated the governor's council, which simultaneously served as the highest court, part of the legislature, and executive adviser to the governor. A cohesive, native-born ruling elite emerged only in the early eighteenth century.

In seventeenth-century Chesapeake, most property-owning white males could vote and chose as their legislators (burgesses) local elites who seemed to be the natural leaders. But because most such men were immigrants lacking strong ties to one another or to the colonies, the assemblies did not create political stability and were contentious.

The Founding of New England

Economic and religious motives drew people to New England. Environmental factors and the Puritans' organization of the New England colonies meant that northern settlements developed very differently from their southern counterparts.

> What were John Winthrop's expectations for the Massachusetts Bay Company colony?

Contrasting Regional Demographic Patterns   Royal bureaucrats in late 1634 ordered port officials in London to collect information on travelers departing for the colonies. The records for 1635 document the departure of 53 vessels—20 to Virginia, 17 to New England, 8 to Barbados, 5 to St. Christopher, 2 to Bermuda, and 1 to Providence Island. Almost 5,000 people set sail, 2,000 for Virginia, about 1,200 for New England, and the rest for island destinations. Nearly three-fifths were between the ages of 15 and 24.

But among those bound for New England, such youths constituted less than one-third of the total; nearly 40 percent were older, and another third were younger. Whereas women made up 14 percent of those going to Virginia, they composed almost 40 percent of New England-bound passengers. New England migrants often traveled in family groups, brought more goods and livestock, and traveled with people from the same region. Their lives in North America must have been less lonely than their southern counterparts.

Contrasting Regional Religious Patterns   Puritan congregations became key institutions in colonial New England, whereas no church had much impact on the early development of the Chesapeake colonies. Spread-out Chesapeake settlement patterns made it difficult to organize a church. Catholic and Anglican bishops in England ignored their coreligionists in America, and Chesapeake congregations languished. Not until the 1690s did the Church of England take firmer root in Virginia; by then, it also replaced Catholicism as the Maryland's established church, and Calvinists were in the minority in both colonies.

In New England and the Chesapeake, religion affected the lives of pious Calvinists, who were expected to reassess the state of their souls regularly. Many devoted themselves to self-examination and Bible study, and families prayed together daily. Yet because even the most pious could never be certain that they were among the elect, anxiety troubled them. It lent an intensity to Calvinists' beliefs and concern with proper behavior—theirs and others'.

Separatists

Separatists who thought the Church of England too corrupt to be salvaged became the first religious dissenters to move to New England. In 1609, a Separatist congregation relocated to Leiden, in the Netherlands, where they found religious freedom—and tolerance for religions and behaviors they abhorred. Hoping to isolate their children from corrupting influences, these people, known today as Pilgrims, received permission from the Virginia Company to colonize its northern territory.

In September 1620, more than one hundred people, only thirty of them Separatists, sailed from England on the crowded *Mayflower*. In November, they landed on Cape Cod, farther north than intended. They moved across Massachusetts Bay to a fine harbor (named **Plymouth** by John Smith in 1614) and into the empty dwellings of a Pautuxet village whose inhabitants had died in the epidemic of 1616–1618.

Plymouth: Colony established by Pilgrims in Massachusetts.

Some scholars now believe that this 1638 painting by Dutch artist Adam Willaerts depicts the Plymouth colony about fifteen years after its founding. The shape of the harbor, the wooden gate, and the houses straggling up the hill all coincide with contemporary accounts of the settlement. No one believes that Willaerts himself visited Plymouth, but people returning from the colony to the Netherlands, where the Pilgrims had lived for years before emigrating, could well have described Plymouth to him.

J. D. Bangs, Courtesy of Leiden American Pilgrim Museum, The Netherlands

Pilgrims and Pokanokets

Because they landed outside the jurisdiction of the Virginia Company, some non-Separatists questioned the authority of the colony's leaders. In response, the **Mayflower Compact**, signed shipboard in November 1620, established a temporary "Civil Body Politic." Male settlers elected a governor and made decisions at town meetings. Later, Plymouth created an assembly to which landowning male settlers elected representatives.

The residents of Plymouth were poorly prepared to subsist in the new environment. Only half of the *Mayflower*'s passengers lived until spring. Survivors owed much to the Pokanokets (a branch of the Wampanoags), who controlled the area. Pokanoket villages had suffered terrible losses in the recent epidemic, so to protect themselves from the powerful Narragansetts of the southern New England coast, the Pokanokets allied themselves with the newcomers. In spring 1621, their leader, Massasoit, agreed to a treaty, and during the colony's first difficult years the Pokanokets supplied the settlers with foodstuffs. The colonists also relied on Squanto, a Pautuxet who served as a conduit between native peoples and Europeans. Captured by fishermen in the early 1610s and taken to Europe, Squanto learned to speak English. After returning, he became the settlers' interpreter and taught them about the environment.

Link to Mayflower Compact.

Mayflower Compact: Agreement signed by *Mayflower* passengers to establish order in their new settlement.

Massachusetts Bay Company

Before the 1620s ended, another group of Puritans (Congregationalists, who hoped to reform the Church of England from within) launched the colonial enterprise that would dominate New England. Charles I, who became king in 1625, attempted to suppress Puritan practices. Some Congregationalist merchants, concerned about their prospects in England, sent colonists to Cape Ann (north of Cape Cod) in 1628. The following year the merchants obtained a royal charter, constituting themselves as the Massachusetts Bay Company.

The new joint-stock company quickly attracted Puritans who feared they would lose the ability to practice their religion freely in their homeland. Committed to reforming the Church of England, they decided to do so from New England. Congregationalist merchants transfered the Massachusetts Bay Company's headquarters there, so they could handle their affairs, secular and religious, as they pleased. Like the Plymouth settlers, they expected to profit from the codfishery and timber exports.

Governor John Winthrop

In October 1629, the Massachusetts Bay Company elected **John Winthrop**, a member of the lesser English gentry, as its governor. Until his death twenty years later, he served continuously in various leadership positions. Winthrop organized the initial segment of the great Puritan migration. In 1630, more than one thousand English men and women moved to Massachusetts—most to Boston. By 1643, nearly twenty thousand more had followed.

On board the *Arbella*, en route to New England in 1630, John Winthrop preached a sermon, "A Model of Christian Charity," outlining his expectations for the colony. He stressed the communal nature of the endeavor, where differences in status or wealth—though retained—would not imply worth. Instead, he explained that, God had planned the world so that "every man might have need of other, and from hence they might be all knit more nearly together." In America, Winthrop asserted, "we shall be as a city upon a hill, the eyes of all people are upon us."

John Winthrop: Governor of Massachusetts Bay colony who wrote "A Model of Christian Charity."

Link to John Winthrop's "A Model of Christian Charity" speech.

Turkeys

Near the end of their first year in North America, Plymouth colonists held a traditional English feast celebrating the harvest. Famously, they invited Massasoit's Pokanokets, and they probably consumed turkey. But why was this bird, originally from America and enjoyed at Thanksgiving today, named for a region of the then-Ottoman Empire? The native peoples of the Americas had their own words for the fowl; Aztecs, for example, called a male bird *huexoloti* and a female *totolin*.

When Columbus carried the birds back to Spain after his first voyage, the Iberian peninsula was a major focal point for Mediterranean commerce, and Spanish mariners sailed frequently to the Middle East. One Spanish vessel took some *huexoloti* and *totolin* to the Ottoman Empire. There, farmers familiar with distant Asian relatives of the bird improved the breed, ultimately producing a plumper, tamer version. By the end of the 1500s, "turkeys" were widely consumed throughout the British Isles.

When Thomas Harriot in his 1588 *Briefe and True Report* mentioned the wild North American version of the birds, he termed them "Turkie cockes and Turkie hennes." He did not use the names native people used because these birds were not new to his audience.

Jamestown and Plymouth settlers also recognized the birds in the colonies as relatives of the fowls they enjoyed in England. But they regarded the North American birds as inferior since they seemingly could not be tamed and ravaged crops. Instead, settlers imported English turkeys to raise for meat.

Were the "turkeys" consumed at the so-called First Thanksgiving the wild American birds, or the tame Ottoman-English variety? It remains a mystery. But that they were termed "turkeys" linked them to the Mediterranean, Europe, and the Middle East as animals in the Columbian Exchange.

Victoria & Albert Museum, London; UK/The Bridgeman Art Library

Turkeys from the Americas quickly traveled around the world, as is illustrated by this Mughal painting from the Islamic empire in India. The local artist Ustad Mansur painted a "turkey-cock" brought to the emperor Jahangir in 1612 from Goa—a Portuguese enclave on the west coast of the Indian subcontinent. Presumably the turkey had been transported from the Iberian peninsula to that European outpost, whence the fowl made its way to Jahangir's court—where it was immortalized by an artist to whom it was an unusual sight.

Winthrop foresaw in Puritan America a true commonwealth in which each person put the good of the whole ahead of him- or herself. Although that society would be characterized by hierarchies of status and power, Winthrop hoped its members would live by the precepts of Christian love. Early Massachusetts and its Caribbean counterpart, Providence Island, had some bitter quarrels and un-Christian behavior, though remarkably, in New England Winthrop's ideal persisted for generations.

Covenant Ideal

Puritans' communal ideal was embodied in the doctrine of the covenant, the notion that God made a contract with them when they were chosen for their special mission to America. They also covenanted with one another to work together. Founders of churches, towns, and colonies in Anglo-America often drafted documents outlining the principles on which their institutions would be based. The Pilgrims' Mayflower Compact was a covenant as was the Fundamental Orders of Connecticut (1639), which defined the basic law for the settlements along the Connecticut River valley beginning in 1636.

The leaders of Massachusetts Bay likewise transformed their company charter into the basis for a covenanted community based on mutual consent. Under pressure from landowning male settlers, they gradually changed the General Court—officially the company's small governing body—into a colonial legislature. They also granted the status of freeman, or voting member, to property-owning adult male church members. Less than two decades after the Puritans arrived in Massachusetts Bay, the colony had a functioning system of self-government composed of a governor and a two-house legislature as well as a judicial system modeled on England's.

New England Towns

The colony's land distribution system furthered the communal ideal. In Massachusetts, groups of men—often from the same English village—applied together for land grants on which to establish towns (novel governance units that did not exist in England). Receiving a grant, these men then determined how the land would be distributed. Understandably, they copied their home villages, first laying out house and church lots. Then they gave each family parcels of land around the town center and reserved the best and largest plots for the most distinguished residents, including the minister. People with low status in England received smaller, less desirable allotments. Still, every man and even a few single women obtained land.

Town centers developed quickly, evolving in three distinctly different ways. Some, chiefly isolated agricultural settlements in the interior, tried to sustain Winthrop's vision of community based on diversified family farms. A second group, the coastal towns like Boston and Salem, became bustling seaports, focal points for trade and places of entry for immigrants. The third category, commercialized agricultural towns, grew up in the Connecticut River valley, where easy water transportation enabled farmers to sell surplus goods.

Pequot War and Its Aftermath

Migration into the Connecticut valley ended the Puritans' relative freedom from clashes with nearby Indians. Relocating under the direction of their minister, Thomas Hooker, their new settlements were remote from other English towns, although the river promised access to the ocean. The site, however, fell within the territory of the powerful Pequots.

Pequot War: Clash in 1637 that resulted as English colonists moved to settle in the Connecticut Valley on land inhabited by the Pequot Indians. The colonists were victorious and took over the Indians' land.

The Pequots' dominance stemmed from their role as primary intermediaries in the trade between New England Algonquians and the Dutch in New Netherland. With the arrival of English settlers, previously subordinate bands could now trade directly with Europeans. Clashes between Pequots and English colonists began earlier, but the establishment of settlements in the Connecticut valley moved them toward war. After two English traders were killed (not by Pequots), the English raided a Pequot village. Pequots then attacked Wethersfield, Connecticut, in April 1637, killing nine and capturing two. To retaliate, an expedition burned the main Pequot town on the Mystic River. The Englishmen and their Narragansett allies slaughtered at least four hundred Pequots, mostly women and children, capturing and enslaving the survivors.

For the next four decades, New England Indians accommodated themselves to the European invasion. They traded with newcomers and sometimes worked for them, but they resisted incorporation into English society. Native Americans persisted in using traditional farming methods, which did not employ plows or fences, and women continued as chief cultivators. When Indian men learned "European" trades, they chose those—like broom making and basket weaving—that most resembled their customary occupations and ensured independence. The one European practice they adopted was keeping livestock, for domesticated animals provided sources of meat once hunting territories became English farms and wild game vanished.

Missionary Activities   Most colonists showed little interest in converting the Algonquians to Christianity. Only a few Massachusetts clerics, notably John Eliot and Thomas Mayhew, seriously undertook missionary work. Eliot insisted that converts reside in towns, farm the land in English fashion, assume English names, wear European-style clothing and shoes, cut their hair, and stop observing their own customs. He met with little success. Only eleven hundred Indians (out of many thousands) lived in the fourteen "Praying Towns" Eliot established, and just 10 percent were baptized.

The missions in New France, however, were more successful. Puritan services lacked Catholicism's beautiful ceremonies and special appeal for women, and the Calvinist Puritans could not offer assurances of a heavenly afterlife. Yet, on the island of Martha's Vineyard, Thomas Mayhew converted many Indians to Calvinist Christianity partly by allowing Wampanoag Christians to lead traditional lives and by training their men as ministers.

While conversion often alienated new Christians from their relatives and traditions, many Indians hoped to use the Europeans' religion to cope with the dramatic changes the intruders had wrought. The combination of disease, alcohol, new trading patterns, and loss of territory disrupted customary ways of life. Shamans had little success in restoring tradition. Many Indians must have concluded that the Europeans' ideas could help them survive.

John Winthrop's description of a great smallpox epidemic that swept through southern New England in the early 1630s reveals the relationship among smallpox, conversion to Christianity, and English land claims. "Divers of them, in their sickness, confessed that the Englishmen's God was a good God; and that if they recovered, they would serve him," he noted in his diary in 1633. But by July, Winthrop observed that most Indians within a 300-mile radius of Boston had died of smallpox. He concluded, "the Lord hath cleared our title to what we possess."

Life in New England

New England's colonizers lived differently than their Algonquian neighbors and Chesapeake counterparts. Algonquian bands usually moved four or five times yearly to maximize their environment. In spring, women planted the fields, but once crops were established, they gathered wild foods while men hunted and fished. Villagers returned for harvest, separated again for fall hunting, and wintered together in a sheltered spot. Women probably determined the timing of these moves, because their activities used the environment more intensively than did men's.

English people lived year-round in the same location. Household furnishings and house sizes resembled those in the Chesapeake, but New Englanders' diets were somewhat more varied. They replowed fields, finding it less arduous to fertilize with manure than to clear new fields every few years. They fenced croplands to keep out cattle, sheep, and hogs that were their chief meat sources. Animal crowding more than human crowding caused New Englanders to spread out across the countryside.

New England Families   Because Puritans commonly moved to America as families, the age range in early New England was wide; and because many more women migrated to New England than to the tobacco colonies, the population could immediately reproduce itself. Lacking tropical diseases, New England was, after the initial difficult years, healthier than the Chesapeake and Britain. Adult male migrants to the Chesapeake lost about a decade from their English life expectancy of fifty to fifty-five years; their Massachusetts counterparts gained five or more years.

Consequently, whereas Chesapeake had few, mostly small families, New England families were numerous, large, and long-lived. Most New England men married; immigrant women married young (at age twenty, on the average); and marriages lasted longer and produced more children likely to live to maturity. Seventeenth-century Chesapeake women raised one to three healthy children; New England women reared five to seven.

The presence of many children combined with Puritans' stress on reading the Bible led to concern for education. Living in towns, colonists could establish small schools; girls and boys were taught basic reading by their parents or a school "dame," and boys could learn writing, arithmetic, and Latin. Whereas early Chesapeake parents commonly died before their children married, New England parents exercised much control over their adult offspring.

What was the impact of religion on colonial life in New England?

Wadsworth Atheneum Museum of Art, Hartford, CT. Gift of Mrs. Walter H. Clark. Endowed by her daughter, Mrs. Thomas L. Archibald/Art Resource, NY

In 1664, an eight-year-old girl, Elizabeth Eggington, became the subject of the earliest known dated New England painting. Her mother died shortly after her birth, perhaps because of childbirth complications; the girl's rich clothing, elaborate jewelry, and feather fan not only reveal her family's wealth but also suggest that she was much loved by her father, a merchant and ship captain. Unfortunately, Elizabeth died about the time this portrait was painted; perhaps it—like some other colonial portraits of young children—was actually painted after her death to memorialize her.

Young men could not marry without acreage and depended on their fathers for that land. Daughters, too, needed a dowry of household goods from parents. Parents relied on children's labor and often seemed reluctant to see them marry. These needs sometimes led to generational conflicts, but generally, children obeyed their parents' wishes.

Impact of Religion

Puritans controlled the governments of Massachusetts Bay, Plymouth, Connecticut, and other early northern colonies. Congregationalism was the only officially recognized religion; except in Rhode Island, other sects had no freedom of worship. In Massachusetts Bay and New Haven, church membership was a prerequisite for voting. Early colonies taxed residents to build churches and pay ministers' salaries, but only New England based criminal codes on the Old Testament. New Englanders were required to attend religious services, and people who expressed contempt for ministers could be punished with fines or whippings.

Strict codes of conduct meant colonists could be tried for drunkenness, card playing, dancing, or idleness—although frequent prosecutions suggest that New Englanders often enjoyed such activities. Couples who had sex during their engagement (as revealed by the birth of a baby less than nine months after their wedding) were fined and publicly humiliated. Men, and a handful of women, who engaged in behaviors that today would be called homosexual were seen as sinful, and some were executed.

In New England, church and state were thus intertwined. Puritans objected to secular interference in religious affairs yet expected the church to influence politics and society. They also believed that the state was obliged to support and protect the one true church—theirs. Although they came to America seeking religious freedom, they saw no contradiction in refusing that freedom to those with different beliefs.

Roger Williams: A minister who advocated complete separation of church and state and religious toleration.

Roger Williams

Roger Williams, a Separatist who migrated to Massachusetts Bay in 1631, quickly ran afoul of Puritan orthodoxy. He told fellow settlers that the king of England had no right to grant them land already occupied by Indians, that church and state should be separate, and that Puritans should not impose their ideas on others. In October 1635, Massachusetts tried Williams for challenging the validity of the colony's charter and for maintaining that New England Congregationalists had not separated sufficiently from England's corrupt institutions and practices.

Convicted and banished, Williams journeyed in early 1636 to the head of Narragansett Bay, where he founded the town of Providence on land he obtained from the Narragansetts and Wampanoags. Providence and other towns in what became Rhode Island tolerated all religions, including Judaism. Along with Maryland, Williams's colony founded presaged the religious freedom that eventually became a hallmark of the United States.

Anne Hutchinson: Dissenter feared not only for her theology but also because she challenged gender roles; banished from Massachusetts.

Anne Hutchinson

Anne Hutchinson presented a more sustained challenge to Massachusetts' leaders. A skilled medical practitioner popular with Boston women, she admired John Cotton, a minister who stressed the covenant of grace, or God's free gift of salvation. Most Massachusetts clerics emphasized the need for good works, study, and reflection for receiving God's grace. (In its extreme form, this doctrine could verge on the covenant of works, meaning that

Blue Laws

Seventeenth-century New England colonies enacted statutes, now called *blue laws*, preventing residents from working or engaging in recreation on Sundays, when they were supposed to attend church. Colonists were fined for plowing fields, pursuing wandering livestock, drinking in taverns, or playing games on the Sabbath. Harsher punishments met thieves who took advantage of church attendance to break into homes.

The term appears to have been coined by the Reverend Samuel Peters, a loyalist, in his *General History of Connecticut*, published in London in 1781. Peters used *blue laws* to refer to Connecticut's early legal code in general, defining it as "bloody Laws; for they were all sanctified with whippings, cutting off the ears, burning the tongue, and death." Eventually, *blue laws* acquired its current meaning of legislation regulating behavior on Sundays. States continued to enact such statutes through the nineteenth century, but as in the colonial period, enforcement varied.

Still, they remained on the books. A 1961 Supreme Court decision, *McGowan v. Maryland*, upheld that state's law restricting what could be sold on Sundays. Whereas colonial legislators were attempting to prevent Sunday work, modern Americans seem more concerned about halting Sunday shopping. Not until 1991 did the last state (North Dakota) repeal a law requiring all stores to be closed on Sundays, and only in 2003 did New York State remove its ban on Sunday liquor sales. During the recession beginning in 2008, remaining blue laws have been challenged by people hoping to stimulate local commercial activity, and the internet campaign—"Keep Sunday Special"—collapsed. Still, persistent pleas to "restore the observance of the Lord's Day in our nation" show the continuing legacy of the seventeenth century.

people could earn their salvation.) Hutchinson began holding women's meetings in her home. Stressing the covenant of grace, she asserted that the elect could be assured of salvation and communicate directly with God, which lessened the importance of the institutional church.

Thus, Hutchinson threatened Puritan orthodoxy. In November 1637, officials charged her with maligning the colony's ministers by accusing them of preaching the covenant of works. For two days, she defended herself, matching scriptural references with John Winthrop. But then Hutchinson boldly declared that God had spoken to her and would curse the Puritans if they harmed her. Excommunicated, she was exiled to Rhode Island in 1638, along with her family and some followers. Years later, after moving to New Netherland, she and most of her children were killed by Indians.

Authorities in Massachusetts perceived Anne Hutchinson as a threat to religious orthodoxy and traditional gender roles. Puritans believed in equality before God, but they considered actual women inferior to men. The magistrates' comments during her trial reveal that they were almost as outraged by her "masculine" behavior as by her religious beliefs. A clergyman told her, "You have stepped out of your place, you have rather been a Husband than a Wife and a preacher than a Hearer."

To New England authorities, an orderly society required the obedience of wives to husbands, subjects to rulers, and ordinary folk to gentry. English people intended to make many changes by colonizing North America, but not the gendered division of labor, the assumption of male superiority, or the maintenance of social hierarchies.

Summary

By the mid-seventeenth century, Europeans had come to North America and the Caribbean to stay, indelibly altering their lives and those of native peoples. Europeans killed Indians with weapons and diseases and had varying success converting them to Christianity. Contacts with indigenous peoples taught Europeans to eat new foods and recognize—however reluctantly—other cultures. The prosperity and survival of many European colonies depended heavily on the cultivation of American crops (maize and tobacco) and an Asian crop (sugar), thus attesting to the importance of post-Columbian ecological exchange.

To a greater extent than their European counterparts, the English transferred the society and politics of their homeland to a new environment. Their sheer numbers, coupled with their need for vast quantities of land for crops and livestock, inevitably produced conflict with Indian neighbors. New England and the Chesapeake differed in the sex ratio and age range of their immigrant populations, their diverse economies, their settlement patterns, and the impact of religion. Yet their expansions engendered similar internal and external tension. Both regions would become embroiled in increasingly fierce rivalries besetting the European powers that would affect Americans of all races until after the mid-eighteenth century, when the Anglo-American colonies won their independence.

Chapter Review

Spanish, French, and Dutch North America

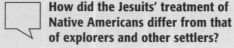

How did the Jesuits' treatment of Native Americans differ from that of explorers and other settlers?

Spanish and other settlers typically sought to dominate the native populations, controlling their labor and often enslaving them, sometimes through the use of violence. The French Jesuits who settled New France (Montreal and Quebec) initially tried to convert Indians to Christianity and convince them to farm in the European style. When that failed, missionaries introduced Catholicism without insisting that Indians abandon their traditions. Missionaries learned Indian languages and lived among potential converts, and while they tried to undermine the authority of shamans, Jesuits also recognized the compatibility of some aspects of native culture with Christianity. This somewhat flexible approach, combined with their lack of interest in land or tribute, made at least some Indians receptive to conversion.

The Caribbean

What made the Caribbean Islands initially desirable for colonization?

European colonizers had different reasons for being drawn to the Caribbean Islands. Spain, which focused on larger islands, saw them as offering the potential for greater wealth with less effort than smaller islands might. Other countries saw the smaller islands as a base to attack Spanish vessels transporting gold, silver, and other valuable commodities from the Americas. The second reason for settling on the smaller islands was sugar cultivation. Sugar was in high demand in Europe, particularly since the sweetener improved the taste of coffee and tea and provided a sweet, yet quick, energy boost.

English Interest in Colonization

What two developments prompted England to consider North American colonization in the early seventeenth century?

First, dramatic population growth in England, partly as a result of more nutritious foods of American origin, increased competition for food, clothing, shelter, and jobs. That, in turn, spurred inflation; wages also fell. Some profited, but those at the lower end of the socioeconomic spectrum—those with little or no land—lapsed into poverty and homelessness. Cities became overcrowded, leading officials to see colonizing North America as a way to reduce England's "surplus" population and related woes. Others hoped to improve their lot in the land-rich colonies. Second, the Protestant Reformation sparked new forms of Christianity that diverged from the Church of England, and while Elizabeth I tolerated such dissent, her successors, the Stuart monarchs, did not. Ultimately, seeking to practice freely their religious beliefs (and avoid imprisonment), some English Puritans, Separatists, and Catholics fled to America.

The Founding of Virginia

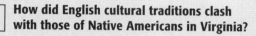

How did English cultural traditions clash with those of Native Americans in Virginia?

While both were religious, Englishmen considered Indian men lazy because they let women cultivate crops while they hunted, which the British regarded as a sport and not work. Native Americans thought Englishmen were effeminate because they farmed, which Indians considered women's work. Political power in Algonquian culture passed through sisters' sons rather through the father, as was the custom in England. Because the British were used to powerful kings, they assumed Indian chiefs held the same autocratic control and ability to make treaties, when in reality, they had limited authority. Most importantly, where the English believed in individual farms and private land ownership, the Algonquians held land communally as a village.

Life in the Chesapeake

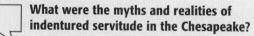

What were the myths and realities of indentured servitude in the Chesapeake?

Chesapeake tobacco farmers filled their extensive demand for labor with indentured servants from England—typically young men who worked for four to seven years in exchange for their passage. Indentured servitude for these young men represented a chance at upward mobility. Most gained "freedom dues" at the completion of their contract, including clothes, tools, livestock, casks of corn and tobacco, and sometimes land. But they worked long hours, six or seven days a week, doing intense physical labor in hot climates. Masters could discipline or sell them, and if indentured servants fled, they faced extreme penalties, although some did win verdicts against cruel masters calling for their transfer or release from indenture. Exposure to disease combined with intense labor so that only 60 percent of indentured men lived to become freedmen, and many who did, lived only another twenty years.

The Founding of New England

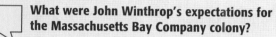

What were John Winthrop's expectations for the Massachusetts Bay Company colony?

First elected governor in 1629, John Winthrop was instrumental in organizing the first Puritan migration from England to the colony. While in transit, he delivered his famous sermon, calling for the new colony to serve as a moral and spiritual example for the rest of the world, a "city upon a hill." He urged colonists of varying ranks to work together, to mediate status differences and to unite around their communal interests. He envisioned a true commonwealth, where people put the common good ahead of their own and were governed by Christian brotherhood.

Life in New England

What was the impact of religion on colonial life in New England?

Although Puritans fled England to practice their faith freely in New England, they offered no such freedom of worship to those who dissented from their beliefs. Puritans controlled the government in many early northern colonies and made Congregationalism the only recognized religion, with church membership and voting rights linked. Colonists were punished with fines or whippings for missing religious services. In addition, strict behavioral codes meant colonists were tried for drunkenness, card playing, dancing, or idleness. Couples who had sex during their engagement were fined and publicly humiliated. People who behaved in ways that today would be called homosexual were sometimes executed. Dissenters such as Roger Williams or Anne Hutchinson, who challenged Puritan orthodoxy, were tried and banished—Williams founded Providence, Rhode Island, based on religious tolerance and was subsequently joined by Hutchinson. Beyond challenging church authority, Hutchinson violated gender norms by preaching.

Suggestions for Further Reading

Virginia DeJohn Anderson, *Creatures of Empire: How Domestic Animals Transformed Early America* (2004)

Richard S. Dunn, *Sugar and Slaves: The Rise of the Planter Class in the English West Indies, 1624–1713* (1972)

David Hackett Fischer, *Champlain's Dream: The European Founding of North America* (2008)

Alison Games, *Migration and the Origins of the English Atlantic World* (1999)

David D. Hall, *Worlds of Wonder, Days of Judgment: Popular Religious Belief in Early New England* (1989)

Karen O. Kupperman, *The Jamestown Project* (2007)

Mary Beth Norton, *Founding Mothers & Fathers: Gendered Power and the Forming of American Society* (1996)

Carla Gardina Pestana, *Protestant Empire: Religion and the Making of the British Atlantic World* (2009)

Helen C. Rountree, *Pocahontas, Powhatan, Opechancanough: Three Indian Lives Changed by Jamestown* (2005)

David J. Weber, *The Spanish Frontier in North America* (1992)

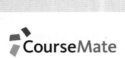

3

North America in the Atlantic World

1650–1720

She was starving. Offered a piece of boiled horse's foot by a compassionate neighbor, the slave gulped it down and grabbed another piece from a child. Later, she recalled that "savoury it was to my taste. . . . Thus the Lord made that pleasant refreshing, which another time would have been an abomination." But Mary Rowlandson's mistress then threatened to kill her, saying that she had "disgraced" the household by begging for food.

What had brought the wife of the Reverend Joseph Rowlandson of Lancaster, Massachusetts, to such distress? On February 10, 1676, a force of Wampanoags, Narragansetts, and Nipmucks had killed fourteen townspeople (including her daughter) and captured twenty-three others in the conflict that New Englanders called King Philip's War. Carried away, she endured their hardships in the wintry countryside of western Massachusetts and southern New Hampshire. She became the slave of Quinnapin, a Narragansett sachem, and his three wives, one of whom, Weetamoo, herself a Wampanoag sachem, was her mistress. Both were eventually killed by the colonists after the death of their leader, the Wampanoag known as King Philip, in August 1676. But months earlier, in May, Mary Rowlandson had been ransomed from her captors for £20— roughly equivalent to $500 today.

Mary Rowlandson's famous 1682 narrative, *The Sovereignty and Goodness of God,* exposes the sufferings she shared with her captors and her inability to sympathize with or understand them. When Weetamoo's baby died, Mary remarked coldly that "there was one benefit in it, that there was more room" in the wigwam. Her narrative illustrates the contentious relationships of Anglo New Englanders and their native neighbors.

Much tension was related to the mainland colonies' involvement in a growing international network. North America, like England, was becoming embedded in a worldwide matrix of trade and warfare. Oceangoing vessels now crisscrossed the globe, carrying European goods to America and Africa, Caribbean sugar to New England and Europe, Africans to the Americas, and New England fish and wood products—and occasionally Indian

Chapter Outline

The Growth of Anglo-American Settlements
New York | New Jersey | Pennsylvania | Carolina | Chesapeake | New England | Colonial Political Structures

A Decade of Imperial Crises: The 1670s
New France and the Iroquois | Pueblo Peoples and Spaniards | King Philip's War | Bacon's Rebellion

The Atlantic Trading System
Why African Slavery? | Atlantic Slave Trade | West Africa and the Slave Trade | New England and the Caribbean | Slaving Voyages

LINKS TO THE WORLD *Exotic Beverages*

Slavery in North America and the Caribbean
African Enslavement in the Chesapeake | African Enslavement in South Carolina | Rice and Indigo | Indian Enslavement in North and South Carolina | Enslavement in the North | Slave Resistance

Imperial Reorganization and the Witchcraft Crisis
Mercantilism and Navigation Acts | Colonial Autonomy Challenged | Glorious Revolution in America | King William's War | The 1692 Witchcraft Crisis | New Imperial Measures

VISUALIZING THE PAST *Debating the Witchcraft Trials*

LEGACY FOR A PEOPLE AND A NATION *Americans of African Descent*

SUMMARY

slaves—to the Caribbean. North American colonies expanded their territorial claims and diversified their economies after the mid-seventeenth century.

Three developments shaped mainland English colonial life between 1640 and 1720: escalating conflicts with Indians and other European colonies; the expansion of slavery; and changes in the colonies' political and economic relationships with England.

The explosive growth of the slave trade significantly altered the Anglo-American economy. Mariners and ship owners profited handsomely from their human cargoes, as did planters who could afford slaves. Initially, the slave trade involved Indians and already enslaved Africans from the Caribbean, but it soon focused on cargoes from Africa. The large influx of West African slaves expanded agricultural productivity, fueled the international trading system, and dramatically reshaped colonial society.

The burgeoning North American economy attracted new attention from colonial administrators. After the Stuarts were restored to the throne in 1660 (having lost it briefly during the English Civil War), London bureaucrats attempted to supervise American settlements so England benefited from their economic growth.

As English settlements expanded, they came into violent conflict with powerful Indian nations, the Dutch, the Spanish, and the French. All European colonies confronted significant crises during the 1670s. By 1720, war—between Europeans and Indians, among Europeans, and among Indians allied with colonial powers—had become a familiar feature of American life. No longer isolated, the people and products of North American colonies had become integral to the world trading system and enmeshed in its conflicts.

As you read this chapter, keep the following questions in mind:

* **What were the consequences of the transatlantic slave trade in North America and Africa?**

* **How did English policy toward the colonies change from 1650 to 1720?**

* **What were the causes and results of new friction between Europeans and native peoples?**

The Growth of Anglo-American Settlements

Why did New York's development lag behind that of other British colonies in the seventeenth century?

Between 1642 and 1646, civil war between supporters of King Charles I and the Puritan-dominated Parliament engulfed England. Parliament triumphed, leading to the execution of the king in 1649 and interim rule by the parliamentary army's leader, Oliver Cromwell, during the so-called Commonwealth period. But after Cromwell's death, Parliament restored the monarchy with Charles I's son and heir agreeing to restrictions on his authority. Assuming the throne in 1660 (see Table 3.1), Charles II rewarded nobles and other supporters with huge tracts of land on the North American mainland, thereby establishing six of the thirteen polities that would form the American nation: New York, New Jersey, Pennsylvania (including Delaware), and North and South Carolina (see Map 3.1). Known as the Restoration colonies, they were proprietorships, where one man or several men owned the soil and controlled the government.

Chronology

1642–46	English Civil War
1649	Charles I executed
1651	First Navigation Act passed to regulate colonial trade
1660	Stuarts (Charles II) restored to throne
1663	Carolina chartered
1664	English conquer New Netherland New York founded New Jersey established
1670s	Marquette, Jolliet, and La Salle explore the Great Lakes and Mississippi valley for France
1675–76	Bacon's Rebellion disrupts Virginia government; Jamestown destroyed
1675–78	King Philip's War devastates New England
1680–1700	Pueblo revolt temporarily drives Spaniards from New Mexico
1681	Pennsylvania chartered
1685	James II becomes king

1686–88	Dominion of New England established, superseding all charters of colonies from Maine to New Jersey
1688–89	James II deposed in Glorious Revolution William and Mary ascend throne
1689	Glorious Revolution in America; Massachusetts, New York, and Maryland overthrow colonial governors
1688–99	King William's War fought on northern New England frontier
1691	New Massachusetts charter issued
1692	Witchcraft crisis in Salem; nineteen people hanged
1696	Board of Trade and Plantations established to coordinate English colonial administration Vice-admiralty courts established in America
1701	Iroquois adopt neutrality policy toward France and England
1702–13	Queen Anne's War fought by French and English
1711–13	Tuscarora War (North Carolina) leads to capture or migration of most Tuscaroras
1715	Yamasee War nearly destroys South Carolina

New York In 1664, Charles II gave his brother James the region between the Connecticut and Delaware Rivers, including the Hudson valley and Long Island. That the Dutch had settled there mattered little; the English and Dutch were engaged in sporadic warfare. In August, James's warships anchored off Manhattan Island, demanding New Netherland's surrender. Although in 1672 the Netherlands briefly retook the colony, the Dutch permanently ceded it in 1674.

In 1664, a significant minority of English people (mostly Puritan New Englanders on Long Island) already lived in the territory James renamed New York, along with the Dutch, Indians, Africans, Germans, Scandinavians, and other Europeans (see Table 3.2). The Dutch West India Company had imported slaves, intending some for resale in the Chesapeake although many remained in New Netherland as laborers. At the time of the English conquest, almost one-fifth of Manhattan's approximately fifteen hundred inhabitants were of African descent.

TABLE 3.1   Restored Stuart Monarchs of England, 1660–1714

Monarch	Reign	Relation to Predecessor
Charles II	1660–1685	Son
James II	1685–1688	Brother
Mary	1688–1694	Daughter
William	1688–1702	Son-in-law
Anne	1702–1714	Sister, sister-in-law

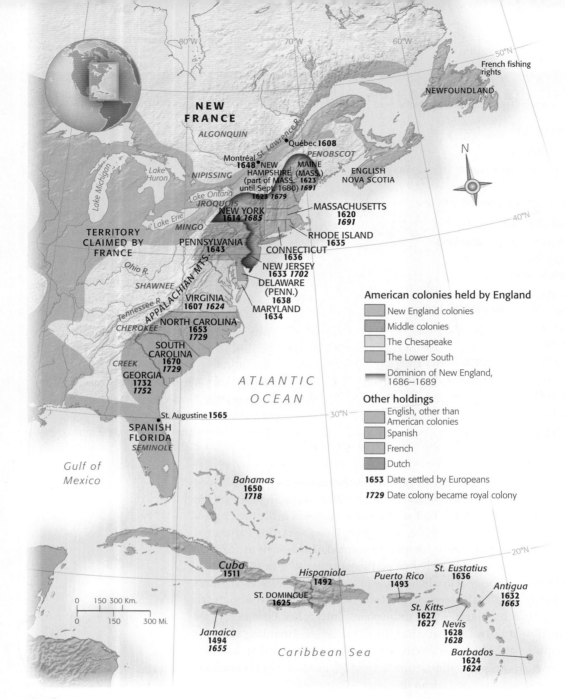

MAP 3.1

The Anglo-American Colonies in the Early Eighteenth Century

By the early eighteenth century, the English colonies nominally dominated the Atlantic coastline of North America. But the colonies' formal boundary lines are deceiving because the western reaches of each colony were still largely unfamiliar to Europeans and because much of the land was still inhabited by Native Americans.

Source: Copyright © Cengage Learning

Recognizing the population's diversity, James's representatives moved cautiously in establishing English authority. The Duke's Laws, a 1665 legal code, applied solely to the English settlements on Long Island, only later extended to the entire colony. James initially maintained Dutch local government, confirmed Dutch land titles, and allowed Dutch residents to maintain customary legal practices. Each

TABLE 3.2   The Founding of English Colonies in North America, 1664–1681

Colony	Founder(s)	Date	Basis of Economy
New York (formerly New Netherland)	James, duke of York	1664	Farming, fur trading
New Jersey	Sir George Carteret, John Lord Berkeley	1664	Farming
North Carolina	Carolina proprietors	1665	Tobacco, forest products
South Carolina	Carolina proprietors	1670	Rice, indigo
Pennsylvania (incl. Delaware)	William Penn	1681	Farming

town could choose which church—Dutch Reformed, Congregational, or Church of England—to support with its taxes. Much to the dismay of English residents, there was no provision for a representative assembly. James distrusted legislative bodies, and not until 1683 did he agree to an elected legislature. The English takeover thus had little immediate effect. The duke did not promote migration, so its population grew slowly, barely reaching eighteen thousand by 1698. Until the 1720s, Manhattan remained a commercial backwater to Boston.

New Jersey
In 1664, the duke of York regranted the land between the Hudson and Delaware Rivers—East and West Jersey—to his friends Sir George Carteret and John Lord Berkeley. That left the duke's own colony hemmed in between Connecticut and the Jerseys, hindering its economic growth. Meanwhile, the Jersey proprietors quickly attracted settlers, promising generous land

National Archives of the Netherlands

The Dutch artist Johannes Vingboons painted this view of New Amersterdam/New York in 1665, shortly after the English takeover. Note the windmill, the tall government buildings, and the small row houses—which made the settlement resemble European villages of its day. The contrast to Plymouth (page 44) is striking.

grants, limited religious freedom, and—without the Crown's authorization—a representative assembly. Many Puritan New Englanders migrated to the Jerseys, along with Barbadians, Dutch New Yorkers, and eventually Scots. By 1726, New Jersey had 32,500 inhabitants, only 8,000 fewer than New York.

Quakers: Members of a religious sect that embraced egalitarianism and rejected traditional religious hierarchies. They believed that the Holy Spirit or the "inner light" could inspire every soul.

Within twenty years, the Society of Friends, also called **Quakers**, purchased Carteret's share (West Jersey) and some of Berkeley's (East Jersey). Rejecting religious hierarchies, Quakers believed that anyone could directly receive God's "inner light" and that all people were equal in God's sight. With no formally trained clergy, Quakers allowed men and women to speak in meetings and become "public Friends" who traveled to spread God's word. Quakers proselytized throughout the Atlantic world in the 1650s. Authorities rejected Quakers' radical egalitarianism, and they encountered persecution everywhere.

Pennsylvania

William Penn: The proprietor of the last unallocated tract of American territory at the king's disposal, which would become Pennsylvania.

In 1681, Charles II granted the region between Maryland and New York to his friend **William Penn**, a prominent Quaker. Penn held the colony as a personal proprietorship, one that earned profits for his descendants until the American Revolution. Penn saw his province as a haven for persecuted coreligionists. Penn offered land to settlers on liberal terms, promising religious toleration, although only Christian men could vote; guaranteeing English liberties, and pledging to establish a representative assembly. He also publicized the availability of land in Pennsylvania through promotional tracts in German, French, and Dutch.

By mid-1683, more than three thousand people—among them Welsh, Irish, Dutch, and Germans—had moved to Pennsylvania, and within five years the population reached twelve thousand. Philadelphia, sited on the easily navigable Delaware River, drew merchants and artisans from throughout the English-speaking world. From mainland and Caribbean colonies alike came Quakers who brought experience on American soil and trading connections. Pennsylvania's fertile lands enabled residents to export surplus flour and other foodstuffs to the West Indies. Philadelphia rapidly acquired more than two thousand citizens and challenged Boston's commercial dominance.

Penn attempted to treat native peoples fairly. He learned to speak the language of the Delawares (or Lenapes), from whom he purchased land to sell to European settlers. Penn also established strict trade regulations and forbade the sale of alcohol to Indians. His policies attracted native peoples who moved to Pennsylvania in the late seventeenth century to escape clashes with English colonists in Maryland, Virginia, and North Carolina. Ironically, however, the same toleration that attracted Native Americans also brought non-Quaker Europeans—Scots-Irish, Germans, and Swiss—who showed little respect for Indian land claims and would clash repeatedly with them.

Carolina

The southernmost proprietary colony, granted by Charles II in 1663, stretched from the southern boundary of Virginia to Spanish Florida. Strategically, a successful English settlement there would prevent Spaniards from pushing farther north. The fertile, semitropical land also promised to yield such exotic and valuable commodities as figs, olives, wines, and silk. The proprietors named their new province Carolina in honor of Charles. The "Fundamental Constitutions of Carolina," which they asked the political philosopher John Locke to draft, outlined a colony governed by landholding aristocrats and characterized by a structured distribution of political and economic power.

But Carolina failed to follow this plan. Instead, it quickly developed two distinct population centers, which in 1729 split into separate colonies under royal rule. Virginia planters settled the Albemarle region that became North Carolina. They established a society like their own, based on cultivating tobacco and exporting forest products. The other population center, which eventually formed South Carolina, developed at Charles Town, founded in 1670. Many of its early residents were sugar planters from overcrowded Barbados who expected to reestablish plantation agriculture and escape hurricanes. They were disappointed: sugar would not grow in Carolina, and a destructive hurricane struck in 1686.

The settlers raised corn and cattle, which they sold to Caribbean planters. They also depended on trade with nearby Indians for commodities they could sell elsewhere, mostly deerskins, sent to Europe, and enslaved Indians, who were shipped to Caribbean islands and northern colonies. During the first decade of the eighteenth century, South Carolina exported an average of 54,000 skins annually, which peaked at 160,000. Before 1715, Carolinians exported 30,000 to 50,000 Indian slaves.

Chesapeake

The English Civil War retarded the development of the earlier English settlements. Struggles between supporters of the king and Parliament caused military clashes in Maryland and political upheavals in Virginia. Once the war ended and immigration resumed, the colonies expanded again. Some settlers, especially those on Virginia's eastern shore and southern border, raised grain, livestock, and flax, to be sold to English and Dutch merchants. Tobacco growers began importing increasing numbers of English indentured servants as farms developed into plantations. Less concerned about Indian attack after the 1646 defeat of the Powhatan Confederacy, colonists sought to enlarge their landholdings.

Chesapeake tobacco planters also started to acquire enslaved workers. Most came from a population that historian Ira Berlin has termed "Atlantic creoles"—people (perhaps of mixed race) who came from other European settlements in the Atlantic world, primarily Iberian outposts. Not all Atlantic creoles arriving in the Chesapeake were bondspeople; some were free or indentured. With them, the Chesapeake became a "society with slaves," where slavery coexisted with various labor systems.

New England

In New England, migration ceased after the Civil War began in 1642. While Puritans were challenging the king and then governing England as a commonwealth, they had little incentive to leave their homeland. Yet the Puritan colonies' population grew dramatically by natural increase. By the 1670s, New England's population more than tripled to approximately seventy thousand, creating pressure on available land. Colonial settlement spread into the Massachusetts and Connecticut interior, and many later generations migrated—north to New Hampshire or Maine, southwest to New York or New Jersey—seeking available farmland. Others learned such skills as blacksmithing or carpentry to support themselves in the growing towns.

Those who remained in the small, densely populated older New England communities experienced witchcraft accusations and trials after 1650. The accused allies of the Devil were thought to harness spirits for good or evil. A witch might engage in fortunetelling, prepare healing potions, or cause the death of a child or animal. Only New England witnessed many witch trials witches (about one hundred in all before 1690). Most of the accused were middle-aged women who had angered their neighbors. Historians have concluded that daily interactions in close-knit communities fostered quarrels that led some colonists to believe others had diabolically caused certain misfortunes. Even so, judges and juries were skeptical: only a few of the accused were convicted, and fewer were executed.

Colonial Political Structures

By the last quarter of the seventeenth century, almost all the Anglo-American colonies had well-established political and judicial structures. In New England, property-holding men or the legislature elected the governors; in other regions, the king or proprietor appointed them. A council, elected or appointed, advised the governor and served as the upper house of the legislature. Each colony had a judiciary with local justices of the peace and county courts, and most had local governing bodies.

A Decade of Imperial Crises: The 1670s

How did settlers' interests collide with those of Native Americans?

Between 1670 and 1680, New France, New Mexico, New England, and Virginia experienced bitter conflicts as their interests collided with those of America's original inhabitants.

New France and the Iroquois

In the mid-1670s, Louis de Buade de Frontenac, the governor-general of Canada, decided to expand New France south and westward to establish a trade route to Mexico and gain control of the valuable fur trade. Accordingly, he encouraged the explorations of Father Jacques Marquette, Louis Jolliet, and René-Robert Cavelier de La Salle in the Great Lakes and Mississippi valley regions. His goal led to conflict with the powerful Iroquois Confederacy, composed of five Indian nations—the Mohawks, Oneidas, Onondagas, Cayugas, and Senecas. (In 1722, the Tuscaroras became the sixth.)

Link to Marquette's account of his exploration of the Mississippi.

Under the terms of a unique defensive alliance forged in the sixteenth century, a representative council made war decisions for the entire Iroquois Confederacy. Before the arrival of Europeans, the Iroquois waged wars primarily for captives to replenish their population. Foreigners brought ravaging disease by 1633, intensifying the need for captives. Simultaneously, Europeans created an economic motive for warfare: the desire to dominate the fur trade and gain unimpeded access to European goods. The 1640s war with the Hurons initiated several conflicts with other Indians known as the **Beaver Wars**, in which the Iroquois fought to control the lucrative peltry trade. Iroquois did not trap beaver; instead, they raided other villages for pelts or attacked Indians carrying furs to European outposts. Then the Iroquois traded that booty for European-made blankets, knives, guns, alcohol, and other items.

Beaver Wars: Series of conflicts between the Hurons (and other Indians) and Iroquois in a quest for pelts.

As Iroquois dominance grew, in the mid-1670s to 1690s, the French repeatedly attacked, seeing the Iroquois as a threat to France's plans to trade with western Indians. Although in 1677 New Yorkers and the Iroquois established a formal alliance known as the Covenant Chain, the English only offered weapons to aid their trading partners. The confederacy held its own and even expanded its reach, enabling it in 1701 to negotiate neutrality treaties with France and other Indians. For the next half-century, the Iroquois maintained their power through trade and diplomacy rather than warfare.

Pueblo Peoples and Spaniards

In New Mexico, too, 1670s events led to a crisis with long-term consequences. Under Spanish domination, Pueblo peoples had added Christianity to their beliefs while retaining traditional rituals. But as decades passed, Franciscans adopted violent tactics to eliminate the native religion. Priests and secular colonists who held *encomiendas* placed heavy labor demands on the people, who were also suffering from Apache raids and food shortages caused by a drought. In 1680, the Pueblos revolted under the leadership of **Popé**, a respected shaman, driving the Spaniards out of New Mexico. Although Spain restored its authority by 1700, Spanish governors now stressed cooperation with the Pueblos, relying on their labor but no longer violating their cultural integrity. The **Pueblo Revolt of 1680** constituted the most successful and longest-sustained Indian resistance movement in colonial North America.

Spanish military outposts (*presidios*) and Franciscan missions offered some protection to Pueblos, but other Indians' desire to obtain horses and guns led to violence throughout the region. Navajos, Apaches, and Utes attacked each other and the Pueblos for captives and hides to trade to the Spanish. Spaniards often kept female and child captives as domestic laborers and sent men to Mexican silver mines. When Comanches migrated west from the Great Plains in the late seventeenth century, Utes allied with them, and after the Pueblo revolt that alliance dominated New Mexico's northern borderlands for several decades.

In the more densely settled English colonies, hostilities developed in the 1670s over land. In New England and Virginia, tensions erupted as settlers increasingly encroached on Native American territories.

Popé: Leader of the Pueblo Revolt against Spanish in 1680.

Pueblo Revolt of 1680: The most successful Indian uprising in American history. Pueblo Indians rebelled against Spanish authority and drove the Spanish from their New Mexico settlements.

King Philip's War

By the early 1670s, the growing settlements in southern New England surrounded Wampanoag ancestral lands on Narragansett Bay. The local chief, Metacom, or King Philip, was troubled by territorial loss and the impact of European culture and Christianity on his people. Philip led attacks on nearby communities in June 1675. Other Algonquian peoples, among them Nipmucks and Narragansetts, joined King Philip's forces. In the fall, they attacked settlements in the northern Connecticut River valley, and the war spread to Maine when the Abenakis entered the conflict. In early 1676, the Indian allies devastated villages like Lancaster, where they captured Mary Rowlandson and others and attacked Plymouth and Providence; later Abenaki assaults forced the abandonment of most Maine settlements. Altogether, the alliance wholly or partially destroyed twenty-seven of ninety-two towns and attacked forty others, pushing the line of English settlement back toward the east and south.

In summer 1676, the Indian coalition ran short of food and ammunition. On June 12, the Mohawks—ancient Iroquois enemies of New England Algonquians—devastated a major Wampanoag encampment while most of the warriors were attacking an English town. After King Philip was killed that August, the southern alliance crumbled. Fighting continued on the Maine frontier for another two years until the English and Abenakis agreed to end the conflict in 1678.

In addition to the Wampanoags, Nipmucks, Narragansetts, and Abenakis who were captured and sold into slavery, still more died of starvation and disease. New Englanders had broken the power of the southern coastal tribes. Thereafter, the southern Indians lived in small clusters, subordinated to the colonists and often working as servants or sailors. Only on Martha's Vineyard did Christian Wampanoags (who had not participated in the war) preserve their cultural identity.

King Philip's War: Major war between Indians and New England settlers.

The settlers paid a terrible price for their victory: an estimated one-tenth of the adult male population was killed or wounded. Proportional to population, it was the most costly conflict in American history. The heavy losses also caused Puritan colonists to question whether God had turned against them. New Englanders did not fully rebuild abandoned interior towns for thirty years, and not until the American Revolution did per capita income reach pre-1675 levels.

Bacon's Rebellion

Bacon's Rebellion: Uprising that resulted from many conflicts, among them mounting land shortage and settlers' desires for Indian lands.

In the early 1670s, conflict wracked Virginia when ex-servants, unable to acquire land, eyed territory reserved by treaty for Virginia's Indians. Governor William Berkeley resisted starting a war, and dissatisfied colonists rallied behind a recent immigrant, the gentleman Nathaniel Bacon, who shared their frustration that desirable land had been claimed. Using as a pretext the July 1675 killing of an indentured servant by Doeg Indians, settlers attacked the Doegs and Susquehannocks, a more powerful nation. In retaliation, Susquehannocks raided outlying farms early in 1676.

Link to Nathaniel Bacon's Manifesto.

The governor outlawed Bacon and his men; the rebels then held Berkeley hostage, forcing him to authorize them to attack the Indians. During the chaotic summer of 1676, Bacon alternately pursued Indians and battled the governor. In September, Bacon's forces burned Jamestown to the ground. But after Bacon died of dysentery the following month, the rebellion collapsed. Even so, a new treaty in 1677 opened much of the disputed territory to settlement. The end of Bacon's Rebellion pushed most of Virginia's Indians west beyond the Appalachians.

The Atlantic Trading System

How was slavery at the center of the expanding trade network between Europe and the colonies?

In the 1670s and 1680s, the Chesapeake's prosperity rested on tobacco, which depended on an ample labor supply. But fewer English men and women proved willing to indenture themselves. Population pressures had eased in England, and the Restoration colonies gave migrants other settlement options. Furthermore, fluctuating tobacco prices and land scarcity made the Chesapeake less appealing. Wealthy Chesapeake tobacco growers found the answer to their labor problem in the Caribbean sugar islands, where Dutch, French, English, and Spanish planters purchased African slaves.

Why African Slavery?

Slavery was practiced in Europe and Islamic lands for centuries. European Christians justified enslaving heathen peoples, especially those of exotic origin, in religious terms, arguing that it might lead to their conversion. Muslims, too, enslaved infidels and imported tens of thousands of black African bondspeople into North Africa and the Middle East. Others believed that wartime prisoners could be enslaved. Consequently, when Portuguese mariners encountered African societies holding slaves, they purchased bondspeople. Indeed, they initially bought slaves in one African nation and sold them in another. From the 1440s on, Portugal imported large numbers of slaves into the Iberian Peninsula; by 1500, enslaved Africans composed one-tenth of the population of Lisbon, Portugal, and Seville, Spain. In 1555, some were taken to England.

Iberians exported African slavery to New Spain and Brazil. Because the Catholic Church prevented the formal enslavement of Indians in those domains and free laborers refused to work in mines or on sugar plantations, African bondspeople became mainstays of the Caribbean and Brazilian economies. The first enslaved Africans in the Americas were imported from Angola, Portugal's early trading partner, and the Portuguese word *Negro* came into use as a descriptor.

English people had few moral qualms about enslaving other humans. Slavery was sanctioned in the Bible and widely practiced by contemporaries. Yet English colonists initially lacked clear categories for "race" and "slave." For example, the 1670 Virginia law that first tried to define the enslaveable declared that "all servants not being christians imported into this colony by shipping shal be slaves for their lives." Such nonracial phrasing reveals that Anglo-American settlers had not yet fully developed the meaning of *race* and *slave* that would come over time.

Atlantic Slave Trade North American mainland planters could not have obtained bondspeople without the rapid development of an Atlantic trading system. Although this elaborate Atlantic economic system has been called the triangular trade, people and products did not move across the ocean in easily diagrammed patterns. Instead, a complicated web of exchange tied the peoples of the Atlantic world together (see Map 3.2).

The expanding trade network between Europe and its colonies was fueled by the sale and transport of slaves, the exchange of commodities produced by slave labor, and the need to feed and clothe bound laborers. By the late seventeenth century, the basis of the European economic system shifted from the Mediterranean and Asia to the Atlantic, with commerce in slaves and the products of slave labor, as its core.

Chesapeake tobacco and Caribbean and Brazilian sugar were shipped to Europe, where they were in demand. The profits paid for African laborers and European manufactured goods. The African coastal rulers received their payment for slaves in European manufactures and East Indian textiles. Europeans purchased slaves from Africa for resale in their colonies, acquired sugar and tobacco from America, and dispatched their manufactures everywhere.

Europeans fought bitterly to control the lucrative trade. The Portuguese, who at first dominated it, were supplanted by the Dutch in the 1630s. In the Anglo-Dutch wars, the Dutch lost to the English, who controlled the trade through the Royal African Company. Holding a monopoly on English trade with sub-Saharan Africa, the company maintained seventeen forts and trading posts, dispatched to West Africa hundreds of ships carrying English goods, and transported about 100,000 slaves to England's Caribbean colonies. After the company's monopoly expired in 1712, independent traders carried most of the Africans imported into the colonies.

West Africa and the Slave Trade Most of the enslaved people carried to North America originated in West Africa, some from the Rice and Grain Coasts, many others from the Gold and Slave Coasts and the Bight of Biafra (modern Nigeria) and Angola. Certain

Colonial Williamsburg Foundation

By the middle of the eighteenth century, American tobacco had become closely associated with African slavery. An English woodcut advertising tobacco from the York River in Virginia accordingly depicted not a Chesapeake planter but rather an African, shown with a hoe in one hand and a pipe in the other. Usually, of course, slaves would not have smoked the high-quality tobacco produced for export, although they were allowed to cultivate small crops for their own use.

coastal rulers served as intermediaries, facilitating permanent slave-trading posts and supplying resident Europeans with slaves. Such rulers simultaneously controlled Europeans' access to bound laborers and desirable trade goods, such as textiles, iron bars, alcohol, tobacco, guns, and cowry shells from the Maldive Islands (in the Indian Ocean), used as currency. At least 10 percent of all slaves exported to the Americas passed through Whydah, Dahomey's major slave-trading port. Portugal, England, and France established forts there, and Europeans had to pay fees to Whydah's rulers before they could begin to acquire cargoes.

The slave trade affected African regions unevenly. It helped to create such powerful eighteenth-century kingdoms as Dahomey and Asante (formed from the Akan States), while rulers in parts of Upper Guinea, especially modern Gambia and Senegal, largely resisted involvement. Traffic in slaves destroyed smaller polities and disrupted traditional economic patterns. Agricultural production intensified, especially in rice-growing areas, to supply slave ships with foodstuffs. Because prisoners of war constituted most of the exported slaves, active traders were also successful warriors. Some nations even initiated conflicts to acquire captives.

MAP 3.2

Atlantic Trade Routes

By the late seventeenth century, an elaborate trade network linked the countries and colonies bordering the Atlantic Ocean. The most valuable commodities exchanged were enslaved people and the products of slave labor.

Source: Copyright © Cengage Learning

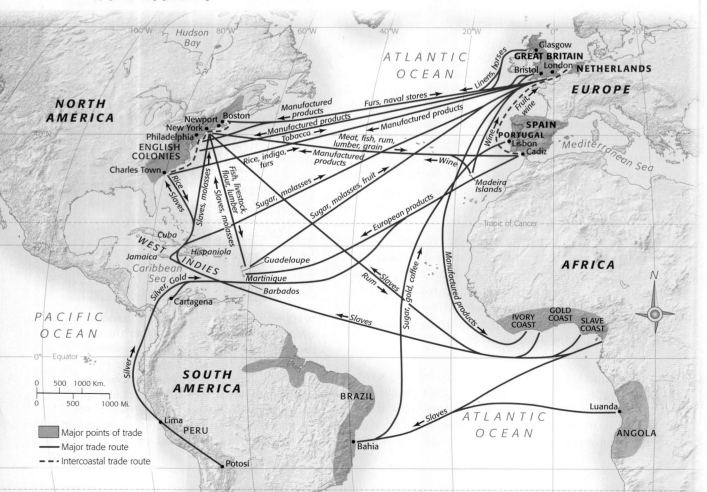

Exotic Beverages

Seventeenth-century colonists developed a taste for tea (from China), coffee (from Arabia), chocolate (from Mesoamerica), and rum. Demand for these once-exotic beverages helped reshape the world economy after the mid-seventeenth century. Approximately two-thirds of the people who migrated across the Atlantic before 1776 were involved, primarily as slaves, in the production of tobacco, calico, and these four drinks. The exotic beverages profoundly affected culture, too, as they moved from luxury to necessity.

Each beverage had its own consumption pattern. Chocolate, brought to Spain from Mexico and consumed hot at intimate gatherings, became the drink of aristocrats. Coffee became the morning beverage of English and colonial businessmen, who praised its caffeine for keeping them focused. Coffee was served in new public coffeehouses, patronized by men, which opened first in London in the late 1660s and in Boston by the 1690s. By the mid-eighteenth century, though, tea—consumed at home in the afternoon at tea tables presided over by women—supplanted coffee in England and America. Tea was genteel; rum was the drink of the masses, made possible by new technology and the increasing production of sugar.

American colonies played a vital role in the production, distribution, and consumption of these beverages. Cacao plantations in South America multiplied to meet the rising chocolate demand. Rum involved Americans in every phase of its production and consumption. The sugar grown on Caribbean plantations was transported to the mainland in barrels and ships made from North American wood. There the syrup was turned into rum at 140 distilleries. Americans drank an estimated four gallons per person annually, but exported much of the rum to Africa, where it could purchase more slaves to produce more sugar to make more rum.

Thus, these beverages linked the colonies to the world and altered their economic and social development.

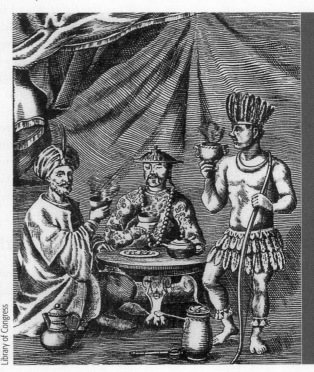

The frontispiece of Peter Muguet, Tractatus De Poto Caphe, Chinesium The et de Chocolata, *1685. Muguet's treatise visually linked the three hot, exotic beverages recently introduced to Europeans. The drinks are consumed by representatives of the cultures in which they originated: a turbaned Turk (with coffeepot in the foreground), a Chinese man (with teapot on the table), and an Indian drinking from a hollowed, handled gourd (with a chocolate pot and ladle on the floor in front of him).*

Library of Congress

New England and the Caribbean

New England had the most complex relationship to the trading system. It produced only one item England wanted: tall trees for masts for sailing vessels. To buy English manufactures, New Englanders needed profits earned elsewhere, especially in the Caribbean. By the late 1640s, decades before the Chesapeake became dependent on *production* by slaves, New England relied on *consumption* by slaves and owners. New England farmers and merchants profited by selling foodstuffs (primarily corn and salt fish) and wood for barrels to Caribbean sugar planters.

Shopkeepers in the interior of New England and middle colonies bartered with local farmers for grains, livestock, and barrel staves, then traded those items to merchants located in port towns. Such merchants dispatched ships to the Caribbean, where they exchanged their cargoes for molasses, sugar, fruit, dyestuffs, and slaves. Fully reloaded, the ships returned to Boston, Newport, New York, or Philadelphia. Americans distilled molasses into rum, the only part of the trade that could be termed triangular. Rhode Islanders took rum to Africa and traded it for slaves, whom they carried to Caribbean islands to exchange for more molasses to produce more rum.

Slaving Voyages

middle passage: The brutal and often fatal journey of slaves from Africa to America.

Tying the system together was the voyage (commonly called the **middle passage**) that brought Africans to the Americas. On shipboard, men were shackled in pairs in the hold except for some exercise on deck, whereas women and children could usually move freely in their daytime work of food preparation and cleaning. Many resisted enslavement by refusing to eat, jumping overboard, or joining in revolts, which rarely succeeded. Their communal singing and drumming, reported by numerous observers, must have lifted their spirits and forged solidarity. Conditions were hellish, as captains often packed people into holds that were hot, crowded, and reeking of vomit.

The traumatic voyage brought heavy fatalities of captives and crew. Roughly 10 to 20 percent of the newly enslaved died en route; on long or disease-ridden voyages, mortality rates were higher. Another 20 percent died before the ships left Africa or shortly after arriving in the Americas. One in every four or five sailors died on voyages, chiefly through exposure to such diseases as yellow fever and malaria.

Sailors signed on to slaving voyages reluctantly. Slave merchants were notoriously greedy and captains brutal—to sailors and captives. Unfortunately, the sailors, often the subject of abuse, in turn abused bondspeople. Yet through intimate contact with the enslaved, they learned the value of freedom, and sailors became known for their fierce attachment to independence.

Slavery in North America and the Caribbean

What skills did African slaves bring to America that proved vital to the development of colonial South Carolina?

Barbados, America's first "slave society" (an economy wholly dependent on enslavement), spawned others. As the island's population expanded, about 40 percent of the early English residents dispersed to other colonies. They carried their laws, commercial contacts, and slaveholding practices with them. A large proportion of the first Africans imported into North America came via Barbados. In addition to the many Barbadians who settled in Carolina, others moved to southern Virginia, New Jersey, and New England.

African Enslavement in the Chesapeake

Newly arrived Africans in the Chesapeake were often assigned to outlying parts of plantations (called quarters) until they learned some English and the routines of American tobacco cultivation. The crop that originated in the Americas was also being grown in various locations in West Africa, so Chesapeake planters, who in the late seventeenth century were still experimenting with curing and processing techniques, could well have drawn on their laborers' expertise Such Africans—mostly men—lived with ten to fifteen workers housed together in one or two buildings, supervised by an Anglo-American overseer. Each man was to cultivate two acres of tobacco a year. Their lives must have been filled with toil and loneliness, for few spoke the same language, and all worked six days a week. Many used their Sunday off to cultivate gardens or to hunt or fish to supplement their meager diet. Only rarely could they form families, because of the scarcity of women.

Slaves usually cost about two and a half times as much as indentured servants, but they could supply a lifetime of service, assuming they survived—which large numbers did not, having been weakened by the voyage and sickened by new diseases. Those with enough money could acquire slaves, accumulate greater wealth, and establish large plantations worked by tens, if not hundreds, of bondspeople, whereas the less affluent could not even afford indentured servants. Anglo-American society in the Chesapeake thus became increasingly stratified as the gap between rich and poor planters widened.

So many Africans were imported into Virginia and Maryland that by 1710 people of African descent composed one-fifth of the population. Even so, a decade later American-born slaves outnumbered their African-born counterparts in the Chesapeake, a trend that continued thereafter.

Link to Colonial Virginia and Maryland slave laws.

African Enslavement in South Carolina

Africans who came with their masters to South Carolina from Barbados in 1670, composing one-quarter to one-third of the early population. The Barbadian slaveowners quickly discovered that African-born slaves' skills were well suited to South Carolina's semitropical environment. African-style dugout canoes became the chief means of transportation in the colony, which was crossed by rivers with large islands. Fishing nets copied from African models proved more efficient. Baskets that enslaved laborers wove and gourds that they hollowed out came into general use as food and drink containers. Finally, Africans adapted their cattle herding techniques in America. Because meat and hides were an early export, Africans contributed to South Carolina's prosperity.

In 1693, as slavery was taking root in South Carolina, Spanish Florida officials began offering freedom to runaways who convert to Catholicism. Hundreds of South Carolina fugitives fled there, although not all gained freedom. Many settled in a town founded for them near St. Augustine, Gracia Real de Santa Teresa de Mose, headed by former slave Francisco Menendez.

After 1700, South Carolinians started importing slaves directly from Africa. In 1710, the African-born constituted a majority of the enslaved population in the colony and, by 1750, bondspeople composed a majority of its residents. The similarity of the South Carolinian and West African environments, coupled with the substantial African-born population, ensured the survival of more aspects of West African culture than elsewhere. Only in South Carolina did enslaved parents give their children African names and develop a dialect that combined English and African terms. (Known as Gullah, it has survived to the present in isolated areas.) In South Carolina, as in Guinea, African women became the primary petty traders, dominating Charles Town markets.

Rice and Indigo

Slave importation coincided with the successful introduction of rice in South Carolina. English people knew nothing about producing rice, but people from Africa's Rice Coast had long worked with the crop. Rice-growing techniques from West Africa, especially cultivation in inland swamps and tidal rivers, were widely adopted. South Carolinians preferred slaves from the Rice Coast, and they preferred women, possibly due to women's crucial role in cultivating rice in West Africa. There, they sowed and weeded the crop, pounded harvested rice with a mortar and pestle to remove the hulls and bran, and then winnowed to separate the grains from the chaff. South Carolinians utilized the West African system of pounding rice by hand until the late eighteenth century.

Every field worker on rice plantations had to cultivate three to four acres a year. Most were female, because enslaved men were assigned to jobs like blacksmithing or carpentry. Planters also expected slaves to grow part of their own food. Under the "task" system of predefined work assignments, experienced slaves could complete their tasks by early afternoon; after that and on Sundays, they were free to work their own gardens or on other projects. One scholar has suggested this unique **task system** used in South Carolina by the early eighteenth century resulted from negotiations between slaves familiar with rice cultivation and masters who desperately needed their expertise.

task system: Each slave had a daily or weekly quota of tasks to complete.

Developers of South Carolina's second cash crop—indigo—also used the task system and drew on slaves' specialized skills. Indigo, the only source of blue dye for the growing English textile industry, was much prized. Eliza Lucas, who managed her father's plantations, experimented with indigo cultivation during the early 1740s. Drawing on the knowledge of slaves and overseers from the Caribbean, she developed the planting and processing techniques later adopted colony-wide. South Carolina indigo never matched the quality of the Caribbean's, but indigo plantations flourished because Parliament offered Carolinians a bounty on every pound exported to Great Britain.

Indian Enslavement in North and South Carolina

In 1708, enslaved Indians composed roughly 14 percent of South Carolina's population. The lucrative traffic in Indian slaves significantly affected South Carolina's relationship with its indigenous neighbors. Native Americans knew they could find a ready market for captive enemies in Charles Town and used it to rid themselves of rivals. Yet as settlers and traders shifted their priorities, first one set of former allies, then another, were enslaved.

The trade in Indian slaves began when the Westos (originally known as the Eries), migrated south from the Great Lakes in the mid-1650s, fleeing their Iroquois enemies after the Beaver Wars. The Westos raided Spain's lightly defended Florida missions and sold Indian captives to Virginians. With the establishment of Carolina, the proprietors monopolized of trade with the Westos, which infuriated settlers shut out of commerce in slaves and deerskins. The planters secretly financed attacks on the Westos, wiping them out by 1682. Southeastern Indians protected themselves from such slave raids by subordination to the English or Spanish, or by coalescing into larger political units, such as those known later as Creeks, Chickasaws, or Cherokees.

At first, the Carolinians did not conflict with neighboring Indians. But in 1711, the Tuscaroras, an Iroquoian people, attacked a Swiss-German settlement at New Bern, North Carolina, which had expropriated their lands, which ignited the **Tuscarora War**. South Carolinians and their Indian allies combined to defeat the Tuscaroras. Afterward, more than a thousand Tuscaroras were enslaved, and the remainder drifted northward, where they joined the Iroquois Confederacy.

Tuscarora War: War in the Carolinas from 1711 through 1713 that pitted Tuscarora Indians against colonists and their Indian allies.

Four years later, the Yamasees, who aided the Carolinians against the Tuscaroras, turned on their English allies. In what seems a long-planned retaliation for abuses by traders and threats to their lands, the Yamasees enlisted the Creeks and other Muskogean peoples to attack outlying English settlements. In spring and summer 1715, English and African refugees by the hundreds streamed into Charles Town. The Yamasee-Creek offensive was thwarted when reinforcements arrived from the north, colonists hastily armed their African slaves, and Cherokees joined the fight. Afterward, Carolinian involvement in the Indian slave trade ceased, because their native neighbors moved away for self-protection. The native peoples of the Carolinas regrouped and rebuilt, for they were no longer subjected to slavers' raids.

Enslavement in the North

Atlantic creoles from the Caribbean and native peoples from the Carolinas and Florida, along with Indians enslaved for crime or debt, composed the bound laborers in the northern mainland colonies. The intricate involvement of northerners in the commerce surrounding the slave trade ensured that many people of African descent lived in America north of Virginia and that "Spanish Indians" became part of the New England population. Some bondspeople resided in urban areas, especially New York, which in 1700 had a larger black population than any other mainland city. Women worked as domestic servants, men as unskilled laborers on the docks.

Yet even in the North, most bondspeople worked in the countryside doing agricultural tasks. Dutch farmers in the Hudson valley and northern New Jersey were likely to rely on enslaved Africans, as were the owners of large landholdings in Rhode Island's Narragansett region. Some toiled in new enterprises, such as ironworks, alongside hired laborers and indentured servants. Although few northern colonists owned slaves, those who did relied heavily on their labor and wanted to preserve the institution of slavery.

The Granger Collection, New York

An advertisement for a sale of slaves of African descent that appeared in the *New York Journal* in 1768. The expertise of two would have appealed to urban buyers: a cooper would have been useful to a barrelmaker or shipper, and the seamstress might have attracted attention from dressmakers. The other bondspeople mentioned could have been purchased by people who wanted house servants or laborers.

Slave Resistance   As slavery grew, so did slaves' resistance. Usually, resistance meant malingering or running away, but occasionally bondspeople planned rebellions. Seven times before 1713, the English Caribbean experienced major revolts. The first mainland slave revolt occurred in New York in 1712. The rebels set a fire and ambushed those who tried to put it out, killing eight and wounding twelve. Of those caught and tried, eighteen were executed. Their decapitated bodies were left rotting outdoors as a warning.

Imperial Reorganization and the Witchcraft Crisis

How did mercantilism benefit some colonies economically and hurt others?

English officials seeking new sources of revenue focused on the expanding Atlantic trade in slaves and the products of slave labor. Parliament and the Stuart monarchs drafted laws to harness the profits of the trade for the mother country.

Mercantilism and Navigation Acts   Like other European nations, England based its commercial policy on mercantilism, the theory that viewed the economic world as a collection of national states, whose governments competed for shares of a finite amount of wealth. What one nation gained, another nation lost. Each nation sought economic self-sufficiency and a favorable balance of trade by exporting more than it imported. Colonies played an important role, supplying the mother country with valuable raw materials and a market for the mother country's manufactured goods.

Parliament's Navigation Acts—passed between 1651 and 1673—established three principles of mercantilist theory. First, only English or colonial merchants could legally trade in the colonies. Second, certain valuable American products could be sold only in the mother country or other English colonies. Initially, these "enumerated" goods included wool, sugar, tobacco, indigo, ginger, and dyes; and later rice, naval stores (masts, pitch, tar, and turpentine), copper, and furs. Third, foreign goods for sale in the colonies had to be shipped through England, paying English import duties. Years later, new laws established a fourth principle: the colonies could not export items (such as wool clothing, hats, or iron) that competed with English products.

These laws adversely affected Chesapeake planters who could not seek foreign markets for their staple crops. The statutes initially helped English Caribbean sugar producers by driving Brazilian sugar from the home market, but later prevented English planters from selling sugar elsewhere. Others benefited: the laws stimulated a lucrative colonial shipbuilding industry, especially in New England. And the northern and middle colonies produced many unenumerated goods—fish, flour, meat and livestock, and barrel staves—that could be traded directly to the French, Spanish, or Dutch Caribbean islands if transported in English or American ships.

English authorities soon learned that enforcing mercantilist laws would be difficult. The American coast's many harbors were havens for smugglers, and colonial officials often looked the other way when illegally imported goods were sold. Because American juries tended to favor local smugglers, Parliament in 1696 established American vice-admiralty courts, which operated without juries and adjudicated violations of the Navigation Acts.

Colonial Autonomy Challenged

By the early 1680s, mainland colonies had become accustomed to a considerable degree of political autonomy. Massachusetts, Plymouth, Connecticut, and Rhode Island operated independently, subject neither to the king nor a proprietor. Whereas Virginia was a royal colony and New Hampshire (1679) and New York (1685) gained that status, all other mainland settlements were proprietorships, over which England exercised little control. In the English colonies, free adult men who owned some property expected to have a voice in their governments, especially about taxation.

After James II became king in 1685, he and his successors sought to tighten the reins of colonial government and reduce the colonies' political autonomy. English officials saw New England as a hotbed of smuggling. Moreover, Puritans denied religious freedom to non-Congregationalists and maintained laws incompatible with English practice. The charters of all colonies from New Jersey to Maine were revoked, and the Crown established a Dominion of New England in 1686. (For the boundaries of the Dominion, see Map 3.1.) Sir Edmund Andros, the governor, had immense power: Parliament dissolved the assemblies, and Andros needed only the consent of an appointed council to make laws and levy taxes.

Glorious Revolution in America

New Englanders endured Andros's **autocratic** rule for more than two years. Then James II's power crumbled when he angered his subjects by levying taxes without parliamentary approval and by converting to Catholicism. In April 1689, Boston's leaders jailed Andros and his associates. The following month they received news of the bloodless coup known as the Glorious Revolution, in which James was replaced in late 1688 by his daughter Mary and her husband, the Dutch prince William of Orange. With Protestants William and Mary in power, the Glorious Revolution affirmed the supremacy of Parliament and Protestantism.

autocratic: Absolute or dictatorial rule.

In other colonies, the Glorious Revolution inspired revolt. In Maryland the Protestant Association overturned the government of the Catholic proprietor, and in New York a militia officer of German origin, Jacob Leisler, assumed control of the government. Bostonians, Marylanders, and New Yorkers saw themselves as carrying out the colonial phase of the English revolt.

But William and Mary also believed that England should exercise tighter control over its unruly American possessions. Consequently, only the Maryland rebellion received royal sanction, primarily because of its anti-Catholic thrust. In New York, Leisler was hanged for treason, and Massachusetts became a royal colony with an appointed governor. The province retained its town meeting system and continued to elect its council, but the 1691 charter eliminated the religious test for voting and office holding. A parish of the Church of England appeared in Boston. The **"city upon a hill,"** as John Winthrop had envisioned it, had ended.

city upon a hill: John Winthrop's vision of the Puritan settlement in New England as a model for the world.

King William's War

A war with the French and their Algonquian allies compounded New England's difficulties. King Louis XIV of France allied himself with the deposed James II, and England declared war on France in 1689—Known today as the Nine Years' War, it was called King William's War by the colonists. Even before war broke out in Europe, Anglo-Americans and Abenakis clashed over English settlements in Maine that had been reoccupied after the 1678 truce and were expanding. Attacks wholly or partially destroyed several towns, and colonial expeditions against Montreal and Quebec in 1690 failed. Even the Peace of Ryswick (1697), which ended the war in Europe, did not bring peace to the northern frontiers. Maine could not be resettled for several decades because of the continuing conflict.

The 1692 Witchcraft Crisis

New Englanders feared a repetition of the devastation of King Philip's War. For eight months in 1692, witchcraft accusations spread through Essex County, Massachusetts— a heavily populated area directly threatened by the Indian attacks in neighboring southern Maine and New Hampshire. Before the crisis ended, fourteen women and five men were hanged, one man was pressed to death with heavy stones, fifty-four people confessed to being witches, and more than 140 people were jailed.

Link to excerpts from the Salem Witchcraft papers.

The crisis began in late February when several children and young women in Salem Village charged older female neighbors with torturing them in spectral form. Other accusers and confessors chimed in, among them female domestic servants orphaned in the Maine war. These young women offered fellow New Englanders a compelling explanation for the troubles afflicting them: their province was under direct assault not only by Indians and the French but also by the Devil and his allied witches.

The so-called afflicted girls accused not just the older women commonly suspected of such offenses but also prominent men from the Maine frontier who had traded with or failed to defeat the Indians. Their leader, accusers declared, was the Reverend George Burroughs, a Harvard graduate who had ministered in Maine and Salem Village and was charged with bewitching soldiers sent to combat the Abenakis. The colony's magistrates, who were also its political and military leaders, were willing to believe such accusations, because it freed them from responsibility for losses on the frontier.

In October, the worst phase of the crisis ended when the governor dissolved the special court established to try the suspects. He and prominent clergymen regarded the descriptions of spectral torturers as "the Devil's testimony," and therefore untrustworthy. Most critics did not think the afflicted were faking, that witches did not exist or that confessions were false. Rather, they questioned whether guilt could be legally established by the evidence presented in court. During the final trials in 1693, almost all the defendants were acquitted, and the governor reprieved the few found guilty.

New Imperial Measures

In 1696, England created the fifteen-member Board of Trade and Plantations, the chief government organ concerned with the American colonies. The board gathered information, reviewed Crown appointments in America, scrutinized colonial legislation, supervised trade policies, and advised ministries on colonial issues. It had no enforcement powers and shared jurisdiction with the customs service, the navy, and a member of the ministry. Although this reform improved colonial administration, supervision of the American provinces remained decentralized and haphazard.

Debating the Witchcraft Trials

By late September 1692, disagreements over the Salem witchcraft trials (which had begun in June) sharply divided the intellectual leaders of Massachusetts Bay. Key among them were the colony's ministers, and especially a father and son: the Reverend Increase Mather and his son Cotton. Both were prolific authors, and both chose to present their views in print. The twenty-nine-year-old Cotton Mather strongly supported the trials and, at the request of the governor, wrote *The Wonders of the Invisible World* to defend the procedures and verdicts. Through its typeface, the title page of his book revealed its subject: DEVILS. On the title page of the related book by his father, *Cases of Conscience*, the less-prominent words were instead "evil Spirits," and rather than language affirming the "Grievous Molestations by Daemons and Witchcrafts" it included the caution that "infallible proofs" would be required to find the accused guilty. Even though Increase inserted an addendum at the end of his text insisting that he agreed with his son, anyone simply comparing the title pages could recognize that he was attempting to conceal competing opinions about the trials within his own family. What other contrasts between the two books are evident in the contents of the title pages?

The Wonders of the Invisible World.

OBSERVATIONS

As well *Historical* as *Theological*, upon the NATURE, the NUMBER, and the OPERATIONS of the

DEVILS.

Accompany'd with,

I. Some Accounts of the Grievous Molestations, by DÆMONS and WITCHCRAFTS, which have lately annoy'd the Countrey; and the Trials of some eminent *Malefactors* Executed upon occasion thereof: with several Remarkable *Curiosities* therein occurring.

II. Some Counsils, Directing a due Improvement of the terrible things, lately done, by the Unusual & Amazing Range of EVIL SPIRITS, in Our Neighbourhood: & the methods to prevent the *Wrongs* which those *Evil Angels* may intend against all sorts of people among us; especially in Accusations of the Innocent.

III. Some Conjectures upon the great EVENTS, likely to befall the WORLD in General, and NEW-ENGLAND in Particular; as also upon the Advances of the TIME, when we shall see BETTER DAYES.

IV. A short Narrative of a late Outrage committed by a knot of WITCHES in *Swedeland*, very much Resembling, and so far Explaining, *That* under which our parts of *America* have laboured!

V. THE DEVIL DISCOVERED: In a Brief Discourse upon those TEMPTATIONS, which are the more Ordinary *Devices* of the Wicked One.

By **Cotton Mather.**

Boston Printed by *Benj. Harris* for *Sam. Phillips.* 1693.

Massachusetts Historical Society

Cases of Conscience

Concerning evil

SPIRITS

Personating Men, Witchcrafts, infallible Proofs of Guilt in such as are accused with that Crime.

All Considered according to the Scriptures, History, Experience, and the Judgment of many Learned men.

By **Increase Mather,** President of Harvard Colledge at Cambridge, and Teacher of a Church at BOSTON in New-England.

Prov. 22. 21. —— *That thou mightest Answer the words of Truth, to them that send unto thee.*

Efficiunt Dæmones, ut quæ non sunt, sic tamen, quasi sint, conspicienda hominibus exhibeant. Lactantius Lib. 2. *Instit.* Cap. 15. *Diabolus Consulitur, cum ijs mediis utimur aliquid Cognoscendi, quæ a Diabolo sunt introducta. Ames. Cas. Consc. L.* 4. *Cap.* 23.

BOSTON Printed, and Sold by *Benjamin Harris* at the London Coffee-House. 1693.

Albert and Shirley Small Special Collections, University of Virginia Library

Americans of African Descent

After the 1670s, the rise of southern economies based on the enslavement of Africans, coupled with employment of enslaved Africans in northern colonies, dramatically altered the American population. By 1775, more than a quarter-million Africans had been imported into the territory that later became the United States; they and their descendants constituted about 20 percent of the population at that time.

According to the 2000 census, 12.5 percent of the Americans now claim descent from African ancestors. Because the legal importation of African slaves ended in 1808 and because the United States attracted relatively few voluntary migrants of African descent until the late twentieth century, most of today's native-born African Americans have colonial ancestors. Conversely, most European Americans are descended in part from the massive European migrations of the nineteenth and early twentieth centuries.

The modern African American population includes people with various skin colors, reflecting past interracial sexual relationships (coerced and voluntary). African Americans, free and enslaved, have had children with Europeans and Indians since the colonial period; more recently, they have intermarried with Asian immigrants. State laws, enacted from the early years of the American republic until 1967—when they were struck down by the Supreme Court—forbade legal marriages between people of European descent and those of other races. Thus, if people of color wanted to wed legally, they had to marry other people of color.

Recently, increasing numbers of interracial unions have produced multiracial children. The 2000 census for the first time allowed Americans to define themselves as members of more than one race. Previous laws defined people with any African ancestry as "black"; on census forms today, people of African descent seem less willing to define themselves as multiracial. Their racial self-definition thus continues to be influenced by a legacy of discrimination.

Most colonists resented alien officials who arrived to implement the policies of king and Parliament, but they adjusted to them and to the Navigation Act's trade restrictions. They fought another of Europe's wars—the War of the Spanish Succession, called Queen Anne's War in the colonies—from 1702 to 1713, without enduring the stresses of the first, despite the heavy economic burdens the conflict imposed. Colonists who allied with the royal government received offices and land grants, and composed "court parties" that supported English officials. Others, who lacked well-placed friends or who defended colonial autonomy, made up the opposition, or "country" interest. By the end of the 1725, most men in both groups were American born. They were from elite families whose wealth derived in the South from staple-crop production and in the North from commerce.

Summary

The years from 1650 to 1720 established the basic economic and political patterns in mainland colonial society. In 1650, two isolated centers of English population, New England and the Chesapeake, existed along the seaboard, along with the Dutch New Netherland. In 1720, nearly the entire North American east coast was in English hands, and Indian control east of the Appalachian Mountains had been broken by King Philip's War, Bacon's Rebellion, the Yamasee and Tuscarora wars, and Queen

Anne's War. West of the mountains, the Iroquois reigned. Most of the population was American-born, except for the African-born people in South Carolina and the Chesapeake. Economies originally based on the fur trade had become more complex and closely linked with the mother country, and political structures had become more uniform. The adoption of large-scale slavery and production of tobacco, rice, and indigo in the Chesapeake and Carolinas distinguished them from northern colonies as true slave societies.

The northern colonies, too, rested on profits from the Atlantic trading system, the key element of which was traffic in slaves. New England sold corn, salt fish, and wood products to the West Indies, where slaves consumed the foodstuffs and whence planters shipped sugar and molasses in barrels. Pennsylvania and New York also found the Caribbean islands a ready market for their livestock, grains, and wheat flour.

Meanwhile, north of Mexico Spanish settlements remained centered on Florida missions and on New Mexican presidios and missions. The French had explored the Mississippi valley but had not yet planted many settlements in the Great Lakes or the west. Both nations' colonists depended on indigenous people's labor and goodwill. Yet the Spanish and French presence to the south and west of English settlements ensured future conflicts among European powers in North America.

By 1720, key elements of the imperial administrative structure that would govern the English colonies until 1775 were in place. Anglo-Americans' commitment to autonomous local government would later lead them into conflict with Parliament and the king.

Chapter Review

The Growth of Anglo-American Settlements

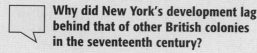

Why did New York's development lag behind that of other British colonies in the seventeenth century?

Granted to James the Duke of York in 1664, New York remained a shadow of Boston until well into the 1720s largely because James, unlike William Penn of Pennsylvania and other proprietors, did not encourage migration with offers of land grants and religious freedom to would-be colonists. Instead, his colony remained hemmed in by Connecticut and New Jersey, which each made successful overtures to draw populations helpful to development. English citizens who might have considered migrating to New York were turned off by James's decision to retain the Dutch local government, land title, and legal practices that had been in place when he assumed control of the former Dutch colony. He also allowed towns to decide which church to support with its taxes and refused a legislative assembly—which many English colonists wanted—until 1683.

A Decade of Imperial Crises: The 1670s

How did settlers' interests collide with those of Native Americans?

Settlers' and Native Americans' interests clashed in two pivotal areas: control of trade and desire for more land. New France and the Iroquois Confederacy clashed over control of the valuable fur trade, which the Iroquois had fought hard to attain. Bitter battles and attacks lasted for twenty years, before culminating in a neutrality treaty. Similarly, in the densely settled New England colonies in the 1670s, hostilities developed as Wampanoags led by King Phillip felt threatened by the Anglo-American communities that surrounded their territory. And in Virginia Nathaniel Bacon and his followers also focused on seizing desirable interior land from Indians, ultimately attacking them and pushing them further west.

The Atlantic Trading System

How was slavery at the center of the expanding trade network between Europe and the colonies?

First, the Chesapeake developed around tobacco farming, which required a vast supply of workers. Fewer English workers were available as population pressures in England eased and Restoration colonies offered land and other opportunities to would-be settlers. Tobacco growers instead turned to slave labor, as did other plantation colonies, thereby expanding the sale and transport of slaves. In addition, commodities produced by slave labor helped boost exports and trade networks, while the need to feed and clothe slaves stimulated new business opportunities for other colonies. New England, for example, profited by selling foodstuffs to feed slaves. The slave trade itself created a global economic network and tensions among European nations seeking to control the lucrative trade.

Slavery in North America and the Caribbean

What skills did African slaves bring to America that proved vital to the development of colonial South Carolina?

African-born slaves had several skills that were crucial to the economic development of South Carolina. From a similarly semi-tropical climate, these slaves adapted dugout canoes from their homeland that became a key means of transportation in the many rivers of the Carolinas. Their fishing nets also proved more efficient. African cattle herding techniques aided in producing the meat and hides that were an early export from the region. Some slaves, particularly women, also knew how to cultivate rice, which was rapidly becoming a staple crop in South Carolina. The area's other crash crop—indigo (the only source of blue dye for the growing English textile industry)—similarly drew on the knowledge of slaves transported to South Carolina from the Caribbean, where indigo plantations flourished.

Imperial Reorganization and the Witchcraft Crisis

How did mercantilism benefit some colonies economically and hurt others?

Mercantilism was grounded in the notion that the world contained a finite amount of wealth, and that if one nation gained, another had to lose. For England, that meant controlling colonial trade and development in ways that benefited the mother country. England passed the Navigation Acts between 1651 and 1673, which allowed only English merchants to trade in the colonies, permitted certain American products to be sold only to England or other English colonies, and required foreign goods bound for the colonies to ship through England and pay related duties. Later, it additionally prevented colonists from exporting anything that competed with English goods. For Chesapeake planters, these policies had a negative effect, preventing them from selling staple crops in foreign markets. English sugar producers in the Caribbean were initially helped, as their Brazilian competitors were driven from the market, but later suffered when they were prevented from selling their sugar elsewhere. New England benefitted from the emergence of a lucrative shipbuilding industry, while the northern and middle colonies gained from trading goods not included the Navigation Acts such as fish, flour, meat, livestock, and barrels.

Suggestions for Further Reading

Ned Blackhawk, *Violence over the Land: Indians and Empires in the Early American West* (2006)

David Eltis, *The Rise of African Slavery in the Americas* (1998)

Alan Gallay, *The Indian Slave Trade: The Rise of the English Empire in the American South, 1670–1717* (2002)

Andrew Knaut, *The Pueblo Revolt of 1680* (1995)

Jill Lepore, *The Name of War: King Philip's War and the Origins of American Identity* (1998)

Edmund S. Morgan, *American Slavery, American Freedom: The Ordeal of Colonial Virginia* (1975)

Jennifer L. Morgan, *Laboring Women: Reproduction and Gender in New World Slavery* (2004)

Mary Beth Norton, *In the Devil's Snare: The Salem Witchcraft Crisis of 1692* (2002)

Marcus Rediker, *The Slave Ship: A Human History* (2007)

Betty Wood, *The Origins of American Slavery* (1997)

Go to the CourseMate website for primary source links, study tools, and review materials for this chapter. www.cengagebrain.com

American Society Transformed

1720–1770

4

The crime was devastating, the punishment terrible. Marie-Joseph Angélique, a Portuguese-born slave of African descent, was hanged in Montréal on June 21, 1734. Judges had convicted Angélique of setting a fire that destroyed the merchant quarter of the town, the Hotel-Dieu, a convent, and a hospital. Under torture, she confessed, insisting she had acted alone. Afterward, her body was left hanging for hours, then it was burned and her ashes scattered.

Angelique had been a slave in an English colony—probably New York—before being purchased nine years earlier by a Montreal wealthy merchant, Sieur de Francheville, and his wife. She worked in their large household with several free laborers and an enslaved Indian boy. She was one of 150 or so bondspeople living among the 3,000 Montreal residents.

Angélique was the immediate suspect. After her master's death in late 1733, she asked her mistress for her freedom, presumably so she could leave Montréal with her lover, Claude Thibault, a former French soldier who was also a Francheville servant. Denied, she threatened to "roast" her mistress, who retaliated by preparing to sell her to a French Caribbean island. She and Claude set fire to another house in January, before attempting unsuccessfully to flee together. Witnesses testified that Angelique had earlier hinted at plans to burn down the Francheville house. Yet until she was tortured, Angelique proclaimed her innocence. She never implicated Claude Thibault, who vanished from New France.

Angélique's tragic story as a woman of African descent who had spent time in the English colonies points up the movement of peoples around the Atlantic world that after 1720 brought new groups to the British colonies. A massive eighteenth-century migration of European and African peoples changed the nature of the North American population. Ethnic diversity was especially pronounced in the small cities of Anglo America, although the colonies south of New England drew the largest number of newcomers, many to the fertile countryside. They swelled the

Chapter Outline

Geographic Expansion and Ethnic Diversity
Spanish and French Territorial Expansion | France and the Mississippi | Involuntary Migrants from Africa | Newcomers from Europe | Scots-Irish, Scots, and Germans | Maintaining Ethnic and Religious Identities

VISUALIZING THE PAST *Slaves' Symbolic Resistance*

Economic Growth and Development in British America
Commerce and Manufacturing in the British Colonies | Wealth and Poverty | Regional Economies

Colonial Cultures
Genteel Culture | The Enlightenment | Oral Cultures | Religious and Civic Rituals | Rituals of Consumption | Tea and Madeira | Rituals on the "Middle Ground"

LINKS TO THE WORLD *Smallpox Inoculation*

Colonial Families
Indian and Mixed-Race Families | European American Families | African American Families | Forms of Resistance | City Life

Politics: Stability and Crisis in British America
Colonial Assemblies | Slave Rebellions in South Carolina and New York | Rioters and Regulators

A Crisis in Anglo-American Religion
George Whitefield | Impact of the Awakening | Virginia Baptists

LEGACY FOR A PEOPLE AND A NATION *"Self-Made Men"*

SUMMARY

79

population, altered political balances, and introduced new religious sects. Unwilling immigrants (slaves and transported convicts), too, clustered primarily in the middle and southern colonies.

Several key themes marked the development of Europe's North American colonies in the mid-eighteenth century: population growth (through natural increase and immigration), new ethnic diversity, the increasing importance of urban centers, the creation of a prosperous urban elite including merchant families like the Franchevilles, rising consumption, and the new significance of internal markets. In the French and British mainland colonies, exports dominated the economy. Settlers along the Atlantic and Gulf coasts were tied to an international commercial system that fluctuated wildly. Yet expanding local populations demanded greater quantities and types of goods, and Europe could not keep up. Therefore, colonists increasingly depended on their own resources. Intermarried networks of wealthy families developed in Europe's American possessions by the 1760s. These well-off, educated colonists participated in transatlantic intellectual life, such as the Enlightenment, whereas some colonists of the "lesser sort" could neither read nor write. Most colonists worked with their hands from dawn to dark. Divisions were most pronounced in British America, the largest and most prosperous settlements. By the last half of the century, social and economic distance among different ranks of Anglo-Americans had widened and produced new conflicts.

In 1720, much of North America was under Indian control. Fifty years later, indigenous peoples still dominated the interior, yet their lives were altered as European settlements expanded. As France moved from the St. Lawrence to the Gulf of Mexico and Spanish outposts expanded east and west from a New Mexican heartland, and as British colonies filled the territory between the Appalachian Mountains and the Atlantic, North America was transformed.

As you read this chapter, keep the following questions in mind:

* **What were the effects of demographic, geographic, and economic changes on Europeans, Africans, and Indian nations alike?**

* **What were the key elements of eighteenth-century colonial cultures?**

* **What developments at midcentury began the process of political and religious change in British North America?**

Geographic Expansion and Ethnic Diversity

What spurred population growth in the British colonies in the thirty years before 1775?

In the mid-eighteenth century, dramatic population growth, along with geographic expansion, characterized British mainland colonies. About 250,000 European-Americans and African Americans resided in the colonies in 1700. Thirty years later, that number had more than doubled, reaching 2.5 million by 1775.

Although migration from Africa, Scotland, Ireland, England, and Germany contributed to population growth, most came from natural increase. Once the difficult early decades of settlement had passed, the American population doubled

Chronology

1690	Locke's *Essay Concerning Human Understanding* published, a key example of Enlightenment thought
1718	New Orleans founded in French Louisiana
1721–22	Smallpox epidemic in Boston leads to first widespread adoption of inoculation in America
1732	Founding of Georgia
1733	John Peter Zenger is tried for and acquitted of "seditious libel" in New York
1739	Stono Rebellion (South Carolina) leads to increased white fears of slave revolts
	George Whitefield arrives in America; Great Awakening broadens
1739–48	King George's War affects American economies
1740s	Black population of the Chesapeake begins to grow by natural increase, contributing to rise of large plantations
1741	New York City "conspiracy" reflects whites' continuing fears of slave revolts
1751	Franklin's *Experiments and Observations on Electricity* published, important American contribution to Enlightenment science
1760–75	Peak of eighteenth-century European and African migration to English colonies
1765–66	Hudson River land riots pit tenants and squatters against large landlords
1767–69	Regulator movement (South Carolina) tries to establish order in backcountry
1771	North Carolina Regulators defeated by eastern militia at Battle of Alamance

approximately every twenty-five years. Women were young when they began childbearing (early twenties for European-Americans, late teens for African Americans), and married women became pregnant every two or three years, having five to ten children. With the colonies' healthy environment, a large proportion of children reached maturity. About half of the population of Anglo America was under sixteen years old in 1775. (Less than one-quarter of the United States population is currently under sixteen.)

Spanish and French Territorial Expansion   British North America's growing population was sandwiched between the Appalachian Mountains (on the west) and the Atlantic coast (on the east). By contrast, Spanish and French territories expanded across North America with modest population increases. At the end of the eighteenth century, Texas had only about three thousand Spanish residents and California fewer than one thousand; the largest Spanish colony, New Mexico, included twenty thousand or so. Mainland French colonies' population increased from approximately fifteen thousand in 1700 to about seventy thousand in the 1760s, clustered in a few scattered locations. Still, French and Spanish geographic expansion dramatically affected native peoples.

Venturing into the Mississippi Valley in the early eighteenth century, the French and Spanish encountered powerful Indian nations like the Quapaws, Osages, and Caddos. A few Europeans—priests, soldiers, farmers, traders, ranchers—met native peoples who wanted access to manufactured goods, and who accordingly sought friendly relations. The Spanish and French invaders had to adapt to Indian diplomatic and cultural practices. French officials, for example, often complained of being forced to endure lengthy calumet ceremonies; and Spaniards, unaccustomed to involving women in diplomacy, had to accede to Texas Indians' use of female representatives. The European nations established neighboring outposts

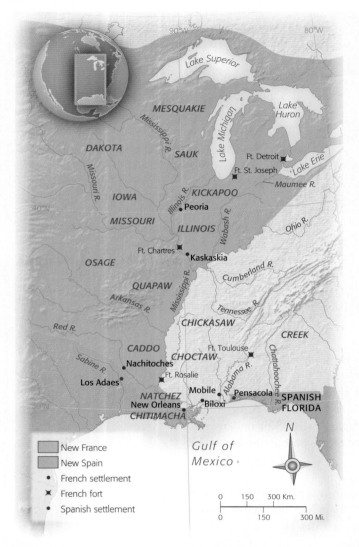

MAP 4.1

Louisiana, ca. 1720

By 1720, French forts and settlements dotted the Mississippi River and its tributaries in the interior of North America. Two isolated Spanish outposts were situated near the Gulf of Mexico.

Source: Copyright © Cengage Learning

Link to Eulalia Perez's account of her work in a California Spanish mission.

in the lower Mississippi region in 1716—the French at Natchitoches (west of the Mississippi), the Spaniards at Los Adaes (see Map 4.1). France had settled Biloxi Bay (in the modern state of Mississippi) in 1699, and strengthened its presence near the Gulf of Mexico by establishing New Orleans in 1718.

Spaniards focused first on Texas (establishing San Antonio in 1718), then the region they called Alta (upper) California. After learning that Russians who hunted sea otters along the northwest coast wanted to colonize the region, they sent expeditions north from their missions in Baja California. From a base at San Diego, where the Franciscan Junipero Serra set up the first mission in Alta California in July 1769, they traveled by land and sea to Monterey Bay, where in April 1770 they claimed Alta California for Spain. Over the next decades, they established presidios and missions along the coast from modern San Francisco to San Diego. There, Spanish Franciscan friars and a few settlers from Mexico lived amid thousands of Indians who had converted to Christianity.

France and the Mississippi

Along the Mississippi, French posts north of New Orleans became the glue of empire. *Coureurs de bois* (literally, "forest runners") used the American interior's waterways to carry goods between Quebec and the new Louisiana territory. Indians traded furs and hides for guns, ammunition, and other items. The Osages were so eager to acquire firearms that they became, in effect, commercial hunters; their women were sometimes so fully occupied processing hides that older men prepared the communities' meals. The largest French settlements, known collectively as *le pays de Illinois* ("the Illinois country"), never totaled much above three thousand people The shortage of European women led to interracial unions between French men and Indian women, creating mixed-race people known as *metís*. French expansion helped reshape native alliances elsewhere. For example, the equestrian Comanches of the Plains, who could now trade with the French, no longer needed Spanish goods or their previous allies, the Utes. Deprived of powerful partners, the Utes negotiated peace with New Mexico in 1752. Once enslaved by Spaniards, Utes enslaved Paiutes and other nonequestrian peoples. They exchanged hides and slaves—mostly young women—for horses and metal goods until the end of Spanish rule in the region.

To French officials, Louisiana's chief function was protection of the valuable Caribbean islands and prevention of Spanish and British expansion. Profit-seeking farmers and Indian traders from Canada demanded slaves from the French government. Officials dispatched more than six thousand Africans, mostly from Senegal, in the decade after 1719. But residents never developed a successful plantation economy. Skins and hides from the Indians, along with tobacco and indigo, composed Louisiana's major eighteenth-century exports. Enslaved Africans were carried north to the Illinois country, where as farm laborers and domestic servants they made up nearly 40 percent of the population in the 1730s.

Louisiana's expansion claimed lands belonging to Natchez Indians. In 1729, the Natchez and newly arrived slaves attacked the colony's northern reaches, killing more than 10 percent of Europeans. The French retaliated, slaughtering the Natchez and their allies, but under French rule, Louisiana remained a fragile colony.

Involuntary Migrants from Africa

Elsewhere in the Americas, slavery took firm hold during the eighteenth century. In all, more Africans than Europeans came to the Americas—the majority as slaves—with half arriving between 1700 and 1800. Most were transported to Brazil or the Caribbean, primarily in British or Portuguese vessels. Of at least 11 million enslaved people brought to the Americas during slavery, only 260,000 were imported by 1775 into the region that became the United States. In South America and the Caribbean, a surplus of enslaved males over females and high mortality rates meant that only a continuing influx of slaves could maintain a consistent work force. On the North American mainland, South Carolina, where rice cultivation was difficult and unhealthful (because malaria-carrying mosquitoes bred in rice swamps), similarly required an inflow of slaves.

Slaves came from various ethnic groups and regions of Africa (see Map 4.2). More than 40 percent embarked from West Central Africa (modern Congo and Angola), nearly 20 percent from the Bight of Benin (modern Togo, Benin, and southwestern Nigeria), about 13 percent from the Bight of Biafra (today's Cameroon, Gabon, and southeastern Nigeria), and approximately 9 percent from the Gold Coast (modern Ghana and neighboring countries). Smaller proportions came from East Africa and the Windward and Rice Coasts (modern Senegal, Gambia, and Sierra Leone).

Standard slave-trading practice—of loading an entire cargo at one port and selling them in another—meant that people from the same area were typically taken to the Americas together. That was heightened by planter partiality for particular ethnic groups. Virginians favored Igbos from the Bight of Biafra, whereas South Carolinians and Georgians selected Senegambians and people from West Central Africa. Rice planters' desire for Senegambians, who were experienced rice cultivators, makes sense, but historians disagree about the reasons behind other preferences.

Possibly tens of thousands of enslaved Africans were Muslims, some of whom were literate in Arabic and came from aristocratic families. The discovery of noble birth could lead to slaves' being returned home. Job Ben Solomon, for example, a slave trader from Senegal, had been captured by raiders while selling bondspeople in Gambia and sent to Maryland in 1732. A letter he wrote in Arabic so impressed his owners that he was liberated the next year. Despite the approximately 260,000 slaves brought to the mainland, after 1740 American-born people of African descent came to dominate the enslaved population because of natural increase.

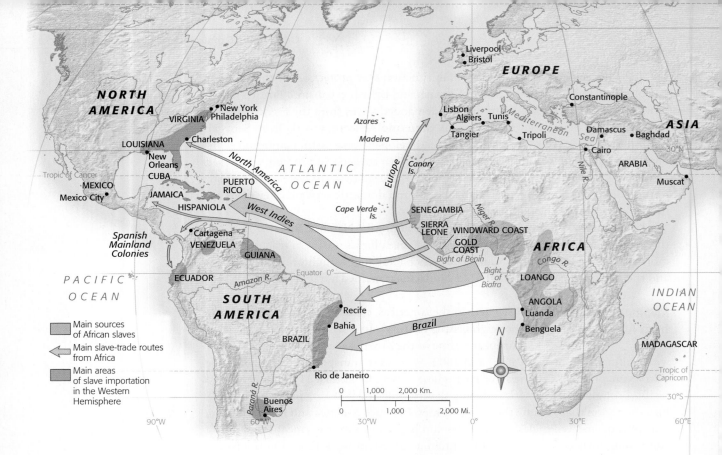

MAP 4.2

Major Origins and Destinations of Africans Enslaved in the Americas

As this schematic map shows, enslaved Africans were drawn from many regions of western Africa (with some coming from the interior of the continent) and were shipped to areas throughout the Americas.

Source: Copyright © Cengage Learning

Although about 40 percent of the Africans were male, women and children composed a majority of slave imports; females were valued for their reproductive and productive capacities. A planter who owned adult female slaves could watch his labor force expand steadily—through the births of their children, designated as slaves in every colony.

In the Chesapeake, the number of bondspeople grew rapidly because imports were added to an enslaved population that also expanded through natural increase. Work routines for cultivating tobacco, coupled with a roughly equal sex ratio, reduced slave mortality and increased fertility. Even in unhealthful South Carolina, American-born slaves outnumbered the African-born by 1750.

Newcomers from Europe

About 500,000 Europeans moved to British North America during the eighteenth century, most after 1730. Influenced by mercantilist thought, British authorities regarded a large, industrious population at home as an asset. They deported "undesirables"—vagabonds and Jacobite rebels (supporters of the deposed Stuart monarchs)—but otherwise discouraged emigration. Instead, they recruited German and French Protestants to the colonies by promising free land and religious

Slaves' Symbolic Resistance

Although revolts and running away have been the focus of many studies of enslaved Africans' resistance to bondage in North America, archaeological finds from the mid-eighteenth-century such as those illustrated here have revealed important aspects of slaves' personal lives and other forms of resistance. The set of objects found in Annapolis constitutes a *minkisi*, or West African spiritual bundle. Africans and African Americans placed such bundles of objects, each with a symbolic meaning (for example, bent nails reflected the power of fire), under hearths or sills to direct the spirits, who entered and left houses through doors or chimneys. Their primary purpose was to protect bondspeople from the power of their masters—for example, by preventing the breakup of a family. The statue of a man was uncovered in an enslaved blacksmith's quarters. It too reflects resistance, but of a different sort: the quiet rebellion of a talented craftsman who used his master's iron and his own time and skill to secretly create a remarkable object. Can students today derive insights about enslaved people's lives from such artifacts as these, even though the illiterate bondspeople left no written records? If so, what?

Private Collection/Picture Research Consultants & Archives

Artifact found in an excavation in Alexandria, Virginia.

Photograph courtesy of Archaeology in Annapolis, University of Maryland, College Park

A minkisi from the eighteenth century found under the floor of the Charles Carroll house in Annapolis, Maryland.

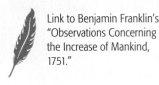

Link to Benjamin Franklin's "Observations Concerning the Increase of Mankind, 1751."

toleration. After 1740, they relaxed citizenship requirements to a small fee, seven years' residence, Protestantism, and an oath of allegiance to the king.

The most successful migrants came well prepared, having learned from earlier migrants that land and resources were abundant and that they would need capital. People who arrived penniless did less well; approximately 40 percent of the newcomers fell into that category, immigrating as bound laborers. Worst off were the 50,000 or so migrants who came as criminals convicted of such offenses as theft and murder. Many unskilled and perhaps one-third female, they were typically dispatched to Maryland to work in tobacco fields, as ironworkers, or as household servants.

Scots-Irish, Scots, and Germans

One of the largest groups of immigrants—over 150,000—were families from Ireland or Scotland. About 70,000 Scots-Irish descendants of Presbyterian Scots who had settled in Northern Ireland during the seventeenth century joined 35,000 who came to America from Scotland (see Table 4.1). Another 45,000 Protestants and Catholics migrated from southern Ireland (often as individuals). High rents, poor harvests, and religious discrimination (in Ireland) pushed people from their homeland. Such immigrants usually landed in Philadelphia or New Castle, Delaware. They moved into the western Pennsylvania backcountry. Later migrants moved to the backcountry of Maryland, Virginia, and the Carolinas. Frequently unable to afford land, they lived illegally on acreage belonging to Indians, land speculators, or colonial governments. They gained a reputation for lawlessness, drinking, and fighting.

Migrants from Germany and German-speaking areas of Switzerland numbered about 85,000 between 1730 and 1755. They, too, usually came in family groups and landed in Philadelphia. Many, like earlier English migrants, contracted to work as servants for several years to pay for their passage. When free, Germans settled together. Many moved west into Pennsylvania and south into the Maryland and Virginia backcountry as well as Charles Town and the southern interior. Germans belonged to various Protestant sects, adding to Pennsylvania's religious diversity. By century's end, Germans were one-third of Pennsylvania's residents. Benjamin Franklin predicted inaccurately in 1751 that they would "Germanize" Pennsylvania.

The most concentrated period of colonial immigration fell between 1760 and 1775, when more than 220,000 free and enslaved people arrived—nearly 10 percent of British North America's population. Tough economic times led many to seek a better life in America; simultaneously, the slave trade burgeoned. Late-arriving free immigrants had little choice but to remain in the cities or move to the edges of settlement; land elsewhere was fully occupied. In the peripheries, they rented or bought property from land speculators.

Maintaining Ethnic and Religious Identities

Huguenots: French Calvinist dissenters from that country's dominant Catholicism.

Half of the colonial population south of New England had non-English origins by 1775. Assimilation into Anglo-American culture depended on settlement patterns, group size, and migrants' cultural ties. The French Protestants (**Huguenots**) who migrated to Charles Town or New York City were unable to sustain their language or religious practices for more than two generations, whereas Huguenots settling in the Hudson Valley remained recognizably French and Calvinist for a

TABLE 4.1   **Who Moved to America from England and Scotland in the Early 1770s, and Why?**

	English Emigrants	Scottish Emigrants	Free American Population
Destination			
13 British colonies	81.1%	92.7%	—
Canada	12.1	4.2	—
West Indies	6.8	3.1	—
Age Distribution			
Under 21	26.8	45.3	56.8%
21–25	37.1	19.9	9.7
26–44	33.3	29.5	20.4
45 and over	2.7	5.3	13.1
Sex Distribution			
Male	83.8	59.9	—
Female	16.2	40.1	—
Unknown	4.2	13.5	—
Traveling Alone or with Families			
In families	20.0	48.0	—
Alone	80.0	52.0	—
Known Occupation or Status			
Gentry	2.5	1.2	—
Merchandising	5.2	5.2	—
Agriculture	17.8	24.0	—
Artisanry	54.2	37.7	—
Laborer	20.3	31.9	—
Why They Left			
Positive reasons (e.g., desire to better one's position)	90.0	36.0	—
Negative reasons (e.g., poverty, unemployment)	10.0	64.0	—

Note: Between December 1773 and March 1776, the British government questioned individuals and families leaving ports in Scotland and England for the American colonies to learn who they were, where they were going, and why they were leaving. This table summarizes just a few of the findings of the official inquiries, which revealed a number of significant differences between the Scottish and English emigrants.

Source of data: Bernard Bailyn, *Voyagers to the West* (New York: Knopf, 1986), Tables 4.1, 5.2, 5.4, 5.7, 5.23, and 6.1.

century. The equally small group of colonial Jews maintained a distinct identity wherever they settled. In places like New York and Newport, Rhode Island, they established synagogues and preserved their religion.

Members of larger migrant groups (Germans, Irish, and Scots) found it easier to sustain European ways. Some ethnicities dominated certain localities. Where migrants from different countries settled the same region, ethnic antagonisms surfaced. One German clergyman in Pennsylvania, for example, claimed that Scots-Irish migrants were "lazy, dissipated and poor." Anglo-American elites fostered antagonisms to maintain their power and frequently subverted naturalization laws to depriving even long-resident immigrants a voice in government.

Ultimately, elites would need the support of non-English Americans. When they moved toward revolution in the 1770s, they deliberately began speaking of "the rights of man," rather than "English liberties," to attract recruits.

Economic Growth and Development in British America

How were the colonies' economic fates increasingly linked to world markets?

The dramatic population increase of Anglo America caused colonial economies to grow, despite the vagaries of international markets. By contrast, the population and economy of New Spain's northern Borderlands stagnated, for the isolated settlements produced few items for export. French Canada exported large quantities of furs and fish, but the government's trade monopoly ensured that profits primarily ended up in the home country. The Louisiana colony required substantial government subsidies to survive. Of France's American possessions, only the Caribbean islands flourished.

Commerce and Manufacturing in the British Colonies

In British North America, the rising population demanded more goods and services, fueling the development of small-scale colonial manufacturing and a complex internal trade network. Roads, bridges, mills, and stores were built to serve new settlements. A lively coastal trade developed; by the late 1760s, more than half of the vessels leaving Boston sailed to other mainland colonies, collecting goods for export and distributing imports and American-made items. Colonies no longer depended wholly on European goods, and the American population generated sufficient demand to support local manufacturing.

Iron making became the largest industry, surpassing England's by 1775. Ironworks in the Chesapeake and middle colonies required sizable investments and substantial workforces—usually indentured servants, convicts, and slaves—who dug the ore, chopped trees for charcoal production, and smelted and refined the ore. Because the work was dirty, dangerous, and difficult, convicts and servants often fled, but enslaved men could learn valuable skills and accumulate property when paid for doing extra assigned tasks.

Colonial prosperity nevertheless depended heavily on overseas demand for tobacco, rice, indigo, fish, and timber products. By selling such items, colonists earned credit to purchase English and European imports. If demand for American exports slowed, the colonists' income and purchasing power dropped, producing economic downswings.

Wealth and Poverty

Despite fluctuations, the American economy grew during the eighteenth century, partly from higher earnings from exports. That produced better living standards for property-owning Americans. Early in the century, as the price of British manufactures fell, households acquired amenities such as chairs and earthenware dishes. Diet also improved as trade brought more varied foodstuffs. After 1750, luxury items could be found in the wealthy's homes, and the "middling sort" imported English ceramics and teapots. Even the poorest property owners had better household goods.

New arrivals did not have the advancement opportunities of their predecessors. Still, at least two-thirds of rural householders owned their own land by 1750. But in the cities, laborers' families lived close to destitution. By the 1760s, applicants for assistance overwhelmed public urban poor-relief systems, and some cities built workhouses or almshouses to shelter growing numbers of elderly and infirm people along with widows and their children.

Regional Economies

Within this overall picture, varying regional patterns emerged, in part because of **King George's War**, also called the War of the Austrian Succession (1739–1748).

New England's export economy rested on trade with the Caribbean: northern forests supplied the timber to build ships that carried salt fish to feed slaves on sugar plantations. The war increased demand for New England's ships and sailors, thus invigorating the economy; but New Englanders suffered major losses of men and materiel in Caribbean battles and in their successful attack on the fortress of Louisbourg (in modern Nova Scotia), which guarded the sea-lanes leading to New France. When the shipbuilding boom ended with the war, the economy stagnated, and widows and orphans crowded relief rolls. Britain even returned Louisbourg to France in the Treaty of Aix-la-Chapelle (1748).

By contrast, King George's War and its aftermath brought prosperity to the middle colonies and the Chesapeake, because the fertile soil and longer growing season in both regions readily produced an abundance of grain. After 1748, when several poor harvests in Europe caused flour prices to skyrocket, Philadelphia and New York took the lead in the foodstuffs trade. Some Chesapeake planters began to convert tobacco fields to wheat and corn. Tobacco remained the largest single export from the mainland colonies, yet grain cultivation significantly changed Chesapeake settlement by encouraging the development of port towns (like Baltimore), where merchants and shipbuilders would handle the new trade.

That South Carolina's staple crop was rice determined its distinctive economic pattern, as did its vulnerability to Atlantic hurricanes. Storms periodically devastated its rice and indigo crops, causing hardship and bankruptcies. Yet after Parliament in 1730 removed rice from the list of enumerated products, South Carolinians prospered by trading directly with Europe. The outbreak of war disrupted that trade, and the colony entered a depression that ended in the 1760s. Overall, though, South Carolina grew faster than other British colonies and had the highest average wealth per freeholder in mainland Anglo America by the American Revolution.

The newest British settlement, Georgia, was chartered in 1732 as a haven for imprisoned English debtors. Its founder, **James Oglethorpe**, envisioned Georgia as a garrison where farmers who would defend the southern flank of English settlement against Spanish Florida. Accordingly, its charter prohibited slavery, but neighboring

King George's War: Also known as the War of Austrian Succession, started out as a conflict between Britain and Spain, but then escalated when France sided with Spain.

James Oglethorpe: Founder of Georgia colony.

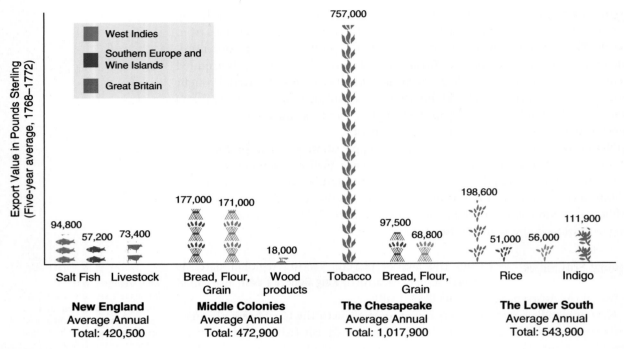

FIGURE 4.1
Regional Trading Patterns

As this figure shows, the different regions of the British mainland colonies had distinct trading patterns: they exported diverse products to different markets. By far the most valuable export was the tobacco grown by Chesapeake slaves.
Source: Adapted from James F. Shepard and Gary M. Walton, *Shipping, Maritime Trade, and the Economic Development of Colonial North America* [Cambridge: University Press, 1972].

Carolina rice planters had the restriction removed in 1751. Thereafter, Georgia developed into a rice-planting slave society resembling South Carolina.

Regional variations highlight the British mainland colonies' disparate experiences within the empire. Despite increasing coastal trade, the colonies' economic fortunes depended on the shifting markets of Europe and the Caribbean. Without an unprecedented crisis in the British imperial system (discussed in Chapter 5), it seems unlikely they could have been persuaded to join in a common endeavor. Even with that impetus, unity proved difficult to maintain.

Colonial Cultures

How did rituals function in colonial America?

By 1750, British America was denser and more diverse than a half-century earlier with new extremes of wealth and poverty, especially in the growing cities. Native-born colonial elites sought to distinguish themselves from ordinary folk as they consolidated their hold on local power.

Genteel Culture

Colonists who acquired wealth through trade, agriculture, or manufacturing spent their money ostentatiously, dressing fashionably, traveling in horse-drawn carriages, and hosting lavish parties. They built large houses containing rooms for dancing, cardplaying, or drinking tea. Sufficiently well-off to enjoy "leisure" time (a first for North America), they attended concerts and the theater, gambled at horse races, and played billiards and other games. They also cultivated polite manners. Although the effects of accumulated wealth were most pronounced in Anglo America, elite families in New Mexico, Louisiana, and Quebec set themselves off from the "lesser sort." Together, these wealthy families deliberately constructed a genteel culture different from that of ordinary colonists.

Men from such families prided themselves on their possessions, their positions in the political and economic hierarchy, their education, and their intellectual connections to Europe. Many had been tutored by private teachers; some attended college. (Harvard, the first colonial college, founded in 1636, was joined by William and Mary in 1693 and Yale in 1701.) In the seventeenth century, only aspiring clergymen attended college, but by the mid-eighteenth century, as colleges broadened their curricula to include mathematics, science, law, and medicine, young men from elite or upwardly mobile families slowly enrolled. American women were mostly excluded from advanced education, except those who joined nunneries in Canada or Louisiana.

Elizabeth Murray, the subject of this 1769 painting by John Singleton Copley, was the wife of James Smith, a wealthy rum distiller. Her fashionable dress and pose would seem to mark her as a lady of leisure, yet both before and during her marriage this Scottish immigrant ran a successful dry goods shop in Boston. She thus simultaneously catered to and participated in the new culture of consumption.

The Enlightenment

The intellectual current known as the **Enlightenment** deeply affected the clergymen who headed colonial colleges and their students. Around 1650, some European thinkers analyzed nature to determine the laws governing the universe. They employed experimentation and abstract reasoning to discover general principles behind phenomena like the motions of planets. Enlightenment philosophers emphasized acquiring knowledge through reason, challenging previously unquestioned assumptions. **John Locke**'s *Essay Concerning Human Understanding* (1690) disputed the notion that human beings are born imprinted with innate ideas. All knowledge, Locke asserted, derived from observations. Belief in witchcraft and astrology and similar phenomena thus were attacked.

The Enlightenment supplied educated, well-to-do people in Europe and America with a common vocabulary and a unified world-view, one that insisted the enlightened eighteenth century was better and wiser than previous ages. It joined them in the common endeavor to make sense of God's creation. Thus American naturalists like John and William Bartram supplied European scientists with information about New World plants and animals for newly formulated classification systems. A prime example of America's participation in the Enlightenment was **Benjamin Franklin**, who retired from a successful printing business in 1748 at age forty-two, devoting himself to scientific experimentation and public service. His *Experiments and Observations on Electricity* (1751) established the basic theory of electricity still used today.

Enlightenment: Intellectual revolution that elevated reason, science, and logic.

John Locke: British philosopher and major Enlightenment thinker; known for his emphasis on the power of human reasoning.

Benjamin Franklin: American who embodied Enlightenment ideas.

Smallpox Inoculation

Smallpox, the world's greatest killer of human beings, repeatedly ravaged North American colonists and Indians. Thus, when the vessel *Seahorse* arrived in Boston from the Caribbean in April 1721 with smallpox-infected people on board, New Englanders feared the worst and quarantined the ship. It was too late: smallpox escaped into the city, and by June several dozen people were afflicted.

But the Reverend Cotton Mather, a member of London's Royal Society (an Enlightenment organization), had read years earlier of a medical technique previously unknown to Europeans but widely employed in North Africa and the Middle East. Called inoculation, it involved taking pus from the pustules (or poxes) of an infected person and inserting it into a small cut on the arm of a healthy individual. With luck, that person would experience a mild case and gain lifetime immunity. Mather's interest was further piqued by his slave Onesimus, a North African who had been inoculated as a youth and who described the procedure in detail.

With the disease coursing through the city, Mather promoted inoculation to the local medical community. But the city's doctors ridiculed his ideas, except for Zabdiel Boylston, a physician and apothecary. The two men inoculated their children and about two hundred others. After the epidemic ended, Bostonians could see the results: of those inoculated, just 3 percent had died; among the thousands who contracted the disease naturally, mortality was 15 percent. Even Mather's most vocal opponents supported inoculation thereafter.

Thus, through transatlantic links forged by the Enlightenment and enslavement, American colonists learned how to combat the deadliest disease. Today, thanks to a successful campaign by the World Health Organization, smallpox has been eradicated.

An Historical

ACCOUNT

OF THE

SMALL-POX INOCULATED

IN

NEW ENGLAND,

Upon all Sorts of Perfons, *Whites, Blacks,* and of all Ages and Conftitutions.

With fome Account of the Nature of the Infection in the NATURAL and INOCULATED Way, and their different Effects on HUMAN BODIES.

With fome fhort DIRECTIONS to the UNEXPERIENCED in this Method of Practice.

Humbly dedicated to her Royal Highnefs the Princefs of WALES, by *Zabdiel Boylfton,* Phyfician.

LONDON:

Printed for S. CHANDLER, *at the* Crofs-Keys *in the* Poultry. M. DCC. XXVI.

Private Collection/Picture Research Consultants & Archives

Several years after he and Cotton Mather combated a Boston smallpox epidemic by employing inoculation, Zabdiel Boylston published this pamphlet in London to spread the news of their success. The dedication to the Princess of Wales was designed to indicate the royal family's support of the procedure.

Enlightenment rationalism affected politics, too. Locke's *Two Treatises of Government* (1691) and works by French and Scottish philosophers challenged a divinely sanctioned, hierarchical political order originating in the power of fathers over families. Men created governments and could alter them, Locke declared. A ruler who broke the social contract and failed to protect people's rights could legitimately be ousted from power peacefully or violently. Enlightenment theorists proclaimed God's natural laws governed even monarchs.

Oral Cultures

The world in which such ideas were discussed was select. Most residents of North America were illiterate. Those who could read often could not write. Books were scarce until the 1750s, and colonial newspapers did not appear until the 1720s. Parents, older siblings, or local widows who needed extra income taught youngsters to read. More fortunate boys (and genteel girls after the 1750s) might learn to write in private schools. Few Americans other than some Church of England missionaries in the South tried to instruct enslaved children. And only the most zealous Indian converts learned Europeans' literacy skills.

Thus, the cultures of colonial North America were primarily oral, communal, and local. Face-to-face conversation was the major means of communication. Different locales developed divergent cultural traditions. Through public rituals colonists forged their cultural identities.

Religious and Civic Rituals

Church attendance was perhaps the most important ritual. In early New England, men and women sat on opposite sides of a central aisle, arranged by age, wealth, and church membership. By the mid-eighteenth century, wealthy husbands and wives sat in privately owned pews; their children, servants, slaves, and the less fortunate sat in sex-segregated fashion at the rear, sides, or balcony of the church. In eighteenth-century Virginia, planter families purchased pews, and in some parishes landed gentlemen strode in as a group before the service, deliberately drawing attention to their exalted position. In Quebec City, formal processions celebrated Catholic feast days; each participant's rank determined his place in the procession. By contrast, Quaker meeting houses in Pennsylvania and elsewhere used an egalitarian but sex-segregated seating system. The various seating and entrance rituals symbolized social rank and local values.

Communal culture also centered on civic involvement. In New England, governments proclaimed official days of thanksgiving (for good harvests, military victories, etc.) and days of fasting and prayer (during difficulties such as droughts or epidemics). Everyone was expected to participate. Because able-bodied men between ages sixteen and sixty were required to serve in local militias, monthly musters also brought the community together.

In the Chesapeake, important rituals occurred on court and election days. When the county court met, men came to file lawsuits, appear as witnesses, or serve as jurors. Court attendance provided civic education; from the proceedings men learned what behavior was expected. Elections served the same purpose, for property-holding men voted in public. An election official, often flanked by the candidates for office, would call each man forward to declare his preference. Voters would then be thanked politely by the gentleman selected, often treated later to rum at nearby taverns.

This trade card (advertisement) issued by a Philadelphia tobacco dealer in 1770 shows a convivial group of wealthy men at a tavern. Both the leisurely activity depicted here and the advertisement itself were signs of the new rituals of consumption. Merchants began to advertise only when their customers could choose among different ways of spending money.

Throughout colonial North America, the public punishment of criminals served to humiliate the offender and remind the community of proper behavioral standards. Public hangings, whippings, and sitting in the stocks expressed community outrage and restored harmony. Judges often assigned penalties that shamed miscreants. When a New Mexico man assaulted his father-in-law, he was directed to pay medical expenses and kneel before him publicly to beg his forgiveness. Even after pardoned of capital offenses, New Englanders were frequently ordered to wear nooses around their necks for years, as a reminder to all of their violation of community norms.

Rituals of Consumption By 1770, Anglo-American households allocated one-quarter of their spending to consumer goods, which fostered new rituals centered on consumption and created what historians have termed "an empire of goods." In the seventeenth century, settlers acquired necessities by bartering with neighbors or ordering from a home-country merchant. By the middle of the eighteenth century, specialized shops selling nonessentials proliferated in cities like Philadelphia and New Orleans. In 1770, Boston had more than five hundred stores, offering millinery, sewing supplies, tobacco, gloves, tableware, and the like. Even small towns had one or two retail establishments. Colonists would set aside time to "go shopping," a novel and pleasurable leisure activity that initiated consumption rituals.

Colonists took pleasure in owning and displaying lovely objects for neighbors and kin to see: a mirror, a ceramic bowl, or clothing made from special fabric. A rich man might hire an artist to paint his family using the objects, thereby creating a record to be admired.

Poor, rural people similarly took pleasure in inexpensive purchases. One Virginia woman traded hens and chickens for a pewter dish. Local slaves exchanged cotton they had grown in their free time for colorful ribbons and hats they must have worn proudly.

Tea and Madeira

Tea drinking, a consumption ritual dominated by women, played an important role throughout Anglo America. Households with aspirations to genteel status sought the necessary items for proper tea consumption: pots, cups, strainers, sugar tongs, bowls, and special tables. Tea provided a focal point for socializing and, because of its cost, served as a status symbol. Wealthy women regularly entertained friends at afternoon tea parties. Tea also appeared healthful; thus even poor households consumed it, although without the fancy equipment of their wealthier neighbors. Another genteel drink was Madeira wine from the Portuguese islands. By 1770, Madeira had become the elite's favored drink, expensive to purchase. Opening the bottle, letting it breathe, decanting and serving it with appropriate glassware were accomplished with elaborate ceremony. After the 1750s, urban dwellers could buy Madeira at specialized stores.

Rituals on the "Middle Ground"

Other rituals allowed the disparate cultures of colonial North America to interact. Particularly important rituals developed on what the historian Richard White has termed the "middle ground"—the psychological and geographical space in which Indians and Europeans encountered each other, primarily via trade or warfare.

When Europeans sought to trade with Indians, they encountered an indigenous exchange system that stressed gift giving over buying and selling. Successful bargaining required French and English traders to present Indians with gifts (cloth, rum, gunpowder, and other items) before negotiating for pelts and skins. Only after those gifts were reciprocated could formal trading begin. For example, Indians in northeastern North America wanted heavy cloths called strouds. Because British manufacturers produced such material in response to natives' demands, British traders acquired an important advantage over their French competitors. Rum became a crucial component, as traders concluded that drunken Indians would sell their furs more cheaply, and some Indians refused to hunt or trade unless they first received rum. Alcohol abuse hastened the deterioration of villages already devastated by disease and dislocation.

Intercultural rituals also developed to deal with murders. Where Europeans sought primarily to punish the murderer, Indians regarded such "eye for an eye" revenge as just one possible response. Compensation could also be accomplished by capturing another Indian or a colonist to take the dead person's place, or by "covering the dead"—providing the deceased's family with goods. Eventually, the French and the Algonquians evolved an elaborate ritual from both societies' traditions: murderers were identified but deaths were usually "covered" by trade goods rather than blood revenge.

Colonial Families

Families constituted the basic units of colonial society, constituting the chief mechanism for production and consumption. Never-married adults were rare. Yet family forms and structures varied widely, and not all were headed by couples.

How did European American families differ from those of Indians or African Americans?

Indian and Mixed-Race Families

As Europeans consolidated their hold on North America, Indians had to adapt. Bands reduced by disease and warfare recombined into new units; for example, the Catawbas emerged in the 1730s in the western Carolinas by merging several earlier peoples, including Yamasees and Guales. Likewise, European authorities reshaped Indian family forms. Whereas many Indian societies had permitted easy divorce, European missionaries frowned on it; societies that had allowed polygynous marriages (including New England Algonquians) redefined them, designating one wife as "legitimate" and others as "concubines."

With continued high mortality, extended kin became increasingly important, with other relatives—sometimes nonkin—assuming child-rearing responsibilities when parents died. Once Europeans established dominance in any region, Indians were unable to pursue traditional modes of subsistence, driving them to unusual family structures and new economic strategies. In New England, for instance, Algonquian husbands and wives survived by working, and sometimes living, separately (perhaps wives as domestic servants, husbands as sailors). Some native women married African American men due to sexual imbalances in both populations. In New Mexico, detribalized Navajos, Pueblos, Paiutes, and Apaches employed as servants by Spanish settlers clustered in the small Borderlands towns. Known as *genizaros,* they lost contact with Indian cultures, instead living on the fringes of Latino society.

Wherever the population contained relatively few European women, sexual liaisons occurred between European men and Indian women. The resulting mixed-race population of *mestizos* and *métis* worked as a familial "middle ground" to ease other cultural interactions. In New France and the Anglo-American backcountry, such families resided in Indian villages and their children sometimes became prominent Native American leaders. By contrast, in the Spanish Borderlands the offspring of Europeans and *genizaros* were shunned. Largely denied legal marriage, they bore generations of "illegitimate" children of various racial mixtures, giving rise in Latino society to multiple labels describing precise degrees of skin color.

European American Families

To eighteenth-century Anglo-Americans, the word *family* meant everyone in one household (including servants or slaves). In 1790, the average home in the United States contained 5.7 free people; few included extended kin, such as grandparents. Family members worked together to produce goods for consumption or sale. The head of the household represented it to the outside world, voting in elections, managing the finances, and holding legal authority over the rest of the family—his wife, children, and servants or slaves.

In English, French, and Spanish America, the vast majority of European families supported themselves by cultivating crops and raising livestock. While the work differed by region or crop, tasks were allocated by sex. The mistress oversaw her female helpers in what Anglo-Americans called "indoor affairs"—preparing food, cleaning the house, doing laundry, and making clothes. Along with cooking, food preparation involved cultivating a garden, harvesting and preserving vegetables, salting and smoking meat, drying apples and pressing cider, milking cows and making butter and cheese. The husband and his male helpers managed "outdoor affairs," cultivating fields, building fences, chopping wood, harvesting and marketing crops, tending livestock, and butchering cattle and hogs. Farm work was so extensive that a married couple could not do it alone; if childless, they needed servants or slaves.

African American Families

Most African American families lived as components of European American households. More than 95 percent of colonial African Americans were held in perpetual bondage. In South Carolina, a majority of the population was of African origin; in Georgia, about half; and in the Chesapeake, 40 percent. Portions of the Carolina low country were nearly 90 percent African American by 1790.

Where African Americans lived determined the shape of their families. In the North, the scarcity of other blacks often made it difficult for bondspeople to form stable households. In the Chesapeake, men and women who regarded themselves as married (slaves could not legally wed) frequently lived on different quarters or different plantations. Children generally resided with mothers. On large Carolina and Georgia rice plantations, enslaved couples usually lived together and accumulated property by working for themselves completing daily "tasks." Some Georgia slaves sold surplus produce, earning money for clothing or such luxuries as tobacco, but rarely enough for their freedom.

Forms of Resistance

Because all British colonies legally permitted slavery, bondspeople had few options for escaping servitude other than fleeing to Florida, where the Spanish offered protection. Some recently arrived Africans stole boats or ran off to join the Indians or establish independent communities on the frontier. Among American-born slaves, family ties strongly affected such decisions. As one South Carolina planter wrote, slaves "love their families dearly and none runs away from the other." Consequently, many owners sought to keep families together. In the Chesapeake, where family members often lived separately, affectionate ties could cause slaves to run away, especially if family members were sold.

Although colonial slaves rarely rebelled collectively, they resisted in other ways. Bondspeople rejected owners' attempts to commandeer their labor on Sundays without compensation. Extended-kin groups protested excessive punishment of relatives and sought to live near one another. If parents and children were separated by sale, other relatives helped with child rearing. Just as among Indians, the extended family served a more important function for African Americans than for European-Americans.

Most slave families carved out some autonomy, especially in their working and spiritual lives, particularly in the Lower South. Some African Americans preserved traditional beliefs or Islamic faith; others converted to Christianity, comforted by its assurances that everyone would be free and equal in heaven. South Carolina and Georgia slaves jealously guarded their ability to control their time after completing their "tasks." Even on Chesapeake tobacco plantations, slaves planted gardens, trapped, or fished to supplement their meager diets. Late in the century, some Chesapeake planters began to hire slaves out, often allowing the workers to keep some of their earnings.

City Life

In cities, African Americans and European Americans resided in neighborhoods together. (In 1760s Philadelphia, one-fifth of the work force was enslaved, and by 1775 blacks composed nearly 15 percent of New York City's population.) Such cities were medium-sized towns by today's standards. In 1750, the largest, Boston and Philadelphia, had just seventeen thousand and thirteen thousand inhabitants, respectively. Unlike their rural

Fire posed a major hazard to colonial cities; several suffered considerable damage in the seventeenth and eighteenth centuries from fires that raged out of control for hours. In the mid-eighteenth-century, cities like New York organized volunteer companies, such as the Hand-in-Hand company pictured here on an unidentified city street about 1750. The firemen are passing buckets of water from the well on the left to the engine on the right, where men on each side operate the pump that directs a stream of water on the fire. The chief is shouting orders through his trumpet at the right of the engine, and the people on the far right are carrying items from the burning building.

counterparts, city dwellers purchased food and wood, and men's jobs frequently took them away from home, giving them more contact with the broader world.

By the 1750s, most major cities had at least one weekly newspaper. Anglo-American newspapers combined local reports with the latest "advices from London" (usually two to three months old). People who could not afford newspapers could either read them (or listen to them read aloud) at taverns and coffeehouses. Contact with the outside world, however, meant sailors sometimes brought deadly diseases into port. Boston, New York, Philadelphia, and New Orleans endured smallpox and yellow fever epidemics, which Europeans and Africans in the countryside largely escaped.

Politics: Stability and Crisis in British America

What were the myths and realities of colonial assemblies?

Early in the eighteenth century, Anglo-American political life exhibited new stability. Despite substantial migration, most mainland residents were born in America. Men from genteel families dominated the political structures, for voters (free male property holders) typically deferred to their well-educated "betters" in election.

Colonial Assemblies

Throughout the Anglo-American colonies, political leaders sought to increase the powers of elected assemblies relative to that of governors and other appointed officials. Assemblies began to claim privileges associated with the British House of Commons, such as initiating tax legislation and controlling the militia. Assemblies also influenced British appointees by threatening to withhold their salaries. In some colonies (Virginia and South Carolina, for example), elite assemblymen presented a united front to royal officials, but in others (such as New York), they fought among themselves bitterly. To win hotly contested elections, New York's genteel leaders began competing for votes. Yet in 1735 the New York government imprisoned newspaper editor **John Peter Zenger**, who vigorously criticized it on the charge of "seditious libel." Arguing that the truth could not be defamatory, his lawyer helped establish a free-press principle in American law.

John Peter Zenger: Central figure in a trial that opened the way for freedom of the press.

Assemblymen saw themselves as acting to prevent encroachments on colonists' liberties—for example, by preventing governors from imposing oppressive taxes. By midcentury, they were comparing the structure of their governments to Britain's balanced polity, equating their governors with the monarch, their councils with the aristocracy, and their assemblies with the House of Commons. All three were believed essential to good government, but Anglo-Americans viewed governors and appointed councils as Britain's representatives and potential threats to colonial ways of life. Many colonists saw the assemblies, however, as the people's protectors. And the assemblies regarded themselves as the people's representatives.

In reality, the assemblies, controlled by dominant families whose members were reelected year after year, rarely responded to poorer constituents' concerns. They also failed to reapportion themselves to provide representation for new settlements; this led to grievances among backcountry dwellers, especially non-English ethnic groups. The colonial ideal of the assembly as the defender of liberty was a myth. In truth, the most ably represented were wealthy male colonists, particularly the assembly members themselves.

At midcentury, the political structures that had stabilized in a period of relative calm confronted a series of crises—ethnic, racial, economic, regional—that exposed internal tensions and foreshadowed the disorder of the revolutionary era. Significantly, they demonstrated that the political accommodations arrived at after the **Glorious Revolution** could no longer adequately govern Britain's American empire.

Glorious Revolution: Overthrow of James II in favor of William and Mary.

Slave Rebellions in South Carolina and New York

Early on Sunday, September 9, 1739, about twenty enslaved men, most likely Catholics from Kongo, gathered near the Stono River south of Charles Town. September fell in the midst of the rice harvest (and thus a stressful time for male Africans, less accustomed than women to rice cultivation), and September 8 was, to Catholics, the birthday of the Virgin Mary. Seizing guns and ammunition, the slaves killed storekeepers and nearby planter families. Then, joined by other bondsmen, they headed toward Florida in hopes of finding refuge. By midday, however, the militia attacked the nearly one hundred fugitives, killing some and dispersing the rest. A week later, most of the remaining conspirators were captured and executed. But for two years, rumors about escaped renegades haunted the colony.

Stono Rebellion: A slave uprising in 1739 in South Carolina.

After the **Stono Rebellion**, laws governing African Americans were stiffened throughout British America. In New York City, the site of the first mainland slave revolt in 1712, the Stono news, coupled with fears of Spain generated by the outbreak of King George's War, set off a reign of terror in the summer of 1741. Colonial authorities suspected a biracial gang of thieves and arsonists of fomenting a slave uprising under the guidance of a European thought to be a Spanish priest. By summer's end, thirty-one blacks and four whites had been executed for participating in the alleged plot. The Stono Rebellion and the New York "conspiracy" confirmed Anglo-Americans' deepest fears about the dangers of slaveholding and revealed the assemblies' inability to prevent internal disorder.

Rioters and Regulators   By midcentury, with most fertile land east of the Appalachians purchased or occupied, conflicts over land titles and conditions of landholding escalated. In 1746, for example, some New Jersey farmers clashed violently with agents of the East Jersey proprietors, who claimed the farmers' land and demanded annual payments, called quit-rents. The most serious land riots occurred along the Hudson River in 1765–1766. Late in the seventeenth century, the governor of New York had granted huge tracts in the lower Hudson Valley to prominent families. They then divided these estates into small farms, which they rented to poor Dutch and German migrants who regarded tenancy as a step toward independence.

After 1740, though, New Englanders and Europeans increasingly migrated to the region, resisting tenancy and often squatting. In the mid-1760s, the Philipse family sued farmers who had lived on Philipse land for two decades. New York courts ordered squatters to make way for tenants with valid leases. Instead, farmers rebelled, terrorizing proprietors and tenants, and on one occasion battling a county sheriff and his posse. The rebellion lasted nearly a year, ending only when British troops captured its leaders.

Violent conflicts erupted in the Carolinas as well. The Regulator movements of the late 1760s (South Carolina) and early 1770s (North Carolina) pitted backcountry farmers against wealthy eastern planters who controlled colonial governments. In South Carolina, Scots-Irish settlers protested their lack of an adequate voice in political affairs. For months, they policed the countryside in vigilante bands known as Regulators, complaining of lax and biased law enforcement. North Carolina Regulators, who objected to heavy taxation, lost a battle with eastern militiamen at Alamance in 1771.

A Crisis in Anglo-American Religion

What was the social and political impact of the Great Awakening?

The most widespread crisis was religious. From the mid-1730s through the 1760s, waves of religious revivalism—today known as the First **Great Awakening**—swept over various colonies, primarily New England (1735–1745) and Virginia (1750s–1760s). Orthodox Calvinists sought to combat Enlightenment rationalism, which denied innate human depravity.

The economic and political uncertainty accompanying King George's War made colonists receptive to **evangelists'** messages. With no prior religious affiliation, many recent immigrants and backcountry residents became potential converts.

The Great Awakening began in New England, where descendants of the Puritan founding generation composed Congregational church memberships. While church members were predominantly female, men and women responded with equal fervor to the Awakening. In the mid-1730s, the Northampton, Massachusetts, preacher and theologian Reverend Jonathan Edwards, gained new youthful followers with Calvinist-based message that individuals could attain salvation only by acknowledging their depraved nature and surrendering completely to God's will.

Great Awakening: Protestant revival movement that emphasized each person's urgent need for salvation by God.

evangelist: A preacher or minister who enthusiastically promotes the Christian gospels.

George Whitefield

The effects of such conversions remained isolated until 1739, when **George Whitefield**, a Church of England clergyman already celebrated for leading revivals in England, arrived in America. A gripping orator, Whitefield toured the British colonies for fifteen months, effectively generating the Great Awakening. One historian has termed him "the first modern celebrity" because of his skillful self-promotion and clever manipulation of his listeners and the newspapers. Everywhere he traveled, his fame preceded him. Readers snapped up books by and about him, the first colonial bestsellers. Thousands of free and enslaved folk from Boston to Savannah heard him speak and experienced conversion. Whitefield's journey created new interconnections among the previously distinct colonies.

George Whitefield: English preacher who toured the colonies and played a major role in the Great Awakening.

Regular clerics initially welcomed Whitefield and his American-born imitators, but many soon concluded that the "revived" religion ran counter to their doctrines. They disliked the emotional style of the revivalists, who took churchgoers away from their usual church services. Particularly troublesome to the orthodox were the female exhorters who publically proclaimed their right to expound God's word.

Link to excerpts from letters to Whitefield from "Deborah Sherman."

Impact of the Awakening

Opposition to the Awakening heightened rapidly, further splintering the already fragmented American Protestantism. Congregationalists and Presbyterians split into "Old Lights"—traditional clerics and their followers—and "New Light" evangelicals. New sects such as Methodists and Baptists gained adherents. Paradoxically, the angry fights and the rapid rise in the number of distinct denominations eventually created an American willingness to tolerate religious diversity. Since no single sect could make an unequivocal claim to orthodoxy, they had to coexist if they were to survive.

Most significantly, the Awakening challenged traditional social patterns, particularly the colonial tradition of deference. Itinerant preachers, only a few of whom were ordained, claimed they understood the will of God better than elite college-educated clerics. They and their followers divided the world into the saved and the damned without respect to gender, age, or status. New Lights also defended the rights of people to dissent from a community consensus, thereby challenging the fundamental tenets of colonial political life. The Awakening's egalitarian themes simultaneously attracted ordinary folk and repelled the elite.

Virginia Baptists

By the 1760s, Baptists had gained a secure foothold in Virginia; inevitably, their beliefs clashed with genteel lifestyles. They dressed plainly, in contrast to the gentry's opulence. They addressed one another as "Brother" and "Sister" regardless of social status, and they elected their

Private Collection/The Bridgeman Art Library

This painting by John Collet shows the charismatic evangelist George Whitefield preaching out of doors in Britain, but the same scene would have been repeated many times in the colonies, especially after the clergy of established churches denied him access to their pulpits, deeming him too radical for their liking. Note the swooning woman in the foreground; women were reputed to be especially susceptible to Whitefield's message. Is the worker offering him a mug of ale derisively or devotedly? The answer is not clear, except that the gesture underscores the diversity of Whitefield's audience—not all were genteel or middling folk.

congregations' leaders. Their monthly meetings, which attracted hundreds of people, introduced new public rituals that rivaled weekly Anglican services.

Strikingly, almost all the Virginia Baptist congregations included free and enslaved members, and some had African American majorities. Church rules applied equally to all members; interracial sexual relationships, divorce, and adultery were forbidden. Congregations forbade masters from breaking up slave couples through sale. Biracial committees investigated complaints about members' misbehavior. Churches excommunicated slaves for stealing from their masters and masters for physically abusing their slaves.

By injecting an egalitarian strain into Anglo-American life at midcentury, the Great Awakening had important social and political consequences, calling into question habitual modes of behavior in the **secular** as well as the religious realm.

secular: Not specifically relating to religion or to a religious body.

"Self-Made Men"

Americans universally celebrate the "self-made man" (always someone explicitly *male*) of humble origins who gains prominence through extraordinary efforts. Most commonly cited examples are Andrew Carnegie (a poor immigrant from Scotland) and John D. Rockefeller (born on a hardscrabble farm in upstate New York).

The initial exemplars of this tradition, though, lived in the eighteenth century. Benjamin Franklin's *Autobiography* chronicled his method for achieving success after beginning life as the seventeenth child of a Boston candle maker. From such humble origins Franklin became a wealthy, influential man active in science, politics, education, and diplomacy. Yet Franklin's tale is rivaled by that of a man apparently born a slave in South Carolina. He acquired literacy, worked as a sailor, purchased his freedom, became an influential abolitionist, married a wealthy Englishwoman, and published a popular autobiography that predated Franklin's. His first master called him Gustavus Vassa, but when publishing his *Interesting Narrative* in 1789, he called himself Olaudah Equiano.

In that *Narrative*, Equiano said he was born in Africa in 1745, kidnapped at age eleven, and transported to Barbados and then to Virginia, where a British naval officer purchased him. For years, scholars have relied on that account for its insights into the middle passage. But evidence recently uncovered by Vincent Carretta, although confirming much of Equiano's autobiography, shows that Equiano twice identified his birthplace as Carolina and was three to five years younger than he claimed. Carretta speculates that the *Narrative* gained its credibility from Equiano's African birth and that admitting his real age would have raised questions about his early life.

Equiano, or Vassa, thus truly "made himself," just as Benjamin Franklin and many others have done. (Franklin typically omitted, rather than altered, inconvenient parts of his history—for example, having an illegitimate son.) Equiano used information undoubtedly gleaned from acquaintances who *had* experienced the middle passage to craft an accurate depiction of its horrors. In the process, he became one of the first Americans to explicitly reinvent himself.

Summary

Over the half-century before 1770, North America was transformed, partly by the dramatic geographic expansion of French and Spanish settlements and partly by newcomers from Germany, Scotland, Ireland, and Africa who brought their languages, customs, and religions. Such transformations affected America's Native residents as well as the newcomers. European immigrants were concentrated in the growing cities and backcountry of British North America. By contrast, slaves from Africa lived and worked within 100 miles of the Atlantic coast. In many colonial South regions, 50 to 90 percent of the population was of African origin.

The economic life of Europe's North American colonies proceeded simultaneously on two levels. On the farms, plantations, and ranches where most colonists resided, arduous labor alike dominated people's lives while providing goods for consumption or sale. Simultaneously, an intricate international trade network affected the economies of the British, French, and Spanish colonies and their Native trading partners and allies. The bitter wars fought by European nations during the eighteenth century inevitably created new opportunities for overseas sales or disrupted traditional markets. The few who reaped the profits of international commerce were the wealthy class of merchants and landowners who dominated colonial life.

A century and a half after European first settled in North America, the colonies mixed diverse European, American, and African traditions into a novel cultural blend. Europeans who interacted regularly with peoples of African and American origin—and with Europeans from other nations—developed new methods of accommodating intercultural differences while also creating ties within their own potentially fragmenting communities. Initially, many colonists continued to identify themselves as French, Spanish, or British rather than as Americans, but in the 1760s some Anglo-Americans began to realize that their interests did not necessarily coincide with Great Britain's and challenged British authority.

Chapter Review

Geographic Expansion and Ethnic Diversity

What spurred population growth in the British colonies in the thirty years before 1775?

Immigration—particularly Scots-Irish and Germans—contributed to some of the population growth among European Americans, but the largest single factor was natural increase (live births). Once the difficult years of early settlement passed and the sex ratio evened out in the South, the population doubled every twenty-five years. Natural increase also boosted the African American enslaved population after 1740, and in some regions the slave population was further augmented by new imports of enslaved people.

Commerce and Manufacturing in British North America

How were the colonies' economic fates increasingly linked to world markets?

As colonies became more entwined in overseas trade, their fortunes were increasingly tied to the ups and downs of those economies. Although colonists developed small-scale manufacturing and broader trade networks to meet increased local demand for goods and services, they nonetheless required external markets for their products—tobacco, rice, indigo, fish, and timber. They used the money made from these items to purchase European and English imports. If demand for American goods fell, so did colonists' income, causing economic downturns. The outbreak of King George's War, for example, increased overseas demand for grain grown in the Chesapeake and led tobacco farmers to convert more of their acreage to the crop, while New England suffered when the shipbuilding boom of the war years ended.

Colonial Cultures

How did rituals function in colonial America?

Cultural rituals played a central role in colonial life, both to create community and to reinforce social status. Church rituals were among the most important, but also the most revealing, with seating arrangements organized by sex, class, age, or wealth. Civic rituals likewise generated community involvement and revealed the behavior communities expected of their members. In New England, everyone was required to participate in official holidays or local militia musters; in the Chesapeake, rituals centered on court or election days; and public punishment of criminals throughout North America was designed to reinforce behavioral standards. Even simple rituals, such as tea-drinking, reinforced gender norms and distinctions of wealth and status. Finally, colonists adapted rituals to facilitate trade with Indians, who had vastly different customs. Europeans seeking to trade with Indians engaged in the gift-giving system typical of native cultures before trade could begin.

Colonial Families

How did European American families differ from those of Indians or African Americans?

Anglo Americans used the word "family" to describe everyone in a household: parents, children, extended kin, and slaves. Families typically supported themselves by farming, with each member assigned a task according to gender norms. (Women did indoor work and related tasks; men did outdoor work.) Indian families were more fluid; before contact with Europeans, they permitted divorce, for example. After contact, extended kin became more important, particularly as families were decimated by disease. Shortages of European women in some colonies led to increased intermarriages, with children raised in Indian villages rather than among settlers. Most African Americans were enslaved, and their families subsumed under European American households. In the Chesapeake, slaves couples who considered themselves married (despite laws prohibiting slave marriage) often lived apart, in different quarters or plantations, with children residing with mothers (and potentially sold off at any time.)

Politics: Stability and Crisis in British America

What were the myths and realities of colonial assemblies?

Anglo-American assemblymen believed they safeguarded colonists' liberties from encroachments by the British government, such as oppressive taxation. Regarding Britain's appointed councils and governors as potential threats, colonists looked to assemblies as their protectors. In truth, elite, wealthy families dominated the assemblies and paid little regard to poorer constituents' concerns, nor did they reapportion themselves so that new settlements would gain representatives, which angered backcountry residents and non-English immigrants.

A Crisis in Anglo-American Religion

What was the social and political impact of the Great Awakening?

Socially, the Great Awakening challenged traditional norms and patterns. Women, for example, began to claim an equal right to preach, and Protestant denominations further split into the "Old Lights"—who followed traditional teachings and ministers—and the "New Light" evangelicals. While initially sparking animosity, ultimately the rise of new denominations promoted greater tolerance for religious diversity. The Great Awakening's egalitarianism also challenged the colonial tradition of deference, in which people knew their place and respected their so-called "betters." New Lights attracted ordinary people as followers and preachers and argued that the world was divided into the saved and the damned without respect to gender, age or status.

Suggestions for Further Reading

Marilyn Baseler, "Asylum for Mankind": America 1607–1800 (1998)

Richard R. Beeman, The Varieties of Political Experience in Eighteenth-Century America (2004)

James F. Brooks, Captives and Cousins: Slavery, Kinship, and Community in the Southwest Borderlands (2002)

William E. Burns, Science and Technology in Colonial America (2005)

Richard Bushman, The Refinement of America: Persons, Houses, Cities (1992)

Kathleen DuVal, The Native Ground: Indians and Colonists in the Heart of the Continent (2006)

Rhys Isaac, The Transformation of Virginia, 1740–1790 (1982)

Jill Lepore, New York Burning: Liberty, Slavery, and Conspiracy in Eighteenth-Century Manhattan (2005)

Harry S. Stout, The Divine Dramatist: George Whitefield and the Rise of Modern Evangelicalism (1991)

Stephanie G. Wolf, As Various as Their Land: The Everyday Lives of 18th Century Americans (1992)

CourseMate

Go to the CourseMate website for primary source links, study tools, and review materials for this chapter.
www.cengagebrain.com

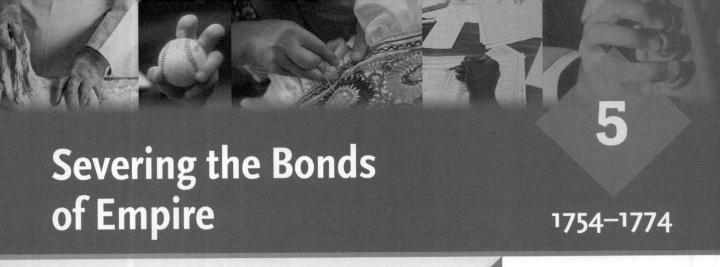

5

Severing the Bonds of Empire

1754–1774

The well-born Scotswoman Janet Schaw chose an inopportune time to visit her older brother in North America. Sailing from Edinburgh in October 1774, she arrived in the West Indies in January 1775, where she visited planter families, some whom were also Scots, and did some shopping before sailing on to meet her brother in North Carolina. There she encountered "rusticks" who had, in her opinion, a "rooted hatred" for the mother country and were forming "schemes" detrimental to Britain and America.

Janet Schaw soon learned that an American congress had forbidden "every kind of diversion, even card-playing." When Wilmington residents held a ball before the ban took effect, she found the event "laughable," like seventeenth-century Dutch paintings of comic, carousing peasants. She also reported that "the Ladies have burnt their tea in a solemn procession," but sniffed, "the sacrifice was not very considerable, as I do not think any one offered above a quarter of a pound." All the "genteel" merchants, she observed, "disapprove of the present proceedings" and were planning to leave. She concluded that the trouble in the colonies had been caused by "mistaken notions of moderation" in parliamentary policy. Schaw returned to Scotland within the year. Her brother's property was later confiscated by the state for his refusing to take an oath of allegiance, but he remained in his new homeland until his death.

In retrospect, John Adams identified the period between 1760 and 1775 as the era of the true American Revolution. The Revolution, Adams declared, ended before the fighting started, for it was "in the Minds of the people," involving not the actual winning of independence but a shift of allegiance from Britain to America. Today, not all historians would concur. But none would deny the importance of the events of those crucial years, in which mainland colonies united against British policies.

During the 1760s and early 1770s, an ever-widening split occurred between Great Britain and Anglo America. In the long history of British settlement in the Western Hemisphere, tension

Chapter Outline

Renewed Warfare Among Europeans and Indians
Iroquois Neutrality | Albany Congress | Seven Years' War

LINKS TO THE WORLD *The First Worldwide War*

1763: A Turning Point
Neolin and Pontiac | Proclamation of 1763 | George III | Theories of Representation | Real Whigs | Sugar and Currency Acts

The Stamp Act Crisis
James Otis's Rights of the British Colonies | Patrick Henry and the Virginia Stamp Act Resolves | Continuing Loyalty to Britain | Anti-Stamp Act Demonstrations | Americans' Divergent Interests | Sons of Liberty | Opposition and Repeal

Resistance to the Townshend Acts
John Dickinson's Farmer's Letters | Rituals of Resistance | Daughters of Liberty | Divided Opinion over Boycotts

VISUALIZING THE PAST *The Revolutionary Symbolism of Female Spinners*

Confrontations in Boston
Boston Massacre | A British Plot? | Samuel Adams and Committees of Correspondence

Tea and Turmoil
Reactions to the Tea Act | Coercive and Quebec Acts

LEGACY FOR A PEOPLE AND A NATION *Women's Political Activism*

SUMMARY

had occasionally marred the relationship between individual provinces and the mother country. Still, it rarely lasted long or was widespread, except during the crisis following the Glorious Revolution in 1689. In the 1750s, however, a series of events beginning with the Seven Years' War drew the colonists' attention toward their relations with Great Britain.

Britain's overwhelming victory in that war, confirmed by treaty in 1763, forever altered the balance of power in North America. France was ousted from the continent and Spain from Florida, with major consequences for interior indigenous peoples and British colonists. Indians, who were experts at playing European powers against one another, lost a major diplomatic tool. Anglo-Americans no longer feared the French on their northern and western borders or the Spanish in the Southeast. The coastal British colonies would never have risked breaking with their mother country, some historians contend, had France controlled the Mississippi River and the Great Lakes in 1776.

The British victory in 1763 left Great Britain with a massive war-related debt. Consequently, Parliament for the first time imposed revenue-raising taxes on the colonies in addition to the customs duties that had long regulated trade. That exposed differences in the political thinking of Americans and Britons that had previously been obscured by a shared political vocabulary.

During the 1760s and early 1770s, Anglo American men and women resisted new tax levies and Britain's attempts to tighten controls over provincial governments. The colonies' elected leaders became increasingly suspicious of Britain's motives. They laid aside old antagonisms to coordinate their responses to the new measures. As late as the summer of 1774, though, most were seeking a solution within the empire; few harbored thoughts of independence.

As you read this chapter, keep the following questions in mind:

* **What were the causes and consequences of the Seven Years' War?**

* **What British policies did Americans protest, and what theories and strategies did they develop to support those protests?**

* **Why did the Tea Act of 1773 cause such a major escalation in tensions between the mainland colonies and Great Britain?**

Renewed Warfare Among Europeans and Indians

What was at stake in the Seven Years' War?

In the mid-eighteenth century, the British colonies along the Atlantic seaboard were surrounded by potentially hostile neighbors: Indians, the Spanish in Florida and the Gulf of Mexico, and the French along the rivers and lakes stretching from the St. Lawrence to the Mississippi. Spanish outposts posed little threat, for Spain was no longer a major power. However, France's forts and settlements dominated the North American interior. In all three Anglo-French wars between 1689 and 1748, Britain could not shake France's hold on the American frontier. Under the Peace of Utrecht, which ended Queen Anne's War in 1713, England won control of such peripheral northern areas as Newfoundland, Hudson's Bay, and Acadia (Nova Scotia)

Chronology

1754	Albany Congress meets to try to forge colonial unity	1766	Stamp Act repealed
	Washington defeated at Fort Necessity, Great Meadows, Pennsylvania		Declaratory Act insists that Parliament can tax the colonies
1755	Braddock's army defeated in Pennsylvania	1767	Townshend Acts lay duties on trade within the empire, send new officials to America
1756	Britain declares war on France; Seven Years' War officially begins	1768	Fort Stanwix treaty opens Kentucky to Anglo-American settlement
1759	British forces take Quebec	1768–70	Townshend duties resisted; boycotts and public demonstrations divide merchants and urban artisans
1760	American phase of war ends with fall of Montreal to British troops		
	George III becomes king	1770	Lord North becomes prime minister
1763	Treaty of Paris ends Seven Years' War		Townshend duties repealed, except for tea tax
	Pontiac's allies attack forts and settlements in West		Boston Massacre kills five colonial rioters
	Proclamation of 1763 attempts to close land west of Appalachians to settlement	1772	Boston Committee of Correspondence formed
1764	Sugar Act lays new duties on molasses, tightens customs regulations	1773	Tea Act aids East India Company
			Bostonians protest the Tea Act
	Currency Act outlaws paper money issued by the colonies	1774	Coercive Acts punish Boston and Massachusetts as a whole
1765	Stamp Act requires stamps on all printed materials in colonies		Quebec Act reforms government of Quebec
	Sons of Liberty formed		First Continental Congress called

and gained access to the Great Lakes region previously dominated by France. But Britain made no territorial gains in King George's War (see Table 5.1.)

Iroquois Neutrality   During Queen Anne's War and King George's War, the Iroquois Confederacy maintained a neutrality policy first developed in 1701. While British and French forces vied for nominal control of North America, the confederacy skillfully manipulated the Europeans, refusing to commit warriors to either side despite gifts from both. The Iroquois continued a long-standing conflict with Cherokees and Catawbas in the South, thus giving their young warriors combat experience and replacing population losses with new captives. They also cultivated peaceful relationships with Pennsylvania and Virginia, partly to obtain the colonists' imprimatur for their domination of the Shawnees and Delawares. And they forged ties with Algonquians of the Great Lakes region, thereby making themselves indispensable go-betweens for commerce between the Atlantic coast and the West. Thus, the Iroquois consolidated their control over the interior north of Virginia and south of the Great Lakes.

But the region inhabited by the Shawnees and Delawares (now western Pennsylvania and Virginia and eastern Ohio) provided the spark that set off a major war. In a significant reversal of previous patterns, that conflict spread from America to Europe, decisively resolving the contest for North America.

As early as the late 1730s, trouble began as British traders pushed west from the Carolinas and Virginia, challenging French power beyond the Appalachians.

TABLE 5.1   The Colonial Wars, 1689–1763

American Name	European Name	Dates	Participants	American Sites	Dispute
King William's War	Nine Years' War	1689–97	England, Holland versus France, Spain	New England, New York, Canada	French power
Queen Anne's War	War of Spanish Succession	1702–13	England, Holland, Austria versus France, Spain	Florida, New England	Throne of Spain
King George's War	War of Austrian Succession	1739–48	England, Holland, Austria versus France, Spain, Prussia	West Indies, New England, Canada	Throne of Austria
French and Indian War	Seven Years' War	1756–63	England versus France, Spain	Ohio country, Canada	Possession of Ohio country

The French had difficulty supplying their settlements during a successful British naval blockade of the St. Lawrence during King George's War. This heightened French colonial officials' fear of British incursions, especially when in the 1740s Iroquois negotiators, claiming to speak for the Delawares and Shawnees, ceded large land tracts to Pennsylvania officials. Squatters (mainly Scots-Irish and Germans) had negotiated agreements with the Delawares for settlement rights. But the agreements reached by the Penn family's agents and the Iroquois ignored local Indians and squatters, all of whom were told to move. Disgruntled Delawares and Shawnees migrated west, where they joined other displaced eastern Indians.

The region to which they moved, claimed by both Virginia and Pennsylvania, was coveted by wealthy Virginians, who, organized as the Ohio Company, received a huge land grant in 1749. The company's agents established trading posts that aimed to dominate the crucial area where the Allegheny and Monongahela Rivers join to form the Ohio (see Map 5.1). But France relied on the Ohio River for access to its posts on the Mississippi. Thus, in the early 1750s, Pennsylvania fur traders, Ohio Company representatives, the French military, squatters, Iroquois, Delawares, and Shawnees jostled for position in the region. A 1752 raid by the French and their native allies on a trading outpost sited at modern Cleveland rid the region of Pennsylvanians, but the Virginians posed a serious challenge. Accordingly, in 1753, the French pushed southward, building fortified outposts at strategic points.

Albany Congress   In response to the French threat, delegates from seven northern and middle colonies gathered in Albany, New York, in June 1754. They sought to persuade the Iroquois to abandon their neutrality and to coordinate plans for colonial defense. The Iroquois saw no reason to change a policy that served them well for half a century. And although the Albany Congress delegates adopted a Plan of Union (which would have established an elected intercolonial legislature with the power to tax), their provincial governments uniformly rejected the plan, fearing a loss of autonomy.

While the Albany Congress delegates deliberated, the war began. Virginia Governor Robert Dinwiddie sent a small militia troop to build a palisade at the forks of the Ohio. When a substantial French force arrived, the Virginia militia surrendered. The French then constructed Fort Duquesne. Learning of the confrontation, the inexperienced young officer who commanded the Virginia reinforcements

MAP 5.1

European Settlements and Indians, 1754

By 1754, Europeans had expanded the limits of the English colonies to the eastern slopes of the Appalachian Mountains. Few independent Indian nations still existed in the East, but beyond the mountains they controlled the countryside. Only a few widely scattered English and French forts maintained the Europeans' presence there.

Source: Copyright © Cengage Learning

pressed on. He encountered a French detachment, and Tanaghrisson, the leader of his Ohio Indian scouts, killed the French commander. Tanaghrisson started a war to force the British to defend the Ohio Country against the French. The Virginians were trapped by pursuing French troops in a crudely built Fort Necessity at Great Meadows, Pennsylvania. After a day-long battle (on July 3, 1754), during which more than one-third of his men were killed or wounded, twenty-two-year-old George Washington surrendered.

Seven Years' War

Washington's blunder and Tanaghrisson's aggression helped ignite a war that eventually encompassed nearly the entire world. In July 1755, a few miles south of Fort Duquesne, the French and Indians attacked British and colonial troops. In the devastating defeat, General Edward Braddock was killed. The Pennsylvania frontier was repeatedly attacked by Delawares for two more years; over a thousand residents were killed. Settlers felt betrayed because the Indians attacking them had once been (an observer noted) "allmost dayly familiars at their houses."

Britain declared war on France in 1756, thus formally beginning the Seven Years' War. Even before then, Britons and New Englanders feared that France would try to retake Nova Scotia, where most of the population descended from seventeenth-century French settlers who had intermarried with local M'ikmaqs. Afraid that the approximately twelve thousand French Nova Scotians would abandon their neutrality policy, British commanders in 1755 forced about seven thousand from their homeland—the first large-scale modern deportation, now called ethnic cleansing. Ships crammed with Acadians sailed to each mainland colony. Many families were separated, some forever. After 1763, the survivors relocated: some returned to Canada, others to France or its Caribbean islands. Many settled in Louisiana, where they became known as Cajuns (derived from *Acadian*).

British officers tried unsuccessfully to coerce the colonies into supplying men and materiel to the army. When William Pitt, the civilian official heading the war effort in 1757, agreed to reimburse the colonies' wartime expenditures and placed recruitment in local hands, he gained greater American support. (Even so, Virginia burgesses appropriated more funds to defend against possible slave insurrections than to fight the French and Indians.) Many colonial militiamen served alongside red-coated regulars from Britain; the two groups maintained an antagonistic relationship, however.

Adding to the tensions were the actions of Anglo-American merchants in Boston, Philadelphia, and New York, who continued trading with the French West Indies. They bribed customs officers to look the other way while cargoes of fish, flour, timber, and other products bound for such neutral ports as Dutch St. Eustatius or Spanish Monte Cristi (on Hispaniola) actually ended up in the French Caribbean, and they acquired valuable French sugar in return. British officials failed to stop the illicit commerce. North America also supplied France with vital materiel during the war.

Nevertheless, in July 1758, British forces recaptured the fortress at Louisbourg, winning control of the entrance to the St. Lawrence River. In the fall, Delawares and Shawnees accepted British peace overtures, and the French abandoned Fort Duquesne. Then, in September 1759, General James Wolfe's regulars defeated the French and

Seven Years' War: Major French-English conflict that was the first worldwide war.

The First Worldwide War

Today, we call two twentieth-century conflicts world wars, but the contest that historians term the "Great War for the Empire" was actually the first worldwide war. It began in spring 1754 in southwestern Pennsylvania, over whether Britain or France would build a fort at the forks of the Ohio. That it eventually involved combatants around the world attests to the growing importance of European nations' overseas empires and the increasing centrality of North America to their struggles for dominance.

The contest at the forks of the Ohio helped to reinvigorate a conflict between Austria and Prussia that sent European nations scrambling for allies. Eventually England, Hanover, and Prussia lined up against France, Austria, Russia, Sweden, and Saxony, and, later, Spain. The war in Europe would last seven years. In 1763, these nations signed a peace treaty that returned the continent to the prewar status, but in the rest of the world Britain had vanquished France and Spain.

In the Caribbean, Britain seized the French islands of Guadeloupe and Martinique, and took Havana from Spain. In North America, the British recaptured the French fortress of Louisbourg and conquered Quebec. In Africa, Britain overwhelmed France's slave-trading posts in Senegambia. In India, British forces won control of Bengal. Late in the war, a British expedition took Manila in the Philippines from Spain.

Thus, the war that started in the American backcountry revealed the steadily growing links between North America and the rest of the world. Winners and losers had to pay for this first worldwide war. Financial struggles in Britain and France produced revolutions abroad (for Britain, in America) and at home (for France).

National Maritime Museum, London

In 1771, artist Dominic Serres, the Elder, depicted British naval vessels attacking the French fortress at Chandernagore in India in 1757 (at left in background). Cannon fire from the warships was critical to the British victory, one of the keys to the conquest of India during the Seven Years' War.

took Quebec. Sensing a British victory, the Iroquois abandoned neutrality, hoping to gain a postwar advantage by allying with Britain. A year later, the British captured Montreal, the last French stronghold, and the American phase of the war ended.

In the **Treaty of Paris** (1763), France ceded its major North American holdings to Britain. Spain, an ally of France toward war's end, gave Florida to the victors. France ceded Louisiana west of the Mississippi to Spain, in partial compensation for its ally's losses elsewhere. The British thus gained control of the continent's fur trade. No longer would the English seacoast colonies have to worry about the threat posed by France's extensive North American territories.

The British triumph stimulated some Americans like Benjamin Franklin to predict a glorious future for British North America. Such men, who would lead the resistance to British measures after 1763, opposed laws that would retard America's growth and supported steps to increase Americans' control over their own destiny.

Treaty of Paris: Treaty by which France ceded most of its holdings to Great Britain and some smaller amounts to Spain.

Link to Benjamin Franklin's "Join or Die" cartoon.

1763: A Turning Point

How did colonists' ideas about government differ from those of the British in the 1760s?

Indigenous peoples of the interior first felt the impact of Britain's victory. After Britain gained the upper hand in the American war in 1758, Creeks and Cherokees lost their ability to force concessions by threatening to turn instead to France or Spain. In desperation and retaliation for British atrocities, Cherokees attacked the Carolina and Virginia frontiers in 1760. Though initially victorious, the Indians were defeated the following year. Late in 1761, a treaty allowed the construction of British forts in Cherokee territories and opened a large tract to European settlement.

Neolin and Pontiac

In the Ohio country, the Ottawas, Chippewas, and Potawatomis reacted angrily when Great Britain, no longer facing French competition, raised prices on trade goods and ended traditional gift-giving practices. As settlers moved into the Monongahela and Susquehanna valleys, a shaman named Neolin urged Indians to oppose European settlement and influence on their culture. Contending that Indian peoples were destroying themselves by dependence on European goods (especially alcohol), Neolin advocated peaceful and armed resistance. If all Indians west of the mountains united to reject the invaders, Neolin declared, the Master of Life would replenish the depleted deer herds and look kindly upon his people.

Heeding Neolin's call, in spring 1763, Ottawa war chief Pontiac forged an unprecedented alliance among Hurons, Chippewas, Potawatomis, Delawares, Shawnees, and Mingoes (Pennsylvania Iroquois). Pontiac besieged Fort Detroit while war parties attacked other British outposts in the Great Lakes. Detroit withstood the siege, but by late June the other forts west of Niagara and north of Fort Pitt had fallen. Indians then raided the Virginia and Pennsylvania frontiers, slaying at least two thousand settlers. They carried off many enslaved African Americans, frightening planters, who feared an Indian-black alliance. In early August, colonial militiamen defeated an Indian force at Bushy Run, Pennsylvania. Pontiac ended the Detroit siege in late October; a treaty ending the war was negotiated three years later.

For nearly eighty years, European settlers and Indians in "Penn's Woods" avoided major conflicts. But the Indian attacks and settlers' response—especially the massacre of several families of defenseless Conestoga Indians in December 1763 by fifty Scots-Irish men known as the Paxton Boys—revealed that violence in the region would become endemic.

Proclamation of 1763

Proclamation of 1763: England's attempt to end Indian problems by preventing westward movement by colonists.

London officials had no experience managing an area as vast as the territory it acquired from France, which included French settlers along the St. Lawrence and many Indian communities. In October, the ministry issued the **Proclamation of 1763,** designating the headwaters of rivers flowing into the Atlantic from the Appalachians as the temporary western boundary for colonial settlement (see Map 5.1). Its promulgators expected to prevent clashes by forbidding colonists to move onto Indian lands. But it infuriated colonists who had squatted west of the line and land speculation companies from Pennsylvania and Virginia.

After 1763, the latter groups (which included such men as George Washington, Thomas Jefferson, Patrick Henry, and Benjamin Franklin) lobbied vigorously to have their claims validated by colonial governments and London administrators. At a treaty conference at Fort Stanwix, New York, in 1768, they negotiated with Iroquois representatives to push the boundary line farther west and south. The Iroquois, still claiming to speak for the Delawares and the Shawnees agreed to the deal, which yielded valuable trade goods and did not affect their own territories. Although the Virginia land companies eventually gained the support of the House of Burgesses, they never made headway in London because administrators worried that western expansion would require funds they did not have.

George III

Financing Britain's debt from the Seven Years' War—and defending newly acquired territories—bedeviled King George III, who in 1760 succeeded his grandfather, George II. During the crucial years between 1763 and 1770, when the rift with the colonies widened and various political crises beset England, the twenty-two-year-old king replaced ministries rapidly. Although determined to assert the power of the monarchy, George III stubbornly regarded adherence to the status quo as the hallmark of patriotism.

Selected as prime minister in 1763, George Grenville confronted a financial crisis: England's indebtedness had nearly doubled since 1754, from £73 million to £137 million. Prewar annual expenditures amounted to no more than £8 million; now the yearly interest on the debt reached £5 million. Grenville's ministry needed funds, but the British were already heavily taxed. Because the colonists benefited from wartime expenditures, Grenville concluded that Anglo-Americans should pay a larger share of the empire's costs.

Ohio Historical Society

Benjamin West, the first well-known American artist, engraved this picture of a prisoner exchange at the end of Pontiac's Uprising, with Colonel Henry Bouquet supervising the return of settlers abducted during the war. In the foreground, a child resists leaving the Indian parents he had grown to love. Many colonists were fascinated by the phenomenon West depicted—the reluctance of captives to abandon their adoptive Indian families.

Theories of Representation

Americans believed they could be represented only by men who lived nearby and for whom they or their property-holding neighbors actually voted. Grenville and his English contemporaries, however, believed that Parliament—king, lords, and commons acting together—represented all British subjects (even overseas) and whether or not they could vote. In Parliament, the particular constituency that chose a member of the House of Commons had no special claim on that member's vote, nor did the member have to live near his constituents. According to this theory, called virtual representation, all Britons—including colonists—were represented in Parliament. Thus, their consent to acts of Parliament could be presumed. In the colonies, by contrast, members of the assemblies' lower houses were viewed as specifically representing the regions that elected them. Before Grenville proposed to tax the colonists, the two notions coexisted. But events of the 1760s revealed their incompatibility.

Real Whigs

Colonists had become accustomed to a central government with limited authority. They believed that a good government was one that largely left them alone, a view matching the theories of British writers known as the Real Whigs. Drawing on a tradition of dissenting thought reaching back to John Locke, Real Whigs stressed the dangers inherent in a powerful government, particularly a monarchy. Some favored republicanism, which proposed to eliminate monarchs and rest power more directly on the people. Real Whigs warned the people to guard constantly against government's attempted encroachments on their liberty and property.

As Britain tightened the reins in the 1760s and early 1770s, many Americans saw parallels in their circumstances and Real Whig ideology. Excessive and unjust taxation, they believed, could destroy their freedoms, and they saw oppressive designs behind the actions of Grenville and his successors. In the mid-1760s, however, colonial leaders merely questioned the wisdom of Grenville's proposed laws.

Sugar and Currency Acts

In 1764, Parliament passed the Sugar and Currency Acts. The **Sugar Act** (also known as the Revenue Act) revised existing customs regulations and laid new duties on some foreign imports into the colonies. Its key provisions, advocated in London by influential Caribbean sugar planters, aimed at discouraging American rum distillers from smuggling French West Indian molasses. Although the Sugar Act resembled the Navigation Acts, it broke with tradition by deliberately seeking to raise revenue rather than channel American trade through Britain. The Currency Act outlawed most colonial paper money, because British merchants had complained that Americans paid debts in inflated local currencies.

Sugar Act: Act passed by British Parliament that sought to raise revenues by taxing colonial imports, notably the sugar trade.

The Sugar and Currency Acts were imposed on an already depressed economy. A business boom accompanied the Seven Years' War, but prosperity ended in 1760 when the war shifted overseas. Urban merchants found few buyers for imported goods, and the loss of military demand for foodstuffs hurt American farmers. The bottom dropped out of the European tobacco market, threatening the livelihood of Chesapeake planters. Sailors and artisans had little work. Thus, the prospect of increased import duties and inadequate currency aroused merchants' hostility.

Without precedent for a united campaign against acts of Parliament, Americans in 1764 took uncoordinated steps. Eight colonial legislatures sent petitions to

Parliament requesting the Sugar Act's repeal. They argued that its commercial restrictions would hurt Britain as well as the colonies and that they had not consented to its passage. Their protests had no effect.

The Stamp Act Crisis

How did the Stamp Act raise issues that would lead to the American Revolution?

The **Stamp Act** (1765), Grenville's most important proposal, required tax stamps on most printed materials, placing the heaviest burden on merchants and the colonial elite, who used printed matter more than ordinary folk. Anyone who purchased a newspaper, made a will, transferred land, accepted a government appointment, or borrowed money would have to pay the tax. Never before had a revenue measure of such scope been proposed for the colonies. The act also required that tax stamps be purchased with scarce sterling coin. Violators would be tried by vice-admiralty courts, where judges rendered decisions, leading Americans to fear the loss of their right to trial by jury. Finally, such a law broke with the colonial tradition of self-imposed taxation.

Stamp Act: Obliged colonists to purchase and use special stamped (watermarked) paper for newspapers, customs documents, various licenses, college diplomas, and legal forms used for recovering debts, buying land, and making wills.

James Otis's *Rights of the British Colonies*

The young Massachusetts attorney James Otis Jr., penned the most important colonial pamphlet protesting the Sugar Act and the proposed Stamp Act: *The Rights of the British Colonies Asserted and Proved.* Otis exposed the dilemma that confounded colonists for the next decade. How could they oppose certain acts of Parliament without questioning Parliament's authority over them? On the one hand, Otis asserted, Americans were "entitled to all the natural, essential, inherent, and inseparable rights" of Britons, including the right not to be taxed without their consent. On the other, Otis admitted that, under the British system since the Glorious Revolution, "the power of parliament is uncontrollable but by themselves, and we must obey . . . till they will be pleased to relieve us."

Link to the Virginia Stamp Act resolutions.

Otis's first contention implied that Parliament could not constitutionally tax the colonies because Americans were not represented in its ranks. Yet his second point accepted the prevailing theory of British government: that Parliament was the sole, supreme authority in the empire. To resolve the dilemma, Otis proposed colonial representation in Parliament, but the British believed that colonists were already virtually represented in Parliament, and Anglo-Americans knew that a handful of colonial delegates to London would easily be outvoted. When Americans learned of the act's adoption in the spring of 1765, they reacted indecisively. Few colonists publicly favored the law, but colonial petitions failed to prevent its adoption. Perhaps Otis was correct: the only course was to pay the stamp tax, reluctantly but loyally.

Patrick Henry and the Virginia Stamp Act Resolves

A twenty-nine-year-old lawyer serving his first term in the Virginia House of Burgesses, Patrick Henry was appalled by his fellow legislators' complacency. "Alone, unadvised, and unassisted, on a blank leaf of an old law book," he wrote the Virginia Stamp Act Resolves.

Little in Henry's earlier life foreshadowed his political success. The son of a prosperous Scots immigrant to western Virginia, Henry had little formal education.

After marrying at eighteen, he failed at farming and storekeeping before turning to the law to support his wife and six children. Henry lacked legal training, but his oratorical skills made him an effective advocate, first for his clients and later for his political beliefs.

Patrick Henry introduced his seven proposals near the end of the legislative session, when many burgesses had already departed. The few burgesses remaining in Williamsburg adopted five of Henry's resolutions by a bare majority. But some colonial newspapers printed Henry's seven original resolutions as if they had been uniformly passed by the House. One was rescinded and two others were never voted on.

The four propositions adopted by the burgesses repeated Otis's arguments, asserting that colonists had never forfeited their rights as British subjects, which included consent to taxation. The other three resolutions went further. The repealed resolution claimed the burgesses had the "exclusive right" to tax Virginians, and the two never considered asserted that Virginians need not obey tax laws passed by other legislative bodies (namely, Parliament).

Continuing Loyalty to Britain

Though contending for their rights, the colonists did not seek independence. Maryland lawyer Daniel Dulany, who's *Considerations on the Propriety of Imposing Taxes on the British Colonies* was the most widely read pamphlet of 1765, expressed the consensus: "The colonies are dependent upon Great Britain, and the supreme authority vested in the king, lords, and commons, may justly be exercised to secure, or preserve their dependence." But, warned Dulany, there was a distinction between a condition of "dependence and inferiority" and one of "absolute vassalage and slavery."

Over the next ten years, America's political leaders searched for a way to control their internal affairs, especially taxation, but remain under British rule. The notion that Parliament could exercise absolute authority over colonial possessions inhered in the British theory of government. Even Britain's harshest critics in the 1760s and 1770s questioned only the wisdom of specific policies, not the principles on which they rested. In effect, the Americans wanted British leaders to revise their fundamental understanding of government.

Anti-Stamp Act Demonstrations

In August, the Loyal Nine, a Boston artisans' social club, organized an anti-Stamp Act demonstration. Hoping to show that people of all ranks opposed the act, they approached leaders of the city's rival laborers' associations, based in Boston's North End and South End neighborhoods. The two groups, composed of unskilled workers and poor tradesmen, often battled each other, but the Loyal Nine convinced them to lay aside their differences for the demonstration.

On August 14, the demonstrators hung an effigy of Andrew Oliver, the province's stamp distributor, from a tree on Boston Common. That night a large crowd led by

In 1795 the artist Lawrence Sully painted the only known life portrait of Patrick Henry. The old man's fierce gaze reflects the same intensity that marked his actions thirty years earlier, when he introduced the Virginia Stamp Act Resolves in the House of Burgesses.

fifty well-dressed tradesmen paraded the effigy around the city. The crowd built a bonfire near Oliver's house and added the effigy to the flames. Demonstrators broke most of Oliver's windows and threw stones at officials. During the melee, the North End and South End leaders toasted their union. Oliver publicly promised not to fulfill the duties of his office.

But another crowd action twelve days later, aimed at Oliver's brother-in-law, Lieutenant Governor Thomas Hutchinson, drew no praise from respectable Bostonians. On August 26, a mob attacked the homes of several customs officers and destroyed Hutchinson's elaborately furnished townhouse. But Hutchinson took some comfort in the fact that "the encouragers of the first mob never intended matters should go this length and the people in general express the utmost detestation of this unparalleled outrage."

Link to Hutchinson's account of the destruction of his house.

Americans' Divergent Interests

Few colonists sided with Britain during the 1760s, but groups had divergent goals. The skilled craftsmen who composed the Loyal Nine and merchants, lawyers, and other educated elites preferred orderly demonstrations. For the city's laborers, economic grievances may have been paramount. Certainly, their "hellish Fury" as they wrecked Hutchinson's house suggests resentment against his display of wealth.

Colonists, like Britons, had a long tradition in which disfranchised people took to the streets to redress grievances. But the Stamp Act controversy for the first time drew ordinary urban folk into transatlantic politics, including recent non-English-speaking immigrants targeted by the double taxation of foreign-language newspapers. Matters that previously concerned only the gentry or colonial legislatures were now discussed everywhere.

The entry of unskilled workers, slaves, and women into imperial politics threatened and aided elite men who wanted to oppose British measures. Anti-Stamp Act demonstrations occurred in cities and towns stretching from Halifax in the north to the Caribbean island of Antigua in the south. They were so successful that, by November 1, when the law was to take effect, not one stamp distributor would carry out his duties. But wealthy men recognized that mobs composed of the formerly powerless could endanger their dominance of society.

Sons of Liberty

They therefore attempted to channel resistance into acceptable forms by creating an intercolonial association, the **Sons of Liberty**. Composed of merchants, lawyers, and prosperous tradesmen, the Sons of Liberty by early 1766 linked protest leaders from New York to those in Charleston, South Carolina, and those in Portsmouth, New Hampshire. With taverns as settings for the exchange of news and opinions, many members were tavern owners.

Sons of Liberty: Groups formed to resist the Stamp Act.

In Charleston (formerly Charles Town) in October 1765, a crowd shouting, "Liberty Liberty and stamp'd paper" forced the resignation of the South Carolina stamp distributor. But the Charleston chapter of the Sons of Liberty was horrified when in January 1766 local slaves paraded through the streets similarly crying, "Liberty!" Freedom from slavery was not what elite slaveowners had in mind.

In Philadelphia, resistance leaders were dismayed when an angry mob threatened to attack Benjamin Franklin's house. Laborers believed Franklin to be partly responsible for the Stamp Act because he had obtained the post of stamp distributor for a friend. But Philadelphia's artisans—the backbone of the opposition movement there and elsewhere—were loyal to Franklin, one of their own who had made good and protected his home. The resulting split between Philadelphia's better-off tradesmen and common laborers prevented an alliance as successful as Boston's.

Opposition and Repeal During fall and winter 1765–1766, Stamp Act opponents pursued various strategies. Colonial legislatures petitioned Parliament to repeal the law, and courts closed because they could not obtain the stamps now required for legal documents. In October, nine colonies sent delegates to a general congress—the first since 1754—in New York to draft a protest stressing the law's adverse economic effects. Meanwhile, the Sons of Liberty held mass meetings to rally public support. Finally, American merchants organized nonimportation associations to pressure British exporters, expecting that since one-quarter of all exports went to the colonies by the 1760s, London merchants whose sales suffered would lobby for repeal.

In March 1766, Parliament repealed the Stamp Act. The nonimportation agreements had created allies for the colonies among wealthy London merchants. But the main factor in winning repeal then was the appointment of a new prime minister. Lord Rockingham, who replaced Grenville in summer 1765, opposed the Stamp Acts an unwise and divisive law. Thus, Rockingham linked repeal to passage of a **Declaratory Act**, which asserted Parliament's authority to tax and legislate Britain's American possessions.

Declaratory Act: Affirmed parliamentary power to legislate its colonies "in all cases whatsoever."

News of the repeal arrived in Newport, Rhode Island, in May, and the Sons of Liberty dispatched messengers throughout the colonies. They organized celebrations commemorating the event and Americans' loyalty to Britain. Their goal achieved, the Sons of Liberty dissolved.

Resistance to the Townshend Acts

In summer 1766, another change in the ministry in London revealed how fragile the colonists' victory had been. The new prime minister, William Pitt, fostered cooperation between the colonies and Britain during the Seven Years' War. But Pitt fell ill, and Charles Townshend became the dominant force in the ministry. An ally of Grenville, Townshend renewed efforts to obtain funds from Britain's American possessions (see Table 5.2).

> How did the Sons of Liberty politicize ordinary Americans during resistance to the Townshend Acts?

The duties Townshend proposed in 1767 seemed to extend the Navigation Acts by focusing on trade goods like paper, glass, and tea. But they differed first by applying to British imports, not to those from foreign countries. Second, the revenues would pay some colonial officials, thereby eliminating assemblies' ability to threaten to withhold salaries from uncooperative officials. Additionally, Townshend's scheme established an American Board of Customs Commissioners and vice-admiralty courts at Boston, Philadelphia, and Charleston. This angered merchants, whose profits would be threatened.

TABLE 5.2   British Ministries and Their American Policies

Head of Ministry	Major Acts
George Grenville	Sugar Act (1764)
	Currency Act (1764)
	Stamp Act (1765)
Lord Rockingham	Stamp Act repealed (1766)
	Declaratory Act (1766)
William Pitt/ Charles Townshend	Townshend Acts (1767)
Lord North	Townshend duties (except for the tea tax) repealed (1770)
	Tea Act (1773)
	Coercive Acts (1774)
	Quebec Act (1774)

John Dickinson's *Farmer's Letters*

Passage of the Townshend Acts drew quick response from the colonies. One series widely-published essays, *Letters from a Farmer in Pennsylvania,* by prominent lawyer John Dickinson, expressed a broad consensus. Dickinson contended that Parliament could regulate colonial trade but could not raise revenue. By distinguishing between trade regulation and taxation, Dickinson avoided the sticky issues of consent and the colonies' relationship to Parliament. But his argument obligated the colonies to assess Parliament's motives in passing trade laws before deciding whether to obey them.

The Massachusetts assembly responded to the Townshend Acts by drafting a letter to the other colonial legislatures, suggesting a joint protest petition. When Lord Hillsborough, recently named to secretary of state for America, learned of the Massachusetts circular, he ordered that colony's Governor Francis Bernard to insist that the assembly recall it. He also directed other governors to prevent their assemblies from discussing it. Hillsborough's order motivated colonial assemblies to unite against this new threat to their prerogatives. In late 1768, the Massachusetts legislature resoundingly rejected recall by a vote of 92 to 17. Bernard immediately dissolved the assembly, and other governors similarly responded.

Rituals of Resistance

John Wilkes: British opponent of King George III who became a hero to American colonists.

The number of votes cast against recalling the circular letter—92—assumed ritual significance for the resistance. The number 45 was already symbolic because **John Wilkes**, a radical Londoner sympathetic to the American cause, had been jailed for publishing an essay entitled *The North Briton*, No. 45. In Boston, the silversmith Paul Revere made a punchbowl weighing 45 ounces that held 45 gills (half-cups). Charleston's tradesmen decorated a tree with 45 lights, set off 45 rockets, and carrying 45 candles, adjourned to a tavern where 45 tables were set with 45 bowls of wine, 45 bowls of punch, and 92 glasses.

Such public rituals taught illiterate Americans about the reasons for resistance. When Boston's revived Sons of Liberty invited hundreds of residents to dine with them each August 14 to commemorate the first Stamp Act demonstration, crowds gathered. Likewise, the public singing of songs supporting the American cause helped spread the word.

The Revolutionary Symbolism of Female Spinners

By the 1760s, middling and well-to-do urban colonists purchased fabric and ordered clothing from tailors and dressmakers. Only the poorer residents of rural America continued to spin wool or flax into yarn, then wove that yarn into cloth and made their own wearing apparel. Urban dwellers, accustomed for decades to following the latest English fashions, had long looked down on rustics who wore homespun—and yet the ability to spin was still seen as a quintessentially feminine occupation, with many young girls being taught that skill. One wealthy Philadelphia poet wrote that working at her wheel reminded her of "a train of Female Hands/ Chearful uniting in Industrious Bands." And so when colonists joined to boycott British goods, one of the key ways in which women could publicize their support for American resistance was to bring their wheels to a public location. What message does the poem convey about the spinners' aims and impact? What was the importance of women undertaking in public a task usually performed in their own homes, if at all?

A

VERSE,

Occasioned by seeing the North-Spinning, in *BOSTON*.

BOSTON, behold the pretty Spinners here,
 And see how gay the pretty Sparks appear:
See Rich and Poor all turn the Spinning Wheel,
All who Compassion for their Country feel,
All who do love to see Industry live,
And see Frugality in *Boston* thrive.

 Britain, behold thy Trade stole from thy Hand,
And carried on in *Boston's* distant Land:
See now thy Trade and Trades men, all expire,
And see them all cut short of their Desire,
Th' Desire they had that *Boston's* Trade should spoil,
That they might reap the Fruit of all our Toil;
... they might take what we've been striving for,
And rule us by the Parlimental Law:
But thanks to GOD, their ill Designs are cropt,
And their Tiramical Designs are stopt.

 Now they have run their Chain's extended Length,
And exhausted all their once encourag'd Strength:
Now have their ill Designs all found an end,
Now they have made a Foe of every Friend:
Now let them starve and die the Death of those,
Who do the Interest of their King oppose.

  BOSTON: Printed and Sold 1769.

A Boston poet in 1769 produced this broadside verse to praise spinners who had gathered in the North End of the City

An eighteenth-century American flax wheel of the sort that would have been used in a public spinning demonstration. Wheels for spinning wool were too large to move easily.

The Sons of Liberty and other American leaders made a deliberate effort to involve ordinary folk in the campaign against the Townshend duties. Most important, they urged colonists of all ranks and both sexes to sign agreements not to purchase or consume British products. The new consumerism that had linked colonists economically now supplied them with a ready method of displaying their allegiance.

Daughters of Liberty

As the primary purchasers of textiles and household goods, women played a central role in the nonconsumption movement. More than three hundred Boston matrons publicly promised not to buy or drink tea, "Sickness excepted." As Janet Schaw later noted, the women of Wilmington, North Carolina, burned their tea after walking through town in a solemn procession. Women exchanged recipes for tea substitutes or drank coffee instead. The best known of the protests, the so-called Edenton Ladies Tea Party, was actually a meeting of prominent North Carolina women who pledged to work for the public good and support resistance to British measures.

In many towns, young women calling themselves Daughters of Liberty met to spin in public squares to persuade other women to make homespun and wear homespun clothing, thereby ending the colonies' dependence on British cloth. These patriotic displays served the same purpose as male rituals involving the numbers 45 and 92. When young ladies from well-to-do families sat outdoors at spinning wheels all day, eating only American food, drinking local herbal tea, and listening to patriotic sermons, they served as political instructors, a role they proudly accepted.

Divided Opinion over Boycotts

Colonists were by no means united in support of nonimportation and nonconsumption. Resistance to the Townshend Acts exposed new splits in American ranks. The most significant rifts divided urban artisans and merchants, allies in 1765.

The Stamp Act boycotts had helped revive a depressed economy by creating demand for local products and reducing merchants' inventories. But in 1768 and 1769, merchants enjoyed boom times and had no incentive to support boycotts. Artisans supported nonimportation enthusiastically, recognizing that the absence of British goods would create a market for their manufactures. Thus tradesmen formed the core of the crowds that coerced importers and their customers by picketing stores, publicizing offenders' names, and sometimes destroying property.

Such tactics were effective: colonial imports from England dropped dramatically in 1769, especially in New York, New England, and Pennsylvania. But the tactics also aroused heated opposition. Some Americans who supported resistance questioned the use of violence to force others to join the boycott. The threat to private property inherent in the campaign frightened wealthier and more conservative men and women. Political activism by ordinary colonists challenged the ruling elite's domination, as many had feared in 1765.

Disclosures that leading merchants had violated the nonimportation agreement caused dissension in the ranks of the boycotters, so Americans were relieved when news arrived in April 1770 that the Townshend duties had been repealed, except for the tea tax. A new prime minister, Lord North, persuaded Parliament that duties on trade within the empire were ill-advised. The other Townshend Acts remained in force, but provisions for paying officials' salaries and tightening customs enforcement appeared less objectionable.

Confrontations in Boston

On the day Lord North proposed repeal of the Townshend duties, a confrontation between civilians and soldiers in Boston led to five Americans' deaths. The decision to base the American Board of Customs Commissioners in Boston ultimately caused the confrontation.

How did Samuel Adams's Committees of Correspondence mark a turning point in Americans' political thinking?

Mobs targeted the customs commissioners from their arrival in November 1767. In June 1768, their seizure of patriot leader John Hancock's sloop *Liberty* on suspicion of smuggling caused a riot in which customs officers' property was destroyed. The ministry brought in troops to maintain order. The assignment of two regiments to their city confirmed Bostonians' worst fears about the oppressive potential of British power. Guards on Boston Neck, the entrance to the city, checked travelers and their goods. Redcoat patrols roamed the city, questioning and

Courtesy of the John Carter Brown Library at Brown University

Shortly after the Boston Massacre, Paul Revere printed this illustration of the confrontation near the customs house on March 5, 1770. Offering visual support for the patriots' version of events, it showed the British soldiers firing on an unresisting crowd (instead of the aggressive mob described at the soldiers' trial) and—even worse—a gun firing from the building itself, which has been labeled "Butchers Hall."

sometimes harassing passersby. Parents feared for the safety of daughters, who were subjected to soldiers' coarse sexual insults. Additionally, many redcoats sought off-duty employment, competing for unskilled jobs with the city's workingmen. The two groups brawled repeatedly in taverns and on the streets.

Boston Massacre:
Confrontation between colonists and British troops in which five colonists where shot and killed.

Link to accounts from the Boston Massacre trial.

Boston Massacre

On the evening of March 5, 1770, a crowd of laborers threw snowballs at soldiers guarding the Customs House. Against orders, the sentries fired on the crowd, killing four and wounding eight, one of whom died a few days later. Reportedly the first to die was Crispus Attucks, a sailor of mixed Nipmuck and African origins. Resistance leaders idealized Attucks and the other dead rioters as martyrs for liberty, holding a solemn funeral and later commemorating March 5 annually.

Despite the political benefits patriots derived from the massacre, they probably did not approve the crowd action that provoked it. Since the destruction of Hutchinson's house in August 1765, men allied with the Sons of Liberty had supported orderly demonstrations. Thus, when the soldiers were tried in November, John Adams and Josiah Quincy Jr., both unwavering patriots, acted as their defense attorneys. Almost all were acquitted, and the two men convicted were released after being branded on the thumb. Undoubtedly, this favorable outcome persuaded London officials not to retaliate against the city.

A British Plot?

For more than two years after the Boston Massacre, a superficial calm emerged. In June 1772, Rhode Islanders, angry with overzealous customs enforcement by the British naval schooner *Gaspée,* attacked and burned it in Narragansett Bay near Providence. Because the perpetrators were never identified, there were no adverse consequences for colonists. The most outspoken newspapers, such as the *Boston Gazette,* the *Pennsylvania Journal,* and the *South Carolina Gazette,* published essays drawing on Real Whig ideology and accusing Great Britain of scheming to oppress the colonies. After the Stamp Act's repeal, the protest leaders praised Parliament; following repeal of the Townshend duties, they warned of impending tyranny. The single ill-chosen stamp tax now seemed part of a plot against American liberties. Essayists pointed to the stationing of troops in Boston and the growing number of vice-admiralty courts as evidence of plans to enslave the colonists. Indeed, patriot writers repeatedly used the word *enslavement.* Most free colonists had direct knowledge of slavery, and the threat of enslavement by Britain must have had peculiar force.

Although some colonists were increasingly convinced that they should seek freedom from parliamentary authority, they continued to acknowledge their British identity and allegiance to George III. They began to envision a system that would enable them to be ruled by their own elected legislatures while remaining subordinate to the king. But any such scheme violated Britons' conception of their government, which posited that Parliament—which they believed encompassed the king as well as lords and commons—wielded sole, undivided sovereignty over the empire. Then, in fall 1772, the North ministry began to implement the Townshend Act that would pay governors and judges from customs revenues. In early November, voters at a Boston town meeting established a **Committee of Correspondence** to publicize the decision by exchanging letters with other Massachusetts towns. Heading the committee was Samuel Adams.

Committees of Correspondence: Local committees established throughout colonies to coordinate anti-British actions.

Samuel Adams and Committees of Correspondence

Fifty-one in 1772, Samuel Adams was about a decade older than the other American resistance leaders. He had been a Boston tax collector, a member and clerk of the Massachusetts assembly, an ally of the Loyal Nine, and one of the Sons of Liberty. Adams drew a sharp contrast between a corrupt, vice-ridden Britain and the colonies, peopled by simple, liberty-loving folk. An experienced political organizer, Adams's Committee of Correspondence sought to create an informed consensus among the residents of Massachusetts.

Until 1772, the protest movement was confined largely to the seacoast and major cities and towns. Adams wanted to widen the movement's geographic scope. Accordingly, the Boston town meeting directed the Committee of Correspondence "to state the Rights of the Colonists and of this Province in particular;" to list "the Infringements and Violations thereof that have been, or from time to time may be made;" and to send copies to other towns.

The statement of colonial rights declared that Americans had absolute rights to life, liberty, and property. The idea that "a British house of commons, should have a right, at pleasure, to give and grant the property of the colonists" was "irreconcileable" with "the first principles of natural law and Justice . . . and of the British Constitution." They complained of taxation without representation, the presence of unnecessary troops and customs officers on American soil, the use of imperial revenues to pay colonial officials, and the expanded jurisdiction of vice-admiralty courts.

The document, which was printed as a pamphlet for distribution to the towns, exhibited none of the hesitation of 1760s' claims against Parliament. No longer were resistance leaders—at least in Boston—preoccupied with defining the limits of parliamentary authority, nor did they mention the necessity of obedience to Parliament. They placed American rights first, loyalty to Great Britain a distant second.

The towns' response to the pamphlet must have thrilled Samuel Adams. While some towns disagreed with Boston's assessment, most aligned with the city. The town of Holden declared that "the People of New England have never given the People of Britain any Right of Jurisdiction over us." The citizens of Petersham commented that resistance to tyranny was "the first and highest social Duty of this people." Beliefs like these made the next crisis in Anglo-American affairs the last.

Tea and Turmoil

> How did the Tea Act push the country to the brink of revolution?

The tea tax was the only Townshend duty still in effect by 1773. After 1770, some Americans continued to boycott English tea; others resumed drinking it. Tea figured prominently in the colonists' diet and social lives, so the boycott meant forgoing a favorite beverage and altering habitual forms of socializing.

Reactions to the Tea Act

In May 1773, Parliament passed the **Tea Act** to save the East India Company from bankruptcy. The company, which held a monopoly on British trade with the East Indies, was important to the British economy and to the prominent British politicians who invested in its stock. Under the act, only the East India Company's agents

Tea Act: England's attempt to bail out East India Company that heightened tensions between the British and the colonies.

could legally sell tea in America. That enabled the company to avoid intermediaries and to price its tea competitively with that of smugglers. Resistance leaders, however, interpreted the measure as designed to make them admit Parliament's right to tax them, for the less expensive tea would still be taxed under the Townshend law. Others saw the Tea Act as the first step in an East India Company monopoly on all colonial trade. Residents of the four cities to receive the first tea shipments prepared to meet this perceived threat to their freedom.

In New York City, tea ships never arrived. In Philadelphia, Pennsylvania's governor persuaded the captain to return to Britain. In Charleston, the tea was unloaded; some was destroyed, the rest sold in 1776 by the new state government. The only confrontation occurred in Boston, where both sides—the town meeting and Governor Thomas Hutchinson, two of whose sons were tea agents—rejected compromise.

The first of three tea ships, the *Dartmouth,* entered Boston harbor on November 28. Customs laws required cargo to be landed and the duty paid within twenty days of a ship's arrival; otherwise, the cargo would be seized and sold at auction. After several mass meetings, Bostonians voted to post guards on the wharf to prevent the tea from being unloaded. Hutchinson refused to permit the vessels to leave the harbor.

On December 16, one day before the cargo would have been confiscated, more than five thousand people (nearly a third of the city's population) crowded into Old South Church. Chaired by Samuel Adams, the meeting hoped to convince Hutchinson to send the tea back. But he refused. In the early evening, Adams reportedly announced "that he could think of nothing further to be done—that they had now done all they could for the Salvation of their Country." Cries then rang out from the crowd: "Boston harbor a tea-pot tonight!" Within minutes, about sixty men crudely disguised as Indians assembled at the wharf, boarded the ships, and dumped the cargo into the harbor. By 9 P.M., 342 chests of tea worth approximately £10,000 floated on the water.

Among the "Indians" were many Boston artisans, including the silversmith Paul Revere. Five masons, eleven carpenters and builders, three leatherworkers, a blacksmith, two barbers, a coachmaker, a shoemaker, and twelve apprentices have been identified as participants. That their ranks also included four farmers from outside Boston, ten merchants, two doctors, a teacher, and a bookseller illustrated the resistance movement's widespread support.

Coercive and Quebec Acts

Coercive (Intolerable) Acts: A series of restrictive laws comprised of the Boston Port Bill, the Massachusetts Government Act, the Justice Act, the Quartering Act, plus the unrelated Quebec Act. Intended by the British Parliament to primarily punish Massachusetts, the acts instead pushed most colonies to the brink of rebellion.

Responding to the tea party, in March 1774, Parliament adopted the first of four laws that became known as the **Coercive, or Intolerable, Acts**. Parliament ordered Boston's port closed until the tea was paid for, prohibiting all but coastal trade in food and firewood. Later in the spring, Parliament passed three other punitive measures. The Massachusetts Government Act altered the province's charter, substituting an appointed council for the elected one, increasing the governor's powers, and forbidding most town meetings. The Justice Act provided that a person accused of committing murder while suppressing a riot or enforcing the laws could be tried outside the colony. Finally, the Quartering Act allowed military officers to commandeer privately owned buildings to house their troops.

Women's Political Activism

In the twenty-first century, female citizens of the United States participate at every level of American public life. Nancy Pelosi was elected Speaker of the House, third in line for the presidency, in January 2007; Hillary Rodham Clinton ran for president in 2008 and became Secretary of State in 2009; and Sonia Sotomayor and Elena Kagan joined the Supreme Court as its second and third current female members in 2009 and 2010, respectively. Nearly one hundred women sit in the House and Senate; many serve in state offices. But before the 1760s, American women were seen as having no appropriate public role. A male essayist expressed the consensus in the mid-1730s: "the Governing Kingdoms and Ruling Provinces are Things too difficult and knotty for the fair Sex, it will render them grave and serious, and take off those agreeable Smiles that should always accompany them."

That changed when colonists resisted new British taxes and laws in the 1760s. Because women made household purchasing decisions, and because with spinning and cloth manufacture their labor could replace imported clothing, their participation was vital. For the first time in American history, women took political stands, deciding whether to boycott British goods. The groups they established to promote home manufactures—dubbed "Daughters of Liberty"—constituted the first American women's political organizations.

Since then, American women have taken part in many political movements, among them antislavery societies, pro- and anti-woman suffrage organizations, the Women's Christian Temperance Union, and the civil rights movement. The legacy of revolutionary-era women continues today. Contemporary Americans would find it impossible to imagine their country without female activists of all affiliations.

Parliament then turned to reforming Quebec's government. Intended to ease strains emerging since the British conquest of the formerly French colony, the Quebec Act granted greater religious freedom to Catholics—alarming Protestant colonists, who equated Roman Catholicism with despotism. It also reinstated French civil law, which had been replaced by British procedures in 1763, and it established an appointed council (rather than an elected legislature). Finally, to protect northern Indians against Anglo-American settlement, the act annexed to Quebec the area west of the Appalachians, east of the Mississippi River, and north of the Ohio River—thereby removing the region from the jurisdiction of seacoast colonies. Wealthy colonists who hoped to develop the Ohio country now faced the prospect of dealing with officials in Quebec.

Members of Parliament who voted for the punitive legislation believed they had solved the problem posed by the troublesome Americans. But to resistance leaders, the Coercive Acts and the Quebec Act proved what they had feared since 1768: that Britain had planned to oppress them.

The Boston Committee of Correspondence urged all colonies to join an immediate boycott of British goods. But Rhode Island, Virginia, and Pennsylvania suggested convening another intercolonial congress to consider an appropriate response, and in mid-June 1774 Massachusetts acquiesced. Even the most ardent patriots hoped for reconciliation. Americans were approaching confrontation but had yet to reach an irrevocable break. So the colonies agreed to send delegates to Philadelphia in September to a Continental Congress.

Summary

At the outbreak of the Seven Years' War in western Pennsylvania, no one could have predicted such dramatic change in Britain's mainland colonies. Yet that conflict simultaneously removed France from North America and created a huge debt that Britain had to repay, developments with major implications for the imperial relationship.

After the war ended in 1763, the number of colonists who defined themselves as political actors increased substantially. Once linked unquestioningly to Great Britain, they began to develop an American identity. Their concept of the political process differed from that of the mother country, and they held a different definition of what constituted representation and consent to government actions. They also came to understand that their economic interests did not necessarily coincide with those of Great Britain. Parliamentary acts such as the Stamp Act and the Townshend Acts elicited colonial responses that produced further responses from Britain. Tensions escalated and climaxed when Bostonians destroyed the East India Company's tea.

In late summer 1774, Americans were committed to resistance but not independence. During the next decade, they would forge a new American nationality.

Chapter Review

Renewed Warfare Among Europeans and Indians

What was at stake in the Seven Years' War?

The Seven Years' War was ultimately a contest over land between the British, French, Native Americans, and some settlers. All parties vied for control of large tracts of western land. The Iroquois, believing themselves the voice of the Delawares and Shawnees, negotiated to cede the land to Pennsylvania; the two tribes then moved west onto land claimed by Virginia and Pennsylvania, while France sought to hold and expand its possessions along the Ohio River, which it relied on for trade. After battling with Indians, France continued to push southward in its land grabbing, and Anglo-American colonists gathered in Albany, New York, to address the French threat. England declared war in 1756 and, after winning the protracted battle, the issue of land between European nations was settled when France ceded most of its North American territories to Britain.

1763: A Turning Point

How did colonists' ideas about government differ from those of the British in the 1760s?

British authorities believed that Parliament—which included the king, lords, and Commons—represented *all* British subjects regardless of where they lived. In this system of virtual representation, the people's consent to Parliament's actions was assumed. Americans, on the other hand, increasingly believed in direct representation, that they could only be represented by men who lived nearby and whom they elected. Moreover, they understood the lower houses as representing the regions that elected them. Living on the other side of the ocean, colonists were also accustomed to a central government with limited authority and embraced the Real Whig notion that good government was one that left them alone to manage their affairs. As England imposed taxes and greater control over the colonies beginning in 1763, many Americans felt their freedom was endangered and questioned whether authority should lie with the monarchy or the people.

The Stamp Act Crisis

How did the Stamp Act raise issues that would lead to the American Revolution?

Angry about the heavy taxes and questioning Britain's right to impose them, colonists began to wonder how they might resist Parliament yet remain British subjects. At issue for essayists such as James Otis was that as British subjects, they possessed the right to consent to taxation—which had not been granted under the Stamp Act. On the other hand, Parliament was a supreme authority to which they must yield. Other leaders, such as Patrick Henry and the Virginia House of Burgesses, were unwilling to relinquish the right to consent to taxation. For ten years, Americans struggled with how to control their internal affairs yet remain under British rule. Protests led to the act's repeal in 1766, but questions about government nonetheless remained.

Resistance to the Townshend Acts

How did the Sons of Liberty politicize ordinary Americans during resistance to the Townshend Acts?

Ordinary Americans were not accustomed to being involved in political affairs, which they understood as handled by elites. But the Sons of Liberty made a conscious effort to draw people from all ranks into their anti-Townshend campaign, partly because they needed widespread participation for their boycott of British products designed in protest to the act. To rally a wider populace, they created rituals that would teach illiterate Americans about the reasons for resistance, including celebrations commemorating previous demonstrations and political songs. Women helped, too, by spinning yarn outdoors in public, symbolically displaying their patriotism for all to see.

Confrontations in Boston

How did Samuel Adams's Committees of Correspondence mark a turning point in Americans' political thinking?

An original member of the Sons of Liberty, Adams wanted to widen the movement's scope beyond its stronghold in New England cities and seacoast towns and create consensus among Massachusetts residents for the cause of liberty. The pamphlet he produced for the Boston Committee of Correspondence in 1772 was widely distributed. It stated the rights of colonists to life, liberty, and property, and it outlined complaints against England for taxation without representation, unnecessary troops and customs officers on American soil, the use of imperial revenues to pay colonial officials, and the expanded jurisdiction of vice-admiralty courts. Far more radical than earlier documents, this one did not seek to define the limits of Parliamentary authority but instead declared colonists' allegiance to America first and England a distant second.

Tea and Turmoil

How did the Tea Act push the country to the brink of revolution?

When Parliament imposed the Tea Act on the colonies in May 1773, it was attempting to save the East India Company from bankruptcy, but colonists thought it was designed to make them admit Parliament's right to tax them. Citizens in several cities wanted to prevent the tea from being unloaded from ships; in Boston, that led to a protest in which the tea was dumped in the harbor by men dressed as Indians. Parliament responded with punitive laws, known as the Coercive or Intolerable Acts, ordering the city to pay for the tea and closing the port until it did. Other acts reorganized the state's government, banned town meetings, and allowed officers to commandeer private buildings to house troops. Colonists saw such measures as proof that Britain would oppress them and sent delegates to a Continental Congress in Philadelphia in 1774 to decide how to respond.

Suggestions for Further Reading

Fred Anderson, *The War That Made America: A Short History of the French and Indian War* (2005)

Bernard Bailyn, *The Ideological Origins of the American Revolution* (1967)

T. H. Breen, *The Marketplace of Revolution: How Consumer Politics Shaped American Independence* (2004)

Benjamin L. Carp, *Rebels Rising: Cities and the American Revolution* (2007)

Gregory Dowd, *War Under Heaven: Pontiac, the Indian Nations, and the British Empire* (2002)

Marc Egnal, *A Mighty Empire: The Origins of the American Revolution* (1988)

Merrill Jensen, *The Founding of a Nation: A History of the American Revolution, 1763–1776* (1968)

Pauline R. Maier, *From Resistance to Revolution: Colonial Radicals and the Development of American Opposition to Britain, 1765–1776* (1972)

Gary B. Nash, *The Unknown American Revolution: The Unruly Birth of Democracy and the Struggle to Create America* (2005)

Peter Silver, *Our Savage Neighbors: How Indian War Transformed Early America* (2008)

Go to the History CourseMate website for primary source links, study tools, and review materials for this chapter. www.cengagebrain.com

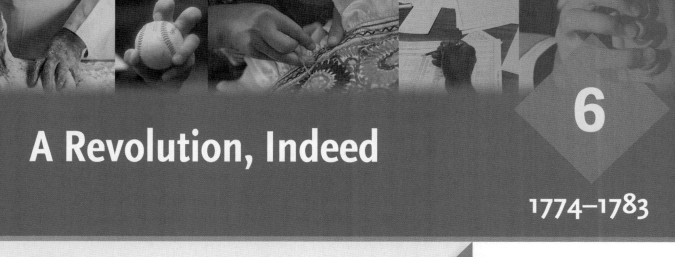

A Revolution, Indeed

6

1774–1783

The Shawnee chief Blackfish named his new captive Sheltowee, or Big Turtle, and adopted him as his son. In February 1778, Blackfish's warriors had caught the lone hunter, Daniel Boone, who then persuaded his fellow frontiersmen to surrender to the Shawnees (British allies). Boone had moved his family from North Carolina to Kentucky three years before as the Revolutionary War began. His contemporaries and some historians have questioned Boone's allegiances during the Revolution. His encounter with the Shawnees highlights ambiguities of revolutionary-era loyalties.

The Shawnees sought captives to cover the death of their chief, Cornstalk, killed months earlier while a prisoner of American militiamen in the Ohio country. Half of the twenty-six men taken were adopted into Shawnee families; those less willing to conform to Indian ways were dispatched as prisoners to the British fort at Detroit. Boone, who assured Blackfish that in the spring he would negotiate the surrender of women and children remaining at his Boonesborough settlement, watched and waited. In June 1778 he escaped, hurrying home to warn the Kentuckians of an impending attack.

When Shawnees and their British allies appeared outside the Boonesborough stockade in mid-September, Boone agreed to negotiate. Although the settlers refused to move back across the mountains, fragmentary evidence suggests that they promised allegiance to the British to avert a battle. But discussions dissolved into a melee, with Indians futilely besieging the fort for a week before withdrawing. That threat gone, Boone was charged with treason and court-martialed by the Kentucky militia. Although he was cleared, questions about the incident and its aftermath haunted him for the rest of his life.

Where did Daniel Boone's loyalties lie? To the British, the Americans, or other Kentuckians? His actions made all three seem possible. Had he betrayed the settlers to Shawnees, seeking to establish British authority in Kentucky? Had he—as he later claimed—twice deceived the Shawnees? Or was the survival of the

Chapter Outline

Government by Congress and Committee
First Continental Congress | Continental Association | Committees of Observation | Provincial Conventions

Contest in the Backcountry
Distrust and Warfare | Frontier Hostilities

VISUALIZING THE PAST *Frontier Refugees*

Choosing Sides
Nova Scotia and the Caribbean | Patriots | Loyalists | Neutrals | African Americans

LINKS TO THE WORLD *New Nations*

War and Independence
Battles of Lexington and Concord | First Year of War | British Strategy | Second Continental Congress | George Washington | British Evacuate Boston | Common Sense | Jefferson and the Declaration of Independence

The Struggle in the North
New York and New Jersey | Campaign of 1777 | Iroquois Confederacy Splinters | Franco-American Alliance of 1778

Life in the Army and on the Home Front
Continental Army | Officer Corps | Hardship and Disease | Home Front

Victory in the South
South Carolina and the Caribbean | Greene and the Southern Campaign | Surrender at Yorktown | Treaty of Paris

LEGACY FOR A PEOPLE AND A NATION *Revolutionary Origins*

SUMMARY

fragile settlements his highest priority? Kentucky was a borderland where British, Indians, and American settlers vied for control. Boone and other Appalachian backcountry residents did not always face clear-cut choices as they struggled under precarious circumstances.

The American Revolution uprooted thousands of families, disrupted the economy, reshaped society by forcing many colonists into permanent exile, and created a nation from thirteen separate colonies. The struggle for independence required revolutionary leaders to accomplish three separate but related tasks. First, they had to transform a consensus favoring loyal resistance into a coalition supporting independence. They pursued various measures (from persuasion to coercion) to enlist European-Americans in the patriot cause, while seeking neutrality from Indians and slaves.

Second, to win independence, patriot leaders needed international recognition and aid, particularly from France. Thus they dispatched to Paris the most experienced American diplomat, Benjamin Franklin, who skillfully negotiated the Franco-American alliance of 1778, crucial to winning independence.

Only the third task directly involved the British. George Washington, commander-in-chief of the American army, soon recognized that his goal should be not to win battles, but to survive to fight another day. The British concentrated on winning and did not consider the difficulties of their main goal, retaining the colonies' allegiance. Americans' triumph owed less to their military powers than to endurance and Britain's mistakes.

As you read this chapter, keep the following questions in mind:

* **What choices of allegiance confronted residents of North America after 1774? Why did people of various descriptions make the choices they did?**

* **What military strategies did the British and American forces adopt?**

* **How did the new nation win independence?**

Government by Congress and Committee

Where did backcountry Indians' loyalties lie at the onset of the Revolution?

Continental Congress: Group of representatives appointed by conventions in most of the North American colonies of Great Britain.

When the fifty-five delegates to the First **Continental Congress** convened in Philadelphia in September 1774, they knew that any measures they adopted would likely enjoy widespread support. That summer, participants at well-publicized open meetings throughout the colonies promised (like some North Carolina men) to "strictly adhere to, and abide by, such Regulations and Restrictions as the Members of the said General Congress shall agree to." Most congressional delegates were selected by extralegal provincial conventions whose members were chosen at local gatherings, because governors had forbidden regular assemblies to conduct formal elections. By designating delegates to Congress, Americans openly defied British authority.

First Continental Congress

The colonies' leading political figures—mostly lawyers, merchants, and planters representing every colony but Georgia—attended the Philadelphia Congress. The

Chronology

1774 First Continental Congress meets in Philadelphia, adopts Declaration of Rights and Grievances	British evacuate Boston
Continental Association implements economic boycott of Britain; committees of observation established to oversee boycott	Declaration of Independence adopted
	New York City falls to British
1774–75 Provincial conventions replace collapsing colonial governments	**1777** British take Philadelphia
	Burgoyne surrenders at Saratoga
1775 Battles of Lexington and Concord; first shots of war fired	**1778** French alliance brings vital assistance to America
Second Continental Congress begins	British evacuate Philadelphia
Washington named commander-in-chief	**1779** Sullivan expedition destroys Iroquois villages
Dunmore's proclamation offers freedom to patriots' slaves who join British forces	**1780** British take Charleston
	1781 Cornwallis surrenders at Yorktown
1776 Paine publishes *Common Sense*, advocating independence	**1782** Peace negotiations begin
	1783 Treaty of Paris signed, granting independence to the United States

Massachusetts delegation included Samuel Adams, the Boston resistance organizer, and his younger cousin John, an ambitious lawyer. New York sent John Jay, a talented young attorney. Virginia elected Richard Henry Lee and Patrick Henry, and George Washington. These men became the chief architects of the new nation.

Congressmen faced three tasks when they convened at Carpenters' Hall on September 5: defining American grievances, developing a resistance plan, and articulating their constitutional relationship with Great Britain. Radical congressmen, like Lee of Virginia, argued that colonists owed allegiance only to George III and that Parliament had no legitimate authority over them. Conservatives, like Pennsylvania's Joseph Galloway and his allies, proposed a union requiring Parliament and a new American legislature to consent jointly to all laws affecting the colonies. Delegates narrowly rejected Galloway's proposal, but they did not embrace the radicals' position either.

Finally, they accepted wording proposed by John Adams. The crucial clauses in the Congress's Declaration of Rights and Grievances declared that Americans would obey Parliament, but only voluntarily, and would resist all taxes in disguise, like the Townshend duties. Remarkably, this position—which would have seemed radical years earlier—represented a compromise in the fall of 1774.

 Link to excerpts from Joseph Galloway's plan of union.

Continental Association The delegates agreed on the laws they wanted repealed (notably the Coercive Acts) and implemented an economic boycott while petitioning the king for relief. They adopted the Continental Association, which called for nonimportation of British goods, effective December 1, 1774; nonconsumption of British products, effective March 1, 1775; and nonexportation of American goods to Britain and the British West Indies, effective September 10, 1775.

More comprehensive than previous economic measures, the Association's provisions appealed to different groups and regions. The nonimportation agreement banned commerce in slaves and manufactures, which accorded with the

Virginia gentry's desire to halt or slow the arrival of enslaved Africans. (Leading Virginians believed slave importations discouraged free Europeans with useful skills from immigrating.) Delaying nonconsumption until three months after implementing nonimportation allowed northern urban merchants time to sell items they acquired before December 1. In 1773, many Virginians had vowed to stop exporting tobacco, to raise prices in a then-glutted market. So they enthusiastically welcomed an Association that banned exportation while permitting them to profit from higher prices for their 1774 crop. It also benefited northern exporters of wood and foodstuffs to the Caribbean with a final selling season before the embargo.

Committees of Observation

To enforce the Continental Association, Congress recommended the election of committees of observation and inspection in every American locality. By specifying that committee members be chosen by all men qualified to vote, Congress guaranteed them a broad popular base. The seven to eight thousand committeemen became local leaders of American resistance.

Initially charged with overseeing implementation of the boycott, within six months these committees became de facto governments. They examined merchants' records, publicizing those who continued to import British goods. They promoted home manufactures, encouraging simple modes of dress and behavior that symbolized Americans' commitment to liberty. Because expensive leisure-time activities were believed to reflect vice and corruption, Congress urged Americans to forgo dancing, gambling, horseracing, and cardplaying.

The committees gradually extended their authority. They attempted to identify opponents of American resistance, developing elaborate spy networks, circulating copies of the Continental Association for signatures, and investigating questionable remarks and activities. Suspected dissenters were urged to support the colonial cause publicly; if they refused, the committees had them watched, restricted their movements, or tried to force them into exile. People engaging in casual political exchanges one day could find themselves charged with "treasonable conversation" the next.

Provincial Conventions

Meanwhile, during the winter and early spring of 1775, colonial governments were collapsing. Only a few legislatures met without challenges to their authority. In most colonies, popularly elected provincial conventions took over the government, sometimes replacing the legislatures or holding concurrent sessions. In late 1774 and early 1775, these conventions approved the Continental Association, elected delegates to the Second Continental Congress (scheduled for May), organized militias, and gathered arms.

Royal officials suffered continuous humiliation. Courts were prevented from meeting; taxes were paid to the conventions' agents rather than to provincial tax collectors; and militiamen would muster only when committees ordered. During the six months preceding the battles at Lexington and Concord, independence was being won at the local level. Still, most Americans proclaimed loyalty to Great Britain.

Contest in the Backcountry

While the committees of observation consolidated their authority in the East, some colonists headed west. Ignoring the Proclamation of 1763, pronouncements by colonial governors, and the threat of Indian attacks, land-hungry folk—many of them recent immigrants from Ireland and soldiers who demobilized in North America after the Seven Years War—swarmed onto lands along the Ohio River and its tributaries after the mid-1760s. Sometimes they purchased property from opportunists with grants of dubious origin; often, they claimed land as squatters. Britain's 1771 decision to abandon (and raze) Fort Pitt removed final restraints on settlement there and rendered the Proclamation of 1763 unenforceable. By late 1775, thousands of new homesteads dotted the backcountry from western Pennsylvania south through Virginia and eastern Kentucky into western North Carolina.

Distrust and Warfare   Few of the backcountry folk viewed the region's native peoples positively. Frontier dwellers had little interest in the small-scale trade that had sustained an uneasy peace; they wanted land for crops and livestock.

In 1774 Virginia, headed by a new governor, **Lord Dunmore**, asserted its title to the developing backcountry. During spring and early summer, tensions mounted as Virginians surveyed Kentucky land on the south side of the Ohio River—territory claimed by the Shawnees. **"Lord Dunmore's War"** consisted of one large-scale confrontation between Virginia militia and some Shawnee warriors. Neither side won, but in the immediate aftermath thousands of settlers—including Boone and his associates—flooded across the mountains.

When war began, the loyalties of Indians and settlers in the backcountry remained, like Boone's, fluid. Hostile to each other, the side each would take in the struggle might depend on which could better serve their interests. Understanding that, the Continental Congress moved to reoccupy Fort Pitt and establish other garrisons in the Ohio country. With this protection, up to twenty thousand settlers poured into Kentucky and western Pennsylvania by 1780.

Native Americans' grievances against European American newcomers predisposed many to ally with Great Britain. Yet some chiefs urged caution: the British abandonment of Fort Pitt (and them) suggested that Britain might not protect them in the future. Furthermore, Britain hesitated to use its potential native allies and initially sought from Indians only neutrality.

Patriots also wanted Indians' neutrality. In 1775, the Second Continental Congress sent a message to Indian communities, describing the war as "a family quarrel between us and Old England" and requesting that they "not join on either side." The Iroquois pledged neutrality. But some Cherokees led by Chief Dragging Canoe hoped to use the "family quarrel" to regain land. In summer 1776, they attacked western Virginia and Carolina settlements. After a militia campaign destroyed many Cherokee towns, Dragging Canoe and his followers fled west, establishing new villages. Other Cherokees agreed to a treaty that ceded more of their land.

Frontier Hostilities   Shawnees and Cherokees continued to attack backcountry settlements, but dissent within their ranks crippled their efforts. The British victory over France in 1763 had destroyed the Indians'

Lord Dunmore: Royal governor of Virginia who promised freedom to slaves who fought to restore royal authority.

Lord Dunmore's War: Confrontation between Virginians and the Shawnee Indians in 1774. During the peace conference that followed, Virginia gained uncontested rights to lands south of the Ohio country in exchange for its claims on the northern side.

Frontier Refugees

As a result of its victory in the Seven Years' War, Great Britain in 1763 took command of Fort Detroit, located on the river that connected Lakes Huron and Erie, shown here in an eighteenth-century watercolor. The strategic site controlled water access to the three western-most Great Lakes; such water travel was crucial in an era with few and poor frontier roads. The American revolutionaries tried twice to capture Detroit, from which Indian raiding parties attacked frontier settlements, but both times the colonial forces were defeated by Britain's Native allies. Thus throughout the war Detroit served as a magnet for loyalist refugees, among them Marie-Therese Berthelet Lasselle, who fled with her family to the fort in 1780 from their trading post at what is now Fort Wayne,

Indiana. Depicted here is her self-portrait in watercolor on silk, with additional silk embroidery. What can we learn about frontier female refugees from such sources? What does this tell us about her priorities, as well as her skills?

Only genteel women learned to produce such works as these, combining embroidery and watercolor. Great artistic skill contributed to this remarkable self-portrait by Marie-Therese Lasselle.

The artist who painted this watercolor of early Detroit is unknown. The view shows both the village and the fort that protected the residents.

ability to maintain their independence: playing European powers against one another. Only a few communities (the Stockbridge Indians of New England and the Oneidas in New York) unwaveringly supported the American revolt; most others either remained neutral or sporadically aligned with the British. In 1778 and early 1779, a frontier militia force under George Rogers Clark captured British posts in modern Illinois (Kaskaskia) and Indiana (Vincennes). Still, the revolutionaries could never overtake the redcoats' stronghold at Detroit.

Backcountry warfare between settlers and Indians persisted long after the Revolution ended. Indeed, the Revolutionary War constituted a brief chapter in the ongoing struggle for control of the region west of the Appalachians, which began in 1763 and continued into the next century.

Choosing Sides

How did colonists choose sides in the conflict with England?

In 1765, Stamp Act protests were supported by most colonists in the Caribbean, Nova Scotia, and the future United States. Demonstrations occurred in Halifax, Nova Scotia, St. Christopher, and Nevis, as well as in Boston, New York, Charleston, and other mainland towns. When the Stamp Act took effect, though, Caribbean islanders loyally paid the duties. In Nova Scotia and the Caribbean, many colonists came to question the aims and tactics of the resistance movement.

Nova Scotia and The Caribbean

Despite the British victory in the Seven Years War, northern mainland and southern island colonies felt vulnerable to French counterattack. Additionally, sugar planters—on some islands outnumbered by their bondspeople twenty-five to one—feared potential slave revolts. Neither region had a large population of European descent or strong local political structures. Fewer people lived in Halifax in 1775 than in the late 1750s, and with successful men heading to England, the sugar islands had only a few resident planters to provide leadership.

Nova Scotians and West Indians had economic reasons for supporting the mother country. In the mid-1770s, the northerners finally broke into the Caribbean market with their dried, salted fish. They reduced New England's domination of the northern coastal trade, and they benefited from Britain's wartime retaliatory measures against the rebels' commerce. British sugar producers relied on their trade monopoly within the empire, for more efficient French planters could sell their sugar for one-third less. Further, the British planters' lobbyists in London won the islands' exclusion from some of the Townshend Act provisions.

Patriots

Many residents of the thirteen colonies supported resistance, then independence. Active revolutionaries accounted for about two-fifths of the European American population and included small and middling farmers, members of dominant Protestant sects, Chesapeake gentry, merchants, city artisans, elected officeholders, and people of English descent. Wives usually, but not always, adopted their husbands' political stance. Although patriots supported the Revolution, they pursued divergent goals within the broader coalition. Some sought limited political reform; others, extensive political change; and still others, social and economic reforms. (The ways their concerns interacted are discussed in Chapter 7.)

Loyalists

About one-fifth of the European American population remained loyal to Great Britain, firmly rejecting independence. Most **loyalists** had long opposed the men who became patriot leaders for varying reasons. British-appointed government officials; Anglican clergy and lay Anglicans in the North; tenant farmers; members of persecuted religious sects; back-country southerners who had rebelled against eastern rule in the late 1760s and early 1770s; and non-English ethnic minorities, especially Scots—all feared the power of those who controlled the colonial assemblies and who had previously shown little concern for their welfare. Joined by merchants whose trade depended on imperial connections and by former British military men who had settled in America after 1763, they formed a loyalist core.

loyalists: Colonists who retained a profound reverence for the British crown and believed that if they failed to defend their king, they would sacrifice their personal honor.

During the war, loyalists congregated in cities held by the British army. When those posts were evacuated at war's end, loyalists scattered throughout the British Empire—Britain, the Bahamas, and especially Canada. In Nova Scotia, New Brunswick, and Ontario, roughly seventy thousand former Americans laid the foundations of British Canada.

Neutrals

Between patriots and loyalists, there remained in the middle perhaps two-fifths of the European American population. Some, like the Quakers, were sincere pacifists. Others opportunistically shifted their allegiance to whatever side happened to be winning. Still others cared little about politics and obeyed whoever was in power. Such colonists resisted British and Americans alike when their demands seemed too heavy—when taxes became too high or when calls for militia service came too often. They made up a large proportion of the backcountry population (including Boone's Kentucky), where Scots-Irish settlers had little love for either the patriot gentry or the English authorities.

To patriots, apathy or neutrality was as heinous as loyalism. By winter 1775–1776, the Second Continental Congress recommended that "disaffected" persons be disarmed and arrested. State legislatures passed laws prescribing severe penalties for suspected loyalists or neutrals. Many began to require voters (or, in some cases, all free adult men) to take oaths of allegiance; refusal usually meant banishment to England or extra taxes. After 1777, many states confiscated the property of banished persons, using it to fund the war. The patriots' policies ensured that their scattered and persecuted opponents could not band together against the revolutionary cause.

African Americans

In New England, with few resident bondspeople, revolutionary fervor was widespread, and free African Americans enlisted in patriot militias. The middle colonies, where bondspeople constituted a small but substantial proportion of the population, were more divided but largely revolutionary. In Virginia and Maryland, where free people constituted a slender majority, the potential for slave revolts raised occasional but not disabling fears. By contrast, South Carolina and Georgia, where slaves composed more than half of the population, were less enthusiastic about resistance. Georgia sent no delegates to the First Continental Congress and reminded its representatives at the second to consider its circumstances, "with our blacks and tories [loyalists] within us," when voting on independence.

Bondspeople faced a dilemma during the Revolution. Their goal was *personal* independence, but how best could they escape from slavery? To most slaves, supporting the British held promise. In late 1774 and early 1775, bondsmen offered to assist the British army in return for freedom.

Slaveowners' worst fears were realized in November 1775, when Virginia's royal governor, Lord Dunmore, offered to free any slaves and indentured servants willing to join the British forces. About one thousand African Americans rallied to the British; although many perished in a smallpox epidemic, three hundred reached occupied New York City under British protection. Because other commanders renewed Dunmore's proclamation, tens of thousands of runaways eventually joined the British. At war's end, at least nine thousand left with the redcoats.

Links to the World

New Nations

The American Revolution created the United States and led to the formation of three other nations: English-dominated Canada, Sierra Leone, and Australia.

In modern Canada before the Revolution, only Nova Scotia had many English-speaking settlers. Largely New Englanders, they were recruited after 1758 to repopulate the region forcibly taken from the exiled Acadians. During and after the Revolution, loyalist families moved to the region that is now Canada, which remained under British rule. Some exiles settled in Quebec as well. In a few years, the loyalist refugees transformed the former French colony, laying the foundation of the modern bilingual (but majority English-speaking) Canadian nation.

Sierra Leone, too, was founded by colonial exiles—African Americans who had fled to the British army during the war, many of whom ended up in London. Seeing the refugees' poverty, charitable merchants—calling themselves the Committee for Relief of the Black Poor—developed a plan to resettle the African Americans elsewhere. The refugees rejected the Bahamas, fearing reenslavement there. They accepted a return to their ancestors' homeland. In early 1787, vessels carrying about four hundred settlers reached Sierra Leone in West Africa, where representatives of the Black Poor Committee acquired land. The first years were difficult, and many died of disease and deprivation. But in 1792, they were joined by several thousand other loyalist African Americans who had originally moved to Nova Scotia. The influx ensured the colony's survival; it remained a part of the British Empire until its independence in 1961.

At the Paris peace negotiations in 1782, American diplomats rejected British suggestions that the United States continue to serve as a dumping ground for convicts. Britain thus needed another destination for people sentenced for crimes such as theft, assault, and manslaughter. It sent them to Australia, claimed for Britain in 1770. Britain continued this practice until 1868, but voluntary migrants also came. The modern nation was created from a federation of separate colonial governments on January 1, 1901.

Thus, the founding event in the history of the United States links the nation to the formation of its northern neighbor and to new nations in West Africa and the Asian Pacific.

Thomas Rowlandson, an English artist, sketched the boatloads of male and female convicts as they were being ferried to the ships that would take them to their new lives in the prison colony of Australia. Note the gibbet on the shore with two hanging bodies—symbolizing the fate these people were escaping.

Miriam and Ira D. Wallach Division of Art, Prints and Photographs, The New York Public Library. Astor, Lenox, and Tilden

National Library of Australia

An early view of the settlement of black loyalists in West Africa, the foundation of the modern nation of Sierra Leone.

Although bondspeople did not pose a serious threat early on, patriots turned rumors of slave uprisings to their advantage. In South Carolina, resistance leaders argued that the Continental Association would protect masters from their slaves. Undoubtedly, many wavering Carolinians were drawn into the revolutionary camp by fear that divisiveness among free people would encourage rebellion by bondspeople.

Patriots could never completely ignore the threats posed by loyalists, neutrals, slaves, and Indians. Occasionally backcountry militiamen refused to turn out for duty on the seacoast because they feared Indian attacks in their absence. Sometimes southern troops refused to serve in the North because they would not leave their regions unprotected against a slave insurrection. But the impossibility of a large-scale slave revolt, coupled with dissension in Indian communities and the patriots' successful campaign to disarm and neutralize loyalists, ensured that the revolutionaries control the countryside.

War and Independence

How did Thomas Paine's *Common Sense* help reshape the war's purpose?

On January 27, 1775, Lord Dartmouth, secretary of state for America, wrote to General Thomas Gage in Boston, urging decisive action. Opposition could not be "very formidable," Dartmouth wrote.

Battles of Lexington and Concord

In response, on April 14 Gage sent an expedition to confiscate colonial military stockpiles at Concord. Bostonians dispatched two messengers, William Dawes and Paul Revere (later joined by Dr. Samuel Prescott), to rouse the countryside. When the British vanguard of several hundred men approached Lexington at dawn on April 19, they found just seventy militiamen—about half of the town's adult male population—mustered on the common. Realizing they could not halt the redcoats' advance, the Americans' commander ordered his men to withdraw. But as they dispersed, a shot rang out; British soldiers then fired. When they stopped, eight Americans lay dead, and another ten wounded. The British moved on to nearby Concord.

There, the militia contingents were larger. At the North Bridge, three British men were killed and nine wounded. Thousands fired from houses and from behind trees as British forces retreated to Boston. By day's end, the redcoats had suffered 272 casualties, including 70 deaths. The arrival of reinforcements and the American militia's lack of coordination prevented heavier British losses. The patriots suffered just 93 casualties.

First Year of War

By the evening of April 20, thousands of American militiamen had gathered around Boston, summoned by local committees. Many stayed only until spring planting, but those who remained were organized into formal units. Officers under the command of General Artemas Ward of the Massachusetts militia ordered that latrines be dug, water supply protected, supplies purchased, military discipline enforced, and defensive fortifications constructed.

For nearly a year, the two armies sat and stared at each other across siege lines. The redcoats attacked only once, on June 17, when they drove the Americans from trenches atop Breed's Hill in Charlestown. In that misnamed Battle of Bunker Hill,

In 1775, an unknown artist painted the redcoats entering Concord. The fighting at North Bridge, which occurred just a few hours after this triumphal entry, signaled the start of open warfare between Britain and the colonies.

Concord Museum, Concord, MA. www.concordmuseum.org.

the British incurred their greatest wartime losses: over 800 wounded and 228 killed. The Americans lost less than half that number.

During the same eleven-month period, patriots captured the British Fort Ticonderoga on Lake Champlain, acquiring much-needed cannon. Trying to bring Canada into the war, patriots also mounted a northern campaign that ended in disaster at Quebec in early 1776 when troops were ravaged by smallpox. But the long lull in fighting between the main armies at Boston during the war's first year gave both sides time to regroup and strategize.

British Strategy

Lord North and his new American secretary, Lord George Germain, made three central assumptions about the war. First, they concluded that patriot forces could not withstand the assaults by trained British regulars. Convinced that the 1776 campaign would decide the war, they dispatched Great Britain's largest force ever: 370 transport ships carrying 32,000 troops and tons of supplies, accompanied by 73 naval vessels and 13,000 sailors. Among them were thousands of professional German soldiers, who had been hired out to Britain.

Second, British officials and army officers adopted a conventional strategy of capturing major American cities and defeating the rebel army with minimal casualties. Third, they assumed that military victory would achieve the colonies' allegiance.

All three assumptions proved false. London officials also missed the significance of the American population's dispersal over an area 1,500 miles long and more than 100 miles wide. Although Britain would control each of America's largest ports at some time during the war, less than 5 percent of the population lived in those cities. Furthermore, with a vast coastline, commerce was easily rerouted. Hence, the loss of cities did little to damage the American cause.

Most of all, London officials did not initially understand that military triumph would not necessarily bring political victory. Securing the colonies would require Americans to return to their original allegiance. After 1778, the ministry strategized to achieve that through the expanded use of loyalist forces and the restoration of civilian authority in occupied areas. But the policy came too late.

Second Continental Congress

Britain had a bureaucracy to supervise the war; Americans had only the Second Continental Congress. The delegates who convened in Philadelphia on May 10, 1775, had to assume the mantle of intercolonial government. As the summer passed, Congress organized the colonies for war. It authorized the printing of money, established a committee to supervise foreign relations, strengthened the militia, and ordered that thirteen frigates be built for a new Continental Navy (eventually, it comprised forty-seven vessels). Most important, it created the Continental Army.

Until Congress met, the Massachusetts provincial congress supervised Ward and the militiamen encamped at Boston. But that army, composed of men from all over New England, heavily drained local resources. Consequently, Massachusetts asked the Continental Congress to direct the army. Initially, Congress had to choose a commander-in-chief. John Adams proposed the appointment of a Virginian "whose Skill and Experience as an Officer, whose independent fortune, great Talents and excellent universal Character, would command the Approbation of all America": **George Washington**. The Congress unanimously concurred.

George Washington: American military leader and the first President of the United States (1789–1797).

George Washington

Washington had not participated prominently in the prerevolutionary agitation. Devoted to the American cause, he was dignified, conservative, and a man of integrity. The younger son of a Virginia planter, Washington did not expect to inherit substantial property and planned to work as a surveyor. But the early death of his older brother and his marriage to the wealthy widow Martha Custis made George Washington one of Virginia's largest slaveholders. After his mistakes early in the Seven Years War, he had repaired his reputation by rallying the troops and maintaining calm during Braddock's defeat in 1755.

Washington had remarkable stamina and leadership ability. More than six feet tall when most men were five inches shorter, he displayed a commanding presence. Even a loyalist admitted that Washington could "atone for many demerits by the extraordinary coolness and caution which distinguish his character."

British Evacuate Boston

Washington took command of the army surrounding Boston in July 1775. By March 1776, when the arrival of cannon from Ticonderoga enabled him to pressure the redcoats, the army was prepared. Yet an assault on Boston proved unnecessary. Sir William Howe, the new commander, wanted to transfer his men to New York City. The patriots' cannon decided the matter. On March 17, the British and many loyalist allies abandoned Boston forever.

At war for months, American leaders denied seeking a break with Great Britain until a pamphlet published in January 1776 advocated that move.

Common Sense

Thomas Paine's **Common Sense** immediately sold tens of thousands of copies. The author, a radical English printer who had lived in America only since 1774, called for independence and challenged many common American assumptions about government and the colonies' relationship to Britain. He advocated the establishment of a republic, a government by the people with no king or nobility. Paine insisted that Britain had exploited the colonies. And for the frequent assertion that an independent America would be weak and divided, he substituted an unlimited confidence in America's strength once freed from European control.

Common Sense: A pamphlet written by Thomas Paine that advocated freedom from British rule.

By late spring, independence had become inevitable. On May 10, the Second Continental Congress recommended that individual colonies form new governments, replacing colonial charters with state constitutions. On June 7, Richard Henry Lee of Virginia, seconded by John Adams, introduced the crucial resolution: "that these United Colonies are, and of right ought to be, free and independent States … that all political connection between them and the State of Great Britain is, and ought to be, totally dissolved." Congress did not immediately adopt Lee's resolution, postponing a vote until early July. Meanwhile, a five-man committee—including Thomas Jefferson, John Adams, and Benjamin Franklin—was directed to draft a declaration of independence.

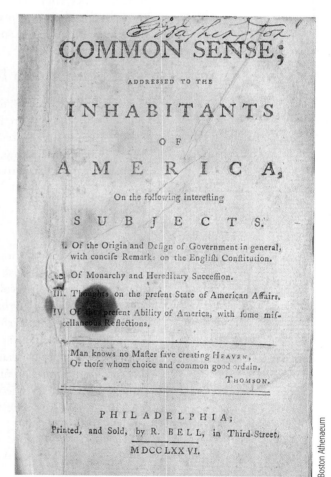

That America's patriot leaders read Thomas Paine's inflammatory *Common Sense* soon after it was published in early 1776 is indicated by this first edition, owned by George Washington himself.

Jefferson and the Declaration of Independence

The committee assigned primary responsibility for writing the declaration to thirty-four-year-old Thomas Jefferson, who was known for his eloquence. A Virginia lawyer and member of the House of Burgesses, Jefferson was educated at the College of William and Mary and in the law offices of a prominent attorney. His knowledge of history and political theory was evident in the declaration and his draft of the Virginia state constitution. While Jefferson wrote and debated in Philadelphia, his beloved wife Martha suffered a miscarriage at their home, Monticello. Not until after her 1782 death from complications following the birth of their sixth (but only third surviving) child, did Jefferson fully commit himself to public service.

Declaration of Independence: Proposed by the Second Continental Congress, this document proclaimed independence of the Thirteen Colonies from British rule.

The draft of the declaration reached Congress on June 28, 1776. The delegates voted for independence four days later, then debated the wording of the declaration for two more days, adopting it with changes on July 4. The **Declaration of Independence** (see Appendix) concentrated on George III, accusing the king of attempting to destroy representative government in the colonies and of oppressing Americans.

The declaration's chief long-term importance lay in the statements of principle that have since as the American ideal: "We hold these truths to be self-evident: That all men are created equal; that they are endowed by their Creator with certain unalienable rights; that among these are life, liberty and the pursuit of happiness; that, to secure these rights, governments are instituted among men, deriving their just powers from the consent of the governed; that whenever any form of government becomes destructive of these ends, it is the right of the people to alter or to abolish it, and to institute new government."

When the delegates in Philadelphia voted to accept the Declaration of Independence, they were committing treason. Therefore, when they concluded with the assertion that they "mutually pledge[d] to each other our lives, our fortunes, and our sacred honor," they spoke the truth.

The Struggle in the North

What was France's role in the American Revolution?

In late June 1776, the first ships carrying Sir William Howe's troops from Halifax appeared off the New York coast (see Map 6.1). On July 2, redcoats landed on Staten Island, but Howe waited for more troops from England before attacking, giving Washington time to march his army of seventeen thousand from Boston to defend Manhattan.

New York and New Jersey

Still inexperienced, Washington and his men made major mistakes, losing battles at Brooklyn Heights and on Manhattan Island. The city fell to the British, who captured nearly three thousand American soldiers. Washington retreated into Pennsylvania, and British forces took most of New Jersey. Occupying troops met little opposition; the revolutionary cause appeared in disarray. "These are the times that try men's souls," wrote Thomas Paine in his pamphlet *The Crisis*.

The British then forfeited their advantage as redcoats in New Jersey went on a rampage of rape and plunder. In retaliation, Washington crossed the Delaware River at night to attack a Hessian encampment at **Trenton** early on December 26. The patriots captured more than nine hundred Hessians and killed another thirty; only three Americans were wounded. Days later, Washington attacked at Princeton. Having gained command of the field, Washington set up winter quarters at Morristown, New Jersey.

Trenton: New Jersey battle where Washington took almost a thousand Hessian prisoners on December 26. It significantly boosted the flailing morale of Washington's troops to fight on.

Campaign of 1777

British strategy for 1777 aimed to isolate New England from the other colonies. General John Burgoyne would lead redcoat and Indian invaders down the Hudson River from Canada to rendezvous near Albany with a similar force moving east. The combined forces would then link up with Howe's troops in New York City. But Howe was planning to capture Philadelphia. In 1777, this independent operation of British armies in America ultimately resulted in disaster.

Howe took Philadelphia, but he delayed before beginning the campaign, took six weeks to transport his troops by sea, and ended up only 40 miles closer to Philadelphia than when he started. This gave Washington time to prepare a defense. At Brandywine Creek and Germantown, the two armies clashed. Although the British won both engagements, the Americans handled themselves well. The redcoats captured Philadelphia in late September, but to little effect. The campaign season was nearly over; the revolutionary army had gained confidence in itself and its leaders; and, far north, Burgoyne was being defeated.

MAP 6.1

The War in the North, 1775–1778

The early phase of the Revolutionary War was dominated by British troop movements in the Boston area, the redcoats' evacuation to Nova Scotia in the spring of 1776, and the subsequent British invasion of New York and New Jersey.

Source: Copyright © Cengage Learning

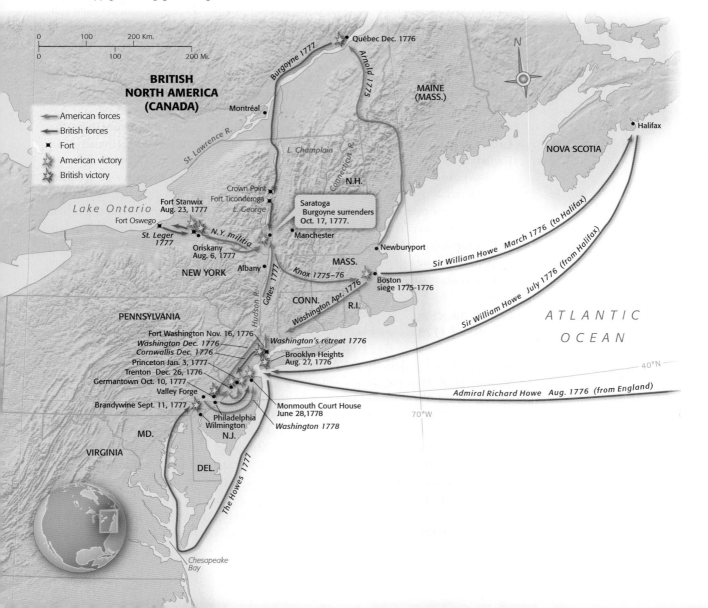

Burgoyne and his men had set out from Montreal in mid-June. An easy triumph at Fort Ticonderoga in July was followed in August by two setbacks—the redcoats and Indians marching east along the Mohawk River turned back after a battle at Oriskany, New York; and in a clash near Bennington, Vermont, American militiamen nearly wiped out eight hundred of Burgoyne's German mercenaries. After several skirmishes, Burgoyne was surrounded near **Saratoga**, New York. On October 17, 1777, he surrendered his force of more than six thousand men.

Saratoga: A turning point in the American Revolution. The American victory in this battle convinced France that Americans could win the war, leading France to ally with the colonists.

Iroquois Confederacy Splinters

The August 1777 battle at Oriskany divided the Iroquois Confederacy. Although the Six Nations had pledged neutrality, two influential Mohawk leaders, the siblings **Mary and Joseph Brant**, believed the Iroquois should ally with the British to protect their territory from land-hungry colonists. The Brants won over the Senecas, Cayugas, and Mohawks, but the Oneidas preferred the American side and brought the Tuscaroras with them. The Onondagas split into three factions, one on each side and one supporting neutrality. At Oriskany, some Oneidas and Tuscaroras joined patriot militiamen in fighting their Iroquois brethren, shattering three hundred years of friendship.

Mary and Joseph Brant: Mohawk leaders who supported the British.

The collapse of Iroquois unity had significant consequences. In 1778, British-allied warriors raided frontier villages in Pennsylvania and New York. The Americans the following summer dispatched an expedition to burn Iroquois crops and settlements. The devastation led many bands to seek food and shelter north of the Great Lakes during the winter of 1779–1780. Many Iroquois settled permanently in Canada.

Burgoyne's surrender at Saratoga overjoyed patriots and discouraged loyalists and Britons. Most important, the American victory at Saratoga drew France into the conflict. The American Revolution gave the French an opportunity to avenge their defeat in the Seven Years' War. Even before Benjamin Franklin arrived in Paris in late 1776, France covertly supplied the revolutionaries with military necessities. Indeed, 90 percent of the gunpowder Americans used during the war's first two years came from France, transported via the French Caribbean island of Martinique.

Franco-American Alliance of 1778

Benjamin Franklin worked tirelessly to strengthen ties between the two nations. Adopting a plain style of dress, Franklin played on the French image of Americans as virtuous farmers. In 1778, the countries signed two treaties. In the Treaty of Amity and Commerce, France recognized American independence and established trade ties. In the Treaty of Alliance, France and the United States promised—assuming that France would declare war on Britain, which it soon did—that neither would negotiate peace without consulting the other. France also abandoned claims to Canada and to North American territory east of the Mississippi River. The most visible symbol of Franco-American cooperation was the Marquis de Lafayette, a young nobleman who volunteered for service with George Washington in 1777 and fought with American forces.

With the alliance, France aided Americans openly, sending troops, naval vessels, arms, ammunition, clothing, and blankets. Second, Britain now had to fight France in the Caribbean and elsewhere. Spain's entry into the war in 1779 as an ally of France (but not of the United States) transformed the Revolution into a global war. The French aided the Americans throughout the conflict, but in its last years that assistance proved vital.

Life in the Army and on the Home Front

How was the Continental Army staffed?

Only in the first months of the war was the revolutionaries' army manned primarily by the semi-mythical "citizen-soldier," who exchanged his plow for a gun. After a few months, early arrivals went home. They reenlisted only briefly when the contending armies neared their farms and towns. In such militia units, elected officers and the soldiers who chose them reflected social hierarchies in their regions of origin, yet also retained a flexibility absent from the Continental Army, composed of men in statewide units led by appointed officers.

Continental Army   Continental soldiers, unlike militiamen, were primarily young, single, or propertyless men who enlisted for long periods or for the war's duration, partly for monetary bonuses or land. They saw in military service an opportunity to assert their masculinity and claim postwar citizenship and property-owning rights. As the fighting dragged on, bonuses grew larger. To meet their quotas, towns and states recruited, including recent immigrants; about 45 percent of Pennsylvania soldiers were of Irish origin, and about 13 percent were German.

Dunmore's proclamation led Congress in January 1776 to modify an earlier policy prohibiting African Americans in the regular army. Recruiters in northern states turned increasingly to bondsmen, who were often promised freedom after the war. Southern states initially resisted, but later all except Georgia and South Carolina enlisted black soldiers. Approximately five thousand African Americans served in the Continental Army, typically in racially integrated units where they were assigned tasks that others shunned, such as burying the dead or foraging for food. Overall, they composed about 10 percent of the regular army, but they seldom served in militia units.

American wives and widows of poor soldiers came to the army with their menfolk because they were too impoverished to survive alone. Such camp followers—roughly 3 percent of the total number of troops—worked as cooks, nurses, and launderers for rations and low wages. The women, along with civilian commissaries and militiamen who floated in and out at irregular intervals, were difficult to manage, especially because they were not subject to military discipline.

Officer Corps   The officers of the Continental Army developed intense pride and commitment to the revolutionary cause. The realities of warfare were often dirty and corrupt, but officers drew strength from a developing image of themselves as professionals who sacrificed for the nation. When Benedict Arnold, an officer who fought heroically for the patriot cause early in the war, defected to the British, they made his name a metaphor for villainy.

Unlike poor women, officers' wives did not travel with the army but made extended visits while the troops were in camp (usually during the winters). They

Courtesy of Mae Theresa Bonitto

Barzillai Lew, a free African American born in Groton, Massachusetts, in 1743, served in the Seven Years' War before enlisting with patriot troops in the American Revolution. An accomplished fifer, Lew fought at the Battle of Bunker Hill. Like other freemen in the north, he cast his lot with the revolutionaries, in contrast to southern bondspeople, who tended to favor the British.

Lord Cornwallis: British general whose surrender at Yorktown in 1781 effectively ended the Revolutionary War.

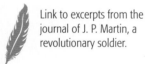

Link to excerpts from the journal of J. P. Martin, a revolutionary soldier.

brought food, clothing, and household furnishings to make their stay more comfortable, and they entertained each other and their menfolk at teas, dinners, and dances. Socializing created friendships later renewed when some of their husbands became the new nation's leaders.

Hardship and Disease   Ordinary soldiers endured more hardships than officers. Wages were low, and often the army could not meet the payroll. Rations (a daily standard allotment of bread, meat, vegetables, milk, and beer) did not always appear, and men had to forage for food. Clothing and shoes were often of poor quality. When conditions deteriorated, troops threatened mutiny (though only a few followed through) or, more often, deserted. Punishments for desertion or offenses such as theft and assault were harsh; convicted soldiers were sentenced to hundreds of lashes, whereas officers were publicly humiliated, deprived of their commission, and discharged in disgrace.

Endemic disease in the camps—dysentery, fevers, and, early in the war, smallpox—made matters worse. Most native-born colonists had neither been exposed to smallpox nor inoculated and were vulnerable when smallpox spread through the northern countryside in early 1774. The disease ravaged Bostonians during the British occupation, troops attacking Quebec in 1775–1776, and the African Americans who fled to join Lord Dunmore (1775) or **Lord Cornwallis** (1781). Most British soldiers had already survived smallpox (which was endemic in Europe), so it posed little threat to redcoats.

Recognizing smallpox's potential to decimate the revolutionaries' ranks, Washington ordered that the regular army be inoculated in 1777. Some would die from the risky procedure and survivors would be incapacitated for weeks. Yet inoculation, coupled with the increasing numbers of foreign-born (and mostly immune) enlistees, helped to protect Continental soldiers later in the war, contributing significantly to the eventual American victory.

American soldiers and sailors captured by the British endured great suffering, especially those held in makeshift prisons or on prison ships near Manhattan. Because Britain refused to recognize the legitimacy of the American government, Redcoat officers regarded the patriots as rebellious traitors rather than as prisoners of war with a right to decent treatment. The meager rations and crowded, unsanitary conditions meant that half to two-thirds of the prisoners fell victim to disease, especially dysentery. Particularly notorious was the hulk *Jersey*; survivors reported fighting over scraps of disgusting food, being covered with "bloody and loathesome filth," and each day having to remove the bodies of five to ten of their dead comrades.

Home Front

Men who enlisted in the army, served in Congress, or were captured were absent for long periods of time. Their womenfolk, who previously had handled only the "indoor affairs" of the household, thus shouldered the "outdoor affairs" as well. John and Abigail Adams took great pride in Abigail's developing skills as a "farmeress." She stopped calling the farm "yours" in letters to her husband and began referring to it as "ours." Most women, like Abigail, did not work in the fields but supervised field workers and managed their families' finances.

Wartime disruptions affected all Americans. People suffered from shortages of necessities like salt, soap, and flour. Severe inflation added to the country's woes. Soldiers on both sides plundered farms and houses, looking for food or salable items; they burned fence rails and took horses and oxen to transport their wagons. Moreover, they carried smallpox and other diseases wherever they went. Women had to decide whether to deliberately risk their children's lives by inoculating them with smallpox or to chance youngsters' contracting the disease "in the natural way." Many, including Abigail Adams, chose the former were relieved when their children survived.

Victory in the South

In early 1778, in the wake of the Saratoga disaster, British military leaders reassessed their strategy. Loyalist exiles in London persuaded them to shift the field of battle southward, contending that loyal southerners would welcome the redcoat army as liberators. Southern colonies that had returned to friendly civilian control could serve as bases for attacking the middle and northern states.

> What risky—but ultimately wise—move did American diplomats make in negotiating peace with England after the American Revolution?

South Carolina and the Caribbean

Sir Henry Clinton, who replaced Howe, oversaw the regrouping of British forces. He ordered the evacuation of Philadelphia in June 1778 and sent a convoy that captured the French Caribbean island of St. Lucia, thereafter a key British base. He also dispatched a small expedition to Georgia. When Savannah and then Augusta fell into British hands, Clinton became convinced that a southern strategy would succeed. In late 1779, he sailed from New York to besiege Charleston, the most important Southern city (see Map 6.2). Although afflicted by smallpox, Americans trapped there held out for months. On May 12, 1780, General Benjamin Lincoln surrendered the entire southern army—fifty-five thousand men. The redcoats then spread through South Carolina, establishing garrisons at key points. Hundreds of South Carolinians proclaimed renewed loyalty to the Crown.

Success of the southern campaign depended on controlling the seas, for the British armies were widely dispersed and travel by land was difficult. The Royal Navy safely dominated the American coastline, but French naval power posed a threat. American privateers infested Caribbean waters, seizing cargoes to and from the British islands. Furthermore, after late 1778 France picked off those islands one by

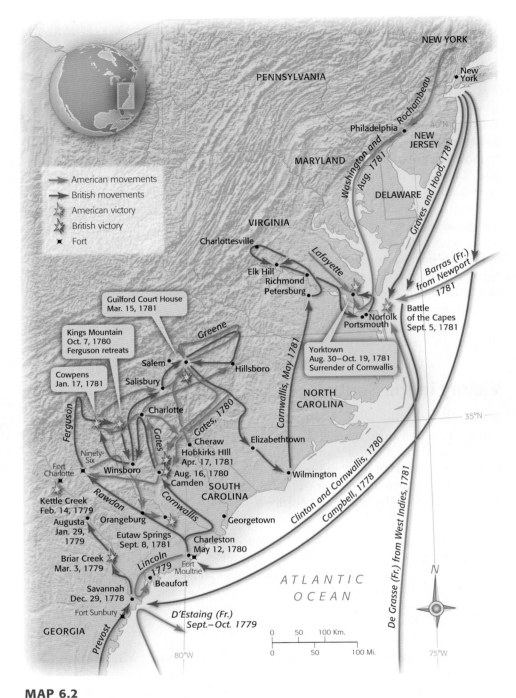

MAP 6.2

The War in the South

The southern war—after the British invasion of Georgia in late 1778—was characterized by a series of British thrusts into the interior, leading to battles with American defenders in both North and South Carolina. Finally, after promising beginnings, Cornwallis's foray into Virginia ended with disaster at Yorktown in October 1781.

Source: Copyright © Cengage Learning

one, including Grenada—second only to Jamaica in sugar production. In early 1781, the British captured St. Eustatius (the Dutch island that was the main conduit for moving military supplies from Europe to America). But the victory might have cost them the war, for Admiral Sir George Rodney failed to pursue the French fleet under Admiral François de Grasse when it sailed from the Caribbean to Virginia, where it played a major role in the **battle at Yorktown**.

The redcoats never established control of the areas they seized in South Carolina or Georgia. Patriot bands operated freely, and the fall of Charleston spurred them to greater exertions. Patriot women in four states formed the Ladies Association, raising money to buy shirts for needy soldiers. Recruiting efforts were stepped up.

Nevertheless, the war in South Carolina went badly for the patriots throughout 1780. At Camden in August, forces under Lord Cornwallis, the new British commander, defeated a reorganized southern army led by Horatio Gates. Thousands of enslaved African Americans joined the redcoats. Running away from their patriot masters individually and as families, they disrupted farming in the Carolinas and Georgia in 1780 and 1781. Tens of thousands of slaves were lost to their owners. Not all of them joined the British or won their freedom. Many served the redcoats as scouts or laborers in camps or occupied cities like New York.

Greene and the Southern Campaign

After the Camden defeat, Washington (who had to remain in the North to contain the British army occupying New York) appointed General Nathanael Greene to command the southern campaign. Greene was appalled by conditions in South Carolina. His troops needed clothing, blankets, and food. He told a friend that incessant guerrilla warfare had "so corrupted the principles of the people that they think of nothing but plundering one another."

Greene moved cautiously. He adopted a conciliatory policy toward the many Americans who had switched sides, an advantageous move in a region where people changed their allegiance up to seven times in less than two years. He ordered his troops to treat captives fairly and not loot loyalist property. He helped the shattered provincial congresses of Georgia and South Carolina reestablish civilian authority in the interior—a goal the British were never able to accomplish. With only sixteen hundred regulars, Greene could not afford to have frontier militia companies occupied in defending their homes from Indian attack. He accordingly pursued diplomacy to keep Indians out of the war. Although royal officials initially won some Indian allies, by war's end only the Creeks remained allied with Great Britain.

Even before Greene took command of the southern army in December 1780, the tide was turning. In October, at King's Mountain, a backcountry force defeated redcoats and loyalists. Then in January 1781, Greene's aide Daniel Morgan routed the British regiment Tarleton's Legion at Cowpens. Greene confronted British troops under Lord Cornwallis at Guilford Court House, North Carolina, in March. Although Cornwallis controlled the field at day's end, most of his army was destroyed. Greene returned to South Carolina, where he forced the redcoats to retire to Charleston.

Surrender at Yorktown

Cornwallis headed north into Virginia, where he joined forces with redcoats commanded by the American traitor Benedict Arnold. He then withdrew to the peninsula between the York and James Rivers, where he fortified Yorktown. Washington moved more than seven

battle of Yorktown: The battle at Yorktown, Virginia, which resulted in the defeat of British military leader Lord Cornwallis and his surrender to George Washington.

Revolutionary Origins

Many historians today would contend that the American Revolution was not truly "revolutionary," if revolution means overturning an earlier power structure. The nation won its independence and established a republic, both radical events in the eighteenth century, but essentially the same men who led the colonies also led the new country (with the exception of British officials and appointees). In contrast, the nearly contemporary French Revolution witnessed the execution of the monarch and many aristocrats and a significant redistribution of authority. So the legacy of the American Revolution appears at once radical and conservative.

Throughout the more than two hundred years since the "Revolution," varying groups have claimed to represent the spirit of the Revolution. People protesting discriminatory policies against women and minorities (usually "liberals") invoke the "created equal" language of the Declaration of Independence. Left-wing organizations rail against concentrations of wealth and power. Those protesting higher taxes (usually "conservatives" wanting a reduced role for government) often adopt the symbolism of the Boston Tea Party, as in the "tea-party" movement opposing Obama administration policies. Right-wing militias arm themselves, preparing to defend their homes and families against a malevolent government, just as they believe the minutemen did in 1775. Indeed, so-called minutemen have formed vigilante groups to guard the United States–Mexico border against illegal aliens. The message of the Revolution can be invoked to support extralegal demonstrations of any description, from invasions of military bases by antiwar protesters to demonstrations outside abortion clinics. But the Revolution can also be invoked to oppose such street protests, because—some would argue—in a republic, change should come peacefully, via the ballot box.

Just as Americans in the eighteenth century disagreed over the meaning of their struggle, so the legacy of revolution remains contested early in the twenty-first century both for the nation.

thousand French and American troops south from New York City. When De Grasse's fleet arrived in time to defeat the Royal Navy vessels sent to relieve Cornwallis, the British general was trapped (see Map 6.2). On October 19, 1781, Cornwallis surrendered.

When news of the defeat reached London, Parliament voted to cease offensive operations in America, authorizing peace negotiations. Washington returned with the main army to the environs of New York, where in March 1783, his underpaid—and, they thought, underappreciated—officers threatened to mutiny unless Congress guaranteed them adequate compensation. Washington, warned in advance of the so-called Newburgh Conspiracy, defused the crisis with a well-reasoned and patriotic speech. At the end of the year, he resigned as commander-in-chief. Still, Washington established an enduring precedent: civilian control of the American military.

The war had been won, but at terrible cost. More than thirty-five thousand American men died, about one-quarter of them from battle and one-half while prisoners of the British. In the South, years of guerrilla warfare and the loss of thousands of runaway slaves shattered the economy. Indebtedness soared, and local governments were crippled, as few people could pay taxes. Some formerly wealthy planters descended into insolvency.

Treaty of Paris

Yet Americans rejoiced when they learned of the signing of the preliminary peace **treaty of Paris** in November 1782. American diplomats—Benjamin Franklin, John Jay, and John Adams—ignored their instructions from Congress to be guided by France and negotiated directly with Great Britain. Their instincts were sound: the French government was more an enemy to Britain than a friend to the United States. French ministers worked secretly to prevent the establishment of a strong, unified government in America. Spain's desire to lay claim to the region between the Appalachian Mountains and the Mississippi River further complicated the negotiations. But the American delegates proved adept at power politics, achieving their main goal: independence as a united nation. Weary of war, the new British ministry made so many concessions that Parliament ousted it shortly after peace terms were approved.

The treaty, signed on September 3, 1783, granted independence to a nation named "the United States of America." Generous boundaries delineated that new nation: to the north, approximately the present-day boundary with Canada; to the south, the 31st parallel (about the modern northern border of Florida); to the west, the Mississippi River. Florida, which Britain had acquired in 1763, reverted to Spain (see Map 7.2). The Americans also gained unlimited fishing rights off Newfoundland. In ceding so much land, Britain ignored the territorial rights of its Indian allies. British diplomats also poorly served loyalists and British merchants. The treaty's ambiguously worded clauses regarding prewar debts and the postwar treatment of loyalists proved impossible to enforce.

treaty of Paris: A treaty signed in 1783 when the British recognized American independence and agreed to withdraw all royal troops from the colonies.

Link to the petition of Connecticut slaves for freedom.

Summary

Having unified the disparate mainland colonies, the victorious Americans had claimed their place in the family of nations and forged a successful alliance with France. With an inexperienced army, they had defeated the world's greatest military power. They won only a few actual victories—most notably, at Trenton, Saratoga, and Yorktown—but their army survived to fight again. Ultimately, the Americans wore their enemy down.

In winning the war, the Americans abandoned their British identity, excluding from their new nation loyalist neighbors unwilling to break with the mother country. They established republican governments at state and national levels and created new national loyalties. They also claimed most of the territory east of the Mississippi River and south of the Great Lakes, thereby greatly expanding land open to settlement and threatening traditional Indian dominance of the interior.

In the future, Americans would face new challenges: ensuring the survival of their republic in a world dominated by the bitter rivalries among Britain, France, and Spain.

Chapter Review

Government by Congress and Committee

How did the first Continental Congress redefine America's relationship to England?

Congressmen meeting at the First Continental Congress in September 1774 were not ready for a complete break from England, but they did outline America's grievances, develop a resistance plan, and define America's relationship to Great Britain. Debate covered the spectrum of opinion from the radical call to obey only the king and not Parliament to the more conservative view that would have Parliament and a new American legislature jointly enacting colonial laws. In the end, the group compromised and agreed in the Declaration of Rights and Grievances to obey Parliament on a voluntary basis (rather than as subjects) and resist all taxes.

Contest in the Backcountry

Where did backcountry Indians' loyalties lie at the onset of the Revolution?

Initially, Indians were inclined to ally with Great Britain, given the hostility they experienced from European American settlers in the backcountry. But other chiefs had their doubts: England had abandoned them in vacating Fort Pitt years earlier. Both the Americans and the British sought a pledge of neutrality, and while some, such as the Iroquois, agreed, others, such as the Cherokees and Shawnees, attacked backcountry settlements in western Virginia and the Carolinas, hoping to use the conflict to regain lost land. A few Indian communities supported the Americans, but most others remained neutral or sporadically sided with the British.

Choosing Sides

How did colonists choose sides in the conflict with England?

Not everyone supported independence from Great Britain. In fact, only two-fifths of the European American population of the thirteen colonies were Patriots seeking to separate from England—among them small and middling farmers, Chesapeake gentry, merchants, city artisans, elected officeholders—and even then, their specific goals varied. Loyalists who opposed the break with England represented one-fifth of the population and included Anglican clergy; parishioners in the North; tenant farmers; members of persecuted religious sects; backcountry southerners; ethnic minorities, especially Scots; and merchants who relied on British trade. Two-fifths of the population remained neutral, including pacifist groups such as the Quakers. Finally, free blacks in the North in the middle colonies took the Patriots' side, while southern bondspeople thought they'd have a better chance at personal freedom by allying with the British, who made such promises to runaway slaves.

War and Independence

How did Thomas Paine's *Common Sense* help reshape the war's purpose?

While Americans had been at war with Great Britain for months, most leaders denied seeking a complete break from England and focused on achieving some autonomy and a redress for various grievances. In January 1776, Paine's widely popular pamphlet called for independence and the establishment of a republic (a government by the people with no king or nobility). He argued that once America broke from European control, it would become strong and prosperous. Within months of its publication, the Second Continental Congress passed a resolution that the colonies should be free and all ties to Great Britain dissolved and charged five men, among them Thomas Jefferson, to write a Declaration of Independence.

The Struggle in the North

What was France's role in the American Revolution?

Initially, France secretly sent military supplies to the Americans and regarded the revolution as a chance to avenge its defeat to Britain in the Seven Years' War. Once Americans won the Battle of Saratoga, the French openly supported them, sending naval vessels, ammunition, and troops. France's assistance proved vital to American victory in the final years of the war. Americans and the French signed two treaties in 1778, the Treaty of Amity and Commerce, which recognized American independence and set up trade relations; and the Treaty of Alliance, which promised neither side would negotiate peace (in conflicts with Britain) without consulting the other. France also abandoned claims to Canada and to North American territory east of the Mississippi River.

Life in the Army and on the Home Front

 How was the Continental Army staffed?

Only in the war's earliest months were battlefields filled by militia men, who left their fields to fight. After that, American leaders organized an army comprising young, single, often propertyless men who enlisted for a period of time for money or land. Towns were required to send their quota of soldiers and did so by enlisting everyone, including recent immigrants. Initially, African Americans were banned from the army, but by 1776, that prohibition was lifted, as northern recruiters promised slaves their freedom after the war. About five thousand enlisted, composing 10 percent of the army, though they were typically in segregated units and often given tasks others rejected, such as burying the dead. Wives and widows of poor soldiers often followed the camps, too, working as cooks, nurses, and launderers for rations or low wages.

Victory in the South

 What risky—but ultimately wise—move did American diplomats make in negotiating peace with England after the American Revolution?

During the signing of a preliminary peace treaty in Paris in 1782 ending the American Revolution, diplomats Benjamin Franklin, John Jay, and John Adams ignored Congress's instructions to let Paris lead the way.

Congress wanted them to follow the terms of the 1778 Treaty of Alliance, in which Americans promised not to make peace with England without consulting France first (and vice versa). Instead, the diplomats trusted their instincts and negotiated on their own. Turns out they were right: French ministers had secretly tried to prevent a strong government from taking hold in America. War-weary Britain not only gave America its independence, but also ceded vast tracts of land and unlimited fishing rights off Newfoundland.

Suggestions for Further Reading

Edwin G. Burrows, *Forgotten Patriots: The Untold Story of American Prisoners during the Revolutionary War* (2008).

Robert McCluer Calhoon, *The Loyalists in Revolutionary America, 1760–1781* (1973)

Colin Calloway, *The American Revolution in Indian Country* (1995)

Stephen Conway, *The War of American Independence, 1775–1783* (1995)

Sylvia Frey, *Water from the Rock: Black Resistance in a Revolutionary Age* (1991)

Pauline Maier, *American Scripture: Making the Declaration of Independence* (1997)

Charles Niemeyer, *America Goes to War: A Social History of the Continental Army* (1997)

Mary Beth Norton, *Liberty's Daughters: The Revolutionary Experience of American Women, 1750–1800* (2nd ed., 1996)

Cassandra Pybus, *Epic Journeys of Freedom: Runaway Slaves of the American Revolution and their Global Quest for Liberty* (2006)

Charles Royster, *A Revolutionary People at War: The Continental Army and American Character, 1775–1783* (1980)

 Go to the CourseMate website for primary source links, study tools, and review materials for this chapter. www.cengagebrain.com

Forging a National Republic

7

1776–1789

On December 26, 1787, a group of Federalists—supporters of the proposed Constitution—gathered in Carlisle, a Pennsylvania frontier town. The men planned to fire a cannon to celebrate their state convention's ratification vote two weeks earlier, but a large crowd of Antifederalists stopped them. First, the Antis blocked the cannon. Then, they attacked the Federalists, who fled as the angry Antis burned a copy of the Constitution.

The next day, Federalists fired their cannon and read the ratification proclamation. Antifederalists paraded and burned effigies of two Federalists. When Federalist officials arrested demonstrators for rioting, the Antifederalist-dominated militia broke them out of jail.

For weeks, participants argued in the Carlisle newspaper about what the demonstrations meant. Federalist proclaimed that the respectable celebrants acted with "good order" and called Antifederalist opponents "worthless ragamuffins." Replying, Antifederalists pronounced the Federalists "an unhallowed riotous mob." Constitution supporters called themselves "friends of government," but through their advocacy of government that aimed to suppress the people's liberties, they revealed they were secretly aristocrats.

The Carlisle riots presaged violent disputes over the new Constitution in Albany (New York), Providence (Rhode Island), and other cities. In a struggle that began in 1775 and persisted until century's end, Americans argued over how to implement republican principles and who best represented the people.

Republicanism—the idea that governments should be based on the consent of the people—originated with theorists in ancient Greece and Rome. Republics, they declared, were desirable yet fragile government forms. Unless citizens were virtuous—sober, moral, and industrious—and agreed on key issues, republics would fail. When Americans left Britain, they abandoned the idea that the best governments balanced participation by a king, the nobility, and the people. Instead, they embraced republicanism, in which the people were sovereign. During and after the war,

Chapter Outline

Creating a Virtuous Republic
Varieties of Republicanism | Virtue and the Arts | Educational Reform | Judith Sargent Murray | Women and the Republic

VISUALIZING THE PAST *Depicting Virtue*

LINKS TO THE WORLD *Writing and Stationery Supplies*

The First Emancipation and the Growth of Racism
Emancipation and Manumission | Growth of Free Black Population | Freedpeople's Lives | Development of Racist Theory | A White Men's Republic

Designing Republican Governments
State Constitutions | Limiting State Governments | Revising State Constitutions | Articles of Confederation

Trials of the Confederation
Financial Affairs | Foreign Affairs | Peace Treaty Provisions

Order and Disorder in the West
Indian Relations | Ordinance of 1785 | Northwest Ordinance

From Crisis to the Constitution
Taxation and the Economy | Shays's Rebellion | Constitutional Convention | Madison and the Constitution | Virginia and New Jersey Plans | Debates over Congress | Slavery and the Constitution | Congressional and Presidential Powers

Opposition and Ratification
Federalists and Antifederalists | Bill of Rights | Ratification | Celebrating Ratification

LEGACY FOR A PEOPLE AND A NATION *The Township and Range System*

SUMMARY

Americans wondered how to ensure political stability, foster consensus, and create and sustain a virtuous republic.

America's leaders attempted to inculcate virtue in their countrymen and countrywomen. After 1776, literature, theater, art, architecture, and education pursued moral goals. Women's education became important, for the mothers of the republic's children would ensure the nation's future. Almost all white men assumed that women, African Americans, and Indians should have no role in politics; men saw the first two groups as household dependents, the last as outside the polity. Still, they disagreed on how many of their number should be included in the political process and how their new governments should be structured.

Then there were Thomas Jefferson's words in the Declaration of Independence: "all men are created equal." Given that statement of principle, how could white republicans justify holding African Americans in perpetual bondage? Some freed their slaves or voted for state laws abolishing slavery. Others denied that blacks were "men" in the same sense as whites.

The most important task facing Americans was constructing a unified national government. Before 1765, many circumstances divided the British mainland colonies: diverse economies, varying religious traditions and ethnic compositions, competing western land claims, and different polities. But the Revolutionary War brought them together, creating a new nationalistic spirit that replaced loyalties to state and region.

Still, America's first national government under the Articles of Confederation proved too weak and decentralized. Political leaders tried another approach in drafting the Constitution in 1787. Some historians have argued that the Articles of Confederation and the Constitution reflect opposing philosophies, the Constitution representing an "aristocratic" counterrevolution against the "democratic" Articles. The two documents are more accurately viewed as successive attempts to solve the same problems—the relationship of states and nation and the extent to which authority should be centralized. Both applied theories of republicanism to problems of governance; neither was entirely successful in resolving those difficulties.

As you read this chapter, keep the following questions in mind:

* **What were the elements of the new national identity? How did women, Indians, and African Americans fit into that identity?**

* **What problems confronted the new nation's leaders as they attempted to establish the first modern republic?**

* **How and why were those problems resolved differently at different times?**

Creating a Virtuous Republic

When the colonies declared independence, John Dickinson recalled years later, "We knew that the people of this country must unite themselves under some form of Government and that this could be no other than the republican form"—in short, self-government by the people. But how should that goal be implemented?

How were notions of republican virtue gendered in post-revolutionary America?

Chronology

1776	Second Continental Congress directs states to draft constitutions	1786	Annapolis Convention meets, discusses reforming government
	Abigail Adams advises her husband to "Remember the Ladies"	1786–87	Shays's Rebellion in western Massachusetts raises questions about future of the republic
1777	Articles of Confederation sent to states for ratification	1787	Royall Tyler's *The Contrast*, first successful American play, performed
	Vermont becomes first jurisdiction to abolish slavery		Northwest Ordinance organizes territory north of Ohio River and east of Mississippi River
1781	Articles of Confederation ratified		Constitutional Convention drafts new form of government
1783	Treaty of Paris signed, formalizing American independence	1788	Hamilton, Jay, and Madison write *The Federalist* to urge ratification of the Constitution by New York
1784	Diplomats sign treaty with Iroquois at Fort Stanwix, but Iroquois repudiate it two years later		Constitution ratified
1785	Land Ordinance of 1785 provides for surveying and sale of national lands in Northwest Territory	1789	William Hill Brown publishes *The Power of Sympathy*, first American novel
1785–86	United States negotiates treaties at Hopewell, South Carolina, with Choctaws, Chickasaws, and Cherokees		Massachusetts orders towns to support public schools
		1800	Weems publishes his *Life of Washington*

Varieties of Republicanism

Three definitions of republicanism emerged in the new United States. Ancient history and political theory informed the first, held by the educated elite (such as the Adamses of Massachusetts). The histories of popular governments in Greece and Rome suggested that republics could succeed only if they were small and homogeneous. According to classical republican theory, unless a republic's citizens were virtuous men willing to sacrifice private interests for the common good, the government would collapse. In return for sacrifices, a republic offered equality of opportunity. Rank would be based on merit rather than inherited status. Society would be governed by members of a "natural aristocracy," men whose talent elevated them from possibly humble beginnings to positions of power.

A second definition, advanced by other elites and some skilled craftsmen, drew on economic theory. This version of republicanism followed Scottish theorist Adam Smith in emphasizing individuals' pursuit of rational self-interest. When republican men sought to improve their own economic and social circumstances, the nation would benefit. Republican virtue would be achieved through the pursuit of private interests, rather than through subordination to communal ideals.

The third notion of republicanism was less influential but more egalitarian than the others. Men who advanced this version, among them Thomas Paine, called for widening men's political participation. They wanted government to respond directly to the needs of ordinary folk, rejecting that the "lesser sort" should defer to their "betters." They were democrats in the modern sense. For them, the untutored wisdom of the people embodied republican virtue.

Depicting Virtue

In the 1780s, American printers began publishing magazines that became important vehicles for promoting their notions of virtue. For monthly or bi-monthly magazines filled with locally written poems and essays publishers needed illustrations—something not required by weekly newspapers. One of the most important and longest lasting of these publications was the *Columbian Magazine*, published in Philadelphia from 1786 to 1792. Seen here are two of the many illustrations its printer commissioned from local artists. *Venerate the Plow* celebrated American agriculture, with the female figure symbolizing America (note the 13 stars in a circle over her head) holding a sheaf of grain. In the other, Columbia presents a girl and a boy (the "rising race") to Minerva (goddess of wisdom), who leans on a pedestal lauding independence as "the reward of wisdom, fortitude, and perseverance." In the background, a farmer plows his field and ships ply the ocean. What future did Americans see for themselves, as represented in these pictures?

Library of Congress

Columbian Magazine, 1786

VENERATE THE PLOUGH

Library of Congress

Columbian Magazine, 1787

All three strands of republicanism contrasted America's industrious virtue with the corruption of Britain and Europe. In the first version, that virtue manifested itself in frugality and self-sacrifice; in the second, it would prevent self-interest from becoming vice; in the third, it was the justification for including propertyless free men as voters. Most agreed that a virtuous country would be composed of hardworking citizens who would dress simply, elect wise leaders, and forgo conspicuous consumption of luxury goods.

Virtue and the Arts

As citizens of the United States constructed their republic, they expected to replace the vices of monarchical Europe—immorality, selfishness, and lack of public spirit—with the virtues of republican America. They sought to embody republican principles in their governments and in their culture, expecting painting, literature, drama, and architecture to convey nationalism and virtue.

Americans faced a contradiction, however. To some republicans, fine arts were manifestations of vice, signaling luxury and corruption. Why did a frugal farmer need a painting or a novel? Why should anyone spend hard-earned wages to see a play in a lavish theater? The first American artists and authors wanted to produce works embodying virtue, but many viewed those works as corrupting, regardless of their content.

Still, authors and artists tried. In Royall Tyler's *The Contrast* (1787), the first successful American play, Colonel Manly's virtuous conduct was contrasted with Billy Dimple's reprehensible behavior. The era's most popular book, Mason Locke Weems's *Life of Washington*, published in 1800 after George Washington's death, was intended to "hold up his great Virtues … to the imitation of Our Youth." The famous tale Weems invented—six-year-old George bravely admitting cutting down his father's favorite cherry tree—ended with George's father exclaiming, "Such an act of heroism in my son, is worth more than a thousand trees."

Painting and architecture, too, were to exemplify high moral standards. Prominent artists Gilbert Stuart and Charles Willson Peale painted portraits of upstanding republican citizens. John Trumbull's canvases sought to inspire patriotism with scenes of historical milestones such as the Battle of Bunker Hill and Cornwallis's surrender at Yorktown. When the Virginia government asked Thomas Jefferson, then minister to France, for advice on designing the state capitol in Richmond, Jefferson recommended copying a simple but noble Roman building, the Maison Carrée at Nîmes. Jefferson's ideals that would guide American architecture for a generation: simplicity of line, harmonious proportions, a feeling of grandeur.

Despite the artists' efforts (or perhaps because of them), some Americans detected signs of luxury and corruption by the mid-1780s. The resumption of European trade after the war brought imported fashions. Elite families again attended balls and concerts. Parties no longer seemed complete without gambling and cardplaying. Social clubs for young people multiplied. Especially alarming was the establishment in 1783 of the Society of the Cincinnati, a hereditary association for Revolutionary War officers and their firstborn sons. Although organizers hoped to advance the citizen-soldier, opponents feared that the group would become the nucleus of a native-born aristocracy. These developments challenged the United States' self-image as a virtuous republic.

Educational Reform

Americans' concern for the infant republic's future focused their attention on children. Education was previously seen as the concern of individual families. Now schooling would serve a public purpose. If young people were to resist vice and become useful citizens, they would need education. The 1780s and 1790s thus witnessed two major changes in educational practice.

Link to Royall Tyler's *The Contrast.*

Links to the World

Writing and Stationery Supplies

In the seventeenth century, colonists stressed teaching children to read the Bible; writing was less necessary, and many people could read but not write. Yet as the eighteenth century progressed, writing skills acquired new significance as family members parted by the Revolutionary War needed to communicate with each other and new opportunities arose for merchants who could handle distant correspondents. After the war, Americans placed greater emphasis on teaching youngsters to write.

Writing drew on materials from around the world. Sheets of paper came from Britain or, increasingly, from American paper mills; more than thirty were built between 1750 and 1780. Quill pens (goose feathers) often originated in Germany or Holland. Penknives to sharpen blunt quills and inkpots (made of brass, glass, or pewter) also came from Britain. But the Americans could not write without additional items from international trade.

For example, to absorb ink properly, paper needed to be treated with pounce, a powder made from gum sandarac (a tree resin from North Africa) and pumice (powdered volcanic glass). Lacking envelopes, eighteenth-century writers folded papers, addressed them on the outside, and sealed them with wax made in Holland or Britain from lac (a resinous secretion of insects, still used today for shellac) from India and cinnabar, a red quartz-like crystal, from Spain. Ink was manufactured from various ingredients: oak galls from Aleppo (in Syria), gum arabic (sap from acacia trees) from Sudan, and alum and copperas (derived from stones) from Britain. Most likely ink was shipped from Britain in powdered form; in America, another key ingredient, urine, would be added so the alum would blend with the other substances.

Therefore, children learning to write in one of the new academies used implements that involved Americans in a commercial chain that linked them to Great Britain, the European continent, North Africa, and the Middle East.

Historic Odessa Foundation

This writing desk, made in Pennsylvania in the mid-to-late eighteenth century, would have been owned by a well-to-do family from the mid-Atlantic states. The pigeon holes would hold incoming and outgoing letters; the many drawers could store paper, ink, seals and sealing wax, and other supplies. The new importance of writing thus produced a perceived need for novel types of furniture.

First, some northern states began using tax money to support public elementary schools. In 1789, Massachusetts became one of the first states requiring towns to offer free public elementary education. Second, since mothers would have to be educated if they were to instruct their children adequately, Massachusetts insisted that elementary schools teach girls as well as boys. Throughout the United States, private academies were founded to provide advanced schooling for teenage girls from well-to-do families. Colleges remained closed to women, but a few fortunate girls could study history, geography, rhetoric, and mathematics.

Judith Sargent Murray

Judith Sargent Murray of Gloucester, Massachusetts, became the chief theorist of women's education in the early republic. Murray argued that women and men had equal intellectual capacities, although inadequate education might make women seem less intelligent. Therefore, concluded Murray, boys and girls should be offered equivalent schooling. She further contended that girls should be taught to support themselves: "Independence should be placed within their grasp."

Murray's ideas were part of a general rethinking of women's position that resulted from the Revolution. Men and women realized that female patriots had made important contributions to independence. Consequently, Americans developed new ideas about women's in republican society.

Judith Sargent Stevens (later Murray), by John Singleton Copley, ca. 1770–1772. The eventual author of tracts advocating improvements in women's education sat for this portrait two decades earlier, during her first marriage. Her clear-eyed gaze suggests both her intelligence and her seriousness of purpose.

Terra Foundation for American Art, Chicago/Art Resource, NY

Link to Judith Sargent Murray's "On the Equality of the Sexes."

Abigail Adams: Wife of Revolutionary figure John Adams (and second U.S. President). Influenced by the ideology of the Revolution, her letter to her husband is considered an early effort for greater rights for women.

Women and the Republic

The best-known expression of those new ideas appeared in a letter **Abigail Adams** addressed to her husband in March 1776. "In the new Code of Laws which I suppose it will be necessary for you to make I desire you would Remember the Ladies," she wrote. "Remember all Men would be tyrants if they could. … If perticuliar care and attention is not paid to the Laidies [sic] we are determined to foment a Rebelion, and will not hold ourselves bound by any Laws in which we have no voice, or Representation." With these words, Abigail Adams applied the ideology developed to combat parliamentary supremacy. She argued that, because men were "Naturally Tyrannical," the United States should reform marriage laws, which subordinated wives to their husbands, giving men control of family property and denying wives the right to independent legal action.

Abigail Adams did not ask for woman suffrage, but others claimed that right, and some authors began to define the "rights of women" in general terms. The New Jersey state constitution in 1776 defined voters carelessly as "all free inhabitants" who met property qualifications. They thereby unintentionally gave the vote to property-holding white spinsters and widows and free black landowners. Qualified women and African Americans regularly voted in New Jersey's local and congressional elections until 1807, when they were disfranchised by the state legislature. That women chose to vote was evidence of how the Revolution altered their perception of their place in the nation's political life.

Even after the war, most European-Americans viewed women in traditional terms, affirming their primary function as wives, mothers, and mistresses of households. Because wives could not own property or participate directly in economic life, women came to be seen as the embodiment of self-sacrificing, republicanism. Through new female-run charitable associations, better-off women assumed public responsibilities among them caring for poor widows and orphans. Thus, men were freed to pursue their economic self-interests, while wives and daughters fulfilled the family's obligation to the common good. The ideal republican man, therefore, was an individualist, seeking advancement for himself and his family. The ideal republican woman put the well-being of others first.

The First Emancipation and the Growth of Racism

What contributed to the growing number of free blacks in America after the revolution?

Revolutionary ideology exposed one of the primary contradictions in American society. There were 700,000 African Americans—roughly 20 percent of the population—residing in the new republic. European-Americans and African Americans saw the irony in slaveholders' claims that they sought to prevent Britain from "enslaving" them. In 1773, Dr. Benjamin Rush called slavery "a vice which degrades human nature," warning ominously that "the plant of liberty is of so tender a nature that it cannot thrive long in the neighborhood of slavery."

African Americans used revolutionary ideology to their advantage. In 1779, a group of slaves from Portsmouth, New Hampshire, addressed the state legislature, pleading "that the name of slave may not more be heard in a land gloriously contending for the sweets of freedom." The same year, several bondsmen in Fairfield, Connecticut, petitioned the legislature for their freedom, characterizing slavery as a "flagrant Injustice." How could men who were "nobly contending in the Cause of Liberty," they asked, continue "this detestable Practice"?

Emancipation and Manumission

Both legislatures responded negatively, but the postwar years witnessed the gradual abolition of slavery in the North. Responding to lawsuits filed by enslaved men and women, Massachusetts courts decided in 1783 that the state constitution prohibited slavery. Other states adopted gradual emancipation laws between 1780 (Pennsylvania) and 1804 (New Jersey). New Hampshire did not formally abolish slavery, but only eight slaves were reported on the 1800 census and none in 1810. Although no southern state adopted emancipation laws, the legislatures of Virginia (1782), Delaware (1787), and Maryland (1790 and 1796) loosened earlier laws restricting slaveowners' ability to free their bondspeople. South Carolina and Georgia never considered such

Private collection, photograph courtesy of Hirschl & Adler Galleries, New York

A sailor of African descent posed proudly for this portrait around 1790. Unfortunately, neither the name of the sailor nor the name of the artist is known today.

acts, and North Carolina insisted that manumissions (emancipations of individual slaves) be approved by county courts.

Revolutionary ideology thus had limited impact on the economic interests of large slaveholders. Only in the northern states—societies with slaves, not slave societies—could state legislatures abolish slavery. Even there, legislators' concern for the *property* rights of slave owners led them to favor gradual over immediate emancipation. For example, New York's law freed children born into slavery after July 4, 1799, but only after they reached their mid-twenties. Laws failed to emancipate the existing slave population. Although emancipation laws forbade the sale of slaves to jurisdictions where slavery remained legal, slaveowners regularly circumvented such provisions. The 1840 census recorded the presence of slaves in several northern states.

Growth of Free Black Population

The number of free people of African descent in the United States grew dramatically in the initial post-Revolution years. Most slaves emancipated before the war were mulattos, born of unions between bondswomen and their masters, who manumitted the children. Wartime escapees from plantations, slaves who served in the American army, and those emancipated by their owners or by state laws, contributed to the nearly 60,000 free people of color in the United States by 1790. Ten years later, they numbered more than 108,000—nearly 11 percent of the total African American population.

In the Chesapeake, manumissions were speeded by economic changes, such as declining soil fertility and the shift from tobacco to grain production. Because grain cultivation was less labor-intensive than tobacco growing, planters had "excess" slaves. They occasionally solved that problem by freeing less productive or more favored bondspeople. The enslaved also negotiated agreements with owners allowing them to live and work independently until they could purchase themselves. Virginia's free black population more than doubled between 1790 and 1810; also by 1810, nearly one-quarter of Maryland's African American population was no longer in bondage.

Freedpeople's Lives

In the 1780s, rural freedpeople headed to northern port cities such as Boston and Philadelphia. With better employment opportunities, especially in domestic service, women outnumbered male migrants by three to two. Some freedmen also worked in domestic service, but larger numbers were unskilled laborers and sailors. A few women and many men (nearly one-third of those in Philadelphia in 1795) were skilled workers or retailers. They exchanged the surnames of former masters for names like Newman or Brown and established independent two-parent families. They also began to occupy distinct neighborhoods, probably due to discrimination.

Even whites who recognized African Americans' right to freedom were unwilling to accept them as equals. Laws discriminated against freedpeople as they had against slaves. Several states—among them Delaware, Maryland, and South Carolina—adopted laws denying property-owning black men the vote. South Carolina forbade free blacks from testifying against whites in court. New Englanders used indenture contracts to control freed youths, who were often denied public education. Freedmen found it difficult to purchase property and find good jobs.

Gradually, freedpeople developed their own institutions. In Charleston, mulattos formed the Brown Fellowship Society, which provided insurance coverage, financed a school, and helped to support orphans. In 1794, former slaves in Philadelphia and Baltimore, led by Reverend Richard Allen, founded societies that eventually formed the **African Methodist Episcopal (AME) church**. AME churches sponsored schools and—along with African Baptist, African Episcopal, and African Presbyterian churches—became cultural centers for free blacks.

African Methodist Episcopal (AME) church: The first black-run Protestant denomination.

Development of Racist Theory

Their endeavors were especially important because the postrevolutionary years witnessed the development of formal racist theory in the United States. Before the Revolution, European-Americans regarded slaves as inferior. Influential writers argued that African slaves' seemingly debased character derived from their enslavement, rather

MAP 7.1

African American Population, 1790: Proportion of Total Population

The first census clearly indicated that the African American population was heavily concentrated in just a few areas of the United States, most notably in coastal regions of South Carolina, Georgia, and Virginia. Although there were growing numbers of blacks in the backcountry—presumably taken there by migrating slaveowners—most parts of the North and East, with the exception of the immediate vicinity of New York City, had few African American residents.

Source: From Lester J. Cappon et al., eds., *Atlas of Early American History: The Revolutionary Era, 1760–1790.* Copyright © 1976 by Princeton University Press.

Percentage of population black

- Majority
- 20–50%
- 5–20%
- Less than 5%
- Other U.S territory

than enslavement's being the consequence of inherited inferiority. After the Revolution, slaveowners needed to defend holding other human beings in bondage against the proposition that "all men are created equal." Consequently, they argued that people of African descent were less than fully human and that the principles of republican equality applied only to European-Americans.

Egalitarian thinking among European-Americans downplayed status distinctions within their own group and differentiated all "whites" from people of color—Indians and African Americans. Decades earlier, Indians began to refer to themselves as "red." Experience as slaves on American soil forged the identity "African" or "black" from the various ethnic and national affiliations of people who survived the transatlantic crossing. Thus, in the revolutionary era "whiteness," "redness," and "blackness"—along with the superiority of the first, the inferiority of the latter two—developed in tandem.

With racism came the assertion that, as Thomas Jefferson insisted in 1781, blacks were "inferior to the whites in the endowments both of body and mind." There followed the belief that blacks were congenitally lazy, even though owners often argued that slaves were "natural" workers. Third was the notion that blacks were sexually promiscuous and that African American men lusted after European American women. The specter of interracial sexual intercourse involving black men and white women haunted early American racist thought. Significantly, the more common sexual exploitation of enslaved women by their masters aroused little concern.

African Americans challenged these racist notions. Benjamin Banneker, a free black mathematical genius, in 1791 sent Thomas Jefferson a copy of his latest almanac (including astronomical calculations) to show blacks' mental powers. Jefferson admitted Banneker's intelligence but said Banneker was exceptional; Jefferson required more evidence if he were to rethink his position on people of African descent generally.

A White Men's Republic

At its birth, leaders defined the republic as a white male enterprise, as laws from the 1770s on linked "whiteness" and male citizenship rights. Some historians have argued that the subjugation of blacks, Indians, and women was a necessary precondition for theoretical equality among white men. Identifying common racial antagonists helped create white solidarity and lessened the threat to gentry power posed by the enfranchisement of poorer men. Moreover, excluding women from politics reserved power for men. After the Revolution, the division of American society between slave and free became a division between blacks—some of whom were free—and whites.

Designing Republican Governments

How did Americans' former experience as British subjects influence the state governments they established?

In May 1776, the Second Continental Congress directed states to devise new republican governments to replace provincial conventions and committees that had met since colonial governments collapsed in 1774 and 1775. Thus American men concentrated on drafting state constitutions and devoted little attention to national government.

State Constitutions

First, state political leaders struggled to define a "constitution" and eventually concluded that legislative bodies should not draft their constitutions. Following Vermont in 1777 and Massachusetts in 1780, they elected conventions exclusively to draft constitutions. Thus, states sought authorization from the people—the theoretical sovereigns in a republic—before establishing new governments. After preparing new constitutions, delegates submitted them to voters for ratification.

Framers of state constitutions concerned themselves primarily with outlining the distribution of and limitations on government power. If authority was not confined within reasonable limits, the states might become tyrannical, as Britain had.

Under colonial charters, Americans learned to fear the power of the governor—usually the appointed agent of the king or proprietor—and to see the legislature as their defender. Accordingly, the first state constitutions typically provided for the governor to be elected annually (commonly by the legislature), limited the number of terms he could serve, and gave him little independent authority. Simultaneously, they expanded the legislature's powers. Every state except Pennsylvania and Vermont retained a two-house structure, with members of the upper house having longer terms and meeting higher property-holding standards than the lower house. They also redrew electoral districts to reflect population patterns. Finally, most states lowered property qualifications for voting. Thus, the revolutionary era witnessed the first deliberate attempt to broaden the base of American government.

Limiting State Governments

But the state constitutions' authors wanted to prevent tyrants from holding office. They consequently included explicit limitations on government authority to protect the inalienable rights of individual citizens. Seven constitutions contained bills of rights, and others had similar clauses. Most guaranteed freedom of the press, rights to fair trials, and protection against general search warrants. An independent judiciary was charged with upholding such rights. Most states also guaranteed freedom of religion, but with restrictions. For example, seven states required that officeholders be Christians, and some supported churches with tax money.

Constitution makers put greater emphasis on preventing state governments from becoming tyrannical than on making them effective wielders of political authority. Establishing such weak political units, especially in wartime, practically ensured that the constitutions would need revision.

Revising State Constitutions

By the mid-1780s, some political leaders concluded that the best way to limit government power was to balance legislative, executive, and judicial powers, a design called checks and balances. The national Constitution drafted in 1787 also embodied that principle.

Yet the constitutional theories applied at the state level did not immediately influence Americans' conception of national government. Because American officials initially focused on the war, the Continental Congress evolved by default. Not until late 1777 did Congress send the **Articles of Confederation**—which outlined the national government—to the states for ratification, and those Articles simply made law the unplanned arrangements of the Continental Congress.

Articles of Confederation: The first document that sought to create the terms of a national government. It reserved substantial powers for the states, granting to each state its "sovereignty, freedom and independence."

**Articles of
Confederation**

The chief organ of national government was a unicameral (one-house) legislature in which each state had one vote. Its powers included conducting foreign relations, mediating interstate disputes, controlling maritime affairs, regulating Indian trade, and valuing state and national coinage. The United States of America was described as "a firm league of friendship" in which each state "retains its sovereignty, freedom and independence, and every Power, Jurisdiction and right, which is not by this confederation expressly delegated to the United States, in Congress assembled."

The Articles required unanimous consent of state legislatures for ratification or amendment, and a clause concerning western lands proved troublesome.

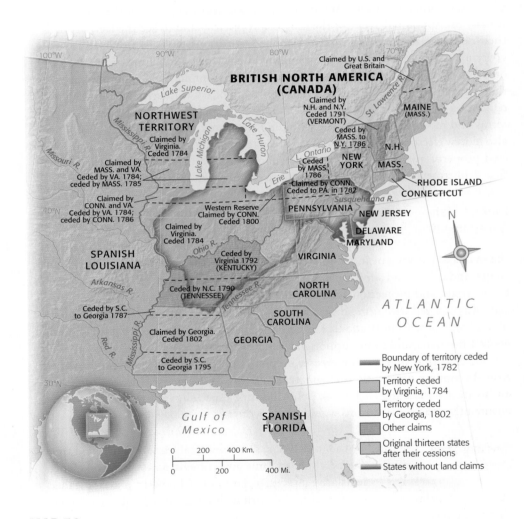

MAP 7.2

Western Land Claims and Cessions, 1782–1802

After the United States achieved independence, states competed with one another for control of valuable lands to which they had possible claims under their original charters. That competition led to a series of compromises among the states or between individual states and the new nation, indicated on this map.

Source: Copyright © Cengage Learning

The draft accepted by Congress allowed states to retain land claims from their original charters. But states with definite western boundaries (such as Maryland and New Jersey) wanted other states to cede to the national government their land-holdings west of the Appalachian Mountains. They feared states with large claims could expand and overpower their smaller neighbors. Maryland refused to accept the Articles until 1781, when Virginia surrendered its western holdings to national jurisdiction (see Map 7.2). Other states followed, establishing the principle that unorganized lands would be held by the nation.

The unicameral legislature, whether it was called the Second Continental Congress (until 1781) or the Confederation Congress (thereafter), was too inefficient to govern effectively. The Articles' authors had not given adequate thought to the distribution of power within the national government or to the relationship between the Confederation and the states. Their Congress was a legislative body and a collective executive (there was no judiciary), but it had no independent income and no authority to compel states to accept its rulings. Under the Articles, national government lurched from crisis to crisis. (See the appendix for the text of the Articles of Confederation.)

Trials of the Confederation

Finance posed the most persistent problem. Because legislators levied taxes reluctantly, Congress and the states first tried to finance the war by printing currency. Although the money was backed only by good faith, it circulated freely and without excessive depreciation during 1775 and most of 1776. Demand for military supplies and civilian goods was high, stimulating trade and local production.

> How did fears of a strong central government ultimately tie the hands of the Confederation Congress?

Financial Affairs

But in late 1776, as the American army suffered reverses in New York and New Jersey, prices rose and inflation set in. State governments fought inflation by controlling wages and prices and requiring acceptance of paper currency equally with specie (coins). States also borrowed funds, established lotteries, and levied taxes. Their efforts were futile, as was Congress's attempt to stop printing currency and rely on state contributions. By early 1780, it took forty paper dollars to purchase one silver dollar. Soon Continental currency was worthless (see Figure 7.1).

In 1781, faced with total collapse of the monetary system, Congress undertook reforms. After establishing a department of finance under the wealthy Philadelphia merchant Robert Morris, it asked states to amend the Articles of Confederation to allow a national duty of 5 percent on imported goods. Morris put national finances on a solid footing, but the customs duty was never adopted. The states' resistance reflected fear of a too-powerful central government.

Foreign Affairs

Because the Articles denied Congress the power to establish a national commercial policy, foreign trade exposed the new government's weaknesses. After the war, Britain, France, and Spain restricted American trade with their colonies. Congress watched helplessly as British goods flooded the United States while American produce could no longer be sold in the British West Indies, once its prime market. Although Americans reopened commerce

FIGURE 7.1
Depreciation of Continental Currency, 1777–1780

The depreciation of Continental currency accelerated in 1778, as is shown in this graph measuring its value against one hundred silver dollars. Thereafter, its value dropped almost daily.
(Source: Data from John J. McCusker, "How Much Is That in Real Money? A Historical Price Index for Use as a Deflator of Money Values in the Economy of the United States," *Proceedings of the American Antiquarian Society*, Vol.101, Pt. 2 [1991], Table C-1.)

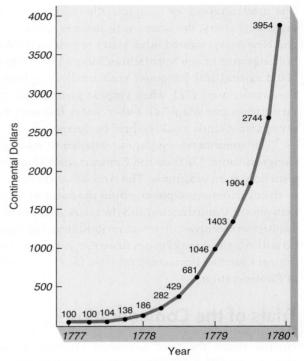

* Currency abandoned in April 1780

with other European countries and started a profitable trade with China in 1784, neither substituted for access to closer and larger markets.

Congress furthermore had difficulty dealing with the Spanish on the nation's southern and western borders. Spain in 1784 closed the Mississippi River to American navigation. Congress, through its Department of Foreign Affairs, opened negotiations with Spain in 1785, but talks collapsed the following year after Congress divided sharply: southerners and westerners insisted on navigation rights, whereas northerners were willing to abandon that claim for commercial concessions in the West Indies.

Peace Treaty Provisions

Provisions of the 1783 Treaty of Paris, too, caused serious problems. Article Four, which promised payment of pre-war debts (most owed by Americans to British merchants), and Article Five, which recommended that states allow loyalists to recover their confiscated property, aroused opposition. States passed laws denying British subjects the right to sue for recovery of debts or property in American courts. Another reason for state opposition was that sales of loyalists' property and possessions had helped finance the war. Because many purchasers were prominent patriots, states hesitated to question the legitimacy of their property titles.

The refusal of state and local governments to comply with Articles Four and Five gave Britain an excuse to maintain military posts on the Great Lakes. Furthermore, Congress's inability to convince states to implement the treaty disclosed its lack of power, even in an area—foreign affairs—in which it had authority under the Articles and undermined the republic's credibility.

Order and Disorder in the West

What was the significance of the Northwest Ordinance?

The United States assumed that the Treaty of Paris cleared its title to all land east of the Mississippi except that held by Spain. Recognizing that land cessions should be obtained from the most powerful tribes, Congress initiated negotiations with northern and southern Indians.

Indian Relations At Fort Stanwix, New York, in 1784, American diplomats negotiated a treaty with chiefs who claimed to represent the Iroquois; and at Hopewell, South Carolina, in late 1785 and early 1786, they negotiated with emissaries from the Choctaw, Chickasaw, and Cherokee nations. In 1786, the Iroquois repudiated the Fort Stanwix treaty, denying that the negotiators were authorized to speak for the Six Nations. The confederacy threatened new attacks on frontier settlements, but the flawed treaty stood. By 1790, the once-dominant confederacy was confined to a few scattered reservations. In the South, too, the United States took the treaties as confirmation of its sovereignty. European-Americans poured over the southern Appalachians, provoking the Creeks to declare war. In 1790, they came to terms with the United States.

Western nations, such as the Shawnees, Chippewas, Ottawas, and Potawatomis, rejected Iroquois hegemony as early as the 1750s. After Iroquois power collapsed, they formed a confederacy and demanded negotiations with the United States. As a united front, they hoped to avoid the piecemeal surrender of land by individual bands and villages. But in the postwar world, Indian nations could no longer play European and American powers against one another. France was gone; Spanish territory lay far to the west and south; and British power was confined to Canada. Only the United States remained.

Ordinance of 1785 Shortly after state land cessions were completed, Congress organized the Northwest Territory, bounded by the Mississippi River, the Great Lakes, and the Ohio River (see Map 7.2). Ordinances passed in 1784, 1785, and 1787 outlined the process through which the land could be sold and governments organized.

Congress in 1785 wanted the land surveyed into townships 6 miles square, each divided into 36 sections of 640 acres (1 square mile). Revenue from the sale of the sixteenth section of each township would support public schools—the first federal aid to education in American history. One dollar was the minimum price per acre; the minimum sale was one section. The resulting minimum outlay, $640, was unaffordable for ordinary Americans, except veterans who received part of their army pay in land warrants. Proceeds from western land sales constituted the first independent revenues available to the national government.

Northwest Ordinance The most important of the three land policies—the Northwest Ordinance of 1787—contained a bill of rights guaranteeing settlers freedom of religion and the right to a jury trial, forbidding cruel and unusual punishments, and nominally prohibiting slavery. Eventually, that prohibition became an important symbol for antislavery northerners, but at the time it had little effect. Some residents already held slaves, and Congress would not deprive them of their property. The ordinance also allowed slaveowners to "lawfully reclaim" runaways who took refuge in the territory—the first national fugitive slave law. It prevented slavery from taking deep root by discouraging slaveholders from moving into the territory, but enslavement was not abolished in the Old Northwest until 1848.

The ordinance of 1787 also specified how territorial residents could organize state governments and seek admission to the Union. Early in the nation's history, therefore, Congress established a policy of admitting new states on the same basis as the old. Having suffered under the rule of a colonial power, congressmen understood the importance of preparing the new nation's first "colony" for eventual self-government. In 1787, the ordinance was purely theoretical. Miamis, Shawnees, and Delawares refused to acknowledge American sovereignty and attacked pioneers who ventured too far north of the Ohio River. In 1788, the Ohio Company, to which Congress had sold a large tract of land, established the town of Marietta at the juncture of the Ohio and Muskingum Rivers. But Indians prevented the company from extending settlement into the interior.

Not until after the Articles of Confederation were replaced with a new constitution could the United States muster sufficient force to implement the Northwest Ordinance. Thus, although the ordinance is often viewed as one of the few lasting accomplishments of the Confederation Congress, it existed within a context of political impotence.

From Crisis to the Constitution

How did the question of slavery become linked to the new U.S. Constitution?

Under the Articles of Confederation, Congress could not levy taxes, force states to establish a uniform commercial policy, or enforce treaties. Partly as a result, the American economy slid into a depression within a year after war's end. Exporters of staple crops (especially tobacco and rice) and importers of manufactured goods suffered from the postwar restrictions that European powers imposed on American commerce. Although recovery began by 1786, some estimates suggest that between 1775 and 1790 America's per capita gross national product declined by nearly 50 percent.

Taxation and the Economy

The near-total cessation of foreign commerce in nonmilitary items during the war stimulated domestic manufacturing. Despite the influx of European goods after 1783, the postwar period witnessed stirrings of American industrial development. Because of continuing population growth, the domestic market assumed greater importance. Moreover, foreign trade patterns shifted from Europe and toward the West Indies. Foodstuffs shipped to the French and Dutch Caribbean islands became America's largest export, replacing tobacco (and thus accelerating the Chesapeake's conversion to grain). South Carolina resumed large-scale slave importation, as planters sought to replace workers lost to wartime disruptions. Yet without British subsidies American indigo could not compete with Caribbean indigo, and rice planters struggled to find new markets.

Representatives of Virginia and Maryland met at Mount Vernon (George Washington's plantation) in March 1785 to negotiate a trade agreement on the Potomac River, which divided the two states. The successful meeting led to an invitation to other states to discuss trade policy at a convention in Annapolis, Maryland. Nine states named representatives to the meeting in September 1786, only five delegations attended. Consequently, they issued a call for another convention in Philadelphia nine months later, "to devise such further provisions as shall … appear necessary to render the constitution of the federal government adequate to the exigencies of the Union."

Initially, few other states responded. But states had huge war debts, issuing securities to soldiers instead of pay and to others for supplies and loans. During the hard times of the early 1780s, many veterans and other creditors sold those securities to speculators, who stood to gain when states taxed the citizenry to pay them off. In 1785, Congress requisitioned more taxes from the states to cover national war bonds. Most states tried to comply, but popular protests led the legislatures to adopt laws relieving taxpayers of some obligations. In Massachusetts, when the state levied heavy taxes at full price in specie, farmers who feared having to sell their land to pay the tax, responded furiously. The actions of men from the state's western counties, many of them veterans from leading families, proved that reform was needed.

Shays's Rebellion

Daniel Shays, a former Continental Army officer, led the disgruntled westerners. On January 25, 1787, about fifteen hundred troops assaulted the Springfield federal armory. The militiamen defending the armory fired on their former comrades-in-arms, who withdrew after suffering twenty-four casualties. Some (including Shays) fled the state; two were hanged; and most escaped punishment by paying small fines and taking oaths of allegiance to Massachusetts. The state legislature reduced the burden on landowners with new import duties and by easing tax collections.

Terming Massachusetts "tyrannical" and styling themselves "Regulators," Shaysites insisted that "whenever any encroachments are made either upon the liberties or properties of the people, if redress cannot be had without, it is virtue in them to disturb government." Thus, they linked their rebellion to the earlier independence struggle.

Constitutional Convention

To political leaders, the rebellion confirmed the need for a stronger federal government. After most states appointed delegates, the Confederation Congress belatedly endorsed the convention, "for the sole and express purpose of revising the Articles of Confederation." In mid-May 1787, fifty-five men, representing every state but Rhode Island, assembled in Philadelphia.

Most delegates to the Constitutional Convention were substantial men of property. They wanted to give the national government new authority over taxation and foreign commerce, but also sought to advance their states' interests. Many had been state legislators, and some helped to draft state constitutions. Most were born in America; more than half had attended college. The youngest delegate was twenty-six, the oldest—Benjamin Franklin—eighty-one. George Washington was elected presiding officer. A dozen men did the bulk of the convention's work; among them Virginia's **James Madison** deserves the title "Father of the Constitution."

Madison and the Constitution

The shy James Madison was thirty-six years old in 1787. A Princeton graduate raised in western Virginia, he served on the local Committee of Safety and was elected to the provincial convention, the state's lower and upper houses, and the Continental

James Madison: Known as the "Father of the Constitution" and was elected President of the United States in 1808.

James Madison (1751–1836), the youthful scholar and skilled politician who earned the title "Father of the Constitution."

Virginia Plan: A proposal calling for the establishment of a strong central government rather than a confederation of states. It gave Congress virtually unrestricted rights of legislation and taxation, power to veto any state law, and authority to use military force against the states.

New Jersey Plan: A proposal calling for a single-chamber congress in which each state had an equal vote, just as the Articles, but strengthened the taxing and commercial powers of Congress.

Congress (1780–1783). Although Madison returned to serve in the Virginia legislature in 1784, he kept up with national politics, partly through correspondence with his friend Thomas Jefferson.

To prepare for the Philadelphia meeting, Madison bought more than two hundred books on history and government, analyzing their accounts of past confederacies and republics. He summed up his research in a paper entitled "Vices of the Political System of the United States." After listing the flaws he perceived in the current government (among them "encroachments by the states on the federal authority" and lack of unity), Madison revealed his belief that the government had to be constructed so it could not become tyrannical or fall under the influence of a particular faction. Rejecting the common assertion that republics had to be small, Madison asserted that a large, diverse republic was preferable. Because the nation would include many factions, no one of them could control the government. Political stability would result from compromises among the contending parties.

Virginia and New Jersey Plans

The so-called **Virginia Plan**, introduced on May 29 by Edmund Randolph, embodied Madison's conception of national government. The plan provided for a two-house legislature, the lower house elected directly by the people and the upper house selected by the lower; representation in both houses proportional to property or population; an executive elected by Congress; a national judiciary; and congressional veto over state laws. Had it been adopted intact, it would have created a government in which national authority reigned unchallenged and state power was diminished. Proportional representation in both houses would also have given large states a dominant voice in the national government.

Many delegates believed the Virginia Plan went too far toward national consolidation. After two weeks of debate, disaffected delegates—particularly those from small states—united under William Paterson of New Jersey. On June 15, Paterson presented an alternative, the **New Jersey Plan**, calling for strengthening the Articles rather than overhauling the government. Paterson proposed retaining a unicameral Congress in which each state had an equal vote, but giving Congress new powers of taxation and regulation. Although the convention initially rejected Paterson's position, he and his allies won several victories in subsequent months.

Debates over Congress

The delegates agreed that the new national government should have a two-house (bicameral) legislature. Further, they concurred that "the people" should be directly represented in at least one house. But they differed on three key questions: Should representation in both houses of Congress be proportional to population? How was representation to be apportioned among the states? How were the members of the two houses to be elected?

The last issue proved the easiest to resolve. Delegates thought it "essential" that the lower branch of Congress be elected directly by the people and "expedient" that members of the upper house be chosen by state legislatures. If the convention had not agreed to allow state legislatures to elect senators, the Constitution would have run into opposition among state leaders. The plan also placed the election of one house of Congress one step removed from the "lesser sort," whose judgment wealthy convention delegates did not trust.

The delegates accepted the principle of proportional representation in the House of Representatives. But small states wanted equal representation in the Senate, which would give them relatively more power at the national level. Large states supported a proportional plan that would give them more votes in the upper house. For weeks, the convention deadlocked. A committee appointed to devise a compromise recommended equal representation in the Senate, with a proviso that all appropriation bills originate in the lower house. But only the absence of several opponents of the compromise during the vote averted a breakdown.

Slavery and the Constitution

The remaining question of how to apportion representation in the lower house divided the nation along sectional lines. Delegates concurred that a census should be conducted every decade to determine the nation's population and that Indians who paid no taxes should be excluded. Delegates from states with large slave populations wanted African and European inhabitants counted equally; delegates from states with few slaves wanted only free people counted. Slavery thus became linked to the new government. Delegates resolved the dispute with a formula developed by the Confederation Congress in 1783 to allocate financial assessments among states: three-fifths of slaves would be included in population totals. (The formula reflected delegates' judgment that slaves were less efficient producers of wealth than free people, not that they were 60 percent human and 40 percent property.) Although the words slave and slavery do not appear in the Constitution, the document contained direct and indirect protections for slavery. The **three-fifths clause**, for example, assured white southern male voters congressional representation out of proportion to their numbers and a disproportionate influence on the selection of the president, because the number of each state's votes in the electoral college was determined by the size of its congressional delegation. In return for southerners' agreement that commercial regulations could be adopted by a simple majority vote (rather than two-thirds), New Englanders agreed that Congress could not end the importation of slaves for twenty years. The fugitive slave clause required states to return runaways to their masters. By guaranteeing national assistance to states threatened with "domestic violence," the Constitution promised aid in putting down future slave revolts and incidents like Shays's Rebellion.

three-fifths clause: Allowed three-fifths of all slaves to be counted for congressional representation and, thereby, in the electoral college that selected the president.

Congressional and Presidential Powers

With issues of slavery and representation resolved, delegates concurred that the national government needed the authority to tax and to regulate foreign and interstate commerce. But instead of giving Congress the wide latitude of the Virginia Plan, delegates enumerated congressional powers and then granting Congress the "necessary and proper" authority to carry them out. Discarding the Virginia Plan's congressional veto, the convention implied but did not explicitly authorize a national judicial veto of state laws. The Constitution plus national laws and treaties would constitute "the supreme law of the land; and the judges in every state shall be bound thereby," Article VI declared ambiguously. Delegates drafted a long list of actions forbidden to states, including impairing contractual obligations—that is, preventing the relief of debtors. And they provided that religious tests could never be required of U.S. officeholders.

The convention placed primary responsibility for foreign affairs with a new official, the president, who was also designated commander-in-chief of the armed forces. That raised the question, unspecified in the Constitution's text, of whether the president or Congress acquired special powers in wartime. With the Senate's consent, the president could appoint judges and other federal officers. To select the president, delegates established the electoral college, whose members would be chosen in each state by legislatures or voters. If a majority of electors failed to unite behind one candidate, the House of Representatives (voting as states, not as individuals) would choose the president. The chief executive would serve for four years but be eligible for reelection.

The key to the Constitution was the distribution of political authority—its **separation of powers** among executive, legislative, and judicial branches of the national government, and division of powers between states and nation (called **federalism**). Two-thirds of Congress and three-fourths of the states had to concur on amendments. The branches balanced one another, their powers entwined to prevent each from acting independently. The president could veto congressional legislation, but that veto could be overridden by two-thirds majorities in both houses, and his treaties and major appointments required the Senate's consent. Congress could impeach the president and federal judges, but courts would have the final say on interpreting the Constitution. These **checks and balances** would keep the government from becoming tyrannical, but at times, they prevented the government from acting quickly and decisively. Furthermore, the Constitution drew such a vague line between state and national powers that the United States fought a civil war in the next century over that issue.

The convention held its last session on September 17, 1787. Of the forty-two delegates present, only three refused to sign the Constitution, two partly because it lacked a bill of rights. Benjamin Franklin encouraged unity, admitting, "I confess that there are several parts of this constitution which I do not at present approve." Yet he urged its acceptance "because I expect no better, and because I am not sure, that it is not the best." Only then was the Constitution made public. (See the appendix for the full text of the Constitution.)

separation of powers: The establishment of three distinct branches of government each with varying political powers.

federalism: System in which states and central governments have distinctive roles and powers.

checks and balances: A separation of powers between the various branches of government, designed to prevent one branch from dominating the others.

Opposition and Ratification

What were the differences between Federalists and Antifederalists in the Constitution debate?

Later the same month, the Confederation Congress submitted the Constitution to the states. The ratification clause provided for the new system to take after approval by special conventions in at least nine states. Thus the national Constitution, unlike the Articles of Confederation, would rest directly on popular authority.

As states elected delegates to the special conventions, newspaper essays and pamphlets defended or attacked the Philadelphia convention's decisions. Every newspaper in the country printed the Constitution, and most supported its adoption. Although most citizens concurred that the national government should have more power over taxation and foreign and interstate commerce, some believed the proposed government held the potential for tyranny. As happened in Carlisle, Pennsylvania, the debate frequently spilled out into the streets.

Federalists and Antifederalists

Supporters of the proposed Constitution called themselves **Federalists**. Building on classical republicanism, they envisioned a virtuous, collectivist, self-sacrificing republic led by a manly aristocracy of talent. They argued that putting good, elite men in charge of a carefully structured government would eliminate the possibility of tyranny. A republic could be large if the government's design prevented any one group from controlling it. The separation of powers among legislative, executive, and judicial branches, and the division of powers between states and nation, would accomplish that.

The Federalists termed those who opposed the Constitution **Antifederalists**, thus casting them negatively. While recognizing the need for a national source of revenue, Antifederalists feared a too-powerful central government. To them, states were the protectors of individual rights; consequently, weakening the states could bring arbitrary power. Antifederalist arguments often listed potential abuses of government authority.

Heirs of the Real Whig ideology of the late 1760s and early 1770s, Antifederalists stressed the need for constant vigilance to avert oppression. Indeed, some of the Antifederalists had originally promulgated those ideas—Samuel Adams, Patrick Henry, and Richard Henry Lee led the opposition to the Constitution. Joining them were small farmers preoccupied with guarding their property against excessive taxation, backcountry Baptists and Presbyterians, and upwardly mobile men who would benefit from an economic and political system less tightly controlled than that the Constitution envisioned.

Federalists: The name supporters of new Constitution gave themselves during the ratification struggle.

Antifederalists: So dubbed by the Federalists, the Antifederalists were opposed to the Constitution because they feared it gave too much power to the central government and it did not contain a bill of rights.

Link to "The Federalist Papers."

Bill of Rights

Antifederalists focused on the Constitution's lack of a bill of rights. Even if the new system weakened the states, people could be protected from tyranny by specific guarantees of rights. The Constitution did contain some prohibitions on congressional power. For example, the writ of habeas corpus, which prevented arbitrary imprisonment, could not be suspended except in "cases of rebellion or invasion." But Antifederalists found such constitutional provisions to be few and inadequate. They wanted a bill of rights.

Letters of a Federal Farmer, perhaps the most widely read Antifederalist pamphlet, listed the rights that should be protected: freedom of the press and religion, trial by jury, and guarantees against unreasonable searches. From Paris, Thomas Jefferson declared, "A bill of rights is what the people are entitled to against every government on earth."

Link to *Letters of a Federal Farmer.*

Ratification

Many states were persuaded when Federalists argued that a national government with the power to tax foreign commerce would lessen the financial burdens that had prompted Shays's Rebellion and similar protests elsewhere. Four of the first five states to ratify did so unanimously, but disagreements then surfaced. Massachusetts, where Antifederalist forces were bolstered by a backlash against the state's heavy-handed treatment of the Shays rebels, ratified by a majority of only 19 of 355 votes cast and recommended amendments

TABLE 7.1   Ratification of the Constitution by State Conventions

State	Date	Vote
Delaware	December 7, 1787	30-0
Pennsylvania	December 12, 1787	46-23
New Jersey	December 18, 1787	38-0
Georgia	January 2, 1788	26-0
Connecticut	January 9, 1788	128-40
Massachusetts	February 6, 1788	187-168
Maryland	April 28, 1788	63-11
South Carolina	May 23, 1788	149-73
New Hampshire	June 21, 1788	57-47
Virginia	June 25, 1788	89-79
New York	July 26, 1788	30-27
North Carolina	November 21, 1789	194-77
Rhode Island	May 29, 1790	34-32

identifying rights. In June 1788, when New Hampshire ratified, the requirement of nine states was satisfied. But New York and Virginia had not yet voted, and the new Constitution could not succeed without those key states.

Pro-Constitution forces won by 10 votes in the Virginia convention, which recommended adding rights specifications. In New York, James Madison, John Jay, and Alexander Hamilton, writing collectively as "Publius," published *The Federalist*, eighty-five essays explaining the theory behind the Constitution and answering critics. Their arguments, coupled with Federalists' promise to add a bill of rights, helped win the battle. On July 26, 1788, New York ratified the Constitution by just 3 votes. Although the last states—North Carolina and Rhode Island—did not join the Union until November 1789 and May 1790, respectively, the new government was a reality. (See Table 7.1 for the details of ratifying convention votes.)

Celebrating Ratification   Americans in many cities celebrated ratification with parades on July 4, 1788, linking the acceptance of the Constitution to the adoption of the Declaration of Independence. The processions dramatized the history and unity of the new nation, seeking to counteract the dissent that had engulfed such towns as Carlisle, Pennsylvania. The processions aimed to educate people about the Constitution's significance and political leaders' hopes for industry and frugality by the American public.

About five thousand people participated in the Philadelphia parade. Floats portraying such themes as "The Grand Federal Edifice" stretched for a mile and a half. More than forty groups of tradesmen sponsored floats, followed by lawyers, doctors, clergymen, and congressmen. Symbolizing the nation's future, students from the University of Pennsylvania and other schools bore a flag labeled "The Rising Generation."

The Township and Range System

Anyone flying over the American countryside west of the Appalachians today can see the township and range system inscribed on the landscape. Roads cross the land in straight lines, meeting at 90-degree angles, carving the terrain into a checkerboard. Originated in the Land Ordinance of 1785, that system organized land sales in the Northwest Territory.

English and native peoples traditionally bounded their lands by natural landmarks such as hills, streams, trees, and rock outcroppings. That system was known as *metes and bounds*. Some early settlers employed surveyors, who created lots of varying sizes divided by lines laid out abstractly on the soil. Sometimes those lines related to natural features, such as the long, narrow lots in French Canada that fronted on the St. Lawrence River.

But because North America was settled piecemeal, no one system dominated until the Land Ordinance of 1785. Thereafter, the ordinance's system became the template for the U.S. government's land distribution.

After a surveyor established an east-west baseline and a north-south meridian on a particular tract, he laid out rectangular townships composed of thirty-six numbered square-mile sections. He ignored natural features; potential buyers would learn for themselves which sections had rivers, hills, or assets like salt licks. The initial policy of selling equally priced sections gave way by 1832 to allow individuals to purchase as few as 40 acres and, after 1854, to price variations. As the United States expanded westward, the township and range system followed, democratizing access to land and opening land for settlement.

The legacy of the Land Ordinance of 1785 for the American people and nation still marks the landscape west of the Ohio River.

Summary

During the 1770s and 1780s, the nation developed an economy independent of the British and attempted to protect the national interest, defend its borders, and promote trade. Some Americans outlined artistic and educational goals for a properly virtuous people. The formulation of American racist thought was also part of the developing Union. Emphasizing race (rather than status as slave or free) as a determinant of African Americans' status allowed men who now termed themselves "white" to define republicanism to exclude most men but themselves. White women, viewed as household dependents, had a limited role in the republic, as mothers of the next generation and as selfless contributors to the nation's welfare.

In 1775, most Americans believed that "that government which governs best governs least," but by the late 1780s many changed their minds. Drafters and supporters of the Constitution concluded that a more powerful central government was needed. During ratification debates, they contended that their proposals were just as "republican" as the Articles of Confederation.

Both sides adhered to republican principles, but Federalists embraced classical republicanism, stressing the community over the individual. Antifederalists wanted a weak central government, formal protection of individual rights, and a loosely regulated economy. The Federalists won when the Constitution was adopted, however narrowly. The 1790s, the first decade under the Constitution, would witness hesitant steps toward creating a true nation, the United States of America.

Chapter Review

Creating a Virtuous Republic

How were notions of republican virtue gendered in post-revolutionary America?

Leaders wanted the new United States to be a republican form of government, and while they debated the specifics, they agreed that in a republic, citizens were virtuous men willing to forgo personal profit for the best interests of the nation. The notion of virtue—the absence of vice or corruption—became increasingly important and inspired educational reform to help children become useful citizens. Some argued that since childrearing was women's role, they, too, would need education to help raise virtuous future citizens. Since women could not own property or participate in politics, their role was as the embodiment of self-sacrificing republicanism, using their nurturing skills to run charitable associations aiding the poor and others. This, in turn, conveyed virtue on their families and freed men to pursue their economic self-interests. The ideal republican male sought upward mobility for himself and his family, while the ideal republican woman put the needs of others first.

The First Emancipation and the Growth of Racism

What contributed to the growing number of free blacks in America after the revolution?

Slaves who escaped plantations during the war, those who served in the military, or those who had been freed by their owners or state laws accounted for many of the 60,000 free people of color in the U.S. by 1790 and 108,000 by 1800. Northern states, which were less reliant on slave labor, increasingly freed slaves and were more likely to adopt laws abolishing slavery. But even there, many states respected owners' "property rights" and preferred gradual manumission over outright abolition. In the courts, too, blacks challenged the contradictions between forced bondage and the ideology of the Revolution, and while often unsuccessful, their actions forced policymakers to grapple with this issue. Postwar economic changes also spurred manumissions, particularly in the Chesapeake, where the shift from tobacco to grain production meant far fewer slaves were required, doubling the free black population in Virginia between 1790 and 1810, for example.

Designing Republican Governments

How did Americans' former experience as British subjects influence the state governments they established?

Coming from their experience under Great Britain, Americans feared the prospect of tyranny developing in the new nation, and as such, early state constitutions sought to limit governors' power through annual elections and term limitations. They further provided little independent authority for governors while expanding that granted to legislatures, typically in a two-house structure. And states put more power in the hands of the people by redrawing election districts to reflect the population and reducing property requirements for voting. To protect citizens' rights, several states included a bill of rights guaranteeing freedom of the press, rights to fair trials, and sometimes freedom of religion even if officeholders had to be Christians. Ultimately, the emphasis on preventing tyranny made states weak politically. Subsequent revisions to state constitutions in the mid-1780s increased the power of the governor and reduced that of the legislature via a system of checks and balances.

Trials of the Confederation

How did fears of a strong central government ultimately tie the hands of the Confederation Congress?

The Articles of Confederation limited congressional power in a number of areas that, in turn, led to financial and policy problems for the new nation. First, because of state resistance to a large central government, a much-needed customs duty was never adopted. Second, Congress's limited ability to establish a national commercial policy left it unable to take action when Britain, France, and Spain restricted American trade. Third, Congress had little power to enforce the 1783 Treaty of Paris's promises that prewar debts (owed by Americans to British merchants) would be repaid and that loyalists would be able to recover confiscated property. States passed various laws prohibiting both, which gave the British an excuse to maintain military posts on the Great Lakes. Worse, the inability to enforce the treaty hurt the republic's credibility in foreign affairs.

Order and Disorder in the West

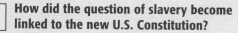

What was the significance of the Northwest Ordinance?

One of the lasting accomplishments of the Confederation Congress, the Northwest Ordinance of 1787 effectively outlined how territory gained in the Treaty of Paris would be organized, how land could be divided and sold, how new states would be admitted to the Union, as well as the rights of people living there. It included a bill of rights guaranteeing freedom of religion and the right to a jury trial, and it forbade cruel and unusual punishments and nominally prohibited slavery. But its ban on slavery was more symbolic than actual because it did not deny slaveholders living in the territory to the right of their property and included the first fugitive slave law. Still, it discouraged slaveholders from moving into the territory and prevented slavery from taking hold on a large scale.

From Crisis to the Constitution

How did the question of slavery become linked to the new U.S. Constitution?

Slavery came into play at the Constitutional Convention as states debated how their populations should be counted in determining the number of representatives each would get in the lower house of Congress. Slave states wanted their bondspeople fully counted, while those from states with few slaves wanted only free people counted. The dispute was resolved by a formula known as the three-fifths compromise, noting that three-fifths of slaves would be included in population totals used to determine congressional districts. While the words *slave* and *slavery* are not used in the Constitution, it nonetheless included direct and indirect protections for slavery, among them assistance in putting down revolts, returning fugitive slaves to masters, and agreeing not to end the importation of bondspeople for twenty years.

Opposition and Ratification

What were the differences between Federalists and Antifederalists in the Constitution debate?

Federalists supported ratification of the Constitution and believed a strong national government led by a talented elite. Moreover, they argued that dividing power between the legislative, executive, and judicial branches, as well as between states and the nation, would prevent one faction from controlling the government or a tyrant from seizing power. Antifederalists, so dubbed by their opponents, feared a too-powerful central government and saw states as protectors of individual rights. As such, they supported state sovereignty, and while they agreed on the need for central currency and taxation, Antifederalists were concerned that the Constitution did not include a bill of rights to safeguard people's individual rights.

Suggestions for Further Reading

Richard Beeman, *Plain, Honest Men: The Making of the American Constitution* (2009)

Ira Berlin and Ronald Hoffman, eds., *Slavery and Freedom in the Age of the American Revolution* (1983)

Cathy N. Davidson, *Revolution and the Word: The Rise of the Novel in America* (1987)

Edith Gelles, *Portia: The World of Abigail Adams* (1992)

Woody Holton, *Unruly Americans and the Origins of the Constitution* (2007)

Peter S. Onuf, *Statehood and Union: A History of the Northwest Ordinance* (1987)

Jack N. Rakove, *Original Meanings: Politics and Ideas in the Making of the Constitution* (1996)

Leonard L. Richards, *Shays's Rebellion: The American Revolution's Final Battle* (2002)

David Waldstreicher, *In the Midst of Perpetual Fetes: The Making of American Nationalism, 1776–1820* (1997)

Gordon S. Wood, *The Creation of the American Republic, 1776–1787* (1969)

Go to the CourseMate website for primary source links, study tools, and review materials for this chapter.
www.cengagebrain.com

The Early Republic: Conflicts at Home and Abroad

8

1789–1800

I n late 1798, wealthy Philadelphia matron Deborah Norris Logan became the target of widespread criticism. Her husband, Jefferson supporter Dr. George Logan, had undertaken a personal peace mission to France, fearing war between the United States and its former ally. When Logan's wife defended his actions, she endured a campaign unlike any experienced by an American woman. That episode suggests the political symbolism now embodied by women, the growing division between the Federalist and Republican factions, and the significance of foreign affairs in the early republic.

First to attack was the Federalist newspaper editor William Cobbett, who observed with sly sexual innuendo in his *Porcupine's Gazette* in July that "it is said that JEFFERSON went to his friend Doctor Logan's farm and spent three days there, soon after the Doctor's departure for France. *Query*: What did he do there?" Later Cobbett suggested that George and Deborah Logan should be publicly shamed—him, presumably, for treason and her, Cobbett implied, for adultery. Republican newspapers leaped to Deborah's defense, attacking the vulgarity of the suggestions about her and Vice President Jefferson.

Although initially Deborah Logan secluded herself at her country estate, on Jefferson's advice she returned to Philadelphia to prove she was "not afraid nor ashamed to meet the public eye." As reports emerged that her husband had had some success in quelling hostilities, she reveled in the praise showered on him. George Logan was enthusiastically welcomed home by Jeffersonian partisans. However, in January 1799, Congress, controlled by Federalists, adopted the so-called Logan Act—still in effect—which forbids private citizens from undertaking unauthorized diplomatic missions.

The Logan controversy was one of many battles in the 1790s. The fight over ratifying the Constitution presaged wide divisions over the major political, economic, and diplomatic questions confronting the republic: the extent to which authority should be centralized; the relationship between national power and states'

Chapter Outline

Building a Workable Government
First Congress | Bill of Rights | Executive and Judiciary | Debate over Slavery

Domestic Policy Under Washington and Hamilton
Washington's First Steps | Alexander Hamilton | National and State Debts | Hamilton's Financial Plan | First Bank of the United States | Interpreting the Constitution | Report on Manufactures | Whiskey Rebellion

The French Revolution and the Development of Partisan Politics
Republicans and Federalists | French Revolution | Edmond Genêt | Democratic Societies

Partisan Politics and Relations with Great Britain
Jay Treaty Debate | Bases of Partisanship | Washington's Farewell Address | Election of 1796

John Adams and Political Dissent
XYZ Affair | Quasi-War with France | Alien and Sedition Acts | Virginia and Kentucky Resolutions | Convention of 1800

VISUALIZING THE PAST *Newspapers of the Early Republic*

The West in the New Nation
War in the Northwest Territory | "Civilizing" the Indians | Iroquois and Cherokees

"Revolutions" at the End of the Century
Fries' Rebellion | Gabriel's Rebellion | Election of 1800

LINKS TO THE WORLD *Haitian Refugees*

LEGACY FOR A PEOPLE AND A NATION *Dissent During Wartime*

SUMMARY

rights; the formulation of foreign policy in an era of continual warfare in Europe; and the limits of dissent. Americans had not anticipated the acrimonious disagreements that rocked the 1790s or the difficulties that would develop as the United States attempted to deal with Indian nations within its borders.

Most important, Americans could not understand the division of citizens into two competing factions. In republics, they believed, the rise of such factions signified decay and corruption. Yet on numerous occasions, as with Deborah and George Logan, Federalist and Republican leaders sought to mobilize their supporters, thereby reworking the nation's political practice if not its theory. As the decade closed, Americans were still grappling with the implications of partisan politics, as evidenced by the hotly contested 1800 election.

As you read this chapter, keep the following questions in mind:

* **What major challenges confronted the new republic?**

* **What disputes divided the nation's citizens?**

* **How did Americans react to those disputes?**

Building a Workable Government

At first, consensus appeared possible. Only a few Antifederalists ran for office in 1788, and even fewer were elected. Thus, most members of the First Congress supported a strong national government. The drafters of the Constitution had deliberately left key issues undecided, so the nationalists' domination of Congress meant that their views prevailed.

> What was the purpose of the Bill of Rights?

First Congress

Congress faced four immediate tasks when it convened in April 1789: raising revenue, responding to states' calls for a bill of rights, setting up executive departments, and organizing the federal judiciary. James Madison, representing Virginia in the House of Representatives, became influential in Congress. He persuaded Congress to adopt the Revenue Act of 1789, imposing a 5 percent tariff on certain imports. Therefore, the First Congress achieved an effective national tax law.

Bill of Rights

Madison opposed additional restrictions on the national government, believing that its limited powers made a **Bill of Rights** unnecessary. But Madison subsequently changed his mind, observing to a friend that "in every Gov[ernmen]t power may oppress." When introducing nineteen proposed amendments in June, he urged fellow congressmen to respond to the people's will, noting in particular that North Carolina refused to ratify the Constitution without a Bill of Rights. After heated debates, Congress approved twelve amendments. The states ratified ten, which became part of the Constitution on December 15, 1791 (see the appendix for the Constitution and all amendments). Their adoption defused Antifederalist opposition.

The First Amendment prohibited Congress from passing any law restricting the right to freedom of religion, speech, press, peaceable assembly, or petition. The

Bill of Rights: The first ten amendments of the Constitution that guaranteed personal liberties.

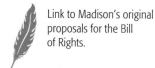

Link to Madison's original proposals for the Bill of Rights.

Chronology

1789 Washington inaugurated as first president	Pinckney's Treaty with Spain establishes southern boundary of the United States
Judiciary Act organizes federal court system	Treaty of Greenville with Miami Confederacy opens Ohio to settlement
French Revolution begins	**1796** First contested presidential election: Adams elected president, Jefferson vice president
1790 Hamilton's *Report on Public Credit* proposes assumption of state debts	
1791 First ten amendments (Bill of Rights) ratified	**1798** XYZ affair arouses American opinion against France
First national bank chartered	Sedition Act penalizes dissent
1793 France declares war on Britain, Spain, and the Netherlands	Virginia and Kentucky Resolutions protest suppression of dissent
Washington's neutrality proclamation keeps the United States out of war	**1798–99** Quasi-War with France
Democratic societies founded, the first grassroots political organizations	Fries's Rebellion in Pennsylvania protests taxation
1794 Whiskey Rebellion in western Pennsylvania protests taxation	**1800** Franco-American Convention ends Quasi-War
	Gabriel's Rebellion threatens Virginia slaveowners
1795 Jay Treaty with England resolves issues remaining from the Revolution	**1801** Thomas Jefferson elected president by the House of Representatives after stalemate in electoral college

Second Amendment guaranteed the right "to keep and bear arms," because of the need for a "well-regulated Militia." The Third Amendment limited the conditions under which troops could be quartered in private homes. The next five pertained to judicial procedures. The Fourth Amendment prohibited "unreasonable searches and seizures"; the Fifth and Sixth established the rights of accused persons; the Seventh specified the conditions for jury trials in civil (as opposed to criminal) cases; and the Eighth forbade "cruel and unusual punishments." The Ninth and Tenth Amendments reserved to the people and the states other unspecified rights and powers.

Executive and Judiciary   Congress also considered the organization of the executive branch. It agreed to continue the three administrative departments established under the Articles of Confederation: War, Foreign Affairs (renamed State), and Treasury. Congress instituted two lesser posts: the attorney general—the nation's official lawyer—and the postmaster general. Controversy arose over whether the president alone could dismiss officials whom he appointed with the Senate's consent. Ultimately, the House and Senate agreed that he had such authority. That established the principle that heads of executive departments are accountable solely to the president.

Judiciary Act of 1789:
Outlined the federal judiciary's jurisdiction and established the Supreme Court, as well as district and appellate courts.

The most far-reaching law, the **Judiciary Act of 1789**, defined the federal judiciary's jurisdiction and established a six-member Supreme Court, thirteen district courts, and three appellate courts. Its most important provision, Section 25, allowed appeals from state to federal courts when cases raised certain types of constitutional questions. It presumed that Article VI of the Constitution, which stated that federal statutes and treaties were "the supreme Law of the Land," implied the right of appeal from state to federal courts, yet the Constitution did not explicitly permit such actions. In the nineteenth century, judges and legislators committed to states' rights would challenge Section 25's constitutionality.

During its first decade, the Supreme Court handled few cases of any importance, and several members resigned. But in a 1796 decision, *Ware v. Hylton*, the Court for the first time declared a state law unconstitutional. It also reviewed the constitutionality of an act of Congress, upholding its validity in the case of *Hylton v. U.S.* The most important case of the decade, *Chisholm v. Georgia* (1793), established that states could be sued in federal courts by citizens of other states. Five years later, the Eleventh Amendment to the Constitution overturned that decision.

Debate over Slavery

Constitutional provisions forbade Congress from prohibiting the importation of slaves for twenty years, but in 1790 three Quaker groups petitioned Congress to end slavery. Legislators insisted, as they would for the next seven decades, that slavery was integral to the Union and that abolition would cause bigger problems, primarily how to deal with a sizable population of freed people.

Some northern congressmen—and Benjamin Franklin—contested the southerners' position. But Congress accepted a committee report denying it the power to halt slave importations before 1808 or emancipate slaves at any time, that authority "remaining with the several States alone."

Domestic Policy Under Washington and Hamilton

> How did the chartering of the Bank of the United States provoke an early constitutional debate?

George Washington did not seek the presidency. In 1783, he returned to Mount Vernon as a Virginia planter. But his fellow countrymen never regarded Washington as just another private citizen. Americans concurred that only George Washington had sufficient stature to serve as the republic's first president, an office designed with him in mind. The unanimous vote of the electoral college formalized that consensus. Washington could not ignore his country's call and headed to New York City, the nation's capital.

Washington's First Steps

Washington acted cautiously during his first months in office in 1789, knowing he would set precedents. When the title by which he should be addressed aroused controversy (Vice President John Adams favored "His Highness, the President of the United States of America, and Protector of their Liberties"), Washington said nothing. The accepted title soon became simply "Mr. President." By using the heads of executive departments as chief advisers, he created the cabinet. Washington also exercised his veto power over congressional legislation sparingly—only if he thought a bill was unconstitutional.

Washington's first major task was to choose the heads of the executive departments. For the War Department, he selected Henry Knox of Massachusetts, who was his artillery general during the war. For the State Department, he selected fellow

Virginian Thomas Jefferson, who had been minister to France. For secretary of the treasury, the president chose the brilliant, ambitious **Alexander Hamilton**.

Alexander Hamilton: Secretary of Treasury under President George Washington.

Alexander Hamilton

The illegitimate son of a Scottish aristocrat and a woman whose husband had divorced her for adultery and desertion, Hamilton was born in the British West Indies in 1757. His early years were spent in poverty, working as a mercantile clerk after his mother's death when he was eleven. In 1773, with financial support from friends, Hamilton enrolled at King's College (later Columbia University). Eighteen months later the seventeen-year-old contributed a pamphlet to the prerevolutionary publication wars. A devoted patriot, Hamilton volunteered for the American army, where in 1777 Washington appointed him as an aide, and they developed great mutual affection.

At twenty-three, Hamilton wed Elizabeth Schuyler, daughter of a wealthy New York family. After the war, he practiced law in New York City and served as a delegate to the Annapolis Convention and the Constitutional Convention. His contributions to *The Federalist* in 1788 revealed him as one of the republic's chief political thinkers.

As treasury secretary and presidential adviser, Hamilton's primary loyalty lay with the nation. Caribbean-born, Hamilton had no natal ties to any state; he neither sympathized with nor fully understood demands for local autonomy. His fiscal policies aimed at consolidating national power, and he favored close ties with Britain.

Second, Hamilton cynically believed people to be motivated by economic self-interest. This set him apart from those Americans who believed public-spirited citizens would pursue the common good rather than private advantage. Hamilton's beliefs influenced the way he tackled the new nation's tangled finances.

National and State Debts

Congress ordered the new treasury secretary to assess the public debt. The country's war debts fell into three categories: those owed by the nation to foreign governments and investors, mostly to France (about $11 million); those owed by the national government to merchants, soldiers, revolutionary bondholders (about $27 million); and, finally, debts owed by state governments (roughly $25 million). On the national debt, Americans recognized that, if their new government was to succeed, it would have to repay financial obligations incurred while winning independence.

State debts were another matter. Some states—notably, Virginia, Maryland, North Carolina, and Georgia—had already paid off most war debts by levying taxes and handing out land grants in lieu of money. They opposed taxing their citizens so the national government could assume other states' debts. Massachusetts, Connecticut, and South Carolina still had sizable unpaid debts and welcomed national assumption. Consolidating state debt in the hands of the national government would help concentrate power at the national level.

National Portrait Gallery, Smithsonian Institution

Alexander Hamilton, by James Sharpless, about 1796. This profile of Hamilton, painted near the end of Washington's presidency, shows the secretary of the treasury as he looked during the years of his first heated partisan battles with Thomas Jefferson and James Madison.

Hamilton's Financial Plan

In his first **Report on Public Credit** in January 1790, Hamilton proposed that Congress assume outstanding state debts, combine them with national obligations, and issue new securities covering principal and accumulated unpaid interest. Hamilton hoped to ensure that holders of the public debt—many of them wealthy merchants and speculators—had a financial stake in the new government's survival. Opposition coalesced around James Madison, whose state of Virginia had mostly eliminated its war debt and who wanted to avoid rewarding wealthy speculators who purchased debt certificates at a small fraction of their value from needy veterans and farmers.

Report on Public Credit: Hamilton's plan to ensure that wealthy merchants, who held the public debt, would be linked to the government's financial survival.

The House initially rejected the assumption of state debts, but the Senate adopted Hamilton's plan largely intact. Compromises followed, linking the assumption bill to another controversial issue: location of the permanent national capital. Deals were struck. A southern site on the Potomac River became the capital, and the first part of Hamilton's program became law in August 1790.

First Bank of the United States

Four months later, Hamilton submitted to Congress a second report on public credit, recommending the chartering of a national bank modeled on the Bank of England. The Bank of the United States, to be chartered for twenty years, was to be capitalized at $10 million. Just $2 million would come from public funds; private investors supplied the rest. The bank would act as collecting and disbursing agent for the Treasury, and its notes would become the nation's currency. But another issue loomed: did the Constitution give Congress the power to establish such a bank?

Interpreting the Constitution

James Madison thought not. He pointed out that Constitutional Convention delegates rejected a clause authorizing Congress to issue corporate charters. President Washington sought other opinions. Attorney General Edmund Randolph and Secretary of State Thomas Jefferson agreed with Madison. Jefferson referred to Article I, Section 8, of the Constitution, which gave Congress the power "to make all Laws which shall be necessary and proper." The key word, Jefferson argued, was *necessary*: Congress could do what was needed, but not what was merely desirable. Thus, Jefferson formulated the strict-constructionist interpretation of the Constitution.

Hamilton's *Defense of the Constitutionality of the Bank*, presented in February 1791, expounded a broad-constructionist view of the Constitution. Hamilton argued that Congress could choose any means not specifically prohibited by the Constitution to achieve a constitutional end. He reasoned if the end was constitutional and the means was not *un*constitutional, then the means was constitutional.

Washington concurred, and the bill became law. The bank proved successful, as did the debt program. The new nation's securities became desirable investments for citizens and wealthy foreigners, especially those in the Netherlands. The influx of capital, coupled with the high prices that American grain now commanded in European markets, eased farmers' debt burdens and contributed to a new prosperity.

Report on Manufactures

In December 1791, Hamilton presented to Congress his *Report on Manufactures*, his third and final prescription for the American economy. Hamilton argued that the nation could never be truly independent as long as it relied heavily on Europe for manufactured goods. He urged Congress to promote the immigration of technicians and laborers and to support industrial development through limited use of protective tariffs. Many of Hamilton's ideas were implemented in later decades, but congressmen in 1791 believed that America's future lay in agriculture and the carrying trade. Congress rejected the report.

That year, Congress tried another of Hamilton's suggestions—an excise tax on whiskey distilled within the United States. Although proceeds from the Revenue Act of 1789 covered the interest on the national debt, the national government required additional income to fund state debts. A tax on whiskey affected few westerners—farmers who grew corn and large distillers who turned it into whiskey—and might also reduce whiskey consumption of whiskey. (Eighteenth-century Americans, notorious for their heavy drinking, consumed about twice as much alcohol per capita as today's rate.) Moreover, western farmers and distillers were Jefferson's supporters, and Hamilton saw the benefits of taxing them rather his merchant supporters.

Whiskey Rebellion   News of the tax sparked protests in the west, where residents were upset that the government that protected them inadequately from Indian attacks was now proposing to tax them disproportionately. Unrest continued for two years on the frontiers of Pennsylvania, Maryland, and Virginia. Large groups drafted petitions protesting the tax, deliberately imitated 1760s' crowd actions, and occasionally harassed tax collectors.

President Washington maintained restraint until violence erupted in July 1794, when western Pennsylvania farmers resisted two excise tax collectors. When about seven thousand rebels convened on August 1 to plot the destruction of Pittsburgh, Washington acted to prevent a repeat of Shays's Rebellion. On August 7, he told insurgents to disperse and summoned nearly thirteen thousand militiamen. By the time federal forces marched westward in October and November, the disturbances ceased. Troops met no resistance and arrested only twenty suspects. Two men were convicted of treason, but Washington pardoned both. The importance of the **Whiskey Rebellion** lay in the forceful message it conveyed. The national government, Washington had demonstrated, would not allow violent resistance to its laws. In the republic, people dissatisfied with laws should try to peacefully amend or repeal them.

Whiskey Rebellion: Tax protest by western farmers that turned violent. Washington's response, sending in troops, demonstrated that only peaceful protests would be tolerated in a republic.

The French Revolution and the Development of Partisan Politics

Why did U.S. leaders find the rise of political factions disturbing?

By 1794, some Americans were beginning to seek change through electoral politics. In a monarchy, formal opposition groups called factions were expected. In a government of the people, however, sustained factional disagreement was considered a sign of corruption. Still, that did not halt partisanship.

Republicans and Federalists   Jefferson and Madison became convinced as early as 1792 that Hamilton's policies favoring wealthy commercial interests at the expense of agriculture would eventually impose a corrupt government on the United States. Characterizing themselves as the true heirs of the Revolution, they charged Hamilton with plotting to subvert republican principles and called themselves and their followers Republicans. Hamilton likewise accused

Jefferson and Madison of attempting to destroy the republic. Hamilton and his supporters called themselves Federalists to link themselves with the Constitution. Newspapers aligned with the two sides published attacks on political opponents.

Washington tried to remain aloof from the political dispute dividing his chief advisers. The growing controversy persuaded him to promote political unity by seeking office again in 1792. But beginning in 1793, developments in foreign affairs magnified the disagreements, for France (America's wartime ally) and Great Britain (America's most important trading partner) resumed the periodic hostilities that originated a century earlier.

French Revolution

In 1789, many Americans welcomed the news of the French Revolution. The French people's success in overthrowing an oppressive monarchy enabled Americans to see themselves as the vanguard of an inevitable trend that would reshape the world in republican terms. By 1793, violence in France continued, and political leaders rapidly succeeded each other. Executions mounted; the king was beheaded early that year. Although many Americans, including Jefferson and Madison, retained sympathy for the revolution, others—among them Alexander Hamilton—cited France as a prime example of the perversion of republicanism.

Debates within the United States intensified when the newly republican France became enmeshed in conflict with other European nations. Seeking to keep neighboring monarchies from intervening and hoping to spread republicanism, French

Erich Lessing/Art Resource, NY

The violence of the French Revolution, especially the guillotining of King Louis XVI, shocked Americans, causing many to question whether the United States should remain that nation's ally.

leaders declared war on Austria and then, in 1793, on Britain, Spain, and Holland. That confronted the Americans with a dilemma. The 1778 Treaty of Alliance with France bound them as allies "forever." Yet the United States was connected to Great Britain through a shared history, language, and renewed economic ties. Americans still purchased most of their manufactured goods from Great Britain and, because U.S. revenues depended heavily on import tariffs, the nation's economic health required uninterrupted trade with England.

Edmond Genêt: French minister to the United States.

Edmond Genêt

The situation intensified in April 1793, when **Edmond Genêt**, a representative of the French government, arrived in Charleston, South Carolina. Genêt's arrival made President Washington wonder. Should he receive Genêt, thus officially recognizing the French revolutionary government? Or should he proclaim neutrality?

Washington resolved his dilemma by receiving Genêt but also issuing a proclamation that the United States would adopt "a conduct friendly and impartial toward the belligerent powers." Federalist newspapers defended the proclamation, while Republicans only reluctantly accepted the enormously popular neutrality policy.

Genêt's faction fell from power in Paris, and he sought political asylum in the United States. But the domestic divisions Genêt helped to widen were perpetuated by clubs called Democratic societies, formed by Americans sympathetic to the French Revolution and worried about the Washington administration.

Democratic Societies

More than forty Democratic societies organized between 1793 and 1800. Members saw themselves as seeking the same goal as the 1760s resistance movement: protecting people's liberties against encroachments by corrupt and self-serving rulers. They protested government fiscal and foreign policy, repeatedly proclaiming their belief in "the equal rights of man," particularly free speech, free press, and free assembly. Like the Sons of Liberty, the Democratic societies comprised chiefly artisans and craftsmen, although professionals, farmers, and merchants also joined. They allied with congressional Republicans.

The rapid spread of citizens' groups outspokenly critical of the administration disturbed Hamilton and Washington. Calling them dangerously subversive, the groups' "real design," a Federalist newspaper asserted, was "to involve the country in war, to assume the reins of government and tyrannize over the people." The counterattack climaxed in the fall of 1794, when Washington accused the societies of fomenting the Whiskey Rebellion. As the first organized political dissenters in the United States, Democratic societies alarmed officials, who had not yet accepted the idea that one component of a free government was organized loyal opposition.

Partisan Politics and Relations with Great Britain

What fueled the growing partisanship in the new republic at the end of the eighteenth century?

In 1794, George Washington dispatched Chief Justice John Jay to London to negotiate unresolved questions in Anglo-American relations. The United States wanted to establish freedom of the seas and to assert its right, as a neutral nation, to trade freely with both combatants. Further, Great Britain still held posts in the American Northwest, thus violating the 1783 peace treaty. Settlers there believed the British were responsible for renewed warfare with neighboring Indians. Americans also wanted a commercial treaty and sought compensation for the slaves who left with the British army after the war.

Jay Treaty Debate

The negotiations proved difficult. Britain agreed to evacuate the western forts and ease restrictions on American trade to England and the Caribbean. The treaty established two arbitration commissions—one to deal with prewar debts Americans owed to British creditors and the other to hear claims for captured American merchant ships—but Britain refused slaveowners compensation for lost bondspeople. Most Americans, including the president, expressed dissatisfaction with some treaty clauses.

The Senate debated the **Jay Treaty** in secret, and the public only learned of its provisions after ratification in late June 1795. Protests followed; newspaper essays and popular gatherings urged Washington to reject the treaty. Southern planters criticized the lack of compensation for runaway slaves and objected to the commission on prewar debts, which might make them pay obligations dating back to the 1760s. Federalists countered with their own meetings and essays, contending that the Jay Treaty would prove preferable to no treaty at all. The president signed the pact in mid-August. One opportunity remained to prevent it from taking effect: Congress had to appropriate funds and, according to the Constitution, appropriation bills had to originate in the House of Representatives.

Washington delayed submitting the treaty to the House until March 1796, futilely hoping the opposition would have dissipated. During the debate, Republicans argued against the appropriations, and they asked Washington to give the House all negotiations documents. In resisting the request, Washington established a power still used today—executive privilege, in which the president may withhold information from Congress if he deems it necessary.

The treaty's opponents initially commanded a congressional majority, but soon pressure mounted for appropriating the necessary funds, fostered by a Federalist campaign targeting middle-state congressmen whose districts would benefit from approval. Petitions contended that failure to fund the treaty would lead to war with Britain, thus endangering Pennsylvania frontier settlements and New York and New Jersey commercial interests. Further, Federalists linked the Jay Treaty with the more popular **Pinckney's Treaty**. In 1795, Thomas Pinckney of South Carolina negotiated a treaty with Spain giving the United States navigation privileges on the Mississippi River and the right to land and store goods at New Orleans tax free. The overwhelming support for Pinckney's Treaty helped to overcome opposition to the Jay Treaty. In late April, the House appropriated the money by 51 to 48. The vote divided along partisan and regional lines: all but two southerners opposed the treaty; all but three congressional Federalists supported it; and a majority of middle-state representatives voted yes.

The Federalists' campaign to sway public opinion ironically violated their fundamental philosophy of government—that ordinary people should defer to the judgment of elected leaders. The Federalists had won the battle, but in the long run they lost the war, for Republicans proved more effective in appealing to the citizenry.

Jay Treaty: Pact that sought to resolve mounting tensions between Britain and the United States in the years after the Revolution. Britain agreed to relinquish control of its western U.S. posts, establish commissions to receive claims for ships damaged by British seizures, and broaden U.S. access to trade with the West and British.

Pinckney's Treaty: Also called the Treaty of San Lorenzo, it won westerners the right of duty-free access to New Orleans and the use of the Mississippi River for commerce.

Bases of Partisanship

The terms used by Jefferson and Madison (the people versus aristocrats) or by Hamilton and Washington (true patriots versus subversive rabble) do not adequately explain growing divisions in the electorate. Differences between agrarian and commercial interests do not cover it either, as more than 90 percent of Americans lived in rural areas. Nor did the divisions in the 1790s simply repeat the Federalist-Antifederalist debate of 1787–1788. Although most Antifederalists became Republicans, the party's leaders, Madison and Jefferson, had supported the Constitution.

Republicans, especially prominent in the southern and middle states, were confident and optimistic about politics and the economy. Southern planters foresaw a prosperous future based partly on westward expansion, which they expected to dominate. Republicans employed democratic rhetoric to win over small farmers south of New England and ethnic groups—especially Irish, Scots, and Germans. Artisans also joined the coalition. Republicans emphasized developing America's resources and remained sympathetic to France.

Federalists, concentrated among the commercial interests of New England, came mostly from English stock. They stressed the need for order, hierarchy, and obedience to authority. Wealthy New England merchants aligned with the Federalists, as did the region's farmers who, prevented from expanding production because of New England's poor soil, gravitated toward the more conservative party. To Federalist eyes, potential enemies—internal and external—threatened the nation, necessitating a protective alliance with Great Britain. Given the dangers posed by European warfare, Federalists' vision of international affairs may have been accurate. But because Federalists offered little hope of a better future, Republicans ultimately prevailed.

Washington's Farewell Address

After the treaty debate, wearied by criticism, George Washington decided to retire. In September, Washington published his Farewell Address, most of which Hamilton wrote. In it Washington outlined two principles that guided American foreign policy until the late 1940s: to maintain commercial but not political ties to other nations and to enter no permanent alliances. He also stressed America's uniqueness—its exceptionalism—and the need for independent action in foreign affairs, today called unilateralism.

Some interpret Washington's desire to end partisan strife as a call for politicians to consider the good of the whole nation. But given the impending presidential election, the Farewell Address appears as an attack on the Republican opposition. Washington advocated unity behind the Federalist banner. Both Federalists and Republicans saw themselves as the true heirs of the Revolution and perceived their opponents as misguided, unpatriotic troublemakers.

Election of 1796

election of 1796: Federalist John Adams won by three votes and, as the second-highest vote-getter in the electoral college, Thomas Jefferson became vice president.

The presidential **election of 1796** saw the first serious contest for the position. Federalists in Congress put forward Vice President John Adams, with the diplomat Thomas Pinckney as his running mate. Congressional Republicans chose Thomas Jefferson as their presidential candidate; the lawyer, Revolutionary War veteran, and politician Aaron Burr of New York ran for vice president.

Most state legislatures appointed electors, and the method of voting in the electoral college did not account for the possibility of party slates. The Constitution's drafters had not foreseen the development of competing political organizations, so there was no way to support one person for president and another for vice president. The electors voted for two people. The man with the highest total became president; the second highest, vice president.

That procedure was the Federalists' undoing. Adams won the presidency with 71 votes, but Jefferson won 68 votes, 9 more than Pinckney, to become vice president. The incoming administration was thus politically divided. The president and vice president, once allies, became bitter enemies.

John Adams and Political Dissent

As president, John Adams never abandoned an outdated notion that the president should be above politics and factionalism. Thus, Adams kept Washington's cabinet intact, despite its key members' allegiance to his chief Federalist rival, Alexander Hamilton. Adams was often passive, letting others (usually Hamilton) lead when he should have. But Adams's detachment did enable him to weather the greatest international crisis yet: the Quasi-War with France.

> What was the underlying purpose of the Alien and Sedition Acts of 1798?

XYZ Affair

The Jay Treaty improved America's relationship with Great Britain, but it provoked France to retaliate by ordering its ships to seize American vessels carrying British goods. In response, Congress authorized ship building and stockpiling weapons and ammunition. President Adams also sent three commissioners to Paris to negotiate a settlement. For months, the commissioners sought talks with Talleyrand, the French foreign minister, but Talleyrand's agents demanded a bribe of $250,000 first. The Americans refused. Adams informed Congress of the impasse and recommended increases in defense appropriations.

Convinced that Adams deliberately sabotaged negotiations, congressional Republicans insisted that the dispatches be turned over to Congress. Adams complied, aware that releasing the reports would work to his advantage. He withheld only the names of the French agents, referring to them as X, Y, and Z. The revelation that the Americans were treated with contempt stimulated anti-French sentiment in the United States and became known as the **XYZ Affair**. Cries for war resounded. Congress abrogated the Treaty of Alliance and authorized American ships to seize French vessels.

XYZ Affair: French demand for bribes from American negotiators that triggered great anger.

Quasi-War with France

Thus began an undeclared war with France fought in Caribbean waters between warships of the U.S. Navy and French privateers. Although Americans initially suffered heavy merchant shipping losses, by early 1799 the U.S. Navy established its superiority. Its ships captured eight French privateers and naval vessels, easing the threat to America's vital Caribbean trade.

Republicans, who opposed war and sympathized with France, could not quell anti-French feelings. Because Agent Y boasted of a "French party in America," Federalists accused Republicans of traitorous designs. A New York newspaper declared that anyone who remained "lukewarm" after reading the XYZ dispatches "must have a soul black enough to be fit for treason Strategems and spoils."

Alien and Sedition Acts

Now that the country seemed to see the truth of what Federalists argued since the Whiskey Rebellion in 1794—that Republicans were subversive foreign agents—Federalists sought to codify that belief into law. In 1798, the Federalist-controlled Congress adopted four laws known as the **Alien and Sedition Acts**, intended to suppress dissent and to prevent further growth of the Republican faction.

Alien and Sedition Acts: A series of laws passed in 1789 under the label of national security but that were intended to suppress dissent and block the rise of the Republican faction.

Three of the acts targeted recently arrived immigrants, whom Federalists accurately suspected of sympathizing with Republicans. The Naturalization Act lengthened the residency period required for citizenship and ordered resident aliens to register with the federal government. The two Alien Acts provided for the detention of enemy aliens in wartime and gave the president authority to deport any alien he deemed dangerous to national security.

The fourth statute, the Sedition Act, outlawed conspiracies to prevent enforcement of federal laws, punishable by five years in prison and a $5,000 fine. And writing, printing, or uttering "false, scandalous and malicious" statements against the government or the president "with intent to defame...or to bring them or either of them, into contempt or disrepute" became a crime punishable by up to two years' imprisonment and a fine of $2,000. Today, a law punishing speech alone would be unconstitutional. But in the eighteenth century, when organized political opposition was suspect, many Americans supported the Sedition Act's free speech restrictions.

Link to William Duane's *A Letter to George Washington, President of the United States.*

The Sedition Act led to fifteen indictments and ten guilty verdicts. Among those convicted were a congressman and former newspaper editor, Matthew Lyon of Vermont; and James Callender, a Scots immigrant and scandalmonger, whose exposés forced Alexander Hamilton to acknowledge an extramarital affair. After turning his attention to President Adams, Callender was convicted, fined, and jailed for nine months. Republican newspaper editors nevertheless continued their criticisms of Federalists, energized rather than quashed by the persecution.

Virginia and Kentucky Resolutions

Link to the Virginia and Kentucky Resolutions.

Jefferson and Madison combated the acts in another way. Petitioning the Federalist-controlled Congress to repeal the laws would fail, and Federalist judges refused to allow accused individuals to question the Sedition Act's constitutionality. Accordingly, the Republican leaders turned to the state legislatures. Concealing their role to avoid being indicted for sedition, Jefferson and Madison drafted resolutions that were introduced into the Kentucky and Virginia legislatures in the fall of 1798. Because a compact among the states created the Constitution, the resolutions contended, people speaking through their states had a right to judge the constitutionality of federal measures. Both pronounced the Alien and Sedition Acts unconstitutional, and thus advanced the doctrine later known as nullification.

Virginia and Kentucky Resolutions: Jefferson's and Madison's response to the Alien and Sedition Acts. The Resolution stressed states' rights and the power of nullification in response to Alien and Sedition Acts.

Although they stood alone, the **Virginia and Kentucky Resolutions** had considerable influence. First, they placed the opposition party in the revolutionary tradition of resistance to tyrannical authority. Second, their theory of union inspired the Hartford Convention of 1814 and southern states' rights advocates in the 1830s and thereafter. Jefferson and Madison identified a key constitutional issue: How far could states go in opposing the national government? The question would not be definitively answered until the Civil War.

Newspapers of the Early Republic

In the 1790s newspaper editors and publishers, unlike today, did not attempt to present news objectively, and indeed, none of their readers expected them to do so. Instead, newspapers were linked to the rapidly expanding political factions of the new nation—the partisan groupings (not yet political parties in the modern sense) terming themselves *Federalists* and *Republicans*. The "official" paper of the Federalists was *The Gazette of the United States* (colonial papers supported by individual governments too had been called *gazettes*—just as the

London Gazette was tied to the English government). Among the Republicans' many allied newspapers was *The New-York Journal, and Patriotic Register*. A reader comparing the front pages of two randomly selected issues could see at a glance the differences between the two. *The Gazette of the United States* filled its first page with sober news articles, whereas the face *The New-York Journal* presented to the world was consumed entirely with advertisements, some headed by intriguing design elements. Which would appeal more directly to America's artisans and forward-thinking agriculturalists: the dull newsprint of the Federalists, or the eye-catching ads of the Republicans?

American Antiquarian Society

American Antiquarian Society

Convention of 1800   Federalists split over France. Hamilton and his supporters called for a declaration legitimizing the undeclared naval war. Adams, though, received private signals—among them George Logan's report—that the French government regretted its treatment of the American commissioners.

Adams dispatched William Vans Murray to Paris to negotiate with Napoleon Bonaparte, France's new leader. The United States sought compensation for ships France had seized since 1793 and abrogation of the treaty of 1778. The Convention of 1800, which ended the Quasi-War, provided the latter but not the former. Still, it freed the United States to follow the independent diplomatic course George Washington urged in his Farewell Address.

The West in the New Nation

How did the new nation begin to expand its boundaries westward?

By the end of the eighteenth century, the nation added three states (Vermont, Kentucky, and Tennessee) and more than 1 million people to the nearly 4 million in the 1790 census. It also nominally controlled the land east of the Mississippi River and north of Spanish Florida. Control of the land north of the Ohio River was achieved only after considerable bloodshed, for the land was dominated by a powerful western confederacy of eight Indian nations led by the Miamis.

War in the Northwest Territory   General Arthur St. Clair, first governor of the Northwest Territory, futilely tried to open more land to settlement through failed treaty negotiations with the western confederacy in early 1789. Subsequently, Little Turtle, the confederacy's war chief, defeated forces led by General Josiah Harmar (1790) and by St. Clair (1791) in battles near the present Indiana and Ohio border. More than six hundred of St. Clair's men died, and more were wounded, in the United States' worst defeat in frontier history.

In 1793, the Miami Confederacy declared that peace would come only if the United States recognized the Ohio River as its northwestern boundary. But the national government refused. A reorganized army under the Revolutionary War hero General Anthony Wayne defeated the confederacy in August 1794 at the Battle of Fallen Timbers (near present-day Toledo, Ohio). Negotiating successfully with the confederacy was crucial for the new nation, because otherwise warfare would continue as American settlers continued west. The United States lacked the resources for a prolonged frontier conflict, so Wayne reached an agreement with the confederacy in August 1795.

The resulting Treaty of Greenville gave the United States the right to settle much of what was to become Ohio. Indians received the acknowledgment they had long sought: American recognition of their rights to the soil. At Greenville, the United States formally accepted the principle of Indian sovereignty, by virtue of residence, over lands native peoples had not ceded. Never again would the U.S. government claim that it acquired Indian territory solely through negotiation with a European or North American country.

Pinckney's Treaty with Spain that year established the 31st parallel as the boundary between the United States and Florida. Spanish influence in the Old Southwest raised questions about the loyalty of American settlers in the region, much of it still unceded and occupied by Creeks, Cherokees, and other Indians. A Southwest Ordinance (1790) attempted to organize the territory; by permitting slavery, it made the region attractive to slaveholders.

"Civilizing" the Indians

Even Indian peoples who lived independent of federal authority came within the orbit of U.S. influence. The nation's stated goal was to "civilize" them. Henry Knox, secretary of war, contended in 1789 that the government should "impart our knowledge of cultivation and the arts to the aboriginals of the country." The first step, Knox suggested, should be to introduce to Indian peoples "a love for exclusive property" by giving livestock to individual Indians. The **Indian Trade and Intercourse Act of 1793** codified Knox's plan, promising that the federal government would supply Indians with animals and agricultural implements, and instructors.

The plan incorrectly posited that Indians' traditional commitment to communal landowning could be overcome, and it ignored their centuries-long agricultural experience. Policymakers focused on Indian men: because they hunted, male Indians were "savages" who should be "civilized" by learning to farm. That women tradi-

Indian Trade and Intercourse Act of 1793: Series of U.S. laws that attempted to "civilize" Indians according to European American standards.

Greenville County Museum of Art

In 1805, an unidentified artist painted Benjamin Hawkins, a trader and U.S. agent to the Indians of the Southeast, at the Creek agency near Macon, Georgia. Hawkins introduced European-style agriculture to the Creeks, who are shown here with vegetables from their fields. Throughout the eastern United States, Indian nations had to make similar adaptations of their traditional lifestyles in order to maintain their group identity.

tionally farmed was irrelevant because, to officials, Indian women—like those of European descent—should confine themselves to child rearing, household chores, and home manufacturing.

Iroquois and Cherokees The Iroquois Confederacy was devastated by the war. Restricted to small reservations increasingly surrounded by Anglo-American farmlands, men could no longer hunt and often spent their days in idle carousing. Quaker missionaries started a demonstration farm among the Senecas to teach men to plow, but women showed greater interest. The same was true among the Cherokees of Georgia. As their southern hunting territories were reduced, Cherokee men did begin to raise cattle and hogs, but they startled reformers by treating livestock like wild game, allowing the animals to run free and shooting them when needed. Men also started to plow the fields, although Cherokee women continued to handle cultivation and harvest.

Iroquois men became more receptive to the Quakers' lessons after the spring of 1799, when a Seneca named Handsome Lake experienced some remarkable visions. Like earlier prophets, Handsome Lake preached that Indian peoples should renounce alcohol, gambling, and other destructive European customs. He directed followers to reorient men's and women's work assignments as the Quakers advocated, as he recognized that only by adopting the European sexual division of labor could the Iroquois retain an autonomous existence.

"Revolutions" at the End of the Century

What gave rise to new potential revolutions in America at the end of the eighteenth century?

Three events at the end of the eighteenth century were real or potential revolutions: Fries's Rebellion, Gabriel's Rebellion, and the election of Thomas Jefferson. Each mirrored the tensions and uncertainties of the young republic. The Fries rebels resisted national authority to tax. Gabriel and his followers challenged the slave system crucial to the Chesapeake economy. And the venomous presidential election of 1800 exposed a structural flaw in the Constitution that had to be corrected.

Fries's Rebellion The tax resistance named for Revolutionary War veteran John Fries arose among German American farmers in Pennsylvania's Lehigh Valley in 1798–1799. To finance the Quasi-War, Congress enacted taxes on land, houses, and legal documents. German Americans, imbued with revolutionary ideals (at least two-fifths were veterans), regarded the taxes as a threat to their liberties and livelihoods. Asserting a right of resistance to unconstitutional laws, they raised liberty poles, signed petitions to Congress, and nonviolently prevented assessors from evaluating their homes. A federal judge ordered the arrest of twenty resisters. In response, in March 1799 Fries led 120 militiamen to Bethlehem, where they surrounded a tavern temporarily housing the prisoners. Fearing a violent confrontation, a federal marshal let the men go. Fries and many of his neighbors were tried; he and two others were convicted of treason; thirty-two more, of violating the Sedition Act. Although Fries and the other "traitors" were sentenced to hang, Adams pardoned them two days before their scheduled execution. Still, the region's residents remained, Republican partisans.

Gabriel's Rebellion

Like their white compatriots, African Americans became familiar with concepts of liberty and equality during the Revolution. They, too, witnessed the benefits of fighting collectively for freedom. Buoyed by news of the successful slave revolt in St. Domingue in 1793, Gabriel, an enslaved Virginia blacksmith, planned the second end-of-the-century revolution.

For months, Gabriel visited Sunday services at black Baptist and Methodist congregations, where bondspeople gathered free of their owners. Gabriel first recruited other skilled African Americans who like himself lived in semi-freedom under minimal supervision. Next, he enlisted rural slaves. The rebels planned to attack Richmond on the night of August 30, 1800; set fire to the city; seize the state capitol; and capture the governor, James Monroe. At that point, Gabriel believed, other slaves and poor whites would join in.

Heavy rain forced a postponement. Several planters then learned of the plot. Gabriel avoided arrest for weeks, but militia troops apprehended and interrogated other rebel leaders. Twenty-six rebels, including Gabriel, were hanged. Ironically, only slaves who betrayed their fellows won freedom as a result of the rebellion.

At his trial, one of Gabriel's followers told his judges that, like George Washington, "I have adventured my life in endeavouring to obtain the liberty of my countrymen, and am a willing sacrifice in their cause." Southern state legislatures responded by increasing the severity of slave laws. Talk of emancipation ceased in the South, and slavery became more firmly entrenched.

Election of 1800

The third end-of-the-century revolution was a Republican "takeover"—the election of Thomas Jefferson as president and a Congress dominated by Republicans. Prior to November 1800, Federalists and Republicans campaigned for congressional seats and maneuvered to control the electoral college. Both sides wanted to avoid reproducing the divided results of 1796. Republicans again nominated Thomas Jefferson and Aaron Burr; Federalists named John Adams, with Charles Cotesworth Pinckney of South Carolina as vice president. The network of Republican newspapers forged in the fires of Sedition Act prosecutions vigorously promoted the Jeffersonian cause. Jefferson and Burr had tied with 73, while Adams had 64 and Pinckney 63. Under the Constitution, the election had to be decided in the existing House of Representatives.

Balloting lasted six days; in the end, a deal was struck that gave Jefferson the presidency on the thirty-sixth ballot. A crucial consequence of the election was the adoption of the Twelfth Amendment, which provided that electors would henceforth cast separate ballots for president and vice president.

The defeated Federalists turned to strengthening their hold on the judiciary. President Adams named his secretary of state, John Marshall, chief justice; his thirty-four years of service left a lasting imprint on constitutional interpretation. Adams spent his last hours in office on March 3, 1801, appointing so-called midnight justices to positions created in the hastily adopted Judiciary Act of 1801. Federalists thus hoped to prevent Jefferson from exerting immediate influence on the judicial branch.

Links to the World

Haitian Refugees

Less than a decade after winning independence, the United States confronted its first immigration crisis. Among the approximately 600,000 residents of St. Domingue in the early 1790s, about 100,000 were free people, almost all of them slaveowners; half were whites, the rest mulattos. When after the French Revolution those free mulattos sought greater social and political equality, slaves seized the opportunity to revolt. By 1793, they triumphed, led by former slave, Toussaint L'Ouverture. In 1804, they ousted the French, establishing the republic of Haiti. Thousands of whites and mulattos, accompanied by as many slaves as they could transport, sought asylum in the United States.

American political leaders nonetheless feared the consequences of their arrival. Southern plantation owners worried that slaves so familiar with ideas of freedom and equality would mingle with their bondspeople. Many were uncomfortable with the immigration of numerous free people of color. Most southern states adopted laws forbidding the entry of Haitian slaves and free mulattos, but they were difficult to enforce, as was a similar congressional act. More than fifteen thousand refugees—white, black, and mixed-race—flooded into the United States and Spanish Louisiana. Many ended up in Virginia or Charleston, Savannah, and New Orleans.

In New Orleans and Charleston, the influx of mulattos aroused a heightened color consciousness that placed light-skinned people at the top of a hierarchy of people of color. After the United States purchased Louisiana in 1803, the number of free people of color there almost doubled in three years, largely because of a final surge of immigration from Haiti. In Virginia, the Haitian revolt inspired slaves in 1800 to plan the incident now known as Gabriel's Rebellion.

The Haitian refugees thus linked European-Americans and African Americans to events in the West Indies.

Louisiana State Museum

A free woman of color in Louisiana early in the nineteenth century, possibly one of the refugees from Haiti. Esteban Rodriguez Mir, named governor of Spanish Louisiana in 1782, ordered all slave and free black women to wear head wraps rather than hats—which were reserved for whites—but this woman and many others subverted his order by nominally complying, but nevertheless creating elaborate headdresses.

Dissent During Wartime

The Quasi-War with France in 1798 and 1799 brought the first attempt to suppress dissent. By criminalizing dissenting speech, the Sedition Act of 1798 tried to quiet the Republicans' criticism of the war and President John Adams. Fifteen men were indicted and ten fined and jailed (including a congressman) after being convicted under the statute.

Although Americans might assume that their right to free speech under the First Amendment—now more fully accepted than two centuries ago—protects dissenters during wartime, history suggests otherwise. Every conflict has stimulated efforts by government and individuals to suppress dissenters. During the Civil War, the Union jailed civilian Confederate sympathizers; during the First World War, the government deported immigrant aliens who too vocally criticized the war effort. World War II brought the silencing of isolationists' voices, denying those who opposed American entry into the war public outlets for their ideas.

Americans remain divided over whether the proper course of action in the 1960s and 1970s was dissent from, or acquiescence to, government policy. The USA PATRIOT Act, adopted after the September 11, 2001 attacks, removed long-standing restrictions on federal government surveillance of citizens, controversially granting access to library records. Criticism of the wars in Iraq and Afghanistan has raised questions: Do newspapers that publish classified information or pictures of abused prisoners overstep their bounds? Can political figures censure the conduct of the wars without seeming unpatriotic?

Freedom of speech is never easy to maintain, and wartime conditions make it tougher. When the nation comes under attack, many patriotic Americans argue that dissent should cease. Others contend that people must always have the right to speak freely. Events in the United States since the 9/11 attacks suggest that this legacy remains contentious for the American people.

Summary

As the nineteenth century began, inhabitants of the United States faced changes. Indians east of the Mississippi River surrendered some traditions to preserve others. Some African Americans struggled unsuccessfully to free themselves from slavery, then confronted more constraints under increasingly restrictive laws.

For European-Americans, the first eleven years under the Constitution established enduring precedents for congressional, presidential, and judicial action—among them establishment of the cabinet, interpretations of key clauses of the Constitution, and stirrings of judicial review of state and federal legislation. Building on successful negotiations with Spain (Pinckney's Treaty), Britain (the Jay Treaty), and France (the Convention of 1800), the United States developed its diplomatic independence.

Yet the 1790s spawned debates over foreign and domestic policy and saw the beginnings of organized factionalism and grassroots politicking, if not yet formal parties. The Whiskey and Fries Rebellions showed that regional conflicts persisted. The waging of an undeclared war against France proved contentious. In 1801, the Jeffersonian ideal of agrarian, decentralized republicanism prevailed over Alexander Hamilton's vision of a powerful centralized economy and strong national government.

Chapter Review

Building a Workable Government

What was the purpose of the Bill of Rights?

Several states threatened not to ratify the Constitution because they feared it would create a too powerful national government. Leaders from states such as North Carolina thought that a bill of rights would expressly state key liberties of the people that should be protected, among them freedom of the press, freedom of speech, freedom of religion, and the right to peaceable assembly. At first, James Madison thought the Bill of Rights was unnecessary, but he changed his mind and submitted nineteen amendments—ten of which the states ratified—that were added to the Constitution on December 15, 1791 and later known as the Bill of Rights.

Domestic Policy Under Washington and Hamilton

How did the chartering of the Bank of the United States provoke an early constitutional debate?

Treasury Secretary Alexander Hamilton asked Congress to charter a national bank, modeled on England's, which would act as a collecting and disbursing agent for the treasury and the source for national currency. Some political leaders were unsure if the Constitution gave it the power to establish a bank. Some, like James Madison and Thomas Jefferson, took a strict-constructionist interpretation of the Constitution, arguing that it allowed Congress only to make laws deemed "necessary"—not merely what was desirable. Hamilton took a broad-constructionist view, stating that Congress could use any means not prohibited by the Constitution to achieve a constitutional end. President Washington agreed, and the bill establishing the Bank of the United States became law.

The French Revolution and the Development of Partisan Politics

Why did U.S. leaders find the rise of political factions disturbing?

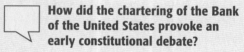

In the new republic, leaders had not yet come to understand or embrace dissent as a natural part of democratic government. Factions were seen as linked to monarchies and deemed a sign of corruption in republics. Washington tried to smooth over discord when Jefferson and Madison critiqued treasury secretary Alexander Hamilton's policies as favoring commercial interests over agriculture. Both sides accused the other of trying to subvert republican principles or destroy the new republic. Similarly, when dozens of Democratic societies sprang up in the 1790s, Washington and Hamilton feared their rapid growth as subversive and dangerous to the unity they believed necessary for the republic's survival.

Partisan Politics and Relations with Great Britain

What fueled the growing partisanship in the new republic at the end of the eighteenth century?

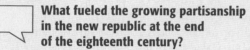

Several different factors divided people and leaders. Debates over who the true patriots were fueled some discord, as did growing differences between agrarian and commercial interests. Republicans optimistically put their faith in the nation's future prosperity, enticing southerners, small farmers, and artisans to ally with them. Federalists, on the other hand, were often New England merchants who sought order and organized authority. Foreign affairs also divided the Republicans and Federalists. As tensions mounted between France and Great Britain in 1793, Americans, too, took sides. Federalists supported an ongoing alliance with Great Britain, which they thought would protect their interests from internal and external enemies, while many others wanted to support France's new revolutionary government.

John Adams and Political Dissent

What was the underlying purpose of the Alien and Sedition Acts of 1798?

Adopted by the Federalist-controlled Congress, these acts were designed to suppress dissent—still seen as dangerous and subversive rather than a natural part of a republic—and weaken the competing Republican faction. Hence, the acts targeted recent immigrants, typically Republican supporters, by lengthening the residency requirement for citizenship among other rules, as well as allowing the president to detain or deport any alien considered dangerous to national security. The Sedition Act outlawed antigovernment conspiracies and curbed free speech by making the writing or uttering of false, malicious or scandalous statements against the government illegal. Although the Federalists expected the acts to weaken their critics, the laws only increased dissent.

The West in the New Nation

How did the new nation begin to expand its boundaries westward?

The United States nominally controlled the land east of the Mississippi and north of Spanish Florida, and later, through warfare and treaty, managed to extend its northernmost boundary to the Ohio River. Initially, leaders attempted to negotiate with Indians living there for the land; when that failed, war with eight Indian nations ensued, culminating in 1795 with the Treaty of Greenville. This agreement allowed the United States to settle most of what would become Ohio in exchange for acknowledging the principle of Indian sovereignty—by virtue of residence—over lands that had not been ceded.

"Revolutions" at the End of the Century

What gave rise to new potential revolutions in America at the end of the eighteenth century?

Three events revealed unresolved issues—and growing tensions—in the new republic. First, Fries's Rebellion questioned the power of the central government to tax, seeing it—much as early revolutionaries had—as a threat to personal liberties and livelihoods. Second, Gabriel's Rebellion of semifree blacks sought to challenge the slave system in the Chesapeake (but ended up inspiring stricter slave laws in the South). And finally the hotly contested 1800 presidential election revealed a structural flaw in the Constitution, which required that presidential electors vote for two men without designating one as president and the other as vice president, thus creating the tie between Jefferson and Burr. It led to the Twelfth Amendment, which provided that electors cast separate ballots for presidential and vice presidential candidates.

Suggestions for Further Reading

Joyce Appleby, *Capitalism and a New Social Order: The Republican Vision of the 1790s* (1984)

Susan Branson, *These Fiery Frenchified Dames: Women and Political Culture in Early National Philadelphia* (2001)

Douglas Egerton, *Gabriel's Rebellion: The Virginia Slave Conspiracies of 1800 and 1802* (1993)

Stanley Elkins and Eric McKitrick, *The Age of Federalism, 1788–1800* (1993)

Joseph J. Ellis, *Founding Brothers: The Revolutionary Generation* (2000)

James Horn, Jan Ellen Lewis, and Peter S. Onuf, eds., *The Revolution of 1800: Democracy, Race, and the New Republic* (2002)

Richard Labunski, *James Madison and the Struggle for the Bill of Rights* (2006)

David Andrew Nichols, *Red Gentlemen & White Savages: Indians, Federalists, and the Search for Order on the American Frontier* (2008)

Jeffrey L. Pasley, *"The Tyranny of Printers": Newspaper Politics in the Early American Republic* (2001)

Thomas P. Slaughter, *The Whiskey Rebellion* (1986)

Go to the CourseMate website for primary source links, study tools, and review materials for this chapter.
www.cengagebrain.com

Defining the Nation

1801–1823

Eager to stand apart from the allegedly aristocratic ways of his Federalist predecessors, President Thomas Jefferson displayed impatience for ceremony. But on his first New Year's Day in office, he awaited the ceremonial presentation of a much-heralded tribute to his commitment, as one gift bearer put it, to "defend Republicanism and baffle all the arts of Aristocracy." Crafted in Massachusetts, the belated inaugural gift weighed more than twelve hundred pounds and measured four feet in diameter, bearing the inscription "THE GREATEST CHEESE IN AMERICA—FOR THE GREATEST MAN IN AMERICA."

The "mammoth cheese" was conceived the previous July and made by the "Ladies" of Cheshire, a Massachusetts farming community as resolutely Jeffersonian-Republican as it was Baptist. As a religious minority in largely Congregationalist New England, the Cheshire Baptists celebrated a president whose vision featured agrarianism and separation of church and state.

Federalist editors joked that the mammoth cheese's maggot-infested condition upon delivery symbolized the nation under Republican rule. Its size represented the excesses of democracy, in which even women and backwoods preachers could play leading roles. Federalists' derision of the mammoth cheese only inspired additional showy expressions of democratic pride. In the following months, a Philadelphia baker sold "Mammoth Bread," while two years later in 1804, a "mammoth loaf" was served in the Capitol to Republicans, including President Jefferson. Behind such symbolism lay serious political ideologies. Jeffersonians believed virtue derived from agricultural endeavors. They thus celebrated the acquisition of the Louisiana Territory, but efforts to expand their agriculturally based "empire of liberty" westward were resisted by Native Americans and their European allies, and sometimes by Federalists. The War of 1812 largely removed such resistance, and the United States began its expansion west. Although that war ended with few issues resolved, it had profound consequences for American development. It secured the United States' sovereignty, opened much of the West to European-Americans and

Chapter Outline

Political Visions
Separation of Church and State | Political Mobilization | The Partisan Press | Limited Government | Judicial Politics | The Marshall Court | Judicial Review | Election of 1804 | Nationalism and Culture

National Expansion Westward
New Orleans | Louisiana Purchase | Lewis and Clark Expedition | Divisions Among Indian Peoples | Tenskwatawa and Tecumseh

The Nation in the Orbit of Europe
First Barbary War | Threats to American Sovereignty | The Embargo of 1807 | International Slave Trade | Election of 1808 | Women and Politics | Failed Policies | Mr. Madison's War

The War of 1812
Invasion of Canada | Naval Battles | Burning Capitals | War in the South | Treaty of Ghent | American Sovereignty Reasserted | Domestic Consequences

VISUALIZING THE PAST *Selling War*

The Nationalist Program
American System | Early Internal Improvements | The Era of Good Feelings | Government Promotion of Market Expansion | Boundary Settlements | Monroe Doctrine

Sectionalism Exposed
Early Industrial Development | Panic of 1819 | Missouri Compromise

LINKS TO THE WORLD *Industrial Piracy*

LEGACY FOR A PEOPLE AND A NATION *States' Rights and Nullification*

SUMMARY

their African American slaves, and helped spur revolutions in transportation and industry.

Contemporary observers hailed postwar nationalism as an "Era of Good Feelings," but when economic boom turned to bust, nationalistic unity faded. No issue proved more divisive than slavery's future in the West, as Missouri's petition for statehood revealed.

As you read this chapter, keep the following questions in mind:

* What characterized the two main competing visions for national development?

* How did America's relationship with Europe influence political and economic developments?

* In what ways did nonvoting Americans—most blacks, women, and Native Americans—take part in defining the new nation?

Political Visions

In his inaugural address, Jefferson addressed the electorate as citizens with common beliefs: "We are all republicans, we are all federalists.... A wise and frugal government, which shall restrain men from injuring one another, which shall leave them free to regulate their pursuits of industry and improvement, and shall not take from the mouth of labor the bread it had earned. This is the sum of good government."

> Was Jefferson's election and political vision truly "the revolution of 1800"?

But outgoing president John Adams did not hear Jefferson's call for unity, having left Washington before dawn. Former friends, the two men now disliked each other. Democratic-Republicans—as the Republicans of the 1790s now called themselves—and Federalists bitterly disagreed on how society and government should be organized. Federalists advocated a strong national government to promote economic development. Democratic-Republicans believed that limited government would foster republican virtue. Nearly two decades later, Jefferson would call his election "the revolution of 1800."

Separation of Church and State

The mammoth cheese symbolized the Cheshire farmers' gratitude for Jefferson's commitment to the separation of church and state. Jefferson believed that "religion is a matter which lies solely between Man & his God." New England Baptists hailed Jefferson as a hero, but New England Federalists thought their worst fears were confirmed. During the 1800 election, Federalists had waged a venomous campaign, incorrectly labeling Jefferson an atheist. Their rhetoric proved so effective that, after Jefferson's election, some New England women hid their Bibles in their gardens and wells to foil Democratic-Republicans allegedly bent on confiscating them.

Jefferson became president during a period of religious revivalism, particularly among Methodists and Baptists, whose democratic preaching—all humans, they said, were equal in God's eyes—encouraged a growing democratic political culture. Thus, the Cheshire Baptists informed the president that their cheese had been made "without a single slave to assist."

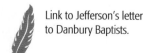

Link to Jefferson's letter to Danbury Baptists.

Chronology

1801	Marshall becomes chief justice		1812	Madison reelected president
	Jefferson inaugurated as president		1812–15	War of 1812
1801–05	United States defeats Barbary pirates		1813	Tecumseh's death
1803	*Marbury v. Madison*			Boston Manufacturing Company starts
	Louisiana Purchase			textile mill in Waltham, Massachusetts
1804	Jefferson reelected president, Clinton vice		1814	Treaty of Ghent
	President		1814–15	Hartford Convention
1804–06	Lewis and Clark expedition		1815	Battle of New Orleans
1805	Tenskwatawa emerges as Shawnee leader		1817	Regular steamboat travel begins on
1807	*Chesapeake* affair			Mississippi
	Embargo Act		1817–1825	Erie Canal constructed
1808	Congress bans slave importation		1819	*McCulloch v. Maryland*
	Madison elected president			Adams-Onis Treaty
1808–13	Tenskwatawa and Tecumseh organize Indian		1819–early 1820s	First major depression
	resistance		1820–1821	Missouri Compromise
1811	National Road begun		1823	Monroe Doctrine

Political Mobilization

The revolution of 1800, which gave the Democratic-Republicans majorities in both houses of Congress along with the presidency, resulted from an electorate limited largely to property-holding men. Under the Constitution, states regulated voting. Nowhere but New Jersey could women vote; that right was granted inadvertently and revoked in 1807. In 1800, free black men meeting property qualifications could vote everywhere but Delaware, Georgia, South Carolina, and Virginia, though local custom often kept them from exercising that right. Partisan politics nonetheless captured Americans' imaginations. Political mobilization took place locally, as candidates rallied popular support on militia training grounds, in taverns and churches, at court gatherings, and during holiday celebrations. Voters and nonvoters expressed their views through parades, petitions, songs and debates. Importantly, they devoured a growing print culture of pamphlets, broadsides (posters), almanacs, and newspapers.

The Partisan Press

Read aloud in taverns, artisans' workshops, and homes, newspapers gave national importance to local events. In 1800, the nation had 260 newspapers; by 1810, it had 396, virtually all of them partisan.

The parties adopted official organs. After his election, Jefferson persuaded the *National Intelligencer* to move from Philadelphia to Washington, where it became the Democratic-Republicans' voice. In 1801, Alexander Hamilton launched the *New York Evening Post* as the Federalist vehicle. Published six or seven times a week, party papers helped feed the growing obsession with partisan politics.

Limited Government

To bring into his administration men sharing his vision of individual liberty, an agrarian republic, and limited government, Jefferson rejected appointments that Adams made in his presidency's last

Courtesy, The Henry Francis du Pont Winterthur Museum

Although most places limited the vote to property-owning white men, elections, such as this one in Philadelphia, drew multi-racial crowds of men, women, and children.

days and dismissed Federalist customs collectors. He awarded treasury and judicial offices to Republicans. Jeffersonians worked to make the government leaner. If Alexander Hamilton had viewed the national debt as the engine of economic growth, Jefferson deemed it the source of government corruption. Secretary of the Treasury Albert Gallatin halved the army budget and reduced the 1802 navy budget by two-thirds. He moved to reduce the national debt from $83 million to $57 million, hoping to retire it altogether by 1817. Jefferson closed two of five diplomatic missions abroad, at The Hague and in Berlin. And the Democratic-Republican–controlled Congress oversaw the repeal of all internal taxes, including the despised whiskey tax of 1791.

Ideas of liberty also distinguished Democratic-Republicans from Federalists. Opposition to the Alien and Sedition Acts of 1798 had united Republicans. Jefferson now declined to use the acts against his opponents, instead pardoning those convicted of violating them.

Congress let the Sedition Act expire in 1801 and the Alien Act in 1802, and repealed the Naturalization Act of 1798, which required fourteen years of residency for citizenship. The 1802 act that replaced it required five years of residency, loyalty to the Constitution, and the forsaking of foreign allegiances and titles. It remained the basis of naturalized American citizenship into the twentieth century.

Judicial Politics   To many Democratic-Republicans, the judiciary represented a centralizing and undemocratic force, since judges were appointed, not elected, and served for life. At Jefferson's prompting, the House impeached (indicted) and the Senate convicted Federal District Judge John Pickering of New Hampshire, whose alleged alcoholism made him an easy mark. The House also impeached Supreme Court Justice Samuel Chase for judicial misconduct. A staunch Federalist, Chase had pushed for prosecutions under the Sedition Act, campaigned for Adams in 1800, and denounced Jefferson's administration. But Democratic-Republicans failed to muster the two-thirds Senate majority necessary for conviction. The failure to remove Chase preserved the Court's independence and established the precedent that criminal actions, not political disagreements, justified removal from office.

The Marshall Court

Although Jefferson appointed three new Supreme Court justices, the Court remained a Federalist stronghold under John Marshall. Even after the Democratic-Republicans achieved a majority of Court seats in 1811, Marshall remained influential as chief justice. Under the Marshall Court (1801–1835), the Supreme Court upheld federal supremacy over the states while protecting commercial interests.

Marshall made the Court an equal branch of government. Marshall strengthened the Court by having it speak with a unified voice; rather than issuing individual concurring judgments, justices now issued joint majority opinions. From 1801 through 1805, Marshall wrote twenty-four of the Court's twenty-six decisions; through 1810 he wrote 85 percent of the opinions.

Judicial Review

In his last hours in office, Adams named Federalist William Marbury a justice of the peace in the District of Columbia. Jefferson's secretary of state, James Madison, declined to certify the appointment, allowing the new president to appoint a Democratic-Republican. Marbury sued, requesting a writ of mandamus (a court order forcing the president to appoint him). If the Supreme Court ruled in Marbury's favor in ***Marbury v. Madison***, the president probably would not comply, and the Court could not force him to do so. Yet, by refusing to issue the writ, the Federalist-dominated bench would hand the Democratic-Republicans a victory.

Marbury v. Madison: Case in which the Supreme Court's power to determine the constitutionality of laws was established.

To avoid both pitfalls, Marshall recast the issue. He ruled that Marbury had a right to his appointment but that the Supreme Court could not compel Madison to honor it because the Constitution did not grant the Court power to issue a writ of mandamus. Without specific mention in the Constitution, Marshall wrote, the section of the Judiciary Act of 1789 authorizing the Court to issue writs was unconstitutional. Thus, the Supreme Court denied itself the power to issue writs of mandamus but established its far greater power to judge the constitutionality of laws. In doing so, Marshall fashioned the theory of judicial review. Because the Constitution was "the supreme law of the land," Marshall wrote, any federal or state act contrary to the Constitution must be null and void. This power of the Supreme Court to determine the constitutionality of legislation and presidential acts enhanced the independence of the judiciary and breathed life into the Constitution.

Election of 1804

In the first election after the Twelfth Amendment's ratification, Jefferson dropped Burr as his running mate and, to have a North-South balance, chose George Clinton of New York. They swamped their opponents—South Carolinian Charles Cotesworth Pinckney and New Yorker Rufus King—in the electoral college by 162 votes to 14, carrying fifteen of the seventeen states. That 1804 election escalated the animosity between Burr and Hamilton, who supported Burr's rival in the New York gubernatorial election. When Hamilton called Burr a liar, Burr challenged Hamilton to a duel. Because New York had outlawed dueling, the encounter happened in New Jersey. Details of the duel remain hazy but the outcome was clear: Hamilton died after being shot by Burr. New York and New Jersey prosecutors indicted Burr for murder.

Burr fled to the West. While historians disagree about his motives, the "Burr Conspiracy" was understood at the time to involve a scheme with Brigadier General James Wilkinson to create a new empire by militarily taking what is now Texas and

Link to a Federalist handbill attacking Aarron Burr.

by persuading existing western territories to leave the United States. Tried for treason in 1807, Burr faced a prosecution aided by President Jefferson but overseen by Jefferson's rival Chief Justice Marshall. Prompted by Marshall to interpret treason narrowly, the jury acquitted Burr, who fled to Europe.

Nationalism and Culture

As statesmen bickered, other Americans conveyed their nationalist visions artistically. Nearly three decades after the Constitution's ratification, painters continued to memorialize great birth scenes of American nationhood, such as the Declaration of Independence's signing, Revolutionary War battles, and the Constitutional Convention. Four of John Trumbull's revolutionary scenes, commissioned in 1817, still hang on the Capitol building rotunda in Washington.

Architecturally, Americans self-consciously constructed an independent nation. Designed by Major Pierre Charles L'Enfant, the city of Washington was meant to embody a "reciprocity of sight": Each of the government's three branches—the legislative, judicial, and executive—should keep an eye on one another. Across America, wealthier people commissioned "federal" style homes, which imitated the simplicity of classical architecture.

The era's best-selling book was Noah Webster's spelling book, which proposed making English more "republican." It sold an estimated 100 million copies by the end of the nineteenth century. Webster advocated a national language that, unlike "King's English," would not require elite training. Words should be spelled as they sound—for example, "honor" should replace "honour." A shared language would unite an increasingly far-flung population.

National Expansion Westward

By 1800, hundreds of thousands of white Americans had settled in the rich Ohio River and Mississippi River valleys, intruding on Indian lands. In the Northwest, they raised foodstuffs, primarily wheat; in the Southwest, they cultivated cotton. During the American Revolution, cotton production was profitable only for the Sea Island planters in South Carolina and Georgia, who grew the long-staple variety. Short-staple cotton, which grew in the interior, was unmarketable because its sticky seeds required removal by hand. After New England inventor **Eli Whitney** designed a cotton gin in 1793, allowing one person to remove the same number of seeds that previously required fifty people, cultivation of short-staple cotton spread rapidly into Louisiana, Mississippi, Alabama, Arkansas, and Tennessee. The cotton gin greatly increased the demand for slaves, who seeded, tended, and harvested cotton fields.

> Why was the Louisiana Purchase among Jefferson's most popular decisions as president?

Eli Whitney: Invented the cotton gin that made cleaning of southern cotton fast and cheap.

American settlers depended on free access to the Mississippi River and its Gulf port, New Orleans. Whoever controlled the port of New Orleans had a hand on the American economy's throat.

New Orleans

Spain, which acquired France's territory west of the Mississippi after the Seven Years' War (1763), secretly transferred it back to France in 1800 and 1801. American officials discovered the transfer in 1802, when Napoleon seemed poised to rebuild a French empire in the New World.

At the time of the Louisiana Purchase in 1803, New Orleans was already a bustling port, though boosters predicted an even brighter future under American "wings."

American concerns intensified when Spanish officials, on the eve of ceding control to the French, violated Pinckney's treaty by denying Americans the privilege of storing their products at New Orleans prior to transshipment to foreign markets. Western farmers and eastern merchants thought Napoleon had closed the port; they talked war.

To relieve the pressure for war and win western farmers' support, Jefferson urged Congress to authorize the call-up of eighty thousand militiamen. He also sent Virginia Governor James Monroe to join Robert Livingston in France to buy the port of New Orleans and as much of the Mississippi valley as possible. Arriving in Paris in April 1803, Monroe learned that France had already offered to sell Louisiana to the United States for a mere $15 million. With St. Domingue torn from French control by revolution and slave revolt, Napoleon abandoned dreams of a New World empire and no longer needed Louisiana as its breadbasket. He urgently needed money to wage war against Britain. On April 30, Monroe and Livingston signed a treaty buying the 827,000-square-mile territory (see Map 9.1).

Louisiana Purchase: The United States bought the Louisiana Territory (the area from the Mississippi River to the Rocky Mountains) from France in 1803 for $15 million. The purchase virtually doubled the area of the United States.

Louisiana Purchase

The **Louisiana Purchase** ensured that the United States would control the Mississippi's mouth, pleasing western settlers who relied on the river to market their goods. It also inspired those who imagined the United States as the nexus of international trade networks reaching between Europe and Asia. Louisiana promised to fulfill easterners' dreams of cheap, fertile lands. Its vast expanse meant, too, that land could be reserved for Indians displaced by white settlers and their black slaves. But some doubted its constitutionality; others worried that it belied the Democratic-Republicans' commitment to debt reduction; and some New England Federalists complained that it undermined their commercial interests and threatened the republic by spreading the population beyond where it could be controlled. Overall, though, the Louisiana Purchase was the most popular achievement of Jefferson's presidency.

When the United States acquired Louisiana, hundreds of thousands of people there became American subjects, including Native Americans from various nations, as well as people of European and African descent—or, often, a complex mixture of the two. Around New Orleans, Louisiana's colonial heritage was reflected in its people: creoles of French and Spanish descent, slaves of African descent, free people of color, and Acadians, or Cajuns (descendants of French settlers in eastern Canada), and some Germans, Irish, and English. The 1810 census reported that 97,000 non-Indians lived in the area. Although Jefferson imagined the West as an "empire of liberty," free people of color and slaves soon discovered they were excluded from the Louisiana Purchase treaty's provision that "the inhabitants of the ceded territory" would gain American citizenship. Denied the right to vote and serve on juries, New Orleans' people of color fought to retain their rights to form families and to bequeath as they pleased, and some succeeded.

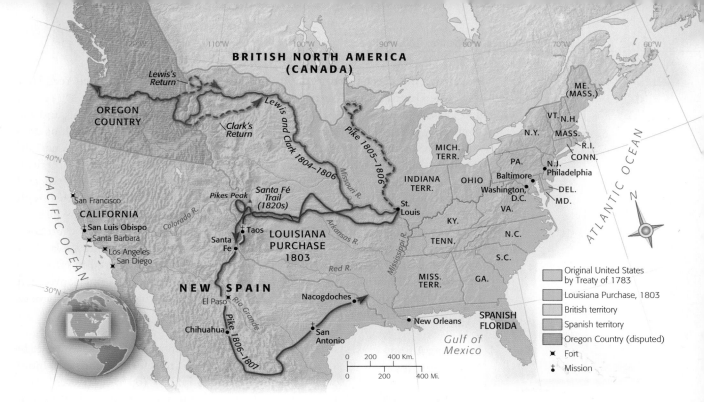

MAP 9.1

Louisiana Purchase

The Louisiana Purchase (1803) doubled the area of the United States and opened the trans-Mississippi West for American settlement.

Source: Copyright © Cengage Learning.

Lewis and Clark Expedition

Jefferson had a long-standing interest in the trans-Mississippi West, fearing that, if Americans did not claim it, the British, who still controlled present-day Canada and parts of the Pacific Northwest, would. He launched a military-style mission to chart the region's commercial possibilities—its water passages to the Pacific and trading opportunities with Indians—while cataloguing its geography, peoples, flora, and fauna.

The expedition, headed by Meriwether Lewis and William Clark, began in May 1804 and lasted for more than two years; it traveled up the Missouri River, across the Rockies, and down the Columbia to the Pacific Ocean—and back. The **Lewis and Clark Expedition** members "discovered" (as they saw it) dozens of previously unknown Indian tribes. Although the Corps of Discovery, as the expedition came to be called, was prepared for possible conflict, its goal was peaceable: to foster trade relations, win political allies, and tap into Indians' knowledge of the landscape. Lewis and Clark brought twenty-one bags of gifts for Native American leaders to establish goodwill and to stimulate interest in trade. Most interactions were cordial, but when Indians were unimpressed by the gifts, tensions arose.

The Corps of Discovery proved democratic in seating enlisted men on courts-martial and allowing Clark's black slave York and the expedition's female guide **Sacagawea** to vote on where to locate winter quarters in 1805. But, unlike other

Lewis and Clark Expedition: Expedition led by Meriwether Lewis and William Clark to explore the Louisiana Territory.

Sacagawea: Female guide who aided Lewis and Clark in exploring the Louisiana Territory.

expedition members, neither York nor Sacagawea drew wages, and when York later demanded his freedom, Clark repaid him with "a severe trouncing."

Lewis and Clark failed to discover a Northwest Passage to the Pacific, and the route they mapped across the Rockies proved perilous, but their explorations contributed to nationalist visions of American expansion. Fossils and Native American artifacts they collected were displayed in Charles Willson Peale's "American Museum," an institution emphasizing the uniqueness of America's geography and its republican experiment. Nationalists overlooked Indians' land claims. Although Jefferson had more sympathy for Indians than did many contemporaries—he took interest in their cultures and believed Indians to be intellectually equal to whites—he lobbied, unsuccessfully, for a constitutional amendment that would transport them west of the Mississippi into Louisiana Territory. He became involved in efforts to pressure the Chickasaws to sell their land, and if legal methods failed, he advocated trickery. Traders, he suggested, might run them into debt, which they would have to repay "by a cessation of lands."

Divisions Among Indian Peoples

Some Indian nations adopted white customs as a means of survival and often agreed to sell their lands and move west. These "accommodationists" (or "progressives") were opposed by "traditionalists," who urged adherence to native ways and refused to relinquish their lands. Distinctions between accommodationists and traditionalists were not always so clear-cut, however.

In the early 1800s, two Shawnee brothers, Tenskwatawa (1775–1837) and **Tecumseh** (1768–1813), led a traditionalist revolt against American encroachment by fostering a pan-Indian federation centered in the Old Northwest and reaching into parts of the South. By the 1800s, the Shawnees lost most of their Ohio land, occupying scattered sites there and in the Michigan and Louisiana territories. Despondent, Lalawethika—Tenskwatawa's name as a youth—turned to a combination of European remedies (particularly whiskey) and Native American ones, becoming a shaman in 1804. But when European diseases ravaged his village, he despaired.

Tecumseh: The Shawnee leader who sought to unite several tribes from Canada to Georgia against encroachment on their lands by American settlers; allied with the British in the War of 1812.

Tenskwatawa and Tecumseh

Lalawethika emerged from an illness in 1805 as a new man, renamed Tenskwatawa ("the Open Door") or—by whites—"the Prophet." Claiming to have died and been resurrected, he traveled in the Ohio River valley as a religious leader, attacking the decline of moral values among Native Americans, warning against whiskey and condemning intertribal battles. He urged Indians to return to the old ways: to hunt with bows and arrows, not guns; to stop wearing hats; and to give up bread for corn and beans.

By 1808, Tenskwatawa and his older brother Tecumseh focused on resisting American aggression. They invited all Indians to settle in pan-Indian towns in Indiana, first at Greenville (1806–1808) and then at Prophetstown (1808–1812). This challenged the treaty-making process by denying the claims of Indians who were given the same land under the Treaty of Greenville of 1795. Younger Indians flocked to Tecumseh, the more political of the two brothers.

Convinced that only an Indian federation could stop white settlement, Tecumseh sought to unify northern and southern Indians from Canada to Georgia. Among southern Indians, only one Creek faction welcomed him, but his efforts alarmed white settlers and government officials. In November 1811, while Tecumseh was in the South, Indiana governor William Henry Harrison moved against Tenskwatawa's followers. During the battle of Tippecanoe, the army burned their town; as they fled, the Indians exacted revenge on white settlers. When Harrison avowed reprisals, Tecumseh allied with the British. This alliance in the West, combined with American neutrality rights on the high seas, was propelling the United States toward war with Britain.

The Nation in the Orbit of Europe

The republic's economy relied heavily on fishing and the carrying trade, with the American merchant marine transporting commodities between nations. Merchants in Boston, Salem, and Philadelphia traded with China, sending cloth and metal to swap for furs with Chinook Indians on the Oregon coast, and then sailing to China to trade for porcelain, tea, and silk. The slave trade lured American ships to Africa. Not long after Jefferson's first inaugural address, the United States was at war with Tripoli—a state along North Africa's Barbary Coast—over a principle that would long be a cornerstone of American foreign policy: freedom of the seas. That is, outside of national territorial waters, the high seas should be open for free transit.

> What led to the War of 1812?

First Barbary War

In 1801, the bashaw (pasha) of Tripoli declared war on the United States for its refusal to pay tribute for safe passage of its ships through the Mediterranean. After two years of stalemate, Jefferson declared a blockade of Tripoli, but when the American frigate *Philadelphia* ran aground in the harbor, its three hundred officers and sailors were imprisoned. Jefferson refused to ransom them, and a small American force accompanied by Arab, Greek, and African mercenaries marched from Egypt to the "shores of Tripoli" to seize the port of Derne. A treaty ended the war in 1805, but the United States continued to pay tribute to the three other Barbary states—Algiers, Morocco, and Tunis—until 1815. In the intervening years, the United States became embroiled in European conflicts.

At first, Jefferson distanced the nation from European turmoil in the wake of the French Revolution. After the Senate ratified the Jay Treaty in 1795, the United States and Great Britain reconciled. Britain withdrew from its western forts on American soil and interfered less in American trade with France. Then, in May 1803, two weeks after Napoleon sold Louisiana to the United States, France was at war against Britain and, later, Britain's allies, Prussia, Austria, and Russia. Initially, the United States benefited, as merchants gained control of most of the West Indian trade. After 1805, when Britain defeated the French and Spanish fleets at Trafalgar, Britain's Royal Navy tightened its control of the oceans. Two months later, Napoleon crushed the Russian and Austrian armies at Austerlitz. Stalemated, France and Britain launched a commercial war, blockading trade and costing the United States dearly.

Threats to American Sovereignty

To replenish their supply of sailors, British vessels stopped American ships and impressed (forcibly recruited) British deserters, British-born naturalized American seamen, and other sailors suspected of being British. Perhaps six to eight thousand Americans were impressed between 1803 and 1812. Alleged deserters—many of them American citizens—faced British courts-martial. Americans saw the principle of "once a British subject, always a British subject" as a mockery of U.S. citizenship and their national sovereignty. Americans also resented the British interfering with their West Indian trade and seizing American vessels within U.S. territorial waters.

In April 1806, Congress responded with the Non Importation Act, barring British manufactured goods from American ports. Because the act exempted most cloth and metal articles, it had little impact on British trade; instead, it warned the British what to expect if they continued to violate American neutral rights. In November, Jefferson suspended the act while Baltimore lawyer William Pinkney joined James Monroe in London to negotiate a settlement. The treaty they carried home did not mention impressments; hence, the president never submitted it for ratification.

Tense Anglo-American relations came to a head in June 1807 when the USS *Chesapeake,* sailing from Norfolk for the Mediterranean, was stopped by the British frigate *Leopard,* whose officers demanded to search the ship for British deserters. Refused, the *Leopard* opened fire, killing three Americans and wounding eighteen others. The British seized four deserters, three of whom held American citizenship; one was hanged. The incident outraged Americans and exposed American military weakness.

The Embargo of 1807

Jefferson responded with what he called "peaceable coercion." In July, the president closed American waters to British warships and increased military and naval expenditures. In December 1807, Jefferson put economic pressure on Great Britain by invoking the Non-Importation Act, followed by the **Embargo Act**. The embargo, which forbade exports from the United States to any country, was a short-term measure to avoid war by pressuring Britain and France to respect American rights and by preventing confrontation between American merchant vessels and European warships.

Embargo Act of 1807: Forbade exports from the United States to any country.

The embargo's biggest economic impact, however, fell on the United States. Exports declined by 80 percent in 1808, squeezing New England shippers and their workers. Manufacturers fared well, as the domestic market became theirs exclusively. Merchants began to shift from shipping to manufacturing. In 1807, there were twenty cotton and woolen mills in New England; by 1813, there were more than two hundred.

International Slave Trade

They had only to look at the vibrant slave trade to see how scarcity bred demand. With Jefferson's encouragement, Congress voted in 1807 to abolish the international slave trade as of January 1, 1808—the earliest date permissible under the Constitution. South Carolina still allowed the legal importation of slaves, but most of the state's planters favored a ban, nervous about adding to the black population of a state where whites were outnumbered. The final bill provided that smuggled slaves would be sold according to the laws of the state or territory in which they arrived, underscoring that even illegal slaves were property. Had the bill not done so, threatened one Georgia congressman, the result might have been "resistance to the authority of the Government," even civil war. During the last four months of 1807, sixteen thousand African slaves arrived at Gadsden Wharf in Charleston, where they were detained by merchants eager to wait out the January 1 deadline. Although many slaves—hundreds, if not thousands—died in the disease-ridden holding pens before they could be sold, merchants calculated the increased value of those who survived until the ban took effect would outweigh the losses. After January 1, 1808, a brisk—and profitable—illegal slave trade took over. In 1819, Congress authorized the president to use force to intercept slave ships along the African coast, but the small American navy could not halt the illicit trade.

Election of 1808

As the 1808 presidential election approached, Democratic Republicans suffered from factional dissent and dissatisfaction in seaboard states hobbled by the trade restrictions. Although nine state legislatures passed resolutions urging Jefferson to run again, the president declined a third term. He supported James Madison, his secretary of state, as the Democratic-Republican standard-bearer. Madison won the endorsement of the party's congressional caucus, and Madison and Vice President George Clinton headed the ticket. Charles Cotesworth Pinckney and Rufus King again ran on the Federalist ticket.

Boarding and Taking of the American Ship Chesapeake (1816) portrays crew from the British frigate *Leopard* fighting to search the USS *Chesapeake* for British navy deserters. The sailors of the *Chesapeake* resisted, but the British overpowered them and seized four deserters, three of them American citizens. Americans were humiliated and angered by the British violation of American rights.

The younger Federalists played up the widespread disaffection with Democratic-Republican policy, especially the embargo. Pinckney received only 47 electoral votes to Madison's 122, but he carried all of New England except Vermont, and won Delaware. Federalists also gained seats in Congress and captured the New York State legislature. Still, the transition from one Democratic-Republican administration to the next went smoothly.

Women and Politics

Wives eased the transition of elected and appointed officials by encouraging political and diplomatic negotiation. Such negotiations often occurred in social settings, even private homes. Women played crucial roles in bridging ideological divides by fostering conversation, providing an ear or a voice for unofficial messages, and—in international affairs—standing as surrogates for their nation. Wives' interactions among themselves served political purposes, too: when First Lady Dolley Madison visited congressmen's wives, she cultivated goodwill for her husband while collecting recipes so she could serve regionally diverse cuisine at White House functions.

Jeffersonians wanted women's support of the embargo. Sympathetic women responded by spurning imported fabric and making (or directing their slaves to make) homespun clothing. Federalists, however, encouraged women to "keep commerce alive," and sympathetic women bought smuggled goods.

Failed Policies

Under domestic opposition, the embargo collapsed. Instead, the Non-Intercourse Act of 1809 reopened trade with all nations except Britain and France, and authorized the president to resume trade with those two nations once they respected American neutral rights. In June

1809, President Madison reopened trade with Britain after its minister to the United States offered assurances that Britain would repeal restrictions on American trade. But his Majesty's government in London repudiated the minister's assurances, leading Madison to revert to nonintercourse.

When the Non-Intercourse Act expired in 1810, Congress substituted Macon's Bill Number 2, reopening trade with Great Britain and France but providing that, when either nation stopped violating American commercial rights, the president would suspend American commerce with the other. When Napoleon accepted, Madison declared nonintercourse on Great Britain in 1811. Although the French continued to seize American ships, Britain became the focus of American hostility because it dominated the seas.

In spring 1812, the British admiralty ordered its ships not to stop, search, or seize American warships, and in June Britain reopened the seas to American shipping. But before word of this policy change reached America, Congress declared war.

Link to President Madison's "War Message" to Congress.

Mr. Madison's War

The House voted 79 to 49 for war; the Senate, 19 to 13. Democratic-Republicans favored war by 98 to 23; Federalists opposed it 39 to 0. Those who favored war, including President Madison, pointed to assaults on American sovereignty and honor: impressment, violation of neutral trading rights, and British alliances with western Indians. Others saw an opportunity to conquer and annex British Canada. Most militant were land-hungry southerners and westerners—the "**War Hawks**"—led by John C. Calhoun of South Carolina and first-term congressman and House Speaker Henry Clay of Kentucky. Most representatives from the coastal states, especially the Northeast, feared trade disruption and opposed "Mr. Madison's War."

War Hawks: Militant Republicans who demanded more aggressive policies and who wanted war with Britain.

Initially, Federalists benefited from antiwar sentiment. They joined renegade Democratic-Republicans in supporting New York City mayor DeWitt Clinton for president in 1812. Clinton lost to Madison by 128 to 89 electoral votes, but Federalists gained some congressional seats and carried many local elections. The pro-war South and the West remained solidly Democratic-Republican.

The War of 1812

What were the consequences of the War of 1812?

Lasting from 1812 to 1815, the war unfolded in skirmishes, for which the U.S. armed forces were ill prepared. The U.S. Military Academy at West Point, founded in 1802, produced only eighty-nine regular officers, and campaigns were executed poorly. Although the U.S. Navy had a corps of experienced officers, it proved no match for the Royal Navy.

The government's efforts to lure recruits—with sign-up bonuses, and promises of three months' pay and rights to purchase 160 acres of western land—met with mixed success. At first, recruitment went well among westerners, motivated by civic spirit, desire for land, anti-Indian sentiment, and fears of Tecumseh's pan-Indian organization. But with pay delays and inadequate supplies, recruitment dwindled. In New England, Federalists discouraged enlistments. Militias in New England and New York often refused to fight outside their states. Desperate, New York offered freedom to slaves who enlisted, and compensation to their owners, and the U.S. Army made the same offer to slaves in the Old Northwest and in Canada. But in the Deep South, fear of arming slaves kept them out of the military except in New Orleans, where a free black militia dated back to Spanish control of Louisiana.

The British recruited slaves by promising freedom in exchange for service. In the end, British forces outnumbered the Americans.

Invasion of Canada

Despite recruitment problems, Americans expected to take Canada easily. Canada's population was sparse, its army small, and the Great Lakes inaccessible to the Royal Navy in the Atlantic. Americans hoped, too, that French Canadians might welcome U.S. forces.

Americans aimed to split Canadian forces and isolate pro-British Indians, especially Tecumseh, whom the British had promised an Indian nation in the Great Lakes region. In July 1812, U.S. general William Hull, territorial governor of Michigan, marched his troops, who outnumbered those of the British, into Upper Canada (modern Ontario), hoping to conquer Montreal. But by abandoning Mackinac Island and Fort Dearborn, and by surrendering Fort Detroit, he left the Midwest exposed. Captain Zachary Taylor provided the only bright spot, giving the Americans a land victory with his September 1812 defense of Fort Harrison in Indiana Territory. By the winter of 1812–1813, the British controlled about half of the Old Northwest.

Naval Battles

Despite victories on the Atlantic by the USS *Constitution* (nicknamed "Old Ironsides"), the USS *Wasp,* and the USS *United States,* the American navy—which began the war with just seventeen ships—could not match the powerful Royal Navy. By 1814, the Royal Navy blockaded nearly all American ports along the Atlantic and Gulf coasts. After 1811, American trade overseas declined by nearly 90 percent, and the lost customs duties threatened to bankrupt the federal government and prostrate New England.

The contest for control of the Great Lakes, the key to the war in the Northwest, evolved as a shipbuilding race. Under Master Commandant Oliver Hazard Perry and shipbuilder Noah Brown, the United States outbuilt the British on Lake Erie and defeated them at the bloody Battle of Put-in-Bay on September 10, 1813, gaining control of Lake Erie.

Burning Capitals

A ragged group of Kentucky militia volunteers, armed with swords and knives, marched 20 to 30 miles a day to join General William Henry Harrison's forces in Ohio. Now 4,500 strong, Harrison's forces took Detroit before crossing into Canada, where at the Battle of the Thames they defeated British, Shawnee, and Chippewa forces in October 1813. Among the dead was Tecumseh. The Americans then razed the Canadian capital of York (now Toronto).

After defeating Napoleon in Europe in April 1814, the British launched a land counteroffensive against the United States, concentrating on the Chesapeake Bay. Royal troops occupied Washington, D.C., in August and set it ablaze. The presidential mansion and parts of the city burned all night. The president and cabinet fled. Dolley Madison stayed to oversee the removal of cabinet documents and to save a Gilbert Stuart portrait of George Washington.

The British intended the attack on Washington as a diversion. The major battle occurred in September 1814 at Baltimore, where the Americans held firm. Francis Scott Key, detained on a British ship, watched the bombardment of Fort McHenry and wrote "The Star-Spangled Banner" (which became the national anthem in 1931). The British inflicted heavy damage but achieved little militarily; their offensive on Lake Champlain also failed. The war reached a stalemate.

Selling War

The War of 1812 was not always a popular war, but in its aftermath many Americans trumpeted the war's successes. To the left, we see a recruitment poster from 1812, in which General William Henry Harrison seeks additional cavalrymen. Hampered in part by transportation difficulties, Harrison is unable to offer much—soldiers are even requested to supply their own bacon as well as their own horses—but he does promise that the expedition will be short, undoubtedly a concern to men eager to return to the fall harvest. To the right, we see a handkerchief made in 1815, after the Treaty of Ghent and the Battle of New Orleans; it features the United States' victories against the world's greatest naval power, Great Britain. Made with a decorative border, the kerchief may have been for display. What similar values do we see promoted in the two images, and what factors—such as their intended audiences, their purposes, and when they were created—might account for any differences between them?

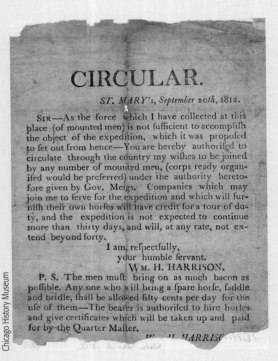

Chicago History Museum

With a tiny regular army, the United States often had to rely on short-term recruits to wage war on the British.

© Collection of the New-York Historical Society, USA/Bridgeman Art Library Ltd.

Made in 1815 from cotton textiles—whose domestic production soared during the War of 1812, with trade cut off from Britain—this handkerchief helps promote American "liberty and independence."

War in the South

To the south, two wars were happening simultaneously. In the Patriots War, a private army of Americans, secretly supported by the Madison administration, tried to seize East Florida from Spain. What started as a settlers' rebellion along the Georgia-Florida border—to grab more land, strike at the Spaniards' Indian allies, and later to protest the Spaniards' arming of black soldiers—turned into a war, with the Patriots backed by U.S. forces and Georgia militia. Federalists condemned the invasion of a neutral territory, and the Senate refused twice (in 1812 and 1813) to support a military seizure of Florida. Embarrassed, Madison withdrew his support, and the movement collapsed in May 1814.

In the war with Britain, the southern theater proved more successful. The final campaign began with an American attack on the Red Stick Creeks along the Gulf of Mexico and the British around New Orleans and ended with Americans gaining new territory. Responding to Tecumseh's call to resist U.S. expansion, in 1813 the Red Sticks attacked Fort Mims, about 40 miles from Mobile, killing hundreds of white men, women, and children. Seeking revenge, General Andrew Jackson of Tennessee rallied his militiamen and Indian opponents of the Red Sticks and crushed the Red Sticks at Horseshoe Bend (in present-day Alabama) in March 1814. This led to the Treaty of Fort Jackson, in which the Creeks ceded 23 million acres, or about half of their holdings, and withdrew to southern and western Mississippi Territory.

Jackson became a major general and continued south toward the Gulf of Mexico. After seizing Pensacola (in Spanish Florida) and then securing Mobile, Jackson's forces marched to New Orleans. Three weeks later, on January 8, 1815, Jackson's poorly trained army held its ground against two British frontal assaults. At day's end, more than two thousand British soldiers lay dead or wounded, while the Americans suffered only twenty-one casualties.

The Battle of New Orleans occurred two weeks after the war's conclusion: word had not yet reached America that British and United States diplomats had signed the **Treaty of Ghent** on December 24, 1814. Still, the Battle of New Orleans catapulted General Andrew Jackson to national political prominence.

Treaty of Ghent: Treaty that ended the War of 1812, restoring the prewar status quo.

Treaty of Ghent

The Treaty of Ghent essentially restored the prewar status quo. It provided for an end to hostilities, release of prisoners, restoration of conquered territory, and arbitration of boundary disputes. But the United States received no satisfaction on impressment, blockades, or other maritime rights for neutrals, and British demands for territorial cessions from Maine to Minnesota went unmet. The British dropped their promise of an independent Indian nation.

Napoleon's defeat allowed the United States to discard its prewar demands, because peace in Europe made impressment and interference with American commerce moot issues. Similarly, war-weary Britain—its treasury nearly depleted—stopped pressing for military victory.

American Sovereignty Reasserted

The War of 1812 affirmed the independence of the American republic and ensured Canada's independence from the United States. Trade and territorial disputes with Great Britain continued, but they never again led to war. The return of peace allowed the United States to again focus on the Barbary Coast, where the dey (governor) of Algiers declared war on the United States. In the Second Barbary War, U.S. forces held hundreds of Algerians while negotiating a treaty in the summer of 1815 that forever freed the United States from paying tributes for passage in the Mediterranean. The Second Barbary War reaffirmed America's commitment to freedom of the seas.

Hartford Convention: Federalist meeting that was perceived as disloyalty during time of war and began the downfall of the party.

Domestic Consequences

The War of 1812 had profound domestic consequences. The Federalists' hopes of returning to national prominence diminished with the **Hartford Convention.** New England delegates—frustrated by the stalemated war and the shattered New England economy—met in Hartford, Connecticut, for three weeks in the winter of 1814–1815 to discuss revising the national compact or pulling out of the republic. Although moderates prevented a resolution of secession—withdrawal from the Union— delegates condemned the war and the embargo while endorsing constitutional changes that would weaken the South's power and make it harder to declare war. When news arrived of Jackson's victory in New Orleans and the Treaty of Ghent, the Hartford Convention made the Federalists look wrong-headed, even treasonous. By the 1820s, the party faded from the national scene.

With Tecumseh's death, midwestern Indians lost their powerful leader; with the British withdrawal, they lost their strongest ally. Some accommodationists, such as the Cherokees, temporarily flourished, but the war effectively disarmed traditionalists bent on resisting American expansion. Although the Treaty of Ghent pledged the United States to end hostilities with Indians and to restore their prewar "possessions, rights, and privileges," Indians could not make the United States honor the agreement.

For American farmers, the war opened formerly Indian land for cultivating cotton in the Old Southwest and wheat in the Old Northwest. It stimulated industry, as Americans could no longer rely on overseas imports, particularly textiles. The War of 1812 thus fueled demand for raw cotton, and the newly acquired lands in the Southwest beckoned southerners who migrated there with slaves, or with expectations of someday owning slaves. The war's conclusion accelerated three trends that would dominate U.S. history for upcoming decades: westward expansion, industrial takeoff, and slavery's entrenchment.

The Nationalist Program

How did the American System mark the triumph of Federalist economic policy?

In his final year as president, James Madison and the Democratic-Republicans absorbed the Federalist idea that the federal government should encourage economic growth. His agenda, which Henry Clay later called the American System, included a national bank, improved transportation, and a protective tariff—a tax on imported goods to protect American manufacturers from foreign competition. Yet true to his Jeffersonian roots, Madison argued that only a constitutional amendment could authorize the federal government to build local roads and canals.

American System

Clay and other congressional leaders, such as Calhoun of South Carolina, believed the American System would ease sectional tension. The tariff would stimulate New England industry, whose goods would find markets in the South and West. The South's and West's agricultural products—cotton and foodstuffs—would feed New England mills and workers. Manufactured and agricultural products would move along roads and canals that tariff revenues would fund. A national bank would handle the transactions.

In 1816, Congress chartered the Second Bank of the United States (the bank's first charter expired in 1811) to serve as a depository for federal funds and to issue currency, collect taxes, and pay the government's debts. The Second Bank of the United States would also oversee state and local banks, ensuring that their paper money had backing in specie (precious metals). Like its predecessor, the bank mixed public and private ownership; the government provided one-fifth of the bank's capital and appointed one-fifth of its directors.

Congress also passed the Tariff of 1816, which taxed imported woolens and cottons, iron, leather, hats, paper, and sugar. The tariff divided the nation. New England and the western and Middle Atlantic states would benefit from it and thus applauded it, whereas many southerners objected that it raised prices on consumer goods and could prompt Britain to retaliate with a tariff on cotton.

Southerners such as Calhoun promoted roads and canals to "bind the republic together." However, on March 3, 1817, the day before leaving office, President Madison, citing constitutional scruples, vetoed Calhoun's "Bonus Bill," which would have authorized federal funding for such public works.

Early Internal Improvements

Federalists and Democratic-Republicans agreed that improved transportation would promote national prosperity. For Federalists, roads and canals were necessary for commercial development; for Jeffersonians, they would spur western expansion and agrarian growth. In 1806, Congress passed (and Jefferson had signed) a bill authorizing funding for the Cumberland Road (later, the National Road), running 130 miles between Cumberland, Maryland, and Wheeling, Virginia (now West Virginia). In 1820, Congress authorized a survey of the National Road to Columbus, Ohio, a project completed in 1833.

Most transportation initiatives received funding from states, private investors, or both. Between 1817 and 1825, New York constructed the **Erie Canal**, linking the Great Lakes to the Atlantic seaboard. Although southern states constructed modest canals, the South's trade depended on river going steamboats after 1817, when steamboats began traveling regularly upriver on the Mississippi. With canals and steamboats, western agricultural products could travel to market faster and less expensively, fueling westward expansion. Canals expanded commercial networks into regions without natural waterways and reoriented midwestern commerce through the North.

Erie Canal: Major canal that linked the Great Lakes to the Atlantic seaboard, opening the upper Midwest to wider development.

The Era of Good Feelings

James Monroe, Madison's successor, was the third Virginian elected president since 1801. A former senator and twice governor of Virginia, he served under Madison as secretary of state and of war and used his association with Jefferson and Madison to attain the presidency. In 1816, he and his running mate, Daniel Tompkins, trounced the last Federalist presidential nominee, Rufus King, garnering all the electoral votes except those of the Federalist strongholds of Massachusetts, Connecticut, and Delaware. A Boston newspaper dubbed this one-party period the **"Era of Good Feelings."**

Led by Federalist chief justice John Marshall, the Supreme Court became the bulwark of the nationalist agenda. In **_McCulloch v. Maryland_** (1819), the Court struck down a Maryland law taxing banks that were not chartered by its legislature—a law aimed at hindering the Baltimore branch of the Second Bank of the United States. At issue was state versus federal jurisdiction. Writing for a unanimous Court, Marshall asserted the supremacy of the federal government over the states. The Court ruled, too, that

Era of Good Feelings: Period of one-party politics during administration of James Monroe.

McCulloch v. Maryland: Supreme Court decision that restated national supremacy over states.

Congress had the power to charter banks. The Marshall Court thus supported the Federalist view that the federal government could promote interstate commerce.

Government Promotion of Market Expansion

Later Supreme Court cases validated government promotion of economic development and encouraged business enterprise. In *Gibbons v. Ogden* (1824), the Supreme Court overturned the New York law granting Robert Fulton and Robert Livingston a monopoly on the New York–New Jersey steamboat trade. Chief Justice Marshall ruled that the federal power to license new enterprises took precedence over New York's grant of monopoly rights and declared that Congress's power under the commerce clause of the Constitution extended to "every species of commercial intercourse." Within two years, the number of steamboats in New York increased from six to forty-three. A later ruling under Chief Justice Roger Taney, *Charles River Bridge v. Warren Bridge* (1837), encouraged new enterprises and technologies by favoring competition over monopoly.

Federal and state courts, in conjunction with state legislatures, encouraged the proliferation of corporations—organizations holding property and transacting business as if they were individuals. Corporation owners, called shareholders, were granted limited liability, or freedom from personal responsibility for the company's debts beyond their original investment.

The government assisted commercial development, too, by expanding the number of U.S. post offices from three thousand in 1815 to fourteen thousand in 1845 and by protecting inventions through patent laws and domestic industries through tariffs on foreign imports.

Boundary Settlements

Monroe's secretary of state, John Quincy Adams, son of John and Abigail Adams, managed the nation's foreign policy from 1817 to 1825. He pushed for expansion of American fishing rights in Atlantic waters, political distance from Europe, and peace. Under Adams's leadership, in 1817 the United States and Great Britain signed the Rush-Bagot Treaty limiting them to one ship each on Lake Champlain and Lake Ontario and to two ships each on the remaining Great Lakes. This first modern disarmament treaty demilitarized the U.S.-Canadian border. Adams then pushed for the Convention of 1818, which fixed the U.S.-Canadian boundary from Lake of the Woods in Minnesota westward to the Rockies along the 49th parallel. They disagreed on the boundary west of the Rockies, so Britain and the U.S. settled on joint occupation of Oregon for ten years (renewed indefinitely in 1827).

Adams's negotiations resulted in the Adams-Onís Treaty, in which the United States gained Florida. Although the Louisiana Purchase omitted reference to Spanish-ruled West Florida, the United States claimed the territory as far east as the Perdido River (the present-day Florida-Alabama border). During the War of 1812, the United States seized Mobile and the remainder of West Florida; after the war, Adams claimed East Florida. In 1819, Don Luís de Onís, the

Travelers, merchants, and livestock clogged portions of the National Road, shown here alongside Milestone 3 in Baltimore in 1829.

Courtesy of the Maryland Historical Society

Spanish minister to the United States, agreed to cede Florida without payment if the United States renounced its dubious claims to northern Mexico (Texas) and assumed $5 million of claims by American citizens against Spain. The Treaty also defined the southwestern boundary of the Louisiana Purchase and divided Spanish Mexico and Oregon Country at the 42nd parallel.

Monroe Doctrine

Adams's desire to insulate the United States and the Western Hemisphere from European conflict brought about his greatest achievement: the **Monroe Doctrine**. Between 1808 and 1822, the United Provinces of Río de la Plata (present-day northern Argentina, Paraguay, and Uruguay), Chile, Peru, Colombia, and Mexico broke from Spain. In 1822, the United States became the first nation outside Latin America to recognize the new states. But with reactionary regimes ascending in Europe and France now occupying Spain, the United States feared that continental powers would attempt to return the new Latin American states to colonial rule.

Monroe's message to Congress in December 1823 became known as the Monroe Doctrine. He announced that the American continents "are henceforth not to be considered subjects for future colonization by any European power." This addressed American anxiety about Latin America and Russian expansion beyond Alaska and its settlements in California. Monroe demanded nonintervention by Europe in the affairs of independent New World nations, and he pledged U.S. noninterference in European affairs, including Europe's existing New World colonies. European nations stayed out of New World affairs because they feared the British Royal Navy, not the United States' proclamations.

Monroe Doctrine: Foreign policy statement that proclaimed that American continents are not to be subjected to European colonization and demanded nonintervention by Europe into the New World nations.

Sectionalism Exposed

The embargo, the War of 1812, and postwar internal improvements encouraged the southern and northern economies to develop in different but interrelated ways. While the South became dependent on cotton, the North underwent an accelerated industrial development. With their commitment to an agrarian nation, Jeffersonians did not promote industry, but some entrepreneurs did.

How did the admission of new states after the War of 1812 ultimately divide the nation?

Early Industrial Development

Despite their separatism, Americans relied on British technology to combine the many steps of textile manufacturing—carding (or disentangling) fibers, spinning yarn, and weaving cloth—under one factory. The first American water-powered spinning mill was established in 1790 by Samuel Slater, a British immigrant who reconstructed from memory the complex machines he had used in England. But Slater's mill only carded and spun yarn; hand-weaving it into cloth was often done by farm women seeking to earn cash. In 1810, Bostonian Francis Cabot Lowell visited the British textile center of Manchester, touring factories and later sketching from memory what he had seen. In 1813, he and his business associates founded the Boston Manufacturing Company, uniting all phases of textile manufacturing under one roof in Waltham, Massachusetts. A decade later, the Boston Manufacturing Company established a model industrial village—named for its now-deceased founder—along the banks of the Merrimack River. At Lowell, Massachusetts, there were boarding houses for workers, a healthy alternative to Manchester's tenements and slums.

When the British flooded the American market with cheap textiles after the War of 1812, Lowell realized the domestic market required protection. He lobbied hard to include cotton textiles in the Tariff of 1816, persuading reluctant South Carolinians to support it.

Northern industrialization was linked to slavery. Much of the capital came from merchants who partly made their fortunes through the trade. Two of the most prominent industries—textiles and shoes—expanded with a growing southern cotton economy. Southern cotton fed northern textile mills, and northern shoe factories sold "Negro brogans" (work shoes) to southern planters.

Panic of 1819

Immediately after the war, the international demand for (and price of) American commodities reached new heights. Poor weather in Europe led to crop failures, increasing demand for northern foodstuffs and Southern cotton, which, in turn, touched off western land speculation. Speculators raced to buy large tracts of land at modest, government-established prices and then to resell them at a hefty profit to would-be settlers.

Prosperity proved short-lived. By the late 1810s, Europeans could grow their own food again, and Britain's new Corn Laws established high tariffs on imports. Cotton prices fell in England. Wars in Latin America interfered with mining and reduced the supply of precious metals, leading European nations to hoard specie. American banks furiously printed paper money and expanded credit even further. Fearful of inflation, the Second Bank of the United States demanded in 1819 that state banks repay loans in specie. State banks then called in the loans and mortgages they had made. Falling commodity prices meant that farmers could not pay their mortgages, and plummeting land values—from 50 to 75 percent in portions of the West—meant they could not meet their debts even by selling their farms. The nation's banking system collapsed, triggering a financial panic.

Foreclosures soared. Unemployment skyrocketed, reaching 75 percent in Philadelphia. Workers and their families could not make it through the winter without charity for food, clothing, and firewood.

Americans everywhere contemplated the virtues and hazards of rapid market expansion, disagreeing on where to place the blame for its shortcomings. Even as the nation's economy rebounded in the early 1820s, amid a flurry of internal improvement projects, no one could predict in what region or sector the nation's fortunes would lie.

Missouri Compromise

America also faced a political crisis in 1819 about slavery's westward expansion. Residents of the Missouri Territory petitioned Congress for admission to the Union with a constitution permitting slavery. Missouri's admission would give slaveholding states a two-vote majority in the Senate and set a precedent for new western states created from the vast Louisiana Purchase.

Following the Louisiana Purchase and especially after the end of the War of 1812, the American population surged westward, leading five new states to join the Union: Louisiana (1812), Indiana (1816), Mississippi (1817), Illinois (1818), and Alabama (1819). Of these, Louisiana, Mississippi, and Alabama permitted slavery. Because Missouri was on the same latitude as free Illinois, Indiana, and Ohio, its admission as a slave state would thrust slavery farther westward and northward.

For two and a half years, the issue dominated Congress. When Representative James Tallmadge Jr. of New York proposed gradual emancipation in Missouri, some

Links to the World

Industrial Piracy

Great Britain, which in the late eighteenth century pioneered mechanical weaving and power looms, knew the value of its head start in the industrial revolution and prohibited the export of textile technology. British-born brothers Samuel and John Slater, their Scottish-born power-loom-builder William Gilmore, and Bostonians Francis Cabot Lowell and Nathan Appleton evaded British restrictions to establish America's first textile factories.

As a supervisor in a British cotton-spinning factory, Samuel Slater had mastered the machinery and the process. To get around British technology laws, Slater emigrated to the United States disguised as a farmer. In 1790 in Pawtucket, Rhode Island, he opened the first water-powered spinning mill in America, rebuilding the complex machines from memory. With his brother John and their Rhode Island partners, Moses and Obadiah Brown and William Almy, Slater later built mills in Rhode Island and Massachusetts. In 1815, he hired a recent immigrant, William Gilmore, to build a water-powered loom like those in Britain. In the 1820s, the Slaters introduced steam-powered looms.

In 1810, while vacationing in Edinburgh, Scotland, Francis Cabot Lowell met fellow Bostonian Nathan Appleton. Impressed by the British textile mills, they planned to introduce water-powered mechanical weaving into the United States. Lowell went to Britain's textile center in Manchester, visiting and observing the factories by day; at night, he sketched the power looms and processes he had seen. Back in the United States, he and others formed the Boston Associates, which created the Waltham-Lowell Mills based on Lowell's industrial piracy. Within a few years, textiles would be a major American industry, and the Boston Associates would dominate it.

Thus, the modern American industrial revolution began with international links, not homegrown American inventions.

This contemporary painting shows the Boston Manufacturing Company's 1814 textile factory at Waltham, Massachusetts. All manufacturing processes were brought together under one roof, and the company built its first factories in rural New England to tap roaring rivers as a power source.

Courtesy of Gore Place Society, Waltham, Massachusetts

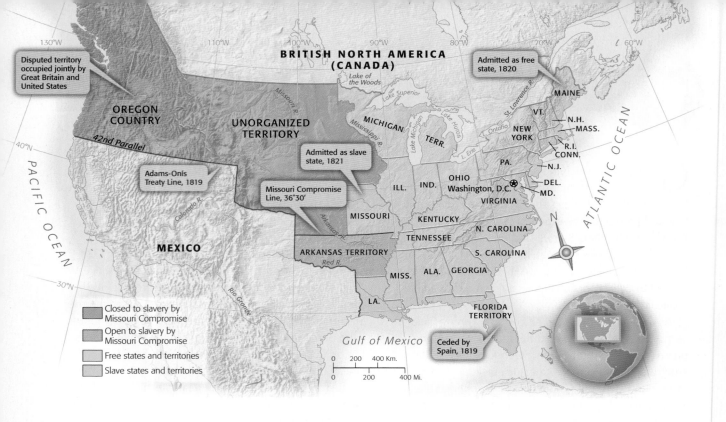

MAP 9.2

Missouri Compromise and the State of the Union, 1820

The compromise worked out by House Speaker Henry Clay established a formula that avoided debate over whether new states would allow or prohibit slavery. In the process, it divided the United States into northern and southern regions.

Source: Copyright © Cengage Learning

Missouri Compromise:
Sought to end the debate over the number of slave and free states admitted to the Union by admitting Missouri as a slave state and Maine as a free state and banned slavery in the Louisiana Territory north of the 36°30′ latitude line.

southerners accused the North of threatening to destroy the Union. The House, which had a northern majority, passed the Tallmadge Amendment, but the Senate rejected it.

House Speaker Henry Clay—himself a western slaveholder—suggested a compromise in 1820. Maine, carved out of Massachusetts, would enter as a free state, followed by Missouri as a slave state, maintaining the balance between slave and free states. In the rest of the Louisiana Territory north of Missouri's southern border of 36°30', slavery would be prohibited forever (see Map 9.2).

The compromise carried but almost unraveled when Missouri submitted a constitution barring free blacks from entering the state. Opponents contended that it violated the federal constitutional provision that citizens of each state were "entitled to all privileges and immunities of citizens in the several States." Proponents countered that many states already barred free blacks. In 1821, Clay proposed a second compromise: Missouri would guarantee that its laws would not discriminate against citizens of other states. (Once admitted to the Union, Missouri twice adopted laws barring free blacks.) For more than three decades, the **Missouri Compromise** would govern congressional policy toward admitting new slave states. But the compromise masked rather than suppressed the simmering political conflict over slavery's westward expansion.

States' Rights and Nullification

Under the Constitution, the exact nature of the relationship between the states and the federal government was initially ambiguous, because Constitutional Convention delegates disagreed on whether states or nation should prevail in an irreconcilable conflict. The Tenth Amendment offered a slight clarification: powers not delegated to the central government, it said, were reserved to the states or to the people.

When New England Federalists met in Hartford at the end of 1814 to prepare a list of grievances against "Mr. Madison's War," they drew on the doctrine of nullification, first announced sixteen years earlier in the Kentucky and Virginia Resolutions, written by Thomas Jefferson and James Madison, respectively. Opposing the Alien and Sedition Acts, these founding fathers asserted that, if the national government assumed powers not delegated to it by the Constitution, states could nullify federal actions—that is, declare them inoperative within state borders. Some New England Federalists discussed taking nullification further by seceding. Their formulation of states' rights to nullify federal authority left a legacy for dissent that was reinvoked in crises up to the present.

In the following decade, South Carolina nullified federal tariffs, and in 1861 southern states threatened by Abraham Lincoln's election as president claimed the right of secession. Although the Civil War supposedly settled the issue—states could neither nullify federal law nor secede—southern states opposing the Supreme Court's 1954 ruling in favor of school integration again claimed the right to nullify "unauthorized" federal policy within their borders. In the early twenty-first century, as the U.S. Congress failed to muster a two-thirds majority to propose a constitutional amendment banning gay marriage, dozens of states ratified their own such constitutional amendments. Symbolically, the threat of secession remains potent. Decrying the 2009 federal stimulus package to aid the ailing national economy, Texas Governor Rick Perry declared that his state might secede rather than face unwanted spending, taxation, and debt. The Hartford Convention's legacy provides Americans who dissent from national policy with a model for using state governments, and threats of secession, as vehicles for their protests.

Summary

The partisanship of the 1790s made the early republic a period of vigorous political engagement. With a vision of an agrarian nation that protected individual liberty, Jeffersonians promoted a limited national government—one that stayed out of religious affairs and spent little on military forces, diplomatic missions, and economic initiatives. The rival Federalists, who exerted their influence through the judiciary, declared federal supremacy over the states even as the judiciary affirmed its own supremacy over other government branches. Federalists hoped a strengthened federal government would promote commerce and industry.

Despite his belief in limited government, Jefferson considered the acquisition of the Louisiana Territory and the Corps of Discovery his greatest presidential accomplishments. Americans soon streamed into the Louisiana Territory. More would have gone if not for Indians (and their British allies) and poorly developed transportation routes.

With its economy focused on international shipping, the greatest threats to the United States came from abroad. In its wars with the Barbary states, the United States sought to guard its commerce and ships on the high seas. Although the War of 1812 was a military stalemate, it inspired a new sense of nationalism and launched an era of American development.

The Treaty of Ghent reaffirmed American independence; thereafter, the nation settled disputes with Great Britain by negotiation. The war also dealt a blow to Indian resistance in the Midwest and Southwest, while accelerating American industrial growth. Federalists' opposition to the war undermined their credibility, and their party faded from the national political scene by 1820. The absence of partisan conflict created what contemporaries called an Era of Good Feelings.

Still, competing visions of America's route to prosperity endured. Under Chief Justice John Marshall, the Supreme Court supported the Federalist agenda, issuing rulings that stimulated commerce and industry. The Democratic-Republicans looked, instead, toward the vast and fertile Louisiana Territory. Fearful of European intentions to reassert influence in the Americas and emboldened by the nation's expanding boundaries, President Monroe proclaimed that the United States would not tolerate European intervention in American affairs. But even as its expanding boundaries strengthened the United States' international presence, territorial expansion threatened newfound political unity at home.

Tensions mounted in 1819, when the postwar economic boom came to a halt and congressmen sharply divided over whether to admit Missouri as a slave state. Henry Clay's compromise temporarily removed the issue of slavery's western expansion from political center stage.

Chapter Review

Political Visions

Was Jefferson's election and political vision truly "the revolution of 1800"?

Jefferson considered his election in 1800 a revolution, since it also gave his Democratic-Republican Party a majority in both houses of Congress. That made it easier to enact his vision of limited government, individual liberty (which required the separation of church and state), and an agrarian (versus commercial) republic. Since Democratic-Republicans viewed national debt as a sign of corruption, he authorized his treasury secretary to cut the federal budget and decrease the national debt (which Federalists saw as a tool to stimulate the economy). Jefferson also pardoned those convicted under the Alien and Sedition Acts, which he regarded as a violation of liberties, and attempted to remove from court appointments people opposed to his brand of politics. (He was ultimately unsuccessful, which maintained the Court's independence).

National Expansion Westward

Why was the Louisiana Purchase among Jefferson's most popular decisions as president?

The purchase of 827,000 square miles of land west of the Mississippi from France doubled the size of the United States, secured American interests from potential European incursion at its inland borders, and opened more land for American settlement (even though Native Americans were already living there). Moreover, by purchasing the land on the other side of the river, the United States controlled access to the Mississippi, which appealed to western settlers who relied on it to get their goods to market. Finally, it fed dreams of cheap, fertile lands for would-be settlers.

The Nation in the Orbit of Europe

What led to the War of 1812?

Freedom of the seas was the main cause. Ongoing hostilities between European nations spilled over onto American ships, as Great Britain often stopped and seized U.S. ships and forced those aboard into military service. Trade embargoes did little to stop the practice and ultimately hurt American merchants and the U.S. economy. Madison pointed to violation of neutral trading rights, British alliances with western Indians, and affronts to American independence as additional causes, while others saw war as an opportunity to annex British Canada. Although Britain reopened the seas and ordered its ships not to disturb American warships by June of 1812, news of the policy change did not reach America until long after Congress declared war.

The War of 1812

What were the consequences of the War of 1812?

Although the Treaty of Ghent ended the fighting and restored the prewar status quo, the United States did not get the results it wanted on impressments, blockades, and maritime rights for neutral parties. The war did, however, affirm American independence and guarantee no future battles with Britain over trade or territory. On the home front, the war shattered the U.S. economy and led some New England Federalists to threaten secession, which contributed to the party's demise when the war soon ended. Indians who had supported the British lost a major ally. And while Indians had their land and rights restored by the Treaty of Ghent, they had no power to enforce it. With the end of war, three trends emerged that were pivotal for the nation's future: westward expansion, the entrenchment of slavery, and industrial development.

The Nationalist Program

How did the American System mark the triumph of Federalist economic policy?

Long opposed to big government, Democratic-Republicans amended this philosophy to adopt the Federalist notion that the central government should aid economic growth. Their program was dubbed the American System, and included a national bank, development of transportation networks, and a protective tariff that would tax imported goods to protect American products from foreign competitors. Advocates of the American System, such as South Carolina leader John C. Calhoun, believed it could bridge sectional divides and expand the nation. Both parties embraced internal improvements for different reasons: Federalists saw them as spurring commercial development, while Jeffersonians (Democratic-Republicans) thought they would lead to western and agrarian expansion.

Sectionalism Exposed

How did the admission of new states after the War of 1812 ultimately divide the nation?

The question of slavery's westward expansion sparked controversy in 1819 when the Missouri Territory asked to be admitted as a slave state. Many feared it would give slaveholding states a two-vote Senate majority and would set a precedent for admitting other western states. And since Missouri was on the same latitude as free Illinois, Indiana, and Ohio, its admission as a slave state would move slavery northward. House Speaker Henry Clay suggested the winning compromise: to maintain the balance between free and slave states, Maine would enter as a free state, Missouri as a slave state, and all future new states north of Missouri's 36°30' border would prohibit slavery. As such, the Missouri Compromise divided the nation into two regions, north and south, according to the politics of slavery.

Suggestions for Further Reading

Stephen Aron, *American Confluence: The Missouri Frontier from Borderland to Border State* (2006)

David Edmunds, *Tecumseh and the Quest for Indian Leadership* (2006)

Joanne B. Freeman, *Affairs of Honor: National Politics in the New Republic* (2001)

Nancy Isenberg, *Fallen Founder: The Life of Aaron Burr* (2007)

John Lauritz Larson, *Internal Improvement: National Public Works and the Promise of Popular Government in the United States* (2001)

Jon Latimer, *1812: War with America* (2007)

Kent Newmyer, *John Marshall and the Heroic Age of the Supreme Court* (2001)

Jeffrey Ostler, *The Plains Sioux and U.S. Colonialism from Lewis and Clark to Wounded Knee* (2004)

Jeffrey Pasley, Andrew Robertson, and David Waldstreicher, eds., *Beyond the Founders: New Approaches to the Political History of the Early American Republic* (2004)

CourseMate   Go to the CourseMate website for primary source links, study tools, and review materials for this chapter. www.cengagebrain.com

The Rise of the South

Thomas Jefferson died, as he had lived, in debt, on July 4, 1826, the same day his long-time rival John Adams died. At Monticello, Jefferson's home in Virginia, anxiety filled his white and black "families."

On January 15, 1827, a five-day estate sale took place at Monticello. Among the paintings, furniture, and mementoes were "130 valuable negroes." Monticello's blacksmith, Joseph Fossett, watched his wife Edith and eight children sold to four different bidders.

Jefferson was reportedly a caring slaveholder, who tried to keep families intact. After his wife, Martha (with whom he had two daughters), died in 1782, Jefferson had six children, four of whom lived beyond infancy, with his slave Sally Hemings. Sally was the half sister of Jefferson's wife and part of an extended family of light-skinned Hemingses.

Joe Fossett, as Jefferson promised, became free one year after his master's death. Jefferson had earlier freed his four children with Sally Hemings: William Beverly Hemings, Harriet Hemings II, James Madison Hemings, and Thomas Eston Hemings. Jefferson never freed Sally; Virginia law would have required him to attain, publicly, a dispensation from the state legislature to free her without removing her from the state. Jefferson wanted no more salacious publicity about his house servant and mistress. Sally died a slave in Charlottesville, Virginia, in 1835 at age sixty-two.

"Thank heaven the whole of this dreadful business is over," wrote Jefferson's granddaughter, Mary, after the auction. She consoled herself that most slaves were sold within the state. Monticello was sold in 1831. But across the South in the 1820s, the "business" of slavery's expansion and cotton production was not over.

In 1815, southern states and territories, with fertile soil and a growing slave labor force, were poised for prosperity and power. New lands were settled, new states were peopled, and the South emerged as the world's most extensive commercial agricultural economy. The Old South's wealth came from export crops, land, and slaves, and its population was almost wholly rural. Racial slavery also affected

Chapter Outline

The "Distinctive" South
South-North Similarity | South-North Dissimilarity | A Southern World-View and the Proslavery Argument | A Slave Society

Southern Expansion, Indian Resistance and Removal
A Southern Westward Movement | Indian Treaty Making | Indian Accommodation | Indian Removal as Federal Policy | Cherokees | Cherokee Nation v. Georgia | Trail of Tears | Seminole Wars

LINKS TO THE WORLD *The Amistad Case*

Social Pyramid in the Old South
Yeoman Farmers | Yeoman Folk Culture | Yeomen's Livelihoods | Landless Whites | Yeomen's Demands and White Class Relations | Free Blacks | Free Black Communities

The Planters' World
The Newly Rich | Social Status and Planters' Values | King Cotton in a Global Economy | Paternalism | Marriage and Family Among Planters

Slave Life and Labor
Slaves' Everyday Conditions | Slave Work Routines | Violence and Intimidation Against Slaves | Slave-Master Relationships

Slave Culture and Resistance
African Cultural Survival | Slaves' Religion and Music | The Black Family in Slavery | The Domestic Slave Trade | Strategies of Resistance | Nat Turner's Insurrection

values, customs, laws, class structure, and the region's relationship to the nation and the world. As slaves were increasingly defined as chattel, they struggled to survive and resist, sometimes overtly, but typically in daily life and culture. By 1860, white Southerners asserted the moral and economic benefits of slavery and sought to advance their power over the national government.

As you read this chapter, keep the following questions in mind:

* **How and why was the Old South a "slave society," with slavery permeating every class and group within it, free or unfree?**

* **How and why did white southerners come to see cotton as "king" of a global economy, and how did the cotton trade's international reach shape southern society from 1815 to 1860?**

* **How did African American slaves build and sustain a meaningful life and a sense of community amid the potential chaos and destruction of their circumstances?**

* **How would you weigh the comparative significance of the following central themes in the history of the Old South: class, race, migration, power, liberty, wealth?**

VISUALIZING THE PAST *Imaging Nat Turner's Rebellion*

LEGACY FOR A PEOPLE AND A NATION *Reparations for Slavery*

SUMMARY

The "Distinctive" South

Not until the first half of the 1800s did slaveholding states from the Chesapeake and Virginia to Missouri, and from Florida to Texas, come to be designated as the South. Today, many consider it America's most distinctive region. Historians have long examined how the Old South was like and unlike the rest of the nation. Because of its unique history, has the South, in the words of poet Allen Tate, always been "Uncle Sam's other province"? Analyzing why the South seems more religious, conservative, or tragic than other regions of America has been an enduring practice.

What made the antebellum South different from the North?

American values, such as materialism, individualism, and faith in progress, have been associated with the North and values such as tradition, honor, and family loyalty, with the South. Stereotype has also labeled the South as static, even "backward," and the North as dynamic in the decades before the Civil War. In truth, there were many Souths: low-country rice and cotton regions with dense slave populations; mountainous regions of small farmers; semitropical wetlands in the Southeast; **plantation** culture in the Cotton Belt and Mississippi valley; tobacco- and wheat-growing regions in Virginia and North Carolina; bustling port cities; wilderness areas with rare hillfolk homesteads.

plantation: Large landholding devoted to a cash crop such as cotton or tobacco.

South-North Similarity The South shared much in common with the rest of the nation. The geographic sizes of the South and the North were roughly the same. In 1815, white southerners and free northerners shared heroes and ideology from the American Revolution and War of 1812. They worshiped the same Protestant God as northerners, lived under the same Constitution, and similarly combined nationalism and localism in their attitudes toward government.

Chronology

1810–20	137,000 slaves are forced to move from the Upper South to Alabama, Mississippi, and other western regions	1845	Florida and Texas gain admission to the Union as slave states
1822	Vesey's insurrection plot is discovered in South Carolina		Publication of Douglass's *Narrative of the Life of Frederick Douglass, an American Slave, Written by Himself*
1830s	Vast majority of African American slaves are native-born in America	1850	Planters' share of agricultural wealth in the South is 90 to 95 percent
1830s–40s	Cotton trade grows into largest source of commercial wealth and America's leading export	1850–60	Of some 300,000 slaves who migrate from the Upper to the Lower South, 60 to 70 percent go by outright sale
1831	Turner leads a violent slave rebellion in Virginia	1857	Publication of Hinton R. Helper's *The Impending Crisis,* denouncing the slave system
1832	Virginia holds the last debate in the South about the future of slavery; gradual abolition is voted down		Publication of George Fitzhugh's *Southern Thought,* an aggressive defense of slavery
	Publication of Dew's proslavery tract *Abolition of Negro Slavery*	1860	405,751 mulattos in the United States, 12.5 percent of the African American population
1836	Arkansas gains admission to the Union as a slave state		Three-quarters of all southern white families own no slaves
1839	Mississippi's Married Women's Property Act gives married women some property rights		South produces largest cotton crop ever

But as slavery and the plantation economy expanded, the South did not become a land of individual opportunity in the same manner as the North.

Research has shown that, despite enormous cruelties, slavery was a profitable labor system for planters. Southerners and northerners shared an expanding capitalist economy. As it grew, the slave-based economy of money-crop agriculture reflected planters' rational choices. More land and slaves generally converted into more wealth.

By the Civil War in 1860, the distribution of wealth and property in the two sections was almost identical: 50 percent of free adult males owned only 1 percent of real and personal property, and the richest 1 percent owned 27 percent of the wealth. North and South had ruling classes. Entrepreneurs in both sections sought their fortunes in an expanding market economy. The southern "master class" was more likely than propertied northerners to move west to make a profit.

South-North Dissimilarity

In terms of differences, the South's climate and longer growing season gave it a rural and agricultural destiny. Many great rivers provided rich soil and transportation routes. The South developed as a biracial society of brutal inequality, where the liberty and wealth of one race depended on the enslavement of another. Cotton growers spread out over large areas to maximize production and income. Consequently, population density in the South was low; by 1860, there were only 2.3 people per square mile in vast and largely unsettled Texas, 15.6 in Louisiana, and 18.0 in Georgia. The Northeast averaged 65.4 people per square mile. Massachusetts had 153.1 people per square mile, and New York City compressed 86,400 people into each square mile.

Where people were scarce, it was difficult to finance and operate schools, churches, libraries, and inns and restaurants. Similarly, the South's rural character and vision of the plantation as self-sufficient meant that the section spent little on public health. Southerners were strongly committed to their churches, and some embraced universities, but these institutions were far less developed than in the North. Factories were rare, because planters invested their capital primarily in slaves. The largest southern "industry" was lumbering, and the largest factories used slaves to make cigars. The South was slower than the North to develop a unified market economy and a regional transportation network and had only 35 percent of the nation's railroad mileage in 1860.

The Old South never developed its own banking and shipping capacity to any degree and relied heavily on the North for both. Most southern bank deposits were in the North, and as early as 1822, one-sixth of all southern cotton cleared for Liverpool or Le Havre from the port of New York and constituted two-fifths of all that city's exports. With cotton constituting two-fifths of New York's exports, merchants and bankers there became interested in the fate of slavery and cotton prices. In economic conventions from 1837 to 1839, southern delegates debated foreign trade, dependence on northern importers and financiers, and other alleged threats to their commercial independence. But nothing came of these conventions.

The South lagged far behind the North in industrial growth. Its urban centers were mostly ports like New Orleans and Charleston, which became crossroads of commerce and small-scale manufacturing. In the interior were small market towns dependent on agricultural trade. As a system of racial control, slavery did not work well in cities. Lacking manufacturing jobs, the South did not attract immigrants as readily the North. By 1860, only 13 percent of the nation's foreign-born population lived in the slave states.

Like most northerners, antebellum southerners embraced evangelical Christianity. Americans from all regions believed in a personal God and in conversion and piety as the means to salvation. But southern Baptists and Methodists concentrated on personal rather than social improvement. By the 1830s in the North, evangelicalism was a wellspring of reform movements (see Chapter 9); but in states where blacks were numerous and unfree, religion, as one scholar has written, preached "a hands-off policy concerning slavery." Moreover, distance and sparse population prevented reform-minded women from developing associations with each other. The reform movements that emerged in the South, such as temperance, focused on personal behavior, not social reform.

A Southern World-View and the Proslavery Argument

In the wake of the American Revolution, Enlightenment ideas of natural rights and equality stimulated antislavery sentiment in the Upper South, produced a brief flurry of manumissions and inspired hope for gradual emancipation. But that confidence waned in the new nation. As slavery spread, southerners vigorously defended it. In 1816, George Bourne, a Presbyterian minister exiled from Virginia for his antislavery sermons and for expulsion of slaveholders from his church, charged that, whenever southerners were challenged on slavery, "they were fast choked, for they had a Negro stuck fast in their throats."

By the 1820s, white southerners justified slavery as a "**positive good**," not merely a "necessary evil." They used the antiquity of slavery, as well as the Bible's

positive good: Southern justification for slavery as beneficial to the larger society, both to white owners and their black slaves.

many references to slaveholding, to foster a historical argument for bondage. But at the heart of the proslavery rationale was a deep and abiding racism. Whites were the more intellectual race, they claimed, and blacks more inherently physical and therefore destined for labor. In an 1851 proslavery tract, John Campbell declared that "there is as much difference between the lowest tribe of negroes and the white Frenchman, Englishman, or American, as there is between the monkey and the negro."

Some southerners defended slavery in practical terms; their bondsmen were economic necessities. In 1845, James Henry Hammond of South Carolina argued that slaveholding was a matter of property rights, protected by the Constitution because slaves were legal property. The deepest root of the proslavery argument was a hierarchical view of the social order with slavery prescribed by God. Southerners cherished tradition, believing social change should come slowly, if at all. As Nat Turner's slave rebellion compelled the Virginia legislature to debate the gradual abolition of slavery in 1831–1832, Thomas R. Dew, a slaveholder and professor at the College of William and Mary, contended that "that which is the growth of *ages* may require ages to remove." Dew's widely read work *Abolition of Negro Slavery* (1832) ushered an outpouring of proslavery writing that would intensify over the next thirty years. As slavery expanded westward and fueled national prosperity, Dew cautioned that gradual abolition threatened the South's "irremediable ruin." Dew declared black slavery the "order of nature," and the basis of the "well-ordered, well-established liberty" of white Americans.

Proslavery advocates invoked natural-law doctrine, arguing that the natural state of humankind was inequality of ability and condition, not equality. Proslavery writers believed that people were born to certain stations in life; they stressed dependence over autonomy and duty over rights as the human condition. As Virginia writer George Fitzhugh put it in 1854, "Men are not born entitled to equal rights. It would be far nearer the truth to say, that some were born with saddles on their backs, and others booted and spurred to ride them."

Many slaveholders saw themselves in a paternal role, as guardians of a familial relationship between masters and slaves. Although contradicted by countless examples of slave resistance and escape, and by slave sales, planters needed to believe in and exerted great energy in constructing the idea of the contented slave.

A Slave Society

In the Old South, whites and blacks grew up, were socialized, married, reared children, worked, conceived of property, and honed their most basic habits of behavior under the influence of slavery. This was true of slaveholding and nonslaveholding whites, as well as slave and free blacks. Slavery shaped the social structure of the South, fueled its economy, and dominated its politics.

The South was interdependent with the North, the West, and Europe in a growing capitalist market system. For its cotton trade, southerners relied on northern banks, northern steamship companies, and northern merchants. But there were elements of that system that southerners increasingly disliked, especially urbanism, the wage labor, a broadening right to vote, and threats to their racial and class order.

Americans have long struggled to define what one historian called the "Dixie difference." "The South is both American and something different," writes another historian, "at times a mirror or magnifier of national traits and at other times a counterculture." Distinctive and national, the South's story begins in what we have come to call the Old South, a term only conceivable after the eviction of native peoples from the region.

Southern Expansion, Indian Resistance and Removal

How did Native Americans living in western territories deal with increasing migration by southern whites?

When the trans-Appalachian frontier opened after the War of 1812, some 5 to 10 percent of the population moved annually, usually westward. In the first two decades of the century, they poured into the Ohio valley; by the 1820s, they were migrating into the Mississippi River valley and beyond. By 1850, two-thirds of Americans lived west of the Appalachians.

A Southern Westward Movement

After 1820, the heart of cotton cultivation and the slave-based plantation system shifted from the coastal states to Alabama and the newly settled Mississippi valley—Tennessee, Louisiana, Arkansas, and Mississippi. Southern slaveholders took slaves with them to the newer areas of the South, and **yeoman** farmers followed, also hoping for new wealth through cheap land and slaves.

yeoman: Independent small farmer, usually nonslaveholding.

A wave of migration was evident across the Southeast. As early as 1817, a Charleston, South Carolina, newspaper reported that migration out of that state had reached "unprecedented proportions." Almost half of the white people born in South Carolina after 1800 left the state, most for the Southwest. The way to wealth for southern seaboard planters was to go west to grow cotton for the booming world markets, by purchasing more land and slaves. The population of Mississippi soared from 73,000 in 1820 to 607,000 in 1850, with African American slaves in the majority. Across the Mississippi River, the population of Arkansas went from 14,000 in 1820 to 210,000 in 1850. By 1835, the American immigrant population in Texas reached 35,000, including 3,000 slaves, outnumbering Mexicans two to one. American settlers declared Texas's independence from Mexico in 1836, spurring further American immigration into the region. By 1845, "Texas fever" boosted the Anglo population to 125,000. Statehood that year opened the floodgates to more immigrants and to a confrontation with Mexico that would lead to war.

As the **cotton kingdom** grew to what southern political leaders dreamed would be national and world dominion, this westward migration, fueled initially by optimistic nationalism, ultimately made migrant planters more sectional and southern. In time, political dominance in the South migrated westward into the Cotton Belt. By the 1840s and 1850s, these capitalist planters, fearful that their slave-based economy was under attack, sought to protect and expand their system. Increasingly, they saw themselves, as one historian has written, less as "landowners who happened to own slaves" than as "slaveholders who happened to own land."

cotton kingdom: A broad swath of territory where cotton was a mainstay that stretched from South Carolina, Georgia, and northern Florida in the east through Alabama, Mississippi, central and western Tennessee, and Louisiana, and from there on to Arkansas and Texas.

But other Americans already occupied much of the desired land. Before 1830, large swaths of upper Georgia belonged to the Cherokees, and huge regions of Alabama and Mississippi were Creek, Choctaw, or Chickasaw land. Indians were also on the move, but in forced migrations. For most white Americans, Indians were in the way of their growing empire. Taking Indian land, so the reasoning went, reflected the natural course of history and progress: the "civilizers" had to displace

Links to the World

The Amistad Case

In April 1839 a Spanish slave ship, *Tecora*, sailed from Lomboko, the region of West Africa that became Sierra Leone. On board were Mende people, sold by their African enemies. In June they arrived in Havana, Cuba, a Spanish colony. Two Spaniards purchased 53 of the Mende and sailed aboard *La Amistad* for their plantations elsewhere in Cuba. After three days, the Africans revolted. Led by a man the Spaniards called Joseph Cinque, they killed the captain and seized control of the vessel. They ordered the two Spaniards to return them to Africa, but the slaveholders tried to reach the American South. Far off course, the Amistad was seized by the USS *Washington* in Long Island Sound and brought ashore in Connecticut.

Joseph Cinque, by Nathaniel Jocelyn, 1840. Cinque led the rebellion aboard "The Amistad," a Spanish ship carrying captive Africans along the coast of Cuba in 1839. They commandeered the ship and sailed it north toward New England where they were rescued off the coast of Connecticut. Cinque, celebrated as a great leader, sat for the painting while he and his people awaited trial. They were freed by a decision of the U.S. Supreme Court in 1841 and returned to their homeland in Sierra Leone in West Africa.

New Haven Colony Historical Society

The "Amistad Africans" soon became a cause for abolitionists and slaveholders, as well as in U.S.-Spanish relations. The Africans were imprisoned in New Haven, and a dispute ensued: Were they slaves and murderers and the property of their Cuban owners, or were they free people exercising their natural rights? Were they Spanish property, seized on the high seas in violation of a 1795 treaty? If a northern state could "free" captive Africans, what did it mean for enslaved African Americans in the South? Connecticut abolitionists went to court, where a U.S. circuit court judge dismissed the mutiny and murder charges but refused to release the Africans because their Spanish owners claimed them as property.

Meanwhile, a Yale professor of ancient languages, Josiah Gibbs, visited the captives and learned their words for numbers. In New York he walked along the docks repeating the Mende words until an African seaman, James Covey, responded. Covey journeyed to New Haven, conversed with the jubilant Africans, and soon their tale garnered sympathy throughout New England.

In a new trial, the judge ruled that the Africans were illegally enslaved and ordered them returned to their homeland. Slave trade between Africa and the Americas was outlawed in a treaty between Spain and Great Britain. Spain's lawyers demanded the return of their "merchandise." Needing southern votes to win reelection, President Martin Van Buren supported Spanish claims and advocated the Africans' return to a likely death in Cuba.

The administration appealed the case to the Supreme Court in February 1841. Arguing the abolitionists' case, former president John Quincy Adams pointed to a copy of the Declaration of Independence on the court wall, invoked the natural rights to life and liberty, and chastised Van Buren. In a 7-to-1 decision, the Court ruled that the Africans were "freeborn."

On November 27, 1841, thirty-five survivors and five American missionaries disembarked for Africa, arriving in Sierra Leone on January 15, 1842.

The Amistad case showed how intertwined slavery was with freedom, and the United States with the world. It poisoned diplomatic relations between America and Spain for a generation, and stimulated Christian mission work in Africa.

the "children of the forest." National leaders provided the rhetoric and justification needed. As president in 1830, Andrew Jackson spoke with certainty about why the Indians must go. "What good man would prefer a country," he asked, "covered with forests and ranged by a few thousand savages to our extensive Republic, studded with cities, towns, and prosperous farms?"

Indian Treaty Making In theory, under the U.S. Constitution, the federal government recognized Indian sovereignty and treated Indian peoples as foreign nations. Agreements between Indian nations and the United States were signed and ratified like other international treaties. In practice, however, fraud dominated the government's approach to treaty making and Indian sovereignty. As the country expanded, new treaties would shrink Indian land holdings.

Although Indian resistance persisted against such pressure after the War of 1812, it only slowed the process. In the 1820s, native peoples in the Middle West, Ohio valley, Mississippi valley, and other parts of the cotton South ceded lands totaling 200 million acres for a pittance.

Indian Accommodation Increasingly, Indian nations east of the Mississippi sought to survive through accommodation. In the first three decades of the century, the Choctaw, Creek, and Chickasaw peoples in the lower Mississippi became suppliers and traders. Under treaty provisions, trading posts and stores provided Indians with supplies and purchased or bartered for Indian-produced goods. The trading posts extended credit to chiefs, who increasingly fell into debt that they could pay off to the federal government only by selling their land.

By 1822, the Choctaw nation had sold 13 million acres but still carried a $13,000 debt. The Indians struggled, increasing agricultural production and hunting, working as farmhands and craftsmen, and selling produce at market stalls in Natchez and New Orleans. As the United States expanded westward, white Americans promoted their assimilation through education and conversion to Christianity. In 1819, in response to missionary lobbying, Congress appropriated $10,000 annually for "civilization of the tribes adjoining the frontier settlements."

Within five years, thirty-two boarding schools enrolled Indian students run by Protestant missionaries. They substituted English for American Indian languages and taught agriculture alongside the Christian gospel. But settlers continued to eye Indian land. Wherever native peoples lived, illegal settlers disrupted their lives. The federal government only halfheartedly enforced treaties, as legitimate Indian land rights gave way to the advance of white civilization.

With loss of land came dependency. The Choctaws relied on white Americans for manufactured goods and even food. Disease further facilitated removal of American Indian peoples to western lands. While other groups increased rapidly, the Indian population fell, some nations declining by 50 percent in three decades. The French traveler and author Alexis de Tocqueville concluded, after observing the tragedy of forced removal in 1831, "as they give way or perish, an immense and increasing people fill their place. There is no instance upon record of so prodigious a growth or so rapid a destruction." As many as 100,000 eastern and southern Indian peoples were removed between 1820 and 1850; about 30,000 died in the process.

Removal had a profound impact on all Shawnees, the people of the Prophet and Tecumseh. After giving up 17 million acres in Ohio in a 1795 treaty, the Shawnees scattered to Indiana and eastern Missouri. Many moved to Kansas territory in 1825. By 1854, Kansas was open to white settlement and the Shawnees had ceded seven-eighths of their land or 1.4 million acres. Men lost their traditional role as providers; their skills hunting woodland animals were useless on the prairies of Kansas. As grain became the tribe's dietary staple, Shawnee women played a greater role as providers, supplemented by government aid under treaty provisions. Remarkably, the Shawnees preserved their language and culture despite these devastating dislocations.

Indian Removal as Federal Policy

Link to the Indian Removal Act.

Cherokees, Creeks, Choctaws, Chickasaws, and Seminoles aggressively resisted white encroachment after the War of 1812. In his last annual message to Congress in late 1824, President James Monroe proposed that all Indians be moved beyond the Mississippi River. Monroe considered this an "honorable" proposal that would protect Indians from invasion and provide them with independence for "improvement and civilization." He believed force would be unnecessary.

But all four tribes unanimously rejected Monroe's proposition. Between 1789 and 1825, the four nations negotiated thirty treaties with the United States, and they reached their limit. Most wished to remain on what little was left of their ancestral land.

Pressure from Georgia had prompted Monroe's policy. In the 1820s, the state had accused the federal government of not fulfilling its 1802 promise to remove the Cherokees and Creeks from northwestern Georgia in return for the state's renunciation of its claim to western lands. In 1826, under federal pressure, the Creek nation ceded all but a small strip of its Georgia acreage, but for Georgians only their complete removal to the West would resolve the conflict.

In an unsuccessful attempt to hold on to the remainder of their traditional lands, which were in Alabama, the Creeks radically altered their political structure. In 1829, they centralized tribal authority and forbade any chief from ceding land.

Indian Removal Act: Authorized Andrew Jackson to exchange public lands in the West for Indian territories in the East and appropriated federal funds to cover the expenses of removal.

In 1830, after extensive debate and a narrow vote, Congress passed the **Indian Removal Act**, authorizing the president to negotiate removal treaties with all tribes living east of the Mississippi. The bill, which provided federal funds for such relocations, would likely not have passed the House without the additional representation afforded slave states due to the Constitution's three-fifths clause.

Cherokees

Link to editorials by Elias Boudinot on Indian Removal.

No people met the challenge of assimilating to American standards more thoroughly than the Cherokees, whose traditional home centered on eastern Tennessee and northern Alabama and Georgia. Between 1819 and 1829, the tribe became economically self-sufficient and politically self-governing; during this Cherokee renaissance the nearly fifteen thousand adult Cherokees regarded themselves as a nation, not a collection of villages. In 1821 and 1822, Sequoyah, a self-educated Cherokee, devised an eighty-six-character phonetic alphabet that made possible a Cherokee-language Bible and a bilingual tribal newspaper, *Cherokee Phoenix* (1828). Between 1820 and 1823, the Cherokees created a formal government with a bicameral legislature, a court system, and in 1827 they adopted a written constitution modeled after that of the United States. They transformed their economy from hunting, gathering, and subsistence agriculture to commodity trade based on barter, cash, and credit. The Cherokee nation, however, collectively owned all tribal land and forbade land sales to outsiders. Nonetheless, many became individual farmers and slaveholders; by 1833, they held fifteen hundred black slaves. Over time, Cherokee racial identity became very complex.

But Cherokee transformations failed to win respect from white southerners. In the 1820s, Georgia pressed them to sell the 7,200 square miles of land they held in the state. Congress appropriated $30,000 in 1822 to buy the Georgia land, but the Cherokees resisted. Impatient, Georgia annulled the Cherokees' constitution, extended the state's sovereignty over them, prohibited the Cherokee National Council from meeting except to cede land, and ordered their lands seized. The discovery of gold on Cherokee land in 1829 further whetted Georgia's appetite for Cherokee territory.

Cherokee Nation v. Georgia

The Cherokees under Chief John Ross turned to the federal courts to defend their treaty with the United States. In *Cherokee Nation v. Georgia* (1831), Chief Justice John Marshall ruled that under the Constitution an Indian tribe was neither a foreign nation nor a state and therefore had no standing in federal courts. Indians were deemed "domestic, dependent nations." Legally, they were in but not of the United States. Nonetheless, said Marshall, the Indians had a right to their lands; they could lose title only by voluntarily giving it up.

A year later, in *Worcester v. Georgia,* Marshall declared that the Indian nation was a distinct political community in which "the laws of Georgia can have no force" and into which Georgians could not enter without permission or treaty. *Phoenix* editor Elias Boudinot called the decision "glorious news." Jackson, however, whose reputation was built as an Indian fighter, did his best to usurp the Court's action. Newspapers widely reported that Jackson had said, "John Marshall has made his decision: now let him enforce it." To open new lands for settlement, Jackson favored expelling the Cherokees.

Georgians, too, refused to comply, and they refused to hear Indians' pleas to share their American dream. A Cherokee census indicated that they owned 33 grist mills, 13 sawmills, 1 powder mill, 69 blacksmith shops, 2 tanneries, 762 looms, 2,486 spinning wheels, 172 wagons, 2,923 plows, 7,683 horses, 22,531 cattle, 46,732 pigs, and 2,566 sheep. "You asked us to form a republican government," declared the Cherokee leader, John Ridge, in 1832. "We did so—adopting your own as a model. You asked us to cultivate the earth, and learn the mechanic arts: We did so. You asked us to learn to read: We did so. You asked us to cast away our idols, and worship your God: We did so." But neither the plow nor the Bible earned the Cherokees respect in the face of the economic, imperial, and racial quests of their fellow southerners (see Map 10.1).

Trail of Tears

The Choctaws made the first forced journey from Mississippi and Alabama to the West in the winter of 1831 and 1832. Alexis de Tocqueville was visiting Memphis when they passed through: "The wounded, the sick, newborn babies, and the old men on the point of death.... I saw them embark to cross the great river," he wrote, "and the sight will never fade from my memory. Neither sob nor complaint rose from that silent assembly." The Creeks in Alabama resisted removal until 1836; a year later, the Chickasaws followed.

Some Cherokees believed that further resistance was hopeless and accepted removal, agreeing in 1835 to exchange their southern home for western land in the Treaty of New Echota. Most wanted to stand firm. John Ross, with petitions signed by fifteen thousand Cherokees, lobbied the Senate against ratification of the treaty. He lost. But when evacuation came in 1838, most Cherokees refused to move. President Martin Van Buren sent federal troops; about twenty thousand Cherokees were evicted, held in detention camps, and marched under military escort to Indian Territory in present-day Oklahoma. Nearly one-quarter died of disease and exhaustion on what came to be known as the **Trail of Tears**.

Trail of Tears: Forced migration in 1838 of Cherokee Indians from their homelands in the southeast to what is now Oklahoma.

When the forced march ended, the Indians had traded about 100 million acres east of the Mississippi for 32 million acres west of the river plus $68 million. Forced removal had a disastrous impact on the Cherokees and other displaced Indian nations. In the West, they encountered an alien environment. Unable to live off the land, many became dependent on government payments. The Cherokees struggled over their tribal government. In 1839, followers of John Ross assassinated the leaders of the protreaty faction. Violence continued sporadically until a new treaty in 1846

MAP 10.1

Removal of Native Americans from the South, 1820–1840

Over a twenty-year period, the federal government and southern states forced Native Americans to exchange their traditional homes for western land. Some tribal groups remained in the South, but most settled in the alien western environment.

Source: Copyright © Cengage Learning

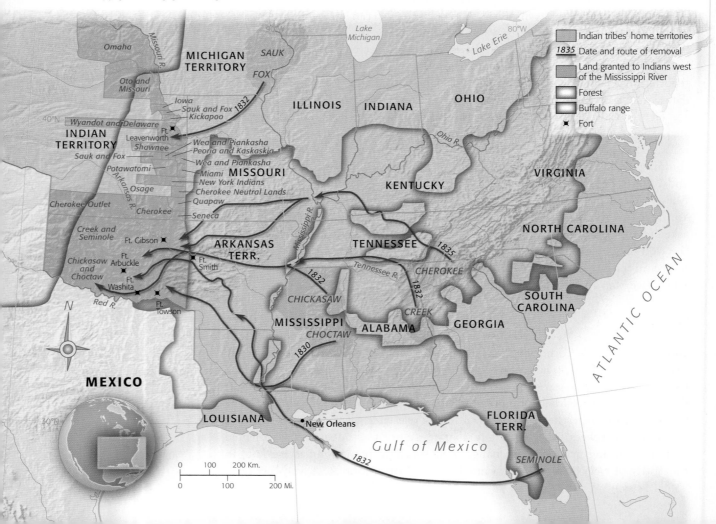

The Trail of Tears, by twentieth-century Pawnee artist Brummet Echohawk. About twenty thousand Cherokees were evicted in 1838–1839, and about one-quarter of them died on the forced march to present-day Oklahoma.

imposed a temporary truce. In time, the Cherokees reestablished their political institutions and a governing body in Tahlequah, in northeastern Oklahoma.

Seminole Wars   In Florida, some Seminole leaders agreed in the 1832 Treaty of Payne's Landing to relocate to the West within three years, but others opposed the treaty. A minority under the charismatic leader Osceola refused to vacate and fought the protreaty group. When federal troops were sent to impose removal in 1835, Osceola waged a guerrilla war against them.

The Florida Indians were a varied group that included many Creeks and mixed Indian–African Americans (ex-slaves or descendants of runaway slaves). The U.S. Army, however, considered them all Seminoles. General Thomas Jesup believed that the runaway slave population was the key to the war. "And if it be not speedily put down," he wrote a friend in 1836, "the South will feel the effects of it on their slave population before the end of the next season."

Osceola was captured and died in an army prison in 1838, but Seminoles fought on under Chief Coacoochee (Wild Cat) and other leaders. In 1842, the United States abandoned removal. Most of Osceola's followers agreed to move west to Indian Territory after another war in 1858, but some remained in the Florida Everglades.

Social Pyramid in the Old South

A large majority of white southerners (three-quarters in 1860) owned no slaves. Most were yeoman farmers who owned their own land and grew their own food. The social distance between poorer whites and the planter class could be great. Still greater was the distance between whites and blacks with free status. White yeomen, landless whites, and free blacks occupied the broad base of the social pyramid in the Old South.

What class tensions emerged in the antebellum South?

Yeoman Farmers

After the War of 1812, white farmers—many with no slaves—moved in waves down the southern Appalachians into the Gulf lands or through the Cumberland Gap into Kentucky and Tennessee. In large sections of the South, especially inland from the coast and away from large rivers, small, self-sufficient farms were the norm. Lured by stories of good land, many men repeatedly uprooted their wives and children.

Their status as a numerical majority did not mean that they set the political or economic direction of the larger society. Self-reliant and often isolated, they operated both apart from and within the slave-based staple-crop economy.

On the southern frontier, men cleared fields, built log cabins, and established farms, while their wives labored in the household and patiently re-created the social ties—to relatives, neighbors, fellow churchgoers—that enriched everyone's experience. Women dreaded the isolation and loneliness of the frontier.

Some yeomen acquired large tracts of level land, purchased slaves, and became planters. They forged part of the new wealth of the cotton boom states of Mississippi and Louisiana, where mobility into the slaveowning class was possible. Others clung to familiar mountainous areas or sought self-sufficiency. As one historian has written, though they owned no slaves, yeomen were jealous of their independence, and "the household grounded their own claims to masterhood."

Yeoman Folk Culture

Yeomen enjoyed a folk culture based on family, church, and local region. Their speech patterns recalled their Scots-Irish and Irish backgrounds. They flocked to religious revivals called camp meetings and got together for house-raisings, logrollings, quilting bees, corn-shuckings, and hunting. Such occasions combined work with fun and fellowship, offering food and liquor in abundance.

Demanding rounds of work and family responsibilities shaped women's lives. They worked in the fields but the preparation of food consumed much of women's time. Household tasks continued during frequent pregnancies and childcare. Nursing and medical care also fell to mothers, who relied on folk wisdom. Women, too, wanted to be masters of their household, although it came at the price of their health.

Yeomen's Livelihoods

At age eighteen in 1841, North Carolinian John F. Flintoff went to Mississippi to seek his fortune. Like other aspiring yeomen, he worked as a slave overseer. Finding it impossible to please his employers, he returned to North Carolina, married, and lived in his parents' house. "Impatient to get along in the world," Flintoff tried Louisiana next and then Mississippi again.

In the Gulf region, routinely, "first rate employment" alternated with "very low wages." Moreover, as a young man on isolated plantations, Flintoff was lonely. His employers found fault with his work, and in 1846 Flintoff concluded that "managing negroes and large farms is soul destroying."

At twenty-six, even before he owned land, Flintoff bought his first slave, "a negro boy 7 years old." Soon he had purchased two more children, the cheapest slaves available. Conscious of his status as a slaveowner, Flintoff resented the low wages he was paid. In 1853, with nine young slaves and a growing family, Flintoff was fired. He returned to North Carolina, sold some of his slaves, and purchased 124 acres with

North Carolina Emigrants: Poor White Folks, oil on canvas, 1845, by James Henry Beard. This depicts a yeoman family, their belongings all on one hungry horse, as they migrate westward in search of new land and livelihood.

help from his in-laws. As he paid off his debts, he hoped to free his wife from labor and send his sons to college. Although Flintoff demonstrated that a farmer could move in and out of the slaveholding class, he never achieved cotton planter status (owning roughly twenty or more slaves).

Probably more typical of the southern yeoman was Ferdinand L. Steel, who as a young man moved from North Carolina to Tennessee to work as a river boatman but eventually took up farming in Mississippi. Steel rose every day at 5 a.m. and worked until sundown. He and his family raised corn and wheat, though cotton was his cash product: he sold five or six bales (about two thousand pounds) a year to obtain money for sugar, coffee, salt, calico, and gunpowder.

Steel's family in Mississippi in the 1840s survived on a household economy. He made the family's shoes; his wife and sister sewed dresses, shirts, and "pantaloons." As the nation fell deeper into crisis over slave labor, this independent southern farmer never came close to owning a slave.

The focus of Steel's life was family and religion. Family members prayed together, and he studied Scripture for an hour after lunch. Steel borrowed histories, Latin and Greek grammars, and religious books from his church. Eventually, he became a traveling Methodist minister.

Landless Whites   A sizable minority of white southerners—from 25 to 40 percent—were hired hands who owned no land and worked for others. Their property consisted of a few household items and some animals—usually pigs. The landless included some immigrants, especially Irish, who did heavy and dangerous work, such as building railroads and digging ditches.

In the countryside, white farm laborers struggled to purchase land in the face of low wages or, if they rented, unpredictable market prices for their crops. Scrimping, some climbed yeoman ranks. When James and Nancy Bennitt of North Carolina succeeded in their ten-year struggle to buy land, they avoided the unstable cotton market and raised extra corn and wheat for cash.

Herdsmen with pigs and other livestock had a desperate struggle. By 1860, as the South anticipated war to preserve its society, between 300,000 and 400,000 white people in Virginia, North and South Carolina, and Georgia—approximately one-fifth of the total white population—lived in poverty. Land and slaves determined wealth in the Old South, and many whites possessed neither.

Yeomen's Demands and White Class Relations

Class tensions emerged in the western, nonslaveholding parts of the seaboard states by the 1830s. There, yeoman farmers resented their underrepresentation in state legislatures and the corruption in local government. Voters in more recently settled states of the Old Southwest adopted white manhood suffrage and other electoral reforms, including popular election of governors, legislative apportionment based on white population only, and locally chosen county government. Slaveowners with new wealth, however, knew that a more open government could permit troubling class conflicts and were determined to hold the reins of power.

Historians have offered several explanations why these tensions did not fuel greater conflict between slaveholders and nonslaveholders. One of the most important factors was race. The South's racial ideology stressed the superiority of all whites to blacks. Thus, slavery became the basis of equality among whites, and white privilege inflated the status of poor whites, giving them a common interest with the rich. The dream of upward mobility blunted class conflict.

Most important, before the Civil War, yeomen worked their farms and avoided debt, largely unhindered by slaveholding planters. Likewise, slaveholders pursued their goals quite independently of yeomen. Suppression of dissent also played an increasing role. After 1830, white southerners who criticized the slave system were intimidated, attacked, or rendered politically powerless in a society held together partly by white racial solidarity.

Still, there were signs of class conflict in the late antebellum period. As cotton lands filled up, nonslaveholders faced narrower economic prospects; meanwhile, wealthy planters enjoyed expanding profits. The risks of entering cotton production were becoming too great and the cost of slaves too high for many yeomen to rise in society. From 1830 to 1860, the percentage of white southern families holding slaves declined steadily from 36 to 25 percent. Although slaveowners were a minority in the white population, planters' share of the South's agricultural wealth remained at 90 and 95 percent.

Anticipating secession, slaveowners stood secure. In the 1850s, they occupied from 50 to 85 percent of the seats in state legislatures and a similarly high percentage of the South's congressional seats. And planters' interests controlled all other major social institutions, such as churches and colleges.

Free Blacks

The nearly quarter-million free blacks in the South in 1860 often fared little better than slaves. Upper South free blacks were usually descendants people manumitted by their owners in the 1780s and 1790s. A remarkable number of slaveholders in Virginia and the Chesapeake had freed their slaves because of religious principles and revolutionary ideals in the wake of American independence (see Chapter 7). Many blacks also became free as runaways, especially by the 1830s.

Some free blacks worked in towns or cities, but most lived in rural areas and struggled to survive. They usually did not own land and labored in someone else's fields, often beside slaves. By law, free blacks could not own guns, buy liquor, violate curfew, assemble except in church, testify in court, or (throughout the South after 1835) vote. Despite obstacles, a minority bought land, and others found jobs as skilled craftsmen, especially in cities.

A few free blacks prospered and bought slaves. In 1830, there were 3,775 free black slaveholders in the South; 80 percent lived in Louisiana, South Carolina, Virginia, and Maryland, and approximately half of the total lived in New Orleans and Charleston. Most purchased their own wives and children, whom they could not free, because laws required newly emancipated blacks to leave their state. To free family members they had purchased, hundreds of black slaveholders petitioned for exemption from the antimanumission laws. At the same time, a few mulattos in New Orleans were active slave traders. Although rare in the United States, the greed and quest for power that lay at the root of slavery could cross any racial or ethnic barrier.

Free Black Communities

In the Cotton Belt and Gulf regions, a large proportion of free blacks were mulattos, the privileged offspring of wealthy white planters. Not all planters freed their mixed-race offspring, but those who did often gave their children a good education and financial backing. In cities like New Orleans, Charleston, and Mobile, extensive interracial sex, as well as migrations from the Caribbean, produced a mulatto population that was recognized as a distinct class.

Free black communities formed in many southern cities by the 1840s, especially around churches. By the late 1850s, Baltimore had fifteen churches, Louisville nine, and Nashville and St. Louis four each—most of them African Methodist Episcopal. Class and race distinctions were important to southern free blacks, but outside a few cities, most mulattos experienced hardship. In the United States, "one drop" of black "blood" made them black, and potentially enslavable.

The Planters' World

> How did paternalism function on southern plantations?

At the top of the southern social pyramid were slaveholding planters. Most lived in comfortable farmhouses, not in the opulence that legend suggests. The grand plantation mansions, with outlying slave quarters, are an enduring symbol of the Old South. But in 1850, 50 percent of southern slaveholders had fewer than five slaves; 72 percent had fewer than ten; 88 percent had fewer than twenty. Thus, the average slaveholder was not a wealthy aristocrat but an aspiring farmer.

The Newly Rich

Link to excerpts from Bennet Barrow's diary.

The newly rich Louisiana cotton planter Bennet Barrow was preoccupied in the 1840s with moneymaking. He worried about his cotton crop, yet to overcome his worries, he hunted frequently and had a passion for racing horses and raising hounds. He could report the loss of a slave without feeling, but became emotional when illness afflicted his sporting animals. His strongest feelings surfaced when his horse Jos Bell—equal to "the best Horse in the South"—"broke down running a mile…ruined for Ever." The same day, Barrow gave his human property a "general Whipping." In 1841, diary entries he worried about a rumored slave insurrection. When a slave named Ginney Jerry "sherked" his cotton-picking duties and was rumored "about to run off," Barrow whipped him one day and the next.

The richest planters used their wealth to model genteel sophistication. Extended visits, parties, and balls to which women wore the latest fashions provided opportunities for friendship, courtship, and display. These entertainments were important diversions for plantation women, who relished social events to break the monotony of their domestic lives. Yet socializing also sustained a rigidly gendered society.

Most of the planters in the cotton-boom states of Alabama and Mississippi were newly rich by the 1840s. As one historian put it, "a number of men mounted from log cabin to plantation mansion on a stairway of cotton bales, accumulating slaves as they climbed." And many did not live like rich men. They put their new wealth into cotton acreage and slaves even as they sought refinement and high social status.

The cotton boom in the Mississippi valley created one-generation aristocrats. A case in point is Greenwood Leflore, a Chocktaw chieftain who owned a plantation in Mississippi with four hundred slaves. After selling his cotton on the world market, he spent $10,000 in France to furnish a single room of his mansion with handwoven carpets, furniture upholstered with gold leaf, tables and cabinets ornamented with tortoise-shell inlay, mirrors, paintings, and a clock and candelabra of brass and ebony.

Social Status and Planters' Values

Slave ownership was the main determinant of wealth in the South. Slaves were a commodity and an investment, much like gold; people bought them on speculation, hoping for a rise in their market value. Many slaveholders mortgaged their slaves and used them as collateral. People who could not pay cash for slaves would ask the sellers to purchase the mortgage, just as banks give mortgages on houses today. The slaveholder would repay the loan in installments with interest. The availability of slave labor tended to devalue free labor: where strenuous work under supervision was reserved for an enslaved race, few free people relished it. When Alexis de Tocqueville crossed from Ohio into Kentucky in his travels of 1831, he observed, "On the right bank of the Ohio [River] everything is activity, industry; labor is honoured; there are no slaves. Pass to the left bank and the scene changes so suddenly that you think yourself on the other side of the world; the enterprising spirit is gone. There, work is not only painful; it is shameful." Aristocratic values—lineage, privilege, pride, honor, and refinement of person and manner—commanded respect throughout the South. Many of those qualities were in short supply, however, in the recently settled portions of the cotton kingdom, where frontier values of courage and self-reliance ruled during the 1820s and 1830s. By the 1850s, a settled aristocratic group of planters did rule, however, in much of the Mississippi valley.

Instead of gradually disappearing, as it did in the North, the Code Duello, which required men to defend their honor through violence, endured in the South. In North Carolina in 1851, wealthy planter Samuel Fleming sought to settle disputes with lawyer William Waightstill Avery by "cowhiding" him in public. Under the code, Avery could redeem his honor violently or to brand himself a coward through inaction. Three weeks later, he shot Fleming dead at point-blank range. A jury took ten minutes to find Avery not guilty, and the spectators gave him a standing ovation.

Aristocratic planters expected to wield power and receive deference from poorer whites. But the independent yeoman class resented infringements of their rights, and many belonged to evangelical faiths that exalted simplicity and condemned the planters' wealth. Much of the planters' power and claims to leadership, after all, were built on their assumption of a monopoly on world cotton and a foundation of black slave labor.

King Cotton in a Global Economy

The American South so dominated the world's supply of cotton that southern planters gained enormous confidence that the cotton boom was permanent and that the industrializing nations of England and France would always bow to **King Cotton**. American cotton production doubled in yield each decade after 1800 and provided three-fourths of the world's supply by the 1840s. Southern staple crops were fully three-fifths of American exports by 1850, and one of every seven workers in England depended on American cotton for his job. Cotton production made slaves the most valuable financial asset in the United States—greater than banks, railroads, and manufacturing combined. In 1860 dollars, the slaves' total value as property equaled an estimated $3.5 billion. (Roughly $70 billion in early twenty-first century dollars.)

King Cotton: Term expressing southern belief that U.S. and British economies depended on cotton making it 'king'.

"Cotton is King," the *Southern Cultivator* declared in 1859, "and wields an astonishing influence over the world's commerce." Until 1840, the cotton trade furnished much of the export capital to finance northern economic growth. After that, the northern economy expanded without dependence on cotton profits. Nevertheless, southern planters and politicians continued to boast of King Cotton's supremacy. "No power on earth dares...to make war on cotton," James Hammond lectured the U.S. Senate in 1858. Although the South produced 4.5 million bales in 1861, its greatest crop ever, such world dominance was about to collapse. Thereafter, cotton became a shackle to the South.

Paternalism

Slaveholding men often embraced a paternalistic ideology that justified their dominance over black slaves and white women. They stressed their obligations, viewing themselves as custodians of society and of the black families they owned. The paternalistic planter saw himself not as an oppressor but as the benevolent guardian of an inferior race.

This comforting self-image let rich planters obscure the harsh dimensions of slave treatment. And slaves—accommodating to the realities of power—encouraged their masters to think their benevolence was appreciated. Paternalism also served as a defense against abolitionist criticism. In reality, paternalism grew as a give-and-take relationship between masters and slaves—owners took labor from the bondsmen, while slaves obligated masters to provide them a measure of autonomy and living space. Relations between men and women in the planter class were similarly defined by paternalism. The upper-class southern woman was raised and educated to be a wife, mother, and subordinate companion to men. South Carolina's Mary Boykin Chesnut wrote of her husband, "He is master of the house. … All the comfort of my life depends upon his being in a good humor." Women found it difficult to challenge society's rules on sexual or racial relations.

Planters' daughters usually attended one of the South's rapidly multiplying boarding schools. Typically, the young woman could entertain suitors whom her parents approved. But she quickly had to choose a husband and commit herself to a man whom she generally had known only briefly. Young women had to follow the wishes of their family, especially their father, even if it left them emotionally empty.

Upon marriage, a planter-class woman ceded to her husband most of her legal rights, becoming part of his family. She was isolated on a large plantation, where she supervised the cooking and preserving of food, managed the house, watched the children, and attended sick slaves. These realities were more confining on the frontier, where isolation was greater. Men on plantations could occasionally escape into the public realm—to town, business, or politics. Women could retreat from rural plantation culture only into kinship and associations with other women.

Marriage and Family Among Planters

A perceptive white woman sometimes approached marriage with anxiety. Lucy Breckinridge, a wealthy Virginia girl of twenty, lamented the autonomy she surrendered at the altar. In her diary, she recorded: "If [husbands] care for their wives at all it is only as a sort of servant, a being made to attend to their comforts and to keep the children out of the way."

Childbearing often involved grief, poor health, and death. In 1840, the birth rate for white southern women was almost 30 percent higher than the national average. The average southern white woman would bear eight children in 1800; by 1860, the figure had decreased to six. Childbirth complications were a major cause of death, occurring twice as often in the hot South as in the Northeast.

Sexual relations between planters and slaves were another problem that white women endured but were not supposed to notice. "Violations of the moral law… made mulattos as common as blackberries," protested a woman in Georgia, but wives had to play "the ostrich game." Such habits produced a large mixed race population by the 1850s.

In the 1840s and 1850s, as abolitionist attacks on slavery increased, southern men published a barrage of articles stressing that women should restrict their concerns to the home. The *Southern Quarterly Review* declared, "The proper place for a woman is at home. One of her highest privileges, to be politically merged in the existence of her husband."

But a study of women in Petersburg, Virginia, a large tobacco-manufacturing town, revealed behavior that valued financial autonomy. Over several decades before 1860, the proportion of women who never married, or did not remarry after the death of a spouse, grew to exceed 33 percent. Likewise, the number of women who worked for wages, controlled their own property, and ran dressmaking businesses increased.

Slave Life and Labor

Slaves knew a life of poverty, coercion, toil, and resentment. They provided the strength and know-how to build an agricultural empire. But they embodied a fundamental contradiction: in the world's model republic, slaves were on the wrong side of a brutally unequal power relationship.

What was the true nature of the master-slave relationship?

Slaves' Everyday Conditions

Southern slaves enjoyed few material comforts beyond the bare necessities. Although they generally had enough to eat, their diet was monotonous and nonnutritious. Clothing was coarse and inexpensive. Few slaves received more than one or two changes of clothing for hot and cold seasons and one blanket each winter. Children of both sexes ran naked in hot weather and wore long cotton shirts in winter. Many slaves went without shoes until December. Conditions were generally better in cities, where slaves frequently lived in the same dwelling as their owners and were regularly hired out, enabling them to accumulate their own money.

The average slave lived in a crude, one-room cabin. Each dwelling housed one or two families. Crowding and lack of sanitation helped spread infection and such contagious diseases as typhoid fever, malaria, and dysentery. White plantation doctors were hired to care for sick slaves, but some "slave doctors" attained a degree of power in the quarters and with masters by healing through herbalism and spiritualism.

Slave Work Routines

Long hours and large work gangs characterized Gulf Coast cotton districts. Overseers rang the morning bell before dawn, and black people, tools in hand, walked toward the fields. Slaves who cultivated tobacco in the Upper South worked long hours picking the sticky, sometimes noxious, leaves under harsh discipline. As one woman recalled when interviewed in the 1930s, "it was way after sundown fore they could stop that field work. Then they had to hustle to finish their night work [such as watering livestock or cleaning cotton] in time for supper, or go to bed without it."

task system: Each slave had a daily or weekly quota of tasks to complete.

Working "from sun to sun" became a norm in much of the South. Profit took precedence over paternalism. Slave women did heavy fieldwork, as much as the men and even during pregnancy. Old people cared for children, doing light chores, or carding, ginning, and spinning cotton.

By the 1830s, planters in the South Carolina and Georgia low country used a **task system** whereby slaves were assigned measured amounts of work to be performed in a given time period. So much cotton per day was to be picked from a designated field, so many rows hoed or plowed in a specified section. Upon completion, slaves' time was their own for working garden plots, tending hogs, even hiring out their own labor. From this experience, many slaves developed a sense of property ownership.

Collection of the J. Paul Getty Museum, Malibu, CA

A portrait of a planter-slaveholder, his two daughters, and their household slave who probably was "nurse" (caretaker) for the children. The picture vividly depicts the attempt at domestic tranquility as well as the prescribed roles of patriarch and slave.

Of the 1860 population of 4 million slaves, half were under age sixteen. "A child raised every two years," wrote Thomas Jefferson, "is of more profit than the crop of the best laboring man." And in 1858, a slaveowner writing in an agricultural magazine calculated that a slave girl he purchased in 1827 for $400 had borne three sons now worth $3,000 as his field hands. Slave children gathered kindling, carried water to the fields, swept the yard, lifted cut sugar-cane stalks into carts, stacked wheat, chased birds away from sprouting rice plants, and labored in cotton and tobacco production.

As slave children matured, they faced psychological traumas, including powerlessness and an awareness that their parents could not protect them. They had to fight to keep from internalizing what whites labeled their inferiority. Many former slaves resented their denial of education. And for girls reaching maturity, the potential trauma of sexual abuse loomed.

Violence and Intimidation Against Slaves

Whites throughout the South believed that slaves "can't be governed except with the whip." One South Carolinian explained to a northern journalist that he whipped his slaves regularly, "the fear of the lash kept them in good order." Evidence suggests that whippings were less frequent on small farms than on large plantations. But beatings symbolized authority to the master and tyranny to the slaves, who used them to evaluate a master. Former slaves said a good owner was one who did not "whip too much," whereas a bad owner "whipped till he's bloodied you and blistered you."

The master wielded virtually absolute authority on his plantation. Slaveholders rarely had to answer to the law or the state. Pregnant women were whipped, and there were burnings, mutilation, torture, and murder. Yet physical cruelty may have been less prevalent in the United States than in other slaveholding parts of the New World, especially some of the sugar islands of the Caribbean, where death rates were so high that the heavily male slave population shrank in size. In the United States, the slave population experienced a steady natural increase, as births exceeded deaths.

The worst evil of American slavery was the nature of slavery itself: coercion, belonging to another person, virtually no hope for mobility or change. Recalling their time in bondage, some former slaves emphasized the physical abuse, memories focused on the tyranny of whipping as much as the pain. Delia Garlic made the essential point: "It's bad to belong to folks that own you soul an' body ... you couldn't guess the awfulness of it." To be a slave was to be the object of another person's will and material gain, as the saying went, "from the cradle to the grave."

Most American slaves retained their mental independence and self-respect despite their bondage. They had to be subservient to their masters, but they talked and behaved differently among themselves. In *Narrative of the Life of Frederick Douglass, an American Slave, Written by Himself* (1845), **Frederick Douglass** wrote that most slaves, when asked about "their condition and the character of their masters, almost universally say they are contented, and that their masters are kind." Slaves did this, said Douglass, because they were governed by the maxim that "a still tongue makes a wise head." Slaves often quarreled over who had the best master, Douglass remarked, when one had a bad master, he sought a better master; and when he had a better one, he wanted to "be his own master."

Frederick Douglass: A former slave who was the leading black abolitionist during the antebellum period.

Slave-Master Relationships

Some former slaves remembered warm feelings between masters and slaves, but the prevailing attitudes were distrust and antagonism. One woman said her mistress was "a mighty good somebody to belong to" but only "'cause she was raisin' us to work for her." Slaves also resented being used as beasts of burden. One man observed that his master "fed us reg'lar on good, 'stantial food, just like you'd tend to your horse, if you had a real good one."

Slaves were alert to the daily signs of their degraded status. One man recalled the general rule that slaves ate cornbread and owners ate biscuits. If blacks did get biscuits, "the flour that we made the biscuits out of was the third-grade sorts." If the owner took his slaves' garden produce to town to sell, slaves often suspected him of pocketing part of the profits.

Link to George and Lucy Skipworth's letters to their master.

Suspicion often grew into hatred. When a yellow fever epidemic struck in 1852, many slaves saw it as God's retribution. An elderly ex-slave named Minnie Fulkes cherished the conviction that God was going to punish white people for their cruelty to blacks. On the plantation, of course, slaves had to keep such thoughts to themselves and created ways to survive and to sustain their humanity in this world of repression.

Slave Culture and Resistance

How did slaves adapt Christianity to make it their own?

The resource that enabled slaves to maintain defiance was their culture: beliefs, values, and practices born of their past and maintained in the present. As best they could, they built a community knitted together by stories, music, a religious world-view, leadership, the smells of their cooking, the sounds of their own voices, and the tapping of their feet. "The values expressed in folklore," wrote African American poet Sterling Brown, provided a "wellspring to which slaves...could return in times of doubt to be refreshed."

African Cultural Survival

Slave culture changed significantly after 1808, when Congress banned further importation of slaves and the generations born in Africa died out. For a few years, South Carolina illegally reopened the international slave trade, but by the 1830s, the majority of slaves in the South were native-born Americans.

Yet African influences remained strong. Some slave men plaited their hair into rows and designs; slave women often wore their hair tied in small bunches secured by string or piece of cloth. A few men and many women wrapped their heads in kerchiefs of the styles and colors of West Africa.

Music, religion, and folktales were parts of daily life for most slaves. Borrowing partly from their African background and forging new American folkways, they developed what scholars have called a sacred world-view, which affected work, leisure, and self-understanding. Slaves made musical instruments with carved motifs that resembled African stringed instruments. One visitor to Georgia in the 1860s described a ritual dance of African origin known as the ring shout: "A ring of singers is formed. ... They then utter a kind of melodious chant, which gradually increases in strength, and in noise, until it fairly shakes the house, and it can be heard for a long distance."

Many slaves continued to believe in spirit possession. While whites believed in ghosts and charms, slaves' belief resembled the African concept of the living dead—deceased relatives visiting the earth for years until the process of dying is complete. Slaves also practiced conjuration and quasi-magical root medicine. By the 1850s, noted conjurers and root doctors were reputed to live in South Carolina, Georgia, Louisiana, and isolated coastal areas with high slave populations.

As they became African Americans, slaves increasingly developed a racial identity. In the colonial period, Africans arrived in America from many states and kingdoms, represented in distinctive languages and traditions. Africans arrived in the New World with virtually no concept of "race"; by the antebellum era, their descendants learned through bitter experience that race was now the defining feature of their lives.

Slaves' Religion and Music

Over time, more and more slaves adopted Christianity, fashioning it into an instrument of support and resistance. Theirs was a religion of justice and deliverance, quite unlike their masters' religious propaganda. "You ought to have heard that preachin,'" said one man. "'Obey your master and mistress, don't steal chickens and eggs and meat,' but nary a word about havin' a soul to save." Slaves believed that Jesus cared about their souls and their plight.

Devout slaves worshiped every day, "in the field or by the side of the road." Some slaves held secret prayer meetings that lasted into the night. Many nurtured an unshakable belief that God would end their bondage. This faith—and the emotional release that accompanied worship—sustained them.

Slaves also adapted Christianity to African practices. In West African belief, devotees are possessed by a god so thoroughly that the god's personality replaces the human personality. In the late antebellum era, Christian slaves experienced possession by the Protestant "Holy Spirit." The combination of shouting, singing, and dancing that seemed to overtake black worshipers formed the heart of their religious faith. "The old meeting house caught fire," recalled an ex-slave preacher. "The spirit was there....God saw our need and came to us." Out in brush arbors or in meetinghouses, slaves thrust their arms to heaven, made music with their feet, and sang away their woes.

Rhythm and physical movement were crucial to slaves' religious experience. In black preachers' chanted sermons, which pulled the sinner into a narrative of meanings and cadences en route to conversion, an American tradition was born. The chanted sermon was a scriptural and patterned form that required audience response punctuated by "yes sirs!" and "amens!" But it was in song that slaves left their most sublime gift to American culture.

Through spirituals, slaves tried to impose order on the chaos of their lives. Often referred to later as the "sorrow songs," lyrics covered many themes, especially imminent rebirth. Sadness could immediately give way to joy: "Oh, Oh, Freedom / Ojh, Oh, Freedom over me— / But before I'll be a slave, / I'll be buried in my grave, / And go home to my Lord, / And Be Free!"

Many songs also express intimacy and closeness with God. Some display rebelliousness, such as the enduring "He said, and if I had my way / If I had my way, if I had my way, / I'd tear this building down!" And some spirituals reached for a collective sense of hope in the black community as a whole.

O, gracious Lord! When shall it be,
That we poor souls shall all be free;
Lord, break them slavery powers—
Will you go along with me?
Lord break them slavery powers,
Go sound the jubilee!

In many ways, American slaves converted the Christian God to themselves. They sought an alternative world—a home other than the one fate had given them on earth. With variations on the Br'er Rabbit folktales—in which the weak survive by wit and power is reversed—and in songs, they fashioned survival from their cultural imagination.

The Black Family in Slavery

Although American law did not recognize slave families, slaveowners *expected* slaves to form families and have children. As a result, there was a normal ratio of men to women, young to old. On some of the largest cotton plantations of South Carolina, when masters allowed their slaves increased autonomy through the task system, the property accumulation in livestock, tools, and garden produce led to more stable and healthier families.

Following African kinship traditions, African Americans avoided marriage between cousins (commonplace among aristocratic slaveowners). By naming their children after relatives of past generations, African Americans emphasized family histories. Kinship networks and extended families held life together in many slave communities.

For slave women, sexual abuse and rape by white masters were ever-present threats. By 1860, there were 405,751 mulattos in the United States, comprising 12.5 percent of the African American population. White planters were sometimes open with their behavior toward slave women, but not in the way they talked about it. Buying slaves for sex was common at the New Orleans slave market. In what was called the "fancy trade" (a "fancy" was a young, attractive slave girl or woman), females were often sold for prices as much as 300 percent higher than the average. At such auctions, slaveholders exhibited some of the ugliest values at the heart of the slave system by paying $3,000 to $5,000 for female "companions."

Slave women like Harriet Jacobs spent years dodging their owners' sexual pursuit. In recollecting her desperate effort to protect her children, Jacobs asked a haunting question: "Why does the slave ever love? Why

This photograph of five generations of a slave family, taken in Beaufort, South Carolina, in 1862, is silent but powerful testimony to the importance that enslaved African Americans placed on their ever-threatened family ties.

Library of Congress

allow the tendrils of the heart to twine around objects which may at any moment be wrenched away by the hand of violence?"

Link to Harriet Jacobs's papers.

The Domestic Slave Trade

Slave families most feared and hated separation by violence from those they loved, sexual appropriation, and sale. Many struggled to keep their children together and, after emancipation, to reestablish contact with loved ones lost by forced migration and sale. Between 1820 and 1860, an estimated 2 million slaves were moved into the region from western Georgia to eastern Texas. When the Union Army registered thousands of black marriages in Mississippi and Louisiana in 1864 and 1865, 25 percent of the men over forty reported that they had been forcibly separated from a previous wife. Thousands of black families were disrupted annually to serve the needs of the expanding cotton economy.

Many antebellum white southerners made their living from the slave trade. In South Carolina by the 1850s, there were over one hundred slave-trading firms selling approximately 6,500 slaves to southwestern states. One estimate from 1858 indicated that slave sales in Richmond, Virginia, netted $4 million that year alone. A market guide to slave sales that same year in Richmond listed average prices for "likely ploughboys," ages twelve to fourteen, at $850 to $1,050; "extra number 1 fieldgirls" at $1,300 to $1,350; and "extra number 1 men" at $1,500.

At slave "pens" in cities like New Orleans, traders promoted "a large and commodious showroom...prepared to accommodate over 200 Negroes for sale." Traders made slaves appear young, healthy, and happy, cutting gray whiskers off men, using paddles as discipline to avoid scarring their merchandise, and forcing people to dance and sing as buyers arrived. When transported to the southwestern markets, slaves were often chained together, making journeys of 500 miles or more on foot.

The complacent mixture of racism and business among traders is evident in their own language. "I refused a girl 20 year[s] old at 700 yesterday," one trader wrote in 1853. "She is very badly whipped but good teeth." Some sales were transacted at owners' requests, often for tragically inhumane reasons. "Bought a cook yesterday that was to go out of state," wrote a trader; "she just made the people mad that was all."

Strategies of Resistance

Slaves brought to their resistance the common sense and determination that characterized their struggle to secure families. The scales weighed against overt revolution, but they seized opportunities to alter work conditions. They sometimes slacked off when they were not watched.

Daily discontent and desperation were also manifest in equipment sabotage; carelessness about work; theft of food, livestock, or crops; or getting drunk on stolen liquor. Some slaves who were hired out hoarded their earnings or became recalcitrant. A woman named Ellen, hired as a cook in Tennessee in 1856, quietly put mercury poison into a roasted apple for her unsuspecting mistress. And some slave women resisted by trying to control their own pregnancy, either by avoiding it or by seeking it to improve their conditions.

Many male, and some female, slaves violently attacked overseers or owners. Southern court records and newspapers contain accounts of resistant slaves who disproved the image of the docile bondsman. Rebels were customarily flogged, sold, or hanged.

Many slaves attempted to run away to the North, and some received assistance from the loose network known as the Underground Railroad (see pages 371–373). But it was more common for slaves to run off temporarily to hide in the woods. Approximately 80 percent of runaways were male; children prevented women from fleeing. Fear, disgruntlement over treatment, or family separation might motivate slaves to flee. Only a minority ever made it to freedom in the North, but these fugitives made slavery an insecure institution by the 1850s.

American slavery also produced some fearless revolutionaries. Gabriel's Rebellion involved about a thousand slaves when it was discovered in 1800, just before it would have exploded in Richmond, Virginia (see pages 213–214). According to controversial court testimony, a similar conspiracy existed in Charleston in 1822, led by a free black named Denmark Vesey. Born a slave in the Caribbean, Vesey won a lottery of $1,500 in 1799, bought his freedom, and became a religious leader. According to one long-argued interpretation, Vesey was a heroic revolutionary determined to free his people. But, in a recent challenge, historian Michael Johnson points out that court testimony is the only reliable source on the alleged insurrection. Might the testimony reveal less of reality than of white South Carolina's fears of slave rebellion? The court, says Johnson, built its case on rumors and intimidated witnesses, and "conjured into being" an insurrection that was not truly about to occur. Whatever the facts, thirty-seven "conspirators" were executed, and more than three dozen others were banished from the state.

Nat Turner's Insurrection

The most famous rebel, **Nat Turner**, struck for freedom in Southampton County, Virginia, in 1831. Turner was a precocious child who learned to read. Encouraged by his first owner to study the Bible, he enjoyed privileges but also endured hard work and changes of masters. His father successfully escaped to freedom.

Young Nat became a preacher known for eloquence and mysticism. After planning for years, Turner led rebels from farm to farm in the predawn darkness of August 22, 1831. The group severed limbs and crushed skulls with axes or killed their victims with guns. Before alarmed planters stopped them, Turner and his followers had in forty-eight hours slaughtered sixty whites. In retaliation, whites randomly killed slaves across the region. Turner was caught and hanged. As many as two hundred African Americans lost their lives as a result of the rebellion.

Nat Turner remains a haunting symbol in America's unresolved history with slavery and discrimination. While in jail, Turner was interviewed by a Virginia lawyer and slaveholder, Thomas R. Gray. Their intriguing creation, *The Confessions of Nat Turner*, became a bestseller within a month of Turner's hanging. Gray called the rebel a "gloomy fanatic," but in a manner that made him fascinating and produced one of the most remarkable documents of American slavery. After Turner's insurrection, many states passed stiffened legal codes against black education and religious practice.

Most importantly, in 1832 a shocked Virginia held a legislative and public debate over gradual emancipation. The plan debated would not have freed any slaves until 1858 and provided that eventually all blacks would be colonized outside Virginia. When the House of Delegates voted, gradual abolition lost, 73 to 58. Virginia merely reinforced its defense of slavery. It was the last time white southerners would debate emancipation.

Nat Turner: A slave who led a bloody rebellion in Southampton County, Virginia, in 1831.

Visualizing the Past

Imaging Nat Turner's Rebellion

Below is the title page from *The Confessions of Nat Turner*, by Thomas R. Gray, 1832. This document of nearly twenty pages was published by the lawyer, Gray, who recorded and likely refashioned Turner's lengthy statement during an interview in his jail cell before his execution. *The Confessions* became a widely sold and sensational documentation of Turner's identity and especially his motivations and methods during the rebellion. It portrayed Turner as a religious mystic

and fanatic and allowed the broad public to imagine the mind of a religiously motivated slave rebel. Below and to the right is "Horrid Massacre in Virginia," 1831, woodcut. This composite of scenes depicts the slaughter of innocent women and children, as well as white men as both victims and resistants. The fear, confusion, and fierce retribution that dominated the aftermath of the Turner rebellion are on display here. Why was Nat Turner's insurrection such a shock to the nation as well as to the South? What kind of impact did Nat Turner's rebellion have on the South's evolving defense of slavery in the coming decades?

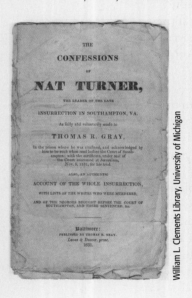

William L. Clements Library, University of Michigan

Library of Congress

Summary

During the four decades before the Civil War, the South grew in land, wealth, and power along with the rest of the country. Although the southern states were enmeshed in the nation's heritage and political economy, they also developed as a distinctive region, ideologically and economically, because of slavery. More than the North, the antebellum South was a biracial society; whites grew up influenced by black folkways and culture; and blacks, the vast majority of whom were slaves, became cobuilders of a rural, agricultural society.

With the cotton boom, as well as state and federal Indian removal policies, the South grew into a slave society. The coercive influence of slavery affected southern life

Reparations for Slavery

How should the United States come to terms with 250 years of racial slavery? Is this period best forgotten as a terrible passage, or does the nation owe a long-overdue debt to black people for their oppression? After emancipation in 1865, and rooted in vague federal promises, many former slaves believed they were entitled to "forty acres and a mule," but these never materialized.

In 1897, Callie House—a poor mother of four born in 1865 in a contraband camp for ex-slaves—organized the National Ex-Slave Pension and Bounty Association, modeled after the soldiers' pension systems. House traveled throughout the South, recruiting 250,000 members at 10-cent dues. Her lobbying of the federal government for slave pensions failed; she was accused of mail fraud and imprisoned for one year in 1916.

More recently, a widespread debate over "reparations" for slavery has emerged. In the rewriting of slavery's history since the 1960s, Americans have learned how slave labor created American wealth: how insurance companies insured slaves, how complicit the U.S. government was in slavery's expansion, and how slaves built the U.S. Capitol while their owners received $5 a month for their labor.

The debate is fueled by analogies: reparations paid to Japanese Americans interned during World War II; reparations paid to Native American tribes for stolen land; reparations paid to Holocaust survivors and victims of forced labor; and a suit settled in 1999 that will pay an estimated $2 billion to some twenty thousand black farmers for discrimination practiced by the Agriculture Department in the early twentieth century.

Some argue that because there are no living former slaves or slaveholders, reparations can never take the form of money. But in 2002, a lawsuit was filed against three major corporations who allegedly profited from slavery, and the National Reparations Coordinating Committee promises a suit against the U.S. government. Some city councils passed resolutions forcing companies in their jurisdictions to investigate possible complicity with slave trading or ownership, prompting some firms to establish scholarship programs for African Americans.

Critics argue that resources would be better spent "making sure black kids have a credible education" and rebuilding inner cities. Advocates contend that, when "government participates in a crime against humanity," it is "obliged to make the victims whole." The movement for reparations has sparked broad public debate. The legacy of slavery for a people and a nation promises to become a test of how to reconcile its history with justice.

and politics and increasingly produced a leadership determined to preserve a hierarchical social and racial order. Despite their shared white supremacy, the democratic values of yeomen often clashed with the profit motives of aristocratic planters. The benevolent self-image and paternalistic ideology of slaveholders was tested by the slaves' own judgments. African American slaves responded by fashioning a rich folk culture and a religion of deliverance. Their experiences could differ from one region and labor type to another. Some blacks were crushed by bondage; others transcended it through survival and resistance.

By 1850, through their own wits and on the backs of African labor, white southerners had aggressively built one of the last profitable, expanding slave societies on earth. North of them and deeply intertwined with them in the same nation, economy, constitutional system, and history, a different kind of society had grown even faster—driven by industrialism and free labor. The clash of these two deeply connected, yet mutually fearful and divided societies would soon explode in political storms over the nation's future.

Chapter Review

The "Distinctive" South

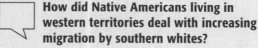

What made the antebellum South different from the North?

Both regions were capitalist and Christian (largely Protestant) and embraced the heroes and causes of the American Revolution. But they differed in their economic development: because of its climate and longer growing season, the South's development was agricultural and rural, whereas the North became increasingly urban and industrial. With a comparatively low population density and people spread out from each other, the South had little income for developing its commercial, educational, and health-related institutions. The South was also slower to develop a regional transportation network or market economy and relied on slaves for labor and the North for banking and other financial institutions. The South had fewer urban areas, and those that existed were primarily port cities such as Charleston that provided a link for commerce and small manufacturing. With few labor opportunities, the South also did not attract as many immigrants as the North.

Southern Expansion, Indian Resistance, and Removal

How did Native Americans living in western territories deal with increasing migration by southern whites?

Indians dealt with white encroachment on their land in several ways. Some embraced accommodation, establishing trading posts to exchange supplies with settlers, often ultimately falling into heavy debt that could only be repaid by selling their land. Others resisted, rejecting removal/relocation plans that whites offered, and holding fast to their land. The Creeks and Cherokees assimilated to American standards—even changed their political structure to more closely resemble that of whites—in an effort to keep their land. When Congress narrowly passed the Indian Removal Act in 1830, which provided funds to relocate Indians to territory further west, the Cherokees refused to leave and sued the state of Georgia in federal court. While the courts found them entitled to their land, President Jackson ignored the ruling and sent in troops to evacuate thousands of Cherokees and march them from Georgia to present-day Oklahoma.

Many refused to go and were imprisoned; others died of disease and exhaustion on the trek known as the Trail of Tears.

Social Pyramid in the Old South

What class tensions emerged in the antebellum South?

Although they were fewer in number, the slaveholding planter class occupied the highest rungs of southern society and dominated its political life (controlling up to 85 percent of legislative posts) as well as churches and colleges. Before the 1830s, the vast socioeconomic differences between rich planters and small, independent, nonslaveholding yeomen farmers were mediated by their shared racial status as white. However, tensions emerged as yeomen began to resent their under-representation in state government and the corruption of local governments. They sought universal manhood suffrage and other reforms, including popular election of governors and legislative apportionment based solely on the white population—all of which planters resisted. Moreover, as cotton farming made land less and less available, nonslaveholders faced fewer opportunities to improve their station, while planters enjoyed greater and greater profits.

The Planters' World

How did paternalism function on southern plantations?

Paternalism was a belief system that enabled slaveholders to justify slaveholding and their dominance over white women. In this view, slave owners portrayed themselves as benevolent guardians over their families, which included slaves. They stressed their obligations to those beneath them—wives, children, and the enslaved. Paternalism denied the truth of slavery's brutality and inhumanity, while providing a counter to abolitionism. As the system developed, it functioned as an exchange in which slaves labored and obligated their owners to provide them with necessities and some autonomy. Between husbands and wives, paternalism gave men control of women's legal rights in marriage—her property became his to manage—and she became his subordinate in every way.

Slave Life and Labor

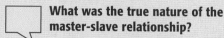
What was the true nature of the master-slave relationship?

Generally speaking, distrust and antagonism were at the core of most master-slave relationships. For slaves, the vulnerability and frustration of being owned and at the mercy of another human being, along with being used for harsh physical labor, sparked much resentment. Slaves did not trust masters to deal fairly with them in their exchanges. There was also much cruelty and brutality—rather than paternalism—on the part of many owners, including whippings and beatings. Slave families were often separated, as one or more members were sold away to other plantations.

Slave Culture and Resistance

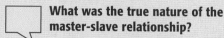
How did slaves adapt Christianity to make it their own?

While many slaves maintained and adapted aspects of the African heritage to their new circumstances, they also embraced and remade Christianity as a form of resistance. In secret prayer meetings, slaves focused on justice and deliverance, believing God would liberate them from their servitude and exact retribution from those who unjustly enslaved or abused them. They also merged their Christianity with African practices, adding shouting, singing, dancing, and other rituals to their religious meetings, along with chanted sermons, which were regarded as vital for the conversion experience. Their religious rituals not only attempted to restore order and meaning to their lives but also establish closeness with God and hope for the future. Finally, while prayer meetings were often held in secret, they helped forge relationships and community in slave quarters.

Suggestions for Further Reading

Ira Berlin, *Generations of Captivity: A History of African American Slaves* (2003)

David Brion Davis, *Inhuman Bondage: The Rise and Fall of Slavery in the New World* (2006)

Steven Deyle, *Carry Me Back: The Domestic Slave Trade in American Life* (2005)

Drew G. Faust, ed., *The Ideology of Slavery: Proslavery Thought in the Antebellum South, 1830–1860* (1981)

Walter Johnson, *Soul by Soul: Life Inside the Antebellum Slave Market* (1999)

Charles Joyner, *Down by the Riverside: A South Carolina Slave Community* (1984)

James D. Miller, *South by Southwest: Planter Emigration and Identity in the Slave South* (2002)

James Oakes, *Slavery and Freedom: An Interpretation of the Old South* (1991)

Michael O'Brien, *Conjectures of Order: Intellectual Life and the American South, 1810–1860*, 2 vols., (2004)

Daniel H. Usner Jr., *American Indians in the Lower Mississippi Valley* (1998)

Annette Gordon-Reed, *The Hemingses of Monticello: An American Family* (2008)

Go to the CourseMate website for primary source links, study tools, and review materials for this chapter. www.cengagebrain.com

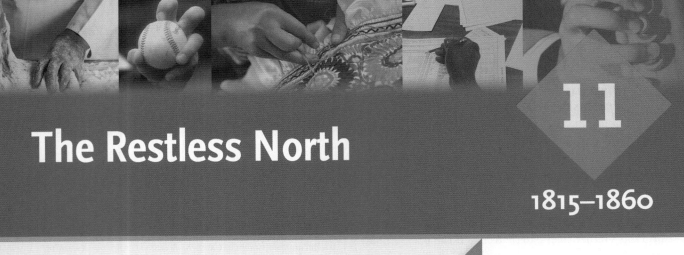

The Restless North

11

1815–1860

After 25 stormy days at sea, Mary Ann and James Archbald and their four children finally arrived in New York on April 17, 1807. The couple left their ancestral homeland in Scotland, envisioning a bright future in which their children would be beholden to no one—neither landlord nor employer. They were pursuing the Jeffersonian dream of republican independence.

The Archbalds bought a farm in central New York, along a Hudson River tributary, where they raised sheep, grew hay and vegetables, skinned rabbits for their meat and fur—and then sold whatever they did not need. From the wool shorn by her husband and sons, Mary Ann and her daughters spun thread and wove cloth for their own use and for sale. They used the cash to pay their mortgage. Twenty-one years after leaving Scotland, Mary Ann Archbald, in anticipation of their last payment, declared, "being out of debt is, in my estimation, being rich." By then, her sons were young adults with visions of wealth that centered on water, not land.

On April 17, 1817—a decade after the Archbalds reached American shores—the New York State legislature authorized construction of a canal connecting Lake Erie to the Hudson River, and surveyors mapped a route through the Archbalds' farm. The sons helped dig the canal, while Mary Ann and her daughters cooked and cleaned for the twenty Irish laborers whom the sons hired. The Archbald sons soon tried commercial speculation, borrowing money to buy wheat and lumber in western New York to resell it at substantial profits to merchants in Albany and New York City. As early as 1808, Mary Ann had reached an unpleasant conclusion about her new home: "We are a nation of traders in spite of all Mr. Jefferson can say or do."

After the War of 1812, the market economy took off in unanticipated ways. In the North, steamboats, canals, and then railroads remapped the young republic's geography and economy, setting off booms in westward migration, industry, commerce, and urban growth.

Chapter Outline

Or Is It the North That Was Distinctive?
Preindustrial Farms | Preindustrial Artisans | Early Industrialization

The Transportation Revolution
Roads | Steamboats | Canals | Railroads | Government Promotion of Internal Improvements | Regional Connections | Ambivalence Toward Progress

LINKS TO THE WORLD *Internal Improvements*

Factories and Industrialization
Factory Work | Textile Mills | Labor Protests | Labor Unions

Consumption and Commercialization
The Garment Industry | Specialization of Commerce | Commercial Farming | Farm Women's Changing Labor | Rural Communities | Cycles of Boom and Bust

VISUALIZING THE PAST *Images of Boom and Bust*

Families in Flux
The "Ideal" Family | Shrinking Families | Women's Paid Labor

The Growth of Cities
Urban Boom | Market-Related Development | Extremes of Wealth | Immigration | Ethnic Tensions | People of Color | Urban Culture | The Penny Press | Cities as Symbols of Progress

LEGACY FOR A PEOPLE AND A NATION *P. T. Barnum's Publicity Stunts*

SUMMARY

Even after the War of 1812, the United States' financial connections to Europe, particularly Britain, remained profound. When Europeans suffered hard times, so, did American merchants, manufacturers, farmers, and workers. For wage-earning Americans, economic downturns often meant unemployment and destitution.

The economy's rapid expansion following the War of 1812 inspired fears that, unless properly controlled, market growth could threaten the nation's moral fiber. It upset family patterns and relied on unskilled workers—often immigrants and free African Americans—who seemed unfit for republican citizenship. Commercially minded Americans saw cities as both exemplars of civilization and breeding grounds of depravity and conflict. Only through faith in progress and upward mobility could Americans remain hopeful that the nation's greatness lay with commercial expansion. They did so partly by articulating a free-labor ideology that rationalized the negative aspects of market expansion while promoting the northern labor system as superior to the South's.

As you read this chapter, keep the following questions in mind:

* **What factors contributed to the commercialization of northern society, and why did they have less of an influence on the South?**

* **How did the daily lives—work, family, leisure—of northerners change between 1815 and 1860?**

* **What factors contributed to rapid urbanization, and how did urban and rural life in the North compare with that in the South?**

Or Is It the North That Was Distinctive?

Historian James McPherson has proposed a new twist to the old question of southern distinctiveness: perhaps it was the *North*—New England, the Middle Atlantic, and the Old Northwest—that diverged from the norm. At the republic's birth, the two regions had much in common: slavery, ethnic homogeneity, a majority of the population engaged in agriculture, a small urban population. But that started to changed with economic development after the War of 1812. State and local governments and private entrepreneurs engaged in development, which happened faster and more extensively in the North. As the North embraced economic progress, it—rather than the South—diverged from the international norm. The North, writes McPherson, "hurtled forward toward a future that many Southerners found distasteful if not frightening." With its continual quest for improvement, the North—much more so than the South—embodied what Frenchman Alexis de Tocqueville, who toured the United States in 1831–1832, called the nation's "restless spirit."

While the South expanded as a slave society during and after the War of 1812, the North transformed, as one historian has put it, from a society with markets to a market society. In the colonial era, settlers lived in a society with markets, one in which they engaged in long-distance trade—selling their surpluses to merchants, who in turn sent raw materials to Europe, using the proceeds to purchase finished goods for resale—but in which most settlers remained self-sufficient. During and after the War of 1812, the North became more solidly a market society, one in which

What happened to the North and South economically after the War of 1812?

Chronology

1824	*Gibbons v. Ogden* prohibits steamboat monopolies		1836	Second Bank of the United States closes
1825	Erie Canal completed		1837	Panic of 1837 begins economic downturn
1827	Construction begins on Baltimore and Ohio (B&O) Railroad		1839–43	Economic depression
			1840s	Female mill workers' publications appear
1830	First locomotive runs on B&O Railroad		1842	*Commonwealth v. Hunt* declares strikes lawful
1830s	Penny press emerges			
1830s–50s	Urban riots commonplace		1844	Federal government sponsors first telegraph line
1834	Women workers strike at Lowell			Lowell Female Reform Association formed
1835	Arkansas passes first women's property law		1845	Massive Irish immigration begins

participation in long-distance commerce fundamentally altered individuals' aspirations and activities. With European trade largely halted during the war, entrepreneurs invested in domestic factories. More men, women, and children began working for wages—rather than on family farms—making the domestic demand for foodstuffs soar. Farming became commercialized, with farmers abandoning self-sufficiency and specializing in crops that would yield cash on the market. Farmers then used the cash to buy goods they once made for themselves, such as cloth and soap, along with some luxuries. Unlike the typical southern yeoman, they were not self-reliant, and isolation was rare. In the North, market expansion altered every aspect of life. Some historians see these rapid and pervasive changes as a market revolution.

Preindustrial Farms

As the nineteenth century dawned, few yeoman farmers, North or South, were entirely independent. Most practiced mixed agriculture, raising a variety of crops and livestock. Their goal was to procure what they called a "competence": everyday comforts and economic opportunities for their children. When they produced more than they needed, they traded the surplus with neighbors or sold it to local storekeepers. Such transactions often transpired without money; farmers might trade eggs for shoes, or they might labor in their neighbor's fields in exchange for hay. Farmers like the Archbalds engaged in long-distance market exchange, selling farm goods for cash to merchants, who sent the

National Gallery of Art, Washington, D.C. Gift of Edgar William and Bernice Chrysler Garbisch

Although separating flax fibers from their woody base could be arduous work, flax-scutching bees—much like corn-husking bees—brought together neighbors for frivolity as well as work.

goods to people far away. But for Mary Ann Archbald, the main reason to earn cash was not to accumulate wealth but to pay off the family's land debt. Although families like the Archbalds indulged in the occasional luxury, security and paying debts mattered more than profit.

Family members provided most farm labor, though some yeoman farmers, North and South, relied on slaves or indentured servants. Men and boys worked in the fields, herded livestock, chopped firewood, fished, and hunted. Women and girls tended gardens, milked cows, spun cloth, processed and preserved food, prepared meals, washed clothes, and watched infants and toddlers.

Farmers cooperated with one another, lending farm tools, harvesting each other's fields, bartering goods, raising their neighbors' barns, and husking their corn. Little cash exchanged hands, mostly because money was scarce. Still, New England farmers kept elaborate account books recording what they owed and were owed, whereas Southern farmers simply made mental notes of debts. In both regions, years might pass without debts being repaid. In the local economy—where farmers exchanged goods with people they knew—a system of "just price" prevailed, in which neighbors calculated value in terms of how much labor was involved. When the same farmers engaged in long-distance trade—selling goods through a network of merchants who eventually resold them as far away as Europe—they set prices based on what the market would bear.

Preindustrial Artisans

Farmers who lived near towns or villages often purchased crafted goods from local cobblers, saddlers, blacksmiths, gunsmiths, silversmiths, and tailors. Most artisans, though, lived in the nation's seaports, where master craftsmen (businessmen who owned shops and tools) employed apprentices and journeymen. Although the majority of craftsmen, North and South, were white, free blacks were well represented in some cities' trades, such as tailoring and carpentry in Charleston, South Carolina. Teenage apprentices lived with masters, who taught, lodged, and fed them in exchange for labor. The master's wife and daughters cooked, cleaned, and sewed for the workers. When their apprenticeship expired, apprentices became journeymen who earned wages, hoping to save money to open their own shops. The workplace had little division of labor or specialization. For example, a tailor measured, designed, and sewed an entire suit.

Men, women, and children worked long days on farms and in workshops, but the pace was uneven and unregimented. When busy, they worked dawn to dusk; work slowed after the harvest or after a large order had been completed. Husking bees and barn raisings brought people together to shuck corn and raise buildings and to eat, drink, and dance. Busy periods did not stop artisans from taking grog breaks or reading the newspaper aloud; they might even close their shops to attend a political meeting. Journeymen craftsmen often staggered in late on Monday mornings, if they showed up at all, after carousing on their day off. In this way, workers exerted a good deal of influence over the workplace.

Early Industrialization

Early industry in the United States reorganized daily work routines and market relationships. In the late eighteenth and early nineteenth centuries, a "putting-out" system developed in the Northeast, particularly in Massachusetts, New Jersey, and Pennsylvania. Women and children continued to produce goods but now a merchant supplied them with raw materials, paid them a wage (usually a price for each piece they produced), and sold their wares in distant markets, pocketing the profits himself. "Outwork," as it is sometimes called, appealed to women eager for cash, whether to secure economic independence or to save for additional land where their children might establish farms. Particularly in New England—where population density, small farms, and tired soil constricted farming opportunities—the putting-out system provided opportunities to earn money with which to buy more fertile western lands.

Drawing on technology from Europe, the earliest factories grew in tandem with the putting-out system. Samuel Slater helped set up the first American water-powered spinning mill in Rhode Island in 1790, using children to card and spin raw cotton into thread. He sent the spun thread to nearby farm families who were paid to weave it into cloth. Although the work remained familiar, women now operated their looms for wages and produced cloth primarily for the market.

The Transportation Revolution

How did the transportation revolution help lay the groundwork for a market economy?

In order to market goods at substantial distances from where they were produced, internal improvements were needed. Before the War of 1812, natural waterways provided the most readily available and cheapest transportation routes for people and goods, but they had limitations. Boatmen poled bateaux (cargo boats) down shallow rivers or floated flatboats down deep ones. Cargo generally moved in one direction—downstream—and most boats were destroyed for lumber at their destination. Upstream commerce was limited.

Roads

Overland transport was limited, too. Although some roads were built during the colonial and revolutionary eras, they often became obstructed by fallen trees, soaked by mud, or clouded in dust. To reduce mud and dust, some turnpike companies built "corduroy" roads, whose tightly lined-up logs resembled the ribbed cotton fabric. But passengers complained of nausea from being continually jolted, and merchants remained wary of transporting fragile wares by wagon. Land transportation was slow and expensive. In 1800, it cost as much to ship a ton of goods 30 miles into the interior as to ship the same goods from New York to England. The lack of cheap, quick transportation impeded westward expansion and industrial growth. With natural water routes unpredictable and roads predictably bad, an urgent need arose for better transportation.

Steamboats

The first major innovation was the steamboat. In 1807, Robert Fulton's Clermont traveled between New York and Albany on the Hudson River in thirty-two hours, demonstrating the feasibility of using steam engines to power boats. After the Supreme Court's ruling against steamboat monopolies in Gibbons v. Ogden (1824), steamboat companies flourished on eastern rivers and, to a lesser extent, on the Great Lakes. They transported settlers to the Midwest, where they would grow grain and raise pigs that fed northeastern factory workers. Along western rivers like the Mississippi and the Ohio, steamboats carried Midwestern timber and grain, and southern cotton to New Orleans, where they were transferred to oceangoing vessels destined for northern and international ports. To travel between Ohio and New Orleans by flatboat in 1815 took several months; in 1840, the same trip by steamboat took just ten days. Privately operated, steamboats became subject to federal regulations after frequent and deadly accidents in which boilers exploded, fires ignited, and boats collided.

Canals

In the late eighteenth and early nineteenth centuries, private companies (sometimes with state subsidies) built small canals to transport goods to and from interior locations. These projects rarely reaped substantial profits, making it difficult to court future investors. In 1815, only three canals measured more than 2 miles long; the longest was 27 miles. After Madison's veto of the Bonus Bill dashed commercially minded New Yorkers' hopes for a canal connecting Lake Erie to the port of New York, Governor DeWitt Clinton pushed successfully for a state-sponsored initiative. The **Erie Canal** was to run 363 miles between Buffalo and Albany and was to be 4 feet deep.

Construction began on July 4, 1817. The canal, its promoters emphasized, would demonstrate how American ingenuity and hard work could overcome any obstacle including the combined ascent and descent of 680 feet between Buffalo and Albany. By so doing, it would help unify the nation and secure its commercial independence from Europe.

Over the next eight years, nine thousand laborers felled forests, shoveled dirt, blasted rock, hauled boulders, rechanneled streams, and molded the canal bed. Stonemasons and carpenters built aqueducts and locks. The work was dangerous, often taking place in malaria- and rattlesnake-infested swamps. Gunpowder explosions blew up some workers along with the rock they blasted. Collapsing canal beds smothered others, while some fell to their death from aqueducts and locks.

The canal's promoters celebrated the waterway as the work of "republican free men," a tribute to the nation's republican heritage. But few of those involved in the canal's construction would have perceived their work as fulfilling Jefferson's notion of republican freedom. Although farmers and artisans provided important labor, unskilled laborers—including immigrants and convicts—outnumbered them. Once completed, the Erie Canal relied on child labor. Boys led the horses that pulled boats between the canal's eighty-three locks, while girls cooked and cleaned on the boats. When the canal froze shut in winter, many workers had neither employment nor shelter.

The Erie Canal's completion in November 1825 brought immediate commercial success. Horse-drawn boats, stacked with bushels of wheat, barrels of oats, and piles of logs, streamed eastward from western New York and Buffalo, where longshoreman transferred shipments to canal boats. Forty thousand passengers in 1825 alone traveled on the new waterway. The canal shortened the journey between Buffalo and New York City from twenty to six days and reduced freight charges by nearly 95 percent—thus securing New York City's position as the nation's preeminent port. Goods that were previously unavailable in the nation's interior now could be had easily and cheaply.

By 1840, canals crisscrossed the Northeast and Midwest, and total canal mileage reached 3,300. Because the South had easily navigable rivers, fewer canals were dug there. None of the new canals enjoyed the Erie's financial success. As the high cost of construction combined with economic contraction, investment in canals slumped in the 1830s. Several midwestern states could not repay their canal loans, leading them to bankruptcy or near-bankruptcy. By mid-century, the canal era had ended, though the Erie Canal (by then twice enlarged and rerouted) continued to prosper and operate until the late twentieth century.

Link to an illustration of Clinton promoting the Erie Canal.

Erie Canal: Major canal that linked Great Lakes to New York City, opening upper Midwest to wider development.

Railroads

The future belonged to railroads. Trains moved faster than canal boats and operated year-round. Railroads could connect the most remote locations to national and international markets. By 1860, the United States had 60,000 miles of track, mostly in the North, and railroads had dramatically reduced the cost and the time involved in shipping goods.

The United States railroad era began in 1830 when Peter Cooper's locomotive, Tom Thumb, steamed along 13 miles of Baltimore & Ohio Railroad track. Not until the 1850s did railroads offer long-distance service at reasonable rates. Even then, lack of a common standard for track width thwarted development of a national system. A journey from Philadelphia to Charleston involved eight different gauges, requiring passengers and freight to change trains seven times. Only at Bowling Green, Kentucky, did northern and southern railroads connect. Despite the race to construct internal improvements, the nation's canals and railroads did little to unite the regions and promote nationalism, as proponents of government-sponsored internal improvements had hoped.

Government Promotion of Internal Improvements

Northern state and local governments and private investors spent more on internal improvements than did southerners. Pennsylvania and New York together accounted for half of all state monies invested. Southern states invested in railroads, but—with smaller free populations—they collected fewer taxes and had less to spend.

For capitalists seeking dividends, southern railroads often seemed a poor bet. To be profitable for investors and affordable for shippers, trains could not ship only one way; if they took agricultural products to market, their cars had to be filled with manufactured or finished goods for the return trip. But slaves and cash-strapped farmers did not provide much of a consumer base. Although planters bought northern ready-made clothes and shoes for their slaves, such purchases—made annually—did not constitute a regular source of incoming freight. Because the wealthiest men lived along rivers and could send their cotton to market on steamboats, they sometimes saw little need for railroads.

The North and South laid roughly the same amount of railroad track per person before the Civil War, but when measured in mileage, the more populous North had tracks that stretched considerably farther, forming an integrated system of local lines branching off major trunk lines. In the South, railroads remained local. Neither people nor goods moved easily across the South, unless they traveled via steamboat or flatboat along the Mississippi River system—and even then, flooded banks often disrupted passage.

Regional Connections

The North's frenzy of canal and railroad building expanded transportation networks far into the hinterlands. In 1815, nearly all produce from the Old Northwest floated down the Mississippi to New Orleans, tying that region's fortunes to the South. By the 1850s, though, canals and railroads strengthened the economic, cultural, and political links between the Old Northwest—particularly the more densely populated northern regions—and the Northeast. (See Map 11.1.)

Internal improvements hastened westward migration, making western settlement more appealing by providing easy access to eastern markets. News, visitors,

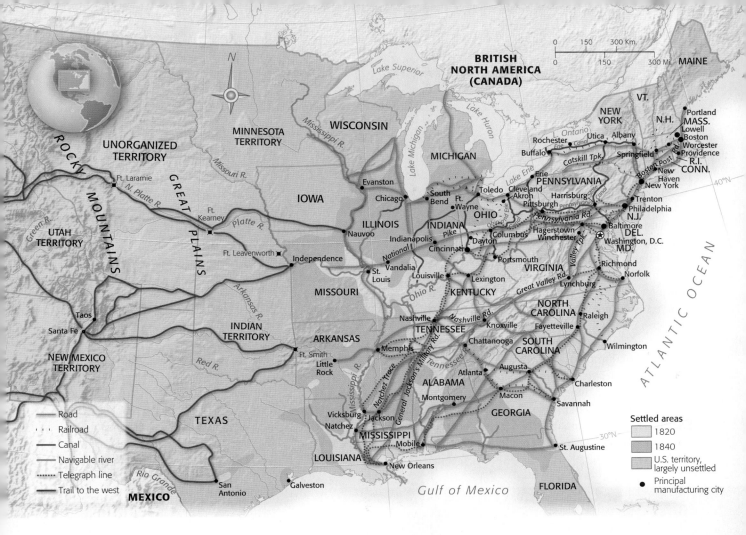

MAP 11.1

Major Roads, Canals, and Railroads, 1850

A transportation network linked the seaboard to the interior. Settlers followed those routes westward, and they sent back grain, grain products, and cotton to the port cities.

Source: Copyright © Cengage Learning

and luxuries now traveled regularly to previously remote areas of the Northeast and Midwest. Delighted that the Erie Canal brought fresh seafood to central New York, Mary Archbald explained that "distance ... is reduced to nothing here."

Samuel F. B. Morse's invention of the telegraph in 1844 allowed news to travel almost instantaneously along telegraph wires. By 1852, more than 23,000 miles of lines were strung nationwide. The telegraph enabled the birth of modern business practices involving the coordination of market conditions, production, and supply across great distances.

Ambivalence Toward Progress

Many northerners hailed internal improvements as symbols of progress. They proclaimed that, by building canals and railroads, they had completed God's design for the North American continent. Practically speaking, canals and railroads allowed them to seek opportunities in the West.

Links to the World

Internal Improvements

On July 4, 1827, ninety-one-year-old Charles Carroll, the only surviving signer of the Declaration of Independence, shoveled the first spadeful of earth on the Baltimore and Ohio Railroad, the nation's first westward railroad. Internal improvements, he and many others believed, would cement the United States' economic independence by supplying the nation's growing industrial centers with food and raw materials, while transporting manufactured goods back to its rural population.

Although boosters championed canals and railroads as the triumph of American republicanism, such projects depended on technology, funding, and labor from abroad. American engineers scrutinized canals and railroads in France, the Low Countries, and England. Railroad companies purchased locomotives from English manufacturers. Foreign investors financed significant portions of projects. Thousands of immigrants, mostly from Ireland, worked blasting boulders, draining malaria-filled swamps, picking at roots and rocks, and heaving dirt. After the Civil War, Chinese immigrants helped build the transcontinental railroad.

Internal improvements allowed people, raw materials, and goods to move inexpensively and quickly across the continent, spurring the nation's growth—but also strengthening its ties to Europe. Cotton and grain moved eastward, with much of it sold overseas. The cotton fed European textile mills; the grain fed their workers. Thus, whenever economic conditions constricted in Europe, American cotton and wheat farmers experienced similar downturns.

Canals and railroads, hailed as great symbols of American independence, linked American farmers to an increasingly complex and volatile international economy.

© Collection of the New-York Historical Society, USA/The Bridgeman Art Library

Workers repair a section of the Erie Canal, near Little Falls, in 1831. While hailed as a great achievement of human progress, the Canal required frequent repairs, frustrating travelers, merchants, boat workers, and people living along its banks.

But people who welcomed such opportunities could find much to lament. Mary Ann Archbald savored fresh seafood dinners but regretted that her sons turned to speculation. Others decried the enormous numbers of Irish canal diggers and railroad track layers, whom they deemed depraved and racially inferior. Still others worried that, by promoting urban growth, transportation innovations fostered social ills.

The degradation of the natural world proved worrisome, too. When streams were rerouted, swamps drained, and forests felled, natural habitats were disturbed, even destroyed. Deprived of water power, mills no longer ran. Without forests, wild animals—on which many rural people (Native American and European American) had relied for protein—sought homes elsewhere. Fishermen, too, found their sources of protein (and cash) dried up when natural waterways were dammed or rerouted to feed canals.

Factories and Industrialization

By dramatically lowering transportation costs, internal improvements facilitated the Northeast's rapid manufacturing and commercial expansion. Western farmers supplied raw materials and foodstuffs for northeastern factories and workers. They also expanded the domestic market for Northeastern manufactured goods. Focused on cultivating their lands, western settlers preferred to buy rather than make cloth, shoes, and other goods. They needed northeastern iron, too, for farm implements, nails, and railroad tracks.

> How was factory work different from the work life people previously knew?

Factory Work   With industrialization, daily life changed dramatically. Much early industrialization involved processing raw materials—milling flour, turning hogs into packaged meat, sawing lumber. The pork-packing industry illustrates how specialization turned skilled craftsmen into laborers. Traditionally, each butcher cut up an entire pig. Under the new industrial organization, each worker was assigned a particular task—such as cutting off the right front leg—as the pig moved down a "disassembly line."

The impersonal nature and formal rules of factory work contrasted with the informal atmosphere of artisan shops and farm households. In large factories, laborers never saw owners, working instead under paid supervisors, nor did they see the final product. Factory workers lost their sense of autonomy in the face of impersonal market forces, as the bell or steam whistle governed their day. Competition from cheaper, less-skilled workers—particularly after European immigration soared in the 1840s—created job insecurity, while opportunities for advancement were virtually nonexistent.

At first Americans imported or copied British machines that would make mass production possible in some industries. Soon, they built their own. The **American System of manufacturing** used precision machinery to produce interchangeable parts. Eli Whitney, the cotton gin's inventor, promoted interchangeable parts in 1798, when he contracted with the federal government to make ten thousand rifles in twenty-eight months. The American System quickly produced the machine-tool industry—the manufacture of machines for the purpose of mass production. The new system permitted large-scale production of inexpensive but high-quality household items.

American System of manufacturing: System of manufacturing that used interchangeable parts.

Textile Mills

Mechanization was most dramatic in textiles, with production centered in New England, near sources of water to power spinning machines and looms. After 1815, New England's rudimentary cotton mills developed into modern factories where machines mass-produced goods. Cotton cloth production rose from 4 million yards in 1817 to 323 million in 1840, and in the mid-1840s, the cotton mills employed approximately eighty thousand "operatives;" more than half were women.

Unable to find enough laborers near mills, managers recruited New England farm daughters, whom they housed in boarding houses in what became known as the **Waltham** or **Lowell** plan of industrialization. People who lived off the land were often suspicious of those who did not—particularly in the United States, where an agrarian lifestyle was associated with virtue. To ease concerns, mill owners offered paternalistic oversight to mill girls; they enforced curfews, prohibited alcohol, and required church attendance. Nonetheless, the Waltham system offered farm girls opportunities to socialize with other women and a sense of independence.

Working conditions in textile mills—the deafening roar of the power looms, the long hours, and regimentation—made young women cling to notions that their jobs were temporary. They used their wages to help their families buy land or send a brother to college, to save for their dowries or education, or to spend on personal items, such as clothing. The average girl arrived at sixteen and stayed five years, usually leaving to get married—often to men they met in town rather than farm boys at home. Although the Waltham plan drew international attention, more common was the Rhode Island (or Fall River) plan employed by **Samuel Slater**, among others. Mills hired entire families, lodging them in company boarding houses. Men often worked farm plots nearby while wives and children worked in the mills, though as the system developed, men worked in the factories, supervising wives and children in family-based work units.

Labor Protests

Mill life got harder over time. To increase productivity, managers sped up machines and required each worker to operate more machines. Between 1836 and 1850, the number of spindles and looms in Lowell increased 150 and 140 percent, respectively, whereas the number of workers increased by only 50 percent. To boost profits, owners lengthened hours, cut wages, and packed boarding houses.

Workers organized, and in 1834, reacting to a 25 percent wage cut, they unsuccessfully "turned out" (struck) against the Lowell mills. As conditions worsened and strikes failed, workers resisted in new ways. In 1844, Massachusetts mill women formed the Lowell Female Reform Association and joined forces with other workers to press, unsuccessfully, for state legislation mandating a ten- instead of fourteen-hour day.

Women aired their complaints in worker-run newspapers: in 1842, the *Factory Girl* appeared in New Hampshire, the *Wampanoag and Operatives' Journal* in Massachusetts. Two years later, mill workers founded the *Factory Girl's Garland* and the *Voice of Industry*, nicknamed "the factory girl's voice." The owner-sponsored *Lowell Offering* faced controversy when workers charged its editors with suppressing articles criticizing working conditions.

Worker turnover weakened organizational efforts. Few militant native-born mill workers stayed to fight the managers and owners, and gradually, fewer New England daughters entered the mills. In the 1850s, Irish immigrant women replaced them. Technological improvements made the work less skilled and more routine, reducing

---

Waltham, Lowell: Sites of early textile mills in New England which were precursors to modern factories. Nearly 80 percent of the workers in Waltham, Lowell, and similar mills were young, unmarried women who had been lured from farms by the promise of wages.

Samuel Slater: British mechanic who carried plans for textile mills to United States.

Link to "Woman's Proper Sphere," published in the *Lowell Offering*.

wages. Male workers, too, protested changes wrought by the **market economy**. As voters, they formed labor political parties first in Pennsylvania, New York, and Massachusetts in the 1820s, and then elsewhere. They advocated free public education and an end to imprisonment for debt, and opposed banks and monopolies. Aspiring to own land, some advocated for free homesteads.

market economy: Newly developing commercial economy that depended on goods and crops produced for sale rather than for personal consumption.

Labor Unions

The courts provided organized labor's greatest victory: protection from conspiracy laws. When journeyman shoemakers organized during the early 1800s, employers accused them of criminal conspiracy. The cordwainers' (shoemakers') cases between 1806 and 1815 left labor organizations in an uncertain position. Although the courts acknowledged journeymen's right to organize, judges viewed strikes as illegal until a Massachusetts case, **Commonwealth v. Hunt** (1842), ruled that Boston journeyman bootmakers could strike "to subserve their own interests."

Commonwealth v. Hunt: A court case in 1842 where the Massachusetts Supreme Judicial Court ruled that labor unions were not illegal monopolies that restrained trade.

The first unions arose among urban journeymen in printing, woodworking, shoemaking, and tailoring. Typically local, the strongest sought protection against competition from inferior workmen by regulating apprenticeships and establishing minimum wages. Umbrella organizations of individual craft unions, like the National Trade Union (1834), arose in several cities in the 1820s and 1830s. But the movement disintegrated amid wage reductions and unemployment in the hard times of 1839–1843.

Permanent labor organizations were difficult to sustain. Skilled craftsmen disdained less skilled workers. Moreover, workers divided along ethnic, religious, racial, and gender lines.

Consumption and Commercialization

Before the 1820s, women sewed most clothing at home, and some people purchased used clothing. Tailors and seamstresses made wealthy men's and women's clothing to order. By the 1820s and 1830s, much clothing was mass-produced for sale in retail clothing stores. Standard sizes replaced measuring, and a division of labor took hold: One worker cut patterns all day, another sewed hems, another affixed buttons. The sewing machine's invention in 1846 sped the process, especially with its wide availability in the 1850s. Many farm families still made their own clothing, yet bought clothes when they could afford to, creating more time for raising crops and children.

How did farm women's work change as the commercial economy expanded?

The Garment Industry

Market expansion created demand for mass-produced clothing. Girls working in factories no longer had time to sew clothes. Young immigrant men, separated from mothers and sisters, bought the crudely made, loose-fitting clothing. But the biggest market for ready-made clothes initially was the cotton South. With the textile industry's success driving up the demand and price for raw cotton, planters bought ready-made shoes and clothes for slaves in whose hands they would rather place a hoe than a needle and thread.

Retailers often bought goods wholesale, though many manufactured shirts and trousers in their own factories. Lewis and Hanford of New York City boasted of cutting more than 100,000 garments in winter 1848–1849. The New York firm did business mostly in the South and owned a retail outlet in New Orleans. While southerners and westerners engaged in the clothing trade, its center remained in New York.

Images of Boom and Bust

The growth of the commercial economy, which saw the mass production of consumer items, also fostered economic boom and bust. Below we see an advertisement from the *Boston Directory* of 1848–1849 for readymade shirts, and we see how *Harper's Weekly* portrayed New York City, the heart of the garment industry, in the heat of the financial panic of 1857, less than a decade later. To what values does F.B. Locke appeal in his choice of imagery for his advertisement? Why does *Harper's Weekly* refer to the discounted goods, and the scramble to purchase them, as an "epidemic"? What is the significance, on the image's left side, of the police officer escorting two children out of the store? What does it indicate about how *Harper's* saw the consequences of the "epidemic"? What else does the picture imply about the social consequences of financial collapse? Do the two images suggest that American values shifted in the intervening decade? Why or why not?

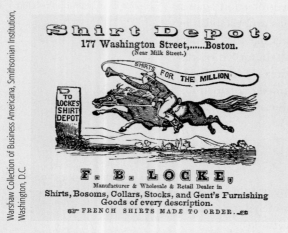

Although F.B. Locke continued to make shirts to order, he adapted to the new market for readymade clothing by becoming a manufacturer, wholesaler, and retailer of men's shirts.

As the nation experienced a serious financial contraction in 1857, prices fell as business languished. But the availability of bargains did not compensate for widespread unemployment and falling wages.

Specialization of Commerce

Commercial specialization transformed some urban traders, especially in New York, into merchant princes. After the Erie Canal opened, New York City became a stop on every major trade route from Europe, southern ports, and the West. Traders sometimes invested in factories, further stimulating urban manufacturing. Some cities specialized: Rochester became a milling center ("The Flour City"), and Cincinnati ("Porkopolis") became the first meatpacking center.

Merchants who engaged in complex commercial transactions required large—mostly male—office staffs. At the bottom were messenger boys, often preteens, who delivered documents. Above them were copyists, who hand-copied documents. Clerks processed documents and did translations. Above them were the bookkeeper and confidential chief clerk. Those seeking employment in such counting houses took a course from a writing master. All hoped to rise to partner, although their chances grew increasingly slim.

Specialization lagged in small towns, where merchants continued to exchange goods with local farm women, and craftsmen continued to sell finished goods, such as shoes. In some rural areas, peddlers were general merchants. But as transportation improved and towns grew, small-town merchants increasingly specialized.

Commercial Farming

Even amid the manufacturing and commercial booms, agriculture remained the northern economy's backbone. But the **transportation revolution** and market expansion transformed semi-subsistence farms into commercial enterprises. Many families stopped practicing mixed agriculture and began to specialize in cash crops. Although most northerners continued to farm, on the eve of the Civil War, their daily lives and relationships often looked very different from those of their parents and grandparents.

transportation revolution: Rapid expansion of canals, steamships, and railroads.

By the 1820s, eastern farmers had cultivated nearly all available land, and their small farms, often with uneven terrains, were not suited for the labor-saving farm implements introduced in the 1830s, such as mechanical sowers, reapers, and threshers. Many northern farmers thus either moved west or quit farming for jobs in merchants' houses and factories. Those who remained, however, proved adaptable, their efforts encouraged by state governments that promoted agricultural innovation.

In 1820, about one-third of northern produce was intended for the market, but by 1850 it surpassed 50 percent. As farmers shifted toward market-oriented production, they invested in additional land (buying farms of neighbors who moved west), new equipment, and new labor sources (hired hands). Many New England and Middle Atlantic farm families faced steep competition from midwestern farmers after the Erie Canal opened. They began abandoning wheat and corn production, shifting to livestock and vegetable and fruit production. Much of what they produced fed the North's growing urban and manufacturing populations.

Farmers financed innovations through land sales and debts. Indeed, increasing land values promised the greatest profit. Farm families who owned land flourished, but by the 1840s it took more than ten years for a laborer in the Northeast to save enough to buy a farm. The number of tenant farmers and hired hands increased, and farmers who had previously employed unpaid family members and enslaved workers now leased portions of their farms or hired waged labor.

Farm Women's Changing Labor

As the commercial economy expanded, farm women added new responsibilities to their substantial duties. Some did outwork. Many increased production of eggs, dairy products, and garden produce for sale; others raised bees or silkworms.

With New England textile mills producing more finished cloth, farm women and children often abandoned time-consuming spinning and weaving, bought factory-produced cloth, and dedicated the saved time to producing additional products, such as butter and cheese, for the market rather than simply for their family's consumption. Some mixed-agriculture farms converted entirely to dairy production, with men taking over formerly female tasks. Canals and railroads carried cheese to eastern ports, where wholesalers sold it worldwide.

Rural Communities

Despite pressure to manage farms like time-efficient businesses, some farmers clung to old practices of gathering at market, general stores, taverns, and church. They continued barn raisings and husking bees, but by the 1830s with young women working in textile mills and young men laboring as clerks or factory hands, there were fewer young people at such events.

While farmers continued to swap labor and socialize with neighbors, they increasingly reckoned debts in dollars. They watched national and international markets more closely. When financial panics hit, cash shortages almost halted business activity, casting many farmers further into debt, sometimes bankruptcy. Faced with potentially losing their land, farmers called in neighbors' debts, sometimes rupturing long-established relationships.

Cycles of Boom and Bust

With market expansion came booms and busts. Prosperity stimulated demand for finished goods, such as clothing and furniture, which led to higher prices and still higher production and to land speculation. Investment money was plentiful as Americans saved and foreign, mostly British, investors bought U.S. bonds and securities. Then production surpassed demand. Prices and wages fell; land and stock values collapsed, and investment money left the United States. This boom-and-bust cycle touched the whole country, but particularly the Northeast.

Although the 1820s and 1830s were boom times, financial panic triggered a bust cycle in 1837, the year after the Second Bank of the United States closed. Economic contraction remained severe through 1843. Many banks could not repay depositors, and states, facing deficits, defaulted on bonds. Because of the **Panic of 1837**, European, especially British, investors became suspicious of U.S. loans and withdrew money from the United States.

Panic of 1837: A severe depression that struck the United States beginning in May 1837.

Hard times had come. "The streets seemed deserted," Sidney George Fisher observed of Philadelphia in 1842. "The largest [merchant] houses are shut up and to rent, there is no business…no money, no confidence." The hungry formed lines at soup societies, and beggars crowded the sidewalks. Laborers demanding their deposits gathered at closed banks. Sheriffs sold seized property at one-quarter of pre-hard-time prices. In smaller cities like Lynn, Massachusetts, shoemakers weathered hard times by fishing and gardening, while laborers scavenged for clams and dandelions. Congress passed the Federal Bankruptcy Law of 1841; by the time the law was repealed two years later, 41,000 bankrupts had sought protection under its provisions.

Families in Flux

What roles did families play in the new industrial era?

Anxieties about economic fluctuations reverberated into northern homes. Sweeping changes in the household economy led to new family ideals. In the preindustrial era, the families were primarily economic units; now they became a moral and cultural institution, though in reality few families could live up to this ideal.

The "Ideal" Family

In the North, the market economy increasingly separated the home from the workplace, leading to a new middle-class ideal in which men functioned in the public sphere, while women oversaw the private or domestic sphere. The home became, in theory, an emotional retreat from the competitive, selfish business world. Men provided and protected, while women nurtured and guarded the family's morality, ensuring that capitalism's excesses did not invade the home. Childhood expanded: children were to remain at home until their late teens or early twenties.

This ideal came to be known as separate-sphere ideology, the cult of domesticity or the cult of true womanhood. Although it rigidly separated the male and female spheres, this ideology elevated domestic responsibilities. In her widely read *Treatise on Domestic Economy* (1841), Catharine Beecher approached housekeeping as a science while trumpeting mothers' role as their family's moral guardian. Beecher maintained that women's natural superiority as moral, nurturing caregivers made them especially suited for teaching (when single) and parenting (once married). Beecher insisted that the private sphere be elevated to the same status as the public.

Shrinking Families

These new domestic ideals depended on smaller families enabling parents, particularly mothers, to give children better attention, education, and financial help. With the market economy, parents could afford to have fewer children because children no longer played a vital economic role. Urban families produced fewer household goods, and commercial farmers, unlike self-sufficient ones, relied on hired laborers. Although smaller families resulted partly from first marriages occurring at a later age, they also resulted from planning, made easier when cheap rubber condoms became available in the 1850s. Some women chose, too, to end accidental pregnancies with abortion.

As they strove to live according to new domestic ideals, middle-class families often relied on African American or immigrant servants, who sacrificed time with their own children in order to care for their employers' children.

In 1800, American women bore seven or eight children; by 1860, they had five or six. This decline occurred even though immigrants with large-family traditions were settling in the United States; thus, the birth rate among native-born women declined more sharply. Although rural families remained larger than urban ones, birth rates among both groups declined comparably.

Few northern women could fulfill the middle-class ideal of **separate spheres**. Most wage-earning women provided essential income for their families and could not stay home. They often saw domestic ideals as oppressive, as middle-class reformers mistook poverty for immorality, condemning working mothers for letting their children work or scavenge rather than attend school. Although most middle-class women could stay home, new standards of cleanliness drained their time. Women's contributions to their families were assessed in moral, not economic terms. Without servants, moreover, women could not devote themselves primarily to their children, making the ideals of the cult of domesticity impossible for many middle-class families.

separate spheres: Middle-class ideology that emerged with the market revolution and divided men's and women's roles into distinct and separate categories based on their perceived gender differences, abilities, and social functions. Men were assigned the public realm of business and politics, while women were assigned to the private world of home and family.

Women's Paid Labor   In working-class families, women left home as early as age twelve, earning wages most of their lives, with short respites for bearing and rearing children. Unmarried girls and women worked primarily as domestic servants or in factories; married and widowed women worked as laundresses, seamstresses, and cooks. Some hawked food and wares on city streets; other did piecework; and some became prostitutes. Few could support themselves or a family comfortably.

If middle-class girls left home to work in New England's textile mills, or in new urban stores as clerks, it was only briefly, before marriage. Otherwise, teaching was the only occupation consistent with genteel femininity. In 1823, Catharine and Mary Beecher established the Hartford Female Seminary, adding history and science to the traditional women's curriculum of domestic arts and religion. A decade later, Catharine Beecher successfully campaigned for teacher-training schools for women. Single, these women need not earn as much as their male counterparts, whom she presumed to be married. Unmarried women earned about half the salary of male teachers. By 1850, schoolteaching had become a woman's profession.

The proportion of single women in the population increased significantly in the nineteenth century. As more young men headed west, some eastern communities had a disproportionate number of young women. Other women chose to remain independent. Because women's work generally paid poorly, those who forswore marriage faced serious challenges, leaving many single women to rely on charitable or family assistance.

The Growth of Cities

How could cities be seen at once as symbols of progress and of moral decay?

No period in American history saw more rapid urbanization than between 1820 and 1860. The percentage of people living in urban areas (defined by a population of 2,500 or more) grew from 7 percent in 1820 to nearly 20 percent in 1860. The greatest growth occurred in the Northeast and Midwest. Although most northerners continued to live on farms or in small villages, cities boomed. Many urban residents were temporary, and many were immigrants.

Urban Boom   In 1820, the United States had 13 places with a population greater than 10,000; in 1860, it had 93. (see Map 11.2). New York City, already the nation's largest city in 1820, saw its population grow from 123,709 that year to 813,669 in 1860. Philadelphia, the nation's second-largest city, saw its population multiply ninefold during that forty-year period. In 1815, Rochester, New York, had just 300 residents. By 1830, the Erie Canal turned the sleepy agricultural town into the nation's twenty-fifth-largest city, with a population of just over 9,000.

Cities experienced geographic expansion too. Until 1830, New Yorkers could walk the entire length of the city in an hour. In 1825, Fourteenth Street was the city's northern boundary. By 1860, Forty-second Street was the city's northern limit. Public transit made city expansion possible. By the 1850s, all big cities had horse-drawn streetcars, allowing wealthier residents who could afford the fare to settle on the cities' outskirts.

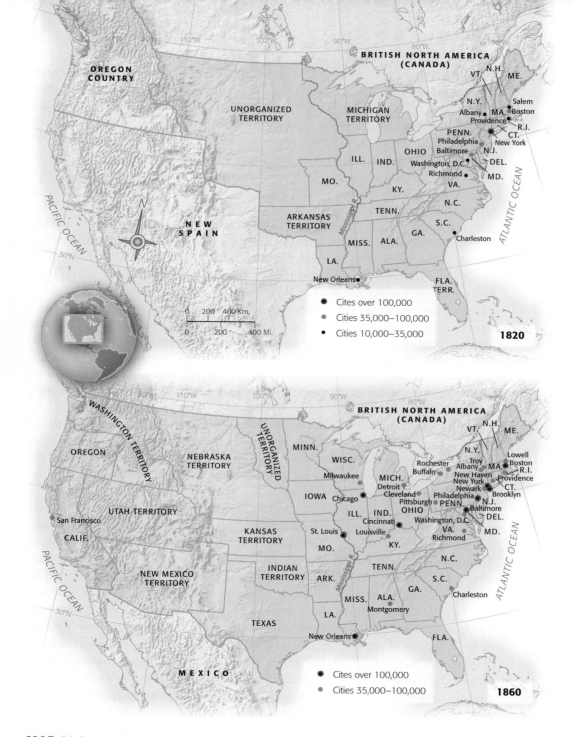

MAP 11.2

Major American Cities in 1820 and 1860

The number of Americans who lived in cities increased rapidly between 1820 and 1860, and the number of large cities grew as well. In 1820, only New York City had a population exceeding 100,000; forty years later, eight more cities had surpassed that level.

Source: Copyright © Cengage Learning

Market-Related Development

Cities sustained the North's market revolution by serving as transportation hubs, commercial centers, and manufacturing sites. Some cities grew up with manufacturing. The Boston Manufacturing Company selected the site for Lowell, Massachusetts, because of its proximity to the Merrimack River, which could power its textile mill. Incorporated in 1826, by the 1850s Lowell was the second-largest city in New England. Although most early manufacturing took place in rural areas, some cities, such as New York, experienced what historians call metropolitan industrialization, which relied on reorganization of labor similar to the earlier putting-out system. Most early ready-made clothing, for example, was produced as outwork by women in tenements throughout New York City. In 1860, 25,000 women worked in manufacturing jobs in New York City, constituting a quarter of the waged labor force; two-thirds worked in the garment industry.

Northern cities developed elaborate municipal services but lacked taxing power to provide services for all. At best, they could tax property adjoining new sewers, paved streets, and water mains. New services and basic sanitation depended on residents' ability to pay. Another solution was to charter private companies to sell basic services. Baltimore first chartered a private gas company in 1816. By mid-century, every major city had done so. Private firms lacked the capital to build adequate water systems, and they laid pipe only in commercial and well-to-do residential areas. Supplying water ultimately fell to city governments.

Extremes of Wealth

Wealth was increasingly concentrated in fewer hands. By 1860, the top 5 percent of American families owned more than half of the nation's wealth, and the top 10 percent owned nearly three-quarters. In the South, income extremes were most apparent on rural plantations, but in the North, cities revealed economic inequities.

A number of factors contributed to widespread poverty in America's industrial cities: poor wages, lack of full-time employment, and the increasingly widespread employment of women and children, which further drove down wages for everyone. Women and children, employers rationalized, did not need a living wage because they were dependent, meaning that they relied on men to support them. In reality, not all women or children had men to support them, nor were men's wages always adequate.

New York provides a striking example of the extremes of wealth accompanying industrialization. Houses built for two families often held four. Some families took in lodgers to pay the rent; such crowding encouraged poorer New Yorkers to head outdoors. But poor neighborhoods were filthy. Excess sewage from outhouses drained into ditches that carried urine and fecal matter into the streets. People piled garbage into gutters, backyards, or alleys. Pigs, geese, dogs, and vultures scavenged the streets, while rats roamed under wooden sidewalks and through large buildings. Typhoid, dysentery, malaria, and tuberculosis regularly visited the poorer sections of cities. Cholera struck in 1831, 1849, and 1866.

Just beyond poverty-stricken neighborhoods were lavish mansions, whose residents escaped to their country estates during summer's brutal heat or epidemics. Much of this wealth was inherited. Rich New Yorkers increased their fortunes by investing in commerce and manufacturing.

The middle class was larger than the wealthy elite but substantially smaller than the working classes. They were businessmen, traders, and professionals, and the rapid turn toward industrialization and commercial specialization made them a larger presence in northern cities than in southern ones. Middle-class families enjoyed new consumer items: wool carpeting, fine wallpaper, and rooms full of furniture. Houses were large, from four to six rooms. By the 1840s and 1850s, middle-class families used indoor toilets that were mechanical, though not yet flushing. These families formed the backbone of urban clubs and societies, filled the family pews in church, and sent their sons to college.

Immigration

Many of the urban poor were immigrants. The 5 million immigrants to the United States between 1830 and 1860 outnumbered the country's population in 1790 (see Figure 11.1). During peak pre-Civil War of immigration (1847–1857), 3.3 million immigrants entered the United States, including 1.3 million Irish and 1.1 million Germans. By 1860, 15 percent of the white population was foreign-born, with 90 percent of immigrants living in northern states.

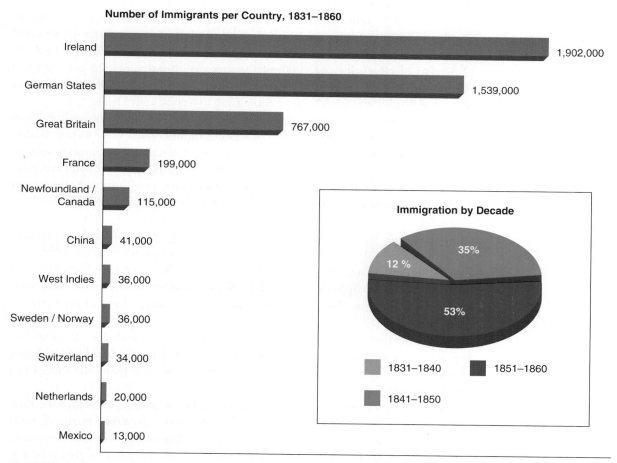

FIGURE 11.1

Major Sources of Immigration to the United States, 1831–1860

Most immigrants came from two areas: Great Britain, of which Ireland was a part, and the German states. These two areas sent more immigrants between 1830 and 1860 than the inhabitants of the United States enumerated at the first census in 1790. By 1860, 15 percent of the white population was of foreign birth.

Source: Data from Stephan Thernstrom, ed., *Harvard Encyclopedia of American Ethnic Groups* (Cambridge, Mass., and London: Harvard University Press, 1980), p. 1047.

Various factors "pushed" Europeans from their homes and "pulled" them to the northern United States. In Ireland, the potato famine (1845–1850)—a period of widespread starvation caused by a diseased potato crop—drove millions from their homeland. Although economic conditions pushed most Germans, some were political refugees—liberals, freethinkers, Socialists, communists, and anarchists—who fled after the abortive revolutions of 1848. Employers, states, and shipping companies promoted opportunities in America with this message: work and prosper in America or starve in Europe. Once in the United States, immigrants soon saw the fallacy of promoters' promises of riches and hundreds of thousands returned home.

Many early immigrants lived or worked in rural areas. Like the Archbalds, a few settled on farms and bought land. Others worked as hired farm hands, canal diggers, or railroad track layers—often hoping to buy land later. By the 1840s and 1850s—when the steady stream of immigration turned into a flood—the prospects of buying land became remote.

By 1860, most immigrants settled in cities, often the port at which they arrived. The most destitute could not afford the fare to places farther inland. Others had resources but fell victim to swindlers. Others liked the cities' ethnic flair. In 1855, 52 percent of New York's 623,000 inhabitants were immigrants, 28 percent from Ireland and 16 percent from the German states. Throughout the 1850s, about 35 percent of Boston was foreign-born; more than two-thirds were Irish.

Most of the new Irish immigrants were young, poor, Roman Catholics from rural districts. Women found work as domestic servants or mill hands, while men worked in construction or transportation. Most Germans came with enough resources to head to states such as Ohio, Illinois, Wisconsin, and Missouri. Although some southern cities like Charleston and Savannah had many Irish immigrants, most European immigrants disliked slavery and semitropical heat and preferred the Northeast or Midwest.

Ethnic Tensions

Tension—often over the era's economic changes—characterized the relationship between native-born Americans and immigrants, particularly Irish Catholics. Native-born workers blamed immigrants for scarce job opportunities and low wages. Middle-class whites blamed them for poverty and crime. They believed immigrants' moral depravity—not poor wages—led to poverty.

White northerners often portrayed Irish immigrants as nonwhite, as African in appearance. But Irish and African Americans did not develop a sense of solidarity. Instead, some of the era's most virulent riots erupted between Irish immigrants and African Americans.

Anti-Catholicism became strident in the 1830s. In Boston, anti-Catholic riots occurred frequently. Nearby Charlestown, Massachusetts, saw a mob burn a convent in 1834. In Philadelphia, a crowd attacked priests and nuns and vandalized churches in 1844, and in Lawrence, Massachusetts, a mob leveled the Irish neighborhood in 1854. Riots between native-born and Irish workers erupted along canals and railroads—but urban riots attracted more newspaper attention, fueling fears that cities were depraved places.

Protestant German immigrants fared better than the Irish. Because Germans generally arrived with resources and skills, Americans stereotyped them as hardworking. But non-Protestant Germans—Catholics and Jews (whom white Americans considered a separate race)—frequently encountered racial and religious prejudice.

Link to the original report of the 1834 convent burning in Charlestown, Massachusetts.

Immigrants often lived in ethnic enclaves, setting up social clubs and mutual aid societies. Irish Catholics had their own neighborhoods, where they established Catholic churches and schools. In larger cities, immigrants from the same German states clustered together.

People of Color

African Americans also forged their own communities and culture. As late as the 1830s, many remained enslaved in New York and New Jersey, but the numbers of free African Americans grew steadily. By 1860, nearly 250,000 (many of them refugees from southern slavery) lived in the urban North. **African Methodist Episcopal churches** and preachers helped forge communities. Churches hosted schools, political reforms, and protest meetings.

African Methodist Episcopal churches: First American denomination established by and for African Americans.

White racism impinged on northern African Americans' lives. Streetcars, hotels, restaurants, and theaters could turn away African Americans without legal penalty. City laws barred African Americans from public buildings. Even where laws were liberal, whites' attitudes constrained African Americans' opportunities. In Massachusetts, for example, African Americans enjoyed more legal rights than anywhere else. Still, whites often refused to shop at black businesses. African Americans were excluded from factory and clerical jobs. Women worked as house servants, cooks, washerwomen, and child nurses. Most African American men worked as construction workers, porters, longshoremen, or day laborers—all jobs subject to frequent unemployment. Others took lower-paying but stable jobs as servants, waiters, cooks, barbers, and janitors. Many African American men became sailors and merchant seamen, jobs offering regular employment and advancement, though not protection from racial taunts.

In the growing cities, African Americans turned service occupations into businesses, opening restaurants, taverns, hotels, barber shops, and employment agencies for domestic servants. Some sold used clothing or were junk dealers. A few became wealthy, invested in real estate, and loaned money. With professionals—ministers, teachers, physicians, dentists, lawyers, and newspaper editors—they formed a small but growing African American middle class.

Still, African Americans became targets of urban violence. White rioters clubbed and stoned African Americans, destroying their houses, churches, and businesses—and sent many fleeing for their lives. Philadelphia experienced five major riots in the 1830s and 1840s. By 1860, hundreds of African Americans had died in urban riots.

Urban Culture

Living in cramped, squalid conditions, working-class families spent little time indoors. In the 1840s, a working-class youth culture developed

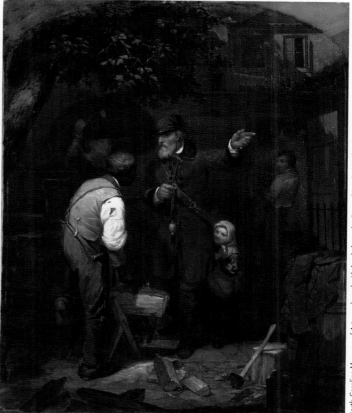

North Carolina Museum of Art, purchased with funds from the State of North Carolina (52.9.2)

Immigrants often considered themselves superior to African Americans, fueling racial tensions. Here, a German immigrant demonstrates his sense of superiority even as he relies on an African American laborer for directions.

Thomas D. Rice playing "Jim Crow" in blackface at the Bowery Theater in New York City, 1833. The rowdy audience climbed onto the stage, leaving Rice little room to perform. In representing African Americans on stage, Rice and other minstrels contributed to establishing both black and white as racial categories.

© Collection of the New York Historical Society

on the Bowery, one of New York's entertainment strips. Lined with theaters, dance halls, and cafés, it became an urban midway. The Bowery boys' greased hair, distinctive clothing, and swagger frightened middle-class New Yorkers, as did the Bowery girls' colorful costumes. Equally scandalous were the middle-class clerks who succumbed to the city's temptations, notably prostitution.

Gangs of garishly dressed young men and women—flaunting their sexuality and drinking to excess—drove respectable citizenry to establish private clubs. Some men joined the Masonic order, which offered members an elaborate code of deference between ranks, while women organized literary clubs and benevolent societies.

Increasingly, urban recreation and sports became commodities. Horseracing, walking races, and, in the 1850s, baseball attracted urban men. Wall Street office workers formed the Knickerbocker Club in 1842 and in 1845 drew up rules for playing baseball. Large cities boasted two or more theaters catering to different classes. Some plays cut across class lines—Shakespeare was so widely performed that even illiterate theatergoers knew his plays.

In the 1840s, singing groups, theater troupes, and circuses traveled from city to city. Minstrel shows were particularly popular, featuring white men (often Irish) in makeup imitating African Americans in song, dance, and patter. In the early 1830s, Thomas D. Rice of New York became famous for portraying Jim Crow, an old southern slave. In ill-fitting patched clothing and torn shoes, the blackface Rice shuffled, danced, and sang. Minstrel performers told jokes mocking economic and political elites and evoked nostalgia for preindustrial work habits and morality. But blackface actors encouraged a racist stereotyping of African Americans as sensual and lazy.

The Penny Press

Accounts of urban culture peppered the penny press, which emerged in the 1830s and swept through northern cities. Made possible by technological advances—the advent of the steam-powered press, improved methods for producing paper, and transportation innovations—the penny press (each newspaper cost one cent) differed greatly from traditional (six-cent) newspapers. Where older papers covered mostly commercial news and identified with a political party, the penny press proclaimed political independence and hired reporters to cover local, national, and international stories. Where six-cent newspapers relied on subscriptions and political contributions for their revenue, penny newspapers were sold by newsboys on the street. They earned money from advertising, and drew an economically diverse readership. Working-class people could now afford to buy newspapers regularly.

Penny newspapers focused on daily life, giving one social class the opportunity to peer into the lives of other classes, ethnicities, and races. Working- and middle-class

P. T. Barnum's Publicity Stunts

Usually remembered for the Ringling Brothers and Barnum & Bailey Circus, P. T. Barnum (1810–1891) left another legacy: the publicity stunt. Using hoaxes and spectacles, Barnum's American Museum in New York City drew tens of millions of visitors between 1841 and 1868, making Barnum the era's second wealthiest American.

Barnum first gained widespread publicity in 1835 with his traveling exhibition of Joice Heth, whom he claimed was the 161-year-old former slave of George Washington. When interest waned, Barnum planted a rumor that she was a machine made of leather and bones. The penny press reveled in the ensuing controversy, swelling admissions and earning Barnum enough to purchase the American Museum, whose "500,000 natural and artificial curiosities" he promoted through similar stunts. Barnum also hosted the nation's first beauty pageant in 1854. Offensive to middle-class sensibilities, it flopped, but Barnum persevered with pageants featuring dogs, babies, and chickens. The baby show attracted 61,000 visitors. Selling more than a million copies, Barnum's autobiography inspired generations of entrepreneurs.

Many cultural icons began as promotional gimmicks, including the Miss America Pageant (1921), the Macy's Thanksgiving Day parade (1924), and the Goodyear blimp (1925). Since 1916, Nathan's has hosted a Fourth of July hotdog eating contest, now attracting forty thousand spectators and a television audience. The *Guinness Book of World Records* began as an Irish beer company's promotional brochure and inspires thousands each year to attempt to break records—and get publicity for it.

By staging stunts for media exposure, today's entrepreneurs reveal the enduring legacy of P. T. Barnum, the self-proclaimed greatest showman on earth.

readers, for example, could read about high society; wealthy readers learned about poorer neighborhoods. The penny press often sensationalized the news, thereby influencing urban dwellers' views of one another and of cities.

Cities as Symbols of Progress

To many northerners, cities symbolized both progress and decay. Cities nurtured churches, schools, civil governments, and museums—all signs of civilization and culture. As canals and railroads opened the West for mass settlement, many white northerners applauded the appearance of church steeples and public buildings in areas that had been "savage wilderness," that is, territory controlled by Native Americans. To many nineteenth-century white Americans, cities represented the moral triumph of civilization over savagery and heathenism.

Yet some middle-class Americans deplored the character of the nation's largest cities, which they saw as havens of disease, poverty, crime, and vice—all signs of moral decline. They considered epidemics to be divine scourges, striking the filthy, intemperate, and immoral. Theft and prostitution provided evidence of moral vice, and wealthy observers perceived these crimes not as by-products of poverty but as signs of individual failing. They pressed for laws against vagrancy and pushed city officials to establish police forces.

How did northerners reconcile urban vices and depravity of the city with their view of cities as symbols of progress? Middle-class reformers focused on purifying cities of disease and vice. If disease was a divine punishment—rather than an offshoot of cramped conditions—then it was within Americans' power to fix things. Middle-class reformers tried to convince the urban working classes that—unlike southern slaves—they could improve their lives by giving up alcohol, working harder, and praying frequently. This belief in upward mobility became central to many north-erners' ideas about progress.

The concept that, in a competitive marketplace, those who worked hard and lived virtuously could improve their status appealed especially to manufacturers and merchants eager to take credit for their own success. Likewise, they hoped factory hands and clerks would embrace the promise of upward mobility and remain opti-mistic despite hardships. Many laborers initially rejected this free-labor ideology as a veiled attempt to tout industrial work habits, rationalize poor wages, and quell worker protest. But by the 1850s, when the question of slavery's westward expansion returned to the political foreground, many northerners embraced free-labor ideol-ogy and regarded slavery as antithetical to it. This way of thinking, perhaps more than anything else, made the North distinctive.

Summary

During the first half of the nineteenth century, the North became enmeshed in commercial culture, as northern states and capitalists invested heavily in internal improvements. Most northerners shifted toward commercial farming or, in smaller numbers, industrial wage labor. Farmers now specialized in cash crops, while their children often worked in factories or countinghouses.

To many northerners, the market economy symbolized progress, bringing eas-ier access to cheap western lands, employment for surplus farm laborers, and the commercial availability of goods that had been time-consuming to produce. But the market economy also led to increased specialization, a depersonalized workplace, and a sharper divide between work and leisure. The market economy also tied north-erners more directly to fluctuating national and international markets, and during economic downturns, many northern families experienced destitution.

With less need for children's labor, northerners began producing smaller fami-lies. Even as working-class children worked, middle-class families created a model of childhood that had parents shielding children from the world's dangers. Mothers, in theory, became moral guardians, keeping the home safe from the new economy's competitiveness and selfishness. Few women, though, could devote themselves entirely to nurturing their families.

Immigrants and free African Americans performed the lowest paying work, and many native-born whites blamed them for problems spurred by rapid economic change. Anti-immigrant (especially anti-Catholic) and antiblack riots became com-monplace. Immigrants and African Americans responded by forming their own communities.

Cities came to symbolize the possibilities and limits of market expansion. Urban areas were marked by extremes of wealth, vibrant working-class cultures as well as poverty, crime, and mob violence. To reconcile the seeming contradictions, middle-class northerners articulated free-labor ideology, touting the possibility for upward mobility in a competitive marketplace. This ideology would become increasingly cen-tral to northern regional identity.

Chapter Review

Or Is It the North That Was Distinctive?

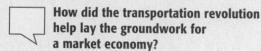 **What happened to the North and South economically after the War of 1812?**

The South continued as an agricultural region and expanded its slave system, while the North transformed quickly into a market economy. With the war cutting off European trade, northern entrepreneurs invested in domestic production and factories. Former artisans and farmers increasingly shifted from producers to wage workers. Early forms of market changes came from piecework or outwork, where manufacturers hired women and children in their homes to produce goods, often paying them for each piece produced. After the first mills were opened in the 1790s, women and children went to work there. People increasingly bought goods—clothes, shoes, and soap—that they once made for themselves. Commercial farming emerged in the North to meet the growing demand for foodstuffs that was created when people shifted from farming to factory jobs. Those farmers who remained in agriculture shifted increasingly to cash crops.

The Transportation Revolution

How did the transportation revolution help lay the groundwork for a market economy?

The lack of inexpensive, quick, and convenient transportation impeded westward expansion and industrial growth until the early nineteenth century. Beginning in the 1800s, however, several innovations—steamboats, canals, and railroads—dramatically reduced the cost and time to transport raw materials, goods, and people. Canals connected regions and shortened travel times, and steamboats reduced trips that previously took months to just days. Faster and less costly to build, railroads soon replaced canals, with transportation costs overall cut by as much as 95 percent. Goods that were previously unavailable in the nation's interior now could be had easily and cheaply. Westward migration expanded, creating new markets and cultural links between previously distant regions, as news, products, and people of various backgrounds fanned out from the Northeast to the Northwest.

Factories and Industrialization

How was factory work different from the work life people previously knew?

The artisan shops and family farms that predated factories had fewer formal rules and less structure than the factories that arose in the late eighteenth and early nineteenth centuries. Artisans and farmers saw themselves as producers, in charge of their labor and its outcome and working side-by-side with hired helpers. In factories, workers infrequently saw owners and worked for wages under the watchful eye of supervisors with strict rules and a clock governing their day. Instead of learning how to make something from start to finish, workers now specialized in only one part of the process and never saw the finished item. There was no job security, and factory workers were often replaced by cheaper immigrant and women workers. Whereas artisan apprentices worked to learn a trade with the hope of setting up their own businesses, there was little or no opportunity for advancement in factories.

Consumption and Commercialization

How did farm women's work change as the commercial economy expanded?

Along with their regular farm and household duties, rural women took on new responsibilities to help pay for some of the items they now bought (such as textiles) instead of bartering for or making on their own. Some took in outwork; others increased production of eggs, milk, butter, and produce and other items for sale in the market. Daughters were often sent to work in textile mills, sending part of their wages home to aid their families.

Families in Flux

What roles did families play in the new industrial era?

Before the rise of the market economy, families were the center of production and economic activity. As industrialization took hold, however, new ideals transformed families into moral and cultural institutions. Men, particularly middle-class men, occupied the public sphere, providing for and protecting their families. In this new "separate spheres" ideology, women's roles were confined to the home, and they were charged with making it a retreat for husbands and children from the harshness of economic life. This ideology, which elevated women's domestic roles, was later dubbed *the cult of domesticity* or *the cult of true womanhood*. However, this ideology was rarely realized in practice.

The Growth of Cities

How could cities be seen at once as symbols of progress and of moral decay?

America experienced rapid urbanization between 1820 and 1860, particularly in the Northeast and Midwest, as some previously agricultural regions—such as Rochester near the Erie Canal—became cities and existing cities grew dramatically in population and size. People flocked to cities seeking opportunities. On the one hand, cities served as transportation and industrial hubs, and nurtured schools, churches, civil governments and museums—all signs of progress. On the other hand, some middle-class Americans regarded them as centers of disease, poverty, crowding, crime, and vice—symbols of moral decline. Prostitution, vagrancy, and theft led reformers to seek to purify cities. They targeted the working class—who many saw as contributing to urban decay—with the promise of

upward mobility and free labor ideology—that those who worked hard, lived virtuous lives, and gave up alcohol—would become successful. Workers initially rejected such notions as an imposition on their lives, but with slavery's potential expansion westward in the 1850s, many embraced free-labor ideology.

Suggestions for Further Reading

Hal Barron, *Those Who Stayed Behind: Rural Society in Nineteenth-Century New England* (1984)

Jeanne Boydston, *Home and Work: Housework, Wages, and the Ideology of Labor in the Early Republic* (1990)

Nancy Cott, *The Bonds of Womanhood: "Women's Sphere" in New England, 1780–1835* (1977)

Daniel Walker Howe, *What Hath God Wrought: The Transformation of America, 1815–1848* (2007)

Bruce Laurie, *Artisans into Workers: Labor in Nineteenth-Century America* (1989)

Mary Ryan, *Cradle of the Middle Class: The Family in Oneida County, New York, 1790–1865* (1981)

Carol Sheriff, *The Artificial River: The Erie Canal and the Paradox of Progress, 1817–1862* (1996)

Christine Stansell, *City of Women: Sex and Class in New York, 1789–1860* (1986)

Melvyn Stokes and Stephen Conway, eds., *The Market Revolution in America: Social, Political, and Religious Expressions, 1800–1880* (1996)

George Rogers Taylor, *The Transportation Revolution, 1815–1860* (1951)

Reform and Politics

12

1824–1845

The twenty-eight-year-old mill hand steadied himself atop a cliff in Paterson, New Jersey, peered down the seventy-foot precipice to the river below, then leapt into the water. He resurfaced to cheers for his death-defying stunt—and what it symbolized. It was September 1827, and Sam Patch—who had worked in textile mills since he was eight years old—wanted to make a point.

Jumping from waterfalls had been a pastime among boys laboring in the mills. But Patch considered it an "art" imbued with political meaning. He timed his Paterson leap to steal the show from Timothy B. Crane, an entrepreneur who had dreamed up Forest Garden, a pleasure park offering "respectable" ladies and gentlemen a respite from the mill town. To reach the park, which was formerly open to everyone, visitors now had to cross a toll bridge. The toll would raise revenue to sustain the park, but it would, as Crane saw it, keep out the riffraff.

Patch and the mill hands understood that the riffraff meant *them*. Forest Garden symbolized a world in which manual labor was devalued, in which artisans became workers, in which industrialists and entrepreneurs increasingly held themselves as morally superior to wage earners. In previous months, town residents attacked (physically and verbally) the park, its workers, its buildings, and Crane. When Crane planned elaborate celebrations marking the toll bridge's completion, Patch determined to assert the pride of workers who made the industrial revolution possible.

In the two years following his Paterson leap—before his last, fatal, jump at the 125-foot Genesee Falls in Rochester, New York—Sam Patch became a professional waterfall jumper. He costumed himself in the symbolic clothing of the textile spinner and associated socially and politically with a raucous crowd of skilled operatives. His flaunting of middle-class values caught the attention of the political press, organs for the era's two main political parties—the Whigs and the Jacksonian Democrats. To Whigs, Patch exemplified what was, in one editor's words, "wrong with

Chapter Outline

From Revival to Reform
Revivals | Moral Reform | Penitentiaries and Asylums | Temperance | Public Schools | Engineering and Science

VISUALIZING THE PAST *Engaging Children*

Utopian Experiments
Mormons | Shakers | Oneidans, Owenites, and Fourierists | American Renaissance

Abolitionism
Early Abolitionism and Colonization | Immediatism | The Lane Debates | The American Antislavery Society | African American Abolitionists | Opposition to Abolitionism | Moral Suasion Versus Political Action

LINKS TO THE WORLD *The International Antislavery Movement*

Women's Rights
Legal Rights | Political Rights

Jacksonianism and Party Politics
Expanding Political Participation | Election of 1824 | Election of 1828 | Democrats | King Andrew

Federalism at Issue: The Nullification and Bank Controversies
Nullification | The Force Act | Second Bank of the United States | Political Violence | Anti-Masonry | Election of 1832 | Jackson's Second Term | Specie Circular

287

The Whig Challenge and the Second Party System

Whigs and Reformers | Election of 1836 | Van Buren and Hard Times | Anglo-American Tensions | William Henry Harrison and the Election of 1840 | President Tyler

LEGACY FOR A PEOPLE AND A NATION *Moral Reformers' Abstinence Campaigns*

SUMMARY

democracy," whereas Jacksonians hailed Patch as a heroic artisan. In 1833, Philadelphia presented President Andrew Jackson with a horse, which the president named Sam Patch.

Like Patch, many Americans tried to reaffirm control over their lives in an era of rapid changes. The market economy, growing wealth and inequality, immigration, the westward thrust of settlement and slavery, and territorial expansion inspired Americans' hopes and fears. Many Americans embraced progress even as they hoped to limit what they saw as its unpleasant side effects. But Americans often divided over what defined progress, what constituted a social ill, and how such ills should be remedied.

To soothe anxieties, many Americans turned to evangelical religion, and, in the North, reform movements. Believing in human perfectibility, reformers worked to free individuals and society from sin. In the Northeast and Midwest in particular, people organized to end prostitution and alcohol abuse, improve prison and asylum conditions, and establish public schools. Other reformers created separate experimental—or utopian—communities. Opponents of slavery and proponents of women's rights, meanwhile, sought to radically alter the application of the revolutionary declaration that "all men are created equal."

Evangelical reformers generally aligned with the Whig Party, but Jacksonian Democrats, too, were concerned with social problems, mostly class inequities. They distrusted middle-class reformers who told working-class men and women how to live, and they opposed special privileges bestowed by government policies and institutions, such as the Second Bank of the United States. Yet when it came to slavery, the national parties often remained silent to keep sectional conflict submerged.

As political rivals, Democrats and Whigs held distinct positions on most other salient issues. Democrats emphasized that the best government is that which governs least, whereas the Whigs championed a strong federal government. Democrats focused on agricultural expansion west, whereas Whigs promoted industrial and commercial growth in the East. They hoped to stimulate growth through their American System of high protective tariffs, centralized banking, and federal funding for internal improvements. Together, Democrats and Whigs constituted what is often called the second party system, characterized by strong organizations, intense loyalty, and religious and ethnic voting patterns.

As you read this chapter, keep the following questions in mind:

* **What were the "evils" in society that reformers hoped to eliminate, and what motivated them to do so?**

* **What was the relationship between reform and politics?**

* **What were the main issues dividing Democrats and Whigs?**

Chronology

1790s–1840s	Second Great Awakening
1820s	Model penitentiaries established
1820s–1840s	Utopian communities founded
1824	No electoral-college majority in presidential election
1825	House of Representatives elects Adams president
1826	American Society for the Promotion of Temperance founded
1828	Tariff of Abominations passed Jackson elected president
1830	Joseph Smith organizes Mormon Church
1830s–40s	Democratic-Whig competition gels in second party system
1831	Garrison first publishes *The Liberator* Antimasons hold first national political convention
1832	Jackson vetoes rechartering Second Bank of the United States Jackson reelected president
1832–33	Nullification Crisis
1836	Specie Circular Van Buren elected president
1837	*Caroline* affair Financial panic ends boom of the 1830s
1837–1842	Croton Aqueduct constructed
1838–39	United States and Canada mobilize militias over border dispute
1839–43	Hard times spread unemployment and deflation
1840	Whigs win presidency under Harrison
1841	Tyler assumes presidency after Harrison's death
1846	Smithsonian Institution founded
1848	Seneca Falls Woman's Rights Convention American Association for the Advancement of Science established

From Revival to Reform

Religious revivals in the late eighteenth and early nineteenth centuries—sometimes called the **Second Great Awakening** for their resemblance to the eighteenth-century Great Awakening—raised people's hopes for the Second Coming of the Christian messiah and the establishment of God's kingdom on earth. Revivalists resolved to speed the millennium, or the thousand years of peace on earth that would accompany Christ's Second Coming, by combating sin. Some believed that the United States had a special mission in God's design and a special role in eliminating evil. Revivalists urged individuals to renounce sins, such as drinking, swearing, and licentiousness, and help combat social evils, including slavery. Not until all Americans were converted would Christ return.

Revivalists strove for large-scale conversions. Rural women, men, and children traveled long distances to camp meetings, where they heard fiery sermons delivered day and night from hastily constructed platforms and tents in forests or fields. In cities, women in particular attended daily services and prayer meetings. Converts vowed to live sanctified lives and help others see the light.

> How did religious revival movements lead to social reform?

Second Great Awakening: Religious revival that swept the country and helped inspire reform movements.

Revivals

The most famous revival was at Cane Ridge, Kentucky, in August 1801. An estimated 25,000 people attended at a time when Kentucky's largest city, Lexington, had barely 2,000 inhabitants. The call to repentance and conversion invigorated southern Protestantism. Although laws often restricted or outlawed black churches and preachers, particularly after Nat Turner's 1831 revolt, black and mixed churches flourished locally. During the 1840s and 1850s, though, as slavery entered public debate, southern Presbyterian, Baptist, and Methodist churches seceded from their denominations' national conferences. For the white leaders of these secessionist churches, slavery did not impede human perfectibility but rather ensured it, as benevolent masters brought Africans to Christ.

Revivalists believed in individual self-improvement, but northern revivalists also emphasized communal improvement. Northern evangelists generated new religious groups and voluntary reform societies. Preachers like Lyman Beecher, who started in New England before moving to Cincinnati, and **Charles Finney**, who traveled the canals and roads linking the Northeast to the Midwest, argued that "God has made man a moral free agent," that Christians were not doomed by original sin, and that anyone could achieve salvation. Revivalism thrived among Methodists and Baptists, whose denominational structures maximized democratic participation and drew ministers from ordinary folk.

Finney achieved his greatest successes in those areas of western New York experiencing rapid changes in transportation and industrialization—what he called the "Burned-Over District" because of the region's intense flames of evangelicalism. Rapid change raised fears of social disorder—family dissolution, drinking, swearing, and prostitution. Many individuals worried, too, about their economic fate during the era's booms and busts.

When northern revivalist preachers emphasized good works—good deeds—they helped ignite social reform movements, first in the Burned-Over District and then in New England, the Middle Atlantic, and the upper Midwest. Evangelically inspired reform associations together constituted what historians call the "benevolent empire." These associations shared a commitment to human perfectibility and often turned to the same wealthy men for financial resources and advice.

Charles G. Finney: A lawyer-turned-Presbyterian minister who conducted revivals in towns like Utica along the Erie Canal and who stressed individual responsibility.

Moral Reform

Those resources enabled reformers to use the era's new technologies—steam presses and railroads. By mass-producing pamphlets and newspapers for distribution into the country's interior, reformers spread their message widely. With canals and railroads making travel easier, reformers could attend conventions and host speakers from distant places. Most reform organizations sponsored weekly newspapers, creating a virtual community of reformers.

While industrialists and merchants provided financial resources for evangelical reform, their wives and daughters solicited new members and circulated petitions. Reformers expanded the cult of domesticity's role for women as moral guardians beyond the home into the public realm. Women helped run reformatories for wayward youth or establish asylums for orphans. Participation in reform movements thus allowed women to exercise moral authority outside the household, giving them new influence. Although some elite women in Upper South cities formed and joined reform societies, moral reform was primarily a northeastern and midwestern phenomenon.

Many female reformers had attended a female academy or seminary. These schools' curriculum included arts of "refinement"—music, dance, penmanship—but focused on science and literature and was modeled on men's colleges. By 1820, roughly equal numbers of men and women attended institutions of higher education. Educated women prepared to influence public opinion even as many maintained domestic responsibilities. A few women became prominent editors and writers, but most influenced society as educators and reformers.

For women and some men, reform represented political influence at a time when only property-owning men could vote. In 1830, as female reformers in New York City organized a shelter for prostitutes, they publicized the names of brothel clients to shame men contributing to women's waywardness. They then organized the Female Moral Reform Society, and by 1840 it had 555 affiliated chapters nation-wide. It soon lobbied successfully for criminal sanctions in New York State against men who seduced women into prostitution.

Link to the Female Moral Reform Society of the City of New York's first annual report.

Penitentiaries and Asylums

A similar belief in perfectibility led reformers to establish penitentiaries that aimed to move beyond punishment into transforming criminals into productive members of society through disciplined regimens. Other reformers sought to improve treatment of the mentally ill, who were frequently imprisoned, often alongside criminals, and put in cages or dark dungeons, chained to walls, and brutalized. **Dorothea Dix**, the movement's leader, exemplifies the reformer who started with a religious belief in human perfectibility and moved into social action. Investigating asylums, petitioning the Massachusetts legislature, and lobbying other states and Congress, Dix encouraged twenty-eight states to build institutions for the mentally ill by 1860.

Dorothea Dix: Leader of movement to improve conditions for the insane.

Temperance

Temperance advocates, who railed against alcoholic beverages, likewise crossed from the personal into the political sphere. Drinking was widespread in the early nineteenth century, when men like Sam Patch gathered in public houses and inns to drink. Politics were discussed, contracts were sealed, celebrations commemorated, and harvests toasted with liquor. "Respectable" women did not drink in public, but many tippled alcohol-based patent medicines promoted as cure-alls.

temperance: Abstinence from alcohol; name of the movement against alcohol.

Evangelicals considered drinking sinful, and forsaking alcohol was often part of conversion. Preachers condemned alcohol for violating the Sabbath—workers' one day off, which some spent at the public house. Factory owners claimed alcohol made workers unreliable. Civic leaders connected alcohol with crime. Middle-class reformers, often women, condemned it for diverting men from family responsibilities and fostering abusive behavior. In the early 1840s, thousands of women formed Martha Washington societies to reform alcoholics, raise children as teetotalers, and spread the temperance message.

Link to an illustration of the Tree of Temperance.

As the temperance movement grew, its goal shifted from moderation to abstinence to prohibition. By the mid-1830s, five thousand state and local temperance societies touted teetotalism, and more than a million people had pledged abstinence. Per capita consumption of alcohol fell from five gallons per year in 1800 to below two gallons in the 1840s. The American Society for the Promotion of Temperance, organized in 1826, pushed for legislation ending alcohol manufacture and sale. In 1851, Maine became the first state to ban alcohol except for medicinal purposes, and by 1855 similar laws were passed throughout New England and in New York, Pennsylvania, and the Midwest.

The temperance campaign had an anti-immigrant and anti-Catholic strain to it. Along the nation's canals, reformers lamented taverns catering to Irish workers, and

Engaging Children

Hundreds of thousands of children joined the temperance movement, often by enlisting in the so-called Cold Water Army. Like adult temperance societies, the Cold Water Army advocated for complete abstinence from alcoholic beverages. On holidays such as George Washington's birthday and the Fourth of July, they marched at public gatherings, singing temperance songs and carrying banners and fans such as the one pictured to the right. Reverend Thomas P. Hunt, a Presbyterian minister, founded the Cold Water Army because he believed that by recruiting children, he stood a much greater chance of eradicating alcohol consumption than if he aimed his temperance efforts directly at adults. What might have been his logic? Why might children have wanted to join a Cold Water Army? Do the images on the certificate and fan offer any clues? What were the benefits of participating in the movement? What were the implied consequences of failing to do so? Why might Hunt have chosen the term "army," and what about that choice might have proved appealing to his young recruits?

Children who participated in a Cold Water Army often received a certificate that acknowledged their commitment to the cause while reiterating the pledge they had taken.

Children in Cold Water Army parades sometimes carried decorative fans, which they may have displayed in their homes as well, as reminders to themselves and their parents of temperance's virtues.

in the cities, they expressed outrage at the Sunday tradition of German families' gathering at beer gardens. Some Catholics heeded the message, pledging abstinence and forming organizations such as the St. Mary's Mutual Benevolence Total Abstinence Society in Boston.

But many workers—Protestants and Catholics—rejected middle-class temperance campaigns. Workers agreed that poverty and crime were problems but blamed poor wages, not drinking habits. Even some who abstained from alcohol opposed prohibition, believing that drinking should be a matter of self-control, not state coercion.

Public Schools

Protestants and Catholics often quarreled over education. Public education usually included religious education, but when teachers taught Protestant beliefs and used the King James Bible, Catholics established their own schools. Some Protestants feared that Catholics would never assimilate into American culture and charged Catholics with plotting to impose papal control. Still, public education touched more Americans than did any other reform movement.

Horace Mann, a Massachusetts lawyer and reformer from humble beginnings, advocated free, tax-supported education to replace church and private schools. Universal education, Mann proposed, would end crime and help Americanize immigrants.

During Mann's tenure as secretary of the Massachusetts Board of Education from 1837 to 1848, Massachusetts led the "common school" movement, establishing teacher training, lengthening the school year, and raising teachers' salaries to make the profession more attractive. Adhering to notions that women had special claims to morality and could be paid less than men, Mann envisioned a system in which women educated future clerks, farmers, and workers with a practical curriculum that emphasized geography, arithmetic, and science. Educational reformers believed that individuals could educate themselves out of their circumstances. Thanks partly to expanding public education, by 1850 the majority of native-born white Americans were literate.

Horace Mann: First secretary of the newly created Massachusetts Board of Education who presided over sweeping reforms to transform schools into institutions that occupied most of a child's time and energy.

Engineering and Science

Public education's emphasis on science reflected a broader belief that engineering and science could help remedy the nation's problems. Scientists and doctors blamed not immorality, but rather unclean, stagnant water for epidemics. After the devastating cholera epidemic of 1832, New York City planned a massive waterworks and, between 1837 and 1842, built the forty-one-mile Croton Aqueduct that brought water from upstate New York to Manhattan.

Several scientific institutions were also founded in this era. After James Smithson, a wealthy British scientist, left his estate to the United States government, Congress established the Smithsonian Institution (1846), which promoted scientific knowledge. Joseph Henry, the Smithsonian's director, was a nationally renowned scientist; his experiments in electromagnetism helped make possible the telegraph and, later in the century, telephone. Like Henry, many nineteenth-century Americans considered religious devotion and scientific inquiry compatible. They saw scientific discoveries as signs of progress, symbolizing that the millennium was approaching. God had created the natural world, they believed, and it was their Christian duty to perfect it in preparation for God's return.

Utopian Experiments

What were the goals of utopian communities?

Some idealists dreamed of an entirely new social order. They established dozens of utopian communities based on religious principles, a resistance to the market economy's excessive individualism, or both. Some groups, like the **Mormons**, arose during the Second Great Awakening. Utopian communities attempted to recapture what they perceived as the past's more communal nature, even while offering radical departures from marriage and child rearing.

Mormons: Members of the Church of Jesus Christ of Latter-Day Saints, the first major denomination founded in 1830 in the United States; members were persecuted for many years.

Joseph Smith: Founder of the Mormon Church.

Mormons

No utopian experiment was more enduring than the Church of Jesus Christ of Latter-day Saints, whose members were known as Mormons. During the 1820s religious ferment in western New York, **Joseph Smith**, a young farmer, reported that an angel called Moroni gave him divinely engraved gold plates. Smith published his revelations as the *Book of Mormon* and organized a church in 1830. The next year, the community moved to Ohio to build a "New Jerusalem" and await the Second Coming of Jesus.

After angry mobs drove the Mormons from Ohio, they settled in Missouri. Anti-Mormons charged that Mormonism was a scam by Joseph Smith and feared Mormon economic and political power. In 1838, Missouri's governor charged Smith with fomenting insurrection and worked to indict him and other leaders for treason. Smith and his followers left for Nauvoo, Illinois. The state legislature gave them a city charter making them self-governing. But again the Mormons met antagonism, especially after Smith introduced polygamy in 1841, allowing men several wives at once. In 1844, after Smith and his brother were charged with treason and jailed, and then murdered, the Mormons left Illinois to seek security in the western wilderness. Under Brigham Young's leadership, they established a cooperative community in the Great Salt Lake valley. There, the Mormons distributed agricultural land according to family size. An extensive irrigation system transformed the arid valley into a rich oasis. As the colony developed, church elders gained control of water, trade, industry, and eventually the territorial government of Utah.

Shakers: Utopian sect that stressed celibacy and emphasized agriculture and handicrafts; became known for furniture designs long after the community itself ceased to exist.

Shakers

The **Shakers**, the largest communal utopian experiment, reached their peak between 1820 and 1860, with six thousand members in twenty settlements in eight states. Shaker communities emphasized agriculture and handcrafts, contrasting with the new factory regime. Founded in England in 1772 by Mother Ann Lee, their name derived from their worship service, which included shaking their bodies. Ann Lee's children died in infancy, and she saw their deaths as retribution for her sin of intercourse; thus she advocated celibacy. After imprisonment in England in 1773–1774, she settled in America.

Shakers lived communally, with men and women in separate quarters; individual families were abolished. Men and women shared leadership equally. Many Shaker settlements became temporary refuges for orphans, widows, runaways, abused wives, and laid-off workers. Their settlements depended on new recruits, partly because celibacy meant no reproduction, but also because some members left, unsuited to communal living or the Shakers' spiritual message.

Oneidans, Owenites, and Fourierists

Other utopian communities joined in resisting social change. John Humphrey Noyes, a lawyer converted by Finney's revivals, established two perfectionist communities: in Putney, Vermont, in 1835, and—after being indicted for adultery—in Oneida, New York, in 1848. Noyes advocated communal property, communal child rearing, and "complex marriage," in which all the community's men were married to all its women, but women could reject a sexual proposition. The Oneida Colony required pregnancies to be planned; couples applied to Noyes for permission to have a child, or Noyes assigned two people to reproduce. Robert Dale Owen's community in **New Harmony**, Indiana (1825–1828), abolished private property and advocated communal child rearing. The Fourierists, named after French philosopher Charles Fourier, established more than two dozen communities in the Northeast and Midwest that resisted individualism and promoted sexual equality.

The most famous Fourier community was Brook Farm, in West Roxbury, Massachusetts. Inspired by **transcendentalism**—the belief that the physical world is secondary to the spiritual realm, which humans can reach only by intuition—Brook Farm's rural communalism combined spirituality, manual labor, intellectual life, and play. Founded in 1841 by Unitarian minister George Ripley, Brook Farm attracted farmers, craftsmen, and writers, among them Nathaniel Hawthorne. The Brook Farm school drew students from outside the community, and Brook Farm residents contributed regularly to the *Dial,* the leading transcendentalist journal. In 1845, Brook Farm's hundred members organized into phalanxes (working-living units), following Fourier's model. As regimentation replaced individualism, membership dropped. A year after a disastrous fire in 1846, the experiment collapsed.

American Renaissance

Ralph Waldo Emerson, a pillar of transcendentalism, was the prime inspiration for a literary outpouring now known as the American Renaissance. He quit his Boston Unitarian ministry in 1831 and spent two years in Europe, before he returned to lecture and write, preaching self-reliance. Widely admired, he influenced Hawthorne, *Dial* editor Margaret Fuller, Herman Melville, and Thoreau. The American Renaissance was distinctively

New Harmony: An important and well-known utopian community, founded in Indiana by Robert Owen.

transcendentalism: The belief that the physical world is secondary to the spiritual realm, which humans can reach only by intuition.

Joslyn Art Museum, Omaha, Nebraska, Gift of Enron Art Foundation

This bucolic image of New Harmony, painted several years after the experiment's collapse, belies the rancorous history of the short-lived community, which attracted many settlers who proved unwilling or unable to commit themselves fully to communitarian life. Pictured here on the far left is the "Hive," which housed the kitchen, office, and meeting rooms; along the hilltop are buildings that housed residents, a laundry, and printing presses.

American and an outgrowth of the European romantic movement. It addressed universal themes using American settings and characters. Hawthorne, for instance, used Puritan New England as a backdrop.

Henry David Thoreau championed individualism. In his 1849 essay on "Resistance to Civil Government" (known after his death as "Civil Disobedience"), Thoreau advocated resistance to a government engaged in immoral acts. During the War with Mexico (see Chapter 14), Thoreau refused to pay taxes, believing they would aid an immoral war to expand slavery, and was briefly jailed. "I cannot for an instant recognize that political organization as my government which is the *slave's* government also," Thoreau wrote.

Abolitionism

How did the Second Great Awakening transform the antislavery movement?

Thoreau joined evangelical abolitionists in trying to eradicate slavery, which they deemed a sin. Inspired by the Second Great Awakening, their efforts built on those of an earlier generation of antislavery activists.

Early Abolitionism and Colonization

From the nation's earliest days—in Philadelphia, New York, Albany, Boston, and Nantucket—free blacks formed societies to petition legislatures, seek judicial redress, stage marches, and publish tracts chronicling slavery's horrors. African American abolitionists wrote about slavery's devastating impact on black and white families, advocated slavery's immediate termination, assisted escaped slaves, and promoted legal equality for free blacks. By 1830, there were fifty African American abolitionist societies. But David Walker, a southern-born free African American, captured white Americans' attention like none other with his *Appeal...to the Colored Citizens* (1829). Walker advocated slavery's violent overthrow, igniting fear throughout the white South and the North.

Violence was not a strategy for early white abolitionists. After the American Revolution, antislavery advocates united in places like Boston and Philadelphia, with its large population of Quakers, whose religious beliefs emphasized human equality. These reformers pressed gradual abolition and an end to the international slave trade. Although they aided African Americans seeking freedom through judicial decisions, their assumptions about blacks' racial inferiority kept them from advocating for equal rights. Early white abolitionists were typically wealthy men whose societies excluded women, African Americans, and non-elites.

Elites were more likely to support colonization, which crystallized in 1816 with the organization of the American Colonization Society. Its members planned to purchase and relocate American slaves and free blacks to Africa or the Caribbean. Supporters included Thomas Jefferson, James Madison, James Monroe, and Henry Clay. In 1824, the society founded Liberia, on Africa's west coast, and began a settlement for African Americans who were willing to go. The society had resettled nearly twelve thousand by 1860. Some colonizationists aimed to strengthen slavery by ridding the South of troublesome slaves or to purge the North of African Americans. Others hoped colonization would improve African Americans' conditions. Although some African Americans supported the movement, black abolitionists generally denounced it.

Links to the World

The International Antislavery Movement

The heart of the international antislavery movement had been in Great Britain, but in the 1830s many of Britain's antislavery societies considered their work finished and disbanded. The international slave trade greatly diminished, and in 1833 Parliament ended slavery in the British Empire.

American abolitionists revived the international antislavery movement. American abolitionism in the 1830s was invigorated by the militancy of black abolitionists and by William Lloyd Garrison's conversion to immediatism. To raise money and pressure the United States to abolish slavery, African American abolitionists in the 1840s toured Britain regularly. Ex-slaves recounted their experiences of slavery and bared their scarred bodies. After fugitive slave Moses Gandy toured England, he published his autobiography, the first of dozens of slave narratives published in London. The next year, 1845,

Frederick Douglass began a nineteen-month tour, giving three hundred lectures in Britain.

In 1849, black abolitionists William Wells Brown, Alexander Crummell, and J. W. C. Pennington were among twenty American delegates at the international Paris Peace Conference. Brown's lecture tour in Britain became a five-year exile because, after passage of the 1850 Fugitive Slave Law, he feared being seized and re-enslaved if he returned to the United States. In 1854, British abolitionists purchased his freedom.

By the early 1850s, abolitionists helped abolish slavery in Colombia, Argentina, Venezuela, and Peru. In the United States, black abolitionists were instrumental in reviving the worldwide antislavery movement, and, as advocates of women's rights, international peace, temperance, and other reforms, in linking Americans to other worldwide reform movements.

Used with Permission of Documenting the American South, The University of North Carolina at Chapel Hill Libraries.

William Wells Brown's autobiography stirred abolitionists in the United States and England. In 1849, Brown was among the American delegates to the Paris Peace Conference, then spent the next five years as an exile in Britain, fearing being sent back to slavery under the 1850 Fugitive Slave Act. He returned to the United States only after British abolitionists purchased his freedom from his former master.

William Lloyd Garrison:
Founder of *The Liberator* and a controversial white abolitionist, he demanded an immediate end to slavery and embraced civil rights for blacks on par with whites.

In the early 1830s, a new group of more radical white abolitionists—most prominently, **William Lloyd Garrison**—demanded immediate, complete, and uncompensated emancipation. Garrison began publishing his abolitionist newspaper, *The Liberator,* in 1831, two years before founding the American Antislavery Society, the era's largest abolitionist organization.

Immediatism

Immediatists believed slavery was a sin needing eradication. They were influenced by African American abolitionist societies and evangelicals' notion that humans, not God, determined their spiritual fate by choosing good or evil. In that sense, all were equal before God's eyes. When all humans had chosen good over evil, the millennium would come. Slavery, however, denied enslaved men and women the ability to make such choices, the ability to act as what Finney called "moral free agents." For every day that slavery continued, the millennium was postponed.

Because the millennium depended on *all* hearts being won over to Christ, Garrison advocated "moral suasion." He and his followers hoped to bring emancipation by winning over slaveowners and others who supported or tolerated slavery. Evangelical abolitionism depended, then, on large numbers of ministers and laypeople spreading the word nationwide.

The Lane Debates

In 1829, Congregationalists and Presbyterians founded the Lane Seminary in Cincinnati to train ministers. With Lyman Beecher as president, it drew northern and southern students and encouraged "people of color" to apply. After Theodore Weld, one of Charles Finney's converts, arrived at Lane in 1833, he organized the Lane Debates, eighteen days of discussion among students and faculty about colonization versus immediatism. Immediatism won.

Led by Weld, the Lane students and faculty founded an antislavery society and tried to reach Cincinnati's growing African American population, which in 1829 had been brutally attacked by white people. Fearful of renewed disorder, white business leaders protested the antislavery society. Lane's trustees, with Beecher's sanction, barred further antislavery activities. The "Lane Rebels" left and enrolled in a new seminary at Oberlin, a northern Ohio town founded as a Christian perfectionist settlement. This seminary became the first college to admit women and one of the first to admit African Americans.

The American Antislavery Society

By 1838, at its peak, the society had 2,000 local affiliates and over 300,000 members. Unlike earlier white abolitionists, the immediatists welcomed men and women of all races and classes. Lydia Maria Child, Maria Chapman, and Lucretia Mott served on its executive committee; Child edited its official paper, the *National Anti-Slavery Standard,* from 1841 to 1843, and Chapman coedited it from 1844 until 1848.

With the "great postal campaign" in 1835, the society flooded the mails with antislavery tracts. Women went door to door collecting signatures on antislavery petitions; by 1838, more than 400,000 petitions were sent to Congress. Abolitionist-minded women met in "sewing circles," making clothes for escaped slaves while organizing activities, such as antislavery fairs at which they sold goods—often handmade items—donating the proceeds to antislavery causes.

African American Abolitionists

Even as white abolitionist societies included African Americans and sponsored speaking tours by former slaves, African Americans continued independent efforts to end slavery and improve free African Americans' status into the 1840s and 1850s. Former slaves—famously, Frederick Douglass, Henry Bibb, Harriet Tubman, and Sojourner Truth—fought slavery through speeches, publications, and participation in a secret network known as the Underground Railroad, which spirited enslaved men, women, and children to freedom. By the thousands, African Americans established churches, founded moral reform societies, published newspapers, created schools and orphanages, and held conventions.

Opposition to Abolitionism

But abolitionists' gains inspired virulent opposition. In the South, mobs blocked the distribution of antislavery tracts. In South Carolina, officials intercepted and burned abolitionist literature, and in 1835 proslavery assailants killed four abolitionists in South Carolina and Louisiana, as well as forty people allegedly plotting a slave rebellion in Mississippi and Louisiana.

White northerners who opposed abolition recognized cotton's vital economic role and feared emancipation would prompt an influx of freed slaves into their region. They believed blacks to be inherently inferior and incapable of the virtue and diligence required of freedom and citizenship.

The North, too, experienced anti-abolitionist violence. In Boston, David Walker died under mysterious circumstances in 1830. Among northerners who despised abolitionists, most were commercial and political elites with strong connections to the southern cotton economy and political connections to leading southerners. Northern gentlemen incited anti-abolitionist riots. Mob violence peaked in 1835, with more than fifty riots aimed at abolitionists or African Americans. In 1837 in Alton, Illinois, a mob murdered white abolitionist editor Elijah P. Lovejoy, and rioters sacked his printing office. In 1838, Philadelphia rioters hurled stones at three thousand black and white women attending the Anti-Slavery Convention of American Women in the new Pennsylvania Hall, constructed to house abolitionist meetings and an abolitionist bookstore, before burning down the building.

Moral Suasion Versus Political Action

Violence made some immediatists question moral suasion as a tactic. James G. Birney, the son of a Kentucky slaveowner, embraced immediatism but believed abolition could be effected only through political action. Involving women violated the natural order of things and detracted from the ultimate goal: freedom for slaves. Thus, when William Lloyd Garrison, an ardent women's rights supporter, endorsed Abby Kelly's appointment to the American Antislavery Society's business committee in 1840, he provoked an irreparable split in the abolitionist movement. Arthur Tappan and Theodore Weld led a dissident group that established the American and Foreign Anti-Slavery Society. That society formed a new political party: the Liberty Party, which nominated Birney for president in 1840 and 1844.

Although committed to immediate abolition, the Liberty Party doubted the federal government's authority to abolish slavery. Only states, they thought, had the jurisdiction to determine slavery's legality. They believed the federal government could act only in western territories, and the party demanded that new territories prohibit slavery. Prominent black abolitionists, including Frederick Douglass, endorsed the party, whose leaders also emphasized combating northern prejudice.

Women's Rights

What inspired the rise of the women's movement in the mid-nineteenth century?

Angelina and Sarah Grimké: Southern-born sisters who were powerful antislavery speakers; later leaders of women's rights movement

At the first World Anti-Slavery Convention in London in 1840, abolitionists Lucretia Mott and Elizabeth Cady Stanton were dismayed when female abolitionists were denied seats in the convention's main hall; eight years later, these women helped organize the first American women's rights convention. Born to a South Carolina slaveholding family, **Angelina and Sarah Grimké** moved north and became active abolitionists. After critics attacked them for speaking to audiences that included men, they became advocates for women's legal and social equality.

The political consciousness of lesser-known women similarly developed from abolitionist activities, particularly petitioning campaigns. After Congress voted to automatically table antislavery petitions in 1836, women defended their right to have their petitions considered. Female petitioners increasingly saw themselves as citizens rather than political subjects.

Religious revivalism helped women see themselves as equal to men, and reform movements brought middle-class women into the public sphere. Female reformers' lobbying helped to effect legal change, making some think the next step was citizenship rights for women.

Legal Rights

After independence, American states carried over traditional English marriage law, giving husbands absolute control over the family. Men owned their wives' property, were their children's legal guardians, and owned whatever family members produced or earned. A father could legally oppose his daughter's choice of husband, though by 1800 most American women chose their spouses.

Married women made modest gains in property and spousal rights after 1830. Arkansas in 1835 passed the first married women's property law, and by 1860 sixteen more states allowed women to own and convey property and write wills. When a wife inherited property, it was hers, though money earned still belonged to her husband. Such laws were popular among wealthy Americans, hoping to protect family fortunes during economic downturns; property in a woman's name was safe from her husband's creditors. In the 1830s, states also added cruelty and desertion as grounds for divorce, but divorce remained rare.

Radical reformers argued that marriage constituted a form of bondage. Lucy Stone, an outspoken critic of marriage, consented to marry fellow abolitionist Henry Blackwell only if she could eschew a vow of obedience and keep her own surname.

Political Rights

Seneca Falls: The location of a women's rights convention in 1848.

The women's movement was launched in July 1848, when Elizabeth Cady Stanton, Lucretia Mott, Mary Ann McClintock, Martha Wright, and Jane Hunt—all abolitionists—organized the first Woman's Rights Convention at **Seneca Falls**, New York.

Three hundred women and men demanded women's social and economic equality. Their Declaration of Sentiments, modeled on the Declaration of Independence, broadcast the injustices suffered by women and proclaimed "All men and women are created equal." The similarities between abolitionism and women's rights led reformers, including former slaves like Sojourner Truth, to work for both movements in the 1850s. The question of female suffrage became divisive. William Lloyd Garrison and Frederick Douglass supported women's right to vote, but most men opposed it. The Seneca Falls' suffrage resolution passed only after Douglass passionately endorsed it. In 1851, **Elizabeth Cady Stanton** joined with temperance advocate **Susan B. Anthony** to become the most vocal suffrage activists.

Elizabeth Cady Stanton, Susan B. Anthony: Vocal advocates of women's suffrage.

Jacksonianism and Party Politics

Like reformers, politicians sought to control the direction of the expanding nation. They reached out to an increasingly broad-based electorate. Hotly contested elections drew the interest of voters and nonvoters alike and fueled bitter rivalries.

How did changing demographics influence the outcome of the 1824 presidential election and the future of political parties?

Expanding Political Participation

Property restrictions for voters, which states began abandoning during the 1810s, remained in only seven of twenty-six states by 1840. Some states even allowed foreign nationals who officially declared their intention of becoming American citizens to vote. The net effect was that between 1824 and 1828 the number of votes cast in presidential elections tripled, from 360,000 to over 1.1 million. The proportion of eligible voters who cast ballots also grew, from about 27 percent in 1824 to more than 80 percent in 1840.

The selection of presidential electors also became more democratic. Previously, a caucus of party leaders picked them in most states, but by 1824 eighteen out of twenty-four states chose electors by popular vote. Consequently, politicians augmented their appeals to voters, and the 1824 election saw the end of the congressional caucus, when House and Senate members of the same political party united to select their candidate.

Election of 1824

As a result, five Democratic-Republican candidates ran for president in 1824. The poorly attended Republican caucus chose William H. Crawford of Georgia, secretary of the treasury, as its candidate. Instead of Congress, state legislatures now nominated candidates, offering the expanded electorate a slate of sectional candidates. John Quincy Adams drew support from New England, while westerners backed House Speaker Henry Clay of Kentucky. Some southerners initially supported Secretary of War John C. Calhoun, who later ran for the vice presidency instead. The Tennessee legislature nominated military hero Andrew Jackson.

Jackson led in electoral and popular votes, but no candidate received an electoral-college majority. Adams finished second. Under the Constitution, the House of Representatives, voting by state delegation, one vote to a state, would select the next president from among the three electoral vote leaders. Clay, with the fewest votes, was dropped. Crawford, disabled from a stroke, never received consideration. Clay backed Adams, who won with thirteen of the twenty-four state delegations and became president (Map 12.1). Adams named Clay as secretary of state, the traditional steppingstone to the presidency.

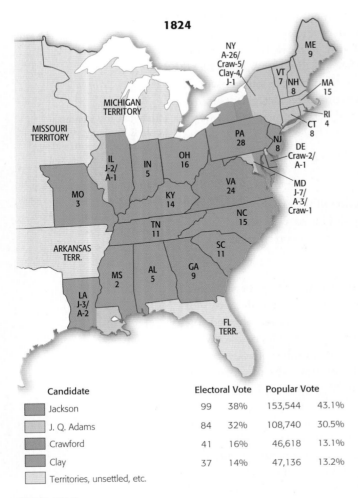

1824

NY
A-26/
Craw-5/
Clay-4/
J-1

ME
9

VT
7

NH
8

MA
15

MICHIGAN
TERRITORY

RI
4

CT
4

MISSOURI
TERRITORY

PA
28

NJ
8

DE
Craw-2/
A-1

IL
J-2/
A-1

IN
5

OH
16

MO
3

KY
14

VA
24

MD
J-7/
A-3/
Craw-1

TN
11

NC
15

ARKANSAS
TERR.

SC
11

MS
2

AL
5

GA
9

LA
J-3/
A-2

FL
TERR.

Candidate	Electoral Vote		Popular Vote	
Jackson	99	38%	153,544	43.1%
J. Q. Adams	84	32%	108,740	30.5%
Crawford	41	16%	46,618	13.1%
Clay	37	14%	47,136	13.2%
Territories, unsettled, etc.				

MAP 12.1

Presidential Election, 1824

Andrew Jackson led in both electoral and popular votes but failed to win a majority of electoral college votes. The House elected John Quincy Adams president.

Source: Copyright © Cengage Learning

Democrats: Members of the party that emerged from Jefferson's Republican party as one of the two dominant parties in the second party system.

Angry Jacksonians denounced the election as a "corrupt bargain," claiming Adams had stolen the election by offering Clay a cabinet position for his votes. The Republican Party split. The Adams wing emerged as the National Republicans, and the Jacksonians became the **Democrats**.

As president, Adams proposed a strong nationalist policy incorporating Clay's American System of protective tariffs, a national bank, and internal improvements. Adams believed the federal government's active role should extend to education, science, and the arts. He proposed a national university in Washington, D.C. Brilliant as a diplomat and secretary of state, Adams fared less well as chief executive.

Election of 1828

The 1828 election pitted Adams against Jackson. Nicknamed "Old Hickory," Andrew Jackson was a tough, ambitious man. Born in South Carolina in 1767, he rose from humble beginnings to become a wealthy Tennessee planter and slaveholder. After leading the Tennessee militia campaign to remove Creeks from the Alabama and Georgia frontier, Jackson gained national acclaim in 1815 as the hero of the Battle of New Orleans. In 1818, his fame increased with his expedition against Seminoles in Spanish Florida. Jackson served as a congressman and senator from Tennessee and the first territorial governor of Florida (1821).

Jackson's supporters accused Adams of stealing the 1824 election and, when he was envoy to Russia, of securing prostitutes for the czar. Anti-Jacksonians countered with reports that Jackson's wife, Rachel, married Jackson before her divorce from her first husband was final. In 1806, while attempting to defend Rachel's integrity, Jackson killed a man during a duel, and the cry of "murderer!" reappeared in the election.

Although Adams kept the states he won in 1824, Jackson swamped him, polling 56 percent of the popular vote and winning in the electoral college by 178 to 83 votes (Map 12.2). Through a lavishly financed coalition of state parties, political leaders, and newspaper editors, a popular movement had elected the president. The Democratic Party became the first well-organized national party.

Democrats

Democrats shared a commitment to the Jeffersonian concept of an agrarian society. They viewed a strong central government as antithetical to individual liberty, and they condemned government intervention in the economy as favoring the rich over the artisan and farmer. When it came to westward expansion, though, Jacksonians called for federal intervention, with Jackson initiating Indian removal despite northeastern reformers' protests.

Like Jefferson, Jackson strengthened the government's executive branch even while advocating limited government. Combining the roles of party leader and chief of state, he centralized power in the White House. He relied on political friends, his "Kitchen Cabinet," for advice, rarely consulting his official cabinet. Rotating officeholders, Jackson claimed, made government more responsive to the public, and he appointed loyal Democrats, a practice his critics called the **spoils system**, in which the victor gives the spoils of victory to his supporters. The spoils system, opponents charged, corrupted the government because it based appointments on loyalty, not competency.

King Andrew

Opponents mocked Jackson as "King Andrew I," charging him with abuse of power by ignoring the Supreme Court's ruling on Cherokee rights, sidestepping his cabinet, and replacing officeholders with his cronies.

Jackson's critics especially disliked his frequent use of the veto to promote limited government. In 1830, he vetoed the Maysville Road bill, which would have funded construction of a 60-mile turnpike from Maysville to Lexington, Kentucky. Constitutionally, he insisted, states bore responsibility for internal improvements within a single state. The veto undermined Clay's American System and embarrassed Clay because the project was in his home district.

The first six presidents vetoed nine bills; Jackson vetoed twelve. Previous presidents believed vetoes were justified only on constitutional grounds; Jackson considered policy disagreements legitimate grounds. He made the veto an effective weapon for controlling Congress, which had to weigh the possibility of a veto as it deliberated.

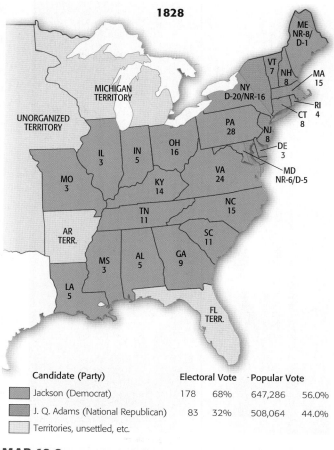

Candidate (Party)	Electoral Vote		Popular Vote	
Jackson (Democrat)	178	68%	647,286	56.0%
J. Q. Adams (National Republican)	83	32%	508,064	44.0%
Territories, unsettled, etc.				

MAP 12.2

Presidential Election, 1828

Andrew Jackson avenged his 1824 loss of the presidency, sweeping the election in 1828.
Source: Copyright © Cengage Learning

spoils system: Practice of rewarding political supporters with public office.

Federalism at Issue: The Nullification and Bank Controversies

The slave South feared federal power. That was especially true for South Carolina, where the planter class was strongest and slavery most concentrated. Southerners resented protectionist tariffs, which in 1824 and 1828 protected manufactures by imposing import duties on manufactured cloth and iron. In protecting northern factories, the tariff raised the costs of manufactured goods to southerners, who labeled the high 1828 tariff the **Tariff of Abominations**.

What was at issue in the Nullification Controversy?

Tariff of Abominations: Protective tariff of 1828 that infuriated southerners; spawned nullification crisis.

The Hermitage: Home of President Andrew Jackson, Nashville, TN

Even as his critics portrayed him as monarchical, Jackson presented himself as the president of the common man. Here he sits atop his prized horse, Sam Patch, named after the disgruntled factory worker and daring waterfall jumper.

Nullification

South Carolina's political leaders rejected the 1828 tariff, invoking the doctrine of nullification, which held that a state had the right to overrule, or nullify, federal legislation. Nullification borrowed from the Virginia and Kentucky Resolutions the idea that the states, representing the people, have a right to judge the constitutionality of federal actions. Jackson's vice president, John C. Calhoun of South Carolina, argued in his unsigned *Exposition and Protest* that, in disagreements between the federal government and a state, a special state convention should decide the conflict by either nullifying or affirming the federal law. As Jackson's running mate in 1828, Calhoun avoided endorsing nullification and embarrassing the Democratic ticket; he also hoped to win Jackson's support as the Democratic presidential heir apparent. Thus, in early 1830, Calhoun presided silently over the Senate when Massachusetts Senator Daniel Webster and South Carolina Senator Robert Y. Hayne debated states' rights. The debate over the tariff soon focused on the nature of the Union, with nullification a subtext. Hayne charged the North with threatening to bring disunity. Webster defended New England and the republic, keeping nullification supporters on the defensive.

Though sympathetic to states' rights and distrustful of the federal government, Jackson rejected state sovereignty. Believing in the Union, he shared Webster's dread of nullification. The president articulated his position at a Jefferson Day dinner with the toast "Our Federal Union, it must and shall be preserved." Vice President Calhoun toasted "The Federal Union—next to our liberty the most dear," revealing his adherence to states' rights. Calhoun and Jackson grew apart, and Jackson looked to Secretary of State Martin Van Buren as his successor.

Tension resumed when Congress passed a new tariff in 1832, reducing some duties but retaining high taxes on imported iron, cottons, and woolens. Although a majority of southern representatives supported the new tariff, South Carolinians did not. They feared the act could set a precedent for congressional legislation on slavery. In November 1832, a South Carolina state convention nullified the 1828 and the 1832 tariffs, declaring it unlawful for federal officials to collect duties in the state.

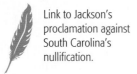

Link to Jackson's proclamation against South Carolina's nullification.

The Force Act

In December, Jackson issued a proclamation opposing nullification. He moved troops to federal forts in South Carolina and prepared U.S. marshals to collect the duties. At Jackson's request, Congress passed the Force Act, authorizing the president to call up troops but offering a way to avoid force by collecting duties before foreign ships reached Charleston's harbor. Jackson also extended an olive branch by recommending tariff reductions.

Calhoun, disturbed by South Carolina's drift toward separatism, resigned as vice president and soon won election to the U.S. Senate, where he worked with Henry Clay on the compromise Tariff of 1833. Quickly passed by Congress and signed by the president, the new tariff lengthened the list of duty-free items and reduced duties over nine years. Satisfied, South Carolina repealed its nullification law. Nullification offered a genuine debate on the nature of the republic. Each side believed it was upholding the Constitution. South Carolina opposed the tyranny of the federal government and manufacturing interests. Jackson fought the tyranny of South Carolina, whose actions threatened to split the republic. It took another crisis, over a central bank, to define the federal powers more clearly.

Second Bank of the United States

At stake was the Second Bank of the United States, whose twenty-year charter would expire in 1836. The bank served as a depository for federal funds and provided business credit. Its bank notes circulated as currency nationwide; they could be readily exchanged for gold. Through its twenty-five branch offices, the Second Bank acted as a clearing-house for state banks, refusing bank notes from state banks lacking sufficient gold reserves. Most state banks saw the central bank's police role as potentially ruinous. Moreover, state banks could not compete equally with the Second Bank, which had more money in reserve.

Many states regarded the national bank as unresponsive to local needs. Westerner settlers and urban workers bitterly remembered the bank's conservative credit policies during the Panic of 1819. As a private, profit-making institution, its policies reflected its owners' interests, especially its president, Nicholas Biddle. An eastern patrician, Biddle symbolized all that westerners resented about the bank, and all that eastern workers disliked about the commercial elite.

Political Violence

Controversy over the Second Bank inflamed longstanding political animosities, bringing violence to the streets. Elections often involved fraud, and with no secret ballot, political parties employed operatives to intimidate voters. New York City had the most powerful political machine, the Democrats' Tammany Hall, and thus in the midst of the Bank controversy, New York's mayoral election of 1834 sparked mayhem.

Three days of rioting began when Democratic operatives stormed Whig headquarters. After beating some **Whigs** unconscious, the Democrats attacked police; eight of them suffered severe wounds, and the mayor was also injured. Vowing revenge, more than five hundred Whigs stole weapons from the armory, but the state militia arrived to restore order.

Whigs: Formerly called the National Republicans; a major political party in the 1830s.

Months later, an election-day riot in Philadelphia left two dead and five buildings burned to the ground. These riots are remarkable for their intensity, but voter intimidation and fraud characterized the second party system.

Antimasonry

Violence was a catalyst for the formation of the Antimason Party, which started in upstate New York in the mid-1820s as a grassroots movement against Freemasonry, a secret male fraternity of middle- and upper-class men prominent in commerce and civic affairs. Opponents claimed Masons colluded to bestow business and political favors on each other, and—in the incident that sparked the organized Antimasonry movement—Masons had obstructed justice in the investigation of the 1826 disappearance and presumed murder of a disgruntled former member who had written an exposé of the society. Evangelicals denounced Masonry, claiming its members neglected their families for alcohol and ribald entertainment. In the 1828 presidential election, the Antimasons opposed Jackson, a Mason. They held their first national political convention in Baltimore in 1831, nominating William Wirt of Maryland for president and Amos Ellmaker of Pennsylvania for vice president.

Election of 1832

Following the Antimasons' lead, the Democrats and National Republicans also held conventions. Democrats reaffirmed Jackson for president and nominated Martin Van Buren of New York for vice president. The National Republican convention selected Clay and John Sergeant of Pennsylvania. The Independent Democrats ran John Floyd and Henry Lee of Virginia.

The Bank of the United States became the election's main issue. Jacksonians denounced it as a vehicle for special privilege, while the Republicans supported it within their plan for economic nationalism. The bank's charter was valid until 1836, but Clay persuaded Biddle to ask Congress for an early rechartering. If Jackson signed the rechartering bill, then Clay could attack the president's inconsistency. If he vetoed it, Clay hoped voters would favor him. The plan backfired. The president vetoed the bill with a message appealing to voters who feared that rapid economic development spread advantages undemocratically. Jackson took a strong stand against special interests that tried to use the government to their own unfair advantage and won 54 percent of the popular vote to Clay's 37 percent. He captured 76 percent of the electoral college. The Antimasons won only Vermont but nonetheless galvanized anti-Jackson opposition.

Jackson's Second Term

Jackson moved in 1833 to dismantle the Second Bank. He deposited federal funds in state-chartered banks. Without federal money, the Second Bank shriveled, becoming a Pennsylvania-chartered private bank in 1836. Five years later, it closed.

Congress passed the Deposit Act of 1836, authorizing the secretary of the treasury to designate one bank per state and territory to provide services formerly performed by the Bank of the United States. The act also provided that federal surplus over $5 million—income derived from the sale of public lands to speculators, who gobbled up land to resell at a profit—be distributed to the states as interest-free loans beginning in 1837.

Eager to use the money for state-funded internal improvements, Democrats joined Whigs in supporting the measure. Fearing that the Act would fuel speculation, promote inflation, and thus undermine farmers' interests, Jackson opposed it. Because support was strong enough to override a veto, Jackson signed the bill but first insisted on a provision prohibiting state banks from issuing or accepting small-denomination paper money. Jackson hoped that by encouraging the use of coins, the provision would prevent unscrupulous businessmen from paying workers in devalued paper bills.

Specie Circular

The president then ordered Treasury Secretary Levi Woodbury to issue the Specie Circular, which provided that after August 1836 only settlers could use paper money to buy land; speculators had to use specie (gold or silver). The policy proved disastrous, significantly reducing public-land sales, which in turn reduced the federal government's surplus and its loans to the states.

Meanwhile, a banking crisis emerged. Fearful that their banknotes would lose value, people redeemed them for specie, creating a shortage that forced banks to suspend payment, further reducing confidence.

Jackson's opponents were irate. Jackson had used his presidential powers to defeat a bill passed by the Senate months earlier that was similar to the Specie Circular. In the waning days of Jackson's administration, Congress repealed the circular, but the president pocket-vetoed the bill by holding it unsigned until Congress adjourned. In May 1838, after Jackson left office, a joint resolution of Congress overturned the circular.

The Whig Challenge and the Second Party System

How did the Whigs and Democrats differ ideologically?

In the 1830s, the Democrats' opponents, including remnants of the National Republican and Antimason parties, united as the Whig Party. Resentful of Jackson's domination of Congress, the Whigs borrowed the name of the eighteenth-century British party that opposed the Hanoverian monarchs' tyranny. From 1834 through the 1840s, the Whigs and the Democrats competed on nearly equal footing, and each drew supporters from all regions. The era's political competition—the second party system—was more intense and better organized than what scholars have labeled as the first party system of Democratic-Republicans versus Federalists.

Whigs and Reformers

Whigs favored economic expansion through an activist government. They supported corporate charters, a national bank, and paper currency; Democrats opposed all three. Whigs professed a belief in progress and perfectibility, and they favored social reforms, prison and asylum reform, and temperance. Jacksonians criticized reform associations for undermining the people's will by giving undue influence to political minorities; Whigs countered they served the common good. Nor did Whigs object to helping special interests if doing so promoted the general welfare. The chartering of corporations, they argued, expanded economic opportunity for everyone. Democrats, distrustful of concentrated economic power, held to the Jeffersonian principle of limited government.

Whigs stressed a "harmony of interests" among all classes along with equal opportunity. Democrats saw society as divided into the "haves" and the "have nots," and embraced "equal rights." They championed "heroic artisans" like Sam Patch, whereas Whigs preferred to see society ruled from the top down. Whigs believed in free-labor ideology and thought that society's wealthy had risen by their own merits. Democrats alleged that, instead, their political opponents had benefited from special favors.

But religion and ethnicity, as much as class, influenced party affiliation. The Whigs' support for moral reform won over evangelical Protestants. Methodists and Baptists were overwhelmingly Whigs, as were the small number of free black voters. In many locales, the membership rolls of reform societies overlapped those of the party. Whigs' rallies resembled camp meetings; their speeches employed pulpit rhetoric; their programs embodied perfectionist beliefs.

By appealing to evangelicals, Whigs alienated other faiths. The evangelicals' ideal Christian state had no room for nonevangelical Protestants, Catholics, Mormons, or religious freethinkers. Those groups opposed Sabbath laws and temperance legislation and preferred to keep religion and politics separate. Consequently, more than 95 percent of Irish Catholics, 90 percent of Reformed Dutch, and 80 percent of German Catholics voted Democratic.

The parties' platforms thus attracted a seemingly odd coalition of voters. Favoring government-sponsored commercial development and fearful of social disorder, the Whigs wanted slower, more controlled settlement of western lands; later, they opposed slavery's westward expansion. Groups as diverse as black New Englanders and slave owners, in the Upper South, liked these ideas; the former, to undercut slavery, and the latter to protect their investments from cheap western competition. Democrats' promises to open additional lands for settlement attracted yeoman farmers, wage earners, frontier slaveowners, and immigrants. With broad voter coalitions, there was room within each party for a spectrum of beliefs, particularly about slavery.

Some politicians went to extremes to keep the potentially divisive issue of slavery out of national political debate. In response to the American Antislavery Society's petitioning campaign, the House of Representatives in 1836 adopted what abolitionists labeled the "gag rule," which automatically tabled abolitionist petitions. Former president John Quincy Adams, now a representative from Massachusetts, defended the right to petition and spoke against the gag rule, which was repealed in 1844.

Election of 1836

Vice President Martin Van Buren headed the Democratic ticket in the 1836 presidential election. A career politician, Van Buren built a political machine—the Albany Regency—in New York and then joined Jackson's cabinet in 1829, first as secretary of state and then as U.S. minister to Great Britain.

Not yet a national party in 1836, Whigs entered three sectional candidates: Daniel Webster (New England), Hugh White (the South), and William Henry Harrison (the West). Van Buren captured the electoral college even though he had only a 25,000-vote lead. No vice-presidential candidate received a majority of electoral votes, and for the only time in American history, the Senate decided a vice-presidential race, selecting Democratic candidate Richard M. Johnson of Kentucky.

Van Buren and Hard Times

Van Buren took office weeks before the American credit system collapsed. With banks refusing to redeem paper currency with gold in response to the Specie Circular, a downward economic spiral began, curtailing bank loans. Credit contraction made things worse. After a brief recovery, hard times persisted from 1839 until 1843.

Van Buren cut federal spending, causing prices to drop further, and opposed a national bank, which would have expanded credit. The president proposed a new regional treasury system for government deposits that became law in 1840. Treasury branches would accept and disperse only gold and silver coin. Increasing the demand for hard coin, it deprived banks of gold and accelerated price deflation. Whigs favored new banks, more paper currency, and readily available corporate and bank charters. As the party of hard money, Democrats favored eliminating paper currency; by the mid-1840s, most favored eliminating bank corporations.

Anglo-American Tensions

Amid hard times came renewed Anglo-American tensions. After the privately owned steamer *Caroline* carried supplies to aid an unsuccessful Canadian uprising against Great Britain, British loyalists burned the ship, killing an American. Britain refused to apologize, and American newspapers called for revenge. Fearing war, President Van Buren posted troops at the border to discourage vigilante retaliation. Tensions subsided in late 1840 when New York arrested a Canadian deemed responsible for the American's death. The alleged murderer was acquitted. Had the verdict gone otherwise, Lord Palmerston, the British foreign minister, might have sought war.

An old border dispute between Maine and New Brunswick also disrupted Anglo-American relations. When Canadian lumbermen cut trees in the disputed region in winter 1838–1839, a Maine posse assembled to expel them. The lumbermen captured the posse, both sides mobilized militias, and Congress authorized a call-up of fifty thousand men. General Winfield Scott was dispatched to Aroostook, Maine, where he arranged a truce. The Webster-Ashburton Treaty (1842) settled the boundaries between Maine and New Brunswick and along the Great Lakes.

Franklin D. Roosevelt Library

Even as the Whigs opposed the Democrats, they adopted many of the Democrats' campaign techniques, appealing to the common man with their "log cabin and cider" campaign of 1840. The band in this street scene is riding a wagon decorated with a log-cabin painting. The campaign's excitement appealed to nonvoters as well as voters, and eighty percent of eligible voters cast ballots.

William Henry Harrison and the Election of 1840

With the nation facing hard times, Whigs confidently approached the 1840 election. Their strategy was simple: maintain supporters and court independents by blaming hardship on Democrats. Whigs rallied behind military hero General William Henry Harrison, conqueror of the Shawnees at Tippecanoe Creek in 1811. Democrats renominated President Van Buren, and the newly formed Liberty Party ran James Birney.

Harrison and his running mate, John Tyler of Virginia, ran a people's crusade against the aristocratic president in "the Palace." Although from a Virginia plantation family, Harrison presented himself as an ordinary farmer. Whigs wooed voters with huge rallies, parades, songs, posters, campaign mementos, and a party newspaper, *The Log Cabin*. Roughly 80 percent of eligible voters cast ballots. Winning the popular vote by a narrow margin, Harrison swept the electoral college, 234 to 60.

Immediately after taking office in 1841, President Harrison convened Congress in special session to pass the Whig program: repeal of the independent treasury system, a new national bank, and a higher protective tariff. But the sixty-eight-year-old

Link to Ellen Kay Bond's speech in support of William Henry Harrison.

Moral Reformers' Abstinence Campaigns

For female moral reformers in the 1830s and 1840s, safeguarding the nation against social ills often meant enforcing a new sexual propriety: premarital celibacy for men and women. Their calls are echoed in today's "purity" movements, which advocate sexual abstinence until marriage.

Moral reformers worried that devastating social byproducts accompanied economic expansion. As young people left home for jobs or schooling, they also moved beyond parental controls that kept them from licentiousness and sin, which could damage the nation's spiritual health. Northern women formed nearly six hundred local reform associations to ward off such threats. They lobbied against prostitution, assisted "fallen" women, preached chastity, and publicly shamed men seeking sexual gratification outside of marriage by visiting brothels or "seducing" virtuous young women. Some men openly criticized reformers' tactics, but few publicly questioned their goals.

Similarly emerging from secular and religious concerns, modern purity campaigns began in the early 1990s, amid escalating AIDS awareness and public outcries over teen pregnancies. Purity activists encourage youth to pledge abstinence to honor "God with your body." Pledging purity, notes one organization's web site, means avoiding pregnancy and sexually transmitted diseases while maintaining "every opportunity to fulfill your dreams." Nineteenth-century reformers, too, reminded youth that their dreams—business ownership, middle-class respectability—depended on sexual propriety. And just as moral reformers offered redemption, today's purity advocates talk about "second virginity."

To foster fellowship and win new pledges, today's purity organizations sponsor concert-like events, modern adaptations of revival-inspired reform meetings. At highly publicized purity balls, daughters and fathers exchange vows: Fathers promise to protect daughters' purity; daughters, to remain chaste until marriage. Young men and women wear purity rings, and pop stars highlight their purity pledges in publicity campaigns. But now as then, purity advocates face criticism for their tactics.

By advocating premarital celibacy as a weapon against society's ills, moral reformers left to a people and a nation an enduring, if controversial, legacy.

Harrison caught pneumonia and died within a month of his inauguration. The Constitution did not stipulate what should happen, but Tyler took full possession of executive powers, setting a precedent that would not be codified in the Constitution until 1967 with the Twenty-fifth Amendment.

TABLE 12.1 United States Presidents, 1824–1845

President	Party	Years in Office
James Monroe	Democratic-Republican	1817–1825
John Quincy Adams	Democratic-Republican	1825–1829
Andrew Jackson	Democratic	1829–1837
Martin Van Buren	Democratic	1837–1841
William Henry Harrison	Whig	1841
John Tyler	elected as Whig, but broke with party	1841–1845

President Tyler   Tyler became more Democrat than Whig. He repeatedly vetoed Clay's protective tariffs, internal improvements, and bills to revive the Bank of the United States. Two days after Tyler's second veto of a bank bill, the cabinet except Secretary of State Daniel Webster resigned; Webster, after negotiating the Webster-Ashburton treaty, followed. Disgusted Whigs referred to Tyler as "His Accidency."

Like Jackson, Tyler expanded presidential powers and emphasized westward expansion. During his presidency, the United States negotiated its first treaties with China, and Tyler expanded the Monroe Doctrine to include Hawaii. But Tyler's vision for national greatness fixed on Texas and the westward expansion of slavery.

Summary

Religion and reform shaped politics from 1824 through the 1840s. Driven by a belief in human perfectibility, many evangelicals, especially women, worked to right the wrongs of American society. They hoped to trigger the millennium, the thousand years of earthly peace accompanying Christ's return. Some utopians joined experimental communities that modeled radical alternatives to existing society. Abolitionists worked to perfect American society by ending slavery. As women entered the public sphere as reformers and abolitionists, some embraced women's rights.

Struggles between the National Republicans and the Democrats, then between the Democrats and the Whigs, stimulated interest in politics. Democrats and Whigs competed for voters by building strong organizations that faced off in national and local elections often characterized by fraud and sometimes violence. Both parties favored economic development, but Whigs advocated centralized government, whereas Democrats advocated limited government and agricultural expansion. Controversies over the Second Bank of the United States and nullification exposed different interpretations of the nation's founding principles.

The late 1830s and early 1840s brought uncertainty: The economy experienced a period of bust, tensions with the British resurfaced, and a president died in office. John Tyler's vision of American greatness depended on westward expansion.

Chapter Review

From Revival to Reform

How did religious revival movements lead to social reform?

Ministers and preachers in the Second Great Awakening raised hope for their audiences that the second coming of Jesus Christ was at hand—as long as listeners were able to renounce sin and purge society of sinful behaviors such as drinking, swearing, and even slavery. Revivalists stressed human perfectibility and promoted self-improvement. They preached that there was a direct link between how people lived and whether they would enter God's Kingdom, and in so doing, inspired social and moral reform. Women were often a major force in reform movements, expanding their domestic roles in the home into efforts to counteract the evils of the market economy. Reform goals included reformatories for wayward youth, orphan asylums, rehabilitation for criminals, temperance, and improvements in education.

Utopian Experiments

What were the goals of utopian communities?

Often inspired by religious revivalism, the utopian movement sought to hold the line on the rapid social change that members found disturbing, in particular, the rising market economy's excessive individualism. Some dreamed of creating a new social order; others wanted to recapture the supposed communal nature of the past and at the same time reshape marriage, child rearing, and other social arrangements. The Shakers, for example, built a profitable community around agriculture and handcrafts, but also abolished individual families in favor of men and women living in separate quarters and sharing leadership. The Oneida community centered on communal property ownership, communal child-rearing, and "complex marriage" in which all men were married to all women. The Fourierists included writers and intellectuals who inspired an American renaissance in literature and the arts, with Brook Farm in West Roxbury, Massachusetts, its most famous community. During its brief existence, the community embraced transcendentalism, the notion that the physical world is secondary to the spiritual realm.

Abolitionism

How did the Second Great Awakening transform the antislavery movement?

Abolitionism dates back to the nation's earliest days, when efforts to end slavery were initiated by both free blacks and elite whites. After 1830, however, evangelical abolitionists seeking to eradicate America's sins focused on slavery with renewed vigor. The activist and newspaper editor William Lloyd Garrison led a new, more radical strain of abolitionism known as "immediatism," which called for the immediate and complete end of slavery without compensating slave owners. Immediatists shared the evangelical belief that people determined their spiritual fate through good or evil acts and that by ending slavery, they could bring about the millennium, or Christ's return to earth. Unlike earlier movements, these abolitionists relied on participation of ministers and many others, and as such encouraged women to not only join but serve on executive committees, a controversial move that ultimately led to the split of the abolitionist movement in 1840.

Women's Rights

What inspired the rise of the women's movement in the mid-nineteenth century?

The religious revivals of the Second Great Awakening provided the first impetus for a later women's movement by encouraging women to see themselves as equal spiritually to men and urging them to take part in reforming society. Women's growing participation in the antislavery movement had many seeing parallels between slave bondage and marriage as a form of bondage as well as women's lack of citizenship rights. Traditional marriage law, borrowed from the English, gave husbands control over the family, including wives' property and earnings. Eight years after being denied a seat at the World Anti-Slavery Convention because of their sex, Elizabeth Cady Stanton and Lucretia Mott joined others in holding the first Woman's Rights Convention in 1848 at Seneca Falls, N.Y. There, three hundred participants outlined their demands for political and social equality, including the right to vote (a controversial issue that was not unanimously approved), in their Declaration of Sentiments, a document that paralleled the Declaration of Independence.

Jacksonianism and Party Politics

How did changing demographics influence the outcome of the 1824 presidential election and the future of political parties?

As suffrage laws changed to eliminate property requirements and allow immigrants to vote, the number of eligible voters tripled from 1824 to 1828. Politicians broadened their outreach to these new voters and successfully urged states to shift from appointing presidential electors to electing them by popular vote. That, combined with the end of candidate selection by congressional caucus, meant that five Democratic-Republican candidates ran for president in 1824. Although Andrew Jackson led in both electoral and popular vote, no one had a clear majority, leaving the House of Representatives to choose the president. Its members chose second-place John Quincy Adams, which led to charges of election-stealing and divided the party into the National Republicans (behind Adams) and the Democrats (behind Jackson). With two parties and only two candidates in the 1828 election, Jackson handily won the presidency, and the Democratic Party became the first well-organized national political party in the United States.

Federalism at Issue: The Nullification and Bank Controversies

What was at issue in the Nullification Controversy?

At the core of the Nullification Controversy were differing interpretations of the Constitution regarding federal power and states' rights. The doctrine of nullification—that states could overrule federal legislation—was based on the Virginia and Kentucky Resolutions of 1798, which argued that states could judge whether federal actions were constitutional, and ultimately nullify federal laws that did not pass the test. President Jackson rejected state sovereignty and saw nullification as leading to disunion. When South Carolina nullified a federal tariff, Jackson threatened force to collect the duties. As a compromise, the tariff was reduced and South Carolina withdrew its nullification. But the debate on the nature of the republic and of federal power continued.

The Whig Challenge and the Second Party System

How did the Whigs and Democrats differ ideologically?

Unlike the Democrats, Whigs advocated for economic growth via an activist government. They were for corporate charters, a national bank and paper currency, and promoted public schools and prison reform. Nor did Whigs worry about government aiding special interests; to them, as long as the public benefited, they saw no problem in it. Democrats believed in the Jefferson model of limited government and worried about government intrusion. Whigs thought government should be ruled from the top down, and they embraced the notion of a meritocracy—that the wealthy obtained their status and power through their own hard work. Democrats saw the world divided into "haves" and "have nots" and sought equal rights for all to restore some form of balance.

Suggestions for Further Reading

Philip F. Gura, *American Transcendentalism: A History* (2007)

Daniel Walker Howe, *What Hath God Wrought: The Transformation of America, 1815–1848* (2007)

Paul E. Johnson, *Sam Patch, the Famous Jumper* (2003)

Mary Kelley: *Learning to Stand and Speak: Women, Education, and Public Life in America's Republic* (2006)

Steven Mintz, *Moralists and Modernizers: America's Pre-Civil War Reformers* (1995)

Richard S. Newman, *The Transformation of American Abolitionism: Fighting Slavery in the Early Republic* (2002)

Susan Zaeske, *Signatures of Citizenship: Petitioning, Antislavery, and Women's Political Identity* (2003)

Harry L. Watson, *Liberty and Power: The Politics of Jacksonian America* (2006)

Go to the CourseMate website for primary source links, study tools, and review materials for this chapter.
www.cengagebrain.com

The Contested West

13

1815–1860

To eight-year-old Henry Clay Bruce, moving west was an adventure. In April 1844, the Virginia boy began a 1,500-mile, two-month trip to his new home in Missouri. Henry marveled at the beautiful terrain, impressive towns, and the steamboat ride from Louisville to St. Louis. Once in Missouri, Henry noticed how much the West differed from the East. Farms were farther apart, and the countryside abounded with wild fruits, game, and fish. Yet rattlesnakes, wolves, and vicious hogs kept Henry and his playmates close to home.

A slave, Henry made the trip with his mother and siblings after his owner, Pettis Perkinson, decided to seek a fresh start in the West. Perkinson and three other white Virginians crammed their families, their slaves, and whatever belongings they could fit into three wagons. In Missouri, Pettis resided with his brother Jack Perkinson, who—according to Henry—yelled at and whipped his slaves. Henry's first year in Missouri was as carefree as a slave child's life could be. The boy fished, hunted (with dogs, not guns), and gathered prairie chickens' eggs. But by age nine, Henry was hired out, first to a brickmaker, then to a tobacco factory. He worked sunup to sundown, and when he failed to satisfy his bosses, he was whipped.

Meanwhile, Pettis Perkinson, unenamored with Missouri, returned to Virginia, later summoning some of his slaves, including Henry. Slaves' work was less rigorous in Virginia, but that did not compensate for leaving loved ones behind in Missouri.

Soon Pettis Perkinson again grew weary of Virginia, and renewed his quest for opportunity in the West, this time, in Mississippi. But cotton plantation life suited neither Henry nor his master, who now decided—to his slaves' joy—to give Missouri another chance.

Two years later, the restless Perkinson decided to head for Texas. Henry, now in his late teens, and his brothers refused to go. Although livid, Pettis Perkinson abandoned his plans rather than deal with recalcitrant slaves. Henry became the foreman on Perkinson's Missouri farm, where he remained until escaping

Chapter Outline

The West in the American Imagination
Defining the West | Frontier Literature | Western Art | Countering the Myths

Expansion and Resistance in the Trans-Appalachian West
Deciding Where to Move | Indian Removal and Resistance | Black Hawk War | Selling the West | Clearing the Land

The Federal Government and Westward Expansion
The Fur Trade | Transcontinental Exploration | A Military Presence | Public Lands

LINKS TO THE WORLD *Gold in California*

The Southwestern Borderlands
Southwestern Slavery | The New Mexican Frontier | The Texas Frontier | The Comanche Empire | American Empresarios | Texas Politics | The Lone Star Republic | Wartime Losses and Profits

VISUALIZING THE PAST *Paintings and Cultural Impressions*

Cultural Frontiers in the Far West
Western Missionaries | Mormons | Oregon and California Trails | Indian Treaties | Ecological Consequences of Cultural Contact | Gold Rush | Mining Settlements

The Politics of Territorial Expansion
Manifest Destiny | Fifty-Four Forty or Fight | Polk and the Election of 1844 | Annexation of Texas

LEGACY FOR A PEOPLE AND A NATION *Descendants of Early Latino Settlers*

SUMMARY

during the Civil War to the free state of Kansas. Finally, Henry Clay Bruce found the opportunity and freedom that led so many to the West.

In 1820, about 20 percent of the nation's population lived west of the Appalachian Mountains. By 1860, nearly 50 percent did. Most whites and free blacks moved west seeking better opportunities. Easterners generally envisioned in the West enormous tracts of fertile, uncultivated land or, beginning in the late 1840s, gold and silver mines that promised quick riches. Some saw opportunities for lumbering or ranching, or selling goods or services to farmers, miners, lumbermen, and cattlemen.

Men often decided to head west without consulting their wives and children, and slaves' wishes received even less consideration. Nor did western settlers consider the impact of their migration on Indian peoples living there. The federal government had displaced many of those Indians from their Eastern homes. It also sponsored westward exploration, made laws regulating settlement and the establishment of territorial governments, surveyed and fixed prices on public lands, and sold land. It invested in transportation routes and established a military presence. In the 1820s, the Mexican government, too, encouraged Anglo-American settlement in the West along its northern borderlands—which it would later regret. U.S. settlers vied with the region's other inhabitants—Indians, Hispanics, and people of mixed heritage—for land and natural resources. A decade later, Mexico's northern province of Texas declared its independence and sought annexation by the United States. Thus began heightened tensions between the United States and Mexico, and within the United States, as Texas's future became entangled with slavery.

For some white Americans, mostly southerners, the ability to own slaves in the West signaled freedom. For others, from the North and the South, slavery's westward expansion frustrated dreams for a new beginning in a region free from slavery's degrading influence on white labor.

Even as Democrats and Whigs skirted the slavery issue, they took distinct stands on westward expansion's role in national economic development. But once the spotlight focused on Texas, political leaders would find it increasingly difficult to disentangle westward expansion from slavery.

With each passing decade, conflict—between expectations and reality, between people with different aspirations and world-views—increasingly defined life in the West. By the mid-1840s, western events would aggravate long-simmering discord between southern and northern political interests.

As you read this chapter, keep the following questions in mind:

* **How did tensions in the East influence western migration and settlement?**

* **How did public, private, and individual initiatives converge to shape the West's development?**

* **What motivated cooperation in the West, and what spurred conflict?**

The West in the American Imagination

What were the myths that helped shape white Americans' perceptions of the West?

For historian Frederick Jackson Turner, writing in the late nineteenth century, the western frontier, with its abundance of free land, was the "meeting point between savagery and civilization." It bred American democracy, shaped the American character, and made the United States exceptional. Modern

Chronology

1812	General Land Office established		U.S. Army Corps of Topographical Engineers established
1820	Price lowered on public lands		
1821	Santa Fe Trail charted	1840–1860	250,000 to 500,000 migrants travel overland
	Mexico's independence	1841	Log Cabin Bill
1823	Mexico allows Stephen Austin to settle U.S. citizens	1844	Presidential campaign features Texas annexation
1824	Congressional General Survey Act	1845	"Manifest destiny" coined
	Jedediah Smith's South Pass publicized		Texas annexed (March 1) and becomes twenty-eighth state (December 29)
	Indian Office established	1846–1848	War with Mexico (see Chapter 14)
1825–1832	*Empresario* contracts signed	1847	Mormons settle Great Salt Lake valley
1826	Fredonia rebellion fails	1848	California gold discovered
1830	Indian Removal Act (see Chapter 10)	1849–50s	Migrants stream into Great Plains and Far West
1832	Black Hawk War	1855	Ash Hollow Massacre
1834	McCormick reaper patented	1857–1858	Mormons and U.S. Army in armed conflict
1836	Lone Star Republic founded	1862	Homestead Act

historians generally eschew the notion of American exceptionalism, stressing instead the complex connections between the United States and the world. Although today's scholars reject the racialist assumptions of Turner's definition of *frontier*, some see value in the term when signifying a meeting place of different cultures. Others see the West as a place, not a process, though they disagree over what delineates it.

Defining the West   For early-nineteenth-century Americans of European descent, the West included anything west of the Appalachian Mountains. It represented the future—a place offering economic and social betterment, typically through land ownership. The West's seeming abundance of land meant that anyone could hope to become an independent farmer. Men who already owned land, like Pettis Perkinson, looked westward for cheaper, bigger, and more fertile landholdings. With the discovery of gold in California in 1848, the West became a place to strike it rich. Others went west by force, including slaves and Indians removed from their eastern homelands by the U.S. military under the Indian Removal Act of 1830.

To others, the notion of the West would have been baffling. Emigrants from Mexico and Central or South America traveled north to get to what European-Americans called the West. Chinese nationals traveled eastward to California. Many Indians considered the West home. Other Indians and French Canadians journeyed southward to the West. All arrived in the western portion of the North American continent because of factors that pushed and pulled them.

Frontier Literature   For European-Americans, Daniel Boone became the archetypical frontiersman, whose daring individualism opened the Eden-like West for hard-working freedom lovers. Through biographies, Boone became a familiar figure in American and European households. The mythical Boone lived in the wilderness and shrank from society. He overpowered bears and

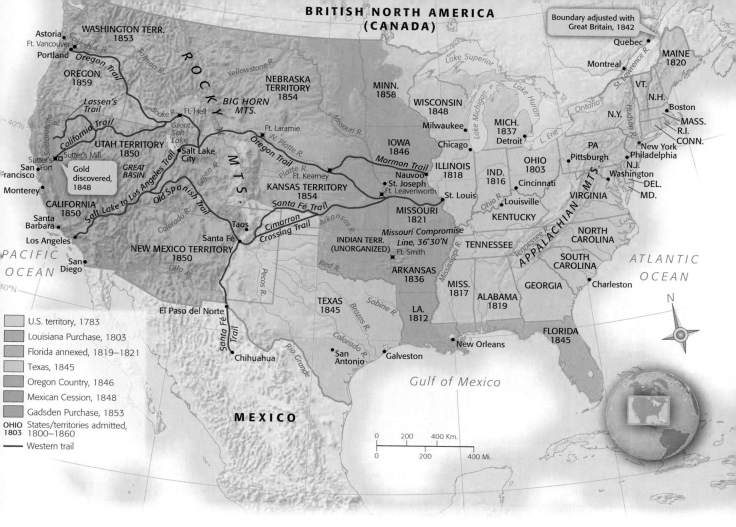

MAP 13.1

Westward Expansion, 1800–1860

Through exploration, purchase, war, and treaty, the United States became a continental nation, stretching from the Atlantic to the Pacific.
Source: Copyright © Cengage Learning

Indians but also became the pathfinder for civilization. As a friend wrote, Boone "has been the instrument of opening the road to millions of the human family… to a Land flowing with milk and honey." By borrowing biblical language—the land of milk and honey denoting the Promised Land—Boone's friend suggested that Boone was Moses-like, leading his people to a land of abundance.

With the invention of the steam press in the early 1830s, western adventure stories became cheap and widely read. Davy Crockett, another real-life figure turned into mythical hero, was featured in many of them. Crockett first fought the Creeks under Andrew Jackson but later championed Indian rights. After losing his life defending the Alamo mission during Texas's fight for independence (1836), Crockett appeared in stories portraying the West as violent, a place where one escaped civilized society and fought Indians and Mexicans. But even in this myth, the American West symbolized what white Americans saw as their nation's core value: freedom.

Western Art

In artists' renderings, the West was sometimes an untamed wilderness inhabited by savages (noble or otherwise), and sometimes a cultivated garden, a land of milk and honey where the Jeffersonian agrarian dream was realized. Such artwork revealed more about white Americans' ideals than about the West itself.

Smithsonian American Art Museum, Washington, DC

In one of his most famous portraits, George Catlin painted Wi-Jun-Jon, an Assiniboine Indian, both before and after he had mingled with white men. In the "before" stance, the Indian is a dignified, peace-pipe-bearing warrior; in the "after" portrait, the "corrupted" Indian has abandoned dignity for vanity and his peace pipe for a cigar.

George Catlin: American painter who traveled throughout the West and produced numerous portraits of Native Americans that reflected his fascination and beliefs about them.

The first Anglo-American artists to travel west were Samuel Seymour and Titian Ramsay Peale, whom the federal government hired to accompany explorer Stephen H. Long to the Rocky Mountains in 1820. They pioneered an influential genre: facsimiles in government reports. Between 1840 and 1860, Congress published nearly sixty works on western exploration, featuring hundreds of lithographs and engravings of plants, animals, and people. Some reports became bestsellers. The government distributed more than fifty-three thousand copies of its popular twelve-volume Pacific Railway Survey (1855–1860), which helped easterners visualize the continent's western reaches.

Sometimes government reports made telling alterations to the paintings they included. When Richard Kern accompanied explorer James H. Simpson in 1849 to the Southwest, he painted a Navajo man in a submissive pose. The reproduction transformed the man's pose into a rebellious one. In other cases, the government reports changed artists' depictions of Indian-occupied landscapes into empty terrain free for the taking.

Artists' cultural assumptions colored their portrayals of the West, too, and commercial artists produced what they thought the public craved. When **George Catlin** traveled west immediately following the Indian Removal Act of 1830, he painted the West with a moral in mind. Indians came in two varieties— those who preserved their original, almost noble qualities of freedom and moderation, and those who, after coming in contact with whites, had become "dissolute." Indians, he implied, benefited from removal from white Americans' corrupting influence.

Countering the Myths

But western realities often clashed with promoters' promises, and disappointed settlers sometimes tried to clarify matters for future migrants. Rebecca Burlend and her son were lured to Illinois by a fellow Englishman's letters extolling "a land flowing with milk and honey." Later, Burlend and her son wrote *A True Picture of Emigration* (1831), which described Illinois' hardships—intemperate weather, difficult working conditions, and swindlers. Her account sought not to discourage emigration, but to substitute a realistic for a rosy description.

Expansion and Resistance in the Trans-Appalachian West

What made the Midwest appealing to white settlers?

In the 1820s and 1830s, settlers streamed into the Old Northwest and the Old Southwest by foot, horseback, wagon, canal boat, steamboat, or a combination of means. Many people, like Pettis Perkinson and his slaves, moved several times, and when opportunities failed to materialize, some returned home.

Both the Old Northwest and the Old Southwest saw population explosions during the early nineteenth century. In 1790, the Northwest region's white population numbered just a few hundred people. By 1860, nearly 7 million people called it home. Between 1810 and 1830, Ohio's population more than quadrupled, while Indiana and Illinois grew fourteenfold and thirteenfold, respectively. Michigan's population multiplied fiftyfold between 1820 and 1850. Migration accounted for most of this growth. Once in the Old Northwest, people did not stay put. Geographic mobility, the search for better opportunities, and connections to the market economy defined the region that became known as the Midwest.

MAP 13.2

Settlement in the Old Southwest and Old Northwest, 1820 and 1840

Removal of Indians and a growing transportation network opened up land to white and black settlers in the regions known as the Old Southwest and the Old Northwest, as the U.S. population grew from 9.6 million in 1820 to 17.1 million in 1840.

Source: Copyright © Cengage Learning

Deciding Where to Move

Moving west meant leaving behind worn-out soil and areas with little land available for purchase, but it also meant leaving family, friends, and communities. The journey promised to be arduous, as did the backbreaking labor of clearing new lands. The West was a land of opportunity but also of uncertainty. What if the soil proved less fertile than anticipated? What if neighbors proved unfriendly, or worse? Settlers tried to control every possible variable. Like Pettis Perkinson, people often relocated where they had relatives or friends and traveled with acquaintances. They chose areas with familiar climates. Migrants also settled in ethnic communities or with people of similar religious affiliations.

The legal status of slavery also influenced where people settled. Some white southerners, tired of the planter elite's power, sought areas free from slavery—or at least where there were few plantations. Many others went west to improve their chances of owning slaves, or of purchasing additional slaves. White northerners also hoped to distance themselves from slavery as well as from free blacks. In the 1850s, many midwestern states passed "black laws" prohibiting African Americans, free or enslaved, from living within their boundaries. Ironically, many free blacks migrated west to free themselves from eastern prejudice.

Between 1815 and 1860, few western migrants settled on the Great Plains, a region reserved for Indians until the 1850s, and few easterners risked the journey to California and Oregon before the transcontinental railroad's completion in 1869. At first, the Southwest appealed most to settlers. But starting in the 1820s, the Midwest drew more settlers with its better-developed transportation routes, democratic access to economic markets, smaller African American population, cheaper average landholding, and climatic similarity to New England and northern Europe. The Old Northwest's thriving transportation hubs also made good first stops for western migrants lacking cash to purchase land. They found work unloading canal boats, planting and harvesting wheat, grinding wheat into flour, sawing trees into lumber or, more often, they cobbled together a combination of these seasonal jobs. With the Old Northwest's population growing quickly, white southerners worried increasingly about congressional representation and laws regarding slavery.

Indian Removal and Resistance

In the Midwest and the Southwest, white settlement depended on Indian removal. Even as the U.S. Army escorted Indians from the Old Southwest (see Chapter 10), the federal government arranged eighty-six treaties between 1829 and 1851 in which northeastern Indian nations relinquished land titles in exchange for lands west of the Mississippi River. Some northern Indians evaded removal, including the Miamis in Indiana, the Ottawas and Chippewas in the upper Midwest, and the Winnebagos in southern Wisconsin. In 1840, Miami chiefs acceded to pressure to exchange 500,000 acres in Indiana for equivalent acreage in Indian Country. Under the treaty, their people had five years to move or be escorted out by federal troops. But about half of the Miami nation dodged the soldiers—and many of those who trekked to Indian Country later returned. In Wisconsin, some Winnebagos eluded removal or returned to Wisconsin after being escorted west by soldiers.

Black Hawk War

In a series of treaties between 1804 and 1830, Sauks (or "Sacs") and Fox leaders exchanged lands in northwestern Illinois and southwestern Wisconsin for lands across the Mississippi River in Iowa

Territory. The Sauk warrior Black Hawk disputed the treaties' validity and in 1832 he led Sauk and Fox families to Illinois, panicking white settlers. The state's governor activated the militia, who were joined by militia from surrounding states and territories and U.S. Army regular soldiers. Over several months, hundreds of Indians and dozens of whites died under gruesome circumstances in the Black Hawk War. As the Sauks and Fox tried to flee across the Mississippi River, American soldiers fired indiscriminately. Those who survived the river crossing met gunfire from Lakota (Sioux), now allied with the Americans.

Black Hawk surrendered, and U.S. officials undertook to impress upon him and other leaders the futility of resistance. After being imprisoned, then sent to Washington, D.C., along a route meant to underscore the United States' immense size and population, and imprisoned again, the Indians were returned to their homes. The Black Hawk War ended militant Indian uprisings in the Old Northwest.

Selling the West

Land speculators, developers of "paper towns" (ones existing on paper only), steamboat companies, and manufacturers of farming implements promoted the Midwest as a tranquil place of unbounded opportunity. Land proprietors emphasized the region's connections to eastern customs and markets. They knew that, when families moved west, they did not seek to escape civilization. Western settlement generally followed connections to national and international markets. Eastern farmers, looking to escape tired soil or tenancy, sought fertile lands for growing commercial crops. Labor-saving devices, such as Cyrus McCormick's reaper (1834) and John Deere's steel plow (1837), made the West more alluring. McCormick, a Virginia inventor, patented a horse-drawn reaper that allowed two men to harvest the same number of acres of wheat that previously required between four and sixteen men. The reaper's efficiency achieved its greatest payoffs on the large, flat prairie lands, so McCormick relocated his factory to Chicago

MCCORMICKS MACHINES.

Wisconsin Historical Society

In his advertisements, Cyrus McCormick portrayed his reapers as making the West into a place of prosperity and leisure.

in 1847. Without John Deere's steel plow, which could break through tough grass and roots without constant cleaning, "breaking the plains" might not have been possible.

Clearing the Land

After locating a suitable land claim, settlers constructed a rudimentary cabin if none already existed. Time did not permit more elaborate structures; settlers first had to clear the land. At the rate of five to ten acres a year, depending on a family's size, the average family needed ten years to clear a farm. Prairie land took less time.

Whereas farming attracted families, lumbering and mining appealed to single young men. By the 1840s, as eastern forests became depleted, northeastern lumber companies and laborers migrated to Wisconsin, Michigan, and Minnesota. Recently arrived Scandinavians and French Canadians also worked in the lumber industry. As the Great Lakes forests thinned, lumbermen moved again—some to the Gulf States' pine forests, some to Canada, and some to the Far West, where Mexicans in California and British in Canada had already established flourishing lumber industries. With the rapid growth of California's cities following the 1849 **Gold Rush**, timber's demand soared, drawing midwestern lumbermen farther west.

Midwestern cities nurtured the surrounding countryside's settlement. Steamboats turned river settlements like Louisville and Cincinnati into commercial centers, while Chicago, Detroit, and Cleveland grew up on the Great Lakes' banks. By the mid-nineteenth century, Chicago, with its railroads, stockyards, and grain elevators, dominated the region's economy; western farmers transported livestock and grain by rail to that city, where pigs became packed meat and grain became flour before being shipped east. The promise of future flour and pigs gave rise to commodities markets. Some of the world's most sophisticated and speculative economic practices began in Chicago.

Gold Rush: After an American carpenter discovered gold in the foothills of California's Sierra Nevada range in 1848, Americans and people from around the world moved to California to look for gold.

The Federal Government and Westward Expansion

How did the federal government sponsor and speed up westward expansion?

Few white Americans considered settling in the West before the region had been explored, surveyed, secured, and "civilized," which meant Indian removal and the establishment of churches, businesses, and American legal structures. Wide-scale settlement depended on the federal government's sponsorship.

The Fur Trade

Fur trappers were among the first white Americans in the trans-Appalachian West, but their lives bore faint resemblance to their mythical representation as mountain men who dared to go where whites never trod. Fur trappers lived among Indians, became multilingual, and often married Indian women. Indian women transformed animal carcasses into finished pelts, and they smoothed trade relations between their husbands and their native communities. The offspring of such marriages—métis or mestizos (people of mixed Indian and European heritage)—added to the West's cultural complexity.

The fur trade was an international business, with pelts from the American interior reaching Europe and Asia. Until the 1820s, British companies dominated the trade, but American ventures prospered in the 1820s and 1830s. Beginning in the 1820s, trappers and traders met annually for a "rendezvous"—a multiday gathering

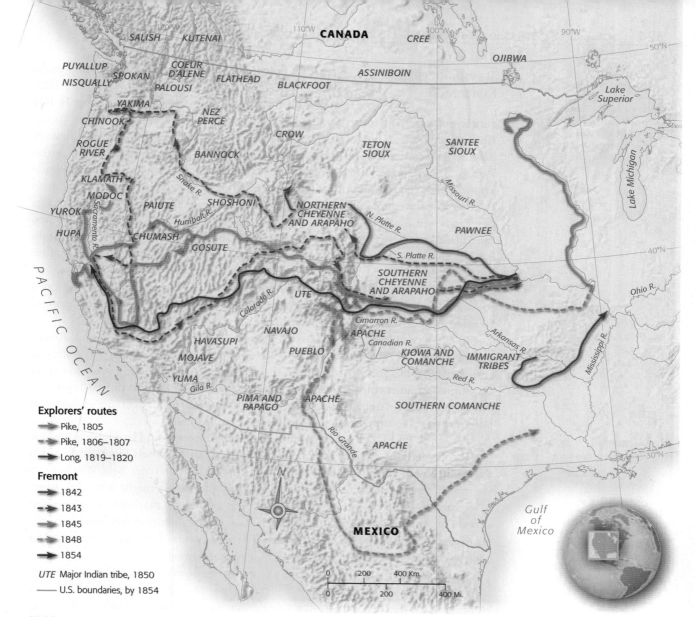

MAP 13.3

Western Indians and Routes of Exploration

Although western explorers believed they were discovering new routes and places, Indians had long lived in most of the areas through which explorers traveled.

Source: Robert Utley, *The Indian Frontier of the American West, 1846–1890*, University of New Mexico Press, 1984. p. 5. Reprinted by permission of the University of New Mexico Press.

where they traded fur for guns, tobacco, and beads that they could later exchange with Indians. Modeled on Indian gatherings that had occurred for generations, the rendezvous united Americans, Indians, Mexicans, and people of mixed heritage from throughout the West to trade and socialize.

By the 1840s, the American fur trade was declining. Beavers had been over-hunted, and fashions shifted toward silk and away from fur for hats. The traders' legacy includes resource depletion, introducing native peoples to devastating diseases, and developing trails across the trans-Mississippi West.

Santa Fe Trail: Trading route from St. Louis, Missouri, to Santa Fe, New Mexico, that enabled commerce to expand its reach farther west.

Transcontinental Exploration

A desire for quicker and safer routes for transporting goods to trading posts drove much early exploration. In 1821, merchant William Becknell helped chart the **Santa Fe Trail** running between Missouri and Santa Fe, New Mexico, where it connected to the Chihuahua Trail running into Mexico, allowing American and Mexican merchants to develop a vibrant trade. In 1824, fur trader Jedediah Smith rediscovered the South Pass, a 20-mile break in the Rocky Mountains in present-day Wyoming previously known only to Native Americans and some Pacific Fur Company trappers. The South Pass became the route followed by most overland travelers to California and Oregon.

Lewis and Clark's Corps of Discovery was the first of many federally sponsored expeditions to chart the trans-Mississippi West. Some expeditions sought to establish cordial relations with Indian groups with whom Americans might trade or enter military alliances. Others were scientific, exploring native inhabitants, flora, and fauna. But they were also commercial. Like Lewis and Clark, later explorers hoped to locate land, water, and rail routes that would allow American businessmen and farmers to trade nationally and internationally.

In 1805, the U.S. Army dispatched Zebulon Pike to find the Mississippi River's source and a navigable route west. He was instructed to research natural resources and native peoples and foster diplomatic relationships with Indian leaders. Before the Supreme Court ruled in *Johnson v. M'Intosh* (1823) that Indians did not own land but merely had a "right of occupancy," government officials instructed Pike and other explorers to purchase lands for military garrisons.

Although Pike failed to identify the Mississippi's source and had limited success in purchasing land, he gathered important information. When Pike and his men wandered into Spanish territory to the south, military officials held Pike captive for months in Mexico, inadvertently showing him areas he might not have otherwise explored. After his release, Pike wrote about a potential market in southwestern cities. The province of Tejas (Texas), with its fertile soil, enchanted him. But Pike dismissed the other northern provinces of Mexico, whose boundaries stretched to present-day Nevada and Utah, as unsuitable for human habitation.

Although nomadic Indians might sustain themselves there, he explained, the region was unfit for cultivation by civilized people. In 1820, army explorer Stephen Long, similarly deemed modern-day Oklahoma, Kansas, and Nebraska as "the Great American Desert," incapable of cultivation. Until the 1850s, when a transcontinental railroad was planned, this "desert" was reserved for Indian settlement. In 1838, Congress established the U.S. Army Corps of Topographical Engineers to systematically explore the West. As a second lieutenant in that corps, **John C. Frémont** undertook three expeditions to the region between the upper Mississippi and Missouri rivers, the Rockies, the Great Basin, Oregon, and California. He helped survey the Oregon Trail. Aided by his wife, Jessie Benton Frémont, he published bestselling accounts of his explorations. The Corps of Topographical Engineers' most significant contributions came in the 1850s with its surveying of possible routes for a transcontinental railroad.

John C. Frémont: Explorer who played a role in a California rebellion against Mexico; later a senator and presidential candidate and force in national politics.

A Military Presence

The army also helped ready the West for settlement. With the General Survey Act of 1824, Congress empowered the military to chart transportation improvements vital to military protection or commercial growth. Army engineers helped design state- and privately sponsored roads,

Links to the World

Gold in California

When James Marshall discovered gold in Sutter's Mill, California, in January 1848, word spread quickly worldwide. Within a year, tens of thousands of adventurers from other countries rushed to California, making it the most cosmopolitan place in North America.

In an era before the telegraph crossed the oceans, the news traveled surprisingly fast. Mexicans heard first. Next, word spread to Chile, Peru, and throughout South America; then across the Pacific to Hawai'i, China, and Australia; and then to Europe—Ireland, France, and the German states. Overland travelers brought the news south to Baja California and Sonora in Mexico. By spring 1849, some six thousand Mexicans were panning for gold; many came seasonally, spreading news of California on every trip home.

The newspaper *Honolulu Polynesian* announced California gold in the kingdom on June 24, 1848. Regular steamship service between Hawai'i and California transported gold seekers as early as 1853.

A ship brought news of California gold discoveries to Valparaiso, Chile, in August 1848. People in Chile's cities talked feverishly about gold, and rumors of California's overnight riches. Before year's end, two thousand Chileans left for California.

Word of gold reached Australia in December 1848, and by 1850 every ship in Sydney Harbour was California-bound. News reached China in mid-1848. Widespread poverty and gold's allure prompted many Chinese to migrate. By the mid-1850s, one in five gold miners was Chinese.

In 1850, the new state of California had nearly 40 percent foreign-born inhabitants, the majority non-European. Through word of mouth, rumor, letters home, and newspaper reports, the 1848 gold discovery linked California to millions of people around the globe.

Collection of the New York Historical Society

This 1855 Frank Marryat drawing of a San Francisco saloon dramatizes the international nature of the California gold rush. Like theater performers, the patrons of the saloon dress their parts as Yankees, Mexicans, Asians, and South Americans.

canals, and railroads, and its soldiers cleared forests and lay roadbeds. A related bill, also in 1824, authorized the army to improve the Ohio and Mississippi rivers; a later amendment did the same for the Missouri.

By the 1850s, 90 percent of the U.S. military was stationed west of the Mississippi River. When Indians refused to relinquish their lands, the army escorted them westward; when they harmed whites, the army waged war. The army sometimes destroyed the crops and buildings of white squatters refusing to vacate lands settled illegally. But, primarily, the army assisted overland migration. Army forts intimidated Indians, defended settlers from Indian attacks, and supplied information and provisions. In theory, the army was also supposed to protect Indians by driving settlers off Indian lands and enforcing laws prohibiting alcohol sales to Indians. Yet the army's small size relative to the territory it regulated made it impossible to do so, even when officers were so disposed.

The Office of Indian Affairs handled the government's other Indian interactions, including treaty negotiations, school management, and trade oversight. Created in 1824 as part of the War Department, the Indian Office cooperated with the military in removing Indians from lands necessary for American expansion and in protecting citizens who relocated west. In 1849, the Indian Office became part of the newly established Department of the Interior and soon shifted from removal to civilization through a reservation system. Whereas some Indians accepted reservations as protection from white incursion, others rejected them, sometimes sparking deadly intratribal disagreements.

Public Lands

The federal government controlled vast tracts of land, procured either from the states' cessions of their western claims after the Revolution or through treaties with foreign powers, including Indian nations. The General Land Office, established in 1812 as part of the Treasury Department, handled those lands' distribution. Its earliest policies divided western lands into 640-acre tracts to be auctioned at a minimum $2 an acre. These policies favored speculators—who bought up millions of acres—over individual, cash-poor farmers. Many settlers became squatters, prompting Congress in 1820 to lower land prices to $1.25 per acre and to sell tracts as small as 80 acres. Twelve years later, it sold 40-acre tracts. Yet it demanded that the land be bought outright; few would-be settlers (particularly after the Panic of 1819) had enough cash to purchase government land. Because speculators sold land on credit, many small-time farmers bought from them at inflated prices.

Farmers pressed for a federal policy of preemption—that is, the right to settle on land without obtaining title, improve it, and buy it later at the legal minimum price ($1.25 an acre). Some states offered lands through preemption, and Congress sometimes authorized preemption of federal lands in the 1820s and 1830s. But the first general preemption law, the so-called Log Cabin Bill, came in 1841, and it applied only to surveyed land. Preemption extended to unsurveyed lands with the **Homestead Act** of 1862, which provided that land would be given free to any U.S. citizen (or foreigner who had declared the intention of becoming a citizen), after residing on it for five years and improving it. Alternatively, settlers could buy land outright at $1.25 an acre after six months of residency, which allowed them to use the land as collateral for loans for additional land, farming supplies, or machinery.

Homestead Act: Passed in 1862, it embodied the Republican party's ideal of "free soil, free labor, free men" by granting 160 acres of public land to settlers who resided on it for five years and improved it.

The Southwestern Borderlands

Along the Louisiana Territory's southwestern border lay vast provinces controlled mostly by the Comanches and other Indians but claimed first by Spain and then—after 1821—by the newly independent nation of Mexico. **New Mexico**, with commercial centers in Albuquerque and Santa Fe, remained under Mexican control until the United States conquered the territory during its War with Mexico. Texas became an autonomous state in 1824, giving it greater independence from federal authorities than New Mexico enjoyed. This situation fostered Texas's struggle for national independence and then annexation to the United States, which returned slavery to the forefront of American political debate.

What factors led white Americans to settle in Texas?

New Mexico: Former Spanish colony in the upper Rio Grande Valley that became part of Mexico after 1821.

Southwestern Slavery

Slavery in the Southwest was centuries-old. Yet as practiced by indigenous peoples—Comanches, Apaches, Kiowas, Navajos, Utes, and Pueblos—and by Spaniards, slavery centered on capturing women and children, who were then assimilated into their captors' communities, where they provided labor and status while fostering economic and diplomatic exchanges with their former communities.

This system was built on racial mixing—a practice anathema to most white Americans. As white slaveholders from the Southeast pushed into Mexican territory during the 1820s and 1830s, they often justified their conquest in racial terms. The region's Hispanic settlers, they reasoned, had been rendered lazy and barbarous by racial intermixing and were thus destined to be supplanted.

The New Mexican Frontier

When Mexico gained independence from Spain in 1821, New Mexico's Hispanic population outnumbered the indigenous Pueblo peoples by three to one. There were twenty-eight thousand Hispanics, including people born in Spain and criollos—people born in New Spain to parents of Spanish descent. Most New Mexicans engaged in irrigated agriculture. To the north of Santa Fe, they farmed small plots, but to the south, larger farms and ranches predominated. Rancheros became wealthy selling wool and corn in distant markets, and from using unpaid laborers: often relatives, bound by debt. Threatened by the province's raiding Indian tribes— Apaches, Utes, Navajos, and Comanches—Hispanics, Pueblos, and mestizos sometimes united in defense. But their numerical superiority allowed Hispanics to seize many Pueblos' villages and lands in the rich northern river valleys.

The Santa Fe Trail caused a commercial explosion in New Mexico, doubling the value of imports in two years. Whereas the Spanish tried to keep foreigners out, the Mexican government offered enormous land grants to Anglo-American and French entrepreneurs, hoping they would develop the region's industry and agriculture and strengthen commercial ties with the United States.

Although commercial relationships grew, few Americans settled in New Mexico during the 1820s and 1830s. The best lands were occupied by Indians and Hispanics. And Americans seeking cheap, fertile land could find it in Texas.

The Texas Frontier

In 1821, indigenous Indians remained the dominant group in Texas, though there were also Hispanics, Anglos, mestizos, and immigrant Indians. Of the thirty thousand indigenous people, most

MAP 13.4

Mexico's Far North

What is now considered the American Southwest was made up of the northern provinces of Mexico until the United States conquered the territory during the Mexican War (1846–1848).

Source: Copyright © Cengage Learning.

were Comanches. Texas was part of what one historian has called the Comanche Empire, an enormous territory from northern Mexico to Louisiana that the Comanches dominated through kinship, trade, diplomacy, and violence. People of European heritage were a small presence in Texas in 1821. Hispanic peoples had been there since the 1500s, establishing missions and presidios, but by 1820 they numbered only five thousand. Most raised livestock on ranches, while others traded (and intermarried) with Indians. They formed a distinctive identity as **Tejanos** (or Texans) rather than as Spaniards.

Tejano: A native Texan of Mexican descent.

After the War of 1812, Anglo-Americans started entering Texas, where they sought furs, silver, or adventure. They traded manufactured goods—guns, ammunition, and kettles—for animal hides, horses, and mules, quickly supplanting the Tejanos as the Indians' trading partners. Although some Anglos settled in Texas, most traveled the Santa Fe and Chihuahua trails without settling.

Paintings and Cultural Impressions

Although few people of Spanish descent settled in Texas, those who did developed a distinctive and proud cultural identity. Calling themselves Tejanos, they adapted their inherited culture—music, dances, and cuisine—to their new surroundings. In the painting below of an 1844 celebration in San Antonio, French-born painter Theodore Gentilz captures the mixture of cultural carryovers and frontier adaptations. Which elements of the scene seem reminiscent of life in Spain or in the colonial capital of Mexico City? Which elements seem to be adaptations to life along a cultural frontier and political borderland? Which elements of the painting seem to celebrate Tejanos' culture, and which, if any, seem critical of it? If you were using this painting as a source of information about Tejano culture and its influence on contemporary music and dance, what else would you want to know about the artist and the scene he has captured?

Although the musician in Gentilz's painting is playing the fiddle, other artistic depictions record the widespread use of the guitar, which helped give rise to the corrido, a folk ballad whose legacy is still apparent in today's country and western music.

Photo by Robert Corwin

Daughters of the Republic of Texas Library

Theodore Gentilz arrived in Texas in the 1840s and soon began portraying the region's culture with his paintbrush. Here, Tejano settlers perform the fandango, a Spanish dance.

The Comanche Empire

As Indians competed for resources, the southwestern borderlands experienced intermittent but brutal violence. Mounted on horses, the Comanches hunted bison, took captives, and stole horses, livestock, and crops from their enemies. Smaller groups, such as the Wichitas and Caddos, grew corn, beans, squash, and pumpkins. When crops failed, farmers often turned to bison hunting as well, sometimes causing conflict with the Comanches.

Tensions increased around the time of Mexican independence, when another ten thousand Indians migrated into the region. From the Old Northwest came Shawnees and Kickapoos—former members of Tecumseh's confederacy. From the Old Southwest came Cherokees, Creeks, Choctaws, Chickasaws, and Seminoles, some with African American slaves. Indian newcomers vied for land and animals, often clashing with established groups. Some immigrant Indians, having adopted Anglo clothing and racial ideologies, dismissed as "savage" the indigenous Indians who hunted buffalo, wore skins, and did not regard land as a commodity.

Because violence threatened Indian removal and disrupted trade, the U.S. government brokered a treaty in 1835: The Comanches would allow immigrants onto their lands in exchange for trade opportunities. Trade quickly boomed. Immigrant Indians swapped agricultural products and manufactured goods, such as rifles and ammunition, for the Comanches' meats, robes, horses, and captives. That same year, the Comanches ended their longstanding war with the Osages. With peace came American traders. Meanwhile, the U.S. government's Indian removal continued, fueling Americans' commitment to cotton cultivation and expansionism.

American *Empresarios*

A decade earlier, before Mexican independence, the Spanish worried about the security of Texas, which they considered a buffer between hostile Indians and the United States. Their solution was to populate it. Thus, when Missouri miner and trader Moses Austin approached Spanish authorities in January 1821 about settling Americans in Texas, they agreed as long as Austin brought Americans willing to assimilate into Texas society. In exchange for promising to bring three hundred Catholic families—and no slaves—Austin would receive 200,000 acres along the Brazos River. Before Austin could act, though, he died, and Mexico won its independence from Spain in September 1821.

Austin's son, Stephen, pursued his father's scheme, pressing the new Mexican government to honor the grant, which it did in 1823, provided that Austin renounce his American citizenship and become a Mexican national. By 1825, Stephen Austin had settled two thousand white people and four hundred "contract laborers" of African descent. With ninety-year contracts, these African Americans were essentially slaves. Austin later brought nine hundred additional families in exchange for more land.

Satisfied with the Austin experiment, in 1824 Mexico passed a Colonization Law providing land and tax incentives to future foreign settlers. Coahuila y Texas specified that the head of a family could obtain up to 4,428 acres of grazing land or 177 acres of farming land. The land was cheap and could be paid for in installments over six years, with nothing due until the fourth year. Foreigners had to be upstanding Christians and permanent residents. To encourage settlers to assimilate into Mexican society, the Coahuila y Texas government provided additional land to those who married Mexican women.

Most U.S. citizens who settled in Mexico did so under an *empresario,* or immigration agent, who selected "moral" colonists, distributed lands, and enforced regulations. In exchange, he received nearly 25,000 acres of grazing land and 1,000 acres of farming land for every hundred families he settled. Between 1825 and 1832, approximately twenty-four *empresario* contracts (seventeen of which went to Anglo-Americans) were signed covering eight thousand families. The land grants covered almost all of present-day Texas.

During the 1820s, some Anglo-Americans who emigrated to Texas felt pushed by the Panic of 1819 and pulled by cheap land and generous credit terms. Despite Mexican efforts to encourage assimilation, these Americans tended to settle in separate communities. Anglo-Americans outnumbered Tejanos two to one. Authorities worried that the transplanted Americans would try to make Texas part of the United States.

Texas Politics In 1826, an *empresario* named Haden Edwards called for an independent Texas, the "Fredonia Republic." Other *empresarios,* seeing advantages in peaceful relations with the Mexican government, resisted Edwards's secessionist movement. Although the Fredonia revolt failed, Mexican authorities dreaded what it might foreshadow.

Consequently, in 1830 Mexican authorities terminated legal immigration from the United States while encouraging immigration from Europe and other parts of Mexico. They prohibited American slaves from entering Texas, which brought Texas in line with the rest of Mexico—where slavery had been outlawed the previous year. Yet these laws did not discourage Americans and their slaves from coming; soon they controlled most of the Texas coastline and its U.S. border. Mexican authorities repealed the anti-immigration law in 1833, reasoning that it discouraged upstanding settlers without deterring undesirables. By 1835, the non-Indian population of Texas was nearly thirty thousand, with Americans outnumbering Tejanos seven to one.

Among white Texans, some, like Stephen Austin, favored staying in Mexico but demanded more autonomy, the legalization of slavery, and free trade with the United States. Others pushed for Texas secession from Mexico and wanted annexation to the United States. In 1835, the secessionists overtook a Mexican military installation charged with collecting taxes at Galveston Bay. Austin advocated a peaceful resolution, but, suspicious, Mexican authorities jailed him for eighteen months, which converted him to the independence cause.

The Lone Star Republic With discontent over Texas increasing throughout Mexico, Mexican president **General Santa Anna** declared himself dictator and marched his army toward Texas. Fearing Santa Anna would free their slaves, Texans rebelled. After initial defeats at the Alamo mission in San Antonio and at Goliad in March 1836, the Texans easily triumphed by year's end. They declared themselves the Lone Star Republic and elected Sam Houston as president. Their constitution legalized slavery and banned free blacks.

Texas then faced the challenge of nation building, which to its leaders involved Indian removal. When the Indians refused to leave, Mirabeau Lamar, the nation's second president, mobilized the Texas Rangers—mounted nonuniformed militia—to drive them out through terror. The Rangers raided Indian villages, where they robbed, raped, and murdered. This "ethnic cleansing," as one historian has labeled it, ultimately cleared the land of native settlers to make room for white Americans and their African American slaves.

General Santa Anna: Mexican president and dictator whose actions led Texans to revolt.

Wartime Losses and Profits

After annexing Texas in 1845, the United States, seeking further territorial expansion, waged war against Mexico from 1846 to 1848 (see Chapter 14). In the borderlands, as in Mexico, some civilians—Indians, Tejanos, californios, and Mexicans—lost their lives, and many more suffered wartime depredations. If they aided the Mexicans, the U.S. Army destroyed their homes; if they refused aid to the Mexicans, the Mexicans destroyed their homes. An 1847 U.S. army report acknowledged that its "wild volunteers…committed…all sorts of atrocities on the persons and property of Mexicans." After the war ended in the borderlands, violence continued, with Texas Rangers slaughtering Indians from 1847–1848.

Some civilians profited from the war. Farmers sold provisions and mules to the armies; peddlers sold alcohol and food to soldiers; and others set up gambling and prostitution businesses near army camps.

Cultural Frontiers in the Far West

How did the gold rush influence the development of the Far West?

Even before the United States seized expansive territory during the War with Mexico, some Americans moved to the Far West, often to California, Utah, and other places Mexico controlled. Some sought religious freedom or to convert others to Christianity, but most wanted fertile farmland.

Western Missionaries

Catholic missionaries maintained a strong presence in the Far West. In Spanish missions, priests introduced Indians to Catholic sacraments; enforced rigid rules about prayer, sexual conduct, and work; and treated them as legal minors. Indians who did not measure up were subject to corporeal punishment. When they ran away, they were forcibly returned. With few options, Indians often responded to abusive practices with armed uprisings, ultimately weakening the mission system.

A Mexican law secularized the California missions in 1833, using them to organize Indian labor. Some Indians stayed at the missions, others left to farm their own land or to find employment, but for almost all, secularization brought enhanced personal freedom despite limited legal rights.

Still, Catholic missionaries—Americans, Europeans, and converted Indians—continued ministering to immigrants, working to convert Indians. Missionaries founded schools, introduced medical services, and even aided in railroad explorations.

In the Pacific Northwest, Catholics vied directly with Protestants for Indian souls. Under the auspices of the American Board of Commissioners for Foreign Missions, two missionary couples—credited as being the first white migrants along the Oregon Trail—traveled to the Pacific Northwest in 1836. Narcissa and Marcus Whitman built a meetinghouse for Cayuse Indians in Waiilatpu, near present-day Walla Walla, Washington, while Eliza and Henry Spalding worked to convert the Nez Percé at Lapwai, in what is now Idaho. With their superior attitude, the Whitmans could not convert the Cayuses. The Whitmans turned their attention to white migrants flowing into Oregon in the 1840s.

Tensions escalated when a devastating measles epidemic struck in 1847, and the Cayuses saw it as a calculated assault. They retaliated by murdering the Whitmans and twelve other missionaries. The Spaldings abandoned their successful mission, blamed Catholics for inciting the massacre, and became farmers in Oregon.

Mormons

Persecuted in Missouri and Illinois, the Mormons in 1847 followed Brigham Young to their "Promised Land" in the Great Salt Lake valley, still under Mexican control but soon to become part of the U.S. territory of Utah. As non-Mormons settled in Utah, Young diluted their influence by attracting new Mormon settlers to what he called the state of Deseret.

The Mormon's arrival in the Great Basin complicated relations among Indians. The Utes, for example, had long traded in stolen goods and captured people, particularly Paiutes. After Mormons tried to curtail the slave trade, Ute slavers tortured Paiute captives, particularly children, calculating that Mormons would buy them. When they did not, Ute slavers sometimes killed the children. The purchased children often worked as servants in Mormon homes. Although the Mormons tried to convert the Paiutes, their condescending treatment caused friction, even violence. Sharing the Utes as a common enemy, the Mormons and Paiutes formed an uneasy alliance in the early 1850s.

With their slave trade threatened and their economy in shambles, the Utes attacked Mormon and Paiute settlements. War erupted in 1853, and although an uneasy truce was reached in 1854, tensions continued between Mormons and Indians.

Mormons also tussled with their white neighbors. Although Mormons prospered from providing services and supplies to California-bound settlers, Young discouraged "gentiles" (his term for non-Mormons) from settling in Deseret and advocated boycotts of gentile businesses. When in 1852 the Mormons openly sanctioned polygamy, anti-Mormon sentiment increased nationwide. In June 1857, President James Buchanan dispatched 2,500 federal troops to suppress an alleged Mormon rebellion.

Anxious over their safety, some Mormons joined Paiutes in attacking a passing wagon train of non-Mormon migrants. Approximately 120 men, women, and children died in the so-called Mountain Meadows Massacre in August 1857. In the next two years, the U.S. Army and the Mormons engaged in armed conflict, with property destruction but no fatalities.

Oregon and California Trails

From 1840 until 1860, between 250,000 and 500,000 people, including children, walked across much of the continent, usually taking seven months. Although they traveled armed, most of their encounters with Indians were peaceful, if tense.

The overland journeys began at one of the so-called jumping-off points—towns such as Independence, St. Joseph, and Westport Landing—along the Missouri River, where migrants bought supplies for the 2,000-mile trip. While miners frequently traveled alone or with fortune-seeking young men, farmers traveled with relatives, neighbors, church members, and other acquaintances.

They timed their departures to be late enough to forage grass for their oxen and livestock, but not so late that they would encounter the treacherous snows of the Rockies and the Sierra Nevada. Not all were successful. From 1846–1847, the Donner Party took a wrong turn, got caught in a blizzard, and resorted to cannibalism. More fortunate overland migrants trudged alongside their wagons roughly 15 miles a day, in weather from freezing cold to blistering heat. Men generally tended livestock, while women set up camp, prepared meals, and tended small children.

Indians were usually peaceful, if cautious. During the trails' early days, Indians provided food and information, or ferried migrants across rivers. In exchange, migrants offered wool blankets, knives, metal pots, tobacco, ornamental beads, and other items. When exchanges went bad—due to misunderstandings or conscious attempts to swindle—tensions escalated.

Link to the overland trail diary of Lucia Eugenia Lamb Everett.

Livestock thefts continuously aggravated migrants, who usually blamed Indians even though whites stole livestock, too. Indians often took livestock when whites failed to offer gifts in exchange for grazing rights. One such incident, the so-called Mormon Cow Incident (or the Grattan Massacre), forever altered relationships along the Oregon Trail.

In August 1854, a Lakota in present-day Wyoming slaughtered a cow that strayed from a nearby Mormon camp. When Lakota leaders offered compensation, U.S. Army Lieutenant John Grattan, intent on making a point, refused. Grattan ordered his men to shoot, and after a Lakota chief fell dead, Indians returned fire, killing Grattan and twenty-nine men. The following year, General William Harney led six hundred soldiers to a village near Ash Hollow, where migrants and Indians had traded for years. When Indian leaders refused to surrender, Harney ordered his men to fire. Thirty minutes later, eighty-seven Indians lay dead, and seventy women and children were taken prisoner. The event disrupted peace along the trail and ignited nearly two decades of warfare between the Lakotas and the U.S. Army.

Indian Treaties

Fort Laramie Treaty: A treaty between the United States and eight northern Plains tribes in which the Indians agreed to maintain intertribal peace, accepted the U.S.-defined territorial regions for each tribe, and allowed the United States to construct roads. In exchange, they received annual payouts of provisions and agricultural necessities.

Still, the Indian Office negotiated treaties to keep Indians—and their intertribal conflicts—from interfering with western migration and commerce. The **Fort Laramie Treaty** of 1851 (or the Horse Creek Council Treaty) was signed by the United States and eight northern Plains tribes—the Lakotas, Cheyennes, Arapahos, Crows, Assiniboines, Gros-Ventres, Mandans, and Arrickaras—who occupied the Platte River valley through which the three great overland routes westward—the Oregon, California, and Mormon Trails—all passed. Two years later, in 1853, the United States signed a treaty with three southwestern nations, the Comanches, Kiowas, and Apaches, who lived near the Sante Fe Trail. Under both treaties, Indians agreed to maintain intertribal peace, recognize government-delineated tribal boundaries, allow the United States to construct roads and forts within those boundaries, refrain from depredations against western migrants, and issue restitution for any depredations nonetheless committed. In return, they would receive annual allotments from the U.S. government for ten years, paid with provisions, domestic animals, and agricultural implements.

Contrary to U.S. expectations, Indian chiefs did not see such treaties as perpetually binding. Government officials, meanwhile, promised allotments but did little to ensure their timely arrival, often leaving Indians starving. Treaties did not end intratribal warfare, nor did they fully secure overlanders' safety. But they represented the U.S. government's efforts to promote expansion and protect its westward-bound citizens.

Ecological Consequences of Cultural Contact

Armed conflict took relatively few lives compared to cholera, smallpox, and other maladies. The trails' jumping-off points bred disease, which migrants inadvertently carried to their Indian trading partners. Fearful of infection, Indians and migrants increasingly shied away from trading.

The disappearance of the buffalo (American bison) from the region further inflamed tensions. The buffalo provided protein to Plains Indians and held spiritual significance. Many Native Americans blamed the migrants for the buffalo's disappearance, even though most overlanders never saw a buffalo. By the time the overland migration peaked in the late 1840s and 1850s, the herds were long overhunted, partly by Native Americans eager to trade their hides. The surviving buffalo scattered to where the grass was safe from the overlanders' livestock. On rare occasions when wagon trains stumbled upon bison herds, men rushed to fulfill their frontier fantasies and shot the animals. For sport, overlanders also hunted antelopes, wolves, bears, and birds—animals that held spiritual significance for many Native Americans.

Gold Rush

Migrants especially intruded on Indian life near the California gold strikes. In January 1848, John Wilson Marshall discovered gold on John Sutter's property along a shallow tributary to the American River near present-day Sacramento, California. During the next year, tens of thousands of "forty-niners" rushed to California, where they practiced placer mining, panning, and dredging for gold in the hope of instant riches.

Some made fortunes. Peter Brown, a black man from Ste. Genevieve, Missouri, wrote his wife in 1851 that "California is the best country in the world to make money. It is also the best place for black folks on the globe." Most forty-niners, however, never found enough gold to pay their expenses. With their dreams dashed, many forty-niners took wage-paying jobs with large mining companies that used dangerous machinery to cut deep into the earth's surface.

As a remote Mexican province, California had small settlements surrounded by military forts (presidios) and missions. It was inhabited mostly by Indians, along with some Mexican rancheros, who raised cattle and sheep on enormous landholdings worked by coerced Indian laborers. With gold strikes, new migrants—from South America, Asia, Australia, and Europe—rushed to California. Although a California Supreme Court ruling—*People v. Hall* (1854)—made it impossible to prevent violence against Chinese immigrants, Chinese citizens continued to seek fortune in California; by 1859, approximately thirty-five thousand Chinese worked in the goldfields.

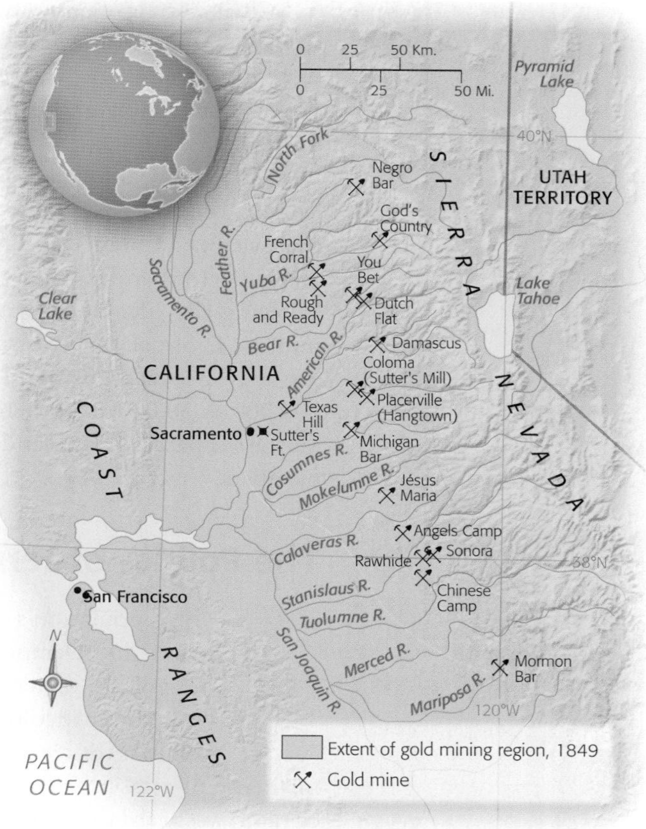

With hungry gold miners to feed, California experienced an agricultural boom. Wheat became the preferred crop: it required minimal investment, was easily planted, and had a short growing season. California's large-scale wheat farming depended on bonded Indian laborers.

Mining Settlements

Mining brought commercial and industrial booms, too, as enterprising merchants rushed to supply new settlers. Among them was Levi Strauss, a German Jewish immigrant, whose tough mining pants found a ready market with prospectors. Because men greatly outnumbered women, women's skills (and company) were in demand. As men set up all-male households and performed traditionally female tasks, women received high fees for cooking, laundering, and sewing. Women also ran boarding houses, hotels, and brothels.

MAP 13.5
The California Gold Rush

Gold was discovered at Sutter's Mill in 1848, sparking the California gold rush that took place mostly along the western foothills of the Sierra Nevada mountains.

Source: Copyright © Cengage Learning

Link to John Sutter's account of discovering gold in California and its consequences.

Link to the original text of "Ahine, Chinaman."

Cities sprang up. In 1848, San Francisco was a small mission settlement of about a thousand Mexicans, Anglos, soldiers, friars, and Indians. With the gold rush, it became a city, ballooning to thirty-five thousand people in 1850. It was the West Coast gateway to the interior, and ships bringing people and supplies jammed the harbor.

Although California was admitted into the Union as a free state in 1850, its legislature soon passed "An Act for the Government and Protection of Indians" that legalized Indians' enslavement. Using enslaved Indians in the mines between 1849 and 1851 ended when newly arrived miners brutally attacked Indian workers, believing they degraded white labor and gave an unfair advantage to established miners. Those slaves who survived the violence became field workers and house servants. Between 1821 and 1860, the Indian population of California fell from 200,000 to 30,000, as Indians died from disease, starvation, and violence. Because masters separated male and female workers, Indians failed to reproduce in large numbers.

The Politics of Territorial Expansion

How did territorial expansion expose political fissures?

The population's westward movement shifted the locus of political power, and Democratic and Whig politicians tried to keep slavery out of the politics of territorial expansion. Westward expansion was central to Democratic ideology, which saw the West's fertile and abundant lands as essential for creating a society of independent white men, freed from the influence of established slaveholders or urban elites. Whigs were more suspicious of rapid westward expansion, though they welcomed the commercial opportunities it might bring. Instead, they pushed for industrial and commercial development within the nation's current boundaries.

Sam Houston: Military and political leader of Texas during and after the Texas Revolution.

The Texas issue, however, made it impossible to disentangle westward expansion and slavery. Soon after establishing the Lone Star Republic, **Sam Houston** approached American authorities to propose annexation as a state. But a new slave state would upset the balance of slave and free states in the Senate. Neither Whigs nor Democrats, wary of causing sectional divisions, were inclined to confront the issue. In the 1830s, Democratic presidents Andrew Jackson and Martin Van Buren—one a strong slavery proponent, the other a mild opponent—sidestepped the issue. But by the mid-1840s—with cotton cultivation expanding rapidly—some Democratic politicians equated Texas annexation with **manifest destiny**.

manifest destiny: Coined by editor John L. O'Sullivan, it was the belief that the United States was endowed by God with a mission to spread its republican government and brand of freedom and Christianity to less fortunate and uncivilized peoples; it also justified U.S. territorial expansion.

Manifest Destiny

The belief that American expansion westward and southward was inevitable, just, and divinely ordained dated to the nation's founding but was first labeled "manifest destiny" in 1845, by John L. O'Sullivan, editor of the *United States Magazine and Democratic Review*. O'Sullivan claimed that Texas annexation would be "the fulfillment of our manifest destiny to overspread the continent allotted by Providence for the free development of our yearly multiplying millions." Manifest destiny implied that Americans had a God-given right, perhaps an obligation, to expand their republican and Christian institutions to less fortunate and less civilized peoples. Implicit in manifest destiny was the belief that American Indians and Hispanics, much like people of African descent, were inferior peoples best controlled or conquered. Manifest destiny provided a political rationale for territorial expansion.

Some, however, felt that an expanding American empire defied God's will. During debates over Texas annexation, Transcendentalist William Ellery Channing argued that the United States should expand its empire by example not conquest: It should be a "sublime moral empire, with a mission to diffuse freedom by manifesting its fruits, not to plunder, crush, and destroy."

In June 1846, impatient expansionists, including John C. Frémont, staged an armed rebellion against Mexican authorities and declared California an independent republic. Because the U.S. military soon conquered California in its War with Mexico, the "Bear Flag Rebellion"—so named for the symbol on the revolutionaries' flag—was short-lived but inflamed racial tensions in California.

Fifty-Four Forty or Fight

To the north, Britain and the United States had jointly occupied the disputed Oregon Territory since 1818. Beginning with John Quincy Adams's administration, the United States tried to fix the boundary at the 49th parallel, but Britain wanted access to Puget Sound and the Columbia River. In the early 1840s, expansionists demanded the entire Oregon Country for the United States, up to its northernmost border at latitude 54° 40'. Soon "fifty-four forty or fight" became their rallying cry.

President Tyler wanted both Oregon and Texas, but was obsessed with Texas. He argued that slavery's expansion would spread the nation's black population more thinly, causing the institution's gradual demise. But when word leaked out that Secretary of State John Calhoun had written to the British minister in Washington justifying Texas annexation to protect slavery, the Senate rejected annexation in 1844 by a vote of 35 to 16.

Polk and the Election of 1844

Worried southern Democrats persuaded their party's 1844 convention to require that the presidential nominee receive two-thirds of the convention votes, effectively giving the southern states a veto and allowing them to block the nomination of Martin Van Buren, who opposed annexation. Instead, the party ran "Young Hickory," House Speaker James K. Polk, an avid expansionist and Tennessee slaveholding cotton planter. The Democratic platform, designed to appeal to voters across regional lines, called for occupation of the entire Oregon Territory and annexation of Texas. The Whigs, who ran Henry Clay, argued that the Democrats' belligerent nationalism would lead to war with Great Britain, Mexico, or both. Clay favored expansion through negotiation, whereas many northern Whigs opposed annexation altogether, fearful it would lead to additional slave states and strain relations with trading partners. Polk won the election by 170 electoral votes to 105, though with a margin of just 38,000 out of 2.7 million votes cast.

Annexation of Texas

Interpreting Polk's victory as a mandate for annexation, President Tyler proposed that Texas be admitted by joint resolution of Congress. The usual method of annexation, by treaty negotiation, required a two-thirds vote in the Senate, which expansionists did not have. Joint

Library of Congress

This 1845 portrayal of Oregon City, the western terminus of the Oregon Trail, was provided by a British army officer sent to investigate the influence of large-scale American immigration into a territory jointly occupied by Great Britain and the United States. After the Oregon Treaty (1846) drew the boundary between British and American territory at the forty-ninth parallel, Oregon City became the capital of the Oregon Territory from 1848 to 1851.

resolution required a simple majority in each house. On March 1, 1845, the resolution passed the House by 120 to 98 and the Senate by 27 to 25. Three days before leaving office, Tyler signed the measure. Mexico, which had never recognized Texas independence, broke relations with the United States. In October, Texas citizens ratified annexation, and Texas joined the Union, with a constitution permitting slavery, in December 1845. The nation was on the brink of war with Mexico. That conflict would lay bare the inextricable relationships among westward expansion, slavery, and sectional discord.

Summary

Encouraged by literary and artistic images of the frontier as a place of natural abundance and opportunity, millions poured into the Old Southwest and Old Northwest in the early nineteenth century. The federal government promoted westward expansion through support for transportation improvements, surveying, cheap land, and protection from Indians. Still, western migrants did not always find what they were seeking. Some returned home, some moved to new locations, and some stayed in the West, abandoning their dreams of economic independence.

Large numbers of African American slaves were moved westward by their owners between 1820 and 1860. Native Americans saw their lands and livelihoods constrict, and their environments drastically altered, threatening their economic and spiritual lives. Some Indians responded to white incursion through accommodation and peaceful overtures; others resisted. For Indians in Texas and California, white incursions brought devastation.

Descendants of Early Latino Settlers

Today, American news media frequently report about Latinos in the United States, for current census figures identify them as the largest racial or ethnic minority. Stories focus on the growing number of documented and undocumented Latino immigrants, their increasing social impact, and their occasionally difficult relationships with African Americans. Yet all the attention to recent arrivals overlooks the sizable number of Latinos who are descended from people whose residency in North America predated the existence of the United States.

When the region stretching from eastern Texas to California was acquired by the United States in the 1840s, its population included indigenous Indian nations and thousands of people with at least partial European ancestry, primarily Spanish or Portuguese. Their descendants have included such U.S. congressmen as Manuel Luján (1969–1988) and such senators as Kenneth Salazar (who served from 2004 to 2009, when he resigned to become Secretary of the Interior). Their families have resided in what is now U.S. territory for twelve or fourteen generations.

Persuasive evidence suggests that many of the early Iberian settlers in New Mexico were *conversos*, or of New Christian descent—that is, people whose Jewish ancestors converted to Catholicism in the fifteenth century to avoid religious persecution. After Jews were expelled from Spain and Portugal in 1492, many fled to the Spanish empire's far corners. Some participated in Juan de Oñate's 1598 expedition to New Mexico. There, some secretly maintained such Jewish customs as Sabbath observances and food restrictions. Today, some Latino residents of New Mexico have acknowledged their *converso* roots and reclaimed a Jewish identity.

These long-standing Latino citizens of the United States, not just those of *converso* descent, have given the nation and its people an important multicultural legacy.

White beliefs about Native Americans' supposed inferiority allowed many to rationalize the Indians' fate; white attitudes toward black people and slavery drove where they settled in the West. Those who believed that slavery degraded white labor headed along a northern trajectory, whereas those who dreamed of slave ownership headed southward, where they clashed with yet another group they deemed racially inferior: Mexicans. When American settlers in Texas achieved independence from Mexico and applied for annexation by the United States, they brought the divisive issue of slavery's westward expansion to the surface. Although Democratic politicians initially tried to maintain a geographic equilibrium by proposing an ambitious territorial agenda in Oregon as well, Texas annexation set the stage for military conflict, the addition of vast territories in the Southwest, and reinvigorated sectional conflict.

Chapter Review

The West in the American Imagination

What were the myths that helped shape white Americans' perceptions of the West?

In dime store novels, artists' paintings, and materials recruiting settlers, the West was depicted as a place of cheap or free, abundant and unoccupied land where anyone could seek to better him- or herself. They often neglected to include that many of these lands were home to native peoples. Artists often depicted Indians as savages (sometimes noble savages) or as docile and easily conquered. Frontiersmen like Daniel Boone were portrayed as having the courage and independent spirit needed to tame the so-called uncivilized wilderness and open the West to freedom-loving white settlers. The West effectively symbolized core American values of freedom, independence, and opportunity.

Expansion and Resistance in the Trans-Appalachian West

What made the Midwest appealing to white settlers?

Migrants who headed west in search of a better life often chose the Midwest because they wanted a region with the same features and conveniences they had come to know. The Midwest, compared to the Old Southwest, had better-developed transportation routes, easier access to markets, a smaller African American population, cheaper landholdings, and a climate similar to New England's. The region proved a good first stop for those who did not yet have enough cash to purchase land; in the Midwest, they could obtain jobs unloading canal boats or working in farms or mills, before moving on.

The Federal Government and Westward Expansion

How did the federal government sponsor and speed up westward expansion?

Federal Indian and land policies, particularly Indian removal from desirable lands, did much to encourage white movement into the West. Many whites, in fact, awaited government efforts to clear lands before moving there. The federal government funded expeditions to chart the trans-Mississippi West, including efforts to find the best location for a transcontinental railroad. Army engineers helped design roads, canals, and railroads, while soldiers cleared forests and did other work. The military also removed Indians from lands that whites desired, defended settlers from Indian attacks, or pushed squatters from land they did not own. Sales of government-controlled land also encouraged settlement.

The Southwestern Borderlands

What factors led white Americans to settle in Texas?

First, the Panic of 1819 pushed some Anglo-Americans to seek cheap land and a fresh start in the Texas territory controlled by Mexico. Beginning in 1824, officials in Mexico also encouraged settlement by offering tax incentives and land grants to foreigners. American Stephen Austin initially settled over two thousand whites, who, contrary to their agreement, brought four hundred slaves. He later brought another nine hundred families. Mexico required settlers be Christians willing to establish permanent residences and to assimilate. But early on, Mexican officials rightly feared that the transplanted Americans would seek to annex Texas to the United States. Beginning in 1826, there were calls for an independent Texas under the name "Fredonia Republic"; and as the proportion of Americans to Tejanos reached seven to one in 1835, calls for secession heightened, culminating in battles and the eventual declaration of Texas as the Lone Star Republic in 1836.

Cultural Frontiers in the Far West

How did the gold rush influence the development of the Far West?

As miners flooded into California seeking gold, an agricultural boom emerged, with wheat becoming the main crop, often farmed by Indian slaves. Wherever mining areas sprung up, a commercial and industrial boom usually followed, as merchants provided necessities and other goods to new settlers. Cities also grew up fast; San Francisco went from one thousand people in 1848 to thirty-five thousand two years later. While California was admitted as a free state that year, it quickly legalized the enslavement of Indians, using them to work in the mines and later in fields or homes.

The Politics of Territorial Expansion

How did territorial expansion expose political fissures?

Efforts to expand the territorial holdings of the United States ultimately magnified sharp regional and political divisions and ended the second party system's cross-sectional alliances. While Democrats embraced westward expansion as part of their vision of a society of independent white farmers, Whigs preferred to focus on commercial development within the nation's existing boundaries. Still, both parties were able to reach compromises with factions in the North and South, until the divisive issue of slavery's role in westward expansion became unavoidable. Those who embraced widening America's territory to the Pacific as its manifest destiny sought to annex Texas—formerly Mexico's holding—and Oregon, which the U.S. jointly occupied with Great Britain. Whigs feared annexation of Texas would widen slavery's reach, tip the balance of free-and-slave states, lead to war with Mexico and strain trade relations. Southern Democrats, including President James Polk, wanted to extend slavery as part of westward expansion, taking the first step by annexing Texas in 1845 as a slave state. The move made regional divisions unavoidable and moved the nation toward a war with Mexico and its own sectional crisis.

Suggestions for Further Reading

Gary Clayton Anderson, *The Conquest of Texas: Ethnic Cleansing in the Promised Land, 1820–1875* (2005)

Stuart Banner, *How the Indians Lost Their Land: Law and Power on the Frontier* (2005)

Ned Blackhawk, *Violence over the Land: Indians and Empires in the Early American West* (2006)

Andrew R. L. Cayton and Peter S. Onuf, *The Midwest and the Nation: Rethinking the History of an American Region* (1990)

Pekka Hämäläinen, *The Comanche Empire* (2008)

Robert V. Hine and John Mack Faragher, *The American West: A New Interpretive History* (2000)

Albert L. Hurtado, *Indian Survival on the California Frontier* (1998)

Susan L. Johnson, *Roaring Camp: The Social World of the California Gold Rush* (2000)

Andrés Reséndez, *Changing National Identities at the Frontier: Texas and New Mexico, 1800–1850* (2005)

Michael L. Tate, *Indians and Emigrants: Encounters on the Overland Trails* (2006)

Go to the CourseMate website for primary source links, study tools, and review materials for this chapter. www.cengagebrain.com

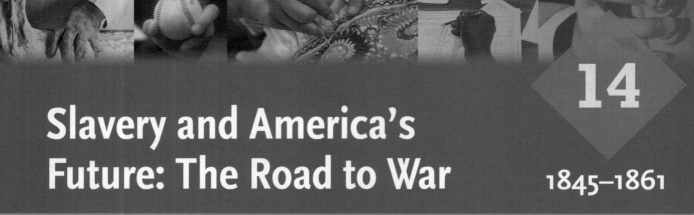

Slavery and America's Future: The Road to War

14

1845–1861

On a stiflingly hot evening, June 16, 1858, former one-term congressman Abraham Lincoln stepped onto the platform of the legislative chamber in the Springfield, Illinois, state house to accept the Republican Party's nomination for the U.S. Senate against America's leading Democrat—the incumbent, Stephen A. Douglas. At six feet, four inches, Lincoln towered over the packed hall. The nation was at a historic crossroads, and he had worked on this speech for weeks, delivering his poetic prose with intellectual power. "Slavery agitation" had convulsed American politics and exploded in guerrilla war in Kansas. "It will not cease," ventured Lincoln, "until a crisis shall have been reached, and passed." Then, in familiar biblical imagery, he gave the crisis its unforgettable metaphor:

> A house divided against itself cannot stand. I believe this government cannot endure permanently half slave and half free....It will become *all* one thing, or *all* the other. Either the *opponents* of slavery will arrest the further spread of it, and place it where the public mind shall rest in the belief that it is in the course of ultimate extinction; or its *advocates* will push it forward, till it shall become alike lawful in *all* the States, *old* as well as *new*—North as well as South.

Lincoln contended that a conspiracy—a "design" led by the Democratic Party's "chief bosses"—sought to make slavery a *national* institution. He charged Douglas with not caring "whether slavery be voted down or voted up."

In the ensuing campaign, Lincoln and Douglas squared off over the issues dividing the country: westward expansion of slavery, the character of federal authority over property in slaves, whether the Declaration of Independence had signaled racial equality, and ultimately the moral integrity and future of the American republic. Reluctantly, Douglas agreed to seven debates, one in each congressional district of Illinois, except Chicago and Springfield, where the candidates had already appeared.

The Lincoln-Douglas debates were three-hour marathons of confrontation, political analysis, and theater, with the candidates speaking in long addresses and rebuttals. Tens of thousands of

Chapter Outline

The War with Mexico and Its Consequences
Oregon | "Mr. Polk's War" | Foreign War and the Popular Imagination | Conquest | Treaty of Guadalupe Hidalgo | "Slave Power Conspiracy" | Wilmot Proviso | The Election of 1848 and Popular Sovereignty

VISUALIZING THE PAST *The Mexican War in Popular Imagination*

1850: Compromise or Armistice?
Debate over Slavery in the Territories | Compromise of 1850 | Fugitive Slave Act | Uncle Tom's Cabin | The Underground Railroad | Election of 1852 and the Collapse of Compromise

Slavery Expansion and Collapse of the Party System
The Kansas-Nebraska Act | Birth of the Republican Party | Know-Nothings | Party Realignment and the Republicans' Appeal | Republican Ideology | Southern Democrats | Bleeding Kansas | Election of 1856

LINKS TO THE WORLD *William Walker and Filibustering*

Slavery and the Nation's Future
Dred Scott Case | Abraham Lincoln and the Slave Power | The Lecompton Constitution and Disharmony Among Democrats

Disunion
John Brown's Raid on Harpers Ferry | Election of 1860 | Secession and the Confederate States of America | Fort Sumter and Outbreak of War | Causation

LEGACY FOR A PEOPLE AND A NATION *Terrorist or Freedom Fighter?*

SUMMARY

people attended these outdoor events, arriving by foot, wagon, or trains. Perhaps never before or since have Americans demonstrated such an appetite for democratic engagement.

As Douglas accused his opponent and Republicans of radicalism—of being "abolitionists" and favoring racial equality—Lincoln was forced to admit that he opposed social equality between whites and blacks. He embraced, however, the natural-rights doctrine of the Declaration of Independence and condemned slavery as an "evil" that must be constrained. Lincoln insisted on stopping slavery's expansion, while maintaining that the federal government could not legally end it in the South. A foot shorter than Lincoln, better dressed, and resplendent in oratorical manner, Douglas appealed to racial prejudice and to a vague unionism. Lincoln cast the election as a moral choice between free-labor—Free-Soil doctrine—and a republic ultimately dominated by slaveholders and their abettors, determined to erase ordinary citizens' liberties.

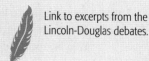

Link to excerpts from the Lincoln-Douglas debates.

Of the quarter-million votes cast, Lincoln received four thousand more than Douglas. But senators were elected by state legislatures in the nineteenth century; due to an outdated apportionment, Democrats maintained a 54-to-46 margin and returned Douglas to the U.S. Senate. Lincoln would be heard from again, however.

Well before 1858, conflict and violence were enveloping the nation. In Kansas Territory, warfare exploded between proslavery and antislavery settlers. In the U.S. Senate, a southern representative had beaten a northern senator senseless. A new fugitive slave law sent thousands of free and fugitive blacks fleeing into Canada in fear for their lives. The Supreme Court issued a dramatic decision about slavery's constitutionality in westward expansion as well as the status of African American citizenship—to the delight of most southerners and the dread of many northerners. And abolitionist John Brown was planning a raid into Virginia to start a slave rebellion.

As the 1850s advanced, divergent economic and political aims, North and South, which had long been held in check, now flew apart over slavery. Political parties fractured, replaced by a realignment that reinforced sectional interests. Each time the nation expanded, it confronted a thorny issue: Should new territories and states be slave or free?

North and South, a feeling grew that America's future was at stake—the character of its economy, its labor system, its definition of constitutional liberty, and its racial self-definition. Blacks could take heart that political strife over slavery might lead to their liberation. In 1855, Frederick Douglass spoke for the enslaved when he wrote, "the thought of only being a creature of the present and the past, troubled me, and I longed to have a future—a future with hope in it."

As you read this chapter, keep the following questions in mind:

* **After 1845, how and why did westward expansion become so intertwined with the future of slavery and freedom?**

* **During the 1850s, why did Americans (white males, virtually all of whom could vote, and blacks, few of whom had the franchise) seem to care so deeply about electoral politics?**

* **What were the long-term and immediate causes of the Civil War?**

Chronology

1846	War with Mexico begins			Buchanan elected president, but Republican Frémont wins most northern states
	Oregon Treaty negotiated		1857	*Dred Scott v. Sanford* endorses southern views on black citizenship and slavery in territories
	Wilmot Proviso inflames sectional divisions			
1847	Cass proposes idea of popular sovereignty			Economic panic and widespread unemployment begin
1848	Treaty of Guadalupe Hidalgo gives United States new territory in the Southwest		1858	Kansas voters reject Lecompton Constitution
	Free-Soil Party formed			Lincoln-Douglas debates attract attention
	Taylor elected president			Douglas contends popular sovereignty prevails over *Dred Scott* decision in territories
	Gold discovered in California, which later applies for admission to Union as free state		1859	Brown raids Harpers Ferry
1850	Compromise of 1850 passes, containing controversial Fugitive Slave Act		1860	Democratic Party splits in two; southern Democrats demand constitutional guarantee for the territories
1852	Stowe publishes *Uncle Tom's Cabin*			Lincoln elected president in divided, sectional election
	Pierce elected president			
1854	Publication of "Appeal of the Independent Democrats"			Crittenden Compromise fails
	Kansas-Nebraska Act wins approval and ignites controversy			South Carolina secedes from Union
	Republican Party formed		1861	Six more Deep South states secede
	Return of fugitive Burns to slavery in Virginia			Confederacy established at Montgomery, Alabama
1856	Bleeding Kansas troubles nation			Attack on Fort Sumter begins Civil War
	Brooks attacks Sumner in Senate chamber			Four states in the Upper South join the Confederacy

The War with Mexico and Its Consequences

Which of Polk's decisions pushed the United States toward war with Mexico?

In the 1840s, territorial expansion surged forward under President **James K. Polk** of North Carolina. The annexation of Texas just before his inauguration did not make war with Mexico inevitable, but several of Polk's decisions did. Mexico broke off relations with the United States, and during the annexation process, Polk urged Texans to seize all land to the Rio Grande and claim the river as their southern and western border. Mexico held that the Nueces River was the border; hence, the stage was set for conflict. In Polk's determination to fulfill the nation's manifest destiny to rule the continent, he wanted Mexico's territory to the Pacific and Oregon Country as well. He and his expansionist cabinet achieved their goals but were unaware of expansionism's price in domestic harmony.

James K. Polk: President from 1845–1849; supporter of immediate annexation of Texas and wanted to gain California and Oregon for the United States as well.

Oregon

During the 1844 campaign, Polk's supporters threatened war with Great Britain to gain Oregon. Not wanting to fight Mexico and Great Britain simultaneously, Polk sought diplomacy in the Northwest, where America and Britain had since 1819 jointly occupied disputed territory. Dropping the demand for a boundary at latitude 54°40', he pressured the British to accept the forty-ninth parallel. In 1846, the Oregon Treaty gave the United

States present-day Oregon, Washington, and Idaho, and parts of Wyoming and Montana. Thus, a new era of land acquisition and conquest began under the eleventh president of the United States, the sixth to be a slaveholder and one who, through an agent, secretly bought and sold slaves from the White House.

"Mr. Polk's War"

Toward Mexico, Polk was more aggressive. In early 1846, he ordered American troops under "Old Rough and Ready," General Zachary Taylor, to defend the contested border of the Rio Grande across from the town of Matamoros, Mexico. Polk saw California as the prize, and he attempted to buy from Mexico a huge tract of land extending to the Pacific. When that failed, Polk waited for war. After a three-week standoff, on April 24, 1846, Mexican cavalry ambushed a U.S. cavalry unit on the north side of the river; eleven Americans were killed, and sixty-three were taken captive. On April 26, Taylor sent a dispatch to Washington, D.C., announcing, "Hostilities may now be considered as commenced."

Polk then drafted a message to Congress: Mexico had "passed the boundary of the United States, had invaded our territory, and shed American blood on American soil." Polk deceptively declared that "war exists by the act of Mexico itself." Two days later, on May 13, the House recognized a state of war with Mexico by a vote of 174 to 14, and the Senate, by 40 to 2. Because Polk withheld key facts, the full reality of what had happened on the distant Rio Grande was not known. Manifest destiny launched the United States into its first major war on foreign territory.

Foreign War and the Popular Imagination

The idea of war unleashed public celebrations in southern and northern cities. After news came of General Taylor's first victories at Palo Alto and Resaca de la Palma, volunteers swarmed recruiting stations. New York, writer Herman Melville remarked that "Nothing is talked of but the Halls of the Montezumas." Publishers rushed books about Mexican geography into print. And new daily newspapers boosted sales by giving the war a romantic appeal.

Here was an adventurous war of conquest, the fulfillment of an Anglo-Saxon—Christian destiny to possess the North American continent, and to civilize the "semi-Indian" Mexicans. Racism fueled the expansionist spirit. In 1846, an Illinois newspaper justified the war by calling Mexicans "reptiles in the path of progressive democracy." Because of newspapers, the War with Mexico became the first national event experienced with immediacy. War correspondents reported on battles, and ships from Vera Cruz on the Gulf Coast of Mexico carried news dispatches to New Orleans. Near war's end, news traveled by telegraph in only three days from New Orleans to Washington, D.C.

The war spawned poetry, song, drama, travel, literature, and lithographs that glorified the conflict. But not everyone cheered. Abolitionist James Russell Lowell considered the war a "national crime committed in behoof of slavery, our common sin." Even proslavery spokesman John C. Calhoun saw the perils of expansionism.

Link to John C. Calhoun's 1850 speech on preserving the Union.

Conquest

Early in the war, U.S. forces made significant gains. In May 1846, Polk ordered Colonel Stephen Kearny and a small detachment to invade the remote provinces of New Mexico and California. Taking Santa Fe, Kearny pushed into California, where he joined forces with two

The Mexican War in Popular Imagination

The War with Mexico was the first American foreign conflict to be covered by the press with actual correspondents and the first to stimulate the creation of widespread promotional popular art and commemorative objects. General Zachary Taylor, the American commander in Mexico, became the hero of the war, and in its wake, was elected president in 1848 in a campaign that featured countless forms of this art. Why was the War with Mexico the first American foreign war to be covered by journalists and so widely depicted in political and military art? Do you think the artistic depictions of the War with Mexico increased or decreased the popularity of the war?

Presentation pitcher: ca. 1848–1850 (porcelain), French School, (19th century) Portrait of Zachary Taylor (1784–1850) on one side, 12th president of the United States (1849–1850); landscape with battle on the other side, hero of the Mexican war (1846–1848); commemorates Taylor's triumph in the 1847 battle of Buena Vista.

Museum of Fine Arts, Houston, Texas, the Bayou Bend Collection, gift of Miss Ima Hogg, Bridgeman Art Library

Chicago History Museum, Bridgeman Art Library

Painting, General Zachary Taylor in command at the Battle of Buena Vista, in Mexico, 1847, oil on canvas, by William Henry Powell (1823–79).

U.S. naval units and American settlers led by Captain John C. Frémont. General Zachary Taylor's forces attacked Monterrey, which surrendered in September, securing northeastern Mexico.

New Mexico did not prove easy for U.S. forces. In January 1847, in Taos, northwest of Santa Fe, Hispanics and Indians led by Pablo Montoya and Tomas Romero rebelled against the Americans and killed government officials. In what became known as the Taos Revolt, some 500 Mexican and Indian insurgents laid siege to a mill in Arroyo Hondo, outside Taos. The U.S. command swiftly suppressed the revolt, and the insurgents retreated to a thick-walled church in Taos Pueblo. With cannon, the U.S. Army killed 150 and captured 400 rebels. After many arrests, approximately 28 insurgent leaders were hanged in the Taos plaza, ending bloody resistance to U.S. occupation.

Before the end of 1846, American forces also established dominion over California. Because losses on the periphery had not broken Mexican resistance, General Winfield Scott carried the war to the enemy's heartland. He led 14,000 men toward Mexico City in what proved to be the war's decisive campaign. Outnumbered and threatened by yellow fever, Scott's men repeatedly discovered flanking routes around their foes. After several hard-fought battles, U.S. troops captured the Mexican capital.

Treaty of Guadalupe Hidalgo

Representatives of both countries signed the **Treaty of Guadalupe Hidalgo** in February 1848. The United States gained California and New Mexico (including present-day Nevada, Utah, and Arizona, and parts of Colorado and Wyoming), and recognition of the Rio Grande as Texas's southern boundary. The American government agreed to settle the claims of its citizens (mostly Texans) against Mexico ($3.2 million) and to pay Mexico a mere $15 million.

The costs of the war included the deaths of thirteen thousand Americans (mostly from disease) and fifty thousand Mexicans. Enmity between Mexico and the United States endured into the twentieth century. Domestically, southwesterners and southern planters were enthusiastic about the war; New Englanders opposed it. Whigs in Congress charged that Polk, a Democrat, had "provoked" an unnecessary war and "usurped the power of Congress." Abolitionists and a minority of antislavery Whigs charged that the war was a plot to extend slavery.

Treaty of Guadalupe Hidalgo: Agreement that ended the U.S. War with Mexico in which Mexico ceded vast amounts of its territory and was forced to recognize the Rio Grande as Texas's southern boundary.

"Slave Power Conspiracy"

These charges fed northern fear of the "Slave Power." Abolitionists had long warned of a slaveholding oligarchy that would dominate the nation through its hold on federal power. Slaveholders gained control of the South by suppressing dissent. They forced the gag rule on Congress in 1836. To many white northerners, even those who saw nothing wrong with slavery, this battle over free speech made the idea of a Slave Power credible. The War with Mexico deepened such fears, as antislavery northerners wondered if it had been launched to acquire vast, new slave territory.

The war's impact on southern opinion was dramatic. Initially, some southern Whigs attacked the Democratic president for causing the war, and few southern congressmen saw slavery as the paramount issue. Many whites, North and South, feared that large land seizures would bring nonwhite Mexicans into the United States and upset the racial order. An Indiana politician did not want "any mixed races in our Union, nor men of any color except white, unless they be slaves." Despite their racism and exaggerations, many statesmen soon saw other potential outcomes of a war of conquest in the Southwest.

Wilmot Proviso

In August 1846, David Wilmot, a Pennsylvania Democrat, proposed an amendment, or proviso, to a military appropriations bill: that "neither slavery nor involuntary servitude shall ever exist" in any territory gained from Mexico. Although the proviso never passed, its repeated introduction by northerners transformed the debate over slavery's expansion. Southerners intensified efforts to protect slavery's future. Alexander H. Stephens declared that slavery was based on the Bible, and John C. Calhoun insisted that slaveholders had a constitutional right to take their slaves (as property) anywhere in the territories.

This position, often called "state sovereignty," was a radical reversal of history. In 1787, the Confederation Congress discouraged if not fully excluded slavery from the Northwest Territory. Article IV of the U.S. Constitution authorized Congress to make "all needful rules and regulations" for the territories, and the Missouri Compromise barred slavery from most of the Louisiana Purchase. Now, southern leaders demanded future guarantees for slavery.

In the North, the **Wilmot Proviso** became a rallying cry for abolitionists. While fourteen northern states endorsed it, not all of its supporters were abolitionists. David Wilmot was neither an abolitionist nor an antislavery Whig. Instead, his goal was to defend "the rights of white freemen" and to obtain California "for free white labor."

As Wilmot demonstrated, it was possible, however, to be a racist and an opponent of slavery. The vast majority of white northerners were not active abolitionists, and their desire to keep the West slavery-free was often matched by their desire to keep blacks from settling there. At stake was the free individual's access to social mobility by acquiring land in the West. Slave labor, thousands of northerners believed, would degrade the toil of free men and render them unemployable. The West therefore must not include slavery.

Wilmot Proviso: A proposed amendment that would have prohibited slavery in territories acquired from Mexico; though it never passed, it transformed the national debate over slavery.

The Election of 1848 and Popular Sovereignty

The divisive slavery question infested national politics. After Polk renounced a second term as president, the Democrats nominated Senator Lewis Cass of Michigan for president and General William Butler of Kentucky for vice president. Cass, a party loyalist who had served in Jackson's cabinet, devised in 1847 the idea of "popular sovereignty"—letting residents in the western territories decide the slavery question for themselves. His party's platform declared that Congress lacked the power to interfere with slavery's expansion. The Whigs nominated General Zachary Taylor, a southern slaveholder and war hero; New York Congressman Millard Fillmore was his running mate. The Whig convention similarly denied that Congress had power over slavery in the territories.

Many southern Democrats distrusted Cass and voted for Taylor because he was a slaveholder. New York Democrats committed to the Wilmot Proviso nominated former president Martin Van Buren. Antislavery Whigs and former Liberty Party supporters joined them to organize the **Free-Soil Party**, with Van Buren as its candidate (see Table 14.1). This party, which sought to restrict slavery expansion to western territories and whose slogan was "Free Soil, Free Speech, Free Labor, and Free Men," won almost 300,000 northern votes. Taylor polled 1.4 million votes to Cass's 1.2 million and won the White House, but the results were ominous.

Free-Soil Party: A political party that sprung from and represented the movement to prevent slavery in the western territories.

TABLE 14.1   New Political Parties

Party	Period of Influence	Area of Influence	Outcome
Liberty Party	1839–1848	North	Merged with other antislavery groups to form Free-Soil Party
Free-Soil Party	1848–1854	North	Merged with Republican Party
Know-Nothings (American Party)	1853–1856	Nationwide	Disappeared, freeing most to join Republican Party
Republican Party	1854–present	North (later nationwide)	Became rival of Democratic Party and won presidency in 1860

Religious denominations, too, severed into northern and southern wings. As the 1850s dawned, the legacies of the War with Mexico and the conflicts of 1848 threatened the nature of the Union.

1850: Compromise or Armistice?

More than eighty thousand Americans flooded into California during the 1849 gold rush. With Congress unable to agree on a governing formula for the territories, President Taylor urged settlers to apply for admission to the Union. They did, proposing a state constitution that banned slavery. Because California's admission as a free state would upset the sectional balance in the Senate (the ratio of slave to free states was fifteen to fifteen), southern politicians wanted to postpone admission and make California a slave territory, or at least extend the Missouri Compromise to the Pacific.

> What were the two troubling issues inherent in the Compromise of 1850?

Debate over Slavery in the Territories
Twice before—in 1820 and 1833—Henry Clay, the Whig leader and "Great Pacificator," had shaped sectional compromise; now he struggled one last time to preserve the nation. In the winter of 1850, Clay and Senator Stephen A. Douglas of Illinois steered their compromise package through debate and amendment.

The problems were numerous. Would California become a free state? How should the territory acquired from Mexico be organized? Texas, which allowed slavery, claimed areas extending as far west as Santa Fe. Southerners complained that fugitive slaves were not returned as the Constitution required, and northerners objected to slave auctions in the nation's capital. Eight years earlier, in *Prigg v. Pennsylvania* (1842), the Supreme Court ruled that enforcement of the Constitution's fugitive slave clause was a federal obligation. Most troublesome, however, was the status of slavery in the territories.

Clay and Douglas discovered in the idea of popular sovereignty what one historian called a "charm of ambiguity." Ultimately, Congress would have to approve statehood for a territory, but "in the meantime," said Lewis Cass, it should allow the people living there "to regulate their own concerns in their own way."

To avoid dissension within their party, northern and southern Democrats explained Cass's statement to constituents in incompatible ways. Southerners claimed that neither Congress nor a territorial legislature could bar slavery. Northerners, however, insisted that Americans living in a territory were entitled to local self-government and thus could outlaw slavery.

Link to the full text of Daniel Webster's March 7, 1850, speech.

The cause of compromise gained a powerful supporter when Senator Daniel Webster committed his prestige and eloquence to Clay's bill. Abandoning his earlier support for the Wilmot Proviso, Webster urged northerners not to "taunt or reproach" the South with antislavery measures. He warned southern firebrands that disunion inevitably would cause violence and destruction. Many of Webster's former abolitionist friends in New England condemned his compromise efforts and accused him of going over to the "devil."

Only three days earlier, Calhoun was carried from his sickbed to oppose the compromise. With Calhoun unable to speak, Senator James Mason of Virginia read his address, which predicted disunion if southern demands went unanswered, frightening some into supporting compromise.

With Clay sick, Douglas reintroduced the compromise measures one at a time. Douglas realized that because southerners favored some bills and northerners the rest, a small majority for compromise could be achieved on each distinct issue. The strategy worked, and the Compromise of 1850 became law.

Compromise of 1850   The compromise had five essential measures:

1. California became a free state.
2. The Texas boundary was set at its present limits (see Map 14.1), and the United States paid Texas $10 million for the loss of New Mexico Territory.
3. The territories of New Mexico and Utah were organized on a basis of popular sovereignty.
4. The fugitive slave law was strengthened.
5. The slave trade was abolished in the District of Columbia.

At best, the Compromise of 1850 was an artful evasion. Douglas found a way to pass the five proposals without convincing northerners and southerners to agree on fundamentals. The compromise bought time, but it did not resolve territorial questions.

MAP 14.1

The Kansas-Nebraska Act and Slavery Expansion, 1854

The vote on the Kansas-Nebraska Act in the House of Representatives (see also Table 14.2 on page 354) demonstrates the sectionalization of American politics due to the slavery question.

Source: Copyright © Cengage Learning

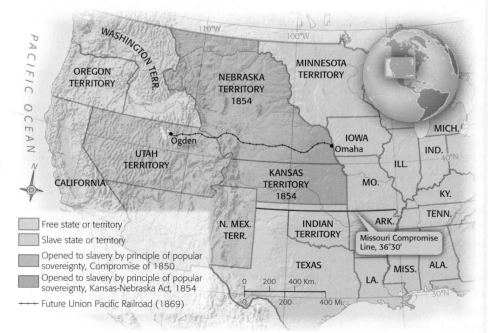

Furthermore, the compromise had two flaws. The first concerned the ambiguity of popular sovereignty. Southerners insisted on no prohibition of slavery during the territorial stage, and northerners declared that settlers could bar slavery whenever they wished. The compromise allowed for the appeal of a territorial legislature's action to the Supreme Court.

Fugitive Slave Act

The second flaw lay in the **Fugitive Slave Act**, which gave new—and controversial—protection to slavery. The law empowered slaveowners to go into state court to present evidence that a slave had escaped. The resulting transcript and a description of the fugitive would serve as legal proof of slave status, even in free states and territories. Court officials adjudicated the identity of the person described, not whether he or she was indeed a slave. The law made it a felony to harbor fugitives and stated that northerners could be summoned to hunt fugitives. The fees paid favored slaveholders: $10 if the alleged fugitive was returned; $5 if not returned.

Abolitionist newspapers attacked the Fugitive Slave Act as a violation of American rights. Why were alleged fugitives denied a trial by jury? Why would northerners be arrested if they harbored runaways? These questions convinced some northerners that free blacks were vulnerable to kidnapping and enslavement. An estimated twenty thousand blacks fled to Canada after the Fugitive Slave Act.

Between 1850 and 1854, protests and violent resistance to slave catchers occurred in northern towns. Sometimes a captured fugitive was broken out of jail by abolitionists, as in the 1851 Boston case of Shadrach Minkins, who was spirited by wagons and trains to Montreal, Canada. That same year, the small black community in Lancaster County, Pennsylvania, defended four escaped slaves from a federal posse charged with reenslaving them. At this "Christiana riot," fugitives killed Edward Gorsuch, the Maryland slaveowner who sought the return of his

Fugitive Slave Act: Part of the Compromise of 1850; controversial measure that gave additional powers to slaveowners in recapturing slaves and angered northerners by requiring them to hunt so-called fugitives.

Link to Frederick Douglass's "What to the Slave is the Fourth of July" speech given at the Rochester Ladies' Anti-Slavery Society in 1852.

Courtesy Amherst College Archives and Special Collections

Eliza crossing the Ohio River, leaping on icebergs, is perhaps the most famous and oft-repeated image from *Uncle Tom's Cabin*. The drawing is from a series by twentieth century Mexican artist Miguel Covarrubias.

"property." A headline reporting the Christiana affair screamed, "Civil War, The First Blow Struck!"

Many abolitionists became convinced that violence was a legitimate means of opposing slavery. In an 1854 column, Frederick Douglass said that the only way to make the fugitive slave law "dead letter" was to make a "few dead slave catchers."

Uncle Tom's Cabin

Uncle Tom's Cabin: Harriet Beecher Stowe's best-selling 1852 novel that aroused widespread northern sympathy for slaves (especially fugitives) and widespread southern anger.

Meanwhile, Harriet Beecher Stowe, whose New England family produced prominent ministers, wrote a novel portraying the humanity and suffering of slaves. Her story, **Uncle Tom's Cabin**, was serialized in 1851 and published as a book in 1852. It touched millions of northerners with its tale of a mother's dash to freedom with her child across the frozen Ohio River. Stowe also portrayed slavery's evil effects on slaveholders, indicting the institution more harshly than southerners caught in its web. Moreover, Stowe exposed northern racism and complicity with slavery by making the worst slaveholder a man of New England birth.

By mid-1853, the book sold over 1 million copies. Its popularity alarmed southern whites, who saw their way of life threatened. Behind southern claims about territorial rights lay the fear that, if nearby areas outlawed slavery, they would become bases from which abolitionism would spread into slave states.

Fifteen to twenty proslavery novels were published in the 1850s as responses to *Uncle Tom's Cabin*. Most paled in comparison to Stowe's masterpiece, but southern writers defended their system as more humane than wage labor. In awkward stories, such as J. W. Page's *Uncle Robin in His Cabin and Tom Without One in Boston,* slaves were induced to run away by visiting abolitionists, and then starved in northern cities.

The Underground Railroad

Underground Railroad: A loosely organized process by which fugitive slaves, often of their own volition, escaped to freedom in the northern United States and Canada.

By the 1850s, slaveholders were especially disturbed by the **Underground Railroad**, a loose, illegal network, spiriting runaways to freedom. Thousands of slaves escaped by these often disorganized routes, but largely through their own wits and courage with assistance from blacks in northern cities. Lewis Hayden in Boston, David Ruggles in New York, William Still in Philadelphia, and Jacob Gibbs in Washington, D.C., were among the many black abolitionists who managed fugitive slave escapes.

Harriet Tubman, herself an escapee in 1848, returned to her native Maryland and to Virginia at least a dozen times, and secretly helped as many as three hundred slaves, some her family members, to freedom. Outraged Maryland planters offered a $40,000 reward for her capture.

In Ohio, white abolitionists, often Quakers, joined with blacks to help slaves cross the river to freedom. The Underground Railroad also had numerous maritime routes, as coastal slaves escaped aboard ships from Virginia, the Carolinas, or New Orleans, and ended up in northern port cities, the Caribbean, or England. Many fugitives from the Lower South and Texas escaped to Mexico, which abolished slavery in 1829. Some joined Seminole communities in Florida, where they fought with them against the U.S. Army in the Seminole Wars of 1835–1842 and 1855–1858.

Slave escapes were a testament to human courage and the will for freedom. They never reached the scale believed by angry slaveholders or claimed by northern towns and local historical societies today. But, in reality and legend, the Underground Railroad applied pressure to the institution of slavery and gave slaves hope.

Election of 1852 and the Collapse of Compromise

The 1852 election gave southern leaders hope that slavery would be secure under a new president. Franklin Pierce, a New Hampshire Democrat, won easily over the Whig presidential nominee, General Winfield Scott. Pierce firmly supported the Compromise of 1850, where Scott's views on the compromise were unknown.

President Pierce's embrace of the compromise appalled many northerners. His enforcement of the Fugitive Slave Act provoked fear especially in the case of the fugitive slave Anthony Burns, who fled Virginia in 1852. In Boston, thinking he was safe, Burns began a new life. But in 1854, federal marshals placed him under guard in Boston's courthouse. An interracial crowd of abolitionists attacked the court-house, killing a jailer while attempting to free Burns.

Pierce telegraphed local officials to "incur any expense to insure the execution of the law" and sent troops to Boston. Soldiers marched Burns to Boston harbor, while Burns's supporters draped the streets in black and hung American flags at half-mast. At a cost of $100,000, a single black man was returned to slavery.

This demonstration of federal support for slavery radicalized opinion, even among many conservatives. Juries refused to convict the abolitionists who stormed the Boston courthouse. New England states passed personal liberty laws that blocked federal enforcement and absolved local judges from enforcing the Fugitive Slave Act, effectively nullifying federal authority. What northerners now saw as evidence of a dominating Slave Power, slaveholders saw as legal defense of their rights.

Pierce confronted sectional conflict at every turn. His proposal for a transconti-nental railroad derailed when congressmen fought over its location, North or South. An annexation treaty with Hawai'i failed because southern senators would not vote for another free state, and efforts to acquire slaveholding Cuba angered northerners.

Events in the Pacific also triggered debate over how far American expansion should extend. With two orchestrated landings in the Bay of Tokyo, in 1853 and 1854, Commodore Matthew Perry established U.S. intentions to trade with Japan. Offended and intrigued, the Japanese were impressed with Perry's steam-powered warships, the first they had seen. Perry's Treaty of Kanagawa in March 1854 negotiated two ports as coaling stations for American ships, but sought-after trad-ing arrangements were slow in coming.

Back home, another territorial bill threw Congress and the nation into greater turmoil, and the Compromise of 1850 collapsed.

Slavery Expansion and Collapse of the Party System

How did the Kansas-Nebraska Act lead to the collapse of existing political parties?

The new controversy began in a surprising way. Stephen A. Douglas intro-duced a bill to establish the Kansas and Nebraska Territories. Ambitious for the presidency, Douglas did not view slavery as a fundamental problem and was willing to risk controversy to economically aid his home state of Illinois. A transcontinental railroad would encourage Great Plains settlement and stimulate the Illinois economy, but no company would build a railroad before Congress orga-nized the territories it would cross. Thus, interest in promoting a railroad drove Douglas to introduce a bill that inflamed sectional passions.

The Kansas-Nebraska Act

The **Kansas-Nebraska Act** exposed conflicting interpretations of popular sovereignty. Douglas's bill left "all questions pertaining to slavery in the Territories...to the people residing therein." Northerners and southerners, however, still disagreed over what territorial settlers could constitutionally do. Moreover, the Kansas and Nebraska Territories lay within the Louisiana Purchase, and the Missouri Compromise prohibited slavery there from latitude 36°30' north to the Canadian border. If popular sovereignty were applied in Kansas and Nebraska, it would mean that the Missouri Compromise was no longer in effect.

Southern congressmen, anxious to establish slaveholders' right to take slaves into any territory, pressed Douglas for an explicit repeal of the 36°30' limitation in exchange for their support. During a carriage ride with Kentucky Senator Archibald Dixon, Douglas conceded: "I will incorporate it in my bill, though I know it will raise a hell of a storm."

Douglas believed that climate and soil conditions would keep slavery out of Kansas and Nebraska. Nevertheless, his bill allowed slavery on land from which it had been prohibited for thirty-four years. Many Free-Soilers and antislavery forces considered this turn of events a betrayal of trust. The bill became law in May 1854 by a vote that demonstrated the dangerous sectionalization of American politics (see Map 14.1 and Table 14.2).

Opposition to the Fugitive Slave Act grew dramatically; between 1855 and 1859, Connecticut, Rhode Island, Massachusetts, Michigan, Maine, Ohio, and Wisconsin passed personal-liberty laws. These laws enraged southerners by providing counsel for alleged fugitives and requiring trial by jury. The Kansas-Nebraska Act had a devastating impact on political parties. The weakened Whig Party broke into northern and southern wings. The Democrats survived, but their support in the North plummeted in the 1854 elections. Northern Democrats lost sixty-six of their ninety-one congressional seats and lost control of all but two free-state legislatures.

Birth of the Republican Party

The beneficiary of northern voters' wrath was a new political party. During debate on the Kansas-Nebraska Act, six congressmen—most prominently, Joshua Giddings, Salmon Chase, and Charles Sumner—published an "Appeal of the Independent Democrats." In it, they attacked Douglas's legislation as a violation of the Missouri Compromise and a "criminal betrayal of precious rights" that would make free

TABLE 14.2   The Vote on the Kansas-Nebraska Act

The vote was 113 to 100 in favor.

	Aye	Nay
Northern Democrats	44	42
Southern Democrats	57	2
Northern Whigs	0	45
Southern Whigs	12	7
Northern Free-Soilers		4

territory a "dreary region of despotism." Their appeal tapped a reservoir of northern concern, cogently expressed by Illinois's Abraham Lincoln.

Although Lincoln did not condemn southerners, he exposed the meaning of the Kansas-Nebraska Act. Lincoln argued that the founders, from love of liberty, banned slavery from the Northwest Territory, kept the word *slavery* out of the Constitution, and treated it as a "cancer" on the republic. Rather than encouraging liberty, the Kansas-Nebraska Act promised to extend slavery. America's future, Lincoln warned, was being mortgaged to slavery.

Thousands of white northerners agreed. During summer and fall 1854, antislavery Whigs and Democrats, Free-Soilers, and reformers throughout the Old Northwest formed the new Republican Party, dedicated to keeping slavery from the territories. Republicans' influence rapidly spread to the East. They won a stunning victory in the 1854 elections, capturing a majority of northern House seats and inspiring roughly a quarter of northern Democrats to desert their party.

For the first time, too, a sectional party gained significant power. The Whigs were gone, and Democrats struggled to maintain national membership. The emergence of the Republican coalition of antislavery interests is the most rapid transformation in party allegiance in American history.

Know-Nothings

Republicans also drew into their coalition a fast-growing nativist movement that called itself the American Party, or Know-Nothings (because initial members kept their purposes secret, answering, "I know nothing" to questions). This group exploited fear of foreigners and Catholics. Between 1848 and 1860, nearly 3.5 million immigrants entered the United States—proportionally the heaviest inflow of foreigners in American history. Democrats courted these new citizens, but many native-born Anglo-Saxon Protestants believed that Irish and German Catholics would owe primary allegiance to the pope in Rome.

Know-Nothings: Anti-Catholic and anti-immigrant party that enjoyed brief surge of popularity in the early 1850s.

In 1854, anti-immigrant fears made the Know-Nothings successful in some northern states, particularly Massachusetts, where they elected 11 congressmen, a governor, all state officers, all state senators, and all but 2 of 378 state representatives. The temperance movement also gained ground early in the 1850s with its promises to stamp out the evils associated with liquor and immigrants (a decidedly anti-Irish campaign). The Know-Nothings strove to reinforce Protestant morality and restrict voting and office holding to the native-born. As the Whig Party vanished, the Know-Nothings filled the void. But, like the Whigs, the Know-Nothings could not keep their northern and southern wings together due to the slavery expansion issue. They dissolved after 1856. Instead, Republicans wooed nativists with temperance ordinances and laws postponing suffrage for naturalized citizens (see Table 14.1).

Party Realignment and the Republicans' Appeal

The Whig Party's demise ensured a major realignment of the political system. Immigration, temperance, homestead bills, the tariff, internal improvements were crucial issues for voters during the 1850s. Commercial agriculture was booming in the Ohio–Mississippi–Great Lakes area, but residents desired more canals, roads, and river and harbor improvements. Because credit was scarce, a homestead program—the idea that western land should be free to individuals who would farm and make a home on it—attracted voters. Republicans appealed to those interested in the economic development of the West.

William Walker and Filibustering

Between 1848 and 1861, the United States was at peace with foreign nations. But that did not stop private citizens, sometimes supported by politicians and businessmen, from launching adventurous attempts to take over foreign lands, especially in Mexico, Central America, and the Caribbean. The 1850s was the heyday of "filibustering," defined in this era as private military expeditions to destabilize or conquer foreign lands in the name of Manifest Destiny, commerce, the spread of slavery and white supremacy, or masculine daring.

At least a dozen filibustering schemes emerged in this era of expansion and sectional crises, all violations of a Neutrality Act of 1818. Such laws did not stop some senators, railroad and shipping entrepreneurs, or the self-styled soldier of fortune, William Walker, from seeking the "Southern dream" of a Latin American empire.

They also did not stop several American presidents from attempting to annex Cuba.

Born in Tennessee, Walker studied in Europe in 1848 before returning to New Orleans for a short stint editing a newspaper. He moved to California, practiced law, and courted conflict by fighting at least three duels. After an ill-fated attempt in 1853 to forcibly create an American "colony" in Sonora and the Baja peninsula in Mexico, Walker turned to Nicaragua, where its isthmus was the fastest route to the California gold fields.

With a small army of mercenaries Walker invaded Nicaragua in 1856, seized its government, declared himself president, and reintroduced slavery, which Nicaragua had banned. Defeated by a coalition of Nicaraguans and British in 1857, Walker returned to the United States and launched a fund-raising and speaking campaign on which he was often treated as a romantic hero. Upon his return to Nicaragua, he was arrested by a U.S. Navy squadron, returned to American soil, tried, and acquitted.

In 1860, Walker published an account of his exploits, *War in Nicaragua*. Famous for his swashbuckling character; Walker was regarded by some as a pirate serving the "Slave Power Conspiracy," and by others as the "grey-eyed man of destiny" advancing slavery and American hegemony. On Walker's third return to Central America in 1860, he was arrested and Honduran authorities executed him by firing squad. These filibustering adventures fired the imagination of Manifest Destiny and were small precursors of a larger United States exploitation and conquest of Latin American in the century to follow. Walker's legend, heroic and notorious, lives on today in Central America and in two American movies, *Burn* (1969), starring Marlon Brando, and *Walker* (1987), starring Ed Harris. Filibusters were links to the world that gave the United States a difficult legacy to overcome with its neighbors from Cuba to Hawaii.

Portrait of William Walker, Tennessee-born filibusterer, a self-styled soldier of fortune who attempted to create his own empire in Nicaragua, where he reinstituted slavery. To some, especially Southerners, he was a romantic hero, but to others, especially Northerners and the U.S. government, he was a notorious villain and arch proponent of the worst aspects of Manifest Destiny.

Library of Congress

Partisan ideological appeals became the currency of the realigned political system. As Republicans preached, "Free Soil, Free Labor, Free Men," they conveyed many northerners' self-image. These phrases resonated with traditional ideals of equality, liberty, and opportunity under self-government—the heritage of republicanism. Invoking that heritage also undercut charges that the Republican Party was radical and abolitionist.

The northern economy was booming, and thousands of migrants moved west to establish farms and communities. Midwesterners multiplied their yields using new machines, such as mechanical reapers. Railroads were carrying their crops to urban markets. And industry was making available goods that had recently been unaffordable for most people.

Republican Ideology

The key to progress appeared, to many people, to be free labor—the dignity of work and the incentive of opportunity. Any hard-working virtuous man, it was thought, could improve his condition and achieve economic independence. Republicans argued that the South, with little industry and slave labor, was backward by comparison.

Traditional republicanism hailed the virtuous common man as the nation's backbone. In Abraham Lincoln, a man of humble origins who became a successful lawyer and political leader, Republicans had a symbol of that tradition. They portrayed their party as the guardian of economic opportunity, giving individuals a chance to work, acquire land, and attain success.

At stake in the crises of the 1850s were two competing definitions of "liberty": southern planters' claims of their liberty to own and transport their slaves nationwide, and northern workers' and farmers' claims of their liberty to seek a new start on free land, unimpeded by a system that defined labor as slave and black.

Opposition to the extension of slavery helped create the Republican Party, but members broadened their appeal by adopting other causes. Their coalition ideology consisted of many elements: resentment of southern political power, devotion to unionism, antislavery based on free-labor arguments, moral revulsion to slavery, and racial prejudice. As *New York Tribune* editor Horace Greeley wrote in 1860, "an Anti-Slavery man per se cannot be elected." But, "a Tariff, River-and-Harbor, Pacific Railroad, Free Homestead man, may succeed although he is Anti-Slavery."

Southern Democrats

In the South, the disintegration of the Whig Party had left many southerners at loose ends politically, including wealthy planters, smaller slaveholders, and urban businessmen. In the tense atmosphere of sectional crisis, southerners were susceptible to strong states' rights positions and the defense of slavery. Hence, most formerly Whig slaveholders became Democrats.

Since Andrew Jackson's day, however, nonslaveholding yeomen had been the heart of the Democratic Party. Democratic politicians, though often slaveowners, lauded the common man and claimed to advance his interests. According to the southern version of republicanism, white citizens in a slave society enjoyed liberty and equality because black people were enslaved. As Jefferson Davis explained in 1851, in the South, slavery elevated every white person to "stand upon the broad level of equality with the rich man." To retain support from ordinary whites, southern Democrats appealed to racism, asking, "Shall negroes govern white men, or white men govern negroes?"

Racial fears and traditional political loyalties kept the political alliance between yeoman farmers and planters intact through the 1850s. Across class lines, white southerners united against what they perceived as the Republican Party's capacity to cause slave unrest. In the South, no viable party emerged to replace the Whigs, and political realignment sharpened sectional identity.

Northern and southern political leaders used race in their arguments about opportunity. The *Montgomery* (Alabama) *Mail* warned southern whites in 1860 that the Republicans intended "to free the negroes" and force amalgamation between them and the children of the poor men of the South. Republicans warned northern workers that, if slavery entered the territories, the great reservoir of opportunity for ordinary citizens would be poisoned.

Bleeding Kansas

The Kansas-Nebraska Act spawned violence as land-hungry partisans clashed in Kansas Territory. Abolitionists and religious groups sent armed Free-Soil settlers; southerners sent reinforcements to establish slavery and prevent "northern hordes" from stealing Kansas. Conflicts led to bloodshed, and soon the nation was talking about "Bleeding Kansas."

Politics in the territory resembled war more than democracy. During 1855 elections for a territorial legislature, thousands of proslavery Missourians—known as Border Ruffians—invaded the polls and ran up a fraudulent majority for proslavery candidates. They murdered and intimidated free state settlers. The resulting legislature legalized slavery. Free-Soilers responded with an unauthorized convention at which they created their own government and constitution.

In May, a proslavery posse sent to arrest the Free-Soil leaders sacked the town of Lawrence, Kansas, killing several people and destroying a hotel. In revenge, the radical abolitionist John Brown and his followers murdered five proslavery settlers along Pottawatomie Creek. The victims' heads and limbs were hacked by heavy broadswords. Brown did not wield a sword, but he fired a fatal shot into the head of one foe. Soon, armed bands of guerrillas battled over land claims and slavery.

Violence reached the U.S. Senate in May 1856, when Charles Sumner of Massachusetts denounced "the Crime against Kansas." Radically opposed to slavery, Sumner assailed the president, the South, and Senator Andrew P. Butler of South Carolina. Butler's cousin, Representative Preston Brooks, approached Sumner, raised his cane in defense of his kin's honor, and beat Sumner on the head. The senator collapsed.

Shocked northerners recoiled from another seeming case of wanton southern violence and assault on free speech. William Cullen Bryant, editor of the *New York Evening Post*, asked, "Has it come to this, that we must speak with bated breath in the presence of our southern masters?" Popular opinion in Massachusetts supported Sumner; South Carolina voters reelected Brooks.

Election of 1856

The election of 1856 showed extreme polarization. For their nominee, Democrats chose James Buchanan of Pennsylvania, who as ambassador to Britain for four years, was uninvolved in territorial controversies. Superior party organization helped Buchanan win 1.8 million votes and the election, but he owed his victory to southern support. Hence, he was dubbed "a northern man with southern principles."

Eleven of sixteen free states voted against Buchanan, and Democrats did not regain those states for decades. The Republican candidate, John C. Frémont, won those eleven free states and 1.3 million votes; Republicans became the dominant party in the North after only two years of existence. The coming battle would pit a sectional Republican Party against an increasingly divided Democratic Party, with voter turnouts as high as 75 to 80 percent in many states.

Slavery and the Nation's Future

For years, Congress tried to settle the issue. In 1857, the Supreme Court attempted to definitively silence controversy.

How did the issue of slavery—and the *Dred Scott* decision—further divide the nation?

Dred Scott Case

A Missouri slave named Dred Scott and his wife, Harriet Robinson Scott, sued for their freedom. Scott argued that his former owner, an army surgeon, had taken him into and kept him for years in Illinois, a free state, and to Fort Snelling in the Minnesota Territory, from which slavery was barred by the Missouri Compromise. Scott first won and then lost his case on appeal in the Supreme Court.

Harriet and Dred Scott were legally married at Fort Snelling in 1836 when Dred was forty and Harriet seventeen. She had lived as a slave on free soil for about five years and had four children, also born on free soil: two sons who died in infancy and two daughters, Eliza and Lizzie, who lived. The quest for "freedom papers" through a lawsuit—begun in 1846 as two separate cases, one in his name and one in hers—possibly came partly from Harriet's desire to protect her teenage daughters from potential sale and sexual abuse. Indeed, her legal case for freedom may have been stronger than Dred's, but lawyers subsumed her case into his during the long appeal process.

After hesitation, the Supreme Court agreed to hear *Dred Scott v. Sanford.* Two northern justices indicated that they would dissent from the assigned opinion and argue for Scott's freedom and the constitutionality of the Missouri Compromise. Their decision emboldened southerners on the Court, who were eager to declare the 1820 geographical restriction on slavery unconstitutional. Several justices felt they should resolve sectional strife once and for all.

In March 1857, Chief Justice Roger B. Taney of Maryland delivered the majority opinion of a divided Court (the vote was 7 to 2). Taney declared that Scott was not a citizen of the United States or Missouri; that residence in free territory did not make Scott free; and that Congress had no power to bar slavery from any territory. The decision not only overturned a thirty-seven year-old sectional compromise, it also invalidated the Wilmot Proviso and popular sovereignty.

The Slave Power seemed to have won a major constitutional victory. African Americans were especially dismayed, for Taney's decision asserted that the founders had never intended for blacks to be citizens. Taney was mistaken, however. African Americans had been citizens in several original states and had voted.

Nevertheless, the ruling seemed to shut the door permanently on black hopes for justice. In northern

Link to excerpts from Chief Justice Roger B. Taney's ruling in the *Dred Scott* case.

Library of Congress

Frank Leslie's *Illustrated Newspaper*, June 27, 1857. Dred Scott and his wife, Harriet, below, and their two children, Eliza and Lizzie, above. Such dignified pictures and informative articles provided Americans broadly with images of the otherwise mysterious Dred Scott and his family in the landmark Supreme Court case.

Dred Scott decision: Controversial 1857 Supreme Court decision that stated that slaves were not U.S. citizens and had no legal right to sue in federal court. It also deemed the Missouri Compromise unconstitutional because Congress lacked the authority to ban slavery in the territories.

black communities, rage and despair prevailed. Many fugitive slaves sought refuge in Canada; others considered the Caribbean or Africa. One black abolitionist said that the **Dred Scott decision** made slavery "the supreme law of the land." In this state of social dislocation and fear, blacks contemplated whether they had any future in the United States.

Northern whites who rejected the decision were suspicious of the circumstances that produced it. Five of the nine justices were southerners; three northern justices dissented or refused to concur in parts of the decision. The only northerner who supported Taney's opinion, Justice Robert Grier of Pennsylvania, was close to President Buchanan. In fact, Buchanan secretly applied improper but effective influence on him.

The decision seemed to confirm every charge against the aggressive Slave Power. The *Cincinnati Freeman* asked, "What security have the Germans and the Irish that their children will not, within a hundred years, be reduced to slavery in this land of their adoption?"

Abraham Lincoln and the Slave Power

Republican politicians used these fears to strengthen their antislavery coalition. Abraham Lincoln declared as early as 1854 that the nation wanted the territories reserved as "homes of free white people. This they cannot be, to any considerable extent, if slavery shall be planted within them."

More important, Lincoln warned of slavery's increasing control over the nation. While the founders recognized slavery's existence, the public, Lincoln argued in the "House Divided" speech of 1858, believed that slavery would die naturally or by legislation. The next step in the unfolding Slave Power conspiracy, Lincoln alleged, would be a Supreme Court decision "declaring that the Constitution does not permit a State to exclude slavery from its limits." Indeed, lawsuits soon challenged state laws that freed slaves brought within their borders.

By endorsing the South's doctrine of state sovereignty, the Court had effectively declared that the Republican Party's central position—no extension of slavery—was unconstitutional. Republicans could only repudiate the decision, appealing to a "higher law," or hope to change the personnel of the Court. They did both and gained politically as fear of the Slave Power grew.

The Lecompton Constitution and Disharmony Among Democrats

Northern voters were alarmed by the prospect that the territories would be opened to slavery. To retain their support, northern Democrats like Stephen Douglas had to reassure these voters. Yet, given his presidential ambitions, Douglas could not alienate southern Democrats.

Douglas chose to stand by popular sovereignty, even if the result angered southerners. In 1857, Kansans voted on a proslavery constitution drafted at Lecompton. It was defeated by more than ten thousand votes in a referendum boycotted by proslavery voters. Kansans did not want slavery, yet President Buchanan tried to force the Lecompton Constitution through Congress to hastily organize the territory.

Never had the Slave Power's influence over the government seemed more blatant; the Buchanan administration and southerners demanded a proslavery outcome, contrary to majority will in Kansas. Douglas threw his weight against the Lecompton Constitution, infuriating southern Democrats like Senator Albert G. Brown of Mississippi. Increasingly, many southerners believed that their sectional rights and slavery would be safe only in a separate nation. And northern Democrats, led by Douglas, found it harder to support the territorial protection for slavery that southern Democrats insisted was a constitutional right.

Disunion

But in the late 1850s, most Americans were not entirely caught up in the slavery crisis. They were preoccupied with personal affairs, especially the economic panic that began in spring 1857. In the Midwest, clerks, mechanics, domestics, railroad hands, and lumber camp workers lost jobs by the thousands. Bankers did not know what to do about a weak credit system caused by frenzied western land speculation earlier in the decade. In parts of the South, such as Georgia, the panic intensified class divisions between upcountry yeomen and coastal slaveholding planters. Farmers blamed the tight money policies of Georgia's budding commercial banking system on wealthy planters who controlled the state's Democratic Party.

> What were the issues leading to secession and the dissolution of the Union?

The panic was caused by several shortcomings of the unregulated American banking system, by speculation in western lands and railroads, and by a weak and overburdened credit system. By 1858, Philadelphia had 40,000 unemployed workers and New York City, nearly 100,000. Fear of bread riots and class warfare gripped many northern cities. Blame for the crisis became sectionalized, as southerners saw their system justified by the temporary collapse of industrial prosperity and northerners feared further incursions of the Slave Power on an insecure future.

John Brown's Raid on Harpers Ferry

Born in Connecticut in 1800, John Brown was raised by staunchly religious antislavery parents. Between 1820 and 1855, he engaged in some twenty business ventures, nearly all of them failures. In his abolitionism, Brown relied on an Old Testament conception of justice—"an eye for an eye"—and he believed that slavery was an "unjustifiable" state of war conducted by one group against another. He also believed that violence in a righteous cause was a holy act. To Brown, the destruction of slavery in America required revolutionary ideology and revolutionary acts.

On October 16, 1859, Brown led a small band of eighteen whites and blacks in an attack on the federal arsenal at Harpers Ferry, Virginia. Hoping to trigger a slave rebellion, Brown failed and was quickly captured. In a celebrated trial in November and a widely publicized execution in December in Charles Town, Virginia, Brown became one of the most enduring martyrs, as well as villains, of American history.

White southerners outrage intensified when they learned that Brown received financial backing from several prominent abolitionists and that such northern intellectuals as Ralph Waldo Emerson and Henry David Thoreau praised Brown as a holy warrior. The South interpreted Brown's attack at Harpers Ferry as an act of terrorism and the fulfillment of their dread of "abolition emissaries" who would infiltrate the region to incite slave rebellion.

When Brown went to the gallows, he handed a note to his jailer with the famous prediction "I John Brown am now quite certain that the crimes of this guilty land will never be purged away, but with blood."

Election of 1860

Many Americans believed that the election of 1860 would decide the Union's fate. Until then, the Democratic Party was the only party that was truly national in scope. But, fatefully, at its 1860 convention in Charleston, South Carolina, the Democratic Party split.

Stephen Douglas wanted his party's presidential nomination, but he feared alienating northern voters by accepting the southern position on the territories. Southern Democrats, however, insisted on recognition of their rights as defined by the *Dred Scott* decision. When Douglas obtained a majority for his version of the

TABLE 14.3   Presidential Votes in 1860 (by State)

Lincoln (Republican)*	Carried all northern states and all electoral votes except three in New Jersey
Breckinridge (Southern Democrat)	Carried all slave states except Virginia, Kentucky, Tennessee, Missouri
Bell (Constitutional Union)	Carried Virginia, Kentucky, Tennessee
Douglas (Northern Democrat)	Carried only Missouri

*Lincoln received only twenty-six thousand votes in the entire South and was not even on the ballot in ten slave states. Breckinridge was not on the ballot in three northern states.

platform, delegates from the Deep South walked out. Compromise efforts failed, and the Democrats presented two nominees: Douglas for the northern wing, and Vice President John C. Breckinridge of Kentucky for the southern.

Republicans nominated Abraham Lincoln, a reflection of the Midwest's growing power. Lincoln was perceived as more moderate on slavery than the early front runner, Senator William H. Seward of New York. A Constitutional Union Party nominated John Bell of Tennessee.

Bell's only issue in the ensuing campaign was preserving the Union. Douglas sought to unite his northern and southern supporters, while Breckinridge backed away from the appearance of extremism, and his supporters in several states stressed his unionism. Although Lincoln and the Republicans denied any intent to interfere with slavery where it existed, they stood firm against its extension into the territories.

The 1860 election was sectional in character, and the only one in American history in which the losers refused to accept the result. Lincoln won, but Douglas, Breckinridge, and Bell together received a majority of the votes. Douglas had broad-based support but won few states. Breckinridge carried nine southern states in the Deep South. Bell won pluralities in Virginia, Kentucky, and Tennessee. Lincoln prevailed in the North, but in the four slave states that remained loyal to the Union (Missouri, Kentucky, Maryland, and Delaware—the border states) he gained only a plurality (see Table 14.3. Lincoln's victory was won in the electoral college. He polled only 40 percent of the total vote and was not on the ballot in ten slave states.

Opposition to slavery's extension was the core issue for Lincoln and the Republican Party. Moreover, northern abolitionists and Free-Soil supporters held them to it. Meanwhile, in the South, proslavery advocates and secessionists whipped up public opinion and demanded that state conventions assemble to consider secession.

Lincoln did not soften his party's position on the territories. Although many conservative Republicans—eastern businessmen and former Whigs who did not feel strongly about slavery—hoped for a compromise, the original and most committed Republicans—old Free-Soilers and antislavery Whigs—held firm on slavery expansion.

In winter 1860–1861, Senator John J. Crittenden of Kentucky offered a late-hour compromise. Hoping to avert disunion, Crittenden proposed that the two sections divide the territories between them at the Missouri Compromise line, 36°30'. When Lincoln ruled out concessions on the territorial issue, Crittenden's peacemaking effort collapsed.

Secession and the Confederate States of America

Meanwhile, on December 20, 1860, South Carolina passed an ordinance of secession. Strategists concentrated on the most extreme proslavery state, hoping that South Carolina's move would induce other states to follow toward disunion.

No longer was secession unthinkable. Secessionists now argued that other states should follow suit and that those favoring compromise could make a better deal outside the Union than in it.

Southern extremists called separate state conventions and passed secession ordinances in Mississippi, Florida, Alabama, Georgia, Louisiana, and Texas. By February 1861, these states joined South Carolina to form a new government in Montgomery, Alabama: the Confederate States of America. The delegates at Montgomery chose Jefferson Davis of Mississippi as their president, and the Confederacy began to function independently of the United States.

This apparent unanimity of action was deceiving. Many southerners—perhaps as much as 40 percent even in the deep South—opposed immediate secession. In some state conventions the secession vote was close, decided by overrepresentation of plantation districts. Four Upper South states—Virginia, North Carolina, Tennessee, and Arkansas—rejected secession and did not join the Confederacy until after fighting began. In border states, popular sentiment was divided; minorities in Kentucky and Missouri tried to secede, but these slave states ultimately came under Union control, along with Maryland and Delaware (see Map 14.2).

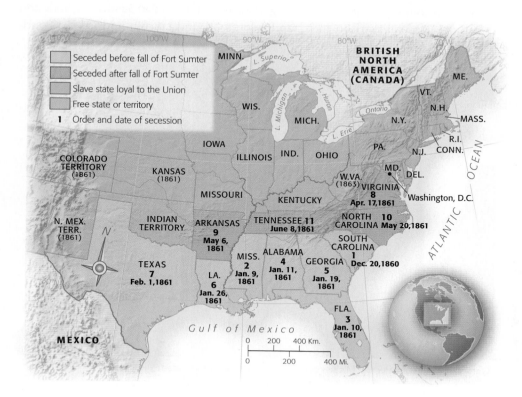

MAP 14.2

The Divided Nation—Slave and Free Areas, 1861

After fighting began, the Upper South joined the Deep South in the Confederacy. How does the nation's pattern of division correspond to the distribution of slavery and the percentage of blacks in the population?

Source: Copyright © Cengage Learning

Secession posed new and troubling issues for southerners. Analysis of election returns from 1860 and 1861 indicates that slaveholders and nonslaveholders were beginning to part company politically. Slaveholding counties strongly supported secession. But nonslaveholding areas proved less willing to support secession" (see Figure 14.1). With war looming, yeomen were beginning to ask themselves how far they would go to support slavery and slaveowners.

In speeches and writings, secession commissioners from the seven seceded states revealed why the Deep South broke away. Repeatedly they stressed independence as the only way to preserve white racial security and the slave system. Upon "slavery," said the Alabama commissioner, Stephen Hale, to the Kentucky legislature, rested "not only the wealth and prosperity of the southern people." Only secession, Hale contended, could sustain the "heaven-ordained superiority of the white over the black race."

Fort Sumter and Outbreak of War

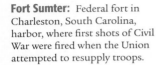

Fort Sumter: Federal fort in Charleston, South Carolina, harbor, where first shots of Civil War were fired when the Union attempted to resupply troops.

The dilemma facing President Lincoln on inauguration day in March 1861 was how to maintain the authority of the federal government without provoking war. By holding onto forts in the states that had left the Union, he could assert federal sovereignty while waiting for a restoration. But Jefferson Davis could not claim to lead a sovereign nation if the Confederate ports were under foreign (that is, U.S.) control. The two sides collided in the early morning of April 12, 1861, at **Fort Sumter** in Charleston harbor. A federal garrison there ran low on food, and Lincoln notified the South

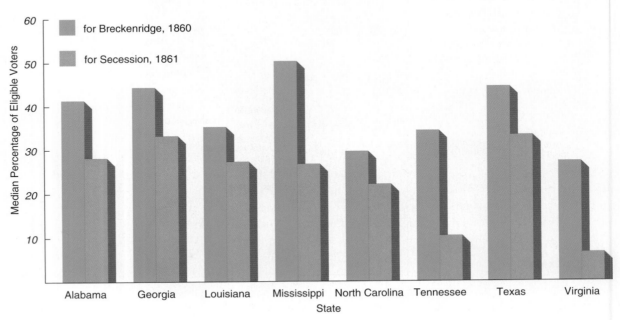

FIGURE 14.1
Voting Returns of Counties with Few Slaveholders, Eight Southern States, 1860 and 1861
This graph depicts voting in counties whose percentage of slaveholders ranked them among the lower half of the counties in their state. How does voters' support for secession in 1861 compare with support for John Breckinridge, the southern Democratic candidate in 1860? Why was their support for secession so weak? At this time, counties with many slaveholders were giving increased support to secession.

Terrorist or Freedom Fighter?

The greatest significance of John Brown's 1859 raid on Harpers Ferry rests in its hold on American memory. Brown has been at once one of the most beloved and loathed figures in American history. In the song that bears his name, "John Brown's Body," a popular marching tune during the Civil War, his "soul goes marching on."

In the wake of his execution, in painting, song, and poetry people constructed a John Brown mythology. Was he a Christ-like figure who died for the nation's sins, who had to commit crimes to expose the nation's larger crime? Or was he a terrorist, who murdered according to his vision of God's will? Brown can be inspiring and disturbing, a warrior saint and a monster. He represents the highest ideals and the most ruthless deeds. He killed for justice and was hanged as a traitor. Over the years, many organizations have adopted John Brown as their justifying symbol, from left-wing students opposing American foreign policy to current anti-abortion groups who target clinics and doctors.

In today's world, terrorism and revolutionary violence are often in the news. Suicide bombers attack buses in Israel; a federal building explodes in Oklahoma City; Al Qaeda operatives blow up trains in Madrid; American embassies are attacked in Africa and Europe; on September 11, 2001, four hijacked passenger airplanes become weapons of death that bring terrorism to American soil as never before; and in Iraq an insurgency resists the American occupation, as a country falls into sectarian civil war between Shi'ites and Sunnis. The story of John Brown's 1859 raid forces us to ask when and how revolutionary violence—for political or spiritual end—is justified. That is his legacy for a people and a nation.

Carolinians that he was sending a supply ship. For the Montgomery government, the alternatives were to attack the fort or acquiesce to Lincoln's authority. The secretary of war ordered local commanders to obtain a surrender or attack the fort. After two days of heavy bombardment, the federal garrison surrendered. Confederates permitted U.S. troops to sail away on unarmed vessels while Charlestonians celebrated. The Civil War—the bloodiest war in America's history—had begun.

Causation Historians have long debated the causes of the Civil War. Some have interpreted it as a clash of two civilizations on divergent historical trajectories. But the issues dividing Americans in 1861 were fundamental to the republic's future. Republican ideology tended toward abolishing slavery, even though Republicans denied such intention. Southern ideology led to establishing slavery everywhere, though southern leaders, too, denied such motives.

Lincoln put these facts succinctly. In a postelection letter to his colleague, Alexander Stephens of Georgia, soon to be vice president of the Confederacy, Lincoln stated, "You think slavery is right and ought to be expanded; while we think it is wrong and ought to be restricted. That I suppose is the rub."

Without slavery, there would have been no war. Many Americans still believe that the war was about states' rights. But the significance of states' rights is always in the cause in which it is employed. To borrow from Frederick Douglass, it is the meaning within the fight that we must understand.

Summary

The War with Mexico fostered massive land acquisition, which forced an open debate about slavery in the West. The Compromise of 1850 attempted to settle the dispute but only exacerbated sectional tensions, leading to the fateful Kansas-Nebraska Act of 1854, which tore asunder the political party system and gave birth to an antislavery coalition. With Bleeding Kansas and the *Dred Scott* decision by 1857, Americans faced clear and dangerous choices about the future of labor and the meaning of liberty in an expanding society. Finally, by 1859, when radical abolitionist John Brown attacked Harpers Ferry to foment a slave insurrection, southerners and northerners regarded each other in conspiratorial terms. Meanwhile, African Americans, slave and free, feared slave catchers and expected violent resolutions to their dreams of freedom in America.

Throughout the 1840s and 1850s, many leaders worked to avert disunion. Secession dismayed northern editors and voters, and it also plunged some planters into depression. Paul Cameron, the largest slaveowner in North Carolina, confessed to being "very unhappy. I love the Union." Many blacks, however, shared Frederick Douglass's outlook. "The contest must now be decided," he wrote in March 1861, "and decided forever, which of the two, Freedom or Slavery, shall give law to this Republic."

Why had all efforts to prevent war failed? The emotions bound up in attacking and defending slavery's future were too powerful, and the interests it affected too vital for a compromise. Advocates of compromise anticipated it would yet again save the Union in 1860, but their hopes were dashed.

During the 1850s, every southern victory in territorial expansion increased fear of the Slave Power, and each new expression of Free-Soil sentiment prompted slaveholders to harden their demands. In the profoundest sense, slavery was the root of the war. As a people and a nation, Americans reached the most fateful turning point in their history. Resolution would now come from the battlefield.

Chapter Review

The War with Mexico and Its Consequences

Which of Polk's decisions pushed the United States toward war with Mexico?

President Polk wanted to expand America's borders to the Pacific during the 1840s and was not going to take "no" for an answer. He supported annexation of Texas and contested the U.S. border with Mexico, urging Texans to claim territory to the Rio Grande. Mexico had considered the Nueces River its border with Texas. While unsuccessfully attempting to buy California from Mexico, Polk also sent troops to defend the Rio Grande dividing line. There, they were met by Mexican cavalry. After a three week stand-off, the Mexican cavalry ambushed a U.S. unit, killing eleven Americans and taking sixty-three captive. Polk informed Congress that Mexico had crossed what he considered the U.S. boundary (the disputed area), and thereby deceptively claimed that Mexico had incited the conflict that would become the war with Mexico.

1850: Compromise or Armistice?

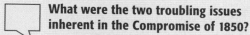

What were the two troubling issues inherent in the Compromise of 1850?

The Compromise of 1850 attempted to resolve the debate between the North and South over slavery in the territories. In the end, it only furthered controversy. First, it left the definition of popular sovereignty unclear so that southerners could interpret it to mean that a region could not ban slavery during the territorial stage, whereas northerners believed it was up to the people to decide. Second, the Fugitive Slave Act enabled slave owners to present evidence in state courts that a slave had escaped, which would then serve as proof of slave status even in free states and territories—and without investigation into its truth. Abolitionists feared that free blacks would be vulnerable to kidnapping and enslavement. Moreover, the law made it a felony to harbor fugitives and said northerners could be compelled to hunt runaway slaves, which further angered northerners and aggravated regional tensions.

Slavery Expansion and Collapse of the Party System

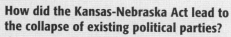

How did the Kansas-Nebraska Act lead to the collapse of existing political parties?

The Kansas-Nebraska Act, which ultimately eroded the 1850 Compromise, prompted sectional divisions within the political parties that led to each party's breakdown. The act established the Kansas and Nebraska territories, but it applied popular sovereignty to let the territories decide what to do about slavery. Northerners argued that since the territories were within the Louisiana Purchase, they were subject to the Missouri Compromise (which prohibited slavery from latitude 36°30 north to the Canadian border). When the Act was passed in 1854, sectional divisions intensified. The weakened Whig Party split into northern and southern wings. Democrats' support in the North plummeted, costing them most of their congressional seats and control of all but two state legislatures. In late 1854, antislavery Whigs and Democrats, Free-Soilers, and reformers throughout the Old Northwest formed the new Republican Party to keep slavery from the territories.

Slavery and the Nation's Future

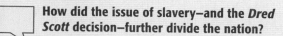

How did the issue of slavery—and the *Dred Scott* decision—further divide the nation?

The *Dred Scott* decision validated northern fears of a southern slave power, and inspired new fears about the territories being open to slavery. The Supreme Court was ultimately stacked in favor of the southern position on slavery and its extension into the new territories. Five of the nine justices were southerners. The court's decision in the *Dred Scott* case—that Scott was a slave despite the fact that he lived in the free territory of Missouri and that Congress could not make any laws that barred slavery—invalidated popular sovereignty, the Wilmot Proviso, and the Missouri Compromise. African Americans were devastated by the court's opinion that the nation's founders had never intended them to be citizens, while white northerners saw the decision as proof of the Slave Power's growing reach.

Disunion

What were the issues leading to secession and the dissolution of the Union?

Abraham Lincoln's contested election by his Democratic rivals, along with the inability to reach a compromise on the extension of slavery in the territories, ultimately fueled the movement to secede. Lincoln, the Republican candidate, won by carrying the North and winning in the Electoral College, but the losing side (with its large southern base) refused to accept the result. Southern Democrats distrusted his claims that he would not interfere with slavery where it existed, and disliked his firm rejection of slavery's expansion into the territories. When President Lincoln rejected a compromise that would divide the territories into slave and free at the Missouri Compromise line (36°30'), hopes for preventing secession collapsed. South Carolina passed the first secession ordinance in December 1860; Mississippi, Florida, Alabama, Georgia, Louisiana, and Texas followed. A month after Lincoln's inauguration, these states established their own national capitol in Montgomery, Alabama, dubbing themselves the Confederate States of America.

Suggestions for Further Reading

Edward L. Ayers, *What Caused the Civil War: Reflections on the South and Southern History* (2005)

Richard J. Carwardine, *Lincoln* (2003)

Charles Dew, *Apostles of Disunion: Southern Secession Commissioners and the Causes of the Civil War* (2001)

Nicole Etcheson, *Bleeding Kansas: Contested Liberty in the Civil War Era* (2004)

Don E. Fehrenbacher, *The Slaveholding Republic: An Account of the United States Government's Relations to Slavery* (2001)

Eric Foner, *Free Soil, Free Labor, Free Men: The Ideology of the Republican Party* (1970)

Robert W. Johannsen, *To the Halls of the Montezumas: The Mexican War and the American Imagination* (1985)

Marc Egnal, *Clash of Extremes: The Economic Origins of the Civil War* (2009)

David S. Reynolds, *John Brown, Abolitionist: The Man Who Killed Slavery, Sparked the Civil War, and Seeded Civil Rights* (2005)

Elizabeth R. Varon, *Disunion! The Coming of the American Civil War, 1789–1859* (2008)

**CourseMate**　Go to the CourseMate website for primary source links, study tools, and review materials for this chapter. www.cengagebrain.com

Transforming Fire: The Civil War

15

1861–1865

Slave pens were the ugly crossroads of American history. Wallace Turnage, a seventeen-year-old slave from a cotton plantation in Pickens County, Alabama, entered wartime Mobile in December 1862 through the slave traders' yard; he would leave Mobile from that same yard twenty months later.

Turnage was born on a tobacco farm near Snow Hill, North Carolina, in 1846. In mid-1860, as the nation teetered toward disunion, he was sold to a Richmond, Virginia, slave trader named Hector Davis. Turnage worked in Davis's three-story slave jail, organizing daily auctions until he was sold for $1,000 in early 1861 to a cotton planter from Pickens County, Alabama. Frequently whipped, the desperate teenager tried four times over the next two years to escape to Union army lines in Mississippi. He was captured each time and returned to his owner.

Frustrated, his owner sold Turnage for $2,000 at the Mobile slave traders' yard to a wealthy merchant in the port city. During 1864, as Mobile came under siege, its slaves were enlisted to build trenchworks. Turnage did many urban tasks for his new owner's family, including driving their carriage on errands.

In early August, Turnage crashed the carriage on a Mobile street. Furious, his owner took him to the slave pen, hiring the jailer to administer thirty lashes in the "whipping house." Stripped naked, his hands tied, Turnage was hoisted up on a hook. When it was over, his owner instructed Wallace to walk home. Instead, Turnage "took courage," as he wrote in his postwar narrative, and walked southwest through the Confederate encampment. The soldiers mistook the bloodied and tattered black teenager for one among hundreds of slaves who did camp labor.

For the next three weeks, Turnage crawled and waded for twenty-five miles through the snake-infested swamps of the Foul River estuary, down the west edge of Mobile Bay. Nearly starved and narrowly escaping Confederate patrols, Turnage made it to Cedar Point, where he could see Dauphin Island, now occupied by Union forces. Alligators swam nearby, as Turnage hid from

Chapter Outline

America Goes to War, 1861–1862
First Battle of Bull Run | Grand Strategy | Union Naval Campaign | War in the Far West | Grant's Tennessee Campaign and the Battle of Shiloh | McClellan and the Peninsula Campaign | Confederate Offensive in Maryland and Kentucky

War Transforms the South
The Confederacy and Centralization | Confederate Nationalism | Southern Cities and Industry | Changing Roles of Women | Human Suffering, Hoarding, and Inflation | Inequities of the Confederate Draft

Wartime Northern Economy and Society
Northern Business, Industry, and Agriculture | The Quartermaster and Military-Government Mobilization | Northern Workers' Militancy | Economic Nationalism and Government-Business Partnership | The Union Cause | Northern Women on Home Front and Battlefront | Walt Whitman's War

The Advent of Emancipation
Lincoln and Emancipation | Confiscation Acts | Emancipation Proclamations | African American Recruits | Who Freed the Slaves? | A Confederate Plan of Emancipation

The Soldiers' War
Hospitals and Camp Life | The Rifled Musket | The Black Soldier's Fight for Manhood

VISUALIZING THE PAST *Black Soldiers in the Civil War*

1863: The Tide of Battle Turns
Battle of Chancellorsville | Siege of Vicksburg | Battle of Gettysburg

Disunity: South, North, and West
Union Occupation Zones | Disintegration of Confederate Unity | Food Riots in Southern Cities | Desertions from the Confederate Army | Antiwar Sentiment, South and North | Peace Democrats | New York City Draft Riots | War Against Indians in the Far West | Election of 1864

1864–1865: The Final Test of Wills
Northern Diplomatic Strategy | Battlefield Stalemate and a Union Strategy for Victory | Fall of Atlanta | Sherman's March to the Sea | Virginia's Bloody Soil | Surrender at Appomattox | Financial Tally | Death Toll and its Impact

LINKS TO THE WORLD *The Civil War in Britain*

LEGACY FOR A PEOPLE AND A NATION *Abraham Lincoln's "Second Inaugural Address"*

SUMMARY

Confederates in a swampy den. He remembered: "It was death to go back and it was death to stay there and freedom was before me."

Then, Turnage noticed an old rowboat that rolled in with the tide. The veteran runaway began to row out into the bay. He suddenly "heard the crash of oars and behold there was eight Yankees in a boat." Turnage jumped into the Union gunboat. For a few moments, he remembered, the oarsmen in blue "were struck with silence" by the frail young black man crouched before them. Turnage looked back at Confederate soldiers on the shore. Then he took his first breaths of freedom.

The Civil War brought astonishing changes to individuals and daily life, North and South. Millions of men were swept into training camps and regiments. Armies numbering in the hundreds of thousands marched over the South, devastating the countryside. Families struggled to survive without men; businesses tried to cope with fewer workers. Women took on extra responsibilities and moved into new work force jobs, with many becoming nurses and hospital workers. But southerners also experienced utter defeat. For most, wealth changed to poverty as countless farms were ruined. Late in the war, many southerners yearned only for an end to inflation, shortages, slave escapes, and the death that visited most families. Southern slaves did not always encounter sympathetic liberators such as those who aided Turnage, fed and clothed him, and took him before a Union general, where the freedman could either join a black regiment or become a white officer's camp servant. Until war's end, Turnage cooked for a Maryland captain.

In the North, farm boys and mechanics would be asked for heretofore unimagined sacrifices. The conflict ensured vast government expenditures and lucrative federal contracts. Businessmen, however, found war profitable. "The battle of Bull Run," predicted an eminent financier in *Harper's Monthly*, "makes the fortune of every man in Wall Street who is not a natural idiot."

Change was most drastic in the South, where secessionists had launched a conservative revolution for their section's independence. Born of states' rights doctrine, the Confederacy had to be transformed into a centralized nation to fight a vast war. Southern whites feared that a peacetime government of Republicans would interfere with slavery and ruin plantation life. Instead, their actions led to a war that turned southern society upside down and imperiled the existence of slavery.

The war created social strains in both North and South. To the alarm of many, the powers of the federal government and of the president increased during the war. Disaffection was strongest, though, in the Confederacy, where poverty and class resentment threatened the South from within. In the North, dissent also flourished, and antiwar sentiment occasionally erupted into violence.

The Civil War forced a social and political revolution regarding race. It compelled leaders and citizens to finally face the question of slavery. And blacks embraced the most fundamental turning point in their experience as Americans.

As you read this chapter, keep the following questions in mind:

* How and why did the Civil War bring social transformations to both South and North?

* How did the war to preserve the Union or for southern independence become the war to free the slaves?

* By 1865, when Americans on all sides searched for the *meaning* of the war they had just fought, what might some of their answers have been?

America Goes to War, 1861–1862

The onset of hostilities sparked patriotic sentiments, speeches, and ceremonies in both North and South. Northern communities raised companies of volunteers eager to save the Union. Southern recruits boasted of whipping the Yankees and returning home before Christmas. Southern women sewed dashing uniforms for men who would soon be lucky to wear drab gray or butternut homespun. Americans went to war in 1861 filled with romantic notions.

> What was the impact of the North's naval victories along the southern coast?

First Battle of Bull Run Through spring 1861, both sides scrambled to organize and train their undisciplined armies. On July 21, 1861, the first battle took place outside Manassas Junction, Virginia, near a stream called **Bull Run**. General Irvin McDowell and thirty thousand Union troops attacked General P. G. T. Beauregard's twenty-two thousand southerners. Federal forces gained ground until they ran into a line of Virginia troops under General Thomas Jackson. Jackson's line held, and the arrival of nine thousand Confederate reinforcements won the day for the South. Union troops fled to Washington.

Bull Run: The location of the first major land battle in the Civil War.

The unexpected rout at Bull Run proved that although the United States enjoyed an advantage in resources, victory would not be easy. Pro-Union feeling was growing in western Virginia, and loyalties were divided in the four border slave states—Missouri, Kentucky, Maryland, and Delaware. But the rest of the Upper South—North Carolina, Virginia, Tennessee, and Arkansas—joined the Confederacy after Fort Sumter. Half a million southerners volunteered to fight—so many that the Confederate government could hardly arm them all. The United States therefore undertook a massive mobilization of troops around Washington, D.C.

Lincoln gave command of the army to General **George B. McClellan**, who proved better at organization and training than fighting. McClellan devoted fall and winter of 1861 to readying a force of a quarter-million men take Richmond, the Confederate capital.

George B. McClellan: Union general very popular with troops who proved better at organization and training than at fighting.

Grand Strategy While McClellan prepared, the Union began to implement other parts of its strategy, which called for a blockade of southern ports and capture of the Mississippi River. Like a constricting snake, this **"Anaconda plan"** would strangle the Confederacy. The Union Navy had too few ships to patrol 3,550 miles of the southern coastline. Gradually, the navy increased the blockade's effectiveness, though it never stopped southern commerce completely.

Anaconda plan: Called for the Union to blockade southern ports, capture the Mississippi River, and, like a snake, strangle the Confederacy.

Chronology

1861 Battle of Bull Run McClellan organizes Union Army Union blockade begins U.S. Congress passes first confiscation act *Trent* affair	African American soldiers join Union Army Food riots occur in southern cities Battle of Chancellorsville ends in Confederate victory but Jackson's death Union wins key victories at Vicksburg and Gettysburg Draft riots take place in New York City
1862 Union captures Fort Henry and Fort Donelson U.S. Navy captures New Orleans Battle of Shiloh shows the war's destructiveness Confederacy enacts conscription McClellan's peninsula campaign fails to take Richmond U.S. Congress passes second confiscation act, initiating emancipation Confederacy mounts offensive in Maryland and Kentucky Battle of Antietam ends Lee's drive into Maryland in September British intervention in the war on Confederate side is averted	**1864** Battles of the Wilderness and Spotsylvania produce heavy casualties on both sides Battle of Cold Harbor continues carnage in Virginia Sherman captures Atlanta Confederacy begins to collapse on home front Lincoln wins reelection, eliminating any Confederate hopes for negotiated end to war Jefferson Davis proposes arming slaves Sherman marches through Georgia to the sea
1863 Emancipation Proclamation takes effect U.S. Congress passes National Banking Act Union enacts conscription	**1865** Sherman marches through Carolinas U.S. Congress approves Thirteenth Amendment Lee abandons Richmond and Petersburg Lee surrenders at Appomattox Court House Lincoln assassinated Death toll in war reaches 620,000

The Confederate strategy was essentially defensive, given the South's claim of independence and the North's resource advantage (see Figure 15.1). But Jefferson Davis called the southern strategy an "offensive defensive," taking advantage of opportunities to attack and using its interior transportation lines to concentrate troops at crucial points. The Confederacy did not need to conquer the North; the Union effort, however, required conquest of the South.

Both sides slighted the importance of the West, that vast expanse between Virginia and the Mississippi River and beyond. Guerrilla warfare broke out in 1861 in the politically divided Missouri, and key locations along the Mississippi and other western rivers would prove crucial prizes in the North's eventual victory. Beyond the Mississippi, the Confederacy hoped to gain an advantage by negotiating treaties with the Creeks, Choctaws, Chickasaws, Cherokees, Seminoles, and smaller groups of Plains Indians. Meanwhile, the Republican U.S. Congress carved the West into territories in anticipation of state making. For most Indians west of the Mississippi, the Civil War was nearly three decades of an enveloping strategy of conquest, relocation, and slaughter.

Union Naval Campaign   The last half of 1861 brought no major land battles, but in late summer, Union naval forces captured Cape Hatteras and Hilton Head, one of the Sea Islands off Port Royal, South Carolina. A few months later, federal naval operations established significant beachheads along the Confederate coastline, including vital points in North Carolina, as well as Fort Pulaski, which defended Savannah.

FIGURE 15.1
Comparative Resources, Union and Confederate States, 1861
The North had vastly superior resources. Although the North's advantages in manpower and industrial capacity proved very important, the South still had to be conquered, its society and its will crushed.
Source: The Times Atlas of World History. Used with permission.

The coastal victories off South Carolina foreshadowed a revolution in slave society. As federal gunboats approached, planters abandoned their land and fled. The Confederate cavalry tried to round up slaves and move them to the interior. But thousands of slaves greeted what they hoped to be freedom with rejoicing and broke the hated cotton gins. Some entered their masters' homes and took clothing and furniture. Many runaways poured into Union lines. Unwilling at first to wage a war against slavery, the federal government did not acknowledge the slaves' freedom—though it used their labor. These emancipated slaves, defined by Union officers as war "contraband" (confiscated enemy property), forced first a debate within the Union Army and government over how to treat the freedmen, and then a forthright attempt to harness their labor and military power.

Spring 1862 brought southerners stronger evidence of the war's gravity. In March, two ironclad ships—the *Monitor* (a Union warship) and the *Merrimack* (a Union ship seized by the Confederacy)—fought off the coast of Virginia. Their battle, though indecisive, ushered in a new era in naval design. In April, Union ships commanded by Admiral David Farragut smashed through log booms blocking the Mississippi River and moved upstream to capture New Orleans. The South's greatest seaport and slave-trading center was now in federal hands.

War in the Far West Farther west, three full Confederate regiments were organized, mostly of Cherokees, but a Union victory at Elkhorn Tavern, Arkansas, shattered southern control of the region. Thereafter, dissension within Native American groups and a Union victory the following year at Honey Springs, Arkansas, reduced Confederate operations in Indian Territory to guerrilla raids.

In the westernmost campaign of the war, from February to May 1862, some three thousand Confederate and four thousand Union forces fought to control New Mexico Territory. The Confederate invasion had aimed to seize the trade riches of the Santa Fe Trail and take possession of gold mines in Colorado and California. But Colorado and New Mexico Unionists fought back, and in a series of battles at Glorieta Pass, 20 miles east of Santa Fe, on March 26 through 28, they blocked the Confederates. By May 1, Confederate forces straggled down the Rio Grande River into Texas, abandoning efforts to take New Mexico.

Ulysses S. Grant: Commander of the Union army.

Battle of Shiloh: The bloodiest battle in American history to that date (April 6–7, 1862).

Grant's Tennessee Campaign and the Battle of Shiloh

Meanwhile, in February 1862, forces in northern Tennessee won significant victories for the Union. A Union commander named **Ulysses S. Grant** saw the strategic importance of Fort Henry and Fort Donelson, the Confederate outposts guarding the Tennessee and Cumberland Rivers. In just ten days, he seized the forts—completely cutting off the Confederates and demanding "unconditional surrender" of Fort Donelson. A path into Tennessee, Alabama, and Mississippi now lay open before the Union Army.

Grant moved into southern Tennessee and the first of the war's shockingly bloody encounters, the **Battle of Shiloh**. On April 6, Confederate general Albert Sidney Johnston caught federal troops with their backs to the Tennessee River awaiting reinforcements. The Confederates attacked and inflicted heavy damage all day. Close to victory, General Johnston was killed. Union reinforcements arrived that night. The next day the battle turned, and after ten hours of combat, the Confederates withdrew.

Neither side won a decisive victory at Shiloh, yet losses were staggering, and the Confederates were forced to retreat into northern Mississippi. Northern troops lost thirteen thousand men (killed, wounded, or captured) out of sixty-three thousand; southerners sacrificed eleven thousand out of forty thousand. Total casualties in this battle exceeded those in all three of America's previous wars combined. Before Shiloh, Grant hoped that southerners would soon tire of the conflict. After Shiloh, he recalled, "I gave up all idea of saving the Union except by complete conquest." Memories of the Shiloh battlefield would haunt the surviving soldiers for the rest of their lives.

Jefferson Davis: President of the Confederacy.

Robert E. Lee: Commander of the Confederate army.

McClellan and the Peninsula Campaign

On the Virginia front, President Lincoln had problems with General McClellan. Only thirty-six, McClellan had achieved success as an army officer and railroad president. Habitually overestimating the size of enemy forces, he called repeatedly for reinforcements and ignored Lincoln's directions to advance. McClellan advocated war of limited aims that would lead to a quick reunion. He intended neither disruption of slavery nor war on noncombatants. McClellan finally sailed his troops down the Chesapeake, landing them on the peninsula between the York and James Rivers, and advanced on Richmond.

After a bloody battle at Fair Oaks on May 31 through June 1, the federal armies moved to within seven miles of the Confederate capital. The Confederate commanding general, Joseph E. Johnston, was wounded at Fair Oaks, and President **Jefferson Davis** placed his chief military adviser, **Robert E. Lee**, in command. The fifty-five-year-old Lee was an aristocratic Virginian, a lifelong military officer, and a veteran of distinction from the War with Mexico. Although he initially opposed secession, Lee gave his allegiance to his state and became a staunch Confederate. He soon foiled McClellan's legions.

First, Lee sent Stonewall Jackson's corps of seventeen thousand northwest into the Shenandoah valley behind Union forces, where they threatened Washington, D.C., and drew some federal troops away from Richmond to protect their own capital. Further, in mid-June, in an extraordinary four-day ride around the entire Union Army, Confederate cavalry under J. E. B. Stuart confirmed the exposed position of McClellan's army north of the Chickahominy River. Then, in the Seven Days Battles, from June 26 through July 1, Lee struck at McClellan's army. Lee's daring move of taking the majority of his army northeast and attacking the Union right flank, while leaving only a small force to defend Richmond, forced McClellan to retreat toward the James River.

During the sustained fighting of the Seven Days, the Union forces suffered 20,614 casualties and the Confederates, 15,849. By August 3, McClellan withdrew his army to the environs of Washington. Richmond remained safe for almost two more years.

Confederate Offensive in Maryland and Kentucky

Buoyed by these results, Jefferson Davis conceived an ambitious plan to gain wartime advantage and recognition of the Confederacy by European nations. He ordered a general offensive, sending Lee into Maryland and Generals Kirby Smith and Braxton Bragg into Kentucky. Calling on residents of Maryland and Kentucky, still slave states, to make a peace with his government, Davis also invited northwestern states like Indiana, which sent much of their trade down the Mississippi to New Orleans, to leave the Union. This was a coordinated effort to take the war to the North and force both a military and a political turning point.

The plan was promising, but the offensive ultimately failed. Lee's forces achieved a striking success at the battle of Second Bull Run, August 29 through 30. The entire Union army retreated to the federal capital. Thousands of wounded occupied schools and churches, and two thousand suffered on cots in the U.S. Capitol rotunda.

But in the bloodiest day of the war, September 17, 1862, McClellan turned Lee back from Sharpsburg, Maryland. In the **Battle of Antietam**, five thousand men died, and another eighteen thousand were wounded. McClellan intercepted a battle order, wrapped around cigars for each Confederate corps commander and lost by a courier. But McClellan moved slowly, failed to use his larger forces in simultaneous attacks,

Battle of Antietam: First major battle on Northern soil.

Library of Congress

In October 1862 in New York City, photographer Mathew Brady opened an exhibition of photographs from the Battle of Antietam. Although few knew it, Brady's vision was very poor, and this photograph of Confederate dead was actually made by his assistants, Alexander Gardner and James F. Gibson.

and allowed Lee's stricken army to retreat to across the Potomac. Lincoln removed McClellan from command.

In Kentucky, Generals Smith and Bragg secured Lexington and Frankfort, but their effort to force the Yankees back to the Ohio River was stopped at the Battle of Perryville on October 8. Bragg's army retreated back into Tennessee, where on December 31, 1862 to January 2, 1863, they fought an indecisive but bloody battle at Murfreesboro. Casualties exceeded even those of Shiloh.

Outnumbered and disadvantaged, the South could not continue the offensive. Davis admitted to Confederate representatives that southerners were entering "the darkest and most dangerous period we have yet had."

Link to reports in *Harper's Weekly* of the Battle of Fredericksburg.

But 1862 also brought painful lessons to the North. On December 13, Union general Ambrose Burnside, now in command of the Army of the Potomac, unwisely ordered his soldiers to attack Lee's army, which held fortified positions at Fredericksburg, Virginia. Lee's men performed efficiently in killing northerners, and Burnside's repeated assaults up Marye's Heights shocked his opponents, killing thirteen hundred and wounding ninety-six hundred Union soldiers. The scale of carnage now challenged people on both sides to question the meaning of such a war.

War Transforms the South

What happened to the South's embrace of state sovereignty during the war?

War disrupted civilian life; one of the first traditions to fall was the southern preference for local and limited government. States' rights had been a formative ideology for the Confederacy, but state governments were weak. To withstand the North's massive power, the South needed to centralize; like the colonial revolutionaries, southerners could unite or die separately.

The Confederacy and Centralization

Jefferson Davis brought arms, supplies, and troops under centralized control. But by early 1862, the scope and duration of the conflict required more recruits. Tens of thousands of Confederate soldiers volunteered for just one year planning to return home in the spring to plant their crops. Faced with a critical manpower shortage, in April 1862 the Confederate government enacted the first national conscription (draft) law in American history.

Davis adopted a firm leadership role toward the Confederate Congress, which raised taxes and later passed a tax-in-kind—paid in farm products. Nearly forty-five hundred agents dispersed to collect the tax. Where opposition arose, the government suspended the writ of habeas corpus (which prevented individuals from being held without trial) and imposed martial law. Still, this tax system proved inadequate for the South's war effort.

To replace the food that men in uniform would have grown, Davis exhorted state governments to require farmers to switch from cash crops to food crops. But army food and labor shortages continued. The War Department impressed slaves to work on fortifications, and after 1861 officers raided farms and carted away grain, meat, wagons, and draft animals to feed the troops. Such raids caused increased hardship and resentment for women managing farms without husbands and sons.

Soon, the Confederate administration in Richmond gained control over the southern economy. The Confederate Congress also gave the central government almost complete control of the railroads. A large bureaucracy of over seventy thousand civilians administered Confederate operations. By the war's end, the southern bureaucracy was larger in proportion to population than its northern counterpart.

Confederate Nationalism

Historians have long argued over whether the Confederacy itself was a "rebellion," a "revolution," or the creation of a genuine "nation." Whatever the label, Confederates created a culture and ideology of nationalism. In flags, songs, language, seals, school readers, and other national characteristics, Confederates created their own story.

Southerners believed the Confederacy was the true legacy of the American Revolution—a bulwark against centralized power that was in keeping with the war. To southerners, theirs was a continuing revolution against the excesses of Yankee democracy, and George Washington (a Virginian) on horseback formed the center of the Confederacy's official seal.

Also central to Confederate nationalism was a refurbished defense of slavery as a benign, protective institution, complete with the image of the "faithful slave." In wartime schoolbooks, children were instructed in the divinely inspired, paternalistic character of slavery. A poem popular among whites captured an old slave's rejection of the Emancipation Proclamation.

> Now, Massa, dis is berry fine, dese words
> You've spoke to me,
> No doubt you mean it kindly, but ole Dinah
> Won't be free…
> Ole Massa's berry good to me—and though I am
> His slave,
> He treats me like I'se kin to him—and I would
> Rather have
> A home in Massa's cabin, and eat his black
> Bread too,
> Dan leave ole Massa's children and go and
> Lib wid you.

This and other forms of Confederate nationalism collapsed in the war's final years. But it would revive in the postwar period in a new ideology of the Lost Cause.

Southern Cities and Industry

Clerks and subordinate officials crowded towns and cities where Confederate departments established offices. "Government girls" staffed the formerly all-male Confederate bureaucracy. The sudden urban migration overwhelmed the housing supply and stimulated new construction. Richmond's population increased 250 percent. Mobile's population jumped from twenty-nine thousand to forty-one thousand; and ten thousand people poured into war-related industries in little Selma, Alabama.

As the Union blockade disrupted imports, the traditionally agricultural South forged new industries. Many planters shared Davis's hope that industrialization would bring "deliverance… from all commercial dependence" on the North or the world. Indeed, the Confederacy achieved tremendous industrial development. Chief of Ordnance Josiah Gorgas increased the capacity of Richmond's Tredegar Iron Works and other factories so that by 1865 his Ordnance Bureau was supplying all Confederate small arms and ammunition. The government constructed new railroad lines and ironworks, using slaves relocated from farms and plantations.

Five Texans in the Confederate cavalry sitting for a formal photograph. Four have the "lone star" on their hats. Like thousands of others, these men posed to send their image to the folks back home, but also perhaps as an act of comradeship at the war front.

Changing Roles of Women

White women, restricted to narrow roles in antebellum society, gained new responsibilities in wartime. The wives and mothers of soldiers now headed households and performed men's work, including raising crops and tending animals. Women in nonslaveowning families cultivated fields, while wealthier women acted as overseers and managed field work. In the cities, white women—previously all but excluded from the labor force—found respectable paying jobs, often in the Confederate bureaucracy. Female schoolteachers appeared in the South for the first time.

Patriotic sacrifice appealed to some women; others resented their new burdens. A Texas woman who had struggled to discipline slaves pronounced herself "sick of trying to do a man's business." Others grew angry over shortages and resented contact with lower-class women. Some scorned the war and demanded that their men return to provide for their families.

Human Suffering, Hoarding, and Inflation

For millions of southerners, the war brought privation and suffering. Mass poverty descended on a large minority of the white population. Many yeoman families lost their breadwinners to the army. Women sought help from relatives, neighbors, friends, anyone. Sometimes they pleaded with the Confederate government to discharge their husbands.

The South was in many places so sparsely populated that the conscription of one craftsman could wreak hardship on an entire county. Often people begged together for the exemption or discharge of the local miller, neighborhood tanner, or wheelwright. Most serious, however, was the loss of a blacksmith, who could repair farming tools.

The blockade of Confederate shipping created shortages of important supplies—salt, sugar, coffee, nails—and speculation and hoarding made shortages worse. Greedy businessmen cornered the supply of some commodities; prosperous citizens stocked up on food. The *Richmond Enquirer* criticized a planter who purchased so many wagonloads of supplies that his "lawn and paths looked like a wharf covered with a ship's loads."

Inflation raged out of control, fueled by the Confederate government's heavy borrowing and inadequate taxes, until prices increased almost 7,000 percent. Inflation particularly imperiled urban dwellers without their own food sources. As early as 1861 and 1862, officials predicted that "women and children are bound to come to suffering if not starvation." Hoarding continued, and a rudimentary relief program organized by the Confederacy failed to meet the need.

Inequities of the Confederate Draft

Not all classes sacrificed equally. The Confederate government's policies decidedly favored the upper class. Until the war's last year, for example, prosperous southerners could avoid military service by hiring substitutes. Well over fifty thousand upper-class southerners purchased such substitutes, despite skyrocketing prices that reached $5,000 or $6,000 per man. Mary Boykin Chesnut knew of one aristocrat who "spent a fortune in substitutes....He is at the end of his row now, for all able-bodied men are ordered to the front."

Anger at such discrimination exploded in October 1862, when the Confederate Congress exempted from military duty anyone who was supervising at least twenty slaves. Protests poured in from across the Confederacy, and North Carolina's legislators condemned the law. Its defenders argued, however, that exemption preserved order and aided food production, and the statute remained on the books.

This "twenty Negro" law is indicative of the racial fears many Confederates felt as the war threatened to overturn southern society. But it also fueled desertion and stimulated Unionism in nonslaveholding regions of the South. In Jones County, Mississippi, a wooded area with few slaves or plantations, Newt Knight, a Confederate soldier, led renegades who took over the county, declared their allegiance to the Union, and called their district the "Free State of Jones." They held out for the remainder of the war as an enclave of Union sympathizers.

The bitterness of letters to Confederate officials suggests the depth of the dissension and class anger. One woman swore to the secretary of war that, unless help was provided to poverty-stricken wives and mothers, "an allwise god...will send down his fury...[on] those that are in power."

Wartime Northern Economy and Society

How did the war affect workers in the North?

War dramatically altered northern society as well. Factories and citizens' associations geared up to support the war, and the federal government and its executive branch gained new powers. Idealism and greed flourished together, and the northern economy proved its awesome productivity.

Northern Business, Industry, and Agriculture

At first, the war was a shock to business. Northern firms lost their southern markets, and many companies changed their products and found new customers. Southern debts became uncollectible, jeopardizing northern merchants and western banks. Farm families struggled with a labor short-age caused by army enlistments. Cotton mills lacked cotton; construction declined; shoe manufacturers sold few of the cheap shoes that planters bought for slaves.

Certain entrepreneurs, such as wool producers, benefited from shortages of competing products, and soaring demand for war-related goods swept some busi-nesses to new success. The Treasury issued $3.2 billion in bonds and paper money called "greenbacks," and the War Department spent over $360 million in revenues from new taxes, including the nation's first income tax.

War-related spending revived business in many northern states. The northern economy also grew because of a complementary relationship between agriculture and industry. Mechanization of agriculture had begun before the war. Wartime recruitment and conscription gave western farmers an added incentive to purchase labor-saving machinery. The shift from human labor to machines created new markets for indus-try and expanded the food supply. Cyrus and William McCormick built an industrial empire in Chicago from the sale of their reapers. Between 1862 and 1864, the manu-facture of mowers and reapers doubled to 70,000 yearly; by war's end, 375,000 reapers were in use, triple the number in 1861. Thus, northern farm families whose breadwin-ners went to war did not suffer as much as their counterparts in the South.

The Quartermaster and Military-Government Mobilization

This government-business marriage emerged from a greatly empowered Quartermaster Department, which became the single largest employer in the United States, issuing thou-sands of manufacturing contracts to hundreds of firms.

Secretary of War Edwin M. Stanton's list of the supplies needed by the Ordnance Department indicates the scope of the demand for government and business coopera-tion: "7,892 cannon, 11,787 artillery carriages, 4,022,130 small-arms… 1,022,176,474 cartridges for small-arms, 1,220,555,435 percussion caps,…26,440,054 pounds of gunpowder,…and 90,416,295 pounds of lead." The government also purchased huge quantities of uniforms, boots, food, camp equipment, saddles, horses, ships, and other necessities. By 1865, the government had purchased some 640,000 horses and 300,000 mules at a cost well over $100 million.

Two-thirds of all U.S. war spending went to supply troops, and President Lincoln appointed West Point–trained engineer, Montgomery Meigs, to command that process. Meigs spent $1.8 billion to wage the war, more than all previous U.S. government expenditures combined since independence. His efforts, argued one his-torian, made the Union army "the best fed, most lavishly supplied army that had ever existed." The success of such military mobilization left an indelible mark on American political-economic history and provided perhaps the oldest root of the modern American "military-industrial state."

The story of Jay Cooke, a wealthy New York financier, best illustrates the wartime partnership between business and government. Cooke earned hefty commissions marketing government bonds to finance the war. But the financier's profit served the Union cause, as the interests of capitalism and government merged in American history's first era of "big government."

Northern Workers' Militancy

Northern industrial and urban workers did not fare as well as. After the initial slump, jobs became plentiful, but inflation ate up much of a worker's paycheck. The price of coffee tripled; rice and sugar doubled; and between 1860 and 1864, consumer prices rose at least 76 percent, while daily wages rose only 42 percent. Workers' families consequently suffered a substantial decline in their standard of living.

Industrial workers also lost job security. To increase production, some employers replaced workers with labor-saving machines. Others urged the government to promote immigration to secure cheap labor. Workers responded by forming unions and sometimes striking. Indeed, thirteen occupational groups—including tailors, coal miners, and railway engineers—formed national unions during the Civil War, and the number of strikes climbed.

Manufacturers viewed labor activism as a threat and formed statewide or craft-based associations to pool information. They shared blacklists of union members and required new workers to sign "yellow dog" contracts (promises not to join a union). To put down strikes, they hired strikebreakers from among blacks, immigrants, and women, and sometimes used federal troops.

Labor militancy, however, did not keep employers from profiting or profiteering on government contracts. With immense demand for army supplies, unscrupulous businessmen sold clothing and blankets made of "shoddy"—wool fibers reclaimed from rags or worn cloth. Shoddy goods often came apart in the rain; most of the shoes purchased early in the war were worthless. Contractors sold inferior guns for double the usual price and passed off tainted meat as good. Rampant corruption led to a year-long investigation by the House of Representatives.

Economic Nationalism and Government-Business Partnership

Legitimate enterprises also made healthy profits. The output of woolen mills increased so dramatically that industry dividends nearly tripled. Some cotton mills made record profits, even while reducing output. Brokerage houses earned unheard-of commissions. Railroads increased their business so much that railroad stocks skyrocketed.

Railroads were a leading beneficiary of government largesse. With southern representatives absent from Congress, the northern route of the transcontinental railroad prevailed. In 1862 and 1864, Congress chartered two corporations, the Union Pacific Railroad and the Central Pacific Railroad, and assisted them financially in connecting Omaha, Nebraska, with Sacramento, California. For each mile of track laid, railroads received a loan of from $16,000 to $48,000 in government bonds plus 20 square miles of land along a free 400-foot-wide right of way. Overall, the two corporations gained approximately 20 million acres and nearly $60 million in loans.

Other businessmen benefited handsomely from the **Morrill Land Grant Act** (1862). To promote public education in agriculture, engineering, and military science, Congress granted each state 30,000 acres of federal land for each of its congressional districts. The law eventually fostered sixty-nine colleges and universities, and enriched a few prominent speculators. Similarly, the Homestead Act of 1862 offered cheap, and sometimes free, land to people who would settle the West and improve their property.

Morrill Land Grant Act: Law in which Congress granted land to states to establish colleges focusing on agriculture, engineering, and military science.

Before the war, banks operating under state charters issued seven thousand different kinds of currency notes. During the war, Congress and the Treasury Department established a national banking system to issue national bank notes, and by 1865 most state banks were forced by a prohibitive tax to join the national system. This created sounder currency but also inflexibility in the money supply and an eastern-oriented financial structure.

In the excitement of wartime moneymaking, an eagerness to display one's wealth flourished in the largest cities. *Harper's Monthly* reported that "the men button their waistcoats with diamonds…and the women powder their hair with gold and silver dust." The *New York Herald* noted: "This war has entirely changed the American character.…The individual who makes the most money—no matter how—and spends the most—no matter for what—is considered the greatest man."

The Union Cause

In the first two years of the war, northern morale remained remarkably high for a cause that today may seem abstract—the Union—but at the time meant the preservation of a social and political order that people cherished.

Secular and church leaders supported the cause, and even ministers who preferred to separate politics and pulpit denounced "the iniquity of causeless rebellion. Abolitionists campaigned to turn the war into a crusade against slavery." Free black communities and churches—both black and white—sent clothing, ministers, and teachers to aid the freedpeople. Indeed, thousands of northern blacks volunteered to join the war effort in spite of the initial rejection they received from the Lincoln administration. Thus, in wartime northern society, materialism and greed flourished alongside idealism, religious conviction, and self-sacrifice.

Northern Women on Home Front and Battlefront

Northern women, like their southern counterparts, took on new roles. They organized over ten thousand soldiers' aid societies, rolled bandages, and raised $3 million for injured troops. Women pressed for the first trained ambulance corps in the Union Army, and they formed the backbone of the **U.S. Sanitary Commission**, a civilian agency recognized by the War Department in 1861, which provided nutritional and medical aid to soldiers. Although most of its officers were men, the bulk of the volunteers who ran its seven thousand auxiliaries were women. Women organized elaborate "Sanitary Fairs" to raise money and awareness for soldiers' health and hygiene.

Approximately thirty-two hundred women also served as nurses in frontline hospitals. Yet women had to fight to serve; the professionalization of medicine since the Revolution created a medical system dominated by men, who often did not want women's aid. Even **Clara Barton**, famous for working in the worst hospitals at the front, was ousted from her post in 1863. But women such as Dorothea Dix, who sought to reform asylums for the insane, and Illinois widow Mary Ann Bickerdyke, who served in Sherman's army in the West, established a heroic tradition for Civil War nurses. They also advanced the professionalization of nursing, as several schools of nursing were established in northern cities during or after the war.

Women also wrote sentimental war poetry, short stories, and novels, and songs that reached thousands of readers in illustrated weeklies, monthly periodicals, and special "story papers." In many stories, female characters seek recognition for their loyalty and Union service, while others probe the suffering and death of loved ones. Louisa May Alcott arrived at her nursing job in Washington, D.C. after the horrific Union defeat at Fredericksburg, in December 1862, and later immortalized her experience in *Hospital Sketches* (1863), providing northern readers a view of the hospitals where loved ones agonized and perished.

U.S. Sanitary Commission: Civilian organization in the North staffed by large numbers of women that was a major source of medical and nutritional aid for soldiers.

Clara Barton: Nurse who worked for the Sanitary Commission and later founded the Red Cross.

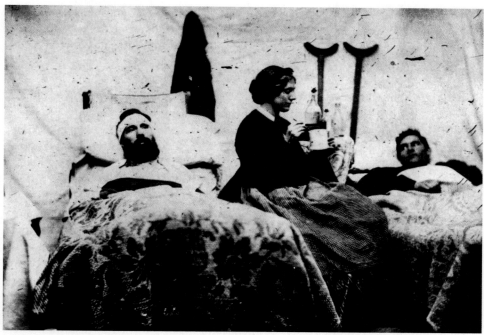

Nurse Anne Bell tending to wounded soldiers in a federal hospital, Nashville, Tennessee, ca. 1863. The distant gaze of the man on the left and the grateful gaze of the one on the right realistically represent agonies of military hospitals.

By 1863, many women found the liberation of slaves an inspiring subject, as Julia Ward Howe did in her immortal "Battle Hymn of the Republic": "As He died to make men holy / Let us die to make men free."

Walt Whitman's War   The poet **Walt Whitman** recorded his experiences as a volunteer nurse in Washington, D.C. As he dressed wounds and comforted suffering men, Whitman found "the marrow of the tragedy concentrated in those Army Hospitals." But he also found inspiration and a deepening faith in American democracy.

In "The Wound Dresser," Whitman meditated unforgettably on the deaths he witnessed:

> On, on I go, (open doors of time! open hospital doors!)
> The crush'd head I dress, (poor crazed hand tear not the bandage away,)
> The neck of the cavalry-man with the bullet through and through I examine,
> Hard the breathing rattles, quite glazed already the eye, yet life struggles hard, (Come sweet death! be persuaded O beautiful death!
> In mercy come quickly.)

Indeed, the scale of death in this war shocked many Americans into believing that the conflict had to be for purposes larger than themselves.

The Advent of Emancipation

Despite the loyalty of soldiers and civilians on both sides, the governments of the United States and the Confederacy lacked clarity about the war's purpose. Throughout the war's early months, Davis and Lincoln avoided

Walt Whitman: Well-known poet and author of *Leaves of Grass*; Whitman wrote about his experiences as a nurse and his renewed faith in democracy.

Why did Lincoln and Davis both avoid the slavery issue in the early days of the war?

references to slavery. Davis realized that emphasis on the issue could increase class conflict in the South. Instead, he told southerners that they were fighting for constitutional liberty: northerners betrayed the founders' legacy, and southerners seceded to preserve it.

Lincoln had his reasons for avoiding slavery. It was crucial at first not to antagonize the Union's border slave states, whose loyalty was tenuous. Lincoln also hoped that a pro-Union majority would assert itself in the South and help coax the South back into the Union. And there were powerful political considerations. Some Republicans burned with moral outrage over slavery; others were frankly racist, dedicated to protecting free whites from the Slave Power and the competition of cheap slave labor. No Republican or northern consensus on slavery existed early in the war.

Lincoln and Emancipation

Lincoln's compassion, humility, and moral anguish during the war were evident in his speeches and writings. But as a politician, Lincoln distinguished between his convictions and his official acts. The latter were calculated for maximum advantage.

Many blacks attacked Lincoln furiously during the war's first year for his refusal to convert the struggle into an "abolition war." When Lincoln countermanded General John C. Frémont's order of liberation for slaves owned by disloyal masters in Missouri in September 1861, the *Anglo-African* declared that the president "hurls back into the hell of slavery thousands…rightfully set free." As late as July 1862, Frederick Douglass characterized administration policy as reconstruction of "the old union on the old and corrupting basis of compromise, by which slavery shall retain all the power that it ever had." Douglass wanted slavery destroyed and the Constitution rewritten in the name of human equality. Within a year, just such a profound result began to take place.

Lincoln first substantively broached the subject of slavery in March 1862, when he proposed that states consider emancipation. He asked Congress to promise aid to any state that emancipated, appealing especially to border state representatives. What Lincoln proposed was gradual emancipation, with compensation for slaveholders and colonization of the freed slaves outside the United States.

Until well into 1864, Lincoln's administration promoted an impractical scheme to colonize 4.2 million freed slaves in Central America or the Caribbean. He was as yet unconvinced that America could become a biracial society, and he feared that white northerners might not support a war for black freedom. Black abolitionists vehemently opposed the Lincoln administration's machinations.

Radical Republicans: A group of Republicans who assailed the U.S. President early in the war for failing to make emancipation a war goal and later making it too easy for defeated rebel states to return to the Union.

A group of Republicans in Congress, known as the **Radical Republicans**—led by George Julian, Charles Sumner, and Thaddeus Stevens—dedicated themselves to a war for emancipation. They were instrumental in creating a special House-Senate committee on the conduct of the war, which investigated Union reverses, sought to improve wartime efficiency, and prodded the president to take stronger measures against slavery.

Confiscation Acts

In August 1861, at the Radicals' instigation, Congress passed its first confiscation act. Designed to punish Confederates, the law confiscated all property used for "insurrectionary purposes." A second confiscation act (July 1862) confiscated the property of anyone who supported the rebellion, even those who merely resided in the South and paid Confederate taxes. Their slaves were declared "forever free of their servitude."

In the summer 1862, Lincoln stood by his proposal of voluntary gradual emancipation and made no effort to enforce the second confiscation act. In protest, Horace Greeley, editor of the powerful *New York Tribune,* published an open letter to the president entitled "The Prayer of Twenty Millions," Greeley declared, "Mr. President, there is not one...intelligent champion of the Union cause who does not feel that all attempts to put down the Rebellion and at the same time uphold its inciting cause are preposterous and futile." Lincoln offered a calculated reply. He disagreed with those who would make slavery the paramount issue of the war and said, "If I could save the Union without freeing any slave I would do it, and if I could save it by freeing all the slaves I would do it; and if I could save it by freeing some and leaving others alone I would also do that. What I do about slavery, and the colored race, I do because I believe it helps to save the Union."

But Lincoln had already decided to issue a presidential **Emancipation Proclamation**. He was waiting for a Union victory so that it would not appear an act of desperation. The letter to Greeley represents Lincoln's concern with conditioning public opinion for the coming social revolution.

Emancipation Proclamation: Lincoln's decree freeing all slaves in Confederate-held territories. It exempted border slave states that remained within the Union.

Emancipation Proclamations

On September 22, 1862, shortly after Union success at the Battle of Antietam, Lincoln issued the first part of his two-part proclamation. Invoking his powers as commander-in-chief, he announced that on January 1, 1863, he would emancipate the slaves in the states "in rebellion" (those lacking legitimate representatives in the U.S. Congress by January). Thus, his September 1862 proclamation was less a declaration of the right of slaves to be free than a threat to southerners: unless they put down their arms and returned to Congress, they would lose their slaves. Lincoln had little expectation that southerners would give up, but he wanted a response.

In the fateful January 1, 1863, proclamation, Lincoln declared that "all persons held as slaves" in areas in rebellion "shall be then, thenceforward, and forever free." But he excepted every Confederate county or city that had fallen under Union control. Those areas, he declared, "are, for the present, left precisely as if this proclamation were not issued." Nor did Lincoln liberate slaves in the border slave states that remained in the Union. "The President has... proclaimed emancipation only where he has notoriously no power to execute it," charged the anti-administration *New York World.*

But Lincoln was worried about the constitutionality of his acts, and he anticipated that after the war southerners might sue for restoration of their "property." Making the liberation of the slaves "a fit and necessary war measure" raised a variety of legal questions: Would it expire with the suppression of a rebellion? The proclamation did little to clarify the status of freed slaves, but did it open the possibility of military service for blacks?

If the Emancipation Proclamation was legally ambiguous, as a moral and political document it had great meaning. Because the proclamation defined the war as a war against slavery, congressional Radicals could applaud it. Yet it also protected Lincoln's position with conservatives, enabling him to retreat and forcing no immediate changes on the border slave states.

Most important, though, thousands of slaves had already reached Union lines across the South. They "voted with their feet" for emancipation well before the proclamation. And now, every advance of federal forces into slave society was a liberating step.

Across the North and in Union-occupied sections of the South, blacks and their white allies celebrated the Emancipation Proclamation. At a large "contraband camp" in Washington, D.C., some six hundred black men, women, and children gathered at the superintendent's headquarters on New Year's Eve and sang through the night. In chorus after chorus of "Go Down, Moses" they announced the magnitude of their painful but beautiful exodus.

African American Recruits

The need for men soon convinced the administration to recruit northern and southern blacks for the Union Army. By the spring of 1863, African American troops were answering the call of a dozen or more black recruiters in northern cities and towns. Lincoln came to see black soldiers as "the great available and yet unavailed of force for restoring the Union."

African American leaders hoped that military service would secure equal rights for their people. Once the black soldier had fought for the Union, wrote Frederick Douglass, "there is no power on earth which can deny that he has earned the right of citizenship in the United States."

In June 1864, with thousands of former slaves in blue uniforms, Lincoln gave his support to a constitutional ban on slavery. On the eve of the Republican national convention, Lincoln called on the party to "put into the platform as the keystone, the amendment of the Constitution abolishing and prohibiting slavery forever." The party promptly called for the **Thirteenth Amendment**, which passed in early 1865 and was sent to the states for ratification. The war to save the Union had become the war to free the slaves.

Thirteenth Amendment: Ended slavery in all U.S. territory.

Who Freed the Slaves?

It has long been debated whether Abraham Lincoln deserved the label (one he never claimed for himself) of "Great Emancipator." Was Lincoln ultimately a reluctant emancipator, following rather than leading Congress and public opinion? Or did Lincoln give essential presidential leadership by going slow but, once moving, never backpedaling on black freedom? Once he focused on the unconditional surrender of the Confederates, Lincoln made slavery's destruction central to the war's purpose.

Others have argued, however, that slaves were central in achieving their own freedom. When they were in proximity to war zones, slaves fled by the thousands. Some worked as camp laborers for the Union armies, and eventually more than 180,000 black men served in the Union Army and Navy. Some found freedom as individuals in 1861, and some not until 1865, as refugees trekking to contraband camps.

Nevertheless, emancipation was a historical confluence of a policy directed by and dependent on the military authority of the president and the will and courage for self-emancipation. Wallace Turnage's escape in Mobile Bay in 1864 demonstrates that emancipation could result from both a slave's own heroism and Union forces. Most blacks comprehended their freedom as given and taken, but also as their human right. "I now dreaded the gun and handcuffs...no more," remembered Turnage. "I could now speak my opinion," Turnage concluded, "to men of all grades and colors."

A Confederate Plan of Emancipation

Before the war was over, the Confederacy, too, addressed emancipation. Late in the war, Jefferson Davis was willing to sacrifice slavery to achieve independence. He proposed that the Confederate government purchase 40,000 slaves to work as army laborers, with a promise of freedom at the end of their service. He then called for the recruitment and arming of slaves as soldiers, who likewise would gain their freedom at war's end, as would their wives and children. Bitter debate over Davis's plan resounded through the Confederacy. When the Confederate Congress finally approved slave enlistments in March 1865, owners had to comply only on a "voluntary" basis. With manpower shortages, General Lee supported the idea of slave soldiers, while most Confederate slaveholders and editors vehemently opposed the enlistment plan. Supporters hoped to fight to a stalemate, achieve independence, and control the postwar racial order through their limited wartime emancipation schemes, but it was too late. By contrast, Lincoln's Emancipation Proclamation stimulated a vital infusion of forces into the Union armies: 134,000 former slaves (and 52,000 free blacks) fought for freedom and the Union. Their participation was pivotal in northern victory.

The Soldiers' War

Military service altered their lives. Enlistment submerged young men in large organizations whose military discipline ignored their individuality. Army life meant tedium, physical hardship, and separation from loved ones, yet it held powerful attractions as well.

> What led previously reluctant white military leaders to accept black soldiers?

Hospitals and Camp Life

Soldiers benefited from certain new products, such as canned condensed milk, but blankets, clothing, and arms were often of poor quality. Hospitals were badly managed at first. Rules of hygiene in large camps were scarcely enforced. Water supplies were unsafe and typhoid common. About 57,000 men died from dysentery and diarrhea; 224,000 Union troops died from disease or accidents, double the 110,100 who died from battle. Confederate troops were less well supplied, and they had no sanitary commission. Still, an extensive hospital network, aided by white female volunteers and black woman slaves, sprang up.

On both sides, troops quickly learned that soldiering was far from glorious. Fighting, wrote a North Carolina volunteer in 1862, taught him "the realities of a soldier's life....Without time to wash our clothes or our persons...the whole army became lousy more or less with body lice." Union troops "skirmished" against lice by boiling their clothes, but to little avail.

War soon exposed them to the blasted bodies of friends and comrades. "It is a sad sight to see the dead and if possible more sad to see the wounded—shot in every possible way you can imagine," wrote one Confederate.

Still, as campaigns dragged on, most soldiers who did not desert grew determined to see the struggle through. "We now, like true Soldiers go determined not to yield one inch," wrote a New York corporal. When at last the war was over, "it seemed like breaking up a family to separate," one man observed.

The Rifled Musket

Advances in technology made the Civil War particularly deadly. The most important were the rifle and the "minie ball." Bullets fired from a smoothbore musket were not accurate at distances over eighty yards. Cutting spiraled grooves inside the barrel gave the projectile greater accuracy, but rifles remained difficult to load and use until the Frenchman Claude Minie and the American James Burton developed a new kind of bullet that expanded on firing and flew accurately. With these bullets, rifles were deadly at four hundred yards.

This meant that soldiers assaulting a position defended by riflemen were in greater peril. While artillery now fired from a safe distance, there was no sub-stitute for the infantry assault or the popular turning movements aimed at an enemy's flank. Thus, advancing soldiers exposed themselves repeatedly to accu-rate rifle fire. Because medical knowledge was rudimentary, even minor wounds often led to amputation and death through infection. Never before in Europe or America had such massive forces pummeled each other with weapons of such destructive power.

The Black Soldier's Fight for Manhood

At the outset of the war, racism in the Union Army was strong. Most white soldiers wanted nothing to do with black people and regarded them as inferior. For many, acceptance of black troops grew only because they could do heavy labor and "stop Bullets as well as white people." A popular song celebrated "Sambo's Right to Be Kilt" as the only justification for black enlistments.

But white officers who volunteered to lead segregated black units to gain pro-motion found that experience altered their opinions. After one month with black troops, a white captain informed his wife, "I have a more elevated opinion of their abilities than I ever had before. I know that many of them are vastly the superiors of those…who would condemn them all to a life of brutal degradation."

Black troops had a mission to destroy slavery and demonstrate their equality. "When Rebellion is crushed," wrote a black volunteer from Connecticut, "who will be more proud than I to say, I was one of the first of the despised race to leave the free North with a rifle on my shoulder." Corporal James Henry Gooding of Massachusetts's black Fifty-fourth Regiment explained that his unit intended "to live down all preju-dice against its color, by a determination to do well in any position it is put."

Indeed, blacks and whites of the Fifty-fourth Massachusetts forged deep bonds. Just before the regiment launched its costly assault on Fort Wagner in Charleston harbor, in July 1863, a black soldier called out to abolitionist Colonel Robert Gould Shaw, who would perish that day, "Colonel, I will stay by you till I die." The Fort Wagner assault was celebrated for demonstrating the valor of black men, but this bloody chapter in the history of American racism also proved that black men had to die in battle to be acknowledged as men.

Such valor emerged despite persistent discrimination. The Union government paid white privates $13 per month plus a clothing allowance of $3.50, whereas black privates earned only $10 per month less $3 for clothing. Outraged, several regiments refused to accept any pay, and Congress eventually remedied the inequity.

Link to Hannah Johnson's letter to President Lincoln asking the government to protect black soldiers.

Black Soldiers in the Civil War

The image below is of the storming of Fort Wagner, July 1863, by the Fifty-fourth Massachusetts regiment, in Charleston, South Carolina, by Chicago printmakers, Kurtz and Allison. Kurtz and Allison issued vivid and colorful chromolithographs in the 1880s, celebrating the military valor of African Americans. This scene depicts the most famous combat action of black troops in the Civil War; the Fifty-fourth was the first northern-recruited black unit, and their bravery and sacrifice served as a measure of African American devotion to the Union cause. At right is a medal for valor won by a member of the 54th Massachusetts Regiment. Why was the 54th Massachusetts regiment such a symbolic test case for the military ability and political meaning of black soldiers in the Civil War? Why did black men have to die on battlefields for many Americans in the Civil War era to consider them fully men and citizens?

Private Collection/Picture Research Consultants & Archives

THE GALLANT CHARGE OF THE FIFTY FOURTH MASSACHUSETTS (COLORED) REGIMENT.
On the Rebel works at Fort Wagner, Morris Island near Charleston, July 18th 1863, and death of Colonel Robt G. Shaw.

The Granger Collection, New York

1863: The Tide of Battle Turns

What turned the tide of war toward Union victory?

The fighting in spring and summer of 1863 did not settle the war, but it suggested the outcome. The campaigns began in a deceptively positive way for Confederates, as Lee's army performed brilliantly in battles in central Virginia.

Vicksburg: Union victory that gave the North complete control of Mississippi River.

Battle of Chancellorsville

On May 2 and 3, west of Fredericksburg, Virginia, some 130,000 members of the Union Army of the Potomac bore down on fewer than 60,000 Confederates. Boldly, Lee and Stonewall Jackson divided their forces, ordering 30,000 men under Jackson on a day-long march westward to prepare a flank attack.

Arriving at their position in late afternoon, Jackson's seasoned "foot cavalry" found unprepared Union troops laughing, smoking, and playing cards. The Confederate attack drove the entire right side of the Union Army back. Eager to press his advantage, Jackson rode forward with a few officers to study the ground. Returning at night, southern troops mistook them for federals and fired, fatally wounding their commander. The next day, Union forces left in defeat. Southern forces won at Chancellorsville, but it cost them Stonewall Jackson, who would remain a legend in Confederate memory.

Siege of Vicksburg

July brought crushing defeats for the Confederacy in two critical battles—**Vicksburg** and **Gettysburg**—that damaged Confederate hopes for independence. Vicksburg was the last major fortification on the Mississippi River in southern hands. General Ulysses S. Grant laid siege to Vicksburg in May, bottling up the defending army of General John Pemberton. If Vicksburg fell, Union forces would control the river, cutting the Confederacy in two and gaining an open path into its interior. To stave off such results, Jefferson Davis put General Joseph E. Johnston in charge and beseeched him to aid Pemberton. Meanwhile, General Robert E. Lee proposed a Confederate invasion of the North, which, though it would not relieve Vicksburg directly, could stun the North and possibly lead to peace. By invading the North a second time, Lee hoped to move away from war-weary Virginia, garner civilian support in Maryland, win a crucial victory on northern soil, threaten major cities, and thereby force a Union capitulation.

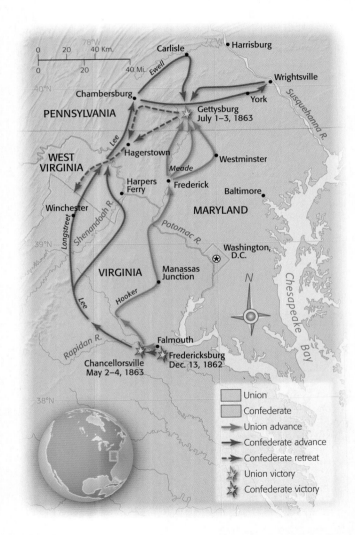

MAP 15.1

Battle of Gettysburg

In the war's greatest battle, fought around a small market town in southern Pennsylvania, Lee's invasion of the North was repulsed. Union forces had the advantage of high ground, shorter lines, and superior numbers. The casulties for the two armies—dead, wounded, and missing—exceeded fifty thousand men.

Source: Copyright © Cengage Learning

As Lee's emboldened army advanced through western Maryland and into Pennsylvania, Confederate prospects along the Mississippi darkened. Davis repeatedly wired General Johnston, urging him to attack Grant's army. Johnston, however, considered "saving Vicksburg hopeless." Grant's men, meanwhile, were supplying themselves from the abundant crops of the Mississippi River valley and could continue their siege indefinitely.

Battle of Gettysburg

Gettysburg: Union victory that halted Confederate invasion of Pennsylvania; turning point in the war in the East.

On July 4, 1863, Vicksburg's commander surrendered. The same day, a battle that had been raging for three days concluded at Gettysburg, Pennsylvania (see Map 15.1). On July 1, Confederate forces hunting for a supply of shoes collided with the Union Army. Heavy fighting on the second day left federal forces in possession of high ground along Cemetery Ridge, where they were shielded by a stone wall and had a clear view of their foe across almost a mile of open field.

Undaunted, Lee believed his reinforced troops could break the Union line, and on July 3 he ordered an assault. Virginians under General George E. Pickett and North Carolinians under General James Pettigrew marched up the slope in a doomed assault known as Pickett's Charge. They breached the enemy's line, but most fell in heavy slaughter. On July 4, Lee had to withdraw, having suffered almost four thousand dead and about twenty-four thousand missing and wounded. The Confederate general blamed himself and offered to resign, but President Davis refused. The Confederacy had reached what many consider its "high water mark" at Gettysburg.

After Gettysburg and Vicksburg, the Confederacy was split; west of the Mississippi, General E. Kirby Smith had to operate on his own, virtually independent of Richmond. Moreover, the heartland of Louisiana, Tennessee, and Mississippi lay exposed to invasion. Lee's northern defeat spelled the end of major southern offensive actions. Severely weakened, the Confederacy henceforth relied on a prolonged defense. By wearing down northern morale, the South might yet win, but its prospects were darker than before.

Disunity: South, North, and West

What were the causes of wartime dissent in the South?

Northern and southern governments waged the final two years of the war with increasing opposition at home. The gigantic costs of a civil war fed the unrest. But protest also arose from stresses in the regions' various social structures.

Union Occupation Zones

Wherever Union forces invaded, they imposed a military occupation consisting of three zones: garrisoned towns, with many troops in control of civilian and economic life; the Confederate frontier, areas still under southern control but with some federal military penetration; and "no man's land," regions between the two armies, beyond Confederate authority and under frequent Union patrols.

About one hundred southern towns were garrisoned, causing severe social disruption. Large regions of Tennessee, Virginia, Louisiana, Mississippi, and Georgia were occupied and suffered food shortages, crop and property destruction, disease, roadway banditry, guerrilla warfare, summary executions, and the random flow of escaped slaves. After two years of occupation, a southern white woman wrote to a kinsman about their native Clarksville, Tennessee: "it is nothing but a dirty hole filled…with niggers and Yankees."

Disintegration of Confederate Unity

Vastly disadvantaged in industrial capacity, natural resources, and labor, southerners felt the cost of the war more painfully than northerners. Worse, internally, the southern class system threatened the Confederate cause.

Planters were increasingly opposed to their own government. Along with new taxation, Confederate military authorities impressed slaves to build fortifications. And when Union forces advanced, Confederate commanders burned cotton stores that lay in the enemy's path, enraging planters about such interference with their agricultural production and finances.

Nor were the centralizing policies of the Davis administration popular. The Confederate constitution granted substantial powers to the central government, especially in war time. But many planters took the position articulated by R. B. Rhett, editor of the *Charleston Mercury,* that the Confederate constitution "leaves the States untouched in their Sovereignty, and commits to the Confederate Government only a few simple objects, and a few simple powers to enforce them."

Confused and embittered planters struck out at Jefferson Davis. Conscription, thundered Governor James E. Brown, was "subversive of [Georgia's] sovereignty, and at war with all the principles for the support of which Georgia entered into this revolution." To frustrate the law, Brown ordered local enrollment officials not to cooperate with the Confederacy.

Southern courts ultimately upheld Davis's power to conscript. Though Davis was devoted to southern independence, some of Davis's actions earned him the hatred of influential citizens.

Food Riots in Southern Cities

Widespread hunger and suffering sparked food riots in spring 1863 in Atlanta, Macon, Columbus, and Augusta, Georgia, and in Salisbury and High Point, North Carolina. On April 2, a crowd assembled in Richmond to demand relief. Responding to a passerby's questions about the group, a young girl replied, "We are starving. We are going to the bakeries and each of us will take a loaf of bread." That action fueled a riot that Davis ordered quelled at gunpoint.

Throughout the rural South, ordinary people resisted more quietly—by refusing to cooperate with conscription, tax collection, and impressments of food. Farmers who did provide food for the army refused to accept payment in certificates of credit or government bonds, as required by law. Conscription officers increasingly found no one to draft. In some areas, tax agents were killed.

Austere and private by nature, Jefferson Davis was ill-equipped to deal with such discontent. His class perspective also distanced him from common people's suffering. While his social circle in Richmond dined on duck and oysters, ordinary southerners went hungry.

Desertions from the Confederate Army

Such discontent affected the Confederate armies. Worried about their loved ones and resentful of what they saw as a rich man's war, large numbers of men abandoned the army, supported by friends and neighbors. Mary Chesnut observed a man being dragged back to the army as his wife looked on. "Desert agin, Jake!" she cried.

Desertion did not become a serious problem for the Confederacy until mid-1862, and stiffer policing solved the problem that year. But from 1863 on, the number of men on duty fell rapidly. By mid-1863, John A. Campbell, the South's assistant secretary of war, estimated that 40,000 to 50,000 troops were absent without leave and that 100,000 were evading duty. By November 1863, one-third of the army could not be accounted for.

The defeats at Gettysburg and Vicksburg dealt a heavy blow to Confederate morale. Desperate, President Davis and several state governors resorted to racial scare tactics to drive southern whites to further sacrifice. Defeat, Davis warned, would mean "extermination of yourselves, your wives, and children." Mississippi Governor Charles Clark predicted "elevation of the black race to a position of equality—aye, of superiority, that will make them your masters and rulers."

Internal disintegration of the Confederacy quickened. A few newspapers began to call for peace. "There has been enough of blood and carnage, enough of widows and orphans," admitted the *Raleigh* (North Carolina) *Daily Progress*. Confederate leaders realized they were losing the people's support. It is remarkable how long and how effectively the Confederacy sustained a military effort facing such internal division.

Antiwar Sentiment, South and North

In North Carolina, William W. Holden, a popular Democratic politician and editor, led a growing peace movement. Over one hundred public meetings supporting peace negotiations took place during summer 1863. In Georgia early in 1864, Governor Brown and Alexander H. Stephens, vice president of the Confederacy, led a similar effort. Ultimately, the lack of a two-party system made questionable the legitimacy of any government criticism.

In the 1863 congressional elections, secessionists and supporters of the administration lost seats to men not identified with the government. In the war's last years, Davis's support in the Confederate Congress dwindled. Some newspaper editors and soldiers, especially in Lee's Army of Northern Virginia, kept the Confederacy alive despite disintegrating popular support.

Link to Alexander H. Stephens's "Slavery is the Cornerstone of the Confederacy" speech.

By 1864, southerners were giving up the struggle. Deserters dominated whole towns and counties. Active dissent was particularly common in upland and mountain regions, where Union support always held fast. Opposition to the war, though less severe, existed in the North as well. Alarm intensified over the growing centralization of government. The draft sparked protest, especially among poor citizens, and the Union Army struggled with a troubling desertion rate. But with vast human resources, the Union government's effectiveness was never threatened.

Moreover, unlike Davis, Lincoln knew how to connect with ordinary citizen. Through public letters to newspapers and private ones to soldiers' families, he reached the common people. The battlefield carnage, political problems, and criticism weighed on him, but his administration never lost control of the war effort.

Peace Democrats

Much of the wartime protest in the North was political. The Democratic Party fought to regain power by blaming Lincoln for the war's death toll, the expansion of federal powers, inflation and the high tariff, and the emancipation of blacks. Its leaders called for an end to the war and reunion on the basis of "the Constitution as it is and the Union as it was." Democrats denounced conscription and martial law, and defended states' rights. They charged repeatedly that Republican policies were designed to flood the North with blacks, threatening white men's privileges. In the 1862 congressional elections, Democrats made a strong comeback, with peace Democrats wielding influence in New York State and majorities in the legislatures of Illinois and Indiana.

Led by outspoken men like Representative Clement L. Vallandigham of Ohio, the peace Democrats became highly visible. Vallandigham criticized Lincoln as a "dictator" who suspended the writ of habeas corpus without congressional authority arrested thousands of innocent citizens, and shut down opposition newspapers (which were true). He urged voters to depose "King Abraham." Vallandigham's attacks seemed so damaging that military authorities arrested him for treason. Lincoln wisely decided against punishment—and martyr's status—for the Ohioan and exiled him to the Confederacy. (Eventually, Vallandigham returned to the North through Canada.)

Some antiwar Democrats did encourage draft resistance, sabotage communications, and plot to aid the Confederacy. Republicans sometimes branded them—and by extension the peace Democrats—as **"Copperheads"** after the poisonous snake. Although some Confederate agents were active in the North and Canada, they never genuinely threatened the Union war effort.

Copperheads: A dangerous snake; Republican nickname for antiwar northern Democrats, some of whom were pacifists, others were activists who encouraged draft resistance, sabotage, and efforts to aid the Confederacy.

New York City Draft Riots

Although many soldiers risked their lives willingly, others sought to avoid service. Under the 1863 draft law, a draftee could stay at home by providing a substitute or paying a $300 commutation fee. Many wealthy men chose these options, and with high demand, clubs, cities, and states provided the money for others to escape conscription. In all, 118,000 substitutes were provided and 87,000 commutations paid before Congress ended the commutation system in 1864.

Urban poor and immigrants in strongly Democratic areas were especially hostile to conscription. The North's poor viewed the system as discriminatory, and many immigrants suspected (wrongly, on the whole) that they were disproportionately called. (Approximately 200,000 men born in Germany and 150,000 born in Ireland served in the Union Army.)

As a result, enrolling officers received rough treatment in many northern areas, and riots occurred in New Jersey, Ohio, Indiana, Pennsylvania, Illinois, and Wisconsin. The most serious violence occurred in New York City in July 1863. The war was unpopular there, and racial, ethnic, and class tensions ran high. Shippers had recently broken a longshoremen's strike by hiring black strikebreakers. Working-class New Yorkers feared an inflow of black labor from the South and regarded blacks as the cause of the war. Poor Irish workers resented being forced to serve in the place of others who could afford to avoid the draft.

Military police officers were attacked first, and then mobs crying, "Down with the rich" looted wealthy homes and stores. But blacks became the special target. Mobs rampaged through African American neighborhoods, beating and murdering people in the streets, and burning an orphan asylum. At least seventy-four people died during three days of violence. Army units dispatched from Gettysburg ended this tragic episode.

War Against Indians in the Far West

A civil war of another kind raged on the Great Plains and in the Southwest. By 1864, U.S. troops under the command of Colonel John Chivington waged full-scale war against the Sioux, Arapahos, and Cheyennes to eradicate Indian title to eastern Colorado. Indian chiefs sought peace, but American commanders had orders to "burn villages and kill Cheyennes." A Cheyenne chief, Lean Bear, was shot as he rode toward U.S. troops, holding papers given him by President Lincoln during a visit to Washington, D.C. Another chief, Black Kettle, was told by the U.S. command that his people would find safe haven in Sand Creek, Colorado. Instead on November 29, 1864, 700 cavalrymen, many drunk, attacked the Cheyenne village. With most men away hunting, the slaughter at the Sand Creek Massacre included 105 Cheyenne women and children and 28 men. American soldiers scalped and mutilated victims, carrying women's body parts on their saddles or hats back to Denver.

In New Mexico and Arizona Territories, an authoritarian and brutal commander, General James Carleton, waged war on the Apaches and Navajos. For generations, both tribes raided the region's Pueblo and Hispanic peoples to maintain their security and economy. During the Civil War years, Anglo-American farms also became Indian targets. In 1863, the New Mexico Volunteers, commanded by former mountain man Kit Carson, defeated the Mescalero Apaches and forced them onto a reservation at Bosque Redondo in the Pecos River valley.

But the Navajos resisted. Carson destroyed their livestock, orchards, and crops, causing the starving Navajos to surrender for food in January 1864. Three-quarters of the 12,000 Navajos were forced to march 400 miles (the "Long Walk") to the Bosque Redondo Reservation, suffering malnutrition and death en route. Permitted to return to a fraction of their homelands later that year, the Navajos never forgot the federal government's ruthless policies of removal and eradication of Indian peoples.

Election of 1864

Back east, war-weariness reached a peak in summer of 1864, when the Democratic Party nominated popular general George B. McClellan for president and inserted a peace plank into its platform. Written by Vallandigham, it called for an armistice and spoke vaguely about preserving the Union. Democrats made racist appeals to white insecurity, calling Lincoln "Abe the nigger-lover." No incumbent president had been reelected since 1832, and some Republicans worked to dump Lincoln from their ticket for Salmon P. Chase or John C. Frémont, although little came of either effort.

With the fall of Atlanta and Union victories in the Shenandoah Valley by early September, Lincoln's prospects rose. A decisive factor: eighteen states allowed troops to vote at the front. Lincoln won 78 percent of the soldier vote. With 55 percent of the popular vote, Lincoln's reelection—a referendum on the war and emancipation—devastated southern morale. Without this political outcome, a Union military victory and a redefined nation might never have happened.

1864–1865: The Final Test of Wills

The Confederates could still have won their version of victory in the war's final year if military stalemate and northern antiwar sentiment had forced a negotiated settlement. But the North prevailed.

> Why was it so crucial to northern military strategy that Europe remain neutral during the Civil War?

Northern Diplomatic Strategy

From the outset, the North had pursued one paramount goal: to prevent recognition of the Confederacy by European nations. Foreign recognition would belie Lincoln's claim that the United States was fighting an illegal rebellion and might lead to the financial and military aid that could ensure Confederate independence. Both England and France stood to benefit from a divided and weakened America. Thus, Lincoln and Secretary of State Seward needed to avoid serious military defeats and controversies with European powers.

Since the textile industry employed one-fifth of the British population, southerners banked on British recognition of the Confederacy. But at the war's start, British mills had a 50 percent surplus of cotton, and they later found new supplies in India, Egypt, and Brazil. The British government flirted with recognition of the Confederacy but awaited southern battlefield successes. France was unwilling to act without Britain. Confederate agents purchased arms and supplies in Europe and obtained loans from European financiers, but they never achieved a diplomatic breakthrough.

An acute crisis occurred in 1861 when the overzealous commander of an American frigate stopped the British steamer *Trent* and removed two Confederate ambassadors, James Mason and John Slidell, to a Boston prison. The British interpreted the capture as a violation of freedom of the seas and demanded the prisoners' release. Lincoln and Seward waited until northern public opinion cooled before releasing them. The incident strained U.S.-British relations.

Then the sale to the Confederacy of warships constructed in England sparked protest from U.S. ambassador Charles Francis Adams. Over twenty-two months, the English-built ship, the *Alabama,* destroyed or captured more than sixty U.S. ships.

Battlefield Stalemate and a Union Strategy for Victory

On the battlefield, northern victory was far from won in 1864. General Nathaniel Banks's Red River campaign to capture more of Louisiana and Texas fell apart, and the capture of Mobile Bay in August did not cause the fall of Mobile. Union general William Tecumseh Sherman soon brought total war to the southern heartland. On the eastern front during winter of 1863–1864, the two armies in Virginia settled into a stalemate awaiting another northern spring offensive.

Military authorities have historically agreed that deep invasion is risky: the farther an army penetrates enemy territory, the more vulnerable its communications and supply lines become. Moreover, observed the Prussian expert Karl von Clausewitz, if the invader encounters a "truly national" resistance, his troops will be "everywhere exposed to attacks by an insurgent population."

General Grant, by now in command of the entire federal army, tested southern will with massive raids. Grant proposed to use armies to destroy Confederate railroads, thus ruining the enemy's transportation and economy. Union troops would live off the land while destroying resources useful to the Confederate military and to the civilian population. After General George H. Thomas's troops won the Battle of Chattanooga in November 1863, Georgia's heartland lay open. Grant entrusted General Sherman with 100,000 men for an invasion toward Atlanta's rail center.

Fall of Atlanta

Jefferson Davis positioned General Joseph E. Johnston's army in Sherman's path. Davis's political strategy for 1864 was to demonstrate Confederate military strength and defend Atlanta. Davis anxiously sought assurances that Atlanta would be held. From a military viewpoint, Johnston maneuvered skillfully. But when Johnston fell silent and continued to retreat, Davis replaced him with the one-legged General John Hood, who knew his job was to fight.

Hood attacked but was beaten, and Sherman's army occupied Atlanta on September 2, 1864. The victory buoyed northern spirits and ensured Lincoln's reelection. Davis exhorted southerners to fight on. Hood's army marched north to

The Civil War in Britain

Because of the direct reliance of the British textile industry on southern cotton (cut off by the war), the American conflict was significant in Britain's economy and domestic politics. The British aristocracy and most cotton mill owners were pro-Confederate and proslavery, whereas clergymen, shopkeepers, artisans, and radical politicians worked for the causes of Union and emancipation. Most British workers saw their future at stake in a war for slave emancipation. "Freedom" to the huge British working class (who could not vote) meant basic political and civil rights, as well as secure jobs in an industrializing economy.

English aristocrats saw Americans as untutored and took satisfaction in America's troubles. Conservatives believed in the superiority of the British system of government and looked askance at America's leveling tendencies. And some aristocratic British Liberals sympathized with the Confederacy's demand for independence. English racism also intensified, exemplified by the popularity of minstrelsy and the employment of science in racial theory.

The British propaganda war over the American conflict was widespread: public meetings organized by both sides were huge affairs, with competing banners, carts and floats, orators and resolutions. In a press war, the British argued over when rebellion is justified, whether secession was right or legal, whether slavery was at the heart of the conflict, and especially over the democratic image of America. This bitter debate became a test of reform in Britain: those eager for a broadened franchise and increased democracy were pro-Union, and those who preferred Britain's class-ridden political system favored the Confederacy.

The nature of the internal British debate was symbolized by the dozens of African Americans who served as pro-Union agents in England. The most popular was William Andrew Jackson, Confederate president Jefferson Davis's former coachman, who escaped from Richmond in September 1862. At British public meetings, Jackson countered pro-Confederate arguments that the war was not about slavery.

In the end, the British government did not recognize the Confederacy, and by 1864 English cotton lords found new sources in Egypt and India. But in this link between America and its English roots at its time of greatest travail, we can see the Civil War's international significance.

Some southern leaders pronounced that cotton was king and would bring Britain to their cause. This British cartoon shows King Cotton brought down in chains by the American eagle, anticipating the cotton famine to follow and the intense debate in Great Britain over the nature and meaning of the American Civil War.

Granger Collection

cut Sherman's supply lines and force him to withdraw, but Sherman marched sixty thousand of his marauding men to the sea (see Map 15.2).

Sherman's March to the Sea

Sherman's army was formidable, composed almost entirely of battle-tested veterans and officers who rose through the ranks from the Midwestern states. Before the march, army doctors weeded out men who were weak or sick. Although many harbored racist attitudes, most now supported emancipation because, as one said, "Slavery stands in the way of putting down the rebellion."

As Sherman's men moved across Georgia, they cut a path 50 to 60 miles wide and more than 200 miles long. The destruction they caused was awesome; indeed, it was Sherman's campaign that later prompted historians to deem this the first modern "total war." A Georgia woman described the "Burnt Country" this way: "The fields were trampled down and the road was lined with carcasses of horses, hogs, and cattle that the invaders, unable either to consume or to carry with them, had wantonly shot down to starve our people." After reaching Savannah in December, Sherman marched his armies into the Carolinas. To his soldiers, South Carolina was "the root of secession." They burned and destroyed as they marched, encountering little resistance. The opposing army of General Johnston was small, but Sherman's men should have faced guerrilla raids and attacks by local defense units. The absence of both led South Carolina's James Chesnut Jr. (a politician and the husband of Mary Chesnut) to write that his state "was shamefully and unnecessarily lost." Southerners lost the will to continue.

MAP 15.2

Sherman's March to the Sea

The deep South proved a decisive theater at the end of the war. From Chattanooga, Union forces drove into Georgia, capturing Atlanta. Following the fall of Atlanta, General Sherman embarked on his march of destruction through Georgia to the coast and then northward through the Carolinas.

Source: Copyright © Cengage Learning

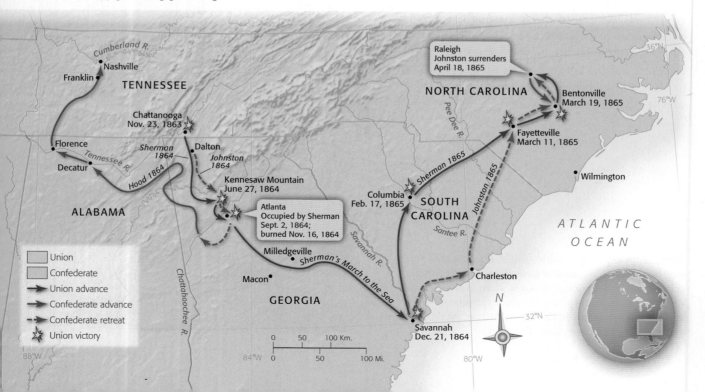

In Georgia alone, as many as nineteen thousand slaves followed the maraud-ing Union troops. Others remained on the plantations to await the war's end, because of either wariness of whites or negative experiences with federal soldiers. The destruction of food harmed slaves as along with white rebels, and many blacks lost livestock, clothing, crops, and other valuables to their liberators.

Virginia's Bloody Soil

Throughout spring and summer 1864, intent on captur-ing Richmond, Grant hurled his troops at Lee's army and suffered appalling losses: almost eighteen thousand casualties in the Battle of the Wilderness; more than eight thousand at Spotsylvania; and twelve thousand in just hours at Cold Harbor.

Before the assault at Cold Harbor, Union troops pinned scraps of paper bearing their names to their backs, certain they would be mowed down as they rushed Lee's trenches. In four weeks in May and June, Grant lost as many men as were enrolled in Lee's entire army. From early May until July, when Union forces fought from forests west of Fredericksburg to Petersburg, south of Richmond, the two armies engaged each other nearly every day. Wagon trains carrying thousands of Union wounded crawled back toward Washington.

Undaunted, Grant kept up the pressure. Although costly, these battles enabled eventual victory: Lee's army shrank until offensive action was no longer pos-sible, while Grant's army kept replenishing itself with new recruits. The siege of Petersburg, with the armies facing each other in miles of trenches, lasted through-out winter 1864–1865.

Surrender at Appomattox

With the numerical superiority of Grant's army now greater than two to one, Confederate defeat was inevita-ble. On April 2, Lee abandoned Richmond and Petersburg. On April 9, he surrendered at **Appomattox Court House**. Grant treated his rival respect-fully and paroled the defeated troops, allowing cavalrymen to keep their horses. Within weeks, Johnston surrendered to Sherman in North Carolina, and Davis, who had fled Richmond, was captured in Georgia. The war was over; the North rejoiced, and most southerners fell into despair.

Appomattox Court House: Site of Lee's surrender to Grant marking the end of the Civil War.

Lincoln lived to see but a few days of the war's aftermath. On the evening of April 14, he accompanied his wife to Ford's Theatre in Washington. There John Wilkes Booth, an embittered southern sympathizer, shot the president in the head at point-blank range. Lincoln died the next day. Twelve days later, troops tracked and killed Booth. Relief at the war's end mingled with a renewed sense of loss and anxiety about the future.

Financial Tally

U.S. loans and taxes during the conflict totaled almost $3 billion, and interest on the war debt was $2.8 billion. The Confederacy borrowed over $2 billion but lost far more in the destruction of homes, crops, livestock, and other property. Union troops looted factories and put two-thirds of the South's railroad system out of service.

Estimates of the total cost of the war exceed $20 billion—five times the total expenditures of the federal government from its creation until 1861. By 1865, the fed-eral government's spending soared to twenty times the prewar level and accounted for over 26 percent of the gross national product. Many changes were more or less

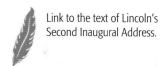

Link to the text of Lincoln's Second Inaugural Address.

Abraham Lincoln's "Second Inaugural Address"

Historian Don Fehrenbacher wrote that "some of Lincoln's words have acquired transcendent meaning as contributions to the permanent literary treasure of the nation." How is this so with the short oration Lincoln delivered at the Capitol on March 4, 1865? In a 701-word prose poem at his second inauguration, Lincoln probed the tragedy of the Civil War and interpreted its meanings. The first paragraph acknowledges the "progress of our arms" over four years of war. In the second paragraph, Lincoln entwines North and South in a mutual fate, but suggests responsibility for which side "would *make* war," and which side "would *accept* war," and leaves it to posterity: "And the war came."

Then Lincoln offers a theological-historical explanation of the war that still resonates today in how Americans interpret this turning point in their history. Lincoln declares that "all knew...somehow" slavery was the "*cause*" of the conflict. Both sides appealed to the "same God." But Lincoln called it "strange that any men should dare to ask a just God's assistance in ringing their bread from the sweat of other men's faces." Lincoln imagined slavery as an "offence" that came "in the providence of God," and brought "this mighty scourge of war" as its awful price.

Suddenly, in rhetoric unusual for presidential inaugurals, Lincoln assumed the prophet's mantle: "Yet if God wills that it [the war] continue, until all the wealth piled by the bond-man's two hundred and fifty years of unrequited toil shall be sunk, and until every drop of blood drawn by the lash, shall be paid by another drawn with the sword, as was said three thousand years ago, so still it must be said 'the judgments of the Lord are true and righteous altogether.'"

Famously, Lincoln ended with a single sentence, where he declared "malice toward none... charity for all" the healing balm for the "nation's wounds." Whether Lincoln was the nation's healer or its war-maker who would demand any sacrifice to restore the Union and destroy slavery has always animated the study of his personal story. The legacy of the Civil War, and Lincoln's own place in it, are forever enmeshed in interpretations of this oratorical masterpiece.

permanent, as wartime measures left the government more deeply involved in manufacturing, banking, and transportation.

Death Toll and its Impact

More men died in the Civil War than in all other American wars combined until Vietnam. The total number of casualties exceeded 1 million—frightfully high for a nation of 31 million people. Approximately 360,000 Union soldiers died, most from disease. Another 275,175 Union soldiers were wounded but survived. On the Confederate side, an estimated 260,000 lost their lives, and almost as many suffered wounds. Not all died on the battlefield: Roughly 30,218 northerners died in southern prisons and 25,976 Confederates died in Union prisons.

The scale and the anonymous nature of death (approximately 620,000 total dead) overwhelmed American culture and led to the establishment of national cemeteries, where the large majority of the fallen were buried without identification. The desperate urge to memorialize individual soldiers in this war, writes historian

Drew Faust, stemmed from "the anguish of wives, parents, siblings, and children who found undocumented, unconfirmed, and unrecognizable loss intolerable."

Summary

The Civil War altered American society forever. Although precise figures on enlistments are unavailable, it appears that 700,000 to 800,000 men served in the Confederate armies. Far more, possibly 2.3 million, served in the Union armies. All were taken from home and family; their lives, if they survived, were permanently altered. During the war, northern and southern women took on new roles to manage the hardships of the home front and to support the war effort.

Industrialization and economic enterprises grew exponentially with the war. Ordinary citizens' futures were increasingly tied to huge organizations. Under Republican leadership, the federal government expanded its power to preserve the Union and extend freedom. A social revolution and government authority emancipated the slaves. It was unclear at war's end how or whether the nation would use its power to protect former slaves' rights. The war left many unanswered questions: How would white southerners, embittered and impoverished, respond to efforts to reconstruct the nation? How would the country care for the maimed, the orphans, the farm widows? What would be the place of black men and women in American life?

In the West, a second civil war resulted in conquest of southwestern Indians by U.S. troops and land-hungry settlers. On the diplomatic front, the Union government managed to keep Great Britain and other foreign powers out of the war. Dissent played a crucial role in the Confederacy's collapse.

In the Civil War, Americans experienced a dramatic transformation. White southerners experienced defeat that few other Americans ever faced. Blacks were moving proudly but anxiously from slavery to freedom. White northerners were self-conscious victors in a massive war for the nation's existence and for new definitions of freedom. The war would leave a compelling memory in American hearts and minds for generations.

Chapter Review

America Goes to War, 1861–1862

What was the impact of the North's naval victories along the southern coast?

In essence, it triggered a revolution in slave society. As federal gunboats drew near the South Carolina coast, planters fled their land. Confederate soldiers were unable to round up slaves, who saw the arrival of the Union navy as a possible door to their freedom. As such, slaves broke cotton gins, stole clothing and furniture from masters' homes, and ran away to join the Union army. While the Union initially did not acknowledge the slaves as free—and instead labeled them war "contraband"—it did put them to work for the Union army.

War Transforms the South

What happened to the South's embrace of state sovereignty during the war?

The state power that had been so sacred to the South before the war was forced—by the need to mobilize—to yield to a central authority. To maintain the war effort, the Confederacy centralized its operations, troops, and supplies, seeing the efforts of individual states as likely to fragment the greater cause. President Jefferson Davis took a firm leadership role toward the Confederate Congress and urged state governments to require farmers to switch from cash crops to food production. The central government assumed control of the southern economy and nearly complete control of the railroads. Much to the dismay of many secessionists, the Southern bureaucracy ironically became larger than its northern counterpart and provided new opportunities for women to work in government jobs.

Wartime Northern Economy and Society

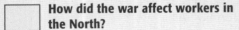

How did the war affect workers in the North?

Northern urban and industrial workers did not fare as well as business owners and merchants during the war. While they enjoyed more job opportunities and higher wages as the wartime economy grew, inflation devoured much of their earnings. Consumer price hikes were nearly twice the rate of workers' salary increases, and workers' families saw their standard of living decline. They also lost job security as employers replaced workers with new labor-saving machines or cheap immigrant workers. Workers in several industries responded by starting unions or going out on strike, but manufacturers fought back with black-lists or by requiring workers to sign "yellow dog" contracts promising not to join a union.

The Advent of Emancipation

Why did Lincoln and Davis both avoid the slavery issue in the early days of the war?

Davis feared the issue would increase class conflict between slaveless yeoman farmers and slave-owning plantation owners in the South. Instead, he preferred to say that southerners were fighting to preserve their constitutional liberties against northerners. Lincoln avoided the topic of slavery to keep from antagonizing the Union's border states, whose loyalty he sought to preserve. He also hoped to inspire a pro-Union majority in the South that might push the region back to the national fold. Avoiding the topic was also politically expedient, since no Republican or northern consensus on slavery existed early in the war—some were strident abolitionists, others were racists who wanted to protect whites from both the Southern Slave Power and the competition of slave labor.

The Soldiers' War

What led previously reluctant white military leaders to accept black soldiers?

At the beginning of the war, the Union army was racist, and many soldiers did not want to fight with blacks, whom they considered inferior. They tolerated them because black recruits would do the jobs white soldiers disliked. White officers' opinions changed when they witnessed the bravery and determination of the segregated black units they led. Black soldiers, too, felt they were fighting prejudice through their military successes, thereby proving their manhood and legitimate claim to freedom. Black soldiers' willingness to die in battle also earned the respect of white men. Many black and white soldiers who fought together did forge deep ties, especially those of the ill-fated fifty-fourth Massachusetts regiment.

1863: The Tide of Battle Turns

What turned the tide of war toward Union victory?

Battles at Vicksburg and Gettysburg changed the course of war from a possible Confederate victory to one assured for the Union. Vicksburg was the last major fortification on the Mississippi River in southern hands, while Gettysburg marked Lee's attempts to break the Union line and invade the North. Both battles produced heavy losses, but also left the Confederate army divided, so that west of the Mississippi General E. Kirby Smith operated alone, while Louisiana, Tennessee, and Mississippi were vulnerable to invasions. After Gettysburg, there were no more Confederate offensive moves; severely weakened, the Confederate army could only act defensively.

Disunity: South, North, and West

What were the causes of wartime dissent in the South?

People across class lines increasingly disliked the actions taken by their government. Planters opposed new taxation and the impressments of their slaves to build fortifications. They also resented that Confederate commanders burned planters' cotton stores as Union soldiers advanced. People universally rejected the increasing size and power of the central government in Richmond and conscription for military service. Many people faced hunger shortages and refused to comply with conscription, taxation, or the demand to provide food for soldiers. The ability of wealthy people to buy their way out of military service by hiring substitutes fueled resentment among soldiers, some of whom abandoned the army.

1864–1865: The Final Test of Wills

Why was it so crucial to northern military strategy that Europe remain neutral during the Civil War?

Lincoln felt that if foreign countries recognized the Confederacy, it would legitimize what Lincoln considered an illegal rebellion. He also feared it could lead to military and financial aid that would facilitate a Confederate victory and its ultimate independence. The president knew that both England and France would gain by a divided America, but France would not act without Britain, and Britain wasn't making a move until there were major southern battlefield successes. While England's relationship with southern textile mills made the confederacy hopeful for an alliance, Britain's large cotton surplus and new supplies in India, Egypt, and Brazil kept it from doing more than selling arms and supplies or offering loans.

Suggestions for Further Reading

Stephen V. Ash, *When the Yankees Came: Conflict and Chaos in the Occupied South* (1995)

Edward L. Ayers, *In the Presence of Mine Enemies: War in the Heart of America, 1859–1863* (2002)

Ira Berlin et al., eds., *Freedom: A Documentary History of Emancipation, 1861–1867*, 3 vols. (1979–1982)

David W. Blight, *Frederick Douglass' Civil War: Keeping Faith in Jubilee* (1989)

Alice Fahs, *The Imagined Civil War: Popular Literature of the North and South* (2001)

Drew G. Faust, *This Republic of Suffering: Death and the American Civil War* (2008)

Chandra Manning, *What This Cruel War Is Over: Soldiers, Slavery, and the Civil War* (2007)

Gary W. Gallagher, *The Confederate War* (1997)

Bruce Levine, *Confederate Emancipation: Southern Plans to Free and Arm Slaves During the Civil War* (2006)

James M. McPherson, *Battle Cry of Freedom: The Civil War Era* (1987)

Philip S. Paludan, *"A People's Contest": The Union and the Civil War* (1989)

Mark R. Wilson, *The Business of Civil War: Military Mobilization and the State, 1861–1865* (2006)

Go to the CourseMate website for primary source links, study tools, and review materials for this chapter. www.cengagebrain.com

Reconstruction: An Unfinished Revolution

1865–1877

The lower half of secession's seedbed, Charleston, South Carolina, lay in ruin when most of the white population evacuated on February 18, 1865. A bombardment by Union forces around Charleston harbor destroyed many of the low-country planters' homes. Fires broke out everywhere, ignited in bales of cotton stockpiled in public squares. To many observers, the flames were the funeral pyres of a dying civilization.

Among the first Union troops to enter Charleston, the Twenty-first U.S. Colored Regiment received the city's surrender from its mayor. For black Charlestonians, who were mostly former slaves, this was a time to celebrate their freedom. Charleston's freedpeople converted Confederate ruin into a vision of Reconstruction based on Union victory and black liberation.

During the war's last year, the Confederates transformed the planters' Race Course, a horseracing track, and its famed Jockey Club, into a prison. Kept outdoors in the middle of the track, 257 Union soldiers died there of exposure and disease and were buried in a mass grave behind the judges' stand. After the city fell, more than twenty black workmen reinterred the dead in marked graves. On the archway over the cemetery's entrance, they painted the inscription "Martyrs of the Race Course."

On the morning of May 1, 1865, a thousand people marched around the planters' Race Course, led by three thousand children carrying roses and singing "John Brown's Body." Black women with flowers and wreaths came next, followed by black men. The parade concluded with black and white Union regiments and white missionaries and teachers. At the gravesite, five black ministers read from Scripture, and a black children's choir sang "America," "The Star-Spangled Banner," and Negro spirituals. After the ceremony, the crowd retired to the Race Course for speeches, picnics, and military festivities.

African Americans founded this "Decoration Day"—now Memorial Day, to remember those lost in battle. In their vision, they were creating the Independence Day of a Second American Revolution.

Chapter Outline

Wartime Reconstruction
Lincoln's 10 Percent Plan | Congress and the Wade-Davis Bill | Thirteenth Amendment | Freedmen's Bureau | Ruins and Enmity

The Meanings of Freedom
The Feel of Freedom | Reunion of African American Families | Blacks' Search for Independence | Freedpeople's Desire for Land | Black Embrace of Education | Growth of Black Churches | Rise of the Sharecropping System

VISUALIZING THE PAST *Sharecropping: Enslaved to Debt*

Johnson's Reconstruction Plan
Andrew Johnson of Tennessee | Johnson's Racial Views | Johnson's Pardon Policy | Presidential Reconstruction | Black Codes

The Congressional Reconstruction Plan
The Radicals | Congress Versus Johnson | Fourteenth Amendment | The South's and Johnson's Defiance | Reconstruction Acts of 1867–1868 | Failure of Land Redistribution | Constitutional Crisis | Impeachment of President Johnson | Election of 1868 | Fifteenth Amendment

Politics and Reconstruction in the South
White Resistance | Black Voters and the Southern Republican Party | Triumph of Republican Governments | Industrialization and Mill Towns | Republicans and Racial Equality | Myth of "Negro Rule" | Carpetbaggers and Scalawags | Tax Policy and Corruption as Political Wedges | Ku Klux Klan

The Civil War and its aftermath wrought unprecedented changes in American society, law, and politics, but economic power, racism, and judicial conservatism limited Reconstruction's revolutionary potential. The nation had to determine the nature of federal-state relations, whether confiscated land could be redistributed, and how to bring justice to freedpeople and aggrieved white southerners. Americans also had to heal psychologically from a bloody and fratricidal war. How they negotiated the relationship between healing and justice would determine the extent of change during Reconstruction.

The turmoil wrought by Reconstruction was most evident in national politics. Lincoln's successor, Andrew Johnson, fought with Congress over Reconstruction policies. Although a southerner, Johnson disliked the South's wealthy planters, and his initial actions suggested that he would be tough on "traitors." By late 1865, however, Johnson became the protector of southern interests.

Johnson imagined a lenient and rapid "restoration" of the South to the Union rather than the fundamental "reconstruction" that Republican congressmen favored. Between 1866 and 1868, the president and Republican leadership in Congress disagreed. Before it ended, Congress impeached the president, enfranchised freedmen, and gave them a role in reconstructing the South. The nation also adopted the Fourteenth and Fifteenth Amendments, ensuring equal protection of the law, citizenship, and universal manhood suffrage. But the cause of equal rights for African Americans fell almost as fast as it had risen.

By 1869, the Ku Klux Klan employed violence to thwart Reconstruction and undermine black freedom. As white Democrats in the South took over state governments, they encountered little opposition. Moreover, the wartime industrial boom created new opportunities and priorities. The West drew American resources like never before. Political corruption became a nationwide scandal, and bribery a part of business.

The white South's desire to reclaim control of its states and of race relations overwhelmed the national interest in stopping it. Thus, Reconstruction became a revolution eclipsed, leaving legacies with which the nation has struggled ever since.

As you read this chapter, keep the following questions in mind:

* **Should the Reconstruction era be considered the Second American Revolution? By what criteria should we make such a judgment?**

* **What were the origins and meanings of the Fourteenth Amendment in the 1860s? What is its significance today?**

* **Reconstruction is judged to have "ended" in 1877. Over the course of the 1870s, what caused its end?**

Retreat from Reconstruction
Political Implications of Klan Terrorism | *Industrial Expansion and Reconstruction in the North* | *Liberal Republican Revolt* | *General Amnesty* | *The West, Race, and Reconstruction* | *Foreign Expansion* | *Judicial Retreat from Reconstruction* | *Disputed Election of 1876 and Compromise of 1877*

LINKS TO THE WORLD *The "Back to Africa" Movement*

LEGACY FOR A PEOPLE AND A NATION *The Lost Cause*

SUMMARY

Chronology

1865	Johnson begins rapid and lenient Reconstruction
	White southern governments pass restrictive black codes
	Congress refuses to seat southern representatives
	Thirteenth Amendment ratified, abolishing slavery
1866	Congress passes Civil Rights Act and renewal of Freedmen's Bureau over Johnson's veto
	Congress approves Fourteenth Amendment
	In *Ex parte Milligan,* the Supreme Court reasserts its influence
1867	Congress passes First Reconstruction Act and Tenure of Office Act
	Constitutional conventions called in southern states
1868	House impeaches and Senate acquits Johnson
	Most southern states readmitted to Union under Radical plan
	Fourteenth Amendment ratified
	Grant elected president
1869	Congress approves Fifteenth Amendment (ratified in 1870)
1871	Congress passes second Enforcement Act and Ku Klux Klan Act
	Treaty with England settles Alabama claims
1872	Amnesty Act frees almost all remaining Confederates from restrictions on holding office
	Grant reelected
1873	*Slaughter-House* cases limit power of Fourteenth Amendment
	Panic of 1873 leads to widespread unemployment and labor strife
1874	Democrats win majority in House of Representatives
1875	Several Grant appointees indicted for corruption
	Congress passes weak Civil Rights Act
	Democratic Party increases control of southern states with white supremacy campaigns
1876	*U.S. v. Cruikshank* further weakens Fourteenth Amendment
	Presidential election disputed
1877	Congress elects Hayes president

Wartime Reconstruction

Which two political acts recognized the centrality of slavery to the war?

How to best reconstruct the Union was an issue as early as 1863, well before the war ended. Specifically, four vexing problems compelled early thinking and would haunt the Reconstruction era. One, who would rule in the South once it was defeated? Two, who would rule in the federal government—Congress or the president? Three, what were the dimensions of black freedom, and what rights under law would the freedmen enjoy? And four, would Reconstruction be a preservation of the old republic or a second Revolution, inventing a new republic?

Lincoln's 10 Percent Plan

Abraham Lincoln had never been anti-southern. His fear was that the war would collapse into guerrilla warfare by surviving Confederates. Lincoln insisted on leniency for southern soldiers once they surrendered. In his Second Inaugural Address, delivered a month before his assassination, Lincoln promised "malice toward none; with charity for all."

Lincoln planned early for a swift and moderate Reconstruction. In his 1863 "Proclamation of Amnesty and Reconstruction," he proposed replacing majority rule with "loyal rule" to reconstruct southern state governments and pardoning ex-Confederates except the highest-ranking military and civilian officers. Once

10 percent of a given state's voting population in the 1860 general election had taken an oath to the United States and established a government, the new state would be recognized. Lincoln did not consult Congress in these plans, and "loyal" assemblies (known as "Lincoln governments") were created in Louisiana, Tennessee, and Arkansas in 1864, states largely occupied by Union troops on which they depended for survival.

Congress and the Wade-Davis Bill

Congress was hostile toward Lincoln's moves to readmit southern states prematurely. Radical Republicans, proponents of emancipation and of aggressively defeating the South, regarded the 10 percent plan a "mere mockery" of democracy. Led by Pennsylvania Congressman Thaddeus Stevens and Massachusetts Senator Charles Sumner, congressional Republicans proposed a harsher approach. Stevens advocated a "conquered provinces" theory, arguing that southerners organized as a foreign nation to war on the United States and, by secession, destroyed their statehood status. They therefore must be treated as "conquered foreign lands" and returned to the status of "unorganized territories" before applying for readmission.

In July 1864, the Wade-Davis bill, sponsored by Ohio Senator Benjamin Wade and Maryland Congressman Henry W. Davis, emerged from Congress with three specific conditions for southern readmission.

Link to the Wade-Davis bill.

1. It demanded a "majority" of white male citizens participating in the creation of a new government.
2. To vote or be a delegate to constitutional conventions, men had to take an "iron-clad" oath (declaring that they never aided the Confederate war effort).
3. All officers above the rank of lieutenant, and all civil officials in the Confederacy, would be disfranchised and deemed "not a citizen of the United States."

Lincoln pocket-vetoed the bill and issued a conciliatory proclamation that he would not commit to any "one plan" of Reconstruction.

This exchange occurred when the war's outcome and Lincoln's reelection were still in doubt. On August 5, Radical Republicans issued the "Wade-Davis Manifesto" to newspapers, accusing Lincoln of usurpation of presidential powers and disgraceful leniency toward an eventually conquered South. Lincoln saw Reconstruction as a means of weakening the Confederacy and winning the war; the Radicals saw it as a transformation of the nation's political and racial order.

Thirteenth Amendment

In early 1865, Congress and Lincoln joined in two important measures that recognized slavery's centrality to the war. On January 31, Congress passed the **Thirteenth Amendment**, which abolished involuntary servitude and declared that Congress shall have the power to enforce this outcome by "appropriate legislation." When the measure passed by 119 to 56, just 2 votes more than the necessary two-thirds, Congress rejoiced.

Thirteenth Amendment: The Constitutional amendment that abolished slavery; passed by Congress in 1865.

But the Thirteenth Amendment had emerged from a congressional debate and considerable petitioning and public advocacy. One of the first and most remarkable petitions for a constitutional amendment abolishing slavery was submitted early in 1864 by Elizabeth Cady Stanton, Susan B. Anthony, and the Women's Loyal National League. Union women accumulated thousands of signatures. It was a long road from the Emancipation Proclamation to the Thirteenth Amendment—through treacherous constitutional theory about individual "property rights," beliefs that the sacred document (the Constitution) ought never to be altered, and partisan politics.

Freedmen's Bureau

On March 3, 1865, Congress created the Bureau of Refugees, Freedmen, and Abandoned Lands—the **Freedmen's Bureau**, an unprecedented agency of social uplift. With thousands of refugees in the South, the government continued what private freedmen's aid societies started in 1862. In its four-year existence, the Freedmen's Bureau supplied food and medical services, built several thousand schools and some colleges, negotiated several hundred thousand employment contracts between freedmen and their former masters, and managed confiscated land.

The Bureau was a controversial aspect of Reconstruction. Southern whites hated it, and politicians divided over its constitutionality. Some bureau agents were devoted to freedmen's rights; others exploited the chaos of the postwar South. The war prompted an eternal question of republics: what are the social welfare obligations of the state toward its people, and what do people owe their governments in return? Apart from their conquest and displacement of the eastern Indians, Americans were inexperienced at the Freedmen's Bureau's task—social reform through military occupation.

Freedmen's Bureau: Created by Congress in March 1865, this agency had responsibility for the relief, education, and employment of former slaves as well as white refugees

Ruins and Enmity

In 1865, with the war's devastation, America was a land with ruins. Some cities lay in rubble, large stretches of the countryside were depopulated and defoliated, and thousands of people, white and black, were refugees. Many white refugees faced genuine starvation. Of the approximately 18,300,000 rations distributed across the South in the Freedmen's Bureau's first three years, 5,230,000 went to whites.

In October 1865, after a five-month imprisonment in Boston, former Confederate Vice President Alexander H. Stephens rode a train southward. When he reached northern Georgia, his native state, his expressed shock: "War has left a terrible impression.... Fences gone, fields all a-waste, houses burnt." Every northern traveler encountered hatred from white southerners. A North Carolina innkeeper told a journalist that Yankees killed his sons, burned his house, stole his slaves and left him "one inestimable privilege ... to hate 'em."

The Meanings of Freedom

Black southerners entered life after slavery with hope and circumspection. A Texas man recalled his father's telling him, "Our forever was going to be spent living among the Southerners, after they got licked." Often the changes freed people valued most were personal—alterations in employer or living arrangements.

How did blacks exert their newfound freedom?

The Feel of Freedom

For former slaves, Reconstruction meant a chance to explore freedom. Former slaves remembered singing into the night after federal troops, who confirmed rumors of their emancipation, reached their plantations. A few people gave in to the desire to do what was formerly impossible. One angry grandmother dropped her hoe and confronted her mistress with, "I'm free! Ain't got to work for you no more!" Another man recalled that he and others "started on the move," either to search for family members or just to move on.

As slaves, they had learned to expect hostility from white people; they did not presume it would instantly disappear. Many freedpeople evaluated potential employers cautiously. After searching for better circumstances, a majority of blacks eventually settled as agricultural workers back on their former farms or plantations. But they relocated their houses and tried to control the conditions of their labor.

Reunion of African American Families

Throughout the South, former slaves focused on reuniting their families, separated during slavery by sale or hardship, and during the war by dislocation. By relying on the black community for help and by placing ads in black newspapers into the 1880s, some succeeded, while others searched in vain.

Husbands and wives who belonged to different masters established homes together to raise their children. When her old master claimed a right to whip her children, a mother replied, "he warn't goin' to brush none of her chilluns no more."

Blacks' Search for Independence

Many black people wanted to minimize contact with whites because, as Reverend Garrison Frazier told General Sherman in January 1865, "There is a prejudice against us … that will take years to get over." As such, blacks abandoned slave quarters and fanned out to distant corners of the land they worked. Some described moving "across the creek" or building a "saplin house … back in the woods." Other rural dwellers established small, all-black settlements that still exist along the South's back roads.

Link to Jourdan Anderson's letter to his former master.

Freedpeople's Desire for Land

In addition to a fair employer, freedpeople wanted to own land, which represented self-sufficiency and compensation for generations of bondage. General Sherman's special Field Order Number 15, issued in February 1865, set aside 400,000 acres of land in the Sea Islands for settlement of freedpeople. Hope swelled among ex-slaves as forty-acre plots and mules were promised to them. But President Johnson ordered them removed in October and the land returned to its original owners under army enforcement.

Most members of both political parties opposed land redistribution to the freedmen. Even northern reformers who administered the Sea Islands during the war showed little sympathy for black aspirations. The former Sea Island slaves wanted small, self-sufficient farms. Northern soldiers, officials, and missionaries brought education and aid to the freedmen but insisted that they grow cotton for competitive market. Ultimately, the U.S. government eventually sold thousands of acres in the Sea Islands, 90 percent of which went to wealthy northern investors.

Black Embrace of Education

Blacks hungered for education that previously belonged only to whites. With freedom, they started schools and filled dirt-floor classrooms, studying day and night. Children brought infants to school, and adults attended at night or after "the crops were laid by." Despite their poverty, many blacks paid tuition, typically $1 or $1.50

African Americans of all ages eagerly pursued the opportunity to gain an education in freedom. This young woman in Mt. Meigs, Alabama, is helping her mother learn to read.

Smithsonian Institution, photo by Rudolf Eickemeyer

a month, which constituted major portions of a person's agricultural wages and totaled more than $1 million by 1870.

In its brief life, the Freedmen's Bureau founded over four thousand schools, and northern reformers established others through private philanthropy. The Yankee schoolmarm—dedicated, selfless, and religious—became an agent of progress in many southern communities. By 1877, more than 600,000 African Americans were enrolled in elementary school.

Blacks and their white allies also established colleges and universities. The American Missionary Association founded seven colleges, including Fisk and Atlanta Universities, between 1866 and 1869. The Freedmen's Bureau helped establish Howard University in Washington, D.C., and northern religious groups, such as the Methodists, Baptists, and Congregationalists, supported seminaries and teachers' colleges.

During Reconstruction, African American leaders often were highly educated members of the prewar elite of free people of color. Francis Cardozo, who held various offices in South Carolina, attended universities in Scotland and England. P. B. S. Pinchback, who became lieutenant governor of Louisiana, was the son of a planter who sent him to school in Cincinnati.

Growth of Black Churches

Freed from slavery's restrictions, blacks could build their own institutions. The secret churches of slavery became public; in communities throughout the South, ex-slaves "started a brush arbor…shelter with leaves for a roof," where freed men and women worshiped.

Within a few years, branches of the Methodist and Baptist denominations attracted most southern black Christians. By 1877 in South Carolina, the African Methodist Episcopal (A.M.E.) Church had a thousand ministers, forty-four thousand members, and a school of theology, while the A.M.E. Zion Church had forty-five thousand members. In these churches, some of which became the wealthiest and most autonomous institutions in black life, freedpeople created enduring communities.

sharecropping: A system where landowners and former slaves managed a new arrangement, with laborers paying with a portion of their crops for the right to work their own land, thereby usually ending up in permanent debt.

Rise of the Sharecropping System

Since most former slaves lacked money to buy land, they preferred the next best thing: renting it. But the South had few sources of credit, and few whites would rent to blacks. Consequently, black farmers and white landowners turned to **sharecropping**, a system in which a landlord or a merchant "furnished" food and supplies, such as draft animals and seed, to farmers who worked the land and received payment from

Sharecropping: Enslaved to Debt

Sharecropping became an oppressive system in the postwar South. A new labor structure that began as a compromise between freedmen who wanted independence and landowners who wanted a stable work force, evolved into a method of working on "halves" and where tenants owed endless debts to the furnishing merchants, who owned plantation stores like this one, photographed in Mississippi in 1868. Merchants recorded in ledger books, like the one at right, the debts that few sharecroppers were able to repay. Why did both former slaves and former slaveowners initially find sharecropping an agreeable, if difficult, new labor arrangement? What were the short- and long-term consequences of the sharecropping system for the freedpeople and for the Southern economy?

Amistad Center for Art & Culture, Hartford, CT. Simpson Collection/Art Resource, New York

This Mississippi plantation store, shown in 1868, is a typical example of the new institution of the furnishing merchant and its power over post-slavery agriculture in the South.

Smithsonian Institution, Division of Community Life

Furnishing merchants kept such ledger books for decades; they became the record of how sharecroppers fell deeper in debt from year to year, and "owed their soul" to the country store.

the crop. White landowners and black farmers bargained with one another; sharecroppers would hold out, or move from year to year. As the system matured during the 1870s and 1880s, most sharecroppers worked "on halves"—half for the owner and half for themselves.

The sharecropping system, which materialized as early as 1868, originated as a compromise between former slaves and landowners. It eased landowners' problems with cash and credit, and provided a permanent, dependent labor force; blacks accepted it because freed them from daily supervision. But sharecropping proved disastrous. Owners and merchants developed a monopoly of control over the agricultural economy, as sharecroppers faced ever-increasing debt (see page 411).

The fundamental problem was that southern farmers still concentrated on cotton. In freedom, black women often stayed away from cotton picking, favoring domestic chores, given the diminishing incentives of the cotton system. Even as the South recovered its prewar share of British cotton purchases, the rewards diminished. Cotton prices began a long decline, as world demand fell off.

Thus, southern agriculture slipped into depression. Black sharecroppers struggled under growing debt that bound them to landowners and to furnishing merchants almost as oppressively as slavery. Many white farmers gradually lost their land and became sharecroppers. By the end of Reconstruction, over one-third of southern farms were worked by sharecropping tenants, white and black.

Link to a sample sharecropping contract.

Johnson's Reconstruction Plan

What was Johnson's vision for Reconstruction?

Many people expected Reconstruction under President Andrew Johnson to be harsh. Throughout his career in Tennessee, he criticized wealthy planters and championed small farmers. When an assassin's bullet thrust Johnson into the presidency, former slaveowners feared Johnson would deal sternly with them. When northern Radicals suggested the exile or execution of ten or twelve leading rebels, Johnson replied, "How are you going to pick out so small a number?"

Andrew Johnson of Tennessee

Like Lincoln, Johnson moved from obscurity to power. With no education, he became a tailor's apprentice. But from 1829, while in his early twenties, he held nearly every office in Tennessee politics: alderman, state representative, congressman, two terms as governor, and U.S. senator by 1857. Although elected as a Democrat, Johnson was the only senator from a seceded state who refused to leave the Union. Lincoln appointed him war governor of Tennessee in 1862; hence his symbolic place on the ticket in the president's 1864 bid for reelection.

Although a Unionist, Johnson's political beliefs made him an old Jacksonian Democrat. Before the war, he supported tax-funded public schools and homestead legislation, fashioning himself as a champion of the common man. Still, Johnson advocated limited government. His philosophy toward Reconstruction: "The Constitution as it is, and the Union as it was."

Through 1865, Johnson alone controlled Reconstruction policy; Congress recessed before he became president and did not reconvene until December. Johnson formed new state governments in the South by using his power to grant pardons and offered easy terms to former Confederates.

Johnson's Racial Views

Johnson had owned house slaves, although he was never a planter. He accepted emancipation but did not believe that black suffrage could be imposed on a southern state by the federal government. This set him on a collision course with the Radicals. On race, Johnson was a white supremacist. He declared in his annual message of 1867 that blacks possessed less "capacity for government than any other race of people … wherever they have been left to their own devices they have shown a constant tendency to relapse into barbarism."

Such racial views affected Johnson's policies. Where whites were concerned, however, Johnson proposed rules that would keep the wealthy planter class at least temporarily out of power.

Johnson's Pardon Policy

White southerners were required to swear an oath of loyalty to gain amnesty, but Johnson barred from the oath former federal officials, high-ranking Confederate officers, and political leaders or graduates of West Point or Annapolis who joined the Confederacy. He also added ex-Confederates whose taxable property was worth more than $20,000. These individuals had to apply to the president for pardon. The president, it seemed, sought revenge on the old planter elite and to promote a new yeoman leadership.

Johnson appointed provisional governors, who began Reconstruction by calling state constitutional conventions. The delegates had to draft new constitutions that eliminated slavery and invalidated secession. After ratification, new governments could be elected, and the states restored to the Union. But only southerners who had taken the oath of amnesty and were eligible voters when the state seceded could participate. Thus, unpardoned whites and former slaves were ineligible.

Presidential Reconstruction

The old white leadership proved resilient; prominent Confederates won elections and turned up in appointive offices. Then Johnson started pardoning planters and leading rebels. By September 1865, hundreds of pardons were issued in one day. These pardons, plus the return of planters' abandoned lands, restored the old elite to power and made Johnson seem the South's champion.

Why did Johnson allow the planters to regain power? He may have enjoyed turning proud planters into pardon seekers. He also sought rapid Reconstruction to deny the Radicals any opportunity for thorough racial and political changes in the South. And Johnson needed southern support in the 1866 elections; hence, he declared Reconstruction complete only eight months after Appomattox. In December 1865, many Confederate congressmen claimed seats in the U.S. Congress, including former Confederate vice president Alexander Stephens, who was now Georgia's senator-elect.

Black Codes

Furthermore, to define the status of freed people and control their labor, some legislatures revised the slave codes by substituting the word *freedmen* for *slaves*. The new black codes compelled former slaves to carry passes, observe a curfew, and live in housing provided by a landowner. Vagrancy laws and restrictive labor contracts bound freedpeople to plantations, and "anti-enticement" laws punished anyone luring these workers to other employment. State-supported schools and orphanages excluded blacks.

It seemed to northerners that the South was intent on returning African Americans to servility and that Johnson's Reconstruction policy held no one responsible for the war. Thus, the Republican majority in Congress halted Johnson's plan. The House and Senate refused to admit newly elected southern representatives. Instead, they bluntly challenged the president's authority and established a joint committee to study a new direction for Reconstruction.

The Congressional Reconstruction Plan

What made Radical Reconstruction different from Johnson's plan?

The Constitution mentioned neither secession nor reunion, but it gave Congress the primary role in admitting states. Moreover, the Constitution declared that the United States shall guarantee to each state a "republican form of government." This provision, legislators believed, gave them the authority to devise Reconstruction policies.

The key question: What had rebellion done to the relationship between southern states and the Union? Congressmen who favored vigorous Reconstruction measures argued that the war had broken the Union and that the South was subject to the victor's will. Moderate congressmen held that the states forfeited their rights through rebellion and thus came under congressional supervision.

The Radicals

Northern Democrats, weakened by their opposition to the war in its final year, denounced racial equality and supported Johnson's policies. Conservative Republicans, despite their party loyalty, favored a limited federal role in Reconstruction. Although a minority, Radical Republicans, led by Thaddeus Stevens, Charles Sumner, and George Julian, wanted to democratize the South, establish public education, and ensure freedpeople's rights. They favored black suffrage, supported some land confiscation and redistribution, and were willing to exclude the South from the Union to achieve their goals.

The Radicals brought a new civic vision; they wanted to create an activist federal government and the beginnings of racial equality. Many moderate Republicans, led by Lyman Trumbull, opposed Johnson's leniency but wanted to restrain the Radicals. They were, however, committed to federalizing the enforcement of civil, if not political, rights for the freedmen.

With the 1866 elections looming, Johnson and the Democrats sabotaged the possibility of a conservative coalition by refusing to cooperate with conservative or moderate Republicans. They insisted that Reconstruction was over, that the new state governments were legitimate, and that southern representatives should be admitted to Congress. The Radicals' influence grew with Johnson's intransigence.

Congress Versus Johnson

Republicans believed they reached a compromise with Johnson in spring 1866. Under its terms, Johnson would modify his program by extending the Freedmen's Bureau for another year and passing of a civil rights bill to counteract the black codes. This would force southern courts to practice equality under the scrutiny of the federal judiciary. Its provisions applied to public, not private, acts of discrimination. The Civil Rights Bill of 1866 was the first statutory definition of the rights of American citizens.

Johnson, however, vetoed both bills; they became law when Congress overrode his veto. Because the civil rights bill defined U.S. citizens as native-born persons who were taxed, Johnson claimed that it discriminated against "large numbers of intelligent, worthy, and patriotic foreigners ... in favor of the negro." Hope of presidential-congressional cooperation was dead. In 1866, newspapers reported daily violations of blacks' rights in the South and carried alarming accounts of anti-Black violence. In Memphis, forty blacks were killed and twelve schools burned by white mobs, and in New Orleans, the toll was thirty-four African Americans dead and two hundred wounded. Violence convinced Republicans, and the northern public, that more needed to be done. A new Republican plan focused on the **Fourteenth Amendment** to the Constitution.

Link to Thaddeus Stevens's reconstruction speech.

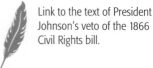

Link to the text of President Johnson's veto of the 1866 Civil Rights bill.

Fourteenth Amendment: Defined U.S. citizens as anyone born or naturalized in the United States, barred states from interfering with citizens' constitutional rights, and stated for first time that voters would be male.

Fourteenth Amendment

Of the five sections of the Fourteenth Amendment, the first would have the greatest legal significance. It conferred citizenship on "all persons born or naturalized in the United States" and prohibited states from abridging their constitutional "privileges and immunities" (see the Appendix for the Constitution and all amendments). It also barred states from taking a person's life, liberty, or property "without due process of law" and from denying "equal protection of the laws." These phrases have become powerful guarantees of African Americans' civil rights and the rights of all citizens, except for Indians, who were not granted citizenship rights until 1924.

Republicans almost universally agreed on the amendment's second and third sections. The fourth declared the Confederate debt null and void, and guaranteed the United States' war debt. Northerners rejected paying taxes to reimburse those who financed a rebellion, and business groups agreed on the necessity of upholding the U.S. government's credit. The second and third sections barred Confederate leaders from holding state and federal office. Only Congress, by a two-thirds vote of each house, could remove the penalty, thereby guaranteeing some punishment for Confederate leaders.

The second section of the amendment also dealt with representation and embodied the compromises that produced it. Northerners disagreed about whether blacks should have the right to vote. In truth, public will, North and South, lagged behind the egalitarianism of enactments that became constitutional cornerstones. Many northern states still maintained black disfranchisement laws during Reconstruction.

Emancipation ended the three-fifths clause for the purpose of counting blacks, which would increase southern representation. Thus, the postwar South stood to gain power in Congress, and if white southerners did not allow blacks to vote, former secessionists would derive the political benefit from emancipation. Consequently, Republicans determined that, if a southern state did not grant black men the vote, their representation would be reduced proportionally. The Fourteenth Amendment specified for the first time that voters were "male." As such, it provoked frustration in the women's rights movement. Advocates of women's equality worked with abolitionists for decades, often subordinating their cause to the slaves'. During the drafting of the Fourteenth Amendment, however, some leaders, such as Elizabeth Cady Stanton and Susan B. Anthony, ended their alliance with abolitionists and fought for women, infusing new life into the women's rights movement. Other female activists, however, argued that it was "the Negro's hour," causing strife among old allies. Many former male abolitionists, white and black, were willing to delay woman suffrage to secure freedmen the vote.

The South's and Johnson's Defiance

Johnson tried to block the Fourteenth Amendment. He urged state legislatures in the South to vote against ratification, and all but Tennessee rejected the amendment by a wide margin.

To present his case to northerners, Johnson organized a National Union Convention. He boarded a special train for a "swing around the circle" that carried his message into the Northeast, the Midwest, and back to Washington. Increasingly, audiences rejected his views, jeering at him. Johnson handed out American flags with thirty-six rather than twenty-five stars, declaring the Union already restored. And he labeled the Radicals "traitors" for attempting to take over Reconstruction.

MAP 16.1

The Reconstruction

This map shows the five military districts established when Congress passed the Reconstruction Act of 1867. As the dates within each state indicate, conservative Democratic forces quickly regained control of government in four southern states. So-called Radical Reconstruction was curtailed in most of the others, as factions within the weakened Republican Party began to cooperate with conservative Democrats.

Source: Copyright © Cengage Learning

In the 1866 elections, radicals and moderates whom Johnson denounced won reelection by large margins, and the Republican majority grew to two-thirds of both congressional houses. The North was clear: Johnson's policies of states' rights and white supremacy were giving the advantage to rebels and traitors. Thus Republican congressional leaders won a mandate to pursue their Reconstruction plan.

But nothing could be accomplished as long as the "Johnson governments" existed and the southern electorate remained exclusively white. Republicans resolved to form new state governments in the South and enfranchise the freedmen.

Reconstruction Acts of 1867–1868

After embittered debate, the First Reconstruction Act passed in March 1867. This plan, under which the southern states were readmitted to the Union, incorporated only a part of the Radical program. Union generals, commanding small garrisons and charged with supervising elections, assumed control in five military districts in the South (see Map 16.1). Confederate leaders designated in the Fourteenth Amendment were barred from voting until new state constitutions were ratified. The act guaranteed freedmen the right to vote and serve in state constitutional conventions. In addition, each southern state was required to ratify the Fourteenth Amendment and its new constitution by majority vote, then submit it to Congress for approval (see Table 16.1).

TABLE 16.1 Plans for Reconstruction Compared

	Johnson's Plan	Radicals' Plan	Fourteenth Amendment	Reconstruction Act of 1867
Voting	Whites only; high-ranking Confederate leaders must seek pardons	Give vote to black males	Southern whites may decide but can lose representation if they deny black suffrage	Black men gain vote; whites barred from office by Fourteenth Amendment cannot vote while new state governments are formed
Officeholding	Many prominent Confederates regain power	Only loyal white and black males eligible	Confederate leaders barred until Congress votes amnesty	Fourteenth Amendment in effect
Time out of Union	Brief	Several years; until South is thoroughly democratized	Brief	3–5 years after war
Other change in southern society	Little; gain of power by yeomen not realized; emancipation grudgingly accepted, but no black civil or political rights	Expand public education; confiscate land and provide farms for freedmen; expansion of activist federal government	Probably slight, depending on enforcement	Considerable, depending on action of new state governments

The Second, Third, and Fourth Reconstruction Acts, passed between March 1867 and March 1868, provided the details for voter registration boards, the adoption of constitutions, and the administration of "good faith" oaths by white southerners.

Failure of Land Redistribution

The Radicals blocked Johnson, but they had hoped Congress could do much more. Thaddeus Stevens, for example, argued that economic opportunity was essential to the freedmen. "He drew up a plan for extensive confiscation and redistribution of land, but it was never realized."

Racial fears and an American obsession with the sanctity of private property made land redistribution unpopular. Thus, black farmers were forced to seek work in a hostile environment in which landowners opposed their acquisition of land.

Constitutional Crisis

To restrict Johnson's influence and safeguard its plan, Congress passed several controversial laws. First, it limited Johnson's power over the army by requiring the president to issue military orders through the General of the Army, Ulysses S. Grant. Then Congress passed the Tenure of Office Act, which gave the Senate power to approve changes in the president's cabinet. Designed to protect Secretary of War Stanton, a Radical sympathizer, this law violated the tradition of presidents controlling cabinet appointments. These measures, along with the Reconstruction Acts, were passed by a two-thirds override of presidential vetoes. In response, Johnson limited the military's power in the South, increasing the powers of the civil governments he created in 1865. Then he removed military officers who were enforcing Congress's new law, preferring commanders who allowed disqualified Confederates to vote. Finally, he tried to remove Secretary of War Stanton, pushing the confrontation to its climax.

Impeachment of President Johnson

Impeachment: Process to remove a president from office; attempted but failed in case of Andrew Johnson.

Impeachment is a political procedure provided for in the Constitution as a remedy for crimes or serious abuses of power by presidents, federal judges, and other high government officials. Those who are impeached (judged or politically indicted) in the House are then tried in the Senate. Historically, this power was not used to investigate and judge the private lives of presidents, although more recently it was used this way against President Bill Clinton.

Twice in 1867, the House Judiciary Committee considered impeachment of Johnson, first rejecting it and then recommending it by a 5-to-4 vote, which was defeated by the House. After Johnson tried to remove Stanton, however, a third attempt to impeach him carried in early 1868. The indictment concentrated on his violation of the Tenure of Office Act, though modern scholars regard his efforts to obstruct enforcement of the Reconstruction Act of 1867 as a more serious offense.

Johnson's trial in the Senate lasted more than three months. The prosecution, led by Radicals, attempted to prove that Johnson was guilty of "high crimes and misdemeanors." But they also argued that the trial was a means to judge Johnson's performance. The Senate rejected such reasoning, which could have made removal from office a political weapon against any chief executive who disagreed with Congress. The prosecution fell one vote short of the necessary two-thirds majority. Johnson remained in office, politically weakened.

Election of 1868

congressional Reconstruction: The process by which the Republican-controlled Congress sought to make the Reconstruction of the ex-Confederate states longer, harsher, and under congressional control.

In the 1868 presidential election, Ulysses S. Grant, running as a Republican, defeated Horatio Seymour, a New York Democrat. Grant was not a Radical, but his platform supported **congressional Reconstruction** and endorsed black suffrage in the South. (Significantly, Republicans stopped short of endorsing black suffrage in the North.) Democrats, meanwhile, denounced Reconstruction and preached white supremacy, conducting the most openly racist campaign to that point in American history. Both sides waved the "bloody shirt," blaming each other for the war's sacrifices. By associating with rebellion and Johnson's repudiated program, Democrats were defeated in all but eight states, though the popular vote was close. Blacks voted en masse for General Grant.

In office, Grant vacillated in dealing with southern states, sometimes defending Republican regimes and sometimes currying favor with Democrats. Occasionally, Grant called out federal troops to stop violence or enforce congressional acts. But he never imposed a military occupation on the South. Rapid demobilization reduced a federal army of more than 1 million to 57,000 within a year of the Appomattox surrender. Thereafter, the number of troops in the South declined, until in 1874 there were only 4,000 in southern states outside Texas. The legend of "military rule," so important to southern claims of victimization during Reconstruction, was steeped in myth.

Fifteenth Amendment

Fifteenth Amendment: Prohibited states from denying the vote to any citizen on account of "race, color, or previous condition of servitude."

In 1869, the Radicals pushed through the **Fifteenth Amendment**, the final major measure in Reconstruction's constitutional revolution. It forbade states to deny the vote "on account of race, color, or previous condition of servitude." Such wording did not guarantee the right to vote. It left states free to restrict suffrage on other grounds so that northern states could continue to deny suffrage to women and certain men—Chinese immigrants, illiterates, and those too poor to pay poll taxes.

The Fifteenth Amendment became law in 1870. Although African Americans rejoiced, it left open the possibility for states to create countless qualification tests to obstruct voting.

Politics and Reconstruction in the South

How did black voters in the early days of Reconstruction transform the South?

From the start, white southerners resisted Reconstruction and opposed emancipation, as evident in the black codes. The former planter class proved especially unbending because of their tremendous financial loss in slaves. For many poor whites who never owned slaves and yet sacrificed in the war, destitution, plummeting agricultural prices, disease, and the uncertainties of a growing urban industrialization drove them off land toward cities and into hatred of black equality.

White Resistance

Some planters attempted to postpone freeing slaves by denying or misrepresenting events. Former slaves reported that their owners "didn't tell them it was freedom" or "wouldn't let [them] go." To retain workers, some landowners claimed control over black children and used guardianship and apprentice laws to bind black families to the plantation.

Adamant resistance by whites soon manifested itself in other ways, including violence. A local North Carolina magistrate clubbed a black man on a public street, and in several states bands of "Regulators" terrorized blacks who displayed independence. And after President Johnson encouraged the South to resist congressional Reconstruction, many white conservatives captured the new state governments, while others boycotted the polls to defeat Congress's plans.

Black Voters and the Southern Republican Party

Enthusiastically, blacks went to the polls, voting Republican, as one man said, to "stick to the end with the party that freed me." Illiteracy did not prohibit blacks (or uneducated whites) from making intelligent choices. Mississippi's William Henry could read only "a little," but he said, "We saw D. Sledge vote; he owned half the county. We knowed he voted Democratic so we voted the other ticket so it would be Republican." Women, who could not vote, encouraged their husbands and sons, and preachers exhorted their congregations to use the franchise.

Cheekwood Museum of Art, Nashville, Tennessee

Thomas Waterman Wood, who had painted portraits of society figures in Nashville before the war, sensed the importance of Congress's decision in 1867 to enfranchise the freedmen. This oil painting, one in a series on suffrage, emphasizes the significance of the ballot for the black voter.

Thanks to a large black turnout and the restrictions on prominent Confederates, a new southern Republican Party came to power in the 1868–1870 constitutional conventions. Republican delegates consisted of a sizable black contingent (265 out of the more than 1,000 delegates throughout the South), northerners who had moved to the South, and native southern whites seeking change. The new constitutions they drafted were more democratic than anything previously adopted in the South. They eliminated property qualifications for voting and holding office, turned many appointed offices into elective posts, and provided for public schools and institutions to care for the mentally ill, the blind, the deaf, the destitute, and the orphaned.

The conventions broadened women's rights in property holding and divorce. Usually the goal was not equality but providing relief to thousands of suffering debtors. Since husbands typically contracted the debts, giving women legal control over their own property provided some protection for families.

Triumph of Republican Governments

Under these new constitutions, southern states elected Republican-controlled governments. For the first time, state legislators in 1868 included black southerners. Contrary to what white southerners later claimed, Republican state governments did not disfranchise ex-Confederates as a group. James Lynch, a leading black politician from Mississippi, saw disfranchising whites as foolish. Landless former slaves "must be in friendly relations with the great body of the whites in the state," he explained. "Otherwise…peace can be maintained only by a standing army." Despised and lacking power, southern Republicans strove for safe ways to gain a foothold in a depressed economy.

Far from vindictive toward the race that enslaved them, most southern blacks appealed to white southerners to be fair. Hence, the South's Republican Party condemned itself to defeat if white voters would not cooperate. Within a few years, most fledgling Republican parties in southern states would be struggling for survival against violent white hostility.

Industrialization and Mill Towns

Reconstruction governments promoted industry via loans, subsidies, and short-term exemptions from taxation. The southern railroad system was rebuilt and expanded, and coal and iron mining made possible Birmingham's steel plants. Between 1860 and 1880, the number of manufacturing establishments in the South nearly doubled.

This emphasis on big business, however, produced higher state debts and taxes, drew money from schools and other programs, and multiplied possibilities for corruption. The alliance between business and government often operated at the expense of farmers and laborers. It also doomed Republicans to failure in building support among poorer whites.

Poverty remained the lot of many southern whites. The war caused a massive loss of income-producing wealth, such as livestock, and a steep decline in land values. From 1860 to 1880, the South's share of per capita income fell to 51 percent of the national average. In many regions, the old planter class still ruled the best land and access to credit or markets.

As poor whites and blacks found farming less tenable, they moved to cities and mill towns. Industrialization did not sweep the South as it did the North, but it laid deep roots. Attracting textile mills to southern towns became a competitive crusade.

In 1860, the South counted some 10,000 mill workers; by 1880, the number grew to 16,741 and by century's end to 97,559. Many poor southerners moved from farmer to mill worker and other low-income wage work.

Republicans and Racial Equality

Whites who controlled the southern Republican Party were reluctant to allow blacks a share of offices proportionate to their electoral strength. Aware of their weakness, black leaders did not push hard for revolutionary change. Instead, they led efforts to establish public schools, although without pressing for integrated facilities. In 1870, South Carolina passed the first comprehensive school law in the South. By 1875, 50 percent of that state's black school-age children were enrolled in school, and approximately one-third of the three thousand teachers were black.

Those African American politicians who did fight for civil rights and integration were typically from cities such as New Orleans or Mobile, where large populations of light-skinned free blacks existed before the war. Their experience made them sensitive to issues of status. Laws requiring equal accommodations won passage but often went unenforced.

Economic progress, particularly land ownership, was a major concern for most freedpeople. Land reform failed because in most states whites were the majority, and former slaveowners controlled the best land and financial resources. Much land did fall into state hands for nonpayment of taxes. Such land was sold in small lots. But most freedmen had too little cash to bid against investors or speculators. Any widespread land redistribution had to arise from Congress, which never supported such action.

Myth of "Negro Rule"

Within a few years, white hostility to congressional Reconstruction increasingly prevailed. Conservatives had always wanted to fight Reconstruction through pressure and racist propaganda began to do so. Charging that the South had been turned over to ignorant blacks, conservatives used "black domination," as a rallying cry for a return to white supremacy.

Such attacks were part of the growing myth of "Negro rule," which would become a central theme in battles over the memory of Reconstruction. African Americans participated in politics but hardly dominated. They were a majority in only two of ten state constitutional conventions. In state legislatures, only in South Carolina's lower house did blacks constitute a majority. Sixteen blacks won seats in Congress before Reconstruction was over. Only eighteen served in a high state office, such as lieutenant governor, treasurer, superintendent of education, or secretary of state.

Some four hundred blacks served in political office during Reconstruction, an enormous achievement. Elected officials, such as Robert Smalls in South Carolina, labored for cheaper land prices, better healthcare, access to schools, and the enforcement of civil rights. For too long, the black politicians of Reconstruction were forgotten heroes of this seedtime of America's long civil rights movement.

Carpetbaggers and Scalawags

Conservative propaganda denounced northern whites as "**carpetbaggers**," greedy crooks planning to pour stolen tax revenues into their luggage made of carpet material. In fact, most northerners who settled in the South came seeking business opportunities, as schoolteachers, or to find a warmer climate; most never entered politics. Those who entered politics generally wanted to democratize the South and to introduce northern ways such as industry and public education.

carpetbaggers: Derogatory nickname southerners gave to northerners who moved south after the Civil War, perceiving them as greedy opportunists who hoped to cash in on the South's plight.

scalawags: Term used by conservative southerners to describe other white southerners who were perceived as aiding or benefiting from Reconstruction.

Conservatives also invented the term **scalawag** to discredit white southerners cooperating with Republicans, as many wealthy men did. Most scalawags were yeoman farmers from mountain areas and nonslaveholding districts who were Unionists under the Confederacy. They hoped to benefit from the education and opportunities Republicans promoted. Sometimes banding with freedmen, they pursued common class interests to make headway against long-dominant planters. Over time, however, most black-white coalitions floundered due to racism.

Tax Policy and Corruption as Political Wedges

Republicans wanted to repair the war's destruction, stimulate industry, and support such new ventures as public schools—all of which required tax money. But the Civil War damaged the South's tax base. One category of valuable property—slaves—had disappeared entirely. Hundreds of thousands of citizens lost much their property—money, livestock, and buildings—to the war. Tax increases (sales, excise, and property) was necessary for even traditional services. Inevitably, Republican tax policies aroused strong opposition, especially among yeomen.

Corruption charges also plagued Republicans. Many carpetbaggers and black politicians engaged in fraudulent schemes or sold their votes, participating in what scholars recognize was a nationwide surge of corruption in an age ruled by "spoilsmen" (see pages 516). Corruption crossed party lines, but Democrats pinned the blame on unqualified blacks and greedy carpetbaggers among southern Republicans.

Ku Klux Klan: A terrorist organization established by six Confederate war veterans that sought to reestablish white supremacy in the South, suppress black voting, and topple Reconstruction governments.

Ku Klux Klan

Republican leaders also allowed factionalism along racial and class lines to undermine party unity. At the same time, the **Ku Klux Klan**, a secret veterans' club that began in Tennessee in 1866, spread through the South, rapidly becoming a terrorist organization. Klansmen sought to frustrate Reconstruction and keep the freedmen in subjection with nighttime harassment, whippings, rapes, and murders.

Although the Klan tormented blacks, its main purpose was political. Lawless nightriders targeted active Republicans, killing leading whites and blacks in several states. After freedmen who worked for a South Carolina scalawag started voting, terrorists visited the plantation and, as one victim noted, "whipped every … [black] man they could lay their hands on." Klansmen also attacked Union League clubs—Republican organizations that mobilized the black vote—and schoolteachers who aided freedmen.

Specific social forces shaped and directed Klan violence, with Alamance and Caswell Counties in North Carolina receiving the worst Klan violence. Slim Republican majorities there rested on cooperation between black voters and white yeomen. Together, these black and white Republicans ousted long-entrenched officials. The wealthy and powerful men who lost their accustomed political control were the Klan's county officers and local chieftains. By intimidation and murder, the Klan weakened the Republican coalition and restored a Democratic majority.

The Granger Collection, New York

Cartoon, depicting a freedman, John Campbell, vainly begging for mercy in Moore County, North Carolina, August 10, 1871. The image evokes the power, fear, and mystery of the Klan without actually showing its bloody deeds.

Klan violence injured Republicans across the South. One of every ten black delegates to the 1867–1868 state constitutional conventions was attacked, seven fatally. In one judicial district of North Carolina, the Ku Klux Klan was responsible for twelve murders, over seven hundred beatings, along with many cases of rape and arson. A single attack on Republicans in Eutaw, Alabama, left four blacks dead and fifty-four wounded. According to historian Eric Foner, the Klan "made it virtually impossible for Republicans to campaign or vote in large parts of Georgia."

Thus Republican mistakes, racial hostility, and terror brought down the Republican regimes. In most states, Radical Reconstruction lasted only a few years (see Map 16.1). The most enduring failure of Reconstruction, however, was that it failed to alter the South's social structure or its distribution of wealth and power.

Retreat from Reconstruction

What led the North to lose interest in reconstructing the South?

During the 1870s, northerners lost the will to sustain Reconstruction, as they confronted economic and social transformations in their regions and the West. Radical Republicans like Albion Tourgée, a former Union soldier who moved to North Carolina and was elected a judge, condemned Congress's timidity. He and many African Americans believed that, during Reconstruction, the North "threw all the Negroes on the world without any way of getting along." As the North lost interest in the South, Reconstruction collapsed.

Political Implications of Klan Terrorism

Whites in the old Confederacy referred to this decline of Reconstruction as "southern redemption." During the 1870s, "redeemer" Democrats claimed to be the South's saviors from alleged "black domination" and "carpetbag rule." Violence and terror emerged as a tactic in politics.

In 1870 and 1871, the Ku Klux Klan's violent campaigns forced Congress to pass two **Enforcement Acts** and an anti-Klan law. These laws made actions by individuals against the civil and political rights of others a federal criminal offense. They also provided for election supervisors and permitted martial law and suspension of the writ of habeas corpus to combat murders, beatings, and Klan threats. In 1872 and 1873, Mississippi and the Carolinas saw many prosecutions; but in other states, the laws were ignored. Southern juries sometimes refused to convict Klansmen; less than half of the 3,310 cases ended in convictions. Although many Klansmen fled their state to avoid prosecution, and the Klan officially disbanded, paramilitary organizations known as Rifle Clubs and Red Shirts often took the Klan's place.

Still, there were ominous signs that the North's commitment to racial justice was fading, as some influential Republicans opposed the anti-Klan laws. Rejecting other Republicans' arguments that the Thirteenth, Fourteenth, and Fifteenth Amendments made the federal government the protector of citizens' rights, dissenters charged that Congress was infringing on states' rights. This foreshadowed a general revolt within Republican ranks in 1872.

Enforcement Acts: Laws that sought to protect black voters and made violations of civil and political rights a federal offense and sought to end Ku Klux Klan violence.

Industrial Expansion and Reconstruction in the North

Immigration and industrialization surged in the North. Between 1865 and 1873, 3 million immigrants entered the country, most settling in the industrial cities of the North and West. Within only eight years, industrial production increased by 75 percent. For the first time, nonagricultural workers outnumbered farmers, and wage earners outnumbered independent craftsmen. Government policies encouraged this rapid growth. Low taxes on investment and high tariffs on manufactured goods helped create a new class of powerful industrialists, especially railroad entrepreneurs.

From 1865 to 1873, 35,000 miles of new track were laid, this fueled the banking industry and made Wall Street the center of American capitalism. Eastern railroad magnates, such as Thomas Scott of the Pennsylvania Railroad, created economic empires with the assistance of huge government subsidies of cash and land. Railroad corporations also bought up mining operations, granaries, and lumber companies. Big business now employed lobbyists to curry favor with government. Corruption ran rampant, with some congressmen and legislators paid retainers by major companies.

As captains of industry amassed unprecedented fortunes, gross economic inequality polarized American society. The work force, worried a Massachusetts business leader, was in a "transition state … living in boarding houses" and becoming a "permanent factory population." In New York or Philadelphia, workers increasingly lived in unhealthy tenement housing. Thousands would list themselves on the census as "common laborer" or "general jobber." Concerned, in 1868 Republicans passed an eight-hour workday bill that applied to federal workers. The "labor question" (see Chapter 18) now preoccupied northerners far more than the "southern" or "freedmen" question.

Then the Panic of 1873 ushered in more than five years of economic contraction. Three million people lost their jobs, especially in large cities. Debtors and the unemployed sought easy-money policies to spur expansion (workers and farmers desperately needed cash). Businessmen, disturbed by the strikes and industrial violence that accompanied the panic, defended property rights and demanded "sound money" policies. The chasm between farmers and workers and wealthy industrialists widened.

Liberal Republican Revolt

Disenchanted with Reconstruction, a largely northern group calling itself the Liberal Republicans bolted the party in 1872 and nominated Horace Greeley, editor of the *New York Tribune,* for president. A varied group, Liberal Republicans included foes of corruption and advocates of a lower tariff. Two popular attitudes united them: distaste for federal intervention in the South and an elitist desire to let market forces and the "best men" determine policy.

Democrats also nominated Greeley in 1872, but it was not enough to keep Grant from reelection. Greeley's campaign for North-South reunion was a harbinger of the future in American politics. Organized Blue-Gray fraternalism (gatherings of Union and Confederate veterans) began as early as 1874. Grant continued to use military force sparingly and in 1875 refused a desperate request from Mississippi's governor for troops to quell racial and political terrorism there.

Grant made a series of poor appointments that fueled public dissatisfaction with his administration. His secretary of war, his private secretary, and officials in the Treasury and Navy Departments were involved in bribery or tax-cheating scandals. Instead of exposing the corruption, Grant defended the culprits. In 1874,

Democrats recaptured the House of Representatives, signaling the end of the Radical Republican vision of Reconstruction.

General Amnesty

Democratic gains in Congress weakened legislative resolve on southern issues. Congress already lifted the political disabilities of the Fourteenth Amendment from many former Confederates. In 1872, it adopted an Amnesty Act, which pardoned most of the remaining rebels. In 1875, Congress passed a **Civil Rights Act**, partly in tribute to the recently deceased Charles Sumner, purporting to guarantee black people equal accommodations in public places, such as inns and theaters, but the bill was watered down and contained no enforcement provisions. (The Supreme Court later struck down this law; see page 523.)

Democrats regained control of four state governments before 1872 and eight by the late January 1876 (see Map 16.1). In the North, Democrats successfully stressed the failure and scandals of Reconstruction governments. Sectional reconciliation now seemed crucial for commerce. The nation was expanding westward, and the South was a new investment frontier.

Civil Rights Act of 1875: Designed to desegregate public places but lacked enforcement provisions.

The West, Race, and Reconstruction

As the Fourteenth Amendment and other enactments granted blacks the beginnings of citizenship, other non-whites faced continued persecution. Across the West, the federal government pursued a containment policy against Native Americans. In California, where white farmers and ranchers often forced Indians into captive labor, some civilians practiced "Indian hunting." By 1880, thirty years of violence left an estimated forty-five hundred California Indians dead at the hands of white settlers.

In Texas and the Southwest, expansionists still deemed Mexicans and other mixed-race Hispanics to be "lazy" and incapable of self-government. In California and the Far West, initially few whites objected to the Chinese who did the dangerous work of building railroads through the Rocky Mountains. But when the Chinese competed for urban, industrial jobs, conflict emerged. Anti-coolie clubs appeared in California in the 1870s, seeking laws against Chinese labor, inciting racism, and organizing vigilante attacks on Chinese workers and the factories that employed them. Western politicians sought white votes by pandering to prejudice, and in 1879 the new California constitution denied Chinese the vote.

Viewing America from coast to coast, the Civil War and Reconstruction years dismantled racial slavery and fostered a volatile new racial complexity, especially in the West. Some African Americans asserted that they were more like whites than "uncivilized" Indians, while others, like the Creek freedmen of Indian Territory, sought an Indian identity. In Texas, whites, Indians, blacks, and Hispanics had mixed for decades, and by the 1870s forced reconsideration in law and custom of exactly who was white.

America was undergoing what one historian has called a reconstruction of the concept of race itself. The turbulence of the expanding West reinforced the new nationalism and the reconciliation of North and South based on a resurgent white supremacy.

Foreign Expansion

In 1867, new expansion pressures led Secretary of State William H. Seward to purchase Alaska from Russia (see Chapter 22). Opponents ridiculed Seward's $7.2 million venture, but Seward convinced congressmen of Alaska's economic potential, and other lawmakers favored the dawning of friendship with Russia.

The "Back to Africa" Movement

In the wake of the Civil War, and especially after the despairing end of Reconstruction, some African Americans sought to leave the South for the American West or North, but also to relocate to Africa. Liberia had been founded in the 1820s by the white-led American Colonization Society (ACS), an organization dedicated to relocating blacks "back" in Africa. Some eleven thousand African Americans had emigrated voluntarily to Liberia by 1860, with largely disastrous results. Many died of disease, and others felt disoriented in the strange new land and ultimately returned to the United States.

Reconstruction reinvigorated the emigration impulse, especially in cotton-growing districts where blacks had achieved political power before 1870 but were crushed by violence and intimidation in the following decade. When blacks felt confident in their future, the idea of leaving America fell quiet; but when threatened or under assault, whole black communities dreamed of a place where they could become an independent "race," a "people," or a "nation" as their appeals often announced. Often that dream, more imagined than realized, lay in West Africa.

Before the Civil War, most blacks had denounced the ACS for its racism and its hostility to their sense of American birthright. But letters of inquiry flooded into the organization's headquarters after 1875. Wherever blacks felt the reversal of the promise of emancipation the keenest, they formed local groups such as the Liberia Exodus Association of Pinesville, Florida, or the Liberian Exodus Arkansas Colony, and many others.

At emigration conventions, and especially in churches, blacks penned letters to the ACS asking for maps or any information about a new African homeland. Some local organizers would announce 80 or 100 recruits "widawake for Liberia," although such enthusiasm rarely converted into an Atlantic voyage. The impulse was genuine, however. "We wants to be a People," wrote the leader of a Mississippi emigration committee; "we can't be it heare and find that we ar compel to leve this Cuntry." Henry Adams, a former Louisiana slave, Union soldier, and itinerant emigration organizer, advocated Liberia, but also supported "Kansas fever" with both Biblical and natural rights arguments. "God ... has a place and a land for all his people," he wrote in 1879. "It is not that we think the soil climate or temperature" elsewhere is "more congenial to us—but it is the idea that pervades our breast 'that at last we will be free,' free from oppression, free from tyranny, free from bulldozing, murderous southern whites."

By the 1890s, Henry McNeal Turner, a freeborn former Georgia Reconstruction politician, and now Bishop of the African Methodist Episcopal Church, made three trips to Africa and vigorously campaigned through press and pulpit for blacks to "Christianize" and "civilize" Africa. Two shiploads of African Americans did sail to Liberia, although most returned disillusioned or ill. Turner's plan of "Africa for the Africans" was as much a religious vision as an emigration system, but like all such efforts then and since, it reflected the despair of racial conditions in America more than realities in Africa. The numbers do not tell the tale of the depth of the impulse in this link to the world: in 1879–1880, approximately twenty-five thousand southern blacks moved to Kansas, whereas from 1865 to 1900, just under four thousand emigrated to West Africa.

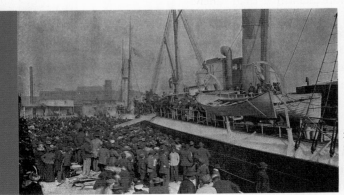

Departure of African American emigrants to Liberia aboard the Laurada, *Savannah, Georgia, March 1896. The large crowd bidding farewell to the much smaller group aboard the ship may indicate both the fascination and the ambivalence for this issue among blacks in the South. (*Illustrated American Magazine, *March 21, 1896).*

© Bettmann/Corbis

Also in 1867 the United States took control of the Midway Islands, a thousand miles northwest of Hawai'i. Through diplomacy, Seward and his successor, Hamilton Fish, resolved wartime grievances with Great Britain by arranging a financial settlement for damage done by the *Alabama* and other cruisers built in England and sold to the Confederacy. Sectional reconciliation in Reconstruction America would serve new ambitions for world commerce and expansion.

Judicial Retreat from Reconstruction

Meanwhile, the Supreme Court played its part in the northern retreat from Reconstruction. During the Civil War, the Court was cautious and inactive. Reaction to the *Dred Scott* decision (1857) was so vehement, and the Union's wartime emergency so great, that the Court had avoided interference with government actions. But that changed in 1866 when *Ex parte Milligan* reached the Court.

Lambdin P. Milligan of Indiana had plotted to free Confederate prisoners of war and overthrow state governments. Consequently, a military court sentenced Milligan, a civilian, to death. Milligan challenged the military tribunal's authority, claiming he was entitled to a civil trial. The Supreme Court declared that military trials were illegal when civil courts were open and functioning.

In the 1870s, the Court renewed its challenge to Congress's actions when it narrowed the meaning of the Fourteenth Amendment. The *Slaughter-House* cases (1873) began in 1869, when the Louisiana legislature granted one company a monopoly on livestock slaughtering in New Orleans. Rival butchers sued, and their attorney, former Supreme Court justice John A. Campbell, argued that Louisiana had violated the rights of some citizens in favor of others. The Fourteenth Amendment, Campbell contended, had brought individual rights under federal protection.

But in the *Slaughter-House* decision, the Supreme Court dealt a blow to the scope of the Fourteenth Amendment. It declared state citizenship and national citizenship separate. National citizenship involved only matters such as the right to travel freely from state to state, and only such narrow rights, held the Court, were protected by the Fourteenth Amendment.

Shrinking from a role as "perpetual censor" for civil rights, the Court's majority declared that the framers of the recent amendments had not intended to "destroy" the federal system, in which the states exercised "powers for domestic and local government, including the regulation of civil rights." Thus, the justices severely limited the amendment's potential for protecting the rights of black citizens—its original intent.

The next day, the Court decided *Bradwell v. Illinois,* a case in which Myra Bradwell, a female attorney, was denied the right to practice law in Illinois because she was a married woman, and hence not a free agent. Using the Fourteenth Amendment, Bradwell's attorneys contended that the state had unconstitutionally abridged her "privileges and immunities" as a citizen. The Supreme Court disagreed, declaring a woman's "paramount destiny ... to fulfill the noble and benign offices of wife and mother."

In 1876, the Court further weakened the Reconstruction era amendments. In *U.S. v. Cruikshank,* the Court overruled the conviction under the 1870 Enforcement Act of Louisiana whites who had attacked a meeting of blacks and conspired to deprive them of their rights. The justices ruled that the Fourteenth Amendment did not give the federal government power to act against these whites. The duty of protecting citizens' equal rights, the Court said, "rests alone with the States." Such judicial conservatism blunted the revolutionary potential of the Civil War amendments.

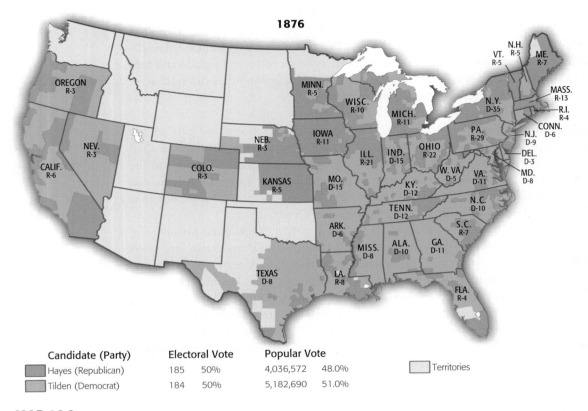

1876

Candidate (Party)	Electoral Vote		Popular Vote	
Hayes (Republican)	185	50%	4,036,572	48.0%
Tilden (Democrat)	184	50%	5,182,690	51.0%
Territories				

MAP 16.2

Presidential Election of 1876 and the Compromise of 1877

In 1876, a combination of solid southern support and Democratic gains in the North gave Samuel Tilden the majority of popular votes, but Rutherford B. Hayes won the disputed election in the electoral college, after a deal satisfied Democratic wishes for an end to Reconstruction.

Source: Copyright © Cengage Learning

Disputed Election of 1876 and Compromise of 1877

As the 1876 presidential election approached, the nation was focused on economic issues, and the North lost interest in Reconstruction. Samuel J. Tilden, the Democratic governor of New York, ran strongly in the South and needed one electoral vote to beat Rutherford B. Hayes, the Republican nominee. Nineteen electoral votes from Louisiana, South Carolina, and Florida (the only southern states not yet under Democratic rule) were disputed; both Democrats and Republicans claimed to have won those states despite fraud committed by their opponents (see Map 16.2).

To resolve this unprecedented situation, Congress established a fifteen-member electoral commission, balanced between Democrats and Republicans. Because the Republicans held the majority in Congress, they prevailed, 8 to 7, on every attempt to count the returns, with commission members voting along strict party lines. Hayes would become president if Congress accepted the commission's findings.

But Democrats controlled the House and could filibuster to block action on the vote. Many citizens feared another civil war, as some southerners vowed, "Tilden or Fight!" The crisis ended when Democrats acquiesced in the election of Hayes

The Lost Cause

All major wars compel a struggle over their historical memory. After the Civil War, white southerners and their northern allies constructed a "Lost Cause" tradition, a racially exclusive version of the war and Reconstruction which persists today.

For ex-Confederates, the Lost Cause served as a psychological response to the trauma of defeat. Over time, it also included reinterpretations of the war's causes, southern resistance to Reconstruction, doctrines of white supremacy, and a mythic popular culture in the North and South. Lost Cause advocates—from officers to soldiers to women leading memorial associations—argued that the war was never about slavery, that the Confederates lost due to Yankee numbers and resources, and that southern and northern sacrifice should be equally honored. In the industrial, multiethnic America of the emerging twentieth century, an Old South of benevolent masters and faithful slaves, of Robert E. Lee as America's truest Christian soldier, provided a sentimentalized road to reunion.

By the 1890s, elite southern white women—among them the United Daughters of the Confederacy—built monuments, lobbied congressmen, delivered lectures, ran contests for schoolchildren, and strove to control the content of history textbooks, to exalt the South. Above all, Lost Causers advocated what one historian has called a "victory narrative" of the nation's triumph over Reconstruction's racial revolution and constitutional transformations. In his 1881 memoir, Jefferson Davis declared: "Well may we rejoice in the regained possession of self-government.... This is the great victory...a total non-interference by the Federal government in the domestic affairs of the States."

These stories endure in Civil War memorabilia, such as the epic *Gone with the Wind*, the 2003 film *Gods and Generals*, and uses of the Confederate flag to oppose civil rights. And the Confederate state rights tradition is employed today by states and advocacy groups to resist federal stimulus money and national healthcare reform.

based on a "deal" between Hayes's supporters and southerners who wanted federal aid to railroads, internal improvements, and removal of troops from southern states. Northern and southern Democrats decided not to contest the election of a Republican who would not continue Reconstruction.

Southern Democrats rejoiced, but African Americans grieved over the betrayal of their hopes for equality. In a Fourth of July speech in Washington, D.C., in 1875, Frederick Douglass reflected on fifteen years of unparalleled change for his people and worried about the hold of white supremacy on America's historical memory: "If war among the whites brought peace and liberty to the blacks, what will peace among the whites bring?"

Summary

Reconstruction left a contradictory record. It was an era of tragic aspirations and failures but also of unprecedented legal, political, and social change. The Union victory brought increased federal power, stronger nationalism, sweeping federal intervention in the southern states, and landmark Constitutional amendments. But northern commitment to make lasting changes eroded, leaving the revolution unfinished. The promise for new lives and liberties among the freedpeople had eroded if not died.

The North embraced emancipation, black suffrage, and constitutional alterations strengthening the central government primarily to defeat the rebellion. As wartime pressures declined, Americans, especially northerners, retreated from Reconstruction. The people and the courts maintained a preference for state authority and distrusted federal power. Free labor ideology stressed respect for property and individual self-reliance. Racism transformed into Klan terror and theories of black degeneration.

New challenges gradually overwhelmed the aims of Reconstruction. Industrialization promised prosperity but also wrought increased exploitation of labor. Moreover, industry increased the nation's power and laid the foundation for an enlarged American role in international affairs. In the wake of the Civil War, Americans faced two profound tasks—healing and dispensing justice. Making sectional reunion compatible with black freedom and equality overwhelmed American politics, and the nation faced this ongoing dilemma more than a century later.

Chapter Review

Wartime Reconstruction

Which two political acts recognized the centrality of slavery to the war?

Passage of the Thirteenth Amendment and establishment of the Freedmen's Bureau in early 1865 sent a clear signal that slavery was a major cause for the Civil War. The Thirteenth Amendment first abolished slavery ("involuntary servitude") and second gave Congress the power to enforce it. Then, a few months later in March, Congress established the Bureau of Refugees, Freedmen and Abandoned Lands, known as the Freedmen's Bureau, to help former slaves. During its four years as a federal agency, it supplied food and medical services, built thousands of schools and colleges, negotiated job contracts between former slaves and masters, and managed confiscated lands.

The Meanings of Freedom

How did blacks exert their newfound freedom?

With emancipation, former slaves sought to reunite families broken apart through slave sales. Community also became important, as they built their own churches that ultimately served to unify racial ties. Seeking greater control over their work lives, African Americans wanted fairer employers and hoped to own land; when that was not possible, they rented land from former masters under the sharecropping system, in which they paid for supplies and rent by giving owners' half their crops on average. Former slaves also embraced the education that had been denied them under slavery and started schools, colleges, and universities throughout the South or attended those launched by the Freedmen's Bureau.

Johnson's Reconstruction Plan

What was Johnson's vision for Reconstruction?

Johnson's approach to Reconstruction could be summed up in a single quote: "The Constitution as it is, and the Union as it was." As president, he controlled Reconstruction policy through 1865, pardoning former Confederates and reestablishing state governments in the South. Despising the planter class, he initially insisted that ex-Confederates with property worth more than $20,000 apply directly to him for pardons. Gradually, Johnson pardoned planters, too, which restored the former elite to power, possibly because he wanted to block Radical Republicans from implementing extensive and racial political changes in the South. Deeply racist, Johnson remained silent when southern states implemented black codes to restrict former slaves' freedom by requiring them to carry passes, obey curfew laws, and live in housing provided by a landowner. Nonetheless, after just eight months, Johnson declared Reconstruction was completed.

The Congressional Reconstruction Plan

What made Radical Reconstruction different from Johnson's plan?

Radical Republicans in Congress were upset at Johnson's moderate approach, which seemed to hold no one responsible for the war and reestablished racial hierarchies and the southern elite. Initially a minority, the Radicals' popularity grew as Johnson increasingly dug in his heels. Radicals wanted to democratize the South through black suffrage, civil rights, and land confiscation and redistribution. They secured passage of the Fourteenth Amendment, which conferred citizenship on "all persons born or naturalized in the United States," and granted voting rights to males. They also passed four strident Reconstruction acts with strict and detailed plans for readmitting southern states to the Union. They barred ex-Confederates from voting until freedmen could and outlined the rules for voter registration boards and the adoption of state constitutions. Unpopular, land redistribution never materialized, but in 1869, Radicals pushed through their final measure, the Fifteenth Amendment, which prohibited states from denying the vote based on "race, color, or previous condition of servitude."

Reconstruction Politics and Economy in the South

How did black voters in the early days of Reconstruction transform the South?

With a large black voter turnout and prominent confederates barred from the polls and political positions, a new southern variant on the Republican Party came to power during the 1868 to 1870 state constitutional conventions. Their constitutions were highly democratic, eliminating property qualifications for voting and political office, shifting some appointed offices to elected ones, and establishing public schools. They also gave women greater rights in terms of property-holding and divorce. Blacks became state legislators for the first time in 1868. Angry whites charged they were being ruled by Negroes, and some resorted to violent resistance. In truth, while blacks did play a greater role in government, they remained a minority.

Retreat from Reconstruction

What led the North to lose interest in reconstructing the South?

During the 1870s, northerners faced economic and social transformations at home and became increasingly disillusioned with Reconstruction. Some northerners thought federal expansion had cut too far into states' rights. Second, while immigration and industrialization made northern economies boom from 1865 to 1873, it also widened the gap between the richest and the poorest and created a powerful new class of industrialists. When the Panic of 1873 brought hard times and job losses, interest in Reconstruction faded beside regional economic concerns. The Supreme Court also played a role, challenging congressional Reconstruction in several decisions. The Court ultimately narrowed the meaning of the Fourteenth Amendment by declaring state and national citizenship as separate issues and limited the amendment's ability to safeguard black citizens, as it was intended to do.

Suggestions for Further Reading

David W. Blight, *Race and Reunion: The Civil War in American Memory* (2001)

W. E. B. Du Bois, *Black Reconstruction in America* (1935)

Eric Foner, *Reconstruction: America's Unfinished Revolution, 1863–1877* (1988)

William Gillette, *Retreat from Reconstruction, 1869–1879* (1980)

Moon-Ho Jung, *Coolies and Cane: Race, Labor, and Sugar in the Age of Emancipation* (2006)

Gerald Jaynes, *Branches Without Roots: The Genesis of the Black Working Class in the American South, 1862–1882* (1986)

Michael Perman, *The Road to Redemption* (1984)

George Rable, *But There Was No Peace* (1984)

Heather Richardson, *West from Appomattox: The Reconstruction of America after the Civil War* (2007)

Elliot West, "Reconstructing Race," *Western Historical Quarterly* (Spring 2003)

Go to the CourseMate website for primary source links, study tools, and review materials for this chapter.
www.cengagebrain.com

17

The Development of the West

In 1893, historian Frederick Jackson Turner delivered a stunning lecture at the World's Columbian Exposition in Chicago that shaped views of the American West for generations. Titled "The Significance of the Frontier in American History," the paper argued that "free land, its continuous recession, and the advancement of American settlement westward" created a distinctive spirit of democracy and egalitarianism. The settlement of several frontier Wests from colonial times onward explained American progress and character.

Across the street, the folk character Buffalo Bill Cody dramatized the conquest of frontiers and the creation of an American identity in a staged extravaganza called "The Wild West." Whereas Turner described a peaceful settlement of empty western land, Cody portrayed violent conquest of territory occupied by savage Indians. Turner's heroes were farmers who tamed the wilderness with plows. Buffalo Bill's heroes were scouts who braved danger and vanquished Indians with firepower. Turner used log cabins, wagon trains, and wheat fields to argue that the frontier fashioned a new, progressive people. Cody depicted the West as a place of brutal aggression and heroic victory.

The American West inspired material progress, and it witnessed the domination of one group over another and over the environment. Turner and Cody believed that by the 1890s, the frontier era had ended. Over time, Turner's theory was abandoned (even by Turner himself) as simplistic, and Buffalo Bill was relegated to the gallery of rogues and showmen. Yet both Wests persisted in the romance of American history, even while they obscured the complex story of western development in the late nineteenth century.

Much of the West was not empty, and its inhabitants utilized resources differently. On the Plains, for example, the Pawnees planted crops in the spring, left their fields in summer to hunt buffalo, then returned for harvesting. They sometimes battled with Cheyennes and Arapahos over access to hunting grounds and crops. In what now is the American Southwest, natives shared the land and sometimes integrated with Hispanic people,

Chapter Outline

The Economic Activities of Native Peoples
Subsistence Cultures | Slaughter of Buffalo | Decline of Salmon

The Transformation of Native Cultures
Western Men | Government Policy and Treaties | Reservation Policy | Native Resistance | Reform of Indian Policy | Zitkala-Sa | Dawes Severalty Act | Ghost Dance | The Losing of the West

VISUALIZING THE PAST *Attempts to Make Indians Look and Act Like "Americans"*

Life on the Natural Resource Frontier
Mining and Lumbering | Complex Communities | Western Women | Significance of Race | Conservation Movement | Admission of New States | Western Folk Heroes

Irrigation and Transportation
Rights to Water | Government Supervision of Water Rights | Newlands Reclamation Act | Railroad Construction | Railroad Subsidies | Standard Gauge, Standard Time

LINKS TO THE WORLD *The Australian Frontier*

Farming the Plains
Settlement of the Plains | Hardship on the Plains | Social Isolation | Mail-Order Companies and Rural Free Delivery | Mechanization of Agriculture | Legislative and Scientific Aids

who were descendants of Spanish colonists. As white immigrants built communities in the West in the late nineteenth century, they exploited the environment for profit more extensively than did Indians. They excavated the earth for minerals, felled forests for construction, built railroads, dammed rivers, and plowed soil with machines. Their goal included buying and selling in regional, national, and international markets. As they transformed the landscape, their market economies transformed the nation.

The West by 1870 spanned from the Mississippi River to the Pacific Ocean and consisted of several regions of varied economic potential. Abundant rainfall along the northern Pacific coast fed forests. Farther south, California's woodlands and grasslands provided fertile valleys for vegetables and oranges. Eastward, from the Cascades and the Sierra Nevada to the Rocky Mountains, gold, silver, and other minerals lay buried. East of the Rockies, the Great Plains divided into a semiarid western side of few trees and buffalo grass and an eastern sector of ample rainfall and tall grasses that could support grain crops and livestock.

Before contact with whites, Indian peoples moved around the region, warring, trading, and negotiating as they searched for food and shelter. In the Southwest, Hispanics moved between Mexican and American territory, establishing towns, farms, and ranches. After the Civil War, white Americans overwhelmed the native and Hispanic peoples, swelling from 7 million to nearly 17 million whites between 1870 and 1890.

The West's abundance of exploitable land and raw materials made white Americans believe that anyone persistent enough could succeed. This confidence rested on a belief that white people were superior and asserted itself at the expense of native people and the environment.

By 1890 farms, ranches, mines, towns, and cities existed throughout present-day continental United States, but vast stretches remained unsettled. Although symbolically important to Turner, the fading frontier had little impact on behavior. Pioneers who failed in one locale tried again elsewhere. A surplus of seemingly uninhabited land gave Americans a feeling that second chances abounded. This belief, more than Turner's theory of frontier democracy or Cody's heroic reenactments left a deep imprint on the American character.

As you read this chapter, keep the following questions in mind:

* How did the interaction between people and the environment shape the physical landscape of the West and the lives of the region's inhabitants?

* How did the U.S. government's relations with Native Americans change over time throughout the late nineteenth century?

* Describe the societal and technological changes that revolutionized the lives of farmers and ranchers on the Great Plains.

The Ranching Frontier
The Open Range | Barbed Wire | Ranching as Big Business

LEGACY FOR A PEOPLE AND A NATION *National Parks*

SUMMARY

Chronology

1862	Homestead Act grants free land to citizens who live on and improve the land
	Morrill Land Grant Act gives states public land to sell in order to finance agricultural and industrial colleges
1864	Chivington's militia massacres Black Kettle's Cheyennes at Sand Creek
1869	First transcontinental railroad completed
1872	Yellowstone becomes first national park
1876	Lakotas and Cheyennes ambush Custer's federal troops at Little Big Horn, Montana
1877	Nez Percé Indians under Young Joseph surrender to U.S. troops
1878	Timber and Stone Act allows citizens to buy timberland cheaply but also enables large companies to acquire huge tracts of forest land
1879	Carlisle School for Indians established in Pennsylvania

1881–82	Chinese Exclusion Acts prohibit Chinese immigration to the United States
1883	National time zones established
1884	U.S. Supreme Court first denies Indians as wards under government protection
1887	Dawes Severalty Act ends communal ownership of Indian lands and grants land allotments to individual native families
1887–88	Devastating winter on Plains destroys countless livestock and forces farmers into economic hardship
1890	Final suppression of Plains Indians by U.S. Army at Wounded Knee
	Census Bureau announces closing of the frontier
	Yosemite National Park established
1892	Muir helps found Sierra Club
1902	Newlands Reclamation Act passed

The Economic Activities of Native Peoples

What factors undermined Native Americans' subsistence in the late nineteenth century?

Native Americans settled the West long before other Americans migrated there; Indians shaped the environment for centuries. Nevertheless, several factors weakened almost all native economic systems in the late nineteenth century.

Subsistence Cultures Western Indian communities varied. Some natives inhabited permanent settlements; others, temporary camps. Most Indians were participants and recipients in a flow of goods, culture, language, and disease carried by migrating bands. Indian economies were based in differing degrees on four activities: crop growing; livestock raising; hunting, fishing, and gathering; and trading and raiding. Corn was the most common crop; sheep and horses, acquired from Spanish colonizers and other Indians, were the livestock; and buffalo (American bison) were the primary prey of hunts. Indians raided one another for food, tools, and horses. When a buffalo hunt failed, they subsisted on crops and hunted buffalo, or stole food and horses when crops failed.

For Indians on the Great Plains, life focused on the buffalo. They cooked and preserved buffalo meat; fashioned hides into clothing, moccasins, and blankets; used sinew for thread and bowstrings; and carved tools from bones and horns. Buffalo were so valuable that Pawnees and Lakotas fought over access to herds. **Plains Indians** periodically set fire to tall-grass prairies, which burned away dead plants, facilitating growth of new grass so horses could feed all summer.

In the Southwest, Indians led varying lifestyles, depending on the environment. For example, in southeastern Arizona and northwestern Mexico, some of the O'odham (in English, "The People") grew irrigated crops in the few river valleys while those who

Plains Indians: Diverse Native American societies inhabiting the region from the Dakotas to Texas.

inhabited the mountainous and desert regions followed a hunter-gatherer existence. The Navaho (or Dine', also meaning "The People") were herders, whose sheep, goats, and horses provided status and security.

What buffalo were to Plains Indians and sheep were to southwestern Indians, salmon were to northwestern Indians. Before the mid-nineteenth century, the Columbia River and its tributaries supported the densest Indian population To harvest fish, the Clatsops, Klamath, and S'Klallams developed technologies of stream diversion, platform construction, and special baskets. Like other natives, they traded for horses, buffalo robes, beads, cloth, and knives.

Slaughter of Buffalo

On the Plains and parts of the Southwest, native worlds gradually dissolved after 1850, when whites competed with Indians for natural resources. Perceiving buffalo and Indians as hindrances, whites endeavored to eliminate both. The U.S. Army refused to enforce treaties that reserved hunting grounds for exclusive Indian use, so railroads sponsored hunts in which eastern sportsmen shot at buffalo from slow-moving trains. Unbeknownst to Indians and whites, however, a combination of circumstances doomed the buffalo before the slaughter of the late 1800s. Natives depleted herds by increasing their kills to trade hides with whites and other Indians. Also, in the dry years of the 1840s and 1850s, Indians relocated to river basins, pushing buffalo out of nourishing grazing territory to face starvation. Whites, too, settled in basin areas, further forcing buffalo away. At the same time, lethal animal diseases, such as anthrax and brucellosis, brought by white-owned livestock, decimated buffalo already weakened by malnutrition and drought. Increasing numbers of horses, oxen, and sheep, owned by white newcomers and some Indians, devoured grasses that buffalo needed. The mass killing only struck the final blow. By the 1880s, a few hundred of the 25 million buffalo estimated on the Plains in 1820 remained.

Denver Art Museum

Using buffalo hides to fashion garments, Indians often exhibited artistic skills in decorating their apparel. This Ute Indian hide dress shows symbolic as well as aesthetic representations.

Decline of Salmon

In the Northwest, salmon suffered a similar fate. White commercial fishermen and canneries moved into the Columbia and Willamette River valleys during the 1860s and 1870s, and by the 1880s they had greatly diminished salmon runs. By the early 1900s, construction of dams on the river and its tributaries further impeded salmon's reproduction. The U.S. government protected Indian fishing rights, and hatcheries restored some salmon supplies, but dams built to provide power, combined with overfishing and pollution, diminished salmon stocks.

The Transformation of Native Cultures

Buffalo slaughter and salmon reduction undermined Indian subsistence, but demographic changes also contributed. Throughout the nineteenth century, white migrants were overwhelmingly young, single males in their twenties and thirties, the age when they were most prone to violent behavior. In 1870, white men outnumbered white women by three

> How did the U.S. government's reservation policy make way for the market economy in the West?

to two in California, two to one in Colorado, and two to one in Dakota Territory. By 1900, preponderances of men remained throughout these places. Indians were most likely to come into contact first with white traders, trappers, soldiers, prospectors, and cowboys—almost all of whom owned guns and would use them on animals and humans who got in their way.

Western Men

Moreover, these men subscribed to prevailing attitudes that Indians were primitive, lazy, and devious. Such contempt made exploiting and killing natives easier, further justified by claims of threats to life and property. When Indians raided white settlements, they sometimes mutilated bodies, burned buildings, and kidnapped women, acts that were embellished in campfire stories and popular fiction to portray Indians as savages. In saloons and cabins, men boasted about fighting Indians and showed off scalps and other body parts from victims.

Indian warriors, too, were young, armed, and prone to violence. Valuing bravery, they boasted of fighting white interlopers. But Indian communities contained excesses of women, the elderly, and children, making native bands less mobile and more vulnerable. They also were susceptible to bad habits of bachelor white society, copying their binges on cheap whiskey and prostitution. The syphilis and gonorrhea that Indian men contracted from Indian women infected by white men killed many and hindered reproduction, which their populations, already declining from smallpox and other white diseases, could not afford. Thus, the age and gender structure of the white frontier population, combined with racist contempt, further threatened western Indians' existence.

Government Policy and Treaties

Government policy reinforced efforts to remove Indians. North American natives were organized not into tribes, as whites believed, but into bands, confederacies, and villages. Two hundred languages and dialects separated these groups, making it difficult for Indians to unite against white invaders. Although a language group could be defined as a tribe, separate bands and clans had different leaders, and seldom did a chief hold widespread power. Moreover, bands often spent more time battling among themselves than with white settlers.

Nevertheless, the U.S. government needed some way of categorizing Indians. After 1795, American officials considered Indian tribes as nations with which they could make treaties ensuring peace and land boundaries. This was a faulty assumption because chiefs who agreed to a treaty did not always speak for the whole band and the group might not abide by it. Moreover, whites seldom accepted treaties as guarantees of Indians' land rights. On the Plains, whites settled wherever they wished, often commandeering choice farmland. In the Northwest, whites considered treaties protecting Indians' fishing rights on the Columbia River to be nuisances and ousted Indians from the best locations.

Reservation Policy

Prior to the 1880s, the federal government tried to force western Indians onto reservations, where they might be "civilized." Reservations usually consisted of areas in a group's previous territory that were least desirable to whites. The government promised protection from white encroachment, along with food, clothing, and other necessities.

Reservation policy helped make way for the market economy. In the early years, trade had benefited Indians and whites equally. Indians acquired clothing, guns, and horses in return for furs, jewelry, and, sometimes, military assistance against other Indians. Over time, Indians became more dependent, and whites increasingly dictated trade. For example, white traders persuaded Navajo weavers in the Southwest to produce heavy rugs for eastern customers and to change designs and colors to boost sales. Meanwhile, Navajos raised fewer crops and were forced to buy food. Soon they were selling land and labor to whites, and their dependency made it easier to force them onto reservations.

Indians had no say over their affairs on reservations. Supreme Court decisions in 1884 and 1886 defined them as wards (like helpless children under government protection) and denied them U.S. citizenship. Thus, they were unprotected by the Fourteenth and Fifteenth Amendments, which extended citizenship to African Americans. Second, pressure from white farmers, miners, and herders who sought Indian lands made it difficult for the government to preserve reservations intact. Third, the government ignored native history, even combining on one reservation enemy bands. Rather than serving as civilizing communities, reservations weakened Indian culture.

Native Resistance

Not all Indians succumbed to market forces and reservation restrictions. Apaches in the Southwest battled whites even after being forced onto reservations. Pawnees in the Midwest resisted disadvantageous deals from white traders. In the Northwest, Nez Percé Indians escaped reservations by fleeing to Canada in 1877. They eluded U.S. troops until, 1,800 miles later in Montana, their leader, Young Joseph, recognized they could not succeed and ended the flight. Sent to a reservation, Joseph unsuccessfully petitioned the government to return his peoples' ancestral lands.

Link to an explanation of the Pima Indian's calendar sticks.

Whites responded to western Indian defiance militarily. In 1860, Navajos reacted by raiding Fort Defiance in Arizona Territory. The army then attacked and starved the Navajo into submission, and in 1863–1864 forced them on a "Long Walk" from their homelands to a reservation at Bosque Redondo in New Mexico. In the Sand Creek region of Colorado in 1864, a militia commanded by Methodist minister John Chivington attacked Cheyennes led by Black Kettle, killing almost every Indian. In 1879, four thousand U.S. soldiers forced surrender from Utes who were resisting further land concessions.

The most publicized battle occurred in June 1876, when 2,500 Lakotas and Cheyennes led by Chiefs Rain-in-the-Face, Sitting Bull, and Crazy Horse annihilated 256 government troops led by the rash Colonel George A. Custer near the Little Big Horn River in southern Montana. Although Indians demonstrated military skill, supply shortages and relentless pursuit by U.S. soldiers eventually overwhelmed armed Indian resistance. Native Americans were not so much conquered as they were harassed and starved into submission.

Reform of Indian Policy

In the 1870s and 1880s, reformers and government officials sought more purposely to "civilize" natives through landholding and education. This meant outlawing customs deemed "savage and pressuring natives to adopt American values of ambition, thrift, and materialism." In doing so, the United States copied other nation's imperialist policies, such as France, which banned native religious ceremonies in its Pacific island colonies.

Others argued for sympathetic—and sometimes patronizing—treatment. Reform treatises, such as George Manypenny's *Our Indian Wards* (1880) and Helen Hunt Jackson's *A Century of Dishonor* (1881), aroused the American conscience.

In the United States, the most active Indian reform organizations were the Women's National Indian Association (WNIA) and the Indian Rights Association (IRA). The WNIA sought to use women's domestic skills and compassion to help the needy and urged gradual assimilation of Indians. The more influential IRA, which had few Native American members, advocated citizenship and landholding by individual Indians. Most white reformers believed Indians were culturally inferior and could succeed economically only by embracing middle-class values of diligence and education.

Reformers deplored Indians' sexual division of labor. Native women seemed to do all the work—tending crops, raising children, cooking, curing hides, making tools and clothes—while being servile to men, who hunted but were otherwise idle. WNIA and IRA wanted Indian men to bear more responsibilities, treat Indian women more respectfully, and resemble male heads of white middle-class households. But when Indian men and women adopted this model of white society, Indian women lost the economic independence and power over daily life they once had.

Zitkala-Sa

Indians like Zitkala-Sa (Red Bird) used white-controlled education to their advantage. Born on South Dakota's Pine Ridge reservation in 1876, at age twelve this Yankton Sioux girl attended an Indiana boarding school and later Earlham College and the Boston Conservatory of Music. An accomplished orator and violinist, her major contribution was her writing on behalf of her people's needs and advocating cultural preservation. In 1901, Zitkala-Sa published *Old Indian Legends,* translating Sioux oral tradition into stories. Zitkala-Sa married a mixed-race army captain who had taken the name Ray Bonnin and became known as Gertrude Bonnin. Subsequently, she was elected the first full-blooded Indian secretary of the Society of American Indians (see page 553).

Dawes Severalty Act

Dawes Severalty Act: U.S. law designed to "civilize" Indians by dividing up and distributing communal tribal lands to individuals.

In 1887, Congress reversed its reservation policy and passed the **Dawes Severalty Act**. It authorized dissolution of community-owned Indian property and granted land to individual Indian families. The government held that land in trust for twenty-five years, so families could not sell their allotments. The law awarded citizenship to those accepting allotments (an act of Congress in 1906 delayed citizenship for those Indians who had not yet taken their allotment). It also entitled the government to sell unallocated land to whites.

Indian policy, under the Interior Department, now embraced two main tactics for assimilating Indians into white American culture. First, under the Dawes Act, the government distributed reservation land to individual families believing that private property would integrate Indians into the larger society as productive citizens. Second, officials believed that Indians would abandon their "barbaric" habits faster if their children were educated in boarding schools.

The Dawes Act represented a Euro-American and Christian worldview that a society of families headed by men was ideal. Government agents, reformers, and educators used schools to create a patriotic, industrious citizenry. Following Virginia's Hampton Institute, founded in 1869 to educate newly freed slaves,

Visualizing the Past

Attempts to Make Indians Look and Act Like "Americans"

Government officials believed that they could "civilize" Indian children in boarding schools by not only educating them to act like white people but also to make them look like white people. Thus the boys in the photograph on the left were given baseball uniforms and the girl on the right was made to wear a dress and carry a purse and umbrella, all of which were foreign to native people. These images convey information about how Indians were treated, but they also suggest attitudes of the photographer and the artist who made the images. What messages about "civilizing" natives did the person who photographed the baseball team and the artist who drew the picture of the girl reuniting with her people want the viewer to receive?

In an attempt to inculcate "American" customs into its native students, the Fort Spokane Indian School in Spokane, Washington, created a baseball team for the young men who boarded there.

University of Washington Libraries, Seattle, Washington

Library of Congress

In an 1884 edition, Frank Leslie's Weekly, one of the most popular illustrated news and fiction publications of the late nineteenth century and early twentieth, depicted an "Americanized" Indian girl dressed as a proper young lady returning from the Carlisle boarding to school to visit her home on Pine Ridge Agency in South Dakota.

439

teachers established the Carlisle School in Pennsylvania in 1879 as the flagship of the government's Indian school system. Boarding schools imposed white-defined sex roles: boys learned farming and carpentry, and girls learned sewing, cleaning, and cooking.

Ghost Dance

Ghost Dance: Ritual where Sioux dancers moved in a circle, accelerating until they reached a trancelike state and experienced visions of the future where white society would vanish from Indian lands.

With resistance suppressed, Lakotas and others turned to the **Ghost Dance** as a spiritual means of preserving native culture. The Ghost Dance involved movement in a circle until dancers reached a trancelike state and envisioned a day when buffalo would return and all elements of white society would disappear.

Ghost Dancers forswore violence, but as the religion spread government agents worried about possible of renewed Indian uprisings. Charging that the cult was anti-Christian, they arrested Ghost Dancers. Late in 1890, the government sent Custer's old regiment, the Seventh Cavalry, to detain Lakotas moving toward Pine Ridge, South Dakota. Although the Indians were starving, the army assumed they were armed for revolt. Overtaking them at a creek called **Wounded Knee**, the troops massacred about three hundred men, women, and children.

Wounded Knee: South Dakota site of a bloody clash between Sioux Indians and whites. Within minutes, white troops—mistakenly assuming the starving Indians were armed for revolt—slaughtered three hundred Indians including seven infants.

The Losing of the West

Indian wars and the Dawes Act effectively accomplished what whites wanted and Indians feared: it reduced native control over land. Between 1887 and the 1930s, native landholdings dwindled from 138 million acres to 52 million. Land-grabbing whites were particularly cruel to the Ojibwas of the northern plains. In 1906, Senator Moses E. Clapp of Minnesota attached to an Indian appropriations bill a rider declaring that mixed-blood adults on the White Earth reservation were "competent" (meaning educated in white ways) enough to sell their land without the Dawes Act's twenty-five-year waiting period. When the bill became law, speculators duped many Ojibwas into signing away their land for counterfeit money and worthless merchandise. The Ojibwas lost more than half their original holdings, and economic ruin overtook them.

Ultimately, political and ecological crises overwhelmed most western Indian groups. Buffalo extinction, enemy raids, and disease, along with military campaigns, hobbled subsistence culture until Native Americans could only yield their lands to market-oriented whites. Believing themselves superior, whites determined to transform Indians by teaching about private property and American ideals, and eradicating their "backward" languages, lifestyles, and religions. Indians tried to retain their culture but by century's end, they lost control of their land and faced increasing pressure to shed their group identity.

Life on the Natural Resource Frontier

What sparked the rise of the conservation movement?

Unlike Indians, who used natural resources for subsistence needs and small-scale trading, whites who migrated to the West and Great Plains saw the vast territory as untapped sources of wealth (see Map 17.1). Extracting its resources advanced settlement, created new markets at home and abroad, and fueled revolutions in transportation, agriculture, and industry across the United States in the late nineteenth century. This same extraction of nature's wealth led to environmental wastefulness and fed racial and sexual oppression.

Mining and Lumbering

In the mid-1800s, the mining frontier drew thousands of people to Nevada, Idaho, Montana, Utah, and Colorado. California's gold rush helped populate a thriving state by 1850 and furnished many of the miners traveling to nearby states. Others followed traditional routes from the East to the West.

Prospectors climbed mountains and trekked across deserts seeking precious metals. They shot game for food and financed their explorations by convincing merchants to advance credit for equipment in return for a share of the as-yet-undiscovered lode. Unlucky prospectors whose credit ran out took jobs and saved up for another search.

MAP 17.1

The Development and Natural Resources of the West

By 1890, mining, lumbering, and cattle ranching had penetrated many areas west of the Mississippi River, and railroad construction had linked together the western economy. These activities, along with the spread of mechanized agriculture, altered both the economy and the people who were involved in them.

Source: Copyright © Cengage Learning

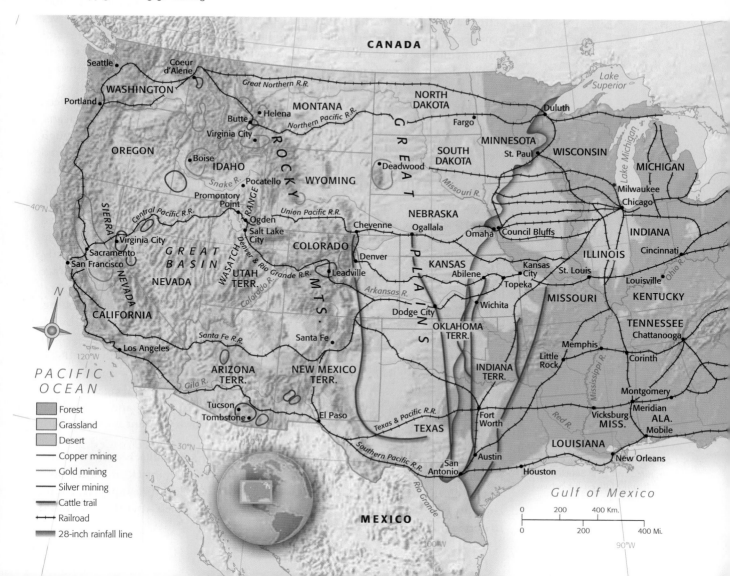

Digging up and transporting minerals was expensive, so prospectors who made discoveries sold their claims to large mining syndicates, such as the Anaconda Copper Company. Financed by eastern capital, these companies brought in engineers, heavy machinery, railroad lines, and work crews, making western mining as corporate as eastern manufacturing. Although discoveries of gold and silver sparked national publicity, mining companies usually exploited equally lucrative lead, zinc, tin, quartz, and copper.

Unlike mining, cutting trees for lumber for construction and heating materials required vast tracts of forest land to be profitable. Because tree supplies in the upper Midwest and South were depleted, lumber corporations moved into northwestern forests. The 1878 Timber and Stone Act sought to stimulate settlement in California, Nevada, Oregon, and Washington by allowing private citizens to buy inexpensive 160-acre plots. Lumber companies grabbed millions of acres by hiring seamen from waterfront boarding houses to register claims to timberland and then transfer them to the companies. By 1900, private citizens had bought over 3.5 million acres, but most of it belonged to corporations.

At the same time, oil companies began drilling wells in the Southwest. In 1900, petroleum came from the Appalachians and the Midwest, but rich oil reserves were discovered in southern California and eastern Texas, turning Los Angeles and Houston into boom cities. Although oil and kerosene were used mostly for lubrication and lighting, oil discovered in the Southwest later became a vital new fuel source.

Complex Communities

As the West developed, it became a multiracial society, including Native Americans, white migrants, Mexicans, African Americans, and Asians. A crescent of territory from western Texas through New Mexico and Arizona to northern California (including Mexico), supported ranchers and sheepherders, descendants of early Spanish settlers. In New Mexico, Spaniards mixed with Indians to form a *mestizo* population. Across the Southwest, Mexican immigrants moved into American territory to find work. Some returned to Mexico seasonally. Although the Treaty of Guadalupe Hidalgo (1848) guaranteed property rights to Hispanics, "Anglo" (the Mexican name for a white American) miners, speculators, and railroads used fraud to steal Hispanic landholdings. Consequently, many Mexicanos moved to cities such as San Antonio and Tucson and became wage laborers.

Before the Chinese Exclusion Act of 1882 prohibited them from immigrating, some 200,000 Chinese—mostly young, single males—entered the United States, building communities in California, Oregon, and Washington. Many came with five-year labor contracts for railroad construction; others labored in the fields. By the 1870s, Chinese composed half of California's agricultural work force, often working in citrus groves. In cities such as San Francisco, they labored in textile and cigar factories.

Japanese and European immigrants also worked in mining and agricultural communities. The region consequently developed its own migrant economy, with workers relocating to take short-term jobs.

Many African Americans were "**exodusters**" who built all-black western towns. Nicodemus, Kansas, for example, was founded in 1877 by black migrants from Lexington, Kentucky. Despite challenges, the town developed newspapers, shops, churches, a hotel, and a bank. It declined when businesses left after the town failed to obtain railroad connections.

exodusters: Freedmen who migrated from the South to the North and Midwest for better opportunities.

The major exodus occurred in 1879, when some six thousand blacks, including former slaves, moved from the South to Kansas, aided by the Kansas Freedmen's Relief Association. Other migrants, encouraged by editors and land speculators, went to Oklahoma Territory, where they founded thirty-two all-black communities in the 1890s and early 1900s.

Western Women

Although unmarried men dominated the frontier, many white women similarly headed west to find fortune. In mining areas, they usually accompanied a husband or father, however. Using their labor as a resource, women earned money by cooking and laundering, and sometimes as sex workers in houses of prostitution. In the Northwest, they worked in canneries, cleaning and salting fish.

Link to Letters of a Woman Homesteader by Elinore Stewart.

White women helped bolster family and community life as members of the home mission movement. They broke from traditional male-dominated Protestant missions. Using the slogan "Woman's work for women," they established missionary societies aiding women—unmarried mothers, Mormons, Indians, and Chinese—who they believed had fallen prey to men or who had not yet adopted Christian virtue.

Significance of Race

For white settlers, race became an important means to control labor and social relations. They classified people into five races: Caucasians (themselves), Indians, Mexicans (both Mexican Americans, who had originally inhabited western lands, and Mexican immigrants), "Mongolians" (a term applied to Chinese), and "Negroes." With these categories, whites imposed racial distinctions on people who, with the possible exception of African Americans, never before considered themselves a "race," and then judged them permanently inferior. In 1878, for example, a federal judge in California ruled that Chinese could not become U.S. citizens because they were not "white persons."

Racial minorities occupied the bottom of a two-tiered labor system and experienced prejudice as whites tried to reserve for themselves the West's riches. Whites dominated the top tier of managerial and skilled positions, while Irish, Chinese, Mexican, and African American laborers held unskilled positions. Anti-Chinese violence erupted during hard times. When the Union Pacific Railroad tried to replace white workers with lower-waged Chinese in Rock Springs, Wyoming, in 1885, whites burned down the Chinese part of town, killing twenty-eight. Mexicans, many of whom were the original landowners in California and elsewhere, saw their property claims ignored or stolen by whites.

Because so many white male migrants were single, intermarriage with Mexican and Indian women was common. Such unions were acceptable for white men, but not for white women, especially with Asian immigrants. Most miscegenation laws passed by western legislatures sought to prevent Chinese and Japanese men from marrying white women.

Conservation Movement

Questions about natural resources caught Americans between desire for progress and fear of spoiling nature. After the Civil War, people eager to protect the natural landscape organized a conservation movement. Sports hunters, concerned about loss of wildlife, opposed commercial hunting and lobbied state legislatures to pass hunting regulations. Artists and tourists in 1864 persuaded Congress to preserve

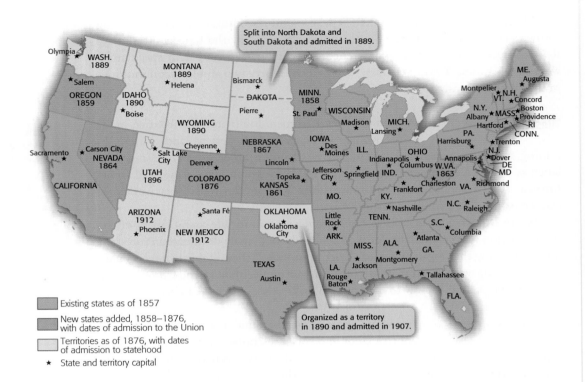

Split into North Dakota and
South Dakota and admitted in 1889.

Organized as a territory
in 1890 and admitted in 1907.

Existing states as of 1857

New states added, 1858–1876,
with dates of admission to the Union

Territories as of 1876, with dates
of admission to statehood

★ State and territory capital

MAP 17.2

The United States, 1876–1912

A wave of admissions between 1889 and 1912 brought remaining territories to statehood and marked the final creation of new states until Alaska and Hawai'i were admitted in the 1950s.

Source: Copyright © Cengage Learning

the Yosemite Valley by granting it to California for public use. In 1872, Congress designated the Yellowstone River region in Wyoming as the first national park. And in 1891 conservationists, led by naturalist John Muir, pressured Congress to authorize President Benjamin Harrison to create forest reserves—public lands protected from private timber companies.

Link to "The Approach to the Valley," from John Muir's, *The Yosemite.*

Despite Muir's activism and efforts by the Sierra Club (which Muir helped found in 1892) and corporations supporting rational resource development, opposition was loudest in the West, where people remained eager to exploit nature. By prohibiting trespass in areas such as Yosemite and Yellowstone, conservation policy deprived Indians and white settlers of wildlife, water, and firewood previously available on federal lands.

Admission of New States

Development of mining and forest regions, along with farms and cities, brought western territories to the threshold of statehood (see Map 17.2). In 1889, Republicans seeking to solidify control of Congress passed an omnibus bill granting statehood to North Dakota, South Dakota, Washington, and Montana. Wyoming and Idaho, which allowed women to vote, were admitted the following year. Congress denied statehood to Utah until 1896, wanting assurances from the Mormons, a majority of the territory's population, that they would prohibit polygamy.

Western states' varied communities flavored American folk culture and fostered a "go-getter" optimism that distinguished the American spirit. The lawlessness of places such as Deadwood, in Dakota Territory, and Tombstone, in Arizona Territory, gave their region notoriety and romance. Legends arose about characters whose lives magnified the western experience, and promoters such as Buffalo Bill enhanced western folklore's appeal.

Western Folk Heroes

Arizona's mining towns, with their free-flowing cash and loose law enforcement, attracted gamblers, thieves, and opportunists who came symbolize the Wild West. Near Tombstone, the infamous Clanton family and their partner John Ringgold (Johnny Ringo) were smugglers and cattle rustlers. The Earp brothers—Wyatt, Jim, Morgan, Virgil, and Warren—and their friends William ("Bat") Masterson and John Henry ("Doc") Holliday operated on both sides of the law as gunmen, gamblers, and politicians. A feud between the Clantons and Earps climaxed on October 26, 1881, in a shootout at the OK Corral, where three Clantons were killed and Holliday and Morgan Earp were wounded.

Writers Mark Twain, Bret Harte, and others captured the flavor of western life, and characters such as Buffalo Bill, Annie Oakley, and Wild Bill Hickok became western folk heroes. But violence and eccentricity were uncommon. Most miners and lumbermen worked long hours, often for corporations, and had little time or money for gambling, carousing, or gunfights. Women worked as teachers, laundresses, storekeepers, and housewives. Only a few were sharpshooters or dance-hall queens. For most, western life was a struggle for survival.

Irrigation and Transportation

Western economic development is the story of how public and private interests used technology and organization to utilize the region's sometimes scarce water resources to make the arid land agriculturally productive.

How did government policies aid the development of the West?

For centuries, Indians irrigated southwestern fields for subsistence farming. When the Spanish arrived, they tapped the Rio Grande River to irrigate farms. Later, they channeled water to San Diego and Los Angeles. The Mormons were the first Americans of northern European ancestry to practice extensive irrigation. Arriving in Utah in 1847, they diverted streams and rivers into canals, enabling them to farm the hard-baked soil. By 1890, Utah boasted over 263,000 irrigated acres supporting more than 200,000 people.

Rights to Water

Efforts at land reclamation through irrigation in Colorado and California sparked conflict over rights to the precious streams that flowed through the West. Americans inherited the English common-law principle of riparian rights, which held that the stream belonged to God; those who lived nearby could take water as needed but should not diminish the river. Intended to protect nature, this principle discouraged economic development by prohibiting property owners from damming or diverting water at the expense of others who lived downstream.

Western settlers rejected riparianism and embraced prior appropriation, which awarded a river's water to the first person claiming it. Westerners, taking cues from eastern Americans who diverted waterways to power mills, asserted that water existed to serve human needs and advance profits. Anyone intending a "reasonable" (economically productive) use of river water should have the right to appropriation. The courts generally agreed.

Government Supervision of Water Rights

Under appropriation, those who dammed and diverted water often reduced its flow downstream. People disadvantaged by such action could either sue or establish a public authority to regulate water usage. Thus in 1879, Colorado created several divisions to regulate water rights. In 1890, Wyoming added a constitutional provision declaring that the state's rivers were public property subject to supervision.

Destined to become the most productive agricultural state, California maintained a mixed legal system that upheld riparianism while allowing for some appropriation. This system disadvantaged irrigators, who sought to change state law. In 1887, the legislature passed a bill permitting farmers to organize into districts that would construct and operate irrigation projects. An irrigation district could purchase water rights, seize private property for irrigation canals, and finance projects through taxation or by issuing bonds. As a result, California became the nation's leader in irrigated acreage, with more than 1 million irrigated acres by 1890, making the state's fruit and vegetable agriculture the most profitable nationwide.

Newlands Reclamation Act

Even so, the federal government owned most western land in the 1890s. Prodded by land-hungry developers, states wanted the federal government to turn over part of public domain lands, claiming they could make them profitable through reclamation—and irrigation. Congress generally refused such transfers because of potential controversies. Who would regulate waterways that flowed through more than one state? If, for example, California controlled the Truckee River, which flowed westward out of Lake Tahoe on the California-Nevada border, how would Nevadans ensure that California would give them sufficient water? Only the federal government had the power to regulate regional water development.

Newlands Reclamation Act: Authorized the U.S. government to sell western public lands to finance dams and irrigation projects in the West.

In 1902, after years of debates, Congress passed the **Newlands Reclamation Act**. It allowed the federal government to sell western public lands to individuals in parcels not to exceed 160 acres and to use proceeds to finance irrigation. The Newlands Act provided for control but not conservation of water, and instead fell within the tradition of development of nature for human profit. It represented a decision by the federal government to aid the agricultural and general economic development of the West.

Railroad Construction

Between 1865 and 1890, railroad expansion boomed, as tracks grew from 35,000 to 200,000 miles, mostly west of the Mississippi River (see Map 17.1). By 1900, the United States contained one-third of all railroad track in the world. The Central Pacific employed thousands of Chinese; the Union Pacific used mainly Irish. Workers lived in shacks and tents that were dismantled, loaded on flatcars, and relocated each day.

After 1880, when steel rails began replacing iron rails, railroads helped to boost the nation's steel industry to international leadership. Railroad expansion also spawned related industries: coal, rail-car manufacturing, and depot construction. Railroads also fueled western urbanization. Transporting people and freight, railroads accelerated the growth of hubs such as Chicago, Omaha, Kansas City, Cheyenne, Los Angeles, Portland, and Seattle.

Links to the World

The Australian Frontier

Australia, founded like the United States as a European colony, had a frontier society that resembled the American West in its mining development, folk society, and treatment of indigenous people. Australia experienced a gold rush in 1851, two years after the United States did, and large-scale mining companies moved into its western regions to extract lucrative mineral deposits.

Promise of mineral wealth lured thousands of mostly male immigrants to Australia in the late nineteenth century. As in the United States, anti-Chinese riots erupted, and beginning in 1854, Australia passed laws restricting Chinese immigration. When the country became an independent British federation in 1901, it implemented a literacy test that terminated Chinese immigration for over fifty years.

Although Australians immortalized folk heroes symbolizing white masculinity and a spirit of personal liberty and opportunism, they considered indigenous peoples, whom they called "Aborigines," as savages. Christian missionaries viewed aborigines as pagan and tried to convert them. In 1869, the government of Victoria Province passed an Aborigine Protection Act that, like American policy toward Indians, encouraging removal of native children from their families to learn European customs in white schools. Aborigines adapted. They formed cricket teams, and those with light skin sometimes told census takers they were white. In the end, Australians resorted to reservations to "protect" Aborigines, much as Americans isolated native peoples on reserved land. Like the Americans, white Australians could not find a place for indigenous people in their land of opportunity.

Much like the American counterpart, the Australian frontier was populated by natives before Anglo colonists arrived. The Aborigines, as the Australian natives were called, lived in villages and utilized their own culture to adapt to the environment. This photo shows a native camp in the Maloga Reserve.

National Library of Australia

Railroad Subsidies   Railroads received some of the largest government subsidies in American history. Promoters argued that because railroads were a public benefit, the government should give them land from the public domain, which they could then sell to finance construction. During the Civil War, Congress, dominated by business-minded Republicans granted railroad corporations over 180 million acres, mostly for interstate routes. Railroads funded construction by using the land as security for bonds or by selling it. State legislators, who often had financial interests in a railroad's, granted some 50 million acres. Cities and towns also assisted, usually via loans or by purchasing railroad bonds or stocks.

Without public help, few railroads could have prospered sufficiently to attract private investment. Although capitalists often opposed government involvement in corporate business, railroads accepted aid and pressured governments for assistance. The Southern Pacific, for example, threatened to bypass Los Angeles unless the city paid a bonus and built a depot. Some laborers and farmers fought subsidies, arguing that companies would become too powerful. Many communities boomed, however, as railroads attracted investment into the West and drew farmers into the market economy.

Standard Gauge, Standard Time   Railroad construction triggered important technological and organizational reforms. By the late 1880s, almost all lines had adopted standard-gauge rails so their tracks could connect. Air brakes, automatic car couplers, and other devices made rail transportation safer and more efficient. The need for gradings, tunnels, and bridges spurred the growth of the American engineering profession. Organizational advances included systems for coordinating passenger and freight schedules, and the adoption of uniform freight-classification systems. However, railroads also reinforced racism by segregating black and white passengers on cars and in stations.

Railroads altered conceptions of time and space. First, instead of expressing the distance between places in miles, people referred to the time it took to travel from place to place. Second, railroad scheduling required the nationwide standardization of time. Before railroads, local clocks struck noon when the sun was overhead, and people set clocks accordingly. But because the sun was not overhead at the same moment everywhere, time varied from place to place. Boston's clocks differed from New York's by almost twelve minutes. In 1883, without authority from Congress, the nation's railroads established four standard time zones for the country. Railroad time became national time.

Farming the Plains

What helped ease farmers' hardships as settlers in the West?

While California led the nation agriculturally, the Great Plains developed rapidly. There, farming in the late 1800s exemplified two important achievements: the transformation of arid prairies into crop-producing land and the transformation of agriculture into big business via mechanization, long-distance transportation, and scientific cultivation. Irrigation and the mechanized agriculture enabled farmers to feed the nation's burgeoning population and turned the United States into the world's breadbasket.

Settlement of the Plains

The number of farms tripled between 1860 and 1910, as hundreds of thousands of hopeful farmers headed to the Plains. The Homestead Act of 1862 and other measures to encourage western settlement offered cheap or free plots to people who would reside on and improve them. Land-rich railroads advertised affordable land, arranging credit terms, and offering reduced fares. Railroad agents—often former immigrants—traveled to Denmark, Sweden, Germany, and other European nations to recruit settlers.

To most families, the West seemed to promise a second chance, a better life. Railroad expansion enabled remote farmers to ship produce to market, and construction of grain elevators eased storage problems. Worldwide and national population growth sparked demand for farm products, and the prospects for commercial agriculture became increasingly favorable.

Hardship on the Plains

Farm life, however, was harder than advertisements and railroad agents insinuated. Migrants often encountered scarcities of essentials they had once enjoyed. Barren prairies contained insufficient lumber so pioneer families built houses of sod and burned buffalo dung for heat. Water was sometimes scarce also. Machinery for drilling wells was expensive, as were windmills for drawing water to the surface.

Weather posed formidable challenges. The climate between the Missouri River and the Rocky Mountains divides along a line running from Minnesota southwest through Oklahoma, then south, bisecting Texas. West of this line, annual rainfall averages less than twenty-eight inches, not enough for most crops or trees (see Map 17.3).

Weather was unpredictable. Weeks of torrid summer heat and parching winds suddenly gave way to violent storms that washed away crops and property. Winter blizzards piled up snowdrifts that halted outdoor movement. Melting snow swelled streams, and floods threatened millions of acres. In fall, a rainless week turned dry grasslands into tinder, and the slightest spark could ignite a prairie fire. Severe drought in Texas between 1884 and 1886 drove many farmers off the land.

Nature could be cruel even under good conditions. Weather favorable for crops also bred insects. In the 1870s and 1880s, grasshopper swarms devoured everything: plants, tree bark, and clothing. One farmer lamented, the "hoppers left behind nothing but the mortgage."

Social Isolation

Settlers also faced social isolation. New England and European farmers lived in villages, traveling daily to nearby fields. In the Plains, the Far West and South, peculiarities of land division compelled rural dwellers to live far apart. Because most plots were rectangular—usually encompassing 160 acres—at most four families could live nearby, but only if they congregated around their shared four-corner intersection. In practice, farm families lived away from boundary lines with a half-mile separating farmhouses. Men might find escape by occasionally traveling to sell crops or buy supplies. Women were more isolated, confined by domestic chores to the household with sporadic trips to exchange food and services with neighbors.

Letters that Ed Donnell, a young Nebraska homesteader, wrote to his family in Missouri reveal how circumstances could dull optimism. In fall 1885, Donnell rejoiced to his mother, "I like Nebr first rate....I have saw a pretty tuff time a part

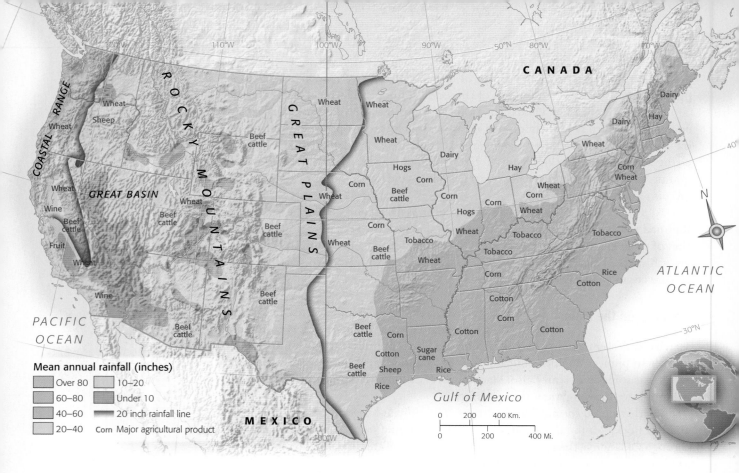

MAP 17.3

Agricultural Regions of the United States, 1890

In the Pacific Northwest and east of the twenty-eight-inch-rainfall line, farmers could grow a greater variety of crops. Territory west of the line was either too mountainous or too arid to support agriculture without irrigation. The grasslands that once fed buffalo herds could now feed beef cattle.

Source: Copyright © Cengage Learning

of the time since I have been out here, but I started out to get a home and I was determined to win or die in the attempt....Have got a good crop of corn, a floor in my house and got it ceiled overhead." But Donnell was lonely. "You wanted to know when I was going to get married. Just as quick as I can get money ahead to get a cow."

A year and a half later, Donnell's dreams were dissolving and, still a bachelor, he was beginning to look elsewhere. By fall, Donnell lamented, "We have been having wet weather for 3 weeks....My health has been so poor this summer and the wind and the sun hurts my head...if I can sell I will...move to town for I can get $40 a month working in a grist mill." Thousands shared Donnell's hardships, and their cityward migration fueled late-nineteenth-century urban growth (see Chapter 19).

Mail-Order Companies and Rural Free Delivery Farm families organized churches and clubs to ease isolation. By 1900, two developments brought rural settlers into closer contact with modern consumer society. First, mail-order companies, such as Montgomery Ward and Sears Roebuck, made new products attainable. Ward and Sears received letters that reported family news and

Montana Historical Society

Evelyn Cameron was a British-born Montana settler whose diaries and photographs portrayed the hardship and beauty of the frontier in the 1890s and early 1900s. Here, she depicted two homesteaders and their simple dwelling with its dirt floor, wood stove, and boxes serving as furniture.

sought advice on needs from gifts to childcare. A Washington man wrote, "As you advertise everything for sale that a person wants, I thought I would write you, as I am in need of a wife, and see what you could do for me."

Second, after farmers petitioned Congress for extension of the postal service, in 1896 the government made Rural Free Delivery (RFD) widely available. Farmers who previously picked up mail in town could now receive letters and catalogs in a roadside mailbox almost daily. In 1913, the postal service inaugurated parcel post, which made shipping costs much cheaper.

Mechanization of Agriculture

Machinery drove the agricultural revolution. When the Civil War took men off farms in the upper Mississippi River valley, women and older men who remained behind began using reapers and other mechanical implements. After the war, demand encouraged farmers to utilize machines, and inventors developed new implements. Seeders, combines, binders, mowers, and rotary plows, improved grain growing on the Plains and in California, while the centrifugal cream separator, patented in 1879, sped the skimming of cream from milk.

TABLE 17.1   **Summary: Government Land Policy**

Railroad land grants (1850–1871)	Granted 181 million acres to railroads to encourage construction and development
Homestead Act (1862)	Gave 80 million acres to settlers to encourage settlement
Morrill Act (1862)	Granted 11 million acres to states to sell to fund public agricultural colleges
Other grants	Granted 129 million acres to states to sell for other educational and related purposes
Dawes Act (1887)	Allotted some reservation lands to individual Indians to promote private property and weaken tribal values among Indians and offered remaining reservation lands for sale to whites (by 1906, some 75 million acres had been acquired by whites)
Various laws	Permitted direct sales of 100 million acres by the Land Office

Source: Goldfield, David; Abbott, Carl E., Anderson, Virginia Dejohn; Argersinger, Jo Ann E.; Argersinger, Peter H.; Barney, William; Weir, Robert M., *American Journey, The*, Volume II, 3rd ed., © 2004. Printed and electronically reproduced by permission of Pearson Education, Inc., Upper Saddle River, New Jersey.

For centuries, farmers planted only what they could harvest by hand. Machines—driven first by animals, then by steam—significantly increased productivity and reduced costs. For example, before mechanization, a farmer working alone could harvest about 7.5 acres of wheat. Using an automatic binder that cut and bundled the grain, he could harvest 135 acres. Machines dramatically reduced the time and cost of farming other crops as well. (See Table 17.1)

Legislative and Scientific Aids

Congress and scientists worked to improve existing crops and develop new ones. The 1862 Morrill Land Grant Act gave states federal lands to sell to finance agricultural research. Consequently new public universities were established in Wisconsin, Illinois, Minnesota, California, and other states. A second Morrill Act in 1890 aided more schools, including several all-black colleges. The Hatch Act of 1887 provided for agricultural experiment stations in every state, further advancing farming science and technology.

Science enabled farmers to use the soil more efficiently. Researchers developed dry farming, a plowing and harrowing technique that minimized evaporation. Botanists perfected varieties of "hard" wheat whose seeds could withstand northern winters. Agriculturists adapted new varieties of alfalfa from Mongolia, corn from North Africa, and rice from Asia. George Washington Carver, a son of slaves who became a chemist and taught at Alabama's Tuskegee Institute, created hundreds of products from peanuts, soybeans, and sweet potatoes. Other scientists combated plant and animal diseases. Technology helped American farmers expand productivity in the market economy.

The Ranching Frontier

How did ranching shift from small, individual-owned endeavors to big business?

Western commercial farming ran headlong into one of the region's most romantic industries—ranching. Beginning in the sixteenth century, Spanish landholders raised cattle in Mexico and what would become the American Southwest. They employed Indian and Mexican cowboys, called *vaqueros,* who tended herds and rounded up cattle.

Anglo ranchers moving into Texas and California in the early nineteenth century hired *vaqueros* to teach them roping, branding, horse training, and saddle making.

By the 1860s, cattle-raising became increasingly profitable, as population growth boosted the demand for beef and railroads simplified food transportation. By 1870, drovers were herding thousands of Texas cattle northward to Kansas, Missouri, and Wyoming (see Map 17.1). At the northern terminus, the cattle were sold or loaded onto trains bound for Chicago and St. Louis slaughterhouses and international markets.

The long drive gave rise to romantic lore of bellowing cattle, buckskin-clad cowboys, and smoky campfires. Trekking 1,000 miles or more for months made cattle sinewy and tough. Herds traveling through Indian territory and farmers' fields were sometimes shot at. When ranchers discovered that crossing Texas longhorns with heavier Hereford and Angus breeds produced sturdier and more profitable animals, cattle raising expanded northward. Herds in Kansas, Nebraska, Colorado, Wyoming, Montana, and Dakota crowded out already declining buffalo.

The Open Range

Cattle raisers minimized expenses by purchasing a few acres bordering a stream and turning their herds loose on adjacent public domain that no one wanted because it lacked water access. By using open-range ranching, cattle raisers could utilize thousands of acres by owning a hundred. Neighboring ranchers often formed associations and allowed herds to graze together, burning an identifying brand into each animal's hide. But as ranchers flowed into the Plains, cattle overran the range, and other groups challenged ranchers over use of the land.

Sheepherders from California and New Mexico were also using the public domain, sparking territorial clashes. Ranchers complained that sheep ruined grassland by eating to the roots and that cattle refused to graze where sheep had been. Occasionally, ranchers and sheepherders resorted to violence rather than settle disagreements in court, where a judge might discover that both were using public land illegally.

More important, the farming frontier generated new land demands. Lacking sufficient timber and stone for traditional fencing, western settlers could not easily define their property. Tensions flared when farmers accused cattle raisers of allowing herds to trespass on cropland and when herders charged that farmers should fence their property.

Barbed Wire

The solution was barbed wire. Invented in 1873 by Joseph F. Glidden, a DeKalb, Illinois, farmer, this inexpensive and mass-produced fencing consisted of wires held in place by sharp spurs. It enabled Plains homesteaders to protect their farms from grazing cattle. It also ended open-range ranching and made roundups unnecessary, as large-scale ranchers enclosed their herds within private property. Similarly, the development of the round silo for storing and making fodder enabled cattle raisers to feed their herds without grazing.

Ranching as Big Business

By 1890, big businesses were taking over the cattle industry and applying scientific methods of breeding and feeding. Corporations also used technology to squeeze larger returns from meatpacking. Every part of a cow had uses: half was meat, but larger profits came from hides for leather, blood for fertilizer, hooves for glue, fat for candles and soap, and the rest for sausages. Cattle processing harmed the environment, as meatpackers and leather tanners dumped unsold goods into waterways. By the late nineteenth century, the Chicago River created a powerful stench that made nearby residents sick.

Open-range ranching made beef a staple of the American diet and created a few fortunes, but it could not survive the rush of history. Overgrazing destroyed Plains grass supplies, and the brutal winter of 1886–1887 destroyed 90 percent of some herds and drove small ranchers out of business. By 1890, large-scale ranchers owned or leased the land they used. Cowboys formed labor organizations and struck for higher pay. The myth of the cowboy's freedom and individualism lived on, but ranching became a corporate business.

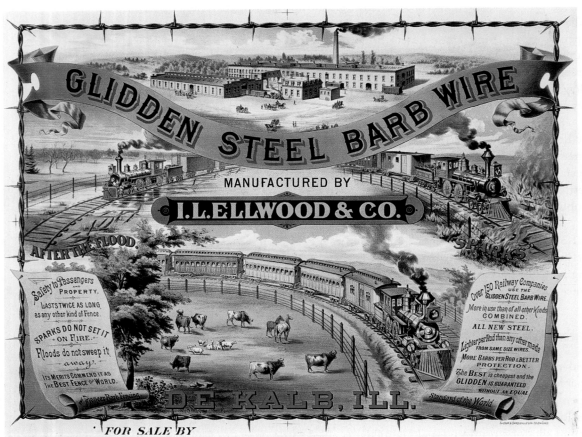

Elwood House Museum, DeKalb, Illinois

Bordered by the product it was promoting, this advertisement conveyed the message that railroads and farmers could protect their property from each other by utilizing a new type of fencing.

National Parks

Embodying greatness in the majesty of national parks is a uniquely American contribution to world culture. Initially, however, Congress did not recognize this possibility: in 1872, it created Yellowstone National Park but appropriated no funds to protect it. In 1886, however, the secretary of the interior was granted cavalry soldiers to supervise the park; meant to be temporary, they stayed until 1922.

Slowly, Congress created other parks, including Yosemite and Sequoia in California in 1890 and sites in Oregon, Utah, Arizona, Montana, and Colorado between 1902 and 1915. But conflicts arose between those who, like naturalist John Muir and the Sierra Club, wished to preserve parks in pristine quality and those, such as Senator William A. Clark of Montana, who wanted to lease the land for logging, mining, railroads, and tourism. Congress in 1916 created the National Park Service (NPS) to conserve natural and historic territory for their enjoyment by Americans. Stephen Mather, head of the service, took preservation seriously but also allowed hotel construction in parks for visitors.

Initially, national parks were in the West, but after 1920 the Park Service established eastern sites, beginning with the Great Smokies in Tennessee and North Carolina and Shenandoah in Virginia. In 1933, President Franklin Roosevelt transferred supervision of all national monuments and historic sites to the NPS, including the Statue of Liberty and Civil War battlefields. A few years later, NPS began adding seashores to its sphere, and from the 1960s onward urban sites such as Golden Gate National Recreation Area near San Francisco were incorporated.

By 1950, 30 million people visited national parks annually. Roads fell into disrepair, campgrounds were dilapidated, and litter was piling up. Moreover, those eager for the economic development of park lands lobbied for permission to dam rivers; expand roads; and build hotels, gas stations, and restaurants. In 1964, Congress passed a bill providing funds for future park land acquisition, but balancing preservation and public use remains controversial. Today, there are almost 400 national park units, encompassing more than 84 million acres. They stand a legacy from the past that poses challenges for the future.

Summary

History revealed that Frederick Jackson Turner's image of the West as the home of democratic spirit and Buffalo Bill's depiction of it as the battlefield of white man's victory were incomplete.

The American West exerted lasting influence on the complex mix of people there. Living mostly in small groups, Indians—the original inhabitants—hunted, farmed, and depended on delicate resources such as buffalo herds and salmon runs. When they came into contact with commerce-minded European-Americans, their resistance to the market economy, diseases, and violence that whites brought into the West failed.

Mexicans, Chinese, African Americans, and Anglos discovered a reciprocal relationship between human activities and the environment. Miners, timber cutters, farmers, and builders extracted raw minerals for eastern factories, used irrigation and machines to yield agricultural abundance, filled pastures with cattle and sheep to expand food sources, and constructed railroads to tie the nation together. But the environment exerted power through climate, insects and parasites, and other hazards.

The West's settlers employed violence and greed that sustained discrimination within a multiracial society, left many farmers feeling cheated, provoked contests over water and pastures, and sacrificed environmental balance for market profits. The region's raw materials and agricultural products raised living standards and hastened industrial progress, but not without costs.

Chapter Review

The Economic Activities of Native Peoples

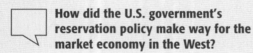

What factors undermined Native Americans' subsistence in the late nineteenth century?

The Native American economic system was increasingly eroded after 1850 by a number of factors, some natural and some resulting from increasing interaction with, and encroachment by, whites. Southwestern and Plains Indian economies were devastated by the declining buffalo herd due to drought, diseases brought by white-owned livestock, excessive Native American hunting and trade, white settlement on Indian lands used for grazing, and whites' efforts to eliminate the buffalo to make way for railroads. Northwestern Indian economies, which relied on salmon fishing, similarly suffered when white commercial fisheries diminished salmon supplies and dammed up rivers and tributaries that were vital for fishing stocks.

The Transformation of Native Cultures

How did the U.S. government's reservation policy make way for the market economy in the West?

U.S. reservation policy before the 1880s forced Indians onto western reservations, promising to protect this territory from white encroachment. Once on reservations, Indians' dependency on whites for trade goods such as clothing, guns, horses, and food made it easier for whites to control Indian affairs. The 1887 Dawes Severalty Act dissolved community-owned Indian land, granting it instead to qualifying individual Indian families. The land was held in trust for twenty-five years and allowed the U.S. government to sell unassigned allotments (typically to whites). The goal of this was to "civilize" Indians and assimilate them into white culture via private property, but in truth it reduced their land holdings by more than half and made way for land sales and further white settlement of the West.

Life on the Natural Resources frontier

What sparked the rise of the conservation movement?

Mining for precious metals, cutting trees for lumber, and drilling for oil drew thousands of people to the West seeking fortune and a better life. It also transformed the natural landscape, contributed to environmental wastefulness and sparked a debate over the desire for progress and the need to preserve nature. This gave rise to a conservation movement after the Civil War.

Recreational hunters and families that depended on wild game for meat lobbied legislatures; artists and tourists pressured Congress to protect Yosemite Valley by granting it to California for public use; and in 1862, the Yellowstone River region in Wyoming became the first national park. Congress also authorized President Benjamin Harrison to create forest reserves, at the urging of a group led by activist John Muir, who founded the environmental group the Sierra Club in 1892.

Irrigation and Transportation

How did government policies aid the development of the West?

Two ways: first, during the Civil War era, government subsidies for railroad construction—among the largest in U.S. history—included massive land grants, which companies could use for interstate routes or sell to finance construction. Federal land grants topped 180 million acres, while states handed over another 50 million acres, and cities and towns helped by offering loans or buying railroad stocks. Second, through the Newlands Reclamation Act (1902), Congress supported the sale of western lands in parcels smaller than 160 acres to individuals, with the funds being used to finance irrigation projects in the region. That, in turn, facilitated the agricultural and economic development.

Farming the Plains

What helped ease farmers' hardships as settlers in the West?

Migrants hoped to find a better life in the West, but often experienced loneliness, isolation, the lack of essential products and services they previously knew, and even shortages of lumber needed to build homes. But the arrival of the railroad, the extension of the postal service into the West, and the advent of the mail-order business ended some of their problems by bringing products and people to the region. New technology and mechanization also made farming easier, and the creation of social clubs, churches and other organizations helped ease social isolation.

The Ranching Frontier

How did ranching shift from small, individual-owned endeavors to big business?

With the increasing demand for beef and expansion of herds, ranchers overgrazed the land, which destroyed grass supplies that fed Plains herds. A brutal winter in 1886 to 1887 killed off 90 percent of some ranchers' herds and drove many out of business. By 1890, big business took over the cattle industry and used scientific methods for breeding and feeding to eliminate dependency on grass and grazing lands.

Suggestions for Further Reading

William Cronon, *Nature's Metropolis: Chicago and the Great West* (1991)

Karl Jacoby, *Crimes Against Nature: Squatters, Poachers, Thieves and the Hidden History of American Conservation* (2001)

Karl Jacoby, *Shadows at Dawn: A Borderlands Massacre and the Violence of History* (2009)

Patricia Nelson Limerick, *The Legacy of Conquest: The Unbroken Past of the American West* (1987)

Eugene P. Moehring, *Urbanism and Empire in the Far West, 1840–1890* (2004)

Robert M. Utley, *The Indian Frontier of the American West, 1846–1890* (1984)

Richard White, *"It's Your Misfortune and None of My Own": A New History of the American* (1991)

Donald Worster, *A Passion for Nature: The Life of John Muir* (2008)

 Go to the CourseMate website for primary source links, study tools, and review materials for this chapter.
www.cengagebrain.com

The Machine Age

18

1877–1920

I n 1911, iron molders at the Watertown Arsenal, a government weapons factory near Boston, went on strike after a coworker, Joseph Cooney, was fired for objecting when an efficiency expert timed his work with a stopwatch. Other molders, fearing that the time study was the first step in management's imposition of new labor standards, defended Cooney. Iron molders' union president John Frey explained, "The workman believes when he goes on strike that he is defending his job."

The army officers who ran the factory thought that they owned the molders' labor and that the output was "one-half what it should be." To increase production, they hired Dwight Merrick, an expert in a new field called "scientific management," to time workers and speed performance.

The day Merrick began his study, a molder named Perkins secretly timed the same task. Merrick reported that the job should take twenty-four minutes and that workers were wasting time and materials; Perkins found that the job required fifty minutes and there was no waste. That evening, the molders discussed how to respond to the discrepancy between Merrick's report and theirs. Cooney argued for resisting scientific management; the workers drew up a petition and the next day walked out.

Eventually, Watertown molders and their bosses compromised, but this incident reveals a significant consequence of industrialization. Four themes characterized the era. First, manufacturers harnessed technology to increase production. Second, they divided work routines into repetitive tasks organized by the clock. Workers who previously felt valued for their skills now struggled to avoid becoming slaves to machines. Third, a new consumer society emerged as new goods such as canned foods and machine-made clothing became common by the late 1800s. Fourth, in their quest for growth and profits, corporation owners amassed power through new forms of organization. Defenders of the new system justified it, while laborers tried to combat what they thought were abuses of power.

Chapter Outline

Technology and the Triumph of Industrialization
Birth of the Electrical Industry | Henry Ford and the Automobile Industry | Carnegie and Steel | The Du Ponts and the Chemical Industry | Technology and Southern Industry | Consequences of Technology | Frederick W. Taylor and Efficiency

LINKS TO THE WORLD *The Atlantic Cable*

Mechanization and the Changing Status of Labor
Mass Production | Restructuring of the Work Force | Industrial Accidents | Freedom of Contract | Court Rulings on Labor Reform

VISUALIZING THE PAST *Impact of the 1913 Triangle Shirtwaist Fire*

Labor Violence and the Union Movement
Railroad Strikes of 1877 | Knights of Labor | Haymarket Riot | American Federation of Labor | Homestead and Pullman Strikes | Labor Violence in the West | IWW | Women Unionists | The Experience of Wage Work

Standards of Living
Commonplace Luxuries | Cost of Living | Supplements to Family Income | Higher Life Expectancy | Flush Toilets and Other Innovations | Dietary Reform | Ready-Made Clothing | Department and Chain Stores | Advertising

In the mid-nineteenth century, an industrial revolution swept through parts of the United States, and its mechanization powered a second round in the late 1800s and early 1900s. Four technological developments propelled this process: electricity, steel production, the internal-combustion engine, and new applications in the use of chemicals. Electricity provided a needed alternative to less efficient steam engines. Steel provided the material for new machines. The demand for transportation beyond railroads spurred progress in automobile manufacture. The textile industry's experiments with dyes, bleaches, and cleaning agents advanced chemical research.

In 1860, only one-fourth of the American labor force worked in manufacturing and transportation; by 1900, over half did. As the twentieth century dawned, the United States was the world's largest producer of raw materials and food, and the most productive industrial nation (see Map 18.1). Between 1877 and 1920, labor-saving machines (see Chapter 19) boosted productivity. Innovations in business organization and marketing also fueled the drive for profits.

Industrialization paralleled and was furthered by extraction of natural resources and agricultural expansion (see Chapter 17). Together, these developments dramatically altered living standards and everyday life. These processes combined people, the environment, and technology in ways that were both constructive and destructive.

As you read this chapter, keep the following questions in mind:

* **How did mechanization affect the lives of average workers and the makeup of the labor force?**

* **In what ways did technological innovation alter the American standard of living?**

* **What ideas did some Americans use to justify industrialization, and how did others criticize it?**

The Corporate Consolidation Movement
Rise of Corporations | *Pools and Trusts* | *Holding Companies* | *Financiers*

The Gospel of Wealth and Its Critics
Government Assistance to Business | *Dissenting Voices* | *Antitrust Legislation*

LEGACY FOR A PEOPLE AND A NATION
Technology of Recorded Sound

SUMMARY

Technology and the Triumph of Industrialization

In 1876, **Thomas Edison** and his associates opened an "invention factory" in Menlo Park, New Jersey, where they intended to turn out "a minor invention every ten days and a big thing every six months or so." Activity at the U.S. Patent Office, created by the Constitution to "promote the Progress of science and useful Arts," reveals how innovative Americans were becoming. Between 1790 and 1860, the government granted 36,000 patents and registered another 1.5 million from 1860 to 1930. Inventions in areas such as electricity, internal combustion, and industrial chemistry often sprang from a marriage between technology and business organization.

How did technological innovations transform American industry?

Thomas A. Edison: Inventor, founder of the first industrial research laboratory.

Chronology

1869	Knights of Labor founded		1893–97	Economic depression causes high unemployment and business failures
1873–78	Economy declines		1894	Workers of Pullman Palace Car Company strike
1877	Widespread railroad strikes protest wage cuts		1895	*U.S. v. E. C. Knight Co.* limits Congress's power to regulate manufacturing
1878	Edison Electric Light Company founded			
1879	George's *Poverty and Progress* argues for taxing unearned wealth		1896	*Holden v. Harcy* upholds law regulating miners' working hours
1881	First federal trademark law begins spread of brand names		1903	Women's Trade Union League (WTUL) founded
1882	Standard Oil Trust founded		1905	*Lochner v. New York* overturns law limiting bakery workers' working hours
1884–85	Economy declines			Industrial Workers of the World (IWW) founded
1886	Haymarket riot in Chicago protests police brutality against labor demonstrations		1908	*Muller v. Oregon* upholds law limiting women to ten-hour workday
	American Federation of Labor (AFL) founded			First Ford Model T built
1890	Sherman Anti-Trust Act outlaws "combinations in restraint of trade"		1911	Triangle Shirtwaist Company fire in New York City leaves 146 workers dead
1892	Homestead (Pennsylvania) steelworkers strike against Carnegie Steel Company		1913	Ford begins moving assembly-line production
			1919	Telephone operators strike in New England

Birth of the Electrical Industry

Most of Edison's one thousand inventions used electricity to transmit light, sound, and images. In 1878, he embarked on a search for an efficient means of indoor lighting. After tedious experiments, Edison perfected the incandescent bulb. His Edison Electric Light Company also devised a system of power generation and distribution to widely provide electricity.

Edison's system of direct current could transmit electricity only a mile or two, losing voltage the farther it traveled. George Westinghouse, an inventor from Schenectady, New York, solved the problem. Westinghouse purchased European patent rights to generators that used alternating current and to transformers that reduced high-voltage power, thus making long-distance transmission efficient.

Other entrepreneurs created new practices to market Edison's and Westinghouse's breakthroughs. Samuel Insull, formerly Edison's private secretary, organized Edison power plants nationwide, amassing an electric utility empire. In the late 1880s and early 1890s, financiers Henry Villard and J. P. Morgan bought up patents in electric lighting and merged small equipment-manufacturing companies into the General Electric Company. General Electric and Westinghouse Electric established research laboratories to create electrical products for everyday use.

Meanwhile, inventors continued to work independently and sell their handiwork and patents to corporations. Granville T. Woods, an engineer sometimes called "the black Edison," patented thirty-five devices vital to electronics and communications. Most were sold to companies such as General Electric, including an automatic

Link to the diary of Thomas Edison.

MAP 18.1

Industrial Production, 1919

By the early twentieth century, each state could boast at least one kind of industrial production. Although the value of goods produced was still highest in the Northeast, states such as Minnesota and California had impressive dollar values of outputs. *Source:* Data from U.S. Bureau of the Census, *Fourteenth Census of the United States, 1920, Vol. IX, Manufacturing* (Washington, D.C.: U.S. Government Printing Office, 1921).

circuit breaker, an electromagnetic brake, and instruments aiding communications between railroad trains.

Henry Ford and the Automobile Industry

In 1885, a German engineer, Gottlieb Daimler, built a light-weight internal combustion motor driven by vaporized gasoline. In the 1890s, **Henry Ford**, an electrical engineer in Detroit's Edison Company, experimented with Daimler's engine to power a vehicle. Applying organizational genius to this invention, Ford spawned a massive industry.

Ford had a scheme as well as a product, declaring in 1909, "I am going to democratize the automobile. When I'm through, everybody will be able to afford one." Ford proposed to mass-produce thousands of identical cars, and engineers set up assembly lines that drastically reduced time and production costs. Instead of performing numerous tasks, each worker did just one, repeatedly, assembling the entire car along a conveyor belt.

Henry Ford: Founder of the Ford Motor Company and pioneer of modern assembly lines used in mass production.

461

Links to the World

The Atlantic Cable

During the late nineteenth century, as American manufacturers expanded their markets overseas, their ability to communicate with customers and investors improved immeasurably because of telegraph cable beneath the Atlantic Ocean. Cyrus Field, who pioneered the idea of laying undersea cable, was an American. Yet most of the engineers and capitalists involved were British. In 1851, a British company laid the first successful undersea telegraph cable from Dover, England, to Calais, France, proving that an insulated wire could carry signals underwater. This venture inspired British and American businessmen to attempt a larger project across the Atlantic.

The first attempts failed, but in 1866 a British ship, funded by British investors, successfully laid a telegraph wire that operated without interruption. Thereafter, England and the United States grew more closely linked in diplomatic relations, and citizens developed greater concern for each other. When American president James Garfield was assassinated in 1881, the news traveled almost instantly to Great Britain, and Britons mourned the death profusely.

Some people lamented the stresses that near-instant international communications created. But financially savvy individuals welcomed the benefits. Rapid availability of stock quotes helped the New York and London stock exchanges boom. Newspaper readers enjoyed reading about events overseas the next day, instead of a week later. By 1902, underwater cables circled the globe. The age of global telecommunications had begun.

Laid by British ships across the ocean in 1866, the Atlantic cable linked the United States with England and continental Europe so that telegraph communications could be sent and received much more swiftly than ever before. Now Europeans and Americans could exchange news about politics, business, and military movements almost instantly, whereas previously such information could take a week or more to travel from one country to another.

In 1913, the Ford Motor Company's first assembly line opened in Highland Park outside Detroit, and the next year, Ford sold 248,000 cars. Soon, other manufacturers entered the field. Rising automobile output created jobs, higher earnings, and greater profits for related industries, too, such as steel, oil, paint, rubber, and glass. Moreover, assembly-line production required new companies to fabricate precision machine tools for making standardized parts.

By 1914, a Ford car cost $490, about one-fourth of its price a decade earlier. Yet that was too expensive for many workers, who earned at best $2 a day. That year, Ford tried to spur productivity, prevent labor turnover, head off unionization, and better enable his workers to buy the cars they produced through his Five-Dollar-Day plan—a combination of wages and profit sharing.

Carnegie and Steel

Many new products required strong, hard metal. Though in use for centuries, steel production was inefficient until British engineer Henry Bessemer developed a process that enabled mass production of inexpensive, high-quality steel from molten iron. American industrialist Andrew Carnegie, who observed the process while in England in 1872, immediately recognized the benefits of the Bessemer process. Carnegie built his Edgar Thompson steel plant near Pittsburgh. Using funds from investors, Carnegie purchased other steel mills, notably the Homestead Steel Company in 1888, and sold steel, initially used to manufacture rails and bridge girders for railroads, to companies using new technologies for plating and pressing steel to make barbed wire, tubing, and other products. In 1892, he formed the Carnegie Steel Company and by 1900 controlled about 60 percent of the steel business. In 1901, Carnegie sold his holdings to a group organized by J. P. Morgan, who formed the huge U.S. Steel Corporation.

The Du Ponts and the Chemical Industry

The du Pont family similarly transformed the chemical industry. In 1902, fearing antitrust prosecution for the company's near monopoly of the explosives industry, three cousins, Alfred, Coleman, and Pierre, took over E. I. du Pont de Nemours and Company and broadened production into fertilizers, dyes, and other chemical products. In 1911, du Pont scientists in the nation's first corporate research laboratory adapted cellulose to produce such consumer goods as photographic film, textile fibers, and plastics. The du Pont company also pioneered methods of management, accounting, and reinvestment of earnings, which contributed to efficient production, better recordkeeping, and higher profits.

Technology and Southern Industry

The South's major staple crops, tobacco and cotton, drew industry to the region after the Civil War. Americans used tobacco mainly for snuff, cigars, and chewing. But in 1876, James Bonsack, an eighteen-year-old Virginian, invented a cigarette-rolling machine. Sales soared after 1885 when North Carolina tobacco magnate James B. Duke mass-produced cigarettes with Bonsack's machine and enticed consumers with free samples, trading cards, and billboard ads. By 1900, his American Tobacco Company was a global business, employing black and white workers (including women), though in separate workrooms.

New technology helped relocate the textile industry to the South. Factories with electric looms were more efficient than New England's water-powered mills, required fewer workers, and provided lighting that expanded production hours.

Investors built new plants in southern communities, where a cheap labor was available. By 1900, the South had more than four hundred textile mills. Women and children earned 50 cents a day for twelve or more hours—about half the wages of northern millworkers. Most mills only hired black workers as janitors. Companies built villages around their mills, where they controlled housing, stores, schools, and churches and banned company criticism and union organization.

Northern and European investors joined southerners in financing other southern industries. During the 1880s, northern capitalists developed southern iron and steel manufacturing, much of it in Birmingham, Alabama. Between 1890 and 1900, northern lumber syndicates moved into the pine forests of the Gulf states, boosting production 500 percent. Southern wood production advanced the construction industry and relocated furniture and paper production from the North to the South. Challenging the power of the planter elite, a business class of manufacturers, merchants, and financiers heralded the emergence of a New South and made southern cities nerve centers of a new economic order.

Consequences of Technology

Machines broadly altered everyday life. Telephones and typewriters made face-to-face communication less important and facilitated correspondence and recordkeeping in growing insurance, banking, and industrial firms. Electric sewing machines made mass-produced clothing. Refrigeration enabled the preservation and shipment of meat, fruit, vegetables, and dairy products. Cash registers and adding machines revamped accounting and created new clerical jobs. At the same time, American universities established programs in engineering.

Technological advances often originated abroad. Europeans made early discoveries in electricity and internal combustion engines. The Bessemer process for producing steel was developed in England, and the du Ponts imported capital and machinery from France for their gunpowder operation. But Americans adapted and advanced these developments, which enabled the United States to surpass other industrializing nations in output by the turn of the century.

Profits resulted from higher production at lower costs. As technological innovations made large-scale production more economical, owners replaced small workshops with large factories. Between 1850 and 1900, average capital investment in a manufacturing firm increased by 250 percent. Only large companies could afford to buy complex machines. And large companies received discounts for buying raw materials and shipping in bulk—advantages economists call economies of scale.

Profitability depended as much on how production was organized. Where once workers such as the Watertown molders controlled the methods of production, by the 1890s engineers and managers with "expert" knowledge planned every task to increase output. Through standardization, they reduced the need for human skills, boosting profits at the expense of worker independence.

Frederick W. Taylor and Efficiency

The most influential advocate of efficient production was Frederick W. Taylor. As foreman and engineer for the Midvale Steel Company in the 1880s, Taylor concluded companies could best reduce costs and increase profits by applying studies of "how quickly the various kinds of work…ought to be done." This meant producing more for lower cost per unit, usually by eliminating unnecessary workers.

In 1898, Taylor took his stopwatch to the Bethlehem Steel Company to illustrate his principles of scientific management. His experiments required studying workers and devising "a series of motions which can be made quickest and best." For shoveling ore, Taylor designed fifteen kinds of shovels and prescribed proper motions for each, thereby reducing a crew of 600 men to 140. Soon other companies, including the Watertown Arsenal, applied Taylor's theories.

Consequently, time, as much as quality, became the measure of acceptable work, and management dictated how things were done. As elements of the assembly line, which divided work into specific time-determined tasks, employees feared they were becoming another interchangeable part.

Mechanization and the Changing Status of Labor

How did mechanization and new systems of management change the nature and status of work?

By 1900, the status of labor shifted dramatically. Technological innovation and assembly-line production created new jobs, but because most machines were labor saving, fewer workers could produce more in less time. Instead of producers, the working class now consisted mainly of employees who

Chicago Historical Society

The combination of machines and workers still required meticulous handwork in some industries. Often women with nimble fingers could find jobs in industries such as jewelry and watchmaking where, as at this room at the Elgin National Watch Company, they could swiftly manipulate tiny production processes.

worked for hire. Producers were paid based on the quality of what they produced; employees received wages for time spent on the job.

Mass Production

With manufacturing subdivided into small tasks, mass production required workers to repeat the same standardized operation all day every day. One investigator found that a worker became "a mere machine." Workers no longer decided when to begin and end the workday or what tools and techniques to use. The clock regulated them. As a Massachusetts factory laborer testified in 1879, "During working hours the men are not allowed to speak to each other . . . on pain of instant discharge. Men are hired to watch and patrol the shop."

Workers such as the Watertown iron molders struggled to retain autonomy. Artisans—glass workers and coopers (barrel makers)—caught in the transition from hand labor to machine production, fought to preserve their work customs, say, by appointing a fellow worker to read a newspaper aloud while they worked. Immigrant factory workers tried to persuade foremen to hire their relatives and friends. After hours, workers enjoyed drinking and holiday celebrations, ignoring employers' attempts to control their social lives.

Employers, concerned with efficiency, wanted behavior standards upheld. Ford Motor Company required workers to satisfy the company's behavior code before becoming eligible for a part of the Five-Dollar-Day plan. To increase worker incentives, some employers established piecework rates, paying per item produced rather than an hourly wage. Employers eager to increase productivity tried to make workers perform like machines.

Restructuring of the Work Force

As machines reduced the need for skilled workers, employers cut labor costs by hiring women and children, and paying them low wages. Between 1880 and 1900, the numbers of employed women soared from 2.6 million to 8.6 million (see Figure 18.1). The proportion of women in domestic service (maids, cooks, laundresses)—the most common and lowest-paid female employment—dropped as jobs opened in other sectors. In manufacturing, women usually held menial positions in textile mills and food-processing plants that paid $1.56 for seventy hours week. (Unskilled men received $7 to $10.) Although the number of female factory hands tripled between 1880 and 1900, the proportion of women workers remained constant.

Expansion of the clerical and retail sectors boosted the numbers and percentages of women who were typists, bookkeepers, and sales clerks—previously male jobs. Inventions, such as the typewriter, cash register, and adding machine, simplified these tasks, and employers replaced males with lower-paid females. By 1920, women filled nearly half of all clerical jobs; in 1880, only 4 percent were women. Although poorly paid, women were attracted to sales jobs because of the respectability, pleasant surroundings, and contact with affluent customers. Nevertheless, sex discrimination persisted. In department stores, only male cashiers handled cash transactions. Women held some low-level supervisory positions, but males dominated managerial ranks.

Meanwhile, the number in nonagricultural occupations tripled between 1870 and 1900. In 1890, over 18 percent of children ages ten to fifteen were employed, particularly in textile and shoe factories (see Figure 18.2). Mechanization created

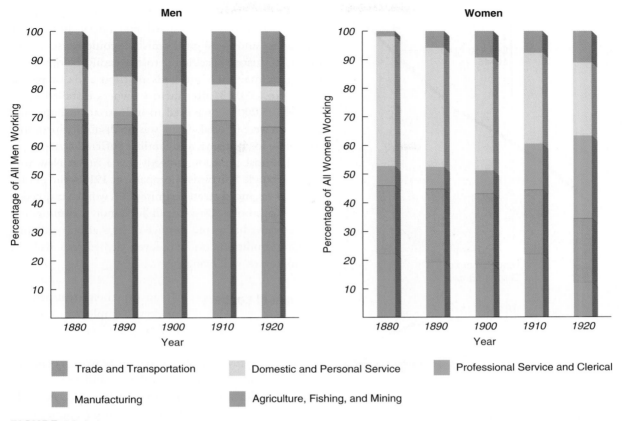

FIGURE 18.1

Distribution of Occupational Categories Among Employed Men and Women, 1880–1920

The changing lengths of the bar segments of each part of this graph represent trends in male and female employment. Over the forty years covered by this graph, the agriculture, fishing, and mining segment for men and the domestic service segment for women declined the most, whereas notable increases occurred in manufacturing for men and professional services (especially store clerks and teachers) for women.

Source: U.S. Bureau of the Census, *Census of the United States, 1880, 1890, 1900, 1910, 1920* (Washington, D.C.: U.S. Government Printing Office).

numerous light tasks, such as running errands, which children could handle cheaply. Conditions were especially hard for child laborers in the South, where mill owners induced desperate white sharecroppers and tenant farmers to bind their children to factories at miserably low wages.

Several states, especially in the Northeast, passed laws specifying minimum ages and maximum hours for child labor. But statutes regulated only firms operating within state borders, not those engaged in interstate commerce. Enforcing age requirements proved difficult because many parents, needing income, lied about their children's ages. After 1900, state laws and automation, along with compulsory school attendance laws, reduced the number of children employed in manufacturing, and Progressive era reformers sought federal legislation restricting child labor (see Chapter 21). Still, many children continued to work at street trades—shining shoes and peddling—while poor children scavenged city streets for coal and wood, discarded clothing, and furniture.

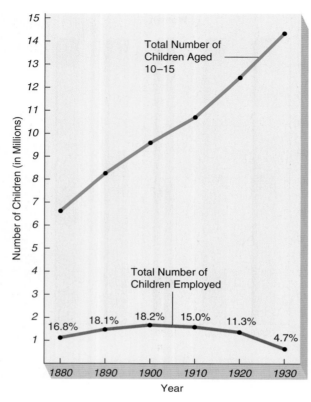

FIGURE 18.2
Children in the Labor Force, 1880–1930
The percentage of children in the labor force peaked around the turn of the century. Thereafter, the passage of state laws requiring children to attend school until age fourteen and limiting the ages at which children could be employed caused child labor to decline.
Source: Data from *The Statistical History of the United States from Colonial Times to the Present* (Stamford, CT.: Fairfield Publishers, 1965).

Industrial Accidents

Repetitive tasks using high-speed machinery dulled concentration, and the slightest mistake could cause serious injury. Industrial accidents rose steadily before 1920, killing or maiming hundreds of thousands of people each year. In 1913, after factory owners installed safety devices, 25,000 people died in industrial mishaps, and 1 million were injured. There was no disability insurance to replace lost income, and families suffered acutely.

The most notorious tragedy was a fire at New York City's Triangle Shirtwaist Company in 1911, which killed 146 workers, mostly teenage immigrant women trapped in locked workrooms. Despite public clamor, prevailing free-market views hampered passage of legislation regulating working conditions, and employers denied responsibility for employees' well-being.

Freedom of Contract

To justify their treatment of workers, employers asserted the principle of "freedom of contract," claiming wages and working conditions resulted from supply and demand. Employers asserted that since workers entered into a contract with bosses, workers could seek another job if they did not like the wages and hours. Actually, employers used supply and demand to set wages as low as laborers would accept. Employees felt trapped. A factory worker told Congress in 1879, "The market is glutted, and…the pay is cut down; our tasks are increased, and if we remonstrate, we are told our places can be filled."

Court Rulings on Labor Reform

Reformers and union leaders lobbied for laws to improve working conditions, but the Supreme Court limited such legislation by narrowly defining which jobs were dangerous and which workers needed protection. In *Holden v. Hardy* (1896), the Court upheld a law regulating miners' working hours, concluding that overly long workdays increase potential injuries. In *Lochner v. New York* (1905), however, the Court voided a law limiting bakery workers to a sixty-hour week and ten-hour day. It ruled that baking was not a dangerous enough occupation to justify restricting workers' right to sell their labor freely. Such restriction, according to the Court, violated the Fourteenth Amendment's guarantee that no state could "deprive any person of life, liberty, or property without due process of law."

In *Muller v. Oregon* (1908), the Court used a different rationale to uphold limiting women in laundries to a ten-hour workday. It set aside its *Lochner* argument to assert that women's well-being as potential childbearers "becomes an object of public interest and care in order to preserve the strength and vigor of the race." The

Visualizing the Past

Impact of the 1911 Triangle Shirtwaist Fire

On March 25, 1911, the worst factory fire in U.S. history occurred at the Triangle Shirtwaist Company, which occupied the top three floors of a building in New York City. Fed by piles of fabric, the fire spread quickly, killing 146 of the 500 young women, mostly Jewish immigrants, employed in the factory. Many of the victims were burned to death because they were locked inside workrooms by their employer; others plunged from windows. These three images show how the public received news of the tragedy, one through friends and relatives who came to identify and claim the bodies of victims, one through a critical cartoon, and the other through the front page of a newspaper. Which of these images seems most powerful and likely to inspire reform? How do mass tragedies get communicated to the public today? What limitations in communications existed in 1911?

Many of the victims of the Triangle Shirtwaist fire of 1911 were lined up in coffins, and their bodies were identified by relatives arriving at a make-shift morgue.

© Bettmann/Corbis

The Granger Collection, New York

John French Sloan, an artist with radical leanings, drew this cartoon in the wake of the Triangle fire. Eager to assert that profit-minded capitalists were responsible for unnecessary deaths, Sloan used stark images to convey his message.

Picture Research Consultants & Archives

Using a large-print headline and grisly photograph, the New York Tribune, one of New York City's and the nation's oldest and most-respected newspapers, filled much of its front page with news of the event.

case represented a victory for reformers seeking government regulation of women's hours and working conditions. As a result of the *Muller* decision, labor laws barred women from occupations, such as in printing and transportation, that required heavy lifting, long hours, or night work, further confining women to low-paying, dead-end jobs.

Labor Violence and the Union Movement

How did employers and others respond to increasing strikes and labor unrest in the late nineteenth century?

Workers adjusted to mechanization as best they could, but anxiety over lost independence and desire for better wages, hours, and working conditions drew disgruntled workers into unions. Trade unions for skilled workers in crafts such as printing and iron molding dated from the early 1800s, but their influence was limited. But by the 1870s, the spread of companies with large labor forces and the tightening of management control spurred a unionization response.

Railroad Strikes of 1877

In the economic slump that followed the Panic of 1873, railroad managers cut wages, increased workloads, and laid off workers, especially union members. Workers responded with strikes and riots. The year 1877 marked a crisis. In July, unionized railroad men organized strikes to oppose wage cuts. Violence spread from Pennsylvania and West Virginia to the Midwest, Texas, and California, derailing trains and burning rail yards. State militias, organized and commanded by employers, broke up picket lines and fired into threatening crowds. Factory workers, wives, and merchants aided the strikers, while railroads enlisted strikebreakers to replace union men.

Pittsburgh experienced the worst violence. On July 21, state troops bayoneted and fired on rock-throwing demonstrators, killing ten and wounding many more. Infuriated, the mob drove the troops into a roundhouse and set fires that destroyed 39 buildings, 104 engines, and 1,245 freight and passenger cars. The next day, the troops shot their way out and killed twenty more citizens before fleeing. After a month, President Rutherford B. Hayes sent in federal soldiers—the first significant use of the army to quell labor unrest.

Knights of Labor

About the same time, the Knights of Labor tried to attract a broad base of laborers. Founded in 1869 by Philadelphia garment cutters, the Knights recruited other workers in the 1870s. In 1879, Terence V. Powderly, a machinist and mayor of Scranton, Pennsylvania, was elected grand master. Under his guidance, Knights membership grew, peaking at 730,000 in 1886. In contrast to most craft unions, Knights welcomed unskilled and semiskilled workers, including women, immigrants, and African Americans (but not Chinese).

The Knights sought a workers' alliance offering an alternative to profit-oriented industrial capitalism. They intended to eliminate conflict between labor and management by establishing a cooperative society in which workers, not capitalists, owned factories, mines, and railroads. The goal, argued Powderly, was to "eventually make every man his own master—every man his own employer." The cooperative idea, attractive in the abstract, was unattainable because employers could outcompete laborers who might try to establish businesses. Strikes might achieve immediate goals, but Powderly and other Knights leaders argued that strikes diverted attention from the long-term goal of a cooperative society and that workers lost more by striking.

Some Knights, however, supported militant action. In 1886, railroad magnate **Jay Gould** refused to negotiate when Knights demanded higher wages and union recognition from Southwest Railroad. A strike began in Texas, then spread to Kansas, Missouri, and Arkansas. Powderly met with Gould and called off the strike, hoping for a settlement. But Gould rejected concessions, and the Knights gave in. Militant craft unions deserted the Knights, upset by Powderly's compromise.

After the Haymarket riot (see next section), Knights membership dwindled, although the union made a brief attempt to unite with Populists in the 1890s (see Chapter 20). Craft unions replaced the Knights' broad-based but often vague appeal, and labor unity faded.

Jay Gould: Captain of industry and owner of the Union Pacific Railroad.

Haymarket Riot

While the Knights were striking, other groups calling for an eight-hour workday generated the largest labor demonstration in the country's history. On May 1, 1886, in Chicago, some 100,000 such workers turned out, including anarchists who believed in using violence. Chicago police, fearing that European radicals were transplanting a tradition of violence to the United States, mobilized. The day passed calmly, but two days later, police stormed an area near the McCormick reaper plant and broke up a battle between striking unionists and nonunion strikebreakers, killing two unionists and wounding others.

The next evening, laborers protested police brutality at Haymarket Square near downtown Chicago. As police approached, a bomb exploded, killing seven and injuring sixty-seven. Authorities made mass arrests, and a court convicted eight anarchists of the bombing, despite questionable evidence. Four were executed, and one committed suicide in prison. The remaining three received pardons in 1893 from Illinois governor John P. Altgeld.

The Haymarket bombing, like the 1877 railroad strikes, heightened fears of labor discontent and of radicalism. The participation of anarchists and socialists, many of them foreign-born, created a feeling that civic leaders act swiftly to prevent social turmoil. Private Chicago donors helped establish a military base near the city. Elsewhere, governments strengthened police forces and armories. Employer associations countered labor militancy by circulating blacklists of union activists whom they would not employ and by hiring private detectives to suppress strikes.

American Federation of Labor

The **American Federation of Labor** (AFL) emerged from the 1886 upheavals as the major workers' organization. An alliance of national craft unions, the AFL had about 140,000 members, mostly skilled workers. Led by **Samuel Gompers**, former head of the Cigar Makers' Union, the AFL pressed for higher wages, shorter hours, and the right to bargain collectively. Unlike the Knights, the AFL accepted capitalism and worked to improve conditions within it.

The AFL avoided party politics, adhering instead to Gompers's dictum of supporting labor's friends and opposing its enemies, regardless of party.

American Federation of Labor (AFL): Skilled craft unions united under leadership of Samuel Gompers.

Samuel Gompers: AFL leader who focused on practical goals like improved wages, hours, and working conditions.

Link to the debate on May 18, 1920, between Samuel Gompers and Henry Justin Allen, the Republican Governor of Kansas.

AFL membership grew to 1 million by 1901 and 2.5 million by 1917, when it consisted of 111 national unions and 27,000 locals. Member unions organized by craft had little interest in recruiting unskilled workers or women. Of 6.3 million employed women in 1910, fewer than 2 percent belonged to unions. Male unionists rationalized women's exclusion by insisting that women should not be employed. According to one labor leader, "The mental and physical makeup of woman is in revolt against wage service. She is competing with the man who is her father or husband or is to become her husband." Mostly, unionists worried that, because women were paid less, men's wages would be lowered or their jobs given to cheaper female workers.

Influenced by nativism and racism, organized labor excluded most immigrants and African Americans, fearing they, too, would depress wages. A few trade unions welcomed immigrants. Blacks were prominent in the coal miners' union and were partially unionized in such trades as construction, barbering, and dock work, which employed numerous African American workers. But they could belong only to segregated unions in the South, and most northern AFL unions had exclusion policies. Long-held prejudices were reinforced when blacks and immigrants, eager for work, replaced striking whites.

Homestead and Pullman Strikes

The AFL and the labor movement suffered setbacks in the early 1890s, when labor violence stirred public fears. In July 1892, the AFL-affiliated Amalgamated Association of Iron and Steelworkers went on strike against pay cuts in Homestead, Pennsylvania. In response to the **Homestead Strike**, Henry C. Frick, president of Carnegie Steel Company, closed the plant. Shortly thereafter, Frick hired three hundred guards from the Pinkerton Detective Agency to protect the factory and floated them in by barge at night. Lying in wait, angry workers attacked and routed the Pinkertons. State troops intervened, and after five months the strikers gave in. By then, public opinion turned against the union.

Homestead Strike: Workers walk out after wage cuts at a Carnegie Steel plant in 1892; officials responded to the strike by shutting down the plant.

In 1894, workers at the Pullman Palace (railroad passenger) Car Company walked out over exploitative policies at the company town near Chicago. The paternalistic owner, George Pullman, provided everything for the twelve thousand residents of the so-called model town named after him. His company controlled all land and buildings, the school, the bank, and the water and gas systems. It paid wages, fixed rents, and spied on disgruntled employees.

One thing Pullman would not do was negotiate with workers. When hard times hit in 1893, Pullman protected profits by cutting wages 25 to 40 percent while holding firm on rents and prices. Hard-pressed workers sent a committee to Pullman to protest. He reacted by firing three committee members. Enraged workers, most of them from the American railway union, called a strike; Pullman closed the factory. The union, led by **Eugene V. Debs**, refused to handle Pullman cars attached to any trains. Pullman rejected arbitration. The railroad owners' association enlisted aid from U.S. Attorney General Richard Olney, a former railroad lawyer, who obtained a court injunction to prevent the union from "obstructing the railways and holding up the mails." President Grover Cleveland ordered federal troops to Chicago. Within a month strikers gave in, and Debs was imprisoned for defying the injunction. The Supreme Court upheld Debs's six-month sentence, arguing that the federal government could legally remove obstacles to interstate commerce.

Eugene V. Debs: Indiana labor leader who organized workers in the Pullman Strike of 1893; would be the Socialist Party of America's presidential candidate five times between 1900 and 1920.

Labor Violence in the West

In the West, unionized miners, led by the Western Federation of Miners (WFM), engaged in highly violent strikes during the 1890s. Membership in the WFM rose, as did antiunion sentiment among employers.

In Idaho, federal troops were called out three times to combat striking miners and protect company property during the 1890s. In 1899, after strikers blew up Bunker Hill Mining Company buildings, soldiers arrested every male in the town, and Governor Frank Steunenberg declared martial law. In 1905, Steunenberg, no longer in office, was assassinated; speculation arose that the WFM had killed him. Investigation by Pinkerton Detective James McParland resulted in the arrest of WFM Secretary-Treasurer William "Big Bill" Haywood and two other WFM officials. Tried for murder in 1907, Haywood was acquitted after his attorney, the famed Clarence Darrow, subverted testimony of a key witness.

IWW

In 1905, rebel unionists formed a new, radical labor organization, the **Industrial Workers of the World (IWW)**. Like the Knights, it strove to unite all laborers of all. Its motto was "An injury to one is an injury to all." But the "Wobblies," as IWW members were known, espoused violence and sabotage. Embracing socialism and the rhetoric of class conflict, Wobblies believed workers should seize and run the nation's industries. Leaders such as Haywood; Mary "Mother" Jones, an Illinois coalfield union organizer; Elizabeth Gurley Flynn, a fiery orator known as the "Joan of Arc of the labor movement"; Italian radical Carlo Tresca; and Swedish-born organizer and songwriter Joe Hill headed a series of strikes. Although the Wobblies' anticapitalist goals and aggressive tactics attracted publicity, the organization collapsed during World War I when federal prosecution sent many of its leaders to jail and local police violently harassed IWW members.

Industrial Workers of the World (IWW): Radical labor organization that sought to unionize all workers; nicknamed Wobblies, the IWW embraced Socialism and led mass strikes of mine workers in Nevada and Minnesota and timber workers in Louisiana, Texas, and the Northwest.

Women Unionists

Despite exclusion from unions, some women organized and fought employers as strenuously as men. The "Uprising of the 20,000" in New York City, a 1909 strike by male and female immigrant members of the International Ladies' Garment Workers' Union (ILGWU), was one of the country's largest strikes. Female trade-union membership grew during the 1910s, but men monopolized national leadership.

Women did dominate one union: the Telephone Operators' Department of the International Brotherhood of Electrical Workers. Organized in Boston in 1912, the union spread throughout the Bell system, the nation's monopolistic telephone company and single largest employer of women. To promote solidarity among their mostly young female members, union leaders organized dances, excursions, bazaars, and educational programs. The union resisted scientific management techniques and rigid supervision. In 1919, several militant union branches paralyzed the phone service of five New England states, but the union collapsed after a failed strike in 1923.

A key organization promoting laboring women's interests was the Women's Trade Union League (WTUL), founded in 1903 and patterned after a similar organization in England. The WTUL sought legislation to improve conditions and reduce hours, sponsored educational activities, and campaigned for woman suffrage.

It helped telephone operators organize, and in 1909 it supported the ILGWU's massive strike against New York City sweatshops. Initially, the WTUL's highest officers were middle-class women, but control shifted in the 1910s to forceful working-class leaders, notably Agnes Nestor, a glove maker, and Rose Schneiderman, a cap maker. The WTUL advocated opening apprenticeship programs to women and training female workers for leadership. It served as a vital link between the labor and women's movements into the 1920s.

The Experience of Wage Work   Dramatic strikes aside, only a small fraction of American wage workers belonged to unions. In 1900, about 1 million of 27.6 million total workers were unionized. By 1920, union membership had grown to 5 million, only 13 percent of the work force. Unionization was strong in construction trades, transportation, communications, and, to a lesser extent, manufacturing. For many workers, getting and keeping a job took priority over higher wages and shorter hours. Job instability and the seasonal nature of work seriously hindered union-organizing. Few companies employed workers year-round; most hired during peak seasons and laid workers off during slack periods. The millions of men, women, and children who were not unionized tried to cope with machine age pressures. Many native-born and immigrant workers joined fraternal societies, such as the Polish Roman Catholic Union, the African American Colored Brotherhood and Sisterhood of Honor, and the Jewish B'nai B'rith. For small contributions these organizations provided life insurance, sickness benefits, and burial costs.

During the machine age, industrial wages rose between 1877 and 1914, boosting purchasing power and creating a mass market for standardized goods. Yet in 1900 most employees worked sixty hours a week at wages averaging 20 cents an hour for skilled work and 10 cents an hour for unskilled. Even as wages rose, living costs increased even faster.

Standards of Living

What was the impact of the new consumer culture on people's lives?

The industrial system improved everyday life. American ingenuity combined with mass production and mass marketing to make available myriad goods that previously had not existed or had been the province of the wealthy. The new material well-being, symbolized by canned foods, ready-made clothing, and home appliances, absorbed Americans into consumer communities and accentuated differences between those who could afford goods and services and those who could not.

Commonplace Luxuries   If a society's affluence is measured by how it converts luxuries into commonplace articles, the United States was becoming affluent between 1880 and 1920. By 1899, manufactured goods and perishable foodstuffs had become increasingly available. That year, Americans consumed 100 crates of oranges for every 1,000 people, bought 2 billion machine-produced cigarettes, and spent about 63 cents per person on soap. By 1921, Americans smoked 43 billion cigarettes (403 per person), ate 248 crates of oranges per 1,000 people, and spent $1.40 on soap.

Data for the period show that incomes rose broadly. By 1920, the richest 5 percent of the population received almost one-fourth of all earned income. Incomes also rose among the middle class. Average pay for clerical workers rose 36 percent between 1890 and 1910 (see Table 18.1). In 1900, federal employees averaged $1,072 a year (around $30,000 in modern dollars). The middle class could afford comfortable housing. A six- or seven-room house cost around $3,000 to buy (about $70,000 in current dollars) and from $15 to $20 per month ($400 to $500 in current dollars) to rent.

Although hourly wages for industrial employees increased, workers spent a disproportionate amount on necessities. Average annual wages of factory laborers rose about 30 percent, from $486 in 1890 (about $12,000 in modern dollars) to $630 in 1910 (about $15,500 in current dollars). In industries with large female work forces, hourly pay rates remained lower than in male-dominated industries. Nevertheless, as Table 18.1 shows, most wages moved upward.

Cost of Living   Wage increases mean little, however, if living costs rise as fast or faster. The weekly cost of living for a typical family of four rose over 47 percent between 1889 and 1913. Goods that cost $68 in 1889 increased, after a slight dip in the mid-1890s, to $100 by 1913.

How, then, could working-class Americans afford goods and services? Many could not. The daughter of a textile worker, recalling her school days, described how "some of the kids would bring bars of chocolate, others an orange.... I suppose they

TABLE 18.1   American Living Standards, 1890–1910

	1890	1910
Income and Earnings		
Annual income		
Clerical worker	$848	$1,156
Public school teacher	256	492
Industrial worker	486	630
Farm laborer	233	336
Hourly wage		
Soft-coal miner	0.18[a]	0.21
Iron worker	0.17[a]	0.23
Shoe worker	0.14[a]	0.19
Paper worker	0.12[a]	0.17
Labor Statistics		
Number of people in labor force	28.5 mil.	41.7 mil.[b]
Average workweek in manufacturing	60 hrs.	51 hrs.

[a]1892
[b]1920

were richer than a family like ours. My father used to buy a bag of candy and a bag of peanuts every payday.... And that's all we'd have until the next payday."

Supplements to Family Income

Still, a family could raise its income and partake modestly in consumer society by sending children and women into the labor market (see pages 466-468). Where a father alone made $600 a year, wages of other family members might lift total family income to $800 or $900. Many families also rented rooms to boarders and lodgers, yielding up to $200 annually. Between 1889 and 1901, working-class families markedly increased expenditures for life insurance and new leisure activities (see Chapter 19), improving their living standard.

More than ever, working Americans lived within a money economy and living in which wages and living standards were closely linked. Between 1890 and 1920, the labor force increased by 50 percent, from 28 million workers to 42 million. These figures represent a change in the nature of work as much as increases in available jobs. In rural households of the nineteenth century, women and children performed crucial tasks of cooking, cleaning, planting, and harvesting—labor absent from employment figures because they earned no wages. As the nation industrialized and the agricultural sector declined, paid employment became more common. The proportion of Americans who worked probably did not increase markedly. What was new was the increase in paid employment, making consumer goods and services more affordable.

Higher Life Expectancy

Medical advances, better diets, and improved housing sharply reduced death rates and extended life. Between 1900 and 1920, life expectancy rose by six years, and the death rate dropped by 24 percent. Notable declines occurred in deaths from typhoid, diphtheria, influenza (except for a harsh pandemic in 1918 and 1919), tuberculosis, and intestinal ailments. There were, however, significantly more deaths from cancer, diabetes, and heart disease, afflictions of an aging population and of new environmental factors, such as smoke and chemical pollution. Homicides and automobile-related deaths also increased dramatically.

Not only were amenities and luxuries more available but upward mobility seemed more accessible, too. Public education, aided by construction of new schools and laws requiring children to stay in school to age fourteen, equipped young people to achieve a living standard higher than their parents'. The creation of managerial and sales jobs helped counter downward mobility when mechanization pushed skilled workers from their crafts. And mass production added greater convenience to workers' lives.

Flush Toilets and Other Innovations

At the vanguard of a revolution in lifestyles stood the toilet. The chain-pull, washdown water closet, invented in England around 1870, reached the United States in the 1880s. Shortly after 1900, the flush toilet appeared. Before 1880, only luxury hotels and wealthy families had private indoor bathrooms. By the 1890s, the germ theory of disease was raising fears about carelessly disposed human waste as a source of infection and water contamination. Middle-class Americans installed modern toilets in urban houses. By the 1920s, toilets were prevalent in working-class homes, too. Edward and Clarence Scott, who manufactured white tissue in perforated rolls, provided Americans a more convenient form of toilet tissue than the rough paper they previously used. Bodily functions took on an unpleasant image, and the home bathroom became a place of utmost privacy.

Before the mid-nineteenth century, Americans typically ate only foods in season. Drying, smoking, and salting could preserve meat for a short time, but the availability of fresh meat and milk was limited due to spoilage. A French inventor developed the cooking-and-sealing process of canning around 1810, and in the 1850s an American man named Gail Borden devised a means of condensing and preserving milk. Sales of canned goods and condensed milk increased during the 1860s, but there were production problems. In the 1880s, inventors fashioned machines to peel fruits and vegetables, and mass-produce cans from tin plate. Now, people everywhere could consume tomatoes, milk, oysters, and other alternatives to previously monotonous diets.

Other inventions broadened Americans' diets. Growing urban populations created demands for more produce. Railroad refrigerator cars enabled growers and meatpackers to ship perishables farther and preserve them longer. By the 1890s, northern city dwellers could enjoy southern and western strawberries, grapes, and tomatoes for several months. Home iceboxes enabled middle-class families to store perishables, and by 1900 the nation had two thousand ice plants, many making home deliveries.

Dietary Reform

Availability of new foods also inspired health advocates to reform American diets. In the 1870s, John H. Kellogg, nutritionist at the Western Health Reform Institute in Battle Creek, Michigan, began serving patients health foods, including peanut butter and wheat flakes. Years later, his brother, William K. Kellogg, invented corn flakes, and another nutritionist, Charles W. Post, introduced Grape-Nuts, replacing eggs, potatoes, and meat with supposedly healthier cereal. Before World War I, scientists discovered the dietetic value of vitamins A and B. Cookbooks and cooking schools increasingly reflected heightened interest in food's possibilities for health and enjoyment.

As in the past, the poorest people still consumed cheap foods, heavy in starches and carbohydrates and little meat. Workers spent almost half of a breadwinner's wages on food, but they never suffered the malnutrition that plagued other developing nations.

Ready-Made Clothing

The sewing machine and standardized sizes sparked a revolution in clothing. Invented in Europe but refined in the mid-nineteenth century by Americans Elias Howe Jr. and Isaac M. Singer, the sewing machine facilitated clothing and shoe manufacture. Demand for uniforms during the Civil War boosted the ready-made clothing industry, and by 1890 annual retail sales reached $1.5 billion. Mass production enabled manufacturers to turn out quality apparel at low cost and to standardize sizes. By 1900, only the poorest families could not afford "ready-to-wear" clothes. Tailors and seamstresses were relegated to repair work. Many women continued to make clothing at home, but commercial dress patterns simplified home production and injected another form of standardization into everyday life.

Mass-produced garments altered clothing styles and tastes. As women's participation in work and leisure activities increased, dress designers shifted from burdensome Victorian designs to more comfortable styles. In the 1890s, hemlines receded, and high-boned collars disappeared. By the 1920s, a dress required three yards of material instead of ten.

Men's clothes, too, became lightweight. Before 1900, men in the middle and well-off working classes would have owned two suits: one for Sundays and special occasions, and one for everyday. After 1900, however, manufacturers produced inexpensive garments from seasonal fabrics. Men replaced derbies with felt hats, and stiff collars and cuffs with soft ones; somber, dark-blue serge gave way to lighter shades and more intricate weaves.

Department and Chain Stores

Department stores and chain stores helped create and serve this new consumerism. Between 1865 and 1900, Macy's Department Store in New York, Wanamaker's in Philadelphia, Marshall Field in Chicago, and the Emporium in San Francisco became urban landmarks. Previously, working classes bought goods in stores with limited inventories, and wealthier people patronized fancy shops; prices, quality of goods, and social custom discouraged each from shopping at the other's establishments. Now, department stores with open displays caused a merchandising revolution, offering home deliveries, exchange policies, and charge accounts.

Meanwhile, the Great Atlantic Tea Company, founded in 1859, became the first grocery chain. Renamed the Great Atlantic & Pacific Tea Company in 1869 (known as A&P), the firm bought in volume and sold to the public at low prices. By 1915, there were eighteen hundred A&P stores, and twelve thousand more over the next ten years.

Advertising

In the late nineteenth century, companies that mass-produced consumer goods hired advertisers to create "consumption communities" of brand-loyal consumers. In 1881, Congress passed a trademark law enabling producers to register brand names. Thousands of companies registered products as varied as Hires Root Beer, Uneeda Biscuits, and Carter's Little Liver Pills. Advertising agencies—a service pioneered by N. W. Ayer & Son of Philadelphia—offered expert advice on cultivating brand loyalty. In 1865, retailers spent about $9.5 million on advertising; $95 million by 1900 and nearly $500 million by 1919. Newspapers served as the prime instrument for advertising, as people read them to find out what was for sale as well as what was happening.

Outdoor billboards and electrical signs were also important selling devices. Billboards on city buildings, in railroad stations, and alongside roads promoted such products as Gillette razors, Wrigley chewing gum, and Budweiser beer. In the mid-1890s, electric lights made billboards exciting. The flashing electrical signs on New York City's Broadway gave the street its label "the Great White Way."

The Corporate Consolidation Movement

What led corporations to increasingly consolidate in the late nineteenth century?

Neither new products nor marketing techniques could mask unsettling economic factors. The huge capital investment for new technology required that factories operate near capacity to recover costs. But the more manufacturers produced, the more they had to sell, which meant spending more on advertising and reducing prices. To compensate, they further expanded production and often reduced wages. To expand, they sold stocks and borrowed money. And to repay loans, they had to produce and sell even more. This spiraling process strangled small firms and thrust workers into constant uncertainty.

In this environment, optimism could dissolve at the hint that debtors could not meet their obligations. Economic downturns occurred regularly—1873, 1884, 1893. Some business leaders blamed overproduction; others, underconsumption; still others blamed lax credit and investment practices. To combat uncertainty, many adopted tighter and larger forms of centralized organization.

Rise of Corporations

Industrialists never questioned the capitalist system. They sought new ways to enlarge the state laws of the early 1800s, which encouraged commerce and industry. Under such laws, anyone could start a company and raise money by selling stock. Stockholders shared in profits without personal risk, because laws limited their liability for company debts to the amount of their investment. Responsibility for company administration rested with its managers.

By 1900, two-thirds of all U.S. manufactured goods were produced by corporations such as General Electric and the American Tobacco Company. In the 1880s and 1890s, the Supreme Court ruled that corporations, like individuals, are protected by the Fourteenth Amendment. States could not deny corporations equal protection nor deprive them of property rights without due process of law. Such rulings insulated corporations from government interference.

Pools and Trusts

Between the late 1880s and early 1900s, business consolidation produced massive conglomerates that have since dominated the nation's economy. At first, such alliances were informal, consisting of cooperative agreements among firms manufacturing the same product or offering the same service. Through these arrangements, called *pools,* competing companies tried to control the market by agreeing how much each should produce and sharing profits. During slow periods, however, pool members secretly reduced prices or sold more than the agreed quota to boost profits.

In 1879, one of **John D. Rockefeller's** lawyers, Samuel Dodd, devised a more reliable means of dominating a market. Dodd suggested adapting a legal device called a *trust,* in which one company could control an industry by luring or forcing stockholders of smaller companies in that industry to yield control of their stock "in trust" to the larger company's board of trustees. This allowed Rockefeller to achieve *horizontal integration*—the control of similar companies—of the profitable petroleum industry in 1882 by combining his corporation with other refineries.

John D. Rockefeller: Creator of Standard Oil and master of the use of pools and trusts to monopolize an industry.

Holding Companies

In 1888, New Jersey adopted laws allowing corporations chartered there to own property in other corporations in other states. This facilitated creation of the *holding company,* which owned a partial or complete interest in other companies and merged assets (buildings, equipment, inventory, and cash) under single management. Rockefeller's Standard Oil combined forty independents. By 1898, Standard Oil refined 84 percent of all oil produced in the nation, controlled most pipelines, and engaged in natural-gas production and ownership of oil-producing properties.

Believing that Rockefeller's Standard Oil monopoly was exercising dangerous power, this political cartoonist depicts the trust as a greedy octopus whose sprawling tentacles already ensnare Congress, state legislatures, and the taxpayer, and are reaching for the White House.

vertical integration: Business strategy in which a holding company would seek to control all aspects of the industry in which it functioned, fusing related businesses together under one management.

To dominate their markets, many holding companies sought control over all aspects of the industry, including raw-materials, manufacturing, and distribution. A model of such **vertical integration**, which fused related businesses under unified management, was Gustavus Swift's Chicago meat-processing operation. During the 1880s, Swift invested in livestock, slaughterhouses, refrigerator cars, and marketing to ensure profits from meat sales at prices he could control.

Mergers provided orderly profits. Between 1889 and 1903, three hundred combinations were formed, mostly trusts and holding companies. Other mammoth combinations included Amalgamated Copper Company, American Sugar Refining Company, and U.S. Rubber Company. These huge companies ruthlessly put thousands of small firms out of business.

Financiers

The merger movement created a new species of businessman, whose vocation was financial organizing. Shrewd investors sought opportunities for combination, formed a holding company, raised money by selling stock and borrowing from banks, then persuaded producers to sell their firms to the new company. Investment bankers such as J. P. Morgan and Jacob Schiff piloted the merger movement, inspiring awe with their financial power.

Corporate growth turned stock and bond exchanges into hubs of activity. In 1886, trading on the New York Stock Exchange passed 1 million shares daily. By 1914, the number of industrial stocks traded reached 511, compared with 145 in

1869. Between 1870 and 1900, foreign investment in American companies rose from $1.5 billion to $3.5 billion. Assets of savings banks, concentrated in the Northeast and the West Coast, rose by 700 percent between 1875 and 1897. These institutions, along with commercial banks and insurance companies, invested heavily in railroads and industrial enterprises.

The Gospel of Wealth and Its Critics

Business leaders used corporate consolidation to minimize competition and justified their tactics with the doctrine of **Social Darwinism**. This ideology loosely grafted Charles Darwin's theory of survival of the fittest onto laissez faire, the doctrine that government should not interfere in private economic matters. Social Darwinists reasoned that, in a free-market economy, wealth would flow naturally to those most capable of handling it. In this view, large corporations represented the natural accumulation of economic power by those best suited for it.

Social Darwinists reasoned, too, that wealth carried moral responsibilities. Steel baron **Andrew Carnegie** asserted "the Gospel of Wealth"—that as guardians of society's wealth, he and other industrialists had a duty to serve society. Carnegie donated more than $350 million to libraries, schools, peace initiatives, and the arts. Such philanthropy, however, also enabled benefactors such as Carnegie to define what was good and necessary for society; it did not translate into paying workers decent wages.

Government Assistance to Business Leaders in the corporate consolidation movement extolled initiative while requesting government assistance. Denouncing efforts to legislate maximum working hours or factory conditions as interference, they nonetheless lobbied for public subsidies and tax relief to encourage business growth. Grants to railroads (see Chapter 17) were one form of such assistance. Tariffs, which benefited American products by placing taxes on imported products, were another. Industrialists argued that tariff protection encouraged the development of new products and enterprises. But tariffs also forced consumers to pay artificially high prices (see page 518).

Dissenting Voices Critics charged that these methods stifled opportunity and originated from greed. Such charges from farmers, workers, and intellectuals, reflected a fear of monopoly—the domination of an economic activity (such as oil refining) by one powerful company (such as Standard Oil). Those who feared monopoly believed that large corporations fixed prices, exploited workers, destroyed opportunity by crushing small businesses, and threatened democracy by corrupting politicians.

By the mid-1880s, some intellectuals challenged Social Darwinism and laissez-faire economics. Philosopher and psychologist William James led this trend, arguing that human will, independent of the environment, could alter existence.

Sociologist Lester Ward, in his book *Dynamic Sociology* (1883), proffered that a system that guaranteed survival only to the fittest was wasteful and brutal. Instead, Ward reasoned, cooperative activity fostered by government intervention

> How did business leaders use Social Darwinism to justify their mergers and consolidations?

Social Darwinism: Extended Charles Darwin's theory of "survival of the fittest" to the free market system, arguing that competition would weed out weaker firms and allow stronger, fitter firms to thrive.

Andrew Carnegie: Scottish immigrant who built an enormous steel company and became a renowned philanthropist.

 Link to the preface of George M. Beard's *American Nervousness: Its Causes and Consequences.*

was fairer. Economists Richard Ely, John R. Commons, and Edward Bemis denounced laissez-faire and praised the assistance that government could offer to ordinary people.

Visionaries such as Henry George and Edward Bellamy questioned why the United States had so many poor people while a few became wealthy. George, a printer with a seventh-grade education, was an avid reader of economic theory. He believed that inequality stemmed from the ability of a few to profit from rising land values, which made landowners rich from high rents. To prevent profiteering, George proposed replacing all taxes with a "single tax" on the "unearned increment"—the rise in property values caused by increased market demand. Argued in *Progress and Poverty* (1879), George's popular plan almost won him the mayoralty of New York City in 1886.

Novelist Edward Bellamy proposed that government own the means of production. In his popular novel, *Looking Backward* (1888), Bellamy depicted Boston in the year 2000 as a peaceful community run by benevolent elders managing the economy so everyone had a job. Bellamy hoped that a "principle of fraternal cooperation" would replace vicious competition and wasteful monopoly. Dubbed "Nationalism," his vision sparked new Nationalist clubs nationwide and kindled appeals for political reform, social welfare measures, and government ownership of railroads and utilities.

Antitrust Legislation   Several states took steps to prohibit monopolies and regulate business. By 1900, twenty-seven states banned pools, and fifteen had constitutional provisions outlawing trusts (see Chapter 20). But state governments lacked the staff and judicial support for an effective attack on big business, and corporations found ways to evade restrictions. Congress moved hesitantly toward legislation but in 1890 passed the Sherman Anti-Trust Act. Introduced by Ohio Senator John Sherman, the law made illegal "every contract, combination in the form of trust or otherwise, or conspiracy in the restraint of trade." Those found guilty of violating the law faced fines and jail terms, and those wronged by illegal combinations could sue for triple damages. However, the law was watered down when rewritten by pro-business eastern senators. It did not clearly define "restraint of trade" and consigned interpretation of its provisions to the often business-allied courts.

Judges used the law's vagueness to blur distinctions between reasonable and unreasonable restraints of trade. When in 1895 the federal government prosecuted the Sugar Trust for owning 98 percent of the nation's sugar-refining capacity, eight of nine Supreme Court justices ruled in *U.S. v. E. C. Knight Co.* that control of manufacturing did not necessarily mean control of trade. According to the Court, the Constitution empowered Congress to regulate interstate commerce, but not manufacturing.

Between 1890 and 1900, the federal government prosecuted only eighteen cases under the Sherman Anti-Trust Act. The most successful involved railroads involved in interstate commerce. Ironically, the act equipped the government to break up labor unions: courts that did not consider monopolistic production a restraint on trade willingly applied antitrust provisions to boycotts by striking unions.

Technology of Recorded Sound

Today's digital recorders and downloadable music derive from technology, chemistry, and human resourcefulness that came together in the late nineteenth century. In 1877, Thomas A. Edison devised a way to preserve and reproduce his voice by storing it on indentations made in tin foil. Edison intended his "speaking machine" to help businesses store dictation. But in 1878, a rivalry with telephone inventor Alexander Graham Bell, who was working on a similar device, drew Edison to invent a phonograph for recorded music. By the 1890s, audiences paid to hear recorded sounds from these machines.

By 1901, companies such as the Columbia Phonograph Company produced machines that played music recorded on cylinders molded from a durable wax compound. Over the next ten years, inventors improved the phonograph so sound played back from a stylus (needle) vibrating in grooves of a shellac disc. Records' playing time increased from two minutes to four.

Phonograph records replaced sheet music as the most popular medium, but soon radio emerged and boosted record sales. Radio's popularity was only possible via another electronic technology: the microphone. This device improved sound quality over megaphones. As phonograph prices declined and sound quality improved, more records became available.

The 1938 invention of the idler wheel, which enabled a phonograph turntable to spin a disk at speeds necessary for the stylus to pick up sound accurately, brought an important advance. Shortly thereafter, significant inventions in sound recording, such as the magnetic tape recorder, allowed for more manipulation of sound in the recording studio. In 1963 Philips, a Dutch electronics firm, introduced the compact audio cassette. Two decades later, Philips joined with the Japanese corporation Sony to adapt digital laser discs, invented by an American for video storage, to hold music The compact disc (CD) was born, and from there it was a short step for the Apple Computer Company to create the iPod, storing CD-quality music on an internal hard drive.

Summary

Mechanization and inventions thrust the United States into the vanguard of industrial nations and altered daily life. By the early twentieth century, American industrial output surpassed that of Great Britain, France, and Germany combined. By 1900, factories, stores, and banks converted America from a debtor, agricultural nation into an industrial, financial, and exporting power.

But aggressive industrial consolidation changed the nature of work from individual activity by skilled producers to mass production by wage earners. Laborers fought to retain control of their work and organized unions. The outpouring of products created a mass society based on consumerism and dominated by technology and the communications media.

The enforcement problems with the Sherman Anti-Trust Act reflected the uneven distribution of power. Corporations consolidated to control resources, production, and politics. Laborers and reformers benefited from material gains that technology and mass production provided, but they accused businesses of acquiring influence and profits at their expense. Some people celebrated the economic transformation. Others struggled with the dilemma of industrialism: whether new accumulations of wealth would undermine the republican ideal of democracy and equality.

Industrial expansion proved unstoppable because so many people were benefiting from it. Moreover, the waves of newcomers pouring into the nation's cities were increasingly furnishing workers and consumers for America's expanding productive capacity.

Chapter Review

Technology and the Triumph of Industrialization

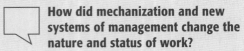

How did technological innovations transform American industry?

New inventions and technological advances made production of goods and services faster and cheaper, which in turn fueled the rise of mass production and consumption. Big factories replaced small workshops as large-scale production became increasingly economical. Thomas Edison's system for inexpensively distributing electricity facilitated the emergence of countless other inventions in the late nineteenth and early twentieth centuries. Henry Ford built on a European invention for engines to create his assembly-line process that would mass produce thousands of identical—ultimately affordable—cars in the early twentieth century. The du Pont family similarly revolutionized the chemical industry; electric looms advanced textile production and relocated it from North to South; while North Carolinian James B. Duke mass-produced cigarettes and remade the tobacco industry.

Mechanization and the Changing Status of Labor

How did mechanization and new systems of management change the nature and status of work?

Innovation created new jobs, but labor-saving machines also meant that fewer workers could produce more in less time. Instead of doing many different tasks, workers now did only one task repeatedly. As workers rather than producers, they lost control over their work days and techniques and instead were regulated by the time clock and the production mandates of bosses. Skill became less important, and as the need for skilled workers

declined, manufacturers saw a way to cut labor costs by hiring women and children, whom they could pay much less. The advent of typewriters and other office machines opened clerical and white collar jobs to women, as well. But in manufacturing, long days and harsh and often hazardous working conditions led to increasing number of accidents as well as labor unrest.

Labor Violence and the Union Movement

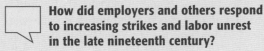

How did employers and others respond to increasing strikes and labor unrest in the late nineteenth century?

Labor activism against long hours, pay cuts, and difficult working conditions became increasingly violent beginning with the Railroad Strike of 1877. After the Haymarket riot of 1886 and other strikes, labor violence and the participation of socialists and anarchists in the labor movement, heightened fears of radicalism. Governments strengthened police forces and armories; employer associations circulated blacklists of union activists, whom they agreed not to employ and they hired private detectives to suppress strikes. State and federal governments also sent in troops, as in the case of the Homestead and Pullman strikes, to break the strikes.

Standards of Living

What was the impact of the new consumer culture on people's lives?

On the one hand, mass production made goods previously deemed luxuries affordable to mainstream Americans, improving everyday life—among them flush toilets, railroad car refrigeration, ready-made clothing, and retail stores. On the other hand, however, workers' wages did not always keep pace with the cost of goods.

Most industrial workers spent a large proportion of their income on necessities. To afford the basics, working families often began to rely on additional sources of income from wives and children, either via factory work or taking in boarders. Advances in nutrition and medical science helped Americans to live longer and healthier lives, although those at the lowest rungs of society still ate diets high in carbohydrates and starches with little meat, and often spent half of the breadwinner's wages even on this meager diet.

The Corporate Consolidation Movement

What led corporations to increasingly consolidate in the late nineteenth century?

Big companies saw consolidation as a way to guarantee profits and control downward economic cycles. They believed the more they pooled resources to set prices and influence profits by determining how much to supply the market, the more they could manage a downturn. Until the 1880s, however, laws made it illegal for companies to own stock in another firm. Instead, businessmen such as John D. Rockefeller turned to trusts, luring stockholders of smaller companies to yield control of their stock "in trust" to the larger company's board of trustees. Once states allowed companies within their borders to own stock in corporations in other states, holding companies emerged, where one firm would own partial or complete interest in another and merge their assets and resources. Holding companies also found it easier to dominate their markets by controlling all aspects of an industry from raw materials to manufacturing to distribution.

The Gospel of Wealth and Its Critics

How did business leaders use Social Darwinism to justify their mergers and consolidations?

Social Darwinism applied Charles Darwin's theory of survival of the fittest to laissez-faire economics, which stressed that government should let the economy manage itself. Social Darwinists argued that in a free-market economy, wealth would flow to those most capable of handling it, and that corporations represented that accumulation of power in the best hands. On the flip side, many believed those with wealth had a moral obligation to use it to improve society; hence, some business leaders such as Andrew Carnegie donated millions to the arts, education, and other worthy causes. Such largesse did not, however, translate into better wages or working conditions for their employees.

Suggestions for Further Reading

Edward L. Ayers, *The Promise of the New South: Life After Reconstruction* (1992)

Ileen A. DeVault, *United Apart: Gender and the Rise of Craft Unionism* (2004)

Steven J. Diner, *A Very Different Age: Americans of the Progressive Era* (1998)

John F. Kasson, *Civilizing the Machine: Technology and Republican Values in America, 1776–1900* (1976)

Alice Kessler-Harris, *Out to Work: A History of Wage-Earning Women in the United States* (2003)

T. J. Jackson Lears and Richard W. Fox, eds., *The Culture of Consumption: Critical Essays in American History, 1880–1980* (1983)

David Montgomery, *The Fall of the House of Labor: The Workplace, the State and American Labor Activism, 1865–1925* (1987)

Jeffrey Sklansky, *The Soul's Economy: Market Society and Selfhood in American Thought, 1820–1920* (2002)

Go to the CourseMate website for primary source links, study tools, and review materials for this chapter.
www.cengagebrain.com

The Vitality and Turmoil of Urban Life

19

1877–1920

Crowds on the street gasped as they looked upward. A man, bound in a straitjacket was hanging by his heels high above New York's Times Square. Suddenly, he wriggled wildly. In seconds Harry Houdini, the early twentieth century's most celebrated showman, was free. As he had done many times, Houdini fed the public's taste for suspense, courage, and entertainment with a death-defying feat.

Born as Erich Weiss in Hungary in 1874, Houdini and his family emigrated to Wisconsin in 1878. After Erich's father lost his job as a rabbi, the family moved to New York City, where father and son worked in a necktie factory. When Erich's father died in 1892, the young man became an entertainer. After a few lackluster years as a magician, Erich discovered his talent as an illusionist and escape artist. He changed his name to Harry Houdini and became one of America's most enthralling performers.

By the early 1900s, "The Great Houdini" was a feature in vaudeville, a new form of urban entertainment. His specialty was escaping from elaborate and dangerous confinements: ropes, manacles, and padlocked containers. Houdini was also a skillful self-publicist, advertising his act with posters and leaflets. Around 1913, Houdini introduced his famous "Chinese water torture cell" escape, in which he extracted himself from being bound and suspended upside down in a water-filled, locked glass-and-steel cabinet. Houdini escaped by manipulating his five-foot-five frame in unusual ways but also by concealing picks and keys, which he sometimes regurgitated. Although he constantly defied death in his act, Houdini could not escape the abdominal infection that took his life in 1926.

Like many people in the late nineteenth and early twentieth centuries, the Weiss family were immigrants who fled poverty and tried to remake themselves in a burgeoning American city. They faced challenges of where to live and work, how to deal with a cash-based economy, how to preserve their ethnic consciousness amid bigotry, how to achieve independence and respectability.

Chapter Outline

Growth of the Modern City

Industrial Development | Mechanization of Mass Transportation | Urban Sprawl | Population Growth | Urban In-Migration | New Foreign Immigration | Geographic and Social Mobility

Urban Neighborhoods

Cultural Retention and Change | Urban Borderlands | Racial Segregation and Violence | Mexican Barrios | Cultural Adaptation

Living Conditions in the Inner City

Inner-City Housing | Housing Reform | New Home Technology | Poverty Relief | Crime and Violence

Managing the City

Water Supply and Sewage Disposal | Urban Engineers | Law Enforcement | Political Machines | Civic Reform | Social Reform | The City Beautiful Movement

VISUALIZING THE PAST: *Street Cleaning and Urban Reform*

Family Life

Family and Household Structures | Declining Birth Rates | Stages of Life | The Unmarried | Boarding and Lodging | Functions of Kinship | Holiday Celebrations

Such challenges made cities places of hope, frustration, achievement, and conflict.

Not until the 1880s did the United States begin to become an urban nation. The technological innovations and industrialization of the late nineteenth century sparked economic and geographical expansion, funneling millions of people cityward. By 1920, the census showed that, for the first time, a majority of Americans (51.4 percent) lived in cities (settlements with more than 2,500 people). Cities were filled with new kinds of consumerism as urban dwellers patronized dance halls, theatrical performances, vaudeville, movies, and sporting events in record numbers. By idolizing Houdini, sports heroes, and movie celebrities, or by benefiting from the largesse of a political boss, ordinary working- and middle-class people could believe in the potential of individuals to free themselves from the uncertainties of an emerging technological and urban society. At the same time, poverty and discrimination haunted the lives of countless urban dwellers, combining the era's opportunities with persistent of inequality and prejudice. Whatever people's personal experiences, cities had become central to American life. How people built cities and adjusted to their environments shaped modern American society.

As you read this chapter, keep the following questions in mind:

* **What were the most important factors contributing to the urban growth of the period 1877–1920?**

* **How did immigrants adjust to and reshape their adopted homeland?**

* **How did industrialization and urbanization affect patterns of family life and leisure time?**

The New Leisure and Mass Culture
Increase in Leisure Time | *Baseball* | *Croquet and Cycling* | *Football* | *Show Business* | *Opportunities for Women and Minorities* | *Movies* | *Yellow Journalism* | *Other Mass-Market Publications* | *Anthony Comstock*

LINKS TO THE WORLD *Japanese Baseball*

LEGACY FOR A PEOPLE AND A NATION *Children and Mass-Produced Toys*

SUMMARY

Growth of the Modern City

Initially, commercial centers cities became the main arenas for industrial development in the late nineteenth century. As labor, transportation, and communication hubs, cities supplied everything factories needed. The further industrialization advanced, the more opportunities it created for jobs and investment, which, in turn drew more people to cities. As workers and consumers, they fueled yet more industrialization.

What fueled urban growth in the late nineteenth century?

Industrial Development   While manufacturing enterprises varied, cities increasingly specialized. Mass production of clothing concentrated in New York City, the shoe industry in Philadelphia, and textiles in New England cities. Other cities created goods derived from surrounding agricultural regions: flour in Minneapolis, cottonseed oil in Memphis, beef and pork in Chicago. Still others

Chronology

1867	First law regulating tenements passes in New York State
1870	One-fourth of Americans live in cities
1876	National League of Professional Baseball Clubs founded
1880s	"New" immigrants from eastern and southern Europe begin to arrive in large numbers
1883	Brooklyn Bridge completed
	Pulitzer buys *New York World,* creating major publication for yellow journalism
1885	Safety bicycle invented
1886	First settlement house opens in New York City
1889	Edison invents motion picture and viewing device
1890s	Electric trolleys replace horse-drawn mass transit
1893	Columbian Exposition opens in Chicago
1895	Hearst buys *New York Journal,* which becomes another popular yellow-journalism newspaper
1898	Race riot erupts in Wilmington, North Carolina
1900–10	Immigration reaches peak
1903	Boston beats Pittsburgh in baseball's first World Series
1905	Intercollegiate Athletic Association, forerunner of National Intercollegiate Athletic Association (NCAA) is formed, restructuring rules of football
1915	Griffith directs *Birth of a Nation,* one of first major technically sophisticated movies
1919	Race riot erupts in East St. Louis, Illinois
1920	Majority (51.4 percent) of Americans live in cities

processed natural resources: gold and copper in Denver, fish and lumber in Seattle, iron in Pittsburgh and Birmingham, oil in Houston and Los Angeles. Such activities increased cities' attraction for people seeking steady employment.

The compact city of the early nineteenth century, where residences mingled among shops, factories, and warehouses, sprawled miles beyond the original settlement. No longer did walking distance determine a city's size. Instead, cities separated into working- and middle-class neighborhoods, commercial strips, downtown, and a ring of suburbs. Two forces were responsible for this: mass transportation, which propelled people and enterprises outward, and economic change, which drew human and material resources inward.

Mechanization of Mass Transportation

By the 1870s, horse-drawn vehicles shared city streets with faster motor-driven conveyances. In the 1880s, cable cars started operating in Chicago, San Francisco, and other cities. In the 1890s, electric-powered streetcars began replacing horse cars and cable cars. In a few cities, companies raised track onto trestles, enabling "elevated" vehicles to travel above jammed downtown streets. In Boston, New York, and Philadelphia, transit firms solved traffic problems by digging underground subway tunnels. Because "els" were expensive to construct, they appeared only in cities with enough riders to ensure profits.

Urban Sprawl

Mass transit launched urban dwellers into remote neighborhoods and created a commuting public. Streetcar lines serviced districts that promised the most riders and increase company revenues. Working-class families, who needed every cent, found streetcars unaffordable. But the growing middle class who could afford the fare—usually 5 cents a ride—could escape to quiet, tree-lined neighborhoods on the outskirts and commute to the inner city for work, shopping, and entertainment.

Picture Research Consultants & Archives

Electric trolley cars and other forms of mass transit enabled middle-class people such as these women and men to reside on the urban outskirts and ride into the city center for work, shopping, and entertainment.

When consumers moved outward, businesses followed, locating near mass transit. Department stores and banks joined groceries, theaters, taverns, and shops to create neighborhood shopping centers. Meanwhile, the urban core became a work zone, where tall buildings loomed over streets clogged with people, horses, and vehicles.

Population Growth Between 1870 and 1920, the number of Americans living in cities increased from 10 million to 54 million. During this period, the number of cities with more than 100,000 people swelled from 15 to 68; those with more than 500,000 rose from two to twelve (see Map 19.1).

American urban growth derived from the annexation of bordering land and people and net migration (excess of in-migrants over out-migrants). For example, in 1898, New York City, previously consisting of Manhattan and the Bronx, merged with Brooklyn, Staten Island, and part of Queens and doubled to 3 million people. Suburbs desired annexation for the schools, water, fire protection, and sewer systems that cities provided.

Link to the 1910 Federal Census Data Information search tool.

Urban In-Migration In-migration from the countryside and immigration from abroad made the greatest contribution to urban population growth. Urban newcomers arrived from two major sources: the American countryside and Europe. Asia, Canada, and Latin America also supplied smaller numbers of immigrants.

1880

Percent of population living in cities
- Over 60%
- 40%–60%
- 20%–40%
- Under 20%
- City with population over 100,000

1920

Percent of population living in cities
- Over 60%
- 40%–60%
- 20%–40%
- Under 20%
- City with population over 100,000

MAP 19.1

Urbanization, 1880 and 1920

In 1880, the vast majority of states were still heavily rural. By 1920, only a few had less than 20 percent of their population living in cities.

Source: Copyright © Cengage Learning

Rural populations declined as urban populations burgeoned. Low crop prices and high debts drove white farmers toward opportunities that cities seemingly offered. Migrants filled major cities, such as Detroit, Chicago, and San Francisco, but also secondary cities, such as Indianapolis, Salt Lake City, Nashville, and San Diego. The thrill of city life beckoned especially to young people. For every four men who migrated cityward, five women did the same, often to escape unhappy homes and enjoy the independence that urban employment offered.

Thousands of rural African Americans also moved cityward, seeking better employment and fleeing crop liens, ravages of the boll weevil on cotton crops, racial violence, and political oppression. Black migration accelerated after 1915, but thirty-two cities already had more than ten thousand black residents by 1900. Because few factories would employ African Americans, most found jobs in the service sector—cleaning, cooking, and driving. Since these were traditionally female jobs, black women outnumbered black men in most cities. In the South, rural black migrants became an important source of unskilled labor in growing cities. By 1900, almost 40 percent of the population of Atlanta, Georgia, and Charlotte, North Carolina, was black.

In the West, Hispanics also moved into cities such as Los Angeles, San Diego, and San Antonio. They took unskilled construction jobs previously held by Chinese laborers driven from Southern California cities by racism. In some Texas cities, native Mexicans (called *Tejanos*) held the majority of unskilled jobs. Mexican men often left home to take temporary jobs in cities, leaving behind female heads of household.

New Foreign Immigration

Most newcomers were foreign immigrants fleeing villages and cities in Europe, Asia, Canada, and Latin America for the United States. Many wanted only to make enough money to return home and live in greater comfort. For every hundred foreigners who entered the country, thirty ultimately left. Still, like Houdini's family, most of the 26 million immigrants arriving between 1870 and 1920 remained, settling largely in cities.

New U.S. immigration was part of a worldwide movement, triggered by population pressures, land redistribution, industrialization, and religious persecution in Europe, Asia, Canada, and Latin America.

Immigrants from northern and western Europe had long made the United States their destination, but after 1880 economic and demographic changes propelled immigrants from other regions. Increased numbers came from eastern and southern Europe, plus smaller groups from Canada, Mexico, and Japan. Between 1900 and 1909, two-thirds of immigrants came from Italy, Austria-Hungary, and Russia. By 1910, arrivals from Mexico outnumbered arrivals from Ireland, and numerous Japanese moved to the West Coast and Hawai'i. Foreign-born blacks, chiefly from the West Indies, also came. (See the Cengage web site for the nationalities of immigrants.)

Many long-settled Americans feared these "**new immigrants**," whose customs, Catholic and Jewish faiths, and poverty made them seem particularly alien. Unlike immigrants from Great Britain and Ireland, new immigrants did not speak English, and often worked in low-skill occupations. Yet old and new immigrants like the Weisses made family the focus of all undertakings. New arrivals usually knew where to go and how to get there from relatives who already immigrated. Workers helped kin obtain jobs, and family members pooled resources to improve their standard of living.

new immigrants: Wave of immigrants after 1880 coming from mainly southern and eastern Europe.

Geographic and Social Mobility

Once they arrived, in-migrants and immigrants rarely stayed put. Each year, millions of families went elsewhere. The Weiss family stayed in Appleton, Wisconsin, only a few years before leaving for New York City. More than half the families residing in a city were gone ten years later. Even within a city, it was common for a family to live at three or more different addresses over a ten- or fifteen-year period. One in every three or four families moved each year (today the rate is one in five). Migration offered one escape to opportunity.

Advancement up the social scale through better jobs was available mostly to white males. Thousands of businesses were needed to supply goods and services to burgeoning urban populations, and as corporations grew and centralized operations, they required new personnel. An aspiring merchant could open a saloon for a few hundred dollars. Knowledge of accounting could qualify workers for white-collar jobs with higher incomes than manual labor.

Such advancement occurred often, but few could accumulate large fortunes. Most of the era's wealthiest businessmen began their careers with advantages: American birth, Protestant religion, education, and affluent parents. Yet considerable movement occurred along the road from poverty to moderate success, from manual to nonmanual work.

Rates of upward occupational mobility were slow but steady between 1870 and 1920. In fast-growing cities such as Atlanta and Los Angeles, approximately one in five white manual workers rose to white-collar or owner's positions within ten years. In older cities such as Boston and Philadelphia, upward mobility averaged closer to one in six workers in ten years. Some men slipped from a higher to a lower rung, but rates of upward movement usually doubled downward rates. Immigrants generally experienced less upward and more downward mobility than the native-born, yet the chances for a white male rising to a higher-status job than his father were good.

The definition of a better job varied. Many immigrant artisans considered an accountant's job unmanly. People who took pride in working with their hands neither desired nonmanual jobs nor encouraged their children to seek them. As one Italian tailor explained, "I want that my oldest boy learn my trade because I tell him that you could always make at least enough for the family."

Failure rates were high among small proprietors in working-class neighborhoods,

Fresh off the boat and wearing homeland clothing, immigrants pose for a photograph outside the federal immigration station at Ellis Island, offshore from New York City. Situated in the shadow of the Statue of Liberty, Ellis Island immigration officials processed millions of newcomers such as these, asking them questions about their background and examining them for health problems.

Records of the Public Health Service. (90-G-125-29)/US GOV National Archives because customers' low incomes made profits uncertain. Many manual workers sought security rather than mobility, preferring a steady wage to risks of ownership.

Many women held paying jobs but since their standing was defined by the men in their lives, their chief means of mobility came from marrying men with wealth or potential. Laws limited what women could inherit; educational institutions blocked their training in such professions as medicine and law; and prevailing assumptions attributed higher aptitude for manual skills and business to men. Assigned to the lowest-paying occupations by prejudice, African Americans, American Indians, Mexican Americans, and Asian Americans made even fewer gains.

A person might achieve social mobility by acquiring property, which was not easily accomplished. Banks and savings-and-loan institutions had strict lending practices, and mortgage loans carried high interest rates and short repayment periods. Nevertheless, some families succeeded in amassing down payments on property. Ownership rates varied regionally—higher in western cities, lower in eastern cities—but 36 percent of all urban American families owned their homes in 1900, the highest homeownership rate of any western nation except for Denmark, Norway, and Sweden.

Many, particularly unskilled workers, did not improve their status; they simply floated from one low-paying job to another. Others found greener pastures. The possibilities for upward mobility tempered people's dissatisfaction with the stresses of city life. For every story of rags to riches, there were myriad small triumphs. Although the gap between rich and poor widened, for those in between, the expanding economies of American cities created room.

Urban Neighborhoods

> How did immigrants adapt to their new lives in U.S. cities?

American cities were characterized by collections of subcommunities where people, most of whom had migrated from somewhere else, coped with daily challenges to their cultures. Rather than yield completely to assimilation, migrants and immigrants interacted with the urban environment to retain their identity while altering their outlook and the social structure of cities.

Cultural Retention and Change

In new surroundings, immigrants first anchored their lives to what they knew: their culture. Old World customs persisted in immigrant districts of Italians from the same province, Japanese from the same island district, and Russian Jews from the same *shtetl.* Newcomers re-created mutual aid societies from their homeland. For example, the Japanese recreated *ken* societies, which organized social celebrations and relief services. The Chinese reproduced loan associations, called *whey,* which raised money to help members acquire businesses, and village associations called *fongs,* which rented apartments to members. Southern Italians transplanted the system whereby a *padrone* (boss) found jobs for unskilled workers by negotiating with—and receiving payoffs from—an employer. All newcomers practiced religion as they always had, held traditional feasts and pageants, and married within their group.

Urban Borderlands

In large cities, such as Chicago, Philadelphia, and Detroit, European immigrants initially clustered in inner neighborhoods where low-skill jobs and cheap housing were most available. These districts often were multi-ethnic, "urban borderlands," where diverse people coexisted. Even within districts identified with a certain group, such as Little Italy, Jewtown, Polonia, or Greektown, rapid mobility undermined homogeneity, as newcomers moved and older inhabitants left. Neighborhoods often housed several ethnic groups, but businesses and institutions, such as bakeries, butcher shops, churches, and club headquarters— operated by and for one ethnic group—gave a neighborhood its identity.

For first- and second-generation immigrants, their neighborhoods acted as havens until individuals were ready to cross from the borderland into the majority society—sometimes within just a few years. The expansion of mass transportation and outward movement of factories enabled people to move to areas where they interspersed with families of their socioeconomic class but not necessarily their ethnicity. European immigrants encountered prejudice, such as the exclusion of Jews from certain neighborhoods, professions, and clubs, but discrimination rarely was systematic. For people of color, however—African Americans, Asians, and Mexicans— discrimination kept them from becoming multiethnic.

Racial Segregation and Violence

Although small numbers of African Americans may have lived near or interspersed with whites in the eighteenth and early nineteenth centuries, by the late nineteenth century rigid racial discrimination forced them into highly segregated ghettos. By 1920, in Chicago, Detroit, Cleveland, and other cities, two-thirds or more of the total black population inhabited only 10 percent of the residential area. Within their neighborhoods, African Americans nurtured institutions to cope with city life: shops, clubs, theaters, dance halls, newspapers, and saloons. Churches, particularly branches of Baptist and African Methodist Episcopal (AME) Protestantism, were especially influential. Pittsburgh blacks boasted twenty-eight such churches in the early 1900s. Membership in Cincinnati's black Baptist churches doubled between 1870 and 1900. In Louisville, blacks built their own theological institute. Black religious activity dominated urban life and represented cooperation across class lines.

The only way blacks could relieve overcrowding from increased migration was to expand residential borders into surrounding, previously white neighborhoods, a process that resulted in harassment and attacks by white residents who feared that blacks would reduce property values. African Americans' increased presence in cities, as well as their competition with whites for housing, jobs, and political influence, sparked race riots. In 1898, white residents of Wilmington, North Carolina, resenting African Americans' involvement in local government and incensed by an African American newspaper editorial accusing white women of loose sexual behavior, rioted and killed dozens of blacks. White supremacists overthrew the city government, expelling black and white officeholders, and instituted restrictions to prevent blacks from voting. An influx of unskilled black strikebreakers into East St. Louis, Illinois, heightened racial tensions in 1917, triggering a riot in which nine whites and thirty-nine blacks were killed and three hundred buildings were destroyed.

Asians also encountered discrimination and segregation. Although Chinese immigrants often preferred to live apart from Anglos in Chinatowns of San Francisco, Seattle, Los Angeles, and New York City, creating their own business, government, and social institutions, Anglos also tried to keep them separated. Using the slogan "The Chinese must go," Irish immigrant Denis Kearney and his followers intimidated employers into refusing to hire Chinese, and drove hundreds of Asians out of the city. San Francisco's government prohibited Chinese laundries from white neighborhoods and banned the wearing of queues, the traditional Chinese hair braid. In 1882, Congress passed the Chinese Exclusion Act, which suspended Chinese immigration and prohibited naturalization of Chinese already residing in the United States. And in 1892, Congress approved the Geary Act, which extended immigration restriction and required Chinese Americans to carry certificates of residence issued by the Treasury Department. The U.S. Supreme Court upheld the Geary Act in 1893 in *Fong Yue Ting v. United States*. Similarly prevented from becoming American citizens, Japanese immigrants, called Issei, also developed communities.

Mexican Barrios

Mexicans in southwestern cities experienced complex residential patterns. In places such as Los Angeles, Santa Barbara, and Tucson, Mexicans had been the original inhabitants; Anglos were newcomers who pushed Mexicans into increasingly isolated districts on the outskirts called *barrios*. Frequently, real-estate covenants, by which property owners pledged not to sell homes to Mexicans (or to African Americans or Jews), kept Mexican families confined in barrios. These areas were outside central-city multiethnic borderlands housing European immigrants. As such, racial bias hindered African Americans', Asians', and Mexicans' opportunities to remake their lives.

Cultural Adaptation

Virtually everywhere immigrants lived, Old World culture mingled with New World realities. Although many foreigners identified themselves by their village or region of birth, native-born Americans categorized them by nationality. People from County Cork and County Limerick, for example, were merged into Irish; those from Calabria and Campobasso into Italians. Immigrant institutions, such as newspapers and churches, had to appeal to the entire nationality to survive.

Moreover, the diversity of American cities prompted foreigners to modify their habits and previous ways of life. Although many immigrants tried to preserve their language, English, taught in schools and needed at work, soon penetrated most communities. Foreigners fashioned homeland styles garments but used American rather than traditional fabrics. Italians went to American doctors but still carried amulets to ward off evil spirits. Polka bands blended American and Polish folk music. Mexican ballads now described border crossing and hardships in the United States.

The influx of so many immigrants between 1870 and 1920 transformed the United States from a basically Protestant nation into a diverse collection of Protestants, Catholics, Orthodox Christians, Jews, Buddhists, and Muslims. Newcomers from Italy, Hungary, Polish lands, and Slovakia joined Irish and Germans to boost the proportion of Catholics in many cities. German and Russian immigrants gave New York City one of the largest Jewish populations in the world.

Many Catholics and Jews tried to accommodate their faiths to the new environment. Catholic and Jewish leaders from earlier immigrant groups supported liberalizing trends—use of English in services, the phasing out of such Old World rituals as saints' feasts, and a preference for public over religious schools. As new immigrants continued to arrive, however, these trends met stiff resistance. Newcomers usually held onto familiar religious practices, whether the folk Catholicism of southern Italy or the Orthodox Judaism of eastern Europe. Despite church attempts to make American Catholicism more uniform, bishops acceded to pressures from predominantly Polish congregations for Polish priests. Eastern

European Jews, convinced that Reform Judaism sacrificed too much to American ways, established the Conservative branch, which retained traditional ritual but abolished the segregation of women in synagogues and allowed English prayers. But, second-generation Catholics and Jews marrying coreligionists of other ethnic groups—an Italian Catholic marrying a Polish Catholic—kept religious identity strong while undercutting ethnic identity.

The cities nurtured rich cultural variety: American folk music and literature, Italian and Mexican cuisine, Irish comedy, Yiddish theater, African American jazz and dance, and much more. Newcomers changed their environment as much as they were changed by it.

Living Conditions in the Inner City

What made cities seem particularly dangerous?

The central sections of American cities were plagued by poverty, disease, crime, and the tensions that occur when manifold people live close together. City dwellers coped, and technology, private enterprise, and public authority achieved some remarkable successes.

Inner-City Housing

In spite of massive construction, population growth outpaced housing supplies. Lack of inexpensive living quarters especially distressed working-class families who, because of low wages, had to rent homes. Landlords exploited housing shortages by splitting up existing buildings to house more people, constructing multiple-unit tenements, and hiking rents. Low-income families adapted to high costs and short supply by sharing space and expenses. A one-family apartment was typically occupied by two or three families, or by one family plus several boarders.

The result was unprecedented crowding. In 1890, New York City's immigrant-packed Lower East Side averaged 702 people per acre, one of the highest population densities in the world.

Conditions were harsh. The largest rooms were barely ten feet wide, and interior rooms either lacked windows or opened onto narrow shafts that bred vermin and rotten odors. Few buildings had indoor plumbing; residents used privies (outdoor toilets) in the back yard or basement. Often, the only source of heat was dangerous, polluting coal-burning stoves.

Housing Reform

Housing problems sparked widespread reform campaigns. New York State led with laws in 1867, 1879, and 1901 that established light, ventilation, and safety codes for new tenement buildings. Reformers, such as journalist Jacob Riis and humanitarian Lawrence Veiller, advocated "model tenements," with spacious rooms and better facilities for low-income families. Model tenements meant lower profits, however—a sacrifice few landlords would make. Reformers and public officials opposed government financing of better housing, fearing it would undermine private enterprise. Still, housing codes and regulatory commissions strengthened local government's power to oversee construction.

New Home Technology

Technology ultimately revolutionized home life. Advanced systems of central heating (furnaces), electric lighting, and indoor plumbing created more comfort, first for middle-class households and

Inner-city dwellers used not only indoor space as efficiently as possible, but also what little outdoor space was available to them. Scores of families living in this cramped block of six-story tenements in New York strung clotheslines behind the buildings. Notice that there is virtually no space between buildings—only rooms at the front and back received daylight and fresh air.

later for most others. Whereas formerly families bought coal or chopped wood for cooking and heating, made candles for light, and hauled bath water, their homes increasingly connected to outside pipes and wires for gas, water, and electricity. Moreover, these utilities helped create new attitudes about privacy. Middle-class bedrooms and bathrooms became private retreats. Scientific and technological advances eventually enabled city dwellers and the nation to live healthier. By the 1880s, doctors began to accept the theory that microorganisms (germs) cause disease. Cities established more efficient water purification and sewage disposal, which control such dread diseases as cholera, typhoid fever, and diphtheria.

Meanwhile, street paving, modernized firefighting equipment, and electric street lighting spread rapidly across urban America. Steel-frame construction, which uses a metal skeleton rather than with masonry walls for building support, enabled the erection of skyscrapers—and thus more efficient vertical use of scarce land. Steel-cable suspension bridges, developed by John A. Roebling and epitomized by his Brooklyn Bridge (completed in 1883), linked metropolitan sections more closely.

Poverty Relief

None of these improvements, however, lightened the burden of poverty. Since colonial days, Americans have disagreed about public responsibility for poor relief. According to traditional beliefs, still widespread in the early twentieth century, anyone could escape poverty through hard work and clean living; moral weakness caused indigence. Such reasoning bred fear that aiding the poor encouraged them to rely on public support rather than their own efforts. As business cycles fluctuated and poverty increased, this attitude hardened, and city governments discontinued direct grants of food, fuel, and clothing to needy families. Instead, cities provided relief in return for work on public projects and sent special cases to state-run almshouses, orphanages, and homes for the blind, deaf, and mentally ill.

Between 1877 and 1892, philanthropists in ninety-two cities formed Charity Organization Societies to make social welfare (like business) more efficient by merging disparate charities into coordinated units. Believing poverty to be caused by personal defects, such as alcoholism and laziness, these organizations visited poor families to identify the "deserving" poor and encourage them to be thriftier and more virtuous. Close observation of the poor, however, prompted some humanitarians to conclude that people's environments, not personal shortcomings, caused poverty and that society should help improve conditions. They believed they could reduce poverty through better housing, education, sanitation, and job opportunities. This fueled campaigns for building codes, factory regulations, and public health measures in the Progressive era of the early twentieth century (see Chapter 21). Still, most middle- and upper-class Americans embraced the creed that only the unfit were poor and that poverty relief should be tolerated but never encouraged.

Crime and Violence

Crime and disorder, as much as crowding and poverty, nurtured fears that cities, especially their slums, threatened the nation. While homicide rates declined in industrialized nations, America's rose alarmingly: 25 murders per million people in 1881; 107 per million in 1898. Domestic violence, muggings, and gang fights made cities turbulent as did pickpockets, swindlers, and burglars. Urban outlaws, such as Rufus Minor, acquired as much notoriety as western desperadoes. Short and bald, Minor resembled a shy clerk, but one police chief labeled him "one of the smartest bank sneaks in America." Minor was implicated in bank heists in New York City, Cleveland, Detroit, Providence, Philadelphia, Albany, Boston, and Baltimore between 1878 and 1882.

Urban crime may have become more conspicuous rather than more prevalent. Undeniably, concentrations of wealth and the mingling of different peoples provided opportunities for larceny, vice, and assault. But urban lawlessness and brutality probably did not exceed that of backwoods mining camps and southern plantations. Nativists were quick to blame immigrants for crime, but the law-breaking population included native-born Americans and foreigners.

Managing the City

What facilitated the rise of political machines in cities?

Burgeoning populations and physical expansion created urgent needs for sewers, police and fire protection, schools, parks, and other services. Such needs strained municipal resources and city governments. In addition to a mayor and a city council, various governmental boards administered health regulations, public works, poverty relief, and other functions. Philadelphia at one time had thirty such boards. State governments also interfered in local matters, appointing board members and limiting cities' abilities to levy taxes and borrow money.

Water Supply and Sewage Disposal

Finding sources of clean water and a way to dispose of waste became increasingly pressing challenges. In the early 1800s, urban households used privies to dispose of human excrement, and factories dumped untreated sewage into rivers, lakes, and bays. By the late nineteenth century, sewer systems and flush toilets, plus use of water as a coolant in factories, overwhelmed waterways, contaminating drinking-water sources. The stench of rivers was often unbearable, and pollution bred disease. In 1878, nineteen thousand people fled a yellow fever epidemic in Memphis. Acceptance in the 1880s of the germ theory of disease prompted cities to reduce chances that human waste and other pollutants would endanger water supplies. Some states legally prohibited discharging raw sewage into rivers and streams, and a few cities began the expensive process of chemically treating sewage. Gradually, water managers installed mechanical filters, and cities, led by Jersey City, began purifying water supplies by adding chlorine. These efforts dramatically reduced deaths from typhoid fever.

But waste disposal remained a thorny problem. Experts in 1900 estimated that every New Yorker generated annually some 160 pounds of garbage (food and bones); 1,200 pounds of ashes (from stoves and furnaces); and 100 pounds of rubbish. Solid waste from factories and businesses included tons of scrap metal and wood. Each of the estimated 3.5 million horses in American cities in 1900 daily dropped about 20 pounds of manure and a gallon of urine that rain washed into nearby water sources. By the twentieth century, this refuse was a health and safety hazard.

Urban Engineers

Citizens' groups, led by women's organizations, began discussing these dilemmas in the 1880s, and by 1900 urban governments began to hire sanitary engineers, to design garbage collection systems, disposing of it in incinerators and landfills. American engineers developed systems and standards of worldwide significance that made cities more livable, such as street lighting, bridge and street construction and fire protection. Elected officials depended on engineers' expertise in aiding urban expansion. Insulated within bureaucratic agencies from tumultuous party politics, engineers made lasting contributions to urban management.

Law Enforcement

After the mid-nineteenth century, urban dwellers increasingly depended on professional police to protect life and property, but law enforcement became complicated and controversial, as various groups differed about how laws should be enforced. Ethnic and racial minorities were more likely to be arrested and police officers applied the law less harshly to members of their own ethnic groups and to people offering bribes.

Often poorly trained and prone to corruption, police were squeezed between demands for swift and severe action on the one hand and for leniency on the other. Some people clamored for police crackdowns on saloons, gambling halls, and houses of prostitution, while those who profited from and patronized such customer-oriented criminal establishments favored loose law enforcement. Achieving balance between criminal law and personal freedom grew increasingly difficult.

Political Machines

Out of the apparent confusion surrounding urban management arose **political machines**, organizations whose main goals were the rewards—money, influence, and prestige—of getting and keeping power. Machine politicians routinely used fraud and bribery to further their ends. But they also provided relief, security, and services to voters.

Machines bred leaders, called **bosses**, who built power bases among working classes, especially immigrants. Most bosses had immigrant backgrounds and grew

political machines: Organizations that emerged in urban, often working-class and immigrant neighborhoods; they solicited votes for particular candidates and promised jobs and other services to supporters; putting their candidates in office gave them power over local government.

bosses: Headed political machines; often of similar background to constituents; popular local figures who exchanged votes for money, support and other favors.

Street Cleaning and Urban Reform

As street cleaning became an ever-increasing necessity in burgeoning cities, the numbers of employees of sanitation departments multiplied and the tools they used on their job became more elaborate. As early as 1896, inventors were designing machines and vehicles with brushes to replace the brooms used by past street-cleaning crews and scrapers for clearing snow. One such inventor, Charles Brooks of Newark, New Jersey, not only patented a street-cleaning and snow-removal truck but also designed a receptacles for storing trash and other litter picked up by his machine. But to the minds of engineers and sanitarians, improving the technology of street cleaning was not enough. The process needed to be organized and controlled in what to their minds was a logical way, giving workers a sense of value and professionalism. These two images reveal an important change in the appearance of the New York City street-cleaning force between 1868 and 1920. What reform attitudes do the contrasting images represent? Given the contrasting dress of the two crews, how would the general public have reacted to each?

Beginning of New York's Street Cleaning Department. Calling the roll, 1868

This shows the great improvements made by Colonel Waring as Street Commissioner. Calling the roll in 1920

Miriam and Ira D. Wallach Division of Art, Prints and Photographs, The New York Public Library. Astor, Lenox and Tilden Foundations

By the early 1900s, the profession of sanitary engineer became an important one to the urban environment. As the human and horse populations of cities grew, garbage, litter, and manure became nagging inconveniences and health hazards. In 1868, street sweepers hired to clean the streets, often consisted of crews hired by political bosses and were required to report to a supervisor for morning roll call.

up in the inner city. They knew their constituents' needs firsthand and gained power by dealing with problems of everyday life. In return for votes, bosses provided jobs, built parks and bathhouses, distributed food and clothing to the needy, and helped when someone ran afoul of the law. New York's "Big Tim" Sullivan, for example, gave out shoes and sponsored annual picnics. Bosses, moreover, made politics a full-time profession. They attended weddings and wakes, joined clubs, and held open houses in saloons where neighborhood folk could speak to them personally. According to George Washington Plunkitt, a neighborhood boss in New York City, "As a rule [the boss]...plays politics every day and night in the year and his headquarters bears the inscription, Never closed."

Link to the *New York Times* article about Tim Sullivan's annual picnic.

To finance their activities and election campaigns, bosses exchanged favors for votes and money. Power over local government enabled machines to control who received public contracts, utility and streetcar franchises, and city jobs. Recipients were expected to repay the machine with a portion of their profits or salaries and to cast supporting votes. Critics called this process graft; bosses called it gratitude.

Bosses such as Philadelphia's "Duke" Vare, Kansas City's Tom Pendergast, and New York's Richard Croker lived like kings, though their official incomes were slim. Yet machines were rarely as dictatorial or corrupt as critics charged. Rather, several machines evolved into tightly structured operations, such as New York's Tammany Hall organization (named after a society that began as a patriotic fraternal club), which blended public accomplishments with personal gain. The system rested on a popular base held together by loyalty and service. Most machines were coalitions of smaller organizations that derived power directly from inner-city neighborhoods. Machine-led governments constructed the urban infrastructure—public buildings, sewer systems, schools, bridges, and mass-transit lines—and expanded urban services—police, firefighting, and health departments.

Machine politics, however, was rarely neutral. Racial minorities and new immigrant groups, such as Italians and Poles, received only token jobs and nominal favors, if any. And bribes and kickbacks made machine projects and services costly to taxpayers. Cities could not ordinarily raise enough revenue for construction projects from taxes and fees, so they financed expansion with loans from the public in the form of municipal bonds, which caused public debts, and then taxes, to soar. And payoffs from gambling, prostitution, and illicit liquor traffic became important sources of machine revenue. But bosses were no guiltier of discrimination and self-interest than were business leaders who exploited workers, spoiled the environment, and manipulated government in pursuit of profits.

Civic Reform

Many middle- and upper-class Americans feared that immigrant-based political machines menaced democracy and wasted municipal finances. Anxious over the poverty and disorder that accompanied city growth, civic reformers organized to install more responsible leaders who would run government efficiently, like a business.

To implement business principles in government, civic reformers supported structural changes, such as city-manager and commission forms of government, which would place administration in the hands of experts rather than politicians, and nonpartisan citywide rather than neighborhood-based election of officials. Reformers believed they could cleanse city government of party politics and weaken bosses' power bases.

A few reform mayors also addressed social problems. Hazen S. Pingree of Detroit, Samuel "Golden Rule" Jones of Toledo, and Tom Johnson of Cleveland worked to provide jobs to poor people, reduce charges by streetcar and utility companies, and promote governmental responsibility for citizens' welfare. They also supported public ownership of gas, electric, and telephone companies, quasi-socialist reforms that alienated their business allies. But Pingree, Jones, and Johnson were exceptions. Civic reformers achieved some successes but rarely held office for long.

Social Reform

Social reformers—mostly young and middle class—also wanted to solve urban problems. Housing reformers pressed local governments for building codes ensuring safety in tenements. Educational reformers sought to use public schools to prepare immigrant children for citizenship by teaching them American values. Health reformers tried to improve medical care for those who could not afford it. And residents of settlement-houses, located in inner-city neighborhoods to bridge the gulf between classes offered vocational classes, lessons in English, and childcare, and they sponsored programs to improve nutrition and housing. Settlement-house workers such as **Jane Addams** and **Florence Kelley** of Chicago and Lillian Wald of New York broadened their scope to fight for school nurses, factory safety codes, and public playgrounds, they became reform leaders in cities and in the nation (see pages 543–544).

Jane Addams: Social worker, pioneer of the settlement house movement and founder of Chicago's Hull House, which provided education, training, and social activities for immigrants and the poor.

Florence Kelley: Settlement-house worker who later became the chief factory inspector for Illinois in 1893.

The City Beautiful Movement

Male reformers similarly worked to improve cities by organizing the City Beautiful movement. Inspired by the 1893 Columbian Exposition, a dazzling world's fair built in Chicago, architects and planners urged the construction of civic centers, parks, and boulevards that would make cities economically efficient and attractive. Projects were underway in Chicago, San Francisco, and Washington, D.C., in the early 1900s. Yet neither government nor private businesses could finance large-scale projects, and planners disagreed among themselves and with social reformers over whether beautification would solve urban problems.

Urban reformers wanted to save cities, but they often failed to realize cities' diverse populations and people's varying visions of reform. To civic reformers, appointing government workers on the basis of civil service exams rather than party loyalty meant progress, but to working-class men, civil service signified reduced employment opportunities. Moral reformers believed that restricting alcoholic beverage sales would prevent breadwinners from squandering wages, but immigrants saw it as interference. Planners saw new streets and buildings as modern necessities, but such structures often displaced the poor. Well-meaning humanitarians criticized immigrant mothers for the way they dressed, did housework, and raised children, without regard for their financial situation. Thus urban reform merged idealism with naiveté and insensitivity.

Family Life

What factors led to declining birth rates in the late nineteenth-century United States?

Urbanization and industrialization strained family life. New institutions—schools, social clubs, political organizations, unions—increasingly competed with the family to provide nurture and education. Clergy and journalists warned that the growing separation between home and work, rising divorce rates, entrance of women into the work force, and loss of parental control over children spelled peril for home and family. Yet the family remained a cushion in an uncertain world.

Family and Household Structures

Until recently, most American households (75 to 80 percent) consisted of nuclear families—usually a married couple, with or without children. Only a few households consisted of extended families—usually a married couple, their children, and one or more relatives. Not many people lived alone.

Several factors explain this pattern. Because immigrants tended to be young, the American population as a whole was young. In 1880, the median age was under twenty-one; by 1920, it was still only twenty-five. (Median age at present is thirty-five.) Moreover, in 1900, the death rate among people aged forty-five to sixty-four was double what it is today. Only 4 percent of the population was sixty-five or older, versus 12 percent today. Thus, few families could form extended three-generation households, and fewer children than today had living grandparents.

Declining Birth Rates

Most of Europe and North America experienced falling birth rates in the nineteenth century. In 1880, the birth rate was 40 live births per 1,000 people; by 1900, it dropped to 32; by 1920, to 28. Although fertility was higher among black, immigrant, and rural women, birth rates of all groups fell.

In part, this decline occurred because, as the United States became more urbanized, the economic value of children lessened. On farms, each child born represented an addition to the family labor force. In the wage-based urban economy, children could not contribute significantly to the family income for many years, and a new child represented a draw on family income. Second, infant mortality fell as diet and medical care improved, and families did not have to bear many children to ensure that some would survive.

Perhaps most importantly, as American society industrialized and urbanized, the idea of a child as an innocent being who needed shelter from society's corruptions spread, first among the middle class and gradually to the working class. A mother's care could be more effective if she had fewer children. That seems to have stimulated decisions to limit family size—either by abstaining from sex or using contraception. Families with six or eight children became rare; three or four became more usual. Birth-control technology—diaphragms and condoms—had been utilized for centuries, but in this era, new materials made devices more convenient and dependable.

Stages of Life

Before the late nineteenth century, stages of life were less distinct than they are today. Childhood, for instance, was regarded as a period during which young people prepared for adulthood by gradually assuming more responsibilities. Subdivisions of youth—toddlers, schoolchildren, teenagers, and the like—were not recognized. Because married couples had more children over a longer time span, parenthood occupied most of adult life. And because few people lived to advanced age, older people were not isolated from other age groups. By the late nineteenth century, however, decreasing birth rates shortened the period of parental responsibility, so more middle-aged couples experienced an "empty nest" when children grew up and left home. Longer life expectancy and a tendency by employers to force aged workers to retire separated the old from the young.

New patterns of childhood also emerged. To be sure, youngsters in working-class families still helped out—working in factories, scavenging streets for scraps of wood and coal, and peddling newspapers. But as states passed compulsory school attendance laws in the 1870s and 1880s, education occupied more of children's daily time than ever, filling nine months of the year until they were teenagers. Schools strengthened peer rather than family influence over behavior. Researchers such as G. Stanley Hall and Luther H. Gulick advocated that teachers and parents match education and play activities to children's changing developmental stages. "Child-saving" advocates asserted that adult-supervised playgrounds would protect children from dangerous activities.

The Unmarried Although marriage rates were high, large numbers of city dwellers were unmarried. In 1890, almost 42 percent of adult American men and 37 percent of women were single, almost twice as high as in 1960 but slightly lower than today. About half still lived with parents, but others inhabited boarding houses. Mostly young, these men and women constituted a separate subculture that supported institutions such as dance halls, saloons, cafés, and the Young Men's Christian Association (YMCA) and Young Women's Christian Association (YWCA).

Some unmarried people were part of the homosexual populations that thrived in large cities such as New York, San Francisco, and Boston. Although difficult to estimate numerically, gay men had their own subculture of clubs, restaurants, coffeehouses, theaters, and support networks. A number of same-sex couples, especially women, formed lasting marital-type relationships, sometimes called "Boston marriages." People in this subculture were categorized more by how they acted—men acting like women, women acting like men—than by who their sexual partners were. The term *homosexual* was not used. Men who dressed and acted like women were called "fairies." Gay women remained more hidden, and a lesbian subculture did not develop until the 1920s.

Boarding and Lodging In every city, boarding houses and lodging hotels were common, but families also took in boarders to occupy rooms vacated by grown children and for additional income. By 1900, as many as 50 percent of city residents, including Erich Weiss's family, had lived either as, or with, boarders at some point. Housing reformers charged that boarding and lodging caused overcrowding and loss of privacy. For people on the move, boarding was a transitional stage, providing a quasi-family environment until they set up their own households. Especially in communities where housing was expensive or scarce, newlyweds sometimes lived temporarily with one spouse's parents. Families also took in widowed parents or unmarried siblings.

Functions of Kinship At a time when welfare agencies were scarce, the family was the institution to which people turned when in need. Relatives often resided nearby and helped with childcare, meals, advice, and consolation. They also obtained jobs for relatives. According to one new arrival, "After two days my brother took me to the shop he was working in and his boss saw me and he gave me the job."

But kinship obligations were not always welcome. Immigrant families pressured last-born daughters to stay home to care for aging parents, a practice that stifled opportunities for education, marriage, and independence. Generational tensions also developed when immigrant parents and American-born children clashed over the abandonment of Old World ways or the amount of wages that employed children should contribute. Nevertheless, kinship helped people cope with stresses of urban-industrial society.

Thus, family life and functions were both changing and holding firm. New institutions were assuming tasks formerly performed by the family. Schools made education a community responsibility. Employment agencies, personnel offices, and labor unions took responsibility for employee recruitment and job security. Age-based peer groups exerted greater influence over people's values and activities. Migration seemed to be splitting families apart. Yet, kinship remained a dependable though not always appreciated institution.

Holiday Celebrations   Family togetherness became especially visible at holiday celebrations. Thanksgiving, Christmas, and Easter were special times for family reunion and child-centered activities. Birthdays, too, became increasingly festive, and served as a milestone for measuring what an individual had experienced and accomplished relative to others of the same age. In 1914, President Woodrow Wilson signed a proclamation designating the second Sunday in May as Mother's Day, capping a six-year campaign by schoolteacher Anna Jarvis, who believed grown children neglected their mothers. Ethnic and racial groups adapted national celebrations to their cultures, preparing special ethnic foods and engaging in special ceremonies.

The New Leisure and Mass Culture

What fueled the rise of commercial leisure?

On December 2, 1889, as workers paraded through Worcester, Massachusetts, seeking shorter working hours, carpenters hoisted a banner proclaiming "Eight Hours for Work, Eight Hours for Rest, Eight Hours for What We Will." That last phrase laid claim to a segment of daily life belonging to the individual. Increasingly, leisure activities filled this time.

Increase in Leisure Time   Mechanization and assembly-line production cut the average manufacturing workweek from sixty-six hours in 1860 to sixty in 1890 and forty-seven in 1920. This meant shorter workdays and freer weekends. White-collar employees spent eight to ten hours a day on the job and often worked only half a day or not at all on weekends. Laborers in steel mills and sweatshops endured twelve- or fourteen-hour shifts with little leisure time. As the economy shifted from production to consumption, more Americans engaged in recreation, and a substantial segment of the economy provided for—and profited from—leisure.

Amusement became a commercial activity, as home entertainment expanded. Mass-produced pianos and sheet music for middle-class families made singing of popular songs a common form of home entertainment. The vanguard of new leisure pursuits, however, was sports. Formerly a fashionable indulgence of elites, organized sports became a favored pastime of all classes.

Baseball

The most popular sport was baseball. Derived from older bat, ball, and base-circling games, in 1845 the Knickerbocker Club of New York standardized the rules of play. By 1860, at least fifty baseball clubs existed, and youths played informal games on city lots and fields nationwide. The National League of Professional Baseball Clubs, founded in 1876, gave the sport a businesslike structure. But as early as 1867, a "color line" excluded black players from professional teams. Still, by the 1880s, professional baseball was big business. In 1903, the National League and competing American League (formed in 1901) began a World Series between their championship teams. The Boston Red Sox beat the Pittsburgh Pirates in that first series.

Croquet and Cycling

Baseball appealed mostly to men. But croquet, also popular, attracted both sexes. Middle- and upper-class people held croquet parties and night contests. Consequently, croquet increased opportunities for social contact between the sexes.

Meanwhile, cycling achieved popularity rivaling baseball, especially after 1885, when the cumbersome velocipede, with its huge front wheel and tall seat, gave way to safety bicycles with pneumatic tires and identical-size wheels. By 1900, Americans owned 10 million bicycles, and clubs petitioned state governments to build more paved roads. African American cyclists were allowed to compete professionally, and one rider, Major Taylor, achieved success in Europe and the United States between 1892 and 1910. Moreover, the bicycle freed women from the constraints of Victorian fashions. To ride the dropped-frame female models, women had to wear divided skirts and simple undergarments. As the 1900 census declared, "Few articles…have created so great a revolution in social conditions as the bicycle."

Football

American football, as an intercollegiate competition, attracted mostly spectators wealthy enough to have access to higher education. By the late nineteenth century, however, the game appealed to a broader audience. The 1893 Princeton-Yale game drew fifty thousand spectators, and informal games were played throughout the country. Soon, however, football became a national scandal because of its violence and use of "tramp athletes," nonstudents hired to help teams win. Critics accused football of mirroring undesirable features of American society. An editor of *The Nation* charged in 1890 that "the lack of moral scruple which pervades the struggles of the business world meets with temptations equally irresistible in the miniature contests of the football field."

The scandals climaxed in 1905, when 18 players died from game-related injuries and 159 were seriously injured. President Theodore Roosevelt, an advocate of athletics, convened a White House conference to discuss ways to eliminate brutality. The gathering founded the Intercollegiate Athletic Association (renamed the National College Athletic Association—NCAA—in 1910) to police college sports. In 1906, the association altered the game to make it less violent and more open.

As more women enrolled in college, they participated in such sports as rowing, track, and swimming. Invented in 1891 as a winter sport for men, basketball—soon women's most popular sport—received women's rules (which limited dribbling and running, and encouraged passing) from Senda Berenson of Smith College.

Links to the World

Japanese Baseball

Baseball, the "national pastime," was one new leisure-time pursuit that Americans took into different parts of the world. The Shanghai Base Ball Club was founded by Americans in China in 1863, but was denounced by the Imperial Court as spiritually corrupting. However, when Horace Wilson, an American teacher, taught baseball rules to his Japanese students around 1870, the game received an enthusiastic reception as a reinforcement of traditional virtues and became a part of Japanese culture.

During the 1870s, scores of Japanese high schools and colleges sponsored organized baseball, and in 1883 Hiroshi Hiraoka, a railroad engineer educated in Boston, founded the first official local team, the Shimbashi Athletic Club Athletics.

Before baseball, the Japanese had no team sports or recreational athletics. Once they learned about baseball, they found the idea of a team sport fit their culture well. But for them, baseball was serious business, involving often brutal training. Practices at Ichiko, one of Japan's two great high school baseball teams in the late nineteenth century, were dubbed "Bloody Urine" because many players passed blood after a day of drilling. There was a spiritual quality as well, linked to Buddhist values. According to one Japanese coach, "Student baseball must be the baseball of self-discipline, or trying to attain the truth, just as in Zen Buddhism." This attitude prompted the Japanese to consider baseball a new method for pursuing the spirit of Bushido, the way of the samurai.

When Americans played baseball in Japan, the Japanese admired their talent but found them lacking discipline and respect. Americans insulted the Japanese by refusing to remove their hats and bow when they stepped up to bat. An international dispute occurred in Tokyo in 1891 when an American professor, late for a game, climbed over a sacred fence and was attacked by Japanese fans. The American embassy lodged a formal complaint. Americans assumed their game would encourage Japanese to become like westerners, but the Japanese transformed baseball into a uniquely Japanese expression of team spirit, discipline, and nationalism.

Replete with bats, gloves, and uniforms, this Japanese baseball team of 1890 very much resembles its American counterpart of that era. The Japanese adopted baseball soon after Americans became involved in their country but also added their cultural qualities to the game.

Japanese Baseball Hall of Fame

Show Business

Three branches of American show business—popular drama, musical comedy, and vaudeville—matured and became popular commercial entertainment. Theatrical performances offered audiences escape into melodrama, adventure, and comedy. For urban people unfamiliar with the frontier, plays made the mythical Wild West and Old South come alive through stories of Davy Crockett, Buffalo Bill, and the Civil War. Virtue and honor always triumphed in melodramas such as *Uncle Tom's Cabin* and *The Old Homestead,* reinforcing faith that, in an uncertain world, goodness would prevail.

George M. Cohan: Singer, dancer, and songwriter who drew on patriotic and traditional values in songs.

The American musical derived from Europe's lavishly costumed operettas. **George M. Cohan**, a singer, dancer, and songwriter born into an Irish family of entertainers, became master of American musical comedy in the early twentieth century. Drawing on patriotism and traditional values in songs such as "Yankee Doodle Boy" and "You're a Grand Old Flag," Cohan boosted morale during the First World War. Initially, American comic operas imitated European musicals, but by the early 1900s composers such as Victor Herbert were writing for American audiences.

Probably the most popular mass entertainment in early-twentieth-century America, vaudeville offered something for everyone. Shows included jugglers, magicians, acrobats, comedians, singers, dancers, and specialty acts like Houdini's escapes. Around 1900, the number of vaudeville theaters and troupes skyrocketed, and operators such as Tony Pastor and the partnership of Benjamin Keith and Edward Albee consolidated theaters and acts under their management. Producer Florenz Ziegfeld brilliantly packaged stylish shows—the Ziegfeld Follies—and gave the nation a new model of femininity, the Ziegfeld Girl, whose graceful dancing and alluring costumes suggested a haunting sensuality.

Link to video and audio of Eva Tanguay singing her theme song "I Don't Care."

Opportunities for Women and Minorities

Show business provided social mobility to female, African American, and immigrant performers, but also encouraged stereotyping and exploitation. Comic opera diva Lillian Russell, vaudeville singer-comedienne Fanny Brice, and burlesque queen Eva Tanguay attracted loyal fans and handsome fees. In contrast to the demure Victorian female, they conveyed pluck and independence. There was something shocking and confident about Eva Tanguay singing, "It's All Been Done Before but Not the Way I Do It." But lesser female performers and showgirls (called "soubrettes") were often exploited by male promoters and theater owners who wanted to profit by titillating the public with scantily clad women.

minstrel shows: Early stage shows in which white men wore blackface makeup and played to the prejudices of white audiences by offering demeaning and caricatured portrayals of African Americans in songs, dances, and skits.

Before the 1890s, the chief form of commercial entertainment employing African Americans was the **minstrel show**, but vaudeville opened new opportunities. Pandering to prejudices of white audiences, composers ridiculed blacks, and black performers were forced to portray demeaning characters. In songs such as "He's Just a Little Nigger, But He's Mine All Mine," blacks were degraded on stage as they were in society. Burt Williams, an educated black comedian and dancer, achieved success by wearing blackface makeup and playing stereotypical roles of a smiling fool and dandy, but the humiliation tormented him.

Like Houdini, many performers were immigrants, and their acts reflected their experiences and daily difficulties. Vaudeville utilized ethnic humor and exaggerated dialects. Skits and songs were fast-paced, replicating the tempo of factories, offices, and the streets. Performances reinforced ethnic stereotypes, but such distortions were more sympathetic than those directed at blacks. A typical scene involving Italians, for example, highlighted a character's uncertain grasp of English, which caused him to confuse *diploma* with *the plumber* and *pallbearer* with *polar bear.* Such scenes allowed audiences to laugh with, rather than at, foibles of the human condition.

Movies

Shortly after 1900, live entertainment yielded to the more accessible motion pictures. Perfected by Thomas Edison in the 1880s, movies began as slot-machine peepshows in arcades and billiard parlors. Eventually, images were projected onto a screen for large audiences. Producers, many of them from Jewish immigrant backgrounds, discovered that a film could tell a story in exciting ways. Using themes of patriotism and working-class experience, early filmmakers helped shift American culture away from its straitlaced Victorian values to a cosmopolitan outlook.

Movies presented controversial social messages as well as innovative technology and styles of expression. *Birth of a Nation* (1915), by director D. W. Griffith, was a stunning but viciously racist epic film about the Civil War and Reconstruction that fanned racial prejudice by depicting African Americans as threats to white moral values. The National Association for the Advancement of Colored People (NAACP), formed in 1909, led organized protests against it. But the film's groundbreaking techniques—close-ups, fade-outs, and battle scenes—heightened its drama.

Technology and entrepreneurship also made news a mass consumer product. Using high-speed printing presses, cheaply produced paper, and profits from growing advertisement revenues, shrewd publishers created an in-demand medium. Increased leisure time seemed to nurture a fascination with the sensational, and from the 1880s onward popular urban newspapers increasingly whetted that appetite.

Yellow Journalism

Joseph Pulitzer, a Hungarian immigrant who bought the *New York World* in 1883, made news a mass commodity. Pulitzer filled the *World* with stories of disasters, crimes, and scandals and featured screaming headlines, set in large, bold type. Pulitzer's journalists sought out news and created it. Reporter Nellie Bly (real name, Elizabeth Cochrane) faked her way into a mental asylum and wrote a brazen exposé of the sordid conditions she found. Other reporters staged stunts and wrote heart-rending human-interest stories. Pulitzer also popularized comics, and the yellow ink in which they were printed gave rise to the term *yellow journalism* as a synonym for sensationalism.

In one year, the *World*'s circulation increased from 20,000 to 100,000, and by the late 1890s it reached 1 million. Other publishers, such as William Randolph Hearst, who bought the *New York Journal* in 1895 and started a newspaper empire, adopted Pulitzer's techniques. Pulitzer, Hearst, and their rivals boosted circulation by featuring sports and women's news. Newspapers previously reported sporting events, but yellow-journalism papers gave such stories greater prominence with separate, expanded sports pages. For women, newspapers added special sections devoted to household tips, fashion, etiquette, and club news.

Other Mass-Market Publications

By the early twentieth century, mass-circulation magazines overshadowed the expensive elitist journals of earlier eras. Publications such as *McClure's, Saturday Evening Post,* and *Ladies' Home Journal* offered human-interest stories, muckraking exposés (see page 542), fiction, photographs, colorful covers, and eye-catching ads. Meanwhile, the number of published books more than quadrupled between 1880 and 1917, reflecting the growing literacy. Between 1870 and 1920, the proportion of Americans over age ten who could not read fell from 20 percent to 6 percent.

Other forms of communication also expanded. In 1891, there was less than 1 telephone for every 100 people in the United States; by 1901, the number reached 2.1, and by 1921, it swelled to 12.6. In 1900, Americans used 4 billion postage stamps; in 1922, they bought 14.3 billion. More than ever before, people in different parts of the country knew about and discussed the same news event. America was becoming a mass society where the same products, technology, and information dominated everyday life.

Anthony Comstock

The new leisure and amusements did not go unopposed. Most prominent among reactionary moralists was **Anthony Comstock**, who made a career of efforts to censor sexually explicit and suggestive literature and entertainment. In 1873, Comstock created the Society for the Supression of Vice and convinced Congress to outlaw the distribution of "lewd and lascivious" material. He secured appointment as a postal inspector and worked to ban marriage manuals and birth control literature from the mails. Between the 1870s and his death in 1915, Comstock constantly campaigned against what he considered indecent performances, especially in New York City. His targets also included paintings of nude women, an exhibition of physical culture, and a play by noted British author George Bernard Shaw that had prostitution among its themes.

But crusaders such as Comstock could not alter cultural change. Mass culture represented democracy because influences flowed upward from the experiences and desires of ordinary people as much as, if not more than, from the rich. The popularity of sports, the themes in movies and on stage, and the content of publications reveal that savvy entrepreneurs understood the need to cater to the new consumers. And producers helped people adapt by providing information about new social and economic conditions and by making some of the disruptive factors more tolerable through drama and humor. The major exception was the portrayal and treatment of African Americans with an unrelenting viciousness.

To some extent, cities' new amusements and media had a homogenizing influence, allowing different social groups to share common experiences. Yet different consumer groups adapted parks, ball fields, vaudeville shows, movies, and feature sections of newspapers to their own cultural needs. To the dismay of reformers who hoped that public recreation and holidays would assimilate newcomers, immigrants used parks for ethnic gatherings and converted picnics and Fourth of July celebrations into occasions for boisterous drinking and sometimes violent behavior. Young working-class men and women resisted parents' and moralists' warnings, and frequented urban dance halls, where they explored forms of courtship and sexual behavior. Thus, leisure—like work and politics—was shaped by the pluralistic forces that thrived in urban life.

Anthony Comstock: Leader of the moral purity crusade against what he saw as vice and corruption; known for his efforts to censor sexually explicit material, including, as postal inspector, seeking to ban birth control literature from the mail.

Children and Mass-Produced Toys

For children, the new form of mass-produced amusement came from commercial toys. Many of the toys and games that remain popular today were created in this era. In the 1880s, George S. Parker, founder of what became Parker Brothers game company, began fashioning board games with entertaining themes to replace previous games with mostly moral lessons.

Many new mass-marketed toys reinforced gender roles. Tinkertoys, erector sets, and model trains anticipated boys' manhood by introducing them to building and mechanics. Baby dolls with more realistic features encouraged girls to practice motherhood tasks of feeding and caring, while paper dolls introduced them to fashion and consumerism. Some dolls, such as Raggedy Ann and Andy and the Campbell Soup Kids, were derived from stories and product advertising.

Most toys reflected a prevailing belief that childhood was a special time in which children should engage in what one educator called "joyous play." But these notions also inspired efforts to provide kids with toys aiding intellectual development, too. Milton Bradley's early games often had educational themes, and Parker Brothers marketed four games on the Spanish-American War.

In the 1920s, 1930s, and 1940s, the toy industry began an interrelationship with mass media such as comics (Katzenjammer Kids and Superman toys), movies (Shirley Temple dolls and Buck Rogers ray guns), and Disney items. In the 1950s, television intensified the links between toys and programming and created an explosion of toy advertising. In the 1970s, the modern electronic toy industry arose, with games such as Pong and Pac-Man. These and other items of children's amusement are legacies of the rise of leisure and child-centeredness from more than a century ago.

Summary

People and technology made the late nineteenth and early twentieth centuries the "age of the city." Flocking cityward, migrants already in America and those from foreign parts remade themselves, like Houdini, and remade the urban environment, too. They brought cultures that in turn enriched American culture. They found escape in new forms of mass leisure and entertainment.

American cities experienced an "unheralded triumph" by the early 1900s. Amid corruption and political conflict, engineers modernized sewer, water, and lighting services, and urban governments made cities safer by expanding professional police and fire departments. When native inventiveness met the traditions of European, African, and Asian cultures, a new society emerged. The jumble of social classes, ethnic and racial groups, and political and professional organizations sometimes lived in harmony, sometimes not.

Optimists envisioned the American nation as a melting pot, where various nationalities would fuse into a unified people. Instead, many ethnic groups proved unmeltable, and racial minorities got burned on the bottom of the pot. Instead, the United States became a pluralistic society in which cultural influences moved in both directions: imposed from above by people with power and influence and adopted from below through the traditions brought to cities by disparate peoples.

By 1920, immigrants and their offspring outnumbered the native-born in many cities, and the national economy depended on these new workers and consumers. Migrants and immigrants transformed the United States into an urban nation. They gave American culture its varied texture and, like Harry Houdini, helped change the course of entertainment and consumerism. Together, they laid the foundations for the liberalism that would characterize American politics in the twentieth century.

Chapter Review

Growth of the Modern City

What fueled urban growth in the late nineteenth century?

Cities grew two ways: by annexing areas that bordered them, as New York City did when it merged with Brooklyn, Staten Island, and parts of Queens, doubling its population to 3 million. Cities also expanded via inmigration from rural areas and immigration from abroad. Within the United States, low crop prices and heavy debts pushed some white farmers from the country to the city; in other cases, young men sought to escape economic hardship for the excitement of cities while young women left unhappy homes for greater independence. Similarly, African Americans headed to cities for better jobs and to escape crop liens and racial violence. Population pressures, land redistribution, industrialization, and religious persecution pushed many immigrants to leave Europe, Asia, Canada, and Latin America for the United States.

Urban Neighborhoods

How did immigrants adapt to their new lives in U.S. cities?

While most immigrants sought to retain old world traditions, once in the United States, those former folkways were changed by, and also helped change, American cities. Traditions held on longer in neighborhoods with immigrants from the same region or district. Immigrants recreated the mutual aid societies, newspapers, and churches that existed in their homelands. While immigrants tried to hold fast to their native languages, English—which children learned in schools—soon dominated ethnic neighborhoods. Foreigners adapted their traditional garments to American fabrics, and their music evolved as well to include American influences or tales of

their adjustment to life here. Catholics and Jews sought to merge their faiths with their new surroundings by liberalizing or eliminating some old world rituals.

Living Conditions in the Inner City

What made cities seem particularly dangerous?

Overcrowding and housing shortages in inner cities, along with poverty and crime, led to fears that cities were dangerous places filled with violence, muggings, gang fights, and even murder. While murder rates did increase fourfold from 1881 to 1898, crime in cities was not greater than that in backwoods mining camps or southern plantations. The high concentrations of people, particularly those of different classes and ethnic/racial backgrounds, mingling in cities simply made urban crime more visible, which in turn made cities seem scarier from the outside looking in.

Managing the City

What facilitated the rise of political machines in cities?

Political machines emerged in typically working class and immigrant neighborhoods to provide relief, security, and services to voters in exchange for votes, money, influence, and prestige. Each machine had a leader, or boss, who helped his constituents obtain jobs, clothing, or legal assistance. Bosses also attended weddings and wakes and had enormous personal appeal with their constituencies. The power they exerted over local government meant machines could control which firms or individuals got public contracts and city jobs and insist that those receiving these awards repay the machine with a share of their profits or salaries. Machine-led governments did build sewer systems, schools, bridges, and transportation lines and expand police and fire, but the bribes and kickbacks they commanded made their projects expensive to taxpayers.

Family Life

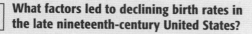

What factors led to declining birth rates in the late nineteenth-century United States?

On farms, children were seen as part of the family's much-needed labor. But as more people left farms for city life, children's economic value lessened. Instead of being need to help with farm work, in cities, they were idle and a drain on family's income. Improvements in health, medicine, and diet lowered the infant mortality rate, which meant families no longer needed to bear more children in the hopes that some might survive. And as the United States became increasingly urbanized, the notion of children needing protection from the city's harsh realities meant that mothers could be more effective caregivers if they had fewer children to raise. Meanwhile, new technology led to better materials for condoms, diaphragms, and other birth control devices, which made them more convenient and reliable.

The New Leisure and Mass Culture

What fueled the rise of commercial leisure?

Mechanization and new, more efficient means of production, along with labor activism, led to shorter work weeks and hours—which, in turn, gave workers more time to use as they saw fit. New mass entertainment rose to fill this need, and included baseball and football leagues, bicycling, and other outdoor activities, as well as theater, vaudeville, and later film. Vaudeville was among the most popular entertainment because its shows tried to appeal to the broadest audiences with jugglers, magicians, comedians, singers, and dancers. Vaudeville, like other forms of show business, also provided new work opportunities for blacks, immigrants, and women, even while reinforcing negative stereotypes of ethnic and racial performers.

Suggestions for Further Reading

John Bodnar, *The Transplanted: A History of Immigrants in Urban America* (1985)

Howard P. Chudacoff and Judith E. Smith, *The Evolution of American Urban Society*, 6th ed. (2005)

John D'Emilio and Estelle Freedman, *Intimate Matters: A History of Sexuality in America* (1988)

Nancy Foner and George M. Frederickson, eds., *Not Just Black and White: Historical and Contemporary Perspectives on Immigration, Race, and Ethnicity in the United States* (2004)

Kenneth T. Jackson, *The Crabgrass Frontier: The Suburbanization of the United States* (1985)

Matthew Frye Jacobson, *Whiteness of a Different Color: European Immigrants and the Alchemy of Race* (1998)

Erika Lee, *At America's Gates: Chinese Immigration During the Exclusion Era, 1882–1943* (2003)

Martin V. Melosi, *The Sanitary City: Urban Infrastructure in America from Colonial Times to the Present* (2000)

Robyn Muncy, *Creating a Female Dominion in American Reform, 1890–1935* (1991)

Kathy Peiss, *Cheap Amusements: Working Women and Leisure in Turn-of-the-Century New York* (1986)

 Go to the CourseMate website for primary source links, study tools, and review materials for this chapter. www.cengagebrain.com

Gilded Age Politics

20

1877–1900

Growing up in rural Wisconsin with no toys except those she made herself, young Frances Willard climbed fences, chopped trees, and once tried to ride a cow. When she turned sixteen in 1855, Frances suddenly had to act and dress like a woman. As she later wrote, "the hampering long skirts were brought, with their hampering corset and high heels... and "[f]rom that time on I always realized and was obedient to the limitations thus imposed." That included living in a supposedly democratic society that refused women the right to vote.

Willard never accepted those limitations. Instead, she advocated combining women's traditional roles with improving society. From 1879 until her death in 1898, Willard served as president of the Women's Christian Temperance Union (WCTU), the nation's largest female organization, making thousands of speeches against alcohol and for women's suffrage.

Not an extremist, Willard believed that giving women voting rights would enable them to use their domestic talents to improve society, especially by removing harmful alcohol. After her sixteenth birthday, she saw the Civil War and its aftermath plus the rise of large corporations big business between 1877 and 1900 influence politics and government. It was an era characterized by greed, special interest, and political exclusion.

The obsession with riches seemed so widespread that, when Mark Twain and Charles Dudley Warner satirized America as a land of money grubbers in their novel *The Gilded Age* (1874), the name stuck and is still used by historians to describe the era.

But economic and political accomplishments occurred at national and state levels. Despite partisan and regional rivalries, Congress achieved legislative landmarks in railroad regulation, tariff and currency reform, civil service, and other important issues. Meanwhile, the judiciary countered reform by supporting big business and defending property rights against state and federal regulation. Exclusion prevented most Americans—including women, southern blacks, Indians, uneducated whites, and unnaturalized immigrants—from voting. This concerned Willard

Chapter Outline

The Nature of Party Politics
Cultural-Political Alignments | Party Factions

Issues of Legislation
Civil Service Reform | Railroad Regulation | Tariff Policy | Monetary Policy | Legislative Accomplishments

Tentative Presidents
Hayes, Garfield and Arthur | Cleveland and Harrison

VISUALIZING THE PAST *The Spectacle of Gilded Age Politics*

Discrimination, Disfranchisement, and Responses
Violence Against African Americans | Disfranchisement | Legal Segregation | African American Activism | Women Suffrage

Agrarian Unrest and Populism
Sharecropping and Tenant Farming in the South | Hardship in the Midwest and West | Grange Movement | The White Hats | Farmers' Alliances | Problems in Achieving Alliance Unity | Rise of Populism | Populist Spokespeople

LINKS TO THE WORLD *Russian Populism*

The Depression and Protests of the 1890s
Continuing Currency Problems | Consequences of Depression | Depression-Era Protests | Socialists | Eugene V. Debs | Coxey's Army

The Silver Crusade and the Election of 1896
Free Silver | Nomination of McKinley | William Jennings Bryan | Election Results | The McKinley Presidency

SUMMARY

LEGACY FOR A PEOPLE AND A NATION *Interpreting a Fairy Tale* and many others, though they were not always willing to create opportunity for all, especially people of color.

Until the 1890s, a stable party system and sectional balance held the political equilibrium. Then, in the 1890s, rural discontent rumbled through the West and South, and a deep economic depression bared the industrial system's flaws. The 1896 presidential campaign stirred Americans, as a new party arose, old parties split, and sectional unity dissolved. The nation emerged from the turbulent 1890s with new economic and political configurations.

As you read this chapter, keep the following questions in mind:

* What were the functions of government in the Gilded Age, and how did they change?

* How did policies of exclusion and discrimination make their mark on the political culture of the age?

* How did the economic climate give rise to the Populist movement?

The Nature of Party Politics

Public interest in elections reached an all-time high between 1870 and 1896. Around 80 percent of eligible voters (white and black males in the North, somewhat lower rates among mostly white males in the South) consistently voted. Featuring parades, picnics, and speeches, politics served as recreation, more popular than baseball or circuses.

> How did factional disputes complicate party politics in the Gilded Age?

Cultural-Political Alignments

In the Gilded Age, party loyalty was fierce. With some exceptions, people who opposed government interference in personal liberty identified with the Democratic Party; those who believed government could be an agent of reform identified with the Republicans. Democrats included foreign-born and second-generation Catholics and Jews. Republicans consisted mostly of native-born Protestants, who believed in the power of legislation for social improvement.

There was also a geographic dimension to these divisions. Northern Republicans capitalized on bitter memories of the Civil War by "waving the bloody shirt" at Democrats. Northern Democrats focused more on urban and economic issues, but southern Democratic candidates waved a different bloody shirt, calling Republicans traitors to white supremacy and states' rights.

Partisan politicians battled over how much government should control people's lives. The most contentious issues were leisure time and celebration of Sunday, the Lord's day. Protestant Republicans tried to keep the Sabbath holy through legislation that closed bars, stores, and commercial amusements on Sundays. Immigrant Democrats, accustomed to feasting after church, fought saloon closings and other restrictions.

Allegiances to national parties were so evenly divided that no faction gained control for long. Between 1877 and 1897, Republicans held the presidency for three terms, Democrats for two. Rarely did one party control the presidency and Congress simultaneously. From 1876 through 1892, presidential elections were close. The outcome often hinged on a few populous northern states—Connecticut, New York, New

Link to a cartoon that shows the political fallout from the Civil War and Reconstruction.

Chronology

1873	Congress ends coinage of silver dollars		"Mississippi Plan" uses poll taxes and literacy tests to prevent African Americans from voting
1873–78	Economic hard times hit		National Woman Suffrage Association formed
1877	Georgia passes poll tax, disfranchising most African Americans	1890s	Jim Crow laws, discriminating against African Americans in legal treatment and public accommodations, passed by southern states
1878	Bland-Allison Act requires Treasury to buy between $2 and $4 million in silver each month	1892	Populist convention in Omaha draws up reform platform
1881	Garfield assassinated; Arthur assumes presidency	1893	Sherman Silver Purchase Act repealed
1883	Pendleton Civil Service Act introduces merit system	1893–97	Major economic depression hits United States
	Supreme Court strikes down 1883 Civil Rights Act	1894	Wilson-Gorman Tariff passes
1886	*Wabash* case declares that only Congress can limit interstate commerce rates		Coxey's Army marches on Washington, D.C.
1887	Farmers' Alliances form	1896	*Plessy v. Ferguson* establishes separate-but-equal doctrine
	Interstate Commerce Commission begins regulating rates and practices of interstate shipping	1898	Louisiana implements "grandfather clause," restricting voting by African Americans
1890	McKinley Tariff raises tariff rates	1899	*Cummings v. County Board of Education* applies separate-but-equal doctrine to schools
	Sherman Silver Purchase Act commits Treasury to buying 4.5 million ounces of silver each month		

Jersey, Ohio, Indiana, and Illinois. Both parties tried to gain advantages by nominating presidential candidates from these states (and by committing vote fraud).

Party Factions   Factional quarrels split both the Republican and the Democratic Parties. Among Republicans, New York's senator Roscoe Conkling led one faction, known as "Stalwarts" and worked the spoils system to win government jobs for supporters. Stalwarts' rivals were the "Half Breeds," led by Maine Congressman James G. Blaine, who also blatantly pursued influence. On the sidelines stood more idealistic Republicans, or "**Mugwumps**" (supposedly an Indian term meaning "mug on one side of the fence, wump on the other"). Mugwumps, such as Missouri Senator Carl Schurz, believed that only righteous, educated men should govern. Republican allies of big business supported gold as the standard for currency, whereas those from mining regions favored silver. Democrats subdivided into white-supremacist southerners, working-class, immigrant-stock supporters of urban political machines, business-oriented advocates of low tariffs and the gold standard, and debtor-oriented advocates of free silver.

Mugwumps: Term used for idealistic Republican reformers.

In each state, one party usually dominated, and often the state "boss" was a senator who doled out jobs and parlayed his clout into national influence. (Until ratification of the Seventeenth Amendment to the Constitution in 1913, state legislatures elected U.S. senators.) These men exercised their power brazenly.

Issues of Legislation

What was at issue in the debate over the gold standard versus free silver?

In Congress, sectional controversies, patronage abuses, railroad regulation, tariffs, and currency provoked heated debates and partisanship. From the end of the Civil War into the 1880s, Congress debated soldiers' pensions. The **Grand Army of the Republic**, an organization of 400,000 Union Army veterans, allied with the Republican Party and cajoled Congress into providing generous pensions for former Union soldiers and their widows. Many were deserved: Union troops were poorly paid. The Union Army spent $2 billion fighting the Civil War, but veterans' pensions cost $8 billion, one of the largest welfare commitments the federal government ever made. By 1900, soldiers' pensions accounted for roughly 40 percent of the federal budget. Confederate veterans were excluded, though some southern states funded small pensions and built old-age homes for ex-soldiers.

Grand Army of the Republic (GAR): A social and political lobbying organization of northern Civil War veterans that convinced Congress to provide $8 billion in pensions for former Union soldiers and widows.

Civil Service Reform

Few politicians dared oppose pensions, but some attempted to dismantle the spoils system, the practice of awarding government jobs to the party faithful regardless of their qualifications. During the Civil War, the federal government expanded considerably, and the spoils system increasingly flourished. As the postal service, diplomatic corps, and other government agencies grew, the number of federal jobs tripled from 53,000 in 1865 to 166,000 in 1891. Elected officials scrambled to control these jobs to benefit their party. In return for short hours and high pay, appointees to federal positions pledged votes and part of their earnings to patrons.

Shocked by corruption, especially after the scandals in the Grant administration, some reformers began advocating appointments based on merit—civil service. Support for change accelerated in 1881 with formation of the National Civil Service Reform League. That year, the assassination of President James Garfield by a distraught job seeker hastened the drive for reform. The **Pendleton Civil Service Act**, passed by Congress in 1882, created the Civil Service Commission to oversee competitive examinations for government positions. The act gave the commission jurisdiction over 10 percent of federal jobs, though the president could expand the list. Because the Constitution barred Congress from interfering in state affairs, civil service at state and local levels developed more haphazardly.

Pendleton Civil Service Act: Attempt to end the spoils system; created the Civil Service Commission to oversee competitive exams for government jobs.

Economic policy was the Gilded Age's main issue. Railroads particularly provoked controversy. In their quest for customers, railroads launched rate wars and angered shippers with inconsistent freight charges. On noncompetitive routes, railroads often boosted charges to compensate for unprofitably low rates on competitive routes. Railroads also played favorites, reducing rates to large shippers and offering free passes to preferred customers and politicians.

Railroad Regulation

Such favoritism stirred farmers, small merchants, and reform politicians to demand rate regulation. By 1880, fourteen states established commissions to limit freight and storage charges of state-chartered lines. Railroads fought back, arguing that the Fourteenth Amendment to the Constitution guaranteed them freedom to acquire and use property without government restraint. But in 1877, in *Munn v. Illinois,* the Supreme Court upheld state regulation, declaring that grain warehouses owned by railroads acted in the public interest and therefore must submit to regulation for "the common good."

Only the federal government could regulate interstate lines, as affirmed by the Supreme Court in the *Wabash* case of 1886. To expand federal regulation, Congress passed the **Interstate Commerce Act** in 1887, which prohibited rebates and rate discrimination, and created the Interstate Commerce Commission (ICC), the nation's first regulatory agency, to investigate railroad rate-making and issue cease-and-desist orders against illegal practices. The legislation's weak enforcement provisions, however, left railroads room for evasion, and judges minimized ICC powers. In the *Maximum Freight Rate* case (1897), the Supreme Court ruled that the ICC lacked power to set rates, and in the *Alabama Midlands* case (1897), it overturned prohibitions against long-haul/short-haul discrimination. Still, regulation, though weakened, remained in force.

Tariff Policy

From 1789 onward, Congress created tariffs, which levied duties (taxes) on imported goods, to protect American products from European competition. But tariffs quickly became a tool special interests used tp enhance profits. By the 1880s, these interests succeeded in obtaining tariffs on more than four thousand items. A few economists and farmers argued for free trade, but most politicians insisted that tariffs were necessary to support industry and preserve jobs.

The Republican Party put protective tariffs at the core of its agenda. Democrats complained that tariffs made prices artificially high by keeping out less expensive foreign goods, thereby benefiting domestic manufacturers while hurting consumers and farmers whose crops were not protected.

During the Gilded Age, revenues from tariffs and other levies created a federal budget surplus. Most Republicans liked that government was earning more than it spent and hoped to keep the surplus as a reserve or use it for projects that would aid commerce. Democrats acknowledged a need for protection of some manufactured goods and raw materials, but they favored lower tariff duties to encourage foreign trade and reduce the Treasury surplus.

Manufacturers and their congressional allies controlled tariff policy. The McKinley Tariff of 1890 boosted already-high rates by 4 percent. When House Democrats passed a bill to trim tariffs in 1894, Senate Republicans, aided by southern Democrats, added six hundred amendments restoring most cuts (the Wilson-Gorman Tariff). In 1897, the Dingley Tariff raised rates further. Attacks on duties made tariffs a symbol of privileged business in the public mind.

Monetary Policy

When increased industrial and agricultural production caused prices to fall after the Civil War, debtors (have-nots) and creditors (haves) had opposing reactions. Farmers suffered because crop prices dropped and because demand for a limited supply of available money raised interest rates on loans, making it costly to borrow funds to pay mortgages and debts. They favored coinage of silver to increase the amount of currency in circulation which in turn would reduce interest rates. Small businessmen, also in need of loans, agreed. Large businesses and bankers favored a stable, limited money supply backed only by gold, fearing currency fluctuations that would threaten investors' confidence in the U.S. economy. The money debate also reflected sectional cleavages: western silver-mining areas and agricultural regions of the South and West against the industrial Northeast.

Before the 1870s, the federal government bought gold and silver to back its paper money (dollars), setting a ratio that made a gold dollar worth sixteen times more than a silver dollar. Discovery and mining of gold in the West, however, increased gold supplies and lowered market prices relative to silver. Consequently, silver dollars disappeared from circulation as owners hoarded them. In 1873, Congress officially halted silver coinage. The United States unofficially adopted the gold standard.

Within a few years, new mines in the West began flooding the market with silver, and its price dropped. Gold now became relatively less plentiful, worth more than sixteen times the value of silver. Silver producers wanted the government to resume buying silver at the old sixteen-to-one ratio. Debtors, hurt by the economic hard times of 1873–1878, saw silver as a means of expanding the currency supply, so they pressed for resumption of silver coinage at the old sixteen-to-one ratio.

With parties split into silver and gold factions, Congress tried to compromise. The Bland-Allison Act (1878) authorized the Treasury to buy $2 million to $4 million worth of silver monthly, and the **Sherman Silver Purchase Act** (1890) increased the government's silver purchase by specifying weight (4.5 million ounces) rather than dollars. Neither measure satisfied various interest groups. Creditors wanted the government to stop buying silver, whereas for debtors, the legislation failed to expand the money supply satisfactorily. The issue would intensify during the 1896 presidential election (see pages 534–535).

Sherman Silver Purchase Act: Law that instructed the treasury to buy, at current market prices, 4.5 million ounces of silver monthly.

Legislative Accomplishments

Members of Congress addressed thorny issues under difficult conditions. They earned small salaries yet had to maintain two residences: in their home district and in Washington. Most Congressmen had no private offices, worked long hours, wrote their own speeches, and paid for staff themselves. Yet, they managed to pass significant legislation.

Tentative Presidents

What actions did American presidents between 1877 and 1900 take to restore authority to their office?

Operating under the cloud of Andrew Johnson's impeachment, Grant's scandals, and doubts about the legitimacy of the 1876 election (see Chapter 16), American presidents between 1877 and 1900 moved to restore authority to their office. Proper and honest, Presidents Rutherford Hayes (1877–1881), James Garfield (1881), Chester Arthur (1881–1885), Grover Cleveland (1885–1889 and 1893–1897), Benjamin Harrison (1889–1893), and William McKinley (1897–1901) tried to act as legislative leaders. Each president cautiously initiated legislation and used vetoes to guide national policy.

Hayes, Garfield, and Arthur

Rutherford B. Hayes had been a Union general and Ohio congressman and governor before his disputed presidential election, which prompted opponents to label him "Rutherfraud." Hayes served as conciliator, emphasizing national harmony over sectional rivalry and opposing racial violence. He tried to overhaul the spoils system by appointing civil service reformer Carl Schurz to his cabinet and battling New York's patronage king, Senator Conkling.

When Hayes declined to run for reelection in 1880, Republicans nominated another Ohio congressman and Civil War hero, James A. Garfield, who won by 40,000 votes out of 9 million cast. By winning the pivotal states of New York and Indiana, Garfield carried the electoral college by 214 to 155. Garfield hoped to reduce the tariff and develop economic relations with Latin America, and he rebuffed Conkling's patronage demands. But in July 1881, Charles Guiteau shot him in a Washington railroad station. Garfield lingered for seventy-nine days before dying on September 19.

Garfield's successor was Vice President Chester A. Arthur, the New York Stalwart whom Hayes had fired. Arthur became a temperate executive. He signed the Pendleton Civil Service Act, urged Congress to modify outdated tariff rates, and supported federal railroad regulation. He wielded the veto aggressively, killing bills that excessively benefited railroads and corporations. Arthur wanted to run for president in 1884 but Republicans nominated James G. Blaine instead.

Democrats picked New York's governor, Grover Cleveland, a bachelor who admitted during the campaign that he had fathered an out-of-wedlock son. Cleveland beat Blaine by only 29,000 popular votes; his tiny margin of 1,149 votes in New York secured that state's 36 electoral votes, enough for a 219-to-182 victory in the electoral college. Cleveland may have won New York thanks to remarks of a Protestant minister, who equated Democrats with "rum, Romanism, and rebellion." Democrats publicized the slur among New York's large Irish-Catholic population, urging voters to support Cleveland.

Cleveland and Harrison Cleveland, the first Democratic president since James Buchanan (1857–1861), expanded civil service, vetoed private pension bills, and urged Congress to cut tariff duties. When advisers worried about his chances for reelection, the president retorted, "What is the use of being elected or reelected, unless you stand for something?" Senate protectionists killed tariff reform, and when Democrats renominated Cleveland in 1888, businessmen convinced him to moderate his attacks on tariffs.

Republicans in 1888 nominated Benjamin Harrison, former Indiana senator and grandson of President William Henry Harrison (1841). Bribery and multiple voting helped him win Indiana by 2,300 votes and New York by 14,000. (Democrats also indulged in frauds, but Republicans proved more successful at them.) Although Cleveland outpolled Harrison by 90,000 popular votes, Harrison carried the electoral college by 233 to 168.

The first president since 1875 whose party had majorities in both Congressional houses, Harrison influenced legislation with everything from threats of vetoes to informal dinners and consultations with politicians. Partly in response, the Congress of 1889–1891 passed 517 bills, 200 more than the average passed by Congresses between 1875 and 1889. Harrison showed support for civil service by appointing reformer Theodore Roosevelt as civil service commissioner. But pressured by special interests, Harrison signed the Dependents' Pension Act, which provided pensions for Union veterans and widows and children, doubling the number of welfare recipients from 490,000 to 966,000.

The Pension Act and other appropriations in 1890 pushed the federal budget past $1 billion for the first time. Democrats blamed the "Billion-Dollar Congress" on spendthrift Republicans and in 1890 voters unseated seventy-eight Republican congressmen. Capitalizing on voter unrest, Democrats nominated Grover Cleveland

The Spectacle of Gilded Age Politics

During the Gilded Age, political events, especially presidential elections, provided opportunity for elaborate spectacle, and politicians occupied the limelight as major celebrities. A presidential campaign functioned as a public festival at a time when mass entertainments such as movies and sports did not exist to offer people outlets for their emotions by attending parades, cheering, watching fireworks, and listening to marching bands. These two images, one an artist's rendering and the other a means for displaying one's preference for a particular candidate, present evidence of how people of the era might have expressed themselves politically. What similarities to modern-day campaign events and symbols do the images represent? In what ways are they different? Did politics and campaigning in the Gilded Age play a different role in the nation's culture than they do at present?

Collection of Janice L. and David J. Frent

© Bettmann/Corbis

The presidential campaign of Rutherford B. Hayes excited strong emotions. The inset image is that of a campaign brooch reminding voters of Hayes's Civil War record, and the drawing illustrates the gala of Haye's inauguration in 1876.

to run against Harrison in 1892. With large business contributions, Cleveland beat Harrison by 370,000 popular votes (3 percent of the total), easily winning the electoral vote.

In office again, Cleveland addressed currency, tariffs, and labor unrest, but his actions reflected political weakness. Cleveland promised sweeping tariff reform, but Senate protectionists undercut his efforts. And he bowed to requests from railroads, sending federal troops to put down the Pullman strike of 1894. In spite of Cleveland's efforts, major events—particularly economic downturn and agrarian ferment—pushed the country in another direction.

Discrimination, Disfranchisement, and Responses

How did southerners find legal means to discriminate against newly enfranchised African Americans in the decades following the Civil War?

Despite speeches about freedom and opportunity during the Gilded Age, policies of discrimination haunted more than half the nation's population. Racial issues long shaped politics in the South, home to the majority of African Americans. Southern white farmers and workers feared that newly enfranchised African American men would challenge their political and social superiority (real and imagined). Wealthy landowners and merchants fanned these fears, keeping blacks and whites from uniting to protest their own economic subjugation.

In the North, discrimination in housing, employment, and access to facilities such as parks, hotels, department stores kept African Americans separate and "in their place." Whether via lower wages or lower crop returns, African Americans felt their imposed inferiority.

Violence Against African Americans

lynching: Vigilante hanging of those accused of crimes; used primarily against blacks.

Ida B. Wells: African American journalist and activist who mounted a national anti-lynching campaign.

Link to a document from an African American mass protest meeting about mistreatment.

In 1880, 90 percent of southern blacks farmed or worked in personal and domestic service—just as they had as slaves. Between 1889 and 1909, more than seventeen hundred African Americans were lynched in the South, often in sparsely populated districts where whites felt threatened by an influx of migrant blacks. Most **lynching** victims were accused of assault—rarely proved—on a white woman.

Blacks did not suffer violence silently. Their most notable activist was **Ida B. Wells**, a Memphis schoolteacher, who was forcibly removed from a railroad car in 1884 when she refused to surrender her seat to a white man. In 1889, Wells became partner of a Memphis newspaper, the *Free Speech and Headlight*, in which she published attacks against white injustice, particularly the case of three black grocers lynched in 1892 after defending themselves against whites. She subsequently toured Europe, drumming up opposition to lynching and discrimination. Unable to return to hostile Memphis, she moved to Chicago and became a powerful advocate for racial justice.

Disfranchisement

Southern white leaders, eager to reassert racial superiority, instituted measures to prevent blacks from voting. Despite threats and intimidation post-Reconstruction, blacks formed the backbone of the southern Republican Party and won numerous elective positions. In North Carolina, for example, eleven African Americans served in the state Senate and forty-three in the House between 1877 and 1890. Unacceptable to racist whites, beginning with Tennessee in 1889 and Arkansas in 1892, southern states levied taxes of $1 to $2 on all voters—prohibitive to most blacks, who were poor and in debt. Other schemes disfranchised—or deprived voting rights to—blacks who could not read.

Furthering disfranchisement, the Supreme Court determined in *U.S. v. Reese* (1876) that Congress had no control over local and state elections other than upholding the Fifteenth Amendment, which prohibits states from denying the vote "on account of race, color, or previous condition of servitude." State legislatures found ways to exclude black voters, however. An 1890 state constitutional convention established the "Mississippi Plan," requiring voters to pay a poll tax eight months before each election, present the tax receipt at election time, and prove they could read and interpret the state constitution. Registration officials applied stiffer standards to blacks than to whites, even declaring black college graduates ineligible due to illiteracy.

Such restrictions proved effective. In South Carolina, 70 percent of eligible blacks voted in the 1880 election; by 1896, the rate dropped to 11 percent. By the 1900s, African Americans effectively lost political rights in the South. Disfranchisement also affected poor whites, few of whom could meet poll tax, property, and literacy requirements. Consequently, total number of eligible voters in Mississippi shrank from 257,000 in 1876 to 77,000 in 1892.

Legal Segregation

Existing customs of racial separation also expanded. In a series of cases during the 1870s, the Supreme Court opened the door to racial discrimination by ruling that the Fourteenth Amendment protected citizens' rights only against infringement by state governments—but not from individuals, businesses, or local governments. These rulings climaxed in 1883 when, in the *Civil Rights* cases, the Court struck down the 1875 Civil Rights Act, which prohibited segregation in facilities, such as streetcars, theaters, and parks. Thus railroads, such as the Chesapeake & Ohio Railroad, could maintain discriminatory policies.

The Supreme Court also upheld legal segregation on a "separate-but-equal" basis in **Plessy v. Ferguson** (1896). This case began in 1892 when a New Orleans organization of African Americans chose Homer Plessy, a dark-skinned creole who was only one-eighth black (but considered black by Louisiana law), to sit in a whites-only railroad car. Plessy was arrested, and the appeal of his conviction reached the U.S. Supreme Court in 1896. The Court affirmed that a state law providing for separate facilities for the two races was reasonable because it preserved "public peace and good order." To the Court, a law separating the races did not necessarily "destroy the legal equality of the races." Although the ruling did not specify the phrase "separate but equal," it legalized separate facilities for black and white people as long as they were equal. In 1899, the Court legitimated school segregation in *Cummins v. County Board of Education*, until it was overturned by *Brown v. Board of Education* in 1954.

Segregation laws—known as Jim Crow laws—multiplied throughout the South, reminding African Americans of inferior status. State and local statutes passed in the 1890 restricted blacks to the rear of streetcars, to separate public drinking fountains and toilets, and to separate sections of hospitals and cemeteries.

Plessy v. Ferguson: Supreme Court ruling validating legal segregation; legalized separate facilities for blacks and whites as long as they were equal.

African American Activism

African American women and men challenged injustice. Some boycotted discriminatory businesses; others promoted "Negro enterprise." In 1898, Atlanta University professor John Hope urged blacks to become their own employers and support Negro Business Men's Leagues. Some blacks used higher education to elevate their status. In all-black teachers' colleges, men and women sought opportunities for themselves and their race.

While disfranchisement pushed African American men from public life, African American women used domestic roles as mothers, educators, and moral guardians to uplift the race and seek improvements. Along with seeking the vote, they successfully lobbied southern governments for cleaner city streets, expanded charity services, and vocational education. Black women and white women sometimes united to achieve their goals, white women often sympathized with white men in supporting racial exclusion.

Women Suffrage

Some women challenged male power structures by seeking the right to vote. An intensely religious woman, Frances Willard believed that (Chrstian) faith would empower women to uplift society, urging women who joined the Women's Christian Temperance Union to sign a pledge to abstain from alcohol to protect families from the evils of drink. But Willard also believed that the WCTU could best do the Lord's work if women could vote. Thus, at its 1884 convention, the WCTU passed a resolution deploring the "disenfranchisement of 12 million people who are citizens." Giving speeches nationwide, Willard became the best-known woman in America.

Courtesy of Heritage Hall, Livingstone College, Salisbury, North Carolina

Livingstone College in North Carolina was one of several institutions of higher learning established by and for African Americans in the late nineteenth century. With a curriculum that emphasized training for educational and religious work in the South and in Africa, these colleges were coeducational, operating on the belief that both men and women could have public roles.

The suffrage crusade was spearheaded by two organizations, the National Woman Suffrage Association (NWSA) and the American Woman Suffrage Association (AWSA). The NWSA, led by Elizabeth Cady Stanton and Susan B. Anthony, advocated women's rights in courts and workplaces as well as at the ballot box.

The AWSA, led by former abolitionists Lucy Stone, focused narrowly on suffrage, particularly at the state level. The two groups merged in 1890 to form the National American Woman Suffrage Association with Stanton as president.

Anthony's effort for a constitutional woman suffrage amendment received little support, with senators claiming suffrage would interfere with women's family obligations. Moreover, the women's suffrage campaign was tainted by racial intolerance, as many movement leaders espoused white superiority and accommodated racial prejudices to retain support. AWSA and NWSA membership was white and mostly middle class. Blacks who joined the WCTU had a separate Department of Colored Temperance. Also, leaders, such as Anthony and Stanton felt humiliated that the Fifteenth Amendment had enfranchised black men but not women. Many believed that "educated" white women should vote and that "illiterate" blacks should not.

The Beautiful Life of Frances E. Willard by Anna A. Gordon, 1898/Picture Research Consultants & Archives

Frances Willard became the second and best-known president of the National Women's Christian Temperance Union (WCTU), founded in 1874. Beyond promoting abstinence from drinking alcohol, Willard and the WCTU also were involved in other reforms, including women's suffrage. In 1893, Willard took her crusade worldwide and became the first president of the International Council of Women. Here Willard's status is symbolized by her seat amid major American and British suffrage leaders, all officers of the World's WCTU.

Women did win partial victories. Between 1870 and 1910, eleven states (mostly in the West) legalized limited woman suffrage. By 1890, nineteen states allowed women to vote on school issues, and three granted suffrage on tax and bond issues. The right to vote in national elections awaited a later generation, but leaders such as Ida B. Wells, Susan B. Anthony, and Lucy Stone proved that women could be politically active even without the vote.

Agrarian Unrest and Populism

How did farmers' discontent crystallize in the Grange movement and Farmers' Alliances?

Economic inequity also sparked a mass movement. Despite rapid industrialization and urbanization in the Gilded Age, the United States remained an agrarian society with 64 percent of the population living in rural areas in 1890. The expression of farmers' discontent with economic hardship—a mixture of strident rhetoric, nostalgic dreams, and hard-headed egalitarianism—began in Grange organizations in the early 1870s. It accelerated when Farmers' Alliances formed in Texas in the late 1870s and spread across the South and Great Plains in the 1880s. The movement flourished where debt, weather, and insects demoralized struggling farmers and inspired visions of a cooperative, democratic society.

Sharecropping and Tenant Farming in the South

Southern agriculture did not benefit much from mechanization. Tobacco and cotton, principal southern crops, required hoeing and weeding by hand. Tobacco leaves matured at different rates and stems were too fragile for machines. Also, mechanical devices were not precise enough to pick cotton. Thus, after the Civil War, southern agriculture remained labor-intensive, and labor lords replaced slaves with sharecroppers and tenant farmers.

Sharecropping and tenant farming—where farmers rented rather than owned their land—entangled millions of black and white southerners in debt and humiliation, weighed down by crop liens. Too poor to have ready cash, most farmers borrowed to buy necessities, offering future crops as collateral. To get supplies, a farmer dealt with a "furnishing merchant," who would exchange provisions for a "lien," or legal claim, on the farmer's forthcoming crop. After the crop was harvested and brought to market, the merchant collected the portion of the crop that would repay the loan. Often, however, the debt exceeded the crop's value. The farmer could pay off only part of the debt but borrowed more for food and supplies for the coming year, sinking deeper into debt.

Merchants frequently took advantage by inflating prices and charging excessive interest on the advances farmers received. Suppose, for example, that a farmer needed a 20-cent bag of seed. The furnishing merchant would sell it to him on credit but for 28 cents. At year's end, that loan would have accumulated interest of 50 percent or more. The farmer, pledging more than his crop's worth against such debts, fell behind and never recovered, risking eviction.

In the southern backcountry, after the Civil War, farmers shifted from diversified and subsistence agriculture to commercial farming, namely cotton. Consequently, yeoman began purchasing supplies such as flour, potatoes, peas, meat, corn, and syrup from merchants. This specialized farming came about for two reasons: constant debt forced farmers to grow crops that would net cash, and railroads enabled them to easily transport cotton to market. As backcountry yeomen devoted more acres to cotton, they raised less of what they needed and were frequently at the mercy of merchants.

Hardship in the Midwest and West

In the Midwest, as growers cultivated more land, as mechanization boosted productivity, and as foreign competition increased, supplies of agricultural products exceeded

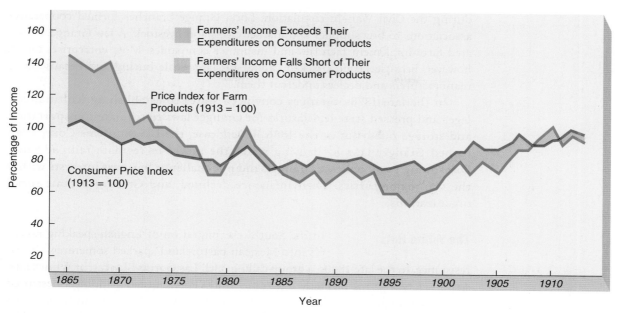

FIGURE 20.1
Consumer Prices and Farm Product Prices, 1865–1913
Until the late 1870s, in spite of falling farm prices, farmers were able to receive from their crops more income than they spent on consumer goods. But beginning in the mid-1880s, consumer prices leveled off and then rose, while prices for farm products continued to drop. As a result, farmers found it increasingly difficult to afford consumer goods, a problem that plagued them well into the twentieth century.

national and worldwide demand. Prices for staple crops dropped steadily. A bushel of wheat that sold for $1.45 in 1866 brought only 80 cents in the mid-1880s and 49 cents by the mid-1890s. Meanwhile, transportation and storage fees remained high. To buy necessities and pay bills, farmers had to produce more. But the more they produced, the lower crop prices dropped (see Figure 20.1).

The West suffered special hardships. In Colorado, absentee capitalists seized control of transportation and water, and concentration of technology by large mining companies pushed out small firms. Charges of monopolistic behavior by railroads echoed among farmers, miners, and ranchers in Wyoming and Montana. In California, Washington, and Oregon, wheat and fruit growers found opportunities blocked by railroads' control of transportation and storage rates.

Grange Movement   With aid from Oliver H. Kelley, a clerk in the Bureau of Agriculture, farmers in almost every state during the 1860s and 1870s founded the Patrons of Husbandry, or the Grange, dedicated to improving economic and social conditions. By 1875, the Grange had twenty thousand branches and a million members. Strongest in the Midwest and South, Granges sponsored meetings and educational events to relieve the loneliness of farm life. Family-oriented local Granges welcomed women's participation.

As membership flourished, Granges turned to economic and political action. Many joined the **Greenback Labor Party**, formed in 1876 to advocate expanding the money supply by keeping "greenbacks"— paper money created by the government

Greenback Labor Party:
Advocated expanding the money supply through the government printing of money not backed by gold.

during the Civil War—in circulation. Local Grange branches formed cooperative associations to buy supplies and market crops and livestock. A few Grangers operated farm-implement factories and insurance companies. Most enterprises failed, however, because farmers lacked capital for large-scale buying and because large manufacturers and dealers undercut them.

In the late 1870s, Granges convinced states to establish agricultural colleges and pressed state legislatures for Granger laws to regulate transportation and storage rates. But in the 1886 *Wabash* case, the U.S. Supreme Court overturned Granger laws by denying states the power to regulate railroad rates. Disavowing party politics, Grangers did not challenge business interests within the two major parties. Their influence declined, and Granges became social organizations.

The White Hats

In the Southwest, migration of English-speaking ranchers into Mexican pastureland sparked sometimes violent resistance. In the late 1880s, a group calling itself Las Gorras Blancas, or White Hats, struggled to control formerly ancestral lands. They burned buildings, destroyed fences that Anglos had erected, and threatened the town of Las Vegas in New Mexico territory. However, they could not halt Anglos from legally buying and using public land. By 1900, many Hispanics had given up farming to work as agricultural laborers or migrate to cities.

Farmers' Alliances

By 1890, two networks of Farmers' Alliances—one in the Great Plains, one in the South—constituted a new mass movement. The first Alliances arose in Texas, where hard-pressed farmers rallied against crop liens, merchants, railroads, and money power. Using traveling lecturers to recruit members, Alliance leaders expanded the movement into other southern states, boasting two million members by 1889. A separate Colored Farmers' National Alliance claimed one million black members. In the late 1880s, the Plains movement organized two million members in Kansas, Nebraska, and the Dakotas. Women participated actively in Alliance activities.

To bypass corporate power and control markets, Alliances, like the Grange, proposed that farmers form cooperatives, joining together to sell crops and livestock and buy supplies. By pooling resources, Alliances reasoned, farmers could exert greater economic pressure and share the benefits of their hard work rather than competing against each other.

To relieve shortages of cash and credit, Alliances proposed a government aid system called a subtreasury. The plan first called for the federal government to construct warehouses where farmers could store nonperishable crops while awaiting higher market prices; the government would then loan farmers Treasury notes amounting to 80 percent of the market price of stored crops. Farmers could use these notes for debts and purchases. Once the crops were sold, farmers would repay the loans plus small interest and storage fees, thereby avoiding the exploitative crop lien system.

The subtreasury plan's second part would provide low-interest government loans to farmers to buy land. These loans, along with the Treasury notes for stored crops, would inject cash into the economy and encourage the kind of inflation that advocates hoped would raise crop prices without raising other prices.

Problems in Achieving Alliance Unity

Had Farmers' Alliances been able to unite politically, they could have wielded formidable power; but racial and sectional differences thwarted merger efforts. Racial voting restrictions weakened Alliance voter strength, and racism blocked acceptance of blacks by white Alliances. Some southern leaders, such as Georgia's Senator Tom Watson, tried to unite distressed black and white farmers, but poor whites held fast to prejudices. Many considered African Americans inferior and took comfort that there always would be people worse off than they were. Regional differences also prevented unity. Northern Alliances favored protective tariffs to keep out foreign grain, whereas white southerners wanted low tariffs to curb costs of imports. However, both favored railroad regulation, equitable taxation, currency reform, an end to alleged election frauds, and prohibition of landownership by foreign investors.

Rise of Populism

By 1890, farmers had elected several sympathetic office-holders, especially in the South, where Alliances controlled four governorships, eight state legislatures, forty-four seats in the House of Representatives, and three in the Senate. In the Midwest, Alliance candidates running on third-party tickets, such as the Greenback Labor Party, won some victories in Kansas, Nebraska, and the Dakotas. Leaders crisscrossed the country to recruit support for a new party. In summer 1890, the Kansas Alliance held a "convention of the people" and nominated candidates who swept the state's fall elections. Formation of this People's Party, or **Populist Party**, gave a title to Alliance political activism. (Populism is the political doctrine that asserts the rights and powers of common people versus elites.) By 1892, southern Alliance members joined northern counterparts in summoning a People's Party convention in Omaha, Nebraska, on July 4 to draft a platform and nominate a presidential candidate.

Charging that inequality (between white classes) threatened to splinter society, the new party's platform declared, "The fruits of the toil of millions are boldly stolen to build up colossal fortunes for a few," and that "wealth belongs to him that creates it." It addressed three central sources of rural unrest: transportation, land, and money. Frustrated with weak regulation, Populists demanded government ownership of railroad and telegraph lines. The monetary plank called on the government to make more money available for farm loans and to restore unlimited coinage of silver. Other planks advocated a graduated income tax, postal savings banks, direct election of U.S. senators, and a shorter workday. As its presidential candidate, the party nominated James B. Weaver of Iowa, a former Union general and supporter of an expanded money supply.

Populist Party: "People's Party;" agrarian-based, third-party challenge to the Republicans and Democrats; advocated for the rights of the common man.

Link to Hamlin Garland's short story, "Under the Lion's Paw," which was read before the audience at the Populist Convention in 1892.

Populist Spokespeople

The Populist campaign featured dynamic personalities such as Mary Lease and "Sockless Jerry" Simpson, an unschooled rural reformer so nicknamed after he ridiculed silk-stockinged wealthy people, causing a reporter to muse that Simpson probably wore no stockings. The South produced leaders, such as Georgia's Tom Watson and North Carolina's Leonidas Polk. Colorado's governor, Davis "Bloody Bridles" Waite, attacked mine owners, and Minnesota's Ignatius Donnelly, pseudoscientist and writer of apocalyptic novels, became chief visionary of the northern plains, penning the Omaha platform's thunderous language.

Russian Populism

Before American Populism, a different form of populism emerged in another largely rural country: Russia. Whereas American Populism came from the Alliance farm organizations, Russian populism was created by intellectuals seeking to educate peasants to agitate for social and economic freedom.

Russian society began to modernize in the mid-nineteenth century. Town governments were given control of local taxation, and education became more widespread. Perhaps most importantly, in 1861 Czar Alexander II signed an Edict of Emancipation, freeing Russian serfs (slaves attached to specific lands) and granting them compensation to buy land. Reforms progressed slowly, prompting some educated Russians, called nihilists, to press for radical reforms, including socialism. The reformers became known as *narodniki*, or populists, from *narod*, the Russian term for "peasant."

Narodniki envisioned a society of self-governing village communes, somewhat like the cooperatives proposed by American Farmers' Alliances. One leader, Peter Lavrov, believed intellectuals must get closer to the people and help them improve their lives. Russian populists believed only an uprising against the czar could realize their goals. When Alexander instituted repressive policies against the *narodniki* in the late 1870s, many turned to terrorism, culminating in Alexander II's assassination in 1881.

Russian peasants remained tied to tradition and could not abandon loyalty to the czar. Arrests and imprisonments after Alexander's assassination discouraged populists' efforts, and the movement declined. Nevertheless, populist ideas became the cornerstone of the 1917 Russian Revolution and of subsequent Soviet social and political ideology.

Bettmann/Corbis

Russian peasants, like American tenant farmers and owners of small landholdings, suffered from poverty and pressures of the expanded market economy. The plight of struggling Russian farm families stirred up empathy from young populist intellectuals, who adopted radical solutions that did not capture as much political fervor among farmers as American populism did.

In the 1892 presidential election, Populist candidate James Weaver garnered 8 percent of the popular vote, majorities in four states, and twenty-two electoral votes. Not since 1856 had a third party done so well in its first national effort. Populists were only successful in the West. The vote-rich Northeast ignored Weaver, and Alabama was the only southern state that gave Populists as much as one-third of its votes.

Still, Populism gave southern and western rural dwellers faith in a future of cooperation and democracy, as they looked toward the 1896 presidential election. Amid hardship and desperation, millions came to believe that a cooperative democracy in which government would ensure equal opportunity could overcome corporate power.

The Depression and Protests of the 1890s

Why did socialism fail to take hold in the United States amid the labor activism of the late nineteenth century?

In 1893, shortly before Grover Cleveland's second presidency began, the Philadelphia & Reading Railroad, once a thriving and profitable line, went bankrupt. Like other railroads, it had borrowed heavily to lay track and build stations and bridges. Overexpansion cut into profits, and ultimately the company could not pay its debts.

The same problem beset manufacturers. Output at McCormick farm machinery factories was nine times greater in 1893 than in 1879, but revenues had only tripled. The company bought more equipment and squeezed more work from fewer laborers, but it only increased debt and unemployment. Jobless workers could not pay their bills. Banks suffered when customers defaulted. The failure of the National Cordage Company in May 1893 sparked a chain reaction of business and bank closings. By year's end, five hundred banks and sixteen hundred businesses failed. Between 1893 and 1897, the nation suffered a devastating economic depression.

Nearly 20 percent of the labor force was jobless during the depression. Falling demand caused prices to drop between 1892 and 1895, but layoffs and wage cuts more than offset declining living costs. Many people could not afford necessities. The New York police estimated that twenty thousand homeless and jobless people roamed city streets.

Continuing Currency Problems

As the depression deepened, the currency dilemma reached a crisis. The Sherman Silver Purchase Act of 1890 had committed the government to use Treasury notes (silver certificates) to buy 4.5 million ounces of silver monthly. Recipients could redeem these certificates for gold, at the ratio of one ounce of gold for every sixteen ounces' of silver. But a western mining boom increased silver supplies, causing its market value to fall and prompting holders of silver certificates and Civil War greenbacks to exchange their notes for more valuable gold. As a result, the nation's gold reserve dwindled, falling below $100 million in early 1893.

If investors believed the country's gold reserve was disappearing, they would lose confidence in America's economic stability and refrain from investing. British capitalists, for example, owned $4 billion in American stocks and bonds and were likely to stop investing if dollars depreciated. The lower the gold reserve dropped, the more people rushed to redeem their money. Panic spread, causing more bankruptcies and unemployment.

To protect the gold reserve, President Cleveland called a special session of Congress to repeal the Sherman Silver Purchase Act. Repeal passed in late 1893, but the run on gold continued. In early 1895, reserves fell to $41 million, and, desperate, Cleveland accepted an offer of 3.5 million ounces of gold for $65 million worth of federal bonds from a banking syndicate led by financier J. P. Morgan. When the bankers resold the bonds, they made a $2 million profit. Cleveland claimed that he had saved the reserves, but discontented farmers, workers, silver miners, and some of Cleveland's Democratic allies saw only humiliation in the president's deal with big businessmen.

The deal between Cleveland and Morgan did not end the depression. After improving slightly in 1895, the economy plunged again. Farm income, declining since 1887, slid further; factories closed; banks restricted withdrawals. The tight money supply depressed housing construction, drying up. Cities like Detroit encouraged citizens to cultivate "potato patches" on vacant land to alleviate food shortages. Urban police stations filled up nightly with homeless people.

Consequences of Depression

In the late 1890s, gold discoveries in Alaska, good harvests, and industrial growth brought relief. But the downturn hastened the crumbling of the old economic system and emergence of a new one. The American economy expanded beyond sectional bases; when western farmers fell into debt, their depressed condition weakened railroads, farm-implement manufacturers, and banks in other regions. Moreover, the corporate consolidation that characterized the new business system tempted many companies to expand too rapidly. When contraction occurred, their reckless debts dragged them down, and they pulled other industries with them.

A new global marketplace was emerging, forcing American farmers to contend with discriminatory transportation rates and falling crop prices at home, along with Canadian and Russian wheat growers, Argentine cattle ranchers, Indian and Egyptian cotton manufacturers, and Australian wool producers. Consequently, one country's economy affected that of other countries. With the glutted domestic market, American businessmen sought new markets abroad (see Chapter 22).

Depression-Era Protests

The depression exposed fundamental tensions in the industrial system. Technological and organizational changes had been widening the gap between employees and employers for half a century. Labor protest began with the railroad strikes of 1877. Their vehemence and support from working-class people raised fears that the United States would experience a popular uprising like the one in France in 1871, which briefly overturned the government and introduced communist principles. The 1886 Haymarket riot, prolonged 1892 strike at the Carnegie Homestead Steel plant, and labor violence among miners in the West heightened anxieties (see Chapter 18). In 1894, there were over thirteen hundred strikes and countless riots. Contrary to accusations of business leaders, few protesters were immigrant anarchists or communists. Rather, they were Americans who believed that in a democracy their voices should be heard.

Socialists

Small numbers of socialists participated in these confrontations. Some socialists believed workers should control factories and businesses; others supported government ownership. All, however, opposed the private enterprise of capitalism. Their ideas derived from Karl Marx (1818–1883), the German philosopher and father of communism, who contended that whoever controls the means of production determines how well people live. Marx wrote that industrial capitalism profits by paying workers less than the value of their labor and that mechanization and mass production alienated workers from their labor. According to Marx, only by abolishing the return on capital—profits—could labor receive its true value, possible only if workers owned the means of production. Marx predicted that workers worldwide would revolt and seize factories, farms, banks, and transportation lines. This revolution would establish a socialist order of justice and equality. Marx's vision appealed to some workers because it promised independence and to some intellectuals because it promised to end class conflict and crass materialism.

In America, socialists disagreed over how to achieve Marx's vision. Much of the movement was influenced by immigrants—first Germans, later Russian Jews, Italians, Hungarians, and Poles. It splintered into small groups, such as the Socialist Labor Party, which failed to attract the mass of laborers because it often focused on doctrine rather than workers' everyday needs. Workers hoped they would benefit through education and acquisition of property; most American workers sought individual advancement rather than the betterment of all.

Eugene V. Debs

In 1894, a new and inspiring Socialist leader emerged. The Indiana-born Eugene V. Debs headed the newly formed American Railway Union, which had carried out that year's strike against the Pullman Company. Jailed for defying the injunction against the strike, Debs read Karl Marx's works in prison. Once released, he became the leading spokesman for American socialism, combining visionary Marxism with Jeffersonian and Populist antimonopolism. Debs captivated audiences with attacks on the free-enterprise system. "Many of you think you are competing," he would lecture. "Against whom? Against Rockefeller?" By 1900, the group soon to be called the Socialist Party of America was uniting around Debs.

Coxey's Army

In 1894, however, a quiet businessman named Jacob Coxey from Massillon, Ohio, captured public attention. Coxey had believed that, to aid debtors, the government should issue $500 million of "legal tender" paper money and make low-interest loans to local governments, which would use the funds to pay unemployed men to build roads and other public works. He planned to publicize his scheme by leading a march from Massillon to Washington, D.C., gathering unemployed workers en route. Coxey's army of about 200 left in March 1894. Hiking across Ohio into Pennsylvania, the marchers received food and housing in depressed industrial towns and rural villages and attracted additional recruits. A dozen similar processions from places such as Seattle, San Francisco, and Los Angeles also trekked eastward. Sore feet prompted some marchers to commandeer trains, but most marches were law-abiding.

Coxey's band of 500 entered Washington on April 30. The next day (May Day, the anniversary of the Haymarket violence), the group, armed with "war clubs of peace," advanced to the Capitol. When Coxey and a few others vaulted a wall surrounding the grounds, mounted police routed the demonstrators. Police dragged Coxey away. As arrests and clubbings continued, Coxey's dream of a demonstration of 400,000 jobless workers dissolved. Unlike socialists, who wished to replace the capitalist system, Coxey's troops merely wanted more jobs and better living standards. The brutal reactions of officials, however, reveal how threatening dissenters like Coxey and Debs seemed to the existing social order.

The Silver Crusade and the Election of 1896

How did Bryan's focus on free silver undermine his presidential campaign and the Populist Party?

Social protest and economic depression made the 1896 presidential election seem pivotal. Debates over money and power were climaxing, Democrats and Republicans battled to control Congress and the presidency. The key question, however, was whether voters would abandon old party loyalties for the Populist party.

Free Silver

The Populist crusade against "money power" settled on the issue of silver, which many believed would solve the nation's complex ills. To them, coinage of silver symbolized an end to special privileges for the rich and the return of government to the people by lifting common people out of debt, increasing the cash in circulation, and reducing interest rates.

As the 1896 election approached, Populists had to decide whether to join with sympathetic factions of the major parties, thus risking a loss of identity, or remain an independent third party. Except in mining areas of Rocky Mountain states, where free coinage of silver had strong support, Republicans were unlikely allies because their support for the gold standard and big-business represented what Populists opposed.

Alliance with northern and western Democrats was more plausible since the party there retained vestiges of antimonopoly ideology and sympathy for a looser currency system, despite the influence of "gold Democrats," such as President Cleveland and Senator David Hill of New York. Linking with Southern Democrats seemed less viable since candidates' failure to carry out their promises left southern farmers feeling betrayed. Whichever option they chose, Populists ensured that the 1896 election would be the most issue oriented since 1860.

Nomination of McKinley

Both major parties were divided. For a year, Ohio industrialist Marcus A. Hanna maneuvered to win the Republican nomination for Ohio's governor, William McKinley, and corralled enough delegates to succeed. The Republicans' only distress occurred when they adopted a platform supporting the gold standard, rejecting a prosilver stance proposed by Colorado senator Henry M. Teller. Teller, a party founder forty years earlier, left the convention in tears, taking a small group of silver Republicans with him.

During the Democratic convention, prosilver delegates wearing silver badges and waving silver banners paraded through the Chicago Amphitheatre. A *New York*

World reporter remarked that "all the silverites need is a Moses." They found one in **William Jennings Bryan**.

William Jennings Bryan

Bryan arrived at the Democratic convention as a member of a contested Nebraska delegation. A former congressman whose support for coinage of silver annoyed President Cleveland, Bryan found the depression's impact on midwestern farmers distressing. Shortly after the convention seated Bryan, he joined the resolutions committee and helped write a platform calling for unlimited coinage of silver. Bryan's now-famous closing words ignited the delegates.

> Having behind us the producing masses of this nation and the world, supported by the commercial interests, the laboring interests, and the toilers everywhere, we will answer [the wealthy classes'] demand for a gold standard by saying to them: You shall not press down upon the brow of labor this crown of thorns, you shall not crucify mankind upon a cross of gold.

After that speech, it took five ballots to win Bryan the nomination, but the magnetic "Boy Orator" proved irresistible. In accepting the silverite goals of southerners and westerners, and repudiating Cleveland's policies, the Democratic Party became more attractive to discontented farmers. But, it alienated a minority wing, who withdrew and nominated their own candidate.

Bryan's nomination presented the Populist party convention with a dilemma. Should Populists join Democrats in support of Bryan or nominate their own candidate? Some reasoned that supporting a separate candidate would split the anti-McKinley vote and guarantee a Republican victory. The convention compromised, first naming Tom Watson as its vice-presidential nominee to preserve party identity (Democrats had nominated Maine shipping magnate Arthur Sewall) and then nominating Bryan for president.

The campaign, as Kansas journalist William Allen White observed, "took the form of religious frenzy." Bryan preached that "every great economic question is in reality a great moral question." Republicans countered Bryan's attacks on privilege by predicting chaos if he won. Hanna invited thousands of people to McKinley's home in Canton, Ohio, where the candidate plied them with homilies on moderation and prosperity, promising something for everyone. In an appeal to working-class voters, Republicans stressed the new jobs that a protective tariff would create.

Election Results

The election revealed that the political standoff had ended. McKinley, symbol of urban and corporate ascendancy, beat Bryan by 600,000 popular votes and won in the electoral college by 271 to 176 (see Map 20.1). Bryan worked hard to rally the nation, but obsession with silver prevented Populists from building the urban-rural coalition that would have expanded their appeal. Urban workers, who might have benefited from Populist goals, feared that silver coinage would shrink the value of their wages. Labor leaders, such as the AFL's Samuel Gompers, though partly sympathetic, would not commit fully because they viewed farmers as businessmen, not workers. And socialists denounced Populists as "retrograde" because they believed in free enterprise. Thus, the Populist crusade collapsed. Although Populists and fusion candidates won a few state and congressional elections, the Bryan-Watson ticket of the Populist party polled only 222,600 votes nationwide.

William Jennings Bryan: Orator, anti-imperialist, champion of farm interests, and three-time Democratic presidential candidate.

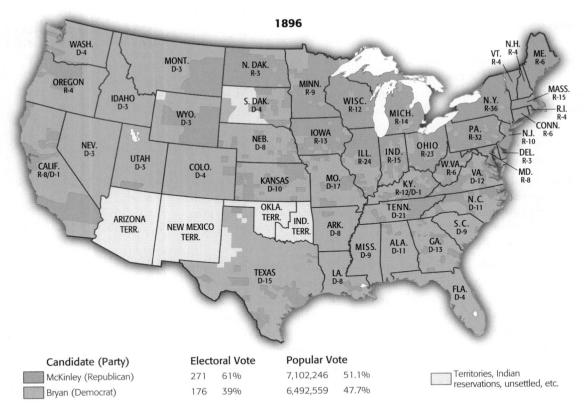

1896

Candidate (Party)	Electoral Vote		Popular Vote	
McKinley (Republican)	271	61%	7,102,246	51.1%
Bryan (Democrat)	176	39%	6,492,559	47.7%

Territories, Indian reservations, unsettled, etc.

MAP 20.1

Presidential Election, 1896

William Jennings Bryan had strong voter support in the South and West, but the numerically superior industrial states, plus California, created majorities for William McKinley.

Source: Copyright © Cengage Learning

The McKinley Presidency

As president, McKinley reinforced his support of business by signing the Gold Standard Act (1900), requiring that all paper money be backed by gold. A seasoned politician, McKinley guided passage of record-high tariff rates as congressman in 1890. He accordingly supported the Dingley Tariff of 1897, which raised duties even higher. A believer in opening new markets abroad to sustain profits at home, McKinley encouraged imperialistic ventures in Latin America and the Pacific. Better times and victory in the Spanish-American War helped him beat Bryan again in 1900.

Summary

Though buffeted by special interests, Gilded Age politicians prepared the nation for the twentieth century. Laws encouraging economic growth with some principles of regulation, measures expanding government agencies while reducing crass patronage, and federal intervention in trade and currency issues evolved during the 1870s and 1880s.

Nevertheless, the United States remained a nation of inconsistencies. Those who supported disfranchisement of African Americans and continued discrimination against blacks and women still polluted politics. People in power could not tolerate

Interpreting a Fairy Tale

The Wizard of Oz, (1939) one of the all-time most popular movies, began as a work of juvenile literature penned by journalist L. Frank Baum in 1900. Originally titled *The Wonderful Wizard of Oz*, the story used memorable characters to create an adventurous quest.

Adults have searched the story for hidden meanings. In 1964, scholar Henry M. Littlefield asserted that Baum intended to write a Populist parable illustrating the conditions of overburdened farmers and laborers. Dorothy, he theorized, symbolized the well-intentioned common person; the Scarecrow, the struggling farmer; the Tin Man, the industrial worker. Hoping for a better life, these friends, along with the Cowardly Lion (William Jennings Bryan), followed a yellow brick road (the gold standard) that led nowhere. The Emerald City was presided over by a wizard, who tried to be all things to all people, but Dorothy revealed him as a fraud. Dorothy was able to leave this muddled society and return to her simple Kansas farm family of Aunt Em and Uncle Henry by using her magical silver slippers (representing coinage of silver, though the movie made them red).

Subsequent theorists identified additional symbols, such as Oz being the abbreviation for ounces (oz.), the chief measurement of gold. The Wicked Witch of the East—who, Baum wrote, kept the little people (Munchkins) "in bondage"—could represent industrial capitalism.

But in 1983, historian William R. Leach asserted that Baum's tale actually was a celebration of urban consumer culture. Its language exalted the opulence of Emerald City, which to Leach resembled the "White City" of the 1893 Chicago World's Fair and Dorothy's optimism symbolized the optimism of industrialism. Baum's career supported this new interpretation. Before writing, he designed display windows and was involved in theater—activities that gave him an appreciation of modern urban life.

The real legacy of *The Wonderful Wizard of Oz* has been its ability to provoke differing interpretations. Baum's fairy tale, the first truly American work of this sort, has bequeathed many fascinating images about the diversity and contradictions of American culture.

radical views like socialism or Populism, but many of those ideas continued to find supporters in the new century.

The 1896 election realigned national politics. The Republican Party, founded in the 1850s amid a crusade against slavery, became the majority party by emphasizing government aid to business, drawing the urban middle class, and playing down moralism. The Democratic Party miscalculated on the silver issue but held its support in the South and in urban political machines. At the national level, however, loyalties lacked their former potency. Suspicion of party politics increased, and voter participation declined. The Populists tried to energize a third-party movement, but their success was fleeting. Still, as the twentieth century progressed, many Populist goals were incorporated by the major parties, including regulation of railroads, banks, and utilities; shorter workdays; a variant of the subtreasury plan; a graduated income tax; and direct election of senators. These reforms succeeded because various groups united behind them. Immigration, urbanization, and industrialization had transformed the United States into a pluralistic society in which compromise had become a political fact of life. As the Gilded Age ended, business was still ascendant, and large segments of the population remained excluded from political and economic opportunity. But the winds of dissent and reform had begun to blow more strongly.

Chapter Review

The Nature of Party Politics

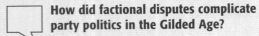

How did factional disputes complicate party politics in the Gilded Age?

Most Democrats sought to restrict government power and included immigrants and Catholics, while most Republicans were native-born Protestants who believed government should play a bigger role in reforming society. Both parties were ultimately divided by factional rifts that kept them from simultaneously controlling the presidency and Congress or holding power in either for very long. Republican factions included Stalwarts and Half Breeds, who each sought to wield influence and jobs toward supporters, and Mugwumps who, thought only the most upstanding men should be allowed in government. Democrats split into white-supremacist southerners, immigrant and working-class advocates of urban political machines, businessmen who sought lower tariffs and the gold standard, and those who embraced free silver. Such divisions within parties made unity difficult.

Issues of Legislation

What was at issue in the debate over the gold standard versus free silver?

The debate over gold versus free silver was in many ways a struggle between debtors and creditors in the late nineteenth century. Farmers and small businessmen (debtors) pushed for silver coinage, which they believed would put more money in circulation and lower interest rates, thereby making it easier for them to repay mortgages and other debts. Large businesses (creditors) preferred money backed by gold, because they considered it more stable, and therefore likely to maintain foreign investors' confidence in the U.S. economy. In effect, the debate became a class struggle, as well as a sectional one: those in the West and South where mining and agriculture dominated, favored silver; those in the industrial Northeast, gold.

Tentative Presidents

What actions did American presidents between 1877 and 1900 take to restore authority to their office?

After Andrew Johnson's impeachment and the scandals plaguing both the Grant administration and the 1876 election, the presidency was tarnished. Presidents Rutherford Hayes (1877–1881), James Garfield (1881), Chester Arthur (1881–1885), Grover Cleveland (1885–1889 and 1893–1897), Benjamin Harrison (1889–1893), and William McKinley (1897–1901) sought to bring integrity back to federal government through various legislative initiatives. They all supported civil service (and its expansion) as a means to end the corruption of the spoils system. With varying success, they addressed currency, tariffs, railroad regulation, and labor unrest.

Discrimination, Disfranchisement, and Responses

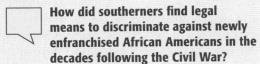

How did southerners find legal means to discriminate against newly enfranchised African Americans in the decades following the Civil War?

To keep blacks from voting, southern leaders instituted measures such as poll taxes, which most blacks could not afford, and literacy tests. These measures were upheld in the Supreme Court, which noted that the Fifteenth Amendment could only prohibit states from denying the vote based on "race, color, or previous condition of servitude," but could not control the local election process. Similarly, Jim Crow, or segregation laws, confined African Americans to separate areas in public places such as streetcars, hospitals, and parks, thereby deliberately reminding them of their inferior status. These laws were upheld by the Supreme Court in *Plessy v. Ferguson*, which allowed that states could legally segregate on a "separate-but-equal" basis. Violence against African Americans—particularly lynching—provided a reminder of the extremes of white racism and hostility.

Agrarian Unrest and Populism

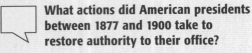

How did farmers' discontent crystallize in the Grange movement and Farmers' Alliances?

As farm prices dropped, farmers found it increasingly difficult to earn a living from their land. Those conditions were made worse by the fact that as smallholders, most could not compete with large firms, which could negotiate lower costs for transportation and supplies by virtue of their size. In response, farmers founded local organizations called Granges in the 1860s and 1870s partly as social clubs and partly to enable them to join forces in cooperatives where they could get the same competitive advantage as larger firms. Granges declined in the late 1870s, replaced a decade later by Farmers' Alliances, which rallied against crop liens, merchants, railroads, and money power. Along with cooperatives, Alliances sought a government aid system called a subtreasury that they hoped would provide low-interest loans to farmers seeking to buy land and would assist farmers in warehousing crops until market prices increased.

The Depression and Protests of the 1890s

Why did socialism fail to take hold in the United States amid the labor activism of the late nineteenth century?

The depression and thousands of strikes beginning with the 1877 railroad strike revealed general worker dissatisfaction that certainly created the conditions ripe for socialism to flourish, particularly once its charismatic leader Eugene V. Debs came to the fore in the 1890s. But American socialists could not agree on how best to implement Marxist strategies for worker control of the means of production and the end of capitalism's inequities. Socialism was also thwarted by that distinctly American celebration of social mobility and individual achievement. While workers found some aspects of socialism attractive, their ultimate aim was individual advancement, which they were unwilling to sacrifice for the greater good of all workers.

The Silver Crusade and the Election of 1896

How did Bryan's focus on free silver undermine his presidential campaign and the Populist Party?

Populists embraced the issue of silver because they believed it would end special privileges for the rich by lifting mainstream Americans from debt, increasing the money in circulation and lowering interest rates. Populists fused these ideas to the Democratic Party by joining forces with them behind William Jennings Bryan for president in 1896. Bryan was singularly focused on silver, but this cost him votes from urban workers, who feared silver coinage would cut their wages. Labor leaders equated farmers with businessmen, and as such, could not join forces with Populists on this issue. Bryan received only 222,600 votes nationwide, and while Populists continued to influence elections, the party itself collapsed.

Suggestions For Further Reading

Edward L. Ayers, *The Promise of the New South: Life After Reconstruction* (1992)
Jean Baker, *Sisters: The Lives of America's Suffragists* (2005)
Glenda Elizabeth Gilmore, *Gender and Jim Crow: Women and the Politics of White Supremacy in North Carolina, 1896–1920* (1996)
Steven Hahn, *A Nation Under Our Feet: Black Political Struggles in the Rural South, from Slavery to the Great Migration* (2003)
Michael Kazin, *The Populist Persuasion: An American History* (1995)
Jean V. Matthews, *The Rise of the New Woman: The Women's Movement in America, 1875–1930* (2003)
Nick Salvatore, *Eugene V. Debs: Citizen and Socialist* (1992)

Go to the CourseMate website for primary source links, study tools, and review materials for this chapter. www.cengagebrain.com

The Progressive Era

21

1895–1920

What Ben Lindsey saw made him furious. As a young Colorado lawyer in the 1890s, a judge asked him to defend two boys, about twelve years old, accused of burglary. The boys had been imprisoned for sixty days without a trial and did not understand what *burglary* meant or how the justice system worked. Visiting them in jail, Lindsay found the youngsters playing poker with two older cellmates—a safecracker and a horse thief. Outraged that children were housed with hardened criminals, Lindsey later wrote, "Here were two boys, neither of them serious enemies of society, who were about to be convicted of burglary and have felony records. . . . I had made up my mind to smash the system that meant so much injustice to youth."

In 1901, Lindsey ran for county judge and began fighting for juvenile protection from criminal prosecution, exploitative labor practices, and burdens of poverty. He and his wife, Henrietta, promoted a separate juvenile court system and aid to families with children at risk of becoming criminals. They wrote reform laws adopted by many states and countries. The Lindseys' efforts showed compassion and middle-class bias as part of a broader movement seeking solutions to modern America's social and economic problems.

During the 1890s, economic depression, labor violence, political upheaval, and foreign entanglements shook the nation. Numerous Americans continued to suffer from poverty and injustice. Some critics regarded industrialists as monsters who controlled markets and prices to maximize profits at the expense of laborers. Others believed government was corroded by bosses who enriched themselves by abusing power. Tensions created by urbanization and industrialization fragmented society into conflicting interest groups.

By 1900, the previous decade's political tumult had calmed, and economic depression subsided. The nation emerged victorious from a war against Spain (see Chapter 22), and a new era of political leaders, including Theodore Roosevelt and Woodrow Wilson, was dawning. A sense of renewal both intensified anxiety over continuing problems and raised hopes that democracy could be reconciled with capitalism.

Chapter Outline

The Varied Progressive Impulse
National Associations and Foreign Influences | The New Middle Class and Muckrakers | Upper-Class Reformers | Settlement Houses | Working-Class Reformers | The Social Gospel | Socialists | Southern and Western Progressivism | Opponents of Progressivism

LINKS TO THE WORLD *Foreign Universities and Study Abroad*

Government and Legislative Reform
Restructuring Government | Labor Reform | Prohibition | Controlling Prostitution

New Ideas in Social Institutions
John Dewey and Progressive Education | Growth of Colleges and Universities | Progressive Legal Thought | Social Science | Eugenics

Challenges to Racial and Sexual Discrimination
Continued Discrimination for African Americans | Booker T. Washington and Self-Help | W. E. B. Du Bois and the "Talented Tenth" | Society of American Indians | "The Woman Movement" | Women's Clubs | Feminism | Margaret Sanger's Crusade | Woman Suffrage

VISUALIZING THE PAST *Heavyweight Boxing Champion Jack Johnson as Race Hero*

Between 1895 and 1920, a complex reform campaign emerged to renovate or restore American society, values, and institutions. By the 1910s, reformers from Republican and Democratic Parties were calling themselves Progressives; in 1912, Progressives formed their own party. Historians have used the term *Progressivism* to refer to the era's spirit, while disagreeing over its meaning and over who actually was Progressive.

The reform impulse had many sources. Industrial capitalism created awesome technology, unprecedented productivity, and copious consumer goods. But it also brought harmful overproduction, domineering monopolies, labor strife, and destruction of natural resources. Burgeoning cities facilitated the distribution of goods and services but also bred poverty, disease, and crime. Rising immigration and a new professional class reconfigured the social order. And the depression of the 1890s forced leading citizens to realize what working people already knew: America's central promise of, equality of opportunity, was elusive.

Middle-class reformers organized around three goals. First, they sought to end abuses of power by making trustbusting, consumers' rights, and good government compelling political issues. Second, Progressives like Ben Lindsey wished to supplant corrupt power with humane institutions, such as schools, courts, and medical clinics. They asserted that society had responsibility and power to improve individual lives and that government must protect the common good and elevate public interest above self-interest. They challenged entrenched views on women's roles, race relations, education, legal and scientific thought, and morality. Third, Progressives wanted to entrust experts who would end wasteful competition and promote social and economic order. Just as corporations applied scientific management to achieve economic efficiency, Progressives advocated expertise and planning to achieve social and political efficiency.

Progressives had faith in humankind's ability to create a better world. Rising incomes, new educational opportunities, and increased availability of goods and services inspired confidence that social improvement would follow. Judge Lindsey expressed the Progressive creed when he wrote, "In the end the people are bound to do the right thing, no matter how much they fail at times."

As you read this chapter, keep the following questions in mind:

* **What were the major characteristics of Progressivism?**

* **In what ways did Progressive reform succeed, and in what ways did it fail?**

* **How did women and racial minorities challenge previous ways of thinking about American society?**

Theodore Roosevelt and Revival of the Presidency

Theodore Roosevelt | Regulation of Trusts | Pure Food and Drug Laws | Race Relations | Conservation | Gifford Pinchot | Panic of 1907 | Taft Administration | Candidates in 1912 | New Nationalism Versus New Freedom

Woodrow Wilson and Extension of Progressive Reform

Woodrow Wilson | Wilson's Policy on Business Regulation | Tariff and Tax Reform | Election of 1916

LEGACY FOR A PEOPLE AND A NATION *Margaret Sanger, Planned Parenthood, and the Birth-Control Controversy*

SUMMARY

Chronology

1895	Booker T. Washington gives Atlanta Compromise speech National Association of Colored Women founded			White Slave Traffic Act (Mann Act) prohibits transportation of women for "immoral purposes" Taft fires Pinchot
1898	*Holden v. Hardy* upholds limits on miners' working hours		1911	Society of American Indians founded
1901	McKinley assassinated; T. Roosevelt assumes presidency		1913	Sixteenth Amendment ratified, legalizing income tax
1904	*Northern Securities* case dissolves railroad trust			Seventeenth Amendment ratified, providing for direct election of senators
1905	*Lochner v. New York* removes limits on bakers' working hours			Underwood Tariff institutes income tax Federal Reserve Act establishes central banking system
1906	Hepburn Act tightens ICC control over railroads Meat Inspection Act passed Pure Food and Drug Act Passed		1914	Federal Trade Commission created to investigate unfair trade practices Clayton Anti-Trust Act outlaws monopolistic business practices
1908	*Muller v. Oregon* upholds limits on women's working hours		1919	Eighteenth Amendment ratified, establishing prohibition of alcoholic beverages
1909	NAACP founded		1920	Nineteenth Amendment ratified, giving women the vote in federal elections
1910	Mann-Elkins Act reinforces ICC powers			

The Varied Progressive Impulse

How did Progressive reform cut across class lines?

After the heated election of 1896, party loyalties eroded and voter turnout declined. In northern states, voter participation in presidential elections dropped from the 1880s' levels of 80 percent to under 60 percent. In southern states, where poll taxes and literacy tests prevented most African American and many poor white males from voting, it fell below 30 percent. At the same time, new interest groups championing their own causes gained influence.

National Associations and Foreign Influences Many formerly local organizations became nationwide after 1890. These included professional associations, such as the American Bar Association; women's organizations, such as the National American Woman Suffrage Association; issue-oriented groups, such as the National Consumers League; civic-minded clubs, such as the National Municipal League; and minority-group associations, such as the National Negro Business League and the Society of American Indians. Because they usually acted outside of parties, such groups made politics more fragmented and issue-focused than in earlier eras.

Reformers also adopted foreign models. Some were introduced by Americans who encountered them while studying in England, France, and Germany; others, by foreigners visiting the United States. Americans copied from England the settlement house, in which reformers lived among and aided the urban poor, and workers' compensation for victims of industrial accidents. Other reforms, such as old-age insurance, subsidized workers' housing, city planning, and rural reconstruction, were modified in America.

Although Populist rural-based goals of moral regeneration, political democracy, and antimonopolism continued after the movement faded, the Progressive quest for social justice, educational and legal reform, and government streamlining had a largely urban quality.

The New Middle Class and Muckrakers

Progressive goals—ending abuse of power, protecting the welfare of all classes, reforming institutions, and promoting social efficiency—existed across society. But a new middle class—men and women in law, medicine, engineering, social service, religion, teaching, and business—formed the reform vanguard. Offended by corruption and immorality in business, government, and human relations, they determined to apply the rational techniques of their professions to social problems. They also believed that they could create a unified nation by "Americanizing" immigrants and Indians through education stressing middle-class customs.

Progressive views were voiced by journalists whom Theodore Roosevelt dubbed **muckrakers** (after a character in the Puritan allegory *Pilgrim's Progress*, who, rather than looking heavenward at beauty, looked downward and raked the muck). Muckrakers fed public tastes for scandal by exposing social, economic, and political wrongs. Investigative articles in popular magazines attacked adulterated foods, fraudulent insurance, prostitution, and political corruption. Lincoln Steffens hoped his exposés of bosses' misrule in *McClure's* would inspire outrage and reform. Other celebrated muckraking works included Upton Sinclair's *The Jungle* (1906), exposing outrages of the meatpacking industry; and Ida M. Tarbell's disparaging history of Standard Oil (first published in *McClure's*, 1902–1904).

muckrakers: Journalists who wrote articles exposing urban political corruption and corporate wrongdoing.

Progressives advocated nonpartisan elections to prevent fraud and bribery bred by party loyalties. To make officeholders more responsible, they urged adoption of the initiative, which permitted voters to propose new laws; the referendum, which enabled voters to accept or reject a law; and the recall, which allowed voters to remove offending officials and judges from office.

Upper-Class Reformers

The Progressive spirit also stirred some businessmen and wealthy women. Executives like Alexander Cassatt of the Pennsylvania Railroad supported some government regulation and political restructuring to protect their interests from more radical reformers. Others, like E.A. Filene, founder of a Boston department store, were humanitarians who worked for social justice. Business-dominated organizations like the U.S. Chamber of Commerce thought that running schools, hospitals, and local government like businesses would stabilize society. Elite women financed settlement houses and organizations like the Young Women's Christian Association (YWCA), which aided unmarried working women.

Settlement Houses

Young, educated middle-class women and men worked to bridge the gap between social classes by living in inner-city settlement houses. Residents envisioned them as places where people could mitigate modern problems through education, art, and reform. Between

1886 and 1910, over 400 settlements were established, mostly in big cities, sponsoring activities such as English-language classes, kindergartens and nurseries, health clinics, vocational training, playgrounds, and art exhibits. The vanguard of progressivism, settlement house workers backed housing and labor reform, offered meeting space to unions, and served as school nurses, juvenile probation officers, and teachers.

Though men helped initiate the settlement movement, women were its most influential participants. Jane Addams of Chicago's Hull House settlement, Lillian Wald of New York's Henry Street settlement, Vida Scudder of Boston's Denison House, and Florence Kelley of Hull House not only broadened traditional female roles as settlement house leaders but used their work a springboard to larger reform roles. Kelley's investigations into the exploitation of child labor prompted Illinois governor John Altgeld to appoint her state factory inspector; she later founded the National Consumers League. Wald helped make nursing a respected profession and co-founded the NAACP. And Addams's efforts toward world peace garnered her the Nobel Peace Prize in 1931.

Working-Class Reformers

Vital elements of what became modern American liberalism derived from working-class urban experiences. By 1900, many urban workers were pressing "bread-and-butter reforms" such as safe factories, shorter workdays, workers' compensation, protection of child and women laborers, better housing, and a more equitable tax structure. Politicians trained in machine politics, and their constituents supported political bosses. Yet bossism was not necessarily incompatible with humanitarianism. "Big Tim" Sullivan, an influential boss in New York's Tammany Hall political machine, said he supported shorter workdays for women because "I had seen me sister go out to work when she was only fourteen and I know we ought to help these gals by giving 'em a law which will prevent 'em from being broken down while they're still young." Working-class advocates opposed prohibition, Sunday closing laws, civil service, and nonpartisan elections, but joined with other reformers to pass laws aiding labor and promoting social welfare.

The Social Gospel

Social Gospel: Movement launched in the 1870s that stressed that true Christianity commits men and women to fight social injustice wherever it exists.

Much of Progressive reform rested on religious values. A movement known as the **Social Gospel**, led by Protestant ministers Walter Rauschenbusch, Washington Gladden, and Charles Sheldon, countered competitive capitalism by interjecting Christian churches into worldly matters, such as arbitrating industrial harmony and improving the conditions of the poor. Believing that helping others provided the way to individual salvation and creating God's kingdom on earth, Social Gospelers governed their lives by asking, "What would Jesus do?"

Others tried to "Americanize" immigrants and Indians by expanding educational, economic, and cultural opportunities. But imposing their values on people of different cultures undermined their efforts. Working-class Catholic and Jewish immigrants, for example, sometimes rejected the Americanization efforts of Social Gospelers and resented middle-class reformers' interference in their child-rearing.

Socialists

Disillusioned immigrant intellectuals, industrial workers, former Populists, and women's rights activists turned to socialism. They wanted the United States to follow the example of Germany,

England, and France, where the government sponsored such socialist goals as low-cost housing, workers' compensation, old-age pensions, public ownership of municipal services, and labor reform. By 1912, the Socialist Party of America claimed 150,000 members, and 700,000 subscribers to its newspaper *Appeal to Reason*.

Politically, socialists united behind Eugene V. Debs, the American Railway Union organizer who drew nearly 100,000 votes as Socialist Party candidate in 1900. A spellbinding orator who appealed to urban immigrants and western farmers alike, Debs won 400,000 votes in 1904 and 900,000 in 1912, at the pinnacle of his and his party's career. Although Debs and other Socialist leaders did not always agree on tactics, they made compelling overtures to reformers.

While some Progressives joined the Socialist Party, most reformers favored capitalism too much to want to overthrow it. Municipal ownership of public utilities represented their limit of drastic change. Some AFL unions supported socialist goals and candidates, but many unions opposed reforms like unemployment insurance because it would increase taxes. Moreover, private real-estate interests opposed government intervention in housing, and manufacturers fought socialism by blacklisting militant laborers.

Southern and Western Progressivism

Progressive reform in the South included the same goals as in the North—railroad and utility regulation, factory safety, pure food and drug legislation, and moral reform. The South pioneered some political reforms; the direct primary originated in North Carolina; the city-commission plan arose in Galveston, Texas; and the city-manager plan began in Staunton, Virginia.

In the West, several politicians championed humanitarianism, putting the region at the forefront of efforts to expand federal and state government functions.

Although their objectives sometimes differed from those of middle-class Progressive reformers, socialists also became a more active force in the early twentieth century. Socialist parades on May Day, like this one in 1910, were meant to express the solidarity of all working people.

Foreign Universities and Study Abroad

The university as a degree-granting institution originated during Medieval times in Islamic Morocco and Egypt. Shortly thereafter, universities arose in Italy, France, England, and Spain. By the end of the nineteenth century, the chief models for the modern university existed in German cities and in British institutions at Oxford and Cambridge. Their academic freedom and dynamic faculty attracted young Americans. German universities were especially inexpensive; with travel costs, they were only a third as much as comparable American institutions.

Their time at British and European universities inspired many Americans with ideas about improving society. The muckraking journalist Lincoln Steffens, for example, received an undergraduate degree from the University of California, then studied at German universities to learn from the great minds that his California professors "quoted and looked up to as their high priests." Scholar and civil rights activist W.E.B. Du Bois pursued graduate work at the University of Berlin. Progressive historian Charles Beard was moved by his studies at Oxford University, and Edith Abbott, who pioneered social work in America, studied welfare policy at the London School of Economics.

Some American students were exposed to the European ideology of social democracy, a movement related to socialism but that emphasized reform through politics rather than revolution. Social democrats aligned with the working class and often called themselves "socialists." But they stressed moral issues rather than pitting one class against another. When these Americans returned home, they brought an opposition to the every-man-for-himself implications of laissez faire and an impetus for using the government for the betterment of all—important underpinnings of Progressive reform.

Corbis

Lincoln Steffens, born in 1866 in Sacramento, California, graduated from the University of California at Berkeley in 1889, then went abroad to "learn culture" by studying at universities in Germany and France. Upon his return to the United States, he became a police reporter in New York City, then wrote articles for the muckraking magazine McClure's, including pieces on corruption in American cities. He compiled the articles into a book, The Shame of the Cities, that became one of the most famous publications of the Progressive Era.

Special Collections Research Center, University of Chicago Library

Edith Abbott grew up in Grand Island, Nebraska, and taught high school before receiving an undergraduate degree from the University of Nebraska and a Ph.D. in economics from the University of Chicago. In 1906, at the age of thirty, she received a fellowship to study in England at the London School of Economics, where she learned new theories about dealing with poverty. After a few years, she joined Jane Addams at Hull House and became a pioneer in progressive reform.

Nevada's Progressive Senator Francis Newlands advocated national planning and federal control of water resources. California Governor Hiram Johnson fought for direct primaries, regulation of child and women's labor, workers' compensation, a pure food and drug act, and educational reform. Southern and western women, white and black, contributed to Progressive causes. In western states, women could vote on state and local matters, but often their reform efforts occurred outside of politics, in racially distinct projects. White women crusaded against child labor, founded social service organizations, and challenged unfair wages. African American women, as homemakers and religious leaders—which whites found more acceptable than political activism—advocated for cleaner streets, better education, and health reforms.

Opponents of Progressivism

It would be incorrect to assume that a Progressive spirit captivated all of America between 1895 and 1920. Defenders of free enterprise opposed regulatory measures believing government programs undermined the initiative and competition basic to a free-market system. "Old-guard" Republicans, such as Senator Nelson W. Aldrich of Rhode Island and House Speaker Joseph Cannon of Illinois, championed this ideology.

Moreover, prominent Progressives were not always "progressive." Their attempts to Americanize immigrants reflected prejudice as well as naiveté. Governor Hiram Johnson promoted discrimination against Japanese Americans, and most southern governors rested their power on appeals to white supremacy. In the South, the disfranchisement of blacks meant that electoral reforms affected only whites. Settlement houses in northern cities kept blacks and whites in separate programs and buildings.

Progressive reformers generally occupied the center of the ideological spectrum, believing on one hand that laissez faire was obsolete and on the other that a radical departure from free enterprise was dangerous. Like Thomas Jefferson, they expressed faith in the will of the people; like Alexander Hamilton, they desired strong central government to act in the interest of conscience.

Government and Legislative Reform

Mistrust of tyranny traditionally prompted Americans to believe that democratic government should be small, interfere in private affairs only in unique circumstances, and withdraw quickly. In the late 1800s, this viewpoint weakened when economic problems led corporations to pursue government aid and protection. Discontented farmers sought government regulation of railroads and other monopolistic businesses. City dwellers, accustomed to favors from political machines, expected government to act on their behalf. Before 1900, state governments had been concerned largely with railroads and economic growth; the federal government had focused primarily on tariffs and the currency. After 1900, public opinion, roused by muckraking media, influenced change.

According to Progressives, what was the government's role in improving society?

Restructuring Government

Middle-class Progressive reformers rejected laissez-faire principles of government, reasoning that in a complex industrial age public authority needed to counteract inefficiency and exploitation. But to tap this power, activists would have to reclaim government from politicians whose greed they believed soiled the democratic system.

Prior to the Progressive era, reformers attacked corruption in city governments through such structural reforms as civil service, nonpartisan elections, and scrutiny of public expenditures. After 1900, campaigns to make cities more efficient resulted in city-manager and commission forms of government, in which urban officials were chosen for professional expertise rather than for political connections. At the state level, Progressives supported several skillful governors. Wisconsin's Robert M. La Follette was one of the most dynamic Progressive governors. A small-town lawyer, La Follette rose through the state Republican Party to become governor in 1900. There, he initiated direct primaries, more equitable taxes, and railroad regulation. After three terms as governor, La Follette became a U.S. senator. "Battling Bob" displayed a rare ability to approach reform scientifically proclaiming that his goal was "not to smash corporations, but to drive them out of politics."

Crusades against corrupt politics made the system more democratic. Political reformers achieved a major goal in 1913 with adoption of the Seventeenth Amendment to the Constitution, which provided for direct election of U.S. senators, replacing election by state legislatures. But party bosses were still able to control elections, and special-interest groups spent large sums to influence voting.

Labor Reform

At the instigation of middle-class/working-class coalitions, many states enacted factory inspection laws, and by 1916 nearly two-thirds of states required compensation for victims of industrial accidents. Some legislatures granted aid to mothers with dependent children. Under pressure from the National Child Labor Committee, nearly every state set a minimum age for employment (varying from twelve to sixteen) and limited hours that children could work. Labor laws were imperfect, however. They seldom provided for the close inspection of factories that enforcement required. And families needing extra income falsified their children's ages to employers.

Several groups also united to achieve restricted working hours for women and aided retirees. After the Supreme Court, in *Muller v. Oregon*, upheld Oregon's ten-hour limit in 1908, more states passed laws protecting female workers. In 1914, the American Association for Old Age Security secured old-age pensions in Arizona. Judges struck down the law, but demand for pensions continued, and in the 1920s many states enacted such laws.

Prohibition

Reformers did not always agree about whether laws should regulate behavior such as drinking habits and sexual conduct. The **Anti-Saloon League**, formed in 1893, allied with the Woman's Christian Temperance Union (founded in 1874) to publicize alcoholism's role in health problems and family distress. The League successfully shifted attention from the immorality of drunkenness to the alleged link between the drinking and accidents, poverty, and poor productivity.

The war on saloons prompted many states and localities to restrict liquor consumption. By 1900, one-fourth of the nation's population lived in "dry" communities, prohibiting liquor sales. But alcohol consumption increased with the influx of immigrants whose cultures included social drinking, convincing prohibitionists that a nationwide ban was needed. In 1918, Congress passed the **Eighteenth Amendment** (ratified in 1919 and implemented in 1920), outlawing the manufacture, sale, and transportation of intoxicating liquors. Not all prohibitionists were Progressive

Anti-Saloon League: Advocacy group founded in 1893 that sought to ban alcohol by publicizing its harmful effects on families and individuals and its link to accidents and health problems.

Eighteenth Amendment: Amendment to the Constitution that established national prohibition of alcohol.

reformers, and vice versa. Nevertheless, the Eighteenth Amendment embodied the Progressive goal to protect family and workplace through reform legislation.

Controlling Prostitution Moral outrage erupted when muckraking journalists charged that international gangs were kidnapping women and forcing them into prostitution, a practice called white slavery. Accusations were exaggerated, but they alarmed moralists who falsely perceived a link between immigration and prostitution, and who feared that prostitutes were producing genetically inferior children. Reformers prodded governments to investigate and pass corrective legislation. The Chicago Vice Commission undertook a "scientific" survey of dance halls and illicit sex and published its findings as *The Social Evil in Chicago* in 1911. The report concluded that poverty, gullibility, and desperation drove women into prostitution. Such investigations publicized rising numbers of prostitutes but failed to prove that criminal organizations lured women into "the trade."

Reformers nonetheless believed they could attack prostitution by punishing those who promoted and practiced it. In 1910, Congress passed the White Slave Traffic Act (Mann Act), prohibiting interstate and international transportation of a woman for immoral purposes. By 1915, nearly every state outlawed brothels and solicitation of sex.

Like prohibition, the Mann Act reflected sentiment that government could improve behavior by restricting it. Middle-class reformers believed the source of evil was not human nature but the social environment. Intervention via laws could help create a heaven on earth, although working classes resented such attempts to control them. Thus, when Chicagoans voted on a referendum to make their city dry before the Eighteenth Amendment was passed, three-fourths of the city's immigrant voters opposed it, and the measure was defeated.

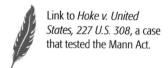
Link to *Hoke v. United States, 227 U.S. 308*, a case that tested the Mann Act.

New Ideas in Social Institutions

What was the impact of Progressive education reforms?

Preoccupation with efficiency and scientific management infiltrated education, law, religion, and social science. Darwin's theory of evolution challenged beliefs in a God-created world; immigration created complex social diversity; and technology made old production habits obsolete. Professionals grappled with how to embrace progress yet preserve the best from the past.

John Dewey and Progressive Education As late as 1870, when families needed children to do farm work, Americans attended school only a few months a year for four years. By 1900, however, the urban-industrial economy and its expanding middle class advanced childhood as a special life stage, sheltering youngsters from society's dangers and promoting their physical and emotional growth. That meant ensuring that youngsters were exposed to age-appropriate educational materials and activities.

Educators argued that expanded schooling produced better adult citizens and workers. In the 1870s and 1880s, laws required children to attend school to age fourteen. The number of public high schools grew from five hundred in 1870 to ten thousand in 1910. By 1900, educational reformers, such as philosopher John Dewey, asserted that schools needed to prepare children for a modern world by making personal development the focus of the curriculum.

Progressive education, based on Dewey's *The School and Society* (1899) and *Democracy and Education* (1916), stressed that learning should involve real-life problems and that children needed to learn from experience, not by rote memorization. Dewey and his wife, Alice, tested these ideas in their Laboratory School at the University of Chicago.

Growth of Colleges and Universities

A more practical curriculum also drove higher education reform. Previously, American colleges resembled their European counterparts: in training a select few for careers in law, medicine, and religion. But in the late 1800s, institutions of higher learning multiplied via state and federal grants. Between 1870 and 1910, American colleges and universities grew from 563 to nearly 1,000. Curricula broadened to make learning more appealing and keep pace with technological and social changes. Harvard University, under President Charles W. Eliot, pioneered new teaching methods and substituted electives for required courses. Many schools considered athletics vital to a student's growth, and men's intercollegiate sports became a permanent feature.

Southern states created segregated colleges for blacks and whites. Although African Americans continued to suffer from inferior educational opportunities, they found intellectual stimulation in all-black colleges and used education to help uplift their race.

Between 1890 and 1910, the number of women attending colleges swelled from 56,000 to 140,000. Roughly 106,000 attended coeducational institutions (mostly state universities); the rest enrolled in women's colleges. By 1920, 283,000 women attended college, accounting for 47 percent of total enrollment. But women were encouraged (and usually sought) to take home education courses, and most medical schools refused to admit women. Separate women's medical schools, such as the Women's Medical College of Philadelphia, trained female physicians, but most of these schools were absorbed or put out of business by larger, male-dominated institutions.

By 1920, 78 percent of children ages five and seventeen were enrolled in public schools; another 8 percent attended private and parochial schools. There were 600,000 college and graduate students in 1920, compared with only 52,000 in 1870. Yet critical analysis seldom tested the faith that schools could promote equality as well as personal growth and responsible citizenship.

Progressive Legal Thought

Harvard law professor Roscoe Pound and Oliver Wendell Holmes Jr., associate justice of the Supreme Court (1902–1932) led an attack on the traditional view of law as universal and unchanging. Their opinion that law should reflect society's needs challenged the practice of invoking inflexible legal precedents. Louis D. Brandeis, a lawyer who later joined Holmes on the Supreme Court, insisted that judges' opinions be based on scientifically gathered information about social realities. Brandeis collected data on harmful effects of long working hours to convince the Supreme Court, in *Muller v. Oregon* (1908), to uphold Oregon's ten-hour limit on women's workday.

Judges raised on laissez-faire economics and strict interpretation of the Constitution overturned laws that Progressives thought necessary. Thus in

1905, the Supreme Court, in *Lochner v. New York*, revoked a state law limiting bakers' working hours. The Court's majority argued that the Fourteenth Amendment protected an individual's right to make contracts without government interference.

Several decisions, beginning with *Holden v. Hardy* (1898), in which the Supreme Court sustained a Utah law regulating miners' working hours, confirmed the use of state police power to protect health, safety, and morals. Judges also affirmed federal police power and Congress's authority over interstate commerce by upholding legislation, such as the Pure Food and Drug Act, the Meat Inspection Act, and the Mann Act.

But even if one agreed that laws should address society's needs, whose needs should prevail? In many localities, a native-born Protestant majority imposed Bible reading in public schools (offending Catholics and Jews), required businesses to close on Sundays, limited women's rights, restricted religious practices of Mormons and others, prohibited interracial marriage, and enforced racial segregation. Justice Holmes asserted that laws should be made for "people of fundamentally differing views," but how to accomplish that continues to spark debates today.

Social Science

Social science—the study of society and its institutions—also changed. Economics scholars used statistics to argue that laws governing economic relationships were not timeless but should reflect prevailing social conditions. A new breed of sociologists led by Lester Ward, Albion Small, and Edward A. Ross agreed, adding that citizens should work to cure social ills.

Meanwhile, historians Frederick Jackson Turner, Charles A. Beard, and Vernon L. Parrington examined the past to explain the present. Beard, like other Progressives, believed that the Constitution was a flexible document. His *Economic Interpretation of the Constitution* (1913) argued that a group of merchants and business-oriented lawyers created the Constitution to defend private property. If the Constitution served special interests in one age, he argued, it could be changed to serve broader interests in another.

In public health, organizations such as the National Consumers League (NCL), founded by Florence Kelley in 1899, joined physicians and social scientists to secure far-reaching Progressive reforms. NCL pursued protection of female and child laborers and elimination of potential health hazards. Local branches united with women's clubs to advance consumer protection measures, such as the licensing of food vendors and inspection of dairies. They urged city governments to fund neighborhood clinics providing medical care to the poor.

Eugenics

The Social Gospel was a response to Social Darwinism, the application of biological natural selection and survival of the fittest to human interactions. But another movement, eugenics, sought to apply Darwinian principles more intrusively. The brainchild of Francis Galton, an English statistician and cousin of Charles Darwin, eugenics rested on the belief that human character and habits could be inherited, including unwanted traits, such as criminality and mental illness. Eugenicists believed society had an obligation to prevent the reproduction of the so-called mentally defective and criminally inclined by preventing them from marrying and, in extreme cases, sterilizing them. Such ideas targeted immigrants and people of color. Supported by such American notables as

Alexander Graham Bell, Margaret Sanger, and W. E. B. Du Bois, eugenics was discredited, especially after it became a linchpin of Nazi racial policies.

Some reformers endorsed eugenics; others embraced immigration restriction to control the composition of American society. Madison Grant's *The Passing of the Great Race* (1916) bolstered theories that immigrants from southern and eastern Europe threatened to weaken American society because they were inferior mentally and morally to earlier Nordic immigrants. Thus many people, including some Progressives, sought to curtail the influx of Poles, Italians, Jews, and other eastern and southern Europeans, and Asians. In the 1920s, restrictive legislation closed the door to "new" immigrants.

Challenges to Racial and Sexual Discrimination

What strategies did women use in their quest for equality in the early twentieth century?

White male reformers of the Progressive era dealt primarily with politics and institutions and ignored issues affecting former slaves, nonwhite immigrants, Indians, and women. Yet these groups caught the Progressive spirit and made strides toward their own advancement. Their efforts, however, posed a dilemma. Should women and nonwhites aim to imitate white men's values and gain their rights? Or was there something unique about racial and sexual cultures worth preserving at the risk of broader gains?

Continued Discrimination for African Americans

In 1900, nine-tenths of African Americans lived in the South, where repressive Jim Crow laws multiplied in the 1880s and 1890s (see page 523). In 1910, only 8,000 out of 970,000 high-school-age blacks were enrolled in southern high schools. Many African Americans moved northward in the 1880s, accelerating their migration after 1900. Although conditions in places like Chicago, Cleveland, and Detroit represented improvement, job discrimination, inferior schools, and segregated housing prevailed.

African American leaders differed over how—and whether—to assimilate. After emancipation, ex-slave Frederick Douglass urged "ultimate assimilation through self-assertion." Others supported emigration to Africa or the establishment of all-black communities in Oklahoma Territory and Kansas. Still others advocated militancy.

Booker T. Washington and Self-Help

Most blacks could neither escape nor conquer white society. Self-help, a strategy articulated by educator **Booker T. Washington**, offered one popular alternative. Born into slavery in Virginia in 1856, Washington obtained an education and in 1881 founded Tuskegee Institute, an all-black vocational school, in Alabama. There he developed a philosophy that blacks' best hopes lay in at least temporarily accommodating whites. Rather than fighting for political rights, Washington counseled African Americans to work hard, acquire property, and prove they were worthy of respect. "Dignify and glorify common labor," he urged in an 1895 speech that became known as the Atlanta Compromise. Washington observed that "in all things that are purely social we can be as separate as the fingers, yet one as the hand in all matters essential to mutual progress."

Booker T. Washington: Leading black activist of the late nineteenth century who advocated education and accommodation with white society as the best strategy for racial advancement.

Because he said what they wanted to hear, white businesspeople, reformers, and politicians regarded Washington as representing all African Americans. Washington endorsed a separate-but-equal policy and never argued that blacks were inferior; rather, he asserted that they could enhance their dignity through self-improvement.

Some blacks, however, concluded that Washington endorsed second-class citizenship. In 1905, a group of "anti-Bookerites" convened near Niagara Falls and pledged militant pursuit of unrestricted voting, economic opportunity, integration, and equality before the law. Representing the Niagara movement was **W. E. B. Du Bois**, an outspoken critic of the Atlanta Compromise.

W. E. B. Du Bois and the "Talented Tenth"

A New Englander and the first black to receive a Ph.D. from Harvard, Du Bois was a Progressive and member of the black elite. While a faculty member at Atlanta University, Du Bois compiled sociological studies of black urban life and wrote in support of civil rights. He treated Washington politely but could not accept accommodation. Du Bois believed an intellectual vanguard of cultured, educated blacks, the "Talented Tenth," should lead in pursuing racial equality. In 1909, he joined white liberals similarly discontented with Washington's accommodationism to form the **National Association for the Advancement of Colored People (NAACP)**. The organization aimed to end racial discrimination, eradicate lynching, and obtain voting rights through legal redress in the courts. By 1914, the NAACP had fifty branch offices and six thousand members.

African Americans struggled with questions about their place in white society. Du Bois voiced this dilemma, observing that "one ever feels his twoness—an American, a Negro, two souls, two thoughts, two unreconciled strivings, two warring ideals in one dark body." As Du Bois wrote in 1903, a black "would not bleach his Negro soul in a flood of white Americanism, for he knows that Negro blood has a message for the world. He simply wishes to make it possible for a man to be both a Negro and an American."

Society of American Indians

In 1911, middle-class Indians formed their own association, the Society of American Indians (SAI), to work for better education, civil rights, and healthcare. It also sponsored "American Indian Days" to cultivate pride and offset the images of savage peoples promulgated in Wild West shows.

SAI's emphasis on racial pride, however, was squeezed between pressures for assimilation and tribal allegiance. Its small membership did not fully represent the diverse and unconnected Indian nations. Individual hard work was not enough to overcome prejudice, and attempts to redress grievances legally faltered for lack of funds. Ultimately, SAI had little effect on poverty-stricken Indians who seldom knew that the organization even existed. Torn by internal disputes, the association folded in the early 1920s.

"The Woman Movement"

Women's groups faced similar struggles about the tactics they should use to achieve rights. Should they try to achieve equality within a male-dominated society? Or use female qualities to create new roles for themselves within society?

W. E. B. Du Bois: African American educator and activist who demanded full racial equality, including the same educational opportunities open to whites, and called on blacks to resist all forms of racism.

National Association for the Advancement of Colored People (NAACP): Organization that called for sustained activism, including legal challenges, to achieve political equality for blacks and full integration into American life.

Link to the chapter "Of Booker T. Washington and Others" in W. E. B Dubois's *The Souls of Black Folk.*

Heavyweight Boxing Champion Jack Johnson as Race Hero

It is probable that more African Americans in the 1910s paid attention to Jack Johnson than they did to either Booker T. Washington or W. E. B. Du Bois. In 1908, Jackson became the first black heavyweight champion of the world by knocking out Tommy Burns. Immediately, white boxing fans began searching for a "Great White Hope" to recapture the title, and in 1910, former champion James J. Jeffries came out of retirement to fight Johnson, boasting that he would "demonstrate that a white man is king of them all." But after fifteen rounds of pummeling from Johnson, Jeffries gave up. African Americans around the nation celebrated their hero's victory, and in some places race riots erupted as angry whites attacked jubilant revelers. Racist reaction was particularly strong because Johnson refused to accept white standards for the way a black man should behave. He courted and married white women, flaunted his consumer tastes, and dealt with opponents and reporters with a pompous attitude. In 1915, Johnson, then thirty-seven years old, lost his title to Jess Willard in Cuba. The fight took place outside the country because in 1913 Johnson had been convicted of violating the Mann Act in transporting Belle Schreiber, a white prostitute, across state lines for "immoral purposes." Sentenced to a year in jail, Johnson fled the country but returned in 1920 to serve a one-year jail sentence. How do these three images reveal racial attitudes, both black and white toward Jack Johnson? What messages do they convey to someone viewing them?

© Bettmann/Corbis

Jack Johnson's first white wife was Etta Terry Duryea, a socialite and former wife of an automobile manufacturer. Their turbulent marriage ended in 1912 when Duryea committed suicide.

Library of Congress

Puck, America's first successful humor magazine, caricatured how "Uncle Tom's Cabin" would have to be performed if Jack Johnson were to beat James Jeffries in 1910. The magazine cover shows Johnson as a large, wealthy man knocking down the slaveholder Simon Legree.

© Stefano Bianchetti/CORBIS

The Italian poster artist Achille Beltrame depicted Jack Johnson's reception by jubilant African Americans in his hometown of Chicago after his triumph over Jim Jeffries in 1910. As a result of that victory, Johnson acquired an international as well as national reputation.

The answers that women found involved a subtle but important shift in their politics. Before 1910, women's rights activists called themselves "the woman movement." Often middle-class, these women strove to move beyond the household into higher education and paid professions. They claimed that women's special, even superior, traits as guardians of family and morality would humanize all of society. Settlement-house founder Jane Addams, for example, endorsed woman suffrage by asking, "If women have in any sense been responsible for the gentler side of life which softens and blurs some of its harsher conditions, may not they have a duty to perform in our American cities?"

Women's Clubs

Originating as literary and educational organizations, women's clubs began taking stands on public affairs in the late nineteenth century. They asserted traditional female responsibilities for home and family as the rationale for reforming society through an enterprise that historians have called social housekeeping. These female reformers worked for factory inspection, regulation of children's and women's labor, improved housing, and consumer protection.

African American women had their own club movement, including the Colored Women's Federation, which sought to establish a training school for "colored girls." Founded in 1895, the National Association of Colored Women was the nation's first African American social service organization; it concentrated on establishing nurseries, kindergartens, and retirement homes. Black women also developed reform organizations within Black Baptist and African Methodist Episcopal churches.

Feminism

Around 1910, some people concerned with women's place in society began using the term *feminism*. Whereas the woman movement spoke of moral purity, feminists emphasized rights and self-development. Charlotte Perkins Gilman, a major figure in the movement, declared in her book *Women and Economics* (1898) that domesticity was obsolete and attacked men's monopoly on economic opportunity. Arguing that paid employees should handle domestic chores, Gilman asserted that modern women must have access to jobs to be independent.

Margaret Sanger's Crusade

Several feminists joined the birth-control movement led by Margaret Sanger. A former visiting nurse who believed in women's rights to sexual pleasure and determining when to have a child, Sanger helped reverse state and federal laws banning publication and distribution of information about sex and contraception. Opposition came from those who saw birth control as a threat to family and morality. Sanger also was a eugenicist who perceived birth control as a means of limiting the numbers of children born to "inferior" immigrant and nonwhite mothers. In 1921, she formed the American Birth Control League, enlisting physicians and social workers to convince judges to allow distribution of birth-control information. Most states still prohibited the sale of contraceptives, but Sanger provoked public debate.

Woman Suffrage

A new generation of Progressive feminists, represented by Harriot Stanton Blatch, daughter of nineteenth-century suffragist Elizabeth Cady Stanton, carried on women's battle for the vote. Blatch linked voting rights to the improvement of women's working conditions. She joined the Women's Trade Union League and founded the Equality League of Self Supporting Women in 1907. Declaring that every woman worked, for wages or unpaid housework, Blatch believed all women's efforts contributed to society's betterment. Thus, women should exercise the vote to promote and protect women's economic roles.

Nine states, all in the West, allowed women to vote in state and local elections by 1912 (see Map 21.1). Suffragists' tactics ranged from persistent letter-writing and publications of the National American Woman Suffrage Association, led by **Carrie Chapman Catt**, to meetings and militant marches of the National Woman's Party, led by Alice Paul and Harriot Stanton Blatch. More decisive, however, was women's service during World War I as factory laborers, medical volunteers, and municipal workers. By convincing legislators that women could shoulder public responsibilities, women's wartime contributions facilitated passage of the national suffrage amendment (the Nineteenth) in 1920.

During the Progressive era, leaders like Blatch, Paul, and Catt helped clarify issues that concerned women and but winning the vote was only a first step. Discrimination in employment, education, and law continued to shadow women for decades. As feminist Crystal Eastman observed after: "women, if I know them, are saying, Now at last we can begin.'. . . Now they can say what they are really after, in common with all the rest of the struggling world, is freedom."

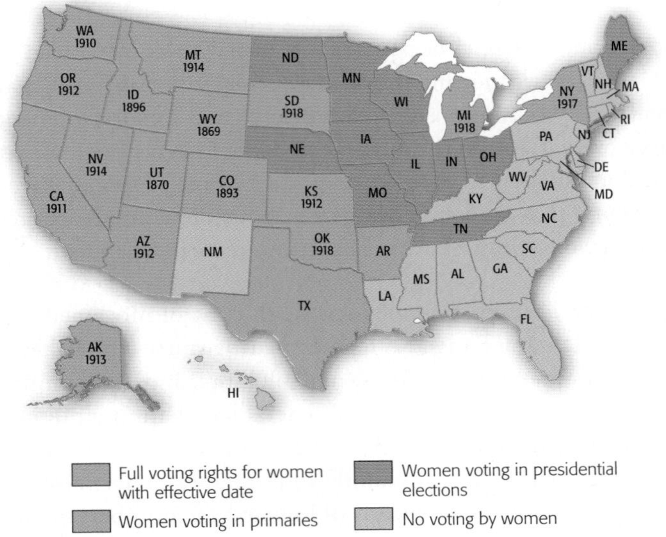

Carrie Chapman Catt: President of the National American Woman Suffrage Association in the early twentieth century.

Full voting rights for women with effective date
Women voting in primaries
Women voting in presidential elections
No voting by women

MAP 21.1

Woman Suffrage Before 1920

Before Congress passed and the states ratified the Nineteenth Amendment, woman suffrage already existed, but mainly in the West. Several midwestern states allowed women to vote only in presidential elections, but legislatures in the South and Northeast generally refused such rights until forced to do so by constitutional amendment.

Source: Copyright © Cengage Learning

Theodore Roosevelt and Revival of the Presidency

The Progressive era' reform focused on the federal government as the foremost agent of change. Although the federal government had notable accomplishments during the Gilded Age, its role was mainly to support rather than control economic expansion. Then, in September 1901, the assassination of President William McKinley by anarchist Leon Czolgosz vaulted **Theodore Roosevelt**, the young vice president, into the White House. As governor of New York, Roosevelt angered state Republican bosses by showing sympathy for regulatory legislation. He would become the nation's most forceful president since Lincoln, one who bestowed the office with much of its twentieth-century character.

> Theodore Roosevelt was known as a trustbuster, but was he?

Theodore Roosevelt: Youthful successor to slain president William McKinley in 1901; U.S. president, 1901–1909; promoted an agenda of progressive reform.

Theodore Roosevelt

Driven by a lifelong obsession to overcome his physical limitations, Roosevelt exerted what he called "manliness"— a zest for action and display of courage. In his teens, he became a marksman and horseman and later competed on Harvard's boxing and wrestling teams. In the 1880s, he lived on a Dakota ranch, roping cattle and brawling with cowboys. Descended from a Dutch aristocratic family, Roosevelt had wealth, but he also inherited a sense of civic responsibility that guided him into public service. He served three terms in the New York legislature, sat on the federal Civil Service Commission, served as New York City's police commissioner, was assistant secretary of the navy, and earned a reputation as a combative, crafty leader. In 1898, he thrust himself into the Spanish-American War by organizing a volunteer cavalry brigade, called the Rough Riders, to fight in Cuba. Although his dramatic act had little impact on the war's outcome, it made him a media hero.

Roosevelt carried his youthful exuberance into the White House. A Progressive, he concurred with allies that a small, uninvolved government would not suffice in the industrial era. Instead, economic progress necessitated a government powerful enough to guide national affairs. Especially in economic matters, Roosevelt wanted government to decide when big business was good and when it was bad.

Regulation of Trusts

The federal regulation of business that characterized twentieth-century America began with Roosevelt's presidency. Although labeled a trustbuster, Roosevelt actually considered

California Museum of Photography, University of California

Theodore Roosevelt (1858–1919) liked to think of himself as a great outdoorsman. He loved most the rugged countryside and believed that he and his country should serve as examples of "manliness."

business consolidation an efficient means to material progress. He believed in distinguishing between good and bad trusts and preventing bad ones from manipulating markets. Thus, he instructed the Justice Department to use antitrust laws to prosecute railroad, meatpacking, and oil trusts, which he believed unscrupulously exploited the public. Roosevelt's policy triumphed in 1904 when the Supreme Court ordered the breakup of Northern Securities Company, the huge railroad combination created by J. P. Morgan. Roosevelt did not attack other trusts, such as U.S. Steel, another of Morgan's creations.

When prosecution of Northern Securities began, Morgan reportedly asked Roosevelt, "If we have done anything wrong, send your man to my man and they can fix it up." The president refused but was more sympathetic to cooperation between business and government than might seem. He urged the Bureau of Corporations (part of the newly created Department of Labor and Commerce) to assist companies in merging and expanding. Through investigation and consultation, the administration cajoled businesses to regulate themselves.

Hepburn Act: Legislation that strengthened regulatory powers of the Interstate Commerce Commission, particularly over railroads, and later other businesses and industries.

Roosevelt also supported regulatory legislation. After a year of wrangling, Roosevelt persuaded Congress to pass the **Hepburn Act** (1906), which gave the Interstate Commerce Commission (ICC) greater authority set railroad freight rates and extend that authority over ferries, express companies, storage facilities, and oil pipelines. The Hepburn Act still allowed courts to overturn ICC decisions, but it now required shippers to prove they had not violated regulations, rather than making the government demonstrate violations.

Pure Food and Drug Laws

Roosevelt showed willingness to compromise to ensure pure food and drug legislation. For decades, reformers urged government regulation of processed meat and patent medicines. Public outrage at fraud flared in 1906 when Upton Sinclair published *The Jungle*, a fictionalized exposé of Chicago meatpacking plants. Sinclair, a socialist who sought to improve working conditions, shocked public sensibilities with vivid descriptions.

> There would be meat stored in great piles; water from leaky roofs would drip over it, and thousands of rats would race about on it…a man could run his hand over these piles of meat and sweep off handfuls of dried dung of rats. These rats were a nuisance, and the packers would put poisoned bread out for them; they would die, and then rats, bread, and meat would go into the hoppers together.

Roosevelt ordered an investigation, and finding Sinclair's descriptions accurate, supported the Meat Inspection Act (1906). This law required government agents monitor the quality of processed meat. But as part of a compromise with meatpackers and their congressional allies, the government had to finance inspections, and meatpackers could appeal adverse decisions. Nor were companies required to provide date-of-processing information on canned meats. Most large meatpackers welcomed legislation because it restored foreign confidence in American meat products.

The Pure Food and Drug Act (1906) also addressed abuses in the patent medicine industry. Makers of tonics and pills had long been making undue claims about their products' effects and used alcohol and narcotics as ingredients. The law required that labels list the ingredients—a goal consistent with Progressive confidence that with information, people would make wiser purchases.

Roosevelt's approach to labor resembled his compromises with business. When the United Mine Workers struck against Pennsylvania coal-mine owners in 1902 over an eight-hour workday and higher pay, the president urged arbitration. Owners refused to recognize the union or arbitrate grievances. As winter approached and fuel shortages loomed, Roosevelt threatened to use federal troops to reopen the mines, thus forcing management to accept. The arbitration commission decided in favor of higher wages and reduced hours and required management to deal with miners' grievance committees. But, it did not mandate recognition of the union. The decision, according to Roosevelt, provided a "square deal" for all. The settlement embodied Roosevelt's belief that the president or his representatives should determine which labor demands were legitimate and which were not.

Race Relations

Although he invited Booker T. Washington to the White House to discuss racial matters, Roosevelt believed in white superiority and was neutral toward blacks only when it helped him politically. Case in point: in 1906 the army transferred African American soldiers from Nebraska to Brownsville, Texas. Anglo and Mexican residents resented their presence and banned them from parks and businesses. On August 14, a battle between blacks and whites broke out, and a white man was killed. Brownsville residents blamed soldiers, but soldiers refused to help investigators identify participants. Consequently, Roosevelt discharged 167 black soldiers without a hearing and prevented them from receiving their pay and pensions. Black leaders were outraged. To preserve black support for Republican candidates in the 1906 elections, Roosevelt waited until after the elections to sign discharge papers.

Conservation

Roosevelt's Progressive impulse for efficiency and love for the outdoors inspired lasting contributions to resource conservation. Government establishment of national parks began in the late nineteenth century. Roosevelt advanced the movement by favoring *conservation* over *preservation*. Thus, he not only exercised presidential power to protect such natural wonders as the Grand Canyon in Arizona by declaring them national monuments, but also backed a policy of "wise use" of forests, waterways, and other resources. Previously, the government transferred ownership of natural resources on federal land to the states and private interests. Roosevelt, however, believed efficient resource conservation demanded federal management over lands in the public domain.

Makers of unregulated patent medicines advertised their products' exorbitant abilities to cure almost any ailment and remedy any unwanted physical condition. Loring's Fat-Ten-U tablets and Loring's Corpula were two such products. The Pure Food and Drug Act of 1906 did not ban these items but tried to prevent manufacturers from making unsubstantiated claims.

Roosevelt used federal authority over resources by protecting waterpower sites from sale to private interests and charging permit fees for users who wanted to produce hydroelectricity. He also supported the Newlands Reclamation Act of 1902, which controlled sale of irrigated federal land in the West (see page 446). Roosevelt tripled the number of national forests and backed conservationist Gifford Pinchot in creating the U.S. Forest Service.

Gifford Pinchot

As principal advocate of "wise use" policy, Pinchot promoted scientific management of the nation's woodlands. He obtained Roosevelt's support for transferring management of the national forests from the Interior Department to his bureau in the Agriculture Department. The Forest Service charged fees for grazing livestock within the national forests, supervised bidding for the cutting of timber, and hired university-trained foresters as federal employees.

Pinchot and Roosevelt did not seek to preserve resources permanently; rather, they wanted to conserve their efficient use and make companies profiting from using public lands pay the government. Many involved in natural-resource exploitation welcomed such a policy because it enabled them to better control products, such as when Roosevelt and Pinchot encouraged lumber companies to engage in reforestation.

Panic of 1907

In 1907, a financial panic caused by reckless speculation forced some New York banks to close to prevent frightened depositors from withdrawing money. J. P. Morgan helped stem the panic by persuading financiers to stop dumping stocks. In return for Morgan's aid, Roosevelt approved a deal allowing U.S. Steel to absorb the Tennessee Iron and Coal Company—a deal at odds with Roosevelt's trustbusting aims.

During his last year in office, Roosevelt retreated from the Republican Party's friendliness to big business. He supported stronger business regulation and heavier taxation of the rich. Promising that he would not seek reelection, Roosevelt backed Secretary of War **William Howard Taft** in 1908. Taft easily defeated three-time Democratic nominee William Jennings Bryan by 1.25 million popular votes and a 2-to-1 margin in the electoral college.

William Howard Taft: Roosevelt's hand-picked successor for president (1909–1913); later served as Supreme Court Justice.

Taft Administration

Taft faced political problems that Roosevelt had postponed, foremost, extremely high tariffs. Honoring Taft's pledge to cut tariffs, the House passed a bill providing numerous reductions. Protectionists in the Senate prepared to amend the bill and revise rates upward. But Senate Progressives attacked the tariff for benefiting special interests, trapping Taft between reformers who claimed to be preserving Roosevelt's antitrust campaign and protectionists who dominated the Republican Party. In the end, Rhode Island Senator Nelson Aldrich restored most cuts, and Taft signed what became known as the Payne-Aldrich Tariff (1909). To Progressives, Taft had failed to fill Roosevelt's shoes.

In reality, Taft was as sympathetic to reform as Roosevelt was. He prosecuted more trusts than Roosevelt, expanded national forest reserves, signed the Mann-Elkins Act (1910), which bolstered regulatory powers of the ICC, and supported such labor reforms as shorter work hours and mine safety legislation. The Sixteenth Amendment, which legalized the federal income tax and the Seventeenth Amendment, which provided for direct election of U.S. senators, were initiated during Taft's presidency (and ratified in 1913). Like Roosevelt, Taft compromised with big business, but unlike Roosevelt, he was unable to manipulate the public with spirited rhetoric. Roosevelt expanded presidential power. Taft believed in the strict restraint of law. He had been a successful lawyer and judge and returned to the bench as chief justice of the United States between 1921 and 1930.

Candidates in 1912

In 1910, when Roosevelt returned from Africa, he found his party torn and tormented. Reformers formed the National Progressive Republican League and rallied behind Robert La Follette for president in 1912, though many hoped Roosevelt would run. Another wing of the party remained loyal to Taft. Disappointed by Taft, Roosevelt spoke out for "the welfare of the people" and stronger business regulation. When La Follette became ill early in 1912, Roosevelt, proclaiming himself fit as a "bull moose," sought the Republican presidential nomination.

Taft's supporters controlled the Republican convention and nominated him for a second term. In protest, Roosevelt's supporters formed a third party—the Progressive, or Bull Moose, Party—and nominated the former president. Meanwhile, Democrats took forty-six ballots to select their candidate, New Jersey's Progressive governor **Woodrow Wilson**. Socialists, by now a growing party, again nominated Eugene V. Debs.

Woodrow Wilson: Democratic president whose election in 1912 ushered in a second wave of progressive reforms on the national level; served as president until 1921.

New Nationalism Versus New Freedom

Central to Theodore Roosevelt's campaign was a scheme called the New Nationalism, which envisioned an era of national unity in which government would coordinate and regulate economic activity. Roosevelt asserted that he would establish regulatory commissions to protect citizens' interests and ensure wise use of economic power. Wilson offered a more idealistic proposal, the "New Freedom." He argued that concentrated economic power threatened individual liberty and that monopolies should be broken up to ensure a free marketplace. But he would not restore laissez faire. Like Roosevelt, Wilson would enhance government authority to protect and regulate. "Without the watchful ... resolute interference of the government, there can be no fair play between individuals and such powerful institutions as the trust," he declared. Wilson stopped short, however, of advocating the cooperation between business and government inherent in Roosevelt's New Nationalism.

Link to Theodore Roosevelt's New Nationalism speech from 1910.

Roosevelt and Wilson stood closer together than their rhetoric implied. Both believed in individual freedom. Both supported equality of opportunity (chiefly for white males), conservation of natural resources, fair wages, and social betterment. Neither would hesitate to expand government intervention through strong leadership and bureaucratic reform.

In the election, the popular vote was inconclusive. The victorious Wilson won just 42 percent, though he did capture 435 out of 531 electoral votes. Roosevelt received 27 percent of the popular vote. Taft polled 23 percent of the popular vote and only 8 electoral votes. Debs won 6 percent but no electoral votes.

Three-quarters of the electorate supported alternatives to Taft's view of restrained government.

Woodrow Wilson and Extension of Progressive Reform

How did participation in World War I alter Wilson's position on business?

Woodrow Wilson

Born in Virginia in 1856 and raised in the South, Wilson was the son of a Presbyterian minister. He earned a B.A. degree at Princeton University, studied law at the University of Virginia, received a Ph.D. degree from Johns Hopkins University, and became a professor of history, jurisprudence, and political economy at Princeton. Between 1885 and 1908, he published several respected books on American history and government.

Wilson was a superb orator who could inspire loyalty with religious imagery and eloquent expressions of American ideals. But he harbored disdain for African Americans, had no misgivings about Jim Crow laws, and opposed admitting blacks to Princeton. At Princeton, he battled against aristocratic elements and earned a reputation as a reformer so that in 1910 New Jersey's Democrats nominated Wilson for governor. Once elected, Wilson repudiated the party bosses and promoted Progressive legislation. A poor administrator, he often lost his temper and refused to compromise. His accomplishments nevertheless won him the 1912 Democratic presidential nomination.

Wilson's Policy on Business Regulation

As president, Wilson blended New Freedom competition with New Nationalism regulation, setting the direction of federal economic policy. Corporate consolidation made restoration of open competition impossible. Wilson sought to prevent abuses by expanding government regulation. He supported congressional passage in 1914 of the Clayton Anti-Trust Act and a bill creating the **Federal Trade Commission** (FTC).

Federal Trade Commission: Agency formed in 1914 to ensure fair trade and practices.

The Clayton Act corrected deficiencies of the Sherman Anti-Trust Act of 1890 by outlawing such practices as price discrimination (lowering prices in some regions but not others) and interlocking directorates (management of two or more competing companies by the same executives). The act also aided labor by exempting unions from its anticombination provision, thereby making peaceful strikes, boycotts, and picketing less vulnerable to government interference. The FTC could investigate companies and issue cease-and-desist orders against unfair practices to protect consumers.

Under Wilson, the Federal Reserve Act (1913), established the nation's first central banking system since 1836. To break the power that syndicates like that of J. P. Morgan held over the money supply, the act created twelve district banks to hold reserves of member banks nationwide. District banks, supervised by the Federal Reserve Board, would lend money to member banks at a low interest rate called the discount rate. By adjusting this rate (and thus the amount a bank could afford to borrow), district banks could increase or decrease the amount of money in circulation, enabling the Federal Reserve Board to loosen or tighten credit, thereby making interest rates fairer.

Tariff and Tax Reform   Wilson and Congress attempted to restore competition with the Underwood Tariff of 1913. By reducing or eliminating certain tariffs, the Underwood Tariff encouraged importation of cheaper foreign goods. To replace revenues lost because of tariff reductions, the act levied a graduated income tax on U.S. residents. Incomes under $4,000 were exempt; thus, almost all factory workers and farmers escaped taxation. Individuals and corporations earning between $4,000 and $20,000 had to pay a 1 percent tax; thereafter rates rose to a maximum of 6 percent on earnings over $500,000.

The outbreak of World War I (see Chapter 23) and the approaching 1916 presidential election prompted Wilson to support stronger reforms. He backed the Federal Farm Loan Act, which created twelve federally supported banks that could lend money at moderate interest to farmers who belonged to credit institutions—a diluted version of the Populists' subtreasury plan proposed a generation earlier (see page 528). To forestall railroad strikes, Wilson in 1916 pushed passage of the Adamson Act, which mandated eight-hour workdays and time-and-a-half overtime pay for railroad laborers. He pleased Progressives by appointing Brandeis, the "people's advocate," to the Supreme Court, though an anti-Semitic backlash almost blocked Senate approval of the Court's first Jewish justice. Wilson also backed laws regulating child labor and providing workers' compensation for federal employees who suffered work-related injuries or illness.

But Wilson never overcame his racism. He fired several black federal officials, and his administration preserved racial separation in restrooms, restaurants, and government office buildings. When the pathbreaking but inflammatory film about the Civil War and Reconstruction, *The Birth of a Nation,* was released in 1915, Wilson allowed a showing at the White House, though he prohibited it during World War I.

Election of 1916   Republicans snubbed Theodore Roosevelt as their candidate in 1916, choosing Charles Evans Hughes, Supreme Court justice and former reform governor of New York. Aware of public anxiety over the world war in Europe since 1914, Wilson ran on neutrality and Progressivism, using the slogan "He Kept Us Out of War." The election was close. Wilson received 9.1 million votes to Hughes's 8.5 million and barely won in the electoral college, 277 to 254. The Socialist candidate drew only 600,000 votes, largely because Wilson's reforms won over some Socialists and because the ailing Eugene Debs was no longer the party's standard-bearer.

During Wilson's second term, U.S. involvement in World War I increased government regulation of the economy. Mobilization and war, he believed, required greater coordination of production and cooperation between the public and private sectors. The War Industries Board exemplified this: private businesses submitted to the board's control on condition that their profit motives would be satisfied. After the war, Wilson's administration dropped such measures, including farm price supports, guarantees of collective bargaining, and high taxes. This retreat from regulation, prompted partly by the election of a Republican Congress in 1918, stimulated a new era of business ascendancy in the 1920s.

Margaret Sanger, Planned Parenthood, and the Birth-Control Controversy

Some Progressive era reforms illustrate how earnest intentions can become tangled in divisive moral issues. Such is the legacy of birth-control advocate Margaret Sanger. In 1912, Sanger produced a column on sex education in the *New York Call* entitled "What Every Girl Should Know." Moralists accused her of writing obscene literature because she publicly discussed venereal disease and contraception. She counseled poor women on New York's Lower East Side about how to avoid frequent childbirth, miscarriage, and bungled abortion. In 1914, Sanger launched *The Woman Rebel*, a monthly newspaper advocating a woman's right to practice birth control. Indicted for distributing obscenity through the mails, she fled to England, where she gave speeches promoting family planning and enjoying sexuality without fear of pregnancy.

Returning to the United States, Sanger opened the country's first birth-control clinic in Brooklyn in 1916. She was arrested, but when a court exempted physicians from a law prohibiting dissemination of contraceptive information, she set up a doctor-run clinic in 1923. Staffed by female doctors and social workers, the Birth Control Clinical Research Bureau became a model for other clinics. Sanger organized the American Birth Control League (1921) and sought support from medical and social reformers, even from the eugenics movement, for legalized birth control. After falling out with some allies, she resigned from the American Birth Control League in 1928.

The movement continued, and in 1938 the American Birth Control League and the Birth Control Clinical Research Bureau merged to form the Birth Control Federation of America, renamed the Planned Parenthood Federation of America (PPFA) in 1942. The organization's mission was to strengthen the family and stabilize society with governmental support, rather than focus on the right to voluntary motherhood. Throughout the 1940s, the PPFA emphasized family planning through making contraceptives more accessible. In 1970, it began receiving federal funds.

In the 1960s, new feminist agitation for women's rights and rising concerns about overpopulation made birth control and abortion controversial. Although PPFA initially dissociated from abortion, the debate between a woman's "choice" and a fetus's "right to life" drew the organization into the fray, especially after 1973, when the Supreme Court validated women's right to an abortion in *Roe v. Wade*. PPFA fought legislative and court attempts to make abortions illegal, and in 1989 it helped organize a women's march on Washington. Some Latino and African American groups attacked the PPFA's stance, charging that abortion was a eugenics program meant to reduce births among nonwhites.

PPFA's involvement in abortion politics resulted in several clinics becoming targets of picketing and violence by those who believe abortion is immoral. PPFA operates nearly nine hundred health centers providing medical services and education. But birth control's legacy to a people and a nation includes disagreement over whose rights and whose morality should prevail.

Summary

By 1920, a quarter-century of reform had wrought momentous changes. Progressives established the principle of public intervention to ensure fairness, health, and safety. Concern over poverty and injustice reached new heights. But reformers could not sustain their efforts indefinitely. Although Progressive values lingered after World War I, a mass-consumer society refocused people's attention from reform to materialism.

Multiple and sometimes contradictory goals characterized the era because there was no single Progressive movement. National programs ranged from Roosevelt's faith in big government as a coordinator of big business to Wilson's promise to dissolve economic concentrations and legislate open competition. At state and local levels, reformers pursued causes as varied as neighborhood improvement, government reorganization, public ownership of utilities, and better working conditions. Women and African Americans developed new consciousness about identify, and although women made some inroads into public life, both groups still found themselves in confined social positions.

Successes aside, the failure of many Progressive initiatives indicates the strength of the opposition, as well as weaknesses within the reform movements. As issues such as Americanization, eugenics, prohibition, education, and moral uplift illustrate, social reform often merged into social control—attempts to impose white, middle-class values on all of society. Courts asserted constitutional and liberty-of-contract doctrines in striking down key Progressive legislation, notably the federal law prohibiting child labor. Federal regulatory agencies rarely had enough resources for thorough investigations; they had to depend on information from the very companies they policed. In 1920, as in 1900, government remained under the influence of business.

Yet Progressive era reforms reshaped the national outlook. Trustbusting, however faulty, made industrialists more sensitive to public opinion. Progressive legislation equipped government with tools to protect consumers against price fixing and dangerous products. Social reformers relieved some ills of urban and industrial life. Although the questions they raised about American life remained unresolved, Progressives made the nation acutely aware of its principles and promises.

Chapter Review

The Varied Progressive Impulse

How did Progressive reform cut across class lines?

The impulse to improve society at the turn of the twentieth century had variants in the working, middle, and wealthier classes. An emerging class of educated male and female professionals stood at the vanguard of Progressivism and sought to apply the techniques of professions such as law, engineering, medicine, social service, and teaching to end the abuse of power and inefficiency in business and government, and to protect the welfare of all classes. They also believed they could unify society through education and Americanization programs for new immigrants and Native Americans. Muckraking journalists exposed corruption and social wrongs, including fraudulent insurance, prostitution, and political corruption, as well as industrial outrages such as Upton Sinclair's exposé of the meatpacking industry. Workers, too, pressed for reforms to improve safety and housing and to include workers' compensation for injuries on the job. There was even a religious component as Protestant ministers sought to counter the negative impact of competitive capitalism and industrialization with a message of Christian salvation known as the "Social Gospel."

Government and Legislative Reform

According to Progressives, what was the government's role in improving society?

Unlike earlier generations of Americans who believed in a limited role for government, Progressives felt the government not only had an obligation to improve society but could protect people and families by restricting behavior. Progressives pushed officials to adopt regulations that would end labor abuses (notably, factory inspection laws), compensation for injured workers, minimum age and wage laws, child labor laws, and protective legislation regulating the hours women could work. Many also supported women's suffrage. Next, Progressives focused on ending vice, pushing for the passage of state laws and later a constitutional amendment (the Eighteenth Amendment, implemented in 1920) banning the manufacture and sale of alcohol—which they believed contributed to accidents, poverty, and poor productivity. Inspired by muckraking articles about gangs forcing white women into prostitution (dubbed "white slavery"), Progressives called for government investigations and new laws. Congress passed the Mann Act in 1910, prohibiting the interstate and international transportation of women for immoral purposes. By 1915 nearly every state outlawed brothels and solicitation of sex.

New Ideas in Social Institutions

What was the impact of Progressive education reforms?

Increasing concerns about the social impact of industrialization, along with a penchant for scientific management and efficiency, drove Progressive approaches to education. Reformers such as John Dewey not only wanted to ensure that children were exposed to age-appropriate materials, but they also focused on preparing children for the modern world by teaching them to use their ingenuity to solve real-life problems. College curricula shifted from their previous nearly exclusive focus on preparing primarily white men for a few professions such as medicine, religion, and law, to a focus on learning that kept pace with technological and social changes. Regarded as vital to a student's growth, athletics became a permanent feature. The number of colleges expanded, including all-black land grant colleges and women's colleges.

Challenges to Racial and Sexual Discrimination

What strategies did women use in their quest for equality in the early twentieth century?

Women's organizations had long struggled over whether to focus on their shared humanity with men or accentuate their unique female qualities in pursuit of equality and new social roles for women. Calling themselves "the woman movement" before 1910, they played up women's special, even superior, traits as guardians of the family and morality. After that date, activists adopted the term *feminism*, emphasizing women's right to citizenship and self-development. Activist styles ranged from moderate to radical, but all saw the vote as a first and vital step to influencing the laws affecting them, be it improving

women's working conditions or assuring their economic roles. Women's participation in the war effort also showed their ability and willingness to serve their country and made it impossible for legislators to continue to justify denying them the vote (which women finally received in 1920).

Theodore Roosevelt and the Revival of the Presidency

Theodore Roosevelt was known as a trustbuster, but was he?

Yes and no. As a Progressive, Roosevelt believed government should guide national affairs and economic development and determine when business was a positive or negative force. But he also thought there were times when business consolidation and mergers could aid economic progress and urged the Bureau of Consolidation to assist them in these efforts. At the same time, he was willing to step in when business consolidation led to corruption and market manipulation, as he did when he had the Justice Department use antitrust laws to prosecute railroad, meatpacking, and oil trusts, which he believed exploited the public. Roosevelt similarly supported regulatory legislation over interstate commerce and the quality of food and drugs. While Roosevelt supported the breakup of J. P. Morgan's Northern Securities Company, he did not break up the huge U.S. Steel Corp and actually allowed it to acquire additional companies during the economic panic of 1907.

Woodrow Wilson and the Extension of Progressive Reform

How did participation in World War I alter Wilson's position on business?

In his first term as president, Wilson was disheartened by the corporate merger movement that seemed to weaken the prospects of fair business competition. To restore that, he increased government regulation of the business sector, supporting the Clayton Antitrust Act and the establishment of the Federal Trade Commission to ensure fair business practices and protect labor. He also established banking regulation with the Federal Reserve Act of 1913 and similarly supported tariff reform and farm loans. With war mobilization a priority in his second term, Wilson sought greater cooperation between the private and public sector. Businesses agreed to submit to the federal War Industry Board's directives in exchange for the promise of profits. After the war, Wilson retreated from the regulation that had been his prewar policy, dropping farm supports, collective bargaining guarantees for labor, and high taxes, thereby inaugurating a new era of big business in the 1920s.

Suggestions for Further Reading

Francis L. Broderick, *Progressivism at Risk: Electing a President in 1912* (1989)

Nancy F. Cott, *The Grounding of Modern Feminism* (1987)

Steven J. Diner, *A Very Different Age: Americans of the Progressive Era* (1998)

Glenda Gilmore, *Who Were the Progressives?* (2002)

Hugh D. Hindman, *Child Labor: An American History* (2002)

Alice Kessler-Harris, *Out to Work: A History of Wage-Earning Women in the United States,* 20th anniversary ed. (2003)

Michael McGerr, *A Fierce Discontent: The Rise and Fall of the Progressive Movement in America, 1870–1920* (2003)

Patricia A. Schecter, *Ida B. Wells and American Reform, 1880–1930* (2001)

David Tyack, *Seeking Common Ground: Public Schools in a Diverse Society* (2003)

Go to the CourseMate website for primary source links, study tools, and review materials for this chapter.
www.cengagebrain.com

The Quest for Empire

22

1865–1914

Chapter Outline

Imperial Dreams
*Foreign Policy Elite | Foreign Trade
Expansion | Race Thinking and the Male
Ethos | The "Civilizing" Impulse*

VISUALIZING THE PAST *Messages in Advertising*

LINKS TO THE WORLD *National Geographic*

Ambitions and Strategies
*Seward's Quest for Empire | International
Communications | Alfred T. Mahan and Navalism*

Crises in the 1890s: Hawai'i, Venezuela, and Cuba
*Annexation of Hawai'i | Venezuelan Boundary
Dispute | Revolution in Cuba |
Sinking of the* Maine *| McKinley's Ultimatum
and War Decision*

The Spanish-American War and the Debate over Empire
*Motives for War | Dewey in the Philippines |
Treaty of Paris | Anti-Imperialist
Arguments | Imperialist Arguments*

**Asian Encounters: War in the Philippines, Diplomacy
in China**
*Philippine Insurrection and Pacification |
China and the Open Door Policy*

TR's World
*Presidential Authority | Cuba and the Platt
Amendment | Panama Canal | Roosevelt
Corollary | U.S.-Mexican Relations |
Peacemaking in East Asia | Dollar Diplomacy |
Anglo-American Rapprochement*

LEGACY FOR A PEOPLE AND A NATION
Guantánamo Bay

SUMMARY

oreign devil!" they shouted at Lottie Moon. The Southern Baptist missionary, half a world away from home, braced herself against the cries of the Chinese "rabble" whom she sought to convert to Christianity in the 1880s. She walked "steadily and persistently" through the hecklers, silently vowing to win their acceptance and their souls.

Born in 1840 in Virginia and educated at what is now Hollins College, Charlotte Diggs Moon volunteered in 1873 for "woman's work" in northern China. There she taught and proselytized, largely among women and children, until her death in 1912.

In the 1870s and 1880s, Lottie Moon (Mu Ladi, or 幕拉第) made sometimes dangerous evangelizing trips to isolated Chinese hamlets. Curious peasant women pinched her, pulled on her skirts, purring, "How white her hand is!" They asked: "How old are you?" "Where do you get money to live on?" Speaking in Chinese, Lottie held a picture book about Jesus Christ, drawing attention to the "foreign doctrine" she hoped would displace Confucianism, Buddhism, and Taoism.

In the 1890s, a "storm of persecution" against foreigners swept China, and missionaries upending traditional ways and authority became hated targets. One missionary conceded that, in "believing Jesus," girls and women alarmed men who worried that "disobedient wives and daughters" would no longer "worship the idols when told." In the Shaling village in early 1890, Lottie Moon's Christian converts were beaten. Fearing for her life, she left China for several months in 1900 during the violent Boxer Rebellion.

Lottie Moon and thousands of missionaries converted only a small minority of Chinese people to Christianity. Although she, like other missionaries, probably never shed the western view that she represented a superior religion and culture, she felt affection for the Chinese. In letters and articles for U.S. audiences, she lobbied to recruit Christian women to stir up "a mighty wave of enthusiasm for Woman's Work for Woman." To this day, the

Lottie Moon Christmas Offering in Southern Baptist churches raises millions of dollars for missions abroad.

Like so many Americans who went overseas in the late nineteenth and early twentieth centuries, Lottie Moon helped spread American culture and influence abroad. Other peoples sometimes adopted and sometimes rejected American ways. American participants likewise were transformed. Lottie Moon, for example, strove to understand the Chinese and learn their language. She assumed their dress and abandoned such derogatory phrases as "heathen Chinese." She reminded less sensitive missionaries that the Chinese rightfully took pride in their ancient history.

Lottie Moon also changed—in her own words—from "a timid self-distrustful girl into a brave self-reliant woman." As she questioned the Chinese confinement of women, most conspicuous in arranged marriages, foot binding, and sexual segregation, she advanced women's rights. She understood that she could not convert Chinese women unless they had the freedom to listen to her appeals. She also challenged male domination of America's religious missions. When the Southern Baptist Foreign Mission Board denied woman missionaries the right to vote in meetings, she resigned. The board soon reversed itself.

Decades later, critics labeled missionaries' activities as "cultural imperialism," accusing them of subverting indigenous traditions and sparking destructive cultural clashes. Defenders of missionary work have celebrated their efforts to break down cultural barriers. Either way, Lottie Moon's story illustrates how Americans in the late nineteenth century interacted with the world; how the categories domestic and foreign intersected; and how Americans expanded abroad not only to seek land, trade, investments, and strategic bases but also to promote American culture.

Between the Civil War and the First World War, an expansionist United States joined the great world powers. Before the Civil War, Americans repeatedly extended the frontier: they bought Louisiana; annexed Florida, Oregon, and Texas; pushed Indians out of the path of white migration westward; seized California and other western areas from Mexico; and acquired southern parts of present-day Arizona and New Mexico from Mexico (the Gadsden Purchase). Americans also developed a lucrative foreign trade with most of the world and promoted American culture everywhere.

By the 1870s, most of Europe's powers were carving up Africa and large parts of Asia and Oceania for themselves. By 1900, they had conquered more than 10 million square miles and 150 million people. As the century turned, France, Russia, and Germany were spending heavily on modern steel navies, challenging an overextended Great Britain. In Asia, a rapidly modernizing Japan was expanding at the expense of China and Russia.

Engineering advances altered the world's political geography through the Suez Canal (1869), the British Trans-Indian railroad (1870), and the Russian Trans-Siberian Railway (1904), while steamships, machine guns, telegraphs, and malaria drugs facilitated the imperialists' task. Simultaneously, European leaders' general optimism in the 1850s and 1860s gave way to a pessimistic sense of impending warfare informed by notions of racial conflict and survival of the fittest.

Observant Americans argued that the United States risked being left behind if it failed to join the scramble for territory and markets. Republican senator Henry Cabot Lodge of Massachusetts argued that "civilization and the advancement of the [Anglo-Saxon] race" were at stake. Such thinking enticed Americans to reach beyond the continental United States for land, markets, cultural penetration, and power.

By 1900, the United States emerged as a great power with particular clout in Latin America, especially as Spain declined and Britain disengaged from the Western Hemisphere. In the Pacific, the new U.S. empire included Hawai'i, American Samoa, and the Philippines. In the decade that followed, President Theodore Roosevelt would seek to consolidate this power.

Most Americans applauded expansionism—the outward movement of goods, ships, dollars, people, and ideas. But many became uneasy whenever expansionism gave way to imperialism—the imposition of control over other peoples, undermining their sovereignty. Abroad, native nationalists, commercial competitors, and other imperial nations tried to block the spread of U.S. influence.

As you read this chapter, keep the following questions in mind:

* **What accounts for the increased importance of foreign policy concerns in American politics in the closing years of the nineteenth century?**

* **What key arguments were made by American anti-imperialists?**

* **How did late-nineteenth-century imperialism transform the United States?**

Imperial Dreams

What drove U.S. expansion overseas in the late nineteenth century?

Foreign policy assumed a new importance for Americans at the end of the nineteenth century. Internal matters such as industrialization, the construction of the railroads, and the settlement of the West still preoccupied many, but political and business leaders now began to advocate an activist approach to world affairs. Their motives were complex, but all emphasized the supposed benefits to the country's domestic health.

These leaders who guided America's expansionist foreign relations also guided the economic development of the machine age, forged the transcontinental railroad, built America's bustling cities and giant corporations, and shaped a mass culture. They unabashedly believed that the United States was an exceptional nation, different from and superior to others because of its Anglo-Saxon heritage and its God-favored and prosperous history.

Along with exceptionalism, American leaders were influenced by nationalism, capitalism, Social Darwinism, and a paternalistic attitude toward foreigners. "They are children and we are men in these deep matters of government," future president Woodrow Wilson announced in 1898. His words reveal the gender and age bias of American attitudes. Where these attitudes intersected with foreign cultures, the result was a mix of adoption, imitation, and rejection.

Chronology

1861–69	Seward sets expansionist course	1899	Treaty of Paris enlarges U.S. empire
1867	United States acquires Alaska and Midway		United Fruit Company forms and becomes influential in Central America
1876	Pro-U.S. Daíz begins thirty-four-year rule in Mexico		Philippine insurrection breaks out, led by Emilio Aguinaldo
1878	United States gains naval rights in Samoa	1901	McKinley assassinated; Theodore Roosevelt becomes president
1885	Strong's Our Country celebrates Anglo-Saxon destiny of dominance	1903	Panama grants canal rights to United States
1887	United States gains naval rights to Pearl Harbor, Hawai'i		Platt Amendment subjugates Cuba
	McKinley Tariff hurts Hawaiian sugar exports	1904	Roosevelt Corollary declares United States a hemispheric "police power"
1893	Economic crisis leads to business failures and mass unemployment	1905	Portsmouth Conference ends Russo-Japanese War
	Pro-U.S. interests stage successful coup against Queen Lili'uokalani of Hawai'i	1906	San Francisco School Board segregates Asian schoolchildren
1895	Cuban revolution against Spain begins		United States invades Cuba to quell revolt
	Japan defeats China in war, annexes Korea and Formosa (Taiwan)	1907	"Great White Fleet" makes world tour
1898	United States formally annexes Hawai'i	1910	Mexican revolution threatens U.S. interests
	U.S. battleship Maine blows up in Havana harbor	1914	U.S. troops invade Mexico
	United States defeats Spain in Spanish-American War		First World War begins
			Panama Canal opens

Foreign Policy Elite It would take time for most Americans to grasp the changes under way. Foreign policy is usually dominated by what scholars have labeled the foreign policy elite—opinion leaders in politics, journalism, business, agriculture, religion, education, and the military. Better read and traveled than most Americans and more politically active in the post-Civil War era, they believed that U.S. prosperity and security depended on the nation's influence abroad. Increasingly in the late nineteenth century, the expansionist-minded elite urged imperialism. They talked about building a bigger navy and digging a canal across Panama, Central America, or Mexico; establishing colonies; and selling surpluses abroad. Among them was Theodore Roosevelt, appointed assistant secretary of the navy in 1897; Senator Henry Cabot Lodge, who joined the Foreign Relations Committee in 1896; and the corporate lawyer Elihu Root, who later served as secretary of war and secretary of state.

These American leaders believed that selling, buying, and investing in foreign marketplaces were important to the United States. One reason was profits from foreign sales. Another was the belief that foreign commerce might serve as a safety valve to relieve overproduction, unemployment, and economic depression since the nation's farms and factories produced more than Americans could consume especially during the 1890s' depression. Economic ties also permitted political influence to be exerted abroad and helped spread the American way of life, especially capitalism.

Messages in Advertising

The American march toward empire was also reflected in advertising. On the front and back covers of this 1901 promotional booklet, the Singer Sewing Machine Company is marketing not only its product but the idea that a sewing machine can unite nations. The image that emerges of the United States is that of peacemaker and unifier. In the 1892 Singer sewing machine advertisement card, the Zulu natives are sewing American-style clothes. What message is being sent here, do you think? How does it compare to the recent advertising campaigns by firms such as Starbucks, Nike, and Subaru that push the product in question only indirectly and instead show people around the world connecting despite their differences?

Sewing machines and therefore world peace?

Rare Book, Manuscript & Special Collections, Duke University Library

Singer sewing machine advertisement card, showing six people from Zululand (South Africa) with Singer sewing machine.

Library of Congress

Foreign Trade Expansion

Foreign trade figured prominently in the United States' economic growth after the Civil War. Foreign commerce stimulated the building of a larger protective navy, the professionalization of the foreign service, calls for more colonies, and an interventionist foreign policy. In 1865, U.S. exports totaled $234 million; by 1900, they climbed to $1.5 billion. By 1914, exports hit $2.5 billion. In 1874, the United States reversed its historically unfavorable balance of trade (importing more than it exported) and began to enjoy a long-term favorable balance. Most of America's products went to Britain, continental Europe, and Canada, but increasing amounts flowed to new markets in Latin America and Asia. Meanwhile, American investments abroad reached $3.5 billion by 1914, placing the United States among the top four investor countries.

Agricultural goods accounted for about three-fourths of total exports in 1870 and about two-thirds in 1900, with grain, cotton, meat, and dairy products topping the list. Farmers' livelihoods thus became tied to world-market conditions and foreign wars. Wisconsin cheesemakers shipped to Britain; the Swift and Armour meat companies exported refrigerated beef to Europe.

In 1913, manufactured goods led U.S. exports for the first time (see Figure 22.1). Substantial proportions of America's steel, copper, and petroleum were sold abroad, making many workers in those industries dependent on American exports.

Race Thinking and the Male Ethos

In expanding U.S. influence overseas, many officials championed a nationalism based on notions of American supremacy. Some found justification for expansionism in racist theories then permeating western thought. For decades, the western scientific establishment classified humankind by race, and students of physical anthropology drew on phrenology and physiognomy—the analysis of skull size and facial features—to produce a hierarchy of superior and inferior races. One French researcher claimed

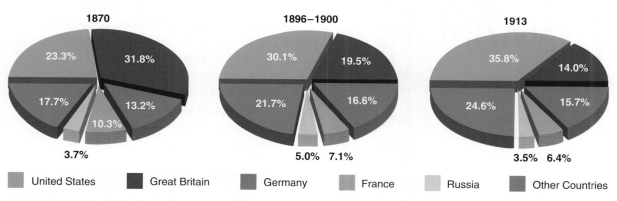

FIGURE 22.1
The Rise of U.S. Economic Power in the World
These pie charts showing percentage shares of world manufacturing production for the major nations of the world demonstrate that the United States came to surpass Great Britain in this significant economic measurement of power.
Source: Friedberg, Aaron L., *The Weary Titan*. © 1988 Princeton University Press, 1989 paperback edition. Reprinted by permission of Princeton University Press.

Links to the World

National Geographic

In early 1888, thirty-three members of Washington, D.C.'s elite Cosmos Club considered "organizing a society for the increase and diffusion of geographical knowledge." The result was the National Geographic Society, the world's largest nonprofit scientific and educational institution.

At the heart of the enterprise was *National Geographic Magazine*, which debuted in October 1888. Early issues were brief and bland, and sales lagged. When Alexander Graham Bell became the society's president in 1898, he shifted emphasis from newsstand sales to society membership, reasoning correctly that belonging to a distinguished fellowship would draw members. He also appointed a talented editor, Gilbert H. Grosvenor, age twenty-three, who commissioned articles and filled eleven pages with photographs.

Early photos showed people posed in their native costumes, displayed as anthropological specimens. By 1908, pictures occupied half of the magazine. In 1910, the first color photographs appeared in a twenty-four-page spread on Korea and China—then the largest collection of color photographs published in a single issue of any magazine. *National Geographic's* other photographic firsts included the first natural-color photos of Arctic life and the undersea world.

The society also sponsored expeditions, such as Robert Peary's and Matthew Henson's 1909 journey to the North Pole and, later, Jacques Cousteau's oceanic explorations and Jane Goodall's observations of wild chimpanzees. These adventures then appeared in the magazine's pages. By the end of Grosvenor's tenure as editor, in 1954, circulation topped 2 million.

Less admirably, Grosvenor's editors pressured photographers for pictures of pretty girls. One photographer recalled, "Hundreds of bare-breasted women, all from poorer countries, were published at a time of booming subscription rates." Editors developed a well-earned reputation for presenting a rosy world-view. An article about Berlin published before the start of World War II, for example, contained no criticism of the Nazi regime and no mention of its persecution of Jews. Recently, the magazine has featured more newsworthy topics—AIDS, stem cell research, Hurricane Katrina, global warming—but in measured tones.

Throughout, the society expanded its reach, producing books, atlases, globes, and television documentaries. Targeting overseas readers, the society in 1995 launched a Japanese-language edition and subsequently twenty-five other foreign editions. *National Geographic*, after a century of linking Americans to faraway places, now connected readers worldwide to the United States.

VOLUME XXI   NUMBER TWO

THE NATIONAL GEOGRAPHIC MAGAZINE

FEBRUARY, 1910

CONTENTS

A Traveler's Notes on Java . . .   HENRY G. BRYANT
WITH 17 ILLUSTRATIONS

An Ancient Capital . . . . .   ISABEL F. DODD
WITH 11 ILLUSTRATIONS

The International Millionth Map of the World
WITH DIAGRAM   BAILEY WILLIS

The Land of the Crossbow . . .   GEORGE FORREST
WITH 15 ILLUSTRATIONS

The Great Natural Bridges of Utah .   BYRON CUMMINGS
WITH 7 ILLUSTRATIONS

The South Polar Expedition
WITH MAP

Wilkes and d'Urville's Discoveries in Wilkes Land
READ ADMIRAL JOHN E. PILLSBURY, U. S. N.

The Barrage of the Nile . . .   DAY ALLEN WILLEY
WITH 14 ILLUSTRATIONS

PUBLISHED BY THE
NATIONAL GEOGRAPHIC SOCIETY
HUBBARD MEMORIAL HALL
WASHINGTON, D.C.

$2.50 A YEAR   25 CTS A COPY

National Geographic Society Image Collection

National Geographic had already gone through five different cover formats when Robert Weir Crouch, an English-born Canadian decorative artist, came up with a design that cemented the magazine's visual identity. Singular and immediately recognizable, the oak-and-laurel frame on the cover of the February 1910 issue would remain largely unchanged for nearly half a century, though the buff-colored border would be replaced with a golden one.

that blacks represented a female race and "like the woman, the black is deprived of political and scientific intelligence."

The language of U.S. leaders was also weighted with words like *manliness* and *weakling*. The warrior and president Theodore Roosevelt viewed people of color (or "darkeys," as he called them) as effeminate weaklings who were unable to govern themselves and could not cope with world politics. Americans debased Latin Americans as half-breeds needing supervision or distressed damsels begging for manly rescue. The gendered imagery in U.S. foreign relations joined race thinking to place women, people of color, and nations weaker than the United States low in the hierarchy of power and, hence, in a dependent status justifying U.S. dominance.

Link to Josiah Strong's *Expansion Under New World Conditions.*

Race thinking—popularized in magazine photos and cartoons, world's fairs, postcards, textbooks, museums, and political orations—reinforced notions of American greatness, influenced the way U.S. leaders dealt with other peoples, and obviated the need to think about the subtle textures of other societies. *National Geographic,* which began publication in 1888, photographically chronicled America's new overseas involvements in Asia and the Pacific, regularly featuring images of exotic, premodern peoples who had not become "Western." Fairs also put so-called uncivilized people of color on display in the "freak" or "midway" section. Dog-eating Filipinos aroused comment at the 1904 St. Louis World's Fair. Such racism downgraded diplomacy and justified domination and war.

Similar thinking permeated attitudes toward immigrants, whose entry into the United States was first restricted in these years. Although the Burlingame Treaty (1868) provided for free immigration between the United States and China, riots against Chinese immigrants continuously erupted in the American West. An 1880 treaty permitted Congress to suspend Chinese immigration to the United States. Tensions continued: in 1885, white coal miners and railway workers in Rock Springs, Wyoming, massacred at least twenty-five Chinese.

In 1906, the San Francisco School Board ordered Chinese, Koreans, and Japanese segregated in special schools. Tokyo protested such discrimination, and President Roosevelt quieted the crisis by striking a "gentleman's agreement" with Tokyo restricting Japanese immigration. San Francisco rescinded its segregation order. Relations with Tokyo worsened again in 1913 when the California legislature denied Japanese residents the right to own property.

The "Civilizing" Impulse

Expansionists believed that empire benefited Americans and those who came under their control. When the United States intervened in weaker states, Americans claimed they were extending liberty and prosperity to less fortunate people. William Howard Taft, as civil governor of the Philippines (1901–1904), described the United States' mission in its new colony as lifting Filipinos up "to a point of civilization" that will make them "call the name of the United States blessed." Later, Taft said about the Chinese that "the more civilized they become ... the wealthier they become, and the better market they become for us."

Missionaries dispatched to Africa and Asia, like Lottie Moon, helped spur the transfer of American culture and power abroad—"the peaceful conquest of the world," as Reverend Frederick Gates put it. In 1915, ten thousand American missionaries worked overseas. In China by 1915, more than twenty-five hundred mostly female American Protestant missionaries taught, preached the gospel, and administered medical care.

Ambitions and Strategies

What happened to Seward's vision of an American empire?

The U.S. empire grew gradually, as American leaders defined guiding principles and built institutions to support overseas ambitions. William H. Seward, one of its chief architects, argued for extension of the American frontier as a senator from New York (1849–1861) and secretary of state (1861–1869). Seward envisioned a large U.S. empire encompassing Canada, the Caribbean, Cuba, Central America, Mexico, Hawai'i, Iceland, Greenland, and the Pacific islands. This empire would result from a natural process of gravitation toward the United States. Commerce would hurry the process, as would a canal across Central America, a transcontinental American railroad, and a telegraph system to speed communications.

Seward's Quest for Empire

Most of Seward's grandiose plans did not reach fruition in his lifetime. In 1867, his efforts for a treaty with Denmark to buy the Danish West Indies (Virgin Islands), was scuttled by Senate foes and a hurricane that wrecked St. Thomas. The Virgin Islanders, who voted for annexation, would wait until 1917 for official U.S. status. Seward's scheme with unscrupulous Dominican Republic leaders to gain a Caribbean naval base at Samaná Bay also failed. The corruption surrounding this deal foiled President Ulysses S. Grant's initiative in 1870 to buy the island nation.

Anti-imperialism, not just politics, blocked Seward. Opponents of empire argued that creating a showcase of democracy and prosperity on unsettled land at home would best persuade other peoples to adopt American principles. Some anti-imperialists, sharing the era's racism, opposed the annexation of territory populated by dark-skinned people.

Seward enjoyed some successes. In 1866, citing the Monroe Doctrine, he sent troops to the Mexico border and demanded that France abandon its puppet regime there. Also facing angry Mexican nationalists, Napoleon III abandoned the Maximilian monarchy that he forcibly installed three years earlier. In 1867, Seward paid Russia $7.2 million for the 591,000 square miles of Alaska—land twice the size of Texas. That same year, Seward claimed the Midway Islands (two small islands and a coral atoll northwest of Hawai'i).

International Communications

In 1866, through the efforts of financier Cyrus Field, an underwater transatlantic cable linked European and American telegraph networks. Backed by J. P. Morgan, communications pioneer James A. Scrymser strung telegraph lines to Latin America, entering Chile in 1890. In 1903, a submarine cable spanned the Pacific to the Philippines; three years later, it reached Japan and China. Information about markets, crises, and war flowed steadily and quickly. Drawn closer to one another through improved communications and transportation, nations found that faraway events had greater impact on them. Increasingly, American diplomats negotiated with their European counterparts as equals—signaling the United States' arrival on the international stage. Washington officials, for example, successfully confronted European powers over Samoa, islands in the South Pacific located 4,000 miles from San Francisco on the trade route to Australia. In 1878, the United States gained exclusive right to a coaling station at Samoa's coveted port of Pago Pago. Eyeing the same prize, Britain and Germany began cultivating ties with Samoan leaders. Tensions grew, and war seemed possible. At the eleventh hour, however, Britain, Germany, and the United States met in Berlin in 1889 and, without consulting the Samoans, devised a three-part protectorate that limited Samoa's independence. Ten years later, the three powers partitioned Samoa: the United States received Pago Pago through annexation of part of the islands (now called American Samoa); Germany took what is today independent Western Samoa; and Britain obtained the Gilbert Islands and Solomon Islands.

Alfred T. Mahan and Navalism

Calling attention to the naval buildup by European powers, notably Germany, U.S. expansionists argued for a bigger, modernized navy, adding the "blue water" command of the seas to its traditional role of "brown water" coastline defense. **Captain Alfred Thayer Mahan**, a popularizer of this New Navy, argued that because foreign trade was essential, the nation required an efficient navy to protect its shipping; and a navy required colonies for bases. Mahan's ideas were published as *The Influence of Sea Power upon History* (1890). Theodore Roosevelt and Henry Cabot Lodge consulted Mahan, sharing his belief in the links between trade, navy, and colonies and his alarm over Germany's aggressive military spirit.

Captain Alfred T. Mahan: Author of *The Influence of Sea Power upon History* (1890) and an advocate of a stronger navy and imperialism.

Moving toward naval modernization, Congress in 1883 authorized construction of the first steel-hulled warships. American factories produced steam engines, high-velocity shells, powerful guns, and precision instruments. The navy shifted from sail power to steam and from wood construction to steel. New Navy ships, such as the *Maine, Oregon,* and *Boston,* thrust the United States into naval prominence.

Crises in the 1890s: Hawai'i, Venezuela, and Cuba

In the depression-plagued 1890s, crises in Hawai'i and Cuba—and the belief that the frontier at home had closed—reinforced the expansionist argument. In 1893, historian Frederick Jackson Turner postulated that the ever-expanding continental frontier, which shaped the American character, was gone. He did not say a new frontier had to be found overseas, but he did claim that "American energy will continually demand a wider field for its exercise."

What typically imperialist actions did the United States take in its dealings with Hawai'i and Venezuela?

Annexation of Hawai'i

Hawai'i, the Pacific Ocean archipelago of eight major islands located 2,000 miles from the West Coast of the United States, emerged as America's new frontier. The Hawaiian Islands had long commanded American attention—commercial, missionary religious, naval, and diplomatic. By 1881, Secretary of State James Blaine already declared the Hawaiian Islands "essentially a part of the American system." By 1890, Americans owned about three-quarters of Hawai'i's wealth and subordinated its economy to that of the United States through sugar exports that entered the U.S. marketplace duty-free.

Hawai'i: Island nation in the Pacific that became an American territory in 1898. It was significant from a military and economic standpoint.

In Hawai'i's multiracial society, Chinese and Japanese nationals far outnumbered Americans, who represented just 2.1 percent of the population. Prominent Americans on the islands organized secret clubs and military units to contest the royal government. In 1887, they forced the king to accept a constitution that granted foreigners the vote and shifted decision making from the monarchy to the legislature. That year, Hawai'i granted the United States naval rights to Pearl Harbor. Many native Hawaiians believed that the *haole* (foreigners)—especially Americans—were stealing their country.

The native government was further undermined when the 1890 McKinley Tariff eliminated the duty-free status of Hawaiian sugar exports in the United States. Suffering declining sugar prices and profits, the American island elite pressed for annexation by the United States, thereby classifying their sugar as domestic. When Princess Lili'uokalani assumed the throne in 1891, she sought to roll back the political power of the *haole*. The next year, the white oligarchy formed the subversive Annexation Club.

The annexationists struck in January 1893 in collusion with John L. Stevens, America's chief American diplomat in Hawai'i, who dispatched troops from the USS *Boston* to occupy Honolulu. The queen, arrested and confined, surrendered. Rather than yield to the new provisional regime, headed by Sanford B. Dole, son of missionaries and a prominent attorney, she relinquished authority to the U.S. government. President Benjamin Harrison hurriedly sent an annexation treaty to the Senate.

Sensing foul play, incoming president Grover Cleveland ordered an investigation, which confirmed a conspiracy that most Hawaiians opposed annexation. But when Hawai'i proved a strategic and commercial way station to Asia and the Philippines during the Spanish-American War, President William McKinley maneuvered annexation through Congress on July 7, 1898. Under the Organic Act of June 1900, the people of Hawai'i became U.S. citizens. Statehood came in 1959.

Venezuelan Boundary Dispute

The Venezuelan crisis of 1895 also saw the United States in an expansive mood. For decades, Venezuela and Great Britain quarreled over the border between Venezuela and British Guiana, a territory containing rich gold deposits and a commercial gateway to northern South America via the Orinoco River. Venezuela sought U.S. help, and in July 1895, Secretary of State Richard Olney brashly lectured the British that the Monroe Doctrine prohibited European powers from denying self-government to nations in the Western Hemisphere. With almost no Venezuelan input, in 1896 an Anglo-American arbitration board divided the disputed territory between Britain and Venezuela. Thus, the United States displayed a typical imperialist trait: disregard for the rights of small nations.

In 1895, Cuba was the site of another crisis. From 1868 to 1878, the Cubans battled Spain for their independence, winning only the end of slavery. While the Cuban economy suffered, repressive Spanish rule continued. Insurgents committed to *Cuba libre* waited for another chance, and José Martí, one of the heroes of Cuban history, collected money, arms, and men in the United States.

Revolution in Cuba

Cuban and American culture intersected in many ways, notably in Baltimore, New York, Boston, and Philadelphia, where many Cubans settled or sent their children to school. When these expatriates returned home, many spoke English, had American names, played baseball, and jettisoned Catholicism for Protestant denominations.

The Cuban and U.S. economies were also intertwined. American investments of $50 million, mostly in sugar plantations, dominated the island. More than 90 percent of Cuba's sugar was exported to the United States, and most island imports came from the United States. Havana's famed cigar factories relocated to Key West and Tampa to evade U.S. tariffs. Martí, however, feared that "economic union means political union," for "the nation that buys, commands" and "the nation that sells, serves."

Martí's fears of a conquering U.S. policy were prophetic. In 1894, the Wilson-Gorman Tariff imposed a duty on Cuban sugar. The Cuban economy, highly dependent on exports, plunged into crisis, hastening the island's revolution against Spain and its further incorporation into the American system. Incorporation into "the American system."

In 1895, from American soil, Martí launched a revolution against Spain. Rebels burned sugar-cane fields and razed mills. U.S. investments were incinerated, and Cuban-American trade dwindled. To separate insurgents from their supporters, Spanish general Valeriano Weyler instituted a policy of "reconcentration." Some 300,000 Cubans were herded into fortified towns and camps, where starvation and disease caused tens of thousands of deaths. As reports of atrocity became headline news in the United States, Americans sympathized with the insurrectionists. In late 1897, a new government in Madrid modified reconcentration and promised some autonomy for Cuba, but the insurgents gained ground.

Sinking of the *Maine*

President William McKinley took office as an imperialist who advocated foreign bases for the New Navy, the export of surplus production, and U.S. supremacy in the Western Hemisphere. Vexed by Cuba's turmoil, he explored purchasing Cuba from Spain for $300 million. In January 1898, when antireform pro-Spanish loyalists and army rioted in Havana, Washington ordered the battleship *Maine* to Havana harbor to demonstrate U.S. concern and to protect American citizens.

On February 15, an explosion ripped the *Maine*, killing 266 of 354 American officers and crew. A week earlier, William Randolph Hearst's inflammatory *New York Journal* published a stolen private letter written by the Spanish minister in Washington, Enrique Dupuy de Lôme, belittling McKinley and suggesting that Spain would fight on. Congress complied unanimously with McKinley's request for $50 million for defense. Vengeful Americans blamed Spain. (Later, official and unofficial studies attributed the sinking to an accidental internal explosion.)

McKinley's Ultimatum and War Decision

Though reluctant to go to war, McKinley sent Spain an ultimatum: accept an armistice, end reconcentration, and designate McKinley as arbiter. Madrid made concessions. It abolished reconcentration and rejected, then accepted, an armistice. The president would no longer tolerate chronic disorder 90 miles off the U.S. coast. On April 11, McKinley asked Congress for authorization to use force "to secure a full and final termination of hostilities between ... Spain and ... Cuba, and to secure in the island the establishment of a stable government, capable of maintaining order." McKinley listed the reasons for war: the "cause of humanity"; the protection of American life and property; the "very serious injury to the commerce, trade, and business of our people"; and, referring to the destruction of the *Maine*, the "constant menace to our peace." On April 19, Congress declared Cuba free and independent and directed the president to use force to remove Spanish authority. The legislators also passed the Teller Amendment, which disclaimed U.S. intention to annex Cuba or control the island except to ensure its "pacification." McKinley blocked a congressional amendment to recognize the rebel government, arguing they were not ready for self-government.

The Spanish-American War and the Debate over Empire

What were the anti-imperialist arguments against U.S. annexation of the Philippines after the Spanish-American War?

By the time the Spanish concessions were on the table, prospects for compromise appeared dim. Cuban insurgents wanted full independence, and no Spanish government could have given up and remained in office. Nor did the United States welcome a truly independent Cuban government that might attempt to reduce U.S. interests.

Motives for War

Mixed motives drove those Americans who favored war. McKinley's April message expressed a humanitarian impulse to stop the bloodletting, a concern for commerce and property. Republicans wanted the Cuba question solved to secure their party's victory in the upcoming congressional elections. Many businesspeople and farmers believed that ejecting Spain from Cuba would open new markets for surplus production. Imperialists,

The Spanish fleet in the Caribbean was commanded by Admiral Pascual Cervera y Topete. His squadron entered Santiago Bay, Cuba, May 19, 1898, where it was immediately blockaded by Admiral William T. Sampson's fleet. On July 3, Cervera—following orders from Madrid—tried a heroic but unsuccessful escape from the U.S. blockade. This painting by Henry Reuterdahl depicts the destruction of the squadron. Cervera survived and became a prisoner of war.

meanwhile, saw the war as an opportunity to fulfill expansionist dreams, while conservatives, alarmed by Populism and labor strikes, welcomed war as a national unifier. One senator commented that "internal discord" was disappearing in the "fervent heat of patriotism." Theodore Roosevelt and others too young to remember the bloody Civil War looked on war as adventure.

More than 263,000 regulars and volunteers served in the army, and another 25,000 in the navy during the war. Most, however, never left the United States. The typical volunteer was young (early twenties), white, unmarried, native-born, and working class. Deaths numbered 5,462, mostly from a typhoid epidemic in Tennessee, Virginia, and Florida. Only 379 died in combat. About 10,000 African American troops in segregated regiments found no relief from racism, even though black troops were central to the victorious battle for Santiago de Cuba. For all, food, sanitary conditions, and medical care were bad. Still, Roosevelt could hardly contain himself. Although his Rough Riders, a motley unit of Ivy Leaguers and cowboys, proved undisciplined and ineffective, Roosevelt's self-serving publicity efforts ensured they received good press.

Dewey in the Philippines

The first war news came from faraway Asia, from the Spanish colony of the Philippine Islands, where Filipinos were also seeking independence. On May 1, 1898, Commodore George Dewey's New Navy ship *Olympia* led an American squadron into Manila Bay and wrecked the Spanish fleet. Dewey received orders from Washington to attack the islands if war broke out. Manila was a choice harbor, and the Philippines sat en route to China's potentially huge market.

Facing Americans and rebels in Cuba and the Philippines, Spanish resistance collapsed rapidly. U.S. ships blockaded Cuban ports and insurgents cut off supplies from the countryside, causing starvation and illness for Spanish soldiers. American troops landed near Santiago de Cuba on June 22 and laid siege to the city. On July 3, U.S. warships sank the Spanish Caribbean squadron in Santiago harbor. American forces assaulted the Spanish colony of Puerto Rico, gaining another Caribbean base for the navy and pushing Madrid to sue for peace.

Treaty of Paris

On August 12, Spain and the United States signed an armistice ending the war. In Paris, in December 1898, they agreed on the peace terms: independence for Cuba from Spain; cession of the Philippines, Puerto Rico, and the Pacific island of Guam to the United States for $20 million. The U.S. empire now stretched deep into Asia, and the annexation of Wake Island (1898), Hawai'i (1898), and Samoa (1899) gave American traders, missionaries, and naval promoters other steppingstones to China.

Link to William Graham Sumner's essay, "The Fallacy of Territorial Expansion" from 1911.

During the war, the *Washington Post* detected that "The taste of empire is in the mouth of the people." But anti-imperialists such as the author Mark Twain, Nebraska politician William Jennings Bryan, reformer Jane Addams, and industrialist Andrew Carnegie argued against annexation of the Philippines. Their concern that a war to free Cuba had led to empire stimulated debate over American foreign policy.

Anti-Imperialist Arguments

Imperial control could be imposed either formally (by military occupation, annexation, or colonialism) or informally (by economic domination, political manipulation, or the threat of intervention). Anti-imperialist ire focused mostly on formal imperial control. Some critics cited the Declaration of Independence and the Constitution, arguing that the conquest of people against their will violated the right of self-determination.

Other anti-imperialists feared that the American character was being corrupted by imperialist zeal. Jane Addams, seeing children play war games on Chicago streets, noted that they were not freeing Cubans but rather slaying Spaniards. Hoping to build a distinct foreign policy constituency from prominent women like Addams championed peace and an end to imperial conquest.

Some anti-imperialists protested that the United States was practicing a double standard—"offering liberty to the Cubans with one hand, cramming liberty down the throats of the Filipinos with the other, but with both feet planted upon the neck of the negro," as an African American politician from Massachusetts put it. Still others warned that annexing people of color would undermine Anglo-Saxon purity and supremacy at home.

For Samuel Gompers and other anti-imperialist labor leaders, the issue was jobs. Might not the new colonials be imported as cheap contract labor to drive down American wages? Would not exploitation of the weak abroad become contagious and lead to further exploitation of the weak at home? The anti-imperialists, however, never launched an effective campaign. Although they organized the Anti-Imperialist League in November 1898, they differed so profoundly on domestic issues that they found it difficult to speak with one voice on a foreign question.

Imperialist Arguments   The imperialists, for their part, appealed to patriotism, destiny, and commerce. They envisioned American merchant ships plying the waters to boundless Asian markets, naval vessels protecting America's Pacific interests, and missionaries uplifting inferior peoples. It was America's duty, they insisted, quoting a then-popular Rudyard Kipling poem, to "take up the white man's burden." Furthermore, Filipino insurgents were beginning to resist U.S. rule, and it seemed cowardly to pull out under fire, especially with Germany and Japan ready to seize the islands.

In February 1899, by a 57-to-27 vote, the Senate passed the Treaty of Paris, ending the war with Spain. Most Republicans voted yes and most Democrats no. An amendment promising independence once the Filipinos formed a stable government lost by only the tie-breaking ballot of the vice president.

Asian Encounters: War in the Philippines, Diplomacy in China

Why was the Open Door policy such a key component of U.S. diplomacy?

The Philippine crisis was far from over. **Emilio Aguinaldo**, the Philippine nationalist leader who battled the Spanish for years, believed that American officials promised independence for his country. But after the victory, U.S. officers ordered Aguinaldo out of Manila. In early 1899, he proclaimed an independent Philippine Republic and took up arms.

Emilio Aguinaldo: Nationalist leader of Filipino war against American occupation.

Philippine Insurrection and Pacification   Both sides fought viciously; American soldiers burned villages and tortured captives, while Filipino forces staged brutal hit-and-run guerilla ambushes. U.S. troops introduced a variant of the Spanish reconcentration policy; in the province of Batangas, for instance, U.S. troops forced residents to live in designated zones to separate insurgents from supporters. Poor sanitation, starvation, and malaria and cholera killed thousands. Outside secure areas, Americans destroyed food supplies to starve out the rebels. At least one-quarter of the population of Batangas died or fled.

Before the Philippine insurrection was suppressed in 1902, some 20,000 Filipinos died in combat, and 600,000 succumbed to starvation and disease. More than 4,000 Americans lay dead. Resistance to U.S. rule, however, continued. When the fiercely independent, often violent Muslim Filipinos of Moro Province refused to knuckle under, the U.S. military threatened extermination. In 1906, 600 Moros, including women and children, were slaughtered at the Battle of Bud Dajo.

U.S. officials soon tried to Americanize the Philippines, instituting a new education system with English as the main language. The architect Daniel Burnham, leader of the City Beautiful movement, planned modern Manila. The Philippine economy grew as an American satellite, and a sedition act sent U.S. critics to prison. In 1916, the Jones Act vaguely promised independence once the Philippines established a "stable government." But the United States did not end its rule until 1946.

China and the Open Door Policy

In China, McKinley successfully focused on a policy emphasizing negotiation. Outsiders had pecked away at China since the 1840s. Taking advantage of the Qing (Manchu) dynasty's weakness, the major imperial powers carved out spheres of influence (regions over which they claimed political control and exclusive commercial privileges): Germany in Shandong, Russia in Manchuria, France in Yunnan and Hainan, and Britain in Kowloon and Hong Kong. Then, in 1895, Japan claimed victory over China in a short war and assumed control of Formosa and Korea and parts of China proper (see Map 22.1). American religious and business leaders petitioned Washington to halt the dismemberment of China before they were closed out.

Secretary of State John Hay knew that missionaries like Lottie Moon had become targets of Chinese nationalist anger and that American oil and textile companies had been disappointed with their investments there. Thus, in September 1899, Hay sent nations with spheres of influence in China a note seeking their respect for the principle of equal trade opportunity—an Open Door. The recipients sent evasive replies, privately complaining that the United States was seeking, for free, the trade rights in China that they had gained at considerable cost.

The next year, the Boxers, a Chinese secret society (so named in the western press because some members were martial artists), sought to expel foreigners. They rioted, killing many outsiders and laying siege to the foreign legations in Beijing in what is known as the **Boxer Rebellion**. The United States joined the other imperial powers in sending troops. Hay also sent a second Open Door note instructing other nations to preserve China's territorial integrity and honor "equal and impartial trade." China continued for years to be fertile soil for foreign exploitation, especially by the Japanese.

The **Open Door policy** became a cornerstone of U.S. diplomacy. While the United States had long opposed barriers to international commerce, after 1900, when the U.S. emerged emerge as the premier world trader, the Open Door policy became an instrument first to pry open markets and then to dominate them. The Open Door also developed as an ideology with several tenets: first, that America's domestic

Boxer Rebellion: Chinese insurgency against Christians and foreigners, defeated by an international force.

Open Door policy: Foreign policy proposed by U.S. Secretary of State John Hay, in which he asked the major European powers to assure trading rights in China by opening the ports in their spheres of influence to all countries.

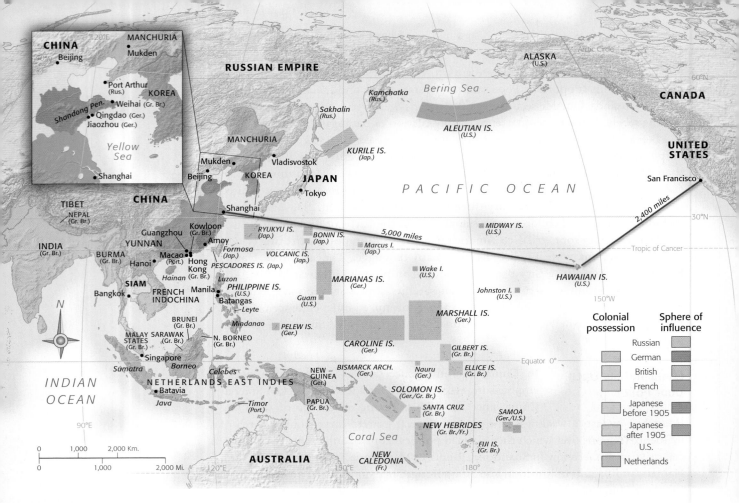

MAP 22.1

Imperialism in Asia: Turn of the Century

China and the Pacific region had become imperialist hunting grounds by the turn of the century. The European powers and Japan controlled more areas than the United States, which nonetheless participated in the imperial race by annexing the Philippines, Wake, Guam, Hawai'i, and Samoa; announcing the Open Door policy; and expanding trade. As the spheres of influence in China demonstrate, that besieged nation succumbed to outsiders despite the Open Door policy.

Source: Copyright © Cengage Learning

well-being required exports; second, that foreign trade would suffer interruption unless the United States intervened abroad; and third, that the closing of any area to American products, citizens, or ideas threatened the survival of the United States.

TR's World

What solidified U.S.–British ties heading into World War I?

Theodore Roosevelt played an important role in shaping U.S. foreign policy in the McKinley administration. As assistant secretary of the navy (1897–1898), as a Spanish-American War hero, and then as vice president in McKinley's second term, Roosevelt worked to make the United States a great power. Long fascinated by power, he also relished hunting and killing. After an argument with a girlfriend in his youth, he vented his anger by shooting a neighbor's dog. Roosevelt justified the slaughtering of American Indians, if necessary, and took his Rough Riders to Cuba, desperate to get in on the fighting.

Like Americans of his day, Roosevelt took for granted the superiority of Protestant Anglo-American culture and believed in using American power to shape world affairs. In TR's world there were "civilized" and "uncivilized" nations; the former, primarily white and Anglo-Saxon or Teutonic, had a right and a duty to intervene in the affairs of the latter (generally nonwhite, Latin, or Slavic, and therefore "backward") to preserve order and stability, even if that meant using violence.

Presidential Authority Roosevelt's love of the good fight caused many to rue his ascension to the presidency after McKinley's assassination in September 1901. But the cowboy was also an astute analyst of foreign policy. Roosevelt understood that American power, though growing, remained limited and that in many parts of the world the United States would have to rely on diplomacy to achieve satisfactory outcomes.

Roosevelt's first efforts were focused on Latin America, where U.S. economic and power towered (see Map 22.2). He also focused on Europe, where repeated disputes

MAP 22.2

U.S. Hegemony in the Caribbean and Latin America

Through many interventions, territorial acquisitions, and robust economic expansion, the United States became the predominant power in Latin America in the early twentieth century. The United States often backed up the Roosevelt Corollary's declaration of a "police power" by dispatching troops to Caribbean nations, where they met nationalist opposition.

Source: Copyright © Cengage Learning

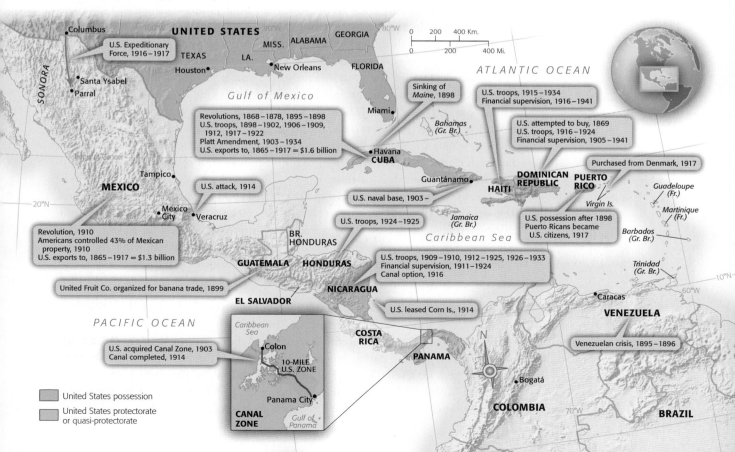

persuaded Americans to develop friendlier relations with Great Britain while avoiding the continent's troubles, which Americans blamed on Germany.

As U.S. economic interests expanded in Latin America, so did U.S. political influence. Exports to Latin America rose from $50 million in the 1870s to more than $120 million in 1901 and $300 million in 1914. Investments by U.S. citizens in Latin America climbed to $1.26 billion in 1914. In 1899, two large banana importers merged to form the United Fruit Company. United Fruit, owning much of the land in Central America (more than a million acres in 1913), and the railroad and steamship lines. The company worked to eradicate yellow fever and malaria while bankrolling favored officeholders.

Cuba and the Platt Amendment

After the destructive war in Cuba, U.S. citizens and corporations dominated the island's economy, controlling the sugar, mining, tobacco, and utilities industries, and most of the rural lands. Private U.S. investments grew from $50 million before the revolution to $220 million by 1913, and U.S. exports to the island rose from $26 million in 1900 to $196 million in 1917. The Teller Amendment outlawed the annexation of Cuba, but Washington officials used its call for "pacification" to justify U.S. control. American troops remained there until 1902.

U.S. authorities restricted voting rights to propertied Cuban males, excluding two-thirds of adult men and all women. American officials also forced Cubans to add the **Platt Amendment** to their constitution. This prohibited Cuba from making treaties that might impair its independence; in practice, this meant all treaties required U.S. approval. Most important, the Platt Amendment granted the United States "the right to intervene" to preserve the island's independence and maintain domestic order. Finally, it required Cuba to lease a naval base to the United States (at Guantánamo Bay, still under U.S. jurisdiction today). Formalized in a 1903 treaty, the amendment governed Cuban-American relations until 1934.

Cubans protested the Platt Amendment, and a rebellion in 1906 prompted another U.S. invasion. The marines stayed until 1909, returned briefly in 1912 and again from 1917 to 1922. U.S. officials helped develop a transportation system, expand the public school system, found a national army, and increase sugar production. When Dr. Walter Reed's experiments, based on the theory of the Cuban physician Carlos Juan Finlay, proved that mosquitoes transmitted yellow fever, sanitary engineers eradicated the disease.

Puerto Rico, the Caribbean island taken as a spoil of war in the Treaty of Paris, first welcomed the United States as an improvement over Spain. But the U.S. military governor, General Guy V. Henry, regarded Puerto Ricans as children who needed "kindergarten instruction in controlling themselves without allowing them too much liberty." Some residents warned against the "Yankee peril"; others applauded the "Yankee model" and futilely anticipated statehood.

Panama Canal

Panama, meanwhile, became the site of a bold U.S. expansionist venture. In 1869, the world marveled when the newly completed Suez Canal facilitated travel between the Indian Ocean and Mediterranean Sea and enhanced the British Empire's power. Surely that feat could be duplicated in the Western Hemisphere, possibly in Panama, a province of Colombia. Business interests joined politicians, diplomats, and navy officers in insisting that the United States control such an interoceanic canal.

Platt Amendment: Added to Cuba's constitution of 1903 under American pressure, it gave the United States the right to intervene if Cuban independence or internal order were threatened, and granted a naval base to the United States at Guantánamo Bay.

Link to the Platt Amendment.

But the Clayton-Bulwer Treaty with Britain (1850) provided for joint control of a canal. The British, recognizing their diminishing influence in the region and cultivating friendship with the United States as a counterweight to Germany, permitted a solely U.S.-run canal in the Hay-Pauncefote Treaty (1901). When Colombia resisted Washington's terms, Roosevelt encouraged Panamanian rebels to declare independence and ordered American warships to back them.

In 1903, the new Panama awarded the United States a canal zone and long-term rights to its control. The treaty also guaranteed Panama its independence. (In 1922, the United States paid Colombia $25 million in "conscience money" but did not apologize.) A technological achievement, the **Panama Canal** was completed in 1914.

Panama Canal: Major waterway built by the United States for $352 million that traverses the Isthmus of Panama in Central America, connecting the Atlantic and Pacific Oceans. Construction began in 1906 and was completed in 1914.

Link to the Roosevelt Corollary to the Monroe Doctrine, in President Roosevelt's fourth annual message to Congress in 1904.

Roosevelt Corollary

Elsewhere in the Caribbean, Roosevelt affirmed U.S. hegemony. Worried that Latin American nations' defaults on debts owed to European banks were provoking European intervention, the president in 1904 issued the Roosevelt Corollary to the Monroe Doctrine. He warned Latin Americans to stabilize their politics and finances or risk "intervention by some civilized nation." Roosevelt's declaration provided the rationale for frequent U.S. interventions in Latin America.

From 1900 to 1917, U.S. presidents ordered American troops to Cuba, Panama, Nicaragua, the Dominican Republic, Mexico, and Haiti to quell civil wars, thwart challenges to U.S. influence, gain ports and bases, and forestall European meddling (see Map 22.2). U.S. authorities ran elections, trained nationals, and shifted foreign debts to U.S. banks. They also controlled tariff revenues and government budgets (as in the Dominican Republic, from 1905 to 1941).

U.S.-Mexican Relations

U.S. officials focused particular attention on Mexico, where long-time dictator Porfirio Díaz (1876–1910) aggressively recruited foreign investors through tax incentives and land grants. American capitalists came to own Mexico's railroads and mines and invested heavily in petroleum and banking, thereby dominating Mexico's foreign trade in the early 1890s. By 1910, Americans controlled 43 percent of Mexican property and produced more than half of the country's oil. The Mexican revolutionaries who ousted Díaz in 1910 wanted to end their economic dependence on the United States.

In a suit and hat, President Theodore Roosevelt occupies the controls of a ninety-five-ton power shovel at a Panama Canal worksite. Roosevelt's November 1906 trip to inspect the massive project was the first time a sitting president left the United States.

AP/Wide World

The revolution descended into a bloody civil war with strong anti-Yankee overtones, and the Mexican government intended to nationalize American-owned properties. President Woodrow Wilson twice ordered troops onto Mexican soil: once in 1914, at Veracruz, to overthrow President Victoriano Huerta, and again in 1916, in northern Mexico, where General John J. "Black Jack" Pershing spent months pursuing Mexican rebel Pancho Villa for raiding an American border town. Failing to capture Villa and facing another nationalistic government, U.S. forces departed in January 1917.

As the United States reaffirmed the Monroe Doctrine, European nations reluctantly honored U.S. hegemony in Latin America. In turn, the United States continued to stand outside European embroilments. Theodore Roosevelt did help settle a Franco-German clash over Morocco by mediating a settlement at Algeciras, Spain (1906), but he drew American criticism this involvement. Americans endorsed the Hague peace conferences (1899 and 1907) and negotiated arbitration treaties, but generally stayed outside the European arena, except for trade.

Peacemaking in East Asia

In East Asia, though, both Roosevelt and his successor, William Howard Taft, sought to preserve the Open Door and to contain Japan's rising power. Many race-minded Japanese interpreted the U.S. advance into the Pacific as an attempt by whites to gain ascendancy over Asians. The United States gradually made concessions to Japan to protect the Philippines and sustain the Open Door policy. Japan continued to plant interests in China and then smashed the Russians in the Russo-Japanese War (1904–1905). President Roosevelt mediated the negotiations at the Portsmouth Conference in New Hampshire and won the Nobel Peace Prize for helping to preserve a balance of power in Asia.

Link to excerpts of notes between the U.S. Secretary of State Elihu Root and Japanese Ambassador Kogoro Takahira.

In 1905, in the Taft-Katsura Agreement, the United States conceded Japanese hegemony over Korea in return for Japan's respect for the U.S. position in the Philippines. Three years later, in the Root-Takahira Agreement, Washington recognized Japan's interests in Manchuria, and Japan again pledged the security of U.S. Pacific possessions and endorsed the Open Door in China. Roosevelt deterred the Japanese with reinforced naval power; in late 1907, he sent the navy's Great White Fleet on a world tour. Impressed, the Japanese expanded their navy.

Dollar Diplomacy

President Taft hoped to counter Japanese advances in Asia through dollar diplomacy—the use of private funds to serve American diplomatic goals while garnering profits for American financiers and bringing reform to developing countries. Taft induced American bankers to join an international consortium to build a railway in China. But it seemed only to embolden Japan to solidify its holdings in China.

In 1914, when World War I broke out in Europe, Japan seized Shandong and some Pacific islands from the Germans. In 1915, Japan issued its Twenty-One Demands, insisting on hegemony over China. The United States lacked power in Asia to block Japan's imperialisms. A new president, Woodrow Wilson, worried about how the "white race" could blunt the rise of "the yellow race."

Guantánamo Bay

Four hundred miles from Miami, near the southeastern corner of Cuba, sits U.S. Naval Base Guantánamo Bay. The oldest American base outside the United States, it is the only one located in a country with which Washington does not have an open political relationship. The United States has occupied Guantánamo since the aftermath of the Spanish-American War, leasing it from Cuba for $4,085 per year (originally $2,000 in gold coins).

Cuban leaders were dissatisfied with the deal early on, and after Fidel Castro's communist takeover in 1959, Guantánamo fueled tensions between the two countries. Castro called it "a dagger pointed at Cuba's heart" and refused to cash the rent checks. That he cashed the very first check, however, enabled Washington to argue that Castro's government accepts the lease.

Since late 2001, "Gitmo" has contained a detainment camp for alleged combatants captured in Afghanistan and, later, Iraq and elsewhere. By 2005, there were more than five hundred detainees from forty countries. The George W. Bush administration called the detainees "unlawful enemy combatants" but promised to follow the Geneva accords governing prisoners of war. Soon, there were allegations of abuse and complaints that holding detainees without trial, charges, or any prospect of release was unlawful. Some detainees committed suicide. For critics, the camp became an international symbol of American heavy-handedness that hurt America's image abroad.

In June 2006, the U.S. Supreme Court ruled that President Bush overstepped his power in establishing procedures for the Guantánamo detainees without congressional authority—and that the procedures violated the Uniform Code of Military Justice and the Geneva accords. Bush said he would like to close the Guantánamo camp but some prisoners were too "darned dangerous" to release or deport. The question for a people and a nation remained: how would the United States balance security with due process and the rule of law?

Anglo-American Rapprochement

British officials shared this concern, though their attention was focused on rising tensions in Europe. Anglo-American cooperation blossomed during the Roosevelt-Taft years. The intense German-British rivalry and the rise of the United States to world power furthered London's quest for friendship with Washington. The two nations shared a common language and respect for private property rights, and Americans appreciated British support in the 1898 war and the Hay-Pauncefote Treaty, London's virtual endorsement of the Roosevelt Corollary, and the withdrawal of British warships from the Caribbean.

British-American trade and U.S. investment in Britain also secured ties. By 1914, more than 140 American companies operated in Britain, including H. J. Heinz's processed foods and F. W. Woolworth's "penny markets." Many decried an Americanization of British culture. Such exaggerated fears, however, gave way to cooperation, especially in 1917 when the United States entered World War I supporting Britain against Germany.

Summary

By 1914, Americans held extensive economic, strategic, and political interests worldwide. The outward reach of U.S. foreign policy from Seward to Wilson sparked opposition from domestic critics, other imperialist nations, and foreign nationalists, but expansionists prevailed, and the trend toward empire endured.

Economic and strategic needs motivated and justified expansion. The belief that the United States needed foreign markets to absorb surplus production joined missionary zeal in reforming other societies through American products and culture. Notions of racial and male supremacy and appeals to national greatness also fed the appetite for foreign adventure. The greatly augmented navy became a primary means for satisfying America's expansionist desires.

Revealing the diversity of America's intersection with the world, missionaries like Moon, generals, companies, and politicians carried American ideas, guns, and goods abroad to a mixed reception. When world war broke out in August 1914, the United States' self-proclaimed greatness and political isolation from Europe were tested.

Chapter Review

Imperial Dreams

What drove U.S. expansion overseas in the late nineteenth century?

American leaders increasingly believed in the decades after the Civil War that the nation's future prosperity and security depended on greater U.S. investment in and influence over other parts of the world. They believed foreign trade could prevent future economic downturns in the U.S.—an increasing concern with the depression of the 1890s—by shipping surplus products made here overseas. Economic ties also permitted political influence to be exerted abroad and helped spread the American way of life, especially capitalism, which fueled dramatic growth of U.S. exports. Leaders also embraced the notion of American "exceptionalism"—that the United States was unique and superior to other regions because of its heritage and God-favored prosperity. Nationalism, capitalism, Social Darwinism, and a paternalistic racism provided rationales for U.S. expansion and imperialism; hence, expansionists argued that when they intervened and sometimes colonized these regions, they were helping to bring prosperity and liberty to weaker, less fortunate peoples.

Ambitions and Strategies

What happened to Seward's vision of an American empire?

Secretary of State William Seward longed for a U.S. empire that would extend the frontier to include Canada, the Caribbean, Cuba, Central America, Mexico, Hawai'i, Iceland, Greenland, and the Pacific islands. He anticipated these areas would naturally gravitate to—and easily become enveloped by—the United States, and that foreign trade and certain infrastructure developments—such as a transcontinental U.S. railroad, a canal across Central America, and a telegraph system—would speed things along. Most of his vision never came to pass, blocked by anti-imperialists, political foes, and failed schemes. He had a few successes, however, including chasing the French puppet government from Mexico in 1866, purchasing Alaska from the Russians in 1867, and claiming the Midway Islands for the United States that year.

Crises in the 1890s: Hawai'i, Venezuela, and Cuba

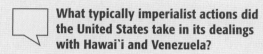

What typically imperialist actions did the United States take in its dealings with Hawai`i and Venezuela?

In both cases, the United States showed disregard for the rights of foreign peoples. Hawai'i was annexed despite the objections of its queen and most Hawaiians because it proved strategically and commercially important to the United States—particularly during the Spanish-American War, when it served as a way station to Asia and the Philippines. Venezuela, meanwhile, sought U.S. assistance in its border dispute with Great Britain over where its boundary with British Guiana should lie. The Anglo-American arbitration board divided up the territory, which was rich with gold and provided a commercial gateway to South America, between Britain and Venezuela, with almost no input from the latter.

The Spanish-American War and the Debate over Empire

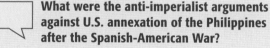

What were the anti-imperialist arguments against U.S. annexation of the Philippines after the Spanish-American War?

Anti-imperialists expressed a wide range of concerns about the potential annexation of the Philippines. For many, it seemed hypocritical for Americans to fight a war for Cuban liberation, only to acquire another small nation in the process. Some argued that it violated the fundamental right of a people to self-determination that Americans themselves embraced in the Declaration of Independence and Constitution. Prominent women such as Jane Addams felt imperialist zeal corrupted the American character, and cited children's playing war games as evidence of this. Racists saw the annexation of nonwhite nation as a potential threat to Anglo-Saxon

purity and supremacy, while labor leaders feared the new colonists might become a cheap labor force to drive down American wages.

Asian Encounters: War in the Philippines, Diplomacy in China

Why was the Open Door policy such a key component of U.S. diplomacy?

The Open Door Policy originated in the late nineteenth century as a solution to U.S. trade difficulties in China. The concept called for nations with spheres of influence in turbulent China to respect the principle of equal trade opportunity in the region. After 1900, when the United States became the world's preeminent trader, the Open Door became the tool by which it could first pry open new markets and then dominate them. As it developed, the Open Door included the following tenets: that America's economy required exports to remain strong; that trade abroad could be interrupted unless the United States intervened; and that any effort to keep U.S. citizens, products, or ideas from other regions threatened U.S. survival.

TR's World

What solidified U.S.-British ties heading into World War I?

Aside from their shared language and respect for private property rights, England and the United States were united by several other factors. Both were concerned about growing Japanese influence in Asia. U.S. investment in Britain, along with increased trade, further strengthened their bonds. British support for the Roosevelt Corollary to Monroe doctrine (granting the United States hegemony in the Western Hemisphere) and the withdrawal of British ships from the Caribbean made relations easier, as did England's respect for the United States' growing status as a world power. Increased tensions between Germany and England, along with British support for the 1898 war, increased cooperation between the two countries and ensured that many Americans would take England's side in the impending global conflict.

Suggestions for Further Reading

Gail Bederman, *Manliness and Cvilization: A Cultural History of Gender and Race in the United States, 1880–1917* (1995)

Kristin L. Hoganson, *Fighting for American Manhood: How Gender Politics Provoked the Spanish-American and Philippine-American Wars* (1998)

Michael H. Hunt, *Ideology and U.S. Foreign Policy* (1987)

Paul A. Kramer, *The Blood of Government: Race, Empire, the United States, and the Philippines* (2006)

Walter LaFeber, *The American Search for Opportunity, 1865–1913* (1993)

Brian M. Linn, *The Philippine War, 1899–1902* (2000)

Eric T. Love, *Race over Empire: Racism and U.S. Imperialism, 1865–1900* (2004)

Stuart Creighton Miller, *"Benevolent Assimilation": The American Conquest of the Philippines, 1899–1903* (1982)

John Offner, *An Unwanted War: The Diplomacy of the United States and Spain over Cuba, 1895–1898* (1992)

Louis A. Perez Jr., *The War of 1898: The United States and Cuba in History and Historiography* (1998)

Americans in the Great War

23

1914–1920

On May 7, 1915, Secretary of State William Jennings Bryan was lunching with cabinet members in Washington when he received a bulletin: the luxurious British ocean liner *Lusitania* had been sunk, apparently by a German submarine. He rushed to his office, and at 3:06 p.m. received confirmation from London: "THE LUSITANIA WAS TORPEDOED OFF THE IRISH COAST AND SANK IN HALF AN HOUR." The giant vessel sank in eighteen minutes; 1,198 people perished, including 128 Americans. With Europe at war, Bryan feared such a calamity. Britain had imposed a naval blockade on Germany, and the Germans had responded with submarine warfare against Allied shipping, proclaiming the North Atlantic a danger zone, then sinking British and Allied ships. As a passenger liner, the *Lusitania* was supposed to be spared, but German officials warned Americans in newspaper notices that they traveled on British or Allied ships at their own risk; passenger liners suspected of carrying munitions or contraband were subject to attack. For weeks, Bryan urged President Woodrow Wilson to stop Americans from booking passage on British ships; Wilson refused.

The *Lusitania,* it soon emerged, *was* carrying munitions. Desperate to keep the United States out of the war, Bryan urged Wilson to condemn Germany and Britain's blockade and to ban Americans from traveling on belligerent ships. Others, including former president Theodore Roosevelt, called the sinking "an act of piracy" and pressed for war. Wilson did not want war, but disagreed with Bryan about treating British and German violations the same. He sent a strong note to Berlin, insisting Germany end its submarine warfare.

As Bryan pressed his case, he became increasingly isolated within the administration. When in early June Wilson refused to ban Americans from travel on belligerent ships and sent a second protest note to Germany, Bryan resigned.

The division between the president and his secretary of state reflected divisions within the American populace over Europe's war. Eastern newspapers charged Bryan with betraying

Chapter Outline

Precarious Neutrality
Outbreak of the First World War | *Taking Sides* | *Wilsonianism* | *Violations of Neutral Rights*

The Decision for War
Peace Advocates | *Unrestricted Submarine Warfare* | *War Message and War Declaration*

Winning the War
The Draft and the Soldier | *Trench Warfare* | *Shell Shock* | *American Units in France* | *The Bolshevik Revolution* | *Fourteen Points* | *Americans in Battle* | *Casualties*

LINKS TO THE WORLD *The Influenza Pandemic of 1918*

Mobilizing the Home Front
Business-Government Cooperation | *Economic Performance* | *Labor Shortage* | *National War Labor Board*

VISUALIZING THE PAST *Eating to Win*

Civil Liberties Under Challenge
The Committee on Public Information | *Espionage and Sedition Acts*

Red Scare, Red Summer
Labor Strikes | *American Legion* | *Palmer Raids* | *Racial Unrest* | *Black Militancy*

The Defeat of Peace
Paris Peace Conference | *League of Nations and Article 10* | *Critics of the Treaty* | *Senate Rejection of the Treaty and League* | *An Unsafe World*

LEGACY FOR A PEOPLE AND A NATION *Freedom of Speech and the ACLU*

SUMMARY

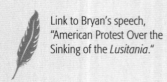

Link to Bryan's speech, "American Protest Over the Sinking of the *Lusitania*."

the country. But in the Midwest and South, Bryan won praise from pacifists and German American groups. Weeks later, speaking to fifteen thousand people at Madison Square Garden, Bryan was applauded when he warned against "war with any of the belligerent nations." Although many Americans agreed with Wilson that honor ranked above peace, others shared Bryan's position that some sacrifice of neutral rights was reasonable to keep the country out of war.

To many, full-scale war seemed unthinkable. The new machine guns, howitzers, submarines, and dreadnoughts were awesome death engines; one social reformer lamented that using them would mean "civilization is all gone, and barbarism come."

For almost three years, President Wilson kept America out of the war, while protecting U.S. trade interests and improving the nation's military posture. But American property, lives, and neutrality fell victim to British and German naval warfare. When, two years after the *Lusitania* went down, the president asked Congress for a declaration of war, he insisted America would not just win but "make the world safe for democracy."

A year and a half later, the Great War would be over. Some 10 million soldiers perished. Europeans experienced the destruction of ideals, confidence, and goodwill, and immense economic damage. The Great War toppled four empires of the Old World—the German, Austro-Hungarian, Russian, and Ottoman Turkish—and left two others, the British and French, drastically weakened.

Losses for the United States were comparatively small, yet American involvement tipped the scales in favor of the Allies by contributing troops, supplies, and loans. The war years also witnessed a massive international transfer of wealth from Europe across the Atlantic, as the United States went from the world's largest debtor nation to its largest creditor. The conflict marked the United States as a world power.

At home, World War I intensified social divisions. Racial tensions accompanied the northward migration of southern blacks, and pacifists and German Americans were harassed. The federal government trampled on civil liberties to silence critics. After Russia's communist revolution, a Red Scare in America repressed radicals and tarnished America's democratic image. Although reformers continued to address issues like prohibition and woman suffrage, the war splintered the Progressive movement.

Abroad, Americans who marched to battle grew disillusioned with the peace process. They recoiled from victors squabbling over the spoils, and they chided Wilson for failing to deliver his promised "peace without victory." After negotiating the Treaty of Versailles at Paris following World War I, the president urged U.S. membership in the new League of Nations, which he believed would reform world politics. The Senate rejected his appeal (the League nonetheless organized without U.S. membership), because many Americans feared the League might threaten the U.S. empire and entangle Americans in Europe's problems.

As you read this chapter, keep the following questions in mind:

* **Why did the United States try to remain neutral and then enter the European war in 1917?**

* **How was American society changed by the war?**

* **What were the main elements of Woodrow Wilson's postwar vision, and why did he fail to realize them?**

Chronology

1914	First World War begins in Europe
1915	Germans sink *Lusitania* off coast of Ireland
1916	After torpedoing the *Sussex*, Germany pledges not to attack merchant ships without warning
	National Defense Act expands military
1917	Germany declares unrestricted submarine warfare
	Russian Revolution ousts the czar; Bolsheviks later take power
	United States enters First World War
	Selective Service Act creates draft
	Espionage Act limits First Amendment rights
	Race riot breaks out in East St. Louis, Illinois
1918	Wilson announces Fourteen Points for new world order
	Sedition Act further limits free speech

	U.S. troops at Château-Thierry help blunt German offensive
	U.S. troops intervene in Russia against Bolsheviks
	Spanish flu pandemic kills 20 million worldwide
	Armistice ends First World War
1919	Paris Peace Conference punishes Germany and launches League of Nations
	May Day bombings help instigate Red Scare
	American Legion organizes for veterans' benefits and antiradicalism
	Wilson suffers stroke after speaking tour
	Senate rejects Treaty of Versailles and U.S. membership in League of Nations
	Schenck v. U.S. upholds Espionage Act
1920	Palmer Raids round up suspected radicals

Precarious Neutrality

> How viable was U.S. neutrality during World War I?

The war that erupted in August 1914 grew from years of European competition over trade, colonies, allies, and armaments. Two powerful alliance systems had formed: the Triple Alliance of Germany, Austria-Hungary, and Italy, and the Triple Entente of Britain, France, and Russia. All had imperial holdings and wanted more. As Germany challenged Great Britain for world leadership, many Americans saw Germany as an excessively militaristic nation that threatened U.S. interests in the Western Hemisphere.

Outbreak of the First World War

Crises in the Balkans triggered events that shattered Europe's delicate balance of power. Slavic nationalists sought to enlarge independent Serbia by annexing regions such as Bosnia, then a province of the Austro-Hungarian Empire. On June 28, 1914, Archduke Franz Ferdinand, heir to the Austro-Hungarian throne, was assassinated by a Serbian nationalist while visiting Sarajevo, the capital of Bosnia. Austria-Hungary consulted its Triple Alliance partner Germany, which urged toughness. When Serbia called on its Slavic friend Russia for help, Russia enlisted France and began mobilizing its armies.

Germany struck first, declaring war against Russia on August 1 and against France two days later. Britain hesitated, but when German forces slashed into neutral Belgium to get at France, London declared war against Germany on August 4. Eventually, Turkey (the Ottoman Empire) joined Germany and Austria-Hungary as the Central Powers, and Italy (switching sides) and Japan teamed up with Britain, France, and Russia as the Allies. Japan seized Shandong, Germany's area of influence in China.

Link to Wilson's Appeal for Neutrality.

President Wilson initially distanced America by proclaiming neutrality—the traditional U.S. policy toward European wars. Privately, he worried that without neutrality, "our mixed populations would wage war on each other."

Taking Sides

Despite Wilson's appeal for unity at home, ethnic groups took opposing sides. Many German Americans and anti-British Irish Americans (Ireland was then trying to break free from British rule) cheered for the Central Powers. Americans with roots in Allied nations championed the Allied cause. Germany's attack on Belgium confirmed for many that Germany was the archetype of unbridled militarism.

The pro-Allied sympathies of Wilson's administration also weakened the U.S. neutrality proclamation. Wilson shared the conviction with British leaders that a German victory would destroy free enterprise and government by law. If Germany won the war, he prophesied, "it would change the course of our civilization and make the United States a military nation."

U.S. economic links with the Allies also rendered neutrality difficult, if not impossible. England, a long-time customer, flooded America with new orders, especially for arms. Sales to the Allies helped end an American recession. Between 1914 and 1916, American exports to England and France grew 365 percent, from $753 million to $2.75 billion. Largely because of Britain's naval blockade, exports to Germany dropped by more than 90 percent, from $345 million to only $29 million. Loans to Britain and France from private American banks—totaling $2.3 billion during neutrality—financed much of U.S. trade with the Allies. Germany received only $27 million in the same period.

To Germans, the links between the American economy and the Allies meant that the United States had become the Allied arsenal and bank. Americans, however, worried that cutting economic ties with Britain would constitute a nonneutral act in favor of Germany. Under international law, Britain—which controlled the seas—could buy both contraband (war-related goods) and noncontraband from neutrals. It was Germany's responsibility, not America's, to stop such trade as international law prescribed by blockading the enemy's territory, seizing contraband from neutral (American) ships, or by confiscating goods from belligerent (British) ships.

Wilsonianism

"Wilsonianism," the cluster of ideas that Wilson espoused, consisted of traditional American principles (such as democracy and the Open Door) and a vision of the United States as a beacon of freedom. Only the United States could lead the convulsed world into a peaceful era of unobstructed commerce, free-market capitalism, democratic politics, and open diplomacy. "America had the infinite privilege of fulfilling her destiny and saving the world," Wilson claimed. Empires had to be dismantled to honor the principle of self-determination. Critics charged that Wilson often violated his own credos while forcing them on others—as his military interventions in Mexico in 1914, Haiti in 1915, and the Dominican Republic in 1916 testified. Nonetheless, his ideals served American commercial purposes.

To say that U.S. neutrality was never a possibility given ethnic loyalties, economic ties, and Wilsonian preferences is not to say that Wilson sought to enter the war. In early 1917, the president remarked that "we are the only one of the great white nations that is free from war today, and it would be a crime against civilization for us to go in." But go in the United States finally did. Why?

Violations of Neutral Rights

The short answer is that Americans got caught in the Allied–Central Power crossfire. The British sought to cripple the German economy by severing neutral trade. They declared a blockade of water entrances to Germany. They seized cargoes and defined a broad list of contraband (including foodstuffs) that they prohibited neutrals from shipping to Germany. Furthermore, to counter German submarines, the British flouted international law by arming their merchant ships and flying neutral (sometimes U.S.) flags. Wilson protested British violations of neutral rights, but London deflected Washington's criticism by paying for confiscated cargoes, while German provocations made British behavior appear less offensive in comparison.

Germany looked for victory at sea by using submarines. In February 1915, Berlin declared a war zone around the British Isles, warned neutral vessels to stay out so as not to be mistakenly attacked, and advised passengers to stay off Allied ships. Wilson informed Germany that it would be held accountable for any losses of American life and property.

Wilson interpreted international law strictly and expected Germans to warn passenger or merchant ships before attacking, so that passengers and crew could disembark safely into lifeboats. The Germans thought that surfacing its slender and sluggish *Unterseebooten* (U-boats) would leave them vulnerable to attack. Berlin protested that Wilson was denying it the one weapon that could break the British economic stranglehold, disrupt the Allies' substantial connection with U.S. producers and bankers, and win the war. To British, Germans, and Americans, naval warfare became a matter of life and death.

The Decision for War

Ultimately, it was the war at sea that doomed the prospects for U.S. neutrality. In early 1915, German U-boats sank ship after ship, notably the *Lusitania* on May 7. Germany's subsequent promise to refrain from attacking passenger liners ended in August when another British vessel, the *Arabic,* was sunk off Ireland. Three Americans died. Germany quickly pledged that an unarmed passenger ship would never again be attacked without warning. But the *Arabic* incident led critics to ask: why not require Americans to sail on American craft? From August 1914 to March 1917, after all, only 3 Americans died on an American ship (the tanker *Gulflight,* sunk by a German U-boat in May 1915), whereas about 190 were killed on belligerent ships.

> How did the Zimmermann telegram finally push Americans to abandon neutrality?

Peace Advocates

In March 1916, a U-boat attack on the *Sussex,* a French vessel crossing the English Channel, injured four Americans and brought the United States close to war. Wilson warned Berlin that the United States would sever diplomatic relations if the attacks continued. Again, the Germans retreated. At the same time, U.S.-British relations soured after Britain's crushing of the Easter Rebellion in Ireland and further British restriction of U.S. trade with the Central Powers.

As the United States became more entangled in the Great War, many Americans urged Wilson to keep the nation out. In early 1915, Jane Addams, Carrie Chapman Catt, and other suffragists helped found the Woman's Peace Party, the U.S. section of the Women's International League for Peace and Freedom. Later that year, pacifist Progressives organized an antiwar coalition, the American Union Against Militarism. The businessmen Andrew Carnegie and Henry Ford financed peace efforts, standing with socialist Eugene Debs.

Antiwar advocates emphasized that war drained a nation of its youth, resources, and reform impulse; that it fostered repression at home; that it violated Christian morality; and that wartime business barons reaped huge profits at the expense of the people. Militarism and conscription, Addams pointed out, were what millions of immigrants left behind in Europe. Although the peace movement was splintered, it articulated several ideas that Wilson, who campaigned on a peace platform in the 1916 election, shared. Wilson futilely labored to bring the belligerents to the conference table, urging them in early 1917 to temper their acquisitive war aims and embrace "peace without victory."

Unrestricted Submarine Warfare

In Germany, Wilson's overture went unheeded. Since August 1916, German leaders debated whether to resume the unrestricted U-boat campaign. Opponents feared a break with the United States, but proponents claimed that only through an all-out attack on Britain's supply shipping could Germany win the war. True, the United States might enter the war, but victory might be achieved before U.S. troops crossed the Atlantic. Consequently, in early February 1917, Germany launched unrestricted submarine warfare, attacking all warships and merchant vessels—belligerent or neutral—in the declared war zone. Wilson quickly broke diplomatic relations with Berlin.

In late February, British intelligence intercepted and passed to U.S. officials a telegram addressed to the German minister in Mexico from German foreign secretary Arthur Zimmermann. Its message: If Mexico joined a military alliance against the United States, Germany would help Mexico recover the territories it lost in 1848. Zimmermann hoped to "set new enemies on America's neck— enemies which give them plenty to take care of over there." Although Mexico City rejected Germany's offer, Wilson judged Zimmermann's telegram "a conspiracy against this country." The prospect of a German-Mexican collaboration turned the tide of opinion in the American Southwest, where antiwar sentiment had been strong.

Soon afterward, Wilson asked Congress for "armed neutrality" to defend American lives and commerce, seeking authority to arm American merchant ships, for example. During the debate, Wilson released Zimmermann's telegram to the press. Americans were outraged. Still, antiwar senators Robert M. La Follette and George Norris, among others, saw the armed-ship bill as a blank check for the president to move the country to war, and they filibustered it to death. Wilson armed America's commercial vessels anyway but acted too late to prevent the sinking of several American ships. War cries escalated.

Link to Wilson's War Message to Congress.

War Message and War Declaration

On April 2, 1917, the president stepped before a hushed Congress and enumerated U.S. grievances: Germany's violation of freedom of the seas, disruption of commerce, interference with Mexico, and breach of human rights by killing innocent Americans.

Congress declared war against Germany on April 6 by a vote of 373 to 50 in the House and 82 to 6 in the Senate. (This vote was for war against Germany only; a declaration of war against Austria-Hungary came months later, on December 7.) Montana's Jeannette Rankin, the first woman to sit in Congress, cast a ringing no vote.

For principle, morality, honor, commerce, security, reform—for these reasons, Wilson took the United States into the Great War. The submarine was certainly the culprit that drew a reluctant president and nation into the maelstrom. Critics blamed Wilson's rigid definition of international law and his contention that Americans should be entitled to travel anywhere, even on a belligerent ship loaded with contraband. Most Americans accepted Wilson's view that the Germans had to be checked to ensure an open, orderly world in which U.S. principles and interests would be safe.

The United States went to war to reform world politics, not to destroy Germany. By early 1917, the president concluded that the United States would not be able to claim a seat at the postwar peace conference unless it became a combatant. At the peace conference, Wilson intended to promote the principles he thought essential to a stable world order, to advance democracy and the Open Door, and to outlaw revolution and aggression. In designating the United States an "Associated" rather than an Allied nation, Wilson tried to preserve part of his country's neutrality, but to no avail.

Winning the War

Even before the U.S. declaration of war, the Wilson administration strengthened the military under the banner of "preparedness." The National Defense Act of 1916 provided for increases in the army and National Guard, and for summer training camps modeled on the one in Plattsburgh, New York, where some of America's elite trained in 1915 as "citizen-soldiers." The Navy Act of 1916 started the largest naval expansion in American history.

> What was the impact of modern, trench warfare on soldiers?

The Draft and the Soldier

To raise an army, Congress in May 1917 passed the **Selective Service Act**, requiring males between age twenty-one and thirty (later changed to eighteen and forty-five) to register. National service, proponents believed, would prepare the nation for battle and instill patriotism and respect for order, democracy, and personal sacrifice. Critics feared it would lead to the militarization of American life.

On June 5, 1917, more than 9.5 million men signed up for the "great national lottery." By war's end, 24 million men were registered by local draft boards. Millions received deferments from military duty because they worked in war industries or had dependents.

The typical soldier was in his early to mid-twenties, white, single, American-born, and poorly educated (most had not attended high school, and perhaps 30 percent could not read or write). Tens of thousands of women enlisted in the army Nurse Corps, served as "hello girls" (volunteer bilingual telephone operators) in the army Signal Corps, and became clerks in the navy and Marine Corps. Some 400,000 African Americans also served in the military. Many southern politicians feared arming blacks, but the army drafted them into segregated units and assigned them

Selective Service Act: Law that required all men between twenty-one and thirty (later expanded to eighteen through forty-five) to register with local draft boards.

to menial labor. They endured abuse and miserable conditions. Ultimately more than 40,000 African Americans would see combat in Europe, and several black units served with distinction in the French army. The all-black 369th Infantry Regiment spent more time in the trenches—191 days—and received more medals than any other American outfit.

Although French officers had their share of racial prejudice and often treated the soldiers from their own African colonies poorly, black Americans serving with the French reported a degree of respect lacking in the American army. The irony was not lost on African American leaders, such as W. E. B. Du Bois, who endorsed the National Association for the Advancement of Colored People's (NAACP) support for the war and urged blacks to volunteer.

Approximately 3 million men evaded draft registration. Some were arrested, others fled to Mexico or Canada, but most stayed home and were never discovered. Another 338,000 men who registered never showed up for induction. According to arrest records, most of these "deserters" and the more numerous "evaders" were lower-income agricultural and industrial laborers. Nearly 65,000 draftees applied for conscientious-objector (CO) status (refusing to bear arms for religious or pacifist reasons), but some changed their minds or failed preinduction examinations. Quakers and Mennonites were numerous among the 4,000 inductees classified as COs. COs who refused noncombat service, such as in the medical corps, faced imprisonment.

Trench Warfare

John J. Pershing: Commander of American Expeditionary Force that fought in Europe.

American Expeditionary Forces: U.S. soldiers who fought in Europe during World War I.

U.S. general **John J. Pershing**, head of the **American Expeditionary Forces** (AEF), insisted that his "sturdy rookies" remain a separate army. He refused to turn over his "soldiers" to Allied commanders, who favored deadly trench warfare. Since fall 1914, zigzag trenches fronted by barbed wire and mines stretched across France. Between the muddy, stinking trenches lay "no man's land," denuded by artillery fire. When ordered out, soldiers would charge enemy trenches only to face machine gun fire and poison gas.

First used by the Germans in April 1915, chlorine gas stimulated overproduction of fluid in the lungs, leading to death by drowning. Gas in a variety of forms (mustard and phosgene, in addition to chlorine) would be used throughout the war, sometimes blistering, sometimes incapacitating, often killing.

The death toll in trench warfare was overwhelming. At the Battle of the Somme in 1916, the British and French suffered 600,000 dead or wounded to earn only 125 square miles; the Germans lost 400,000 men. At Verdun that year, 336,000 Germans perished, and at Passchendaele in 1917 more than 370,000 British men died to gain about 40 miles of mud and barbed wire.

Shell Shock

Not long after arriving on the French front, U.S. units faced the horrors caused by advanced weaponry. Some suffered shell shock, a mental illness also known as war psychosis. Symptoms included a fixed, empty stare; violent tremors; paralyzed limbs; listlessness; jabbering; screaming; and haunting dreams. The illness could strike anyone; even soldiers who appeared courageous cracked after days of incessant shelling and inescapable human carnage. Red Cross canteens, staffed by women volunteers, provided relief and offered haircuts, food, and recreation.

A U.S. soldier of Company K, 110th Infantry Regiment, receives aid during fighting at Verennes, France.

National Archives

In Paris, where forty large houses of prostitution thrived, venereal disease became such a problem that French prime minister Georges Clemenceau offered licensed, inspected prostitutes to the U.S. army. Still, by war's end, about 15 percent of America's soldiers contracted venereal disease, costing the army $50 million and 7 million days of active duty. Periodic inspections, chemical prophylactic treatments, and the threat of court-martial for infected soldiers kept the problem from being greater.

American Units in France

Soldiers filled their diaries and letters with descriptions of local customs and "ancient" architecture, and noted how the grimy and war-torn French countryside bore little resemblance to the groomed landscapes in paintings. "Life in France for the American soldier meant marching in the dirt and mud, living in cellars in filth, being wet and cold and fighting," the chief of staff of the Fourth Division remarked. "He had come to help...but these French people did not seem to appreciate him at all."

With both sides exhausted, the Americans tipped the balance toward the Allies. But not right away. Initially, the U.S. Navy battled submarines and escorted troop carriers and pilots in the U.S. Air Service, flying mostly British and French aircraft, saw limited action. American flying "aces" like Eddie Rickenbacker defeated their German counterparts in aerial "dogfights" and became heroes in France and their own country. But only ground troops could make a decisive difference, and American units did not engage in much combat until after the harsh winter of 1917–1918.

The Bolshevik Revolution

The military and diplomatic situation changed dramatically as a result of the Bolshevik Revolution in Russia. In November 1917, the liberal-democratic government of Aleksander Kerensky, which led the country since the czar's abdication early in the year, was overthrown by by V. I. Lenin's radical socialists. Lenin vowed to change world politics and end imperial rivalries on terms that challenged Wilson's. To Lenin, the war signaled the impending end of capitalism and the rise of a global revolution of workers. For western leaders, the prospect of Bolshevik-style revolutions worldwide was too frightening to contemplate.

In the weeks following their takeover, the Bolsheviks attempted to embarrass the capitalist governments and incite world revolution. They published Allied secret agreements for dividing up the colonies and other territories of the Central Powers if Allies were victorious. Wilson confided to Colonel House that he wanted to tell the Bolsheviks to "go to hell," but he accepted the colonel's argument that he would have to address Lenin's claims that there was little to distinguish the two warring sides and that socialism represented the future.

Fourteen Points: President Wilson's program for world peace; presented to Congress in a 1918 speech, in the midst of World War I.

Link to Wilson's Fourteen Points delivered to the Joint Session of Congress.

Fourteen Points

In the **Fourteen Points**, unveiled in January 1918, Wilson reaffirmed America's commitment to an international system governed by laws and renounced territorial gains as a legitimate war aim. The first five points called for diplomacy "in the public view," freedom of the seas, lower tariffs, armament reductions, and the decolonization of empires. The next eight points specified the evacuation of foreign troops from Russia, Belgium, and France and appealed for self-determination for nationalities in Europe, such as the Poles. For Wilson, the fourteenth point was the mechanism for achieving the others: "a general association of nations," or League of Nations.

Lenin was unimpressed and called for an immediate end to the fighting, the eradication of colonialism, and self-determination for all peoples. Lenin also made a separate peace with Germany—the Treaty of Brest-Litovsk, signed on March 3, 1918. The deal erased centuries of Russian expansion, as Poland, Finland, and the Baltic states were taken from Russia and Ukraine was granted independence. One of Lenin's motives was to allow Russian troops loyal to the Bolsheviks to return home to fight anti-Bolshevik forces attempting to oust his government.

Americans in Battle

In March 1918, the Germans launched a major offensive. By May, they were within 50 miles of Paris. U.S. First Division troops helped blunt the German advance at Cantigny (see Map 23.1). In June the Third Division and French forces held positions along the Marne River at Château-Thierry, and the Second Division attacked the Germans in the Belleau Wood. American soldiers won the battle after three weeks of fighting, but thousands died or were wounded in sacrificial frontal assaults against German machine guns.

Allied victory in the Second Battle of the Marne in July 1918 stemmed German advances. In September, French and American forces took St. Mihiel

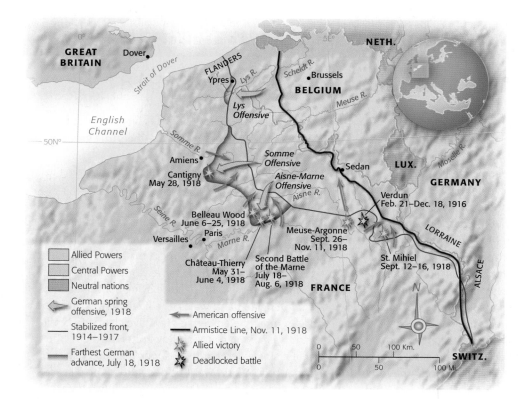

MAP 23.1

American Troops at the Western Front, 1918

America's 2 million troops in France met German forces head-on, ensuring the defeat of the Central Powers in 1918.

Source: Copyright © Cengage Learning

in a ferocious battle. Then, in the Meuse-Argonne offensive, over 1 million Americans joined British and French troops in weeks of combat; some twenty-six thousand Americans died before the Allies claimed the Argonne Forest on October 10. For Germany—its ground and submarine war stymied, its troops and cities mutinous, its allies Turkey and Austria dropping out, its Kaiser abdicating—peace became imperative. The Germans accepted a punishing armistice effective November 11, 1918.

Casualties

The cost of the war is impossible to compute: the belligerents counted 10 million soldiers and 6.6 million civilians dead and 21.3 million people wounded. Fifty-three thousand American soldiers died in battle, and another 62,000 died from disease, mainly a virulent strain of influenza that ravaged the world in late 1918. Economic damage was colossal and output dwindled, contributing to widespread starvation in Europe in the winter of 1918–1919.

The German, Austro-Hungarian, Ottoman, and Russian empires were gone. For a time, it appeared the Bolshevik Revolution might spread westward, as communist

The Influenza Pandemic of 1918

In summer and fall 1918, a terrible plague swept the earth. It claimed more than twice as many lives as the Great War itself—between 25 and 40 million people. In the United States, 675,000 people died.

The first cases were identified in Midwestern military camps in early March. At Fort Riley, Kansas, forty-eight men died. Soldiers shipped out to Europe in large numbers (eighty-four thousand in March), some unknowingly carrying the virus. The illness appeared on the western front in April. By June, an estimated 8 million Spaniards were infected, giving the disease its name, the Spanish flu.

In August, a second, deadlier form of the influenza erupted simultaneously in three cities on three continents: Freetown, Sierra Leone, in Africa; Brest, France, and Boston, Massachusetts. In September, the disease swept down the East Coast, killing twelve thousand Americans.

People could be healthy at the start of the weekend and dead by the end of it. Some experienced rapid accumulation of fluid in the lungs and literally drowned.

Others died slowly. Mortality rates were highest for twenty- to twenty-nine-year-olds—the same group dying in the trenches.

In October, the epidemic hit full force, spreading to Japan, India, Africa, and Latin America. In the United States, 200,000 perished. There was a nationwide shortage of caskets and gravediggers, and funerals were limited to fifteen minutes. Bodies were left in gutters or on front porches, to be picked up by trucks that drove the streets.

Suddenly, in November, for reasons still unclear, the epidemic eased, though the dying continued into 1919. In England and Wales, the final toll was 200,000, while in India the epidemic may have claimed 20 million. It was, in the historian Roy Porter's words, "the greatest single demographic shock mankind has ever experienced." World War I helped spread the disease. Americans, accustomed to thinking that two great oceans isolated them, were reminded that they were immutably linked to the rest of humankind.

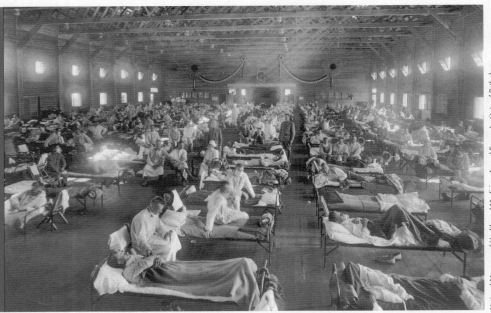

National Museum of Health and Medicine, Armed Forces Institute of Pathology

The influenza pandemic of 1918 perhaps started in earnest here, at Camp Funston, Kansas, in the spring of that year. Soldiers were struck with a debilitating illness they called "knock me down fever."

uprisings shook Germany and parts of central Europe. Before the armistice, revolutionaries temporarily took power in the German cities of Bremen, Hamburg, and Lübeck. In Moscow, the new Soviet state sought to consolidate its power.

Mobilizing the Home Front

Though the United States was belligerent for only nineteen months, the war had a tremendous impact on America. The federal government expanded its power over the economy to meet war needs and intervened in American life as never before. The enlarged Washington bureaucracy managed the economy, labor force, military, and public opinion. The government spent more than $760 million a month from April 1917 to August 1919. As tax revenues lagged, the administration resorted to deficit spending (see Figure 23.1). To Progressives of the New Nationalist persuasion, the wartime expansion and centralization of government power were welcome, but others worried about the dangers of concentrated federal power.

How did wartime labor shortages create new opportunities for American workers?

Business-Government Cooperation

The federal government and private business became partners during the war. Early on, the government relied on industrial committees for advice on purchases and prices. But evidence of businesspeople cashing in on the national interest aroused public protest. The head of the aluminum advisory committee, for example, was also president of the largest aluminum company. Consequently, committees were

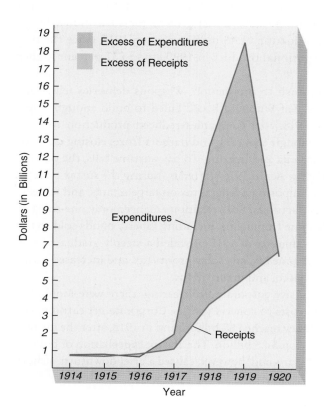

FIGURE 23.1
The Federal Budget, 1914–1920

During the First World War, the federal government spent more money than it received from increased taxes. It borrowed from banks or sold bonds through Liberty Loan drives. To meet the mounting costs of the war, in other words, the federal government had to resort to deficit spending. Expenditures topped receipts by more than $13 billion in 1919. Given this wartime fiscal pattern, moreover, the U.S. federal debt rose from $1 billion in 1914 to $25 billion in 1919.

Source: U.S. Department of Commerce, *Historical Statistics of the United States: Colonial Times to 1957* (Washington, D.C.: Bureau of the Census, 1960), p. 711.

War Industries Board:
Government agency established
to coordinate military
purchasing, ensure production
efficiency, and provide weapons
and supplies to the military.

Link to "Recipe for Victory:
Food and Cooking in
Wartime," a collection of
books and government
publications documenting
the national effort to promote
and implement a plan to
make food the key to
winning World War I.

replaced in July 1917 with a single manager, the **War Industries Board**. The
government also suspended antitrust laws and signed cost-plus contracts, guaranteeing companies healthy profits and a means to head off labor strikes with
higher wages. Competitive bidding was virtually abandoned, and big business
grew bigger.

Hundreds of new government agencies, staffed primarily by businesspeople,
used economic controls to shift the nation's resources to the Allies, the AEF, and
war-related production. The Food Administration, led by engineer and investor
Herbert Hoover, urged Americans to grow "victory gardens" and eat meatless and
wheatless meals—but it also set prices and regulated distribution. The Railroad
Administration took over the railway industry. The Fuel Administration controlled
coal supplies and rationed gasoline. When strikes threatened the telephone and telegraph companies, the federal government seized and ran them.

The largest of the superagencies was the War Industries Board (WIB), headed
by the financier Bernard Baruch. This Wall Streeter told Henry Ford that he would
dispatch the military to seize his plants unless the automaker accepted WIB limits
on car production. Designed to coordinate the national economy, the WIB made
purchases, allocated supplies, and fixed prices at levels that business requested. The
WIB also ordered the standardization of goods to streamline production. The varieties of automobile tires, for example, were reduced from 287 to 3.

Economic Performance   About one-quarter of American production was diverted
to war needs. As farmers enjoyed boom years, they put
more acreage into production and mechanized. Gross farm income from 1914 to
1919 increased more than 230 percent. Although manufacturing output leveled
off in 1918, wartime demand fueled substantial growth for such industries as
steel, which reached a peak production of 45 million tons in 1917, twice the prewar figure. Overall, the gross national product in 1920 stood 237 percent higher
than in 1914.

Mistakes happened in the rush to production. Weapons deliveries fell short;
the bloated bureaucracy of the War Shipping Board failed to build enough ships.
In the severe winter of 1917–1918, coal companies reduced production to raise
prices; railroads did not have enough coal cars; and harbors froze, closing out coal
barges. People died from pneumonia and freezing. To pay wartime bills, the government increased taxes. The Revenue Act in 1916 started by raising the surtax on high
incomes and corporate profits, imposing a federal tax on large estates, and increasing the tax on munitions manufacturers. Still, taxation financed only one-third of
the war. The other two-thirds came from loans, including Liberty bonds sold to the
American people. The War Revenue Act of 1917 provided a steeply graduated personal income tax, a corporate income tax, an excess-profits tax, and increased excise
taxes on alcoholic beverages, tobacco, and luxury items.

Although taxes curbed excessive corporate profiteering, there were loopholes.
Sometimes companies inflated costs to conceal profits. Corporate net earnings for
1913 totaled $4 billion; in 1917 they reached $7 billion; and in 1918, after the tax bite
and the war's end, they still stood at $4.5 billion. The abrupt cancellation of billions
of dollars' worth of contracts at war's end, however, caused a brief downturn, a short
boom, and then an intense decline (see Chapter 24).

Eating to Win

The war effort mobilized Americans as never before and also demanded that they make sacrifices. Hebert Hoover's Food Administration used colorful posters to persuade Americans to change their eating habits. The poster below uses bold type and a man standing over a fallen German soldier to send a patriotic message to eat less and save food for the troops. The poster at right has a 1940s Uncle Sam as teacher with a book promoting City and Farm Gardens and asking folks to learn more. The poster below and to the right uses religion (and guilt) to motivate the public. Which poster do you find most effective, and why? How are Americans persuaded today to change their eating habits?

In this colorful 1917 poster, Uncle Sam, posing as a teacher, says, "Garden to cut food costs." The poster offers a free Department of Agriculture "bulletin on gardening—it's food for thought."

Hispanic artist Francis Luis Mora used strong graphics for his 1918 poster showing a man standing over a fallen German soldier.

This 1917 poster showing a bounty of fall harvest fruits and vegetables—"This is what God gives us"—uses richly detailed illustration and colorful red type to get attention and ask the question, "What are you giving so that others may live?"

DON'T FORGET THE SALVATION ARMY

MY DOUGHNUT GIRL

WORDS BY
ELMORE LEFFINGWELL
AND JAMES LUCAS

MUSIC BY
ROBERT BROWN AND
WILLIAM FRISCH

THIS SONG
OFFICIALLY ENDORSED
AND ADOPTED BY

THE
SALVATION
ARMY

(OFFICIAL SEAL)

BROADWAY MUSIC CORPORATION
WILL VON-TILZER PRESIDENT
145 WEST 45 U ST NEW YORK

Picture Research Consultants & Archives

Stella Young (1896–1989), a Canadian-born woman from Chelsea, Massachusetts, became widely known as the "Doughnut Girl" because of her service during the First World War with the American branch of the Salvation Army, an international organization devoted to social work. She arrived in France in March 1918 and worked in emergency canteens near the battle front, providing U.S. troops with coffee, cocoa, sandwiches, doughnuts, pie, and fruit. Stella Young became famous when this picture of her wearing a khaki uniform and a "doughboy" steel helmet was widely circulated as a postcard. A piece of sheet music was even written about her. She served again in World War II. Chelsea named a city square in her honor in 1968.

Labor Shortage

For American workers, the full-employment wartime economy increased earnings. With the higher cost of living, however, workers saw minimal improvement. Turnover rates escalated as workers switched jobs for better pay and conditions. Some employers sought to overcome labor shortages by expanding social programs and by establishing personnel departments.

To meet the labor crisis, the Department of Labor's U.S. Employment Service matched laborers with job vacancies, attracting workers from the South and Midwest to war industries in the East. The department also temporarily relaxed the literacy-test and head-tax provisions of immigration law to attract farm labor, miners, and railroad workers from Mexico. As workers crammed into cities, the U.S. Housing Corporation and Emergency Fleet Corporation built row houses in Newport News, Virginia, and Eddystone, Pennsylvania.

The tight wartime labor market meant new job opportunities for women. In Connecticut, a special motion picture, *Mr. and Mrs. Hines of Stamford Do Their Bit*, appealed to housewives' patriotism, urging them to take factory jobs. Although the number of women in the work force increased slightly, many women moved into formerly male jobs, trading domestic service or textile jobs for those in factories, offices or firearms plants. At least 20 percent of employees in the wartime electrical-machinery, airplane, and food industries were women. For the first time, department stores employed African American women as elevator operators and cafeteria waitresses. But most working women were single and remained in the sex-segregated occupations of typists, nurses, teachers, and domestic servants.

Women also participated in the war effort as volunteers, making clothing for refugees and soldiers, serving at Red Cross facilities, and teaching French to nurses assigned to the war zone. Many worked for the Women's Committee of the Council of National Defense, a network of state and local organizations publicizing government mobilization programs, encouraging home gardens, sponsoring drives to sell Liberty bonds, and promoting social welfare reforms. This patriotic work improved prospects for passing the Nineteenth Amendment granting woman suffrage. "We have made partners of women in this war," Wilson said as he endorsed woman suffrage in 1918. "Shall we admit them only to a partnership of suffering and sacrifice . . . and not to a partnership of privilege and right?"

War mobilization encouraged a great migration of southern African Americans to northern cities to work in railroad yards, packing houses, steel mills, shipyards, and coal mines. Between 1910 and 1920, Cleveland's black population swelled by more than 300 percent, Detroit's by more than 600 percent, and Chicago's by 150 percent. All told, about a half-million African Americans moved to the North, with families pooling savings or selling household goods to fund the journey. Most migrants were unmarried and skilled or semiskilled males in their early twenties. Northern wartime jobs provided an escape from low wages, sharecropping, tenancy, crop liens, debt peonage, lynchings, and political disfranchisement. One African American wrote to a friend in Mississippi, "I just begin to feel like a man…. I don't have to humble to no one … Will vote the next election."

National War Labor Board

To keep factories running smoothly, Wilson instituted the National War Labor Board (NWLB) in early 1918. The NWLB discouraged strikes and lockouts and urged management to negotiate with unions. In July, after the Western Union Company fired eight hundred union members for trying to organize the firm's workers, the president nationalized the telegraph lines and put the laborers back to work. But in September the NWLB ordered striking Bridgeport, Connecticut, machinists back to munitions factories, threatening to revoke the draft exemptions they received for working in an essential industry.

Labor leaders hoped the war would offer opportunities for recognition and better pay through partnership with government. Samuel Gompers threw the AFL's loyalty to Wilson, promising to deter strikes. He and other moderate labor leaders accepted appointments to federal agencies. The antiwar Socialist Party blasted the AFL for becoming a "fifth wheel on [the] capitalist war chariot," but union membership climbed from roughly 2.5 million in 1916 to more than 4 million in 1919.

The AFL, however, could not curb strikes by the radical Industrial Workers of the World (IWW, also known as Wobblies) or rebellious AFL locals, especially those controlled by socialists. In the nineteen war months, more than six thousand strikes expressed workers' demands for a living wage and improved working conditions. Unions sought to create industrial democracy, a more representative workplace with labor helping to determine job categories and content. Defying the AFL, labor parties sprung up in twenty-three states by 1920.

Civil Liberties Under Challenge

How did free speech come under fire during World War I?

Wilson and his advisers enjoyed the support of newspapers, religious leaders, and public officials. They were less certain, however, about ordinary Americans. An official and unofficial campaign soon began to silence dissenters who questioned Wilson's decision for war or who protested the draft. The Wilson administration compiled one of the worst civil liberties records in American history.

Targets of governmental and quasi-vigilante repression included hundreds of thousands of Americans and aliens: pacifists, conscientious objectors, socialists, radical labor groups, the debt-ridden Oklahoma tenant farmers who staged the Green Corn Rebellion against the draft, the Non-Partisan League, reformers like Robert La Follette and Jane Addams, and others. In the wartime debate over democratic free speech, the concept of "civil liberties" emerged for the first time as a major public policy issue (see "Legacy for a People and a Nation," page 616)

Committee on Public Information: Wartime propaganda agency, headed by journalist George Creel. While claiming merely to combat rumors with facts, the Creel committee in reality publicized the government's version of events and discredited all who questioned that version.

Espionage Act: Law that set fines and prison sentences for a variety of loosely defined antiwar activities.

The Committee on Public Information

Spearheading the administration's war campaign war was the **Committee on Public Information** (CPI), formed in April 1917 and headed by Progressive journalist George Creel. Employing talented writers and scholars, the CPI used propaganda to mobilize public opinion. Pamphlets and films demonized the Germans, and CPI "Four-Minute Men" spoke at movie theaters, schools, and churches to pump up patriotism. Encouraged by the CPI, film companies and the National Association of the Motion Picture Industry produced documentaries, newsreels, and anti-German movies, such as *The Kaiser, the Beast of Berlin* (1918).

The committee also urged the press to practice self-censorship and encouraged people to spy on neighbors. Ultrapatriotic groups, such as the Sedition Slammers and the American Defense Society, used vigilantism. In Hilger, Montana, citizens burned history texts mentioning Germany. To avoid trouble, the Kaiser-Kuhn grocery in St. Louis changed its name to Pioneer Grocery. Townspeople in Berlin, Iowa, henceforth hailed from Lincoln. The German shepherd became the Alsatian shepherd.

With Liberty Loan quotas to fill, towns sometimes bullied "slackers" into purchasing bonds. Nativist advocates of "100% Americanism" exploited the atmosphere to exhort immigrants to throw off their Old World cultures. Companies offered English language and naturalization classes and refused jobs and promotions to those who did not learn English. Even labor's drive for compulsory health insurance, which before the war gained advocates in several states, became victimized by the poisoned atmosphere. Many physicians and insurance companies previously denounced health insurance as "socialistic"; after the United States entered the war, they discredited it as "Made in Germany."

Even institutions that had prided themselves on tolerance became contaminated. Wellesley College economics professor Emily Greene Balch was fired for her pacifist views (she won the Nobel Peace Prize in 1946). Three Columbia University students were apprehended in mid-1917 for circulating an antiwar petition. Columbia fired Professor J. M. Cattell, a distinguished psychologist, for his antiwar stand. His colleague Charles Beard, a historian with a prowar perspective, resigned in protest. Local school boards also dismissed teachers who questioned the war.

Espionage and Sedition Acts

The Wilson administration guided through an obliging Congress the **Espionage Act** (1917) and the Sedition Act (1918), giving the government wide latitude to crack down on critics. The first statute forbade "false statements" designed to impede the draft or promote military insubordination, and it banned from the mails materials considered treasonous. The Sedition Act made it unlawful to obstruct the sale of war

Chicago History Museum

A member of the Eighth Regiment of the Illinois National Guard with his family, circa 1918. Originally organized as a volunteer regiment during the Spanish-American War in 1898, the Eighth Regiment achieved its greatest fame during World War I. The only regiment to be entirely commanded by blacks and headquartered at the only black armory in the U.S., the "Fighting 8th" served with distinction in France, with 143 of its members losing their lives.

bonds and to use "disloyal, profane, scurrilous, or abusive" language to describe the government, the Constitution, the flag, or the military uniform. More than two thousand people were prosecuted under the acts, with many others intimidated into silence.

Progressives and conservatives used the war emergency to throttle the Industrial Workers of the World and the Socialist Party. Government agents raided IWW meetings, and the army put down IWW strikes. By war's end, most of the union's leaders were in jail. In summer 1918, the Socialist Party leader Eugene V. Debs was arrested by federal agents for an oration extolling socialism and freedom of speech—including the freedom to criticize Wilson on the war. Debs told the court what many thought of the Espionage Act: it was "a despotic enactment in flagrant conflict with democratic principles and with the spirit of free institutions." Handed a ten-year sentence, Debs remained in prison until he was pardoned in late 1921.

The Supreme Court endorsed such convictions. In *Schenck v. U.S.* (1919), the Court upheld the conviction of a Socialist Party member who mailed pamphlets urging draft resistance. In wartime, Justice Oliver Wendell Holmes wrote, the First Amendment could be restricted when words "are of such a nature as to create a clear and present danger that they will bring about the substantial evils that Congress has a right to prevent."

Red Scare, Red Summer

The line between wartime suppression of dissent and the postwar Red Scare is not easily drawn. Together they stabbed at the Bill of Rights and wounded radicalism in America. While wartime fears focused on subversion, after the armistice it was revolution; and while the prewar target was often German Americans, in 1919 it was frequently organized labor. Alarmed by the Russian Revolution and the communist uprisings in Europe, American fears grew in 1919 when the Soviet leadership formed the Communist International (or Comintern) to export revolution worldwide. Terrified conservatives sought out pro-Bolshevik sympathizers (or "Reds," from the red flag used by communists) in the United States, especially in immigrant groups and labor unions.

How did the Red Scare that took place after World War I dash hopes for a more egalitarian postwar America?

Labor Strikes

Labor union leaders emerged from the war determined to secure higher wages and retain wartime bargaining rights. Employers instead rescinded benefits they were forced to grant to labor during the war, including recognition of unions. The result more than 3,300 strikes involving 4 million laborers in 1919. On May 1, a day of celebration for workers worldwide, bombs were sent to prominent Americans, though most were intercepted and dismantled. Police never captured the conspirators, but many blamed anarchists and others bent on destroying the American way of life. When the Boston police went on strike in September, some claimed a Bolshevik conspiracy, but others thought it ridiculous to label Boston's Irish American, Catholic cops "radicals."

Unrest in the steel industry in September stirred more ominous fears. Many steelworkers worked twelve hours a day, seven days a week, and lived in squalid housing, counting on the National Committee for Organizing Iron and Steel Workers to improve their lives. When postwar unemployment in the industry climbed and the U.S. Steel Corporation refused to meet with committee representatives, 350,000 workers walked off the job, demanding the right to collective bargaining, a shorter workday, and a living wage. The steel barons hired strikebreakers and sent agents to club strikers. The strike collapsed in early 1920.

Political and business leaders dismissed the steel strike as a foreign threat orchestrated by American radicals. There was no conspiracy, and the American left was splintered. Two defectors from the Socialist Party, John Reed and Benjamin Gitlow, founded the Communist Labor Party in 1919. The rival Communist Party of the United States of America, composed largely of aliens, was launched the same year. But their combined membership did not exceed 70,000—and in 1919 the harassed Socialist Party could muster barely 30,000 members.

American Legion

Although divisiveness signified radicals' weakness, Progressives and conservatives interpreted the advent of new parties as strengthening the radical menace. Organized in May 1919 to lobby for veterans' benefits, the American Legion soon preached an antiradicalism that fueled the Red Scare. By 1920, 843,000 Legion members, mostly middle- and upper-class, embraced an impassioned Americanism demanding conformity.

Wilson's attorney general, A. Mitchell Palmer, also insisted that Americans think alike. A Progressive reformer, Quaker, and ambitious politician, Palmer appointed J. Edgar Hoover to head the Radical Division of the Department of Justice. Hoover compiled index cards naming allegedly radical individuals and organizations. During 1919, agents jailed IWW members; Palmer made sure that 249 alien radicals, including anarchist Emma Goldman, were deported to Russia.

States passed peacetime sedition acts and arrested hundreds of people. Vigilante groups and mobs flourished once again, their numbers swelled by returning veterans. In November 1919, in Centralia, Washington, American Legionnaires broke from a parade to storm the IWW hall. Several were wounded, others arrested, and one ex-soldier was taken from jail by a mob, then beaten, castrated, and shot. The New York State legislature expelled five elected Socialist Party members in early 1920.

Palmer Raids

The Red Scare reached a climax in January 1920 in the Palmer Raids. Planned and directed by J. Edgar Hoover, government agents in thirty-three cities broke into meeting halls and homes without search warrants, jailing four thousand people without counsel. In Boston, four hundred people were detained on bitterly cold Deer Island; two died of pneumonia, one leaped to his death, and another went insane. Because of court rulings and the courageous efforts of Assistant Secretary of Labor Louis Post, most of the arrestees were released, although in 1920–1921 nearly six hundred aliens were deported.

Palmer's disregard for elementary civil liberties drew criticism, with many charging that his tactics violated the Constitution. When Palmer called for a peacetime sedition act, he alarmed liberal and conservative leaders. His prediction that pro-Soviet radicals would incite violence on May Day 1920 proved mistaken—no disturbances occurred anywhere. Palmer, who called himself the "Fighting Quaker," was jeered as the "Quaking Fighter."

Racial Unrest

Palmer also blamed communists for the racial violence that gripped the nation, though the charge was baseless. African Americans realized well before the war ended that their participation did little to change discriminatory white attitudes. The Ku Klux Klan was reviving, and racist films like D. W. Griffith's *The Birth of a Nation* (1915) fed prejudice with its celebration of the Klan and demeaning depiction of blacks. Despite wartime declarations of humanity, between 1914 and 1920, 382 blacks were lynched, some of them in military uniform.

Northern whites who resented "the Negro invasion" rioted, as in East St. Louis, Illinois, in July 1917 and a month later in Houston. During the bloody Red Summer of 1919 (so named by African American author James Weldon Johnson for the blood that was spilled), race riots rocked two dozen cities and towns. The worst violence occurred in Chicago, a favorite destination for migrating African Americans. In the hot days of July 1919, an African American youth swimming at a segregated white beach was hit by a thrown rock and drowned. Soon African Americans and whites were battling each other. Stabbings, burnings, and shootings continued for days until state police restored some calm. Thirty-eight people died, twenty-three African Americans and fifteen whites.

A disillusioned W. E. B. Du Bois vowed a struggle: "We return. We return from fighting. We return fighting." Or, as poet Claude McKay put it after the Chicago riot in a poem he titled "If We Must Die,"

> Like men we'll face the murderous cowardly pack.
> Pressed to the wall, dying, but fighting back.

Black Militancy   Du Bois and McKay reflected a newfound militancy among African American veterans and northern African American communities. Editorials in African American newspapers subjected white politicians to increasingly harsh criticism and implored readers to embrace their prowess and beauty. The NAACP stepped up its campaign for civil rights and equality, vowing in 1919 to publicize the terrors of lynching and seek legislation against it. Other blacks, doubting the potential for equality, turned to the charismatic Jamaican immigrant Marcus Garvey, who called on African Americans to seek a separate black nation.

The crackdown on laborers and radicals, and the resurgence of racism in 1919, dashed wartime hopes. Although the passage of the **Nineteenth Amendment** in 1920, guaranteeing women the right to vote, showed that reform could happen, it was the exception. Unemployment, inflation, racial conflict, labor upheaval, a campaign against free speech inspired disillusionment in the immediate postwar years.

Nineteenth Amendment: Amendment to the Constitution that granted women the right to vote.

The Defeat of Peace

What kept the United States out of the League of Nations?

President Wilson seemed focused on confronting the threat of radicalism more abroad than at home. He revealed his ardent anti-Bolshevism when he ordered five thousand American troops to northern Russia and ten thousand more to Siberia, where they joined other Allied contingents in fighting what was now a Russian civil war. Wilson did not consult Congress. He said the military expeditions would guard Allied supplies and Russian railroads from German seizure and would also rescue Czechs who wished to fight the Germans.

Seeking to smash the infant Bolshevik government, Wilson backed an economic blockade of Russia, sent arms to anti-Bolshevik forces, and refused to recognize Lenin's government. The United States also secretly passed military information to anti-Bolshevik forces and used food relief to shore up Soviet opponents in the Baltic region. Later, at the Paris Peace Conference, Soviets were denied a seat. U.S. troops did not leave Russia until spring 1920, after the Bolsheviks demonstrated their staying power. Wilson faced a monumental task in securing a postwar settlement, though some critics said his own actions did not help. During the 1918 congressional elections, Wilson misstepped in suggesting that patriotism required the election of a Democratic Congress; Republicans blasted the president for questioning their love of country. The GOP gained control of both houses, and Wilson aggravated his political problems by not naming a senator to his advisory American Peace Commission. He also refused to take any prominent Republicans to Paris or to consult with the Senate Foreign Relations Committee before the conference.

Wilson was greeted by adoring crowds in Paris, London, and Rome, but their leaders—Georges Clemenceau of France, David Lloyd George of Britain, and Vittorio Orlando of Italy (with Wilson, the Big Four)—became formidable adversaries. After four years of war, the Allies were not going to be cheated out of the fruits of victory. The late-arriving Americans had not suffered as France and Great Britain had. Germany would have to pay big for the calamity it caused.

Paris Peace Conference   The Big Four tried to work out an agreement, mostly behind closed doors. The victors demanded that Germany (which had been excluded from the proceedings) pay a huge reparations bill. Wilson instead called for a small indemnity, fearing that an economically hobbled Germany might turn to Bolshevism. Unable to moderate the Allied position, the president reluctantly agreed to a clause blaming the war on Germany and to the creation of a commission to determine reparations (later set at $33 billion). Wilson acknowledged that the peace terms were hard, but he also believed that "the German people must be made to hate war."

As for dismantling empires and the principle of self-determination, Wilson could only deliver some of his goals. The conferees created a League-administered "mandate" system that placed former German and Turkish colonies under the control of other imperial nations. Japan gained authority over Germany's Pacific colonies, while France obtained what became Lebanon and Syria, while the British received the three former Ottoman provinces that became Iraq. Britain also secured Palestine, on the condition that it promote "the establishment in Palestine of a national home for the Jewish people" without prejudice to "the civil and religious rights of existing non-Jewish communities"—the so-called Balfour Declaration of 1917.

Elsewhere in Europe, Wilson's prescriptions fared better. Out of Austria-Hungary and Russia came the newly independent states of Austria, Hungary, Yugoslavia, Czechoslovakia, and Poland. Wilson and his colleagues also built a *cordon sanitaire* (buffer zone) of new westward-looking nations (Finland, Estonia, Latvia, and Lithuania) around Russia, to quarantine the Bolshevik contagion.

League of Nations: Wilson's plan for an international deliberative body, viewed as necessary to keep the peace; rejected by the U.S Senate; the U.S. never joined.

League of Nations and Article 10   Wilson worked hardest on the charter for the **League of Nations**, the centerpiece of his plans for the postwar world. He envisioned the League as having power over disputes among states; as such, it could transform international relations. Even so, the great powers would have preponderant say: the organization would have an influential council of five permanent members and elected delegates from smaller states, an assembly of all members, and a World Court.

Wilson identified Article 10 as the "kingpin" of the League covenant: "The Members of the League undertake to respect and preserve as against external aggression the territorial integrity and existing political independence of all Members of the League." Wilson insisted that there could be no future peace with Germany without a league to oversee it.

German representatives initially refused to sign the punitive treaty but submitted in June 1919. They gave up 13 percent of Germany's territory, 10 percent of its population, all of its colonies, and a huge portion of its national wealth. Many people wondered how the League could function in the poisoned postwar atmosphere of humiliation and revenge.

Critics of the Treaty

Critics in the United States were not so sure. In March 1919, thirty-nine senators (enough to deny the treaty the necessary two-thirds vote) signed a petition stating that the League's structure did not adequately protect U.S. interests. Wilson denounced his critics as "pygmy" minds, but he persuaded the peace conference to exempt the Monroe Doctrine and domestic matters from League jurisdiction. Wilson would budge no more. Could his critics not see that membership in the League would give the United States "leadership in the world"?

By summer, criticism intensified: Wilson had bastardized his own principles. He conceded Shandong to Japan and killed a provision affirming the racial equality of all peoples. The treaty ignored freedom of the seas, and tariffs were not reduced. Reparations promised to be punishing on Germany. Critics on the left protested that the League would perpetuate empire. Conservative critics feared that the League would limit American freedom of action in world affairs, stymie U.S. expansion, and intrude on domestic questions. And Article 10 raised serious questions: Would the United States be obligated to use armed force to ensure collective security? And would the League feel compelled to crush colonial rebellions, such as in Ireland or India?

Henry Cabot Lodge of Massachusetts led the Senate opposition to the League. A Harvard-educated Ph.D. and partisan Republican who disliked Wilson, Lodge packed the Foreign Relations Committee with critics and introduced several reservations to the treaty, most importantly that Congress had to approve any obligation under Article 10.

In September 1919, Wilson embarked on a speaking tour of the United States. Growing more exhausted, he dismissed antagonists as "contemptible quitters." While doubts about Article 10 multiplied, Wilson highlighted neglected features of the League charter—such as the arbitration of disputes and an international conference to abolish child labor. In Colorado, the president awoke to nausea and uncontrollable facial twitching. Days later, he suffered a massive stroke that paralyzed his left side. He became peevish and more stubborn, increasingly unable to conduct presidential business. Advised to placate Lodge and other "Reservationist" senatorial critics so the Versailles treaty might receive Congressional approval, Wilson rejected "dishonorable compromise."

Link to Henry Cabot Lodge's reservations regarding the Treaty of Versailles.

Freedom of Speech and the ACLU

Before World War I, those with radical views often received harsh treatment for exercising their freedom of speech. During the war, however, the Wilson administration's suppression of dissidents led some Americans to reformulate the traditional definition of allowable speech. Roger Baldwin, a conscientious objector, and Crystal Eastman, a woman suffrage activist, were among the first to advance the idea that the content of political speech could be separated from the identity of the speaker and that patriotic Americans could—indeed should—defend the right of others to express political beliefs abhorrent to their own. After defending conscientious objectors, Baldwin and Eastman—joined by activists such as Jane Addams, Helen Keller, and Norman Thomas—formed the American Civil Liberties Union (ACLU).

Since 1920, the ACLU, which today has some 300,000 members, has aimed to protect the basic civil liberties of all Americans. It has been involved in almost every major civil liberties case in U.S. courts, among them the landmark *Brown v. Board of Education* case (1954), which ended federal tolerance of racial segregation. More recently, the ACLU was involved in the 1997 Supreme Court case, ruling that the 1996 Communications Act banning "indecent speech" violated First Amendment rights.

Conservatives have long criticized the ACLU for its opposition to official prayers in public schools and its support of legal abortion, as well as its decisions on whose freedom of speech to defend. ACLU proponents counter that it has also defended those on the right, such as Oliver North, a key figure in the 1980s Iran-contra scandal.

Either way, the principle of free speech is today broadly accepted by Americans. Membership in the ACLU skyrocketed since the September 11, 2001, terrorist attacks, due to concern about government policies eroding privacy and legal protections, not only for Americans and foreign detainees at the Guantánamo Bay. Ironically, the Wilson administration's crackdown on dissent produced an expanded commitment to freedom of speech for a people and a nation.

Senate Rejection of the Treaty and League

Twice in November the Senate rejected the Treaty of Versailles and thus U.S. membership in the League. In March 1920, the Senate again voted; this time, a majority (49 for and 35 against) favored the treaty with reservations, but the tally fell short of the two-thirds needed. Had Wilson permitted Democrats to compromise—to accept reservations—he could have achieved his goal of membership in the League, which, despite the U.S. absence, came into being.

At the core of the debate lay a basic foreign policy issue: whether the United States would endorse collective security or continue the more solitary path articulated in George Washington's Farewell Address and the Monroe Doctrine. In a world dominated by imperialist states unwilling to subordinate their strategic ambitions to an international organization, Americans preferred their traditional nonalignment and freedom of choice over binding commitments to collective action. Wilson countered that the League promised something better than the status quo for the United States and the world; collective security in place of the frail protection of alliances and the instability of a balance of power.

An Unsafe World　　　Ultimately, World War I did not make the world safe for democracy, but it did make the United States a greater world power. By 1920, the United States was the world's leading economic power, producing 40 percent of its coal, 70 percent of its petroleum, and half of its pig iron. It also ranked first in world trade. American companies used the war to nudge Germans and British out of foreign markets, especially in Latin America. Meanwhile, the United States shifted from a debtor to a creditor nation, becoming the world's leading banker.

After the disappointment of Versailles, the peace movement revitalized, and the military became more professional. The Reserve Officers Training Corps (ROTC) became permanent; military colleges provided upper-echelon training; and the Army Industrial College, founded in 1924, pursued business-military cooperation in logistics and planning. The National Research Council, created in 1916 with government money and Carnegie and Rockefeller funds, continued a defense research alliance. Tanks, quick-firing guns, armor-piercing explosives, and oxygen masks for high-altitude-flying pilots were among the technological advances emerging from World War I.

The international system born in these years was fragmented. Nationalist leaders active during World War I, such as Ho Chi Minh of Indochina and Mohandas K. Gandhi of India, vowed independence for their peoples. Communism became a disruptive force in world politics, and the Soviets bore a grudge against those who tried to thwart their revolution. The new states in central and eastern Europe proved weak. Germans bitterly resented the harsh peace settlement, and German war debts and reparations problems dogged international order for may years.

Summary

The war years marked the emergence of the United States as a world power, and Americans could take justifiable pride in their contribution to the Allied victory. But the war exposed deep divisions among Americans: white versus black, nativist versus immigrant, capital versus labor, men versus women, radical versus Progressive and conservative, pacifist versus interventionist, nationalist versus internationalist.

During the war, the federal government intervened in the economy and influenced people's everyday lives as never before. Although the Wilson administration shunned reconversion plans (war housing projects, for example, were sold to private investors) and quickly dismantled the many government agencies, the World War I experience of the activist state served as guidance for 1930s reformers battling the Great Depression (see Chapter 25). The partnership of government and business in managing the wartime economy advanced the development of a mass society through the standardization of products and the promotion of efficiency. Wilsonian wartime policies also nourished the concentration of corporate ownership by suspending anti-trust laws. Business power dominated the next decade, while labor entered lean years.

Although the disillusionment evident after Versailles did not cause the United States to adopt isolationism (see Chapter 26), skepticism about America's ability to right wrongs abroad marked the postwar American mood. People recoiled from photographs of shell-shocked faces and of bodies dangling from barbed wire. American soldiers, tired of idealism, craved regular jobs. Many Progressives lost their enthusiasm for crusades, disgusted by the bickering of the victors. By 1920, idealism faded. Americans were sure what their country's newfound status as a leading world power meant for the nation. With uneasiness and a mixed legacy from the Great War, the country entered the 1920s.

Chapter Review

Precarious Neutrality

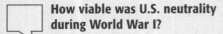 **How viable was U.S. neutrality during World War I?**

President Woodrow Wilson, like most Americans, not only embraced neutrality, he took pride in being one of the few western nations to be free from the war for its first three years. Still, U.S. economic links with Allied nations and Wilson's shared belief with the British that a German victory would spell the end of free enterprise and the rule of law made pure neutrality less believable to the outside world and less possible in the long run. The United States relied on sales to Allied nations to end its recession. It was also difficult to claim U.S. neutrality while American banks made extensive loans to Britain and France and sold arms to the Allies. Indirectly, or at least via commerce, the United States was engaged in the war even before officially entering the battlefields.

The Decision for War

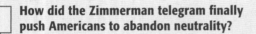 **How did the Zimmerman telegram finally push Americans to abandon neutrality?**

For months in early 1917, Germany had launched a submarine attack on both warships and commercial vessels regardless of stated neutrality or whether the ships were commercial or warships. Americans were already outraged by this when British intelligence passed on to the United States an intercepted telegram in which the German minister in Mexico, Arthur Zimmerman, promised to help Mexico regain the territories it lost to the United States in 1848 if it united with Germany against the United States. The idea was to bring an enemy into America's back yard, but Mexico refused. Wilson released the telegram to the press, and anti-German sentiment skyrocketed. When several American ships were sunk shortly thereafter, war cries heightened, and Wilson asked Congress to declare war against Germany.

Winning the War

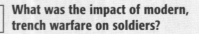 **What was the impact of modern, trench warfare on soldiers?**

Aside from an increased risk of casualty or fatality, trench warfare was mentally debilitating. Battles would be fought in zigzag, muddy, vile-smelling trenches fronted by barbed wire and mines across France. Soldiers would charge enemy trenches, often facing machine gun fire or poison gas. Many surviving soldiers suffered a mental illness dubbed "shell shock." Though not labeled as such at the time, its victims faced a kind of post-traumatic stress disorder, with symptoms including a fixed stare, violent tremors, paralyzed limbs, listlessness, jabbering, screaming, and nightmares. Trench warfare also produced extraordinarily high casualty rates.

Mobilizing the Home Front

How did wartime labor shortages create new opportunities for American workers?

A full employment economy during the war not only meant that workers saw salaries increase (albeit sometimes only slightly ahead of inflation), but they also could easily leave jobs with low salaries or harsh conditions for something better. Worker shortages enabled women to move into higher-paying, formerly male jobs, trading domestic service for factories, shifting from clerking in department stores to stenography and typing, or leaving textile mills for firearms plants. Blacks made gains, too, as war mobilization pushed a half million African Americans to migrate to northern cities, leaving behind low-paid sharecropping and tenant farming for better wages in railroad yards, packing houses, steel mills, shipyards, and coal mines.

Civil Liberties Under Challenge

How did free speech come under fire during World War I?

Passage of the Espionage Act (1917) and the Sedition Act (1918) empowered the federal government to legally prosecute its critics (nearly 20,000 were prosecuted), while others were intimidated into silence. Federal agents arrested Socialist Party leader Eugene V. Debs when he spoke out about socialism and freedom of speech, including the freedom to criticize Wilson's move to war. Professors who articulated pacifist views found themselves fired or forced to resign. Labor unions were similarly quashed. Outside government, ultrapatriotic groups employed vigilantism, burning textbooks that mentioned Germany or bullying people to buy war bonds.

Red Scare, Red Summer

 How did the Red Scare that took place after World War I dash hopes for a more egalitarian postwar America?

Fears of a communist invasion began shortly after the Bolshevik Revolution and heightened when the Communist Party promised to spread its message worldwide. As membership in both the Socialist and Communist Parties in the United States grew, nationwide crackdowns began against radicals, with labor a particular target. The passage of the Nineteenth Amendment granting women the right to vote in 1920 provided a glimmer of hope for postwar social improvement, but it was the rare exception. Instead, violations of the Bill of Rights and freedom of speech combined with unemployment, inflation, resurgent racism, and a revitalized Ku Klux Klan to dampen hopes for a more promising, egalitarian postwar America.

The Defeat of Peace

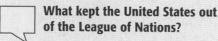 **What kept the United States out of the League of Nations?**

While the League of Nations was Wilson's brainchild, the United States never joined. To Wilson, the League promised a more stable world based on collective security. But this notion of collectivity was problematic for a people used to operating independently in world affairs. Critics on the left feared that the League would perpetuate empire. Conservative critics worried that it might limit America's freedom to act as it saw fit in world affairs, block U.S. expansion, and intrude on domestic concerns. Worse, critics at home worried about being compelled to participate in collective action deemed necessary by the League.

Suggestions for Further Reading

John Milton Cooper Jr., *Breaking the Heart of the World: Woodrow Wilson and the Fight for the League of Nations* (2001)

Alan Dawley, *Changing the World: American Progressives in War and Revolution, 1914–1924* (2003)

David S. Foglesong, *America's Secret War Against Bolshevism* (1995)

James B. Grossman, *Land of Hope: Chicago, Black Southerners, and the Great Migration* (1989)

Michael Kazin, *A Godly Hero: The Life of William Jennings Bryan* (2006)

Jennifer D. Keene, *Doughboys, the Great War, and the Remaking of America* (2001)

David M. Kennedy, *Over Here: The Home Front in the First World War* (1980)

Thomas J. Knock, *To End All Wars: Woodrow Wilson and the Quest for a New World Order* (1992)

Margaret MacMillan, *Paris 1919: Six Months That Changed the World* (2002)

Robert H. Zieger, *America's Great War: World War I and the American Experience* (2000)

 Go to the CourseMate website for primary source links, study tools, and review materials for this chapter.
www.cengagebrain.com

The New Era

24

1920–1929

Beth and Robert Gordon were incompatible marriage partners. Beth was frumpy and demanding; Robert liked to party. One evening at a nightclub, he met Sally Clark, who liked to party, too. When Robert came home smelling of perfume, the couple argued, and then subsequently divorced. Soon, however, he missed Beth's intellect. Meanwhile, Beth bought new clothes and makeup, turning herself into a glamorous beauty. Beth and Robert coincidentally visited the same summer resort and rekindled their romance. When Robert was injured in an accident, Beth nursed him back to health, much to Sally's disappointment. In the end, Beth and Robert remarried.

This story is the plot of the 1920 motion picture *Why Change Your Wife?*—one of dozens of films directed by Cecil B. DeMille. DeMille gave audiences what they fantasized about doing. Beth, Robert, and Sally dressed stylishly, went out dancing, listened to phonograph records and visited resorts. Although DeMille's films and others of the 1920s usually ended by reinforcing marriage, ruling out premarital sex, and supporting the work ethic, they also exuded a new morality. Male and female characters shed old-style values for the pursuit of luxury, fun, and sexual freedom, just as actors such as Gloria Swanson and Thomas Meighan, stars of *Why Change Your Wife?* did in their off-screen lives. In this way, the film was a harbinger of a new era.

During the 1920s, consumerism flourished. Although poverty beset small farmers, workers in declining industries, and non-whites in inner cities, most other people enjoyed a high standard of living relative to previous generations. Spurred by advertising and installment buying, Americans acquired radios, automobiles, real estate, and stocks. As in the Gilded Age, the federal government nurtured a favorable climate for business. In contrast to the Progressive era, few people worried about abuses of power. Yet state and local governments undertook important reforms.

It was an era in which people embraced new technology while trying to preserve long-held values. New forms of

Chapter Outline

Big Business Triumphant
New Economic Expansion | Associations and "New Lobbying" | Setbacks for Organized Labor | Languishing Agriculture

Politics and Government
Scandals of the Harding Administration | Coolidge Prosperity Extensions of Progressive Reform | Indian Affairs and Politics | Women and Politics

A Consumer Society
Effects of the Automobile | Advertising | Radio

Cities, Migrants, and Suburbs
African American Migration | Marcus Garvey | Newcomers from Mexico and Puerto Rico | Suburbanization

New Rhythms of Everyday Life
Household Management | Health and Life Expectancy | Older Americans and Retirement | Social Values | Women in the Work Force | Employment of Minority Women | Alternative Images of Femininity | Gay and Lesbian Culture

LINKS TO THE WORLD *Pan American Airways*

VISUALIZING THE PAST *Expansion of the Suburbs in the 1920s*

Lines of Defense
Ku Klux Klan | Immigration Quotas | Fundamentalism | Scopes Trial | Religious Revivalism

amusement coincided with creativity in the arts and advances in science and technology. Changes in work habits, family responsibilities, and healthcare fostered new uses of time and new attitudes about behavior, including encouragements to "think young." While many people experienced material bounty, others continued to endure hardship. The decade's modernism and materialism were appealing to many but unsettling to those who clung to tradition.

The glitter of consumer culture that dominated DeMille's films blinded Americans to rising debt and uneven prosperity. A devastating depression would bring the era to a brutal close.

As you read this chapter, keep the following questions in mind:

* How did developments in technology and the workplace stimulate social change during the 1920s?

* What were the benefits and costs of consumerism, and how did people deal with challenges to old-time values?

* What caused the stock market crash and the ensuing deep depression that signaled the end of the era?

The Age of Play
Movies and Sports | Sports Heroes | Movie Stars and Public Heroes | Prohibition

Cultural Currents
Literature of Alienation | Harlem Renaissance | Jazz

The Election of 1928 and the End of the New Era
Herbert Hoover | Al Smith | Hoover's Administration | Stock Market Crash | Declining Demand | Corporate Debt and Stock Market Speculation | Economic Troubles Abroad; Federal Failures at Home

LEGACY FOR A PEOPLE AND A NATION
Intercollegiate Athletics

SUMMARY

Big Business Triumphant

What helped turn the economy around in the 1920s?

The 1920s began with economic decline. After World War I, industrial output dropped as wartime orders evaporated. In the West, railroads and the mining industry suffered, and layoffs spread through New England as textile companies abandoned outdated factories for the South's convenient raw materials and cheap labor. When demobilized soldiers flooded the work force, unemployment, around 2 percent in 1919, passed 12 percent in 1921. Consumer spending dwindled, causing more contraction and joblessness.

New Economic Expansion

Electric energy prompted a recovery in 1922 that continued unevenly until 1929. Electric motors replaced steam engines, producing goods more cheaply and efficiently.

Most urban households now had electric service, enabling them to utilize new appliances, such as refrigerators and vacuum cleaners. The growing economy gave Americans more spending money for new services, too, such as restaurants, beauty salons, and movie theaters. Installment, or time-payment, plans drove the new consumerism. Of 3.5 million automobiles sold in 1923, 80 percent were bought on credit.

Although Progressive era trust-busting had reined in big business, it had not eliminated oligopoly, the control of an entire industry by one or a few large firms. By the 1920s, a few sprawling companies, such as U.S. Steel and General Electric, dominated basic industries, and oligopolies controlled marketing, distribution, and finance.

Chronology

1920	Volstead Act implements prohibition (Eighteenth Amendment)
	Nineteenth Amendment ratified, legalizing vote for women in federal elections
	Harding elected president
	KDKA transmits first commercial radio broadcast
1920–21	Postwar deflation and depression
1921	Federal Highway Act funds national highway system
	Emergency Quota Act establishes immigration quotas
	Sacco and Vanzetti convicted
	Sheppard-Towner Act allots funds to states to set up maternity and pediatric clinics
1922	Economic recovery raises standards of living
	Coronado Coal Company v. United Mine Workers rules that strikes may be illegal actions in restraint of trade
	Bailey v. Drexel Furniture Company voids restrictions on child labor
	Federal government ends strikes by railroad shop workers and miners
	Fordney-McCumber Tariff raises rates on imports
1923	Harding dies; Coolidge assumes presidency
	Adkins v. Children's Hospital overturns a minimum wage law affecting women
1923–24	Government scandals (Teapot Dome) exposed
1924	Snyder Act grants citizenship to all Indians not previously citizens
	National Origins Act revises immigration quotas
	Coolidge elected president
1925	Scopes trial highlights battle between religious fundamentalists and modernists
1927	Lindbergh pilots solo transatlantic flight
	The Jazz Singer, first movie with sound, released
1928	Stock market soars
	Hoover elected president
1929	Stock market crashes; Great Depression begins

Associations and "New Lobbying"

Business and professional organizations also expanded in the 1920s. Retailers and manufacturers formed trade associations to swap information, and professionals expanded their organizations. Farm bureaus promoted scientific agriculture and tried to stabilize markets. These special-interest groups participated in what is called the "new lobbying." With government playing an increasingly influential role, hundreds of organizations sought to convince legislators to support their interests.

Government policies helped business thrive, and legislators depended on lobbyists' expertise. Prodded by lobbyists, Congress cut taxes on corporations and wealthy individuals in 1921 and passed the Fordney-McCumber Tariff Act in 1922. Presidents Warren G. Harding, Calvin Coolidge, and Herbert Hoover appointed cabinet officers who were favorable toward business. Regulatory agencies, such as the Federal Trade Commission and the Interstate Commerce Commission, cooperated with corporations more than they regulated them. Key Supreme Court decisions sheltered business from government regulation and hindered organized labor. In *Coronado Coal Company v. United Mine Workers* (1922), Chief Justice and former president William Howard Taft ruled that a striking union, like a trust, could be prosecuted for illegal restraint of trade, yet in *Maple Floor Association v. U.S.* (1929), the Court decided that trade associations that distributed anti-union information were not acting in restraint of trade. The Court also voided restrictions on child labor (*Bailey v. Drexel Furniture Company,* 1922), and overturned a minimum wage law affecting women because it infringed on liberty of contract (*Adkins v. Children's Hospital,* 1923).

Setbacks for Organized Labor

Public opinion turned against organized labor in the 1920s, linking it with communism brought to America by radical immigrants. Using Red Scare tactics, the Harding administration in 1922 obtained a sweeping court injunction to quash a strike by 400,000 railroad workers. State and federal courts issued injunctions to prevent other strikes and permitted businesses to sue unions for damages suffered from labor actions.

Some companies imposed yellow dog contracts, which made refusal to join a union a condition of employment. Companies also countered the appeal of unions by offering pensions, profit sharing, and company-sponsored picnics and sporting events—a policy known as welfare capitalism. State legislators aided employers by prohibiting closed shops (workplaces where union membership was mandatory) and permitting open shops (where employers could hire nonunion employees). As a result of court action, welfare capitalism, and ineffective leadership, union membership fell from 5.1 million in 1920 to 3.6 million in 1929.

Languishing Agriculture

Agriculture languished during the 1920s, as farmers faced international competition and went into debt when they tried to increase productivity by investing in machines, such as harvesters and tractors. Irrigation and mechanization made large-scale farming so efficient that fewer farmers could produce more crops than ever before. As a result, crop prices plunged, big agribusinesses took over, and small landholders and tenants struggled, especially as incomes plummeted and debts rose.

Politics and Government

A series of Republican presidents extended Theodore Roosevelt's government-business cooperation, but they made government a compliant coordinator rather than the active manager Roosevelt advocated. President **Warren G. Harding**, elected in 1920, was a symbol of government's good will toward business. He captured 16 million popular votes to 9 million for the Democratic nominee, Ohio governor James M. Cox. (The total vote in the 1920 presidential election was 36 percent higher than in 1916, reflecting the first-time participation of women voters.)

What happened to Progressive reform in the 1920s?

Warren G. Harding:
29th President of the United States in office from 1921 to 1923.

Scandals of the Harding Administration

A small-town newspaperman and senator from Ohio, Harding appointed assistants who promoted business growth, notably Secretary of State Charles Evans Hughes, Secretary of Commerce Herbert Hoover, Secretary of the Treasury Andrew Mellon, and Secretary of Agriculture Henry C. Wallace. Harding also backed reforms. But he had personal weaknesses, notably, his extramarital affairs and poor judgment in appointments. In 1917, he began a relationship with Nan Britton, thirty-one years his junior, that resulted in a daughter in 1919. Britton revealed the secret in a book, *The President's Daughter* (1927), although Harding never acknowledged his illegitimate offspring.

Of greater consequence, Harding appointed cronies who used office holding for personal gain. Charles Forbes, head of the Veterans Bureau, went to federal prison, convicted of fraud and bribery in government contracts. Notoriously, a

Teapot Dome: Scandal that rocked the Harding administration after Harding's Secretary of the Interior was found guilty of secretly leasing government oil reserves to two oilmen in exchange for a bribe.

Calvin Coolidge: 30th President of the United States; took office after the death of President Warren Harding in 1923.

congressional inquiry in 1923 and 1924 revealed that Secretary of the Interior Albert Fall accepted bribes to lease government property to oil companies. Fall was fined $100,000 and spent a year in jail for his role in the so-called **Teapot Dome** scandal, named for the Wyoming oil reserve he handed to the Mammoth Oil Company.

By mid-1923, Harding had become disillusioned by these scandals. On a speaking tour that summer, he became ill and died in San Francisco on August 2. Although his death preceded revelation of the Teapot Dome scandal, some speculated that Harding committed suicide to avoid impeachment or was poisoned by his wife. Most evidence, however, points to death from natural causes, probably heart disease.

Coolidge Prosperity

Vice President **Calvin Coolidge**, who became president, was less outgoing than Harding. As governor of Massachusetts, Coolidge attracted national attention in 1919 with his stand against striking Boston policemen and won business support and the vice-presidential nomination in 1920.

Respectful of private enterprise and aided by Andrew Mellon, who was retained as treasury secretary, Coolidge's administration reduced federal debt, lowered income-tax rates (especially for the wealthy), and began construction of a national highway system. With farm prices falling, Congress twice passed bills to establish government-backed price supports for staple crops (the McNary-Haugen bills of 1927 and 1928). Resembling the 1890s Farmers' Alliances subtreasury scheme, these bills would have established a system whereby the government would buy surplus farm products and either hold them until prices rose or sell them abroad. Coolidge, however, vetoed the measures as improper government interference in the market economy.

"Coolidge prosperity" was the decisive issue in the 1924 presidential election. Both major parties ran candidates who favored private initiative over government intervention. At their national convention, Democrats voted 542 to 541 against condemning the revived Ku Klux Klan, and deadlocked for 103 ballots between southern prohibitionists, who supported former treasury secretary William G. McAdoo, and antiprohibition easterners, who backed New York's governor, Alfred E. Smith. They finally compromised on John W. Davis, a New York corporate lawyer.

Remnants of the Progressive movement, along with farm, labor, and socialist groups, formed a new Progressive Party and nominated Robert M. La Follette, the aging Wisconsin reformer. The new party stressed public ownership of railroads and power plants, conservation of natural resources, aid to farmers, rights for organized labor, and regulation of business. Coolidge beat Davis by 15.7 million to 8.4 million popular votes and 382 to 136 electoral votes. La Follette received 4.8 million popular votes and 13 electoral votes.

Extensions of Progressive Reform

The urgency for political and economic reform that inspired the previous Progressive generation faded in the 1920s. Much reform, however, occurred at state and local levels. Following pre–World War I initiatives, thirty-four states instituted or expanded workers' compensation laws and public welfare programs in the 1920s. By 1926, every major city and many smaller ones had planning and zoning commissions to harness physical growth to the common good. A new generation of reformers who later influenced national affairs acquired experience in statehouses, city halls, and universities.

Indian Affairs and Politics

Organizations such as the Indian Rights Association, the Indian Defense Association, and the General Federation of Women's Clubs worked to obtain justice and social services for Native Americans, including better education and return of tribal lands. But like other minorities, Indians met discrimination and pressure to assimilate. Severalty, the federal policy created by the Dawes Act of 1887, allotting land to individuals rather than to tribes, failed to make Indians self-supporting. Attached to their land, they showed little inclination to move to cities. Whites still hoped to convert native peoples into "productive" citizens, typically ignoring indigenous cultures. Reformers were especially critical of Indian women, who rejected middle-class homemaking habits and balked at sending their children to boarding schools.

Citizenship status remained unclear. The Dawes Act had conferred citizenship on Indians who accepted land allotments, but not those who remained on reservations. After several court challenges, Congress passed an Indian Citizenship Act (Snyder Act) in 1924, granting citizenship to all Indians. President Hoover reinforced this measure's intent by stating that citizenship was the best means for Indians to assimilate.

Women and Politics

Ratification of the Nineteenth Amendment in 1920 gave women the vote, but they remained excluded from local and national power structures. Instead, they worked through voluntary organizations to lobby legislators on issues such as birth control, peace, education, Indian affairs, or opposition to lynching.

In 1921, women's groups persuaded Congress to pass the **Sheppard-Towner Act**, allotting funds to states to create maternity and pediatric clinics to reduce infant mortality. (The measure ended in 1929, when Congress, pressured by physicians, canceled funding.) The Cable Act of 1922 reversed the law under which an American woman who married a foreigner assumed her husband's citizenship, allowing her to retain U.S. citizenship. At the state level, women achieved some rights, such as the ability to serve on juries.

Sheppard-Towner Act: Sought to reduce infant mortality by providing matching funds to states to create prenatal and child health clinics. It was repealed in 1929.

As new voters, however, women pursued diverging goals. Women in the National Association of Colored Women, for example, fought for the rights of minorities. Other groups, such as the National Woman's Party, pressed for an equal rights amendment to ensure women's equality under the law. But such activity alienated the National Consumers League, the Women's Trade Union League, the League of Women Voters, and other organizations that supported protective legislation to limit hours and improve conditions for employed women.

A Consumer Society

How did the emergence of a consumer society change American life?

The consumerism depicted in *Why Change Your Wife?* reflected important economic changes affecting the nation. Between 1919 and 1929, the gross national product—the total value of goods and services produced in the United States—swelled by 40 percent. Wages and salaries also grew (though not as drastically), while the cost of living remained stable. People had more purchasing power (see Table 24.1). By 1929, two-thirds of all Americans had electricity, compared with one-sixth in 1912. In 1929, one-fourth of all families owned vacuum cleaners. Many could afford such goods as radios, cosmetics, and movie tickets because several

TABLE 24.1   Consumerism in the 1920s

1900	
2 bicycles	$ 70.00
Wringer and washboard	5.00
Brushes and brooms	5.00
Sewing machine (mechanical)	25.00
TOTAL	$ 105.00
1928	
Automobile	$ 700.00
Radio	75.00
Phonograph	50.00
Washing machine	150.00
Vacuum cleaner	50.00
Sewing machine (electric)	60.00
Other electrical equipment	25.00
Telephone (per year)	35.00
TOTAL	$1,145.00

Source: From an article in *Survey Magazine* in 1928 reprinted in *Another Part of the Twenties*, by Paul Carter. Copyright 1977 by Columbia University Press. Reprinted with permission of the publisher.

family members worked or because the breadwinner took a second job. Nevertheless, new products and services were available to more than just the rich.

Effects of the Automobile

During the 1920s, automobile registrations soared from 8 million to 23 million, and by 1929 there was one car for every five Americans. Mass production and competition made cars affordable. A Ford Model T cost less than $300, and a Chevrolet sold for $700 by 1926—when factory workers earned about $1,300 a year and clerical workers about $2,300. At those prices, people could consider the car a necessity rather than a luxury.

Cars altered American life. Owners abandoned crowded streetcars; roads became cleaner as autos replaced horses. Women drivers achieved newfound independence. By 1927, most autos were enclosed (they previously had open tops), creating new private space for courtship and sex. Mostly, the car was the ultimate social equalizer. As one writer observed in 1924, "It is hard to convince Steve Popovich, or Antonio Branca, or plain John Smith that he is being ground into the dust by Capital when at will he may drive the same highways…and get as much enjoyment from his trip as the modern Midas."

After World War I, motorists joined farmers and bicyclists in their decades-old campaign for improved roads. In 1921, Congress passed the Federal Highway Act, providing funds for state roads, and in 1923 the Bureau of Public Roads planned a national highway system. Roadbuilding inspired such technological developments as mechanized graders and concrete mixers. The oil-refining industry, which produced gasoline, became powerful. In 1920, the United States produced about 65 percent of the world's oil. Public officials to pay more attention to traffic control, with General Electric Company producing the first timed stop-and-go traffic light in 1924.

Advertising

By 1929, more money was spent on advertising than on formal education. Blending psychological theory with practical cynicism, advertising theorists asserted that any people's tastes could be manipulated. For example, cosmetics manufacturers like Max Factor, Helena Rubenstein, and African American entrepreneur Madame C. J. Walker used movie stars and beauty advice in magazines to entice female customers. Other advertisers hired baseball star Babe Ruth to endorse food and sporting goods.

Radio

Radio became an influential advertising medium. By 1929, over 10 million Americans owned radios, spending $850 million annually on radio equipment. In the early 1920s, Congress decided that broadcasting should be a private enterprise, not a tax-supported public service as in Great Britain. American programming focused on entertainment rather than educational content, because entertainment attracted larger audiences and therefore higher advertising profits. Station KDKA in Pittsburgh, owned by Westinghouse Electric Company, pioneered commercial radio in 1920. In 1922, an AT&T-run station in New York City broadcast advertisements—commercials. By late 1922, there were 508 commercial stations.

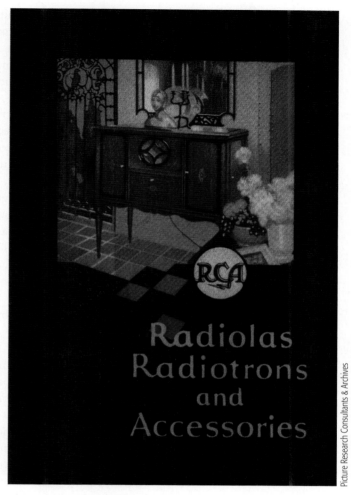

As large as today's big-screen television sets, luxury radios served as both entertainment machines and decorative furniture. The RCA "Radiola" was an early radio receiver combined with speakers and housed in an attractive wood cabinet.

Radio transformed American society. In 1924, both political parties broadcast their presidential nominating conventions, enabling candidates to reach more Americans. And radio's mass marketing and standardized programming blurred ethnic boundaries and helped create a homogeneous American culture, which television and other mass media expanded throughout the twentieth century.

Cities, Migrants, and Suburbs

The 1920 federal census revealed that, for the first time, a majority of Americans lived in urban areas (places with 2,500 or more people). Growth in manufacturing and services helped propel urbanization. Industries like steel, oil, and auto production energized Birmingham, Houston, and Detroit; services and retail trades boosted Seattle, Atlanta, and Minneapolis.

What fueled the growth of cities in the 1920s?

During the 1920s, 6 million Americans left farms for the city. Many young people, seeking excitement and openness, moved to regional centers like Kansas City or to the West. Between 1920 and 1930, California's population increased 67 percent, and California became a highly urbanized state while retaining its status as a leader in agricultural production.

African American Migration

African Americans, in what has come to be called the Great Migration, made up a sizable portion of people on the move during the 1920s. Pushed from cotton farming by a boll weevil plague and lured by industrial jobs, 1.5 million blacks moved, doubling the African American populations of New York, Chicago, Detroit, and Houston. They found jobs not unlike those in the South—janitors, longshoremen, and domestic servants for whites.

Forced by low wages and discrimination to seek cheap housing, black newcomers squeezed into ghettos like Chicago's South Side. But blacks found better neighborhoods closed to them. They could either crowd into densely populated black neighborhoods or spill into nearby white neighborhoods. Fears of "invasion" sparked violence and prompted neighborhood associations to adopt restrictive covenants, whereby white homeowners pledged not to sell or rent to blacks.

Marcus Garvey

In response to discrimination and violence, thousands of urban blacks joined movements that glorified racial independence. The most influential of these black nationalist groups was the Universal Negro Improvement Association (UNIA), led by **Marcus Garvey**, a Jamaican immigrant who believed blacks should separate from corrupt white society. Unlike the NAACP, formed by elite African American and white liberals (see page 553), the UNIA was comprised exclusively of blacks, largely from the lower classes.

Marcus Garvey: Charismatic black leader who promoted racial pride and independence and believed blacks should separate from white society.

Garvey furthered Booker T. Washington's ideas of economic independence (see page 552) by promoting black-owned businesses that would manufacture and sell products to black consumers. His newspaper, *Negro World,* preached black independence, and he founded the Black Star steamship line to transport manufactured goods among black businesses in North America, the Caribbean, and Africa. In 1919, the U.S. Bureau of Investigation (BOI), forerunner to the FBI, began monitoring Garvey's radical activities, and the BOI's deputy head, J. Edgar Hoover, proclaimed Garvey to be one of the most dangerous blacks in America.

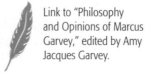

Link to "Philosophy and Opinions of Marcus Garvey," edited by Amy Jacques Garvey.

The UNIA declined in the mid-1920s after mismanagement plagued Garvey's plans. In 1923, Garvey was deported for mail fraud involving the bankrupt Black Star line. His prosecution, however, was politically motivated. Middle-class African American leaders, such as W. E. B. Du Bois, opposed the UNIA, fearing that its extremism would undermine their efforts. Nevertheless, for years the UNIA attracted a large following (contemporaries estimated 500,000; Garvey claimed 6 million), and Garvey's speeches instilled in many African Americans a heightened sense of racial pride.

Newcomers from Mexico and Puerto Rico

The newest immigrants came from Mexico and Puerto Rico, where declining fortunes pushed people off the land. During the 1910s, Anglo farmers' associations encouraged Mexicans to provide cheap labor, and by the 1920s Mexican migrants constituted three-fourths of farm labor in the American West. Growers treated Mexican laborers as slaves, paying them extremely low wages. Although some achieved middle-class status, most crowded into urban low-rent districts plagued by poor sanitation, poor police protection, and poor schools. Mexicans moved back and forth across the border, creating a way of life that Mexicans called *sin fronteras*—without borders.

The 1920s also witnessed an influx of Puerto Ricans to the mainland, as a shift in the island's economy from sugar to coffee production created a labor surplus. Attracted by contracts from employers seeking cheap labor, they created *barrios* (communities) and found jobs in factories, hotels, restaurants, and domestic service. Like Mexicans, Puerto Ricans maintained customs and developed businesses—*bodegas* (grocery stores), cafés, boarding houses—and social organizations to help them adapt to American society. Educated elites—doctors, lawyers, and business owners—became community leaders.

Suburbanization   As urbanization peaked, suburban growth accelerated. Prosperity and automobile transportation in the 1920s made suburbs more accessible to those wishing to leave urban neighborhoods. Between 1920 and 1930, suburbs of Chicago (such as Oak Park and Evanston), Cleveland (Shaker Heights), and Los Angeles (Burbank and Inglewood) grew five to ten times faster than nearby central cities. Los Angeles builders alone erected 250,000 homes for auto-owning suburbanites. Most suburbs were middle- and upper-class bedroom communities; some, like Highland Park (near Detroit) were industrial satellites.

Suburbanites wanted to escape big-city crime, grime, and taxes, and they fought to preserve control over police, schools, and water and gas services. Particularly in the Northeast and Midwest, the suburbs' independence prevented central cities from accessing the resources and tax bases of wealthier suburban residents. Population dispersal spread the environmental problems of city life—trash, pollution, noise—across the metropolitan area.

Most of the consumers who jammed shops, movie houses, and sporting arenas, and who embraced fads like crossword puzzles and miniature golf, lived in or around cities. People defied older morals by patronizing speakeasies (illegal saloons during prohibition), wearing outlandish clothes, and dancing to jazz, while others reminisced about the simplicity of a world gone by.

New Rhythms of Everyday Life

How did technological advances impact social life in America in the 1920s?

Amid changes, people increasingly split their day into distinct time compartments: work, family, and leisure. For many, mechanization and higher productivity enabled employers to shorten the work week for many industrial laborers from six days to five and a half. White-collar employees often worked a forty-hour week, enjoyed the weekend off, and received annual vacations.

Family size decreased between 1920 and 1930 as birth control became more widely practiced. Over half the women married in the 1870s and 1880s had five or more children; in the 1920s, only 20 percent did. Meanwhile, divorce rates rose from 1 divorce for every 7.5 marriages in 1920 to 1 in 6 by 1929.

Pan American Airways

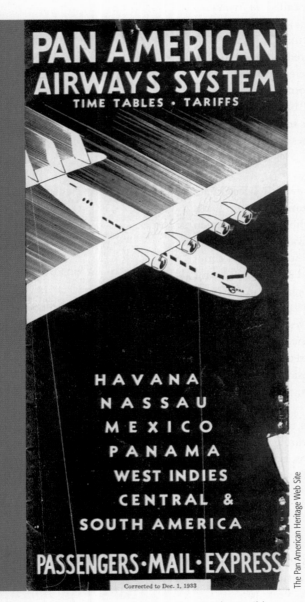

HAVANA
NASSAU
MEXICO
PANAMA
WEST INDIES
CENTRAL &
SOUTH AMERICA

PASSENGERS · MAIL · EXPRESS

The Pan American Heritage Web Site

Providing air transport connections to the Caribbean, Central America, and South America, Pan American Airways established the first major passenger and cargo links between the United States and other nations. By the early 1930s, flights were so numerous that the timetable announced in this illustration consisted of twelve pages.

Air transportation and airmail service between the United States and Latin America began in the 1920s, but anti-American hostility in the region made establishing connections difficult. In 1926, the U.S. government, fearful that German aircraft might bomb the Panama Canal in future conflicts, signed a treaty with Panama giving American airplanes exclusive rights to Panamanian airports. Charles Lindbergh (see page 639) and a formerly obscure pilot, Juan Trippe, played key roles in expanding American air service throughout Latin America.

With help from his father-in-law, a banking partner of J. P. Morgan, Trippe established Pan American Airways (informally known as Pan Am) in 1927 and won a contract to carry mail between Florida and Cuba. In December of that year, Lindbergh charmed the Mexicans into accepting airline links to the United States. The next year, Lindbergh joined Pan Am and began flying company planes to Central and South America, helping Trippe initiate mail and passenger service to Panama, Mexico, and other Latin American countries in 1929. Trippe advertised to wealthy Americans the opportunity to escape prohibition and enjoy Caribbean beaches via Pan Am.

Pan Am built airports that became essential connections between Latin America and the rest of the world. Trippe's employees created aerial maps that provided navigational aids. Pan Am linked Latin America more closely with the United States and helped unite parts of Latin America that had previously been divided by impenetrable mountain ranges. Yet Pan Am would resort to almost any tactic to build an airport: it cooperated with unsavory dictators, engaged in bribery, and violated human rights, in one case helping Bolivian police corral local Indians behind barbed wire for days to clear land for an airport.

Still, Pan Am enabled Americans (mostly the wealthy) to travel abroad and brought more foreigners to the United States. In 1942, its aircraft became the first to fly around the world. In the 1940s, the company began offering flights to Europe and Africa. Until its demise in 1991, Pan Am provided a leading link between the United States and the rest of the world.

Expansion of Suburbs in the 1920s

An outburst of housing and highway construction made possible the rapid growth of suburbs in the 1920s. The Chicago suburb of Niles Centre, later renamed Niles Center and ultimately called the Village of Skokie, was incorporated in 1888. Aided by the service of commuter railroads, the village began to grow in the early 1900s, and in 1913 the first permanently paved road in Cook County was built in Niles Center. After 1920, a real estate boom began, and by the mid 1920s the village had its own water, sewer, and street lighting services, along with many more paved roads. Wealthy Chicagoans such as utilities and railroad investor Samuel Insull built lavish homes in Niles Center, and soon commercial and office buildings sprang up along the major thoroughfares. Population grew so rapidly that the community boasted that it was "The World's Largest Village." The Great Depression halted the boom in 1929, but significant growth resumed after the Second World War. How do you think daily life changed as a result of the growth of suburbs?

Skokie Historical Society

In some areas, real estate developers laid out streets and blocks in burgeoning suburbs, enticing offices, stores, and institutions before residences were even built. This photograph of Niles Center, Illinois, taken from an airplane around 1927, reveals how roads and automobiles had become essential to suburban expansion.

Skokie Historical Society

As the 1920s proceeded, suburban housing construction accelerated. These private homes, one still under construction, along Brown Street in Niles Center, Illinois, in 1926 reveal how an open prairie was converted into a residential community. Note the presence of autos, a flatbed truck, and electrical wires, all critical to suburban life.

631

Household Management

Machines lightened some household tasks. Especially in middle-class households, electric irons and washing machines simplified wives' chores. Gas- and oil-powered central heating and hot-water heaters eliminated the hauling of wood, coal, and water; maintaining a kitchen fire; and removing ashes.

But technology and economic change also created new demands on women's time. Daughters of working-class families stayed in school longer, making them less available to help with housework. Advertisers of washing machines, vacuum cleaners, and commercial soap tried to make women feel guilty for homes that weren't spotlessly clean. No longer a producer of food and clothing as her ancestors were, a housewife became the family's shopper and chauffeur. One survey found that urban housewives spent seven and one-half hours per week driving to shop and transport children.

Health and Life Expectancy

With the discovery of vitamins between 1915 and 1930, nutritionists advocated certain foods to prevent illness, and giant companies advertised products as filled with vitamins and minerals. Producers of milk, canned fruits and vegetables, and other foods made claims that were hard to dispute because little was known about these invisible, tasteless ingredients. Welch's Grape Juice, for example, avoided mentioning its excess sugars when it advertised that it was "Rich in Health Values."

Better diets and improved hygiene made Americans healthier. Life expectancy at birth increased from fifty-four to sixty years between 1920 and 1930, and infant mortality decreased by two-thirds. Public sanitation and research in bacteriology reduced life-threatening diseases, such as tuberculosis and diphtheria. But medical progress did not benefit everyone equally; infant mortality rates were 50 to 100 percent higher among nonwhites than among whites, and tuberculosis in inner-city slums remained alarmingly common. Nevertheless, the total population over age sixty-five grew 35 percent between 1920 and 1930.

Older Americans and Retirement

Industrialism put premiums on youth and agility, pushing older people into poverty from forced retirement and reduced income. Most European countries established state-supported pension systems in the early 1900s. Many Americans, however, believed that pensions smacked of socialism and that individuals should prepare for old age by saving in their youth.

Most inmates in state poorhouses were older people, and almost one-third of Americans age sixty-five and older depended financially on someone else. Few employers, including the federal government, provided for retired employees. Resistance to pension plans broke at the state level in the 1920s. Led by the physician Isaac Max Rubinow and the journalist Abraham Epstein, reformers persuaded voluntary associations, labor unions, and legislators to endorse old-age assistance. By 1933, almost every state provided at least minimal support to needy elderly, opening the door to a national program of old-age insurance.

Social Values

New influences altered habits and values. Women and men wore more casual and colorful styles than their parents' generation. The line between acceptable and inappropriate behavior blurred as smoking, drinking, and frankness about sex became fashionable. Birth control gained a large following in respectable circles. Newspapers, magazines, motion pictures (such as *Why Change Your Wife?*), and popular songs (such as "I Don't Care") made certain that Americans did not suffer from "sex starvation."

Because state child-labor laws and compulsory-attendance rules kept children in school longer, peer groups played a more influential role in socializing youngsters than parents. School classes, sports, and clubs constantly brought together children of the same age, separating them from the influence of adults.

Between 1890 and the mid-1920s, ritualized middle- and upper-class courtship, consisting of men's formally "calling on" women and chaperoned social engagements, faded in favor of "dating," without supervision. Unmarried young people, living away from family restraints, eagerly went on dates to new commercial amusements, such as movies and nightclubs. Automobiles made dating more extensive. A woman's job seldom provided sufficient income for entertainments, but she could enjoy them if a man "treated" her. Romance, and at times sexual exploitation, accompanied the practice, especially when a woman was expected to trade sexual favors for being treated. Under the courtship system, a woman controlled who could "call" on her, but reliance on a man's money for entertainment presented difficult moral choices.

Women in the Work Force

After World War I, women continued to stream into the labor force. By 1930, 10.8 million women held paying jobs, an increase of 2 million since war's end. Although the proportion of women working in agriculture shrank, their proportion in categories of urban jobs grew or held steady (see Figure 24.1). Sex segregation persisted; most women took jobs that men seldom sought. Thus, over 1 million women worked as teachers and nurses. Some 2.2 million women were typists, bookkeepers, and filing clerks, a tenfold increase since 1920. Another 736,000 were store clerks,

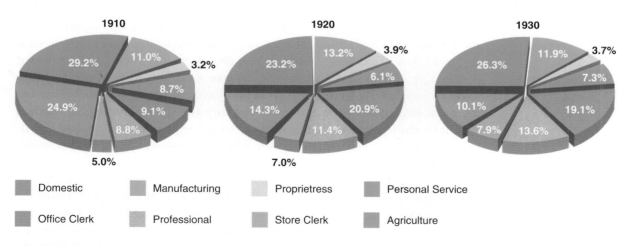

FIGURE 24.1

Changing Dimensions of Paid Female Labor, 1910–1930

These charts reveal the extraordinary growth in clerical and professional occupations among employed women and the accompanying decline in agricultural labor in the early twentieth century. Notice that manufacturing employment peaked in 1920 and that domestic service fluctuated as white immigrant women began to move out of these jobs and were replaced by women of color.

George Eastman House

The expansion of service-sector jobs and new technology opened new opportunities for women in the 1920s. This telephone operator handled scores of phone calls and monitored a huge switchboard at the same time. Her dress and jewelry contrasted with the simpler styles worn by factory women, who had to be more careful in working with dangerous machines.

and growing numbers were personal service workers, such as waitresses and hairdressers. Although almost 2 million women worked in manufacturing, their numbers grew little over the decade. Women's wages seldom exceeded half of those paid to men.

Family economic needs were paramount among women's reasons for working. Consumerism tempted working- and middle-class families to live beyond their means or expand their incomes with women's wages. Although most married women did not hold paying jobs (only 12 percent were employed in 1930), married women as a proportion of the work force rose by 30 percent during the 1920s, and the number of employed married women swelled from 1.9 million to 3.1 million.

Employment of Minority Women

The proportion of nonwhite women in paid labor was double that of white women. Often, they entered the work force because husbands were unemployed or underemployed. The majority of employed African American women held domestic jobs. The few who held factory jobs performed the least desirable, lowest-paying tasks. Some opportunities opened for educated African American women in social work, teaching, and nursing, but these women also faced discrimination and low incomes. More than white mothers, employed black mothers called on female relatives to help with childcare.

Next to African American women, Japanese American women were the most likely to hold paying jobs, similarly working as field hands and domestics, facing racial bias and low pay. Economic necessity also drew thousands of Mexican American women into the labor force, although their traditions resisted female employment. Most worked as domestic servants, operatives in garment factories, and agricultural laborers.

Alternative Images of Femininity

Women remade the image of femininity, casting aside the heavy, floor-length dresses and long hair of previous generations. Instead, many opted for the independence and sexual freedom of the 1920s flapper with her short skirts and bobbed hair. Although few women lived the flapper life, office workers, store clerks, and college coeds adopted the look. As Cecil B. DeMille's movies showed, new female icons included movie temptresses, such as Clara Bow, known as the "It Girl," and Gloria Swanson, notorious for torrid love affairs on and off the screen. Many women asserted new social equality with men. One observer described "the new woman" as intriguingly independent.

She takes a man's point of view as her mother never could....She will never make you a hatband or knit you a necktie, but she'll drive you from the station…in her own little sports car. She'll don knickers and go skiing with you,…she'll dive as well as you, perhaps better, she'll dance as long as you care to…

Gay and Lesbian Culture

The era's sexual openness enabled the underground homosexual culture to surface somewhat. In nontraditional city neighborhoods, such as New York's Greenwich Village, cheap rents and a relative tolerance attracted gay men and lesbians, who patronized dance halls, speakeasies, and cafés. Still, gay establishments remained targets for police raids, demonstrating that there was little acceptance from the larger society.

These trends represented a break with the nineteenth century's more restrained culture. But social change rarely proceeds smoothly. As the decade advanced, groups mobilized to defend older values.

Lines of Defense

Early in 1920, the leader of a newly formed organization hired two public relations experts, Edward Clarke and Elizabeth Tyler. They canvassed the South, Southwest, and Midwest, where they found countless people eager to pay a $10 membership fee and $6 for a white uniform. Clarke and Tyler pocketed $2.50 from each membership and secured 5 million members by 1923.

> How did various groups seek to hold the line on social change in the 1920s?

Ku Klux Klan

This was the Ku Klux Klan, a revived version of the hooded order that terrorized southern communities after the Civil War. Reconstituted in 1915 by William J. Simmons, an Atlanta, Georgia, evangelist and insurance salesman, the Klan adopted the hoods, intimidating tactics, and the mystical terminology of its forerunner (its leader was the Imperial Wizard; its book of rituals, the Kloran).

The new Klan fanned outward from the Deep South, wielding power in places as diverse as Oregon, where Portland's mayor was a Klan member, and Indiana, where Klansmen held the governorship and several legislative seats. Members included many from the urban middle class who feared losing social and economic gains and were nervous about a new youth culture that eluded family control. It included a women's adjunct with roughly a half-million members.

One phrase summed up Klan goals: "Native, white, Protestant supremacy." *Native* meant no immigration, no mongrelization of American culture. According to Imperial Wizard Hiram Wesley Evans, "The world has been so made so that each race must fight for its life, must conquer, accept slavery, or die." Evans accused the Catholic Church of discouraging assimilation and enslaving people to priests and a foreign pope.

Using threatening assemblies, violence, and political and economic pressure, the Klan meted out vigilante justice to suspected bootleggers, wife beaters, and adulterers; forced schools to stop teaching evolution; campaigned against Catholic and Jewish political candidates; and fueled racial tensions against Mexicans in Texas border cities. Klan women promoted native white Protestantism but also worked for moral reform and prohibition. Because the KKK vowed to protect women's virtue, housewives sometimes appealed to the Klan to punish abusive or irresponsible husbands. The Klan's method of justice was flogging.

By 1925, however, scandal undermined the Klan's moral base. Indiana grand dragon David Stephenson was convicted of second-degree murder after he kidnapped and raped a woman who later died. Eventually, the Klan's negative brand of patriotism and purity could not compete in a pluralistic society.

Intolerance pervaded American society in the 1920s. Nativists charged that Catholic and Jewish immigrants clogged city slums, flouted community norms, and stubbornly embraced alien religious and political beliefs. Fear of immigrant radicals also fueled a dramatic 1921 trial of two Italian anarchists, **Nicola Sacco and Bartolomeo Vanzetti**, convicted of murdering a paymaster and guard in Braintree, Massachusetts. Evidence for their guilt was flimsy.

Nicola Sacco and Bartolomeo Vanzetti: Italian immigrants found guilty of a Massachusetts murder and sentenced to death. Sacco and Vanzetti were also anarchists and much of their murder trial focused on their radicalism.

Immigration Quotas

Efforts to restrict immigration gathered support. Labor leaders warned that aliens would depress wages and raise unemployment. Business executives, who formerly desired cheap immigrant laborers, now realized that mechanization would keep wages low. Drawing support from such groups, Congress set yearly immigration allocations for each nationality in the Emergency Quota Act of 1921. By restricting annual immigration of a given nationality to 3 percent of immigrants from that nation already residing in the United States in 1910, the Act favored Anglo-Saxon Protestant immigrants. It discriminated against Catholics and Jews from southern and eastern Europe, whose numbers were comparatively small in 1910.

In 1924, Congress replaced the Quota Act with the **National Origins Act**. This law limited annual immigration to 150,000 people and set quotas at 2 percent of each nationality residing in the United States in 1890, except for Asians, who were banned completely. The act further restricted southern and eastern Europeans, since fewer of those groups lived in the United States in 1890 than in 1910, although it allowed foreign-born wives and children of U.S. citizens to enter as nonquota immigrants.

In 1927, a revised National Origins Act redefined quotas to be distributed among European countries in proportion to the national origins (country of birth or descent) of American inhabitants in 1920. People from the Western Hemisphere did not fall under the quotas (except for those whom the Labor Department defined as potential paupers) and became the largest immigrant groups (see Figure 24.2).

National Origins Act of 1924: Restricted annual immigration from any foreign country to two percent of each nationality residing in the United States in 1890 (but barred Asians); also limited total annual immigration to 150,000.

Fundamentalism

The pursuit of spiritual purity stirred religious fundamentalists, as millions sought salvation from what they perceived as the irreverence of a materialistic, hedonistic society. Resolutely believing that God's miracles created the world, they condemned the theory of evolution as heresy. Wherever fundamentalists constituted a majority of a community, they sought to determine what schools taught. Their enemies were modernists, who used social sciences, such as psychology, to interpret behavior. To modernists, God was important to the study of culture and history, but science advanced knowledge.

fundamentalism: Twentieth century movement within Protestantism that taught literal interpretation of the Bible.

Scopes trial: Trial that took place after high school teacher John Scopes challenged a Tennessee law that banned teaching the theory of evolution in public schools.

Scopes Trial

In 1925, Christian **fundamentalism** clashed with modernism in the **Scopes Trial** in Dayton, Tennessee. The state legislature banned public schools from teaching the theory that humans evolved

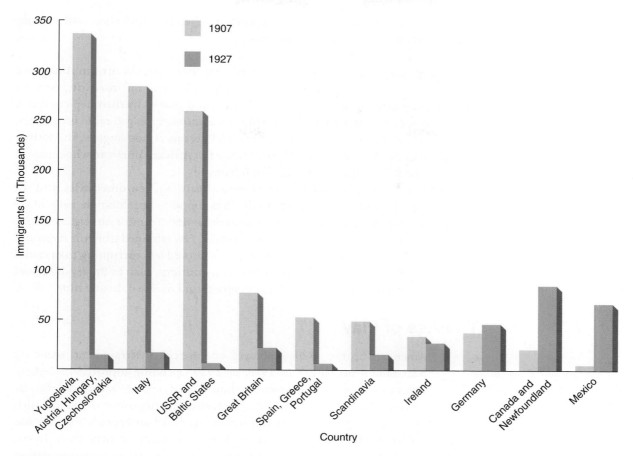

FIGURE 24.2
Sources of Immigration, 1907 and 1927
Immigration peaked in 1907 and 1908, when newcomers from southern and eastern Europe poured into the United States. After immigration restriction laws were passed in the 1920s, the greatest number of immigrants came from the Western Hemisphere (Canada and Mexico), which was exempted from the quotas, and the number coming from eastern and southern Europe shrank.

from lower forms of life rather than descending from Adam and Eve. High school teacher John Thomas Scopes volunteered to serve as a test case and was arrested for violating the law. William Jennings Bryan, former secretary of state and three-time presidential candidate, argued for the prosecution, and civil liberties lawyers headed by Clarence Darrow represented Scopes. News correspondents crowded into town, and radio stations broadcast the trial.

Although Scopes was convicted—clearly he had broken the law—modernists claimed victory. The testimony, they believed, showed fundamentalism to be illogical. The trial's climax occurred when Bryan testified as an expert on the Bible. He asserted that Eve really had been created from Adam's rib, that the Tower of Babel was responsible for the diversity of languages, and that Jonah had actually been swallowed by a big fish. Spectators in Dayton cheered Bryan, but the liberal press mocked him. Nevertheless, fundamentalists continued to pressure schools to stop teaching evolution and created an independent subculture with their own schools, radio ministries, and missionary societies.

Religious Revivalism   Urban Pentecostal churches attracted African Americans and whites struggling with economic insecurity, nervous about modernism's attack on old-time religion, and swayed by their depiction of a personal Savior. Using modern advertising and elaborately staged radio broadcasts, magnetic preachers, such as Aimee Semple McPherson of Los Angeles, the former baseball player Billy Sunday, and Father Divine (an African American who amassed an interracial following) stirred revivalist fervor.

Clergy and teachers of all faiths condemned dancing, new dress styles, and sex in movies and parked cars. Many urban dwellers supported prohibition, believing it would win the battle against poverty, vice, and corruption. Yet most Americans sought balance as they tried to adjust to the modern order. Few refrained from the radio and movies like *Why Change Your Wife?*—activities that proved less corrupting than critics feared. Americans sought fellowship in civic organizations, such as Rotary, Elks, and women's clubs. Perhaps most important, people found release in leisure time.

The Age of Play

Why did movie and sports heroes become so important during the 1920s?

Americans in the 1920s embraced commercial entertainment, spending $2.5 billion on leisure in 1919; by 1929, spending topped $4.3 billion. Spectator amusements—movies, music, and sports—accounted for 21 percent of the 1929 total; the rest involved participatory recreation such as games, hobbies, and travel. Entrepreneurs fed an appetite for fads and spectacles. Early in the 1920s, mahjong, a Chinese tile game, was the craze. In the mid-1920s, devotees popularized crossword puzzles, printed in mass-circulation newspapers and magazines. By 1930, the nation boasted thirty thousand miniature golf courses. Dance crazes like the Charleston and recorded music on radio boosted the growing popularity of jazz.

Movies and Sports   Americans embraced movies and sports. In total capital investment, motion pictures became one of the nation's leading industries. In 1922, movies attracted 40 million viewers weekly; by 1929, nearly 100 million—at a time when the nation's population was 120 million and total weekly church attendance was 60 million. Between 1922 and 1927, the Technicolor Corporation developed a means of producing movies in color. That, along with the introduction of sound in 1927's *The Jazz Singer*, made movies more exciting.

Although DeMille's romantic comedies like *Why Change Your Wife?* explored worldly themes, his most popular films—*The Ten Commandments* (1923) and *The King of Kings* (1927)—were biblical. Lurid dramas like *Souls for Sale* (1923) and *A Woman Who Sinned* (1924) also drew big audiences, as did slapstick comedies starring Harold Lloyd and Charlie Chaplin. In 1927, producers—bowing to pressure from legislators and religious leaders—instituted self-censorship, forbidding nudity, rough language, and plots that did not end with justice and morality triumphant. Movies also reproduced social prejudices—the few black actors were limited to playing maids and butlers.

Spectator sports drew millions every year. In an age when technology and mass production robbed experiences of their uniqueness, sports provided the unpredictability that people craved. Newspapers and radio magnified this tension, glorifying events with such dramatic narrative that promoters did not need advertising.

Baseball's drawn-out suspense, diverse plays, and potential for keeping statistics attracted a huge following. After the 1919 "Black Sox scandal"—when eight members of the Chicago White Sox were banned for allegedly throwing the World Series to the Cincinnati Reds (even though a jury acquitted them)—baseball transformed itself. A record 300,000 people attended the six-game 1921 World Series between the New York Giants and New York Yankees. Millions enjoyed professional games on the radio. Although African American ballplayers were prohibited from the major leagues, they formed their own teams, and in 1920 the first successful Negro League was founded in Kansas City, Missouri.

Sports Heroes

As technology and mass society made the individual less significant, people clung to heroic personalities. Athletes like Bill Tilden in tennis, Gertrude Ederle in swimming (in 1926, she became the first woman to swim across the English Channel), and Bobby Jones in golf were famous. But boxing, football, and baseball produced the most popular sports heroes. Heavyweight champion Jack Dempsey, the "Manassa (Colorado) Mauler," attracted the first of several million-dollar gates in his fight with Frenchman Georges Carpentier in 1921.

Baseball's foremost hero was George Herman "Babe" Ruth, who began as a pitcher but broke records hitting home runs. Ruth hit twenty-nine homers in 1919, fifty-four in 1920 (the year the Boston Red Sox traded him to the New York Yankees), fifty-nine in 1921, and sixty in 1927—each year a record. His talent and boyish grin endeared him to millions. Known for overindulgence in food, drink, and sex, he charmed fans into forgiving his excesses with by visiting hospitalized children.

Link to a video showing the success of Gertrude Ederle swimming the English Channel.

Link to a video of the boxing match between Jack Dempsey and Georges Carpentier.

Movie Stars and Public Heroes

Americans fulfilled their yearning for romance and adventure through movie idols. One of the decade's most adored movie personalities was Rudolph Valentino, whose image exploited the era's sexual liberalism. In his most famous film, Valentino played a passionate sheik who carried away beautiful women to his tent. When he died at thirty-one of complications from ulcers and appendicitis, the press turned his funeral into a public extravaganza.

The era's most celebrated hero, however, was **Charles A. Lindbergh**, an indomitable aviator who in May 1927 flew a plane solo from New York to Paris. The flight riveted America, as newspaper and telegraph reports followed Lindbergh's progress. After the pilot landed successfully, President Coolidge dispatched a warship to bring "Lucky Lindy" home, where he was greeted with a parade. Lindbergh received the Distinguished Flying Cross and the Congressional Medal of Honor. Promoters offered him millions of dollars to tour the world and $700,000 for a movie contract. His flight epitomized individual achievement and courage—old-fashioned values that attracted public respect.

Charles A. Lindbergh: Popular aviator who flew solo across the Atlantic in his small single engine plane, the "Spirit of St. Louis," in May 1927.

Prohibition

The Eighteenth Amendment (1919) and subsequent federal law (the Volstead Act of 1920) prohibited the manufacture, sale, and transportation of alcoholic beverages. It worked well at first. Per capita consumption of liquor dropped, as did arrests for drunkenness. But it was barely enforced: in 1922, Congress gave the Prohibition Bureau less than $7 million for nationwide enforcement, and by 1927 most state budgets omitted funds to enforce prohibition.

After 1925, prohibition broke down as thousands made their own wine and gin illegally and bootleg importers evaded the few patrols that existed. Moreover, drinking was a business with willing customers, and criminal organizations capitalized on public demand. The most notorious of such mobs belonged to Al Capone, who seized control of illegal liquor and vice in Chicago, maintaining power over politicians and the vice business through intimidation, bribery, and violence. Americans wanted liquor, and until 1931, when a federal court convicted and imprisoned Capone for income-tax evasion (the only charge for which authorities could obtain hard evidence), he supplied them.

Cultural Currents

How did discontent with 1920s conformity give rise to important creative cultural movements?

Intellectuals were quick to expose the era's hypocrisies. Writers and artists felt at odds with society, and their rejection of materialism and conformity was biting and bitter.

Literature of Alienation

Several writers from the so-called Lost Generation, including novelist Ernest Hemingway and poets Ezra Pound and T. S. Eliot, abandoned the United States for Europe. Others, like novelists William Faulkner and Sinclair Lewis, remained in America but expressed disillusionment with the materialism they witnessed. F. Scott Fitzgerald's novels, *This Side of Paradise* (1920) and *The Great Gatsby* (1925), and Eugene O'Neill's plays scorned Americans' preoccupation with money. Edith Wharton explored the clash of old and new moralities in novels such as *The Age of Innocence* (1920). Hemingway's *A Farewell to Arms* (1929) interwove antiwar sentiment with critiques of the emptiness in modern relationships.

Harlem Renaissance

Discontent inspired a new generation of African American artists. Middle-class, educated, and proud of their African heritage, black writers rejected white culture and exalted the militantly assertive "New Negro." In the "Negro Mecca" of New York's Harlem, black intellectuals and artists, aided by a few white patrons, celebrated black culture during what became known as the Harlem Renaissance.

The popular 1921 musical comedy *Shuffle Along* is often credited with launching the Harlem Renaissance and showcased talented African American artists, such as the composer Eubie Blake and the singer Josephine Baker. The Harlem Renaissance also fostered several gifted writers, among them poets Langston Hughes, Countee Cullen, and Claude McKay and novelists Zora Neale Hurston, Jessie Fauset, and Alain Locke. Though cherishing their African heritage and folk culture of the slave

Collection of Archie Motley and Valerie Gerrard Browne. Photo courtesy of The Art Institute of Chicago

This painting by African American artist Archibald Motley represented the "Ash-Can" style, which considered no subject too undignified to paint, as well as the sensual relationship between jazz music and dancing in African American culture.

South, these artists and intellectuals realized that blacks had to come to terms with being free Americans. Langston Hughes wrote, "We younger Negro artists who create now intend to express our individual dark-skinned selves without fear or shame. If white people are pleased, we are glad. If they are not, it doesn't matter. We know we are beautiful."

Jazz

The Jazz Age, as the 1920s is sometimes called, owes its name to the music of the African American culture. Evolving from African and African American folk music, early jazz communicated exuberance, humor, and autonomy that African Americans seldom experienced in their public and political lives. Jazz's emotional rhythms and improvisation blurred the distinction between composer and performer. Urban dance halls and nightclubs, some of which included interracial audiences, featured performers like trumpeter Louis Armstrong and blues singer Bessie Smith. Music recorded by African American artists and aimed at African American consumers (sometimes called "race records") gave African Americans a place in commercial culture. More important, jazz endowed America with its own distinctive art form.

In many ways, the 1920s were the nation's most creative years. Painters such as Georgia O'Keeffe, Aaron Douglas, and John Marin forged a uniquely American style of visual art. Composer Henry Cowell pioneered electronic music, and Aaron Copland built orchestral works around native folk motifs. George Gershwin blended jazz rhythms, classical forms, and folk melodies in serious works (*Rhapsody in Blue,* 1924, and Piano Concerto in F, 1925, and hit tunes such as "The Man I Love"). In architecture, skyscrapers drew worldwide attention to American forms. The "emotional and aesthetic starvation" that essayist Harold Stearns lamented early in the decade were gone by 1929.

The Election of 1928 and End of the New Era

What were the early signs that the prosperity of the 1920s was coming to an end?

Intellectuals' uneasiness about materialism seldom affected the confident rhetoric of politics. Herbert Hoover voiced that confidence when he accepted the Republican nomination for president in 1928. "We in America today," Hoover boasted, "are nearer to the final triumph over poverty than ever before in the history of any land."

Herbert Hoover

As the Republican candidate in 1928 (Coolidge chose not to seek reelection), Hoover fused the traditional value of individual hard work with modern emphasis on corporate action. A Quaker from Iowa, orphaned at age ten, Hoover put himself through Stanford University and became a wealthy mining engineer. During and after World War I, he distinguished himself as U.S. food administrator.

As secretary of commerce under Harding and Coolidge, Hoover promoted associationalism. Recognizing that nationwide associations dominated commerce and industry, Hoover sought business and government cooperation. He made the Commerce Department a center for the promotion of business, encouraging trade associations, holding conferences, and issuing reports, all aimed at improving productivity and profits.

Al Smith

In sharp contrast, Democrats in 1928 chose New York's governor Alfred E. Smith. Hoover had rural, native-born, Protestant, and business roots, but had never run for public office. Smith was an urbane politician of Irish stock with a career embedded in New York City's Tammany Hall political machine. He relished the give-and-take of city streets.

Smith was the first Roman Catholic to run for president on a major party ticket. His religion enhanced his appeal among urban ethnics, who increasingly voted, but intense anti-Catholic sentiments lost him southern and rural votes. Smith had a strong record on Progressive reform and civil rights, but his campaign stressed issues unlikely to unite these groups, particularly his opposition to prohibition.

Hoover, who emphasized national prosperity under Republican administrations, won the popular vote by 21 million to 15 million and the electoral vote by 444 to 87. Smith carried the nation's twelve largest cities, formerly Republican strongholds. For the next forty years, the Democratic Party solidified this urban base, which in conjunction with its traditional strength in the South made the party a formidable force in national elections.

Hoover's Administration

At his inaugural, Hoover proclaimed a New Day, "bright with hope." His cabinet featured mostly businessmen, including six millionaires. To lower ranking posts, Hoover appointed young professionals who agreed that a scientific approach could solve national problems. Like Hoover, Americans widely believed that individual effort led to success and that poverty suggested personal weakness. Prevailing opinion also held that fluctuations of the business cycle were natural and therefore not to be tampered with by government.

Stock Market Crash

This trust dissolved on October 24, 1929, later known as Black Thursday, when stock market prices suddenly plunged, wiping out $10 billion in value (worth around $100 billion today). Panic set in. Prices of many stocks hit record lows; some sellers could find no buyers. At noon, leading bankers put up $20 million and ceremoniously began buying stocks. The mood brightened, and some stocks rallied.

But as news spread, frightened investors sold off to avoid further losses. On Black Tuesday, October 29, prices plummeted again. Hoover assured Americans that "the crisis will be over in sixty days." He shared the popular assumptions that the economy was strong enough to endure until the market righted itself. Instead, the crash ultimately unleashed a devastating worldwide depression.

In hindsight, the depression began long before the stock market crash. Prosperity in the 1920s was not as widespread as optimists believed. Agriculture had languished for decades, and many areas, especially in the South, were outside the new bounty of consumer society. Industries such as mining and textiles failed to sustain profits throughout the decade, and even the automotive and household goods industries had been stagnant since 1926. The fever of speculation included rash investment in California and Florida real estate, as well as in the stock market, and masked what was unhealthy in the national economy.

Declining Demand

The economic weakness that underlay the Great Depression had several interrelated causes. Since mid-1928, demand for new housing had faltered, reducing sales of building materials and unemployment. In growth industries, such as automobiles and electric appliances, demand leveled off, so factory owners cut production and workers. Retailers had amassed large inventories that were going unsold and started ordering less. Farm prices continued to sag, leaving farmers with less income for new machinery and goods. As wages and employment fell, families could not afford to buy consumer goods. Thus, by 1929, a sizable population of underconsumers was causing serious repercussions.

As the rich grew richer, middle- and lower-income Americans barely made modest gains. Although average per capita disposable income (income after taxes) rose about 9 percent between 1920 and 1929, income of the wealthiest 1 percent rose 75 percent. Much of this increase was put into stock market investments, not consumer goods.

Intercollegiate Athletics

In 1924 brutality, academic fraud, and illegal payments to recruits prompted the Carnegie Foundation for the Advancement of Higher Education to undertake a five-year investigation of college sports. Its 1929 report recommended the abolition of football and condemned coaches and alumni but had minimal effect. Football was immensely popular, and colleges and universities built stadiums to attract spectators, bolster alumni allegiance, and enhance revenues.

From the 1920s to the present, intercollegiate sports ranked as a major commercial entertainment. Still, American higher education has struggled to reconcile conflicts between the commercialism of athletic competition and the ideals of amateurism. But the economic potential of college sports coupled with expanding athletic departments—elaborate facilities as well as staffs—has created programs that compete with and sometimes overshadow an institution's academic mission.

Since the 1920s, recruiting scandals, academic fraud, and felonious behavior sparked controversy in college sports. In 1952, after revelations of point-shaving (fixing the outcome) of basketball games at several colleges, the American Council on Education undertook its own study. Its recommendations, including the elimination of football bowl games, went largely unheeded. In 1991, further abuses prompted the Knight Foundation Commission on Intercollegiate Athletics to urge college presidents to reform intercollegiate athletics. Few significant changes resulted, even after a follow-up study in 2001.

The most sweeping reforms followed court rulings in the 1990s, mandating that women's sports be treated equally with men's under Title IX of the Educational Amendments Act of 1972. Enforcement, however, provoked a backlash that resulted in efforts to prevent men's teams from being cut to satisfy Title IX. In recent years, the National College Athletic Association (NCAA) has attempted to regulate academic standards in college athletics, but its success depends on cooperation from member institutions. With millions of dollars involved, the system established in the 1920s has withstood most pressures for change.

Corporate Debt and Stock Market Speculation

Furthermore, many businesses overloaded themselves with debt. To obtain loans, they misrepresented their assets in ways that hid their inability to repay. Such practices, overlooked by lending agencies, put the nation's banking system on precarious footing.

Risky stock market speculation also precipitated the depression. Individuals and corporations bought millions of stocks on margin, meaning that they invested with a down payment of only a fraction of a stock's actual price and then used these partially paid-for stocks as collateral for more stock purchases. When stock prices stopped rising, investors tried to unload what they bought on margin. But with numerous investors selling simultaneously, prices plunged. Brokers demanded full payment for stocks bought on margin. The more obligations went unmet, the more the system tottered. Inevitably, banks and investment companies collapsed.

Economic Troubles Abroad; Federal Failures at Home

International economic conditions also contributed to the Depression. During and after World War I, Americans loaned billions to European nations. By the late 1920s, however, American investors instead kept their money in the lucrative U.S. stock market. Europeans, unable to borrow more or sell goods in the American market because of high tariffs, bought less from the United States. Moreover, the Allied nations depended on German war reparations to pay their debts to the United States, and the German government depended on American bank loans to pay those reparations. When the crash choked off American loans, the western economy ground to a halt.

The government refrained from regulating speculation. In supporting business expansion, the Federal Reserve Board pursued easy credit policies, charging low discount rates (interest on its loans to member banks) even though such loans were financing the speculative mania.

Neither experts nor people on the street realized what really happened in 1929. Conventional wisdom, based on previous depressions, held that economic problems had to run their course. So in 1929 people waited for the tailspin to ease, never realizing that the new era had ended and that the economy, politics, and society would have to be rebuilt.

Summary

Two critical events, the end of World War I and beginning of the Great Depression, marked the boundaries of the 1920s. After the war, traditional customs weakened as women and men sought new forms of self-expression and gratification. Modern science and technology touched the lives of rich and poor alike through mass media, movies, sports, automobiles, and electric appliances. Moreover, the decade's freewheeling consumerism enabled ordinary Americans to emulate wealthier people purchasing more and engaging in stock market speculation.

Beneath the new era's materialism, prejudice and ethnic tensions tainted the American dream. Klansmen and immigration restrictionists encouraged discrimination against racial minorities and ethnic groups. Meanwhile, the distinguishing forces of twentieth-century life—technological change, bureaucratization, mass culture, and growth of the middle class—accelerated, making the decade truly "new."

Chapter Review

Big Business Triumphant

What helped turn the economy around in the 1920s?

Two factors helped transform the initial postwar World War I recession into recovery: the advent of electric energy in 1922 and new government pro-business initiatives. Electricity enabled goods to be produced more inexpensively, thereby driving consumer demand and stimulating the economy across the board. New installment or credit plans for purchasing big items such as cars also drove consumption. Business organizations successfully used new lobbying techniques to prompt government to implement pro-business policies that also stimulated growth. Congress cut taxes on corporations and wealthy individuals in 1921, and passed the Fordney-McCumber Tariff Act (1922). The Federal Trade Commission and the Interstate Commerce Commission tended to cooperate with corporations rather than regulate them. And several Supreme Court decisions sheltered business from government regulation and hindered organized labor.

Politics and Government

What happened to Progressive reform in the 1920s?

While Progressivism faded on a national level, its reform spirit continued to inspire local and state initiatives as well as those by women and ethnic groups. After the war, many states adopted or expanded workers' compensation laws and public welfare programs. Native American groups worked for better education and return of tribal lands, while white reformers held out hope of getting Indians to adopt white middle-class standards of work, family, and citizenship. Although women got the right to vote in 1920, their voluntary organizations became the tools for lobbying for various issues from birth control to protective labor legislation to questions of citizenship and equality.

A Consumer Society

How did the emergence of a consumer society change American life?

In the 1920s, incomes increased, while new mass production methods kept the price of goods stable or made them more affordable. Consequently, greater numbers of Americans could afford products such as automobiles that once were the province of the wealthy. Car ownership led consumers to join with farmers in seeking improved roadways. At the same time, the emergence of advertising as a tool helped manipulate purchases and increasingly erased ethnic differences to create a more homogenous consumer society. And the growth of the radio, with its mass marketing and standardized programs, further blurred differences and heightened immigrants assimilation into American culture and ways of life.

Cities, Migrants, and Suburbs

What fueled the growth of cities in the 1920s?

In 1920, for the first time in U.S. history, more people lived in urban areas than rural areas. In part, the shift was driven by young people, who left farms for the more exciting and varied life of cities. The demographic change was also driven by the migration of African Americans from poverty and a boll weevil plague on southern farms to seek better paying factory jobs in the North. Once there, they faced discrimination in housing. Immigrants from Mexico and Puerto Rico were similarly pushed off their land due to agricultural changes to find better opportunities in America. Many Mexicans became underpaid and exploited farm laborers in the West, while Puerto Ricans found jobs in factories and restaurants or as domestic servants. Both maintained customs and developed local businesses or social clubs to help them adapt.

New Rhythms of Everyday Life

How did technological advances impact social life in America in the 1920s?

First, improved productivity and mechanization led to shorter workweeks, permitting the expansion of leisure activities and greater freedom, especially for young people. Industrialism privileged youth and agility over experience and forced older people to retire, which often meant economic hardship or poverty. Second, new appliances made housework less arduous and time-consuming and shifted women's roles from producer within the home to consumer for the family. Third, advances in nutrition helped people live longer and healthier lives. Birth control also enabled families to separate sexuality from reproduction, and family size decreased. Finally, as products and services became more widely available, an increasing number of married women moved into the work force to expand their families' purchasing power.

Lines of Defense

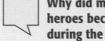 **How did various groups seek to hold the line on social change in the 1920s?**

Troubled by the liberal social influences of the era, several groups emerged seeking to restore what they considered to be traditional American values. The Ku Klux Klan was reconstituted in 1915 to re-establish native white American supremacy in the face of increasing immigration and black migration and to protect white women's virtue against so-called corrupting influences. They were joined in their anti-immigration sentiment by other nativist groups, who pressed Congress to establish immigration quotas. Similarly, fundamentalist Christian groups sought to replace the modern emphasis on science with a renewed centrality of God's role in creation and daily life. Hence, the Tennessee legislature banned the teaching of the theory of evolution, resulting in the pivotal Scopes trial in 1925. Religious revivalism likewise condemned the new social practices of dating, dancing, and fashion and the hint of sex in movies.

The Age of Play

Why did movie and sports heroes become so important during the 1920s?

As mass consumption took hold, Americans felt robbed of a sense of individual distinctiveness. To recover that lost sensibility, Americans gravitated toward leisure activities that celebrated individual achievement or that inspired a sense of adventure or romance. Sports provided drama, unpredictability, and a chance to celebrate a particular player's talent. Motion pictures not only let viewers live vicariously through the exciting lives of characters, but also inspired the hope for adventure in their own lives. Finally, national heroes such as aviator Charles Lindbergh made the possibility of greatness seem real and attainable, even if most Americans would never personally experience it for themselves.

Cultural Currents

 How did discontent with 1920s conformity give rise to important creative cultural movements?

Many artists and writers felt disillusioned with the materialism they witnessed in America during this age of mass consumption and innovation. While some, like Ernest Hemingway, left for Europe, others remained in the United States and transformed these feelings into novels and other creative works that explored the problems of modern society or proffered a particular political view. Middle-class, educated African Americans rejected white culture and celebrated their heritage in novels, poems, plays, and art, creating the literary and artistic movement known as the Harlem Renaissance. Black culture also produced the Jazz Age, creating a distinctly American musical form.

The Election of 1928 and the End of the New Era

What were the early signs that the prosperity of the 1920s was coming to an end?

While the 1929 stock market crash put a definitive ending on the era's seeming prosperity, in truth, the seeds of recession were sown many years before. First, so-called prosperity had never reached farmers; agriculture had lagged for decades. Mining, textiles, and other industries did not remain profitable the entire decade, and even the automobile industry was stagnant after 1926. As demand faltered, factories cut back on production and workers, which in turn meant less disposable income to purchase consumer goods, triggering further cutbacks in retail orders and production. Housing demand dropped off after mid-1928, and at the same time, businesses were overloaded with debt. Together, this made for a perfect economic storm when the market crashed in 1929.

Suggestions for Further Reading

Lynn Dumenil, *The Modern Temper: American Culture and Society in the 1920s* (1995)

Colin Grant, *Negro with a Hat: The Rise and Fall of Marcus Garvey* (2008)

Maury Klein, *Rainbow's End: The Crash of 1929* (2003)

Roland Marchand, *Advertising the American Dream: Making Way for Modernity, 1920–1940* (1985)

Nathan Miller, *New World Coming: The 1920s and the Making of Modern America* (2004)

David Montgomery, *The Fall of the House of Labor: The Workplace, the State, and American Activism, 1865–1925* (1987)

Mae M. Ngai, *Impossible Subjects: Illegal Aliens and the Making of Modern America* (2004)

George Sanchez, *Becoming Mexican American: Ethnicity, Culture and Identity in Chicano Los Angeles, 1900–1945* (1993)

Susan Thistle, *From Marriage to the Market: The Transformation of Women's Lives and Work* (2006)

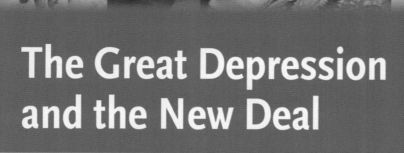

The Great Depression and the New Deal

25

1929–1941

I n 1931, the rain stopped in the Great Plains. Montana and North Dakota became as arid as the Sonora Desert. Temperatures reached 115 degrees in Iowa. The soil baked. Farmers watched rich black dirt turn to gray dust.

Then the winds began to blow. Farmers had stripped the Plains of native grasses in the 1920s, plowing up 50,000 acres of new land daily. Now, with nothing to hold the earth, it began to blow away. The dust storms began in 1934—and worsened in 1935. Dust obscured the sun. Cattle, blinded by blowing grit, ran in circles until they died. Clouds of dust filled the skies of Kansas, Colorado, Oklahoma, Texas, and New Mexico—the Dust Bowl.

In late 1937, on a farm near Stigler, Oklahoma, Marvin Montgomery counted his assets: $53 and a 1929 Hudson car. On December 29, 1937, Montgomery and his wife and four children—along with their furniture, bedding, pots, and pans—squeezed into the Hudson. Traveling west on Route 66, the Montgomerys headed for California.

At least a third of farms in the Dust Bowl were abandoned in the 1930s, and many families headed west, lured by advertisements promising work in California fields. Some 300,000 people migrated to California in the 1930s; many were white-collar workers seeking better opportunities in California's cities. But the plight of families like the Montgomerys, captured in federal government-sponsored Farm Security Administration (FSA) photographs, came to represent the human suffering of the Great Depression.

The Montgomerys ran out of money in Arizona and worked in the cotton fields there for five weeks before moving on. In California, wages were low and migrant families felt unwelcome. As they took over the agricultural labor formerly done by Mexicans and Mexican Americans, they forfeited their "whiteness" in the eyes of many Californians. "Negroes and Okies' upstairs," read a sign in a San Joaquin valley movie theater.

Most migrants to rural California lived in squalid camps, but the Montgomerys secured housing provided by the Farm

Chapter Outline

Hoover and Hard Times, 1929–1933
Farmers and Industrial Workers | Marginal Workers | Middle-Class Workers and Families | Hoover's Limited Solutions | Protest and Social Unrest | Bonus Army

Franklin D. Roosevelt and the Launching of the New Deal
Banking Crisis | First Hundred Days | National Industrial Recovery Act | Agricultural Adjustment Act | Relief Programs

Political Pressure and the Second New Deal
Business Opposition | Demagogues and Populists | Left-Wing Critics | Shaping the Second New Deal | Works Progress Administration | Social Security Act | Roosevelt's Populist Strategies

Labor
Rivalry Between Craft and Industrial Unions | Sit-Down Strikes | Memorial Day Massacre

VISUALIZING THE PAST *The Women's Emergency Brigade and the General Motors Sit-Down Strike*

Federal Power and the Nationalization of Culture
New Deal in the West | New Deal for Native Americans | New Deal in the South | Mass Media and Popular Culture

LINKS TO THE WORLD *The 1936 Olympic Games*

The Limits of the New Deal
*Court-Packing Plan | Roosevelt
Recession | Election of 1940 |
Race and the Limits of the New
Deal | African American Support |
An Assessment of the New Deal*

LEGACY FOR A PEOPLE AND A NATION *Social
Security*

SUMMARY

Security Administration. The FSA camp had 240 tents and 40 small houses. For nine months, the Montgomery family lived in a fourteen-by-sixteen-foot tent, which rented for 10 cents a day plus four hours of volunteer labor a month. Then they moved into an FSA house, "with water, lights, and everything, yes sir; and a little garden spot furnished." Soon, employment opportunities emerged in California's aircraft factories and shipyards mobilizing for World War II.

The Montgomerys' experience shows the human costs of the Great Depression that plunged the world into an economic crisis. Between 1929 and 1933, the U.S. gross national product was cut in half. Corporate profits fell from $10 billion to $1 billion; 100,000 businesses closed. Four million workers were unemployed in January 1930; by November, unemployment reached 6 million. When President Herbert Hoover left office in 1933, 13 million workers—about one-fourth of the labor force—were idle, and millions worked only part-time. There was no national safety net: no welfare system, no unemployment compensation, no Social Security. And, as thousands of banks failed, with no federally guaranteed deposit insurance, families' savings disappeared.

Herbert Hoover, who was elected president in the prosperous late 1920s, looked first to private enterprise for solutions. By the end of his term, he extended the federal government's role in managing an economic crisis further than his predecessors had. Still, the depression deepened, and Americans became desperate. The economic catastrophe exacerbated existing racial and class tensions in the United States, while in Germany, it propelled Adolf Hitler to power. By late 1932, many feared the depression was a crisis of capitalism, even of democracy itself.

In 1932, voters replaced Hoover with a man who promised a New Deal. Franklin Delano Roosevelt's programs did not end the depression (only the massive mobilization for World War II did that), but they did alleviate suffering. For the first time, the federal government assumed responsibility for the nation's economy and its citizens' welfare, thus strengthening its power in relation to states.

Although some Americans saw the depression as an opportunity for major economic change—even revolution—Roosevelt's goal was to save capitalism. New Deal programs increased federal government regulation without fundamentally altering the system or distribution of wealth. Despite pressure to attack racial discrimination, Roosevelt never directly challenged southern legal segregation—partly because he relied on southern Democrats in Congress to pass New Deal legislation.

Despite its limits, the New Deal preserved America's democratic experiment through uncertainty and crisis. By decade's end, a world war shifted America's focus from domestic to foreign policy. But the changes begun by the New Deal continued to transform the United States for decades.

As you read this chapter, keep the following questions in mind:

* How did economic hard times during the 1930s affect Americans, and what differences were there in the experiences of specific groups and regions?

* How and why did the power of the federal government expand during the Great Depression?

* What were the successes and the failures of the New Deal?

Link to photographs taken by FSA photographer Dorothea Lange that capture the suffering of the depression.

Hoover and Hard Times, 1929–1933

Why was Hoover reluctant to implement relief programs during the Great Depression?

By the early 1930s, as the depression deepened, tens of millions of Americans were desperately poor. In cities, the hungry lined up at soup kitchens; some scratched through garbage cans for food. In West Virginia and Kentucky, widespread hunger and limited resources led the American Friends Service Committee to distribute food only to those weighing 10 percent below the normal weight for their height. In November 1932, *The Nation* told readers that one-sixth of the American population risked starvation.

Families were evicted. The new homeless poured into shantytowns, called "Hoovervilles" in ironic tribute to the formerly popular president. Over a million men took to the road or the rails in search of work. Couples delayed marriage and married people put off having children. In 1933 the birth rate sank below replacement rates. More than a quarter of women ages twenty to thirty during the Great Depression never had children.

Farmers and Industrial Workers

The agricultural sector, which employed almost one-quarter of American workers and missed the good times of the 1920s, was hit hard. As urbanites cut spending and foreign competitors dumped agricultural surpluses into the global market, farm prices hit bottom. Farmers tried to compensate by producing more, thus adding to the surplus and further depressing prices. By 1932, a bushel of wheat that cost North Dakota farmers 77 cents to produce brought only 33 cents. Cash-strapped farmers could not pay property taxes or mortgages. Banks foreclosed. In Mississippi, on a single day in April 1932 approximately one-fourth of the states' farmland was auctioned to meet debts. By the middle of the decade, the Dust Bowl would also drive thousands of farmers from their land.

America's industrial workers had seen their standard of living improve during the 1920s, and their consumer spending bolstered the nation's economic growth. But as incomes declined, sales of manufactured goods plummeted and factories closed—more than seventy thousand went out of business by 1933. As car sales dropped from 4.5 million in 1929 to 1 million in 1933, Ford laid off more than two-thirds of its Detroit workers. Almost one-quarter of industrial workers were unemployed, and those with jobs saw the average wage fall by almost one-third.

Marginal Workers

For workers on the lowest rungs of the employment ladder, the depression was crushing. In the South, where African Americans faced the greatest discrimination, jobs that white men had considered below their dignity—bellhop, garbage collector—seemed suddenly

Chronology

1929 Stock market crash (October); Great Depression begins	Indian Reorganization (Wheeler-Howard) Act restores lands to tribal ownership
1930 Hawley-Smoot Tariff raises rates on imports	**1935** National Labor Relations (Wagner) Act guarantees workers' right to unionize
1931 "Scottsboro Boys" arrested in Alabama	Social Security Act establishes insurance for the aged, the unemployed, and needy children
1932 Banks fail throughout nation	Works Progress Administration (WPA) creates jobs in public works projects
Bonus Army marches on Washington	Revenue (Wealth Tax) Act raises taxes on business and the wealthy
Hoover's Reconstruction Finance Corporation tries to stabilize banks, insurance companies, railroads	**1936** 9 million Americans unemployed
Roosevelt elected president	United Auto Workers win sit-down strike against General Motors
1933 13 million Americans unemployed	**1937** Roosevelt's court-packing plan fails
"First Hundred Days" of Roosevelt administration offer major legislation for economic recovery and poor relief	Memorial Day massacre of striking steelworkers
National bank holiday halts run on banks	"Roosevelt recession" begins
Agricultural Adjustment Act (AAA) encourages decreased farm production	**1938** 10.4 million Americans unemployed
National Industrial Recovery Act (NIRA) attempts to spur industrial growth	80 million movie tickets sold each week
Tennessee Valley Authority (TVA) established	**1939** Marian Anderson performs at Lincoln Memorial
1934 Long starts Share Our Wealth Society	Social Security amendments add benefits for spouses and widows
Townsend proposes old-age pension plan	

desirable. In 1930, a short-lived fascist-style organization, the Black Shirts, recruited forty thousand members with the slogan "No Jobs for Niggers Until Every White Man Has a Job!" And as industry cut production in the North, blacks were typically the first fired. By 1932, African American unemployment reached almost 50 percent.

Mexican Americans and Mexican nationals in the Southwest were also hit hard. Their wages on California farms fell from a miserable 35 cents an hour in 1929 to 14 cents an hour by 1932. Throughout the Southwest, campaigns against "foreigners" hurt Mexican immigrants and American citizens of Hispanic descent whose families had lived in the Southwest for centuries, long before the land belonged to the United States. In 1931, the Labor Department announced plans to deport illegal immigrants to free jobs for Americans. This policy fell hardest on people of Mexican origin. Even those who immigrated legally often lacked full documentation. The U.S. government deported eighty-two thousand Mexicans between 1929 and 1935. Almost half a million people repatriated to Mexico during the 1930s. Some left voluntarily, but many were tricked into believing they had no choice.

Even before the economic crisis, women of all classes and races were barred from many jobs and paid significantly less than men. Most Americans believed that men should be breadwinners and women homemakers and worried that women who worked took jobs from men. In fact, men laid off from U.S. Steel would not have been hired as secretaries, "salesgirls," or maids. Nonetheless, when a 1936 Gallup poll asked whether wives should work if their husbands had jobs, 82 percent of respondents (including 75 percent of the women) answered no. Such beliefs influenced policy. In 1930 and 1931, 77 percent of urban school systems refused to hire married women as teachers.

The depression had a mixed impact on women workers. At first, women workers lost jobs faster than men. Women in low-wage manufacturing jobs were laid off before male employees. Almost one-quarter of domestic workers—many of them African American—lost jobs as middle class families economized. Despite discrimination and a poor economy, however, women's employment increased during the 1930s. "Women's jobs," such as teaching and clerical work, were not hit as hard as "men's jobs" in heavy industry, and women increasingly sought employment to keep their families afloat. Still, by 1940 only 15.2 percent of married women were employed.

Middle-Class Workers and Families

Although unemployment climbed to 25 percent, most Americans did not lose homes or jobs during the depression. Professional and white-collar workers fared better than industrial workers and farmers. Many middle-class families, however, "made do" with less. Women economized, using cheap ingredients to extend food further ("Cracker-Stuffed Cabbage"). Although most families' incomes fell, the impact was cushioned by the falling cost of consumer goods. Men who could no longer provide well for their families often deemed themselves "failures." But even for the relatively affluent, the psychological impact of the depression was inescapable. The human toll of the depression was visible everywhere, and no one took economic security for granted any more.

Hoover's Limited Solutions

Although **Herbert Hoover**, "the Great Engineer," had a reputation as a problem solver, no one, including Hoover, knew what to do about the crisis. Experts disagreed about the depression's causes and about potential solutions. Many business leaders believed financial panics and depressions, though painful, were part of a natural "business cycle." Economic depressions, according to this theory, brought down inflated prices and cleared the way for real growth.

Herbert Hoover: 31st President of the United States, 1929–1933.

Herbert Hoover disagreed. "The economic fatalist," he said, "believes that these crises are inevitable.... I would remind these pessimists that exactly the same thing was once said of typhoid, cholera, and smallpox." Hoover had faith in "associationism": business and professional organizations, coordinated by the federal government, uniting to solve the nation's problems. The federal government would serve as a clearing-house for ideas that state and local governments and private industry could voluntarily implement.

While many Americans thought Hoover was doing nothing, in truth he stretched his beliefs about the role of government to their limit. He tried voluntarism, exhortation, and limited government intervention. First, he sought voluntary pledges from business groups to keep wages stable and renew investment. But when businesspeople looked at their own bottom lines, few could honor those promises.

As unemployment climbed, Hoover continued to encourage voluntary responses, creating the President's Organization on Unemployment Relief (POUR) to generate private contributions to aid the destitute. Although 1932 saw record charitable contributions, they were inadequate. By mid-1932, one-quarter of New York's private charities, funds exhausted, closed their doors. State and city officials found their treasuries drying up, too. Hoover feared that government "relief" would destroy self-reliance in the poor. Thus, he authorized federal funds to feed the drought-stricken livestock of Arkansas farmers but rejected a smaller grant providing food for impoverished farm families. Many Americans became angry at Hoover's seeming insensitivity. Two short years after his election, Hoover was the most hated man in America.

Hoover eventually endorsed limited federal action to combat the crisis, but it was too little. Federal public works projects, such as the Grand Coulee Dam in Washington, created some jobs. The Federal Farm Board, established in 1929, supported crop prices by lending money to cooperatives to buy crops and keep them off the market. But the board ran short of money, and unsold surpluses jammed warehouses.

Hoover also signed into law the Hawley-Smoot Tariff (1930) to support American farmers and manufacturers by raising import duties to a staggering 40 percent. Instead, it hampered international trade as other nations created their own protective tariffs. And, as other nations sold less to the United States, they had less money to repay their U.S. debts or buy American products. Fearing the collapse of the international monetary system, Hoover in 1931 announced a moratorium on the payment of First World War debts and reparations.

In January 1932, the administration took its most forceful action. The **Reconstruction Finance Corporation** (RFC) provided federal loans to banks, insurance companies, and railroads, which Hoover hoped would shore up those industries and halt the disinvestment in the American economy. Here, Hoover compromised his ideological principles. This was direct government intervention, not "voluntarism." If he would support direct assistance to private industries, why not relief to the millions of unemployed?

Reconstruction Finance Corporation: Agency set up under the Hoover administration during the Great Depression to make loans to shore up banks and other industries.

Protest and Social Unrest

More and more Americans asked that question. Social unrest and violence surfaced as the depression deepened. This raised the specter of popular revolt, and Chicago mayor Anton Cermak told Congress that if the federal government did not send his citizens aid, it would have to send troops instead.

Tens of thousands of farmers took the law into their own hands. Angry crowds forced auctioneers to accept just a few dollars for foreclosed property, and then returned it to the original owners. In August 1932, a new group, the Farmers' Holiday Association, encouraged farmers to hold back agricultural products to limit supply and drive prices up. In the Midwest, farmers barricaded roads to stop other farmers' trucks, and then dumped the contents in roadside ditches. In cities, the most militant actions came from Unemployed Councils, local groups for unemployed workers that were created and led by Communist Party members. Communist leaders believed that the depression demonstrated capitalism's failure and offered an opportunity for revolution. Few of the quarter-million Americans joining the local Unemployed Councils sought revolution, but they did demand

National Archives

In the summer of 1932, unemployed veterans of the First World War gathered in Washington, D.C. to demand payment of their soldiers' bonuses. After Congress rejected the appeal of the "Bonus Army," some refused to leave and President Hoover sent U.S. Army troops to force them out. Here, police battle Bonus Marchers in July 1932.

action. When three thousand members of Detroit Unemployment Councils marched on Ford's River Rouge plant in 1932, Ford security guards opened fire on the crowd, killing four men and wounding fifty. As social unrest spread, so did racial violence. Vigilante committees offered bounties to force African Americans off the Illinois Central Railroad's payroll: $25 for maiming and $100 for killing black workers. Ten men were murdered and at least seven wounded. The Ku Klux Klan reemerged, and white mobs tortured, hanged, and mutilated thirty-eight black men during the depression's early years. Racial violence was not restricted to the South; lynchings took place in Pennsylvania, Minnesota, Colorado, and Ohio as well.

Bonus Army   The worst confrontation happened in summer 1932. More than fifteen thousand unemployed World War I veterans and their families converged on the nation's capital as Congress debated a bill authorizing immediate payment of cash "bonuses" that veterans were scheduled to receive in 1945. Calling themselves the Bonus Army, they set up a sprawling "Hooverville" shantytown across the river from the Capitol. Concerned about the impact on the federal budget, President Hoover opposed the bonus bill, and the Senate voted it down.

Most of the Bonus Marchers left Washington, but several thousand stayed. Calling them "insurrectionists"—though many were simply destitute—the president set a deadline for their departure. On July 28, Hoover sent in the U.S. Army, led by General Douglas MacArthur. Four infantry companies, four troops of cavalry, a machine gun squadron, and six tanks converged on the veterans and their families. What followed shocked Americans: men and women chased by horsemen; children tear-gassed; shacks set afire. Hoover was unrepentant, insisting in a campaign speech, "Thank God we still have a government that knows how to deal with a mob."

As the depression worsened, the appeal of a strong leader—someone who would take decisive action—grew. In February 1933, the U.S. Senate passed a resolution calling for newly elected president **Franklin D. Roosevelt** to assume "unlimited power." The rise to power of Hitler and his National Socialist Party in depression-ravaged Germany was an obvious parallel.

Franklin D. Roosevelt: 32nd President of the United States, 1933–1945.

Franklin D. Roosevelt and the Launching of the New Deal

How did the federal government take on new roles during the period dubbed "The First Hundred Days"?

In the 1932 presidential campaign, Democratic challenger Franklin Delano Roosevelt insisted that the federal government had to play a greater role. Roosevelt supported direct relief payments for the unemployed, declaring that such governmental aid was "a matter of social duty." He pledged "a new deal for the American people," though he was never very explicit about its outlines. His most concrete proposals, in fact, were sometimes contradictory. But Roosevelt committed to use the power of the federal government to combat the paralyzing economic crisis. Voters chose Roosevelt over Hoover overwhelmingly.

Franklin Roosevelt, the twentieth-century president most beloved by America's "common people," was born into upper-class privilege. After graduating from Harvard College and Columbia Law School, he married **Eleanor Roosevelt**, Theodore Roosevelt's niece and his own fifth cousin, once removed. He served in the New York State legislature, was appointed assistant secretary of the navy by Woodrow Wilson, and, at age thirty-eight, ran for vice president in 1920 on the Democratic Party's losing ticket.

Eleanor Roosevelt: Widely popular and influential First lady of the United States from 1933 to 1945.

In 1921, Roosevelt was stricken with polio and was bedridden for two years. He lost the use of his legs but gained, according to his wife Eleanor, a new strength of character. By 1928, Roosevelt was sufficiently recovered to run for—and win—the governorship of New York, and then to accept the Democratic Party's presidential nomination in 1932.

Elected in November 1932, Roosevelt would not take office until March 4, 1933. (The Twentieth Amendment to the Constitution shifted future inaugurations to January 20.) In this long interregnum, the American banking system reached the verge of collapse.

Banking Crisis

The origins of the banking crisis lay in the flush years of World War I and the 1920s, when American banks made risky loans. After real-estate and stock market bubbles burst in 1929 and agricultural prices collapsed, these loans soured, leaving many banks without sufficient funds to cover customers' deposits. Fearful of losing their savings, depositors withdrew money from banks and put it into gold or under mattresses.

"Bank runs," in which crowds of frightened customers demanded their money, became common.

By the 1932 election, the bank crisis was escalating rapidly. Hoover, the lame-duck president, refused to take action without Roosevelt's support, while Roosevelt refused to endorse actions he could not control. By Roosevelt's inauguration on March 4, every state had either suspended banking operations or restricted depositors' access to their money. The new president understood that the total collapse of the U.S. banking system would threaten the nation's survival.

Roosevelt vowed in his inaugural address to face the crisis "frankly and boldly." The lines best remembered from his speech are words of comfort: "the only thing we have to fear is fear itself—nameless, unreasoning, unjustified terror." But the only loud cheers came when Roosevelt asserted that, if need be, "I shall ask the Congress for the one remaining instrument to meet the crisis—broad Executive power to wage a war against the emergency, as great as the power that would be given to me if we were in fact invaded by a foreign foe."

The next day Roosevelt, using powers legally granted by the World War I Trading with the Enemy Act, closed the nation's banks for a four-day "holiday" and summoned Congress to an emergency session. He introduced the Emergency Banking Relief Bill, which was passed sight unseen by unanimous House vote, approved 73 to 7 in the Senate, and immediately signed into law. It provided federal authority to reopen solvent banks and reorganize the rest, and authorized federal money to shore up private banks. Roosevelt had attacked "unscrupulous money changers," and critics of the failed banking system hoped he planned to remove the banks from private hands. Instead, Roosevelt's banking policy was like Hoover's—a fundamentally conservative approach that upheld the status quo.

The banking bill could save the U.S. banking system only if Americans were confident enough to deposit money in the reopened banks. In the first of his radio "Fireside Chats," Roosevelt asked Americans for support. The next morning when banks opened, people lined up to deposit money. It was an enormous triumph for the new president. It also demonstrated that Roosevelt, though unafraid to take bold action, was not as radical as some wished or as others feared.

Link to the video and transcript of FDR's first inaugural address.

First Hundred Days

During the ninety-nine-day-long special session of Congress, dubbed by journalists "The First Hundred Days," the federal government took on dramatically new roles. Roosevelt, aided by advisers—lawyers, university professors, and social workers collectively nicknamed "the Brain Trust"—and by the capable First Lady, sought to revive the American economy. These "New Dealers" had no single plan, and Roosevelt fluctuated between balancing the budget and massive deficit spending (spending more than is taken in in taxes and borrowing the difference). But with a mandate for action and the support of a Democrat-controlled Congress, the new administration produced a flood of legislation. Two basic strategies emerged during the First Hundred Days. New Dealers experimented with national economic planning, and they created a range of "relief" programs for the needy.

National Industrial Recovery Act

At the heart of the New Deal experiment were the **National Industrial Recovery Act (NIRA)** and the **Agricultural Adjustment Act (AAA)**. The NIRA was based on the belief

National Industrial Recovery Act (NIRA): Agency that brought together business leaders to draft codes of "fair competition" for their industries. These codes recognized workers' rights to establish unions, set production limits, prescribed wages and working conditions, and forbade pricecutting and unfair competitive practices.

Agricultural Adjustment Act (AAA): New Deal program that sought to curb the surplus farm production that depressed crop prices by offering payments for reducing production of seven farm products.

National Recovery Administration: Agency responsible for administering the National Industrial Recovery Act and establishing fair-trade codes for industries with the goal of stimulating the economy.

that "destructive competition" worsened industry's economic woes. Skirting anti-trust regulation, the NIRA authorized competing businesses to cooperate in crafting industrywide codes that allowed manufacturers to establish industry-wide prices and wages. With wages and prices stabilized, the theory went, consumer spending would increase, thus allowing industries to rehire workers. Significantly, Section 7(a) guaranteed industrial workers the right to "organize and bargain collectively"—in other words, to unionize. Individual businesses' participation in this **National Recovery Administration** (NRA) program was voluntary, so though it was larger than previous government–private sector cooperation, it was not very different from Hoover-era "associationalism."

As small-business owners feared, big business dominated the NRA-mandated cartels. NRA staff lacked the experience to stand up to corporate representatives. The twenty-six-year-old NRA staffer who oversaw the creation of the petroleum industry code was "helped" by twenty highly paid oil industry lawyers. The majority of the 541 codes approved by the NRA reflected the interests of major corporations, not small-business owners, labor, or consumers. Fundamentally, the NRA did not deliver economic recovery. In 1935, the Supreme Court ended the fragile, floundering system when it ruled that the NRA extended federal power past its constitutional bounds.

Agricultural Adjustment Act

The Agricultural Adjustment Act (AAA) had a more enduring effect. Establishing a national system of crop controls, it offered subsidies to farmers who agreed to limit production of specific crops. (Overproduction drove crop prices down.) In 1933, the nation's farmers destroyed 8.5 million piglets and plowed under crops in the fields. Millions of hungry Americans found it difficult to understand this waste of food.

Government crop subsidies proved a disaster for tenant farmers and sharecroppers, who were turned off their land as landlords cut production. In the South, the number of sharecropper farms dropped by almost one-third between 1930 and 1940 and dispossessed farmers—many of them African American—headed to cities and towns. But the subsidies did help many. In the Dakotas, government payments accounted for almost three-quarters of the total farm income for 1934.

In 1936, the Supreme Court found that the AAA, like the NRA, was unconstitutional. But the AAA (unlike the NRA) was too popular with its constituency, American farmers, to disappear. The legislation was rewritten to meet the Supreme Court's objections, and farm subsidies continued into the twenty-first century.

Relief Programs

Roosevelt moved quickly to implement poor relief: $3 billion in federal dollars were allocated in 1935. New Dealers—like many other Americans—disapproved of direct relief payments. Thus, New Deal programs emphasized "work relief." By January 1934, the Civil Works Administration hired 4 million people, most earning $15 a week. And the **Civilian Conservation Corps** (CCC) paid unmarried young men $1 a day to do hard outdoor labor: building dams and reservoirs, creating trails in national parks. By 1942, the CCC employed 2.5 million men, including eighty thousand Native Americans working on western Indian reservations.

Work relief programs rarely included poor women. Mothers of young children were usually classified as "unemployable" and offered "mother's-aid" grants that,

Civilian Conservation Corps: Relief program that employed jobless young men in such government projects as reforestation, park maintenance, and erosion control.

as historian Linda Gordon explains, were miniscule compared to wages in federal works programs. While federal relief programs rejected the poor-law tradition that distinguished between the "deserving" and the "undeserving" poor, local officials did not. Journalist Lorena Hickok reported to Harry Hopkins that "a woman who isn't a good housekeeper is apt to have a pretty rough time of it."

The **Public Works Administration** (PWA), created by Title II of the National Industrial Recovery Act, appropriated $3.3 billion for PWA projects in 1933. New Deal public works programs built infrastructure nationwide, especially in underdeveloped regions.

But the PWA's main purpose was to pump federal money into the economy. As federal revenues for 1932 had totaled only $1.9 billion, this huge appropriation shows that the Roosevelt administration was willing to use the controversial technique of deficit spending to stimulate the economy.

In the three months until Congress adjourned on June 16, 1933, Roosevelt delivered fifteen messages proposing major legislation, and Congress passed fifteen significant laws (see Table 25.1). The United States rebounded from near collapse. As New Deal programs were implemented, unemployment fell steadily from 13 million in 1933 to 9 million in 1936. Farm prices rose, along with wages and salaries, and business failures abated (see Figure 25.1).

> **Public Works Administration:** New Deal relief agency that appropriated $3.3 billion for large-scale public works projects to provide jobs and stimulate the economy.

TABLE 25.1 New Deal Achievements

Year	Labor	Agriculture and Environment	Business and Industrial Recovery	Relief	Reform
1933	Section 7(a) of NIRA	Agricultural Adjustment Act Farm Credit Act	Emergency Banking Relief Act Economy Act Beer-Wine Revenue Act Banking Act of 1933 (guaranteed deposits) National Industrial Recovery Act	Civilian Conservation Corps Federal Emergency Relief Act Home Owners Refinancing Act Public Works Administration Civil Works Administration	TVA Federal Securities Act
1934	National Labor Relations Board	Taylor Grazing Act			Securities Exchange Act
1935	National Labor Relations (Wagner) Act	Resettlement Administration Rural Electrification Administration		Works Progress Administration National Youth Administration	Social Security Act Public Utility Holding Company Act Revenue Act (wealth tax)
1937		Farm Security Administration		National Housing Act	
1938	Fair Labor Standards Act	Agricultural Adjustment Act of 1938			

Source: Adapted from Charles Sellers, Henry May, and Neil R. McMillen, *A Synopsis of American History*, 6th ed. Copyright © 1985 by Houghton Mifflin Company. Reprinted by permission.

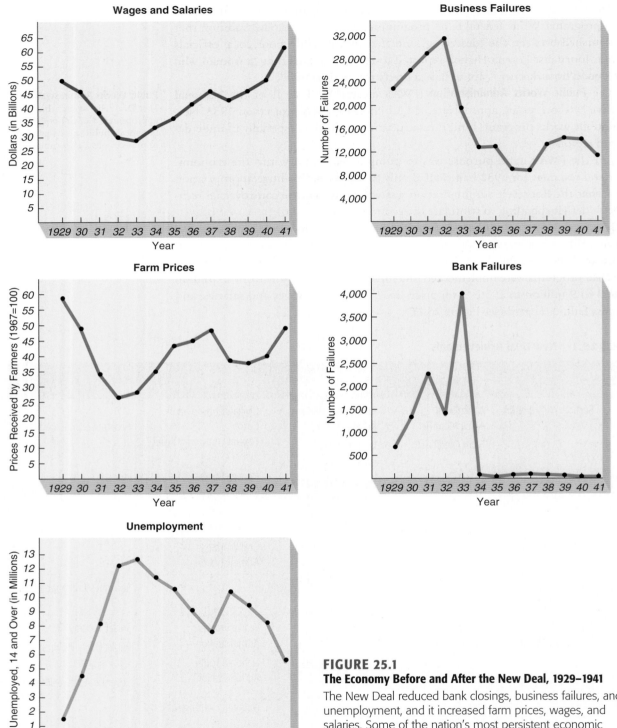

FIGURE 25.1

The Economy Before and After the New Deal, 1929–1941

The New Deal reduced bank closings, business failures, and unemployment, and it increased farm prices, wages, and salaries. Some of the nation's most persistent economic problems, however, did not disappear until the advent of the Second World War.

Political Pressure and the Second New Deal

The unprecedented popular and congressional support for Roosevelt's New Deal did not last. The seeming unity of the First Hundred Days masked deep divides within the nation, and once the immediate crisis was averted the struggle over solutions began. Some tried to stop the expansion of government power, others pushed for increased governmental action to combat continuing poverty and inequality.

What were the hallmarks of the Second New Deal?

Business Opposition

As the economy partially recovered, many wealthy business leaders criticized the New Deal. They condemned government regulation and taxation, along with the use of deficit financing for public works. In 1934, several corporate leaders joined former presidential candidate Al Smith and disaffected conservative Democrats to establish the American Liberty League to campaign against New Deal "radicalism." Hoping to turn southern whites against the New Deal and splinter the Democratic Party, the Liberty League also secretly channeled funds to a racist group in the South, which tried to foster protest by circulating pictures of the First Lady with African Americans.

Demagogues and Populists

Other Americans (sometimes called "populists") thought the government favored business over the people. Unemployment decreased—but 9 million people were still jobless. In 1934, a wave of strikes involving 1.5 million workers hit the nation. In 1935, enormous dust storms enveloped the southern plains, killing livestock and driving families like the Montgomerys from their land. As their dissatisfaction mounted, so did the appeal of various demagogues, who played to people's prejudices.

Father Charles Coughlin, a Roman Catholic priest whose weekly radio sermons reached 30 million listeners, spoke to those who felt they had lost control of their lives to distant elites. Increasingly anti–New Deal, he was also anti-Semitic, telling listeners that an international conspiracy of Jewish bankers caused their problems.

Another challenge came from Dr. Francis E. Townsend, a public health officer in Long Beach, California, who lost his job at age sixty-seven with only $100 in savings. His situation was common. With social welfare left to the states, only about 400,000 of the 6.6 million elderly Americans received any state-supplied pensions. As employment and savings disappeared, many older people fell into poverty. Townsend proposed that Americans over age sixty should receive a government pension of $200 a month, financed by a new "transaction" (sales) tax. Townsend's plan was fiscally impossible (almost three-quarters of working Americans earned $200 a month or less) and profoundly regressive (because sales tax rates are the same for everyone, they take a larger share of income from those who earn least). Nonetheless, 20 million Americans, or 1 in 5 adults, signed petitions supporting this plan.

Then there was Huey Long, perhaps the most successful populist demagogue in American history. As a U.S. senator, Long initially supported the New Deal but soon decided that Roosevelt had fallen captive to big business. In 1934, Long proposed that the government seize (by taxation) all income exceeding $1 million a year and wealth in excess of $5 million per family and use those funds to provide each American family an annual income of $2,000 and a one-time homestead allowance of $5,000. By mid-1935, Long's movement claimed 7 million members, and few doubted that he aspired to the presidency. But Long was killed by a bodyguard's bullet during an assassination attempt in September 1935.

Left-Wing Critics

The political left also gained ground. Socialists and communists alike criticized the New Deal for trying to save capitalism instead of lessening the inequality of power and wealth in America. In California, muckraker and socialist Upton Sinclair won the Democratic gubernatorial nomination in 1934 with the slogan "End Poverty in California" and the left-wing Progressive Party provided seven of Wisconsin's ten representatives to Congress. Even the U.S. Communist Party found new support as it campaigned for social welfare and relief. Disclaiming any intention of overthrowing the U.S. government, the party proclaimed that "Communism Is Twentieth Century Americanism" and cooperated with left-wing labor unions, student groups, and writers' organizations in a "**Popular Front**" against fascism abroad and racism at home. In the late 1920s, it established the League of Struggle for Negro Rights to fight lynching, and from 1931 on provided critical legal and financial support to the "Scottsboro Boys," who were falsely accused of raping two white women in Alabama (see page 673). In 1938, the party had fifty-five thousand members.

Popular Front: Coalition of communist and politically left groups against fascism and racism.

Shaping the Second New Deal

It was not only external critics who pushed Roosevelt to focus on social justice. Due to Eleanor Roosevelt's influence, the president's administration included many progressive activists. **Frances Perkins**, America's first woman cabinet member, came from a social work background, as did Roosevelt's close adviser Harold Ickes. Women social reformers who coalesced around the First Lady played important roles, and African Americans had an unprecedented voice in this White House. By 1936, at least fifty black Americans held relatively important positions in New Deal agencies and cabinet-level departments. Journalists called these officials—who met on Friday evenings at the home of Mary McLeod Bethune, Director of Negro Affairs for the National Youth Administration—the "black cabinet."

Frances Perkins: Served as Secretary of Labor from 1933 to 1945, former Progressive reformer, and first woman cabinet member.

As the election of 1936 neared, Roosevelt knew he had to appeal to seemingly contradictory desires. Americans hit hard by the depression looked to the New Deal for help. Those with a tenuous hold on the middle class wanted security and stability. Still others, frightened by populist promises of people like Long and Coughlin, wanted the New Deal to preserve American capitalism. With this in mind, Roosevelt took the initiative again.

During the period historians call the Second New Deal, Roosevelt introduced progressive programs aimed at providing "greater security for the average man than he has ever known before in the history of America." The first triumph of the Second New Deal was a law that Roosevelt called "the Big Bill." The Emergency Relief Appropriation Act provided $4 billion in new deficit spending, primarily for massive public works programs for the jobless. It also established the Resettlement Administration, which resettled destitute families and organized rural homestead communities and suburban greenbelt towns for low-income workers; the Rural

Electrification Administration, which brought electricity to isolated areas; and the National Youth Administration, which sponsored work-relief programs for young adults.

Works Progress Administration

The largest and best-known program was the **Works Progress Administration** (WPA), later renamed the Work Projects Administration. The WPA employed more than 8.5 million people who built 650,000 miles of highways and roads, and 125,000 public buildings, as well as bridges, reservoirs, irrigation systems, sewage treatment plants, parks, playgrounds, and swimming pools nationwide. WPA workers built or renovated schools and hospitals, operated nurseries for pre-school children, and taught 1.5 million adults to read and write.

The WPA also employed artists, musicians, writers, and actors in cultural programs. The WPA's Federal Theater Project brought vaudeville, circuses, and theater, including African American and Yiddish plays, to cities and towns. Its Arts Project hired painters and sculptors to teach in rural schools and commissioned artists to decorate post office walls with murals depicting American life. Perhaps the most ambitious program, the WPA's Federal Writers' Project (FWP) hired authors such as John Steinbeck and Richard Wright to create guidebooks for every state and write about the people of the United States. More than two thousand elderly former slaves told their stories to FWP writers as "slave narratives." Life stories of sharecroppers and textile workers were published as *These Are Our Lives* (1939). WPA arts projects were controversial, for many of the WPA artists, performers, and writers sympathized with the political struggles of workers and farmers, and some were communists.

The Works Progress Administration commissioned twenty-six artists to create a mural depicting scenes of life in modern California for San Francisco's Coit Tower, which had been completed in 1933. "The Woman with Calla Lilies," a detail from the large fresco that filled the lobby, was painted by Maxine Albro.

Works Progress Administration: Massive public works program that hired people to construct highways, roads, buildings; it also provided jobs for artists, actors, and writers in cultural programs.

Social Security Act

Big Bill programs were part of a short-term "emergency" strategy, but Roosevelt's long-term strategy centered on the **Social Security Act**. This measure created, for the first time, a federal system to provide for the social welfare of American citizens. Its key provision was a pension system in which eligible workers paid Social Security taxes on wages and their employers contributed an equivalent amount; these workers then received federal retirement benefits. The Social Security Act also created welfare programs, including a cooperative federal-state system of unemployment compensation and Aid to Dependent Children (later renamed Aid to Families with Dependent Children, AFDC) for needy children in families without fathers present.

Social Security Act: New Deal relief measure that launched a federal retirement benefits system as well as unemployment compensation, aid to needy children and other welfare benefits.

Compared with the national systems of social security in most western European nations, the U.S. system was fairly conservative. First, the government did not pay for old-age benefits; workers and their bosses did. Second, the tax was regressive in that the more workers earned, the less they were taxed proportionally. Finally, the law did not cover agricultural labor, domestic service, and "casual labor not in the course of the employer's trade or business" (for example, janitorial work at a hospital). Thus, a disproportionately high number of people of color, who worked as farm laborers, domestic servants, or in service jobs, received no benefits. The act also excluded public-sector employees, so many teachers, nurses, librarians, and social workers (mostly women) went uncovered. (Although the original Social Security Act provided no retirement benefits for spouses or widows of covered workers, Congress added these benefits in 1939.) Despite these limitations, the federal government took some responsibility for the economic security of the aged, the temporarily unemployed, dependent children, and people with disabilities.

Link to a transcript of FDR's 1936 Democratic Party nomination acceptance speech.

Roosevelt's Populist Strategies

As the 1936 election approached, Roosevelt adopted the populist language of his critics. Denouncing the "unjust concentration of wealth and power," he proposed that government should "cut the giants down to size" through antitrust suits and heavy corporate taxes. He also supported the Wealth Tax Act, which helped redistribute income (see Figure 25.2).

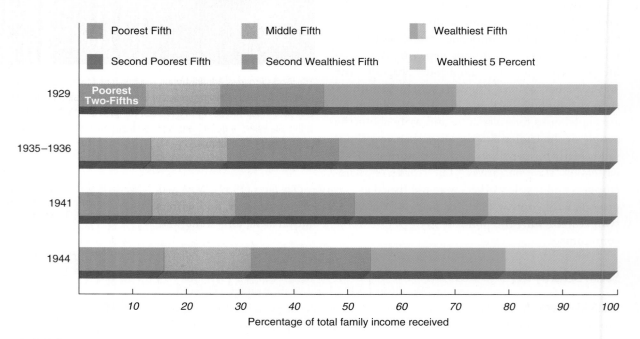

FIGURE 25.2
Distribution of Total Family Income Among the American People, 1929–1944 (percentage)
Although the New Deal provided economic relief to the American people, it did not, as its critics so often charged, significantly redistribute income downward from the rich to the poor.
Source: Adapted from U.S. Bureau of the Census, *Historical Statistics of the United States, Colonial Times to 1970*. Bicentennial Edition, Washington, D.C.: U.S. Government Printing Office, 1975, page 301.

In November 1936, Roosevelt won the presidency by a landslide. Democrats won such huge majorities in the House and Senate that some worried the two-party system might collapse. In fact, Roosevelt and the Democrats had forged a powerful "New Deal coalition," consisting of the urban working class (especially immigrants from southern and eastern Europe), organized labor, the eleven states of the Confederacy (the "Solid South"), and northern blacks. African Americans in northern cities now constituted voting blocs, and New Deal benefits drew them away from the Republican Party, which they had long supported as the party of Lincoln. This New Deal coalition ensured that Democrats would occupy the White House for most of the next thirty years.

Labor

How did Roosevelt provide support for labor?

During the depression's worst years, American workers struggled for the rights of labor. Management, however, resisted unionization, with some refusing to recognize unions and others hiring armed thugs to intimidate workers. When workers walked off the job, employers replaced them with strike-breakers. Workers tried to keep the strikebreakers from crossing picket lines, and the situation often turned violent. Local police or National Guard troops frequently intervened for management. As strikes spread, violence erupted in the steel, automobile, and textile industries, among lumber workers in the Pacific Northwest, and among teamsters in the Midwest.

The Roosevelt administration supported labor with the 1935 **National Labor Relations (Wagner) Act**. It guaranteed workers the right to organize unions and bargain collectively. It outlawed "unfair labor practices," such as firing workers who joined unions, prohibited management from sponsoring company unions, and required employers to bargain with labor's elected union representatives on wages, hours, and working conditions. The Wagner Act created an enforcement mechanism: the National Labor Relations Board (NLRB). By decade's end, the NLRB played a key role in mediating disputes. With federal protection, union membership grew from 3.6 million in 1929 to 7 million in 1938.

National Labor Relations (Wagner) Act: Guaranteed workers the rights to organize and bargain collectively and outlawed unfair labor practices.

The Wagner Act further alienated business leaders from the New Deal. "No Obedience," proclaimed an editorial in a leading business magazine.

Rivalry Between Craft and Industrial Unions

The growth and increasing militancy of the labor movement exacerbated an existing division between "craft" and "industrial" unions. Craft unions represented labor's elite: skilled workers in a particular trade, such as carpentry. Industrial unions represented all the workers, skilled and unskilled, in a given industry. In the 1930s, industrial unions grew dramatically.

Craft unions dominated the American Federation of Labor, the powerful umbrella organization for specific unions. Most AFL leaders offered little support for industrial organizing. Many looked down on industrial workers, disproportionately immigrants from southern and eastern Europe. Skilled workers had economic interests different from those of unskilled workers, and more conservative craft unionists were alarmed at what they saw as the radicalism of industrial unions.

The Women's Emergency Brigade and the General Motors Sit-Down Strike

During the 1937 sit-down strike by automobile workers in Flint, Michigan, a women's "emergency brigade" of wives, daughters, sisters, and sweethearts demonstrated daily at the plant. When police tried to force the men out of Chevrolet Plant No. 9 by filling it with tear gas, the women used clubs to smash the plant's windows and let in fresh air. Sixteen people were injured that day in the riot between police and strikers. The following day the Women's Emergency Brigade marched again. Using this photograph as visual evidence, how did these women attempt to demonstrate the respectability and mainstream nature of their protest? How does that message fit with the clubs several still carry?

© Bettmann/Corbis

Gerenda Johnson, wife of a striker, leads a march past the GM Chevrolet small parts plant on the day following a violent conflict between police and strikers.

Congress of Industrial Organizations: 3.7 million member association of industrial unions; included women and people of color.

In 1935, John L. Lewis, head of the United Mine Workers and the nation's most prominent labor leader, resigned as vice president of the AFL. He and other industrial unionists created the Committee for Industrial Organization (CIO); the AFL then suspended all CIO unions. In 1938, the slightly renamed **Congress of Industrial Organizations** had 3.7 million members, slightly more than the AFL's 3.4 million. Unlike the AFL, the CIO included women and people of color, giving these "marginal" workers greater employment security and the benefits of collective bargaining.

666

Sit-Down Strikes

The most decisive labor conflict came when the United Auto Workers (UAW) demanded recognition from General Motors (GM), Chrysler, and Ford. When GM refused, UAW organizers and workers at the Fisher Body plant in Flint, Michigan, held a "sit-down strike" on December 30, 1936 *inside* the factory. Refusing to leave, they immobilized GM production. GM tried to force them out by turning off the heat. When police tried tear gas; strikers turned water hoses on them.

As the sit-down strike spread to adjacent plants, auto production plummeted. General Motors obtained a court order to evacuate the plant, but the strikers stood firm, risking imprisonment and fines. In a critical decision, Michigan's governor refused to send in the National Guard. After forty-four days, GM agreed to recognize the union, and Chrysler followed. Ford held out until 1941.

Link to songs, photographs, and video from the GM sit-down strike of 1936–1937.

Memorial Day Massacre

On the heels of this triumph, however, came a reminder of the costs of labor's struggle. On Memorial Day 1937, picnicking workers and their families marched toward the Republic Steel plant in Chicago, intending to support strikers picketing there. Police ordered them to disperse. One marcher threw something, and the police attacked. Ten men were killed, seven shot in the back. Thirty marchers were wounded, including a woman and three children. Many Americans, fed up with labor strife and violence, showed little sympathy for the workers.

Gradually violence receded, as the National Labor Relations Board successfully mediated disputes. Unionized workers—about 23 percent of the nonagricultural work force—saw their standard of living rise. By 1941, the average steelworker could afford to buy a pair of shoes for his children every other year.

Federal Power and the Nationalization of Culture

In the 1930s, national media, politics, and the federal government played an increasingly important role in the lives of Americans from different regions, classes, and ethnic backgrounds. In 1930, with the single exception of the post office, Americans had little direct contact with the federal government. By the end of the 1930s, almost 35 percent of the population received some federal government benefit, whether crop subsidies through the federal AAA or a WPA job or relief payments through FERA. Beginning with the New Deal, Americans expected the federal government to play a major role in the life of the nation.

In what ways did the Depression inspire the emergence of a youth culture?

New Deal in the West

The New Deal changed the American West more than any other region, as federally sponsored construction of dams and other public works projects reshaped the region's economy and environment. The Boulder Dam (later renamed for Herbert Hoover) harnessed the Colorado River, providing water to southern California municipalities and using hydroelectric power to produce electricity for Los Angeles and southern Arizona. The water from such dams opened new areas to agriculture and allowed western cities to expand; the cheap electricity they produced attracted industry. After the completion of Washington State's Grand Coulee Dam in 1941, the federal government controlled a great deal of water and hydroelectric power in the region, which effectively meant control over the region's future.

The federal government also brought millions of acres of western land under its control in the 1930s. To combat the environmental disaster of the Dust Bowl and keep agriculture prices from falling further, federal programs worked to limit production. In 1934, the Taylor Grazing Act imposed new restrictions on ranchers' use of public lands for grazing stock. Federal stock reduction programs probably saved the western cattle industry, but they destroyed the Navajos' traditional economy by forcing them to reduce the size of sheep herds on federally protected reservation lands. Large western farms and ranches benefited from federal subsidies and crop supports, but such programs also increased federal government control in the region.

New Deal for Native Americans

New federal activism also extended to the West's people. Previous federal policy toward Native Americans, especially those on reservations, were disastrous. The Bureau of Indian Affairs (BIA) was riddled with corruption; in its attempts to "assimilate" Native Americans, it separated children from parents, suppressed native languages, and outlawed tribal religious practices. Division of tribal lands failed to promote individual land ownership. In the early 1930s, Native Americans were the poorest group in the nation, plagued with an infant mortality rate twice that of white Americans.

In 1933, Roosevelt named one of the BIA's most vocal critics to head the agency. John Collier, founder of the American Indian Defense Agency, meant to completely reverse America's Indian policy. The **Indian Reorganization Act** (1934) worked toward ending forced assimilation and restoring Indian lands to tribal ownership. Indian tribes regained their status as semisovereign nations, guaranteed "internal sovereignty" in matters not limited by acts of Congress.

Indian Reorganization Act: 1934 measure that sought to restore Indian lands to tribal ownership and provided federal recognition of tribes as semisovereign nations.

Some Indians denounced the IRA as a "back-to-the-blanket" measure based on romantic notions of "authentic" Indian culture. The tribal government structure specified by the IRA was culturally alien to tribes such as the Papagos, whose language had no word for "representative." The Navajo nation refused to ratify the IRA. Eventually, however, 181 tribes organized under the IRA, which laid the groundwork for future economic development and limited political autonomy among native peoples.

New Deal in the South

New Dealers did not set out to transform the American West, but they did intend to transform the South, which was long mired in poverty. In 1929, the South's per capita income of $365 per year compared to $921 in the West. More than half of southern farm families were tenants or sharecroppers. Almost 15 percent of South Carolina's people could not read or write.

Tennessee Valley Authority: Ambitious plan of economic development that centered on creating an extensive hydroelectric power project in the poor Appalachian area.

The largest federal intervention in the South was the **Tennessee Valley Authority** (TVA), authorized by Congress during Roosevelt's First Hundred Days. The TVA was created to develop a water and hydroelectric power project similar to the West's multipurpose dams of the West (see Map 25.1). However, confronted with the poverty

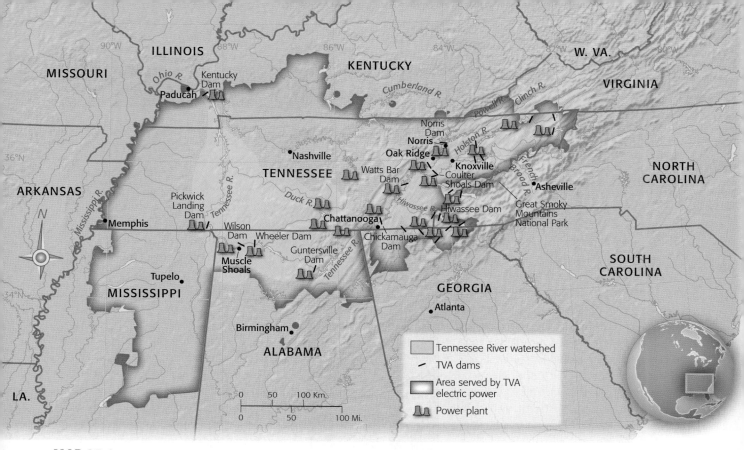

MAP 25.1

The Tennessee Valley Authority

To control flooding and generate electricity, the Tennessee Valley Authority constructed dams along the Tennessee River and its tributaries from Paducah, Kentucky, to Knoxville, Tennessee.

Source: Copyright © Cengage Learning

of the Tennessee River Valley region (which included parts of Virginia, North Carolina, Tennessee, Georgia, Alabama, Mississippi, and Kentucky), the TVA expanded to promote economic development, bring electricity to rural areas, restored fields worn out from overuse, and fight malaria.

Although it benefited many southerners, the TVA proved to be an environmental disaster. TVA strip mining caused soil erosion. Its coal-burning generators released sulfur oxides, which combined with water vapor to produce acid rain. Above all, the TVA degraded the water by dumping untreated sewage, toxic chemicals, and metal pollutants from strip mining into streams and rivers.

Southern senators benefited from federal dollars to their states. But they were also suspicious of federal intervention. When federal action threatened the South's racial hierarchy, they resisted. As the nation's poorest and least educated region, the South would not easily be integrated into the national culture and economy. But New Deal programs began that process and improved the lives of at least some of the region's people.

Mass Media and Popular Culture

America's national popular culture helped break down regional boundaries and foster national connections.

The 1936 Olympic Games

The 1936 Olympic Games, scheduled in Berlin under the Nazi regime, created a dilemma for the United States and other nations. Would participation in the Nazi-orchestrated spectacle lend credence to Hitler? Or would victories by other nations undermine Hitler's claims about the superiority of Germany's "Aryan race"?

From the first modern Olympic Games in 1896, international politics were always near the surface. Germany was excluded in 1920 and 1924 following its World War I defeat. The International Olympic Committee's choice (in 1931) of Berlin for the XI Olympiad was intended to welcome Germany back into the world community. However, with Hitler's rise to power in 1933, Germany determined to use the games as propaganda for the Nazi state. Soon thereafter, campaigns to boycott the Berlin Olympics emerged in several nations, including the United States.

Americans were divided over the boycott. Some U.S. Jewish groups led campaigns against U.S. participation in Berlin, while others took no public position, concerned

Leonard de Selva/Corbis

that their actions might lead to increased anti-Semitic violence within Germany. African Americans opposed the boycott and looked forward to demonstrating in Berlin how wrong Hitler's notions of Aryan superiority were. Some also pointed out the hypocrisy of American officials who criticized Germany while ignoring U.S. discrimination against black athletes.

The United States sent 312 athletes to Berlin; 18 were African Americans who won 14 medals, almost one-quarter of the U.S. total of 56. Track and field star Jesse Owens earned 4 gold medals. Jewish athletes won 13. But German athletes won 89. Despite the controversy, the XI Olympiad was a public relations triumph for Germany. The *New York Times*, impressed by the Germans' hospitality, proclaimed that the XI Olympiad put Germany "back in the fold of nations."

The idealistic vision of nations linked in peaceful athletic competition hit a low point at the 1936 Olympics. The 1940 Olympic Games, scheduled for Tokyo, were cancelled because of the escalating world war.

Corbis-Bettmann

The eleventh summer Olympic Games in Berlin were carefully crafted as propaganda for the Nazi state. And the spectacle of the 1936 games, as represented in the poster above, was impressive. But on the athletic fields, Nazi claims of Aryan superiority were challenged by athletes such as African American Jesse Owens, who is shown at left breaking the Olympic record in the 200-meter race.

Radio filled the days and nights of the depression era. As cheaper models became available, by 1937 people were buying radios at the rate of twenty-eight a minute. By decade's end, 27.5 million households owned radios, and families listened on average five hours a day. Roosevelt used radio to speak directly to the American people with "Fireside Chats."

In a time of uncertainty, radio gave citizens immediate access to political news and the actual voices of elected leaders. During hard times, radio offered escape: for children, the adventures of *Flash Gordon;* for housewives, new soap operas, such as *The Romance of Helen Trent.* Families gathered to listen to the comedy of ex-vaudevillians Jack Benny, George Burns, and Gracie Allen.

Listeners were carried to New York City for performances of the Metropolitan Opera on Saturday afternoons; to the Moana Hotel on the beach at Waikiki through the live broadcast of *Hawaii Calls;* to major league baseball games (begun by the St. Louis Cardinals in 1935) in distant cities. Millions shared the horror of the kidnapping of aviator Charles Lindbergh's son in 1932; black Americans in the urban North and rural South experienced the triumphs of African American boxer Joe Louis ("the Brown Bomber"). Radio lessened isolation and helped create a more homogeneous mass culture across class and regional lines.

The shared popular culture of 1930s America also centered on Hollywood movies. The film industry suffered in the initial years of the depression, but it rebounded after 1933. In a nation of fewer than 130 million people, between 80 and 90 million movie tickets were sold weekly by the mid-1930s, as Americans sought escape at the movies. Comedies were especially popular, from the slapstick of the Marx Brothers to the sophisticated banter of *My Man Godfrey.*

Link to clips from the Marx Brothers' film *Duck Soup.*

Yet as gangster movies (including *Little Caesar* and *Scarface*) drew crowds in the early 1930s, many Americans worried about their glamorization of crime. Faced with a boycott organized by the Roman Catholic Legion of Decency, in 1934 the film industry established a production code that would determine what American film audiences saw—and did not see—for decades.

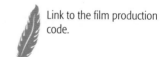

Link to the film production code.

Finally, in an unintended consequence, federal policies to channel jobs to male heads of households strengthened the power of national popular culture. During Roosevelt's first two years in office, 1.5 million youths lost jobs; many young people who would have gone to work at age fourteen in better times decided to stay in school. By decade's end, three-quarters of American youth went to high school—up from one-half in 1920—and graduation rates doubled. As more young people went to high school, more participated in national youth culture, increasingly listening to the same music and adopting similar clothing, dances, and speech. Paradoxically, the hard times of the depression caused youth culture to spread more widely among America's young.

The Limits of the New Deal

Roosevelt began his second term with a strong mandate for reform. Almost immediately, however, the president's actions undermined his New Deal agenda. Labor strife and racial issues divided America. As the world inched toward war, domestic initiatives lost ground to foreign affairs and defense. By late 1938, New Deal reform ground to a halt.

How did Roosevelt undermine his New Deal agenda?

Court-Packing Plan

Following his landslide victory in 1936, Roosevelt sought to safeguard his progressive agenda. He saw the U.S. Supreme Court as its greatest threat. In ruling unconstitutional both the National Industrial Recovery Act (in 1935) and the Agricultural Adjustment Act (in 1936), the Court rejected specific legislative provisions and the expansion of presidential and federal power such legislation entailed. Only three of the nine justices were consistently sympathetic to New Deal "emergency" measures, and Roosevelt was convinced the Court would invalidate most of the Second New Deal legislation. Citing the advanced age and heavy workload of the nine justices, he asked Congress for authority to appoint up to six new justices. But in an era that had seen the rise of Hitler, Mussolini, and Stalin, many Americans saw Roosevelt's plan as an attack on constitutional government. Congress rebelled, and Roosevelt experienced his first major congressional defeat.

Ironically, during the long public debate over court packing, key swing-vote justices began to support pro–New Deal rulings. The Court upheld both the Social Security Act and the Wagner Act (*NLRB v. Jones & Laughlin Steel Corp.*), extending Congress's power to regulate interstate commerce. Moreover, a new judicial pension program encouraged older judges to retire, and the president appointed seven new associate justices. In the end, Roosevelt got what he wanted from the Supreme Court, but the court-packing plan damaged his credibility.

Roosevelt Recession

Another New Deal setback was the recession of 1937–1939, sometimes called the Roosevelt recession. In 1937, confident that the depression had reversed, Roosevelt reduced government spending. The Federal Reserve Board, concerned about a 3.6 percent inflation rate, tightened credit. These two actions sent the economy into a tailspin: unemployment climbed from 7.7 million in 1937 to 10.4 million in 1938.

New Dealers struggled over the direction of liberal reform. Some urged trust-busting; others advocated the resurrection of national economic planning. But Roosevelt instead chose deficit financing to stimulate consumer demand and create jobs. And in 1939, with conflict over the world war that had begun in Europe commanding more U.S. attention, the New Deal came to an end. Roosevelt sacrificed further domestic reforms in return for conservative support for his programs of military rearmament and preparedness.

Election of 1940

No president had served more than two terms, and Americans speculated about whether Franklin Roosevelt would seek a third term in 1940. Roosevelt seemed undecided until spring, when Adolf Hitler's military advances in Europe convinced him to stay on. Roosevelt promised Americans, "Your boys are not going to be sent into any foreign wars."

Roosevelt did not win this election in a landslide, but the New Deal coalition held. Roosevelt again won in the cities, supported by blue-collar workers, ethnic Americans, and African Americans. He also carried every southern state.

Race and the Limits of the New Deal

While the New Deal benefitted many Americans, it fell short of equality for people of color. National programs were implemented locally. In the South, African Americans received lower relief payments than whites and were paid less for WPA jobs. And in Tucson, Arizona, Federal Emergency Relief Agency officials divided applicants into four groups—Anglos, Mexican Americans, Mexican immigrants, and Indians—and allocated relief payments in descending order.

Such discriminatory practices were rooted in racism and served the economic interests of whites/Anglos. The majority of African American and Mexican American workers were paid so poorly that they *earned* less than impoverished whites got for "relief." Why would these workers take low-paying private jobs if government relief or government work programs provided more income? Local communities understood that federal programs threatened a political, social, and economic system based on racial hierarchies.

The case of the Scottsboro Boys illustrates racism in conflicts between local and national power in 1930s America. One night in March 1931, young black and white "hobos" starting fighting on a Southern Railroad freight train as it passed through Alabama. The black youths won and tossed the whites off the train. Afterward, a posse stopped the train, and threw the black youths in the Scottsboro, Alabama, jail. Two white women "riding the rails" claimed that the men raped them. Medical evidence later showed that the women were lying. But within two weeks, eight of the so-called Scottsboro Boys were convicted of rape by all-white juries and sentenced to death. The ninth, a boy of thirteen, was saved from the death penalty by one vote. The case—clearly a product of southern racism—became a cause célèbre, nationally and through the efforts of the Communist Party, worldwide.

The Supreme Court intervened, ruling that Alabama deprived black defendants of equal protection under the law by excluding African Americans from juries and denying defendants counsel. Alabama, however, staged new trials, convicting five of the young men (four would be paroled by 1950, and one escaped from prison). On issues of race, the South would not yield easily to federal power.

© Bettmann/Corbis

Marchers in Washington, D.C. demand freedom for the "Scottsboro Boys," young African American men who were falsely accused and convicted of raping two white women in Alabama in 1931. This 1933 march was organized by the International Labor Defense, the legal arm of the Communist Party of the United States of America, which waged a strong campaign on behalf of the nine young men.

Second, the gains made by people of color under the New Deal were limited by the political realities of southern resistance. For example, in 1938 southern Democrats blocked an antilynching bill with a six-week filibuster in the Senate. Roosevelt refused to use his political capital to break the filibuster and pass the bill. He knew that blacks would not desert the Democratic Party, but without southern senators, his legislative agenda was dead. Roosevelt wanted all Americans to experience democracy, but he had no strong commitment to civil rights.

African American Support

Why, then, did African Americans support Roosevelt and the New Deal? Because, despite discriminatory policies, the New Deal helped African Americans. By 1939, almost one-third of African American households survived on income from a WPA job. African Americans held significant positions in the Roosevelt administration, and the First Lady publically showed her commitment to racial equality. When the Daughters of the American Revolution refused to allow acclaimed black contralto Marian Anderson to perform in Washington's Constitution Hall, Eleanor Roosevelt arranged for Anderson to sing at the Lincoln Memorial instead.

Nonetheless, given the limits of New Deal reform, some African Americans concluded that self-help and direct-action movements were a surer alternative. In 1934, black tenant farmers and sharecroppers joined with poor whites to form the Southern Tenant Farmers' Union. In the North, African American consumers boycotted white merchants who refused to hire blacks. Their slogan was "Don't Buy Where You Can't Work." And the Brotherhood of Sleeping Car Porters, led by A. Philip Randolph, fought for the rights of black workers. Such actions helped improve the lives of black Americans during the 1930s.

An Assessment of the New Deal

Any analysis of the New Deal must begin with Roosevelt himself. Assessments of him varied widely during his presidency: he was passionately hated, and passionately loved. When he spoke to Americans in his Fireside Chats, hundreds of thousands wrote to him, asking for help and offering advice.

Eleanor Roosevelt played an unprecedented role in the Roosevelt administration. As First Lady, she worked for social justice, bringing reformers, trade unionists, and advocates for the rights of women and African Americans to the White House. Sometimes described as the New Deal's conscience, she took public positions—especially on African American civil rights—far more progressive than those of her husband's administration. She served as a lightning rod, deflecting conservative criticism from her husband to herself. And she cemented the allegiance of such groups as African Americans to the New Deal.

Most historians and political scientists consider Franklin Roosevelt a truly great president, citing his courage, his willingness to experiment, and his capacity to inspire the nation. Some, who see the New Deal as a squandered opportunity for true change, charge that Roosevelt lacked vision. They judge Roosevelt by goals that were not his own: Roosevelt was a pragmatist whose goal was to preserve the system. But even critics agree that he transformed the presidency. Some find this troubling, tracing the roots of "the imperial presidency" to the Roosevelt administration.

During his more than twelve years in office, Roosevelt strengthened the presidency and the federal government. Through New Deal programs, the government

Social Security

The New Deal's Social Security system has created a secure old age for millions of Americans. Although Social Security initially excluded some of America's neediest citizens such as farm and domestic workers, amendments expanded eligibility. Today, almost 99 percent of American workers are covered by Social Security. But today's Social Security system faces an uncertain future. Its troubles are due partly to decisions made during the 1930s. President Franklin Roosevelt did not want Social Security to be confused with poor relief. Instead, he created a system financed by payments from workers and employers. This system, however, presented a short-term problem. If benefits came from their contributions, workers who began receiving Social Security payments in 1940 would have received less than $1 a month. Therefore, Social Security payments from current workers paid the benefits of those already retired.

Over the years, this financing system has become increasingly unstable. In 1935, average life expectancy was under sixty-five years, the age one could collect benefits. Today, American men live almost sixteen years past the retirement, and women come close to twenty years past retirement age. In 1935, there were 16 current workers paying into the system for each person receiving benefits. In 2000, there were fewer than 3.5 workers per retiree. Unless the system is reformed, many argue, the retirement of the baby-boom cohort could even bankrupt the system.

While the stock market rose rapidly during the 1990s, some proposed that, because Social Security paid only a fraction of what individuals might have earned by investing their Social Security tax payments in stocks, let Americans do just that. Opponents declared this proposal too risky; others asked if current workers kept their money to invest, where would benefits for current retirees come from? The stock market's huge drop in 2001 and then in 2008 (and the losses sustained by private pension funds) slowed the push for privatization. Nonetheless, with the oldest baby boomers beginning to retire, questions about the future of Social Security remain an important part of the system's legacy.

expanded its regulatory responsibilities, including overseeing the nation's financial systems. For the first time, the federal government offered relief to the jobless and needy and used deficit spending to stimulate the economy. Millions of Americans benefited from government programs still operating today, among them Social Security.

However, as late as 1939, more than 10 million people remained jobless, and the nation's unemployment rate stood at 19 percent. It was not until 1941, as the nation mobilized for war that unemployment declined to 10 percent. By 1944, only 1 percent of the labor force was jobless. World War II, not the New Deal, reinvigorated the American economy.

Summary

In the 1930s, a major economic crisis threatened the nation. By 1933, almost one-quarter of America's workers were unemployed. Millions were hungry or homeless. Herbert Hoover, elected president in 1928, believed that government should play a limited role in managing the economy. He tried to solve the nation's economic problems through "associationalism," a voluntary partnership of businesses and the federal government. In the 1932 presidential election, voters turned to the candidate who promised them a "New Deal," Franklin Delano Roosevelt.

The New Deal was a liberal reform program that developed within America's capitalist and democratic system. It expanded the power of the federal government. New Deal reforms forced banks, utilities, stock markets, farms, and most businesses to adhere to federal rules. The government guaranteed workers' right to join, and federal law required employers to negotiate with workers' unions on wages, hours, and working conditions. Many unemployed workers, elderly and disabled Americans, and dependent children were protected by a national welfare system administered through the federal government. The New Deal had its detractors. Business leaders attacked its new regulations and support of organized labor. As the federal government expanded its role, tensions between national and local authority sometimes flared, and differences in regional social and economic structures challenged policymakers. Both the West and the South were transformed by federal government action, but citizens there were suspicious of federal intervention, and white southerners resisted challenges to the racial system of Jim Crow. The political realities of a fragile New Deal coalition and strong opposition shaped—and limited—New Deal programs. However, the New Deal fundamentally changed the way that the U.S. government would deal with future economic downturns and with the needs of its citizens.

Chapter Review

Hoover and Hard Times, 1929–1933

 Why was Hoover reluctant to implement relief programs during the Great Depression?

Hoover believed in limited government and was afraid that government relief would promote entitlement and weaken self-reliance among the poor. When he made federal funds available to feed livestock, but not people, he was reviled by Americans everywhere. By the time he finally initiated federal jobs programs, it was too late to change public opinion. His public works projects, such as the Grand Coulee Dam, created some jobs, but nowhere near enough to have an impact. While the Federal Farm Board, established in 1929, supported farm prices and lent money to coops, it was poorly funded. Hoover's most direct government program—the Reconstruction Finance Corporation implemented at the end of his presidency in 1932—offered relief to businesses, but still provided no direct relief for the unemployed.

Franklin D. Roosevelt and the Launching of the New Deal

How did the federal government take on new roles during the period dubbed "The First Hundred Days"?

During this special session of Congress held just after his election in 1932, Roosevelt sought to revive the flagging economy through two types of federal initiatives: national economic planning and relief programs. Both would ultimately expand federal power. The planning portion of this "New Deal" focused on the National Industrial Recovery Act (NIRA) and the Agricultural Adjustment Act (AAA). The NIRA encouraged industries to adopt wage and price standards that could erase competition and increase consumer spending and, therefore, demand for workers. The AAA established crop controls and offered farm subsidies. Roosevelt also spent $3 billion on work relief programs, such as the Civilian Conservation Corps, which hired young men to help build dams, reservoirs, and trails in national parks; and the Public Works Administration, whose workers completed the Grand Coulee Dam and built New York City's Triborough Bridge and hundreds of other public facilities. Fifteen laws were passed, helping the United States to recover and unemployment to drop from 13 million in 1933 to 9 million in 1936.

Political Pressure and the Second New Deal

What were the hallmarks of the Second New Deal?

Responding to political pressure, the Roosevelt administration increased direct economic support for hard-hit and vulnerable Americans. The Emergency Relief Appropriation Act allocated $4 billion in deficit spending to provide public works jobs through the Works Progress Administration (WPA)—building roads, bridges, and parks and renovating schools and hospitals. It also implemented initiatives to teach illiterate Americans to read and write and employed artists, writers, and actors. The Resettlement Administration relocated poor families and organized homestead communities, while the Rural Electrification Administration brought electricity to rural areas. The hallmark of the "Second New Deal" was the Social Security Act, which created a federal pension system, unemployment benefits, and welfare for needy families.

Labor

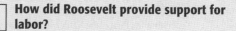

How did Roosevelt provide support for labor?

Labor unrest and dissatisfaction with dwindling wages and harsh working conditions increased throughout the 1930s. Public support for strikes waned as violence escalated throughout the decade. But Roosevelt bolstered labor's rights with the 1935 National Labor Relations (Wagner) Act, which guaranteed workers the right to organize unions and bargain collectively. The Act made it illegal for businesses to fire workers who joined unions and banned management from sponsoring company unions. It also required firms to bargain with union representatives about wages, hours, and working conditions and created a National Labor Relations Board to mediate disputes. As the NLRB took hold, violence dissipated and workers' wages increased.

Federal Power and the Nationalization of Culture

In what ways did the Depression inspire the emergence of a youth culture?

Government policies focused on channeling jobs to the male heads of household. That meant that young boys who, at age 14, under normal economic conditions would have gone to work, could not find jobs. Hence, they stayed in school longer, and high school graduation rates by the end of the decade doubled. As young people spent more time in school, they developed a shared youth culture reflected in shared choices of music, clothing, and behavior.

The Limits of the New Deal

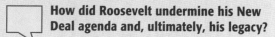

How did Roosevelt undermine his New Deal agenda and, ultimately, his legacy?

Roosevelt made two moves with serious consequences for the New Deal. Concerned that the Supreme Court, which had ruled both the NIRA and the AAA unconstitutional, would also rule against future initiatives, Roosevelt asked Congress to give him the authority to appoint six new justices, arguing that the present nine were getting old and were overworked. Congress refused and, although FDR was able to name seven new associate justices when a new pension program encouraged older judges to retire, his political credibility was damaged by his court-packing scheme. Second, in 1939, with war intensifying in Europe, Roosevelt traded further domestic reform for conservatives' support for military rearmament.

Suggestions for Further Reading

Anthony J. Badger, *The New Deal: The Depression Years, 1933–1940* (1989)

Alan Brinkley, *The End of Reform: New Deal Liberalism in Recession and War* (1995)

Alan Brinkley, *Voices of Protest: Huey Long, Father Coughlin, and the Great Depression* (1982)

Lizabeth Cohen, *Making a New Deal: Industrial Workers in Chicago* (1990)

Blanche Wiesen Cook, *Eleanor Roosevelt, Vols. 1 and 2* (1992, 1999)

Timothy Egan, *The Worst Hard Time* (2005)

Sidney Fine, *Sitdown: The General Motors Strike of 1936–37* (1969)

James E. Goodman, *Stories of Scottsboro* (1994)

David M. Kennedy, *Freedom from Fear: The American People in Depression and War* (1999)

Robert McElvaine, *The Great Depression: America, 1929–1941* (1984)

Donald Worster, *Dust Bowl: The Southern Plains in the 1930s* (2004)

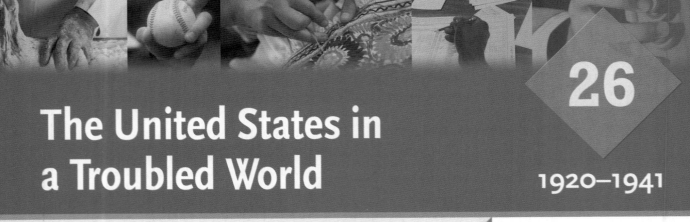

In 1921, the Rockefeller Foundation dedicated several million dollars for projects to control yellow fever in Latin America, beginning in Mexico. Carried by mosquitoes, the virus caused severe headaches, vomiting, jaundice (yellow skin), and often death. Learning from the pioneering work of Carlos Juan Finlay of Cuba, Oswaldo Cruz of Brazil, and U.S. Army surgeon Walter Reed, scientists sought to destroy the mosquito in its larval stage, before it became an egg-laying adult.

U.S. diplomats, military officers, and business executives agreed that the disease threatened public health, which in turn disturbed political and economic order. When outbreaks occurred, ports were closed and quarantined, disrupting trade and immigration. The infection struck American officials, merchants, investors, and soldiers stationed abroad. It incapacitated workers, reducing productivity. Throughout Latin America, insufficient official attention to yellow-fever epidemics stirred public discontent against regimes the United States supported. When the Panama Canal opened in 1914, leaders feared the disease would spread, even reinfecting the United States, which suffered its last epidemic in 1905.

Gradually overcoming strong local anti-U.S. feelings, Rockefeller personnel inspected breeding places and deposited larvae-eating fish in public waterworks. In 1924, La Fundación Rockefeller declared yellow fever eradicated in Mexico. Elsewhere in Latin America, the foundation's antimosquito campaign proved successful in maritime and urban areas but less so in rural and jungle regions. Politically, Rockefeller Foundation efforts in the 1920s and 1930s strengthened central governments by providing a public health infrastructure and diminished anti-U.S. sentiment.

The Rockefeller Foundation's campaign offers insights into Americans' fervent but futile effort to build a stable international order after World War I. Despite the "isolationist" tag sometimes applied to U.S. foreign relations during the interwar decades, Americans remained active in world affairs in the 1920s and

Chapter Outline

Searching for Peace and Order in the 1920s
Peace Groups | Washington Naval Conference | Kellogg-Briand Pact

The World Economy, Cultural Expansion, and Great Depression
Economic and Cultural Expansion | War Debts and German Reparations | Decline in Trade | U.S. Recognition of the Soviet Union

U.S. Dominance in Latin America
American Economic Muscle | Good Neighbor Policy | Clash with Mexican Nationalism

The Course to War in Europe
German Aggression Under Hitler | Isolationist Views in the United States | Nye Committee Hearings | Roosevelt's Evolving Views | Poland and the Outbreak of World War II

VISUALIZING THE PAST *German Blitzkrieg in Poland*

Japan, China, and a New Order in Asia
Jiang Jieshi | Manchurian Crisis | Roosevelt's Quarantine Speech

U.S. Entry into World War II
The German Advance | First Peacetime Military Draft | Atlantic Charter | U.S. Demands on Japan | Surprise Attack on Pearl Harbor | Explaining Pearl Harbor

LINKS TO THE WORLD *Radio News*

LEGACY FOR A PEOPLE AND A NATION
Presidential Deception of the Public

SUMMARY

1930s—from gunboats on Chinese rivers, to negotiations in European financial centers, to marine occupations in Haiti and Nicaragua, to oil wells in the Middle East, to campaigns against diseases in Africa and Latin America. President Wilson rightly said after World War I that the United States had "become a determining factor in the history of mankind."

The most apt description of interwar U.S. foreign policy is "independent internationalism." Notwithstanding the nation's overseas projects—colonies, spheres of influence, naval bases, investments, trade, missionary activity, humanitarian projects—many Americans regarded themselves as isolationists, meaning they wanted no part of Europe's political squabbles, military alliances, or the League of Nations, which might drag them into war. Internationalist-minded Americans—including most senior officials—also wanted to stay out of future European wars but were more willing than isolationists to work to shape the world.

A stable world would better facilitate American prosperity and security. In the interwar years, American diplomats increasingly sought to exercise U.S. power through conferences, humanitarian programs, cultural penetration (Americanization), moral lectures and calls for peace, nonrecognition of disapproved regimes, arms control, and economic and financial ties under the Open Door principle.

But a stable world order proved elusive. Public health projects saved countless lives but could not address the low living standards and staggering poverty of dependent peoples around the globe. World War I debts and reparations bedeviled the 1920s. The Great Depression shattered world trade and threatened America's prominence in international markets. It also spawned political extremism, militarism, and war in Europe and Asia. As Nazi Germany marched to war, the United States adopted a neutrality policy. The United States sought to defend its interests in Asia against Japanese aggression by invoking the Open Door policy.

In the late 1930s, and especially after the outbreak of European war in September 1939, many Americans came to agree with President Franklin D. Roosevelt that Germany and Japan imperiled U.S. interests because they were building self-sufficient spheres of influence on the basis of military and economic domination. Roosevelt first pushed for U.S. military preparedness and then favored aiding Britain and France. A German victory, he reasoned, would destroy traditional economic ties, threaten U.S. influence in the Western Hemisphere, and place at the pinnacle of European power Adolf Hitler, whose ambitions and barbarities seemed limitless.

Meanwhile, Japan seemed determined to dismember America's Asian friend China, to destroy the Open Door principle, and endanger a U.S. colony—the Philippines. To deter Japanese expansion in the Pacific, the United States cut off supplies of vital American products, such as oil. Japan's surprise attack on Pearl Harbor, Hawai'i, in December 1941 brought the United States into World War II.

As you read this chapter, keep the following questions in mind:

* **Why and by what means did Americans try to facilitate a stable world order in the interwar period?**

* **How did the Roosevelt administration respond to the growing Nazi German threat in the second half of the 1930s?**

* **Why did the United States enter World War II?**

Chronology

1921–22	Washington Conference limits naval arms
	Rockefeller Foundation begins battle against yellow fever in Latin America
1922	Mussolini comes to power in Italy
1924	Dawes Plan eases German reparations
1928	Kellogg-Briand Pact outlaws war
1929	Great Depression begins
	Young Plan reduces German reparations
1930	Hawley-Smoot Tariff raises duties
1931	Japan seizes Manchuria
1933	Adolf Hitler becomes chancellor of Germany
	United States extends diplomatic recognition to Soviet Union
	United States announces Good Neighbor policy for Latin America
1934	Fulgencio Batista comes to power in Cuba
1935	Italy invades Ethiopia
	Congress passes first Neutrality Act
1936	Germany reoccupies Rhineland
	Spanish Civil War breaks out

1937	Sino-Japanese War breaks out
	Roosevelt makes "quarantine speech" against aggressors
1938	Mexico nationalizes American-owned oil companies
	Munich Conference grants part of Czechoslovakia to Germany
1939	Germany and Soviet Union sign nonaggression pact
	Germany invades Poland; Second World War begins
1940	Germany invades Denmark, Norway, Belgium, the Netherlands, and France
	Selective Training and Service Act starts first U.S. peacetime draft
1941	Lend-Lease Act gives aid to Allies
	Germany attacks Soviet Union
	United States freezes Japanese assets
	Roosevelt and Churchill sign Atlantic Charter
	Japanese flotilla attacks Pearl Harbor, Hawai'i; United States enters Second World War

Searching for Peace and Order in the 1920s

How did the peace movement influence U.S. foreign policy in the interwar years?

World War I left Europe in shambles. Between 1914 and 1921, Europe suffered tens of millions of casualties from world war, civil wars, massacres, epidemics, and famine. Germany and France lost 10 percent of their workers. The American Relief Administration and private charities delivered food to needy Europeans, including Russians wracked by famine in 1921 and 1922. Through food relief, Americans hoped to dampen any appeal political radicalism might have overseas. Secretary of State Charles Evans Hughes and other leaders expected U.S. economic expansion to promote international stability, believing prosperity would eliminate ideological extremes, revolution, arms races, aggression, and war.

Collective security, as envisioned by Woodrow Wilson (see page 615), elicited little enthusiasm among Republican leaders. Senator Henry Cabot Lodge gloated in 1920 that "we have destroyed Mr. Wilson's League of Nations." Not quite. The Geneva-headquartered League of Nations, envisioned as a peacemaker, proved feeble, not just because the United States did not join but also because members failed to utilize it to settle disputes. Still, starting in the mid-1920s, U.S. officials participated discreetly in League meetings on public health, prostitution, drug and arms trafficking, counterfeiting of currency, and other questions. The Rockefeller Foundation donated $100,000 a year to the League's public health ventures.

Peace Groups

Wilson's legacy was felt in other ways as well. During the interwar years, peace groups worked for international stability and drew widespread public support. Women gravitated to their own organizations because of the popular assumption that women—as nurturing mothers—had a unique aversion to war. Carrie Chapman Catt's moderate National Conference on the Cure and Cause of War, formed in 1924, and the U.S. section of the Women's International League for Peace and Freedom (WILPF), organized in 1915 by Jane Addams and Emily Greene Balch, became the largest women's peace groups. When Addams won the Nobel Peace Prize in 1931, she transferred her award money to the League of Nations.

Peace groups differed over strategies to ensure world order. Some urged cooperation with the League of Nations and the World Court. Others championed arbitration, disarmament and arms reduction, the outlawing of war, and strict neutrality during wars. The WILPF called for an end to U.S. economic imperialism, which it claimed compelled the United States to intervene militarily in Latin America to protect U.S. business interests. The Women's Peace Union (organized in 1921) lobbied for a constitutional amendment requiring a national referendum on a declaration of war. Quakers, YMCA officials, and Social Gospel clergy in 1917 created the American Friends Service Committee to identify pacifist alternatives to warmaking.

Washington Naval Conference

Peace advocates influenced Warren G. Harding's administration to convene the **Washington Naval Conference** of November 1921–February 1922. Delegates from Britain, Japan, France, Italy, China, Portugal, Belgium, and the Netherlands joined a U.S. team led by Secretary of State Charles Evans Hughes to discuss limiting naval armaments. American leaders worried that an expansionist Japan, with the world's third largest navy, would overtake the United States, ranked second behind Britain.

Washington Naval Conference: Multi-national conference led by U.S. Secretary of State Hughes to address the problem of the United States, Great Britain, and Japan edging toward a dangerous (and costly) naval-arms race.

Hughes opened the conference with the stunning proposal to scrap thirty major U.S. ships, totaling 846,000 tons. He urged the British and Japanese delegations to do away with smaller amounts. The final limit was 500,000 tons each for the Americans and the British, 300,000 tons for the Japanese, and 175,000 tons each for the French and the Italians. These limits were agreed to in the Five-Power Treaty, which also set a ten-year moratorium on building capital ships (battleships and aircraft carriers). The governments further pledged not to build new fortifications in their Pacific possessions (such as the Philippines). Next, the Nine-Power Treaty reaffirmed the Open Door in China, recognizing Chinese sovereignty. Finally, in the Four-Power Treaty, the United States, Britain, Japan, and France agreed to respect one another's Pacific possessions. These treaties did not limit submarines, destroyers, or cruisers, nor did they provide enforcement powers for the Open Door. Still, Hughes achieved arms limitation and improved America's strategic position vis-à-vis Japan in the Pacific.

Kellogg-Briand Pact

Peace advocates also welcomed the Locarno Pact of 1925, a set of agreements among European nations that sought to reduce tensions between Germany and France, and the Kellogg-Briand Pact of 1928. In the latter document, sixty-two nations agreed to "condemn recourse to war for the solution of international controversies, and renounce it as an instrument of national policy." The Kellogg-Briand Pact passed the U.S. Senate 85 to 1, but it lacked enforcement provisions. Although weak, it reflected popular opinion that war was barbaric. But arms limitations, peace pacts, and efforts by peace groups and international institutions failed to muzzle the dogs of war, which fed on the economic troubles that upended world order.

The World Economy, Cultural Expansion, and Great Depression

How did the Great Depression help push the world to the brink of war?

While Europe struggled to recover after World War I, the international economy wobbled and then collapsed. The Great Depression set off a political chain reaction that carried the world to war. Cordell Hull, U.S. secretary of state from 1933 to 1944, argued that political extremism and militarism sprang from maimed economies. Hull proved right.

Economic and Cultural Expansion

Because of World War I, the United States became a creditor nation and the financial capital of the world (see Figure 26.1). From 1914 to 1930, private investments abroad grew fivefold, to more than $17 billion. By the late 1920s, the United States produced nearly half of the world's industrial goods and ranked first among exporters ($5.2 billion worth of shipments in 1929). Britain and Germany lost ground to American businesses in Latin America, where Standard Oil operated in eight nations and the United Fruit Company became a huge landowner.

America's economic prominence facilitated the export of American culture. Hollywood movies saturated the global market and stimulated interest in all things American. Although some foreigners warned against Americanization, others aped U.S. mass-production methods and emphasis on efficiency and modernization. Coca-Cola opened a bottling plant in Essen, Germany; Ford built an automobile assembly plant in Cologne.

Adolf Hitler: German chancellor and Nazi dictator whose efforts to restore his nation's prominence included a brutal program to purify it of Jews and others he deemed "inferior race."

Germans marveled at Henry Ford's industrial techniques (*Fordismus*). In the 1930s, Nazi leader **Adolf Hitler** sent German car designers to Detroit before launching the Volkswagen. The Phelps-Stokes Fund further advertised the American capitalist model, exporting to black Africa Booker T. Washington's Tuskegee philosophy of education, while the Rockefeller Foundation supported colleges to train doctors in Lebanon and China and funded medical research in Europe.

The U.S. government assisted this expansion. The Webb-Pomerene Act (1918) excluded from antitrust prosecution those combinations set up for export trade; the Edge Act (1919) permitted American banks to open foreign-branch banks; and the overseas offices of the Department of Commerce distributed market information. The federal government also stimulated foreign loans by American investors. U.S. government support for the expansion of the telecommunications industry helped International Telegraph and Telephone (IT&T), Radio Corporation of America (RCA), and the Associated Press (AP) become international giants by 1930.

War Debts and German Reparations

Some Europeans branded the United States stingy for its handling of World War I debts and reparations. Twenty-eight nations became entangled in inter-Allied government debts totaling $26.5 billion ($9.6 billion of them owed to the U.S. government). Europeans owed private American creditors another $3 billion and urged Americans

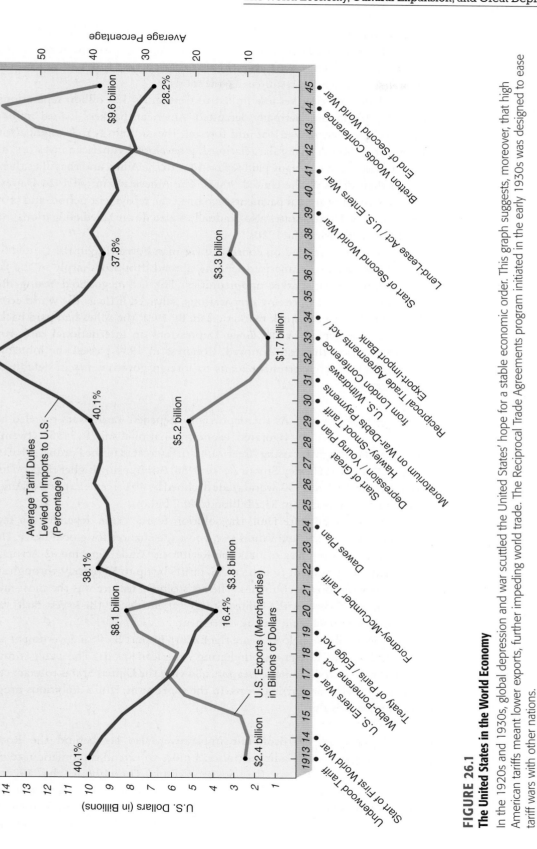

FIGURE 26.1
The United States in the World Economy

In the 1920s and 1930s, global depression and war scuttled the United States' hope for a stable economic order. This graph suggests, moreover, that high American tariffs meant lower exports, further impeding world trade. The Reciprocal Trade Agreements program initiated in the early 1930s was designed to ease tariff wars with other nations.

Source: U.S. Bureau of the Census, *Historical Statistics of the United States, Colonial Times to 1970* (Washington, D.C., 1975).

to erase government debts as a magnanimous contribution to the war effort. During the war, they angrily charged, Europe bled while America profited. American leaders insisted on repayment, some pointing out that the victorious European nations gained vast territory and resources as war spoils.

The debts question became linked to Germany's $33 billion reparations bill. Hobbled by inflation, Germany defaulted. American bankers loaned millions of dollars to keep Germany afloat and forestall the radicalism that might thrive on economic troubles. A triangular relationship developed: American investors' money flowed to Germany, Germany paid reparations to the Allies, and the Allies then paid some of their debts to the United States. The American-crafted 1924 Dawes Plan reduced Germany's annual payments, extended the repayment period, and provided more loans. The United States also gradually scaled down Allied obligations, cutting the debt by half during the 1920s.

But everything hinged on continued German borrowing in the United States, and in 1928 and 1929 American lending abroad dropped sharply in the face of more lucrative stock market opportunities. The U.S.-negotiated Young Plan of 1929, which reduced Germany's reparations, salvaged little as the world economy collapsed following the stock market crash. By 1931, the Allies had paid back only $2.6 billion. Staggered by the Great Depression—an international catastrophe— they defaulted on the rest. Annoyed, Congress in 1934 passed the Johnson Act, which forbade U.S. government loans to foreign governments in default to the United States.

Decline in Trade

As the depression deepened, tariff wars revealed a reinvigorated economic nationalism. By 1932, twenty-five nations retaliated against rising American tariffs (created in the Fordney-McCumber Act of 1922 and the Hawley-Smoot Act of 1930) by imposing higher rates on foreign imports. From 1929 to 1933, world trade declined by 40 percent. Exports of American merchandise slumped from $5.2 billion to $1.7 billion.

For Secretary of State Hull, the solution to the crisis depended on reviving world trade; this he insisted would also boost the chances for global peace. He successfully pressed Congress to pass the Reciprocal Trade Agreements Act in 1934, empowering the president to reduce U.S. tariffs by up to 50 percent through special agreements with foreign countries. The act's central feature was the most-favored-nation principle, whereby the United States was entitled to the lowest tariff rate set by any nation with which it had an agreement.

In 1934, Hull also helped create the Export-Import Bank, a government agency providing loans to foreigners purchasing American goods. The bank stimulated trade and became a diplomatic weapon, allowing the United States to exact concessions by approving or denying loans. In the short term, Hull's ambitious programs brought mixed results.

U.S. Recognition of the Soviet Union

Economic imperatives also lay behind the Roosevelt administration's move to extend diplomatic recognition to the Soviet Union. Throughout the 1920s, the Republicans refused diplomatic relations with the Soviet government, which failed to pay $600 million for confiscated American-owned property and repudiated preexisting Russian debts. Nonetheless, in the late 1920s American businesses, such as

General Electric and International Harvester, entered the Soviet marketplace, and Henry Ford signed a contract to build an automobile plant there. By 1930, the Soviet Union was the largest buyer of American farm and industrial equipment.

Upon becoming president, Roosevelt speculated that closer Soviet-American relations might help the economy while deterring Japanese expansion. In 1933, he granted U.S. diplomatic recognition to the Soviet Union in return for Soviet agreement to discuss its debts and grant Americans in the Soviet Union religious freedom and legal rights.

U.S. Dominance in Latin America

> How was Roosevelt's Good Neighbor policy different from past dealings in Latin America?

Through the Platt Amendment, the Roosevelt Corollary, the Panama Canal, military intervention, and economic preeminence the United States had thrown an imperial net over Latin America in the early twentieth century. U.S. dominance in the hemisphere grew after World War I. A prominent State Department officer patronizingly remarked that Latin Americans were of "low racial quality" and "easy people to deal with if properly managed."

U.S.-made schools, roads, telephones, and irrigation systems dotted Caribbean and Central American nations. American "money doctors" in Colombia and Peru helped reform tariff and tax laws and invited U.S. companies to build public works. Washington forced private high-interest loans on the Dominican Republic and Haiti. Republican administrations curtailed U.S. military intervention in the hemisphere, withdrawing troops from the Dominican Republic (1924) and Nicaragua (1925). But marines returned to Nicaragua in 1926 to end fighting between conservative and liberal Nicaraguans and protect American property. In Haiti, the U.S. troop commitment lasted from 1915 until 1934, with soldiers there to keep pro-Washington governments in power.

PRIVATE WHARF, W. F. McLAUGHLIN & CO., SANTOS, BRAZIL.

© Curt Teich Postcard Archives, Lake County Museum

Among the U.S. companies with large holdings in Latin America in the interwar period was F. W. McLaughlin & Co. of Chicago. Here, workers on a private company wharf in Santos, Brazil, prepare to load coffee for shipment to the United States.

Link to a transcript of FDR's speech at the Inter-American Conference for the Maintenance of Peace in Buenos Airies, 1937.

Good Neighbor policy: Implemented by President Roosevelt, this Latin American policy stated that no nation had the right to intervene in the affairs of another; it substituted direct U.S. intervention with diplomacy and support for various leaders, businesses, and other programs.

Link to a political cartoon of the United States as the Good Neighbor.

American Economic Muscle

By 1929, American investments in Latin America (excluding bonds and securities) totaled $3.5 billion, and U.S. exports dominated the region's trade. Country after country experienced the repercussions of U.S. economic and political decisions. For example, the price that Americans set for Chilean copper determined the health of Chile's economy. Latin American nationalists protested that their resources were being drained away by U.S. companies, leaving many nations in a disadvantageous position. Unapologetic Americans believed they were bringing material improvements and the blessings of liberty to Latin American neighbors. Two years later, a Chilean newspaper warned that the American "Colossus" had "financial might" without "equal in history" and that its aim was "Americas for the Americans—of the North." In the United States, Senator William Borah of Idaho urged that Latin Americans be granted the right to decide their own futures.

Good Neighbor Policy

Renouncing unpopular military intervention, the United States tried new methods to maintain its influence in Latin America: Pan-Americanism (a fifty-year-old concept strengthening ties between North and South America), support for strong local leaders, the training of national guards, economic and cultural penetration, Export-Import Bank loans, financial supervision, and political subversion. Dubbed the **Good Neighbor policy** by Roosevelt in 1933, it meant that the United States would be less blatant in its domination—less willing to defend exploitative business practices and to launch military expeditions and less reluctant to consult with Latin Americans.

Most notably, Roosevelt ordered home the U.S. military forces stationed in Haiti (since 1915) and Nicaragua (since 1912, with a hiatus in 1925–1926), and he restored some sovereignty to Panama and increased that nation's income from the canal. Roosevelt's popularity in Latin America grew when, in a series of pan-American conferences, he joined in pledging that no nation in the hemisphere would intervene in the "internal or external affairs" of any other.

Roosevelt promised more than he was prepared to deliver. His administration continued to support dictators in the region, believing they would preserve U.S. economic interests. When a revolution brought a radical government to power in Cuba in 1933, FDR instructed the American ambassador in Havana to work with conservative Cubans to replace the new government with one friendlier to U.S. interests. With Washington's support, army sergeant Fulgencio Batista took power in 1934.

During the Batista era, which lasted until Fidel Castro ousted Batista in 1959, Cuba protected U.S. investments and aligned itself with U.S. foreign policy. In return, the United States provided military aid and Export-Import Bank loans, abrogated the unpopular Platt Amendment, and gave Cuban sugar a favored position in the U.S. market. American tourists flocked to Havana's nightlife of rum, rhumba, prostitution, and gambling. Nationalistic Cubans protested that their nation had become a mere extension of the United States.

Clash with Mexican Nationalism

In Mexico, Roosevelt again showed the restraint that his predecessors lacked. Since Woodrow Wilson sent troops to Mexico in 1914 and 1916, U.S.-Mexican relations struggled as the two governments wrangled over U.S. economic interests. Still, by 1934 the United States was Mexico's chief trading partner, accounting for 61 percent of

Mexico's imports and taking 52 percent of its exports. That year, however, a new government under Lázaro Cárdenas pledged "Mexico for the Mexicans" and strengthened trade unions to strike against foreign corporations.

In 1937, workers struck foreign oil companies for higher wages and recognition, but the companies, including Standard Oil, rejected union appeals, hoping to send a message across the hemisphere that economic nationalism could never succeed. The following year, the Cárdenas government expropriated the property of all foreign-owned petroleum companies, calculating that the approaching war in Europe would restrain the United States from attacking Mexico. The United States countered by reducing purchases of Mexican silver and promoting a multinational business boycott. But Roosevelt rejected appeals to intervene militarily, fearing that Mexicans would increase oil sales to Germany and Japan. Tense negotiations led to a 1942 agreement whereby the United States conceded that Mexico owned and controlled its raw materials, and Mexico compensated the companies for their lost property.

While the United States remained the dominant power in the hemisphere, the Good Neighbor policy filled Latin Americans with hope that a new era had dawned. The sober-minded nationalists in the region knew that deepening tensions in Europe and Asia might have influenced Washington's restraint. But these threats also created a sense that nations in the Western Hemisphere should stand together.

The Course to War in Europe

On March 5, 1933, one day after Roosevelt's inauguration, Germany's parliament granted dictatorial powers to the new chancellor, Adolf Hitler, leader of the **Nazi Party**. It was a stunning rise to power for Hitler, whose Nazis probably would have remained a fringe party had the Great Depression not hit Germany so hard. Production plummeted 40 percent, and unemployment ballooned to 6 million, meaning that two out of five people were jobless. A disintegrating banking system, which robbed millions of their savings, and widespread German resentment over the Versailles peace settlement fueled mass discontent. While the communists preached a workers' revolution, German businessmen and property owners supported Hitler and the Nazis, believing they could manipulate him once he had thwarted the communists. They were wrong.

Like Benito Mussolini, who gained control of Italy in 1922, Hitler was a fascist. Fascism (called Nazism, or National Socialism, in Germany) celebrated supremacy of the state over the individual, dictatorship over democracy, authoritarianism over freedom of speech, a state-regulated economy over a free market, and militarism over peace. The Nazis vowed to revive Germany, cripple communism, and "purify" the German "race" by destroying Jews and others, such as homosexuals and Gypsies, whom Hitler deemed inferior. The Nuremberg Laws of 1935 stripped Jews of citizenship and outlawed Jewish intermarriage with Germans. Half of all German Jews were without work.

German Aggression Under Hitler Determined to get out from under the Versailles treaty, Hitler withdrew Germany from the League of Nations, ended reparations payments, and began to rearm. While secretly laying plans to conquer neighboring states, he watched admiringly as Mussolini's troops invaded Ethiopia in 1935. The next year, Hitler ordered his troops into the Rhineland, an area demilitarized by the Versailles treaty.

> Why did many Americans support isolationism at the outbreak of World War II?

Nazi Party: National Socialist German Workers' Party founded in Germany in 1919; it rose to prominence under the leadership of Adolf Hitler; stressed facism and anti-Semitism.

Link to excerpts from General Smedley Butler's, "War is a Racket."

In 1936, Italy and Germany formed an alliance called the Rome-Berlin Axis. Shortly thereafter, Germany and Japan united against the Soviet Union in the Anti-Comintern Pact. Britain and France responded with a policy of **appeasement**, hoping to curb Hitler's expansionism by permitting him a few territorial nibbles. Instead, the German leader continually raised his demands.

The Spanish Civil War in 1936 upped the ante for Hitler. Beginning in July, about three thousand American volunteers, known as the Abraham Lincoln Battalion of the International Brigades, joined Spanish Loyalists in defending Spain's elected republican government against Francisco Franco's fascist movement. The Soviet Union also aided the Loyalists. Hitler and Mussolini sent military aid to Franco, who won in 1939, tightening fascism's grip on the European continent.

Early in 1938, Hitler again tested European tolerance when he sent soldiers to annex his birth nation, Austria. In September, he seized the Sudeten region of Czechoslovakia. France and Britain, without consulting the Czechs, agreed to allow Hitler this territorial bite, in exchange for a pledge that he would not take more. British Prime Minister Neville Chamberlain returned home proclaiming, "peace in our time." In March 1939, Hitler swallowed the rest of Czechoslovakia (see Map 26.2).

appeasement: The process of making concessions to pacify, quiet, or satisfy the other party.

Isolationist Views in the United States

Many Americans sought to distance themselves from the tumult by embracing isolationism—which signified abhorrence of war and opposition to U.S. alliances with other nations. Americans learned powerful negative lessons from World War I: that war damages reform movements, undermines civil liberties, dangerously expands federal power, disrupts the economy, and accentuates racial and class tensions. In a 1937 Gallup poll, nearly two-thirds thought U.S. participation in World War I was a mistake.

Conservative isolationists feared higher taxes and increased executive power if the nation went to war. Liberal isolationists worried that domestic problems might go unresolved with increased military spending. Many isolationists predicted that, in attempting to spread democracy, Americans would lose freedoms at home. The vast majority of isolationists opposed fascism, but they did not think the United States should do what Europeans themselves refused to do: block Hitler.

Nye Committee Hearings

A congressional committee headed by Senator Gerald P. Nye held hearings from 1934 to 1936 on the role of business in the U.S. decision to enter World War I. The Nye committee did not prove that American munitions makers dragged the nation into that war, but it uncovered evidence that bribed foreign politicians to bolster arms sales in the 1920s and 1930s.

Isolationists grew suspicious of American business ties with Nazi Germany and fascist Italy. Twenty-six of the top American corporations, including DuPont, Standard Oil, and General Motors, had contracts in 1937 with German firms. After Italy attacked Ethiopia in 1935, American petroleum, copper, scrap iron, and steel exports to Italy increased substantially, despite Roosevelt's call for a moral embargo. Other businesses, such as the Wall Street law firm of Sullivan and Cromwell, severed lucrative ties with Germany to protest the Nazi persecution of Jews.

Reflecting the popular desire for distance from Europe's distress, Roosevelt signed a series of **neutrality acts**. The Neutrality Act of 1935 prohibited arms shipments to either side in a war, once the president declared the existence of belligerency.

neutrality acts: Laws passed in mid-thirties to keep the United States out of any European wars.

The Neutrality Act of 1936 forbade loans to belligerents. The Neutrality Act of 1937 introduced the cash-and-carry principle, which required warring nations to pay cash for nonmilitary purchases and carry goods from U.S. ports in their own ships. The act also forbade Americans from traveling on the ships of belligerent nations.

Roosevelt's Evolving Views
President Roosevelt shared isolationist views in the early 1930s. Although prior to World War I, he was an expansionist and interventionist, during the interwar period he talked more about the horrors of war. In a speech in August 1936 at Chautauqua, New York, Roosevelt appealed to pacifist voters in the upcoming election. The United States, he promised, would remain unentangled in the European conflict. During the crisis over Czechoslovakia in 1938, Roosevelt endorsed appeasement.

Meanwhile, Roosevelt grew troubled by the arrogance of Germany, Italy, and Japan—aggressors he tagged the "three bandit nations." He condemned the Nazi persecution of the Jews and Japan's expansionist actions in East Asia. In November 1938, Hitler launched *Kristallnacht* (or "Crystal Night," named for the shattered glass that littered the streets after the attack on Jewish synagogues, businesses, and homes) and sent tens of thousands of Jews to concentration camps. Shocked, Roosevelt recalled the U.S. ambassador to Germany and allowed fifteen thousand refugees on visitor permits to remain longer in the United States. But he would not break trade relations with Hitler or push Congress to loosen tough immigration laws. Congress rejected all measures, including a bill to admit twenty thousand children under the age of fourteen. Motivated by economic concerns and widespread anti-Semitism, more than 80 percent of Americans supported Congress's decision to uphold immigration restrictions.

Even the tragic voyage of the *St. Louis* did not change government policy. The vessel left Hamburg in mid-1939 carrying 930 desperate Jewish refugees. Denied entry to Havana, the *St. Louis* headed for Miami, where Coast Guard cutters prevented it from docking and forced it to return to Europe. Some refugees took shelter in countries that later were overrun by Hitler's legions.

Quietly, Roosevelt began readying for war. In early 1938 he successfully pressured the House of Representatives to defeat a constitutional amendment that would require a majority vote in a national referendum before a congressional declaration of war could take effect (unless the United States were attacked). Later, in the wake of the Munich crisis, Roosevelt asked Congress for funds to fortify the air force, which he believed essential to deter aggression. In January 1939, the president secretly decided to sell bombers to France. Although these five hundred combat planes did not deter war, French orders spurred the growth of the U.S. aircraft industry.

Hitler's swallowing of Czechoslovakia in March 1939 proved a turning point for Western leaders. Until then, they could explain away Hitler's actions by saying he was only trying to reunite German-speaking peoples. They now realized it would take force to stop him. When Hitler began eyeing Poland, London and Paris stood by the Poles. Undaunted, Berlin signed a nonaggression pact with Moscow in August 1939, including a top-secret protocol that carved eastern Europe into German and Soviet zones, and let the Soviets grab the eastern half of Poland and the three Baltic states of Lithuania, Estonia, and Latvia, formerly part of the Russian Empire.

German *Blitzkrieg* in Poland

World War II in Europe would drag on for almost six years. It began suddenly, however, with Nazi Germany's invasion of Poland in the predawn hours of September 1, 1939. The thundering tanks, the long line of German soldiers, and the headlines all present visual information about the German *blitzkrieg*. Together, these images convey Germany's technological and manpower superiority as well as the momentous consequences of the invasion. Which one speaks to you most powerfully, and why? How would you receive information about an important event like this today?

© Michael Nicholson/Corbis

German propaganda postcard showing Panzer tanks during the blitzkrieg.

STF/AFP/Getty Images

German troops entering Poland after the blitzkrieg.

Hulton Archive/Getty Images

The front page of London's Evening Standard newspaper on September 1, 1939, announcing the German invasion of Poland.

Poland and the Outbreak of World War II

Early on September 1, 1939, German tanks rolled into Poland. German fighter planes covered the advance, thereby launching a new type of warfare, the *blitzkrieg* ("lightning war")—highly mobile land forces and armor combined with tactical aircraft. Within forty-eight hours, Britain and France declared war on Germany.

When Europe descended into war in September 1939, Roosevelt declared neutrality and pressed for repeal of the arms embargo. After much debate, Congress in November lifted the embargo on contraband and approved cash-and-carry exports of arms. Using methods short of war, Roosevelt thus began to aid the Allies. Hitler sneered that a "half Judaized ... half Negrified" United States was "incapable of conducting war."

Japan, China, and a New Order in Asia

How did the United States perceive its interests to be threatened by Japanese expansionism?

Meanwhile, Asia suffered the aggressive march of Japan. The United States had interests at stake in Asia: the Philippines and Pacific islands, religious missions, trade and investments, and the Open Door in China. In missionary fashion, Americans believed they were China's special friend and protector. Pearl Buck's bestselling novel and subsequent film, *The Good Earth* (1931), countered prevailing images of "heathen Chinee" by representing the Chinese as noble peasants. By contrast, the aggressive Japan loomed as a threat to American interests. The Tokyo government seemed bent on subjugating China and unhinging the Open Door doctrine of equal trade and investment.

The Chinese were uneasy about the U.S. presence in Asia and shared Japan's desire to reduce western influence. The 1911 Chinese Revolution still rumbled in the 1920s, as antiforeign riots damaged U.S. property and imperiled American missionaries. Chinese nationalists criticized the American imperialist practice of extraterritoriality (the exemption from Chinese legal jurisdiction of foreigners accused of crimes), and they demanded respect for Chinese sovereignty.

Jiang Jieshi

In the late 1920s, civil war broke out in China when Jiang Jieshi (Chiang Kai-shek) ousted Mao Zedong and his communist followers from the ruling Guomindang Party. Americans applauded this anti-Bolshevism and Jiang's conversion to Christianity in 1930. Jiang's new wife, American-educated Soong Meiling, won their hearts with her flawless English and western fashion. Warming to Jiang, U.S. officials signed a treaty in 1928 restoring control of tariffs to the Chinese.

Japan grew suspicious of U.S. ties with China. In the early twentieth century, Japanese-American relations deteriorated as Japan gained influence in Manchuria, Shandong, and Korea. The Japanese sought to dominate Asian territories that produced the raw materials that their import-dependent island nation required. The Japanese also resented the discriminatory immigration law of 1924, which excluded them from emigrating to the United States. Secretary Hughes called the law "a lasting injury" to Japanese-American relations. Despite the Washington Conference treaties, naval competition continued, as did commercial rivalry. In the United States the importation of inexpensive Japanese goods spawned "Buy America" campaigns and boycotts.

Manchurian Crisis   Relations further soured in 1931 after the Japanese military seized Manchuria from China (see Map 26.1). Larger than Texas, Manchuria served Japan both as a buffer against the Soviets and as a vital source of coal, iron, timber, and food. More than half of Japan's foreign investments rested in Manchuria. Although the seizure of Manchuria violated the Nine-Power Treaty and the Kellogg-Briand Pact, the United States lacked the power to compel Japanese withdrawal, and the League of Nations merely condemned the Tokyo government. The American response came as a moral lecture known as the Stimson Doctrine: the United States would not recognize any impairment of China's sovereignty or of the Open Door policy, Secretary Stimson declared in 1932.

Japan continued to pressure China, triggering the Sino-Japanese War in mid-1937. Japanese forces seized Beijing and several coastal cities. The bombing of Shanghai intensified anti-Japanese sentiment in the United States. To help China by permitting it to buy American arms, Roosevelt refused to declare the existence of war, thus avoiding activation of the Neutrality Acts.

Roosevelt's Quarantine Speech   On October 5, 1937, the president called for a quarantine to curb the "epidemic of world lawlessness." People who thought Washington had been too gentle with Japan cheered, while isolationists warned that Roosevelt was edging toward war.

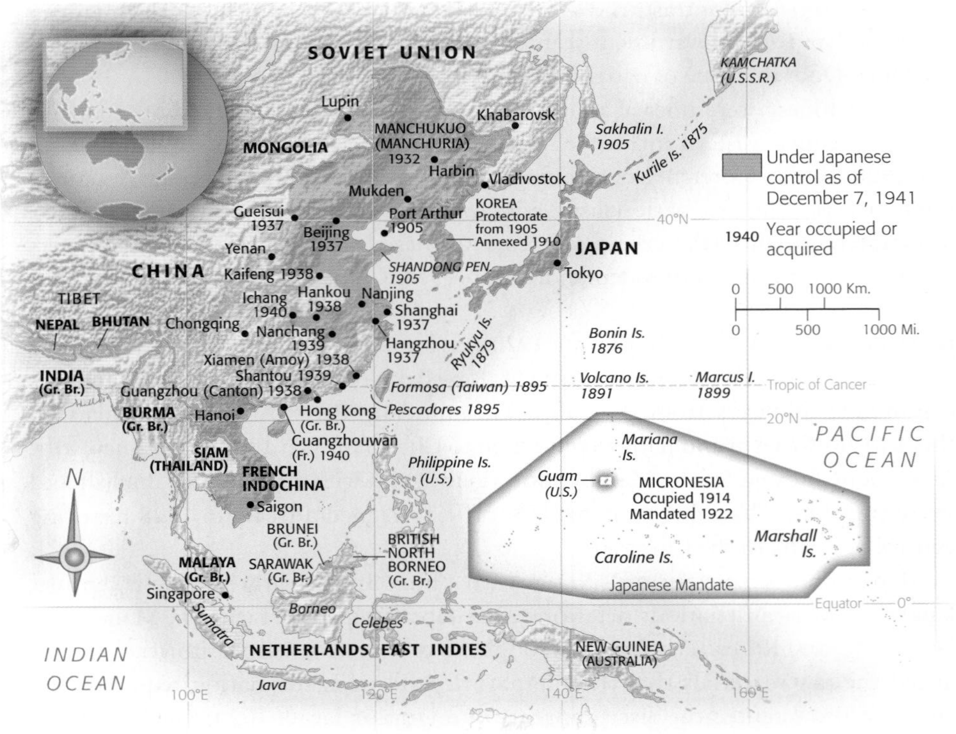

MAP 26.1

Japanese Expansion Before Pearl Harbor

The Japanese quest for predominance began at the turn of the century and intensified in the 1930s. China suffered the most at the hands of Tokyo's military. Vulnerable U.S. possessions in Asia and the Pacific proved no obstacle to Japan's ambitions for a Greater East Asia Co-Prosperity Sphere.

Source: Copyright © Cengage Learning

On December 12, Japanese aircraft sank the American gunboat *Panay*, an escort for Standard Oil Company tankers on the Yangtze River, killing two American sailors. Roosevelt was relieved when Tokyo apologized and offered to pay for damages.

Japan's declaration of a New Order in Asia, in the words of one American official, "banged, barred, and bolted" the Open Door. Alarmed, the Roosevelt administration during the late 1930s gave loans and sold military equipment to Jiang's Chinese government. In mid-1939, the United States abrogated its trade treaty with Tokyo, yet Americans continued to ship oil, cotton, and machinery to Japan. The administration hesitated to initiate economic sanctions because it might spark a Japanese-American war at a time when Germany posed a more serious threat and the United States was unprepared for war. When war broke out in Europe in late summer 1939, Japanese-American relations were stalemated.

U.S. Entry into World War II

A stalemate was fine with many Americans if it kept the United States out of war. But could it stay out? Roosevelt remarked in 1939 that the United States could not "draw a line of defense around this country and live completely and solely to ourselves." Polls showed that Americans favored the Allies and supported aid to Britain and France, but the great majority emphatically wanted the United States to remain at peace. Troubled by this conflicting advice—oppose Hitler, aid the Allies, but stay out of the war—the president gradually moved the nation from neutrality to undeclared war against Germany and then, after the Japanese attack on Pearl Harbor, to full-scale war.

> In what way did Roosevelt gradually move America into World War II?

Because the stakes were so high, Americans vigorously debated the direction of foreign policy from 1939 through 1941. The widespread use of radio, the nation's chief news source, helped stimulate public interest. So did ethnic affiliations with the various belligerents and victims. The American Legion, the League of Women Voters, labor unions, and local chapters of the Committee to Defend America by Aiding the Allies and of the isolationist America First Committee (both organized in 1940) provided outlets for citizen participation in the national debate. African American churches organized anti-Italian boycotts to protest Mussolini's pummeling of Ethiopia.

In March 1940, the Soviet Union invaded Finland. In April, Germany conquered Denmark and Norway (see Map 26.2). On May 10, 1940, Germany attacked Belgium, the Netherlands, and France, ultimately pushing French and British forces back to the English Channel. At Dunkirk, France, between May 26 and June 6, more than 300,000 Allied soldiers frantically escaped to Britain on a flotilla of small boats. The Germans occupied Paris a week later. A new French government in the town of Vichy collaborated with the Nazis and, on June 22, surrendered France to Berlin. The German Luftwaffe (air force) launched massive bombing raids against Great Britain.

Alarmed by the swift defeat of one European nation after another, Americans gradually shed their isolationism. Promising that New Deal reforms would not be sacrificed for military preparedness, the president aided the beleaguered Allies to prevent the fall of Britain. In May 1940, he ordered the sale of old surplus military equipment to Britain and France. In July, he cultivated bipartisan support by naming Republicans Henry L. Stimson and Frank Knox, backers of aid to the Allies, secretaries of war and the navy, respectively. In September, the president traded fifty

MAP 26.2

The German Advance

Hitler's drive to dominate Europe pushed German troops deep into France and the Soviet Union. Great Britain took a beating but held on with the help of American economic and military aid before the United States itself entered the Second World War in late 1941.

Source: Copyright © Cengage Learning

over-age American destroyers for leases to eight British military bases, including Newfoundland, Bermuda, and Jamaica.

First Peacetime Military Draft

Selective Training and Service Act: Law that required all men between twenty-one and thirty (later expanded to eighteen through forty-five) to register with local draft boards.

Lend-Lease bill: Program proposed by Roosevelt to supply war material to cash-strapped Britain.

Two weeks later, Roosevelt signed the hotly debated and narrowly passed **Selective Training and Service Act**, the first peacetime military draft in American history. The law called for the registration of all men between the ages of twenty-one and thirty-five; more than 16 million men signed up. Meanwhile, Roosevelt won reelection in November 1940 with promises of peace: "Your boys are not going to be sent into any foreign wars."

Roosevelt claimed that the United States could avoid war by enabling the British to win. In January 1941, Congress debated the president's **Lend-Lease bill**. Because Britain was broke, the president explained, the United States should lend rather than sell weapons. In March 1941, with pro-British sentiment running high, the House passed the Lend-Lease Act by 317 votes to 71; the Senate followed with a 60-to-31 tally. The initial appropriation was $7 billion, but by war's end, it reached $50 billion, more than $31 billion of it for Britain.

To ensure delivery of Lend-Lease goods, Roosevelt ordered the U.S. Navy to patrol halfway across the Atlantic, and he sent American troops to Greenland.

Links to the World

Radio News

In radio's early years, network executives believed their job was to entertain Americans and that left current affairs to newspapers. Yet radio could report news as it happened, something no previous medium could do.

Franklin Roosevelt was among the first to grasp radio's potential. As governor of New York, he occasionally went on the air, and after becoming president, he commenced his Fireside Chats, reassuring Americans during the depression that the government was working to help them. The broadcasts were so successful that one journalist remarked, "The President has only to look toward a radio to bring Congress to terms."

Across the Atlantic, Adolf Hitler also used the radio to carry speeches directly to the German people. His message: Germany had been wronged by enemies abroad and by Marxists and Jews at home. But under Hitler, the Nazis promised to restore the country's former greatness. As *Sieg Heil!* thundered over the airwaves, millions of Germans saw Hitler as their salvation.

In 1938, as events in Europe escalated, American radio networks increased news coverage. When Hitler annexed Austria in March, NBC and CBS broke into scheduled programs to deliver bulletins. Then, on March 13, CBS broadcast the first international news roundup, a half-hour show featuring live reports. A new era in American radio was born. In the words of author Joseph Persico, what made the broadcast revolutionary "was the listener's sensation of being on the scene" in far-off Europe. When leaders from France and Britain met with Hitler in Munich later that year, millions of Americans listened intently to live radio updates.

Correspondents became well known, none more than Edward R. Murrow of CBS. During the Nazi air blitz of London in 1940–1941, Murrow's understated, nicotine-scorched voice kept Americans spellbound, as he tried to "report suffering to people [Americans] who have not suffered."

Undoubtedly, Murrow's reports strengthened the interventionist voices in Washington by emphasizing Winston Churchill's greatness and England's bravery. And radio reports from Europe made Americans feel closely linked to people living an ocean away.

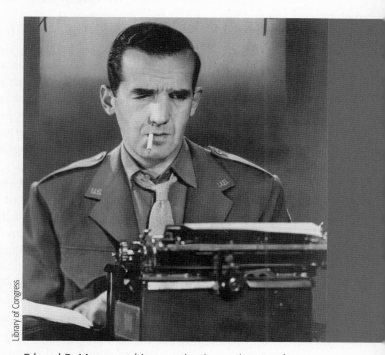

Library of Congress

Edward R. Murrow at his typewriter in wartime London.

In July, the president dispatched marines to Iceland, arguing that it was essential for safeguarding the Western Hemisphere. He also sent Lend-Lease aid to the Soviet Union, which Hitler attacked in June (thereby shattering the 1939 Nazi-Soviet nonaggression pact). If the Soviets could hold off two hundred German divisions in the east, Roosevelt calculated, Britain would gain some breathing time.

Atlantic Charter

In August 1941, **Winston Churchill** and Roosevelt met for four days on a British battleship off the coast of Newfoundland. The two leaders issued the **Atlantic Charter**, a set of war aims reminiscent of Wilsonianism: collective security, disarmament, self-determination, economic cooperation, and freedom of the seas. Churchill later recalled that the president told him that he could not ask Congress to declare war against Germany, but "he would wage war" and "become more and more provocative."

On September 4, a German submarine launched torpedoes at (but did not hit) the American destroyer *Greer*. Henceforth, Roosevelt said, the U.S. Navy would fire first when under threat. He also made good on a private promise that American warships would convoy British merchant ships across the ocean. Thus, the United States entered into an undeclared naval war with Germany. When in early October a German submarine torpedoed the U.S. destroyer *Kearny* off the coast of Iceland killing one hundred Americans, the president announced that "the shooting has started." Congress scrapped the cash-and-carry policy and revised the Neutrality Acts to permit transport of munitions to Britain on armed American merchant ships. The United States was edging close to being a belligerent.

U.S. Demands on Japan

It seems ironic, therefore, that World War II came to the United States by way of Asia. Roosevelt wanted to avoid war with Japan to concentrate on defeating Germany. In September 1940, after Germany, Italy, and Japan signed the Tripartite Pact (to form the Axis powers), Roosevelt slapped an embargo on shipments of aviation fuel and scrap metal to Japan. After Japanese troops occupied French Indochina in July 1941, Washington froze Japanese assets in the United States, virtually ending trade (including oil) with Japan. "The oil gauge and the clock stood side by side" for Japan, wrote one observer.

Tokyo recommended a summit meeting between President Roosevelt and Prime Minister Prince Konoye, but American officials insisted that the Japanese first agree to respect China's sovereignty and honor the Open Door policy. Roosevelt supported Secretary Hull's hard line against Japan's pursuit of the Greater East Asia Co-Prosperity Sphere—the name Tokyo gave to the vast Asian region it intended to dominate.

Roosevelt told his advisers to string out ongoing Japanese-American talks to gain time to fortify the Philippines and check the fascists in Europe. By deciphering intercepted messages through Operation MAGIC, American officials learned that Tokyo's patience with diplomacy was dissipating. In late November, the Japanese rejected American demands to withdraw from Indochina. An intercepted message decoded on December 3 instructed the Japanese embassy in Washington to burn codes and destroy cipher machines—suggesting that war was coming.

Surprise Attack on Pearl Harbor

In a daring raid on Pearl Harbor in Hawai'i, an armada of sixty Japanese ships, including six carriers bearing 360 airplanes, crossed 3,000 miles of the Pacific Ocean. To avoid detection, they maintained radio silence. Early on December 7, some 230 miles northwest of Honolulu, the carriers unleashed their planes, dropping torpedoes and bombs on an unsuspecting American naval base and nearby airfields.

The stricken USS *West Virginia* was one of eight battleships caught in the surprise Japanese attack at Pearl Harbor, Hawai'i, on December 7, 1941. In this photograph, sailors on a launch attempt to rescue a crew member from the water as oil burns around the sinking ship.

The battleship USS *Arizona* fell victim to a Japanese bomb that ignited explosives below deck, killing more than 1,000 sailors. The USS *Nevada* tried to escape by heading out to sea, but was hit in a second aerial attack. Altogether, the invaders sank or damaged eight battleships, many smaller vessels, and more than 160 aircraft on the ground. A total of 2,403 died; 1,178 were wounded. The Pearl Harbor tragedy, from the perspective of the war's outcome, amounted to a military inconvenience more than a disaster.

Explaining Pearl Harbor

American cryptanalysts may have broken the Japanese diplomatic code, but the intercepted messages never revealed naval or military plans and never mentioned Pearl Harbor specifically. Roosevelt did not, as some critics charged, conspire to leave the fleet vulnerable to attack so that the United States could enter World War II through the back door of Asia. The base at Pearl Harbor was not on red alert

Presidential Deception of the Public

Before U-652 launched two torpedoes at the *Greer*, heading for Iceland on September 4, 1941, the U.S. destroyer had stalked the German submarine for hours. After the attack, which missed its mark, the *Greer* also released depth charges. But when President Roosevelt described the encounter in a radio Fireside Chat on September 11, he declared that the German submarine fired the first shot and accused Germany of violating freedom of the seas.

Roosevelt misled the American people about the events of September 4. The incident had little to do with freedom of the seas—which related to merchant ships, not to U.S. warships in a war zone. Roosevelt's words were a call to arms, yet he never asked Congress for a declaration of war against Germany. The president believed that deceiving Americans would move them toward war as noble and necessary. The practice worked: polls showed that most Americans approved Roosevelt's shoot-on-sight policy following the *Greer* incident.

Over time, even those who agreed that Germany had to be stopped, questioned Roosevelt's methods as dangerous to the democratic process, which cannot work in an environment of dishonesty and a usurping of congressional powers. In the 1960s, during the Vietnam War, Senator J. William Fulbright of Arkansas recalled the *Greer* incident: "FDR's deviousness in a good cause made it easier for LBJ to practice the same kind of deviousness in a bad cause." In the mid-1980s, Reagan administration officials consciously lied about U.S. arms sales to Iran and covert aid to the Nicaraguan rebels. After the March 2003 U.S. invasion of Iraq, there were charges that President George W. Bush and his aides did the same in claiming that Iraq had weapons of mass destruction, which its leader, Saddam Hussein, intended to use. Bush, critics charged, had used "weapons of mass deception" to justify the invasion of Iraq.

Following Roosevelt, presidents have found it easier to distort, withhold, or lie about foreign relations to shape a public. One result: the growth of the "imperial presidency"—grabbing power from Congress and using questionable means to support presidential objectives. The practice of deception—even for a noble end—was one of Roosevelt's legacies for a people and a nation.

---

because a message from Washington warning of the imminence of war was transmitted by a slow method and arrived too late. Base commanders believed Hawai'i too far from Japan to be a target. Like Roosevelt's advisers, they expected an assault on British Malaya, Thailand, or the Philippines. The Pearl Harbor calamity stemmed from mistakes and insufficient information, not from conspiracy.

 Link to the transcript, audio, and commentary of President Roosevelt's December 8, 1941, "Day of Infamy" speech.

On December 8, referring to the previous day as "a date which will live in infamy," Roosevelt asked Congress for a declaration of war against Japan. He noted that Japan had also attacked Malaya, Hong Kong, Guam, the Philippines, Wake, and Midway. A unanimous vote in the Senate and a 388-to-1 vote in the House thrust America into war. Representative Jeannette Rankin of Montana voted no, as she had for World War I. Britain declared war on Japan, but the Soviet Union did not. Three days later, Germany and Italy, honoring the Tripartite Pact they had signed with Japan in September 1940, declared war against the United States.

A fundamental clash of systems explains why war came. Germany and Japan preferred a world divided into closed spheres of influence. The United States sought a liberal capitalist world. American principles manifested respect for human rights; fascists in Europe and militarists in Asia did not. The United States prided itself on democracy; Germany and Japan embraced authoritarian regimes. When the United States protested against German and Japanese expansion, Berlin and Tokyo charged that Washington conveniently ignored its sphere of influence in Latin America and its history of military and economic aggrandizement. Such incompatible objectives obstructed diplomacy and made war likely.

Summary

In the 1920s and 1930s, Americans could not create a peaceful and prosperous world order. The Washington Conference treaties failed to curb a naval arms race or protect China, and both the Dawes Plan and the Kellogg-Briand Pact proved ineffective. U.S. trade policies, shifting from protectionist tariffs to reciprocal trade agreements, only minimally improved U.S. or international commerce during the Great Depression. Recognition of the Soviet Union barely improved relations. Most ominous, the aggressors Germany and Japan ignored repeated U.S. protests. Even where U.S. policies seemed to satisfy Good Neighbor goals in Latin America, nationalist resentments simmered and Mexico challenged U.S. dominance.

During the late 1930s and early 1940s, President Roosevelt hesitantly but steadily moved the United States from neutrality to aiding the Allies, to belligerency, and finally to war after the Pearl Harbor attack. Congress gradually revised and retired the Neutrality Acts in the face of growing danger.

World War II offered another opportunity for Americans to set things right in the world. As publisher Henry Luce wrote in *American Century* (1941), the United States must "exert upon the world the full impact of our influence." Isolationists joined the president's calls for victory. "We are going to win the war, and we are going to win the peace that follows," Roosevelt predicted.

Chapter Review

Searching for Peace and Order in the 1920s

How did the peace movement influence U.S. foreign policy in the interwar years?

In the wake of World War I, several peace organizations—some formed by female activists—emerged to ensure world order and prevent another war. Their strategies varied: some embraced alliances with the League of Nations and the World Court; others looked to arbitration, disarmament, arms reduction, making wars illegal, and observing strict neutrality. Peace activism helped lead President Harding to convene the Washington Naval Conference from November 1921 to February 1922 in which delegates from Britain, Japan, France, Italy, China, Portugal, Belgium, and the Netherlands agreed to limit naval armaments and set a ten-year moratorium on ship-building. Other policy developments included the Nine-Power Treaty, which reaffirmed the Open Door in China and recognized Chinese sovereignty; the Locarno Pact of 1925, which sought to reduce tensions between Germany and France; and the Kellogg-Briand Pact of 1928, in which sixty-two nations agreed to condemn war as the solution to international disputes.

The World Economy, Cultural Expansion, and Great Depression

How did the Great Depression help push the world to the brink of war?

Economic tensions existed among world powers after World War I. The United States emerged as a creditor nation and Europeans—particularly Germany—largely as debtors. Europeans often accused the United States of stinginess and profiting from Europe's hardships. When the stock market crashed in 1929, Europeans defaulted on a large portion of what they owed. The Great Depression not only created an international economic crisis, it also inspired economic nationalism in countries that were already pushed financially to the edge. Secretary of State Charles Hull aptly predicted that maimed economies inspired militarism and extremism, and no country's economy was as hard-pressed as Germany's.

U.S. Dominance in Latin America

How was Roosevelt's Good Neighbor policy different from past dealings in Latin America?

Prior to Roosevelt, U.S. leaders were quick to resort to military intervention in dealing with Latin America. The Good Neighbor policy took a more subtle approach: it centered on building friendship ties through Pan-Americanism; supporting strong local leaders; training national guards; penetrating the region through economic and cultural means; providing financial supervision and loans; and relying on political subversion. Roosevelt withdrew troops from Haiti and Nicaragua restored some sovereignty to Panama, and increased that nation's income from the canal. While the administration backed dictators who seemed supportive of U.S. economic interests, the Good Neighbor policy nonetheless convinced many Latin Americans that a new, more cooperative era had begun.

The Course to War in Europe

Why did many Americans support isolationism at the outbreak of World War II?

Americans had long embraced isolationism largely because their long history of political independence that did not necessitate alliances with other nations.

That was fortified by the experience of World War I, which damaged reform movements at home, disrupted the U.S. economy, and expanded federal power. In fact, two-thirds of Americans surveyed thought entry into World War I had been a mistake. Many Americans similarly feared tax increases, the loss of freedom at home, and the shift of federal funds away from domestic problems toward military spending. Some also distrusted the role of business in pushing the nation toward war.

Japan, China, and a New Order in Asia

How did the United States perceive its interests to be threatened by Japanese expansionism?

As Japan moved to lessen—and eliminate—western influence in the East and to dominate Asian territories producing beneficial raw materials, the United States worried about what this would mean to its geopolitical and economic interests in East Asia, including in the Philippines and the Pacific Islands. They also feared it portended Japanese control of China and Southeast Asia. The Japanese viewed the U.S. presence in the region as an intolerable check on their ambitions, and the two nations remained locked in a stalemate as World War II loomed.

U.S. Entry into World War II

In what way did Roosevelt gradually move America into World War II?

Like most Americans, Roosevelt remained wary of intervening actively in the growing crisis, but as one European nation after another succumbed to the Nazis, staying out of the conflict proved increasingly difficult. Roosevelt was horrified by Germany's treatment of Jews and Japan's expansionism in East Asia, but Hitler's 1939 takeover of Czechoslovakia proved the turning point. FDR quietly began preparing for war, even while hoping that he could keep the United States out of it by ensuring that Britain did not fall. In May 1940 he ordered the sale of surplus military equipment to Britain and France. Because England had no money to pay for weapons, the president urged Congress to let it borrow the necessary arms. The president also signed the Selective Training and Service Act, the first peacetime military draft.

Suggestions for Further Reading

H. W. Brands, *Traitor to His Class: The Privileged Life and Radical Presidency of Franklin Delano Roosevelt* (2008)

Patrick Cohrs, *The Unfinished Peace After World War I: America, Britain and the Stabilization of Europe, 1919–1932* (2006)

Frank Costigliola, *Awkward Dominion: American Political, Economic, and Cultural Relations with Europe* (1984)

Justus D. Doenecke, *Storm on the Horizon: The Challenge to American Intervention, 1939–1941* (2000)

Akira Iriye, *The Origins of the Second World War in Asia and the Pacific* (1987)

David M. Kennedy, *Freedom from Fear: The American People in Depression and War, 1929–1945* (1999)

Walter LaFeber, *Inevitable Revolutions: The United States in Central America,* 2nd and extended ed. (1993)

Fredrick B. Pike, *FDR's Good Neighbor Policy* (1995)

Emily S. Rosenberg, *Spreading the American Dream: American Economic and Cultural Expansion, 1890–1945* (1982)

Linda A. Schott, *Reconstructing Women's Thoughts: The Women's International League for Peace and Freedom Before World War II* (1997)

Go to the CourseMate website for primary source links, study tools, and review materials for this chapter. www.cengagebrain.com

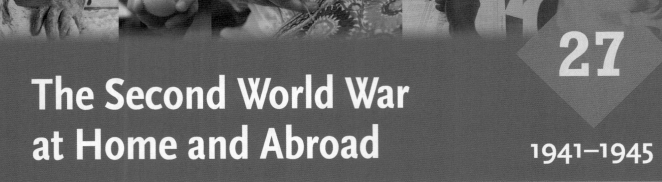

The Second World War at Home and Abroad

27

1941–1945

William Dean Wilson was only sixteen in 1942 when U.S. Marine Corps recruiters came to Shiprock, New Mexico, where he attended the Navajo boarding school. Five years too young to be drafted and a year too young to volunteer, he lied about his age, dropped out of school, and joined the Marine Corps.

Wilson was recruited for one of the most important projects of the war. Battles were won or lost because nations broke the codes enemies used to transmit messages. The marines were developing a code based on Diné, the highly complex Navajo language. In 1942, there was no written form and fewer than thirty non-Navajos in the world—none of them Japanese—who understood it. This code promised to be unbreakable.

Wilson and other Navajo recruits helped devise a basic code. Navajo words represented the first letter of their English translations; thus *wol-la-chee* ("ant") stood for the letter *A*. Each also memorized Navajo words that represented 413 basic military terms. *Dah-he-tih-hi* ("hummingbird") meant fighter plane; *ne-he-mah*, "our mother," was the United States.

Beginning with the Battle of Guadalcanal, Wilson and others of the 420 code talkers participated in every Marine assault in the Pacific. Usually, two code talkers were assigned to a battalion, one going ashore with assault forces and the other receiving messages on ship. Often under hostile fire, code talkers set up their equipment and transmitted enemy sightings or directed shelling by American detachments. "Were it not for the Navajos," declared Major Howard Conner, Fifth Marine Division signal officer, "the Marines would never have taken Iwo Jima. The entire operation was directed by Navajo code…."

Wartime service changed the Navajo code talkers' lives. For some, it broadened horizons and deepened ambitions; William Dean Wilson became a tribal judge. But in 1945 most Navajo war veterans simply wanted to return to their homes and traditional culture. They participated in purification ceremonies to dispel battlefield ghosts and invoke blessings for the future.

Chapter Outline

The United States at War
A Nation Unprepared | War in the Pacific | "Europe First" Strategy

The Production Front and American Workers
Businesses, Universities, and the War Effort | Manhattan Project | New Opportunities for Workers | Women at Work | Organized Labor During Wartime | Success on the Production Front

Life on the Home Front
Supporting the War Effort | Propaganda and Popular Culture | Wartime Prosperity | A Nation in Motion | Racial Conflicts | Families in Wartime

VISUALIZING THE PAST *Portraying the Enemy*

The Limits of American Ideals
Internment of Japanese Americans | African Americans and "Double V" | A Segregated Military | America and the Holocaust

LINKS TO THE WORLD *Tokyo Rose*

Life in the Military
Selective Service | Fighting the War

Winning the War
Tensions Among the Allies | War in Europe | Yalta Conference | Harry Truman | War in the Pacific | Bombing of Japan

LEGACY FOR A PEOPLE AND A NATION *Nuclear Proliferation*

SUMMARY

World War II marked a turning point in the lives of Americans and the history of the United States. Although the war began badly for the United States, by mid-1942 the Allies halted the Axis powers' advance. In June 1944, American troops, together with Canadian, British, and Free French units, launched a massive invasion across the English Channel, landing at Normandy and pushing into Germany the following spring. Battered by bombing raids, leaderless after Adolf Hitler's suicide, and pressed by a Soviet advance, the Nazis capitulated in May 1945. In the Pacific, Americans drove Japanese forces back toward Japan. America's devastating conventional bombing of Japanese cities, followed by the atomic bombs that demolished Hiroshima and Nagasaki in August 1945 and the Soviet Union's declaration of war on Japan, led to Japan's surrender. At war's end, prospects for international cooperation seemed bleak. The "Grand Alliance"—Britain, the Soviet Union, and the United States—had different visions of the postwar world, and the advent of the atomic age frightened everyone.

The war was fought far from the United States, but it had a major impact on American society. America's leaders committed the United States to become the "arsenal of democracy," producing vast quantities of arms. All economic sectors—industry, finance, agriculture, labor—were mobilized. America's big businesses got bigger, as did labor unions and farms. The federal government, which had the monumental task of managing the war, expanded its reach and power.

During the war, nearly one of every ten Americans moved to another state. Most headed for war-production centers, especially in northern and West Coast cities. Japanese Americans were forced from their homes and incarcerated in remote "relocation centers." While the war encouraged African Americans to demand full citizenship rights, competition for jobs and housing spawned race riots. For women, the war offered new job opportunities in the armed forces and war industries.

On the home front, the American people supported the war effort by collecting scrap iron, rubber, and newspapers for war use and planting "victory gardens." At war's end, although many Americans grieved for lost loved ones and worried about the postwar order, the United States had unprecedented power and prosperity.

As you read this chapter, keep the following questions in mind:

* **What military, diplomatic, and social factors influenced decisions about how to fight the Second World War?**

* **Was the generation of Americans that fought World War II "the greatest generation"?**

* **How did World War II transform the United States?**

The United States at War

As Japanese bombs fell on the U.S. territory of Hawai'i, American antiwar sentiment evaporated. Franklin Roosevelt declared war on Japan on December 8, 1941. When Germany declared war on the United States three days later, America joined British and Soviet Allied nations in battling the Axis powers of Japan, Germany, and Italy. Although the attack on Pearl Harbor was a surprise, America's embargo of shipments to Japan and refusal to accept Japan's expansionist policies had helped bring the two nations to the brink of war, and the United States was deeply involved in an undeclared naval war with Germany before Japan's attack

Was the United States prepared for war when it finally entered World War II?

Chronology

1941	Japan attacks Pearl Harbor United States enters World War II
1942	War Production Board created to oversee conversion to military production Allies losing war in Pacific to Japan; U.S. victory at Battle of Midway in June is turning point Office of Price Administration creates rationing system for food and consumer goods United States pursues "Europe First" war policy; Allies reject Stalin's demands for a second front and invade North Africa West Coast Japanese Americans relocated to internment camps Manhattan Project set up to create atomic bomb Congress of Racial Equality established
1943	Soviet army defeats German troops at Stalingrad Congress passes War Labor Disputes (Smith-Connally) Act following coal miners' strike "Zoot suit riots" in Los Angeles; race riots break out in Detroit, Harlem, and other cities
	Allies invade Italy Roosevelt, Churchill, and Stalin meet at Teheran Conference
1944	Allied troops land at Normandy on D-Day, June 6 Roosevelt elected to fourth term as president United States retakes Philippines
1945	Roosevelt, Stalin, and Churchill meet at Yalta Conference British and U.S. forces firebomb Dresden, Germany Battles of Iwo Jima and Okinawa result in heavy Japanese and American losses Roosevelt dies; Truman becomes president Germany surrenders; Allied forces liberate Nazi death camps Potsdam Conference calls for Japan's "unconditional surrender" United States uses atomic bombs on Hiroshima and Nagasaki Japan surrenders

on Pearl Harbor. By December 1941, Roosevelt had instituted an unprecedented peacetime draft, created war mobilization agencies, and commissioned war plans for simultaneous struggle in Europe and the Pacific.

A Nation Unprepared   Nonetheless, the nation was not ready for war. Throughout the 1930s, military funding was a low priority. In September 1939 (when Hitler invaded Poland and began World War II), the U.S. Army ranked forty-fifth in size among the world's armies and could fully equip only one-third of its 227,000 men. A peacetime draft instituted in 1940 expanded the U.S. military to 2 million men, but Roosevelt's 1941 survey of war preparedness estimated that the United States could not be ready to fight before June 1943.

In December 1941, the Allies were losing the war (see Map 26.1). Hitler claimed Austria, Czechoslovakia, Poland, the Netherlands, Denmark, and Norway. Romania was lost, then Greece and Bulgaria. France fell in 1940. Britain fought on, but German planes rained bombs on London. More than 3 million German-led soldiers penetrated the Soviet Union and Africa. German U-boats controlled the Atlantic from the Arctic to the Caribbean. Within months of America's entry into the war, German submarines sank 216 vessels—some so close to American shores that people could see the glow of burning ships.

War in the Pacific   In the Pacific, the war was largely America's. The Soviets had not declared war on Japan, and there were too few British troops protecting England's Asian colonies to make much difference. By late spring 1942, Japan had captured most European colonial possessions in Southeast Asia. The Japanese attacked the Philippines hours after Pearl Harbor and destroyed U.S. air capability in the region. American and Filipino troops retreated to the Bataan Peninsula, hoping to hold the main island, Luzon, but Japanese forces were superior. In March 1942, General Douglas MacArthur, the commander of U.S. forces in the Far East, departed the Philippines, proclaiming, "I shall return."

Left behind were almost eighty thousand American and Filipino troops. Starving and sick, they held on for almost another month before surrendering. Japanese troops, lacking supplies, were unprepared to deal with this large number of prisoners, and most believed the prisoners forfeited honorable treatment by surrendering. In what came to be known as the Bataan Death March, the Japanese force-marched their captives to prison camps 80 miles away, denying them food and water and bayoneting or beating to death those who fell behind. Ten thousand Filipinos and six hundred Americans died on the march. Tens of thousands of Filipino civilians died under Japanese occupation.

The United States stuck back. On April 18, sixteen American B-25s appeared over Japan. The Doolittle raid (named after the mission's leader) did little harm but pushed Japanese commander Yamamoto to bold action. Japan moved to lure the weakened United States into a "decisive battle." The target was Midway—two tiny islands about 1,000 miles northwest of Honolulu, where the U.S. Navy had a base. If Japan could take Midway, it would have a secure defensive perimeter far from the home islands (see Map 27.2). By using Guam, the Philippines, and even Australia as hostages, Japan believed, it could negotiate a favorable peace agreement with the United States.

General Yamamoto did not know that America's MAGIC code-breaking machines could decipher Japanese messages. When the Japanese fleet arrived, it found the U.S. Navy lying in wait. The Battle of Midway in June 1942 was a turning point in the Pacific war. Japan's hope to force the United States to withdraw, leaving Japan to control the Pacific, vanished. Now Japan was on the defensive.

"Europe First" Strategy Despite the importance of these early Pacific battles, America's war strategy was "Europe First." American war planners believed that if Germany conquered the Soviet Union, it might directly threaten the United States. Roosevelt also feared that the Soviet Union, suffering heavy losses against Hitler, might pursue a separate peace with Germany and so undo the Allied coalition. Therefore, the United States would work with Britain and the USSR to defeat Germany, then deal with an isolated Japan.

British prime minister Winston Churchill and Soviet premier **Joseph Stalin** disagreed over strategy. By late 1941, German troops nearly reached Moscow and Leningrad (present-day St. Petersburg) and slashed into Ukraine, taking Kiev, claiming the lives of over a million Soviet soldiers. Stalin pressed for British and American troops to attack Germany from the west to draw Germans away from the Soviet front. Roosevelt agreed and promised to open a "second front" before the end of 1942. Churchill, however, blocked this plan. Churchill wanted to control the North Atlantic shipping lanes first and promoted air attacks on Germany. He also pushed for an attack on Axis positions in North Africa; halting the Germans there would protect British imperial possessions in the Mediterranean and the oil-rich Middle East.

Joseph Stalin: Soviet premier and dictator of the Soviet Union who came to power after the death of Vladimir Lenin in 1924 and ruled until his death in 1953.

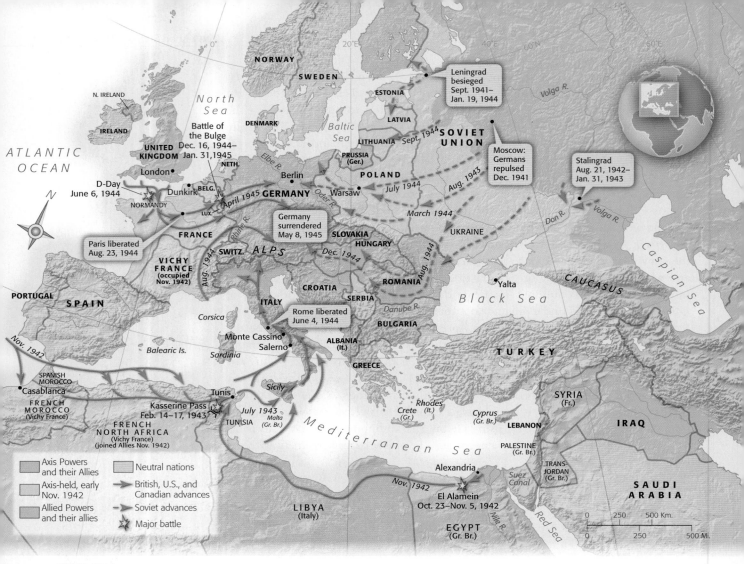

MAP 27.1

The Allies on the Offensive in Europe, 1942–1945

The United States pursued a "Europe First" policy: first defeat Germany, then focus on Japan. American military efforts began in North Africa in late 1942 and ended in Germany in 1945 on May 8 (V-E Day).

Source: Copyright © Cengage Learning

Against his advisers' advice, Roosevelt accepted Churchill's plan. The U.S. military was not ready for a major campaign, and Roosevelt needed to show the American public some success in the European war. Thus, instead of rescuing the USSR, the British and Americans landed in North Africa in November 1942, winning quick victories in Algeria and Morocco. In Egypt, the British confronted General Erwin Rommel and his Afrika Korps in a struggle over the Suez Canal and the Middle East oil fields, with Rommel's army surrendering after six months. Meanwhile, the Soviet army hung on. The Soviet Union lost 1.1 million men in the Battle of Stalingrad but defeated the German Sixth Army there in early 1943. By spring 1943, Germany, like Japan, was on the defensive. Relations among the Allies remained precarious as the United States and Britain continued to resist Stalin's demand for a second front.

The Production Front and American Workers

How did wartime production needs create a new relationship between government and business and government and science?

Although the war would be fought on the battlefields of Europe and the Pacific, America's strategic advantage lay on the "production front" at home. By making the machines that would win the war for the Allies, the United States would prevail through a "crushing superiority of equipment," Roosevelt told Congress.

Goals for military production were staggering. In 1940, American factories built only 3,807 airplanes. Following Pearl Harbor, Roosevelt wanted 60,000 aircraft in 1942 and twice that in 1943. Plans called for the manufacture of 16 million tons of shipping and 120,000 tanks. The military needed supplies for a force that would reach almost 16 million men. During the war, military production superseded the manufacture of civilian goods. Automobile plants built tanks and airplanes instead of cars; dress factories sewed military uniforms. The **War Production Board**, established in early 1942, allocated resources and coordinated production among thousands of independent factories.

War Production Board: Government agency established during WWII which allocated resources, coordinated production among thousands of independent factories, and awarded government contracts for wartime production.

Businesses, Universities, and the War Effort

During the war, American businesses overwhelmingly cooperated with government war-production plans, inspired by patriotism and generous financial incentives. In 1940, as the United States produced armaments for the Allies, the American economy recovered from the depression. Rising consumer spending built industrial confidence. Auto manufacturers, for example, expected to sell 25 percent more in 1941 than in 1939. The massive retooling necessary to produce planes or tanks instead of cars would be expensive and leave manufacturers dependent on a single client—the federal government. The federal government, however, paid for retooling and factory expansions; it guaranteed profits by allowing corporations to charge the government for production costs plus a fixed profit. It created generous tax write-offs and exemptions from antitrust laws. Consequently, corporations doubled their net profits between 1939 and 1943.

Most military contracts went to America's largest corporations, which had the facilities to guarantee rapid production. From mid-1940 through September 1944, the government awarded contracts totaling $175 billion, with about two-thirds going to the top hundred corporations. General Motors received 8 percent of the total. This approach made sense for a nation that wanted enormous quantities of war goods manufactured quickly; most small businesses lacked the necessary capacity. However, wartime government contracts further consolidated American manufacturing in the hands of giant corporations.

GM GENERAL MOTORS

PRODUCING MORE FOR VICTORY

Folks

"UNITED WE STAND"

JULY, 1942
VOL. 5   NO. 7

Dayton Presents Arms for Victory Pageant "Plowshares"...Pages 2-5

Courtesy, Collection of Peter Kreitler

Unprepared to fight a war of such magnitude, the U.S. government turned to the nation's largest and most efficient corporations to produce the planes and ships and guns that would make America the "great arsenal of democracy," and General Motors received 8 percent of the value of all government war contracts. With no new cars to sell, GM continued to advertise in national magazines, proclaiming "Victory Is Our Business." Pictured here is GM's in-house magazine for employees, reminding these "production soldiers" of the importance of their work.

Manhattan Project

Wartime needs also created a new relationship between science and the U.S. military. Millions of dollars funded university research programs, which developed new technologies of warfare, such as vastly improved radar systems. The most important government-sponsored research program was the **Manhattan Project**, a $2 billion secret effort to build an atomic bomb. Roosevelt was convinced by scientists fleeing the Nazis in 1939 that Germany was developing an atomic weapon, and he resolved to beat them to it. The Manhattan Project achieved the world's first sustained nuclear chain reaction in 1942 at the University of Chicago. In 1943, the federal government established a secret community for atomic scientists and their families at Los Alamos, New Mexico, to develop the weapon that would change the world.

Manhattan Project: Secret program to develop the atomic bomb.

New Opportunities for Workers

America's new defense factories required millions of workers. At first workers were plentiful: 9 million Americans were still unemployed in 1940 when war mobilization began. But the armed forces took almost 16 million men, forcing industry to look more broadly for workers. Women, African Americans, Mexican Americans, and poor whites from Appalachia and the Deep South streamed into defense jobs.

In some cases, federal action eased their path. As many industries refused to hire African Americans, **A. Philip Randolph**, head of the Brotherhood of Sleeping Car Porters, proposed a march on Washington, D.C., to demand equal access to defense jobs. Roosevelt, fearing race riots, offered a deal. In exchange for canceling the march, the president issued Executive Order No. 8802, which prohibited discrimination in war industries and government jobs. Although enforcement was uneven, hundreds of thousands of black Americans migrated from the South to northern and western industrial cities on the strength of this guarantee of job equality.

A. Philip Randolph: Labor leader whose threatened march on Washington led to the creation of Executive Order No. 8802, which prohibited racial discrimination in war industries and government jobs.

Through the **bracero program**, Mexican workers also filled wartime jobs in the United States. About 200,000 Mexican farm workers, or *braceros,* were offered short-term contracts to fill vacant agricultural jobs as Americans sought well-paid war work. Mexican and Mexican American workers faced discrimination and segregation, but they seized these new economic opportunities. In 1941 not a single Mexican American worked in the Los Angeles shipyards; by 1944, 17,000 worked there.

bracero program: Wartime "temporary worker" measure that brought in seasonal farm laborers from Mexico.

Women at Work

Employers initially insisted that women were not suited for industrial jobs, but labor shortages changed their position. Posters and billboards urged women to "Do the Job HE Left Behind, and the government's War Manpower Commission glorified the invented worker **"Rosie the Riveter."**

Rosie the Riveter was an inspiring, albeit inaccurate, image of working women. Only 16 percent of women workers held defense plant jobs, and only 4.4 percent held "skilled" jobs (such as riveting). Nonetheless, during the war years, more than 6 million women entered the labor force, and the number of working women increased by 57 percent. More than 400,000 African American women left domestic service for higher-paying industrial jobs, often with union benefits.

Rosie the Riveter: Symbol of the woman war worker; the bulging muscles represented her strength as she aided the nation's war effort by taking jobs vacated by men who fought in the war.

Workers in defense plants were often expected to work ten days for every day off or to accept difficult night shifts. Businesses and the federal government provided workers new support to keep them on the job. The West Coast Kaiser shipyards offered high pay, childcare, subsidized housing, and healthcare: the Kaiser Permanente Medical Care Program, a forerunner of the health maintenance organization (HMO), supplied medical care for a weekly payroll deduction of 50 cents. The federal government also funded childcare centers, which 130,000 preschoolers and 320,000 school-age children attended.

Organized Labor During Wartime

Because America's war strategy relied on industrial production, the federal government attempted to ensure that labor strikes would not interrupt production. Days after Pearl Harbor, a White House labor-management conference agreed to a no-strike/no-lockout pledge. In 1942, Roosevelt created the National War Labor Board (NWLB) to settle disputes. The NWLB forged a temporary compromise between labor union demands for a "closed shop," in which only union members could work, and management's desire for "open" shops. Workers could not be required to join a union, but unions could enroll as many members as possible. Between 1940 and 1945, union membership ballooned from 8.5 million to 14.75 million.

The government did restrict union power if it threatened war production. When coal miners in the United Mine Workers union went on strike in 1943, following an NWLB attempt to limit wage increases to a cost-of-living adjustment, coal shortages halted railroads and closed steel mills. Few Americans supported this strike. As anti-labor sentiment grew, Congress passed the War Labor Disputes (Smith-Connally) Act, granting the president authority to seize and operate any strike-bound plant deemed necessary to the national security.

Success on the Production Front

For nearly four years, American factories operated twenty-four hours a day, seven days a week, turning out roughly 300,000 airplanes, 102,000 armored vehicles, 77,000 ships, 20 million small arms, 40 billion bullets, and 6 million tons of bombs. By war's end, the United States was producing 40 percent of the world's weaponry. This feat depended on transforming formerly skilled work into assembly-line mass production. Henry Ford, now seventy-eight years old, created a massive bomber plant outside Detroit with assembly lines almost a mile long producing one B-24 Liberator bomber every hour. On the West Coast, William Kaiser cut construction time for Liberty ships—the huge, 440-foot-long cargo ships transporting tanks, guns and bullets overseas—from 355 to 56 days. The ships were not well made; welded hulls sometimes split in rough seas. However, as the United States struggled to produce cargo ships faster than German U-boats could sink them, production speed counted more than quality.

Life on the Home Front

What was the impact of the war on family life?

The United States, protected by two oceans from its enemies, was spared the war that other nations experienced. Americans grieved the loss of loved ones abroad, but bombs did not fall on U.S. cities; invading armies did not burn and rape and kill. Instead, war mobilization ended the Great Depression and brought prosperity. American civilians experienced the paradox of good times amid global conflagration.

Supporting the War Effort

Still the war was a constant presence for Americans on "the home front." Civilians supported the war effort, though Americans were never as committed to shared sacrifice as images of "the greatest generation"—widely circulated in early twenty-first century popular history and culture—suggest. During the war, however, families planted 20 million "victory gardens" to free up food supplies for the military. Housewives saved cooking fat, which yieleded glycerin to make black powder used in shells or bullets. Children collected scrap metal; the iron in one old shovel blade could make four hand grenades.

Many consumer goods were rationed or unavailable. To save wool for military use, the War Production Board directed that men's suits would have narrow lapels, shorter jackets, and no vests or pant cuffs. Bathing suits, the WPB specified, must shrink by 10 percent. When silk and nylon were diverted from stockings to parachutes, women used makeup on their legs. The Office of Price Administration (OPA), created by Congress in 1942, established a nationwide rationing system for such goods as sugar, coffee, and gasoline. By early 1943, the OPA instituted a point system for rationing food. Every citizen received two ration books each month, and feeding a family required complex calculations. Sugar was tightly rationed, and people saved for months to make a birthday cake. A black market existed, but most Americans understood that sugar produced alcohol for weapons manufacture and meat fed "our boys" overseas.

Propaganda and Popular Culture

Despite near-unanimous support for the war, government leaders worried that, over time, public willingness to sacrifice might lag. In 1942, Roosevelt created the Office of War Information (OWI), which hired Hollywood filmmakers and New York copywriters to sell the war at home. OWI posters exhorted Americans to sacrifice, and reminded them to watch what they said, for "loose lips sink ships."

Link to World War II propaganda posters.

Popular culture also reinforced wartime messages. A *Saturday Evening Post* advertisement for vacuum cleaners (unavailable for the duration) urged women war workers to fight "for freedom and all that means to women everywhere. You're fighting for a little house of your own, and…the right to bring up your children without the shadow of fear." Songs urged Americans to "Remember December 7th" or to "Accentuate the Positive." Others made fun of America's enemies ("You're a sap, Mr. Jap / Uncle Sam is gonna spanky").

Link to World War II era anti-Axis cartoons.

Movies drew 90 million viewers a week in 1944—out of a total population of 132 million. During the war and Hollywood tried to meet Eleanor Roosevelt's challenge to "Keep 'em laughing." *A WAVE, a WAC, and a Marine* promised "no battle scenes, no message, just barrels of fun." Others, such as *Bataan* or *Wake Island,* portrayed actual—if sanitized—events. Even in comedies, however, the war was always present. Theaters held "plasma premieres," offering free admission to anyone donating blood to the Red Cross. Audiences rose to sing "The Star Spangled Banner," then watched newsreels with censored combat footage before the feature film. In movie theaters, Americans saw the horror of Nazi death camps in May 1945.

Wartime Prosperity

The war demanded sacrifices from Americans, but between 1939 and the end of the war, per capita income rose from $691 to $1,515, and salaries increased more than 135 percent. Price controls kept inflation down so that wage increases did not disappear to higher costs. With little to buy, savings rose.

Portraying the Enemy

Racial stereotyping affected how both the Americans and the Japanese waged war. The Americans badly underestimated the Japanese, leaving themselves open for the surprise attack on Pearl Harbor and American forces in the Philippines. And the Japanese, believing Americans were barbarians who lacked a sense of honor, mistakenly expected that the United States would withdraw from East Asia once confronted with Japanese power and determination. This cover for *Collier's* magazine, appearing shortly after the first anniversary of Japan's attack on Pearl Harbor, shows some of the most extreme racial imagery of the war, but it was scarcely alone. How is Japan portrayed here? How might the fact that Japan had launched an immensely successful surprise attack on the United States have shaped this image, or Americans' reactions to it?

Private Collection/Picture Research Consultants & Archives

American propaganda caricatured all the Axis powers, but the Japanese were most likely to be portrayed as subhuman.

World War II cost approximately $304 billion (more than $3 trillion in today's dollars), which the United States financed through deficit spending, borrowing money by selling war bonds. The national debt skyrocketed, from $49 billion in 1941 to $259 billion in 1945 (and was not paid off until 1970). However, wartime revenue acts increased the number of Americans paying personal income tax from 4 million to 42.6 million—at rates ranging from 6 to 94 percent—and introduced a new system in which employers "withheld" taxes from employee paychecks. For the first time, individual Americans paid more in taxes than corporations.

A Nation in Motion Despite hardships and fears, the war offered home-front Americans new opportunities. More than 15 million civilians moved during the war (see Map 27.2), including seven hundred thousand black Americans who left the South during the war years. The rapid influx of war workers to cities and towns strained community resources. Migrants crowded into substandard housing—even woodsheds, tents, or cellars—and into trailer parks without adequate sanitary facilities. Disease spread: scabies and ringworm, polio, tuberculosis. Many long-term residents found the newcomers—especially the unmarried male war workers—a rough bunch. In and around Detroit, where car factories now produced tanks and planes, residents called war workers freshly arrived from southern Appalachia "hillbillies" and "white trash." Many migrants knew little about urban life. One young man from rural Tennessee, unfamiliar with traffic lights and street signs, navigated by counting trees between his home and the war plant where he worked. Some Appalachian "trailer-ites" appalled their neighbors by building outdoor privies.

Racial Conflicts

As people from different backgrounds confronted one another under difficult conditions, tensions rose. In 1943, almost 250 racial conflicts exploded in forty-seven cities. In Detroit, white mobs—undeterred by police—roamed the city attacking blacks. Blacks hurled rocks at police and dragged white passengers off streetcars. After thirty hours of rioting, twenty-five blacks and nine whites lay dead.

In Los Angeles in 1943, young Mexican American gang members, or *pachucos,* wore zoot suits: long jackets with wide padded shoulders, loose pants "pegged" below the knee, wide-brimmed hats, and dangling watch chains. With cloth rationed, wearing pants requiring five yards of fabric was a political statement, and although a high percentage of Mexican Americans served in the military, many white servicemen believed otherwise. Rumors that *pachucos* had attacked white sailors set off four days of violence as mobs of white men—mainly soldiers and sailors—roamed the streets attacking and stripping zoot-suiters. Los Angeles outlawed zoot suits, but the riots ended only when naval personnel were removed from the city.

Families in Wartime

War profoundly transformed families. Despite policies exempting married men and fathers from the draft during most of the war, almost 3 million families were broken up. The divorce rate of 16 per 1,000 marriages in 1940 almost doubled to 27 per 1,000 in 1944. Still, the number of marriages rose from 73 per 1,000 unmarried women in 1939 to 93 in 1942. Some couples scrambled to marry before the man was sent overseas; others sought military deferments. Total births climbed from 2.4 million babies in 1939 to 3.1 million in 1943. Many were "goodbye babies," conceived to guarantee the family's continuation if the father died in war.

On college campuses, women complained, along with the song lyrics, "There is no available male." But other young women found plenty of male company, sparking concern about wartime threats to sexual morality. *Youth in Crisis,* a 1943 newsreel, featured a girl with "experience far beyond her age" necking with a soldier on the street. These "victory girls" were said to support the war effort by giving their all to men in uniform. Many young men and women behaved as they never would in peacetime, which often meant hasty marriages to virtual strangers, especially if a baby was on the way. Despite changes in behavior, taboos against unwed motherhood remained strong, and only 1 percent of births during the war were to unmarried women. Wartime mobility also increased opportunities for same-sex relationships, and gay communities grew in such cities as San Francisco.

In many ways, the war reinforced traditional gender roles that had weakened during the depression, when many men lost the breadwinner role. Now men defended their nation while women "kept the home fires burning," sometimes filling jobs vacated by soldiers "for the duration" of the war. Women who worked were frequently blamed for neglecting their children and creating an "epidemic" of juvenile delinquency Nonetheless, millions of women took on new responsibilities in wartime and enjoyed greater independence, and many husbands returned to find that their families' lives seemed complete without them.

The Limits of American Ideals

The U.S. government worked hard to explain to its citizens the reasons for their sacrifices. In 1941 Roosevelt had pledged America to defend "four essential human freedoms"—freedom of speech, freedom of religion, freedom from want, and freedom from fear. Government-sponsored films contrasted democracy and totalitarianism, freedom and fascism, equality and oppression.

> In what ways were American notions of civil liberties and basic freedoms tested during the war years?

As America fought the totalitarian regimes of the Axis powers, the nation confronted tough questions. What limits on civil liberties were justified in the interest of national security? How freely could information flow without revealing military secrets and costing American lives? How could the United States protect itself against spies or saboteurs, especially from German, Italian, or Japanese citizens living in the United States? And what about America's ongoing race problem? The answers revealed tensions between the nation's democratic claims and its wartime practices.

Regarding civil liberties, American leaders embraced a "strategy of truth," declaring that citizens required a truthful accounting of the war's progress. However, the government closely controlled military information, as even seemingly unimportant details might tip off enemies about troop movements. While government-created propaganda sometimes dehumanized the enemy, especially the Japanese, such hate mongering was used much less than during World War I.

More complex was how to handle dissent and guard against enemy agents potentially operating within the nation's borders. The 1940 Alien Registration (Smith) Act made it unlawful to advocate the overthrow of the U.S. government by force or violence. After Pearl Harbor, the government arrested thousands of Germans, Italians, and other Europeans as suspected spies and potential traitors. The government interned 14,426 Europeans in Enemy Alien Camps and prohibited ten thousand Italian Americans from living or working in restricted zones along the California coast.

Internment of Japanese Americans

In March 1942, Roosevelt ordered that all 112,000 foreign-born Japanese and Japanese Americans living in California, Oregon, and the state of Washington (the vast majority of the mainland population) be removed from the West Coast to "relocation centers." There were no individual charges, as was the case with Italian and German nationals; Japanese and Japanese Americans were imprisoned, under suspicion solely because they were of Japanese descent.

American anger at Japan's "sneak attack" on Pearl Harbor fueled calls for internment, as did fears that West Coast cities might be attacked. Long-standing racism was evident, but people in economic competition with Japanese Americans also supported internment. Although Japanese nationals were forbidden U.S. citizenship or property ownership, American-born Nisei (second generation) and Sansei (third

Tokyo Rose

Thousands of American soldiers fighting the Japanese in the Pacific found their closest link to home in American popular music on Japanese airwaves. Far less comforting, however, many servicemen wrote home about Tokyo Rose, the sultry-voiced, English-speaking announcer who taunted them with tales of wives' and girlfriends' infidelity and predicted, with alarming certainty, devastating attacks on American forces.

An American government investigation in summer 1945 concluded that Tokyo Rose did not exist. Most probably, historians have argued, Tokyo Rose was the creation of American servicemen rather than of Japanese propagandists. Tales of Tokyo Rose enabled soldiers to discuss fears that were too difficult to confront directly.

On the first day of September, however, Iva Toguri as "Tokyo Rose" held a press conference in Japan, most likely prompted by reporters' promise of $2000

for an exclusive interview (money she never received). An American citizen visiting a sick aunt in Japan when the war began, Toguri did host a radio show aimed at American servicemen during the war but as Orphan Ann, not Tokyo Rose. She threatened listeners to "creep up and annihilate them with [her] nail file" rather than with military bombardment and attacks with poison gas that American servicemen remembered hearing.

In this interview, Toguri had, by claiming the identity of Tokyo Rose, seemingly confessed to treason. The U.S. government imprisoned her for a year while they investigated her story. Released for lack of evidence, she attempted to return to the United States, prompting widespread protests. Veterans demanded a trial of the woman who had "betrayed" or caused American servicemen's deaths. In 1949, Toguri was convicted on the basis of perjured testimony and imprisoned for ten years. Toguri's conviction was shaped by the new cold war between the United States and the Soviet Union, as Americans worried about the loyalty of American citizens. America's new superpower status created links to a larger world that shaped national opinions and fears.

© Corbis

When reporters offered $2000 for an interview with "Tokyo Rose," recently married Iva Toguri D'Aquino stepped forward— even though Tokyo Rose did not exist. Shown here being interviewed by U.S. correspondents in Yokohama following the end of the war, Toguri never received the promised funds but was instead arrested and held in custody while the U.S. government investigated her actions during the war.

generation), all U.S. citizens, were successful in business and agriculture. The eviction order forced Japanese Americans to sell property valued at $500 million for a fraction of its worth.

The internees were sent to camps in Arkansas's Mississippi River floodplain; to Wyoming's intermountain terrain; the western Arizona desert; and to other desolate spots in the West. The camps were bleak: Behind barbed wire, families lived in a single room furnished only with cots, blankets, and a bare light bulb. Most had no running water. Toilets and dining and bathing facilities were communal. People nonetheless attempted to sustain community life, setting up schools, consumer cooperatives, and sports leagues. Betrayed by their government, many internees were ambivalent about their loyalty to the United States. Some sought legal remedy, but the Supreme Court upheld the government's action in *Korematsu v. U.S.* (1944). Almost 6,000 of the 120,000 internees renounced U.S. citizenship and demanded to be sent to Japan. Others sought to demonstrate their loyalty. The all–Japanese American 442nd Regimental Combat Team, drawn heavily from internees, was the most decorated unit of its size, receiving a Congressional Medal of Honor, 47 Distinguished Service Crosses, 350 Silver Stars, and more than 3,600 Purple Hearts. In 1988, Congress apologized and paid $20,000 to each of the 60,000 surviving Japanese American internees.

African Americans and "Double V"

African American leaders wanted the nation to confront the parallels between Nazi racist doctrines and Jim Crow segregation in the United States. Proclaiming a "Double V" campaign (victory at home and abroad), groups such as the National Association for the Advancement of Colored People (NAACP) hoped to "persuade, embarrass, compel and shame our government and our nation into a more enlightened attitude toward a tenth of its people." The NAACP, 50,000 strong in 1940, had 450,000 members by 1946. And in 1942, civil rights activists founded the Congress of Racial Equality (CORE), which stressed "nonviolent direct action" and staged sit-ins to desegregate restaurants and movie theaters in Chicago and Washington, D.C.

Military service was a key issue for African Americans, who understood the link between the military service and citizenship. But the U.S. military remained segregated by race and resisted using black units as combat troops. As late as 1943, less than 6 percent of the armed forces were African American. The marines initially refused to accept African Americans, and the navy approximated segregation by assigning black men to service positions in which they would rarely interact with nonblacks as equals or superiors.

A Segregated Military

The federal government and War Department decided that the world war was no time to integrate the military. The majority of Americans (approximately 89 percent of Americans were white) opposed integration. Racism was so entrenched that the Red Cross segregated blood plasma during the war. Integration of military installations, the majority of which were in the South, would have provoked a crisis as federal power contradicted state law. Government and military officials argued that wartime integration would create disorder within the military and hinder America's war effort. General George C. Marshall, Army Chief of Staff, proclaimed "The army is not a sociological laboratory." Hopes for racial justice, so long deferred, were another casualty of the war.

Link to the letter from James Thompson to the *Pittsburgh Courier* about the "Double V" campaign.

National Archives

During World War II, for the first time, the War Department sanctioned the training and use of African American pilots. These members of the 99th Pursuit Squadron—known as "Tuskegee Airmen" because they trained at Alabama's all-black Tuskegee Institute—joined combat over North Africa in June 1943. Like most African American units in the racially segregated armed forces, the men of the 99th Pursuit Squadron were under the command of white officers.

Despite discrimination, African Americans stood up for their rights. Lt. Jackie Robinson refused to move to the back of the bus at the army's Camp Hood, Texas, in 1944—and faced court-martial, even though military regulations forbade discrimination on military vehicles. Black sailors disobeyed orders to return to work after an explosion—caused by the navy practice of assigning untrained men to load bombs onto Liberty ships—destroyed two ships and killed 320 men. When they were court-martialed, future Supreme Court justice and chief counsel for the NAACP Thurgood Marshall claimed that "This is not fifty men on trial for mutiny. This is the Navy on trial for its whole vicious policy toward Negroes."

African American servicemen did eventually fight on the front lines. The "Tuskegee Airmen," pilots trained at the Tuskegee Institute in Alabama, saw heroic service in all-black units, such as the Ninety-ninth Pursuit Squadron, which won eighty Distinguished Flying Crosses. After the war, African Americans called on their wartime service to claim their civil rights. African Americans' wartime experiences were mixed, but the war was a turning point for equal rights.

America and the Holocaust

America's inaction in what we now call the Holocaust is tragic, though the consequences are clearer now than at the time. As the United States turned away refugees on the *St. Louis* (page 689) in early 1939 and refused to relax immigration quotas to admit European Jews and others fleeing Hitler's Germany, almost no one foresaw death camps like Auschwitz. Americans knew they were turning away people fleeing dire persecution, and anti-Semitism played a significant role, but it was not unusual to refuse those seeking refuge, especially during a major economic crisis.

In 1942, American newspapers reported the "mass slaughter" of Jews and other "undesirables" (Gypsies, homosexuals, the physically and mentally handicapped) under Hitler. Many Americans, having been duped by manufactured atrocity tales during World War I, wrongly discounted these stories. But Roosevelt knew about Nazi death camps capable of killing up to two thousand people an hour using the gas Zyklon-B.

In 1943, British and American representatives met in Bermuda but took no action. Appalled, Secretary of the Treasury Henry Morgenthau Jr. charged that the State Department's foot dragging made the United States an accessory to murder. In 1944, Roosevelt created the War Refugee Board, establishing refugee camps in Europe and helping to save 200,000 Jews. But it came too late. By war's end, the Nazis had systematically murdered almost 11 million people.

Life in the Military

More than 15 million men and approximately 350,000 women served in the U.S. armed forces during World War II. Eighteen percent of American families had a father, son, or brother in the military. Some men (and all of the women) volunteered. But more than 10 million were draftees. By presidential order, the military stopped accepting volunteers in December 1942 in an attempt to fill military positions while maintaining war production. The draft extended broadly and mostly equitably across the population during World War II.

> How did racial and gender norms play out in the military during World War II?

Selective Service The Selective Service Act allowed deferments, but they did not disproportionately benefit the wealthy. Almost ten thousand Princeton students or alumni served—as did all four of Franklin and Eleanor Roosevelt's sons. The small number of college deferments was balanced by deferments for many "critical occupations," including war workers and almost 2 million agricultural workers. Most exemptions were for men deemed physically or mentally unqualified to serve. Army physicians discovered the depression's impact as draftees arrived with rotted teeth and deteriorated eyesight—signs of malnutrition. Almost one-third of African American draftees were functionally illiterate, Forty-six percent of African Americans and almost one-third of European-Americans called for the draft were classified "4-F"—unfit for service.

Nonetheless, almost 12 percent of America's population served in the military. Ethnic and regional differences were profound, and northerners and southerners often could not understand one another. Differences among whites were often profound, and although African Americans and Japanese Americans served in separate units, Hispanics, Native Americans, and Chinese Americans served alongside whites. The result was often tension, but many Americans became less prejudiced as they served with men unlike themselves.

Fighting the War Although military service was widespread, the burdens of combat were not equally shared. Women's roles in the U.S. military were much more restricted than in the British or Soviet militaries, where women served in combat-related positions. U.S. women served as nurses, in communications offices, and as typists or cooks. The recruiting slogan for the WACs (Women's Army Corps) was "Release a Man for Combat." However, most men never saw combat either; one-quarter never left the United States. One-third of U.S. military personnel served in clerical positions, filled mainly by well-educated men. African Americans, though assigned dirty and dangerous tasks, were largely kept from combat service. In World War II, lower-class, less-educated white men did most of the fighting.

Combat in World War II was horrible. Hollywood war films depicted men dying bravely, shot cleanly and comforted by buddies in their last moments. In reality, less than 10 percent of casualties were caused by bullets. Most men were killed or wounded by mortars, bombs, or grenades. Seventy-five thousand American men remained missing in action at war's end, blown into fragments too small to identify. Combat meant sliding down a mud-slicked hill into a pile of putrid corpses and using flamethrowers that burned at 2,000 degrees Fahrenheit on other human beings. It meant steering a landing craft through floating body parts, knowing that if you made it ashore, you could be blown apart by artillery. Service was for the war's duration. Only death, serious injury, or victory offered release.

Close to 300,000 American servicemen died in combat, and almost 1 million were wounded, half of them seriously. Medical advances, such as the development of penicillin and the use of blood plasma to prevent shock, helped wounded men survive—but many never fully recovered. Between 20 and 30 percent of combat casualties were psychoneurotic. The federal government censored images of American combat deaths, consigning them to a secret file known as "the chamber of horrors." Americans at home rarely understood what combat had been like.

Winning the War

Why did Truman opt to use the atomic bomb to help end the war, rather than negotiate a peace with Japan?

Axis hopes for victory depended on a short war. German and Japanese leaders knew that, if the United States had time to fully mobilize, flooding the theaters of war with armaments and reinforcing Allied troops with fresh, trained men, the war was lost, but many believed the United States would concede if met with early, decisive defeats. By mid-1942, the Axis powers understood that they had underestimated American resolve and other Allies' willingness to sacrifice their citizens to stop the Axis's advance (see Map 27.1). The chance of an Axis victory grew slim as months passed, but though the outcome was virtually certain after spring 1943, two years of fighting lay ahead.

Tensions Among the Allies

The Allies' suspicions of one another undermined cooperation. The Soviets pressed Britain and the United States to open a second front to draw German troops away from the USSR. The United States and Britain, however, continued to delay. With the alliance badly strained, the three Allied leaders met in Tehran, Iran, in December 1943. Stalin and Roosevelt dismissed Churchill's proposal for another peripheral attack, this time through the Balkans to Vienna. The three agreed to launch **Operation Overlord**—the cross-channel invasion of France—in early 1944. And the Soviet Union promised to aid the Allies against Japan once Germany was defeated.

Operation Overlord: Allied troops stormed a sixty-mile stretch of the Normandy coast in the largest amphibious invasion in history.

War in Europe

The second front opened in the dark morning hours of June 6, 1944: D-Day. In the largest amphibious landing in history, more than 140,000 Allied troops commanded by American general Dwight D. Eisenhower scrambled ashore at Normandy, France. Landing craft and soldiers immediately encountered the enemy; they triggered mines and were pinned down by fire from cliffside pillboxes. Although heavy bombardment and the clandestine work of saboteurs had softened the German defenses, the fighting was ferocious.

By late July, 1.4 million Allied troops spread across the countryside, liberating France and Belgium by the end of August, but leaving a path of devastation. Almost thirty-seven thousand Allied troops died in that struggle, and up to twenty thousand French civilians were killed, most by Allied bombing. German armored divisions counterattacked in Belgium's Ardennes Forest in December, hoping to reach Antwerp to halt Allied supplies through that Belgian port. After weeks of heavy fighting in the **Battle of the Bulge**, the Allies gained control in late January 1945.

Battle of the Bulge: Military offensive led by Germany. Named for the eighty-mile-long and fifty-mile-wide "bulge" that the German troops drove inside the American lines.

By that point, "strategic" bombing destroyed Germany's war production and devastated its economy. In early 1945, the British and Americans began "morale" bombing, killing tens of thousands of civilians in aerial attacks on Berlin and then Dresden. Meanwhile, Soviet troops marched through Poland to Berlin. American forces crossed the Rhine River in March 1945 and captured the industrial Ruhr valley. Several units entered Austria and Czechoslovakia, where they met Soviet soldiers.

Yalta Conference

In early 1945, Franklin Roosevelt, by this time very ill, called for a summit meeting to discuss plans for the postwar world. The three Allied leaders met at Yalta, in the Russian Crimea, in February 1945. Britain, its formerly powerful empire now vulnerable and shrinking, sought to protect its colonial possessions and limit Soviet power. The Soviet Union, with 21 million dead, wanted German reparations for its massive rebuilding effort. The Soviets hoped to expand their sphere of influence throughout eastern Europe and guarantee national security; Germany, Stalin insisted, must be permanently weakened.

The United States also sought to expand its influence and control the peace. Roosevelt lobbied for the United Nations Organization, approved in principle the previous year at Dumbarton Oaks in Washington, D.C., through which the United States hoped to exercise influence. The United States wanted to avoid the debts-reparations fiasco that plagued Europe after World War I. U.S. goals included self-determination for liberated peoples; gradual decolonization; and management of world affairs by what Roosevelt called the Four Policemen: the Soviet Union, Great Britain, the United States, and China. (Roosevelt hoped China might help stabilize Asia after the war. The United States abolished the Chinese Exclusion Act in 1943 to consolidate ties between the two nations.) The United States also wanted to limit Soviet influence in the postwar world.

Military positions during the Yalta conference helped shape the negotiations. Soviet troops occupied eastern European nations, including Poland, where Moscow installed a pro-Soviet regime despite a British-supported Polish government-in-exile in London. With Soviet troops in place, Britain and the United States were limited in negotiating this region's future. The Big Three agreed that some eastern German territory would be transferred to Poland and the remainder divided into four zones—the fourth to be administered by France. Berlin, within the Soviet zone, would also be divided among the four victors. In exchange for U.S. promises to support Soviet claims on territory lost to Japan in the Russo-Japanese War of 1904–1905, Stalin agreed to a treaty of friendship with Jiang Jieshi (Chiang Kai-shek), America's ally in China, rather than with the communist Mao Zedong (Mao Tse-tung), and to declare war on Japan within three months of Hitler's defeat.

Harry S Truman

Franklin D. Roosevelt, reelected to an unprecedented fourth term in November 1944, died on April 12, 1945, and Vice President Harry S Truman became president. Truman, who replaced former vice president Henry Wallace as Roosevelt's running mate in 1944, was inexperienced in foreign policy and was not informed about the top-secret atomic weapons project until he became president. Eighteen days into Truman's presidency, Adolf Hitler killed himself in a bunker in bomb-ravaged Berlin. On May 8, Germany surrendered.

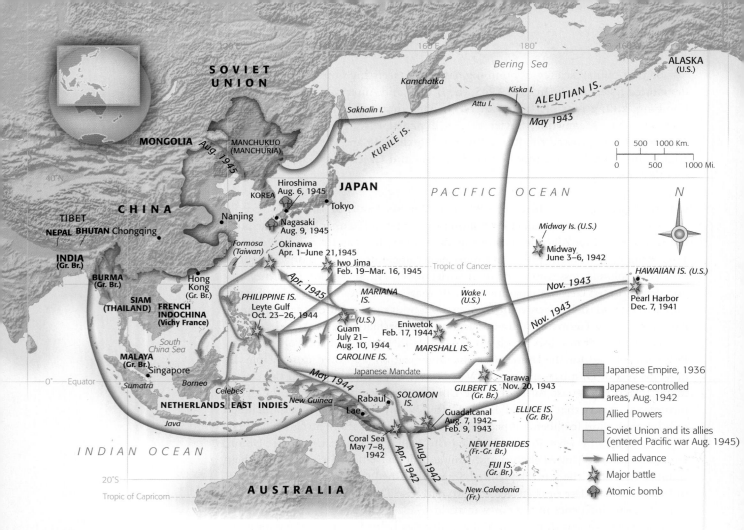

MAP 27.2

The Pacific War

The strategy of the United States was to "island-hop"—from Hawai'i in 1942 to Iwo Jima and Okinawa in 1945. Naval battles were also decisive, notably the Battles of the Coral Sea and Midway in 1942. The war in the Pacific ended with Japan's surrender on August 15, 1945 (V-J Day).

Source: Copyright © Cengage Learning

As the great powers jockeyed for influence after Germany's surrender, the Grand Alliance began to crumble. At the Potsdam Conference in mid-July, Truman was less patient with the Soviets than Roosevelt had been. Truman learned during the conference that a test of the new atomic weapon had been successful. The United States no longer needed the Soviet Union's help in the Pacific war. The Allies did agree that Japan must surrender unconditionally. But with the end of the European war, wartime bonds among the Allies were strained.

War in the Pacific

In the Pacific, the war continued. Since the Battle of Midway in June 1942, American strategy had been to "island-hop" toward Japan, skipping the most fortified islands whenever possible and taking the weaker ones, aiming to strand Japanese armies. To cut off supplies, Americans targeted the Japanese merchant marine. By 1944, Allied troops—from the United States, Britain, Australia, and New Zealand—secured the Solomon, Gilbert, Marshall, and Mariana Islands. General Douglas MacArthur landed at Leyte to retake the Philippines for the United States in October 1944.

In February 1945, while the Big Three were meeting at Yalta, U.S. and Japanese troops battled for Iwo Jima, a small island about 700 miles south of Tokyo. Twenty-one thousand Japanese defenders occupied the island's high ground. Hidden in a caves, trenches, and underground tunnels, they were protected from U.S. aerial bombardment supporting an amphibious landing. The island offered no cover, and marines were slaughtered as they came ashore. For twenty days, U.S. forces fought their way up Mount Suribachi, the highest and most heavily fortified point on Iwo Jima. Iwo Jima claimed 6,821 American and more than twenty thousand Japanese lives.

A month later, American troops landed on Okinawa, an island at the southern tip of Japan, from which Allied forces planned to invade the main Japanese islands. Fighting raged for two months. The monsoon rains began in May, turning battle-fields into seas of mud filled with decaying corpses. The supporting fleet endured mass kamikaze (suicide) attacks, as Japanese pilots intentionally crashed bomb-laden planes into American ships. On Okinawa, 7,374 American soldiers and marines died in battle. Almost the entire Japanese garrison of 100,000 was killed. More than one-quarter of Okinawa's people, or approximately 80,000 civilians, perished.

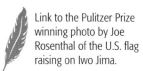

Link to the Pulitzer Prize winning photo by Joe Rosenthal of the U.S. flag raising on Iwo Jima.

Bombing of Japan

With American forces just 350 miles from Japan's main islands, a powerful Japanese military faction was determined to preserve the emperor's sovereignty and avoid an unconditional surrender. On the night of March 9, 1945, 333 American B-29 Superfortresses dropped explosives on a 4-by-3-mile area of Tokyo. They created a firestorm, a fierce blaze that sucked the oxygen from the air, creating hurricane-force winds and growing hot enough to melt concrete and steel. Almost 100,000 people were incinerated, suffocated, or boiled to death hiding in canals. Over the following five months, American bombers attacked sixty-six Japanese cities, leaving 8 million people homeless, killing almost 900,000.

Japan, meanwhile, was attempting to bomb the U.S. mainland. Thousands of bomb-bearing high-altitude balloons, constructed from rice paper and potato-flour paste by schoolgirls, were launched into the jet stream. Those that reached the United States fell on unpopulated areas, occasionally starting forest fires. The only mainland U.S. casualties in the war were five children and an adult on a Sunday school picnic in Oregon who accidentally detonated a balloon bomb. As General Yamamoto had realized at the war's beginning, American resources would far out-last Japan's.

Early in the summer of 1945, Japan put out peace feelers through the Soviets. Japan was not, however, willing to accept the "unconditional surrender" terms the Allied leaders agreed to at Potsdam, and Truman chose not to pursue a negotiated peace. U.S. troops were mobilizing to invade the Japanese home islands, but the Manhattan Project's success offered another option, and Truman took it. Using atomic bombs on Japan, Truman believed, would end the war quickly and save American lives. Concern about the postwar order also influenced Truman's decision;

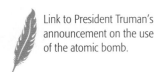

Link to President Truman's announcement on the use of the atomic bomb.

Potsdam Declaration: Ultimatum Truman gave to Japan to surrender unconditionally or face "prompt and utter destruction."

the atomic bomb demonstrated American power and prevented the Soviets from entering the Pacific war and playing a role in the peace that followed.

Some historians argue that Japan was on the verge of unconditional surrender; others that the antisurrender faction was strong enough to prevail. No matter which is true, bombing (whether conventional or atomic) fit the established U.S. strategy of using machines rather than men whenever possible. The decision to use the atomic bomb did not seem as momentous to Truman as it does in retrospect. The moral line had already been crossed with wholesale bombing of civilian populations: the Japanese bombed Shanghai in 1937. Germans "terror-bombed" Warsaw, Rotterdam, and London. British and American bombers purposely created firestorms in German cities, killing 225,000 people on a single night in Dresden, Germany. The American bombing of Japanese cities with conventional weapons already killed nearly a million people. What distinguished the atomic bombs from conventional bombs was their power and efficiency—not that they killed huge numbers of civilians in unspeakably awful ways.

On July 26, 1945, the Allies delivered an ultimatum to Japan: promising that the Japanese people would not be "enslaved," the **Potsdam Declaration** called for

John Launois/Black Star

U.S. Air Force

This scorched watch, found in the rubble at Hiroshima, stopped at the time of the blast—8:16. The shock waves and fires caused by the atomic bomb leveled great expanses of the city. Radiation released by the bomb caused lingering deaths for thousands who survived the explosion. The photo of Hiroshima shown above was taken eight months after the attack.

Nuclear Proliferation

Virtually from the moment of the Hiroshima and Nagasaki atomic bombings, American strategists grappled with the problem of keeping others from the "nuclear club," particularly the Soviet Union. On September 23, 1949, President Truman informed shocked Americans that the Soviets had successfully tested an atomic device.

In the years thereafter, membership in the nuclear club grew, through huge national investments, espionage, and a black market selling raw materials and technologies. There were successful detonations by Great Britain (1952), France (1960), China (1964), India (1974), and Pakistan (1998). Israel crossed the nuclear weapon threshold on the eve of the 1967 Six-Day War but to this day has refused to confirm that it has the bomb. Recently, creditable reports indicate that North Korea has a small nuclear arsenal and that Iran is working to get one.

Still the number of nuclear states is fewer than experts predicted in the 1960s, when analysts warned that thirty nations might be so armed by the 1990s. It did not happen because the five existing nuclear powers committed themselves in the mid-1960s to promoting nonproliferation. Subsequently, twenty-two of thirty-one states that started down the nuclear path changed course and renounced the bomb. By late 2006, the Treaty on the Non-Proliferation of Nuclear Weapons (NPT), enacted on July 1, 1968, had 187 signatories and was hailed as one of the great international agreements of the post-1945 era.

Skeptics took a different view, noting that three states outside the NPT (Israel, India, and Pakistan) became nuclear powers. They charged the "original five" with preventing others from obtaining nuclear arms while keeping large stockpiles themselves. With the world in 2009 awash in some twenty-three thousand nuclear weapons (97 percent belonging to the United States and Russia), critics feared terrorist groups or other nonstate actor getting bombs. In that nightmare scenario, they warned, the de facto post-Nagasaki international moratorium on the use of nuclear weapons would be literally blown away.

unconditional surrender or "prompt and utter destruction." Tokyo radio announced that the government would respond with *mokusatsu* (literally, "kill with silence," or ignore the ultimatum). On August 6, 1945, a B-29 bomber, the *Enola Gay,* dropped an atomic bomb above Hiroshima, igniting a firestorm and killing 130,000 people. Tens of thousands more would suffer from radiation poisoning.

On August 8, the Soviet Union declared war on Japan. On August 9, the United States used a second atomic bomb on Nagasaki, killing sixty thousand people. Five days later, Japan surrendered. Recent histories argue that the Soviet declaration of war played a more significant role in Japan's surrender than America's use of atomic weapons. In the end, the Allies promised that the Japanese emperor could remain as the nation's titular head. World War II was over.

Summary

Hitler once prophesied, "We may be destroyed, but if we are, we shall drag a world with us." World War II devastated much of the globe. In Asia and Europe, ghostlike people wandered through rubble, searching for food. One out of nine people in the Soviet Union had perished: at least 21 million civilian and military war dead. The Chinese lost 10 million; the Germans and Austrians, 6 million; the Japanese,

2.5 million. Up to 1 million died of famine in Japanese-controlled Indochina. Almost 11 million people were murdered in Nazi death camps. Across the globe, World War II killed at least 55 million people.

War required Allied nations with different goals to cooperate. Tensions remained high, as the United States and Britain resisted Stalin's demands for a second front to draw Germans away from the Soviet Union. The United States, meanwhile, was fighting the Japanese in the Pacific. When Japan surrendered in August 1945, the strains between the Soviet Union and its English-speaking Allies made postwar stability unlikely.

American servicemen covered the globe, while on the home front, Americans worked around the clock to make weapons. Despite wartime sacrifices, many Americans found the war had improved their lives. Mobilization ended the Great Depression. Americans moved to war-production centers. The influx of workers strained community resources and sometimes led to social friction and violence. But many Americans—African Americans, Mexican Americans, women, poor whites from the South—found new opportunities in well-paid war jobs. The federal government became a stronger presence, regulating business and employment; overseeing military conscription, and even controlling what people could buy to eat or to wear.

At war's end, only the United States had the economic resources to spur international recovery; only the United States was more prosperous than when war began. In the coming struggle to fashion a new world—the Cold War—the United States held a commanding position. For better or worse—and clearly there were elements of each—World War II was a turning point in the nation's history.

Chapter Review

The United States at War

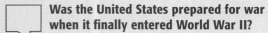

Was the United States prepared for war when it finally entered World War II?

No. The Roosevelt administration had begun efforts to prepare the nation to enter the war, despite strong opposition from much of the public, but those changes—including the institution of the first peacetime draft in the nation's history—were minor compared to the scale of the challenge ahead. The United States did not maintain a large standing army before World War II, and in 1939, the U.S. Army ranked forty-fifth among world armies, and there was only enough equipment for one-third of its troops. President Roosevelt's study of U.S. preparedness determined that the country would not be up to fighting before 1943—a luxury it would not have after the December 7, 1941 attack on Pearl Harbor pulled America officially into the war.

The Production Front and American Workers

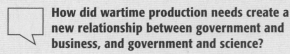

How did wartime production needs create a new relationship between government and business, and government and science?

Mobilizing for war required that factories shift from producing consumer goods to wartime necessities such as uniforms, arms, tanks, and so forth. The federal government enticed businesses to cooperate by offering generous tax write-offs and exemptions from antitrust laws. It also paid to retool or expand factories for war production and guaranteed the bottom line by allowing corporations to charge production costs plus a fixed profit. This enabled companies to double their net profits from 1939 to 1944. The government ensured that labor strikes would not disrupt production by having the newly formed National War Labor Board settle disputes. The government spent millions on university research programs that would develop new war technologies, most importantly, the $2 billion secret Manhattan Project to build an atomic bomb.

Life on the Home Front

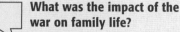 **What was the impact of the war on family life?**

Family life was transformed by the war. Nearly three million families were broken up during the war years, despite government policies that exempted married men and fathers from the draft. Although divorce rates doubled, marriage rates also increased from 73 per 1,000 unmarried women in 1939 to 93 in 1942—with couples scrambling to tie the knot before draftees were sent overseas. Birth rates rose, too, from 2.4 million babies in 1939 to 3.1 million in 1943, as families had children in the hopes of continuing the family should the father not return from war. Despite fears about the erosion of sexual mores, taboos against unwed motherhood remained strong, and only 1 percent of births during the war were to unmarried women. Wartime mobility also increased opportunities for same-sex relationships, and gay communities grew in such cities as San Francisco. Still, the war reinforced traditional gender roles—men served as the nation's defenders while women were to "keep the home fires burning," sometimes filling jobs vacated by soldiers, albeit just "for the duration." Nonetheless, millions of women enjoyed the independence that came with their new responsibilities, and many men returned to families that functioned without them.

The Limits of American Ideals

 In what ways were American notions of civil liberties and basic freedoms tested during the war years?

Without question, tensions emerged between wartime practices and America's democratic ideals. Government propaganda films contrasted American democracy and freedom with totalitarianism and fascism. While U.S. leaders embraced a "strategy of truth" that promised to honestly report the war's progress to the public, the government nonetheless tightly controlled military information—even seemingly unimportant details. Freedoms were in fact curbed, as evident in passage of the 1940 Alien Registration (Smith Act), which made it illegal to advocate overthrowing the U.S. government. But the most grievous civil liberties violation was the treatment of ethnic Americans and resident aliens, notably the internment

of the Japanese. In March 1942, Roosevelt ordered that all 112,000 foreign-born Japanese and Japanese Americans living in California, Oregon, and the state of Washington be removed from the West Coast to "relocation centers"— camps in Arkansas, Wyoming, and Arizona. There were no individual charges; they were imprisoned under suspicion solely because they were of Japanese descent. In 1988, Congress issued a public apology, with included a $20,000 payment to each of the surviving 60,000 Japanese American internees.

Life in the Military

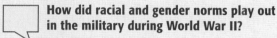 **How did racial and gender norms play out in the military during World War II?**

More than 15 million men and approximately 350,000 women served in the U.S. armed forces during World War II. The discrimination that existed throughout American society was replicated in the armed services: African Americans and Japanese Americans served in units segregated from whites (although Hispanics, Native Americans, and Chinese Americans were part of "white" units). African Americans were given the dirtiest and most dangerous assignments, though they were largely kept from combat service. Less-educated, lower-class white men did most of the fighting. Women who volunteered for the Women's Army Corps and other female military organizations served as nurses, in communications offices, as typists, and as cooks—all military extensions of their traditional gender roles.

Winning the War

 Why did Truman opt to use the atomic bomb to help end the war, rather than negotiate a peace with Japan?

Historians continue to debate this question. From a military standpoint, Truman would only agree to an unconditional surrender of the Japanese, something the Japanese were unlikely to accept. Truman believed that using the atomic bomb would end the war quickly and save U.S. soldiers' lives. He was also concerned about the postwar order and believed the atomic bomb would demonstrate American power and keep the Soviets both from entering the Pacific war and later playing a role in the peace process. Because extensive bombing of Japanese civilian areas had already occurred, Truman did not see the use of the bomb as crossing a moral line the way it would later come to be understood. What distinguished the atomic bombs from conventional bombs, as Truman saw it, was their power and efficiency—not that they killed huge numbers of civilians in unspeakably awful ways.

Suggestions for Further Reading

Michael C. C. Adams, *The Best War Ever: America and World War II* (1993)

Tsuyoshi Hasegawa, *Racing the Enemy: Stalin, Truman, and the Surrender of Japan* (2005)

William I. Hitchcock, *The Bitter Road to Freedom: A New History of the Liberation of Europe* (2008)

John Howard, *Concentration Camps on the Homefront: Japanese Americans in the House of Jim Crow* (2008)

David M. Kennedy, *Freedom from Fear: The American People in Depression and War, 1929–1945* (1999)

Warren F. Kimball, *Forged in War: Roosevelt, Churchill, and the Second World War* (1997)

Nelson Lichtenstein, *Labor's War at Home: The CIO in World War II* (1983)

Gerald F. Linderman, *The World Within War: America's Combat Experience in World War II* (1997)

Leisa Meyers, *Creating G.I. Jane: Sexuality and Power in the Women's Army Corps During World War II* (1996)

George Roeder, Jr., *The Censored War: American Visual Experience During World War II* (1993)

Barbara Dianne Savage, *Broadcasting Freedom: Radio, War, and the Politics of Race, 1938–1948* (1999)

Ronald Takaki, *Double Victory: A Multicultural History of America in World War II* (2000)

 CourseMate   Go to the CourseMate website for primary source links, study tools, and review materials for this chapter. www.cengagebrain.com

28

The Cold War and American Globalism

1945–1961

On July 16, 1945, the "Deer" Team leader parachuted into northern Vietnam, near Kimlung, a village in a valley of rice paddies. Colonel Allison Thomas and five other members of his Office of Strategic Services (OSS) unit could not know that the end of the Second World War was weeks away. Their mission: to work with the Vietminh, a nationalist Vietnamese organization, to sabotage Japanese forces that in March seized Vietnam from France. A banner proclaimed, "Welcome to Our American Friends." Ho Chi Minh, head of the Vietminh, offered the OSS team supper. The next day, Ho denounced the French but remarked "We welcome 10 million Americans." "Forget the Communist Bogy," Thomas radioed OSS headquarters in China.

A communist dedicated to winning his nation's independence from France, Ho joined the French Communist Party after World War I. For the next two decades, living in China, the Soviet Union, and elsewhere, he planned and fought to free his nation from French colonialism. During World War II, Ho's Vietminh warriors harassed French and Japanese forces and rescued downed American pilots. In March 1945, Ho met with U.S. officials in China. Receiving no aid from his ideological allies in the Soviet Union, Ho hoped the United States would favor his nation's quest for liberation.

Other OSS personnel soon parachuted into Kimlung, including a male nurse who diagnosed Ho's ailments as malaria and dysentery. Quinine and sulfa drugs restored his health, but Ho remained frail. Everywhere the Americans went, impoverished villagers thanked them with gifts of food and clothing, interpreting the foreigners' presence as a sign of U.S. anticolonial and anti-Japanese sentiments. In early August, the Deer Team offered Vietminh soldiers weapons training. Ho hoped young Vietnamese could study in the United States and that U.S. technicians could help build an independent Vietnam.

A second OSS unit, the "Mercy" Team, headed by Captain Archimedes Patti, arrived in the city of Hanoi on August 22. But, unbeknownst to these OSS members, who believed that President Franklin D. Roosevelt's sympathy for eventual Vietnamese

Chapter Outline

From Allies to Adversaries
Decolonization | Stalin's Aims | U.S. Economic and Strategic Needs | Stalin and Truman | The Beginning of the Cold War | Atomic Diplomacy | Truman Doctrine | Inevitable Cold War?

VISUALIZING THE PAST *Stalin: Ally to Adversary*

Containment in Action
Lippmann's Critique | Marshall Plan | National Security Act | Berlin Blockade and Airlift | Twin Shocks

The Cold War in Asia
Chinese Civil War | Vietnam's Quest for Independence

The Korean War
U.S. Forces Intervene | Chinese Entry into the War | Truman's Firing of MacArthur | Peace Agreement | Consequences of the War

Unrelenting Cold War
"Massive Retaliation" | CIA as Foreign Policy Instrument | Nuclear Buildup | Rebellion in Hungary | U-2 Incident | Formosa Resolution

LINKS TO THE WORLD *The People-to-People Campaign*

The Struggle for the Third World
Interests in the Third World | Racism and Segregation as U.S. Handicaps | Development and Modernization | Intervention in Guatemala

The Cuban Revolution and Fidel Castro | Arab-Israeli Conflict | Suez Crisis | Eisenhower Doctrine | Geneva Accords on Vietnam | National Liberation Front

LEGACY FOR A PEOPLE AND A NATION
The National Security State

SUMMARY

independence remained U.S. policy, the new Truman administration had decided to let France decide Vietnam's fate. That policy change explains why Ho never received answers to the letters and telegrams he sent to Washington beginning August 30, 1945.

On September 2, 1945, with OSS personnel present, Ho Chi Minh read his declaration of independence for the Democratic Republic of Vietnam: "All men are created equal; they are endowed by their Creator with certain unalienable Rights; among these are Life, Liberty, and the pursuit of Happiness." Borrowing from the internationally renowned 1776 American document, Ho itemized Vietnamese grievances against France.

In a last meeting with Captain Patti, Ho expressed sadness that the United States armed the French to reestablish their colonial rule in Vietnam. Sure, Ho said, U.S. officials in Washington judged him a Moscow puppet because he was a communist. But Ho claimed that he drew inspiration from the American struggle for independence. Ho insisted the Vietnamese would go it alone. And they did—first against the French and eventually against more than half a million U.S. troops in what became the United States' longest war.

Because Ho Chi Minh and many of his nationalist followers declared themselves communists, U.S. leaders rejected their appeal. Endorsing the containment doctrine against communism, American presidents from Truman to George H. W. Bush believed that a ruthless Soviet Union directed a worldwide communist conspiracy against peace, free-market capitalism, and democracy. Soviet leaders from Joseph Stalin to Mikhail Gorbachev protested that a militarized, economically aggressive United States sought world domination. This protracted contest between the United States and the Soviet Union acquired the name Cold War.

The primary feature of world affairs for more than four decades, the Cold War was fundamentally a contest between the United States and the Soviet Union over spheres of influence. The contest between the capitalist West and the communist East dominated international relations and eventually took the lives of millions, cost trillions of dollars, spawned doomsday fears, and destabilized several nations. Occasionally, the two superpowers negotiated and signed agreements to temper their dangerous arms race; at other times, they went to the brink of war and armed allies to fight vicious Third World conflicts. Sometimes these allies had their own ambitions and resisted pressure from one or both superpowers.

Vietnam was part of the *Third World,* a term for nations that in the Cold War era wore neither the West (the First World) nor the East (the Second World) label. Sometimes called developing countries, Third World nations were generally nonwhite, nonindustrialized, and located in the southern half of the globe—in Asia, Africa, the Middle East, and Latin America. Many had been colonies of European nations or Japan and were vulnerable to the Cold War rivalry. U.S. leaders often interpreted their anticolonialism as Soviet inspired rather than as expressions of indigenous nationalism. Vietnam became one among many sites where Cold War fears and Third World aspirations intersected, prompting U.S. intervention and a globalist foreign policy that regarded the world as the appropriate sphere for America's influence.

Critics in the United States challenged Cold War exaggerations of threats from abroad, meddlesome interventions in the Third World, and militarization of foreign policy. But when leaders like Truman described the Cold War as a life-and-death struggle against a monstrous enemy, critics were drowned out by charges that dissenters were soft on communism, if not un-American. U.S. leaders successfully cultivated a Cold War consensus that stifled debate and shaped the mindset of generations of Americans.

As you read this chapter, keep the following questions in mind:

* **Why did relations between the Soviet Union and the United States turn hostile soon after their victory in World War II?**

* **When and why did the Cold War expand from a struggle over the future of Europe and central Asia to one encompassing virtually the entire globe?**

* **By what means did the Truman and Eisenhower administrations seek to expand America's global influence in the late 1940s and the 1950s?**

From Allies to Adversaries

Was the Cold War inevitable?

World War II unsettled the international system. Germany was in ruins. Great Britain was overstrained, France was rent by internal division, and Italy was weakened. Japan was decimated and occupied, and China was headed toward renewed civil war. Throughout Europe and Asia, factories, transportation, and communications links were reduced to rubble, and agricultural production plummeted. The United States and the Soviet Union offered different solutions. The collapse of Germany and Japan, moreover, created power vacuums that drew the two major powers into collision as they sought influence where Axis aggressors had once held sway. For example, in Greece and China, where civil wars raged between leftists and conservative regimes, the two powers supported opposite sides.

Decolonization   With empires disintegrating, a new Third World emerged. Financial constraints and nationalist rebellions forced the imperial states to set their colonies free. Britain exited India (and Pakistan) in 1947 and Burma and Sri Lanka (Ceylon) in 1948. The Philippines gained independence from the United States in 1946. After four years of battling nationalists in Indonesia, the Dutch left in 1949. In the Middle East, Lebanon (1943), Syria (1946), and Jordan (1946) gained independence, while in Palestine British officials faced pressure from Zionists intent on creating a Jewish homeland and from Arab leaders opposed to it. In Iraq, nationalist agitation increased against the British-installed government. Washington and Moscow saw these new or emerging Third World states as potential allies that might provide military bases, resources, and markets. Some new nations, however, chose nonalignment in the Cold War.

Chronology

1945	Roosevelt dies; Truman becomes president Atomic bombings of Japan		1951	United States signs Mutual Security Treaty with Japan
1946	Kennan's "long telegram" criticizes USSR Vietnamese war against France erupts		1953	Eisenhower becomes president Stalin dies United States helps restore shah to power in Iran Korean War ends
1947	Truman Doctrine seeks aid for Greece and Turkey Marshall offers Europe economic assistance National Security Act reorganizes government		1954	Geneva accords partition Vietnam CIA-led coup overthrows Arbenz in Guatemala
1948	Communists take power in Czechoslovakia Truman recognizes Israel United States organizes Berlin airlift		1955	Soviets create Warsaw Pact
			1956	Soviets crush uprising in Hungary Suez crisis sparks war in Middle East
1949	NATO founded as anti-Soviet alliance Soviet Union explodes atomic bomb Mao's communists win power in China		1957	Soviets fire first ICBM and launch *Sputnik*
			1958	U.S. troops land in Lebanon Berlin crisis
1950	NSC-68 recommends major military buildup Korean War starts in June; China enters in fall		1959	Castro ousts Batista in Cuba
			1960	Eighteen African colonies become independent

Stalin's Aims

The United States and Soviet Union assessed their most pressing tasks differently. The Soviets, though committed to victory over capitalist countries, were most concerned about preventing another invasion of their homeland. Its land mass was three times that of the United States, but it had only 10,000 miles of seacoast, which was under ice for much of the year. Russian leaders before and after the revolution made increased maritime access a chief foreign policy aim.

Worse, the USSR's geographical frontiers were hard to defend. Siberia, vital for mineral resources, lay 6,000 miles east of Moscow and was vulnerable to encroachment by Japan and China. In the west, the border with Poland generated violent clashes since World War I, and 25 million Russians died after Hitler's invasion in 1941. Henceforth, Soviet leaders wanted no dangers along their western borders.

Overall, however, Soviet territorial objectives were limited. Although Americans were quick to compare Stalin to Hitler, Stalin's aims were more limited and resembled those of tsars before him: he wanted to push the Soviet Union's borders to include the Baltic states of Estonia, Latvia, and Lithuania, along with the eastern part of prewar Poland. To the south, Stalin wanted a presence in northern Iran, and he pressed the Turks for naval bases and free access out of the Black Sea. Economically, the Soviets did not promote rapid rebuilding of the region's war-ravaged economies or expanded world trade.

U.S. Economic and Strategic Needs

The United States, by contrast, came out of the war secure in its borders. Separated from other world powers by two oceans, the U.S. home base was virtually immune from attack during the fighting. American casualties were fewer than any of the other major combatants. With its fixed capital intact, its resources more plentiful than

Stalin: Ally to Adversary

These two *Look* magazine portrayals of Soviet leader Stalin indicate how quickly the Grand Alliance of World War II disintegrated into the superpower confrontation of the Cold War. In the first piece, from mid 1944, correspondent Ralph Parker writes that Stalin spends half his time writing poetry and the other half reading it to the school children who clamor to sit on his knee. "Stalin," Parker adds, "is undoubtedly among the best-dressed of all world leaders making Churchill in his siren suit look positively shabby." Four years later, Louis Fischer paints a very different picture. "This small man with drooping shoulders tyrannizes one-fifth of the world," Fischer writes of the Soviet leader, adding that neither Hitler nor any Russian czar were as powerful or as menacing as the "Great Red Father." What do these two items suggest about American attitudes toward the outside world? What do they suggest about the role of the press in U.S. society?

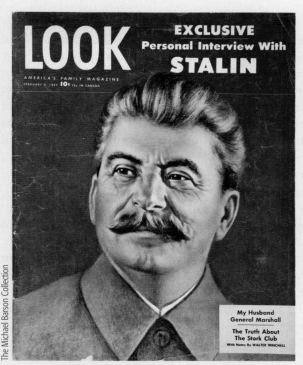

"A Guy named Joe" cover story of Look Magazine by Ralph Parker, June 27, 1944.

"Life Story of Stalin" by Louis Fischer in Look Magazine, June 8, 1948

The Michael Barson Collection

ever, and in lone possession of the atomic bomb, the United States was the strongest power in the world at war's end.

But Washington officials worried about complacency. Some other power—almost certainly the Soviet Union—could take advantage of instability in war-torn Europe and Asia and seize control of these areas, with dire implications for the United States' security. Therefore, Washington sought bases overseas to keep an airborne enemy at bay. To enhance U.S. security, U.S. planners sought the quick reconstruction of nations—including former enemies Germany and Japan—and a world economy based on free trade.

The Soviets, on the other hand, refused to join the new World Bank and International Monetary Fund (IMF), created at the July 1944 Bretton Woods Conference by forty-four nations to stabilize trade and finance. They held that the United States dominated both institutions and used them to promote private investment and open international commerce, which Moscow saw as capitalist tools. With the United States as its largest donor, the World Bank opened in 1945 and made loans to finance members' reconstruction projects; the IMF, also heavily U.S.-backed, helped members meet their balance-of-payments problems through currency loans.

Stalin and Truman

Joseph Stalin, though hostile to the western powers and capable of ruthlessness against his people (his periodic purges since the 1930s took the lives of millions), did not want war. He was aware of his country's weakness vis-à-vis the United States and believed he must try to achieve his aspirations through cooperation. Stalin believed that Germany and Japan would eventually threaten the Soviet Union, and his suspicion of capitalist powers was boundless. Many concluded that Stalin was clinically paranoid. As historian David Reynolds has noted, this alleged paranoia, coupled with Stalin's xenophobia (fear of anything foreign) and his Marxist-Leninist ideology, created in him a mental map of them versus us that influenced his approach to world affairs.

Harry Truman had none of Stalin's capacity for ruthlessness, but to a lesser degree he, too, was also prone to a "them versus us" world-view. He often glossed over nuances, ambiguities, and counterevidence, preferring an either/or answer. Truman exaggerated, as when he declared in his undelivered farewell address that he "knocked the socks off the communists" in Korea. When Truman protested in 1945 during a meeting at the White House that the Soviets were not fulfilling the Yalta agreement on Poland, the Soviet commissar of foreign affairs, V. M. Molotov, stormed out. Truman self-consciously developed what he called his tough method, which became a trademark of U.S. Cold War diplomacy.

The Beginning of the Cold War

No precise start for the Cold War's beginning can be given. It resulted from an ongoing process that arguably began in 1917 with the Bolshevik Revolution and the western powers' hostile response. But in a more meaningful sense, it began in mid-1945, as World War II ended. By spring 1947, certainly, the struggle had begun.

One of the first Soviet-American clashes came in Poland in 1945, when the Soviets blocked the Polish government-in-exile in London from becoming part of the communist government that Moscow sponsored. The Soviets also extinguished civil liberties in Romania, arguing that the United States similarly manipulated Italy.

Moscow initially allowed free elections in Hungary and Czechoslovakia, but as the Cold War accelerated and U.S. influence in Europe expanded, the Soviets encouraged communist coups in Hungary (1947) and Czechoslovakia (1948). Yugoslavia was unique: its independent communist government, led by Josip Broz Tito, broke with Stalin in 1948.

To defend their actions, Moscow officials noted that the United States was reviving their traditional enemy, Germany, and was meddling in eastern Europe. The Soviets cited clandestine American meetings with anti-Soviet groups, repeated calls for elections likely to produce anti-Soviet regimes, and the use of loans to gain political influence (financial diplomacy). Moscow charged that the United States was pursuing a double standard—intervening in eastern Europe but demanding that the Soviet Union stay out of Latin America and Asia. The United States called for free elections in the Soviet sphere, Moscow noted, but not in the U.S. sphere in Latin America.

Atomic Diplomacy

The Soviets believed the United States was practicing "atomic diplomacy"—maintaining a nuclear monopoly to scare the Soviets into diplomatic concessions. Secretary of State James F. Byrnes thought that the atomic bomb could deter Soviet expansion, but Secretary of War Henry L. Stimson disagreed in 1945. If Americans continued to have "this weapon rather ostentatiously on our hip," he warned Truman, the Soviets' "suspicions and their distrust of our purposes and motives will increase."

In this atmosphere, Truman refused to turn over the weapon to an international authority. In 1946, he backed the Baruch Plan, named after its author, financier Bernard Baruch, which provided for U.S. abandonment of its atomic monopoly only after the world's fissionable materials were controlled by an international agency. The Soviets retorted that it would require them to shut down their atomic-bomb development project while the United States continued its own. Washington and Moscow soon became locked in a frightening nuclear arms race.

By the middle of 1946, Soviets and Americans clashed on every front. When the United States refused a Soviet request for a reconstruction loan but gave one to Britain, Moscow upbraided Washington for using its dollars to manipulate foreign governments. The two Cold War powers also backed different groups in Iran, where the United States helped bring the pro-West shah to the throne. Unable to agree on the unification of Germany, the former allies built up their zones independently.

After Stalin gave a speech in February 1946 depicting the world as threatened by capitalist acquisitiveness, the U.S. chargé d'affaires in Moscow, **George F. Kennan**, sent a pessimistic long telegram to Washington. His widely circulated report fed a growing belief among U.S. officials that only toughness would work with the Soviets. The following month, in Fulton, Missouri, former British prime minister Winston Churchill warned that a Soviet-erected iron curtain cut off eastern European countries from the West. With an approving Truman nearby, Churchill called for Anglo-American partnership to resist the new menace.

The growing Soviet-American tensions had major implications for the United Nations. The delegates who gathered in San Francisco in April 1945 to sign the U.N. charter agreed on an organization that included a General Assembly of all member states and a smaller Security Council spearheading peace and security issues. Five great powers were given permanent seats on the council—the United States, the Soviet Union, Great Britain, China, and France—and could each exercise a veto

George F. Kennan: American diplomat in Moscow, architect of the Cold War policy of containment.

against any proposed action. To be effective on the major issues of war and peace, therefore, the U.N. needed great power. Of the fifty-one founding states, twenty-two came from the Americas and another fifteen from Europe, which effectively gave the United States a large majority in the assembly. In retaliation, Moscow exercised its veto in the Security Council.

Some high-level U.S. officials were dismayed by the administration's harsh anti-Soviet posture. Secretary of Commerce Henry A. Wallace charged that Truman's get-tough policy substituted atomic and economic coercion for diplomacy. Wallace told a Madison Square Garden audience in September 1946 that "getting tough never brought anything real and lasting—whether for schoolyard bullies, or businessmen or world powers." Truman fired Wallace, blasting him privately as "a real Commy."

Truman Doctrine

East-West tensions escalated further in early 1947, when Britain requested American help in Greece defending their conservative client-government (a government dependent on the economic or military support of a more powerful country) in a civil war against leftists. The Republican Eightieth Congress wanted less spending; many of its members had little respect for the Democratic president who voters repudiated in the 1946 elections by giving the GOP ("Grand Old Party," the Republican Party) majorities in both houses of Congress. Republican senator Arthur Vandenberg of Michigan, a bipartisan leader, told the president that he would have to "scare hell out of the American people" to gain congressional approval.

Link to the Truman Doctrine.

Thus, the president delivered a speech laced with alarmist language staking out the United States' role in the postwar world. Truman claimed that communism imperiled the world. "If Greece should fall under the control of an armed minority," he concluded in an early version of the domino theory, "the effect upon its neighbor, Turkey, would be immediate and serious. Confusion and disorder might well spread throughout the entire Middle East." Truman articulated what became known as the **Truman Doctrine**: "It must be the policy of the United States to support free peoples who are resisting attempted subjugation by armed minorities or by outside pressures."

Truman Doctrine: U.S. policy designed to contain the spread of communism; began with President Truman's 1947 request to Congress for economic and military aid to the struggling countries of Greece and Turkey to prevent them from succumbing to Soviet pressure.

Critics correctly pointed out that the Soviet Union was little involved in the Greek civil war, that the communists in Greece were more pro-Tito than pro-Stalin, and that the resistance movement had noncommunist as well as communist members. Truman countered that, should communists gain control of Greece, they might open the door to Soviet power in the Mediterranean. The Senate approved Truman's request by 67 to 23 votes. Using U.S. dollars and military advisers, the Greek government defeated the insurgents in 1949, and Turkey became a U.S. ally on the Soviets' border.

Inevitable Cold War?

In the months after Truman's speech, the term *Cold War* slipped into the lexicon as a description of the Soviet-American relationship. Within two years of the victory over the Axis powers, the two Grand Alliance members were locked in a struggle for world dominance that would last almost half a century. Even before World War II ended, observers anticipated that the United States and the Soviet Union would seek to fill the power vacuum. The two countries had a history of hostility and were militarily powerful. Most of all, they were divided by sharply differing political economies with divergent needs and by a deep ideological chasm.

It is far less clear that the conflict had to result in a Cold War. The "cold peace" that had prevailed from the revolution in 1917 through World War II could conceivably have continued into the postwar years. Neither side's leadership wanted war. Both hoped—at least initially—that cooperation could be maintained. The Cold War resulted from decisions by individuals who might have done more to maintain diplomatic dialog and negotiate solutions to international problems. For decades, Americans would wonder if the high price they were paying for victory in the superpower confrontation was necessary.

Containment in Action

To counter Soviet and communist expansion, the Truman team chose a policy of **containment**. George Kennan, now at the State Department in Washington, published an influential statement of the containment doctrine. Writing as Mr. X in the July 1947 issue of *Foreign Affairs* magazine, Kennan advocated a "policy of firm containment, designed to confront the Russians with unalterable counterforce at every point where they show signs of encroaching upon the interests of a peaceful and stable world." Such counterforce, Kennan argued, would check Soviet expansion. Kennan's X article joined the Truman Doctrine as a key manifesto of Cold War policy.

Was the U.S. containment policy successful?

containment: U.S. policy uniting military, economic, and diplomatic strategies to prevent the spread of Soviet communism and to enhance America's security and influence abroad.

Lippmann's Critique

The veteran journalist Walter Lippmann took issue with the containment doctrine in his powerful book *The Cold War* (1947), calling it a "strategic monstrosity" that failed to distinguish between areas vital and peripheral to U.S. security. Nor did Lippmann share Truman's conviction that the Soviet Union was plotting to take over the world. Ironically, Kennan agreed with much of Lippmann's critique and soon distanced himself from the doctrine he helped create.

Invoking the containment doctrine, the United States in 1947 and 1948 began to build an international economic and defensive network to protect American prosperity and security and to advance U.S. hegemony. In western Europe, the region of primary concern, American diplomats pursued economic reconstruction, the ouster of communists from governments, as occurred in 1947 in France and Italy, and blockage of "third force" or neutralist tendencies. Officials also kept the decolonization of European empires orderly. Meanwhile, American culture—consumer goods, music, consumption ethic, and production techniques—permeated European societies. Some Europeans resisted Americanization, but transatlantic ties strengthened.

Marshall Plan

Americans, who already spent billions of dollars on European relief and recovery by 1947, remembered too well the troubles of the 1930s: global depression, political extremism, and war born of economic discontent. Such cataclysms could not be allowed to happen again; communism must not replace fascism. Hence, in June 1947, Secretary of State George C. Marshall announced that the United States would finance a massive European recovery program. Launched in 1948, the **Marshall Plan** sent $12.4 billion to western Europe until 1951 (see Map 28.1). To stimulate business at home, the legislation required that Europeans spend this aid on American-made products. The Marshall Plan proved a mixed success; it caused inflation, failed to solve a balance-of-payments problem, took only tentative steps toward economic integration, and further divided Europe

Marshall Plan: The Truman administration's proposal for massive U.S. economic aid to speed the recovery of war-torn Europe.

MAP 28.1

Divided Europe

After the Second World War, Europe broke into two competing camps. When the United States launched the Marshall Plan in 1948, the Soviet Union countered with its own economic plan the following year. When the United States created NATO in 1949, the Soviet Union answered with the Warsaw Pact in 1955. On the whole, these two camps held firm until the late 1980s.

Source: Copyright © Cengage Learning

Map legend:

$ Participants in the Marshall Plan

Member of NATO,* formed in 1949

Member of COMECON,** formed in 1949, and the Warsaw Pact, organized in 1955

● Member of the European Common Market, formed in 1958

Iron Curtain

* North Atlantic Treaty Organization
** Council for Mutual Economic Assistance

ICELAND — Reykjavík
Joined Common Market, 1973

IRELAND — Dublin

UNITED KINGDOM — London
U.S. loan of $3.5 billion, 1946
Exploded first atomic bomb, 1952
Joined Common Market, 1973

NORWAY — Oslo

SWEDEN — Stockholm

FINLAND — Helsinki

DENMARK — Copenhagen
Joined Common Market, 1973

NETHERLANDS — Amsterdam

BELGIUM — Brussels

LUX.

FRANCE — Paris
Exploded first atomic bomb, 1960
Withdrew from NATO, 1966

WEST GERMANY — Bonn

EAST GERMANY — East Berlin
West Berlin
Berlin blockade, 1948–1949

SWITZ. — Bern

POLAND — Warsaw

CZECHOSLOVAKIA — Prague
Communist coup, 1948
U.S.S.R. invasion, 1968

AUSTRIA — Vienna
Joined NATO, 1955
Zones of occupation ended, 1955

HUNGARY — Budapest
Revolution, 1956

ITALY — Rome

YUGOSLAVIA — Belgrade
Tito-Stalin schism, 1948

ROMANIA — Bucharest

BULGARIA — Sofia

ALBANIA — Tiranë
Left COMECON, 1961
Withdrew from WP, 1968

GREECE — Athens
Truman Doctrine, 1947
Joined NATO, 1952
Joined Common Market, 1981

TURKEY — Ankara
Truman Doctrine, 1947
Joined NATO, 1952

CYPRUS — Nicosia

PORTUGAL — Lisbon
Joined Common Market, 1986

SPAIN — Madrid
Joined NATO, 1982
Joined Common Market, 1986

UNION OF SOVIET SOCIALIST REPUBLICS — Moscow
Exploded first atomic bomb, 1949

Volga R.
Don R.
Dnieper R.
Danube R.

Caspian Sea
Black Sea
Baltic Sea
North Sea
Mediterranean Sea
ATLANTIC OCEAN

Corsica
Sardinia
Sicily
Balearic Is.

Arctic Circle

400 Mi.
400 Km.
200
0

20W 0 20E 40E 60E
40N 50N 60N

between "East" and "West." But the program spurred impressive western European industrial production and investment, started the region toward self-sustaining economic growth, and—from the American perspective—contained communism.

National Security Act

Truman streamlined U.S. defense by working with Congress on the **National Security Act of July 1947**. The act created the Office of Secretary of Defense (which became the Department of Defense two years later) to oversee the armed services, the National Security Council (NSC) of high-level officials to advise the president, and the Central Intelligence Agency (CIA) to conduct spy operations and information gathering overseas. By the early 1950s, the CIA expanded to include covert (secret) operations aimed at overthrowing unfriendly foreign leaders. The National Security Act gave the president increased powers regarding foreign policy.

In response, Stalin forbade communist satellite governments in eastern Europe to accept Marshall Plan aid and ordered communist parties in western Europe to work to thwart it. He also created the Cominform, an organization designed to coordinate communist activities around the world. Whereas U.S. planners saw the Marshall Plan as protecting their European friends against a potential Soviet threat, to Stalin it raised anew the specter of capitalist penetration. He tightened his grip on eastern Europe—most notably, engineering a coup in Czechoslovakia in February 1948 that ensured full Soviet control, which heightened anxiety in the United States.

National Security Act of July 1947: Act that unified the armed forces under a single agency, later called the Department of Defense. It also established the National Security Council to advise the president on matters of national security and created the Central Intelligence Agency (CIA).

Berlin Blockade and Airlift

In June 1948, the Americans, French, and British agreed to fuse their German zones, and integrate West Germany (the Federal Republic of Germany) into the western European economy. Fearing a resurgent Germany tied to the American Cold War camp, the Soviets cut off western land access to the jointly occupied city of Berlin, located inside the Soviet zone. President Truman then ordered the **Berlin airlift**, a massive airlift of food, fuel, and other supplies to Berlin. The Soviets finally lifted the blockade in May 1949 and founded the German Democratic Republic, or East Germany.

The successful airlift may have saved Truman's political career; he narrowly defeated Republican Thomas E. Dewey in the November 1948 presidential election. Truman next formalized the military alliance among the United States, Canada, and western Europe. In April 1949, twelve nations signed a mutual defense treaty, agreeing that an attack on any one of them would be considered an attack on all, and establishing the **North Atlantic Treaty Organization** (NATO; see Map 28.1).

Berlin airlift: American program to deliver food and supplies to the people of the blockaded city of Berlin, Germany.

Not since 1778 had the United States entered a formal European military alliance, and some critics, such as Senator Robert A. Taft, Republican of Ohio, claimed that NATO would provoke rather than deter war. Administration officials responded that should the Soviets ever probe westward, NATO would bring the full force of the United States to bear on the Soviet Union. Truman officials also hoped that NATO would keep western Europeans from embracing communism or even neutralism in the Cold War. The Senate ratified the treaty by 82 votes to 13, and the United States began to spend billions of dollars under the Mutual Defense Assistance Act.

By summer 1949, Truman and his advisers were basking in the successes of their foreign policy. Containment was working, West Germany was recovering, the Berlin

North Atlantic Treaty Organization: A mutual defense pact between the United States and eleven other nations—including Europe and Canada—promising to stand united in the face of military aggression, specifically by the Soviet Union.

Mao Zedong: Chinese military and political leader who established the communist People's Republic of China.

Link to William Faulkner's Nobel Prize speech about nuclear war, fear, and the artist.

NSC-68: Secret report by the National Security Council that would characterize U.S. Cold War strategy for decades; it saw the clash between the United States and the Soviet Union as a fight between good and evil and reversed post World War military demobilization, focusing instead on military build-up.

How did the Cold War turn "hot" in Asia?

blockade had been defeated, and NATO had been formed. True, there was trouble in China, where the communists under **Mao Zedong** were winning a civil war. But that struggle would likely wax and wane for years to come. Just possibly, some dared to think, Harry Truman was on his way to winning the Cold War.

Twin Shocks

Then, suddenly, in late September, came two momentous developments that made Americans feel in even greater danger than ever before. First, a U.S. reconnaissance aircraft detected unusually high radioactivity in the atmosphere: the Soviets had exploded an atomic device. With the U.S. nuclear monopoly erased, western Europe seemed more vulnerable. Second, the communists in China completed their conquest sooner than many expected. Now the world's largest and most populous countries were ruled by communists, and one of them had the atomic bomb.

Rejecting calls for high-level negotiations, Truman in early 1950 gave the go-ahead for production of a hydrogen bomb, the "Super." Kennan bemoaned the militarization of the Cold War and was replaced at the State Department by Paul Nitze. The National Security Council delivered to the president in April 1950 a significant top-secret document tagged **NSC-68**. Predicting continued tension with expansionistic communists, the report, authored primarily by Nitze, urged a much enlarged military budget and the mobilization of public support. The Cold War was about to become vastly more expensive and far-reaching.

The Cold War in Asia

Asia gradually became ensnared in the Cold War. Indeed, the consequences of an expansive containment doctrine would exact its heaviest price on the United States, in the bloody wars in Korea and Vietnam. Though less important to both superpowers than Europe, Asia would be the continent where the Cold War most often turned hot.

From the start, Japan was crucial to U.S. strategy. The United States monopolized Japan's reconstruction through a military occupation directed by General Douglas MacArthur. Truman disliked "Mr. Prima Donna, Brass Hat" MacArthur, but MacArthur wrote a democratic constitution, gave women voting rights, revitalized the economy, and destroyed the nation's weapons. U.S. authorities Americanized Japan by censoring films critical of the United States (for the destruction of Hiroshima, for example) or depicting Japanese customs, such as suicide, arranged marriages, and swordplay. In 1951, the United States and Japan signed a separate peace that restored Japan's sovereignty and ended the occupation. A Mutual Security Treaty that year provided for the stationing of U.S. forces in Japan, including a U.S. base on Okinawa.

Chinese Civil War

The administration had less success in China. The United States had long backed the Nationalists of Jiang Jieshi (Chiang Kai-shek) against Mao Zedong's communists. But after World War II, Generalissimo Jiang's government had become corrupt, inefficient, and out of touch with discontented peasants, whom the communists enlisted with promises of land reform. Jiang also subverted American efforts to negotiate a cease-fire and a coalition government.

American officials divided on the question of whether Mao was an Asian Tito—communist but independent—or, as most believed, part of an international communist movement that might give the Soviets a springboard into Asia. Thus, when Chinese communists made secret overtures to the United States for diplomatic talks in 1945 and 1949, American officials rebuffed them. Mao leaned to the Soviet side in the Cold War. Because of China's fierce independence, a Sino-Soviet schism opened.

With his victory in September 1949, Mao proclaimed the People's Republic of China (PRC). Truman hesitated to extend diplomatic recognition to the new government. U.S. officials became alarmed by the 1950 Sino-Soviet treaty of friendship and the harassment of Americans in China. Truman also chose nonrecognition because vocal Republican critics, the so-called China lobby, pinned Jiang's defeat on Truman. The president argued that despite billions of dollars in American aid, Jiang proved a poor instrument of containment. Not until 1979 did official Sino-American relations resume.

Vietnam's Quest for Independence

Mao's victory in China drew urgent American attention to Indochina, the southeast Asian peninsula held by France for the better part of a century. The Japanese wrested control over Indochina during World War II, but the Vietnamese nationalists grew stronger. Their leader, Ho Chi Minh, hoped to use Japan's defeat to assert Vietnamese independence, and he sought U.S. support. American rejected Ho's appeals in favor of restoring French rule, mostly to ensure France's cooperation in the emerging Soviet-American confrontation. Ho, the State Department declared, was an "agent of international communism" who would assist Soviet and, after 1949, Chinese expansionism. Overlooking the native roots of the nationalist rebellion against French colonialism, Washington officials interpreted events in Indochina through a Cold War lens.

When war between the Vietminh and France broke out in 1946, the United States initially took a hands-off approach. But when Jiang's regime collapsed in China three years later, the Truman administration in February 1950 recognized the French puppet government of Bao Dai, a playboy and former emperor. To many Vietnamese, the United States thus became in essence a colonial power, an ally of the hated French. Second, in May, the administration agreed to send weapons and assistance to sustain the French in Indochina. From 1945 to 1954, the United States gave $2 billion of the $5 billion that France spent to keep Vietnam within its empire—to no avail (see Chapters 30 and 31). How Vietnam became the site of the United States' longest war is one of the most tragic stories of modern history.

The Korean War

Early on June 25, 1950, a large military force of the Democratic People's Republic of Korea (North Korea) moved into the Republic of Korea (South Korea). Colonized by Japan since 1910, Korea was divided in two after Japan's defeat in 1945. Although the Soviets armed the North and the Americans armed the South (U.S. aid had reached $100 million a year), the **Korean War** began as a civil war. Since its division, the two parts had been skirmishing while antigovernment (and anti-U.S.) guerrilla fighting flared in the South.

What were the consequences of the Korean War for the United States?

Korean War: War between North Korea and South Korea with heavy U.S. and Soviet involvement (1950–1953) with each seeking to undermine the other with economic pressure and military raids.

Both the North's communist leader, Kim Il Sung, and the South's president, Syngman Rhee, sought to reunify their nation. Kim's military gained strength when tens of thousands of Koreans returned home in 1949 after serving in Mao's army. Though President Truman claimed the Soviets had masterminded the North Korean attack, Stalin reluctantly approved the attack after Kim predicted an early victory and after Mao backed Kim. When the U.N. Security Council voted to defend South Korea, the Soviet representative was not present to veto because the Soviets were boycotting the United Nations for its refusal to admit the People's Republic of China. During the war, Moscow gave limited aid to North Korea and China, reneging on promised Soviet airpower. Aware of his strategic inferiority vis-à-vis the United States, Stalin did not want war.

U.S. Forces Intervene

The president first ordered General Douglas MacArthur to send arms and troops to South Korea. He did not seek congressional approval—fearing lawmakers would initiate a lengthy debate—and thereby set the precedent of waging war on executive authority alone. After the Security Council voted to assist South Korea, MacArthur became commander of U.N. forces in Korea. Sixteen nations contributed troops, but 40 percent were South Korean and about 50 percent American. In the war's early weeks, North Korean tanks and superior firepower sent the South Korean army into retreat. The first American soldiers, taking heavy casualties, could not stop the North Korean advance. Within weeks, the South Koreans and Americans were pushed into the tiny Pusan perimeter at South Korea's tip.

General MacArthur planned a daring amphibious landing at heavily fortified Inchon, several hundred miles behind North Korean lines. After U.S. bombs pounded Inchon, marines sprinted ashore on September 15, 1950, liberating the South Korean capital of Seoul and pushing the North Koreans back. Truman meanwhile redefined the U.S. war goal from the containment of North Korea to the reunification of Korea by force.

Chinese Entry into the War

In September, U.N. forces drove deep into North Korea, and American aircraft began strikes against bridges on the Yalu River, the border between North Korea and China. Mao publicly warned that China could not permit the bombing of its transportation links with Korea and would not accept annihilation of North Korea. MacArthur shrugged off the warnings, and Washington officials agreed, confident that the Soviets were not preparing for war.

MacArthur was right about the Soviets, but wrong about the Chinese. On October 25, the Chinese sent soldiers into the war near the Yalu River. Perhaps to lure U.S. forces into a trap or to signal willingness to negotiate, they pulled back after a successful offensive against South Korean troops. Then, on November 26, tens of thousands of Chinese troops surprised U.S. forces and drove them southward. One U.S. officer described "the men of a whole United States Army fleeing from a battlefield, abandoning their wounded, running for their lives."

Truman's Firing of MacArthur

By 1951, the front had stabilized around the 38th parallel. Both Washington and Moscow welcomed negotiations, but MacArthur called for an attack on China and Jiang's return. Denouncing the concept of limited war (war without nuclear weapons, confined to one place), MacArthur hinted that the president was practicing appeasement. In April, backed by the Joint Chiefs of Staff (the heads of the various armed services), Truman fired MacArthur, who nonetheless returned home a hero. Truman's popularity sagged, but he weathered scattered demands for his impeachment.

Armistice talks began in July 1951, but the fighting continued for two more years. Defying the Geneva Prisoners of War Convention (1949), U.S. officials announced that only those North Korean and Chinese prisoners of war (POWs) who wished to go home would be returned. While Americans resisted forced repatriation, the North Koreans denounced forced retention. Both sides undertook "reeducation" or "brainwashing" on POWs.

Peace Agreement   As the POW issue stalled negotiations, U.S. officials made deliberately vague public statements about using atomic weapons in Korea. Not until July 1953 was an armistice signed. Stalin's death in March and new leaders in Moscow and Washington facilitated a settlement. The combatants agreed to hand over the POW question to a special panel of neutral nations, which later gave prisoners their choice of staying or leaving. The North Korean–South Korean borderline was set near the 38th parallel, the prewar boundary, and a demilitarized zone was created between them.

American casualties totaled 54,246 dead and 103,284 wounded. Nearly 5 million Asians died: 2 million North Korean civilians and 500,000 soldiers; 1 million South Korean civilians and 100,000 soldiers; and at least 1 million Chinese soldiers—ranking Korea as one of the costliest wars of the twentieth century.

© Bettmann/Corbis

Soldiers from Company D First Marine Division, mounted on a M-26 tank, spearheaded a patrol in search of guerrillas during the Korean War.

Consequences of the War

The Korean War carried major domestic political consequences. The failure to achieve victory and the public's impatience undoubtedly helped to elect Republican Dwight Eisenhower to the presidency in 1952, as the former general promised to end the war. The powers of the presidency grew as Congress repeatedly deferred to Truman. The president never asked Congress for a declaration of war, believing that, as commander-in-chief, he had the authority to send troops wherever he wished. He saw no need to consult Congress, except to get the $69.5 billion Korean War bill paid. In addition, Republican lawmakers, including Wisconsin senator Joseph McCarthy, accused Truman and Secretary of State Dean Acheson of being soft on communism; this pushed the administration into an uncompromising position in the negotiations.

Moreover, the Sino-American hostility generated by the war made U.S. reconciliation with the Beijing government impossible and made South Korea and Formosa major recipients of American foreign aid. The alliance with Japan strengthened as its economy boomed after filling large U.S. procurement orders. Australia and New Zealand joined the United States in a mutual defense agreement, the ANZUS Treaty (1951). The U.S. Army sent four divisions to Europe and initiated plans to rearm West Germany. The military budget jumped from $14 billion in 1949 to $44 billion in 1953; it remained between $35 billion and $44 billion a year throughout the 1950s. The Soviet Union matched this military buildup, resulting in an arms race. Truman's legacy was a highly militarized U.S. foreign policy on a global scale.

Unrelenting Cold War

How did Dulles and Eisenhower raise the stakes in the Cold War?

President Eisenhower and Secretary of State **John Foster Dulles** largely sustained Truman's Cold War policies. As a World War II general, Eisenhower negotiated with world leaders. After the war, he served as army chief of staff and NATO supreme commander. Dulles had been closely involved with U.S. diplomacy since the first decade of the century.

John Foster Dulles: Secretary of State under Dwight D. Eisenhower. He spoke of a holy war against "atheistic communism" and rejected the policy of containment.

Eisenhower and Dulles accepted the Cold War consensus about the threat of communism and the need for global vigilance. Although Democrats promoted an image of Eisenhower as a bumbling, passive, aging hero, deferring most foreign policy matters to Dulles, the president in fact commanded the policymaking process and occasionally tamed the more hawkish proposals of Dulles and Vice President Richard Nixon. Even so, the secretary of state was influential. Few Cold Warriors rivaled Dulles's impassioned anticommunism, often expressed in biblical terms. Though articulate, he impressed people as arrogant and hectoring and averse to compromise, an essential ingredient in successful diplomacy. His assertion that neutrality was an "immoral and short-sighted conception" did not sit well with Third World leaders, who resented being told they had to choose between East and West.

"Massive Retaliation"

Considering containment too defensive, Dulles called instead for liberation, freeing eastern Europe from Soviet control. *Massive retaliation* was the administration's plan for the nuclear obliteration of the Soviet state or its assumed client, the People's Republic of China, if either one took aggressive action.

Militarily, Eisenhower and Dulles emphasized airpower and nuclear weaponry. The president's preference for heavy weapons stemmed partly from his desire to trim the federal budget (and get "more bang for the buck," as the saying went). Galvanized by the successful test of the world's first hydrogen bomb in November 1952, Eisenhower oversaw a massive stockpiling of nuclear weapons—from 1,200 at the start of his presidency to 22,229 at the end. With this huge military arsenal, the United States could practice "brinkmanship": not backing down in a crisis, even if it meant taking the nation to the brink of war. Eisenhower also popularized the "**domino theory**": that small, weak, neighboring nations would fall to communism like dominoes if they were not supported by the United States.

domino theory: Eisenhower's prediction that if Vietnam went communist, then smaller, neighboring communities of Thailand, Burma, Indonesia, and ultimately all of Asia would fall like dominos.

CIA as Foreign Policy Instrument

Eisenhower increasingly utilized the Central Intelligence Agency as an instrument of foreign policy. The CIA put foreign leaders (such as King Hussein of Jordan) on its payroll; subsidized foreign labor unions, newspapers, and political parties; planted false stories in newspapers through disinformation projects; and trained foreign military officers in counterrevolution. It hired American journalists and professors, used business executives as fronts, and conducted experiments on unsuspecting Americans to determine the effects of mind control drugs (the MKULTRA program). The CIA also launched covert operations (including assassination schemes) to subvert Third World governments, helping to overthrow the governments of Iran (1953) and Guatemala (1954), but failing in attempts to topple regimes in Indonesia (1958) and Cuba (1961).

The U.S. intelligence community followed the principle of plausible deniability: covert operations should be conducted in such a way and the decisions that launched them concealed so well that the president could deny any knowledge of them. Thus, President Eisenhower disavowed any U.S. role in Guatemala, even though he ordered the operation. He and his successor, John F. Kennedy, also denied instructing the CIA to assassinate Cuba's Fidel Castro, whose regime after 1959 became stridently anti-American.

Nuclear Buildup

Leaders in Moscow quickly became aware of Eisenhower's covert actions, as well as his stockpiling of nuclear weapons. They increased their intelligence and tested their first H-bomb in 1953. Four years later, they fired the world's first intercontinental ballistic missile (ICBM) and propelled the satellite **Sputnik** into outer space. Americans felt more vulnerable to air attack, even though in 1957 the United States had 2,460 strategic weapons and a nuclear stockpile of 5,543, compared with the Soviet Union's 102 and 650. The administration deployed intermediate-range missiles in Europe, targeted against the Soviet Union. At the end of 1960, the United States added Polaris missile-bearing submarines to its navy. To foster future technological advancement, the National Aeronautics and Space Administration (NASA) was created in 1958.

Sputnik: Soviet satellite that was the world's first successful launch in space in 1957; it dashed the American myth of unquestioned technological superiority.

Overall, though, Eisenhower sought to avoid military confrontation with the Soviet Union and China, content to follow Truman's *containment* of communism. Eisenhower refused to use nuclear weapons and proved more reluctant than other Cold War presidents to send soldiers into battle. Convinced that the struggle against Moscow would be largely decided by international public opinion, he wanted to win the "hearts and minds" of people overseas. The "People-to-People" campaign, launched in 1956, used ordinary Americans and nongovernmental organizations to enhance the international image of the United States.

The People-to-People Campaign

Just after the Cold War began, U.S. officials determined that the Soviet-American confrontation was as much psychological and ideological as military and economic. One result was the People-to-People campaign, a state-private venture initiated by the United States Information Agency (USIA) in 1956, which aimed to win the "hearts and minds" of people around the world. In this program, American propaganda experts used ordinary Americans, businesses, civic organizations, labor groups, and women's clubs to promote confidence abroad in American goodness. The People-to-People campaign, one USIA pamphlet said, made "every man an ambassador."

Campaign activities resembled the home-front mobilization efforts of World War II. Americans were told that $30 could send a ninety-nine-volume portable library of American books to schools and libraries overseas. Publishers donated magazines and books for free distribution to foreign countries. People-to-People committees organized sister-city affiliations and pen-pal letter exchanges, hosted exchange students,

and organized travelling People-to-People delegations. The travellers were urged to behave like goodwill ambassadors and "help overcome any feeling that America is a land that thinks money can buy everything."

Camp Fire Girls in more than three thousand communities took photographs on the theme "This is our home. This is how we live. These are my People." The photographs were sent to girls in Latin America, Africa, Asia, and the Middle East. The Hobbies Committee connected people with interests in radio, photography, coins, stamps, and horticulture.

The persistence to this day of the widespread impression that Americans are a provincial, materialistic people prompts skepticism about the People-to-People campaign's success. But alongside this negative image is a positive one that sees Americans as admirably open, friendly, optimistic, and pragmatic. Whatever role the People-to-People campaign played in the larger Cold War struggle, it certainly linked ordinary Americans more closely to people around the world.

Dwight D. Eisenhower Library

"Make a friend this trip," urges this framed People-to-People poster, delivered to President Eisenhower in May 1957, "for yourself, for your business, for your country." With the president are two of the campaign's leaders, John W. Hanes Jr. and Edward Lipscomb.

Sometimes the propaganda war was waged on the Soviets' turf. In 1959, Vice President Richard Nixon traveled to Moscow for a U.S. products fair. In the display of a modern American kitchen, Nixon extolled capitalist consumerism, while Soviet premier Nikita Khrushchev, Stalin's successor, touted the merits of communism. The encounter became famous as the kitchen debate.

Rebellion in Hungary   In February 1956, Khrushchev called for peaceful coexistence between capitalists and communists, denounced Stalin, and suggested that Moscow would tolerate different brands of communism. Testing Khrushchev's permissiveness, revolts erupted in Poland and Hungary. After a new Hungarian government in 1956 withdrew from the Warsaw Pact (the Soviet military alliance formed in 1955 with communist countries of eastern Europe), Soviet troops and tanks crushed the rebellion.

Although the Eisenhower administration's propaganda encouraged liberation efforts, U.S. officials could not aid the rebels without igniting a world war. Instead, they promised only to welcome more Hungarian immigrants than American quota laws allowed. The West could have reaped some propaganda advantage had not British, French, and Israeli troops—U.S. allies—invaded Egypt during the Suez crisis just before the Soviets smashed the Hungarian uprising (see page 750).

The turmoil had hardly subsided when the divided city of Berlin again became a Cold War flash point. The Soviets railed against American bombers capable of carrying nuclear warheads in West Germany, and they complained that West Berlin had become an escape route for disaffected East Germans. In 1958, Khrushchev announced that the Soviet Union would recognize East German control of all of Berlin unless the United States and its allies began talks on German reunification and rearmament. The United States refused; Khrushchev backed down but promised to press the issue again.

U-2 Incident   Two weeks before a summit in Paris on May 1, 1960, a U-2 spy plane carrying high-powered cameras crashed 1,200 miles inside the Soviet Union. Moscow admitted shooting down the plane and promptly displayed captured CIA pilot Francis Gary Powers and the pictures he had snapped of Soviet military sites. Khrushchev demanded an apology for the U.S. violation of Soviet airspace. When Washington refused, the Soviets left the Paris summit.

Meanwhile, both sides kept a wary eye on the People's Republic of China. Despite evidence of a widening Sino-Soviet split, most U.S. officials treated communism as a monolithic movement. In 1954, in a dispute over Jinmen (Quemoy) and Mazu (Matsu), two tiny islands off the Chinese coast, the United States and the People's Republic of China lurched toward the brink. Taiwan's Jiang Jieshi used these islands to raid the mainland. Communist China bombarded the islands in 1954. Thinking that U.S. credibility was at stake, Eisenhower defended the outposts, hinting that he might use nuclear weapons. "Let's keep the Reds guessing," advised John Foster Dulles.

Formosa Resolution   In early 1955, Congress passed the Formosa Resolution, authorizing the president to deploy troops to defend Formosa and adjoining islands. In so doing, Congress formally surrendered to the president what it informally gave up in the 1950 Korea decision: the constitutional power to declare war. The crisis passed, but war loomed again in 1958 over Jinmen and Mazu. This time, as Jiang withdrew some troops, China relaxed its bombardments. But Eisenhower's nuclear threats persuaded the Chinese that they, too, needed nuclear arms. In 1964, China exploded its first nuclear bomb.

The Struggle for the Third World

How did racism in America interfere with U.S. leaders' ability to win Cold War allies among developing nations?

In much of the Third World, the process of decolonization that began during the World War I accelerated after World War II, when the economically wracked imperial countries proved incapable of resisting their colonies' demands for freedom (see Map 28.2). From 1943 to 1994, a total of 125 countries became independent (including the former Soviet republics that departed the USSR in 1991). The emergence of so many new states after the 1940s shook the foundations of the international system. In the traditional U.S. sphere of influence, Latin America, nationalists once again challenged Washington's dominance.

Interests in the Third World

By the late 1940s, Soviet-American rivalry shifted increasingly to the Third World. The new nations could buy U.S. goods, supply strategic raw materials, and invite investments (more than one-third of the United States' private foreign investments were in Third World countries in 1959). Both great powers looked to these new states for votes in the United Nations and for military and intelligence bases. But many new nations sought to end the economic, military, and cultural hegemony of the West and played the two superpowers against each other to garner more aid and arms. U.S. interventions—military and otherwise—in the Third World, American leaders believed, became necessary to impress Moscow with Washington's might and to counter other potential threats to U.S. interests.

To thwart nationalist, radical, and communist challenges, more than 90 percent of U.S. foreign aid was going to developing nations by 1961. Washington also allied with undemocratic but anticommunist regimes, meddled in civil wars, and unleashed CIA covert operations. When some of the larger Third World states—notably India, Ghana, Egypt, and Indonesia—refused to take sides in the Cold War, Secretary of State Dulles declared that neutralism was a step toward communism, insisting with Eisenhower that every nation should take sides in this life-or-death struggle.

American leaders argued that technologically "backward" Third World countries needed western-induced capitalist development to enjoy economic growth and political moderation U.S. officials often ascribed stereotyped race-, age-, and gender-based characteristics to Third World peoples, seeing them as dependent and irrational, and therefore dependent on the fatherly tutelage of the United States.

Racism and Segregation as U.S. Handicaps

Racism influenced U.S. relations with Third World countries. In 1955, G. L. Mehta, the Indian ambassador to the United States, was refused service in the whites-only section of a restaurant at Houston International Airport. The insult stung, as did similar indignities experienced by other Third World diplomats. Dulles apologized to Mehta and thought racial segregation in the United States was a "major international hazard," spoiling U.S. efforts to win friends in Third World countries and giving the Soviets a propaganda advantage.

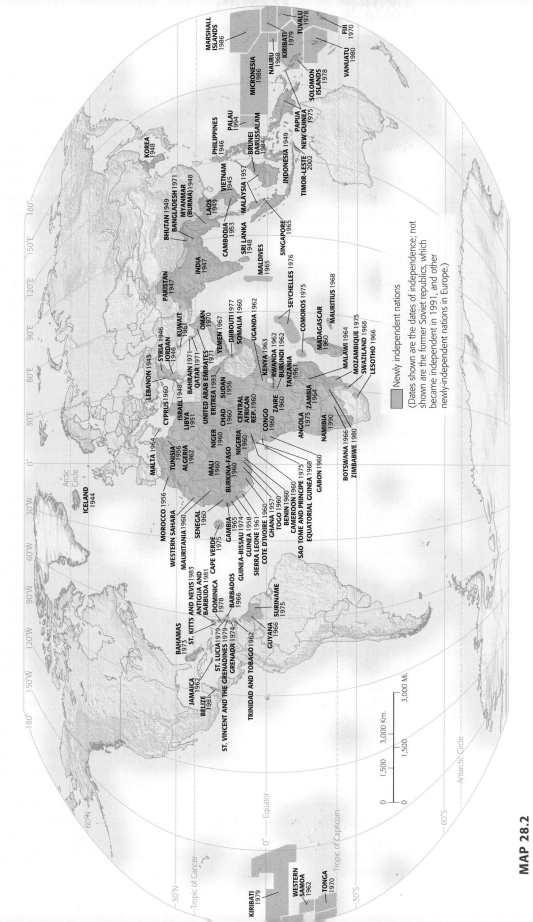

MAP 28.2

The Rise of the Third World: Newly Independent Nations Since 1943

Accelerated by the Second World War, decolonization liberated many peoples from imperial rule. New nations emerged in the postwar international system dominated by the Cold War rivalry of the United States and the Soviet Union. Many newly independent states became targets of great-power intrigue but chose nonalignment in the Cold War.

Source: Copyright © Cengage Learning

Thus, as the U.S. attorney general noted, race relations "furnished grist for the Communist propaganda mills." When the Court announced its *Brown* decision in 1954, the government quickly broadcast news of the desegregation order around the world in thirty-five languages on its *Voice of America* overseas radio network. But the problem did not go away. For example, after the 1957 Little Rock crisis, Dulles remarked that racial bigotry was "ruining our foreign policy." Still, when a Department of State office countered Soviet propaganda with a 1958 World's Fair exhibit in Brussels titled "The Unfinished Work"—on U.S. strides toward desegregation—southern conservatives kicked up such a furor that the Eisenhower administration closed the display.

American hostility toward revolution also obstructed the quest for influence in the Third World. In the twentieth century, the United States opposed revolutions in Mexico, China, Russia, Cuba, Vietnam, Nicaragua, and Iran, among other nations. Many Third World revolutions arose against America's Cold War allies and threatened American investments, markets, and military bases. Preferring to maintain the status quo, the United States usually supported its European allies or the conservative, propertied classes in the Third World.

Development and Modernization

Yet idealism also inspired U.S. policy. Believing that Third World peoples craved modernization and the U.S. economic model of private enterprise, U.S. policymakers launched various development projects. Such projects promised sustained economic growth, prosperity, and stability, which the benefactors hoped would undermine radicalism. In the 1950s, the Carnegie, Ford, and Rockefeller Foundations worked with the U.S. Agency for International Development (AID) to sponsor a Green Revolution promoting agricultural production. The Rockefeller Foundation supported foreign universities' efforts to train national leaders committed to nonradical development.

To persuade Third World peoples to abandon radical doctrines, U.S. leaders created propaganda campaigns. The United States Information Agency (USIA), founded in 1953, used films, radio broadcasts, the magazine *Free World*, exhibitions, and libraries (in 162 cities worldwide by 1961) to trumpet the theme of People's Capitalism. Citing the United States' economic success—contrasted with "slave-labor" conditions in the Soviet Union—it showcased well-paid U.S. workers, political democracy, and religious freedom. To counter ugly pictures of segregation, the USIA applauded success stories of individual African Americans, such as boxers Floyd Patterson and Sugar Ray Robinson. In 1960, some 13.8 million people visited U.S. pavilions abroad.

Undoubtedly, the American way of life had appeal for some Third World peoples. Hollywood movies offered enticing glimpses of middle-class materialism, and U.S. films dominated many overseas markets. Blue jeans, advertising billboards, and soft drinks flooded foreign societies. Foreigners often envied and resented Americans for having and wasting so much and for allowing their corporations to extract high profits from overseas. Americans were often blamed for the persistent poverty of the developing world, even though the leaders of those nations made decisions that hindered their own progress, such as pouring millions of dollars into their militaries while their people needed food. Nonetheless, anti-American resentments manifested in the late 1950s in attacks on USIA libraries in Calcutta, India; Beirut, Lebanon; and Bogotá, Colombia.

Intervention in Guatemala

When the more benign techniques of containment—aid, trade, cultural relations—proved insufficient to get Third World nations to line up on the American side in the Cold War, the Eisenhower administration often showed a willingness to press harder, by covert or overt means. Guatemala was an early test case. In 1951, leftist Jacobo Arbenz Guzmán was elected president of Guatemala, a poor country whose largest landowner was the American-owned United Fruit Company. United Fruit was an economic power throughout Latin America, where it owned 3 million acres of land and operated railroads, ports, ships, and telecommunications facilities. To fulfi ll his promise of land reform, Arbenz expropriated United Fruit's uncultivated land and offered compensation. The company dismissed the offer and charged that Arbenz posed a communist threat—a charge that CIA officials had already fl oated because Arbenz employed some communists in his government. The CIA began a secret plot to overthrow Arbenz. He turned to Moscow for military aid, thus reinforcing American suspicions. The CIA airlifted arms into Guatemala, dropping them at United Fruit facilities, and in mid-1954, CIA-supported Guatemalans struck from Honduras. U.S. planes bombed the capital city, and the invaders drove Arbenz from power. The new pro-American regime returned United Fruit's land, but an ensuing civil war staggered the Central American nation for decades.

The Cuban Revolution and Fidel Castro

Eisenhower also worried as turmoil gripped Cuba in the late 1950s. In early 1959, Fidel Castro's rebels, or *barbudos* ("bearded ones"), driven by anti-American nationalism, ousted Fulgencio Batista, a long-time U.S. ally whose corrupt, dictatorial regime turned Havana into a haven for gambling, prostitution, and organized crime. Cubans resented U.S. domination since the early twentieth century, when the Platt Amendment compromised their independence. Castro sought to break the U.S. grasp on Cuban trade and roll back American business, which had invested some $1 billion on the island.

In early 1960, after Cuba signed a trade treaty with the Soviet Union, Eisenhower ordered the CIA to organize Cuban exiles to overthrow the Castro government. The agency also plotted the Cuban leader's assassination. When the president drastically cut U.S. sugar purchases, Castro seized North American–owned companies that had not yet been nationalized. Castro appealed to the Soviet Union, which offered loans and expanded trade. Before leaving office in early 1961, Eisenhower broke diplomatic relations with Cuba and advised president-elect John F. Kennedy to advance plans for the invasion, which came—and failed—in early 1961 (see page 791).

Arab-Israeli Conflict

In the Middle East, meanwhile, ongoing tensions between Arabs and Jews posed additional challenges (see Map 33.1). Before the end of World War II, only France and Britain had been concerned with this region of the world. But the dissolution of empires and the rise of Cold War tensions drew Washington in, as did tensions in British-held Palestine. From 1945 to 1947, Britain tried to enlist U.S. officials to help resolve how to split Palestine between Arabs and Jews. The Truman administration declined, and the British in 1947 turned the issue over to the United Nations, which voted to partition Palestine into separate Arab and Jewish states. Arab leaders opposed the decision, but in May 1948 Jewish leaders announced the creation of Israel.

The United States, which lobbied to secure the U.N. vote, extended recognition to the new state mere minutes after its founding. A moral conviction that Jews deserved a homeland after the Holocaust and that Zionism would create a democratic Israel influenced Truman, as did the belief that Jewish votes might swing some states to the Democrats in the 1948 election. These beliefs trumped concerns that Arab oil producers might turn against the United States. The Soviet Union recognized the new nation, but Israel kept Moscow at arm's length. Palestinian Arabs, displaced from land they considered theirs, joined with Israel's Arab neighbors to make immediate war on the new state. The Israelis fought for six months until a U.N.-backed truce was called.

Thereafter, U.S. Middle East policy centered on ensuring Israel's survival and cementing ties with Arab oil producers. U.S. companies produced about half of the region's petroleum in the 1950s. Oil-rich Iran became a special friend as its shah granted American oil companies a 40 percent interest in a new petroleum consortium in return for CIA help in the successful overthrow, in 1953, of his rival, Mohammed Mossadegh.

American officials faced a more formidable foe in Egypt's Gamal Abdul Nasser, a towering figure in a pan-Arabic movement, who vowed to expel the British from the Suez Canal and the Israelis from Palestine. The United States wished neither to anger the Arabs, for fear of losing valuable oil supplies, nor to alienate its ally Israel, supported at home by politically active American Jews. When Nasser declared neutrality in the Cold War, Dulles lost patience.

Suez Crisis

In 1956, the United States reneged on its offer to help Egypt finance the Aswan Dam, which would provide inexpensive electricity and water for Nile valley farmland. Nasser responded by nationalizing the British-owned Suez Canal, intending to use its profits to build the dam. Fully 75 percent of western Europe's oil came from the Middle East, most of it via the Suez Canal. Fearing an interruption, the British and French conspired with Israel to bring down Nasser. On October 29, 1956, the Israelis invaded Suez, joined two days later by British and French forces.

Eisenhower fumed. Washington's allies had not consulted him, and the president feared the invasion would cause Nasser to seek help from the Soviets, inviting them into the Middle East. Eisenhower sternly demanded that London, Paris, and Tel Aviv pull their troops out, and they did. Egypt took possession of the canal, the Soviets built the Aswan Dam, and Nasser became a hero. The United States countered Nasser by supporting the notoriously corrupt conservative King Ibn Saud of Saudi Arabia, who renewed America's lease of an air base.

Eisenhower Doctrine

Washington officials worried that a power vacuum existed in the Middle East and that the Soviets might fill it. To protect U.S. interests, the president proclaimed in the 1957 **Eisenhower Doctrine** that the United States would intervene in the Middle East if any government threatened by a communist takeover asked for help. In 1958 fourteen thousand American troops scrambled to quell an internal political dispute in Lebanon that Washington feared might be exploited by pro-Nasser groups or communists.

Cold War concerns also drove Eisenhower's policy toward Vietnam. Despite substantial U.S. aid, the French lost steadily to the Vietminh. Finally, in early 1954, Ho's forces surrounded the French fortress at Dienbienphu in northwest Vietnam (see Map 30.1). Some advisers advocated military intervention, but Eisenhower

Eisenhower Doctrine: 1957 proclamation that the United States would send military aid and, if necessary, troops to any Middle Eastern nation threatened by "Communist aggression."

The National Security State

For decades, America's Cold War religion has been national security; its texts, the Truman Doctrine, the X article, and NSC-68; and its cathedral, the national security state. The word *state* in this case means "civil government." During the Cold War, embracing preparedness for total war, the U.S. government essentially transformed itself into a huge military headquarters that interlocked with corporations and universities.

Overseen by the president and his National Security Council, the national security state's core—once called the National Military Establishment—in 1949 became the Department of Defense. This department is a leading employer; its payroll by 2007 included 1.4 million people on active duty and almost 600,000 civilian personnel. Almost 700,000 of these troops and civilians served overseas, in 177 countries. Although national defense spending declined after the Cold War, it never fell below $290 billion. In the aftermath of the 9/11 terrorist attacks and the invasion of Iraq, the military budget rose again, reaching $439 billion in 2007. That does not include tens of billions of dollars in supplementary funds allocated by Congress to pay for operations in Afghanistan and Iraq.

Joining the Department of Defense as instruments of national security policy were the Joint Chiefs of Staff, the Central Intelligence Agency, and dozens more government bodies. The focus of these entities was finding the best means to combat real and potential threats from foreign governments. But what about threats from within? The terrorist attacks of September 2001 made starkly clear that enemies existed who, while perhaps beholden to a foreign entity, launched their attacks from inside the nation's borders.

Accordingly, in 2002 President George W. Bush created the Department of Homeland Security (DHS), with 170,000 employees encompassing all or part of twenty-two agencies, including the Coast Guard, the Customs Service, the Federal Emergency Management Administration (FEMA), and the Internal Revenue Service. It would involve the biggest overhaul of the federal bureaucracy since the Department of Defense was created, and it signified a more expansive notion of national security. By 2008, the number of DHS employees had risen to 208,000.

In 1961, President Eisenhower warned against a military-industrial complex, while others feared a warfare state. Still, the national security state remained vigorous in the early twenty-first century, a lasting legacy of the initial Cold War period for a people and a nation.

---

moved cautiously. The United States had advised and bankrolled the French, but had not committed troops to the war.

Eisenhower pressed the British to help form a coalition to address the Indochinese crisis, but they refused. At home, influential members of Congress—including Lyndon Baines Johnson of Texas, who as president would wage large-scale war in Vietnam—told Eisenhower they wanted "no more Koreas" and warned him against any U.S. military commitment. The issue became moot on May 7, when the weary French defenders at Dienbienphu surrendered.

Link to the Eisenhower Doctrine.

Geneva Accords on Vietnam

Peace talks, already under way in Geneva, brought Cold War and nationalist contenders together—the United States, the Soviet Union, Britain, the People's Republic of China, Laos, Cambodia, and the competing Vietnamese regimes of Bao Dai and Ho Chi Minh. The 1954 Geneva accords, signed by France and Ho's Democratic Republic of Vietnam, temporarily divided Vietnam at the 17th parallel; Ho's government was confined to the North, Bao Dai's to the South. The 17th parallel was meant as a truce line, not a national boundary; the country was scheduled to be reunified after national elections in 1956. Meanwhile, neither North nor South was to join a military alliance or permit foreign bases on its soil.

National Liberation Front

Diem proved a difficult ally. He abolished village elections and appointed people beholden to him. He threw dissenters in jail and shut down newspapers that criticized him. Noncommunists and communists alike struck back at Diem's repressive government. In Hanoi, Ho's government in the late 1950s sent aid to southern insurgents, who assassinated hundreds of Diem's village officials. In late 1960, southern communists, acting at Hanoi's direction, organized the National Liberation Front (NLF), known as the Vietcong. The Vietcong attracted other anti-Diem groups in the South. The Eisenhower administration, aware of Diem's shortcomings, affirmed its commitment to an independent, noncommunist South Vietnam.

Summary

The United States emerged from World War II as the preeminent world power. Washington officials nevertheless worried that the unstable international system, an unfriendly Soviet Union, and the decolonizing Third World could upset U.S. plans for the postwar peace. Locked with the Soviet Union in a Cold War, U.S. leaders marshaled their nation's superior resources to influence other countries. Foreign economic aid, atomic diplomacy, military alliances, client states, covert operations, propaganda, and cultural infiltration became the instruments of the Cold War, which began as a conflict over the Europe's future but soon encompassed the globe.

The United States' international leadership was welcomed by those who feared Stalin's intentions. The reconstruction of former enemies Japan and West Germany helped those nations recover swiftly and become staunch members of the western alliance. But U.S. policy also sparked resistance. Communist countries condemned financial and atomic diplomacy, while Third World nations sought to undermine the United States' European allies and sometimes identified the United States as an imperial coconspirator. Occasionally, even the United States' allies bristled at a United States that boldly proclaimed itself economic master and global policeman.

At home, critics protested that Presidents Truman and Eisenhower exaggerated the communist threat, wasting U.S. assets on immoral foreign ventures. Still, these presidents and their successors held to creating a nonradical, capitalist, free-trade international order. Determined to contain Soviet expansion, fearful of domestic charges of being soft on communism, they enlarged the U.S. sphere of influence and held the line against the Soviet Union and the People's Republic of China and against revolution everywhere. One consequence was a dramatic increase in presidential power over foreign affairs—what the historian Arthur M. Schlesinger Jr. called "the Imperial Presidency."

The United States' globalist perspective prompted Americans to interpret troubles in the developing world as Cold War conflicts, inspired by Soviet-backed communists. The intensity of the Cold War obscured for Americans the indigenous roots of most Third World troubles, as the wars in Korea and Vietnam attested. Nor could the United States abide developing nations' drive for economic independence—for controlling their own raw materials and economies. Intertwined in the global economy as importer, exporter, and investor, the United States read challenges from this periphery as threats to the American standard of living. Overall, the rise of the Third World introduced new actors to the world stage, challenging the bipolarity of the international system. All the while, the threat of nuclear war unsettled Americans and foreigners alike.

Chapter Review

From Allies to Adversaries

Was the Cold War inevitable?

Historians have long debated this question. Aside from their alliance during World War II, the United States and Soviet Union had a tense relationship dating back to the 1917 Bolshevik Revolution. Since leaders of each country did not want war, their decades-old "cold peace" arguably could have continued and inspired future cooperation. Some believe, however, that each nation's desire to fill the power vacuum left by the World War II defeat of Germany and Japan, along with their disparate goals and political ideologies, led individual leaders to make decisions that exacerbated tensions to the point of Cold War. While both nations clashed on most fronts by 1946, some argue that leaders could have done more to keep diplomatic negotiations open. Both countries backed different groups in Iran, could not agree on German reunification, and took many other opposing foreign policy positions. And the U.S. nuclear monopoly only escalated strife, first because the Soviets believed the United States used their nuclear superiority to bully them into concessions, and later when the Soviets had their own nuclear bomb, by advancing an arms race.

Containment in Action

Was the U.S. containment policy successful?

In 1947, Truman and his aides adopted what they called the containment policy, which meant challenging the Soviets every time they attempted to spread communism beyond their borders. The policy was successful in building an international network by aiding European reconstruction and having communists removed from governments, as in Italy and France. The policy also led the

United States to a twelve-nation mutual defense treaty in 1949 and the establishment of NATO (the North Atlantic Treaty Organization). Truman hoped NATO would keep Europeans from turning communist and would deter Soviets from expansion. But containment failed when China, the world's most populous nation, became communist in 1949. Containment similarly could not keep the Soviet Union from becoming a nuclear power.

The Cold War in Asia

How did the Cold War turn "hot" in Asia?

U.S. foreign policy sought to keep communism from spreading to Asia. That often led to decisions that alienated potential allies. The United States rejected an offer for diplomatic talks with China, and later refused diplomatic recognition to the People's Republic of China in 1949, fearing the nation was ultimately a likely Soviet ally. The U.S. also intervened militarily in Korea, to thwart what it saw a Soviet-sponsored attack by the North against the South. After the Sino-Soviet treaty of friendship in 1950, U.S. policy focused on keeping Indochina from falling to the communists. Rather than recognizing tensions in Vietnam as a rebellion against French colonial rule, Truman and his aides blamed the Soviets for stirring up insurrection to expand communism. As such, the United States lent military aid to the French, becoming increasingly engaged in what would develop into the Vietnam War.

The Korean War

What were the consequences of the Korean War for the United States?

Along with heavy casualties (54,246 Americans died and 103,284 were wounded), the conflict greatly influenced politics in the United States. First, the powers of the U.S. president expanded, as Truman never sought congressional permission to declare war, believing that as commander-in-chief, he could dispatch troops at will. Consequently, he only turned to Congress for funding, and Congress also deferred to Truman rather than exercise its authority. As Republicans accused Truman of being soft on communism, he took an increasingly uncompromising position in negotiations for peace. But public frustration over U.S. failure in the war led to Eisenhower's election in 1952. Finally, the war generated increased hostilities between the United States and China, stoked the arms race with the Soviet Union, and strengthened the U.S. alliance with Japan.

Unrelenting Cold War

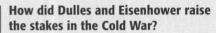

How did Dulles and Eisenhower raise the stakes in the Cold War?

While President Eisenhower and Secretary of State Dulles continued the containment policy, they also added more aggressive tactics to their Cold War politics. Militarily, Eisenhower increased the nuclear arsenal, seeing it as a way to get more bang for the buck. Possessing the atomic bomb and the hydrogen bomb enabled the United States to practice brinkmanship, not backing down against the spread of communism, even to the brink of war. Eisenhower also popularized the domino theory—that neighboring countries would fall to communism like dominoes without U.S. assistance. At the same time, however, Eisenhower worked to avoid engaging in hot war. Instead, he increasingly utilized the Central Intelligence Agency, training foreign military officers in counter-revolutions, subverting Third World governments, and attempting to influence international opinion with disinformation and pro-U.S. campaigns. Brinkmanship and espionage prompted a similar Soviet response, as the USSR tested its own H-bomb in 1953, fired the first intercontinental ballistic missile in 1957, and increased

intelligence operations—all of which made Americans feel increasingly vulnerable to attack.

The Struggle for the Third World

How did racism in America interfere with U.S. leaders' ability to win Cold War allies among developing nations?

Racism influenced U.S. relations with Third World countries, whose leaders were often people of color. With segregation and discrimination persisting in the United States, it was difficult for U.S. leaders to claim a moral advantage over communism and win friends in new and developing nations. Matters were made worse when there were incidents of discrimination against visiting leaders, as when Indian ambassador G. L Mehta was refused service in the whites-only section of a Houston restaurant. To counter this image, the U.S. government broadcast the positive news of the Supreme Court's desegregation ruling in the *Brown vs. Board of Education* in 1954, using its Voice of America overseas radio network to get the word out around the world in thirty-five languages.

Suggestions for Further Reading

Campbell Craig and Fredrik Logevall, *America's Cold War: The Politics of Insecurity* (2009)

Nick Cullather, *Secret History: The CIA's Classified Account of Its Operations in Guatemala, 1952–1954* (1999)

Mary L. Dudziak, *Cold War Civil Rights: Race and the Image of American Democracy* (2000)

John Lewis Gaddis, *Strategies of Containment*, 2nd ed. (2005)

Walter LaFeber, *America, Russia, and the Cold War, 1945–2006*, 10th ed. (2006)

Douglas Little, *American Orientalism: The United States and the Middle East Since 1945* (2002)

Robert J. McMahon, *The Limits of Empire: The United States and Southeast Asia Since World War II* (1999)

Geoffrey Roberts, *Stalin's Wars: From World War to Cold War, 1939–1953* (2007)

Marc Trachtenberg, *A Constructed Peace: The Making of the European Settlement, 1945–1963* (1999)

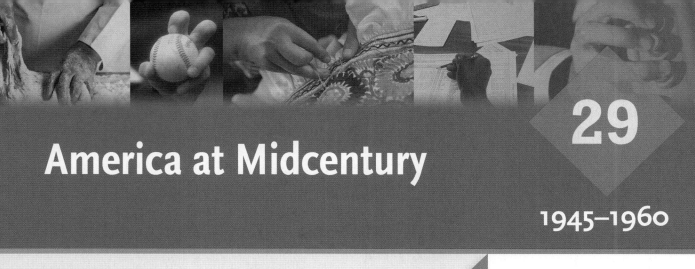

America at Midcentury

29

1945–1960

Isaac and Oleta Nelson wrapped themselves in blankets that morning in late January, 1951 as they joined a hundred or so friends and neighbors from Cedar City, Utah, to watch the first atomic test on U.S. soil since the end of World War II. "We wanted to…show our patriotism," Isaac remembered. The red-orange flare of the bomb lit up the trees across the valley, more than ten miles away.

In the years immediately following World War II, the United States tested atomic weapons on isolated islands in the south Pacific. U.S. officials knew the dangers of radioactivity. But as the USSR developed an atomic weapon and hostilities in Korea escalated the Cold War, Atomic Energy Commission (A.E.C.) members argued that testing outside the national borders might compromise national security. The danger to American public health and safety, they concluded (in a phrase from 1957 legal testimony), was offset by the threat of "total annihilation" by the Soviet enemy.

President Truman selected land in Nevada, already a bombing and gunnery range, for nuclear testing. Advisors portrayed the land, which stretched across portions of Nevada, Arizona, and Utah and was downwind of Los Angeles and Las Vegas, as "virtually uninhabitable." Yet almost 100,000 people lived there, including descendants of Mormons who had arrived in the 1840s and members of the Western Shoshone Nation, on whose land the test site lay. As radioactive clouds drifted over the towns and farms, children played in the fallout as if it were snow.

After fallout from "Harry," a 32-kiloton blast, saturated the region in 1953, 4,500 of the 14,000 sheep on local ranches died. The A.E.C. blamed the "unprecedented cold weather." Lambs were born that spring without wool or skin, their organs covered only by a thin membrane. The commission suppressed veterinary reports documenting lethal levels of radiation. In 1955, A.E.C. medical staff told residents that radiation from tests was only "about one-twentieth of that in an X-ray." Within hours of watching a fallout cloud, Oleta Nelson became nauseous, with violent

Chapter Outline

Shaping Postwar America
The Veterans Return | The G.I. Bill | Economic Growth | Baby Boom | Suburbanization | Inequality in Benefits

Domestic Politics in the Cold War Era
Harry S Truman and Postwar Liberalism | Postwar Strikes and the Taft- Hartley Act | 1948 Election | Truman's Fair Deal | Eisenhower's Dynamic Conservatism | Growth of the Military-Industrial Complex

Cold War Fears and Anticommunism
Espionage and Nuclear Fears | Politics of Anticommunism | McCarthyism and the Growing "Witch Hunt" | Anticommunism in Congress | Waning of the Red Scare

The Struggle for Civil Rights
Growing Black Political Power | Supreme Court Victories and School Desegregation | Montgomery Bus Boycott | White Resistance | Federal Authority and States' Rights

Creating a Middle-Class Nation
Prosperity for More Americans | Sunbelt and Economic Growth | A New Middle-Class Culture | Whiteness and National Culture | Television | Consumer Culture | Religion

VISUALIZING THE PAST *Moving to Levittown*

Men, Women, and Youth at Midcentury
Marriage and Families | Gender Roles in 1950s Families | Women and Work | "Crisis of Masculinity" | Sexuality | Youth Culture | Challenges to Middle-Class Culture

LINKS TO THE WORLD *Barbie*

755

The Limits of the Middle-Class Nation

Critics of Conformity |
Environmental Degradation |
Continuing Racism | *Poverty in an*
Age of Abundance

LEGACY FOR A PEOPLE AND A NATION *The*
Pledge of Allegiance

SUMMARY

diarrhea; her exposed skin turned bright red. A month later, her hair fell out. Oleta was diagnosed with a brain tumor in 1962. She died in 1965. By that time, the cancer rate for "downwinders" was one and a half times the rest of the U.S. population.

The Cold War did not affect most Americans so directly. Nonetheless, Cold War fears and policies shaped American life during the postwar era, even as many people labored to leave the difficult years of depression and war behind and create good lives for their families.

The United States emerged from World War II stronger and more prosperous. Europe and Asia had been devastated, but America's farms, cities, and factories were intact. U.S. production capacity had increased during the war, and fighting fascism gave Americans a unified purpose. But memories of sixteen years of depression and war would continue to shape the choices Americans made in their private lives, their domestic policies, and their relations with the world.

In the postwar era, the federal government's actions and individuals' choices profoundly reconfigured American society. Postwar social policies—often shaped by Cold War concerns—that sent millions of veterans to college on the GI Bill, linked the nation with high-speed interstate highways, fostered the growth of suburbs and the Sunbelt, and disrupted regional isolation helped to create a national middle-class culture encompassing an unprecedented majority of citizens. Countless individual decisions—to go to college, marry young, have a large family, move to the suburbs, start a business—were made possible by federal initiatives. Americans in the postwar era defined a new American Dream—one that centered on the family, greater material comfort and consumption, and a shared sense of a common culture. Elite cultural critics roundly denounced this ideal of suburban comfort as "conformism," but many Americans found satisfaction in this new way of life.

Nonetheless, almost one-quarter of Americans did not share in the postwar prosperity. Rural poverty continued, and inner cities became increasingly impoverished as more-affluent Americans moved to the suburbs and new migrants—poor black and white southerners, immigrants from Mexico and Puerto Rico, and Native Americans resettled by the federal government from tribal lands—arrived.

As class and ethnicity became less important in suburbia, race continued to divide Americans. African Americans faced discrimination nationwide, but the war marked a turning point in the struggle for equal rights. African Americans' initiatives led to important federal actions, including the Supreme Court's school desegregation decision in *Brown v. Board of Education*. In 1955, the year-long Montgomery bus boycott launched the modern civil rights movement.

Postwar domestic politics took second place to the foreign policy challenges of the Cold War and anticommunism shaped domestic politics. Truman pledged to expand the New Deal but was stymied by a conservative Congress, and Eisenhower offered a solid Republican platform, seeking—though rarely attaining—a balanced budget, reduced taxes, and lower levels of government spending. The economic boom that began after World War II lasted twenty-five years, bringing new prosperity to Americans. Although fears—of nuclear war, of returning hard times—lingered, prosperity bred complacency by the late 1950s. At decade's end, people sought satisfaction in their families and in the consumer pleasures newly available to so many.

As you read this chapter, keep the following questions in mind:

* **How did the Cold War affect American society and politics?**

* **How did federal government actions following World War II change the nation?**

* **During the 1950s, many people began to think of their country as a middle-class nation. Were they correct?**

Shaping Postwar America

What drove the mass migration of Americans to the suburbs after World War II?

Americans faced many challenges at the end of World War II. The nation had to reintegrate war veterans into civilian society and transform a wartime economy to peacetime functions. It also had to contend with the Cold War and new global balance of power. Though unemployment rose and a wave of strikes rocked the nation, the economy soon flourished. This strong economy, along with new federal programs, transformed American society.

The Veterans Return

In 1945, as Germany and Japan surrendered, the United States faced a new challenge: demobilizing almost 15 million servicemen. Veterans' homecomings were often joyful, but not always easy. Many veterans returned to wives whose lives had gone on without them, to children they barely knew. Some had serious physical injuries. Almost half a million veterans were diagnosed with neuropsychiatric disabilities, and the National Mental Health Act of 1946 passed largely because of the war's psychological toll on veterans.

Americans also worried about how the economy would absorb millions of returning veterans. As the end of the war approached, factories began to lay off workers. Ten days after the Allied victory over Japan, 1.8 million people nationwide received pink slips, and 640,000 filed for unemployment compensation.

The GI Bill

The federal government planned for demobilization during the war. In the spring of 1944, Congress unanimously passed the Servicemen's Readjustment Act, known as the **GI Bill** of Rights. It showed the nation's gratitude to servicemen but also attempted to keep demobilized veterans from swamping the U.S. economy. Approximately half of all veterans received unemployment benefits, meant to stagger their entry into the job market. The GI Bill also provided low-interest home or business loans and stipends to cover the cost of college or technical school tuition and living expenses.

GI Bill: Popular name for the Servicemen's Readjustment Act (1944), which sought to aid returning veterans—and maintain economic stability—by providing college tuition, job training, unemployment benefits, low-interest home and farm loans.

Chronology

1945	World War II ends
1946	Marriage and birth rates skyrocket
	More than 1 million veterans enroll in colleges under GI Bill
	More than 5 million U.S. workers go on strike
1947	Taft-Hartley Act limits power of unions
	Truman orders loyalty investigation of 3 million government employees
	Mass-production techniques used to build Levittown houses
1948	Truman issues executive order desegregating armed forces and federal government
	Truman elected president
1949	Soviet Union explodes atomic bomb
1950	Korean War begins
	McCarthy alleges communists in government
	"Treaty of Detroit" creates model for new labor-management relations
1951	Race riots in Cicero, Illinois, as white residents oppose residential integration
1952	Eisenhower elected president

1953	Korean War ends
	Congress adopts termination policy for Native American tribes
	Rosenbergs executed as atomic spies
1954	*Brown v. Board of Education* decision reverses "separate but equal" doctrine
	Senate condemns McCarthy
1955	Montgomery bus boycott begins
1956	Highway Act launches interstate highway system
	Eisenhower reelected
	Elvis Presley appears on *Ed Sullivan Show*
1957	King elected first president of Southern Christian Leadership Conference
	School desegregation crisis in Little Rock, Arkansas
	Congress passes Civil Rights Act
	Soviet Union launches *Sputnik*
1958	Congress passes National Defense Education Act
1959	Alaska and Hawai'i become forty-ninth and fiftieth states

The GI Bill applied equally to all veterans, regardless of race or gender, as long as they were not less-than-honorably discharged. But because of congressional wrangling, implementation fell to state and local agencies, which enabled racial discrimination to occur. And because people charged with homosexuality were not honorably discharged, they were denied benefits.

Nonetheless, almost half of returning veterans used GI education benefits. Roughly 2.2 million veterans attended college, graduate, or professional school. In 1947, about two-thirds of America's college students were veterans. While racial segregation persisted, Negro colleges grew. The flood of students and federal dollars into colleges and universities created a golden age for higher education, and the resulting increase in educated workers benefited the economy.

Education created social mobility: children of menial laborers became white-collar professionals. The G.I. Bill fostered a new national middle-class culture. As colleges exposed people to new ideas, students became less rooted in ethnic or regional cultures.

Economic Growth

American concerns that economic depression would return with war's end proved unfounded. The postwar economy recovered quickly, fueled by consumer spending. Although Americans brought home steady paychecks during the war, there was little to buy. No new cars, for example, had been built since 1942. Americans saved for four years, and they were ready to spend. Companies like General Motors, which expanded operations after the war, found millions of eager customers. Because most factories around the world were in ruins, U.S.

corporations expanded their global dominance. Farming was also revolutionized. New machines, such as crop dusting planes and mechanical cotton, tobacco, and grape pickers, along with increased use of fertilizers and pesticides greatly increased the total value of farm output, as the productivity of farm labor tripled. The potential for profit drew large investors, and the average size of farms increased from 195 to 306 acres.

Baby Boom

During the Great Depression, people delayed marriage, and America's birth rate plummeted. War's end brought a boom in marriage and birth rates. In 1946, the U.S. marriage rate was higher than that of any record-keeping nation (except Hungary). The soaring birth rate reversed the downward trend of the previous 150 years. "Take the 3,548,000 babies born in 1950," wrote Sylvia F. Porter in her syndicated newspaper column. "Bundle them into a batch, bounce them all over the bountiful land that is America. What do you get?" Porter's answer: "Boom. The biggest, boomiest boom ever known in history. Just imagine how much these extra people, these new markets, will absorb—in food, clothing, in gadgets, in housing, in services." Although the **baby boom** peaked in 1957, more than 4 million babies were born every year until 1965 (see Figure 29.1). As this vast cohort aged, it had successive impacts on housing, nursery schools, grade schools, and high schools, fads and popular music, colleges, the job market, and retirement funds, including Social Security.

baby boom: The soaring birth rate that occurred in the United States from 1946 through the early 1960s.

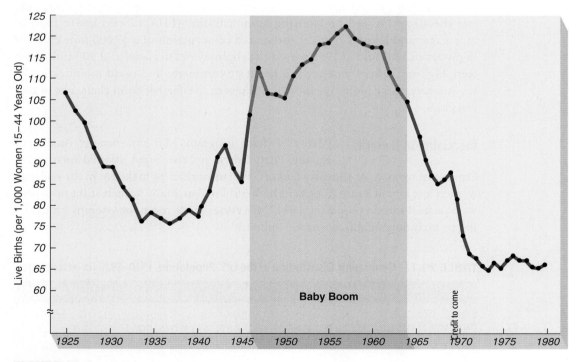

FIGURE 29.1
Birth Rate, 1945–1964
The birth rate began to rise in 1942 and 1943, but it skyrocketed during the postwar years beginning in 1946, reaching its peak in 1957. From 1954 to 1964, the United States recorded more than 4 million births every year.

Source: Adapted from U.S. Bureau of the Census, Historical Statistics of the United States, Colonial Times to 1970, *Bicentennial Edition (Washington, D.C.: U.S. Government Printing Office, 1975), p. 49.*

Scarcely any new housing had been built since the 1920s. Almost 2 million families were doubled up with relatives in 1948; 50,000 people lived in quonset huts, and in Chicago housing was so tight that 250 used trolley cars were sold as homes.

Suburbanization

A combination of market forces, government actions, and individual decisions solved the housing crisis and, in so doing, changed the way large numbers of Americans lived. In the postwar years, white Americans moved to the suburbs. Some white families moved out of urban neighborhoods because African American families were moving in. Most, however, simply wanted their own home, and suburban developments were affordable. Although suburban development predated World War II, the massive migration of 18 million Americans to the suburbs between 1950 and 1960 was on a wholly different scale (see Table 29.1).

In 1947, builder William Levitt adapted Henry Ford's assembly-line methods to revolutionize home building. By 1949, instead of four or five custom homes per year, Levitt's company built 180 houses a week. They were very basic—four and a half rooms on a 60-by-100-foot lot, all with identical floor plans disguised by four different exteriors. By rotating seven paint colors, Levitt guaranteed that only 1 in every 28 houses would be identical. The basic house sold for $7,990. Other homebuilders quickly adopted Levitt's techniques.

Suburban development happened on such a large scale because federal policies encouraged it. Federal Housing Administration (FHA) offered low-interest GI mortgages and loans. Congress authorized construction of a 37,000-mile chain of highways in 1947 and in 1956 passed the Highway Act to create a 42,500-mile interstate highway system. Intended to facilitate commerce and rapid mobilization of the military, these highways allowed workers to live farther from their jobs in central cities.

Inequality in Benefits

Postwar federal programs did not benefit Americans equally. First, federal policies often assisted men at the expense of women. As industry laid off civilian workers to make room for veterans, women lost jobs at a rate 75 percent higher than men. Many women still worked but were pushed into lower-paying jobs. Universities made room for veterans on the GI Bill by excluding qualified women students.

TABLE 29.1   Geographic Distribution of the U.S. Population, 1930–1970 (in percentages)

Year	Central Cities	Suburbs	Rural Areas and Small Towns
1930	31.8	18.0	50.2
1940	31.6	19.5	48.9
1950	32.3	23.8	43.9
1960	32.6	30.7	36.7
1970	31.4	37.6	31.0

Source: Adapted from U.S. Bureau of the Census, *Decennial Censuses,* 1930–1970 (Washington, D.C.: U.S. Government Printing Office).

Inequities were also based on race. Like European American veterans, African American, Native American, Mexican American, and Asian American veterans received educational benefits and hiring preference in civil service jobs. But war workers from these groups were among the first laid off. Federal loan officers and bankers often labeled African American or racially mixed neighborhoods "high risk," denying mortgages to racial minorities regardless of individual creditworthiness. This practice, called "redlining" because such neighborhoods were outlined in red on lenders' maps, kept African Americans and many Hispanics from sharing the postwar economic explosion. White families who bought homes with federally guaranteed mortgages saw their investments grow dramatically over the years.

Domestic Politics in the Cold War Era

What happened to New Deal style liberalism after World War II?

The United States' social and economic transformations in the postwar era were largely due to federal policies and programs, but politically, foreign affairs were paramount, given the challenges of the expanding Cold War. Domestically, Truman attempted to build on the New Deal's liberal agenda, while Eisenhower sought balanced budgets and business-friendly policies. Neither administration approached the level of political and legislative activism of the 1930s New Deal.

Harry S Truman and Postwar Liberalism

Harry Truman, the plain-spoken former haberdasher from Missouri, never expected to be president. In 1944, when Franklin Roosevelt asked him to be his vice-presidential candidate, Truman almost refused. With the war in its fourth year, the president had little time for his new vice president and left Truman in the dark about everything from the Manhattan Project to plans for postwar domestic policy. When Roosevelt died, suddenly, in April 1945, Truman was left unprepared.

Truman stepped up, however, placing a sign on his desk that proclaimed, "The Buck Stops Here." Most of Truman's presidency focused on foreign relations, as he led the nation through the end of World War II and into the Cold War with the Soviet Union. Domestically, he oversaw reconversion from war to peace and attempted to keep a liberal agenda—the legacy of Roosevelt's New Deal—alive.

In his 1944 State of the Union address, President Roosevelt offered Americans a "Second Bill of Rights": the right to employment, healthcare, education, food, and housing. This declaration of government responsibility for citizens' welfare was the cornerstone of postwar liberalism. Truman's legislative program similarly promoted the federal government's active role in guaranteeing social welfare, promoting social justice, managing the economy, and regulating business. Truman proposed an increase in the minimum wage and the **Full Employment Act**, introduced by congressional Democrats in the winter of 1945, which guaranteed work to the able and willing, through public-sector employment if necessary. Truman's gamble that full employment would generate sufficient tax revenue and that consumer spending would fuel

Full Employment Act: Postwar liberal initiative that sought to stimulate economic growth by raising the minimum wage and guaranteeing jobs to those willing and able to work, through public-sector employment if necessary. The act passed without either of these provisions, which were blocked in Congress.

economic growth paid off, but a conservative coalition of Republicans and southern Democrats in Congress refused to raise the minimum wage and gutted the Full Employment Act, which passed in 1946 without provisions regarding guaranteed work. But it did create a Council of Economic Advisers to help the president prevent economic downturns.

Postwar Strikes and the Taft-Hartley Act

Converting to a peacetime economy hit workers hard, as inflation skyrocketed once wartime price controls were lifted. More than 5 million workers walked off the job. Unions shut down the coal, automobile, steel, and electric industries, and halted railroad and maritime transportation. The strikes were so disruptive that Americans began hoarding food and gasoline.

By the spring of 1946, Americans grew impatient with the strikes and partly blamed the Democratic administration. When unions threatened a national railway strike, President Truman announced that if strikers in an industry deemed vital to national security refused a presidential order to return to work, he would ask Congress to draft them into the armed forces. The Democratic Party would not offer unlimited support to organized labor.

Then, in 1947 in an effort to restrict the power of labor unions, pro-business Republicans and conservative Democratic allies passed the **Taft-Hartley Act**. It allowed states to adopt right-to-work legislation outlawing "closed shops," in which all workers were required to join the union if a majority favored a union shop. The law also mandated an eighty-day cooling-off period before unions initiated strikes imperiling national security. These restrictions limited unions' ability to expand their membership. Truman did not want to see union power limited, but Congress passed the Taft-Hartley Act over his veto.

As Truman presided over the rocky transition from a wartime to a peacetime economy, he had to deal with massive inflation (briefly hitting 35 percent), shortages of consumer goods, and postwar strikes that slowed production of consumer goods and further increased prices. Truman's approval rating plunged from 87 percent in late 1945 to 32 percent in 1946.

1948 Election

By 1948, it seemed that Republicans would win the White House in November. The party nominated Thomas Dewey, the man Roosevelt defeated in 1944, as its candidate. Republicans hoped schisms in the Democratic Party would ensure victory. Former New Dealer Henry A. Wallace was running on the **Progressive Party** ticket, advocating friendly relations with the Soviet Union, racial desegregation, and nationalization of basic industries. And when the Democratic Party adopted a pro-civil rights plank in 1948, some white southerners created the States' Rights Democratic Party (the Dixiecrats), which nominated the fiercely segregationist governor Strom Thurmond of South Carolina.

Truman refused to give up. He resorted to red-baiting, denouncing "Henry Wallace and his communists." He also sought support from African American voters in northern cities, becoming the first presidential candidate to campaign in Harlem. Truman prevailed, with the help of African American voters. Roosevelt's New Deal coalition—African Americans, union members, northern urban voters, and most southern whites—endured.

Taft-Hartley Act: 1947 law that amended some of the pro-labor provisions of the 1935 Wagner Act. It permitted states to outlaw the closed shop—workplaces where only union members could be hired—outlawed secondary boycotts, required union officials to sign loyalty oaths, and permitted the president to call a cooling-off period to delay any strike that might endanger national safety or health.

Progressive Party: Party formed from a splintering within the Democratic Party in 1948 by those dissatisfied with Truman. It advocated friendly relations with the Soviet Union, racial desegregation, a ban on monopolies, and nationalization of basic industries.

Truman's Fair Deal

In his 1949 State of the Union message, Truman stated: "I expect to give every segment of our population a **fair deal**." Truman, unlike Roosevelt, pushed legislation supporting African American civil rights, including antilynching bills. He proposed a national health insurance program and federal aid for education. Southern conservatives in Congress destroyed his civil rights legislation. The American Medical Association denounced his health insurance plan as "socialized medicine," and the Roman Catholic Church opposed educational assistance because it would not include parochial schools.

When Truman ordered troops to Korea in June 1950, many reservists and national guardsmen resented being called to active duty. Inflation rose, as people—remembering the previous war's shortages—stockpiled sugar, coffee, and canned goods. Charges of influence peddling by Truman's cronies, along with the unpopular war, pushed the president's approval rating to an all-time low of 23 percent in 1951.

fair deal: Agenda proposed by President Truman that included civil rights, national healthcare legislation, and federal aid to education.

Eisenhower's Dynamic Conservatism

"It's Time for a Change" was the Republican presidential campaign slogan in 1952, and voters agreed. Americans hoped that Republican candidate General **Dwight D. Eisenhower**, the popular World War II hero, could end the Korean War. And Eisenhower appealed to moderates in both parties (Democrats tried to recruit him as their presidential candidate).

With a Republican in the White House for the first time in twenty years, conservatives hoped to roll back such New Deal liberal programs as Social Security. As a moderate, Eisenhower embraced what he called "dynamic conservatism": being "conservative when it comes to money and liberal when it comes to human beings." In 1954, Eisenhower signed legislation that raised Social Security benefits and added 7.5 million workers, mostly self-employed farmers, to its rolls. Eisenhower's administration, motivated by Cold War fears, also increased funding for education. In 1957, when the Soviet Union successfully launched *Sputnik*, the first earth-orbiting satellite, and America's first satellite exploded seconds after liftoff, politicians and policy makers worried about the nation's scientific vulnerability. The resulting National Defense Education Act (NDEA) funded elementary and high-school programs in mathematics, foreign languages, and the sciences and offered fellowships and loans to college students.

Dwight D. Eisenhower: Republican President of United States (1953–1961) known for his moderate politics, steering a middle course between Democratic liberalism and traditional Republican conservatism.

Growth of the Military-Industrial Complex

Overall, however, Eisenhower's administration was fiscally conservative and pro-business. The president tried to reduce federal spending and to balance the budget. However, faced with three recessions (in 1953–1954, 1957–1958, and 1960–1961) and the cost of America's global activities, Eisenhower turned to deficit spending. In 1959, federal expenditures climbed to $92 billion, about half of which went to support a large standing military of 3.5 million men and to develop new weapons.

Eisenhower, however, feared the impact of such developments. In his farewell address in early 1961, the outgoing president condemned this new "conjunction of an immense military establishment and a large arms industry" and warned that its "total influence—economic, political, even spiritual" threatened the nation's democratic process. Eisenhower, the former five-star general and war hero, urged Americans to "guard against…the **military-industrial complex**."

Link to text and audio excerpts of Eisenhower's farewell address.

military-industrial complex: Term made famous by President Eisenhower's farewell speech in 1961; it refers to the U.S. military, arms industries, and related government and business interests, which together grew in power, size, and influence in the decades after World War II.

Cold War Fears and Anticommunism

How did Cold War fears inspire a Red Scare in the United States?

International relations had a profound influence on America's domestic politics after World War II. Americans were frightened by the Cold War tensions between the United States and the Soviet Union, but such reasonable fears spilled over into anticommunist demagoguery and witch hunts, which trampled civil liberties, suppressed dissent, and resulted in the persecution of thousands of innocent Americans.

Anticommunism was not new: a Red Scare swept the nation following the 1917 Russian Revolution, and opponents of America's labor movement used charges of communism to block unionization through the 1930s. Many saw the Soviet Union's virtual takeover of eastern Europe in the late 1940s as an alarming parallel to Nazi Germany's takeover of neighboring states. People remembered the failure of "appeasement" at Munich and worried about being "too soft" toward the Soviet Union.

Espionage and Nuclear Fears

U.S. intelligence officers in a top-secret project, code-named "Venona," decrypted almost three thousand Soviet telegraphic cables that proved Soviet spies had infiltrated U.S. government agencies and nuclear programs. (The United States also had spies within the Soviet Union). Intelligence officials withheld this evidence from the American public so that the Soviets would not realize their codes had been compromised.

Fear of nuclear war also contributed to American anticommunism. In 1949, when the Soviet Union joined the United States in possessing atomic weapons, President Truman initiated a national atomic civil defense program, advising Americans, "I cannot tell you when or where the attack will come or that it will come at all. I can only remind you that we must be ready." Children practiced "duck-and-cover" positions in classrooms, learning how to shield their faces from the atomic flash. *Life* magazine featured backyard fallout shelters. Americans worried that the United States was newly vulnerable to attack.

Link to the 1961 *Twilight Zone* episode, "The Shelter."

Politics of Anticommunism

American leaders did not always draw a sufficient line between attempts to prevent Soviet spies from infiltrating government agencies and anticommunist scare-mongering. Republican politicians "red-baited" Democratic opponents, eventually targeting the Truman administration. In 1947, President Truman ordered investigations into the loyalty of more than 3 million government employees. As anticommunist hysteria grew, the government discharged people deemed "security risks," among them alcoholics, homosexuals, and debtors thought susceptible to blackmail. Leading the anticommunist crusade was the **House Un-American Activities Committee** (popularly known as HUAC). Created in 1938 to investigate "subversive and un-American propaganda," the committee lost credibility by charging that film stars—including eight-year-old Shirley Temple—were Communist Party dupes. In 1947, HUAC attacked Hollywood again, using Federal Bureau of Investigation (FBI) files and the testimony of people like Screen Actors Guild president Ronald Reagan (a secret FBI informant). Screenwriters and directors known as the "Hollywood Ten" were sent to prison for contempt of Congress when they refused to "name names" of suspected communists.

House Un-American Activities Committee (HUAC): Influential Congressional committee, originally created in 1938, which investigated communist influence in America and contributed to anti-communist hysteria in the postwar United States.

At least a dozen others committed suicide. Studios blacklisted hundreds of actors, screenwriters, directors, even makeup artists suspected of communist affiliations. With no evidence of wrongdoing, people's careers were ruined.

McCarthyism and the Growing "Witch Hunt"

University professors became targets of the growing "witch hunt" in 1949, when HUAC demanded lists of textbooks used at eighty-one universities. When the board of regents at the University of California, Berkeley, instituted a loyalty oath for faculty, firing twenty-six who resisted on principle, protests nationwide forced the regents to back down. But many professors began to downplay controversial material in their courses. In the labor movement, the CIO expelled eleven unions, with more than 900,000 members, for alleged communist domination. The red panic reached its nadir in February 1950, when **Joseph R. McCarthy**, a relatively obscure, Republican U.S. senator from Wisconsin, charged that the U.S. State Department was "thoroughly infested with Communists." Not an especially credible source, McCarthy first claimed that there were 205 communists in the State Department, then 57, then 81. He had a severe drinking problem and a record of dishonesty as a lawyer and judge. But McCarthy crystallized Americans' anxieties, and such anticommunist excesses came to be known as McCarthyism.

Joseph R. McCarthy: Wisconsin senator who launched a massive public campaign against Communism and the Soviet spies and sympathizers that he claimed were inside the federal government. He was later discredited.

Anticommunism in Congress

In such a climate, most public figures found it risky to stand up against McCarthyist tactics. In 1950, Congress passed the Internal Security (McCarran) Act, which

Senator Joseph McCarthy's downfall came in 1954 during the televised Army-McCarthy hearings, when army counsel Joseph Welsh (left) confronted McCarthy on national TV. McCarthy's wild accusations and abusive treatment of witnesses disgusted millions of viewers.

required members of "Communist-front" organizations to register with the government and prohibited them from holding government jobs or traveling abroad. In 1954, the Senate passed the Communist Control Act, sponsored by Democratic senator Hubert H. Humphrey of Minnesota, which effectively made membership in the Communist Party illegal.

Ethel and Julius Rosenberg:
Couple found guilty of conspiracy to commit espionage and executed in 1953.

In 1948, Congressman Richard Nixon of California, a member of HUAC, was propelled onto the national stage when he accused former State Department official Alger Hiss of espionage. That same year, **Ethel and Julius Rosenberg** were arrested for passing atomic secrets to the Soviets; they were found guilty of treason and executed in 1953. For decades, many historians believed the Rosenbergs were victims of a witch hunt, but there was strong evidence of Julius Rosenberg's guilt uncovered at the time (and evidence that Ethel Rosenberg was less involved). This evidence was not presented at trial for national security reasons and remained top secret until 1995, when a Clinton administration initiative opened the files.

Waning of the Red Scare

Link to the video of the exchange between Joseph Welch and McCarthy.

The worst excesses of Cold War anticommunism waned when Senator McCarthy was discredited on national television in 1954. McCarthy was a master at using the press, making sensational accusations—front-page material—just before reporters' deadlines. When McCarthy's charges proved untrue, retractions appeared in the back pages of the newspapers. But McCarthy's crucial mistake was charging on television that the U.S. Army was shielding communists, citing the case of one army dentist. In the so-called Army-McCarthy hearings, held by a Senate subcommittee in 1954, McCarthy, apparently drunk, alternately ranted and slurred his words. In December 1954, the Senate voted to "condemn" McCarthy for sullying the dignity of the Senate. He remained a senator, but exhaustion and alcohol took their toll and he died in 1957 at age forty-eight. With McCarthy discredited, the most virulent anticommunism had run its course. However, the use of fear tactics for political gain, and the narrowing of American freedoms and liberties were chilling legacies of the Cold War.

The Struggle for Civil Rights

What facilitated the emergence of a renewed civil rights movement?

The Cold War also shaped African American struggles for social justice and the nation's responses to them. As the Soviet Union pointed out, the United States could hardly pose as the leader of the free world or condemn the denial of human rights in eastern Europe and the Soviet Union while practicing segregation. Nor could the United States convince new African and Asian nations of its dedication to human rights if African Americans were subjected to segregation, discrimination, disfranchisement, and racial violence. Many Americans viewed any criticism of the United States as a Soviet-inspired attempt to weaken the nation. In this heated environment, African Americans struggled to seize the political initiative.

Link to the 1950s documentary on racism in Levittown, Penn., focusing on the African American Myers family.

Growing Black Political Power

African Americans who helped win World War II were determined to enjoy better lives in postwar America, and politicians like Harry Truman were heeding black aspirations, especially as black voters in some urban-industrial states began to influence the political balance of power.

President Truman supported African American civil rights because he genuinely believed that every American should enjoy equal citizenship rights. Truman was disturbed by a resurgence of racial terrorism, as a revived Ku Klux Klan burned crosses and murdered blacks seeking civil rights after World War II. But what really horrified Truman was the report that police in Aiken, South Carolina, gouged out the eyes of a black sergeant three hours after his army discharge. In December 1946, Truman signed an executive order establishing the President's Committee on Civil Rights. Its report, *To Secure These Rights,* would become the civil rights movement agenda for the next twenty years. It called for antilynching and antisegregation legislation and for laws guaranteeing voting rights and equal employment opportunity.

In 1948, Truman issued two executive orders. One proclaimed a policy of "fair employment throughout the federal establishment" and created the Employment Board of the Civil Service Commission to hear discrimination charges. The other ordered the racial desegregation of the armed forces. Despite strong opposition to desegregation within the military, segregated units were being phased out by the beginning of the Korean War.

Changing social attitudes and experiences in postwar America facilitated these changes. A new and visible black middle class was emerging, composed of college-educated activists, war veterans, and union workers. White awareness of social injustice was heightened by Gunnar Myrdal's social science study *An American Dilemma* (1944) and by Richard Wright's novel *Native Son* (1940) and autobiography *Black Boy* (1945). Blacks and whites worked together in CIO unions and service organizations, such as the National Council of Churches. In 1947, a black baseball player, **Jackie Robinson**, broke the major league color barrier and electrified Brooklyn Dodgers fans.

Jackie Robinson: First African American to play major-league baseball (1947).

Supreme Court Victories and School Desegregation

African Americans were successfully challenging racial discrimination in the courts and in state and local legislatures. Northern state legislatures, pressured by civil rights activists, passed prohibitions against employment discrimination in the 1940s and 1950s. During the 1940s, Thurgood Marshall, head of the NAACP's Legal Defense and Educational Fund, and his colleagues worked to destroy the separate-but-equal doctrine established in *Plessy v. Ferguson* (1896). In higher education, the NAACP calculated, the cost of equality in racially separate schools would be prohibitive. "You can't build a cyclotron for one student," acknowledged one university president. Through NAACP lawsuits, African American students won admission to professional and graduate schools at formerly segregated state universities. The NAACP also won victories through the Supreme Court in *Smith v. Allwright* (1944), which outlawed the whites-only primaries held by the Democratic Party in some southern states; *Morgan v. Virginia* (1946), which struck down segregation in interstate bus transportation; and *Shelley v. Kraemer* (1948), which held that racially restrictive covenants (private agreements among white homeowners not to sell to blacks) could not legally be enforced.

Even so, blacks continued to suffer disfranchisement, job discrimination, and violence. But in 1954, the NAACP won a historic Supreme Court victory:

Brown v. Board of Education of Topeka: Landmark Supreme Court case (1954) that overturned *Plessy v. Ferguson* (1896); it desegregated public schools by arguing that racially separate schools are inherently unequal.

Martin Luther King, Jr.: African American minister whose philosophy of civil disobedience fused the spirit of Christianity with the strategy of achieving racial justice by nonviolent resistance.

Link to Martin Luther King's words and legacy.

Brown v. Board of Education of Topeka. Written by Chief Justice Earl Warren, the court's unanimous decision concluded that "Separate educational facilities are inherently unequal." But the ruling that overturned *Plessy v. Ferguson* did not demand immediate compliance. A year later, the Court ordered school desegregation, but only "with all deliberate speed."

Montgomery Bus Boycott

By the mid-1950s, African Americans were engaged in a grassroots struggle for civil rights in both the north and the south, though southern struggles drew the most national attention. In 1955, Rosa Parks, a department store seamstress and NAACP activist, was arrested for refusing to give up her seat to a white man on a public bus in Montgomery, Alabama. Her arrest enabled local black women's organizations and civil rights groups to organize a boycott of the city's bus system. They selected **Martin Luther King Jr.**, a twenty-six year-old, recently ordained Baptist minister with a Ph.D. from Boston University, as their leader. Schooled in the teachings of India's leader Mohandas K. Gandhi, King believed in nonviolent civil disobedience as a vehicle to focus the nation's attention on the immorality of Jim Crow.

During the year-long Montgomery bus boycott, blacks rallied in their churches. They maintained their boycott through heavy rains and the steamy summer heat, often walking miles a day. With the bus company near bankruptcy and downtown merchants suffering from declining sales, city officials adopted harassment tactics to end to the boycott. But the black people of Montgomery persevered: thirteen months later, the Supreme Court declared Alabama's bus segregation laws unconstitutional.

White Resistance

White reactions to civil rights gains varied. Some communities in border states like Kansas and Maryland quietly implemented school desegregation, and southern moderates advocated a gradual rollback of segregation. But others urged defiance. The Klan experienced another resurgence, and white violence against blacks increased. In 1955, white men in Mississippi beat, mutilated, and murdered Emmett Till, a fourteen-year-old from Chicago, because they took offense at how he spoke to a white woman; an all-white jury took only 67 minutes to acquit those charged with the crime. Business and professional people created White Citizens' Councils (known familiarly as "uptown Ku Klux Klans") to resist school desegregation and use economic power against civil rights activists. When FBI director J. Edgar Hoover briefed President Eisenhower on southern racial tensions in 1956, he warned of communist influences among civil rights activists and suggested that Citizens' Councils might "control the rising tension."

White resistance also mounted in large northern cities. Chicago's African American population increased from 275,000 in 1940 to 800,000 in 1960, and their numbers gave them political power. Though most found good jobs in industry, they also found racism and housing segregation. So racially divided was Chicago that the U.S. Commission on Civil Rights in 1959 described it as "the most residentially segregated city in the nation." Other northern cities were not far behind.

Federal Authority and States' Rights

Although he disapproved of racial segregation, President Eisenhower objected to "compulsory federal law," for he believed that race relations would improve "only if [desegregation] starts locally." He also feared that rapid desegregation would jeopardize Republican inroads in the South. Thus, Eisenhower did not state forthrightly that the federal government would enforce the *Brown* decision as the nation's law.

Events in Little Rock, Arkansas, forced the president to act. In September 1957, Arkansas governor Orval E. Faubus defied a court-supported desegregation plan for Little Rock's Central High School, saying on television that "blood would run in the streets" if black students tried to enter the high school. On the second day of school, eight black teenagers tried to enter Central High, but they were turned away by Arkansas National Guard troops. The ninth student was surrounded by jeering whites and narrowly escaped the mob with the help of a sympathetic white woman.

The "Little Rock Nine" first entered Central High more than two weeks later and only after a federal judge intervened. As an angry crowd surrounded the school television broadcast the scene to the world, Eisenhower decided to nationalize the Arkansas National Guard (placing it under federal, not state, control) and dispatch one thousand army paratroopers to guard the students for the rest of the year. Eisenhower's use of federal power was a critical step toward racial equality, for he directly confronted the conflict between federal authority and states' rights. However, state power triumphed the following year, when Faubus closed public high schools in Little Rock rather than desegregate them.

In 1957, Congress passed the first Civil Rights Act since Reconstruction, creating the Commission on Civil Rights to investigate systemic discrimination, such as in voting. Although this measure was not fully effective, it lent federal recognition

For leading the movement to gain equality for blacks riding city buses in Montgomery, Alabama, Martin Luther King Jr. (1929–1968) and other African Americans, including twenty-three other ministers, were indicted by an all-white jury for violating an old law banning boycotts. In late March 1956, King was convicted and fined $500. A crowd of well-wishers cheered a smiling King (here with his wife, Coretta) outside the courthouse, where King proudly declared, "The protest goes on!" King's arrest and conviction made the bus boycott front-page news across America.

to civil rights. Most important, however, was growing grassroots activism. In 1957, Martin Luther King Jr. became the first president of the Southern Christian Leadership Conference (SCLC), organized to coordinate civil rights activities. With the success in Montgomery and gains through the Supreme Court, African Americans were poised to launch a national civil rights movement.

Creating a Middle-Class Nation

What led to the emergence of a middle-class culture in the 1950s?

Despite resistance to civil rights during the 1950s, the United States was becoming increasingly inclusive. National prosperity offered ever greater numbers of Americans material comfort and security through entrance into an economic middle class. Old European ethnic identities faded, as an ever smaller percentage of America's people were first- or second-generation immigrants.

In the new suburbs, people from different backgrounds created communities. Middle-class Americans increasingly looked to national media for advice on matters ranging from how to celebrate Thanksgiving to how to raise children. New opportunities for consumption—whether teenage fads or suburban ranch-style homes—also tied disparate Americans together. In the postwar years, a new middle-class way of life transformed the United States.

Prosperity for More Americans

During the 1950s, strong economic growth made more Americans than ever economically secure. This economic boom was driven by consumer spending, as Americans bought consumer goods unavailable during the war, and industries expanded production. As the Cold War deepened, government defense spending created jobs and stimulated the economy.

Cold War military and aerospace programs fueled the need for highly educated scientists, engineers, and other white-collar workers. Universities received billions of dollars to fund research, expanding their roles in American life. Government-funded research went beyond military weapon systems and the space race: the transistor, invented during the 1950s, was used in radios and sparked the computer revolution.

A new era of labor relations helped bring economic prosperity to more Americans. The United Auto Workers (UAW) and General Motors led the way for other corporations in providing workers with health insurance, pension plans, and guaranteed cost-of-living adjustments, or COLAs. A 1950 agreement gave GM's workers a five-year contract with regular wage increases tied to corporate productivity. With wage increases tied to corporate productivity, labor cast its lot with management: workplace stability and efficiency, not strikes, would bring higher wages. During the 1950s, wages and benefits propelled union families into the economic middle class.

Sunbelt and Economic Growth

In the 1930s, Roosevelt called the South "the nation's No. 1 economic problem." During World War II, new defense plants and military training camps channeled federal money to the region, stimulating economic growth. In the postwar era, massive defense spending continued to shift economic development to the South and Southwest—the **Sunbelt** (see Map 29.1). Government actions—including tax breaks

Sunbelt: Southern and southwestern states whose rapid economic development brought many new residents during the postwar years.

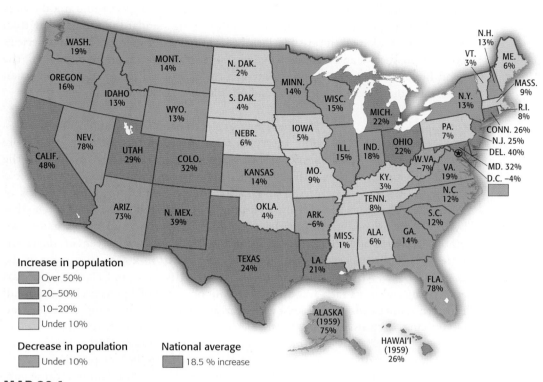

MAP 29.1

Rise of the Sunbelt, 1950–1960

The years after the Second World War saw a continuation of the migration of Americans to the Sunbelt states of the South, Southwest, and West Coast.

Source: Copyright © Cengage Learning

for oil companies, siting of military bases, and defense and aerospace contracts—were crucial to the region's new prosperity.

The Sunbelt's spectacular growth was also due to agribusiness, the oil industry, real-estate development, and recreation. Sunbelt states successfully sought foreign investment and drew industry with lower taxes and heating bills, along with right-to-work laws banning closed shops. The development of air conditioning was also crucial, making the hottest days bearable. Houston, Phoenix, Los Angeles, San Diego, Dallas, and Miami all boomed, and by 1963 California was the most populous state in the Union.

A New Middle-Class Culture

By the 1950s, it seemed that America was becoming a middle-class nation. Unionized blue-collar workers gained middle-class incomes, and veterans with GI Bill college educations swelled the managerial and professional class. In 1956, for the first time, the United States had more white-collar than blue-collar workers, and 60 percent of families had incomes in the middle-class range (approximately $3,000 to $9,000 a year in the mid-1950s).

Paradoxically, the strength of unions in the postwar era contributed to a decline in working-class identity: as large numbers of blue-collar workers participated in suburban middle-class culture, the lines separating working class and middle class seemed less important. Increasingly, a family's living standard mattered more than what sort of work made it possible. People of color did not share equally in America's postwar prosperity and were usually invisible in American representations of "the good life." However, many middle-income African Americans, Latinos, and Asian Americans did participate in the broad middle-class culture.

Whiteness and National Culture

The emergence of a national middle-class culture was possible partly because America's population was more homogeneous in the 1950s than before or since. In the nineteenth and early twentieth centuries, the United States restricted or prohibited immigration from Asia, Africa, and Latin America while accepting millions of Europeans. This large-scale European immigration was shut off in the 1920s, so that by 1960 only 5.7 percent of Americans were foreign-born (compared with approximately 15 percent in 1910 and 12.4 percent in 2005). In 1950, 88 percent of Americans were of European ancestry (compared with 69 percent in 2000); 10 percent of the population was African American; 2 percent was Hispanic; and Native Americans and Asian Americans each accounted for about one-fifth of 1 percent. But almost all European Americans were at least a generation removed from immigration. Instead of "Italians" or "Russians" or "Jews," they were increasingly likely to describe themselves as "white." In 1959, the addition of two new states, Alaska and Hawai'i, brought more people of native, Asian, or Pacific origin to the U.S. population.

Although the new suburbs were peopled mostly by white families, these suburbs were more diverse than the communities from which their residents had come. America's small towns and urban ethnic enclaves were homogeneous and usually intolerant of challenges to tradition. In the suburbs, many people encountered different customs and beliefs. But new suburbanites often traded the provincial homogeneity of specific ethnic or regional cultures for a new sort of homogeneity: a national middle-class culture.

Television

Because many white Americans were new to the middle class, they were uncertain about what was expected of them. They found instruction in the national mass media. Women's magazines helped housewives replace ethnic dishes with "American" recipes created from national brandname products—such as casseroles made with Campbell's Cream of Mushroom soup. Television also fostered America's shared culture. Although television sets cost about $300—the equivalent of $2,000 today—almost half of American homes had TVs by 1953. Television ownership rose to 90 percent by 1960, when more American households had a television set than a washing machine.

On television, suburban families like the Cleavers (*Leave It to Beaver*) ate dinner at a properly set dining room table. June Cleaver did housework in a carefully ironed dress. Every crisis was resolved through paternal wisdom. These popular family situation comedies reinforced the suburban middle-class ideal many American families sought.

The "middle-classness" of television programming was due partly to advertising. Corporations buying airtime did not want to offend potential consumers. Thus, although African American musician Nat King Cole drew millions of viewers to his NBC television show, it never found a sponsor. National corporations feared being linked to a black performer would hurt sales among whites—especially in the South. Because African Americans made up about 10 percent of the population and many had little disposable income, they had little influence. The *Nat King Cole Show* was canceled within a year; it was a decade before the networks again anchored a show around a black performer.

With only network television available—ABC, CBS, and NBC (and, until 1956, DuMont)—70 percent or more of all viewers might be watching the same popular program. (In the early twenty-first century, the most popular shows might attract 12 percent of the audience.) Television gave Americans shared experiences and helped create a more homogeneous, white-focused, middle-class culture.

Consumer Culture

Americans also found common ground through con-sumer goods. After decades of scarcity, Americans had a dazzling array of choices, and even the most utilitarian objects got two-tone paint jobs or rocket-ship details. People used purchases to express their personal identities and claim status. Cars more than anything else embodied consumer fantasies. Expensive Cadillacs were the first to develop tail fins, soon added to midrange Chevys, Fords, and Plymouths. Americans spent $65 billion on automobiles in 1955—a figure equivalent to almost 20 percent of the gross national product. To pay for cars, suburban houses and modern appliances, consumer debt rose from $5.7 billion in 1945 to $58 billion in 1961.

Religion

Church membership (primarily in mainline Christian churches) doubled between 1945 and the early 1960s. The mass media probably played a role, as preachers like Billy Graham created national congregations from television audiences with a message combining the promise of salvation with Cold War patriotism. But local churches and synagogues also offered new suburbanites a sense of community, celebrating life's rituals and supporting those far from their extended families.

Men, Women, and Youth at Midcentury

> How did the economic and social structure of the 1950s influence gender roles?

Having survived the Great Depression and a world war, many Americans sought fulfillment in private life. They saw their commitment as an expression of faith in the future. Despite the satisfactions many found in family life, men and women found their life choices limited by social pressures to conform to narrowly defined gender roles.

Marriage and Families

During the 1950s, few Americans remained single, and most people married young. By 1959, almost half of American brides were under age nineteen; their husbands were usually only a year or so older. Early marriage was endorsed by experts and approved by most parents, partly to prevent premarital sex. One popular women's magazine argued, "When two people are ready for sexual intercourse at the fully human level they are ready for marriage.... And society has no right to stand in their way."

Many young couples found freedom from parental authority by marrying. Most newlyweds quickly had babies—an average of three—completing their family while in their twenties. Birth control (condoms and diaphragms) was widely available and

Moving to Levittown

Builder William Levitt's assembly-line methods created affordable homes for young families—although initially only "Caucasians" were allowed to buy homes in Levittown. This family, shown here on their moving day, would have received a copy of the Levittown *Homeowner's Guide,* which contained a list of "dos" and "don'ts": for example, residents were not to hang laundry on Sundays, when their neighbors were "most likely to be relaxing on the rear lawn." What does this photograph reveal about the new Levittown family, and why might the community rule book promise to help residents "enjoy their new home"? From looking carefully at the map, including street names and public spaces, how did developers try to create neighborhood and community in a development of inexpensive and virtually identical homes?

Urban Archives, Temple University, Philadelphia

The State Museum of Pennsylvania, Pennsylvania Historical and Museum Commission

HOMEOWNERS GUIDE

- SOME INFORMATION FOR RESIDENTS OF LEVITTOWN TO HELP THEM ENJOY THEIR NEW HOMES

The State Museum of Pennsylvania, Pennsylvania Historical and Museum Commission widely used, as couples planned family size. Two children were the American ideal in 1940; by 1960, most couples wanted four. About 88 percent of children under eighteen lived with two parents (in 2000, the figure was 69 percent). Fewer children were born outside marriage; only 3.9 percent of births were to unmarried women in 1950 (compared with more than one-third of births in 2000). As late as 1960, there were only 9 divorces per 1,000 married couples.

Gender Roles in 1950s Families

In 1950s families, men and women usually took distinct roles, with male breadwinners and female homemakers. Contemporary commentators insisted this was based on essential differences between the sexes. In truth, the economic and social structure and cultural values of postwar America determined what choices were available to American men and women.

During the 1950s, it was possible for many families to live in modest middle-class comfort on one (male) salary. There were incentives for women to stay home, especially while children were young. Good child-care was rarely available, and fewer families lived close to relatives. Childcare experts, including **Dr. Spock**, whose 1946 *Baby and Child Care* sold millions of copies, insisted that a mother's full-time attention was necessary for her children's well-being. Because of hiring discrimination, women who could afford to stay home often did not find the available jobs attractive enough to justify juggling paid employment with housework. Instead, schools and religious institutions benefited from women's volunteer labor.

Dr. Spock: Physician and author of *Baby and Child Care*, the bestselling childrearing manual for parents of the baby boom generation.

Women and Work

Suburban domesticity left many women feeling isolated from the larger world their husbands inhabited. The popular belief that one should find complete emotional satisfaction in private life put unrealistic pressures on marriages. And finally, despite near-universal celebration of women's domestic roles, many women were managing both job and family responsibilities (see Figure 29.2). Twice as many women were employed in 1960 as in 1940, including 39 percent of women with children between age six and seventeen. Most worked part-time for a specific family goal: a new car; college tuition. They saw these jobs as service to the family, not independence from it.

Still, women faced discrimination in the work force. Want ads were divided into "Help Wanted—Male" and "Help Wanted—Female" categories. Female full-time workers earned, on average, 60 percent of what men were paid and were restricted to lower-paid "female" fields, as maids, secretaries, teachers, and nurses. A popular book, *Modern Woman: The Lost Sex,* claimed that ambitious women and "feminists" suffered from "penis envy." College psychology

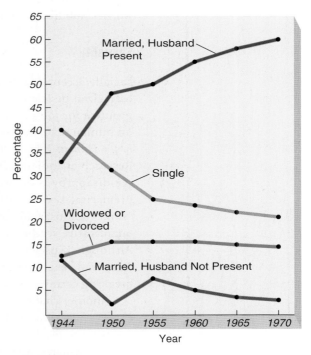

FIGURE 29.2
Marital Distribution of the Female Labor Force, 1944–1970
The composition of the female labor force changed dramatically from 1944 to 1970. In 1944, 41 percent of women in the labor force were single; in 1970, only 22 percent were single. During the same years, the percentage of the female labor force who had a husband in the home jumped from 34 to 59. The percentage who were widowed or divorced remained about the same from 1944 to 1970.
Source: Adapted from U.S. Bureau of the Census, Historical Statistics of the United States, Colonial Times to 1970, *Bicentennial Edition (Washington, D.C.: U.S. Government Printing Office, 1975) p. 133.*

textbooks warned women not to "compete" with men; magazine articles described "career women" as a "third sex." Medical schools commonly limited female admission to 5 percent of each class. In 1960, less than 4 percent of lawyers and judges were female. When future Supreme Court Justice Ruth Bader Ginsburg graduated at the top of her Columbia Law School class in 1959, she could not find a job.

"Crisis of Masculinity"

Academics and mass media critics devoted equal attention to the plight of the American male. American men faced a "crisis of masculinity," proclaimed the nation's mass-circulation magazines. In a bestselling book, sociologist William H. Whyte explained that postwar corporate employees had become "organization men," succeeding through cooperation and conformity, not initiative and risk. Experts claimed women's "natural" desire for security and comfort was stifling men's instinct for adventure. Men who did not conform to standards of male responsibility—husband, father, breadwinner—were socially condemned. Some linked concerns about masculinity to the Cold War, arguing that unless American men recovered masculinity diminished by white collar work or suburban family life, the nation's future was at risk.

Sexuality

Sexuality was complicated terrain in postwar America. Only heterosexual intercourse within marriage was socially acceptable. Women who became pregnant outside marriage were often ostracized by friends and family and expelled from school. Homosexuality was grounds for job dismissal, expulsion from college, even jail. In his major works on human sexuality, *Sexual Behavior in the Human Male* (1948) and *Sexual Behavior in the Human Female* (1953), Dr. Alfred Kinsey, director of the Institute for Sex Research at Indiana University, noted that, while 80 percent of his female sample disapproved of premarital sex on "moral grounds," half of them had had premarital sex. He also reported that 37 percent of American men had had "some homosexual experience." Americans made bestsellers of Kinsey's dry, quantitative studies, while the *Chicago Tribune* called him a "menace to society." Although Kinsey's research did not provide a completely accurate picture of American sexual behavior, it told many Americans that they were not alone in breaking certain rules.

Another challenge to the sexual rules came from Hugh Hefner, who launched *Playboy* magazine in 1953. Within three years, its circulation reached 1 million. Hefner saw *Playboy* as an attack on America's "ferocious anti-sexuality" and his nude "playmates" as a means for men to combat what he considered the increasingly "blurred distinctions between the sexes" in American life.

Youth Culture

The sheer numbers of "baby boom" youth made them a force in American society. As this group moved from childhood to youth, a distinctive youth culture developed. Its customs and rituals were created within peer groups and shaped by national media—teen magazines, movies, radio, advertising, and music. America's corporations quickly learned the power of youth, as children's fads launched multimillion-dollar industries. Mr. Potato Head—probably the first toy advertised on television—had $4 million in sales in 1952. In the mid-1950s, when Walt Disney's television show *Disneyland*

Links to the World

Barbie

Barbie, the all-American doll, is—like many Americans—an immigrant. Although introduced in 1959 by the American toy company Mattel, Barbie's origins lie in Germany, where she was called Lilli.

The German Lilli doll was a novelty toy for adult men (as evidenced by her proportions, equivalent to 39-21-31 in human terms and her sexy outfits). She was based on a character that cartoonist Reinhard Beuthien drew for the German tabloid *Das Bild* in 1952. Lilli was so popular that she became a regular feature, later made three-dimensional as *Bild* Lilli, an eleven-and-a-half-inch-tall blonde doll with the figure Barbie would make famous.

Lilli came to America with Ruth Handler, one of the founders and codirectors of the Mattel toy company. When she glimpsed Lilli while vacationing in Europe, Handler bought three—and gave one to her daughter Barbara, after whom Lilli would be renamed. Mattel bought the rights to Lilli and unveiled Barbie in March 1959. Despite mothers' hesitations about buying a doll that looked like Barbie, within the year Mattel had sold 351,000 Barbies at $3 each (or about $17 in 2000 dollars). The billionth Barbie was sold in 1997.

Within the United States, Barbie has been controversial—at least among adults. Some have worried that Barbie's wildly unrealistic figure fosters girls' dissatisfaction with their own body—a serious problem in a culture plagued with eating disorders. Others claim that, despite Barbie's 1980s "Girls Can Do Anything" makeover, Barbie represents empty-headed femininity, focused on endless consumption. And many have noted that blonde, blue-eyed Barbie fails to represent the diversity of America's people.

In 2002, international labor-rights groups called for a boycott of Barbie. They cited studies showing that half of all Barbies are made by exploited young women in mainland China: of the $10 retail, Chinese factories receive only 35 cents per doll to cover their costs, including labor. Saudi Arabia banned Barbie in 2003, arguing that her skimpy outfits and the values she represents are not suitable for a Muslim nation. Still, the eleven-and-a-half-inch doll remains popular worldwide, selling in more than 150 countries. Today, the average American girl has ten Barbies—and the typical German girl owns five. For better or worse, Barbie continues to link the United States and the rest of the world.

Before Barbie became an American child's toy, she was "Lilli," a German sex symbol. Mattel transformed the doll into a wholesome American teenager with a new wardrobe to match.

Foto: © Ivan Steiger, Toy Museum Munich & Prague

featured Davy Crockett, "King of the Wild Frontier," every child (and more than a few adults) *had* to have a coonskin cap. As these baby-boom children grew up, their buying power shaped American popular culture.

By 1960, America's 18 million teenagers were spending $10 billion a year. Seventy-two percent of movie tickets in the 1950s were sold to teenagers, and Hollywood created teen films ranging from forgettable B-movies to controversial films such as James Dean's *Rebel Without a Cause*. Adults worried that teens would copy the delinquency romanticized in *Rebel Without a Cause,* and teenage boys did emulate Dean's rebellious look. The film, however, blamed parents for teenage confusion, drawing on popular psychological theories about sexuality and the "crisis of masculinity." Nothing defined youth culture as much as music. Young Americans were electrified by the driving energy of Bill Haley and the Comets, Chuck Berry, Little Richard, and Buddy Holly. **Elvis Presley**'s 1956 appearance on TV's *Ed Sullivan Show* touched off a frenzy of teen adulation—and a flood of letters from parents scandalized by his "gyrations." Although few white musicians acknowledged it, the roots of rock 'n' roll lay in African American rhythm and blues. The raw energy and sometimes sexually suggestive lyrics of early rock music faded as the music industry sought white performers, like Pat Boone, to do blander, more acceptable "cover" versions of music by black artists.

This distinct youth culture made many adults uneasy. Parents worried that "going steady" might encourage teens to "go too far" sexually. Juvenile delinquency was a major concern. Crime rates for young people had risen dramatically after World War II, but much of it was "status" crime—curfew violations, sexual experimentation, underage drinking—activities that were criminal because of the person's age. Congress held hearings on juvenile delinquency, with experts testifying to the corrupting power of youth-oriented popular culture, comic books in particular. Most youthful behavior, however, fit squarely into the consumer culture that youth shared with their parents. "Rebellious youth" rarely questioned the logic of postwar American culture.

Elvis Presley: Popular rock 'n' roll musician who melded country, gospel, and rhythm and blues influences; his sexually charged style drew young fans and alarmed many adults.

Challenges to Middle-Class Culture

The growth of middle-class culture inspired pockets of cultural dissent. **Beat** (a word that suggested both "down and out" and "beatific") writers rejected middle-class social decorum and contemporary literary conventions. The Beat Generation embraced spontaneity in their art, sought escape from the demands of everyday life, and enjoyed open sexuality and drug use. Perhaps the most significant beat work was Allen Ginsberg's angry, incantational poem "Howl" (1956), the subject of an obscenity trial whose verdict opened American publishing to a broader range of works. The mainstream press ridiculed the beats, dubbing them "beatniks" (after *Sputnik,* suggesting their un-Americanness). Still, they laid the groundwork for the 1960s counterculture.

Beats: Nonconformist writers, such as Allen Ginsberg and Jack Kerouac, who expressed scorn for the middle-class ideals of conformity, religion, family values, and materialism.

The Limits of the Middle-Class Nation

What were the limits of middle class culture that began to emerge?

During the 1950s, America's popular culture and mass media celebrated new opportunities. But influential critics condemned middle-class culture as a wasteland of conformity, homogeneity, and ugly consumerism.

Critics of Conformity These critics were not lone figures crying out in the wilderness. Americans, obsessed with self-criticism even as most participated wholeheartedly in the celebratory "consensus" culture of their age, rushed to buy books like J.D. Salinger's *The Catcher in the Rye* and Norman Mailer's *The Naked and the Dead,* which were profoundly critical of American society. Americans even made bestsellers of difficult academic works, such as David Riesman's *The Lonely Crowd* (1950) and William H. Whyte's *The Organization Man* (1955), both of which criticized conformity. These critiques also appeared in mass-circulation magazines like *Ladies' Home Journal* and *Reader's Digest.* Steeped in such cultural criticism, many Americans understood *Invasion of the Body Snatchers*—a 1956 film in which zombielike aliens grown in pods gradually replace a town's human inhabitants—as criticism of suburban conformity and of postwar cultural homogeneity.

Most critics were attempting to understand large-scale and significant changes in American society. Americans did lose some autonomy in work as large corporations replaced smaller businesses; they experienced the homogenizing force of mass production and a national consumer culture; they saw distinctions among ethnic groups and even among socioeconomic classes fade. Critics, however, were often elitist and antidemocratic, seeing only bland conformity and sterility in the emerging middle-class suburban culture and not understanding that inexpensive suburban housing gave healthier, possibly happier, lives to millions raised in dank, dark tenements or ramshackle farmhouses without indoor plumbing.

Environmental Degradation The new consumer culture encouraged wasteful habits and harmed the environment. *BusinessWeek* noted that corporations need not rely on "planned obsolescence," purposely designing a product to wear out. Americans replaced products because they were "out of date," not because they did not work, and automakers, encouraging the trend, revamped designs annually. America's new consumer society used an ever larger share of the world's resources. By the 1960s, the United States, with only 5 percent of the world's population, consumed more than one-third of its goods and services.

The rapid economic growth exacted environmental costs. Steel mills, coal-powered generators, and internal-combustion car engines burning lead-based gasoline polluted the atmosphere and imperiled people's health. As suburbanites commuted greater distances to work and neighborhoods were built without public transportation, Americans relied on private automobiles, consuming the nonrenewable resources of oil and gasoline and filling cities and suburbs with smog. Water was diverted from lakes and rivers to service burgeoning Sunbelt cities, including the swimming pools and golf courses that dotted parched Arizona and southern California.

Defense contractors and farmers were among the country's worst polluters. Refuse from nuclear weapons facilities at Hanford, Washington and at Colorado's Rocky Flats arsenal poisoned soil and water resources. Agriculture used pesticides and other chemicals. DDT, a chemical used on Pacific islands during the war to kill mosquitoes and lice, was used widely in the United States until after 1962, when wildlife biologist Rachel Carson indicted DDT for the deaths of mammals, birds, and fish in her bestselling book *Silent Spring.*

In the midst of prosperity, few understood the consequences of the economic transformation taking place. The nation was moving toward a postindustrial economy in which providing goods and services to consumers was more important than producing goods. Therefore, though union members prospered during the 1950s, union membership grew slowly—because most new jobs were created in the union-resistant white-collar service trades. Technological advances increased productivity and also pushed people from well paid blue-collar jobs into the growing and lower-paid service sector.

Continuing Racism   Racial discrimination stood unchallenged in most of 1950s America. Suburbs, North and South, were almost always racially segregated. Many white Americans had little or no contact with people of different races, in part because the relatively small populations of nonwhite Americans were not dispersed equally nationwide. In 1960, there were 68 people of Chinese descent and 519 African Americans living in Vermont; 181 Native Americans lived in West Virginia; and Mississippi had just 178 Japanese American residents. Most white Americans in the 1950s—especially those outside the South—gave little thought to race. Instead, they regarded the emerging middle-class culture not as "white," but as "American," marginalizing people of color in image as in reality.

In an age of abundance, more than one in five Americans lived in poverty. One-fifth of the poor were people of color, including almost half of the nation's African Americans and more than half of all Native Americans. Two-thirds of the poor lived in households headed by a person with an eighth-grade education or less, one-fourth in households headed by a single woman. More than one-third of the poor were under age eighteen; one-fourth were over age sixty-five. Social Security payments helped, but many retirees were not yet covered, and medical costs drove many older Americans into poverty.

Poverty in an Age of Abundance   As millions of Americans (most of them white) settled in suburbs, the poor were concentrated in inner cities. African American migrants from the South were joined by poor whites from the southern Appalachians, moving to Chicago, Cincinnati, Baltimore, and Detroit. Latin Americans arrived in growing numbers from Mexico, the Dominican Republic, Colombia, Ecuador, and Cuba. Because of the strong economy, many newcomers gained a higher standard of living. But discrimination limited their advances, and they endured crowded and decrepit housing and poor schools. Federal programs that helped middle-class Americans sometimes made the lives of poor people worse. For example, the National Housing Act of 1949, passed to make available "a decent home . . . for every American family," provided for "urban redevelopment." Redevelopment meant slum clearance, replacing poor neighborhoods with luxury high-rise buildings, parking lots, and even highways.

In rural areas, the growth of large agribusinesses pushed tenant farmers and small farm owners off the land. From 1945 to 1961, the nation's farm population declined from 24.4 million to 14.8 million. When the harvesting of cotton in the South was mechanized in the 1940s and 1950s, more than 4 million people were displaced. Southern tobacco growers dismissed tenant farmers, bought tractors, and hired migratory workers. In the West and Southwest, Mexican citizens became cheap migrant labor under the *bracero* program. Almost 1 million Mexican workers came

After the war, American Indians lost sacred land to both big corporations and the federal government. In 1948 George Gillette (*left*), chairman of the Fort Berthold, North Dakota, Indian Tribal Council, covers his face and weeps as Secretary of the Interior J. A. Krug signs a contract buying 155,000 acres of tribal land for a reservoir.

legally to the United States in 1959. Entire families labored, enduring conditions little better than in the Great Depression.

Native Americans were America's poorest people, with an average annual income barely half that of the poverty level. Conditions worsened under termination, a federal policy implemented during Eisenhower's administration. Termination reversed the Indian Reorganization Act of 1934, allowing Indians to terminate their tribal status and remove reservation lands from federal protection prohibiting their sale. Sixty-one tribes were terminated between 1954 and 1960. Termination could only occur with a tribe's agreement, but pressure was sometimes intense—especially when reservation land was rich in natural resources. Enticed by cash payments, almost four-fifths of the Klamaths of Oregon voted to sell their shares of the forest land. Many Indians left reservation land for the city. By the time termination ceased in the 1960s, observers compared the situation of Native Americans to the devastation their forebears had endured in the nineteenth century.

Overall, many Americans enjoyed relative prosperity in the postwar era. But those who had made it to the comfortable middle class often ignored the plight of those left behind. Their children—the baby-boom generation—would see racism, poverty, and the self-satisfaction of postwar suburban culture as a failure of American ideals.

The Pledge of Allegiance

The Pledge of Allegiance Americans recite today was shaped by the Cold War. Congress added the phrase "under God" to the pledge in 1954 to emphasize the difference between the god-fearing United States and the "godless communists" of the Soviet Union.

The Pledge of Allegiance was not always an important part of American life. The original version was written in 1892 by Francis Bellamy, editor of *The Youth's Companion*, to commemorate the four-hundredth anniversary of Columbus's arrival in North America. In 1942, Congress officially adopted a revised version as an act of wartime patriotism. The Supreme Court ruled in 1943, however, that schoolchildren could not be forced to say the Pledge to the Flag.

During the Cold War years, the pledge became an increasingly important symbol of U.S. loyalty. Cold War fears fueled a campaign by the Knights of Columbus, a Catholic men's service organization, to include "under God" in the pledge. Supporting the bill, President Eisenhower proclaimed that

in this way we shall constantly strengthen those spiritual weapons which forever will be our country's most powerful resource in peace and war. From this day forward, the millions of our schoolchildren will daily proclaim in every city and town, every village and every rural schoolhouse, the dedication of our nation and our people to the Almighty.

Some Americans, citing the doctrine of separation of church and state, have protested including "under God." In June 2002, the Ninth District Court (covering California and eight western states) sparked a controversy by ruling that the 1954 pledge was unconstitutional because it conveyed "state endorsement" of a religious belief. Questions about the proper role of religion in the United States remain controversial, a legacy for a people and a nation becoming more diverse in the twenty-first century.

Summary

In the years following World War II, Americans married and had children in record numbers. Millions of veterans used the GI Bill to attend college, buy homes, and start businesses. Although American leaders feared that the nation would lapse back into economic depression after wartime government spending ended, consumer spending brought growth. Sustained economic growth lifted a majority of Americans into an expanding middle class.

The Cold War presidencies of Truman and Eisenhower focused more on international relations than on domestic politics. Within the United States, Cold War fears provoked an extreme anticommunism that stifled political dissent and diminished Americans' civil liberties and freedoms.

The continuing African American struggle for civil rights drew national attention during the Montgomery bus boycott. African Americans won victories in the Supreme Court, including the landmark *Brown v. Board of Education* decision. Truman and Eisenhower used federal power to guarantee the rights of African Americans, as a national civil rights movement coalesced.

Despite continued racial divisions, the United States became a more inclusive nation in the 1950s, as a majority of Americans participated in a national, consumer-oriented, middle-class culture. This culture largely ignored the poverty in the nation's cities and rural areas, but for the growing number in the middle-class, the American Dream seemed a reality.

Chapter Review

Shaping Postwar America

What drove the mass migration of Americans to the suburbs after World War II?

Two factors facilitated massive migration to the suburbs: first, demand for affordable, single-family homes, and second, federal policies. Few new houses or apartments were built during the Great Depression and World War II, and many young couples were forced to move in with relatives or find creative solutions to the housing shortage. In the postwar years, developers applied assembly-line techniques to home construction, creating new suburbs on relatively inexpensive land outside cities. At the same time, the Federal Housing Authority offered low-interest mortgages and loans, and Congress authorized the construction of major roadways and interstate highways in the late 1940s and 1950s. These roads linked the new suburbs to jobs in the cities.

Domestic Politics in the Cold War Era

What happened to New Deal style liberalism after World War II?

President Harry S Truman embraced the same government responsibility for citizens' welfare that drove FDR's New Deal programs, but with limited success. He sought an increase in the minimum wage, national housing legislation offering mortgage loans, national health insurance, and federal aid for education. He additionally supported the Full Employment Act and civil rights legislation for African Americans. But conservative Republicans and southern Democrats in Congress gutted the Full Employment Act and refused to raise the minimum wage, while southern conservatives destroyed his civil rights legislation. His medical insurance and educational funding also met with resistance. A moderate Republican, Eisenhower signed amendments to the Social Security Act that increased benefits and made 7.5 million workers eligible for the program. He also increased government funding for education. Still, neither Truman nor Eisenhower came close to the liberalism of the New Deal.

Cold War Fears and Anticommunism

How did Cold War fears inspire a Red Scare in the United States?

In the 1940s and 1950s, as Cold War tensions escalated between the U.S. and its rival superpower, the Soviet Union, Americans became increasingly nervous that communist power might reach their shores. Many Americans regarded the Soviet Union's virtual takeover of eastern Europe in the late 1940s as frighteningly similar to Nazi Germany's takeover of neighboring states during the war. Fear of a nuclear war with the Soviets also inspired anticommunism in the United States, especially after 1949 when the Soviet Union possessed atomic weapons. Normal fears, however, were replaced by irrational ones at every level of society, fueling anticommunist venom and witch hunts that violated people's civil rights and led to the persecution of thousands of innocent Americans. Mainstream Americans built bomb shelters; government employees could be deemed "security risks" (and fired) for such flimsy reasons as alcoholism, homosexuality, and high levels of debt—often without evidence of disloyalty. The House Un-American Activities Committee (HUAC) conducted public investigations that targeted Hollywood, university professors, and others. Consequently, studios blacklisted actors, screenwriters, and others suspected of communist affiliations, and university professors were fired based on the books they used or their unwillingness to take a loyalty oath. Fears drove the CIO to purge itself of eleven unions—900,000 labor union members—for alleged, but unproven, communist domination. The red scare waned after 1954 when Republican Senator Joseph McCarthy was discredited on national television for his claims about communist party members infiltrating the state department.

The Struggle for Civil Rights

What facilitated the emergence of a renewed civil rights movement?

African Americans who helped win World War II were determined to improve their status and end discrimination in the United States. That sentiment, along with the growth of a new and visible black middle class of college educated activists, war veterans, and union workers, helped reinvigorate civil rights activism among blacks and raise awareness of social injustice among white politicians and mainstream Americans. President Truman established the President's Commission on Civil Rights in 1946, which produced a report that became the civil rights' movement agenda for the next twenty years—calling for legislation to end lynching and segregation and guarantee voting rights and equality in employment. Academics and authors such as Gunnar Myrdal and Richard Wright produced powerful works that educated Americans about ongoing racial injustice. African Americans mounted successful challenges to racial discrimination in the courts, most notably the end of segregated schools in the 1954 landmark *Brown v. Board of Education of Topeka* case. At the grassroots level, blacks fought discrimination, most visibly in the year-long Montgomery Bus Boycott, which began in 1955 when Rosa Parks, a seamstress and NAACP activist, was arrested for refusing to give up her seat on a city bus to a white man. Martin Luther King, Jr., a recently ordained minister, led the successful boycott and in 1957 became the first president of the Southern Christian Leadership Conference (SCLC), organized to coordinate civil rights activities.

Creating a Middle-Class Nation

What led to the emergence of a middle-class culture in the 1950s?

In the postwar era, Americans enjoyed national prosperity on an unprecedented level. That meant that there were more and better-paying jobs that enabled greater numbers of people to move into the ranks of middle class, complete with its material comfort and security. Veterans who took advantage of G.I. Bill educational opportunities were able to swell the professional and managerial job classifications, while previously blue-collar manufacturing jobs now paid well-enough to make these families middle class, too. People of varying ethnic backgrounds came together via home ownership in the new suburbs, which, although still largely white, were far more diverse than the communities where people previously resided. An assortment of newly affordable goods from cars to clothing reached a wider segment of the population. And an emerging national mass media—magazines, newspapers, film, and television—taught all Americans how to behave and live like a single, unified, national middle-class—with American foods replacing ethnic dishes, national brands

replacing homemade products, and nationalized notions about how to raise children. Television shows reinforced ideas about how proper people dressed, arranged their homes, and raised children, thereby reinforcing white middle-class ideals to those watching across class, racial, and ethnic lines.

Men, Women, and Youth at Midcentury

How did the economic and social structure of the 1950s influence gender roles?

In the 1950s, men and women occupied separate gender roles. Economically, middle-class families could survive on one income, typically the man's. Most Americans believed that men should be breadwinners and women homemakers. Culturally, women's domestic roles were hailed as their true vocation, even though in reality they left many feeling isolated and unfulfilled. While many married women did work outside the home, it was often part-time and for a specific goal, such as a new car. There were other disincentives that kept many women from seeking full-time work or careers: childcare was virtually nonexistent; popular childcare experts such as Dr. Spock argued that children required a mother's full-time care; and hiring discrimination meant that there were few well-paying jobs open to women to make it worth juggling home and work responsibilities. Employment ads were sex segregated into Help Wanted—Male and Help Wanted—Female categories, and on average women earned only 60 percent of what men earned. Men who did not conform to standards of male responsibility—husband, father, breadwinner—were also socially condemned, and experts worried about the crisis in masculinity of a new generation of "organization men," corporate employees who succeeded through cooperation and conformity rather than initiative and risk.

The Limits of the Middle-Class Nation

What were the limits of middle class culture that began to emerge?

Influential critics pointed out several negative consequences of the middle class culture that emerged in the 1950s. First, consumerism encouraged wasteful and environmentally unsound purchasing habits. Instead of Americans replacing products when they wore out, now they replaced them when they seemed outdated. Worse, by the 1960s the United States, with only 5 percent of the world's population, consumed more than one-third of its goods and services. All of this production generated increased pollution and health concerns. Americans' growing dependence on the automobile to led to increased reliance on gasoline, and water was shifted from lakes to swimming pools as the Sunbelt developed. Even in the age of affluence, more than one-fifth of Americans were poor, often people of color (especially Native Americans and African Americans), many of whom were concentrated in inner cities. Racial discrimination continued, resulting in racially segregated suburbs. Programs that helped the middle class often hurt the poor, such as the National Housing Act of 1949, which promised decent housing via urban redevelopment; for the poor, that meant slum clearance, replacing their neighborhoods with luxury high-rise buildings, parking lots, and even highways.

Suggestions for Further Reading

Glenn C. Altschuler and Stuart M. Blumin, *The GI Bill: A New Deal for Veterans* (2009)

Taylor Branch, *Parting the Waters: America in the King Years, 1954–1963* (1988)

Lizabeth Cohen, *A Consumer's Republic: The Politics of Mass Consumption in Postwar America* (2003)

Stephanie Coontz, *The Way We Never Were: American Families and the Nostalgia Trap* (1992)

Thomas Patrick Doherty, *Cold War, Cool Medium: Television, McCarthyism, and American Culture* (2003)

Mary Dudziak, *Cold War Civil Rights: Race and the Image of American Democracy* (2000)

James Gregory, *The Southern Diaspora: How the Great Migrations of Black and White Southerners Transformed the Nation* (2007)

Thomas Hine, *Populuxe* (1986)

Grace Palladino, *Teenagers* (1996)

Michael Sherry, *In the Shadow of War* (1995)

Thomas J. Sugrue, *Sweet Land of Liberty: The Forgotten Struggle for Civil Rights in the North* (2008)

Go to the CourseMate website for primary source links, study tools, and review materials for this chapter.
www.cengagebrain.com

The Tumultuous Sixties

30

1960–1968

It was late, and Ezell Blair had an exam the next day. But he and his friends in the dormitory sat talking—as they often did—about injustice, about living in a nation that proclaimed equality for all but denied full citizenship to some because of the color of their skin. They were complaining about the do-nothing adults, condemning the black community of Greensboro when Franklin McCain said, as if he meant it, "It's time to fish or cut bait." Joe McNeil and McCain's roommate, David Richmond, agreed.

The next day, February 1, 1960, after their classes at North Carolina Agricultural and Technical College, the four freshmen walked into town. At the F.W. Woolworth's on South Elm Street, one of the most profitable stores in the national chain, each bought a few small things. Then, nervously, they sat down at the lunch counter and tried to order coffee. These seventeen- and eighteen-year-olds were prepared to be arrested, even physically attacked. But nothing happened. The counter help ignored them as long as possible; finally one worker reminded them, "We don't serve colored here." An elderly white woman told the boys how proud she was of them. The store closed; the manager turned out the lights. After forty-five minutes, the four men who began the sit-in movement left the store.

They returned the next day with twenty fellow students. By February 3, sixty-three of the sixty-five seats were taken. On February 4, the sit-in spread to the S.H. Kress store across the street. By February 7, there were sit-ins in Winston-Salem; by February 8, in Charlotte; on February 9, in Raleigh. By the third week in February, students were picketing Woolworth's stores in the North. On July 26, 1960, they won. F.W. Woolworth's ended segregation in all its stores.

The sit-in at the Greensboro Woolworth's signaled the beginning of a decade of public activism unmatched in U.S. history. During the 1960s, millions of Americans—many of them young—marched for civil rights or against the war in Vietnam. Passion over contemporary issues revitalized democracy and threatened to tear the nation apart.

Chapter Outline

Kennedy and the Cold War
John Fitzgerald Kennedy | Election of 1960 | Nation Building in the Third World | Soviet-American Tensions | Bay of Pigs Invasion | Cuban Missile Crisis

Marching for Freedom
Students and the Movement | Freedom Rides and Voter Registration | Kennedy and Civil Rights | Birmingham and the Children's Crusade | "Segregation Forever!" | March on Washington | Freedom Summer

Liberalism and the Great Society
Kennedy Assassination | Johnson and the Great Society | Civil Rights Act | Election of 1964 | Improving American Life | War on Poverty

VISUALIZING THE PAST *"Project C" and National Opinion*

Johnson and Vietnam
Kennedy's Legacy in Vietnam | Tonkin Gulf Incident and Resolution | Decision for Escalation | Opposition to Americanization | American Soldiers in Vietnam | Divisions at Home

A Nation Divided
Urban Unrest | Black Power | Youth and Politics | Free Speech Movement | Student Activism | Youth and the War in Vietnam | Youth Culture and the Counterculture

LINKS TO THE WORLD *The British Invasion*

John F. Kennedy, the nation's youngest president, told Americans as he took office in 1961, "The torch has been passed to a new generation." Despite his inspirational language, Kennedy had only modest success implementing his domestic agenda. In his third year as president, however, Kennedy offered greater support for civil rights and proposed ambitious domestic policies. When Kennedy was assassinated in November 1963, his death seemed, to many, the end of an era of hope.

Lyndon Johnson, Kennedy's successor, invoked the memory of the martyred president to launch an ambitious program of civil rights and liberal legislation. Calling his vision the Great Society, Johnson meant to use federal power to eliminate poverty and guarantee equal rights to all Americans.

Despite liberal triumphs and civil rights gains, social tensions escalated during the mid-1960s. A revitalized conservative movement emerged, and Franklin Roosevelt's old New Deal coalition fractured as white southerners abandoned the Democratic Party. Angry that poverty and discrimination persisted despite landmark civil rights laws, many African Americans rioted. White youth culture increasingly rejected the values and lifestyle of its elders, creating what Americans have called the generation gap.

Developments overseas also contributed to a growing national instability. After the 1962 Cuban missile crisis brought the Soviet Union and the United States close to nuclear disaster, President John F. Kennedy and Soviet leader Nikita Khrushchev moved to reduce bilateral tensions in 1963. Cold War pressures in Europe lessened appreciably. Everywhere else, however, the superpowers competed frantically. Throughout the 1960s, the United States tried various of approaches—including foreign aid, CIA covert actions, military assaults, cultural penetration, economic sanctions, and diplomacy—to win the Cold War. In Vietnam, Kennedy expanded U.S. involvement significantly. Johnson "Americanized" the war, increasing U.S. troops to more than half a million in 1968.

By 1968, the war in Vietnam divided Americans and undermined Johnson's Great Society. With the assassinations of Martin Luther King Jr. and Robert Kennedy—two of America's brightest leaders—with cities in flames and tanks in Chicago streets in August, the fate of the nation seemed to hang in the balance.

As you read this chapter, keep the following questions in mind:

* **What were the successes and failures of American liberalism in the 1960s?**

* **Why did the United States expand its participation in the war in Vietnam and continue in the war so long?**

* **By 1968, many believed the fate of the nation hung in the balance. What did they think was at stake? What divided Americans, and how did they express their differences?**

1968
The Tet Offensive | Johnson's Exit | Assassinations | Chicago Democratic National Convention | Global Protest | Nixon's Election

LEGACY FOR A PEOPLE AND A NATION *The Immigration Act of 1965*

SUMMARY

Chronology

1960	Sit-ins begin in Greensboro Birth-control pill approved John F. Kennedy elected president Young Americans for Freedom write Sharon Statement
1961	Freedom Rides protest segregation in transportation
1962	Students for a Democratic Society issues Port Huron Statement Cuban missile crisis courts nuclear war
1963	Civil rights March on Washington for Jobs and Freedom draws more than 250,000 South Vietnamese leader Diem assassinated following U.S.-sanctioned coup d'état John F. Kennedy assassinated; Lyndon B. Johnson becomes president
1964	Civil Rights Act passed by Congress Race riots break out in first of the "long, hot summers" Gulf of Tonkin Resolution passed by Congress Free Speech Movement begins at University of California, Berkeley Lyndon B. Johnson elected president
1965	Lyndon Johnson launches Great Society programs United States commits ground troops to Vietnam and initiates bombing campaign Voting Rights Act outlaws practices preventing most African Americans from voting in southern states Immigration and Nationality Act lowers barriers to immigration from Asia and Latin America Malcolm X assassinated
1966	National Organization for Women founded
1967	"Summer of love" in San Francisco's Haight-Ashbury district Race riots erupt in Newark, Detroit, and other cities
1968	Tet Offensive deepens fear of losing war in Vietnam Martin Luther King Jr. assassinated Robert Kennedy assassinated Violence erupts at Democratic National Convention Richard Nixon elected president

Kennedy and the Cold War

How was the Cuban missile crisis a watershed in U.S.–Soviet relations?

John F. Kennedy: President from 1961 until his assassination in 1963.

Young, handsome, and intellectually curious, **John F. Kennedy** brought wit and sophistication to the White House. His Irish American grandfather had been mayor of Boston, and his millionaire father, Joseph P. Kennedy, served as ambassador to Great Britain. In 1946, the young Kennedy returned from World War II a naval hero (the boat he commanded was sunk by a Japanese destroyer in 1943, and Kennedy saved his crew) and campaigned to represent Boston in the U.S. House of Representatives. He served three terms, and in 1952 was elected to the Senate.

John Fitzgerald Kennedy

As a Democrat, Kennedy inherited the New Deal commitment to America's social welfare system. He generally voted with the pro-labor sentiments of his low-income, blue-collar constituents. But he avoided controversial issues, such as civil rights and the censure of Joseph McCarthy. Kennedy won a Pulitzer Prize for his *Profiles in Courage* (1956), a study of principled politicians, but he shaded the truth in claiming sole authorship, as it was written largely by aide Theodore Sorensen (from more than one hundred pages of notes dictated by Kennedy). In foreign policy, Senator

Kennedy endorsed the Cold War policy of containment. Despite an unimpressive legislative record, he enjoyed an enthusiastic following, especially after his landslide reelection to the Senate in 1958.

Kennedy cultivated an image as a happy, healthy family man. But he was a chronic womanizer, even after his 1953 marriage to Jacqueline Bouvier. Nor was he the picture of physical vitality: as a child he nearly died of scarlet fever and later developed severe back problems, worsened by his participation in World War II. Kennedy was diagnosed with Addison's disease, an adrenalin deficiency that required daily cortisone injections and often left him in pain. As president he would require plenty of bed rest and frequent therapeutic swims in the White House pool.

Election of 1960

Kennedy beat Republican Richard Nixon in the 1960 presidential election by a narrow 118,000 votes of nearly 69 million cast. Kennedy achieved mixed success in the South but ran well in the Northeast and Midwest. His Roman Catholic faith hurt him in states where voters feared he would take direction from the pope, but helped in states with large Catholic populations. As the sitting vice president, Nixon had to answer for sagging economic figures and the Soviet downing of a U-2 spy plane. In televised debates against the telegenic Kennedy, Nixon looked nervous and surly, and the camera made him appear unshaven. Perhaps worse, when asked to list Nixon's significant decisions as vice president, Eisenhower replied, "If you give me a week, I might think of one."

The new president surrounded himself with young advisers whom writer David Halberstam called "the best and the brightest." Secretary of Defense Robert McNamara (age forty-four) was an assistant professor at Harvard at twenty-four and later the whiz-kid president of the Ford Motor Company. Kennedy's special assistant for national security affairs, McGeorge Bundy (age forty-one) became a Harvard dean at thirty-four with only a bachelor's degree. Secretary of State Dean Rusk (fifty-two) had been a Rhodes scholar in his youth. Kennedy was only forty-three, and his brother Robert, the attorney general, was thirty-five.

Kennedy gave top priority to waging the Cold War. In the campaign, he accused Eisenhower of pursuing an unimaginative foreign policy that failed to reduce the threat of nuclear war with the Soviet Union and weakened America's standing in the Third World.

Many Americans were enchanted with the youthful and photogenic Kennedys. Here, the president and his family pose outside the Palm Beach, Florida, home of the president's father after a private Easter Service, April 14, 1963.

Nation Building in the Third World

Kennedy understood, sooner than his advisers, that there were limits to American power abroad. More than his predecessor, he proved willing to initiate dialog with the Soviets, sometimes using his brother Robert as a secret channel to Moscow. Yet Kennedy also sought victory in the Cold War. After Soviet leader Nikita Khrushchev endorsed "wars of national liberation," such as the one in Vietnam, Kennedy called for "peaceful revolution" through nation building. The administration helped developing nations with aid to improve agriculture, transportation, and communications. Kennedy thus oversaw the creation of the multibillion-dollar Alliance for Progress in 1961 to spur economic development in Latin America. That year, too, he created the Peace Corps, dispatching American teachers, agricultural specialists, and health workers to assist authorities in developing nations.

Cynics then and later dismissed the Alliance and the Peace Corps as Kennedy's Cold War tools for countering anti-Americanism and defeating communism in the developing world. True enough, but the programs were also born of genuine humanitarianism. As the historian Elizabeth Cobbs Hoffman has written, "the Peace Corps broached an age-old dilemma of U.S. foreign policy: how to reconcile the imperatives and temptations of power politics with the ideals of freedom and self-determination for all nations."

The Alliance for Progress was only partly successful; infant mortality rates improved, but Latin American economies registered unimpressive growth and class divisions widened, exacerbating political unrest. Although many foreign peoples welcomed U.S. economic assistance and craved American material culture, they resented interference. And because aid was usually transmitted through a self-interested elite, it often never reached the poor.

Although Kennedy and his aides were supportive of social revolution in the Third World, they disapproved of communist involvement in these uprisings. Therefore, the administration relied on counterinsurgency to defeat revolutionaries who challenged pro-U.S. Third World governments. U.S. military and technical advisers trained native troops and police to quell unrest.

Soviet-American Tensions

The new president struggled in relations with the Soviet Union. A summit meeting with Soviet leader Nikita Khrushchev in Vienna in June 1961 went poorly, as the two leaders disagreed over preconditions for peace and stability in the world. Consequently, the administration's first year witnessed little movement on controlling the nuclear arms race or getting a superpower ban on testing nuclear weapons in the atmosphere or underground. Instead, both superpowers accelerated their arms production. In 1961, the U.S. military budget shot up 15 percent; by mid-1964, U.S. nuclear weapons increased by 150 percent. Government advice to citizens to build fallout shelters in their backyards intensified public fear of devastating war.

If war occurred, many believed Berlin would be the cause. In mid-1961, Khrushchev demanded an end to western occupation of West Berlin and a reunification of East and West Germany stood by U.S. commitment to West Berlin and West Germany. In August the Soviets, at the urging of the East German regime, erected a concrete and barbed-wire barricade to halt the exodus of East Germans into the more prosperous and politically free West Berlin. The Berlin Wall inspired protests throughout the noncommunist world, but Kennedy privately sighed that "a wall is a hell of a lot better than a war." The barrier shut off the flow of refugees, and the crisis passed.

Bay of Pigs Invasion

Yet Kennedy knew that Khrushchev would continue to press for advantage elsewhere, and he was particularly rankled by growing Soviet assistance to Fidel Castro's Cuban government. The Eisenhower administration contested the Cuban revolution and bequeathed to the Kennedy administration a partially developed CIA plan to overthrow Fidel Castro: CIA-trained Cuban exiles would land and secure a beachhead; the Cuban people would rise up against Castro and welcome a new U.S.-backed government.

The attack took place on April 17, 1961, as twelve hundred exiles landed at the swampy Bay of Pigs in Cuba. Instead of meeting discontented Cubans, they were greeted by Castro's troops and quickly captured. Kennedy tried to keep the U.S. participation in the operation hidden but the CIA's role swiftly became public. Anti-American sentiment swept through Latin America. Castro, concluding that the United States might launch another invasion, looked increasingly toward the Soviet Union for military and economic assistance.

Embarrassed by the Bay of Pigs fiasco, Kennedy vowed to bring Castro down. The CIA soon hatched a project called Operation Mongoose to disrupt the island's trade, support raids on Cuba from Miami, and kill Castro. The agency's assassination schemes included providing Castro with cigars laced with explosives and poison. The United States also tightened its economic blockade and undertook military maneuvers in the Caribbean. The Joint Chiefs of Staff sketched plans to spark a rebellion in Cuba that would be followed by an invasion of U.S. troops.

Cuban Missile Crisis

Both Castro and Khrushchev believed an invasion was coming, which partly explains the Soviet leader's risky decision in 1962 to secretly deploy nuclear missiles in Cuba as a deterrent. But Khrushchev also hoped the move would improve the Soviet position in the nuclear balance of power and force Kennedy to finally resolve the German problem. Khrushchev wanted the West out of Berlin, and he worried that Washington might provide West Germany with nuclear weapons. He thought he could prevent it by putting Soviet missiles just 90 miles off the coast of Florida. The world soon faced brinkmanship at its most frightening.

In mid-October 1962, a U-2 plane flying over Cuba photographed missile sites. The president immediately organized a special Executive Committee (ExComm) to force the missiles and their nuclear warheads out of Cuba. Options considered ranged from full-scale invasion to limited bombing to quiet diplomacy. Defense Secretary Robert McNamara proposed a solution acceptable to the president: a naval quarantine of Cuba.

Kennedy addressed the nation on television on October 22, demanding that the Soviets retreat. U.S. warships began crisscrossing the Caribbean, while B-52s with nuclear bombs took to the skies. Khrushchev agreed to withdraw the missiles if the United States pledged never to attack Cuba and removed Jupiter missiles aimed at the Soviet Union from Turkey. For days the world teetered on the brink of disaster. Then, on October 28, came a compromise. The United States agreed to Soviet demands in exchange for the withdrawal of Soviet offensive forces from Cuba. Fearing Castro might make matters worse, Khrushchev settled without consulting the Cubans.

Cuban missile crisis:
Confrontation between the Soviet Union and the United States in 1962 regarding the Soviet deployment of nuclear missiles in Cuba. It put the world on the brink of nuclear disaster until the two nations reached a compromise.

The **Cuban missile crisis** was a watershed in the Soviet-American relationship. Kennedy and Khrushchev acted with greater prudence in its aftermath, taking steps toward improved relations. In August 1963, the adversaries signed a treaty banning nuclear tests in the atmosphere, the oceans, and outer space. They also installed a coded wire-telegraph "hot line" staffed around the clock to allow near-instant communication between the capitals. They refrained from further confrontation in Berlin.

Together, these small steps began to build much-needed mutual trust. By autumn 1963, the Cold War in Europe was fading as both sides accepted the status quo of a divided continent and fortified border. Still, the arms race continued and accelerated, and the superpower competition in the Third World remained intense.

Marching for Freedom

What was Kennedy's reaction to growing civil rights activism?

President Kennedy regarded the Cold War as the most important issue Americans faced. But in the early 1960s, young civil rights activists seized the national stage and demanded that the federal government mobilize behind them.

Students and the Movement

In 1960, six years after the *Brown* decision declared "separate but equal" unconstitutional, only 10 percent of southern public schools had begun desegregation. Fewer than one in four adult African Americans in the South could vote, and water fountains were still labeled White Only and Colored Only. But within one year after the young men sat down at the all-white lunch counter in Greensboro, more than seventy thousand Americans—mostly college students—had participated in sit-ins.

Student Nonviolent Coordinating Committee (SNCC): Civil rights organization founded by young people that played a key role in grassroots organizing in the south in the early 60s.

The young people who created the **Student Nonviolent Coordinating Committee (SNCC)** in spring 1960 to coordinate the sit-in movement were committed to nonviolence. In the years to come, such young people would risk their lives in the struggle for social justice.

Freedom Rides and Voter Registration

On May 4, 1961, thirteen members of the Congress of Racial Equality (CORE), a nonviolent civil rights organization formed during World War II, purchased bus tickets in Washington, D.C., for a 1,500-mile trip through the South to New Orleans. Calling themselves Freedom Riders, this racially mixed group meant to demonstrate that, despite Supreme Court rulings ordering the desegregation of interstate buses, Jim Crow still ruled in the South. They knew they were risking their lives. One bus was firebombed outside Anniston, Alabama. Riders were badly beaten in Birmingham. In Montgomery, a thousand whites attacked riders with baseball bats and steel bars. Police stayed away; the police commissioner called the freedom riders troublemakers.

News of the violent attacks made headlines worldwide. Soviet commentators highlighted the "savage nature of American freedom and democracy." One southern business leader, in Tokyo to promote Birmingham as a site for international business development, saw Japanese interest evaporate when photographs of the Birmingham attacks appeared in Tokyo newspapers.

In America, the violence forced many to confront racial discrimination and hatred in their nation. Many middle- and upper-class white southerners resisted integration following the *Brown* decision, and the Freedom Rides made some think differently. The *Atlanta Journal* editorialized: "[I]t is time for the decent people…to muzzle the jackals." The global outcry pushed a reluctant President Kennedy to send federal marshals to safeguard Freedom Riders in Alabama. But bowing to white southern pressure, he allowed the Freedom Riders to be arrested in Mississippi.

Beginning in 1961, thousands of SNCC volunteers, many of them high school and college students, risked their lives encouraging African Americans in rural Mississippi to register to vote. Some SNCC volunteers were white, and some were northerners, but many were black southerners, often from low-income families. They experienced first-hand the intersection of racism, powerlessness, and poverty.

Kennedy and Civil Rights

Kennedy was sympathetic—though not terribly committed—to the civil rights movement, and he realized that racial oppression hurt the United States in the Cold War struggle for international opinion. However, like Franklin D. Roosevelt, he understood that if he alienated conservative southern Democrats in Congress, his legislative programs would founder. Thus, he appointed five die-hard segregationists to the federal bench in the Deep South and delayed fulfilling his campaign pledge to end segregation in federally subsidized housing (by executive order) until late 1962. He allowed FBI director J. Edgar Hoover to harass Martin Luther King and other activists, using wiretaps and surveillance to gather personal information and circulating rumors of communist connections and personal improprieties to discredit them.

But grassroots civil rights activism—and the violence of white mobs—forced Kennedy's hand. In September 1962, the president ordered 500 U.S. marshals to protect James Meredith, the first African American to attend the University of Mississippi. Thousands of whites attacked the marshals with guns, gasoline bombs, bricks, and pipes, killing two and seriously wounding 160 federal marshals. The marshals did not back down, nor did James Meredith.

Birmingham and the Children's Crusade

In 1961, the Freedom Riders captured the attention of the nation and the larger Cold War world. Martin Luther King Jr., having risen through the Montgomery bus boycott to leadership in the movement, concluded that only by provoking a crisis would the civil rights struggle advance. King and the SCLC planned a 1963 campaign in Birmingham, Alabama. Anticipating a violent response, they called their plan Project C—for confrontation. King wanted Americans to see the racist hate and violence that marred their nation.

Through April 1963, nonviolent protests in Birmingham led to hundreds of arrests. Then, on May 2, in a controversial action, King and Birmingham parents put children on the front lines. As about a thousand African American children, some as young as six, marched, police commissioner Eugene "Bull" Connor ordered police to train "monitor" water guns—powerful enough to strip bark from a tree at 100 feet—on them. The water guns mowed the children down, and police loosed attack dogs as the nation watched in horror on TV. President Kennedy demanded that Birmingham's white business and political elite negotiate a settlement. The Birmingham movement won and, more importantly, pushed civil rights to the fore of Kennedy's agenda.

"Segregation Forever!"   On June 11, defiant Alabama governor George C. Wallace fulfilled a promise to "bar the schoolhouse door" himself to prevent desegregation of the University of Alabama. Hearing echoes of Wallace's inaugural pledge "Segregation now, segregation tomorrow, segregation forever!" and facing a nation rocked by civil rights protests, Kennedy committed the federal government to guarantee racial justice—even over the opposition of individual states. On June 12, in a televised address, Kennedy said, "Now the time has come for this nation to fulfill its promise." Hours later, civil rights leader Medgar Evers was murdered in his driveway in Jackson, Mississippi. The next week, the president asked Congress to pass a comprehensive civil rights bill ending legal racial discrimination.

March on Washington   On August 28, 1963, a quarter-million Americans gathered on the Washington Mall to show support for Kennedy's civil rights bill. Behind the scenes, organizers from major civil rights groups—SCLC, CORE, SNCC, the NAACP, the Urban League, and A. Philip Randolph's Brotherhood of Sleeping Car Porters—grappled with growing tensions within the movement. SNCC activists saw Kennedy's proposed legislation as too little, too late. King and other older leaders counseled moderation. The movement was splintering.

What most Americans saw, however, was a celebration of unity. Black and white celebrities joined hands; folk singers sang freedom songs. Television aired Martin Luther King Jr.'s prophesy of a day when "all God's children, black men and white men, Jews and Gentiles, Protestants and Catholics, will be able to join hands and sing in the words of the old Negro spiritual, Free at last! Free at last! Thank God Almighty, we are free at last!" The 1963 March on Washington for Jobs and Freedom was a triumph, powerfully demonstrating African Americans' commitment to equality and justice. Days later, white supremacists bombed the Sixteenth Street Baptist Church in Birmingham, killing four black girls.

Freedom Summer   During the summer of 1964, more than one thousand white students joined the voter mobilization project in Mississippi. They formed Freedom Schools, teaching literacy and constitutional rights, and helped organize the Mississippi Freedom Democratic Party as an alternative to the white-only Democratic Party. SNCC organizers also believed that large numbers of white volunteers would focus national attention on Mississippi repression and violence. Project workers were arrested over a thousand times and were shot at, bombed, and beaten. On June 21, local black activist James Cheney and two white volunteers, Michael Schwerner and Andrew Goodman, were murdered by a Klan mob. That summer, black and white activists risked their lives together, challenging the Deep South's racial caste system.

Liberalism and the Great Society

What made the War on Poverty controversial?

By 1963, Kennedy seemed to be taking a new path. Campaigning in 1960, he promised to lead Americans into a New Frontier, with the federal government working to eradicate poverty, guarantee healthcare to the elderly, and provide decent schools for all children. But few of Kennedy's domestic initiatives were passed into law. Lacking a popular mandate in the 1960 election, fearful of alienating southern Democrats in Congress, Kennedy let his social policy agenda languish.

"Project C" and National Opinion

This photograph of a police dog attacking a 17-year-old demonstrator during a civil rights march in Birmingham, Alabama, appeared on the front page of the *New York Times* on May 4, 1963, just above a second photograph of a fireman spraying a group that included three teenage girls with a high pressure fire hose. The following day President Kennedy discussed this photo in a meeting in the White House. Some historians argue that photographs not only document history, they make it. Is that statement true in this case? How does this photograph fit into Martin Luther King's plans for "Project C" (see page 793)? What difference might it make that the *New York Times* editors chose to run this photograph rather than one of the many others taken that day?

AP Photo/Bill Hudson

Mass media coverage helped galvanize public opinion in support of civil rights protesters.

Instead, Kennedy focused on the economy, believing that continued prosperity would solve social problems. Kennedy's vision was perhaps best realized in the United States's space program. As the Soviets moved ahead in the space race, Kennedy vowed in 1961 to put a man on the moon before decade's end. With billions in new funding, the National Aeronautics and Space Administration (NASA) began the Apollo program. And in February 1962, astronaut John Glenn orbited the earth in the space capsule *Friendship 7.*

Kennedy Assassination

The nation would not learn what sort of president John Kennedy might have become. On November 22, 1963, riding with his wife, Jackie, in an open-top limousine in Dallas, Texas, Kennedy was cheered by thousands along the motorcade's route. Suddenly, shots rang out. The president crumpled, shot in the head. Tears ran down the cheeks of CBS anchorman Walter Cronkite as he told the nation the president was dead.

That same day, police captured a suspect: Lee Harvey Oswald, a former U.S. marine (dishonorably discharged) who once attempted to gain Soviet citizenship. Two days later, Oswald was shot dead by nightclub owner Jack Ruby. Shocked Americans wondered if Ruby was silencing Oswald to prevent him from implicating others. The seven-member Warren Commission, headed by U.S. Supreme Court Chief Justice Earl Warren, concluded that Oswald acted alone. Millions of Americans watched their president's funeral: the brave young widow; a riderless horse; three-year-old "John-John" saluting his father's casket. In one awful moment in Dallas, the reality of the Kennedy presidency had been transformed into myth, the man into martyr. In the post-assassination national grief, **Lyndon Johnson** invoked Kennedy's memory to push through the most ambitious legislative program since the New Deal.

Lyndon Johnson: 36th President of the United States; champion of civil rights legislation and the war on poverty.

Link to President Johnson's "Great Society" speech.

The Great Society: President Johnson's vision for America; LBJ believed the federal government must act to alleviate poverty, end racial injustice, and improve the lives of all Americans.

Civil Rights Act of 1964: The most significant civil rights law in U.S. history; ended legal discrimination and segregation in public accommodations.

Johnson and the Great Society

Where Kennedy came from wealth and was educated at Harvard, Johnson grew up in modest circumstances in the Texas hill country and graduated from Southwest Texas State Teachers' College. He was as earthy as Kennedy was elegant, prone to curses and willing to use his physical size to his advantage. Johnson first came to Congress in 1937. As Senate majority leader from 1954 to 1960, he learned how to manipulate people and wield power. As president, he used these skills to unite the nation.

Johnson, a liberal in the style of Franklin D. Roosevelt, believed the federal government must actively improve Americans' lives. In a 1964 University of Michigan commencement address, he described his vision of "abundance and liberty for all…demand[ing] an end to poverty and racial injustice…where men are more concerned with the quality of their goals than the quantity of their goods." Johnson called this vision **"The Great Society."**

Civil Rights Act

Johnson signed into law the **Civil Rights Act of 1964**, which ended *legal* discrimination on the basis of race, color, religion, or national origin, in federal programs, voting, employment, and public accommodation. The original bill did not include sex discrimination; that was introduced by a southern congressman who hoped it would engender opposition to torpedo the bill. But a bipartisan group of women members of the House of Representatives ensured its passage with sex as a protected category. Significantly, the Civil Rights Act of 1964 gave the government authority to withhold federal funds from public agencies or federal contractors that discriminated and established the Equal Employment Opportunity Commission (EEOC) to investigate and judge job discrimination claims. However, the EEOC largely ignored sex discrimination, prompting women's equality activists in 1966 to form the **National Organization for Women (NOW)**.

Many Americans did not believe it was the federal government's job to end racial discrimination or poverty. Many white southerners resented federal intervention in local customs and, millions of conservative Americans believed that since the New Deal the federal government had overstepped its constitutional boundaries. They sought a return to local control and states' rights. In the 1964 election, this conservativism was championed by Republican candidate, Arizona senator Barry Goldwater.

Election of 1964

Goldwater voted against the 1964 Civil Rights Act and opposed Social Security. Like many conservatives, he believed that individual *liberty,* not equality, mattered most. Goldwater further believed that the United States needed a more powerful national military to fight communism; in campaign speeches, he suggested that the United States should use tactical nuclear weapons against its enemies.

Goldwater's campaign slogan, "In your heart you know he's right," was turned against him by Lyndon Johnson supporters: "In your heart you know he's right...far right," one punned. Johnson campaigned on an unemployment rate below 4 percent and economic growth above 6 percent. But, as he told an aide, his support for African American civil rights had "delivered the south to the Republican Party for my lifetime and yours."

Tensions exploded at the 1964 Democratic National Convention. Two delegations from Mississippi demanded to be seated. The Democratic Party's official delegation was exclusively white; the Mississippi Freedom Democratic Party (MFDP) was racially mixed. White southern delegates threatened to leave if the MFDP delegates were seated. Johnson sought a compromise, but the MFDP declined. "We didn't come all this way for no two seats," MFDP delegate Fannie Lou Hamer said, and the delegation walked out.

Johnson won the election by a landslide, but he lost the Deep South—the first Democrat since the Civil War to do so. Voters also elected the most liberal Congress in history. With the mandate provided by a record 61.1 percent of the popular vote, Johnson launched his Great Society. Congress passed the most sweeping reform legislation since 1935.

In late 1964, the SCLC made voting rights its top priority. Martin Luther King Jr. and other leaders turned to Selma, Alabama, seeking another public confrontation that would mobilize national support and federal action. It came on March 6, when state troopers turned electric cattle prods, chains, and tear gas against peaceful marchers. On March 15, the president supported a second monumental civil rights bill, the **Voting Rights Act**. It outlawed practices that prevented most blacks in the Deep South from voting and provided for federal election oversight in districts with evidence of past discrimination. Within two years, African Americans registered to vote in Mississippi jumped from 7 percent to almost 60 percent. Black elected officials became increasingly common in southern states over the following decade.

National Organization for Women (NOW): Civil-rights group for women that lobbied for equal opportunity, filed lawsuits against gender discrimination, and mobilized public opinion against sexism. (see page 820).

Voting Rights Act: Law that outlawed practices that prevented blacks in the South from voting.

Improving American Life

Immigration Act of 1965: Law that abolished the national-origins quotas of the 1920s and transformed America's racial and ethnic kaleidoscope.

Seeking to improve American life, the Johnson administration established new student loan and grant programs to help low- and moderate-income Americans attend college, and created the National Endowment for the Arts and the National Endowment for the Humanities. The **Immigration Act of 1965** ended racially based quotas. And Johnson supported consumer protection legislation, including the 1966 National Traffic and Motor Vehicle Safety Act, inspired by Ralph Nader's expos of the automobile industry, *Unsafe at Any Speed* (1965). Johnson signed "preservation" legislation protecting America's wilderness and supported laws addressing environmental pollution.

War on Poverty

War on Poverty: Name of campaign launched by Lyndon B. Johnson to bring the poor into mainstream society by promoting greater opportunity through public works and training programs.

At the heart of Johnson's Great Society was the **War on Poverty**, which included major legislation beginning in 1964. Johnson and other liberals believed that, in a time of affluence, the nation should use its resources to end "poverty, ignorance and hunger as intractable, permanent features of American society." (see Table 30.1).

Johnson's goal was "to offer the forgotten fifth of our people opportunity, not doles." Municipalities and school districts received billions of federal dollars to improve opportunities for the poverty-stricken, from preschoolers (Head Start) to high schoolers (Upward Bound) to young adults (Job Corps). The Model Cities program offered federal funds to upgrade employment, housing, education, and health in targeted urban neighborhoods, and Community Action Programs involved poor Americans in creating local grassroots antipoverty programs.

TABLE 30.1   Great Society Achievements, 1964–1966

	1964	1965	1966
Civil Rights	Civil Rights Act Equal Employment Commission Twenty-fourth Amendment	Voting Rights Act	
War on Poverty	Economic Opportunity Act Office of Economic Opportunity Job Corps Legal Services for the Poor VISTA		Model Cities
Education		Elementary and Secondary Education Act Head Start Upward Bound	
Environment		Water Quality Act Air Quality Act	Clean Water Restoration Act

New Government Agencies		Department of Housing and
		   Urban Development
		National Endowments for the
		   Arts and Humanities
			Department of Transportation

Other		Medicare and Medicaid Immigration and Nationality Act	

Note: The Great Society of the mid-1960s saw the biggest burst of reform legislation since the New Deal of the 1930s.

The Johnson administration also expanded the Food Stamp program and earmarked billions for constructing public housing and subsidizing rents. Two new federal programs guaranteed healthcare: **Medicare** for those sixty-five and older, and **Medicaid** for the poor. Finally, Aid to Families with Dependent Children (AFDC), the welfare program created during the New Deal, broadened benefits and eligibility.

The War on Poverty was controversial. Leftists believed that the government was doing too little to change structural inequality. Conservatives argued that Great Society programs created dependency among America's poor. Policy analysts noted that specific programs were ill conceived and badly implemented. Decades later, most historians judge the War on Poverty a mixed success. Its programs improved the quality of housing, healthcare, and nutrition available to the poor. Between 1965 and 1970, federal spending for Social Security, healthcare, welfare, and education more than doubled, with the number of Americans receiving food stamps increasing from 600,000 (in 1965) to 17 million in 1975. Poverty among the elderly fell from 40 percent in 1960 to 16 percent in 1974, due largely to increased Social Security benefits and Medicare. The War on Poverty improved many Americans' lives (see Figure 30.1).

But War on Poverty programs less successfully addressed the causes of poverty. Neither the Job Corps nor Community Action Programs showed significant results. Economic growth was primarily responsible for the dramatic decrease in poverty rates during the 1960s—from 22.4 percent of Americans in 1959 to 11 percent in 1973.

Political compromises created long-term problems. For example, Congress accommodated doctors and hospitals in its Medicare legislation by allowing federal reimbursements of hospitals' "reasonable costs" and doctors' "reasonable charges" in treating elderly patients. With no incentives for doctors or hospitals to hold prices down, national healthcare expenditures as a percentage of gross national product rose by almost 44 percent from 1960 to 1971. Problems aside, Johnson's Great Society was a moment in which many Americans believed they could and should solve the problems of poverty, disease, and discrimination.

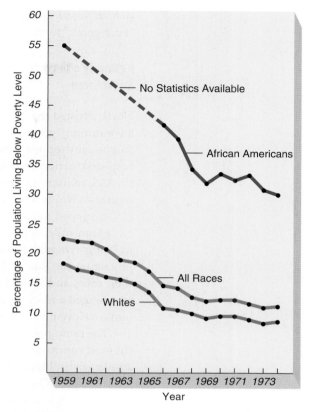

FIGURE 30.1

Poverty in America for Whites, African Americans, and All Races, 1959–1974

Because of rising levels of economic prosperity, combined with the impact of Great Society programs, the percentage of Americans living in poverty in 1974 was half as high as in 1959. African Americans still were far more likely than white Americans to be poor. In 1959, more than half of all blacks (55.1 percent) were poor; in 1974, the figure remained high (30.3 percent). The government did not record data on African American poverty for the years 1960 through 1965.

Source: © Cengage Learning

Medicare: Program created by President Johnson to provide government health insurance for those sixty-five and older.

Medicaid: Program created by President Johnson to provide health care for the poor.

Johnson and Vietnam

In foreign policy, Johnson upheld ideas about U.S. superiority and the communist menace. International affairs had never much interested him, and he had little appreciation for foreign cultures. At the Taj Mahal in India, Johnson tested the monument's echo with a Texas cowboy yell. On a trip to Senegal, he ordered

How did the war in Vietnam become Americanized?

that an American bed, a special showerhead, and cases of Cutty Sark be sent with him. "Foreigners," Johnson quipped, only half-jokingly, "are not like the folks I am used to."

Kennedy's Legacy in Vietnam

Yet Johnson knew that foreign policy, especially regarding Vietnam, would demand his attention. Since the late 1950s, hostilities in Vietnam increased, as Ho Chi Minh's North assisted the Vietcong guerrillas in the South in reunifying the country under a communist government. President Kennedy increased aid to the Diem regime in Saigon, airdropped more raid teams into North Vietnam, and launched herbicide crop destruction to starve the Vietcong out of hiding. Kennedy also strengthened the U.S. military presence in South Vietnam: by 1963, more than sixteen thousand military advisers were there, some authorized to participate in combat alongside the U.S.-equipped Army of the Republic of Vietnam (ARVN).

Meanwhile, opposition to Diem's repressive regime increased. Peasants objected to being removed from their villages for their own safety, and Buddhist monks, protesting the Roman Catholic Diem's religious persecution, poured gasoline over their robes and ignited themselves in the streets of Saigon. Eventually U.S. officials encouraged ambitious South Vietnamese generals to remove Diem. They murdered him on November 1, 1963, just three weeks before Kennedy was killed.

The timing of Kennedy's assassination weeks later ensured that Vietnam would be the most controversial aspect of his legacy. He expanded U.S. involvement and approved a coup against Diem, but despite the urgings of top advisers, he refused to commit U.S. ground forces. Over time he became skeptical about South Vietnam's prospects and hinted he would end the U.S. commitment after winning reelection in 1964. What he would have done had he lived can never be known, but what seems clear is that Kennedy arrived in Dallas that fateful day uncertain about how to solve the Vietnam problem.

Tonkin Gulf Incident and Resolution

Lyndon Johnson, too, was unsure on Vietnam, wanting to do nothing there that could jeopardize his chances of winning the 1964 election. Yet Johnson also sought victory in the struggle, and throughout 1964 the administration secretly planned to expand the war to North Vietnam.

In early August 1964, U.S. destroyers reported coming under attack twice in three days from North Vietnamese patrol boats in the Gulf of Tonkin (see Map 30.1). Despite a lack of evidence that the second attack occurred, Johnson ordered retaliatory air strikes against North Vietnamese patrol boat bases and an oil depot. By a vote of 416 to 0 in the House and 88 to 2 in the Senate, Congress quickly passed the Gulf of Tonkin Resolution, giving the president the authority to "take all necessary measures to repel any armed attack against the forces of the United States and to prevent further aggression." In so doing, Congress essentially surrendered its war-making powers to the executive branch.

Decision for Escalation

President Johnson also appreciated how the Gulf of Tonkin affair boosted his public approval ratings and removed Vietnam as a campaign issue for GOP presidential nominee Barry Goldwater. On the ground in South Vietnam, however, the outlook remained grim. As the Vietcong made gains, U.S. officials secretly planned to escalate U.S. involvement.

In February 1965, in response to Vietcong attacks on U.S. installations in South Vietnam that killed thirty-two Americans, Johnson ordered Operation Rolling Thunder, a bombing program that continued, more or less uninterrupted, until

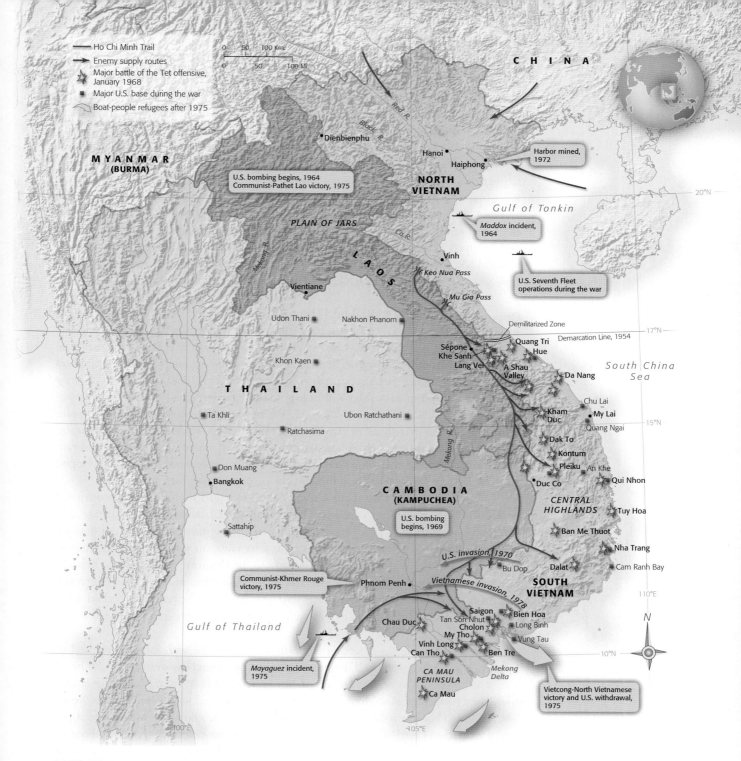

MAP 30.1

Southeast Asia and the Vietnam War

To prevent communists from coming to power in Vietnam, Cambodia, and Laos in the 1960s, the United States intervened massively in Southeast Asia. The interventions failed, and the remaining American troops made a hasty exit from Vietnam in 1975, when the victorious Vietcong and North Vietnamese took Saigon and renamed it Ho Chi Minh City

Source: Copyright © Cengage Learning

October 1968. On March 8, the first U.S. combat battalions came ashore near Danang. The North Vietnamese responded by increasing infiltration into the South. In Saigon, meanwhile, coups and countercoups by self-serving military leaders undermined U.S. efforts.

In July 1965, Johnson convened a series of high-level discussions about U.S. policy. Though the escalation of the war had by then already begun, these deliberations confirmed that America's commitment would be more or less open-ended. On July 28, Johnson publicly announced a significant troop increase, with others to follow. By the end of 1965, more than 180,000 U.S. ground troops were in South Vietnam. In 1966 the figure climbed to 385,000. In 1967 alone, U.S. warplanes flew 108,000 sorties and dropped 226,000 tons of bombs on North Vietnam. In 1968 U.S. troop strength reached 536,100. Each American escalation brought a new North Vietnamese escalation and increased assistance to Hanoi from the Soviet Union and China.

Opposition to Americanization

Rolling Thunder and the U.S. troop commitment Americanized the war, transforming it from a civil war between North and South into a U.S. war against the communist Hanoi government. In the key months of decision, Democratic leaders in the Senate, major newspapers such as the *New York Times* and the *Wall Street Journal,* and columnists such as Walter Lippmann warned against deepening involvement, as did Vice President Hubert H. Humphrey and Undersecretary of State George W. Ball. Virtually all of the United States's allies—including France, Britain, Canada, and Japan—cautioned against escalation and urged a political settlement. Remarkably, top U.S. officials knew that the odds of success were small but hoped new measures would cause Hanoi to end the insurgency in the South.

U.S. leaders feared that if the United States failed in Vietnam, other countries would find U.S. power less credible. The Soviets and Chinese would challenge U.S. interests elsewhere, and allied governments might conclude they could not depend on Washington. Johnson worried that failure in Vietnam would harm his domestic agenda and cause personal humiliation. As for the stated objective of helping a South Vietnamese ally repulse external aggression, that did not figure into the equation as much as it would have had the Saigon government—racked with infighting and possessing little popular support—done more in its own defense.

American Soldiers in Vietnam

To minimize publicity about the war, Johnson refused to call up reserve forces. This forced the military to rely heavily on the draft, which made Vietnam a young man's war—the average age of soldiers was twenty-two, compared with twenty-six in World War II. It also became a war of the poor and the working class. Through the years of heavy escalation (1965–1968), college students could get deferments, as could teachers and engineers. (In 1969, the draft was changed so that some students were called up through a lottery system.) The armed services recruited hard in poor communities, many of them heavily African American and Latino, advertising the military as an avenue of training and advancement; very often, the pitch worked. Once in uniform, those with fewer skills were far more likely to see combat, and hence to die.

Infantrymen maneuvered into thick jungles, where booby traps and land mines were a constant threat. Boots and human skin rotted from the rains, which alternated with the withering suns. The enemy was hard to find, often burrowed into elaborate underground tunnels or melded into the population, where any Vietnamese might be a Vietcong.

Larry Burrows/Getty Images

Wounded American soldiers after a battle in Vietnam.

The American forces fought well, and their entry helped stave off a South Vietnamese defeat, thereby achieving Americanization's most immediate and basic objective. But as the North Vietnamese matched each U.S. escalation with their own, the war became a stalemate. The U.S. commander, General William Westmoreland, mistakenly believed that a strategy of attrition represented the key to victory. Thus, the measure of success became the body count, the number of North Vietnamese and Vietcong corpses found after battle. But counts were manipulated by officers eager to demonstrate an operation's success. Worse, the U.S. reliance on massive military technology—including carpet bombing, napalm (jellied gasoline), and crop defoliants that destroyed forests— alienated many South Vietnamese and brought new recruits to the Vietcong.

Divisions at Home   As television coverage brought the war into homes nightly, the number of opponents grew. College professors and students organized debates and lectures on American policy, which became a form of protest, called "teach-ins" after the sit-ins of the civil rights movement. Pacifist groups, such as the American Friends Service Committee and the Women's International League for Peace and Freedom, organized early protests.

In early 1966, Senator William Fulbright held televised hearings on whether the national interest was served by the war. To the surprise of some, George F. Kennan testified that his containment doctrine was meant for Europe, not volatile Southeast Asia. America's "preoccupation" with Vietnam, Kennan asserted, was undermining its global obligations. The Fulbright hearings provoked Americans to think about the conflict and the nation's role in it and revealed deep divisions on Vietnam among public officials.

Defense secretary Robert McNamara, who championed the Americanization of the war in 1965, became increasingly troubled by the killing and bombing. In November 1965, he expressed skepticism that victory could ever be achieved. American credibility, far from being protected by the commitment, was suffering grievous damage, McNamara feared. But Johnson was determined to prevail in Vietnam. Although he occasionally halted the bombing to encourage Ho Chi Minh to negotiate (on America's terms), and to disarm critics, such pauses often were accompanied by increases in American troop strength. Ho steadfastly rejected American terms, which amounted to abandonment of his lifelong dream of an independent, unified Vietnam.

A Nation Divided

What were the hallmarks of the youth movement in the 1960s?

As Johnson struggled in Vietnam, his Great Society faced challenges at home. The United States was fracturing along many lines: black and white, youth and age, radical and conservative.

Urban Unrest

In 1964, shortly after President Johnson signed the landmark Civil Rights Act, racial violence erupted in northern cities. Angry Harlem residents took to the streets after a white police officer shot a black teenager. The following summer, in the predominantly black Watts section of Los Angeles, crowds burned, looted, and battled police for five days. The riot, which began when a white police officer attempted to arrest a black resident on suspicion of drunken driving, left thirty-four dead. In July 1967, twenty-six people were killed in street battles between African Americans and police and army troops in Newark, New Jersey. A week later, in Detroit, forty-three died as 3 square miles of the city went up in flames. In 1967 alone, there were 167 violent outbreaks in 128 cities.

The "long, hot summers" of urban unrest differed from previous race riots, which were typically started by whites. Here, black residents exploded in anger and frustration over the conditions of their lives. They looted and burned stores, most of them white-owned, while also devastating their own neighborhoods.

In 1968, the National Advisory Commission on Civil Disorders, chaired by Governor Otto Kerner of Illinois, warned that America was "moving towards two societies, one white, one black—separate and unequal," and blamed white racism for the riots. "What white Americans have never fully understood—but what the Negro can never forget—is that white society is deeply implicated in the ghetto. White institutions created it, white institutions maintain it, and white society condones it," concluded the Kerner Commission. Some white Americans disagreed, while others wondered why African Americans were venting their frustration just when they were making real progress in civil rights.

The answer stemmed partly from regional differences. The civil rights movement focused mostly on fighting *legal* disenfranchisement and discrimination in the South and largely ignored problems in the North. Increasingly concentrated in the deteriorating inner-city ghettos, most northern African Americans faced discrimination in housing, credit, and employment. The median income of northern African Americans was roughly half that of northern whites, and their unemployment rate was twice as high. Many northern African Americans had given up on the civil rights movement and the Great Society.

Black Power

In this climate, a new voice urged African Americans to seize freedom "by any means necessary." Malcolm X, a onetime pimp and street hustler who converted in prison to the Nation of Islam faith, offered African Americans new leadership. Members of the Nation of Islam, known as Black Muslims, espoused black pride and separatism from white society. Their faith combined traditional Islam with a belief that whites were subhuman devils whose race would soon be destroyed and emphasized sobriety, thrift, and social responsibility. By the early 1960s, Malcolm X had become the Black Muslims' chief spokesperson. But his murder in 1965 by members of the Nation of Islam who felt betrayed when he started his own, more racially tolerant organization, transformed Malcolm X into a powerful symbol of black defiance and self-respect.

A year after Malcolm X's death, Stokely Carmichael, SNCC chairman, denounced "the betrayal of black dreams by white America." To end white oppression, Carmichael proclaimed, blacks had to "stand up and take over" by electing black candidates, and organizing their own schools and institutions to embrace "**Black Power**." That year, SNCC expelled its white members and repudiated nonviolence and integration. CORE followed suit in 1967.

The best-known black radicals were the Black Panthers, an organization formed in Oakland, California, in 1966. Blending black separatism and revolutionary communism, the Panthers focused on destroying capitalism and its "military arm," the police. Male Panthers dressed in commando gear, carried weapons, and talked about killing "pigs" and did kill eleven police officers by 1970. Police responded in kind; most infamously, Chicago police murdered the local Panther leader Fred Hampton in his bed. However, the Panthers also worked to improve life in their neighborhoods by instituting free breakfast and healthcare programs for ghetto children, offering courses in African American history, and demanding jobs and housing. Before the end of the decade, a vocal minority of the United States's young would join in calls for revolution.

Black Power: Advocated in 1966 by SNCC president Stokley Carmichael; it advocated black nationalism, self-determination and greater militance as a means of self-defense.

Youth and Politics

By the mid-1960s, 41 percent of the American population was under age twenty. These young people spent more time with peers than any previous generation, as three-quarters of them graduated from high school (up from one-fifth in the 1920s) and almost half of them went to college (up from 16 percent in 1940). As this large baby-boom generation came of age, many believed they must provide democratic leadership for their nation. Inspired by the sit-in movement at black colleges, some white college students—from both political left and right—committed to changing the system.

In fall 1960, a group of conservative college students met at William F. Buckley's estate in Sharon, Connecticut, to form Young Americans for Freedom (YAF). Their manifesto, the Sharon Statement, endorsed Cold War anticommunism and a vision of limited government directly opposed to New Deal liberalism. The YAF planned to capture the Republican Party and move it to the political right; Goldwater's selection as the Republican candidate for president in 1964 demonstrated their early success.

Link to the Sharon Statement.

At the other end of the political spectrum, an emerging "New Left" also rejected liberalism. Whereas conservatives believed liberalism's activist government encroached on individual liberty, the New Left believed that liberalism was not enough to bring equality to all Americans. Meeting in Port Huron, Michigan, in 1962, founding members of Students for a Democratic Society (SDS) drafted their "Port Huron Statement," condemning racism, poverty in the midst of plenty, and

Link to the Port Huron Statement.

the Cold War. Calling for "participatory democracy," SDS sought to wrest power from the corporations, the military, and the politicians and return it to "the people."

Free Speech Movement

The rise of activist white youth crystallized at the University of California, Berkeley. In the fall of 1964, the university administration banned political activity—including recruiting volunteers for civil rights work in Mississippi—from its traditional place along a university-owned sidewalk bordering the campus. When police tried to arrest a CORE worker who defied the order, four thousand students surrounded the police car. Berkeley graduate student and Mississippi Freedom Summer veteran Mario Savio encouraged the students: "You've got to put your bodies upon the levers...[and] you've got to indicate to the people who run it, to the people who own it, that unless you're free, the machine will be prevented from working at all."

Student political groups, left and right, united to create the **Free Speech Movement (FSM)**. The FSM won back the right to political speech, but not before state police had arrested almost eight hundred student protesters. Many saw the administration's actions as a failure of America's democratic promises, but the FSM also demonstrated to students their potential power. By decade's end, the activism born at Berkeley would spread to hundreds of colleges and universities.

Student Activism

Student protesters sought greater control over their education, demanding more relevant class offerings, more freedom in course selection, and a greater voice in the running of universities. Students protested against the doctrine of in loco parentis, which put universities legally "in the place of parents," allowing control over student behavior that went beyond the law. In loco parentis fell heaviest on women, who had strict curfew regulations called parietals, while men did not. Along with an end to sex discrimination, protesters like those at the University of Kansas wanted administrators to explain how statements that "college students are assumed to have maturity of judgment necessary for adult responsibility" squared with the minute regulation of students' nonacademic lives. One young man complained that "a high school dropout selling cabbage in a supermarket" had more rights and freedoms than successful university students.

Youth and the War in Vietnam

It was the war in Vietnam, however, that mobilized a nationwide student movement. Believing that learning and speaking out about issues was their civic duty, in 1965 university students and faculty held teach-ins about U.S. involvement in Vietnam. SDS sponsored the first major antiwar march that year, drawing twenty thousand protesters to Washington, D.C. On campuses everywhere, students borrowed civil rights movement tactics, picketing ROTC buildings and protesting military research and recruiting done on their campuses. Despite the antiwar protests' visibility, most students did not yet oppose the war: in 1967, only 30 percent of male students were **doves** on Vietnam, while 67 percent were **hawks**. But as the war escalated, more students distrusted the government as well as the seemingly arbitrary authority of university administrations.

Youth Culture and the Counterculture

The large baby-boom generation changed the nation's culture more than its politics. Although many protested the war and marched for social justice, most did not.

Link to Mario Savio's "Machine" speech.

Free Speech Movement (FSM): Coalition of student groups that insisted on the right to campus political activity. Began at the University of California, Berkeley.

doves: Term for opponents of American military involvement in Vietnam.

hawks: Term for those who supported American goals in the Vietnam War.

Pictorial Press

Hundreds of thousands of young people came together for the Woodstock Music and Art Fair in August 1969. In its coverage, *Time* magazine warned adults that "the children of the welfare state and the atom bomb do indeed march to the beat of a different drummer, as well as to the tune of an electric guitarist," but the local sheriff called them "the nicest bunch of kids I've ever dealt with."

Fraternity and sorority life stayed strong even as radicalism flourished. And although there was some crossover, black, white, and Latino youth had different cultural styles, music, and clothes. Nonetheless, as potential consumers, young people exercised tremendous cultural authority and drove American popular culture in the late 1960s.

The most unifying element of youth culture was music. The Beatles captured American teenagers—73 million viewers watched their first television appearance on the Ed *Sullivan Show* in 1964. Bob Dylan promised revolutionary answers in "Blowin' in the Wind"; Janis Joplin brought the sexual power of the blues to white youth; James Brown and Aretha Franklin proclaimed black pride; and the psychedelic rock of Jefferson Airplane and the Grateful Dead—along with hallucinogenic drugs—redefined reality. At the Woodstock Festival in upstate New York in 1969, more than 400,000 people reveled in the music and a world of their own making, living in rain and mud for four days without shelter and without violence.

Some hoped to turn youth rebellion into social revolution, rejecting what they saw as hypocritical middle-class values. They crafted an alternative way of life, or **counterculture**, liberated from competitive materialism and celebrating pleasure. "Sex, drugs, and rock 'n' roll" became a mantra of sorts, offering these hippies

counterculture: Youth movement that promoted drugs, free love and an alternative way of life opposing what it saw as the materialism and conformity of mainstream American society.

Links to the World

The British Invasion

The British invasion began in earnest on February 7, 1964. Three thousand screaming American teenagers were waiting when Pan Am's *Yankee Clipper* touched down at Kennedy Airport with four British "moptops" aboard. "I Want to Hold Your Hand" was at the top of the U.S. charts, and the largest television audience in history watched the Beatles on the *Ed Sullivan Show* the following Sunday night.

Although the Beatles led the invasion, they did not conquer America alone. The Rolling Stones' first U.S. hit single also came in 1964. The Dave Clark Five appeared on *Ed Sullivan* eighteen times. And there were many others, Herman's Hermits, the Animals, the Yardbirds, the Hollies, the Kinks, and Petula Clark.

The British invasion was, at least partly, the triumphal return of American music, a transatlantic exchange that reinvigorated both nations. American rock 'n roll had lost much of its early energy by the early 1960s,

and the London-centered popular music industry was pumping out a saccharine version of American pop. But by the late 1950s, young musicians in England's provincial cities were listening to the music of African American bluesmen Muddy Waters and Howlin' Wolf; and the early rock 'n' roll of Buddy Holly and Chuck Berry. None of this music had a large audience in the United States, where *Billboard* magazine's number one hit for 1960 was Percy Faith's "Theme from *A Summer Place*" (a movie starring Sandra Dee and Troy Donahue).

Young British musicians, including John Lennon, Eric Clapton, and Mick Jagger, re-created American musical forms and reinvented rock 'n' roll. By the mid-1960s, the Beatles and the other British invasion bands were at the heart of a youth culture that transcended national boundaries. This music linked America's youth with young people throughout the world.

The Beatles perform on the Ed Sullivan Show *in February 1964. Although Britain's Queen Mother thought the Beatles "young, fresh, and vital," American parents were appalled when the "long" Beatles haircut swept the nation.*

a path to a new consciousness. Many did the hard work of creating communes and intentional communities, whether in cities or in hidden stretches of the rural United States. Although the New Left criticized the counterculture as apolitical, many hippies did envision revolutionary change through mind-altering drugs, sex, or music.

The nascent counterculture first entered the national consciousness during summer 1967, when tens of thousands poured into the Haight-Ashbury district of San Francisco, the heart of the United States's psychedelic culture, for the summer of love. As an older generation of "straight" (or establishment) Americans watched with horror, white youth adopted countercultural ways. Coats and ties disappeared, as did stockings and bras. Young men grew long hair, and parents complained, "You can't tell the boys from the girls." Millions used marijuana or hallucinogenic drugs, read underground newspapers, and thought of themselves as alienated from straight culture even though as high school or college students, they were not completely dropping out.

Some of the most lasting cultural changes involved attitudes about sex. The mass media were fascinated with "free love," and while some people embraced promiscuous sexuality, more importantly, premarital sex no longer destroyed a woman's "reputation." The birth-control pill, widely available to single women by the late 1960s, greatly lessened the risk of unplanned pregnancy, and venereal diseases were easily cured by antibiotics. The number of couples living together increased 900 percent from 1960 to 1970. While many young people no longer hid that they were sexually active, 68 percent of American adults disapproved of premarital sex in 1969.

The adult generation that grew up in the hard decades of depression and war and saw middle-class respectability as crucial to success and stability did not understand. How could young people risk their futures by having sex without marriage, taking drugs, or protesting the war in Vietnam?

1968

By 1968, it seemed that the nation was coming apart. Divided over the war in Vietnam, frustrated by the slow pace of social change, or angry about racial violence, Americans faced the most serious domestic crisis of the postwar era.

What made 1968 distinctive?

The Tet Offensive

On January 31, 1968, the first day of the Vietnamese New Year (Tet), Vietcong and North Vietnamese forces struck South Vietnam, capturing provincial capitals (see Map 30.1). During the carefully planned offensive, the Saigon airport, the presidential palace, and the ARVN headquarters were attacked. U.S. and South Vietnamese units eventually regained control, inflicting heavy casualties and devastating villages.

Although the Tet Offensive was not the resounding battlefield victory its strategists sought, the heavy fighting called into question U.S. military leaders' predictions that the war would soon be won. Had not the Vietcong and North Vietnamese demonstrated that they could strike when and where they wished? If the United States's airpower, dollars, and half a million troops could not now defeat the Vietcong, could they ever do so? Top presidential advisers sounded notes of despair. Clark Clifford, the new secretary of defense, told Johnson the war could not be won, even with the 206,000 additional soldiers Westmoreland requested. Aware that the nation was suffering a financial crisis prompted by rampant deficit spending, Johnson's advisors knew that taking the initiative in Vietnam would cost billions more, further derail the budget, panic foreign owners of dollars, and wreck the economy.

Lyndon Johnson, 1968. The war in Vietnam gradually destroyed his presidency and divided the nation.

Lyndon B. Johnson Presidential Library

Johnson's Exit

Controversy over the war split the Democratic Party, just as a presidential election loomed in November. Senator Eugene McCarthy of Minnesota and Robert F. Kennedy (now a senator from New York), both strong opponents of Johnson's war policies, forcefully challenged the president in early primaries. During a March 31 television address, Johnson announced a halt to most of the bombing, asked Hanoi to negotiate, and stunned listeners by withdrawing from the presidential race. His presidency had become a casualty of war. Peace talks began in May in Paris, but the war ground on.

Assassinations

Days after Johnson's shocking announcement, Martin Luther King Jr. was murdered in Memphis. It remains unclear why James Earl Ray, a white forty-year-old drifter and petty criminal, shot King or whether he acted alone. King had become an outspoken critic of the Vietnam War and of U.S. capitalism by 1968, and while some Americans hated what he stood for, most Americans mourned his death, and African American rage and grief exploded in 130 cities. The violence provoked a backlash from whites—primarily urban, working-class people who were had no sympathy for African Americans' increasing demands. In Chicago, Mayor Richard Daley ordered police to shoot rioters.

An already shaken nation watched in disbelief only two months later when antiwar Democratic presidential candidate Robert Kennedy was shot and killed after winning the California primary. His assassin, Sirhan Sirhan, an Arab nationalist, targeted Kennedy because he supported Israel.

Chicago Democratic National Convention

Violence erupted again in August at the Democratic National Convention in Chicago. Thousands of protesters converged on the city: students who'd gone Clean for Gene, cutting long hair and donning "respectable" clothes to campaign for antiwar candidate Eugene McCarthy; members of the United States's counterculture, drawn

The Immigration Act of 1965

When President Johnson signed the 1965 Immigration Act in a ceremony at the Statue of Liberty, he believed its importance was that it "repair[ed] a very deep and painful flaw in the fabric of American justice" by ending national-origins quotas that all but excluded "Polynesians, orientals, and Negroes." Nevertheless, the president mistakenly saw it as primarily symbolic. In fact, this act may have had greater long-term impact on Americans than any other Great Society legislation.

The 1965 Immigration Act ended blatant discrimination against potential immigrants from Asia, Africa, and Third World nations by substituting Eastern and Western Hemispheric "caps" for national quotas and allowing family reunification. The architects of the Immigration Act did not expect immigration to change, but world events decreed otherwise. Political instability, along with rapidly growing population in many poorer nations, created a large pool of potential immigrants who were drawn by U.S. prosperity.

By the 1990s, immigration accounted for almost 60 percent of America's population growth. By 2000, more Americans were foreign-born than at any time since the 1930s. The majority now came not from Europe but from Mexico, the Philippines, Vietnam, China, the Dominican Republic, Korea, India, the former USSR, Jamaica, and Iran.

More than two-thirds of the new immigrants settled in six states—New York, California, Florida, New Jersey, Illinois, and Texas—and later diversified other regions. By the late twentieth century, Spanish-language signs appeared in South Carolina, and Hmong farmers from the mountains of southeast Asia offered produce at the farmers' market in Missoula, Montana. The legacy of the 1965 Immigration Act was unintended but profound: the people and the nation are today more diverse than they otherwise would have been.

by the anarchist Yippies' promise of a Festival of Life to counter the Convention of Death; and antiwar groups. Mayor Daley assigned twelve thousand police to twelve-hour shifts and had twelve thousand army troops with bazookas, rifles, and flamethrowers as backup. Police attacked peaceful antiwar protesters and journalists. "The whole world is watching," chanted protesters, as police beat people.

Global Protest   Upheavals spread around the world that spring and summer. In France, university students protested rigid academic policies and the Vietnam War. They received support from French workers, who occupied factories and paralyzed public transport; the turmoil contributed to the collapse of Charles de Gaulle's government the following year. In Italy, Germany, England, Ireland, Sweden, Canada, Mexico, Chile, Japan, and South Korea, students held similar protests. In Czechoslovakia, hundreds of thousands of demonstrators flooded Prague streets, demanding democracy and an end to Soviet repression. This so-called Prague Spring developed into a full-scale national rebellion before being crushed by Soviet tanks.

Why so many uprisings occurred simultaneously is unclear. The postwar baby boom produced by the late 1960s a huge mass of young adults, many who grew up in relative prosperity with high expectations for the future. Technological advances allowed the nearly instantaneous transmittal of televised images worldwide, so protests in one country could readily inspire similar actions in others. Demonstrations might have occurred in any case, but news footage showing the wealthiest nation carpet bombing a poor country surely helped fuel the agitation.

Nixon's Election   The presidential election of 1968 did little to heal the nation. Democratic nominee Hubert Humphrey, Johnson's vice president, seemed a continuation of old politics. Republican candidate Richard Nixon appealed to people tired of social unrest. He reached out to those he called "the great, quite forgotten majority—the nonshouters and the nondemonstrators." On Vietnam, Nixon vowed he would "end the war and win the peace." Governor George Wallace of Alabama, a segregationist who proposed using nuclear weapons on Vietnam, ran as a third-party candidate. Wallace carried five southern states, drawing almost 14 percent of the popular vote. Nixon won with slim margins. Divisions among Americans deepened.

Yet on Christmas Eve 1968—in a step toward fulfilling John Kennedy's pledge—*Apollo 8* entered lunar orbit. Looking down on a troubled world, the astronauts broadcast photographs of a fragile blue orb floating in darkness and read aloud the opening passages of Genesis, "In the beginning, God created the heaven and the earth…and God saw that it was good." Many listeners found themselves in tears.

Summary

The 1960s began with high hopes for a more democratic United States. Civil rights volunteers, often risking their lives, carried the quest for racial equality across the nation. The 1964 Civil Rights Act and the 1965 Voting Rights Act were major milestones. The United States was shaken by the assassination of President John Kennedy in 1963, but under President Johnson, the liberal vision of government working to improve citizens' lives inspired legislation designed to create a Great Society.

The Cold War between the United States and the USSR intensified during the 1960s, and the 1962 Cuban missile crisis almost brought nuclear war. Determined not to let Vietnam "fall" to communists, the United States sent military forces to prevent the victory of communist Vietnamese nationalists led by Ho Chi Minh. By 1968, there were more than half a million American ground troops in Vietnam, which divided Americans at home, undermined Great Society programs, and destroyed Lyndon Johnson's presidency.

Despite civil rights gains, many African Americans turned away from the movement, seeking more immediate change. Poor African American neighborhoods burned as riots spread nationwide. Vocal young people—and some of their elders—questioned whether democracy truly existed in the United States. Large numbers of the nation's white youth rebelled by embracing a "counterculture" that rejected white middle-class respectability. 1968 was a year of crisis, of assassinations and violence in the streets. The decade that started with promise ended in fierce political polarization.

Chapter Review

Kennedy and the Cold War

How was the Cuban missile crisis a watershed in U.S.–Soviet relations?

Tensions had long existed between the two super-powers, which both had nuclear weapons and disagreed over preconditions for peace and disarmament. In 1962, when the Soviets moved to place nuclear missiles in Cuba, 90 miles from the Florida coast, the U.S. and Soviet Union were on the brink of a nuclear disaster. Stressful negotiations between the two countries eventually led the Soviets to remove the missiles if the United States promised never to attack Cuba and remove missiles aimed at the Soviet Union from Turkey. The event forced both leaders to take small steps toward improving their relationship and operating with greater trust. In August 1963, they signed a treaty banning nuclear tests in the atmosphere, oceans, and outer space.

Marching for Freedom

What was Kennedy's reaction to growing civil rights activism?

President Kennedy was sympathetic to civil rights and recognized that U.S. racism damaged the nation's international reputation. But he also worried about alien-ating southern white Democrats in Congress. He kept their allegiance—and thwarted civil rights—by appointing segregationist judges to federal courts in the Deep South and held off signing an executive order forbidding segrega-tion in federally subsidized housing. He also permitted the FBI to harass civil rights leaders—Martin Luther King Jr. in particular—with wiretaps, surveillance, and efforts to dam-age their reputations. But continued African American activism and the often-violent responses of whites to actions such as the Freedom Rides and voter registration efforts—all of which were covered by national and interna-tional media—helped push Kennedy to finally and formally support the civil rights struggle. He ordered U.S. marshals to protect James Meredith, the first African American to attend the University of Mississippi, and in 1963, he asked Congress to pass a comprehensive civil rights bill.

Liberalism and the Great Society

What made the War on Poverty controversial?

As part of his Great Society programs, President Johnson believed he could use the nation's prosperity to end poverty once and for all. War on Poverty programs included public housing and subsidized rents, Medicare and Medicaid, Food Stamps, Head Start, Job Corps, and Community Action Programs to involve the poor in cre-ating antipoverty efforts. While a noble idea, the War on Poverty triggered intense reactions on both sides of the political spectrum. Those on the left felt the government had treated the surface-level problems resulting from poverty, without analyzing poverty's causes or address-ing the structural inequalities that caused it in the first place. Those on the right feared the programs would cre-ate dependency rather than inspire initiative among the poor. Analysts, too, thought many of the programs were poorly implemented.

Johnson and Vietnam

How did the war in Vietnam become Americanized?

In 1965, with the South Vietnamese govern-ment teetering on the brink of defeat, Lyndon Johnson dramatically expanded U.S. involvement in the conflict. Specifically, he launched Operation Rolling Thunder, a sustained bombing program that would last for three years, and he dispatched U.S. ground forces to the con-flict; by the end of the year, 180,000 U.S. troops were on the ground, and the number would reach more than half a million by 1968. As the U.S. presence in South Vietnam grew, so did that of North Vietnam, and so did the assistance to the North from the Soviet Union and China.

A Nation Divided

What were the hallmarks of the youth movement in the 1960s?

Whether via politics or culture, the baby boom generation of young Americans came of age determined to make a difference in shaping the future of the nation. Some were inspired by the civil rights movement. Many committed themselves to political change, both on the left and right. Conservative college students met in 1960 at William F. Buckley's family estate to form Young Americans for Freedom, with a goal of limited govern-ment and opposition to New Deal style liberalism. On the left, students who felt that liberalism had not gone far enough to bring equality to all Americans, founded the Students for a Democratic Society (SDS) in 1962.

Students protested a range of issues, from efforts to block free speech on campus to gender inequality and sexism to—most significantly—the Vietnam War. Other young Americans hoped to turn youth rebellion into social revolution, rejecting what they saw as hypocritical middle-class values. They crafted an alternative way of life, or counterculture, liberated from competitive materialism and celebrating pleasure and personal freedom.

1968

What made 1968 distinctive?

Around the world, 1968 was a year of violent protest and political disillusionment. In the United States, people became increasingly frustrated with the war in Vietnam, as the Tet Offensive demonstrated that the war's end was nowhere in sight.. Two national leaders—Martin Luther King and Robert Kennedy—were assassinated, dousing the hopes held by African Americans, political activists, and young voters for a different, more progressive America, and sparking violent protests in 130 cities. Demonstrations at the Democratic National Convention in Chicago turned violent, as police and army troops attacked peaceful antiwar protesters and journalists. Upheavals in

the U.S. spread worldwide. In France, students protested the war and rigid school policies, supported by workers who occupied factories and shut down public transportation. Within a year, similar student rebellions occurred in Italy, Germany, England, Ireland, Sweden, Canada, Mexico, Chile, Japan, and South Korea, while in Prague, Czechoslovakia, thousands of protesters demanded democracy and an end to Soviet repression, before their rebellion was crushed by Soviet tanks.

Suggestions for Further Reading

Beth Bailey, *Sex in the Heartland* (1999)

David Farber, *Chicago '68.* (1988)

Lawrence Freedman, *Kennedy's Wars: Berlin, Cuba, Laos, and Vietnam* (2000)

George C. Herring, *LBJ and Vietnam: A Different Kind of War* (1994)

Michael Kazin and Maurice Isserman, *America Divided: The Civil War of the 1960s* (1999)

Fredrik Logevall, *Choosing War: The Lost Chance for Peace and the Escalation of War in Vietnam* (1999)

Lisa McGirr, *Suburban Warriors: The Origins of the New American Right* (2001)

Charles Payne, *I've Got the Light of Freedom: The Organizing Tradition and the Mississippi Freedom Struggle* (1995)

 **CourseMate**   Go to the CourseMate website for primary source links, study tools, and review materials for this chapter. www.cengagebrain.com

Continuing Divisions and New Limits

31

1969–1980

In 1969, Daniel Ellsberg was a thirty-eight-year-old former aide to Assistant Secretary of Defense John McNaughton. At the Pentagon, Ellsberg worked on a top-secret study of U.S. decision making in Vietnam. When he left office after Richard Nixon's election, Ellsberg accessed a copy of the study stored at the Rand Corporation, where he would resume his pregovernment research career. He spent six months poring over the seven thousand pages that comprised the Pentagon Papers.

Initially supportive of U.S. military intervention in Vietnam, Ellsberg had grown disillusioned. A Harvard-trained Ph.D., former marine officer, and Cold Warrior, he spent from 1965 to 1967 in South Vietnam, assessing the war's progress for his superiors in Washington. He went on combat patrols and interviewed military officials, U.S. diplomats, and Vietnamese leaders. The war, he concluded, was—in military, political, and moral respects—a lost enterprise.

Loyal to the president, Ellsberg was initially reluctant to act. But when in 1969 it became clear that Nixon had no intention of ending the war, Ellsberg boldly decided to risk imprisonment by making the Pentagon Papers public. The study, he believed, showed that presidents had escalated the American commitment in Vietnam despite pessimistic estimates from advisers—and that they had repeatedly lied to the public about their actions and the results. Ellsberg hoped disclosing this information would generate sufficient uproar to force a dramatic policy change.

Aided by a Rand colleague, Ellsberg surreptitiously photocopied the study, then spent months pleading with antiwar senators and representatives to release it. When they refused, he went to the press. On June 13, 1971, the *New York Times* published a front-page article on the Pentagon Papers. Other newspapers soon published excerpts, too.

Ellsberg's leak became controversial. Nixon tried to stop the papers' publication—among the first efforts to muzzle the press since the American Revolution—and to discredit Ellsberg and deter other leakers through the illegal actions of petty operatives. Many Americans saw Ellsberg as a hero who acted to shorten an illegitimate war. To others, he was a publicity-seeking traitor.

Chapter Outline

The New Politics of Identity
African American Cultural Nationalism | Mexican American Activism | Chicano Movement | Native American Activism | Affirmative Action

The Women's Movement and Gay Liberation
Liberal and Radical Feminism | Accomplishments of the Women's Movement | Opposition to the Women's Movement | Gay Liberation

The End in Vietnam
Invasion of Cambodia | Protests and Counter-demonstrations | Morale Problems in Military | Paris Peace Accords | Costs of the Vietnam War | Debate over the Lessons of Vietnam | Vietnam Veterans

VISUALIZING THE PAST *The Image of War*

Nixon, Kissinger, and the World
Nixon Doctrine | Détente | Opening to China | Wars in the Middle East | Antiradicalism in Latin America and Africa

LINKS TO THE WORLD *OPEC and the 1973 Oil Embargo*

Presidential Politics and the Crisis of Leadership
Nixon's Domestic Agenda | Enemies and Dirty Tricks | Watergate Cover-up and Investigation | Impeachment and Resignation | Ford's Presidency | Carter as "Outsider" President

Economic Crisis
Stagflation and Its Causes | Attempts to Fix the Economy | Impacts of the Economic Crisis | Tax Revolts | Credit and Investment

An Era of Cultural Transformation
*Environmentalism | Technology |
Religion and the Therapeutic
Culture | Sexuality and the
Family | Youth | Diversity*

Renewed Cold War and Middle East Crisis
*Carter's Divided Administration | Camp
David Accords | Soviet Invasion of
Afghanistan | Iranian Hostage Crisis | Rise
of Saddam Hussein*

LEGACY FOR A PEOPLE AND A NATION *The All-
Volunteer Force*

SUMMARY

The 1970s would be, for Americans, a decade of division and limits. The chaos of 1968 continued in Nixon's early presidency. Antiwar sentiment became more extreme, and as government deceptions were exposed, Americans were increasingly divided over Vietnam. The movements for racial equality and social justice also became more radical by the early 1970s. Although some continued to work for racial integration, many embraced cultural nationalism and sought separatist cultures and societies. Even the women's movement, which won victories against sex discrimination in the 1970s, had a polarizing effect. Opponents, many of them women, understood feminism as an attack on their way of life and mobilized a conservative grassroots movement that would gain political importance in subsequent decades.

This divided America faced great challenges abroad. Richard Nixon and his national security adviser, Henry Kissinger, understood that the United States and the Soviet Union, weakened by the costs of their competition and challenged by other nations, faced a world where power was diffused. Accordingly, even as they stubbornly sought victory in Vietnam, Nixon and Kissinger sought improved relations with the People's Republic of China and the Soviet Union.

Ultimately, Richard Nixon's illegal acts in the political scandal known as "Watergate" shook the faith of Americans. By the time Nixon, under threat of impeachment, resigned, Americans were cynical about politics. Neither of Nixon's successors, Gerald Ford or Jimmy Carter, could restore that lost faith. Carter's presidency was undermined by international events beyond his control. In the Middle East—a region of increasing importance in U.S. foreign policy—Carter helped broker a peace between Egypt and Israel but proved powerless to end a lengthy hostage crisis in Iran. Meanwhile, the Soviet invasion of Afghanistan in 1979 revived Cold War tensions.

A deepening economic crisis added to Carter's woes. In the 1970s, middle-class Americans saw their savings disappearing to double-digit inflation and their jobs vanishing overnight. The downturn was largely caused by changes in the global economy and international trade, worsened by the oil embargo launched by Arab members of the Organization of Petroleum Exporting Countries in 1973. Americans realized their vulnerability to decisions made in far-off lands.

As you read this chapter, keep the following questions in mind:

* How did American foreign policy change as a result of involvement in Vietnam?

* Why did Americans see this era as an age of limits?

* Some historians describe the period between 1968 and 1980 as a time when many Americans lost faith—in their government, in the possibility of joining together in a society that offered equality to all, in the possibility of consensus instead of conflict. Do you agree, or were the struggles and divisions of this era similar to those of previous decades?

Chronology

1969	Stonewall Inn uprising begins gay liberation movement
	Apollo 11 Astronaut Neil Armstrong becomes first person to walk on moon's surface
	National Chicano Liberation Youth Conference held in Denver
	"Indians of All Tribes" occupy Alcatraz Island
	Nixon administration begins affirmative-action plan
1970	United States invades Cambodia
	Students at Kent State and Jackson State Universities shot by National Guard troops
	First Earth Day celebrated
	Environmental Protection Agency created
1971	Pentagon Papers published
1972	Nixon visits China and Soviet Union
	CREEP stages Watergate break-in
	Congress approves ERA and passes Title IX, which creates growth in women's athletics
1973	Peace agreement in Paris ends U.S. involvement in Vietnam
	OPEC increases oil prices, creating U.S. energy crisis

	Roe v. Wade legalizes abortion
	Agnew resigns; Ford named vice president
1974	Nixon resigns under threat of impeachment; Ford becomes president
1975	In deepening economic recession, unemployment hits 8.5 percent
	New York City saved from bankruptcy by federal loan guarantees
	Congress passes Indian Self-Determination and Education Assistance Act in response to Native American activists
1976	Carter elected president
1978	*Regents of the University of California v. Bakke* outlaws quotas but upholds affirmative action
	California voters approve Proposition 13
1979	Three Mile Island nuclear accident raises fears
	Camp David accords signed by Israel and Egypt
	American hostages seized in Iran
	Soviet Union invades Afghanistan
	Consumer debt doubles from 1975 to hit $315 billion

The New Politics of Identity

> How did identity politics reshape political activism in the late 1960s and 1970s?

By the end of the 1960s, as divisions among Americans deepened, movements for social justice and racial equality became stronger, louder, and often more radical. The civil rights movement, begun in a quest for equality and integration, splintered, as many young African Americans rejected nonviolence and integration in favor of separatism, and embraced a distinct African American culture. Mexican Americans and Native Americans, inspired by the civil rights movement, created powerful "Brown Power" and "Red Power" movements by the early 1970s. They, too, demanded equal rights and cultural recognition. These movements fueled a new "identity politics," which saw group identity as the basis for political action and argued that social policy should be based on the needs, not of individuals, but of different identity-based groups.

African American Cultural Nationalism

By 1970, most African American activists no longer sought political power and racial justice by emphasizing the shared humanity of all people. Instead, they attracted a large following by highlighting the distinctiveness of black culture. Many African Americans, disillusioned by the racism that outlasted the end of legal segregation, believed that integration would mean subordination in a white-dominated society.

In the early 1970s, though mainstream groups like the NAACP continued to seek equality through the courts and ballot boxes, many African Americans looked to culture rather than to narrow political action for social change. Rejecting current European American standards of beauty, young people let their hair grow into "naturals" and "Afros," claiming the power of black "soul." Seeking strength in their cultural heritage, black students and faculty fought successfully to create black studies departments in universities. African traditions were reclaimed—or sometimes invented. The new holiday Kwanzaa, created in 1966 by Maulana Karenga, a professor of black studies, celebrated African heritage.

United Farm Workers leaders César Chávez and Dolores Huerta talk during the 1968 grape pickers' strike. The statue of the Virgin Mary, poster for presidential candidate Robert Kennedy, and photograph of Mahatma Gandhi suggest the guiding religious, political, and philosophical understandings of the movement.

Arthur Schatz/Time Life Pictures/Getty Images

Mexican American Activism

In 1970, the nation's 9 million Mexican Americans (4.3 percent of the United States's population) were concentrated in the Southwest and California. Although the federal census counted all Hispanics as white, discrimination in hiring, pay, housing, schools, and the courts was commonplace. Almost half of Mexican Americans were functionally illiterate, and in 1974, only 21 percent of Mexican American males graduated high school. Although more Mexican Americans were middle class, almost one-quarter remained below the poverty level in the 1970s.

The national Mexican American movement for social justice began with migrant farm workers. From 1965 to 1970, labor organizers **César Chávez** and Dolores Huerta led migrant workers in a strike (*huelga*) against large grape growers in California's San Joaquin Valley.

Chávez and the AFL-CIO–affiliated United Farm Workers (UFW) drew national attention to the working conditions of migrant laborers, who received as little as 10 cents an hour (the minimum wage in 1965 was $1.25) and were often lodged by employers in squalid housing without running water or indoor toilets. A national consumer boycott of table grapes brought the growers to the bargaining table, and in 1970 the UFW won better wages and working conditions. The union resembled nineteenth-century Mexican *mutualistas*, or cooperative associations. Its members founded cooperative groceries, a Spanish-language newspaper, and a theater group.

César Chávez: Labor leader who founded the United Farm Workers and was the driving force in creating the Latino civil rights movement of the 1960s and 1970s; he fused nonviolence (using boycotts, strikes and demonstrations) with the dignity of farm workers and of Hispanic heritage.

Chicano Movement

During the same period, in northern New Mexico, Reies Tijerina created the Alianza Federal de Mercedes (Federal Alliance of Grants). The group wanted the return of land it claimed belonged to local *hispano* villagers, whose ancestors occupied the territory before the United States annexed it under the 1848 Treaty of Guadalupe Hidalgo. In Denver, former boxer Rudolfo "Corky" Gonzáles drew more than one thousand Mexican Americans for the National Chicano Liberation Youth Conference in 1969. They adopted a manifesto, *El Plan Espiritual de Aztlan*, condemning the "brutal 'Gringo' invasion of our territories."

Link to *El Plan Espiritual de Aztlan*.

These young activists called for the liberation of *La Raza* (from *La Raza de Bronze*, "the brown people") from oppressive U.S. society, not for equal rights. They also rejected a hyphenated Mexican-American identity. The "Mexican American," they explained in *El Plan Espiritual de Aztlán*, "lacks respect for his culture." Instead, they called themselves Chicanos or Chicanas—barrio slang associated with *pachucos*, the hip, sometimes criminal young men who symbolized what "respectable" Mexican Americans despised.

Many middle-class and older Mexican Americans never embraced the term *Chicano* or the separatist, cultural agenda of *el movimiento*. Younger activists succeeded in introducing Chicano studies into local high school and college curricula and in creating a unifying cultural identity for Mexican American youth. La Raza Unida (RUP), a Southwest-based political party, registered tens of thousands of voters and won local elections. Although never as influential nationally as the African American civil rights movement, the Chicano movement effectively challenged discrimination locally and created a basis for political action.

Native American Activism

Between 1968 and 1975, Native American activists forced American society to hear their demands and to reform U.S. government policies toward native peoples. Young Native American activists were influenced by cultural nationalist beliefs. Seeking a return to the "old ways," they joined with "traditionalists" to challenge tribal leaders who advocated assimilation.

In November 1969, an activist group called Indians of All Tribes occupied Alcatraz Island in San Francisco Bay, demanding that the land be returned to native peoples for an Indian cultural center. The protest, which lasted nineteen months and involved more than four hundred people from fifty different tribes, marked the consolidation of pan-Indian activism, which claimed a shared "Indian" identity that transcended tribal differences. Although the protesters did not reclaim Alcatraz Island, they drew attention to the growing Red Power movement. In 1972, the radical U.S. Indian Movement occupied a Bureau of Indian Affairs office in Washington, D.C., and then in 1973 a trading post in Wounded Knee, South Dakota, where U.S. Army troops had massacred three hundred Sioux men, women, and children in 1890.

Link to photos from the 1969–1971 occupation of Alcatraz Island by Indians of All Tribes.

Meanwhile, moderate activists, working through such pan-tribal organizations as the National Congress of American Indians and the Native American Rights Fund, lobbied Congress for greater rights and resources to govern themselves. In response, Congress and the federal courts returned millions of acres of land, and in 1975 Congress passed the **Indian Self-Determination and Education Assistance Act**. Still, during the 1970s and 1980s, American Indians had a higher rate of tuberculosis, alcoholism, and suicide than any other group. Nine of ten lived in substandard housing, and unemployment approached 40 percent.

Indian Self-Determination and Education Assistance Act: 1975 act that granted Native American tribes control of federal aid programs on the reservations and oversight of their own schools.

Affirmative Action

As activists made Americans aware of inequality, policymakers struggled to frame remedies. As early as 1965, President Johnson acknowledged the limits of civil rights legislation, calling for "not just legal equality…but equality as a fact and equality as a result." Johnson joined his belief that the federal government must help *individuals* attain competitive skills to a new concept: equality could be measured by *group* outcomes.

Practical issues helped shift emphasis to group outcomes. The 1964 Civil Rights Act outlawed discrimination but seemingly stipulated that action could be taken only when an employer "intentionally engaged" in discrimination against an individual. The tens of thousands of cases filed with the Equal Employment Opportunity Commission (EEOC) suggested a pervasive pattern of racial and sexual discrimination in education and employment, but each required proof of "intentional" actions against an individual. Some argued that it was possible, instead, to prove discrimination by "results"—by the relative number of African Americans or women an employer hired or promoted.

In 1969, the Nixon administration implemented the first major government affirmative action program. The Philadelphia Plan (so called because it targeted government contracts in that city) required businesses contracting with the federal government to show (in Nixon's words) "affirmative action to meet the goals of increasing minority employment" and set specific numerical "goals," or quotas, for employers. All major government contracts soon required affirmative action for women and racial and ethnic minorities, and many corporations and educational institutions began similar programs.

Supporters saw affirmative action as a remedy for the effects of past discrimination. Critics argued that creating proportional representation for women and minorities meant discrimination against others who had not created past discrimination and that group-based remedies violated the principle of judging individuals on their merits. As programs to bring members of underrepresented groups into college classrooms, law firms, and firehouses nationwide, a deepening recession made jobs scarce. Thus, increasing the number of minorities and women hired often meant reducing the number of white men, which triggered resentment.

The Women's Movement and Gay Liberation

What were the successes of the women's movement?

During the 1960s, a "second wave" of the American women's movement emerged, and by the 1970s mainstream and radical activists waged a multifront battle for "women's liberation." In 1963, the popularity of Betty Friedan's *The Feminine Mystique* signaled fuel for a revived women's movement. Writing as a housewife (though she had a long history of political activism), Friedan described "the problem with no name," the dissatisfaction of educated, middle-class wives and mothers like herself, who—looking at their homes and families—wondered guiltily if that was all there was to life. Instead of blaming women for failing to adapt to women's proper role, as 1950s magazines often did, Friedan blamed the role itself and the society that created it.

Liberal and Radical Feminism

The organized, liberal wing of the women's movement emerged in 1966, with the founding of the **National Organization for Women** (NOW). Consisting

National Organization for Women (NOW): Women's rights organization founded in 1966 that lobbied for equal opportunity, filed lawsuits against gender discrimination, and mobilized public opinion against sexism.

primarily of educated, professional women, NOW began as a lobbying group seeking to pressure the EEOC to enforce the 1964 Civil Rights Act. (Racial discrimination was the EEOC's focus, and sex discrimination a low priority.) By 1970, NOW had one hundred chapters with more than three thousand members nationwide.

Another strand of the women's movement developed from the nation's increasingly radical social justice movements. Many women working for civil rights or against the Vietnam War were treated as second-class citizens, making coffee, not policy. As they analyzed inequality, these women recognized women's oppression. In 1968, a group of women protested the "degrading mindless-boob girlie symbol" represented by the Miss America Pageant in Atlantic City. Although nothing was burned, the pejorative term for feminists, *bra-burners*, came from this event, in which women threw items of "enslavement" (girdles, high heels, curlers, and bras) into a Freedom Trashcan.

Feminism was never a single set of beliefs. Most radical feminists, however, practiced "personal politics," believing, as feminist author Charlotte Bunch explained, that "there is no private domain of a person's life that is not political, and there is no political issue that is not ultimately personal." In the early 1970s, women meeting in suburban kitchens, college dorm rooms, and churches or synagogues created consciousness-raising groups, where they explored topics such as power relationships in marriage, sexuality, abortion, healthcare, work, and family.

Accomplishments of the Women's Movement

During the 1970s, the women's movement claimed significant achievements: the right of a married woman to obtain credit in her own name; the right of an unmarried woman to obtain birth control; the right of women to serve on juries; the end of sex-segregated help wanted ads. They challenged attitudes about rape that blamed the victim for the attack and established rape crisis centers, educated police and hospital officials about procedures for protecting rape survivors, and changed laws.

In 1971, the Boston Women's Health Collective published *Our Bodies, Ourselves* to help women understand and take charge of their sexual and reproductive health. Women who sought the right to safe and legal abortions won a major victory in 1973 when the Supreme Court, in a 7-to-2 decision on **Roe v. Wade**, ruled that privacy rights protected a woman's choice to end a pregnancy.

Women's organizations united to promote an **Equal Rights Amendment**, ending discrimination on the basis of sex, first proposed in the 1920s. On March 22, 1972, the Senate approved the amendment, which stated that "equality of rights under the law shall not be denied or abridged by the United States or by any State on account of sex" by a vote of 82 to 8. By the end of the year, 22 states (of the 38 necessary to amend the Constitution) ratified the ERA. Also in 1972, Congress passed Title IX of the Higher Education Act, which barred federal funds from colleges or universities that discriminated against women. Universities began channeling money to women's athletics, and women's participation in sports boomed.

Women's applications to graduate programs also boomed. In 1970, only 8.4 percent of medical school graduates and 5.4 percent of law school graduates were women. By 1979, those figures climbed to 23 percent and 28.5 percent respectively.

Roe v. Wade: 1973 Supreme Court ruling that privacy rights protected a woman's decision to end a pregnancy.

Equal Rights Amendment: Proposed constitutional amendment guaranteeing equal rights for women was passed with strong support of both Democrats and Republicans in Congress but fell short of ratification by the states by the 1982 deadline.

Link to Army recruitment ads for women in the 1970s.

The 1940s comic book heroine Wonder Woman appeared on the cover of *Ms.* magazine's first regular issue in July 1972. Wonder Woman represented feminist belief in "womanpower," but the choice of Wonder Woman had a practical justification as well: The main financial investor in *Ms.*, Warner Communications, was about to re-launch Wonder Woman comics.

Opposition to the Women's Movement

The women's movement met with powerful opposition, much of it from women. Many did not want equality if that meant giving up traditional gender roles in marriage or working at low-wage jobs. African and Hispanic American women, many of whom were active in movements for the liberation of their people and some of whom helped create second-wave feminism, often regarded feminism as a white movement that ignored their cultural traditions and diverted attention from the fight for racial equality.

Organized opposition to feminism came primarily from conservative, often religiously motivated men and women. As one conservative Christian writer claimed,

"The Bible clearly states that the wife is to submit to her husband's leadership." Such beliefs, along with fears about changing gender roles, fueled the STOP-ERA movement led by Phyllis Schlafly, a lawyer and conservative political activist. Schlafly attacked the women's movement as "a total assault on the role of the American woman as wife and mother." Schlafly's group argued that the ERA would decriminalize rape, force Americans to use unisex toilets, and make women subject to the military draft.

In fighting the ERA, tens of thousands of women became politically experienced; they fed a growing grassroots conservative movement that would blossom in the 1980s. By the mid-1970s, the STOP-ERA movement stalled the Equal Rights Amendment. Despite Congress's deadline extension, the amendment fell three states short of ratification and expired in 1982.

Gay Liberation

In the early 1970s, gay men and lesbians faced widespread discrimination. Consensual sexual intercourse between people of the same sex was illegal in almost every state, and until 1973 the American Psychiatric Association labeled homosexuality a mental disorder. Homosexual couples did not receive partnership benefits, such as health insurance; they not could adopt children. The issue of gay and lesbian rights divided even progressive organizations: in 1970, the New York City chapter of NOW expelled its lesbian officers. Gay men and lesbians could avoid harassment and discrimination by hiding their sexual identity, but that also made it difficult to organize politically.

There were small homophile organizations, such as the Mattachine Society and the Daughters of Bilitis, that worked for gay rights since the 1950s. But the symbolic beginning of the gay liberation movement came on June 28, 1969, when New York City police raided the Stonewall Inn, a gay bar in Greenwich Village, for violating a city law that made it illegal for more than three homosexual patrons to occupy a bar at the same time. That night, patrons stood up to the police, and hundreds joined them. The next morning, New Yorkers found a new slogan spray-painted on neighborhood walls: Gay Power.

Inspired by the Stonewall riot, some people worked openly and militantly for gay rights. They focused on legal equality and the promotion of Gay Pride. Some rejected the notion of fitting into straight (heterosexual) culture and created distinctive gay communities. By 1973, there were about eight hundred gay organizations in the United States. Centered in big cities and on college campuses, most organizations created supportive environments for gay men and lesbians to come out of the closet and push for reform. By decade's end, gay men and lesbians were a political force in cities including New York, Miami, and San Francisco.

The End in Vietnam

No issue divided Americans as pervasively as the Vietnam War. Although Richard Nixon said he was going to end the war fast, he did not. Like Johnson, he feared that a precipitous withdrawal would harm U.S. credibility on the world stage, as well as his own standing at home. Anxious to get American troops out of Vietnam, Nixon was equally committed to preserving an independent, noncommunist South Vietnam. Hence, he adopted a policy that at once contracted and expanded the war.

What kept Nixon from ending the Vietnam War as quickly as he had hoped?

Invasion of Cambodia

Nixon's policy centered on Vietnamization—building up South Vietnamese forces to replace U.S. forces. Accordingly, the president decreased U.S. troops from 543,000 in the spring of 1969 to 156,800 by the end of 1971, and to 60,000 by the fall of 1972. Vietnamization helped limit domestic dissent, but it did not end the stalemate in the Paris peace talks underway since 1968. Therefore, Nixon intensified the bombing of North Vietnam and enemy supply depots in neighboring Cambodia, hoping to pound Hanoi into concessions (see Map 30.1 on page 801).

The bombing of neutral Cambodia commenced in March 1969. For fourteen months, B-52 pilots flew 3,600 missions and dropped over 100,000 tons of bombs, initially in secret. When the North Vietnamese refused to buckle, Nixon turned up the heat: in April 1970, South Vietnamese and U.S. forces invaded Cambodia. The president announced publicly that he would not allow "the world's most powerful nation" to act "like a pitiful, helpless giant."

Protests and Counter-Demonstrations

Instantly, the antiwar movement emerged, as students on about 450 college campuses went out on strike and hundreds of thousands of demonstrators in various cities protested the administration's policies. The crisis atmosphere intensified on May 4, when National Guardsmen in Ohio fired into a crowd of fleeing students at Kent State University, killing 4 and wounding 11. Ten days later, police armed with automatic weapons blasted a women's dormitory at the historically black Jackson State University in Mississippi, killing 2 and wounding 9 students. Police claimed they had been shot at, but no such evidence could be found. Nixon's widening of the war sparked outrage, and in June the Senate terminated the 1964 Tonkin Gulf Resolution. After two months, U.S. troops withdrew from Cambodia.

Although a majority of Americans told pollsters they thought the original troop commitment to Vietnam was a mistake, 50 percent said they believed Nixon's claim that the Cambodia invasion would shorten the war, and some were angered by antiwar protests. In Washington, an "Honor America Day" program attracted more than 200,000 people who heard Billy Graham and Bob Hope laud administration policy. Nevertheless, the tumult over the invasion reduced Nixon's options on the war. Henceforth, solid majorities opposed any new missions for U.S. ground troops in Southeast Asia.

Morale Problems in the Military

Equally troubling, morale and discipline among troops was declining before Nixon took office. There were reports of drug addiction, desertion, racial discord, even the murder of unpopular officers by enlisted men (called fragging). The 1971 court-martial and conviction of Lieutenant William Calley, charged with overseeing the killing of more than three hundred unarmed South Vietnamese civilians in **My Lai** in 1968, got particular attention when an army photographer captured the horror in graphic pictures.

Paris Peace Accords

The Nixon administration, meanwhile, stepped up efforts to pressure Hanoi into a settlement. When the North Vietnamese launched a major offensive into South Vietnam in March 1972, Nixon responded with a massive aerial onslaught. In December 1972, after an apparent

My Lai: South Vietnamese village and site of an intended search-and-destroy mission by U.S. soldiers that evolved into a brutal massacre of more than 300 unarmed civilians, including women and children; some were lined up in ditches and shot, with their village then burned to the ground.

peace agreement collapsed, the United States launched another air strike on the North—the so-called Christmas bombing.

A diplomatic agreement was close. Months earlier, Kissinger and his North Vietnamese counterpart, Le Duc Tho, resolved many outstanding issues. Notably, Kissinger agreed that North Vietnamese troops could remain in the South after the settlement, while Tho abandoned Hanoi's insistence that the Saigon government of Nguyen Van Thieu be removed. On January 27, 1973, Kissinger and Le Duc Tho signed a cease-fire agreement, and Nixon compelled a reluctant Thieu to accept it by threatening to cut off U.S. aid. The United States promised to withdraw its troops within sixty days. North Vietnamese troops could stay in South Vietnam, and a coalition government that included the Vietcong would be formed in the South.

The United States pulled its troops out of Vietnam, leaving behind some military advisers. Soon, full-scale war erupted again. Just before the South Vietnamese surrendered, hundreds of Americans and Vietnamese who worked for them were hastily evacuated from Saigon. On April 29, 1975, the South Vietnamese government collapsed, and Vietnam was reunified under a communist government in Hanoi. Saigon was renamed Ho Chi Minh City for the persevering patriot who died in 1969.

Costs of the Vietnam War

More than 58,000 Americans and between 1.5 and 2 million Vietnamese died in the war. Civilian deaths in Cambodia and Laos reached hundreds of thousands. The war cost the United States at least $170 billion, and billions more in subsequent veterans' benefits. Money spent on the war was unavailable for domestic programs. The nation suffered inflation, political schism, and abuses of executive power. The war also delayed accommodation with the Soviet Union and the People's Republic of China, fueled friction with allies, and alienated Third World nations.

In 1975, communists established repressive governments in Vietnam, Cambodia, and Laos, but beyond Indochina the domino effect once predicted by U.S. officials never occurred. Acute hunger afflicted the people of those devastated lands. Soon refugees—boat people—crowded aboard unsafe vessels to escape. Many emigrated to the United States, where they were received with mixed feelings by Americans reluctant to be reminded of defeat and their responsibility for the plight of the southeast Asian peoples.

Debate over the Lessons of Vietnam

Americans seemed angry and confused about the war. Hawkish observers claimed that failure in Vietnam undermined the nation's credibility. They pointed to a "Vietnam syndrome"—an American suspicion of foreign entanglements—which they feared would inhibit the future exercise of U.S. power. America lost in Vietnam, they asserted, because Americans lost their guts at home.

Dovish analysts, meanwhile, blamed the war on an imperial presidency that permitted strong-willed men to act without restraint and on a weak Congress that conceded too much power to the executive branch. Make the president adhere to the checks-and-balances system—make him go to Congress for a declaration of war—these critics counseled. This view found expression in the War Powers Act of 1973, which limited the president's warmaking freedom and required Congressional approval before committing U.S. forces to combat lasting more than sixty days.

The Image of War

The Vietnam War has been called the first "television war." More than ever before (or arguably since) news clips and photos brought Americans and others around the world face-to-face with the fighting and its victims. On June 8, 1972, as children and their families fled the village of Trang Bang, their bodies seared by napalm, Huynh Cong "Nick" Ut took this iconic photograph that became an antiwar rallying point and symbol of hope. The girl in the center, Phan Thi Kim Phuc, survived the attack but had to endure fourteen months of painful rehabilitation to treat the third-degree burns that covered more than half of her body. Kim later became a Canadian citizen and a Goodwill Ambassador for the United Nations Educational, Scientific and Cultural Organization (UNESCO). Some analysts have argued that a single image can become the voice of popular protest; others say that even indelible images such as this one cannot have that power. What do you think?

AP Images/Huynh Cong 'Nick' Ut

Vietnam Veterans   Veterans' calls for help in dealing with posttraumatic stress disorder, which afflicted thousands of the 2.8 million Vietnam veterans, stimulated public discussion. Doctors reported that the disorder, which included nightmares and extreme nervousness, stemmed from soldiers having seen many children, women, and elderly killed. Some GIs inadvertently killed these people; some killed them vengefully and later felt guilt. Other veterans publicized their deteriorating health from the defoliant Agent Orange and other herbicides they handled or were accidentally sprayed with in Vietnam.

Nixon, Kissinger, and the World

The difficulties of the Vietnam war signified to Nixon and Kissinger that American power was limited and, in relative terms, in decline. This reality necessitated a new approach to the Cold War. In particular, they believed the United States had to adapt to a new, multipolar international system no longer defined by the Soviet-American rivalry. Western Europe was becoming a major player in its own right, as was Japan. The Middle East loomed increasingly large, due largely to America's growing dependence on oil. Mostly, Americans had to come to grips with China by rethinking its policy of hostile isolation.

> How did the Vietnam War influence Nixon's approach to foreign policy?

They were an unlikely duo—the reclusive, ambitious Californian, born of Quaker parents, and the sociable Jewish intellectual who fled Nazi Germany as a child. Nixon, ten years older, was a career politician, while Kissinger made his name as a Harvard professor and foreign policy consultant. What the two men shared was a paranoia about rivals and a capacity to think in broad conceptual terms about America's place in the world.

Nixon Doctrine   In July 1969, Nixon and Kissinger acknowledged the limits of American power and resources in the Nixon Doctrine. The United States, they said, would provide economic aid to allies, but these allies should not count on American troops. Washington could not afford to sustain its overseas commitments and would have to rely on regional allies—including authoritarian regimes—to maintain an anticommunist world order. Nixon's doctrine partially retreated from the 1947 Truman Doctrine's promise to support noncommunist governments facing threats.

Détente   The other pillar of the new foreign policy was **détente**: measured cooperation with the Soviets through negotiations within an environment of rivalry. Détente's primary purpose, like that of containment, was to check Soviet expansion and limit the Soviet arms buildup, but through diplomacy and mutual concessions. The second part of the strategy sought to curb revolution and radicalism in the Third World and quash threats to U.S. interests. Specifically, expanded trade with friendlier Soviets and Chinese might reduce the huge U.S. balance-of-payments deficit. Improving relations with both communist giants, when Sino-Soviet tensions were increasing, might weaken communism.

détente Nixon's foreign policy initiative with the Soviet Union; it focused on mutual cooperation and sought to check expansion and reduce arms buildup through diplomacy and negotiation.

The Soviet Union, too, found that the Cold War drained its resources, with defense needs and consumer demands at odds. Improved ties with Washington would also allow the USSR to focus on its increasingly fractious relations with China and might generate progress on outstanding European issues, including the status of Germany and Berlin. In May 1972, the United States and the USSR agreed in the ABM Treaty (officially the Treaty on the Limitation of Anti-Ballistic Missile Systems) to slow the arms race by limiting intercontinental ballistic missiles and antiballistic missile defenses.

Opening to China   Meanwhile, the United States took dramatic steps to end two decades of Sino-American hostility. The Chinese wanted to spur trade and hoped that friendlier Sino-American relations would make their onetime ally and now enemy, the Soviet Union, more cautious. In early 1972, Nixon made a historic trip to Red China, where he and the venerable Chinese leaders Mao Zedong and Zhou Enlai agreed to disagree on many issues, except one: the Soviet Union should not be permitted to make gains in Asia. Sino-American relations improved slightly, and official diplomatic recognition came in 1979.

The opening to communist China and the policy of détente with the Soviet Union reflected Nixon's and Kissinger's belief in the importance of maintaining stability among the great powers. In the Third World, too, they sought stability, though there they hoped to get it by maintaining the status quo. As it happened, events in the Third World would provide the Nixon-Kissinger approach with its greatest test.

Nixon Presidential Materials Project, National Archives and Record Administration

This was the week that changed the world, " Richard Nixon said of his visit to China in February 1972. Many historians agree and consider the China opening Nixon's greatest achievement as president. When he and wife Pat visited the Great Wall the president reportedly remarked: "This is a great wall."

OPEC and the 1973 Oil Embargo

If one date can mark the decline of American power in the Cold War era and the arrival of Arab nations on the world stage, it would be October 20, 1973. That day, the Arab members of the Organization of Petroleum Exporting Countries (OPEC)—Saudi Arabia, Iraq, Kuwait, Libya, and Algeria—imposed an embargo on oil shipments to the United States and other Israeli allies. The move was in retaliation against U.S. support of Israel in the two-week-old Yom Kippur War. The embargo followed an OPEC price hike days earlier from $3.01 to $5.12 per barrel. In December, the five Arab countries, joined by Iran, raised prices again, to $11.65 per barrel, almost a fourfold increase from early October.

Gasoline prices surged across America, and some dealers ran low on supplies. Americans endured endless lines at the pumps and shivered in underheated homes. When the embargo ended in March 1974, oil prices stayed high, and the aftereffects of the embargo would linger through the decade. It confirmed how much America's economic destiny was beyond its control.

Just twenty years before, in the early 1950s, Americans produced at home all the oil they needed. By the early 1960s, the picture changed, as Americans depended on foreign sources for one of every six barrels of oil they used. As author Daniel Yergin has put it, "The shortfall struck at fundamental beliefs in the endless abundance of resources... that a large part of the public did not even know, up until October 1973, that the United States imported any oil at all."

When the embargo ended, Americans resumed their wastefulness, but in a changed world the United States had become a dependent nation, its economic future linked to decisions by Arab leaders half a world away.

In 1976, OPEC sharply raised the price of oil a second time, prompting this editorial cartoon by Don Wright of the Miami News.

Wars in the Middle East

In the Middle East, the situation grew more volatile after the Arab-Israeli Six-Day War in 1967. Israel scored victories against Egypt and Syria, seizing the Sinai Peninsula and the Gaza Strip from Egypt, the West Bank and East Jerusalem from Jordan, and the Golan Heights from Syria (see Map 33.1). Israel gained 28,000 square miles and could henceforth defend itself against invading forces. But with Gaza and the West Bank as the ancestral home to hundreds of thousands of Palestinians (see Chapter 28), Israel found itself governing people who wanted to see it destroyed. When the Israelis established Jewish settlements in their newly won areas, Arab resentment grew. Terrorists associated with the Palestinian Liberation Organization (PLO) made hit-and-run raids on Jewish settlements, hijacked jetliners, and murdered Israeli athletes at the 1972 Olympic Games in Munich, West Germany. The Israelis retaliated by assassinating PLO leaders.

In October 1973, on the Jewish High Holy Day of Yom Kippur, Egypt and Syria attacked Israel, primarily seeking revenge for the 1967 defeat. Surprised, Israel reeled before launching an effective effective counteroffensive against Soviet-armed Egyptian forces in the Sinai. To punish Americans for their pro-Israel stance, the Organization of Petroleum Exporting Countries (OPEC), a group of mostly Arab nations that united to raise oil prices, embargoed oil shipments to the United States and other Israeli supporters. An energy crisis rocked the nation. Kissinger arranged a cease-fire in the war, but OPEC did not lift the oil embargo until March 1974. The next year, Kissinger persuaded Egypt and Israel to accept a U.N. peacekeeping force in the Sinai. But Arabs still vowed to destroy Israel, and Israelis built more Jewish settlements in occupied lands.

Antiradicalism in Latin America and Africa

In Latin America, meanwhile, the Nixon administration sought to thwart radical leftist challenges to authoritarian rule. In Chile, after voters in 1970 elected a Marxist president, Salvador Allende, the CIA secretly encouraged military officers to stage a coup. In 1973, a military junta ousted Allende and installed an authoritarian regime under General Augusto Pinochet. (Allende was subsequently murdered.) Washington publicly denied any role.

In Africa, too, Washington preferred the status quo, backing the white-minority regime in Rhodesia (now Zimbabwe) and activating the CIA in a failed effort to defeat a Soviet- and Cuban-backed faction in Angola's civil war. In South Africa, Nixon tolerated the white rulers who imposed segregationist apartheid on blacks and mixed-race "coloureds" (85 percent of the population), keeping them poor, disfranchised, and ghettoized in prisonlike townships. After the leftist government assumed power in Angola, however, Washington paid attention to the rest of Africa, building economic ties and sending arms to friendly black nations, such as Kenya and the Congo, while distancing the United States from the white governments of Rhodesia and South Africa.

Presidential Politics and the Crisis of Leadership

How did Watergate bring down the Nixon administration?

Nixon's foreign policy accomplishments were overshadowed by domestic failures. He betrayed the public trust and broke laws. That, combined with Americans' belief that their leaders had lied repeatedly about the war in Vietnam, shook Americans' faith in government. This new mistrust joined with conservatives' traditional suspicion of big, activist government to create a crisis of leadership and undermine liberal policies that governed the nation since the New Deal. Suspicion of the government, exacerbated by Watergate, would limit what Nixon's successors, Gerald Ford and Jimmy Carter, could accomplish.

Nixon's Domestic Agenda

Richard Nixon was brilliant, politically cunning, yet also crude, prejudiced against Jews and African Americans, happy to use dirty tricks and presidential power against his enemies, and driven by a resentment that bordered on paranoia. The son of a grocer from an agricultural region of southern California, Nixon loathed the liberal establishment, which loathed him back, and his presidency was driven by that as much as by strong philosophical commitment to conservative principles.

Any of Nixon's domestic policy initiatives seemed liberal. The Nixon administration pioneered affirmative action. It doubled the budgets of the new National Endowment for the Humanities (NEH) and National Endowment for the Arts (NEA). Nixon supported the ERA, signed major environmental legislation, created the Occupational Safety and Health Administration (OSHA), used deficit spending to manage the economy, and proposed a guaranteed minimum income for all Americans.

Yet, Nixon pursued a conservative agenda that involved devolution, shifting federal government authority to states and localities. He promoted revenue-sharing programs that distributed federal funds back to the states, thus appealing to those who saw high taxes as supporting liberal giveaway programs for poor and minority Americans. Nixon worked to equate the Republican Party with law and order and the Democrats with permissiveness, crime, drugs, radicalism, and the hippie lifestyle. He used his outspoken vice president, Spiro Agnew, to attack war protesters as "naughty children." He appointed four conservative justices to the Supreme Court: Warren Burger, Harry Blackmun, Lewis Powell Jr., and William Rehnquist.

Determining whether Nixon was liberal, conservative, or simply pragmatic is complicated. For example, when the Nixon administration proposed a guaranteed minimum income for all Americans, his larger goal was to dismantle the welfare system and its liberal bureaucracy of social workers. And though Nixon doubled NEA funding, he redirected awards from the northeastern art establishment—the "elite" that he considered an enemy—toward local and regional art groups.

Nixon additionally sought to attract white southerners to the Republican Party. He nominated two southerners to the Supreme Court—one of whom had a segregationist record. When Congress declined to confirm either nominee, Nixon protested angrily. After the Supreme Court upheld a school desegregation plan requiring a highly segregated North Carolina school system to achieve racial integration by busing both black and white children throughout the county (*Swann v. Charlotte-Mecklenburg,* 1971), Nixon denounced busing. (Resistance to busing was not purely southern, as Boston residents protested—sometimes violently—court-ordered busing to combat school segregation in 1974.)

Enemies and Dirty Tricks

Nixon was almost sure of reelection in 1972. His Democratic opponent was **George McGovern**, a progressive senator from South Dakota and strong opponent of the Vietnam War, who appealed to the left. Alabama governor George Wallace, running on a third-party ticket, withdrew after an assassination attempt left him paralyzed. The Nixon campaign, however, took no chances. On June 17, five men from the

George McGovern: Liberal Senator from South Dakota and Democratic candidate for president in 1972.

Committee to Re-elect the President, or CREEP were caught breaking into Democratic National Committee offices at the Watergate complex in Washington, D.C. The break-in got little attention, and Nixon swept into office in November with 60 percent of the popular vote. McGovern carried only Massachusetts and the District of Columbia. But as Nixon triumphed, his downfall had begun.

From the beginning of his presidency, Nixon obsessively believed he was surrounded by enemies. On Nixon's order, his aide Charles Colson formed a secret group called "the Plumbers." Their first job was to break into the office of the psychiatrist treating Daniel Ellsberg, the former Pentagon employee who made the **Pentagon Papers** public, looking for material to discredit him. During the 1972 presidential campaign, the Plumbers bugged phones, infiltrated campaign staffs, and wrote anonymous letters falsely accusing Democratic candidates of sexual misconduct. They were going back to plant more surveillance equipment at the Democratic National Committee offices when they were caught by the D.C. police at the Watergate complex.

Pentagon Papers: 47-volume U.S. government study from the end of WW II to the Vietnam War, and tracing U.S. involvement in Southeast Asia. Released to the press by former Pentagon employee Daniel Ellsberg, they revealed military mistakes and a long history of White House lies to Congress, foreign leaders and the American people.

Link to "The Watergate Files" from the Ford Library and Museum.

Watergate Cover-Up and Investigation

Nixon was not directly involved in the Watergate affair. But instead of distancing himself and firing those responsible, he covered up their connection to the break-ins. He had the CIA stop the FBI's investigation, claiming it imperiled national security. At this point, Nixon obstructed justice—a felony and an impeachable crime—but he also halted the investigation. However, two relatively unknown reporters for the *Washington Post,* Carl Bernstein and Bob Woodward, stayed on the story. Aided by an anonymous, highly placed government official whom they code-named Deep Throat (the title of a notorious 1972 X-rated film), they followed a money trail leading straight to the White House. (W. Mark Felt, second in command at the FBI in the early 1970s, identified himself as Watergate's Deep Throat in 2005.)

From May to August 1973, the Senate held televised public hearings on the Watergate affair. White House Counsel John Dean, fearful that he was becoming the fall guy for the Watergate fiasco, gave damning testimony. On July 13, a White House aide told the Senate Committee that Nixon regularly recorded his conversations in the Oval Office. Nixon refused to turn the tapes over to Congress.

Link to *The Washington Post's* collection of Nixon's White House tapes.

Impeachment and Resignation

Nixon faced scandals on other fronts. In October 1973, Vice President Spiro Agnew resigned, following charges that he accepted bribes while governor of Maryland. Nixon appointed and Congress approved Michigan's **Gerald Ford**, the House minority leader, as Agnew's replacement. Meanwhile, Nixon's staff was increasingly concerned about his excessive drinking and seeming mental instability. Then, on October 24, 1973, the House of Representatives began impeachment proceedings.

Gerald Ford: Michigan Congressman who took the place of Vice President Spiro Agnew when Agnew resigned following charges of corruption. Ford became the 38th president of the nation when Nixon resigned in 1974.

Under court order, Nixon released edited portions of the Oval Office tapes. Although the first tapes revealed nothing criminal, the public was shocked by Nixon's obscenities and racist slurs. In July 1974, the Supreme Court ruled that Nixon must release all the tapes. Despite erasures on two key tapes, the House Judiciary Committee found evidence to impeach Nixon on three grounds: obstruction of justice, abuse of power, and contempt of Congress. On August 9, 1974, facing certain impeachment and conviction, Richard Nixon became the first president of the United States to resign.

The Watergate scandal shook Americans' confidence in government. It also prompted Congress to pass several bills aimed at restricting presidential power, including the War Powers Act.

Ford's Presidency

Gerald Ford, the nation's first unelected president, faced a cynical nation. The presidency was discredited. The economy was in decline. Ford was an honorable man who tried to end the long national nightmare. But when he issued a full pardon to Richard Nixon, his approval ratings plummeted from 71 to 41 percent.

Ford accomplished little domestically during his two and a half years in office. The Democrats gained a large margin in the 1974 congressional elections, and after Watergate, Congress was willing to exercise its power. Ford almost routinely vetoed its bills—thirty-nine in one year—but Congress often overrode his veto. Ford was often portrayed as a buffoon and klutz in political cartoons, comedy monologs, and on the new hit television show *Saturday Night Live*. Ford caught the fallout of disrespect that Nixon's actions had unleashed. No longer would respect for the presidency prevent the media from reporting presidential stumbles or misconduct.

Carter as "Outside" President

Jimmy Carter, who was elected in 1976 by a slim margin, initially benefited from Americans' suspicion of politicians. Carter was a one-term Georgia governor, one of the new southern leaders committed to racial equality. He grew up on his family's peanut farm in rural Plains, Georgia, graduated from the Naval Academy, then served as an engineer in the navy's nuclear submarine program. Carter, a born-again Christian, promised Americans, "I will never lie to you."

Jimmy Carter: 39th President of the United States (1977–1981).

From his inauguration, when he broke with the convention of a motorcade and walked down Pennsylvania Avenue holding hands with his wife and close adviser, Rosalynn, and their daughter, Amy, Carter emphasized his populist, outsider appeal. But that status proved problematic as president. Though an astute policymaker, he scorned the deal-making that was necessary to pass legislation in Congress.

Carter faced problems that would have challenged any leader: continued economic decline, unabated energy shortages, and public distrust of government. More than any other postwar U.S. leader, Carter was willing to tell Americans things they did not want to hear. As shortages of natural gas forced schools and businesses to close during the bitterly cold winter of 1977, Carter, wearing a cardigan sweater, called for sacrifice and implemented energy conservation measures at government buildings. In the defining speech of his presidency, Carter told Americans that the nation suffered from a crisis of the spirit. He talked about the false lures of self-indulgence and consumption. He called for a "new commitment to the path of common purpose." But he offered few solutions for the national malaise.

Carter eased burdensome government regulations without destroying consumer and worker safeguards and created the Departments of Energy and Education. He also established a $1.6 billion "superfund" to clean up abandoned chemical-waste sites and placed more than 100 million acres of Alaskan land under federal protection as national parks, forests, and wildlife refuges.

Economic Crisis

What were the long-term effects of the 1970s recession?

Since World War II, except for a few brief downturns, prosperity dominated American life. Prosperity made possible the great liberal initiatives of the 1960s and improved the lives of America's poor and elderly. But in the early 1970s, that long period of economic expansion ended. In 1974 alone, the gross national product dropped 2 percentage points. Industrial production fell 9 percent. Inflation—the increase in costs of goods and services—skyrocketed, and unemployment grew.

Stagflation and Its Causes

Throughout most of the 1970s, the U.S. economy floundered in what economists dubbed "stagflation": a stagnant economy characterized by high unemployment combined with out-of-control inflation. Stagflation was almost impossible to manage with traditional economic remedies. When the federal government increased spending to stimulate the economy and reduce unemployment, inflation grew. When it tried to control inflation by cutting government spending or tightening money supply, the recession deepened and unemployment escalated.

The causes of the economic crisis were complex. President Johnson created inflationary pressure by waging an expensive war in Vietnam while greatly expanding domestic spending in his Great Society programs. But fundamental problems also came from the United States' changing role in the global economy. By the early 1970s, both of the United States's wartime adversaries, Japan and Germany, had become major economic powers and competitors in global trade that the United States once dominated. In 1971, for the first time since the nineteenth century, the United States imported more than it exported, beginning an era of U.S. trade deficits.

Corporate actions also contributed to the growing trade imbalance. During the years of global dominance, few U.S. companies improved production techniques or educated workers. Consequently, U.S. productivity—the average output of goods per hour of labor—declined. But wages rarely did. The combination of falling productivity and high labor costs meant that U.S. goods became increasingly expensive. Worse, U.S. companies allowed the quality of their goods to decline. From 1966 to 1973, for example, U.S. car and truck manufacturers recalled almost 30 million vehicles because of serious defects.

The United States's global economic vulnerability was driven home by the energy crisis in 1973. The country depended on imported oil for almost one-third of its energy. When OPEC cut off shipments to the United States, prices rose 350 percent and increased heating costs, shipping costs, and manufacturing costs, as well as the cost of goods and services. Inflation jumped from 3 percent in 1973 to 11 percent in 1974. Sales of gas-guzzling U.S. cars plummeted as people switched to energy-efficient subcompacts from Japan and Europe. GM laid off 6 percent of its domestic work force and put larger numbers on rolling unpaid leaves. As the ailing automobile industry quit buying steel, glass, and rubber, manufacturers of these goods laid off workers, too.

Attempts to Fix the Economy

American leaders tried desperately to manage the economic crisis, but their actions often exacerbated it. As America's rising trade deficit undermined international confidence in the dollar, the Nixon administration ended the dollar's link to the gold standard; free-floating exchange rates increased prices of foreign goods in the United States and stimulated inflation. President Ford followed the tenets of monetary theory, which held that, with less money available to "chase" the supply of goods, price increases would gradually slow down, ending the inflationary spiral. He curbed federal spending and encouraged the Federal Reserve Board to tighten credit, which prompted the worst recession in forty years. In 1975, unemployment reached 8.5 percent.

Carter's larger economic policies, including his 1978 deregulation of airline, trucking, banking, and communications industries, would eventually foster economic growth—but not soon enough. After a decade of decline, Americans were losing faith in the economy and their leaders' ability to manage it.

Impacts of the Economic Crisis

The 1970s economic crisis accelerated the transition from an industrial to a service economy. During the 1970s, the American economy "deindustrialized." Automobile companies laid off workers. Steel plant closings left communities devastated. Other manufacturing concerns moved overseas, seeking lower labor costs and fewer government regulations. New jobs were created—27 million of them—overwhelmingly in the "service sector": retail sales, restaurants, and other service providers. These jobs paid much lower wages than union manufacturing and often lacked healthcare benefits.

Formerly successful blue-collar workers saw their middle-class standards of life slipping away. More married women joined the work force because they had to. High school or college graduates in the 1970s, raised with high expectations, found limited possibilities, if they found jobs at all.

As the old industrial North and Midwest regions declined, people headed for the Sunbelt, which was booming (see Map 31.1). The federal government invested heavily in the South and West during the postwar era, especially in military and defense industries. The Sunbelt was primed for the rapid growth of modern industries and services—aerospace, defense, electronics, transportation, research, banking and finance, and leisure. City and state governments competed for business dollars, partly by preventing the growth of unions. Atlanta, Houston, and other southern cities marketed themselves as cosmopolitan and racially tolerant; they bought sports teams and built museums.

This population shift south and west, combined with the flight of middle-class taxpayers to the suburbs, created disaster in northern and midwestern cities. New York City, near financial collapse by late 1975, was saved only when the House and Senate Banking Committees approved federal loan guarantees. Cleveland defaulted on its debts in 1978, the first major city to do so since Detroit declared bankruptcy in 1933.

Tax Revolts

Meanwhile, a tax revolt movement emerged in the West. In California, inflation had driven property taxes up rapidly, hitting middle-class taxpayers hard. Instead of calling for wealthy citizens and major corporations to pay a larger share, voters rebelled against taxation itself. California's Proposition 13, passed by a landslide in 1978, rolled back property taxes and restricted future increases. Thirty-seven states similarly cut property taxes, and twenty-eight lowered their state income taxes.

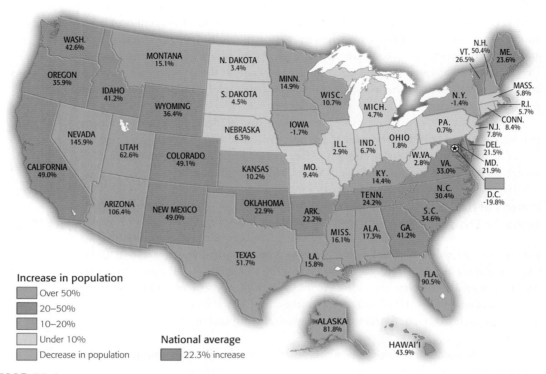

MAP 31.1

The Continued Shift to the Sunbelt in the 1970s and 1980s

Throughout the 1970s and 1980s, Americans continued to leave economically declining areas of the North and East in pursuit of opportunity in the Sunbelt. States in the Sunbelt and in the West had the largest population increases.

Source: Copyright © Cengage Learning.

The impact of Proposition 13 and similar initiatives was initially cushioned by state budget surpluses, but as those turned to deficits, states cut services—closing fire stations and public libraries, ending or limiting mental health services and programs for the disabled. Public schools were hit especially hard.

Credit and Investment Before the runaway inflation of the 1970s, home mortgages and auto loans were the only major debt most Americans had. National credit cards had become common only in the late 1960s, and few Americans—especially those who remembered the Great Depression—were willing to spend money they did not have. In the 1970s, however, double-digit inflation rates made it economically smarter to buy goods before prices went up, even if it meant borrowing the money. Because debt was paid off later with devalued dollars, the consumer came out ahead. In 1975, consumer debt hit a high of $167 billion; it almost doubled to $315 billion by 1979.

In the 1970s, Americans became investors rather than savers. Because banking regulations capped interest paid on individual savings accounts, with inflation, a savings account bearing 5 percent interest actually *lost* more than 20 percent of its value from 1970 through 1980. That same money, invested at market rates, would have grown dramatically. Fidelity Investments, a mutual fund company, saw an opportunity: its money market accounts combined many smaller investments to purchase large-denomination Treasury bills and certificates of deposit, thus providing small investors the high interest rates normally available only to major investors. Money market investments grew from $1.7 billion in 1974 to $200 billion in 1982. Deregulation of the New York Stock Exchange spawned discount brokerage houses, whose low commission rates were affordable for middle-class investors.

An Era of Cultural Transformation

As Americans struggled with economic recession, governmental betrayal, and social division, major strands of late-twentieth-century culture developed. The current environmental movement, the growth of technology, the rise of born-again Christianity and a "therapeutic culture," contemporary forms of sexuality and the family, and America's emphasis on diversity all have roots in this odd decade sandwiched between the political vibrancy of the 1960s and the conservatism of the 1980s.

How did the new social mores of the 1970s impact family life?

Environmentalism   A series of ecological crises drove home the fragility of the environment. In 1969, a major oil spill took place off the coast of Santa Barbara, California; that same year, the polluted Cuyahoga River, flowing through Cleveland, caught fire. In 1979, human error contributed to a nuclear accident at the Three Mile Island nuclear power plant near Harrisburg, Pennsylvania, and in 1980 President Carter declared a federal emergency at New York State's Love Canal, a dump site for a local chemical manufacturer, after it was discovered that 30 percent of local residents had suffered chromosome damage. Public activism produced major environmental initiatives, from the Environmental Protection Agency (EPA), created (under strong public pressure) in 1970 by the Nixon administration, to eighteen major environmental laws enacted by Congress during the decade.

When almost 20 million Americans—half of them schoolchildren—celebrated the first Earth Day on April 22, 1970, they signaled the triumph of a new understanding of environmentalism. Central to this movement was a recognition that the earth's resources were finite and must be conserved and protected. Many also identified rapid global population growth as a problem, and state public health offices frequently dispensed contraceptives to stem this new "epidemic."

Ken Regan/Regan Pictures, Inc.

Celebrants of the first Earth Day, on April 22, 1970, gather in an urban park. More than 20 million Americans across the nation participated in local teach-ins, celebrations, and protests to draw attention to environmental issues. By 1990, Earth Day was celebrated globally, drawing 200 million participants from 141 countries.

Technology

Neil Armstrong: First man to set foot on the moon.

During these years, Americans became uneasy about the science and technology that had been one source of America's might. Americans watched with pride as astronaut **Neil Armstrong** stepped onto the lunar surface on July 20, 1969, but technology could not cope with earth-bound problems of poverty, crime, pollution, and urban decay. The failure of technological warfare to deliver victory in Vietnam came as antiwar protesters were questioning the morality of such technology. Although some Americans joined a movement for human-scale development, the nation depended on complex technological systems. And it was during the 1970s that America's computer revolution began: the integrated circuit was created in 1970, and by 1975 the MITS Altair 8800—boasting 256 bytes of memory and taking about thirty hours to assemble—could be mail-ordered from Albuquerque, New Mexico.

Religion and the Therapeutic Culture

As Americans confronted material limits, they increasingly sought spiritual fulfillment Although Methodist, Presbyterian, and Episcopalian churches lost members during this era, evangelical and fundamentalist Christian churches grew dramatically. Protestant evangelicals, describing themselves as "born again," emphasized the daily presence of God in their lives. Even some Catholics, such as the Mexican Americans who embraced the *cursillo* movement (a "little course" in faith), sought a personal relationship with God. The New Age movement drew from and often combined nonwestern spiritual and religious practices, including Zen Buddhism, yoga, and shamanism, along with insights from western psychology and spiritually oriented environmentalism.

During the 1970s, the United States saw the emergence of a therapeutic culture. Although some were disgusted with the self-centeredness of the Me-Decade, bestselling books by therapists and self-help gurus insisted that individual feelings offered the ultimate measure of truth. Self-help books with titles like *I'm OK—You're OK* made up 15 percent of all bestselling books.

Sexuality and the Family

Link to news coverage of the 1979 Disco Demolition night at Comiskey Park in Chicago.

One such self-help book was *The Joy of Sex* (1972), which sold 3.8 million copies in two years. Sex became more visible in public culture during the 1970s, as television loosened its regulation of sexual content. In the early 1960s, married couples in television shows were required to occupy twin beds; in the 1970s, hit television shows included *Three's Company*, a comedy based on the then-scandalous premise that a single man shared an apartment with two beautiful female roommates—and got away with it by pretending he was gay. Donna Summers's 1975 disco hit "Love to Love You Baby" contained sixteen minutes of sexual moaning. Discos were sites of sexual display, both for gay men and for macho working-class cultures. Though few Americans participated in heterosexual orgies at New York City's Plato's Retreat, many read about them in *Time* magazine.

Sexual behaviors also changed. The seventies were the era of singles bars and gay bathhouses, but for most Americans, the sexual revolution meant broader public acceptance of premarital sex and limited acceptance of homosexuality, especially among educated Americans. More heterosexual young people lived together without marriage during the 1970s; the Census Bureau even coined the term *POSSLQ* (persons of opposite sex sharing living quarters) to describe the relationship.

Changes in sexual mores and women's roles altered the American family, too. By the late 1970s, the birth rate dropped 40 percent from its 1957 peak. Almost one-quarter of young single women in 1980 said they did not plan to have children. And a rising percentage of babies were born to unmarried women, as the number of families headed by never-married women rose 400 percent. The divorce rate also rose, partly because states implemented "no fault" divorce. Americans also developed greater acceptance of various family forms (symbolized by the blended family of television's *Brady Bunch*).

Youth

Young people gained new freedoms and responsibilities in American society during the 1970s. In 1971, recognizing that the 18-year-old men who were eligible for the draft could not vote, Congress passed and the states quickly ratified the 26th Amendment, which lowered the voting age to 18. Similarly, 29 states lowered their drinking age. Marijuana use skyrocketed, and several states moved toward decriminalization. In the early 1970s, some young people established communes and attempted to create countercultural worlds outside "the system." Later in the decade, others created the punk movement, which offered new physical and cultural spaces for youth through music and its do-it-yourself ethic.

Diversity

The racial-justice and identity movements of the late 1960s and 1970s made Americans more aware of differences among the nation's peoples, as an influx of new immigrants from Latin America and Asia increased the visibility of Hispanic and Asian Americans. The challenge was figuring out how to acknowledge the new importance of "difference" in public policy. The 1970s solution was the idea of "diversity." Difference was not a problem but a strength; the nation should not seek policies to diminish differences among its peoples but should instead seek to foster the "diversity" of its schools, workplaces, and public culture.

The 1978 Supreme Court decision in *Regents of the University of California v. Bakke* was a crucial early step. Allan Bakke, a thirty-three-year-old white man with a strong academic record, was denied admission to the medical school of the University of California at Davis. Bakke sued, charging he had been denied equal protection because the medical school's affirmative-action program reserved 16 percent of its slots for racial-minority candidates, who were held to lower standards. In 1978, the Supreme Court, in a split decision, decided in favor of Bakke. Four justices argued that any race-based decision violated the Civil Rights Act of 1964; four saw affirmative-action programs as constitutionally acceptable. The deciding vote, though for Bakke, contained an important qualification. A "diverse student body," Justice Lewis Powell wrote, is "a constitutionally permissible goal for an institution of higher education." To achieve diversity, educational institutions could consider race in admissions.

 Link to the Supreme Court's decision in *Regents of the University of California v. Bakke*.

Renewed Cold War and Middle East Crisis

When Jimmy Carter took office in 1977, he asked Americans to abandon their "inordinate fear of Communism." Carter vowed to reduce the U.S. military presence overseas, to cut back arms sales, and slow the nuclear arms race. More than 400,000 U.S. military personnel were stationed abroad, the United States had military links with ninety-two nations, and the CIA was active on every

What was Carter's record regarding the Middle East?

continent. Carter promised to avoid new Vietnams and give more attention to environmental issues. He especially determined to improve human rights abroad—the freedom to vote, worship, travel, speak out, and get a fair trial. Like his predecessors, however, Carter identified revolutionary nationalism as a threat to the United States's global prominence.

Carter's Divided Administration

Carter spoke and acted inconsistently, partly because in the post-Vietnam years no consensus existed in foreign policy and partly because his advisers squabbled among themselves. One source of the problem was Zbigniew Brzezinski, a Polish-born political scientist who became Carter's national security adviser. An old-fashioned Cold Warrior, Brzezinski blamed foreign crises on Soviet expansionism. Carter gradually listened more to Brzezinski than to Secretary of State Cyrus Vance, an experienced public servant who advocated quiet diplomacy. Under Carter, détente deteriorated and the Cold War deepened. Initially, Carter maintained fairly good relations with Moscow and secured some foreign policy successes. The United States signed two treaties with Panama in 1977. One provided for the return of the Canal Zone to Panama in 2000, and the other guaranteed the United States the right to defend the canal after that time. With conservatives denouncing the deal as a sellout, the Senate narrowly endorsed both agreements in 1978. The majority agreed with Carter's argument that relinquishing the canal would improve U.S. relations with Latin America.

Egyptian president Anwar al-Sadat, U.S. President Jimmy Carter, and Israeli Prime Minister Menachem Begin sit together outside the White House on March 26, 1979, ready to sign the peace treaty based on the Camp David Accords of September 1978. The treaty ended the longstanding state of war between Egypt and Israel.

Wally McNamee/CORBIS

Camp David Accords

The crowning accomplishment of Carter's presidency was the **Camp David accords**, the first mediated peace treaty between Israel and an Arab nation. In September 1978, the president persuaded Israel and Egypt to agree to a peace treaty, gained Israel's promise to withdraw from the Sinai Peninsula, and forged a provisional agreement that provided for continued negotiations on the future status of Palestinians living in the occupied territories of Jordan's West Bank and Egypt's Gaza Strip. Other Arab states denounced the agreement for not requiring Israel to relinquish all occupied territories and not guaranteeing a Palestinian homeland. But the accord, signed on March 26, 1979, by Israeli prime minister Menachem Begin and Egyptian president Anwar al-Sadat, at least ended warfare along one frontier.

Camp David accords:
Agreements that were signed by Egypt's President Sadat and Israel's Prime Minister Begin following twelve days of secret negotiations—arranged by President Carter—at Camp David.

Soviet Invasion of Afghanistan

Meanwhile, relations with Moscow deteriorated. U.S. and USSR officials sparred over the Kremlin's reluctance to lift restrictions on Jewish emigration and over the Soviet decision to deploy new intermediate-range ballistic missiles aimed at western Europe. Then, in December 1979, the Soviets invaded Afghanistan, a remote country whose strategic position made it a source of great-power conflict. Following World War II, Afghanistan struggled with ongoing ethnic and factional squabbling; in the 1970s, it spiraled into anarchy. In late 1979, the Red Army entered Afghanistan to shore up a faltering communist government under siege by Muslim rebels. Moscow officials calculated they could be in and out of the country before anyone noticed, including the Americans.

Carter not only noticed but reacted forcefully. He suspended shipments of grain and high-technology equipment to the Soviet Union, withdrew a major arms control treaty from Senate consideration, and initiated an international boycott of the 1980 Summer Olympics in Moscow. He also secretly authorized the CIA to distribute aid, including arms and military support, to the Mujahidin (Islamic guerillas) fighting the communist government and sanctioned military aid to their backer, Pakistan. Announcing the Carter Doctrine, the president asserted that the United States would intervene, unilaterally and militarily, should Soviet aggression threaten the petroleum-rich Persian Gulf. Carter warned aides that the Soviets, unless checked, would likely attack elsewhere in the Middle East, but declassified documents confirm what critics said: that the Soviet invasion was limited and did not presage a push into the Persian Gulf.

Iranian Hostage Crisis

Carter simultaneously faced a tough foreign policy test in neighboring Iran. The shah, long favored by the United States, was dethroned by a coalition of Iranians, who resented the dislocation of their traditional ways by the shah's attempts at modernization. Riots led by anti-American Muslim clerics erupted in late 1978. The shah went into exile, and in April 1979 Islamic revolutionaries, led by the Ayatollah Khomeini, an elderly cleric who denounced the United States as the stronghold of capitalism and western materialism, proclaimed a Shi'ite Islamic Republic. In November, with the exiled shah in the United States for medical treatment, mobs stormed the U.S. embassy in Teheran. They took American personnel as hostages, demanding the return of the shah to stand trial. The Iranians eventually released a few American prisoners, but fifty-two others suffered solitary confinement, beatings, and terrifying mock executions.

The All-Volunteer Force

On June 30, 1973, the United States ended its military draft and turned to an all-volunteer force (AVF). The nation never had a peacetime draft before 1940, when it began looking ahead to the coming war. But as the country embraced global leadership after World War II and faced a heightened Cold War, the draft became part of American life. More than 50 million American men had been inducted into the military between World War II's end and 1973.

Richard Nixon promised to end the draft during his 1968 presidential campaign, realizing that it was a focus for widespread protest against the Vietnam War. Ending the draft was not feasible during the war, but Nixon began planning for an all-volunteer force once in office. Many Americans supported the shift because they believed a president could not rely on a draft to compel people to fight a war they did not support.

The military, however, disliked Nixon's plan. The war in Vietnam shattered morale and left the military—particularly the army—in disarray. Public opinion of the military was at an all-time low. How would they attract volunteers?

As the largest of the four services, the army required the most volunteers. To draw volunteers, it ended make-work ("chickenshit") tasks and enhanced professionalism. It also turned to market research and advertising. Discovering that many men were afraid to lose their individuality, the army launched a campaign telling potential volunteers, "Today's Army Wants to Join You."

The army needed about 225,000 recruits annually (compared to about 65,000 per year in 2009) and had difficulty attracting them. Within a decade, however, America's military boasted a higher rate of high school graduates than the comparable age population. During an era of relative peace, many young people found opportunities for education and training through military service, particularly the economically disadvantaged, a high percentage of whom were African American.

The proportion of women in the military increased from 1.9 percent in 1972 to about 15 percent currently, with a wider range of available roles. The nation's understanding of military service changed from an obligation of (male) citizenship to a voluntary choice. The implications seemed less urgent in peacetime. But in wartime, the legacy of the move to an AVF raises the question: What does it mean when only a small number of volunteers bears the burden of warfare and most Americans never have to consider the possibility of going to war?

Unable to gain the hostages' freedom through diplomatic intermediaries, Carter took steps to isolate Iran economically, freezing Iranian assets in the United States. When the hostage takers paraded their blindfolded captives before television cameras, Americans felt taunted and humiliated. In April 1980, Carter broke diplomatic relations with Iran and ordered a daring rescue mission. But equipment failed and two aircraft collided, killing eight American soldiers. The hostages were not freed until January 1981, after Carter left office.

The Iranian revolution, together with the rise of the Mujahidin in Afghanistan, signified the emergence of Islamic fundamentalism as a force in world affairs. Socialism and capitalism, the answers that the two superpowers offered to the problems of modernization, failed to solve the problems in Central Asia and the Middle East. Consequently, Islamic orthodoxy found growing support for its message: that secular leaders such as Nasser in Egypt and the shah in Iran had taken their peoples down the wrong path, necessitating a return to conservative Islamic values and Islamic law. The Iranian revolution expressed a deep and complex mixture of discontents within many Islamic societies.

Rise of Saddam Hussein

U.S. officials took some consolation from Iran's troubles with the avowedly secular government in neighboring Iraq. Ruled by the Ba'athist Party, Iraq won favor in Washington for its pursuit and execution of Iraqi communists. When a Ba'athist leader named Saddam Hussein took over as president of Iraq in 1979 and threatened the Teheran government, U.S. officials worried that Saddam could offset the Iranian danger in the Persian Gulf. As border clashes between Iraqi and Iranian forces escalated into war 1980, Washington policymakers were officially neutral but soon tilted toward Iraq.

Carter earned some diplomatic successes in the Middle East, Africa, and Latin America, but the revived Cold War and prolonged Iranian hostage crisis hurt the administration politically. Contrary to Carter's goals, more U.S. military personnel were stationed overseas in 1980 than in 1976; the defense budget climbed and arms sales grew to $15.3 billion in 1980. On human rights, the president practiced a double standard, applying the human-rights test to some nations (the Soviet Union, Argentina, and Chile) but not to U.S. allies (South Korea, the shah's Iran, and the Philippines). Still, Carter's human-rights policy saved the lives of some political prisoners and institutionalized concern for human rights worldwide. But his inability to restore economic and military dominance dashed his reelection prospects. He lost in 1980 to the hawkish Ronald Reagan, former Hollywood actor and governor of California.

Summary

From the crisis year of 1968 on, Americans were increasingly polarized—over the Vietnam War, over the best path to racial equality and equal rights, and over the meaning of America itself. As many activists turned to "cultural nationalism," or group-identity politics, notions of American unity seemed a relic of the past. And though a new women's movement won victories against sex discrimination, powerful opposition arose in response.

During this era, Americans became increasingly disillusioned with politics and presidential leadership. Richard Nixon's abuses of power in the Watergate scandal and cover-up, combined with growing awareness that the administration had lied repeatedly about the United States's role in Vietnam, produced a profound suspicion of government. A major economic crisis ended the post–World War II expansion, and Americans struggled with the effects of stagflation: rising unemployment rates coupled with high inflation.

Overseas, a string of setbacks—defeat in Vietnam, the oil embargo, and the Iranian hostage crisis—signified the waning of U.S. power. Détente with the Soviet Union had flourished for a time; however, by 1980 Cold War tensions escalated. And the Middle East became an increasing focus of U.S. foreign policy.

Plagued by political, economic, and foreign policy crises, by the late 1970s America's age of liberalism was over; the elements for a conservative resurgence were in place.

Chapter Review

The New Politics of Identity

How did identity politics reshape political activism in the late 1960s and 1970s?

By the late 1960s, social justice movements were becoming more vocal and radical; they were also shifting their activist agendas to focus on racial, ethnic, and cultural distinctiveness. Younger, newer members to the struggle for black, Hispanic, and Native American civil rights wanted more than simply integration into mainstream U.S. society—they also wanted to embrace and celebrate the cultural heritage and history that made them distinct and find acceptance for these differences within society writ large. As such, their activism shifted to "identity politics," which saw group identity as the basis of social action. Through the Black Power movement, for example, African Americans embraced a black standard of beauty, celebrated their heritage, and founded black studies programs in universities—all while seeking social and political equality, too. Most importantly, movements like Black Power, Red Power (Native American), or Brown Power (Mexican American), which embraced identity politics as their modus operandi, argued that social policy should be based not on what might empower an individual, but rather on what would most benefit an entire identity group.

The Women's Movement and Gay Liberation

What were the successes of the women's movement?

The women's movement made major gains in the 1960s and 1970s: the right of a married woman to obtain credit in her own name; the right of an unmarried woman to obtain birth control; women's right to serve on juries; and the end of sex-segregated help wanted ads. Activists established rape crisis centers, educated law enforcement, and challenged definitions of rape that blamed the victim for the attack. Many worked for legalized abortion at the state level and won a major victor with the 1973 Supreme Court decision in *Roe v. Wade,* which ruled that privacy rights protected a woman's decision not to continue a pregnancy. The women's movement also achieved greater opportunities for women in sports via passage of Title IX of the Higher Education Act, which barred federal funds from colleges or universities discriminating against women. Likewise, the movement sparked the creation of women's studies programs in colleges nationwide.

The End in Vietnam

What kept Nixon from ending the Vietnam War as quickly as he had hoped?

Nixon's policy in Vietnam was driven by a goal to end the war fast, partly so that it would not ruin his political career as it had Johnson's. But at the same time, he did not want to hurt American credibility as a world leader, and he still sought to prevent South Vietnam's defeat. Consequently, although he dramatically decreased the number of American troops from 543,000 in 1969 to 60,000 in 1970, he increased bombing of North Vietnam and neutral Cambodia, hoping to force the enemy into concessions. The North Vietnamese stood firm. A ceasefire was agreed to in 1973, and shortly after U.S. troops left, a large-scale war developed between North and South Vietnam, with the latter falling and the communists claiming control of the entire country in 1975.

Nixon, Kissinger, and the World

How did the Vietnam War influence Nixon's approach to foreign policy?

The drawn-out struggle in Vietnam signified to Nixon that American power was limited. The war must be wound down, and similar commitments must be avoided in the future. Accordingly, he adopted the Nixon Doctrine, which said the United States would provide economic aid but not troops to allies. In addition, he implemented détente, a policy aimed at creating improved Soviet-American relations and a reduced arms race within an environment of rivalry. With his historic trip to China in early 1972, he moved to end two decades of Sino-American hostility. Chinese leaders Mao Zedong and Zhou Enlai agreed with Nixon that the Soviet Union should be kept from making gains in Asia.

Presidential Politics and the Crisis of Leadership

How did Watergate bring down the Nixon administration?

Sometimes paranoid, Nixon kept long lists of so-called enemies and directed aide Charles Colson to form a secret group called the Plumbers to dig up dirt on various groups, individuals and political rivals. During Nixon's 1972 reelection campaign, the Plumbers were arrested while breaking into the Democratic National Campaign headquarters in the Watergate complex to plant surveillance equipment. While Nixon was not directly involved in this effort, he made the mistake of blocking the CIA and FBI investigations into it—which constituted an obstruction of justice (an impeachable offense). He also initially refused to turn over his audiotape conversations to congressional hearings. Eventually, he relinquished the tapes, although several contained significant gaps. Congress began impeachment hearings, and facing certain conviction and impeachment, on August 9, 1974, Nixon became the first U.S. president to resign from office.

Economic Crisis

What were the long-term effects of the 1970s recession?

The 1970s recession accelerated the nation's shift from an industrial to a service-based economy. As manufacturers in leading industries, such as automobiles and steel, laid off large numbers of workers or shifted to cheaper overseas production, new jobs opened in the lower-paid service sector, such as cashiers and waiters. Increasing numbers of married women went to work to keep their families afloat. Older industrial cities suffered decay, while the Sunbelt was well-positioned to prosper with the growth of modern industries such as defense, aerospace, and finance. Double-digit inflation in the 1970s led people to buy up goods before prices would rise, often on credit, fueling a major rise in consumer indebtedness. Finally, with interest rates capped on savings accounts, people increasingly shifted to new forms of investment in mutual funds and the stock market.

An Era of Cultural Transformation

How did the new social mores of the 1970s impact family life?

Increasing tolerance and openness about sex in the 1970s facilitated major changes in traditional notions of what constituted a family. There was a broader acceptance of premarital sex and limited acceptance of homosexuality. As a result, more heterosexual couples opted to live together without marrying. Though most did still marry, they married later and had fewer children.

By decade's end, the birth rate dropped nearly 40 percent from its all-time high, and roughly 25 percent of single women said they did not intend to have children at all. Divorce rates also shot up as a result of new no-fault laws that enabled couples to end their marriages without proving adultery, abandonment, or other cause. Americans also developed a greater acceptance for a variety of family forms, including new blended families resulting from divorce and remarriage.

Renewed Cold War and Middle East Crisis

What was Carter's record regarding the Middle East?

On the one hand, Carter achieved great success in mediating a peace treaty between Israel and Egypt in 1978. Although Arab states felt it fell short in not providing a Palestinian homeland and allowing Israel to maintain some of its occupied territories, it was a major first step toward a lasting settlement in the region. On the other hand, Carter angered Iranians when he provided protection for the exiled shah in the United States to seek medical treatment. Mobs stormed the U.S. embassy in Iran and took hostages to press for the shah to stand trial. Carter's inability to free the U.S. hostages contributed to his political downfall and defeat in his reelection bid in 1980.

Suggestions for Further Reading

Donald T. Critchlow, *Phyllis Schlafly and Grassroots Conservatism: A Woman's Crusade* (2005)

Daniel Ellsberg, *Secrets: A Memoir of Vietnam and the Pentagon Papers* (2002)

David Farber, *Taken Hostage: The Iran Hostage Crisis and America's First Encounter with Radical Islam* (2004)

Nancy MacLean, *Freedom Is Not Enough: The Opening of the American Workplace* (2006)

Rick Perlstein, *Nixonland: The Rise of a President and the Fracturing of America* (2008)

Ruth Rosen, *The World Split Open: How the Modern Women's Movement Changed America* (2000)

Hal Rothman, *The Greening of a Nation: Environmentalism in the U.S. Since 1945* (1997)

Edward D. Berkowitz, *Something Happened: A Political and Cultural Overview of the Seventies* (2007)

John D. Skrentny, *The Minority Rights Revolution* (2002)

Odd Arne Westad, *The Global Cold War: Third World Interventions and the Making of Our Times* (2005)

Go to the History CourseMate web site for primary source links, study tools, and review materials.
www.cengage.com/Norton

Conservatism Revived

32

1980–1992

I t was hot and there was a lot of desert," Luisa Orellana remembered about crossing the Mexican border into the United States in the early 1980s. "All of us started running, each one with a child in our arms.... It rained so hard we couldn't see where we were going, but it helped because the Border Patrol couldn't see us either."

Three months earlier Luisa's father was murdered. Tanis Stanislaus Orellana had worked in El Salvador with Archbishop Óscar Romero, the most powerful critic of the ruling military dictatorship whose death squads killed thirty thousand Salvadorans between 1979 and 1981. Romero was assassinated in 1980—shot as he consecrated the Eucharist during Mass. The civil war that followed lasted twelve years, leading an estimated 4 million Salvadorans to seek refuge elsewhere from the threat of torture, rape, and murder.

Luisa's family joined that exodus; after Orellana's murder, they fled, leaving almost everything behind. Taking a bus through Guatemala, they crossed illegally into Mexico and, sheltered by churches, made their way from Chiapas to Mexico City to Agua Prieta, on the U.S.-Mexico border.

There, Luisa's family ran two miles through blinding rain. Cold, hungry, and scared, they were met by the Sanctuary movement, Americans who believed that the U.S. government's refugee policy, which offered asylum to those fleeing violent repression and possible death or torture, must include those who escaped the deadly civil wars ravaging Central America in the 1980s. The U.S. government instead designated them "economic refugees" and denied them asylum.

The U.S. Sanctuary movement used church networks and human rights groups to investigate Central American refugees' stories of rape, torture, and murder. Many members belonged to faith-based communities, although secular institutions, including universities and the state of New Mexico, also participated. Some movement members went to prison, charged with transporting or harboring fugitives.

Chapter Outline

Reagan and the Conservative Resurgence
Ronald Reagan | The New Conservative Coalition | Reagan's Conservative Agenda | Attacks on Social Welfare Programs | Pro-Business Policies and the Environment | Attacks on Organized Labor | The New Right

Reaganomics
Supply-Side Economics | Harsh Medicine for Inflation | "Morning in America" | Deregulation | Junk Bonds and Merger Mania | The Rich Get Richer

Reagan and the World
Soviet-American Tension | Reagan Doctrine | Contra War in Nicaragua | Iran-Contra Scandal | U.S. Interests in the Middle East | Terrorism | Enter Gorbachev | Perestroika and Glasnost

American Society in the 1980s
Growth of the Religious Right | "Culture Wars" | The New Inequality | Social Crises in American Cities | The AIDS Epidemic | New Immigrants from Asia | The Growing Latino Population | New Ways of Life

VISUALIZING THE PAST *Combating the Spread of AIDS*

The End of the Cold War and Global Disorder
George Herbert Walker Bush | Pro-Democracy Movements | Collapse of Soviet Power | Costs of Victory | Saddam Hussein's Gamble | Operation Desert Storm | Domestic Issues | Clarence Thomas Nomination

Luisa's family went from the sanctuary offered by Tucson churches at the center of the movement to live in the basement of a Spokane, Washington, Catholic church. In 1989, the U.S. government granted protection and work permits to Central American refugees. Luisa stayed in Washington, where she became a teacher of English as a second language. Luisa Orellana's family were part of the "new immigration" that began in the early 1970s and grew throughout the 1980s, as record numbers of immigrants came to the United States from Asia, Mexico, Central and South America, and the Caribbean. Many from Central America, Vietnam, the Soviet Union, and Cuba were political refugees. The Orellanas found safety and peace in the United States, but not all immigrants—or all Americans—fared so well in the 1980s. Divisions between rich and poor increased; social problems—drugs, violence, homelessness, the growing AIDS epidemic—made life more difficult for the urban poor, while those on the other side of the economic divide, enjoyed an era of luxury and ostentation.

Ronald Reagan's election in 1980 began twelve years of Republican rule, as Reagan was succeeded by his vice president, George H. W. Bush, in 1988. Reagan was a popular president who seemed to restore the confidence shaken by the 1970s social, economic, and political crises. Wealthy people liked Reagan's pro-business economic policies; the religious New Right shared his vision of "God's America"; white middle- and working-class Americans admired Reagan's charisma and his embrace of "old-fashioned" values.

Reagan supported New Right social issues: he was anti-abortion, embraced prayer in schools, and reversed the GOP's support of the Equal Rights Amendment. Most important, Reagan appointed Supreme Court and federal judges whose rulings strengthened social-conservative agendas. Reagan's primary focus was on the conservative issues of reducing the size and power of the federal government and creating favorable conditions for business. The U.S. economy recovered from the 1970s stagflation and boomed through much of the 1980s. But corruption flourished in financial institutions freed from government oversight. By the end of the Reagan-Bush era, a combination of tax cuts and massive increases in defense caused the budget deficit to jump fivefold.

Overseas, meanwhile, the Cold War intensified, then ended. The key figure in the intensification was Reagan, who promised to stand up to the Soviet Union. The key figure in ending the Cold War was Soviet leader Mikhail Gorbachev, who came to power in 1985 determined to end the USSR's economic decline, which required a more amicable superpower relationship. Gorbachev hoped to reform the Soviet system, not eradicate it, but lost control of events as revolutions in eastern Europe toppled one

LINKS TO THE WORLD *CNN*

LEGACY FOR A PEOPLE AND A NATION *The Americans with Disabilities Act*

SUMMARY

communist regime after another. In 1991, the Soviet Union itself disappeared. The Persian Gulf War of that same year demonstrated America's unrivaled world power and the unprecedented importance of the Middle East.

As you read this chapter, keep the following questions in mind:

* Ronald Reagan, campaigning for president in 1984, told voters, "It's morning again in America." How might Americans from different backgrounds judge the accuracy of his claim?

* What issues, beliefs, backgrounds, and economic realities divided Americans in the 1980s, and how do those divisions shape the culture and politics of contemporary America?

* Why did the Cold War intensify and then wane during the decade of the 1980s?

Reagan and the Conservative Resurgence

What groups made up the new Republican coalition of the 1980s?

The 1970s were hard for Americans: defeat in Vietnam, the resignation of a president in disgrace, the energy crisis, economic stagflation, and the Iranian hostage crisis. In 1980, President Carter's approval rating stood at 21 percent, lower than Richard Nixon's during the Watergate crisis. The time was ripe for a challenge to Carter's leadership, the Democratic Party, and the liberalism that had essentially governed the United States since Franklin Roosevelt's New Deal.

Ronald Reagan: Former actor and California governor (1967–1975) who became the 40th President of the United States from 1981–1989.

Ronald Reagan

In 1980, several conservative Republican politicians entered the presidential race, including **Ronald Reagan**, former movie star and two-term governor of California. In the 1940s, as president of Hollywood's Screen Actors Guild, Reagan was a New Deal Democrat. But in the 1950s, as a corporate spokesman for General Electric, he became increasingly conservative. In 1964, Reagan's televised speech supporting Republican presidential candidate Barry Goldwater catapulted him to the forefront of conservative politics.

Elected governor of California two years later, Reagan became known for his right-wing rhetoric: The United States should "level Vietnam, pave it, paint stripes on it, and make a parking lot out of it." And in 1969, when student protestors occupied People's Park near the University of California in Berkeley, he threatened a "bloodbath," dispatching National Guard troops. Reagan was often pragmatic; he denounced welfare but presided over reform of the state's social welfare bureaucracy. And he signed one of the nation's most liberal abortion laws.

neoconservatives: A small but influential group of intellectuals—typically former Democrats disillusioned with the party after Vietnam—who became part of Republican Ronald Reagan's conservative coalition.

The New Conservative Coalition

In the 1980 election, Reagan contrasted incumbent Jimmy Carter with an optimistic vision for America's future. With his Hollywood charm, he forged different sorts of American conservatives into a new coalition. Political conservatives wanted to strengthen national defense, limit federal power, and roll back the liberal programs of the 1930s New Deal and 1960s Great Society. Reagan similarly attracted economic conservatives, promising deregulation and tax policies benefiting corporations, wealthy investors, and entrepreneurs. He also drew **neoconservatives**, a small but

Chronology

1980	Reagan elected president
1981	AIDS first observed in United States
	Economic problems continue; prime interest rate reaches 21.5 percent
	"Reaganomics" plan of budget and tax cuts approved by Congress
1982	Unemployment reaches 10.8 percent, highest rate since Great Depression
	ERA dies after STOP-ERA campaign prevents ratification in key states
1983	Reagan introduces SDI
	Terrorists kill U.S. marines in Lebanon
	U.S. invasion of Grenada
1984	Reagan aids contras despite congressional ban
	Economic recovery; unemployment rate drops and economy grows without inflation
	Reagan reelected
	Gorbachev promotes reforms in USSR
1986	Iran-contra scandal erupts
1987	Stock market drops 508 points in one day
	Palestinian *intifada* begins
1988	George H. W. Bush elected president
1989	Tiananmen Square massacre in China
	Berlin Wall torn down
	U.S. troops invade Panama
	Gulf between rich and poor at highest point since 1920s
1990	Americans with Disabilities Act passed
	Communist regimes in eastern Europe collapse
	Iraq invades Kuwait
	South Africa begins to dismantle apartheid
1991	Persian Gulf War
	USSR dissolves into independent states
	United States enters recession
1992	Annual federal budget deficit reaches high of $300 billion at end of Bush presidency

influential group of intellectuals—typically former Democrats disillusioned with the party after Vietnam.

Reagan further tapped into the sentiments that fueled the 1970s tax revolt movement, drawing voters from traditionally Democratic constituencies, such as labor unions and urban ethnic groups. Many middle- and working-class whites resented what they saw as tax-funded welfare for people who did not work. These "Reagan Democrats" found the Republican critique of tax-funded social programs and "big government" appealing, even though Reagan's policies would benefit the wealthy at their expense.

Finally, Reagan drew the increasingly powerful, religiously based New Right. Many of them were evangelical Christians who believed (in Moral Majority founder Jerry Falwell's words) that America's "internal problems are the direct result of her spiritual condition."

Reagan's Conservative Agenda

Reagan won the election with 51 percent of the popular vote. Jimmy Carter carried only six states. Reagan served two terms as president, and like Franklin Roosevelt, defined the era over which he presided. Reagan was not especially focused on the details of governing. When Carter briefed him on foreign and domestic policy, Reagan took no notes. Critics argued that his lack of knowledge could prove dangerous—as when he insisted that intercontinental ballistic missiles carrying nuclear warheads could be called back once launched.

But supporters insisted that Reagan focused on the big picture. When he spoke to the American people, he offered what seemed to be simple truths. While even supporters winced at his willingness to reduce complex policy issues to basic (and often misleading)

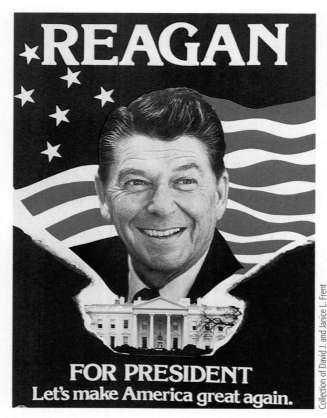

REAGAN
FOR PRESIDENT
Let's make America great again.

Collection of David J. and Janice L. Frent

Ronald Reagan, the Republican presidential candidate in 1980, campaigned for "family values," an aggressive anti-Soviet foreign and military policy, and tax cuts. He also exuded optimism and appealed to Americans' patriotism. This poster issued by the Republican National Committee included Reagan's favorite campaign slogan, "Let's make America great again."

stories, Reagan was to most Americans the Great Communicator. He won admiration for his courage after he was seriously wounded in an assassination attempt sixty-nine days into his presidency. Most important, Reagan had a clear vision for the United States' future. He wanted to roll back the liberalism of the past fifty years that made government responsible for the nation's economic health and the social welfare of its citizens.

Attacks on Social Welfare Programs

Reagan, like traditional conservatives, believed that the federal government could not solve social problems. He tapped into a backlash against such Great Society programs. Many Americans who struggled to make ends meet during the economic crises of the 1970s and early 1980s resented paying taxes that, they believed, funded government handouts. Lasting racial tensions also fueled public resentment: Reagan fed a stereotype of welfare recipients as unwed, black, teenage mothers who kept having babies to collect larger checks.

In 1981, the administration cut social welfare funding by $25 billion. But welfare programs benefiting the poor (Aid to Families with Dependent Children and food stamp programs) were small compared with Social Security and Medicare—welfare programs benefiting Americans across income levels. The Reagan administration did shrink the *proportion* of the federal budget devoted to social welfare programs (including Social Security and Medicare) from 28 to 22 percent by the late 1980s, but only because of a $1.2 trillion increase in defense spending.

Pro-Business Policies and the Environment

Reagan also attacked federal environmental, health, and safety regulations as reducing business profits and discouraging economic growth. Administration officials claimed that removing government regulation would restore the creativity of America's free-market system. However, they did not so much end government's role as deploy government power to aid corporate America. The president even appointed opponents of federal regulations to head agencies charged with enforcing them.

Environmentalists were appalled when Reagan appointed James Watt, a well-known antienvironmentalist, as secretary of the interior. Watt was a leader in the Sagebrush Rebellion, which sought the return of publicly owned lands in the West, such as national forests, to state control. The federal government controlled more than half of western lands, including 83 percent of the land in Nevada, 66 percent in Utah, and 50 percent in Wyoming. But state control was not the sole issue; Watt's group wanted to open western public lands to businesses for logging, mining, and ranching.

Telling Congress in 1981, "I don't know how many generations we can count on until the Lord returns," Watt dismissed concerns about protecting resources and public lands and allowed private corporations to acquire oil, mineral, and timber rights to federal lands for minuscule payments. He was forced to resign in 1983 after he referred to a federal advisory panel as "a black...a woman, two Jews, and a cripple." Even before Watt's resignation, his actions reenergized the nation's environmental movement and provoked opposition from business leaders in western states who understood that uncontrolled strip-mining and clear-cut logging could destroy lucrative tourism and recreation industries.

Attacks on Organized Labor

The pro-business Reagan administration undercut organized labor's ability to negotiate wages and working conditions. Union power was already waning; labor union membership declined in the 1970s as jobs in heavy industry disappeared, and efforts to unionize the high-growth electronics and service sectors failed. In August 1981, Reagan intervened in a strike by the Professional Air Traffic Controllers Organization (PATCO). The air traffic controllers—federal employees, for whom striking was illegal—protested working conditions they believed compromised the safety of air travel. Forty-eight hours into the strike, Reagan fired the 11,350 strikers, stipulating that they could never be rehired by the Federal Aviation Administration.

With the support of Reagan appointees to the National Labor Relations Board, businesses took an increasingly hard line with labor during the 1980s, and unions failed to mount effective opposition. Yet roughly 44 percent of union families voted for Reagan in 1980, drawn to his espousal of old-fashioned values and vigorous anticommunist rhetoric.

The New Right

It is surprising that the religious New Right was drawn to Reagan, a divorced man without strong ties to religion or, seemingly, his own children. But Reagan supported New Right social issues: the anti-abortion cause and prayer in public schools.

Reagan's judicial nominations also pleased the religious New Right. The Senate, in a bipartisan vote, refused to confirm Supreme Court nominee Robert Bork, but Congress eventually confirmed Anthony M. Kennedy. Reagan also appointed Anton Scalia, who would become a key conservative force, and Sandra Day O'Connor (the first woman appointee), and elevated Nixon appointee William Rehnquist to chief justice. In 1986, the increasingly conservative Supreme Court upheld a Georgia law that punished consensual sex between men with up to twenty years in jail (*Bowers v. Hardwick*); in 1989, justices ruled that a Missouri law restricting the right to an abortion was constitutional (*Webster v. Reproductive Health Services*), thus encouraging further challenges to *Roe v. Wade*. Overall, however, the Reagan administration did not push a conservative social agenda as strongly as some in the new Republican coalition had hoped.

Reaganomics

The centerpiece of Reagan's domestic agenda was the economic program that took his name: Reaganomics. The U.S. economy was faltering in the early 1980s. Stagflation proved resistant to traditional remedies: when the government increased spending to stimulate a stagnant economy, inflation skyrocketed; when it cut spending or tightened the money supply to reduce inflation, the economy plunged deeper into recession and unemployment jumped.

> Why was the 1980s' economic boom a mixed blessing?

Reagan offered a simple answer. Instead of focusing on the complexities of global competition, deindustrialization, and OPEC's control of oil, Reagan argued that U.S. economic problems were caused by intrusive government regulation of business and industry, expensive social programs, high taxes, and deficit spending—in short, government itself. Reagan sought to unshackle the free-enterprise system from government regulation, slash social programs, and balance the budget by reducing the role of the federal government.

Supply-Side Economics   Reagan's economic policy was based largely on supply-side economics, the theory that tax cuts (rather than government spending) stimulate growth. Economist Arthur Laffer proposed one hypothesis—his soon-to-be-famous Laffer curve. It stated that at some point rising tax rates discourage people from engaging in taxable activities (such as investing). As people invest less, the economy slows, and there is less tax revenue to collect. Cutting taxes, in contrast, reverses the cycle.

Although economists accepted the larger principle behind Laffer's curve, almost none believed that U.S. tax rates approached the point of disincentive. Even conservative economists were suspicious of supply-side principles. Reagan and his staff, however, sought a massive tax cut, arguing that American corporations and individuals would invest funds freed up by lower tax rates, producing new plants, jobs, and products. And as prosperity returned, profits at the top would "trickle down" to the middle classes and even to the poor.

David Stockman, head of the Office of Management and Budget, proposed a five-year plan to balance the federal budget through economic growth (created by tax cuts) and deep spending cuts, primarily in social programs. Congress cooperated with a three-year, $750 billion tax cut, the largest in American history. Stockman's plan assumed $100 billion in cuts from government programs, including Social Security and Medicare, which Congress rejected. Reagan, meanwhile, canceled out gains from domestic spending cuts by dramatically increasing defense spending.

Major tax cuts, big increases in defense spending, small cuts in social programs: the federal budget deficit exploded from $59 billion in 1980 to more than $100 billion in 1982 to almost $300 billion by the end of George Bush's presidency in 1992. The federal government borrowed money to make up the difference, transforming the United States from the world's largest creditor to its largest debtor (see Figure 32.1). The national debt grew to almost $3 trillion.

Harsh Medicine for Inflation   In 1981, the Federal Reserve Bank, an autonomous federal agency, raised interest rates for bank loans to an unprecedented 21.5 percent, battling inflation by tightening the money supply and slowing the economy. The nation plunged into recession. By year's end, the gross national product (GNP) fell 5 percent and sales of cars and houses dropped sharply. Unemployment soared to 8 percent.

By late 1982, unemployment reached 10.8 percent, the highest rate since 1940. For African Americans, it was 20 percent. Reagan promised that consumers would lift the economy from the recession by spending their tax cuts. But as late as April 1983, unemployment remained at 10 percent, and people were angry.

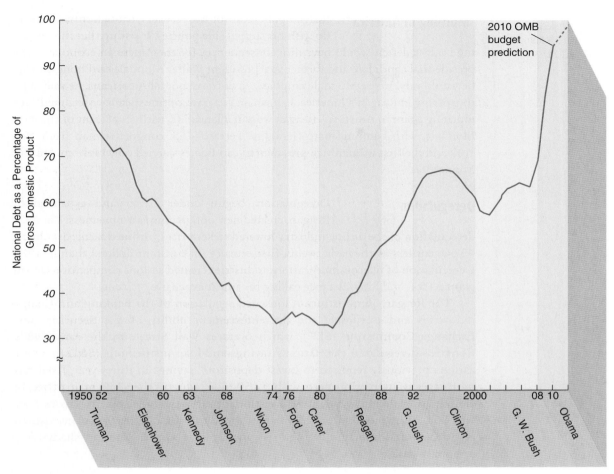

FIGURE 32.1
America's Rising National Debt, 1974–1989

America's national debt, which rose sporadically throughout the 1970s, soared to record heights during the 1980s. Under President Reagan, large defense expenditures and tax cuts caused the national debt to grow by $1.5 trillion.

Source: Adapted from U.S. Bureau of the Census, *Statistical Abstract of the United States* (Washington, D.C.: 1992), p. 315.

Along with industries such as steel and automobiles, agriculture, too, was faltering as farmers suffered from falling crop prices, floods, droughts, and burdensome debts at high interest rates. Many lost their property through mortgage foreclosures; others filed for bankruptcy. As the recession deepened, poverty rose to its highest level since 1965.

It was harsh medicine, but the Federal Reserve Bank's plan to end stagflation worked. High interest rates helped drop inflation from 12 percent in 1980 to less than 7 percent in 1982. The economy also benefited from OPEC's 1981 decision to increase oil production, thus lowering prices. In 1984, the GNP rose 7 percent, the sharpest increase since 1951, and midyear unemployment fell to a four-year low of 7 percent.

Link to a collection of campaign ads from the 1984 election.

"Morning in America"

Reagan got credit for the recovery, though it had little to do with his supply-side policies. Insisting that the escalating budget deficit would have dire consequences for the American economy, 1984 presidential candidate and former vice president Walter Mondale said honestly that he would raise taxes. Mondale emphasized fairness; not all Americans, he said, were prospering in Reagan's America. Reagan, in contrast, optimistically proclaimed, "It's morning again in America." Reagan won in a landslide, with 59 percent of the vote. Mondale, with running mate Geraldine Ferraro—U.S. congresswoman from New York and the first woman vice-presidential candidate—carried only his home state of Minnesota.

Deregulation

Deregulation, begun under Carter and expanded by Reagan, created new opportunities for business. The 1978 deregulation of the airline industry lowered ticket prices; airline tickets cost almost 45 percent less in the early twenty-first century (in constant dollars) than in 1978. Deregulation of telecommunications industries created serious competition for the giant AT&T, and long-distance calling became inexpensive.

The Reagan administration loosened regulation of the banking and finance industries and purposely cut the enforcement ability of the Securities and Exchange Commission (SEC), which oversees Wall Street. In the early 1980s, Congress deregulated the nation's savings-and-loan institutions (S&Ls), organizations previously required to invest depositors' savings in thirty-year, fixed-rate mortgages secured by property within a 50-mile radius of the S&L's main office. By ending government oversight of investment practices, while covering losses from bad S&L investments, Congress left no penalties for failure. S&Ls increasingly put depositors' money into high-risk investments and engaged in shady—even criminal—deals.

Junk Bonds and Merger Mania

Risky investments typified Wall Street as well, as Michael Milken, a reclusive bond trader, pioneered the junk bond industry and created lucrative investment possibilities. Milken offered financing to debt-ridden corporations unable to get traditional, low-interest bank loans, using bond issues that paid investors high interest rates because they were high-risk (thus junk bonds). Many of these corporations were attractive targets for takeover by other corporations or investors, who, in turn, could finance takeovers with junk bonds. Such predators could use the first corporation's existing debt as a tax write-off, sell off unprofitable units, and lay off employees to create a more profitable corporation.

By the mid-1980s, hundreds of major corporations—including giants Walt Disney and Conoco—fell prey to merger mania and hostile takeovers. Profits for investors were staggering, and by 1987 Milken, the guru of junk bonds, was earning $550 million a year—about $1,046 a minute.

Deregulation helped smaller corporations challenge the virtual monopolies of giant corporations in fields like telecommunications. And the American economy boomed. Although the stock market plunged 508 points on a single day in October 1987—losing 22.6 percent of its value, or almost double the percentage loss in the 1929 crash—it rebounded quickly. The high-risk boom of the 1980s, however, had

S & L s' new drive-through window

UNITED STATES TREASURY

George Fisher/Arkansas Democrat Gazette

The 1980s savings-and-loan crisis led to the greatest collapse of U.S. financial institutions since the Great Depression. The federal bailout of S&Ls would cost American taxpayers at least $124 billion.

significant costs. Corporate downsizing meant layoffs for white-collar workers and management personnel, many of whom had difficulty finding comparable positions. The wave of mergers and takeovers left American corporations increasingly burdened by debt. It also helped to consolidate sectors of the economy—such as the media—under the control of a few players.

The Rich Get Richer   The high-risk, deregulated boom of the 1980s was rotten with corruption. By the late 1980s, insider trading scandals—in which people used "inside" corporate information unavailable to the general public to make huge profits trading stocks—rocked financial markets and sent some of the most prominent Wall Street figures to jail. Savings and loans lost billions in bad investments, sometimes turning to fraud to cover them up. Scandal reached to the White House: Vice President Bush's son Neil was involved in shady S&L deals. The Reagan-Bush administration's bailout of the S&L industry cost taxpayers half a trillion dollars.

During the 1980s, the rich got richer, and the poor got poorer (see Figure 32.2). The number of Americans reporting an annual income of $500,000 increased tenfold between 1980 and 1989. The average compensation of corporate executive officers increased from 35 times an average worker's pay in 1978 to 71 times workers' average pay in 1989 (in 2005 the ratio was 262 to 1). In 1987, the United States had forty-nine billionaires—up from one in 1978. Middle-class incomes, however, remained stagnant.

Percentage Increase in Pretax Income, 1977–1989

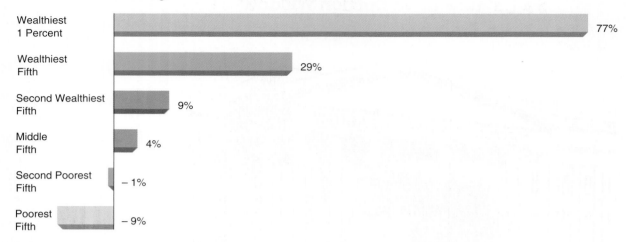

Wealthiest 1 Percent	77%
Wealthiest Fifth	29%
Second Wealthiest Fifth	9%
Middle Fifth	4%
Second Poorest Fifth	– 1%
Poorest Fifth	– 9%

FIGURE 32.2
While the Rich Got Richer in the 1980s, the Poor Got Poorer
Between 1977 and 1989, the richest 1 percent of American families reaped most of the gains from economic growth. In fact, the average pretax income of families in the top percentage rose 77 percent. At the same time, the typical family saw its income edge up only 4 percent. And the bottom 40 percent of families had actual declines in income.
Source: Data from the *New York Times*, March 5, 1992.

Reagan's economic policies benefited the wealthy at the expense of other Americans. Reagan's tax policies decreased the total effective tax rates—income taxes plus Social Security taxes—for the top 1 percent of American families by 14.4 percent. But they increased taxes for the poorest 20 percent of families by 16 percent. By 1990, the richest 1 percent controlled 40 percent of the nation's wealth.

Reagan and the World

What characterized Reagan's approach to foreign policy?

A key element in Reagan's winning strategy in the 1980 election was his call for the United States to assert itself in the world. Though lacking a firm grasp of world issues, history, and geography, Reagan adhered to a few core principles. One was a deep anticommunism; a second was an underlying optimism about the United States' power and ability to positively affect the world. Together, these elements help explain Reagan's aggressive anticommunist foreign policy and his positive response in his second term to Soviet leader Mikhail Gorbachev's call for "new thinking" in world affairs.

Soviet-American Tension

Initially, embracing the strident anticommunism of early U.S. Cold War foreign policy, Reagan rejected Nixon's détente and Carter's human rights focus. Where Nixon and Carter perceived an increasingly multipolar international system, the Reagan team reverted to a bipolar perspective defined by the Soviet-American relationship. When Poland's pro-Soviet leaders in 1981 cracked down on an independent labor organization, Solidarity, Washington restricted Soviet-American trade and hurled angry words at Moscow. In March 1983, Reagan told evangelical Christians in Florida that the Soviets were "an evil empire." That year, Reagan restricted commercial flights to the Soviet Union after a Soviet fighter pilot mistakenly shot down a South Korean commercial jet that strayed 300 miles off course into Soviet airspace, killing 269 passengers.

Reagan believed that a substantial military buildup would thwart the Soviet threat. Accordingly, the administration launched the largest peacetime arms buildup in history. In 1985, when the military budget hit $294.7 billion (a doubling since 1980), the Pentagon spent an average of $28 million an hour. Assigning low priority to arms control talks, Reagan announced in 1983 his desire for a space-based defense shield against incoming ballistic missiles: the **Strategic Defense Initiative** (SDI). His critics tagged it "Star Wars" and said such a system could never work—some enemy missiles would get through. Moreover, the critics warned, SDI would elevate the arms race to dangerous levels. Still, SDI research and development consumed tens of billions of dollars.

Strategic Defense Initiative (SDI): Reagan's proposed program for developing a high-tech, space-based defense shield that would protect the United States against incoming ballistic missiles; nicknamed "Star Wars" by critics.

Reagan Doctrine

Because he attributed Third World disorders to Soviet intrigue, the president declared the Reagan Doctrine: the United States would openly support anticommunist movements—freedom fighters battling the Soviets or Soviet-backed governments. In Afghanistan, Reagan continued providing covert assistance, through Pakistan, to the Mujahidin rebels fighting Soviet occupation. When the Soviets stepped up the war in 1985, the Reagan administration sent more high-tech weapons, particularly anti-aircraft Stinger missiles. Easily transportable and fired by a single soldier, the Stingers turned the tide in Afghanistan by making Soviet jets and helicopters vulnerable below eleven thousand feet.

The administration also applied the Reagan Doctrine aggressively in the Caribbean and Central America (see Map 32.1). In October 1983, the president sent troops into the tiny Caribbean island of Grenada to oust a pro-Marxist government. In El Salvador, he provided military and economic assistance to a military-dominated government struggling with left-wing revolutionaries. The regime used right-wing death squads, from which Luisa Orellana and her family fled. By decade's end, the death squads had killed forty thousand dissidents and citizens, as well as several U.S. missionaries. By the late 1980s, the United States spent more than $6 billion there in a counterinsurgency war. In January 1992, the Salvadoran combatants finally negotiated a U.N.-sponsored peace.

Contra War in Nicaragua

The Reagan administration also meddled in the Nicaraguan civil war. In 1979, leftist insurgents overthrew Anastasio Somoza, a long-time U.S. ally. The revolutionaries called themselves Sandinistas in honor of César Augusto Sandino, who headed the anti-imperialist Nicaraguan opposition against U.S. occupation in the 1930s and was finally assassinated by Somoza supporters. When the Sandinistas aided rebels in El Salvador, bought Soviet weapons, and invited Cubans to help reorganize the Nicaraguan army, Reagan officials charged that Nicaragua was becoming a Soviet client. In 1981, the CIA began to train, arm, and direct more than ten thousand counterrevolutionaries, known as contras, to overthrow the Nicaraguan government.

Many Americans, including Democratic leaders in Congress, were skeptical about the communist threat and warned that Nicaragua could become another Vietnam. Congress in 1984 voted to stop U.S. military aid to the contras. Secretly, the Reagan administration lined up other countries, including Saudi Arabia, Panama, and South Korea, to funnel money and weapons to the contras, and in 1985 Reagan imposed an economic embargo against Nicaragua. Reagan rejected a plan from Costa Rica's president Oscar Arias Sanchez in 1987 to obtain a cease-fire in Central America through negotiations and cutbacks in military aid to rebel forces. (Arias won the 1987 Nobel Peace Prize.) Three years later after Reagan left office, Central American presidents brokered a settlement; in the national election that followed, the Sandinistas lost to a U.S.-funded party. After a decade of civil war, thirty thousand Nicaraguans had died, and the ravaged economy was one of the poorest in the hemisphere.

Oliver North: U.S. Marine colonel who became a central figure in the Iran-Contra, arms-for-hostages scandal.

Iran-Contra Scandal

Reagan's obsession with defeating the Sandinistas almost caused his political undoing. In November 1986 it became known that the president's national security adviser, John M. Poindexter, and an aide, Marine lieutenant colonel **Oliver North**, in collusion with CIA director Casey, covertly

MAP 32.1

The United States in the Caribbean and Central America

The United States has often intervened in the Caribbean and Central America. Geographical proximity, economic stakes, political disputes, security links, trade in illicit drugs, and Cuban leader Fidel Castro's long-time defiance of Washington have kept U.S. eyes fixed on events in the region.

Source: Copyright © Cengage Learning

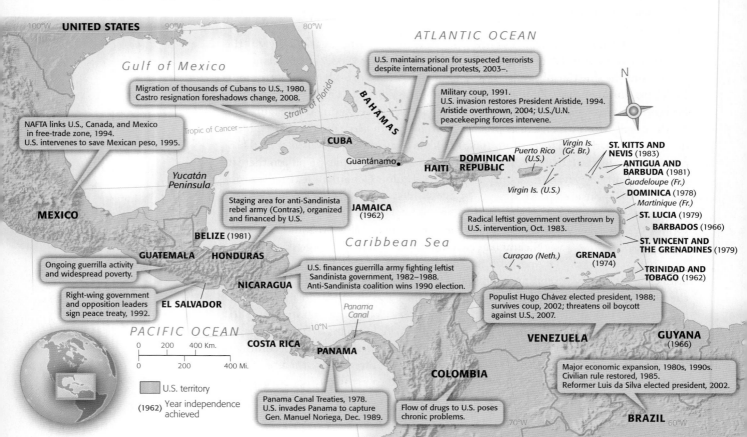

sold weapons to Iran in an unsuccessful attempt to win the release of Americans held hostage by Islamic fundamentalist groups in the Middle East. Washington had condemned Iran as a terrorist nation and demanded that allies cease trade there. More damaging was the revelation that money from the Iran arms deal was illegally diverted to the contras. North later admitted that he illegally destroyed government documents and lied to Congress to keep the operation clandestine.

Although Reagan survived the **Iran-contra scandal**, his popularity declined, and Congress reasserted its authority over foreign affairs. In late 1992, outgoing president George W. H. Bush pardoned several former government officials convicted of lying to Congress. Critics smelled a cover-up, for Bush himself, as vice president, participated in high-level meetings on Iran-contra deals. As for North, his conviction was overturned on a technicality.

Iran-contra scandal: Scandal in which Reagan administration illegally sold weapons to Iran to finance contras in Nicaragua.

U.S. Interests in the Middle East

Iran-contra also pointed to the increased importance in U.S. foreign policy of the Middle East and terrorism (see Map 33.1). The main U.S. goals in the Middle East remained preserving access to oil and supporting its ally Israel, while checking Soviet influence. In addition, American leaders faced new pressures from a deepened Israeli-Palestinian conflict and an anti-American and anti-Israeli Islamic fundamentalist movement that spread after the 1979 ouster of the shah of Iran.

The 1979 Camp David accords between Israel and Egypt raised hopes of a lasting settlement involving self-government for the Palestinian Arabs living in the Israeli-occupied Gaza Strip and West Bank. Instead, Israel and the Palestinian Liberation Organization (PLO) remained at odds. In 1982, in retaliation for Palestinian shelling of Israel from Lebanon, Israeli troops invaded Lebanon. The beleaguered PLO and various Lebanese factions called on Syria to contain the Israelis. Thousands of civilians died. Soon after Reagan sent Marines to Lebanon to join a peacekeeping force, U.S. troops became embroiled in a war between Christian and Muslim factions. In October 1983, terrorist bombs demolished a barracks, killing 241 U.S. servicemen. Four months later, Reagan pulled the remaining Marines out.

Terrorism

The attack on the Marine barracks showed the growing danger of terrorism to the United States and other western countries. In the 1980s, numerous otherwise powerless groups, many of them associated with the Palestinian cause or with Islamic fundamentalism, relied on terrorism to further their aims. Often they targeted U.S. citizens and property, because of Washington's support of Israel and U.S. involvement in the Lebanese civil war. Of the 690 hijackings, kidnappings, bombings, and shootings around the world in 1985, for example, 217 were against Americans, most originating in Iran, Libya, Lebanon, and the Gaza Strip. Three years later, a Pan American passenger plane was destroyed over Scotland, and many suspected pro-Iranian terrorists.

Washington, allied with Israel, continued to propose plans for Israelis to give back occupied territories and for Arabs to stop trying to push the Jews out of the Middle East. As the peace process stalled in 1987, Palestinians in the West Bank began an *intifada* (Arabic for "uprising") against Israeli forces. Israel refused to negotiate, but the United States talked with PLO chief Yasir Arafat after he renounced terrorism and accepted Israel's right to live in peace. For the PLO to recognize Israel and the United States to recognize the PLO were major developments in the Arab-Israeli conflict.

In South Africa, too, American diplomacy became more aggressive. At first, the Reagan administration followed a policy of constructive engagement, asking the increasingly isolated government to reform its white supremacist apartheid system. But many Americans demanded cutting off imports from South Africa and pressuring 350 U.S. companies to cease operations there. Some U.S. cities and states passed divestment laws, withdrawing dollars from U.S. companies active in South Africa. Public protest and congressional legislation forced the Reagan administration in 1986 to impose economic restrictions. Within two years, about half of the U.S. companies in South Africa left.

Enter Gorbachev

Many on the right disliked the South Africa sanctions policy; they believed the main black opposition group, the African National Congress (ANC), was dominated by communists, and they doubted the efficacy of sanctions. They also balked when Reagan, his popularity declining, entered negotiations with the Soviet Union. At a 1985 Geneva summit meeting, Reagan agreed in principle with new Soviet leader Mikhail S. Gorbachev's contention that strategic weapons should be substantially reduced, and at a 1986 Reykjavik, Iceland, meeting, they came close to a major reduction agreement. SDI stood in the way: Gorbachev insisted it should be shelved, and Reagan refused.

But Reagan and Gorbachev got along well. As General Colin Powell commented, though the Soviet leader was far superior to Reagan in mastery of specifics, he understood that Reagan was, as Powell put it, "the embodiment of his people's down-to-earth character, practicality, and optimism." And Reagan toned down his strident anti-Soviet rhetoric.

Perestroika and *Glasnost*

The turnaround in Soviet-American relations stemmed more from changes abroad than from Reagan's decisions. Under Gorbachev, a younger generation of Soviet leaders came to power in 1985. They modernized the highly bureaucratized, decaying economy through a reform program known as *perestroika* ("restructuring") and liberalized the authoritarian political system through *glasnost* ("openness"). For these reforms to work, Soviet military expenditures had to be reduced.

In 1987, Gorbachev and Reagan signed the **Intermediate-Range Nuclear Forces (INF) Treaty** banning all land-based intermediate-range nuclear missiles in Europe. About 2,800 missiles were destroyed. Gorbachev also reduced his nation's armed forces, helped settle regional conflicts, and began the withdrawal of Soviet troops from Afghanistan. The Cold War was coming to an end.

Intermediate-Range Nuclear Forces (INF) Treaty: Treaty signed by U.S. President Reagan and Soviet leader Mikhail Gorbachev banning all land-based intermediate-range nuclear missiles in Europe, and resulting in the destruction of 2,800 missiles.

What divided Americans in the 1980s?

American Society in the 1980s

As the Cold War waned, the belief in a United States united by shared middle-class values also lost its force. By the 1980s, after years of social struggle and division, few Americans believed in the reality of that vision; many rejected it as undesirable. Although the 1980s were never as contentious as the 1960s and 1970s, deep social divides split Americans. A newly powerful group of Christian conservatives challenged the secular culture. A growing class of affluent Americans seemed a society apart from the urban poor, whom sociologists and journalists began calling the underclass. And the composition of the

U.S. population was changing dramatically, as people immigrated to the United States from more and different nations than ever before.

Growth of the Religious Right

Since the 1960s, America's mainline liberal Protestant churches—Episcopalian, Presbyterian, Methodist—had lost members, while Southern Baptists and other denominations offering the experience of being "born again" through belief in Jesus Christ and the literal truth of the Bible (fundamentalism) grew rapidly. Fundamentalist preachers reached out through television: by the late 1970s, televangelist Oral Roberts was drawing 3.9 million viewers. Nearly 20 percent of Americans self-identified as fundamentalist Christians in 1980.

Most fundamentalist Christian churches stayed out of the social and political conflicts of the 1960s and early 1970s. But in the late 1970s, some influential preachers mobilized for political struggle. In a 1980 Washington for Jesus rally, fundamentalist leader Pat Robertson told crowds, "We have enough votes to run the country." The Moral Majority, founded in 1979 by Jerry Falwell, sought to create a Christian America, partly by supporting political candidates. Falwell's defense of socially conservative values and his condemnation of feminism (he called NOW the National Order of Witches), homosexuality, pornography, and abortion resonated with many Americans.

Throughout the 1980s, the coalition of conservative Christians known as the New Right campaigned against America's secular culture. Rejecting "multiculturalism"—that different cultures and lifestyle choices were equally valid—the New Right worked to make "God's law" the basis for American society. Concerned Women for America, founded by Beverly LaHayes in 1979, wanted elementary school readers containing "unacceptable" religious beliefs (including excerpts from *The Diary of Anne Frank* and *The Wizard of Oz*) removed from classrooms, and fundamentalist Christian groups again challenged teaching evolutionary theory in public schools. The Reagan administration frequently turned to James Dobson, founder of the conservative Focus on the Family organization, for policy advice.

Link to President Reagan's remarks at the Baptist Fundamentalism Annual Convention on April 13, 1984.

"Culture Wars"

Many Americans vigorously opposed the New Right's seeming intolerance and threat to basic freedoms, including freedom of religion for those whose beliefs differed from the conservative Christianity of the New Right. In 1982, politically progressive television producer Norman Lear, influential former congresswoman Barbara Jordan, and other prominent figures from the fields of business, religion, politics, and entertainment founded People for the American Way to support American civil liberties, the separation of church and state, and the values of tolerance and diversity. The struggle between the religious right and their opponents for the nation's future came to be known as the culture wars.

Many beliefs of Christian fundamentalists ran counter to the way most Americans lived—especially regarding women's roles. By the 1980s, a generation of girls had grown up expecting opportunities their mothers never had. Legislation such as the Civil Rights Act of 1964 and Title IX opened both academic and athletic programs to females. By 1985, more than half of married women with children under three worked outside the home—many from economic necessity. The religious right's insistence that women's place was in the home, subordinated to her husband, contradicted the gains made toward sexual equality and the reality of many women's lives.

The New Inequality

As Americans fought the "culture wars" of the 1980s, another social divide threatened the nation. A 1988 national report on race relations looked back to the 1968 Kerner Commission report to claim, "America is again becoming two separate societies," white and black. The majority of the United States' poor were white, and the black middle class was expanding. But people of color were disproportionately poor. In 1980, 33 percent of African Americans and 26 percent of Hispanic Americans lived in poverty, compared with 10 percent of whites (see Figure 32.3).

Reasons for poverty varied. The legacies of racism played a role. The changing job structure was partly responsible, as well-paid jobs decreased, replaced by lower-paid service jobs. In addition, families headed by a single mother were five times more likely to be poor than families maintained by a married couple. By 1992, 59 percent of African American children and 17 percent of white children lived in female-headed households, and almost half of African American children lived in poverty.

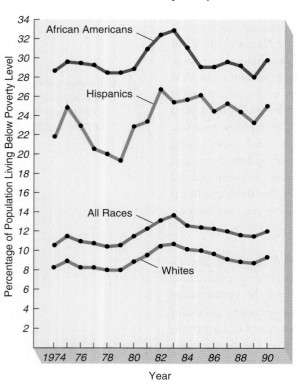

FIGURE 32.3
Poverty in America by Race, 1974–1990
Poverty in America rose in the early 1980s but subsided afterward. Many people of color, however, experienced little relief during the decade. Notice that the percentage of African Americans living below the poverty level was three times higher than that for whites. It was also much higher for Hispanics.
Source: Adapted from U.S. Bureau of the Census, *Statistical Abstract of the United States* (Washington, D.C.: 1992), p. 461.

Social Crises in American Cities

In impoverished inner-city neighborhoods, violent crime—particularly homicides and gang warfare—grew alarmingly, as did school dropout rates, crime rates, and child abuse. Some people sought escape in drugs, especially crack, a derivative of cocaine, which first struck New York City's poorest neighborhoods in 1985. Gang shootouts over drugs were deadly: the toll in Los Angeles in 1987 was 387 deaths, more than half of them innocent bystanders. Many states instituted mandatory prison sentences for possessing small amounts of crack equivalent to those for 100 grams of cocaine, the drug of more-affluent, white Americans. Such policies increased America's prison population almost fourfold from 1980 to the mid-1990s, with black and Latino youth arrested in disproportionate numbers. By 2000, young black men were more likely to have been arrested than to have graduated from college.

Homelessness also grew during the 1980s. Some homeless were impoverished families; many had drug or alcohol problems. About one-third were former psychiatric patients. By 1985, 80 percent of the total number of beds in state mental hospitals had been eliminated on the premise that neighborhood programs would better serve people than state institutions. Such local programs never materialized. Consequently, many of America's mentally ill citizens wandered the streets.

The AIDS Epidemic

Another social crisis confronting Americans in the 1980s was the global spread of acquired immune deficiency syndrome,

Combating the Spread of AIDS

During the 1960s and 1970s, with penicillin offering a quick and painless cure for venereal diseases and dependable contraceptives, such as the birth control pill, widely available, non-monogamous sex had fewer physical risks than at any time in history. But new sexually transmitted diseases appeared during the 1980s. By far the most serious was HIV/AIDS (Human Immunodeficiency Virus/Acquired Immune Deficiency Syndrome). Because AIDS initially was diagnosed in communities of gay men, many heterosexual Americans were slow to understand that they, too, might be at risk. Public health agencies and activist groups worked to raise awareness and promote safe sex. How is the couple in this ad portrayed? How does this image complicate widespread assumptions about who is at risk? And how does this public service advertisement make the case for "safe sex"?

Campaigns for "safe sex," such as this New York City subway ad, urged people to use condoms.

or **AIDS**. Caused by the human immunodeficiency virus (HIV), AIDS leaves its victims susceptible to deadly infections and cancers. The human immunodeficiency virus is spread through the exchange of blood or body fluids, often through sexual intercourse or needle sharing by intravenous drug users.

AIDS was first diagnosed in the United States in 1981. Between 1981 and 1988, of the 57,000 AIDS cases reported, nearly 32,000 resulted in death. Politicians were slow to devote resources to AIDS, partly because it was initially perceived as a "gay man's disease." "A man reaps what he sows," declared the Reverend Jerry Falwell of the Moral Majority. AIDS, and other sexually transmitted diseases such as genital herpes and chlamydia, ended an era defined by penicillin and "the pill," in which sex was freed from the threat of serious disease or unwanted pregnancy.

AIDS: Acquired Immune Deficiency Syndrome first diagnosed in the United States in 1981; had a very high mortality rate in the 1980s.

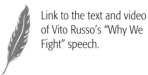

Link to the text and video of Vito Russo's "Why We Fight" speech.

New Immigrants from Asia

Social divisions were further complicated by the arrival of new immigrants from regions barely represented in the United States. Between 1970 and 1990, the United States absorbed more than 13 million new arrivals, most from Latin America and Asia. Before the 1965 immigration reforms, Americans of Asian ancestry made up less than 1 percent of the population; by 1990, that figure tripled.

Before 1965, most Asian Americans were of Japanese ancestry (about 52 percent in 1960), followed by Chinese and Filipino. There were only 603 Vietnamese residents of the United States in 1964. By 1990, the United States had absorbed almost 800,000 refugees from Indochina, casualties of the Vietnam war. Immigrants flooded in from South Korea, Thailand, India, Pakistan, Bangladesh, Indonesia, Singapore, Laos, Cambodia, and Vietnam. Japanese Americans were now only 15 percent of the Asian American population.

Immigrants from Asia were typically highly skilled or unskilled. Unsettled conditions in the Philippines in the 1970s and 1980s created an exodus of well-educated Filipinos to the United States. India's abundance of physicians and healthcare workers increasingly emigrated, as did educated, skilled workers from Korea, Taiwan, and China. Other Chinese immigrants, however, had few job skills and spoke little English. Many crowded into neighborhoods like New York City's Chinatown, where women worked under terrible conditions in the city's nonunion garment industry.

But even highly educated immigrants had limited options. A 1983 study found that Korean Americans owned three-quarters of the approximately twelve hundred greengroceries in New York City. Though often cited as a success story, Korean greengrocers usually descended the professional ladder: 78 percent had college or professional degrees.

The Growing Latino Population

Unprecedented immigration coupled with a high birth rate made Hispanic Americans the fastest-growing group of Americans. In 1970, Hispanic Americans made up 4.5 percent of the nation's population; that jumped to 9 percent by 1990, when one out of three Los Angelenos and Miamians were Hispanic. Mexican Americans, concentrated in California and the Southwest, made up most of this population, but Puerto Ricans, Cubans, Dominicans, and other Caribbean immigrants also lived in the United States, clustered principally in East Coast cities.

During the 1980s, people from Guatemala and El Salvador, like Luisa Orellana, fled civil war and government violence for the United States. Although the U.S. government commonly refused them political asylum (about 113,000 Cubans received political refugee status during the 1980s, compared with fewer than 1,400 El Salvadorans), a national Sanctuary movement of Christian churches defied the law to protect refugees from deportation. Economic troubles in Mexico and throughout Central and South America also produced a flood of undocumented workers who crossed the poorly guarded 2,000-mile border between the United States and Mexico, seeking economic opportunities. Some were sojourners, who moved back and forth across the border. A majority meant to stay.

Many Americans believed new arrivals threatened jobs and economic security, and nativist violence and bigotry increased. In 1982 twenty-seven-year-old Vincent Chin was beaten to death in Detroit by an unemployed auto worker and his uncle. American automobiles were losing to Japanese imports, and the two men seemingly mistook the Chinese American Chin for Japanese. In New York, Philadelphia, and Los Angeles, inner-city African Americans boycotted Korean groceries. Riots broke out in Los Angeles schools between black students and newly arrived Mexicans. In Dade County, Florida, voters passed an antibilingual measure that removed Spanish-language signs on public transportation, while at the state and national level people debated declaring English the "official" U.S. language. Public school classrooms, however, struggled with practical issues: in 1992, more than one thousand school districts in the United States enrolled students from at least eight different language groups.

Concerned about illegal aliens, Congress passed the **Immigration Reform and Control (Simpson-Rodino) Act** in 1986. Its purpose was to discourage illegal immigration by imposing sanctions on employers who hired undocumented workers, but it also provided amnesty to millions who immigrated illegally before 1982.

New Ways of Life

Many Americans found their lifestyles transformed during the 1980s due to new technologies and new models of distribution and consumption. American businesses made huge capital investments in technology as computers became workplace staples. With new communications technology, large office parks could be located outside cities, where building costs were low, fostering "edge cities" or "technoburbs" filled with residents who lived, worked, and shopped beyond the old city centers. New single family homes grew larger; home prices rose from two and a half times the median household salary in 1980 to more than four times the median salary in 1988.

While the rich embraced ostentation (Donald Trump's $29 million yacht had gold-plated bathroom fixtures), people of more modest means also consumed more. Between 1980 and 1988, Walmart's sales jumped from $1.6 billion to $20.6 billion. The number of American shopping malls increased by two-thirds. Eating out became common. The percentage of overweight or obese Americans increased dramatically during the 1980s, even as more people began to run marathons, take aerobics classes or buy actress Jane Fonda's aerobics exercise videos.

Almost half of American families owned a home computer by 1990. About half of all families subscribed to cable television by the mid 1980s. MTV (Music Television), launched in 1981, quickly became a national phenomenon. Early MTV stars included Michael Jackson, whose fourteen-minute "Thriller" video premiered there in 1983, and Madonna, whose creative manipulation of her image, from "Boy Toy" sexuality to "Express Yourself" celebration of female empowerment, infuriated both sides in the decade's culture wars. Movie attendance dropped as Americans bought newly affordable VCRs and rented movies.

The End of the Cold War and Global Disorder

The end of Ronald Reagan's presidency coincided with world events that brought the dawn of a new international system. Reagan's vice president, **George H.W. Bush**, would become president and oversee the transition. The scion of a Wall Street banker and U.S. senator from Connecticut, Bush attended an exclusive boarding school and then Yale. He had the advantage in seeking the Republican presidential nomination in having been a loyal vice president. And he possessed a

Immigration Reform and Control (Simpson-Rodino) Act: 1986 law that sought to discourage illegal immigration by fining employers who hired undocumented workers, but that also provided amnesty and a path to citizenship for millions who immigrated illegally before 1982.

 Link to the 1984 *Time* magazine article "Here Come the Yuppies."

What were the highs and lows of Bush's presidency?

George H.W. Bush: 41st president (1989-1993).

formidable résumé, including ambassador to the United Nations, chairman of the Republican Party, special envoy to China, and director of the CIA. He had also been a war hero, flying fifty-eight combat missions in the Pacific in World War II and receiving the Distinguished Flying Cross.

George Herbert Walker Bush

Bush entered the 1988 presidential campaign trailing his Democratic opponent, Massachusetts governor Michael Dukakis. Republicans turned that around by waging one of the most negative campaigns in U.S. history. Dukakis, while not personally attacking Bush, ran an uninspired campaign. Bush won by 8 percentage points in the popular vote and received 426 electoral votes to Dukakis's 112. The Democrats, however, retained control of both houses of Congress.

Bush's main interest was foreign policy, but he was naturally cautious and reactive in world affairs, much to the chagrin of neoconservatives. Mikhail Gorbachev's reforms in the Soviet Union were now stimulating reforms in eastern Europe that ultimately led to revolution. In 1989, thousands in East Germany, Poland, Hungary, Czechoslovakia, and Romania startled the world by repudiating their communist governments and staging mass protests for increased freedom. In November 1989, Germans scaled the Berlin Wall and tore it down; the following October, the two Germanys reunited. By then, other eastern European communist governments had fallen or were near collapse.

Pro-Democracy Movements

Challenges to communist rule in China met with less success. In June 1989, Chinese armed forces slaughtered hundreds—perhaps thousands—of unarmed students and citizens holding peaceful pro-democracy rallies in Beijing's Tiananmen Square. The Bush administration, anxious to preserve influence in Beijing, simply denounced the action, allowing the Chinese government to emphatically reject political liberalization.

Elsewhere, however, democratization efforts proved too powerful to resist. In South Africa, a new government under F. W. de Klerk began a cautious retreat from apartheid. In February 1990, de Klerk legalized all political parties in South Africa, including the ANC, and released Nelson Mandela, a hero to black South Africans, after a twenty-seven-year imprisonment. Then, the government repealed its apartheid laws over several years, allowing all citizens to vote. Mandela, who became South Africa's first black president in 1994, called the transformation a small miracle.

AP Images/John Parkin

African National Congress (ANC) leader Nelson Mandela gestures after casting his vote at Ohlange High School hall in Inanda, on April 27, 1994, for South Africa's first all-race elections. When results were announced later in the week, Mandela had been elected South Africa's first black president.

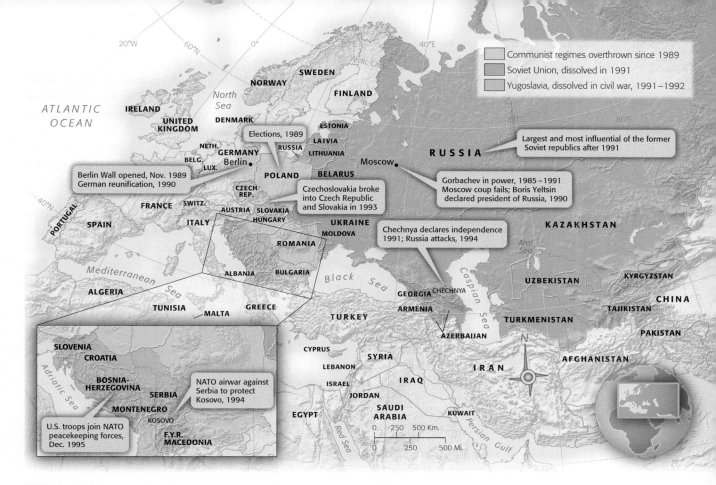

MAP 32.2

The End of the Cold War in Europe

When Mikhail Gorbachev came to power in the Soviet Union in 1985, he initiated reforms that ultimately undermined the communist regimes in eastern Europe and East Germany and led to the breakup of the Soviet Union itself, ensuring an end to the Cold War.

Source: Copyright © Cengage Learning

Collapse of Soviet Power

In 1990, the Soviet Union began to disintegrate. First the Baltic states of Lithuania, Latvia, and Estonia declared independence from Moscow. The following year, the Soviet Union ceased to exist, disintegrating into successor states—Russia, Ukraine, Tajikistan, and many others (see Map 32.2). Muscled aside by Russian reformers who thought he was moving too slowly toward democracy and free-market economics, Gorbachev lost power. The breakup of the Soviet empire, the dismantling of the Warsaw Pact (the Soviet military alliance formed in 1955 with communist countries of eastern Europe), the repudiation of communism by its leaders, German reunification, and a significantly reduced risk of nuclear war signaled the end of the Cold War.

The United States and its allies had won. The containment policy followed by nine presidents—from Truman through Bush—had many critics over the years, but succeeded at containing communism for four-plus decades without blowing up the world and obliterating freedom at home. Over time, the Soviet socialist economy proved less able to compete with the American free-market, less able to cope with the demands of the Soviet and eastern European citizenry.

Yet the Soviet empire might have survived longer had it not been for Gorbachev, one of the most influential figures of the twentieth century. Through unexpected overtures and decisions, Gorbachev fundamentally transformed the superpower relationship in ways that could scarcely have been anticipated before. Ronald Reagan's role was less central but still important because of his later willingness to negotiate and treat Gorbachev more as a partner than as an adversary. Just as personalities mattered in starting the Cold War, they mattered in ending it.

Costs of Victory

The victory in the Cold War elicited little celebration among Americans. The confrontation may never have become a hot war globally, but the period after 1945 nevertheless witnessed numerous Cold War–related conflicts claiming millions of lives. In the Vietnam War alone, up to 2 million people died, more than 58,000 of them Americans. Military budgets ate up billions of dollars, shortchanging domestic programs. Some Americans wondered whether the communist threat was ever as grave as officials had claimed.

Bush proclaimed a new world order and signed important arms reduction treaties with the Soviet Union in 1991 and with the post-breakup Russia in 1993. But the United States sustained a large defense budget and stationed large numbers of military forces overseas. As a result, Americans were denied the peace dividend that they hoped would reduce taxes and free up funds for domestic problems.

In Central America, the Bush administration cooled the zeal with which Reagan meddled, but showed no reluctance to intervene to further U.S. aims. In December 1989, American troops invaded Panama to oust military leader Manuel Noriega. A long-time drug trafficker, Noriega stayed in Washington's favor in the mid-1980s by providing logistical support for the Nicaraguan contras. In the early 1990s, exposés of his sordid record changed Bush's mind. Noriega was captured and taken to Miami, where, in 1992, he was convicted of drug trafficking and imprisoned. Devastated Panama, meanwhile, became increasingly dependent on the United States.

Saddam Hussein's Gamble

The strongest test of Bush's foreign policy came in the Middle East. The Iran-Iraq War ended inconclusively in August 1988, after eight years and almost 400,000 dead. The Reagan administration assisted the Iraqis with weapons and intelligence, as had many NATO countries. In mid-1990, Iraqi president Saddam Hussein, facing massive war debts, invaded neighboring Kuwait, hoping to enhance his regional power and oil revenues. George Bush condemned the invasion and vowed to defend Kuwait, partly fearing that Iraq might threaten U.S. oil supplies in Kuwait and petroleum-rich Saudi Arabia.

Within weeks, Bush convinced every important government, including most Arab and Islamic states, to economically boycott Iraq. Then, in Operation Desert Shield, Bush dispatched more than 500,000 U.S. forces to the region, joined by more than 200,000 from allied countries. Likening Saddam to Hitler and declaring it the first post–Cold War "test of our mettle," Bush rallied a deeply divided Congress to authorize "all necessary means" to oust Iraq from Kuwait (a vote of 250 to 183 in the House and 52 to 47 in the Senate). Many Americans believed that economic

In the Persian Gulf War of early 1991, Operation Desert Storm forced Iraqi troops out of Kuwait. Much of that nation's oil industry was destroyed by bombs and by the retreating Iraqis, who torched oil facilities as they left. Oil wells burned for months, darkening the sky over these American forces and causing environmental damage.

sanctions should be given more time to work, but Bush would not wait. Victory would come swiftly and cleanly.

Operation Desert Storm

Operation Desert Storm began on January 16, 1991, with the greatest air armada in history pummeling Iraqi targets. U.S. missiles reinforced round-the-clock bombing raids on Baghdad, Iraq's capital. It was a television war, in which CNN reporters broadcast live from a Baghdad hotel as bombs fell. In late February, coalition forces under General Norman Schwartzkopf launched a ground war that quickly routed the Iraqis from Kuwait. When the war ended on March 1, at least 40,000 Iraqis had been killed, while allied troops lost 240 (148 of them Americans).

Bush rejected suggestions from advisers to take Baghdad and topple Hussein's regime. Coalition members would not have agreed to such a plan, and it was unclear who would replace Iraq's dictator. So Saddam Hussein remained, though with his authority curtailed. The United Nations maintained an arms and economic embargo, and the Security Council issued Resolution 687, demanding full disclosure of Iraq's program to develop weapons of mass destruction and ballistic missiles. In Resolution 688, the Security Council condemned the Iraqi regime's brutal crackdown against Kurds in northern Iraq and Shi'ite Muslims in the south and demanded access for humanitarian groups. The United States, Britain, and France seized on Resolution 688 to create a northern no-fly zone, prohibiting Iraqi aircraft flights. A similar no-fly zone was set up in southern Iraq in 1992 and expanded in 1996.

Links to the World

CNN

When Ted Turner launched CNN, his Cable News Network, on June 1, 1980, few people took it seriously. CNN, with a staff of three hundred—mostly young, mostly inexperienced—operated from the basement of a converted Atlanta country club. CNN was initially known for its on-air errors, as when a cleaning woman emptied anchor Bernard Shaw's trash during his live newscast. But by 1992, CNN was seen in more than 150 nations, and *Time* magazine named Ted Turner its "Man of the Year."

Throughout the 1980s, CNN built relations with local news outlets worldwide. Millions watched as CNN reporters broadcast live from Baghdad in the 1991 Gulf War. When the Soviet Union wanted to denounce the 1989 U.S. invasion of Panama, officials called CNN's Moscow bureau instead of the U.S. embassy. During the Gulf War, Saddam Hussein reportedly kept televisions in his bunker tuned to CNN, and in 1992 President George H. W. Bush noted, "I learn more from CNN than I do from the CIA."

Despite its global mission, CNN's American origins were often apparent. During the U.S. invasion of Panama, CNN cautioned correspondents not to refer to the American military forces as "our" troops. What CNN offered was a global experience: people throughout the world watching the major moments in contemporary history as they unfolded. America's CNN created new links among the world's people. But, as *Time* magazine noted (while praising Turner as the "Prince of the Global Village"), such connections "did not produce instantaneous brotherhood, just a slowly dawning awareness of the implications of a world transfixed by a single TV image."

© Bettmann/Corbis

An employee at the CNN studios in Jerusalem dons a gas mask after an alarm sounds indicating an Iraqi missile attack on Israeli targets, January 19, 1991. CNN changed media history in the way its live coverage reported events as they unfolded.

The Americans with Disabilities Act

The Americans with Disabilities Act (ADA), passed by large bipartisan majorities in Congress and signed into law by President George H.W. Bush on July 26, 1990, built on the legacy of the United States' civil rights movement. Beyond prohibiting discrimination, it mandated that public and private entities—schools, stores, restaurants and hotels, government provide "reasonable accommodations" to allow people with disabilities to participate fully in the life of their communities and their nation.

The equal-access provisions of the ADA have changed the U.S. landscape. Steep curbs and stairs once blocked access to wheelchair users; now ramps and lifts are common. Buses "kneel" for passengers with limited mobility; crosswalks and elevators use audible signals for the sight-impaired; colleges and universities offer qualified students a wide range of assistance. People with various disabilities have traveled into the Grand Canyon and other parks, thanks to the National Park Service's accessibility programs.

At the same time, ADA employment regulations have generated difficult legal questions. Which conditions are covered by the ADA? (The Supreme Court ruled that asymptomatic HIV infection is a covered disability and carpal tunnel syndrome is not.) Employers may not discriminate against qualified people who can, with "reasonable" accommodation, perform the "essential" tasks of a job—but what is "reasonable" and what is "essential"? The specific provisions of the ADA will likely continue to be contested and redefined in the courts. But as Attorney General Janet Reno noted, as she celebrated the ADA's tenth anniversary, its true legacy is the determination "to find the best in everyone and to give everyone equal opportunity."

Although many would later question President Bush's decision to stop short of Baghdad, initially there were few objections. In the wake of Desert Storm, the president's popularity soared to 91 percent, beating the record 89 percent set by Harry Truman in June 1945 after Germany surrendered. Cocky advisers thought Bush could ride his popularity through the 1992 election.

Domestic Issues

Bush could also claim domestic achievements that seemed to affirm his pledge to lead a "kinder, gentler nation." In 1990, for example, Bush signed the **Americans with Disabilities Act**. Also in 1990, the president signed the Clean Air Act, which sought to reduce acid rain by limiting factory and automobile emissions.

Yet Bush's poll numbers started falling and kept falling, largely because of his ineffectual response to the weakening economy. He was slow to grasp the implications of the national debt and massive federal deficit. When the nation entered a full-fledged recession after the Gulf War, Bush merely proclaimed that things were not that bad. Business shrank, despite low interest rates that theoretically should have encouraged investment. Real-estate prices plummeted. American products faced tougher competitors, especially Japan and Asian nations. As unemployment climbed to 8 percent, consumer confidence sank. By late 1991, fewer than 40 percent of the American people felt comfortable about the nation's direction.

Americans with Disabilities Act: Law that barred discrimination against disabled persons in employment, transportation, public accommodation, communications, and governmental activities.

871

Clarence Thomas: 1991
African American nominee for
the Supreme Court who was
appointed despite accusations of
sexual harassment by an attorney
he had supervised. As a justice, he
has interpreted the Constitution
narrowly, championing
conservative social issues.

Clarence Thomas Nomination

Bush's credibility was diminished further in fall 1991 by the confirmation hearings for **Clarence Thomas**, his Supreme Court nominee. The Bush administration hoped that those who opposed the nomination of another conservative to the high court might support an African American justice. But in October, Anita Hill, an African American law professor at the University of Oklahoma, charged that Thomas had sexually harassed her when she worked for him during the early 1980s. The televised Judiciary Committee hearings turned ugly, and some Republican members suggested that Hill was either lying or mentally ill. Thomas described himself as the "victim" of a "high-tech lynching." However, Hill's testimony focused the nation's attention on issues of power, gender, race, and the workplace. And the Senate's confirmation of Thomas, along with the attacks on Hill, angered many, further increasing the gender gap in American politics.

Summary

When Ronald Reagan left the White House in 1988, the *New York Times* wrote: "Ronald Reagan leaves no Vietnam War, no Watergate, no hostage crisis. But he leaves huge question marks—and much to do." George H.W. Bush met the foreign policy promises of the 1980s, as the Soviet Union collapsed and America won the Cold War. He also led the United States into war with Iraq, which ended swiftly but left Saddam Hussein in power.

During the 1980s, the United States moved from recession to economic prosperity. However, deep tax cuts and massive increases in defense spending boosted the national debt from $994 billion to more than $2.9 trillion. Pro-business policies, such as deregulation, created opportunities for economic growth but also opened the door to corruption. Policies that benefited the wealthy at the expense of middle-class or poor Americans widened the gulf between the rich and everyone else. Drug addiction, crime, and violence grew, especially in impoverished areas. The 1980s also saw the coalescence of "culture wars" between fundamentalist Christians who sought to "restore" America to God and opponents who championed separation of church and state and embraced liberal values. The nation shifted politically to the right, though the coalitions of economic and social conservatives that supported Reagan were fragile.

Finally, during the 1980s, America became more racially and ethnically varied. The nation's Latino and Asian population grew in size and visibility. During the Reagan-Bush years, America became more divided and more diverse. In the years to come, Americans and their leaders would struggle with the legacies of the "Reagan era."

Chapter Review

Reagan and the Conservative Resurgence

What groups made up the new Republican coalition of the 1980s?

In his 1980 and 1984 presidential campaigns (and as president), Ronald Reagan appealed to, and ultimately united, a broad range of previously fragmented groups nationwide, transforming them into a strong Republican base. First, Reagan drew those who wanted to strengthen the military, minimize federal power, and weaken liberal social programs stemming from the 1930s New Deal and 1960s Great Society. Second, Reagan attracted economic conservatives with his stand on deregulation, weaker unions, and tax policies benefiting corporations and investors. Third, Reagan drew support from disillusioned Democrats—intellectual neoconservatives who fell away from the party after Vietnam as well as members of unions and ethnic groups who resented what they saw as their hard-earned tax dollars funding welfare hand-outs to those who did not work. Finally, though divorced, Reagan also drew the growing religious New Right into his coalition by embracing causes that were important to them, such as the anti-abortion movement and prayer in public schools.

Reaganomics

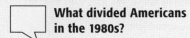

Why was the 1980s' economic boom a mixed blessing?

On the one hand, by 1984, the Federal Reserve's policy of increasing interest rates and tightening money supply ended stagflation and reversed the economic downturn. And President Reagan's pro-business policies and deregulation helped smaller companies make inroads into fields previously dominated by major corporations. On the other hand, deregulation allowed many businesses—particularly the financial services industry—to operate without accountability to governing authorities such as the SEC. Consequently, corruption was widespread, as some investors became rich via insider trading, the illegal practice of buying stocks with information not available to the public. Shady deals in the savings and loan industry caused its collapse and required a federal bail-out of half a trillion dollars. The high-risk investment climate of the latter half of the decade not only fueled a stock market crash in 1987, but also led to corporate downsizing and layoffs for middle managers. Finally, Reagan's tax cuts and other policies benefited the rich at the expense of other Americans, enabling the rich to get richer while the poor became poorer.

Reagan and the World

What characterized Reagan's approach to foreign policy?

In foreign policy, Reagan was both aggressive and flexible. In dealing with the Soviets, he initially adopted a strident anticommunist position, implementing the Reagan Doctrine to aid anticommunist freedom fighters around the world. He branded the Soviet Union as "an evil empire" and helped arm counter-revolutionaries to overthrow the Nicaraguan government when he thought it

was becoming communist. Believing that a solid defense would thwart the Soviet threat, Reagan launched the largest peacetime arms buildup in U.S. history, spending $294.7 billion in 1985 (twice as much as in 1980). But his optimism about the power of the United States to positively affect world events also led him in his second term to accept Soviet leader Mikhail Gorbachev's call for disarmament and new thinking in world affairs that led to the end of the Cold War.

American Society in the 1980s

What divided Americans in the 1980s?

Americans continued to feel the tug of unresolved racial and ethnic tensions, especially as the immigrant groups who arrived in the 1960s and 1970s (the majority from Asia and Latin America) changed the demographic composition of American society. The gulf—both economic and cultural—widened between well-off Americans and the urban poor. New lines were also being drawn between secular and religious forces, as a powerful new group of Christian conservatives sought to reverse what they regarded as society's increased permissiveness, restore conservative family values, and shape the nation's future around their core Christian beliefs. The resulting battle, dubbed the culture wars, pitted those who supported the separation of church and state and celebrated tolerance and diversity against this new religious right.

The End of the Cold War and Global Disorder

What were the highs and lows of Bush's presidency?

George H. W. Bush's popularity ratings soared to 91 percent after the United States' success in Operation Desert Storm. He scored kudos for passing the Americans with Disabilities Act, banning job discrimination against those with disabilities who can reasonably perform a job's task with minor accommodations. He also signed the Clean Air Act in 1990, which sought to reduce acid rain by restricting factory and auto emissions. But his blind-spot about the weakening economy and recession that emerged after the Gulf War turned voters off. He dismissed the rising jobless rates, shrinking number of businesses, and plummeting real estate prices as not that bad, leading many Americans to distrust the nation's future in Bush's hands.

Suggestions for Further Reading

Elijah Anderson, *Streetwise: Race, Class, and Change in an Urban Community* (1992)

Lou Cannon, *President Reagan: The Role of a Lifetime* (2000)

Robert M. Collins, *Transforming America: Politics and Culture During the Reagan Years* (2006)

John Ehrman, *The Eighties: America in the Age of Reagan* (2005)

Jack F. Matlock, *Reagan and Gorbachev: How the Cold War Ended* (2004)

John Micklethwait and Adrian Wooldridge, *The Right Nation: Conservative Power in America* (2004)

James A. Morone, *Hellfire Nation: The Politics of Sin in American History* (2003)

James Patterson, *The Restless Giant: The United States from Watergate to Bush vs. Gore* (2005)

Mary Elise Sarotte, *1989: The Struggle to Create Post-Cold War Europe* (2009)

Into the Global Millennium

33

America Since 1992

At 8:46 a.m. on that fateful Tuesday morning, Jan Demczur, a window washer, stepped into an elevator in the North Tower of the World Trade Center in New York City. The elevator started to climb, but before it reached its next landing, one of the six occupants recalled, "We felt a muted thud. The whole building shook. And the elevator swung from side to side like a pendulum." None of the occupants knew it, but American Airlines Flight 175 had just crashed into the building, at a speed of 440 miles per hour.

The elevator started plunging. Someone pushed the emergency stop button, and the descent stopped. Then a voice came over the intercom: there had been an explosion. As smoke seeped into the elevator, several men used the wooden handle of Demczur's squeegee to force open the doors but discovered they were on the fiftieth floor, where this elevator did not stop. In front of them was a wall.

Demczur, a Polish immigrant and former builder, saw that the wall was made of sheetrock, a plasterboard he knew could be cut. Using the squeegee, the men took turns scraping and poking, and finally burst through to a men's bathroom. Startled firefighters guided them to a stairwell. They finally reached the street at 10:23 a.m. Five minutes later, the tower collapsed.

It was September 11, 2001.

Later that day, Demczur learned that terrorists had hijacked four airliners and turned them into missiles. Two were flown into the World Trade Center; one slammed into the Pentagon in Washington, D.C.; and one crashed in a Pennsylvania field after passengers tried to retake the plane from the hijackers. Both World Trade Center towers collapsed, killing nearly three thousand people.

It was the deadliest attack the United States ever suffered on its soil. The events sent shock waves around the globe, revealing how interconnected the world had become in the early twenty-first century. At the World Trade Center alone, nearly five hundred foreigners from more than eighty countries perished.

Chapter Outline

Social Strains and New Political Directions

Turmoil in L.A. | *Clinton's Victory* | *Clinton and the "New Democrats"* | *"Republican Revolution" and Political Compromise* | *Political Partisanship and Scandal* | *Politics, the Media, and Celebrity Culture* | *Violence and Anger in American Society* | *Clinton's Diplomacy* | *Balkan Crisis* | *Agreements in the Middle East* | *Bin Laden and Al Qaeda*

Globalization and Prosperity

Digital Revolution | *Globalization of Business* | *Critics of Globalization* | *Target: McDonald's* | *The Bush-Gore Race* | *The Contested Election of 2000*

9/11 and the War in Iraq

9/11 | *Afghanistan War* | *PATRIOT Act* | *Economic Uncertainty* | *International Responses* | *Why Iraq?* | *Congressional Approval* | *Fall of Baghdad* | *Election of 2004* | *America Isolated*

Domestic Politics in Post-9/11 America

The Presidency of George W. Bush | *Hurricane Katrina* | *Economic Recession* | *Election of 2008* | *Barack Obama*

Americans in the First Decade of the New Millennium

Race and Ethnicity in Recent America | *The Changing American Family* | *Medicine, Science, and Religion* | *Century of Change* | *Globalization and World Health* | *Confronting Terrorism*

LINKS TO THE WORLD *The "Swine Flu" Pandemic*

LEGACY FOR A PEOPLE AND A NATION *The Internet*

VISUALIZING THE PAST *Arizona's Immigration Law*

SUMMARY

Many of the victims were, like Demczur, immigrants who came to New York seeking a better life; others were on temporary work visas. But all made the World Trade Center a kind of global city within a city, where some 50,000 people worked and another 140,000 visited daily.

A symbol of U.S. financial power, the World Trade Center towers also represented the globalization of trade that marked the 1980s and 1990s. The towers housed the offices of more than four hundred businesses, including the world's leading financial institutions—Bank of America, Switzerland's Credit Suisse Group, Germany's Deutsche Bank, and Japan's Dai-Ichi Kangyo Bank.

Globalization was a 1990s buzzword and went beyond trade and investment to include connections in commerce, communications, and culture. While terrorists—tied to a radical Islamic group called Al Qaeda—sought to bring down that globalization, their attack used the same international technological, economic, and travel infrastructure that fueled global integration. Cell phones, computers, intercontinental air travel—all instruments of globalization—were crucial in the terrorists' plot to turn four jetliners into lethal weapons.

Islamic militants had bombed the World Trade Center's underground parking garage before, in 1993, but Americans at the time paid only fleeting attention. President Bill Clinton took office in 1993 and concentrated less on foreign policy and more on domestic issues such as healthcare and deficit reduction. Clinton also sought to harness globalization to the United States' benefit.

For most Americans, the 1990s brought good times. The stock market soared, unemployment dropped, and more Americans owned homes. But the 1990s were also marked by violence and cultural conflict—the first multiethnic uprising in Los Angeles, domestic terrorism in Oklahoma City, school shootings, and hate crimes.

These were also politically volatile years. From the first days of Clinton's presidency, conservative Republicans blocked Democrats' legislative programs, and the GOP routed Democrats in the 1994 midterm elections. But Republicans alienated voters by shutting down the federal government during the winter of 1995–1996 in a budget standoff, and Clinton was reelected in 1996. However, scandal plagued the Clinton White House, compromising the president's ability to lead.

Clinton's successor, George W. Bush, successful in a close and controversial election, responded to the 9/11 attacks by declaring a "war on terrorism." Bush ordered U.S. forces into large-scale military action, first in Afghanistan, where Al Qaeda was headquartered with the blessing of the ruling Taliban regime, then in Iraq to oust Saddam Hussein's government. Militarily, the Taliban and the Iraqi government were quickly beaten. Al Qaeda, however, remained a threat, and in Afghanistan fighting resumed.

In Iraq, U.S. occupying forces battled a major insurgency. Bush's high approval ratings dropped, and though he won reelection in 2004, his second term was undermined by continued bloodshed in Iraq and scandal at home. In 2008, Democratic candidate Barack Obama won the presidency on a platform of hope and change. As the nation's first African American president, his election was symbolically important, but Obama, who inherited two wars and a major recession, struggled to deliver the domestic transformations he had promised.

As you read this chapter, keep the following questions in mind:

* **What was "The New Economy" of the 1990s, and how did it contribute to the globalization of business?**

* **Did the attacks of September 11, 2001, change America in fundamental ways? Explain.**

* **Why did the United States invade Iraq in 2003, and why did its occupying forces subsequently face a drawn-out and bloody insurgency?**

Social Strains and New Political Directions

Although the 1990s would be remembered for relative peace and prosperity, the decade did not start that way. Drugs, homelessness, and crime plagued U.S. cities. Racial tensions worsened; the gulf between rich and poor widened. The economy tipped into recession. Public disillusionment with political leaders ran strong. As the 1992 presidential election began, Americans wanted a change.

Turmoil in L.A.   Racial tensions that troubled the nation erupted in the South Central neighborhood of Los Angeles in 1992. There was an immediate cause: A jury with no African American members had acquitted four white police officers charged with beating a black man, Rodney King, who fled a pursuing police car at speeds exceeding 110 miles per hour.

The roots of the violence, however, went deeper. Almost one-third of South Central residents lived in poverty—a rate 75 percent higher than for the city as a whole—after well-paid jobs disappeared during the deindustrialization of the 1970s and 1980s. Tensions increased as new immigrants arrived—Latinos from Mexico and Central America, who competed with African Americans for jobs, and Koreans who established small businesses such as grocery stores. Outside the legitimate economy, the 40 Crips (an African American gang) and the 18th Street gang (Latino) struggled over territory as the crack epidemic further decimated the neighborhood and the homicide rate soared. Many African American and Latino residents saw high prices in Korean-owned shops as exploitation, while Korean shopkeepers complained of frequent shoplifting, robberies, even beatings.

The violence in Los Angeles was a multiethnic uprising that left at least fifty-three people dead and symbolized fundamental conflicts in American society. In addition, the economy had grown slowly or not at all during the Bush administration. In 1978, California's Proposition 13—the first in a series of tax revolts nationwide—cut property taxes while the population boomed, and the state faced bankruptcy in mid-1992. Thirty states were in financial trouble in the early 1990s. Factory employment plummeted, and corporate downsizing cost well-educated

Chronology

1992	Violence erupts in Los Angeles over Rodney King verdict	2000	Nation records longest economic expansion in its history
	Major economic recession		Supreme Court settles contested presidential election in favor of Bush
	Clinton elected president	2001	Economy dips into recession; period of low growth and high unemployment begins
1993	Congress approves North American Free Trade Agreement (NAFTA)		Bush becomes president
1994	Contract with America helps Republicans win majorities in House and Senate		Al Qaeda terrorists attack World Trade Center and Pentagon
	Genocide in Rwanda		United States attacks Al Qaeda positions in Afghanistan, topples ruling Taliban regime
	U.S. intervention in Haiti	2003	United States invades Iraq, ousts Saddam Hussein regime
1995	Domestic terrorist bombs Oklahoma City federal building	2004	Bush reelected
	U.S. diplomats broker peace for Bosnia	2005	Hurricane Katrina strikes Gulf Coast
1996	Welfare reform bill places time limits on welfare payments	2006	Iraq War continues; by end of year, U.S. deaths reach three thousand
	Clinton reelected		Democrats take both houses of Congress in midterm elections
1998	House votes to impeach Clinton	2007	Major economic recession begins in December
1999	Senate acquits Clinton of impeachment charges	2008	Barack Obama elected president
	NATO bombs Serbia over Kosovo crisis	2009	Obama announces increased U.S. military commitment to Afghanistan; U.S. continues troop drawdown in Iraq
	Antiglobalization demonstrators disrupt World Trade Organization (WTO) meeting in Seattle		

white-collar workers their jobs, too. In 1991, median household incomes severely declined; in 1992, the number of poor people in America reached the highest level since 1964.

Clinton's Victory

As the American economy suffered, so did President George H. W. Bush's approval rating. Despite the credit Bush gained for ending the Cold War and the quick victory in the Gulf War, economic woes and a lack of what he once called the "vision thing" left him vulnerable in the 1992 presidential election.

The Democratic nominee, Arkansas governor **Bill Clinton**, offered a profound contrast to Bush. Clinton's campaign headquarters bore signs with the four-word reminder "It's the economy stupid." In a town hall–format presidential debate, a woman asked how the economic troubles affected each candidate, and Clinton replied, "Tell me how it's affected you again?" George Bush was caught on camera looking at his watch.

On election day, Clinton and his running mate, Tennessee Senator Al Gore, swept New England, the West Coast, and much of the industrial Midwest, even making inroads into an almost solidly Republican South and drawing "Reagan Democrats" back to the fold.

Bill Clinton: 42nd U.S. President, from 1993–2001. Clinton served as the Governor of Arkansas for twelve years prior to his election to the U.S. Presidency.

Presidential candidate Bill Clinton campaigns in Jackson, Mississippi, in 1992. Describing Clinton's campaign appearance the night before the election, a *New York Times* journalist wrote: "Bill Clinton, a middling amateur saxophonist, is playing his true instrument, the crowd."

Clinton and the "New Democrats"

A journalist described Bill Clinton in a 1996 *New York Times* article as "one of the biggest, most talented, articulate, intelligent, open, colorful characters ever to inhabit the White House," while noting that Clinton "can also be an undisciplined, fumbling, obtuse, defensive, self-justifying rogue." Larger than life, Clinton was a born politician from a small town called Hope who had wanted to be president most of his life. At Georgetown University in Washington, D.C., during the 1960s he protested the Vietnam War and (like many of his generation) maneuvered to keep himself out of it. Clinton won a Rhodes scholarship to Oxford, earned his law degree from Yale, and returned to his home state of Arkansas, where he was elected governor in 1978 at age thirty-two. Bill Clinton's wife, **Hillary Rodham Clinton**, was the first First Lady to have a significant career of her own. They met when they were both law students at Yale, where Hillary Rodham had made Law Review (an honor not shared by her husband).

Politically, Bill Clinton was a "new Democrat," advocating a more centrist—though still socially progressive—position for the Democratic Party. Clinton and his colleagues emphasized private-sector economic development, focusing on job training and other policies they believed would promote opportunity, not dependency. They championed a global outlook in foreign policy and economic development, along with an ethic of "mutual responsibility" and "inclusiveness."

Hillary Rodham Clinton: Wife of President Bill Clinton, she was directly involved in policymaking during her husband's presidency. She later served as a New York senator (2001–2009), ran for president, and served as Secretary of State.

Clinton began his presidency with an ambitious program of reform and revitalization, including appointing a cabinet that "looks like America" in all its diversity. Republicans did not allow Clinton the traditional honeymoon period and maneuvered him into fulfilling his pledge to end the ban on gays in the military before he secured congressional or military support. Amid controversy, Clinton accepted a "don't ask, don't tell" compromise that alienated liberals and conservatives, the gay community and the military.

Clinton's major goal was affordable healthcare. But special interests mobilized in opposition: the insurance industry worried about lost profits; the business community feared higher taxes; the medical community worried about more regulation, lower government reimbursement rates, and reduced healthcare quality. The healthcare task force, cochaired by Hillary Rodham Clinton, could not defeat these forces and healthcare failed.

"Republican Revolution" and Political Compromise

New-style Republicans challenged the beleaguered Clinton. In September 1994, more than three hundred Republican candidates for the House of Representatives endorsed the Contract with America. Developed under the leadership of Georgia representative **Newt Gingrich**, the Contract promised "the end of [big] government… [and] the beginning of a Congress that respects the values and shares the faith of the American family." It called for a balanced-budget amendment to the Constitution, reduction of the capital gains tax, a two-year limit on welfare payments (while making unmarried mothers under eighteen ineligible), and increased defense spending.

In the midterm elections, the Republican Party mobilized socially conservative voters to take control of both houses of Congress for the first time since 1954. Many Republicans believed attempts to weaken federal power and dismantle the welfare state would succeed.

But while they supported reducing government spending, many Americans opposed cuts to specific programs, including Medicare and Medicaid, education and college loans, highway construction, farm subsidies, veterans' benefits, and Social Security. Republicans made a bigger mistake when they issued Clinton an ultimatum on the federal budget and forced the government to suspend all nonessential action during the winter of 1995–1996.

Such struggles led Clinton to make compromises that moved American politics to the right. For example, he signed the 1996 Personal Responsibility and Work Opportunity Act, a welfare reform measure mandating that heads of families on welfare must find work within two years (though states could exempt 20 percent of recipients), limiting welfare benefits to five years over an individual's lifetime, and making many legal immigrants ineligible. The Telecommunications Act of 1996, signed by Clinton, reduced diversity in media by permitting companies to own more television and radio stations.

Clinton was reelected in 1996 (defeating Republican Bob Dole and Reform Party candidate Ross Perot), partly because Clinton stole some of the conservatives' thunder. He declared that "the era of big government is over" and invoked family values, a centerpiece of the Republican campaign. Sometimes Clinton's actions were true compromises; other times, he reclaimed issues from the conservatives, as when he redefined family values as "fighting for the family-leave law."

Newt Gingrich: Republican Congressman who co-authored the 1994 "Contract with America" pledging tax cuts, congressional term limits, tougher crime laws, anti-pornography measures, a balanced-budget amendment, and other reforms.

Link to the 1994 Republican Party's "Contract with America."

Clinton's legislative accomplishments were modest but included the Family and Medical Leave Act, guaranteeing 91 million workers the right to take time off to care for ailing relatives or newborn children. The Health Insurance Portability and Accountability Act ensured that, when Americans changed jobs, they would not lose health insurance because of preexisting medical conditions. Clinton created national parks that protected 3.2 million acres of American land and made progress cleaning up toxic waste dumps. However, the 1990s will most likely be remembered for its prosperity and economic growth.

Political Partisanship and Scandal

Political battles were divisive and ugly as the political right attacked Clinton with vehemence. Hillary Clinton was a frequent target; when she told a hostile interviewer during her husband's first presidential campaign, "I suppose I could have stayed home and baked cookies ... But what I decided to do was pursue my profession." The *New York Post* called her "an insult to most women." And an independent counsel's office headed by Kenneth Starr, a conservative Republican and former judge, would spend $72 million investigating allegations of wrongdoing by the Clintons. Starr was originally charged with investigating Whitewater, a 1970s Arkansas real-estate deal in which the Clintons had invested. He found no evidence against the Clintons, but Starr expanded his investigation and proved that Clinton lied to a grand jury when he testified that he had not engaged in sexual relations with twenty-two-year-old White House intern Monica Lewinsky.

In a 445-page report to Congress, Starr outlined eleven possible grounds for impeachment, accusing Clinton of lying under oath, obstruction of justice, witness tampering, and abuse of power. In December 1998, the House of Representatives, voting along party lines, concluded that the president committed perjury and obstructed justice. Clinton became the second president to face a trial in the Senate, which has the constitutional responsibility to decide (by two-thirds vote) whether to remove a president from office.

But the American people did not want Clinton removed from office. Polls showed that large majorities approved of his job performance, even while condemning his personal behavior. Many did not believe his actions constituted "high crimes and misdemeanors" (normally acts such as treason) required by the Constitution for impeachment. The Republican-controlled Senate, responding partly to popular opinion, did not vote to convict Clinton.

Politics, the Media, and Celebrity Culture

Clinton was not the first president to engage in illicit sex. President John F. Kennedy had numerous sexual affairs, including one with a nineteen-year-old intern. But after the 1970s Watergate scandals, the media no longer turned a blind eye to presidential misconduct. The fiercely competitive news networks relied on scandal, spectacle, and crisis to lure viewers. The 1990s partisan political wars created a take-no-prisoners climate. Both Republican Speaker of the House Newt Gingrich and his successor, Robert Livingston, resigned when evidence of their extramarital affairs surfaced. Finally, as former Clinton aide Sidney Blumenthal writes, the impeachment struggle was part of the culture wars: "a monumental battle over ... cultural mores and the position of women in American society, and about the character of the American people."

Violence and Anger in American Society

Political extremism exploded on April 19, 1995, when 168 people were killed in a bomb blast that destroyed the nine-story Alfred P. Murrah Federal Building in Oklahoma City.

At first, many blamed Middle Eastern terrorists. But a charred piece of truck axle two blocks away, with a still legible vehicle identification number, revealed that the bomber was Timothy McVeigh, a white American and Persian Gulf War veteran. He sought revenge for the deaths of Branch Davidian religious sect members, whom he believed the FBI deliberately slaughtered in a standoff over firearms charges two years before in Waco, Texas.

In subsequent months, reporters and investigators discovered militias, tax resisters, and white-supremacist groups nationwide. These groups believed that the federal government was controlled by "sinister forces," including Zionists, cultural elitists, and the United Nations. After McVeigh's act of domestic terrorism, many groups lost members.

On April 20, 1999, eighteen-year-old Eric Harris and seventeen-year-old Dylan Klebold opened fire on classmates and teachers at Columbine High School in Littleton, Colorado, killing thirteen before killing themselves. No clear reason why two academically successful students in a middle-class suburb would commit mass murder emerged. Students in Paducah, Kentucky; Springfield, Oregon; and Jonesboro, Arkansas, also massacred classmates.

Then, two hate crimes shocked the nation. In 1998, James Byrd Jr., a forty-nine-year-old African American, was murdered by three white supremacists who dragged him with a chain from the back of a pickup truck in Jasper, Texas. Later that year, Matthew Shepherd, a gay college student, was beaten and left tied to a wooden fence in freezing weather outside Laramie, Wyoming. His killers said they were humiliated when he flirted with them at a bar. To some, these murders signified the strength of racism and homophobia in the United States. Others saw Americans' horror over these murders as a sign of positive change.

Clinton's Diplomacy

Internationally, the United States occupied a uniquely powerful position in the 1990s. The demise of the Soviet Union created a one-superpower world in which the United States stood far above other powers in political, military, and economic might. Yet in his first term Clinton was more wary in traditional aspects of foreign policy—great-power diplomacy, arms control, regional disputes—than in facilitating American cultural and trade expansion. Recalling the public's impatience in the Vietnam debacle, he was suspicious of foreign military involvements.

Clinton's mistrust of foreign interventions was cemented by the difficulties in Somalia. In 1992, Bush sent U.S. Marines to the East African nation as part of a U.N. effort to ensure that humanitarian supplies reached starving Somalis. But in summer 1993, when Americans were attacked there, Clinton withdrew U.S. troops. And he did not intervene in Rwanda, where in 1994 the majority Hutus butchered 800,000 of the minority Tutsis in a brutal civil war.

Balkan Crisis

Many administration officials argued for using America's power to contain ethnic hatreds, support human rights, and promote democracy worldwide. That notion was tested in the Balkans, where

Bosnian Muslims, Serbs, and Croats were killing one another. Clinton talked tough against Serbian aggression and atrocities in Bosnia-Herzegovina, especially the Serbs' "ethnic cleansing" of Muslims through massacres and rape camps. He occasionally ordered air strikes, but he primarily emphasized diplomacy. In late 1995, American diplomats brokered a fragile peace.

But Yugoslav president Slobodan Milosevic continued the anti-Muslim and anti-Croat fervor. When Serb forces moved to violently rid Kosovo of its majority ethnic Albanians, reports of Serbian atrocities and a major refugee crisis stirred world opinion and pressed Clinton to intervene. In 1999, U.S.-led NATO forces launched a massive aerial bombardment of Serbia. Milosevic withdrew from Kosovo, where U.S. troops joined a U.N. peacekeeping force.

Agreements in the Middle East

In the Middle East, Clinton tried to help the PLO and Israel settle their differences. In September 1993, the PLO's Yasir Arafat and Israel's prime minister, Yitzhak Rabin, signed an agreement at the White House for Palestinian self-rule in the Gaza Strip and the West Bank's Jericho. The following year Israel signed a peace accord with Jordan, further reducing the chances of another Arab-Israeli war. Radical anti-Arafat Palestinians, however, continued terrorist attacks on Israelis, while extremist Israelis killed Palestinians and, in November 1995, Rabin himself. Only after American-conducted negotiations and renewed violence in the West Bank did Israel agree in early 1997 to withdraw troops from the Palestinian city of Hebron. Thereafter, the peace process alternately sagged and spurted.

International environmentalism also gathered pace in the 1990s. The George H. W. Bush administration had opposed many provisions of the 1992 Rio de Janeiro Treaty protecting the diversity of plant and animal species and resisted stricter rules to reduce **global warming**. Clinton, urged on by his environmentalist vice president Al Gore, signed the 1997 Kyoto protocol, which aimed to combat carbon dioxide and other emissions. But facing strong opposition, Clinton never submitted the protocol for ratification to the Republican-controlled Senate.

global warming: Worldwide surge in average temperatures most scientists attribute to greenhouse-gas emissions.

Bin Laden and Al Qaeda

Meanwhile, the threat to U.S. interests by Islamic fundamentalism loomed. Senior White House officials worried **Al Qaeda** (Arabic for "the base"), an international terrorist network led by Osama bin Laden, wanted to purge Muslim countries of what it considered the profane influence of the West.

The son of a Yemen-born construction tycoon in Saudi Arabia, bin Laden had supported the Afghan Mujahidin in their struggle against Soviet occupation. He then founded Al Qaeda and financed terrorist projects with his substantial inheritance. Then he focused on American targets. In 1995, a car bomb in Riyadh killed 7 people, 5 of them Americans. In 1998, bombings at the American embassies in Kenya and Tanzania killed 224 people, including 12 Americans. In Yemen in 2000, a boat laden with explosives hit the destroyer USS *Cole,* killing 17 American sailors. Although bin Laden masterminded and financed these attacks, he eluded U.S. attempts to apprehend him. In 1998, Clinton approved a plan to assassinate bin Laden, but it failed.

Al Qaeda: A radical Islamic group founded in the late 1980s and headed by Osama bin Laden; it relies on an international network of cells to carry out terrorist attacks against the West, particularly the United States and its allies, in the name of Islamic fundamentalism.

Globalization and Prosperity

For most Americans, the late 1990s marked unprecedented peace and prosperity. Between 1991 and 1999, the Dow Jones Industrial Average climbed from 3,169 to a high of 11,497. The booming market benefited the middle class and the wealthy, as mutual funds, 401(k) plans, and other new investment vehicles drew a majority of Americans into the stock market. In 1952, only 4 percent of U.S. households owned stocks; by 2000, almost 60 percent did.

At the end of the 1990s, unemployment was 4.3 percent—the lowest peacetime rate since 1957. That made it easier to implement welfare reform, and welfare rolls declined 50 percent. Both the richest 5 percent and poorest 20 percent of American households saw their incomes rise almost 25 percent. That translated to an average gain of $50,000 for the top 5 percent and only $2,880 for the bottom 20 percent, further widening the gap between rich and poor. Still, by 1999, more than two-thirds of Americans were homeowners—the highest percentage in history.

The roots of the 1990s boom were in the 1970s, when corporations began investing in new technologies, retooling plants, and cutting labor costs. Specifically, companies reduced the influence of organized labor by moving operations to the union-weak South and West and to countries such as China and Mexico, with cheap labor and lax pollution controls.

Digital Revolution   The rapid development of information technology— computers, fax machines, cell phones, and the Internet— had a huge economic impact in the 1980s and 1990s. New companies and industries sprang up, many headquartered in California's Silicon Valley. By the late 1990s, the *Forbes* list of the 400 Richest Americans featured high-tech leaders such as Microsoft's

Students and their teacher gather around a laptop at an elementary school in Hebei Province, China. This innovative tool for learning connects these students to resources that were not easily accessible in the past.

Bill Gates, the wealthiest person in the world with worth approaching $100 billion, as his company produced the operating software for most personal computers.

The heart of this technological revolution was the microprocessor. Introduced in 1970 by Intel, it miniaturized a computer's central processing unit, enabling small machines to perform calculations previously requiring large machines. Computing chores that took a week in the early 1970s took only a minute by 2000; the cost of storing one megabyte of information fell from $5,000 in 1975 to $.17 in 1999.

Clinton and his advisers helped further spur economic growth by abandoning the middle-class tax cut and making deficit reduction a top priority. White House officials rightly concluded that, if the deficit—which topped $500 billion—could be brought under control, interest rates would drop and the economy would rebound. And that is what happened. By 1997, the budget deficit had been erased, and the gross national product rose by an average of 3.5–4 percent annually.

Globalization of Business

The journalist Thomas L. Friedman asserted that the post–Cold War world was the age of **globalization**, characterized by the integration of markets, finance, and technologies. U.S. officials lowered trade and investment barriers, completing the **North American Free Trade Agreement (NAFTA)** with Canada and Mexico in 1993, and in 1994 concluding the Uruguay Round of the General Agreement on Tariffs and Trade (GATT), which lowered tariffs for the seventy member nations that accounted for about 80 percent of world trade. The Clinton administration also endorsed the 1995 creation of the **World Trade Organization** (WTO), to administer and enforce agreements made at the Uruguay Round. Finally, the president formed a National Economic Council to promote trade missions around the world.

Multinational corporations were the hallmark of this global economy. By 2000, there were 63,000 parent companies worldwide and 690,000 foreign affiliates. Some, such as Nike and Gap, Inc., subcontracted some production to developing countries with the lowest labor costs. World exports totaled $5.4 trillion in 1998, twice that of 1978. U.S. exports reached $680 billion in 1998, but imports rose to $907 billion (for a trade deficit of $227 billion). Sometimes the multinationals affected foreign policy, as when Clinton in 1995 extended full diplomatic recognition to Vietnam under pressure from such corporations as Coca-Cola, Citigroup, General Motors, and United Airlines, which wanted to enter that emerging market.

globalization: The removal of barriers to flow of capital, goods, and ideas across national borders.

North American Free Trade Association (NAFTA): Pact that admitted Mexico to the free-trade zone that the United States and Canada had created earlier.

World Trade Organization: International organization that regulates the global trading system and provides dispute resolution between member nations.

Critics of Globalization

While the administration promoted open markets, labor unions argued that free-trade agreements exacerbated the trade deficit and exported American jobs. Average wages for American workers declined after 1973, from $320 per week to $260 by the mid-1990s. Other critics maintained that globalization widened the gap between rich and poor countries, creating a mass of "slave laborers" in poor countries working under conditions that would be intolerable in the West. Environmentalists charged that globalization exported pollution to countries unprepared to deal with it. Still others warned about the power of multinational corporations over traditional cultures.

Antiglobalization fervor reached a peak in the fall of 1999, when thousands of protesters disrupted the WTO meeting in Seattle. In the months that followed, there were sizable protests at meetings of the International Monetary Fund (IMF) and the World Bank.

Target: McDonald's

Activists also targeted corporations, such as the Gap, Starbucks, Nike, and, especially, McDonald's, which by 1995 was serving 30 million customers daily in over one hundred countries. Critics assailed the company's alleged exploitation of workers, its high-fat menu, and its role in creating an increasingly homogeneous world culture. For six years starting in 1996, McDonald's endured hundreds of often-violent protests, including bombings in Rome, Prague, London, Macao, Rio de Janeiro, and Jakarta.

Others decried the violence and the arguments of the antiglobalization campaigners. True, some economists acknowledged, statistics showed that global inequality had grown. But if one included quality-of-life measurements, such as literacy and health, global inequality had declined. Some studies found that wage and job losses for U.S. workers were caused not primarily by globalization factors, such as imports, production outsourcing, and immigration, but by technological change that made production more efficient. Some researchers saw no evidence that governments' sovereignty had been compromised or that there was a "race to the bottom" in labor and environmental standards from globalization.

As for creating a homogeneous global culture, McDonald's, others said, tailored its menu and operating practices to local tastes. And although American movies, TV programs, music, computer software, and other intellectual property dominated world markets, foreign competition also arrived in the United States. American children were gripped by the Japanese fad Pokemon, for example, and satellite television created a worldwide following for European soccer teams.

The Bush-Gore Race

The strong economy should have given Vice President **Al Gore** an advantage in the 2000 presidential election. But Gore failed to inspire voters. Earnest and highly intelligent, with a resume that included service in Vietnam and six terms in Congress, he appeared to be a well-informed policy wonk rather than a charismatic leader.

Gore's Republican opponent was the son of former president George H. W. Bush. An indifferent student, **George W. Bush** graduated from Yale in 1968 and pulled strings to jump ahead of a one-and-a-half-year waiting list for the Texas Air National Guard, thus avoiding service in Vietnam. He had a rocky career in the oil business, but Bush's fortunes improved during his father's presidency, and in 1994 he was elected to the first of two terms as governor of Texas.

Al Gore: Long-time Democratic Senator from Tennessee and vice president under Bill Clinton (1993–2001); unsuccessfully ran for president in the highly contested 2000 race; won a 2007 Nobel Peace Prize for his advocacy and expertise on environmental issues, particularly global warming.

George W. Bush: 43rd President of the United States, from 2001 to 2008; son of 41st president George H. W. Bush

The Contested Election of 2000

Al Gore narrowly won the popular vote, but not the presidency. It all came down to Florida (where Bush's brother Jeb was governor) and its twenty-five electoral votes. In the initial tally, Bush narrowly edged Gore out in Florida, but the close margin legally required a recount. In several heavily African American counties, tens of thousands of votes went uncounted because voters failed to fully dislodge the "chads," small perforated squares, when punching the paper ballots. Lawyers struggled over whether "hanging chads" (partially detached) and "pregnant chads" (punched but not detached) were sufficient signs of voter intent. In Palm Beach County, many elderly Jewish residents were confused by a poorly designed ballot and accidentally selected the allegedly anti-Semitic Pat Buchanan instead of Gore. After thirty-six days, with court cases at the state and federal levels, the Supreme Court voted 5 to 4 along narrowly partisan lines to end the recount process. Florida's electoral votes—and the presidency—went to George Bush. Struggles over the election further polarized the nation.

With the close election, many believed Bush would govern from the center. Some also thought he moved to the right during the election only to ensure conservative evangelical Christian votes. But Bush governed from the right, arguably further to the right than any other modern administration.

9/11 and the War in Iraq

In international affairs, the administration charted a unilateralist course. Given America's preponderant power, senior Bush officials reasoned, it did not need other countries' help. Accordingly, Bush withdrew the United States from the 1972 Anti-Ballistic Missile Treaty with Russia to develop a National Missile Defense system similar to Reagan's "Star Wars." The White House renounced the 1997 **Kyoto protocol** on controlling global warming and opposed a protocol strengthening the 1972 Biological and Toxin Weapons Convention. These decisions and the administration's hands-off policy toward the Israeli-Palestinian peace process caused consternation in Europe.

Kyoto protocol: A protocol setting strict emission targets for industrialized nations. President Bush refused to sign the agreement, making the United States one of only four nations that declined participation.

9/11

Then came September 11, 2001. On that sunny Tuesday morning, nineteen hijackers seized control of four commercial jets departing from East Coast airports. At 8:46 a.m. one plane crashed into the 110-story North Tower of the World Trade Center in New York City. At 9:03 a.m., a second plane flew into the South Tower. In under two hours, both buildings collapsed, killing thousands of office workers, firefighters, and police officers. At 9:43, the third plane crashed into the Pentagon. The fourth plane was also headed toward Washington, but several passengers, learning of the World Trade Center attacks through cell-phone conversations, stormed the cockpit; in the scuffle, the plane crashed in Somerset County, Pennsylvania, killing all aboard.

More than three thousand people died in the deadliest act of terrorism in history. The hijackers—fifteen Saudi Arabians, two Emiratis, one Lebanese, and an Egyptian—had ties to Al Qaeda. Officials in the Clinton and Bush administrations had warned that an Al Qaeda attack was inevitable, but neither administration made counterterrorism a foreign policy priority.

Afghanistan War

In an instant, counterterrorism was priority number one. President Bush responded with military force. Al Qaeda operated out of Afghanistan with the blessing of the ruling Taliban, a repressive Islamic fundamentalist group that gained power in 1996. In early October, the United States launched a sustained bombing campaign against Taliban and Al Qaeda positions, and sent special operations forces to help a resistance organization in northern Afghanistan. Within two months, the Taliban was driven from power, although bin Laden and top Taliban leaders eluded capture.

As administration officials acknowledged, military victory did not end the terrorist threat. Bush spoke of a long struggle against evil forces, in which the nations of the world were either with the United States or against it. Some questioned whether a war on terrorism could ever be won in a meaningful sense, given that the foe was a nonstate actor. Stunned by September 11, most Americans experienced a renewed sense of national unity and pride. Flag sales soared, and Bush's approval ratings skyrocketed.

AFP/Getty

The attacks on 9/11 brought forth an outpouring of sympathy for the victims and their families, and for the United States generally, from people around the world. Here firefighters in Taipei, Taiwan, attend a prayer service during a global day of mourning.

PATRIOT Act

USA PATRIOT Act: Controversial anti-terrorist law that extended the government's legal surveillance power to allow monitoring of telephone and internet communications and library searches.

But the new patriotism had a dark side. Congress passed the **USA PATRIOT Act** (Uniting and Strengthening America by Providing Appropriate Tools Required to Intercept and Obstruct Terrorism), making it easier for law enforcement to conduct searches, wiretap telephones, and obtain electronic records on individuals. Attorney General John Ashcroft approved giving FBI agents new powers to monitor the Internet, mosques, and rallies. Civil libertarians charged that the Justice Department overstepped, and some judges ruled against the tactics. Yet, according to a June 2002 Gallup poll, 80 percent of Americans were willing to exchange some freedoms for security.

Weeks after the attacks, 71 percent surveyed said that they felt depressed, and one-third had trouble sleeping. Yet people continued shopping in malls, visiting amusement parks, and working in skyscrapers. Although airline bookings dropped significantly early on, people returned to the skies. In Washington, Democrats and Republicans again sparred over judicial appointments, energy policy, and the proposed new **Department of Homeland Security**, approved by Congress in November 2002 to coordinate defense against terrorism.

Department of Homeland Security: Cabinet-level department created by Congress to coordinate anti-terrorism efforts. Various agencies were placed under its jurisdiction including the Coast Guard, the Customs Service, the Federal Emergency Management Agency (FEMA), and the Immigration and Naturalization Service.

Economic Uncertainty

Economically, the months before September 11 witnessed a collapse of the "dot-coms," Internet companies that were the darlings of Wall Street in the 1990s. In 2001, some five hundred dot-coms declared bankruptcy or closed. There were other economic warning signs as well, notably a meager 0.2 percent growth rate in goods and services for 2001's second quarter. Corporate revenues were also down.

Economic concerns deepened after 9/11 with a four-day closing of Wall Street and sharp drop in stock prices. The Dow Jones Industrial Average plunged 14.26 percent. The markets eventually rebounded, but questions remained about the economy's health. Neither economic uncertainty nor the failure to capture **Osama bin Laden** dented Bush's popularity. In the 2002 midterm elections, Republicans retook the Senate and increased their majority in the House.

International Responses

Overseas, the president's standing was not nearly so high. Immediately after September 11, governments worldwide announced they would work with Washington against terrorism. But within a year, Bush's good-versus-evil stance put off foreign observers. When the president hinted that the United States might unilaterally strike Saddam Hussein's Iraq or deal forcefully with North Korea or Iran—Bush's "axis of evil"—many allied governments strongly objected.

Bush and other top officials argued that in an age of terrorism, the United States would not wait for a potential security threat to become real; it would strike first. Americans, Bush declared had to be "ready for preemptive action when necessary to defend our liberty and to defend our lives." Critics, among them world leaders, called it recklessly aggressive and contrary to international law.

But Bush was determined, particularly on Iraq. Several of his top advisers, including Secretary of Defense Donald Rumsfeld and Vice President Dick Cheney, had wanted to oust Saddam Hussein since the 1991 Gulf War. After the Twin Towers fell, they folded Iraq into the war on terrorism—even though counterterrorism experts saw no link between Saddam and Al Qaeda. Initially, Secretary of State **Colin Powell**, the first African American in that post, kept the focus on Afghanistan, but gradually the White House shifted. By spring 2002 a secret consensus was reached: Saddam Hussein would be removed by force.

Why Iraq?

In September 2002, Bush challenged the United Nations to enforce its resolutions against Iraq, or the United States would act itself. He and his aides offered shifting reasons for getting tough with Iraq. They said Saddam was a major threat to the United States and its allies, a leader who possessed and would use banned biological and chemical "weapons of mass destruction" (WMDs) and who sought nuclear weapons. They claimed, contrary to their own intelligence, that he had ties to Al Qaeda and could be linked to the 9/11 attacks.

But there were other motivations as well. Neoconservatives claimed that ousting Saddam would enhance the security of Israel, the United States' key Middle East ally, and start a chain reaction extending democracy throughout the region. White House political strategists believed a swift removal of a hated dictator would assure Bush's reelection. And Bush wanted to prevent an Iraq armed with WMDs from destabilizing an oil-rich region.

Congressional Approval

Bush claimed he did not need congressional authorization for military action against Iraq, but sought it anyway. In early October 2002, the House of Representatives voted 296 to 133 and the Senate 77–23 to authorize force against Iraq. Many who voted in favor were unwilling to

Osama bin Laden: A wealthy Islamic fundamentalist militant who had been expelled from his native Saudi Arabia in 1991 and took refuge in Sudan, where he financed large-scale construction and agricultural projects and amassed followers to his Al Qaeda terrorist organization, masterminding several attacks, among them September 11, 2001, attack on the United States.

Colin Powell: Four-star general who served as National Security Adviser (1987–1989), Chairman of the Joint of Chiefs of Staff (1989–1993), and Secretary of State (2001–2005).

defy Bush so close to midterm elections, even though they opposed military action without U.N. sanction. Critics complained that the president had not presented evidence that Saddam Hussein constituted an imminent threat or was connected to the 9/11 attacks. Bush switched to a less hawkish stance, and in early November, the U.N. Security Council unanimously approved Resolution 1441, imposing rigorous arms inspections on Iraq.

But the Security Council was divided over the next move. In late January 2003, the weapons inspector's report castigated Iraq for failing to complete "the disarmament that was demanded of it" but also said it was too soon to tell whether inspections would succeed. Whereas U.S. and British officials said the time for diplomacy was up, France, Russia, and China called for more inspections. As the U.N. debate continued, Bush sent about 250,000 soldiers to the region. Britain sent about 45,000 troops.

Fall of Baghdad

In late February, the United States floated a resolution to the U.N. that proposed issuing an ultimatum to Iraq, but only three of the fifteen Security Council members agreed. Bush abandoned the resolution and diplomatic efforts on March 17, when he ordered Saddam Hussein to leave Iraq within forty-eight hours or face an attack. Saddam ignored the ultimatum, and on March 19 the United States and Britain launched an aerial bombardment of Baghdad and other areas. A ground invasion followed (see Map 33.1). On April 9, Baghdad fell.

Thus, when violence soon erupted, U.S. planners seemed powerless to respond. The plight of ordinary Iraqis deteriorated as the occupation authority proved unable to maintain order. Decisions by the Coalition Governing Council (CPA), headed by Ambassador Paul Bremer, made matters worse, notably Bremer's move in May to disband the Iraqi army. A multisided insurgency of Saddam loyalists, Iraqi nationalists, and foreign Islamic revolutionaries took shape; soon, U.S. occupying forces faced frequent ambushes. By October 2003, more troops died from these attacks than had perished in the initial invasion.

The chaos in Iraq and the failure to find weapons of mass destruction had critics questioning the war's validity. Prewar claims of a "rush to war" resounded again. Even defenders of the invasion castigated the administration for its failure to anticipate the occupation problems. In spring 2004, photos showing Iraqi detainees being abused by American guards at Abu Ghraib prison were broadcast worldwide, generating international condemnation.

Election of 2004

John Kerry: Senator from Massachusetts and Vietnam War veteran; Democratic nominee for president in 2004.

Facing reelection, President Bush expressed disgust at Abu Ghraib and denied charges that he and top aides condoned the abuse. The White House also claimed the transfer of sovereignty to an interim Iraqi government in June would flatten the insurgency. Bush's Democratic opponent, Senator **John Kerry** of Massachusetts, a Vietnam veteran who had voted for the Iraq resolution, never articulated a clear alternative strategy on the war. Bush won reelection with 51 percent of the popular vote to Kerry's 48 percent and 279 electoral votes to Kerry's 252. The GOP also increased its majorities in the House and Senate.

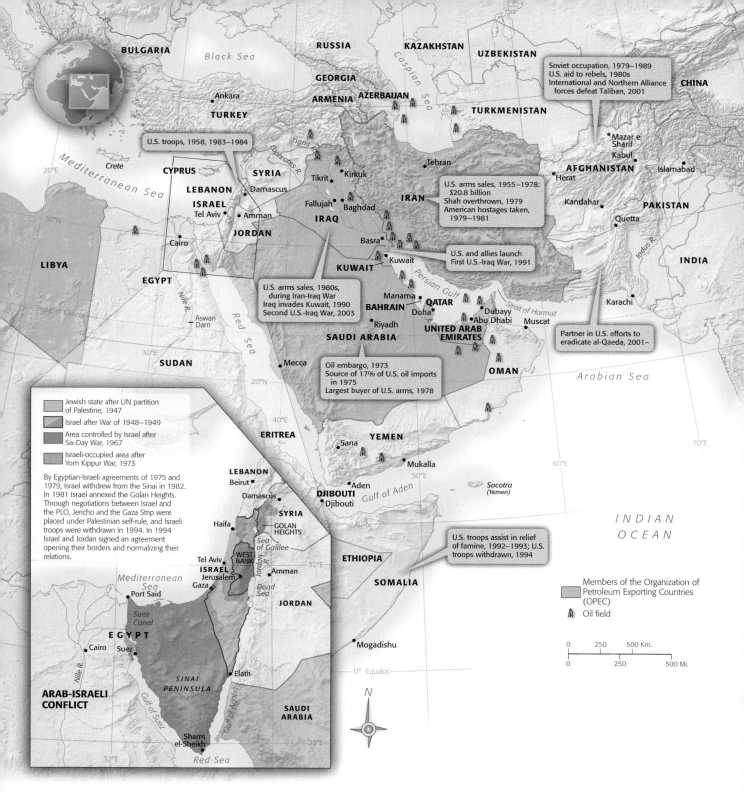

Black Sea

BULGARIA

RUSSIA

KAZAKHSTAN

UZBEKISTAN

Caspian Sea

CHINA

Soviet occupation, 1979–1989
U.S. aid to rebels, 1980s
International and Northern Alliance
forces defeat Taliban, 2001

GEORGIA

ARMENIA

AZERBAIJAN

TURKMENISTAN

Ankara

TURKEY

Mazar e
Sharif

Kabul

Islamabad

Mediterranean Sea

Crete

20°E

CYPRUS

U.S. troops, 1958, 1983–1984

SYRIA

Tigris R.

Euphrates R.

Tehran

AFGHANISTAN

Herat

LEBANON

Damascus

Tikrit

Kirkuk

ISRAEL

Tel Aviv

Amman

Fallujah

Baghdad

30°N

IRAQ

IRAN

U.S. arms sales, 1955–1978:
$20.8 billion
Shah overthrown, 1979
American hostages taken,
1979–1981

Kandahar

PAKISTAN

Quetta

Cairo

JORDAN

Basra

30°N

LIBYA

EGYPT

Nile R.

KUWAIT

Kuwait

U.S. and allies launch
First U.S.-Iraq War, 1991

Persian Gulf

Strait of Hormuz

INDIA

Karachi

Aswan
Dam

U.S. arms sales, 1980s,
during Iran-Iraq War
Iraq invades Kuwait, 1990
Second U.S.-Iraq War, 2003

Manama

BAHRAIN

Doha

QATAR

Dubayy

Abu Dhabi

Muscat

Partner in U.S. efforts to
eradicate al-Qaeda, 2001–

Red Sea

SUDAN

30°E

Riyadh

UNITED ARAB
EMIRATES

Tropic of Cancer

Mecca

SAUDI ARABIA

Oil embargo, 1973
Source of 17% of U.S. oil imports
in 1975
Largest buyer of U.S. arms, 1978

OMAN

Arabian Sea

40°E

20°N

Jewish state after UN partition
of Palestine, 1947

Israel after War of 1948–1949

Area controlled by Israel after
Six-Day War, 1967

Israeli-occupied area after
Yom Kippur War, 1973

By Egyptian-Israeli agreements of 1975 and
1979, Israel withdrew from the Sinai in 1982.
In 1981 Israel annexed the Golan Heights.
Through negotiations between Israel and
the PLO, Jericho and the Gaza Strip were
placed under Palestinian self-rule, and Israeli
troops were withdrawn in 1994. In 1994
Israel and Jordan signed an agreement
opening their borders and normalizing their
relations.

ERITREA

LEBANON

Beirut

Damascus

SYRIA

Haifa

GOLAN
HEIGHTS

Sea
of Galilee

YEMEN

Sana

Mukalla

60°E

70°E

50°E

Aden

Gulf of Aden

Socotra
(Yemen)

DJIBOUTI

Djibouti

ETHIOPIA

U.S. troops assist in relief
of famine, 1992–1993; U.S.
troops withdrawn, 1994

INDIAN
OCEAN

Tel Aviv

WEST
BANK

ISRAEL

Jerusalem

Gaza

Jordan R.

Dead
Sea

SOMALIA

32°E

Mediterranean
Sea

Port Said

JORDAN

Amman

Members of the Organization of
Petroleum Exporting Countries
(OPEC)

Oil field

Nile R.

Suez
Canal

EGYPT

Cairo

Suez

0   250   500 Km.

0   250   500 Mi.

Mogadishu

0° Equator

ARAB-ISRAELI
CONFLICT

SINAI
PENINSULA

Elath

Gulf of Suez

Gulf of Aqaba

SAUDI
ARABIA

28°N

N

Sharm
el-Sheikh

32°E

36°E

Red Sea

MAP 33.1

The Middle East

Middle East nations maintained precarious relations with the United States. To protect its interests, the United
States extended large amounts of economic and military aid and sold them weapons. The Arab-Israeli
dispute particularly upended order, although the peace process moved forward intermittently.

Source: Copyright © Cengage Learning

America Isolated   Internationally, Bush faced criticism because of Iraq, Abu Ghraib, his administration's lack of engagement in the Israeli-Palestinian dispute, and seeming disdain for diplomacy generally. The White House, critics said, rightly sought to prevent North Korea and Iran from joining the nuclear club but seemed incapable of making it happen. In Europe, Bush continued to be depicted as a gun-slinging cowboy whose aggressive policies threatened world peace.

Iraq, though, remained the chief problem. The bill for the war now exceeded $1 billion per week. In March 2005, American war dead reached 1,500; in December 2006, it reached 3,000. Meanwhile, by mid-2006, estimates of Iraqi civilian deaths ranged from 60,000 to 655,000. Iraqi casualties resulted from insurgent suicide attacks, U.S. bombing of suspected insurgent hideouts, and increasing sectarian violence between Sunnis and Shi'ites.

The Bush administration denied that Iraq had degenerated into civil war or that the struggle had become a Vietnam-like quagmire, but it seemed uncertain how to end the fighting. In Congress and the press, calls for withdrawal from Iraq multiplied, but skeptics cautioned it could make things worse, triggering sectarian bloodshed and a collapse of the Baghdad government. The power and regional influence of neighboring Iran would increase, and American credibility would be undermined throughout the Middle East. The 2007 "surge" of increased U.S. forces in Iraq contributed to a drastic reduction in violence, as commanders shifted to a counterinsurgency strategy emphasizing protection of the population. But the surge did little to promote political reconciliation among competing Iraqi factions. That objective remained elusive when Bush left office in early 2009.

Domestic Politics in Post 9/11 America

The centerpiece Bush's domestic agenda, achieved before the 9/11attacks, was a $1.3 trillion tax cut—the largest in U.S. history. As Bush intended, it wiped out the $200 billion budget surplus he inherited from the Clinton administration.

The Presidency of George W. Bush   Much of Bush's agenda fit with conservative principles. Religious conservatives liked the newly prominent role of religion in politics. The president spoke frequently of his faith; Attorney General John Ashcroft, a Pentecostal Christian, held prayer meetings every morning in the Justice Department. And Bush appointed the medical director of a Christian pregnancy-counseling center whose website claimed that the "distribution of birth control is demeaning to women … and adverse to human health and happiness" to head the nation's federal family planning program.

Bush also advocated economic deregulation. His administration dismantled environmental restrictions on the oil, timber, and mining industries, and as Wall Street developed an array of risky financial instruments, he remained hands-off. While his plan to partially privatize Social Security or reform immigration failed, Bush did reshape the Supreme Court. Fifty-year-old conservative U.S. Circuit Court judge John Roberts was confirmed as chief justice after Chief Justice William Renquist died, and another strong conservative, 55-year-old Samuel Alito, became junior associate justice when Sandra Day O'Connor resigned.

But Bush often turned to a form of "big government" conservatism. Bush dramatically increased the federal government's role in public education through his "**No Child Left Behind**" initiative. Meant to fix a "broken system of education that dismisses certain children and classes of children as unteachable," the legislation linked federal funding to state action: to receive federal education dollars, states had to set "high standards," evaluating students through standardized tests and holding schools accountable. While conservatives traditionally argued against federally subsidized medical care, the Bush administration created an expensive entitlement program covering prescription drugs for American seniors under Medicare.

No Child Left Behind: Label for Bush law mandating standardized testing in reading and math in grades four and eight.

Hurricane Katrina

Growing perceptions of administrative incompetence began to undermine Americans' confidence in Bush's administration. In late August, 2005, a major hurricane hit the U.S. Gulf Coast and New Orleans. **Hurricane Katrina** destroyed the levees that kept low-lying parts of New Orleans from being swamped by Lake Pontchartrain and surrounding canals. Floodwater covered 80 percent of New Orleans, and more than eighteen hundred people died.

Tens of thousands of people who lacked the resources to flee New Orleans sought shelter at the Superdome. Food and water quickly ran low and toilets backed up; people wrapped the dead in blankets and waited for rescue. Those outside the Gulf region, watching the suffering crowd of mainly poor, black New

Hurricane Katrina: Worst natural disaster in U.S. history; resulting flooding destroyed much of New Orleans and Gulf Coast in August 2005; poor handling of the crisis fueled cries of racism and tarnished the Bush administration.

AP Photo/Ben Sklar

Rescuers save a family from floodwaters in Bay St. Louis, Mississippi, after Hurricane Katrina. Katrina destroyed not only New Orleans, but much of the U.S. Gulf Coast from Louisiana into Alabama. The federal government designated 90,000 square miles as disaster area. More than 1,800 people lost their lives in the storm.

Orleanians at the Superdome, discussed what Democratic party leader Howard Dean called the "ugly truth": that poverty remains linked to race. The public also worried about administrative mismanagement and the president's seeming indifference.

Economic Recession

But larger troubles were brewing: American home prices—a "housing bubble"—were about to collapse. After initial deregulation in the 1980s, financial institutions sought new ways to expand their profits and experimented with "subprime" mortgages for people who previously would not have qualified for credit. By 2006, one-fifth of all home loans were subprime. As demand for homes kept rising, so did prices. Because housing prices kept going up, lenders saw little risk. If a family defaulted on their mortgage and lost their house, the property could be sold for more than it was worth. Wall Street firms bought up mortgages, bundling them together, good and bad, into multibillion dollar packages to sell to investors. These mortgage-backed securities—made possible by deregulation—were complex and risky.

This unstable structure began to fail in 2007, as more borrowers defaulted on mortgages. People tried to escape unaffordable mortgages by selling their houses, but housing prices plummeted. Increasingly, mortgages were larger than a home's value. And the financial institutions that gambled on mortgage-backed securities did not have enough capital to sustain such losses. Worldwide, banks were on the verge of collapse.

This crisis paralyzed the credit markets. Businesses couldn't get loans to buy raw materials or inventory; consumers couldn't get credit to buy large items, such as cars. Many Americans were already deeply in debt. In 2005, the average family spent more than it earned—and for those under 35, the savings rate was minus 16 percent. As credit tightened, people bought less. Businesses laid off workers, and unemployment climbed. The Bush administration attempted to prevent the financial system's collapse by bailing out those deemed "too big too fail." The Troubled Asset Relief Program (TARP) eventually provided $700 billion dollars in loans to failing institutions, but Americans on "main street" were angry that tax dollars rescued wealthy bankers on "Wall Street."

Election of 2008

In the 2008 presidential election, the hard-fought Democratic primary pitted New York senator Hillary Clinton against Illinois senator **Barack Obama**, forcing Americans to confront the meaning of race and gender in American society. Obama, who won the Democratic nomination, ran against Arizona senator John McCain, a Vietnam veteran who survived five years in a P.O.W. camp. McCain never drew enthusiastic support from socially conservative Republicans, though some embraced his choice of running mate, Alaska Governor Sarah Palin. Obama mobilized the grassroots: young people, African Americans, people who had never voted before. More than any previous candidate, he used technology to reach voters, who contributed millions of dollars through his website.

Republican vice presidential candidate Sarah Palin drew crowds, but appeared uninformed on key issues. Critics argued that McCain's choice of Palin showed weak judgment that could be disastrous in the presidency. The economy was the deciding

Barack Obama: 44th president (elected 2008) and the nation's first African American president who took office in the midst of the worst economic crisis since the Great Depression.

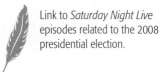

Link to *Saturday Night Live* episodes related to the 2008 presidential election.

factor: McCain's claim, in the midst of Wall Street's September 2008 meltdown, that "the fundamentals of our economy are strong" backfired, giving Obama victory in November.

Barack Obama

Link to the March 18, 2008, "Race Speech" by, at the time, presidential candidate, Barack Obama.

Barack Hussein Obama, the nation's forty-fourth president, was born in Hawai'i in 1961. His mother was a white woman from Kansas; his father a Kenyan graduate student at the University of Hawai'i. (The couple divorced when their child was two years old and each married again, giving Barack both African and Indonesian half-siblings.) Obama spent part of his childhood in Indonesia with his mother and attended high school in Hawai'i. After graduating from Harvard Law School, Obama became a community organizer in Chicago. He married fellow Harvard Law graduate Michelle Robinson, working as a civil rights lawyer and law professor at the University of Chicago before entering state politics in 1997. He gained national acclaim as a first-term senator for his keynote speech at the 2004 Democratic national convention.

Obama began his presidency with ambitious goals. He vowed to pass a comprehensive healthcare reform bill within the year, but he also had to confront his inheritance: two unresolved wars, a massive federal deficit, and a major recession. In February 2009, Obama signed legislation creating a $787 billion economic stimulus package to jumpstart the economy and supported expanding TARP and bailing out failing auto giants GM and Chrysler. The economy began a slow recovery in 2009, but unemployment rates remained high, reaching 10.2 percent. One in eight Americans received food stamps from the government, and Walmart pointed to evidence of hard times: a big jump in the purchase of kitchen storage containers for leftovers.

More than 75,000 people gathered in Chicago's Grant Park to celebrate Barack Obama's election on November 4, 2008.

Fierce partisan bickering stalled healthcare reform and job creation. Some saw the gridlock as proof that U.S. leaders were unable to address long-term social and economic challenges; others countered that the system was designed by the Founders to function slowly and cautiously.

In foreign affairs, Obama had more latitude. In Iraq, U.S. casualty figures continued to decline in 2009, and Obama planned to withdraw combat forces from the country by August 2010. After deliberating in fall 2009, Obama announced that he would boost U.S. troop numbers in Afghanistan by about 30,000, bringing the total to 100,000. To allay concerns that the war would stretch on indefinitely, Obama simultaneously declared that the United States would begin withdrawing its forces in 2011. Critics were unmoved, calling Afghanistan "Obama's War."

Link to President Obama's West Point speech announcing troop increase in Afghanistan.

Americans in the First Decade of the New Millennium

At the beginning of the twenty-first century, the United States is a nation of extraordinary diversity. Immigration reform in the mid-1960s opened U.S. borders to people from a wider variety of nations than previously. At the same time, new technologies—the Internet, cable and satellite television—replaced mass markets with niche markets. Everything from television shows to cosmetics to cars could be targeted toward specific groups defined by age, ethnicity, class, gender, or lifestyle choices. These changes helped to make Americans' understandings of identity more fluid and complex.

Race and Ethnicity in Recent America

In the 2000 U.S. government census, for the first time Americans could identify themselves as belonging to more than one race. The change acknowledged the growing number of Americans born to parents of different racial backgrounds. Critics, however, worried that, because census data are used for allocating resources, the new "multiracial" option would reduce the clout of minority groups. Thus, the federal government counted those who identified both as white and a racial or ethnic minority as belonging to the minority group. Consequently, the official population of some groups increased. Others rejected racial and ethnic categories altogether: 20 million people identified themselves simply as "American."

On October 17, 2006, the United States population passed 300 million. During the 1990s, the population of people of color grew twelve times as fast as the white population, fueled by immigration and birth rates. In 2003, Latinos passed African Americans to become the second largest ethnic or racial group (after non-Hispanic whites), making the United States the fifth largest "Latino" country in world (see Figure 33.1). Immigration from Asia also remained high, and in 2007, 5 percent of the U.S. population was Asian or Asian American. Most of this immigration is legal, but in 2005 an estimated 11.1 million people were in the United States without official documentation, up from 3 million in 1980.

The Changing American Family

Americans were increasingly divided over changing family structure (see Figure 33.2). The median age at marriage continued to rise, reaching 28.1 for men and 25.9 for women in 2009. In 2006, when households composed of married couples slipped below 50 percent for the first time, unmarried, opposite-sex partners made up about

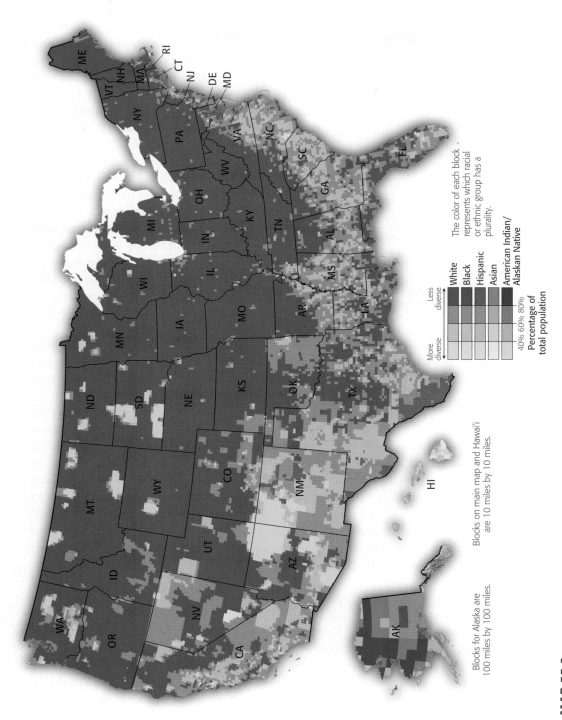

MAP 33.2

Mapping America's Diversity

Aggregate figures (more than 12 percent of the U.S. population was African American and about 4 percent Asian American in 2000, for example) convey America's ethnic and racial diversity. However, as this map shows, members of racial and ethnic groups are not distributed evenly throughout the nation.

Source: Adapted from the *New York Times National Edition,* April 1, 2001, "Portrait of a Nation," p. 18. Copyright 2001 by The New York Times Co. Reprinted with permission.

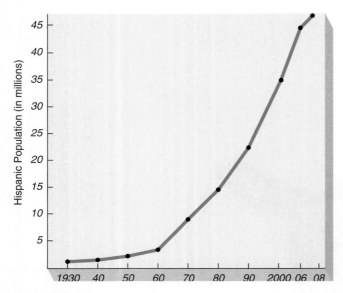

FIGURE 33.1
The Growth of the U.S. Hispanic Population

"Hispanic" combines people from a wide variety of national origins or ancestries—including all the nations of Central and South America, Mexico, Cuba, Puerto Rico, the Dominican Republic, Spain—as well as those who identify as Californio, Tejano, Nuevo Mexicano, and Mestizo.

Source: Adapted from the U.S. Department of Commerce, Economics and Statistics Information, Bureau of the Census, 1993 report "We, the American...Hispanics"; also recent Census Bureau figures for the Hispanic population.

5 percent of households, and same-sex couples accounted for just under 1 percent. One-third of female-partner households and one-fifth of male-partner households had children, and in 2002 the American Academy of Pediatrics endorsed adoption by gay couples. An antigay movement coexisted with support for the legal equality of gay, lesbian, transgendered, and bisexual Americans. Although many states and corporations extended domestic-partner benefits to gay couples, the federal Defense of Marriage Act, passed in 1996, defined marriage as a union between one man and one woman.

The birth rate to unmarried women increased to four of every ten babies in 2007. (In Sweden, the rate was 55 percent; in Japan 2 percent.) In the majority of married-couple families with children under eighteen, both parents held jobs. Although almost one-third of families with children had only one parent present—usually the mother—children also lived in blended families created by second marriages or moved between parents with joint custody. In 2006, the leading edge of the baby-boom generation turned sixty. As life expectancy increases, the growing number of elderly Americans will put enormous pressure on the nation's healthcare system and strain Social Security and Medicare.

Other health issues have become increasingly important. More than two-thirds of American adults are now overweight or obese—conditions linked to hypertension, cardiovascular disease, and diabetes. In 1995, no state had an adult obesity rate that hit 20 percent. By 2009, only Colorado fell below that 20 percent mark. Childhood obesity rates exceeded 30 percent in twenty-nine states. Cigarette smoking continues to slowly decline. About one-fifth of adults smoked in 2008, down from about one-third in 1980. Approximately 440,000 people die annually from smoking-related illnesses, and medical costs and lost productivity total about $157 billion a year.

Medicine, Science, and Religion

Rapid advances in biogenetics offer new possibilities and raise ethical conundrums. During in vitro fertilizations—in which sperm and egg combine in a sterile dish and the fertilized egg or eggs are then transferred to the uterus—five- or six-cell blastocytes are formed. These blastocytes contain stem cells, unspecialized cells that can be induced to become cells with specialized functions. For example, stem cells might become insulin-producing cells of the pancreas, and thus a cure for diabetes.

President Bush in 2001 called embryonic stem cell research "the leading edge of a series of moral hazards," because extracting stem cells destroys the blastocyte's

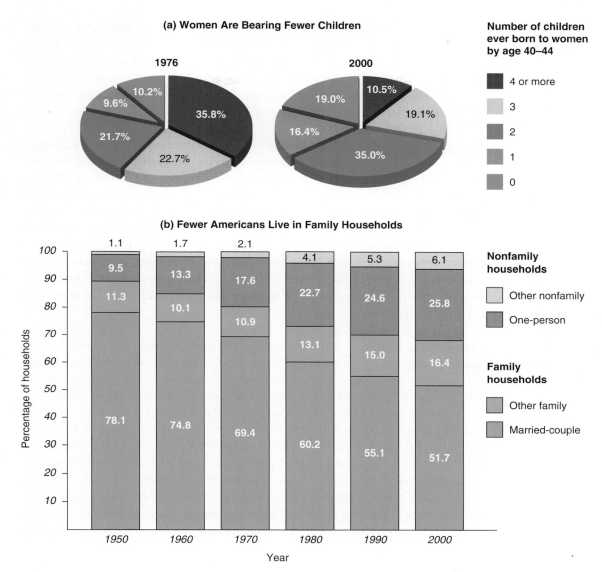

FIGURE 33.2
The Changing American Family

American households became smaller in the latter part of the twentieth century, as more people lived alone and women had, on average, fewer children.

Source: Adapted from U.S. Bureau of the Census, www.census.gov/prod/2002pubs/censr-4.pdf and www.census.gov/population/pop-profile/2000/chap04.pdf.

"potential for life." He limited federally funded research to the existing seventy-eight stem cell lines, most of which turned out not to be viable. However, most Americans support stem cell research, believing that the moral good of curing diseases outweighs the moral good of preserving the potential life of blastocytes. In early 2009, President Obama signed an executive order ending the Bush restrictions.

Still, for many there remains a conflict between religious belief and scientific study. Fundamentalist Christians sought to prevent the teaching of evolution in the nation's science classes or to introduce instruction of biblical creationism or intelligent design, which holds that an intelligent creator is behind the development of life on earth. The percentage of Americans who accept scientific evidence for evolution is lower than that in any other major nation except Turkey.

Century of Change

The twentieth century witnessed momentous changes, some bringing benefits, others threatening the existence of the human species. Research in the physical and biological sciences provided insight into the structure of matter and the universe. Technology enabled Americans to be more connected to other people worldwide than ever. This was perhaps the most powerful product of globalization. In 1955, 51 million people a year traveled by plane. By the turn of the century, 1.6 billion were airborne annually, and 530 million—or about 1.5 million each day—crossed international borders. This permeability of national boundaries brought many benefits, as did the integration of markets and the spread of information that occurred alongside it.

Globalization and World Health

On the flip side, the rapid increase in international air travel was a potent force for the spread of global disease, as flying enabled people to reach the other side of the world in less time than the incubation period for many ailments. Worse, in 2003 the World Health Organization (WHO) estimated that nearly one-quarter of global disease and injury was related to environmental degradation. For example, 90 percent of diarrheal diseases (such as cholera), which were killing 3 million people a year, resulted from contaminated water. According to WHO, more than thirty infectious diseases were identified in humans for the first time from 1980 to 2000—including AIDS, Ebola virus, hantavirus, and hepatitis C and E. Environmentalists, meanwhile, insisted that the growing global exchange was having a deleterious impact on the ecosystem through climate change, ozone depletion, hazardous waste, and damage to fisheries.

Confronting Terrorism

The 9/11 attacks brought home what Americans had previously only dimly perceived: that globalization shrunk the buffers that distance and two oceans provided the United States. Al Qaeda used the increasingly open, globalized world to expand its reach. It had shown that small terrorist cells could become transnational threats without a state sponsor or home base. According to U.S. intelligence, Al Qaeda operated in more than ninety countries.

How would one go about vanquishing such a foe? Was a decisive victory even possible? These remained open questions nine years after the World Trade Center collapsed. Unchallenged militarily, the United States felt few constraints about intervening in Afghanistan and then Iraq. It continued to spend colossal sums on its military. (The Pentagon in 2010 spent more than $680 billion, or roughly $77 million dollars per hour.) America had military commitments around the globe, from the Balkans and Iraq to Afghanistan and Korea (see Table 33.1).

Links to the World

The "Swine Flu" Pandemic

When United flight 803 from Washington DC landed at Tokyo's Narita airport on May 20, 2009, Japanese health officials boarded the plane. Wearing respirator masks, goggles, and disposable scrubs, they used thermal scanners to check passengers for elevated temperatures. If any symptoms were discovered, the plane would be quarantined. Japan had already closed its borders to travelers from Mexico, where the H1N1 "swine flu" virus emerged about three weeks earlier. Mexico closed schools and businesses. Nevertheless, the H1N1 virus had, by mid-May, already spread to more than 22 countries.

After several deaths in Mexico in late April, the World Health Organization raised its alert level to stage 5, expecting the virus to create the first major flu pandemic in more than forty years. Health analysts believed that the "right" pathogen emerging in the "right" place might spread worldwide in a day.

But global connections also offered new tools to combat pandemics. Global surveillance of disease might head off developing health threats, for example, and individual nations and global organizations can pool expertise as they develop vaccines and techniques to cope with pandemics. In addition, some believe that a global culture where borders present little barrier may facilitate the growth of global immunities to infectious diseases.

People everywhere were relieved when swine flu was ultimately no more deadly than a seasonal flu. Previously, SARS (severe, acute respiratory syndrome) and the H5N1 "bird flu" also failed become worldwide heath threats. But the World Heath Organization and the U.S. Centers for Disease Control and Prevention cautioned that the emergence of a major pandemic was simply a matter of time. In the era of globalization, diseases do not stop at borders or respect wealth and power, and the links between Americans and the rest of the world's peoples cannot be denied.

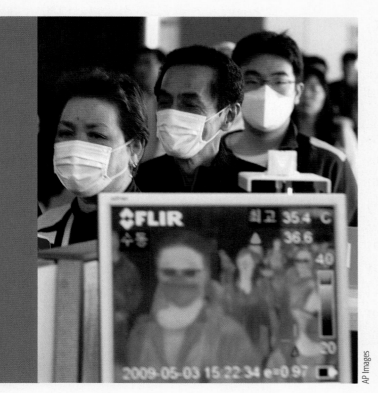

As the H1N1 virus—"swine flu"—spread rapidly in the spring of 2009, nations around the world attempted to prevent the spread of infection. Here, thermal cameras check the body temperatures of passengers arriving at Incheon International Airport in South Korea.

AP Images

TABLE 33.1   U.S. Military Personnel on Active Duty in Foreign Countries, 2009[1]

Region/Country[2]	Personnel	Region/Country[2]	Personnel
United States and Territories		Diego Garcia	253
Continental U.S.	959,508	Egypt	265
Alaska	21,597	Iraq	164,000
Hawai'i	36,890	Israel	45
Guam	2,970	Oman	34
Puerto Rico	179	Pakistan	39
Europe		Qatar	463
Belgium*	1,267	Saudi Arabia	269
France*	58	United Arab Emirates	105
Germany*	52,658	**Sub-Saharan Africa**	
Greece*	361	Djibouti	1,207
Greenland*	144	Kenya	41
Hungary	60	South Africa	30
Italy*	9,707	**Western Hemisphere**	
Netherlands*	510	Bahamas, The	45
Norway*	70	Brazil	37
Portugal*	716	Canada	128
Russia	57	Chile	30
Spain*	1,365	Colombia	77
Turkey*	1,616	Cuba (Guantanamo)	926
United Kingdom*	9,199	Honduras	416
East Asia and Pacific		Peru	45
Australia	139	**Total Foreign Countries[2]**	262,793
China (includes Hong Kong)	68	**Ashore**	242,291
Japan	35,965	**Afloat**	20,502
Korea, Rep. of	[Figures not available]	**Total Worldwide[2]**	1,418,542
Philippines	117	**Ashore**	1,313,308
Singapore	125	**Afloat**	105,234
Thailand	95		
North Africa, Near East, and South Asia			
Afghanistan	66,400		
Bahrain	1,507		

*NATO countries

[1]Only countries with 30 or more U.S. military personnel are listed.

[2]Includes all regions/countries, not simply those listed.

Source: U.S. Department of Defense, Defense Manpower Data Center.

The Internet

"Google it"—the phrase, essentially unknown before the new century, had within its first years become a household expression. Google was the popular Internet search engine that went from obscurity in the mid-1990s to handling more than 300 million queries daily from around the world—almost 40 percent of all Internet search requests.

While widespread Internet use was a recent phenomenon, its history went back four decades. In the mid-1960s, the U.S. military's Advanced Research Projects Agency (ARPA) wanted a communications network for government and university researchers across the nation. In 1969, early portions of the experimental system, called ARPANET, went online at UCLA; the University of California, Santa Barbara; Stanford Research Institute; and the University of Utah. By 1971, twenty-three computers were connected, and the numbers reached a thousand by 1984. Renamed the Internet, this system transmitted only words, but in 1990 computer scientists developed the World Wide Web to send graphic and multimedia information. Then in 1993, the first commercial "browser" for Web navigation hit the market, followed in 1994 and 1995 by two superior browsers: Netscape and Internet Explorer.

By the end of 2009, there were more than 1.7 billion Internet users worldwide, including 230 million Americans. With technological advances and new forms of "broadband" access with high-speed connections, users could send and receive e-mail, join online discussion groups, read newspapers, download books and music, shop, and do their banking—all through a computer at home. For Americans in the new globally connected millennium, the Internet was a fitting legacy of the twentieth century.

Summary

The 1990s were, for most Americans, good times. A digitized revolution in communications and information generated prosperity and transformed life in America and worldwide. The longest economic expansion in American history—from 1991 to 2001—meant that most Americans who wanted jobs had them, that the stock market boomed, that the nation had a budget surplus, and that more Americans owned homes. And with no formidable rival, the United States stood as the world's lone superpower.

Yet unsettling events troubled the nation. Minutes before midnight on December 31, 1999, President Clinton called on Americans not to fear the future, but to "welcome it, create it, and embrace it." The challenges ahead would include the contested 2000 presidential election that was decided by the Supreme Court in a partisan 5-to-4 vote and the end of a ten-year economic expansion in 2001.

Then, on September 11, 2001, radical Islamic terrorists attacked the World Trade Center and the Pentagon, killing thousands. The new president, George W. Bush, declared a war on terrorism. While U.S. forces went after targets in Afghanistan, Congress created the Department of Homeland Security and passed the USA PATRIOT Act, expanding the federal government's surveillance powers. In March 2003, Bush initiated a war in Iraq, not expecting the full-blown insurgency that followed. Bush won reelection in 2004, but his fortunes waned. Two costly wars abroad and a severe economic crisis paved the way for Barack Obama's historic election in 2008.

Visualizing the Past

Arizona's Immigration Law

In April 2010, the state of Arizona enacted a controversial immigration law, by far the toughest in the nation. Intended to help identify and deport undocumented immigrants, it required immigrants to carry their immigration documents and authorized police to question anyone suspected of wrongdoing about his or her immigration status. Those without papers could be detained until their status was verified. Opponents of the bill argued that it would lead to harassment of Hispanics, whether they were undocumented, legal immigrants, or US citizens, and President Obama called it a threat to "basic notions of fairness that we cherish as Americans." This bill—one of 222 state immigration laws enacted between 2007 and early 2010—provoked a national debate. What case against the law does this editorial cartoon make? How does the cartoonist use iconic images? Does the cartoon suggest problems with the wording of the law or with its possible implementation?

"I CAN TELL BY THE COLOR OF YOUR SKIN YOU'RE NOT FROM AROUND HERE, ARE YOU?"

© 2010 Joe Heller, The Green Bay Press-Gazette, and PoliticalCartoons.com

Dozens of editorial cartoons took on the Arizona Immigration law. This one, by Joe Heller, appeared in the Green Bay Press.

The first decade of the twenty-first century was different from what Americans imagined on New Year's Eve 1999. The terror attacks of September 11, 2001, shook America to its core. Then came two lengthy wars, followed by the most severe economic downturn since the Great Depression. By decade's end, Americans were deeply divided over how to respond to the nation's problems. As a new decade dawned, Americans continued to struggle over foreign and domestic priorities with the passion and commitment that keeps democracy alive.

Chapter Review

Social Strains and New Political Directions

What political struggles complicated Bill Clinton's first presidency?

As a "New Democrat" or centrist, Bill Clinton faced members of his own party who found some of his policies—such as his emphasis on private sector economic development—too conservative. Worse, from the start, a new breed of conservative Republicans challenged many of Clinton's campaign goals, and ultimately took control of both houses of Congress after the mid-term elections in 1994. This group successfully blocked Clinton's attempts at healthcare reform and compromised his position on gays in the military. These increasing partisan roadblocks led the beleaguered president to make compromises that pushed the nation further to the right—most notably, signing the 1996 Personal Responsibility and Work Opportunity Act (also known as "Welfare Reform"), which limited federal assistance for the needy to two years, and the Telecommunications Act, which allowed greater concentration of media ownership in fewer hands.

Globalization and Prosperity

What concerns did critics raise about globalization?

The so-called "age of globalization" that emerged in the late 1990s was characterized by greater worldwide integration of markets, finance, and technology. Labor unions feared losing jobs to less expensive overseas production, while critics argued that globalization widened the gap between rich and poor nations, fueling the creation of an underclass of "slave laborers" in poor countries and a race to the bottom. Environmentalists charged that globalization resulted in greater pollution of developing countries, and others feared the power of multinational corporations over traditional cultures. Anti-global protests targeted McDonald's as symbolizing the creation of a homogeneous global culture, and demonstrations turned violent at World Trade Organization meetings in 1999 and those of the International Monetary Fund in 2001.

9/11 and the War in Iraq

How did the events of Sept. 11 change America's relationship to the world?

Immediately after the attacks, the world community united in support of the United States, promising to work with Washington to fight terrorism. But before long, as President Bush took a firm good-vs.-evil stance that dictated countries were either with the United States or against it, he began to alienate allies and other friendly nations. Bush and his aides felt that the United States could not wait for threats to materialize; they had to strike first. And Bush differed with much of the U.N. Security Council over how to deal with Saddam Hussein's Iraq. The Council wanted to give arms inspections more time to succeed; the United States, backed by Britain, felt the time for diplomacy was over. The discord increased when Bush opted to launch an invasion. Bush also faced sharp international criticism for the military's abuse of war prisoners at Abu Ghraib.

Domestic Politics in Post-9/11 America

What was the decisive factor in the 2008 election?

In a word, the economy. While Americans were increasingly unhappy about the war in Iraq and disliked the Bush administration's handling of Hurricane Katrina, the biggest issue fueling voters rejection of the Republican Party and its presidential candidate John McCain was the deepening economic crisis. Years of deregulation led to risky investment practices in America's financial sector—particularly in housing and credit—that ultimately triggered a dangerous spiral of plummeting home values, foreclosures, and banking and credit problems. As credit tightened, businesses laid off workers and unemployment skyrocketed. The Bush administration provided $700 billion in loans to failing institutions, angering many Americans. When John McCain misspoke in the midst of the financial meltdown that "the fundamentals of our economy are strong," many questioned how in touch he was, and elected Barack Obama.

Americans in the First Decade of the New Millennium

What demographic changes are Americans beginning to face in the 21st century?

As the American population reached the 300 million mark in 2006, the country was more racially and ethnically diverse than ever. The population of people of color grew twelve times faster than that of whites, and Latinos became the second largest ethnic or racial group after non-Hispanic whites. Family structure has become increasingly varied, with households composed of married couples representing less than 50 percent of the population, and one-third of all children born to single women. The country also faces an aging population, as the leading edge of the baby boom generation turned 60 in 2006. That, combined with greater life expectancy, presents new concerns of healthcare and additional family pressures. Meanwhile, debates about balancing science and religion—particularly over the teaching of evolution and biblical creationism—continue to divide the nation.

Suggestions for Further Reading

Derek Chollet and James Goldgeier, *America Between the Wars: From 11/9 to 9/11* (2008)

Barbara Ehrenreich, *Nickled and Dimed: On (Not) Getting by in America* (2002)

David Halberstam, *War in a Time of Peace: Bush, Clinton, and the Generals* (2001)

John F. Harris, *The Survivor: Bill Clinton in the White House* (2005)

Jennifer L. Hochschild, *Facing up to the American Dream: Race, Class, and the Soul of the Nation* (1995)

James Mann, *Rise of the Vulcans: The History of Bush's War Cabinet* (2004)

Alejandro Portes and Reuben G. Rumbaut, *Immigrant America: A Portrait,* 3d ed. (2006)

Thomas E. Ricks, *The Gamble: General David Paterus and the American Military Adventure in Iraq, 2006-2008* (2009)

Joseph E. Stiglitz, *Globalization and Its Discontents* (2002)

Appendix

Declaration of Independence in Congress, July 4, 1776

When, in the course of human events, it becomes necessary for one people to dissolve the political bonds which have connected them with another, and to assume, among the powers of the earth, the separate and equal station to which the laws of nature and of nature's God entitle them, a decent respect to the opinions of mankind requires that they should declare the causes which impel them to the separation.

We hold these truths to be self-evident: That all men are created equal; that they are endowed by their Creator with certain unalienable rights; that among these are life, liberty, and the pursuit of happiness; that, to secure these rights, governments are instituted among men, deriving their just powers from the consent of the governed; that whenever any form of government becomes destructive of these ends, it is the right of the people to alter or to abolish it, and to institute new government, laying its foundation on such principles, and organizing its powers in such form, as to them shall seem most likely to effect their safety and happiness. Prudence, indeed, will dictate that governments long established should not be changed for light and transient causes; and accordingly all experience hath shown that mankind are more disposed to suffer, while evils are sufferable, than to right themselves by abolishing the forms to which they are accustomed. But when a long train of abuses and usurpations, pursuing invariably the same object, evinces a design to reduce them under absolute despotism, it is their right, it is their duty, to throw off such government, and to provide new guards for their future security. Such has been the patient sufferance of these colonies; and such is now the necessity which constrains them to alter their former systems of government. The history of the present King of Great Britain is a history of repeated injuries and usurpations, all having in direct object the establishment of an absolute tyranny over these states. To prove this, let facts be submitted to a candid world.

He has refused his assent to laws, the most wholesome and necessary for the public good.

He has forbidden his governors to pass laws of immediate and pressing importance, unless suspended in their operation till his assent should be obtained; and, when so suspended, he has utterly neglected to attend to them.

He has refused to pass other laws for the accommodation of large districts of people, unless those people would relinquish the right of representation in the legislature, a right inestimable to them, and formidable to tyrants only.

He has called together legislative bodies at places unusual, uncomfortable, and distant from the depository of their public records, for the sole purpose of fatiguing them into compliance with his measures.

He has dissolved representative houses repeatedly, for opposing, with manly firmness, his invasions on the rights of the people.

He has refused for a long time, after such dissolutions, to cause others to be elected; whereby the legislative powers, incapable of annihilation, have returned to the people at large for their exercise; the state remaining, in the mean time, exposed to all the dangers of invasions from without and convulsions within.

He has endeavored to prevent the population of these states; for that purpose obstructing the laws for naturalization of foreigners; refusing to pass others to encourage their migration hither, and raising the conditions of new appropriations of lands.

He has obstructed the administration of justice, by refusing his assent to laws for establishing judiciary powers.

He has made judges dependent on his will alone, for the tenure of their offices, and the amount and payment of their salaries.

He has erected a multitude of new offices, and sent hither swarms of officers to harass our people and eat out their substance.

He has kept among us, in times of peace, standing armies, without the consent of our legislatures.

He has affected to render the military independent of, and superior to, the civil power.

He has combined with others to subject us to a jurisdiction foreign to our constitution, and unacknowledged by our laws, giving his assent to their acts of pretended legislation:

For quartering large bodies of armed troops among us;

For protecting them, by a mock trial, from punishment for any murders which they should commit on the inhabitants of these states;

For cutting off our trade with all parts of the world;

For imposing taxes on us without our consent;

For depriving us, in many cases, of the benefits of trial by jury;

For transporting us beyond seas, to be tried for pretended offenses;

For abolishing the free system of English laws in a neighboring province, establishing therein an arbitrary government, and enlarging its boundaries, so as to render it at once an example and fit instrument for introducing the same absolute rule into these colonies;

For taking away our charters, abolishing our most valuable laws, and altering fundamentally the forms of our governments;

For suspending our own legislatures, and declaring themselves invested with power to legislate for us in all cases whatsoever.

He has abdicated government here, by declaring us out of his protection and waging war against us.

He has plundered our seas, ravaged our coasts, burned our towns, and destroyed the lives of our people.

He is at this time transporting large armies of foreign mercenaries to complete the works of death, desolation, and tyranny already begun with circumstances of cruelty and perfidy scarcely paralleled in the most barbarous ages, and totally unworthy the head of a civilized nation.

He has constrained our fellow-citizens, taken captive on the high seas, to bear arms against their country, to become the executioners of their friends and brethren, or to fall themselves by their hands.

He has excited domestic insurrection among us, and has endeavored to bring on the inhabitants of our frontiers the merciless Indian savages, whose known rule of warfare is an undistinguished destruction of all ages, sexes, and conditions.

In every stage of these oppressions we have petitioned for redress in the most humble terms; our repeated petitions have been answered only by repeated injury. A prince, whose character is thus marked by every act which may define a tyrant, is unfit to be the ruler of a free people.

Nor have we been wanting in our attentions to our British brethren. We have warned them, from time to time, of attempts by their legislature to extend an unwarrantable jurisdiction over us. We have reminded them of the circumstances of our emigration and settlement here. We have appealed to their native justice and magnanimity; and we have conjured them, by the ties of our common kindred, to disavow these usurpations, which would inevitably interrupt our connections and correspondence. They, too, have been deaf to the voice of justice and of consanguinity. We must, therefore, acquiesce in the necessity which denounces our separation, and hold them, as we hold the rest of mankind, enemies in war, in peace friends.

We, therefore, the representatives of the United States of America, in General Congress assembled, appealing to the Supreme Judge of the world for the rectitude of our intentions, do, in the name and by the authority of the good people of these colonies, solemnly publish and declare, that these United Colonies are, and of right ought to be, FREE AND INDEPENDENT STATES; that they are absolved from all allegiance to the British crown, and that all political connection between them and the state of Great Britain is, and ought to be, totally dissolved; and that, as free and independent states, they have full power to levy war, conclude peace, contract alliances, establish commerce, and do all other acts and things which independent states may of right do. And for the support of this declaration, with a firm reliance on the protection of Divine Providence, we mutually pledge to each other our lives, our fortunes, and our sacred honor.

Articles of Confederation

Whereas the Delegates of the United States of America in Congress assembled did on the fifteenth day of November in the Year of our Lord One Thousand Seven Hundred and Seventy seven, and in the Second Year of the Independence of America agree to certain articles of Confederation and perpetual Union between the States of Newhampshire, Massachusetts Bay, Rhode Island and Providence Plantations, Connecticut, New York, New Jersey, Pennsylvania, Delaware, Maryland, Virginia, North Carolina, South Carolina and Georgia in the Words following, viz. "Articles of Confederation and perpetual Union between the states of Newhampshire, Massachusetts Bay, Rhode Island and Providence Plantations, Connecticut, New York, New Jersey, Pennsylvania, Delaware, Maryland, Virginia, North Carolina, South Carolina and Georgia.

Article I

The Stile of this confederacy shall be "The United States of America."

Article II

Each state retains its sovereignty, freedom and independence, and every Power, Jurisdiction and right, which is not by this confederation expressly delegated to the United States, in Congress assembled.

Article III

The said states hereby severally enter into a firm league of friendship with each other, for their common defence, the security of their Liberties, and their mutual and general welfare, binding themselves to assist each other, against all force offered to, or attacks made upon them, or any of them, on account of religion, sovereignty, trade, or any other pretence whatever.

Article IV

The better to secure and perpetuate mutual friendship and intercourse among the people of the different states in this union, the free inhabitants of each of these states, paupers, vagabonds and fugitives from Justice excepted, shall be entitled to all privileges and immunities of free citizens in the several states; and the people of each state shall have free ingress and regress to and from any other state, and shall enjoy therein all the privileges of trade and commerce, subject to the same duties, impositions and restrictions as the inhabitants thereof respectively, provided that such restriction shall not extend so far as to prevent the removal of property imported into any state, to any other state of which the Owner is an inhabitant; provided also that no imposition, duties or restriction shall be laid by any state, on the property of the united states, or either of them.

If any Person guilty of, or charged with treason, felony, or other high misdemeanor in any state, shall flee from Justice, and be found in any of the united states, he shall upon demand of the Governor or executive power, of the state from which he fled, be delivered up and removed to the state having jurisdiction of his offence.

Full faith and credit shall be given in each of these states to the records, acts and judicial proceedings of the courts and magistrates of every other state.

Article V

For the more convenient management of the general interests of the united states, delegates shall be annually appointed in such manner as the legislature of each state shall direct, to meet in Congress on the first Monday in November, in every year, with a power reserved to each state, to recall its delegates, or any of them, at any time within the year, and to send others in their stead, for the remainder of the Year.

No state shall be represented in Congress by less than two, nor by more than seven Members; and no person shall be capable of being a delegate for more than three years in any term of six years; nor shall any person, being a delegate, be capable of holding any office under the united states, for which he, or another for his benefit receives any salary, fees or emolument of any kind.

Each state shall maintain its own delegates in a meeting of the states, and while they act as members of the committee of the states.

In determining questions in the united states, in Congress assembled, each state shall have one vote.

Freedom of speech and debate in Congress shall not be impeached or questioned in any Court, or place out of Congress, and the members of congress shall be protected in their persons from arrests and imprisonments, during the time of their going to and from, and attendance on congress, except for treason, felony, or breach of the peace.

Article VI

No state without the Consent of the united states in congress assembled, shall send any embassy to, or receive any embassy from, or enter into any conference, agreement, or alliance or treaty with any King, prince or state; nor shall any person holding any office of profit or trust under the united states, or any of them, accept of any present, emolument, office or title of any kind whatever from any king, prince or foreign state; nor shall the united states in congress assembled, or any of them, grant any title of nobility.

No two or more states shall enter into any treaty, confederation or alliance whatever between them, without the consent of the united states in congress assembled, specifying accurately the purposes for which the same is to be entered into, and how long it shall continue.

No state shall lay any imposts or duties, which may interfere with any stipulations in treaties, entered into by the united states in congress assembled, with any king, prince or state, in pursuance of any treaties already proposed by congress, to the courts of France and Spain.

No vessels of war shall be kept up in time of peace by any state, except such number only, as shall be deemed necessary by the united states in congress assembled, for the defence of such state, or its trade; nor shall any body of forces be kept up by any state, in time of peace, except such number only, as in the judgment of the united states, in congress assembled, shall be deemed requisite to garrison the forts necessary for the defence of such state; but every state shall always keep up a well regulated and disciplined militia, sufficiently armed and accoutred, and shall provide and constantly have ready for use, in public stores, a due number of field pieces and tents, and a proper quantity of arms, ammunition and camp equipage.

No state shall engage in any war without the consent of the united states in congress assembled, unless such state be actually invaded by enemies, or shall have received certain advice of a resolution being formed by some nation of Indians to invade such state, and the danger is so imminent as not to admit of a delay, till the united states in congress assembled can be consulted: nor shall any state grant commissions to any ships or vessels of war, nor letters of marque or reprisal, except it be after a declaration of war by the united states in congress assembled, and then only against the kingdom or state and the subjects thereof, against which war has been so declared, and under such regulations as shall be established by the united states in congress assembled, unless such state be infested by pirates, in which case vessels of war may be fitted out for that occasion, and kept so long as the danger shall continue, or until the united states in congress assembled shall determine otherwise.

Article VII

When land-forces are raised by any state for the common defence, all officers of or under the rank of colonel, shall be appointed by the legislature of each state respectively by whom such forces shall be raised, or in such manner as such state shall direct, and all vacancies shall be filled up by the state which first made the appointment.

Article VIII

All charges of war, and all other expences that shall be incurred for the common defence or general welfare, and allowed by the united states in congress assembled, shall be defrayed out of a common treasury, which shall be supplied by the several states, in proportion to the value of all land within each state, granted to or surveyed for any Person, as such land and the buildings and improvements thereon shall be estimated according to such mode as the united states in congress assembled, shall from time to time direct and appoint. The taxes for paying that proportion shall be laid and levied by the authority and direction of the legislatures of the several states within the time agreed upon by the united states in congress assembled.

Article IX

The united states in congress assembled, shall have the sole and exclusive right and power of determining on peace and war, except in the cases mentioned in the sixth article—of sending and receiving ambassadors—entering into treaties and alliances, provided that no treaty of commerce shall be made whereby the legislative power of the respective states shall be restrained from imposing such imposts and duties on foreigners, as their own people are subjected to, or from prohibiting the exportation or importation of any species of goods or commodities whatsoever—of establishing rules for deciding in all cases, what captures on land or water shall be legal, and in what manner prizes taken by land or naval forces in the service of the united states shall be divided or appropriated—of

granting letters of marque and reprisal in times of peace— appointing courts for the trial of piracies and felonies committed on the high seas and establishing courts for receiving and determining final appeals in all cases of captures, provided that no member of congress shall be appointed a judge of any of the said courts.

The united states in congress assembled shall also be the last resort on appeal in all disputes and differences now subsisting or that hereafter may arise between two or more states concerning boundary, jurisdiction or any other cause whatever; which authority shall always be exercised in the manner following. Whenever the legislative or executive authority or lawful agent of any state in controversy with another shall present a petition to congress, stating the matter in question and praying for a hearing, notice thereof shall be given by order of congress to the legislative or executive authority of the other state in controversy, and a day assigned for the appearance of the parties by their lawful agents, who shall then be directed to appoint by joint consent, commissioners or judges to constitute a court for hearing and determining the matter in question: but if they cannot agree, congress shall name three persons out of each of the united states, and from the list of such persons each party shall alternately strike out one, the petitioners beginning, until the number shall be reduced to thirteen; and from that number not less than seven, nor more than nine names as congress shall direct, shall in the presence of congress be drawn out by lot, and the persons whose names shall be so drawn or any five of them, shall be commissioners or judges, to hear and finally determine the controversy, so always as a major part of the judges who shall hear the cause shall agree in the determination: and if either party shall neglect to attend at the day appointed, without showing reasons, which congress shall judge sufficient, or being present shall refuse to strike, the congress shall proceed to nominate three persons out of each state, and the secretary of congress shall strike in behalf of such party absent or refusing; and the judgment and sentence of the court to be appointed, in the manner before prescribed, shall be final and conclusive; and if any of the parties shall refuse to submit to the authority of such court, or to appear to defend their claim or cause, the court shall nevertheless proceed to pronounce sentence, or judgment, which shall in like manner be final and decisive, the judgment or sentence and other proceedings being in either case transmitted to congress, and lodged among the acts of congress for the security of the parties concerned: provided that every commissioner, before he sits in judgment, shall take an oath to be administered by one of the judges of the supreme or superior court of the state, where the cause shall be tried, "well and truly to hear and determine the matter in question, according to the best of his judgment, without favour, affection or hope of reward:" provided also that no state shall be deprived of territory for the benefit of the united states.

All controversies concerning the private right of soil claimed under different grants of two or more states, whose jurisdictions as they may respect such lands, and the states which passed such grants are adjusted, the said grants or either of them being at the same time claimed to have originated antecedent to such settlement of jurisdiction, shall on the petition of either party to the congress of the united states, be finally determined as near as may be in the same manner as is before prescribed for deciding disputes respecting territorial jurisdiction between different states.

The united states in congress assembled shall also have the sole and exclusive right and power of regulating the alloy and value of coin struck by their own authority, or by that of the respective states—fixing the standard of weights and measures throughout the united states—regulating the trade and managing all affairs with the Indians, not members of any of the states, provided that the legislative right of any state within its own limits be not infringed or violated—establishing and regulating post-offices from one state to another, throughout all the united states, and exacting such postage on the papers passing thro' the same as may be requisite to defray the expences of the said office—appointing all officers of the land forces, in the service of the united states, excepting regimental officers—appointing all the officers of the naval forces, and commissioning all officers whatever in the service of the united states—making rules for the government and regulation of the said land and naval forces, and directing their operations.

The united states in congress assembled shall have authority to appoint a committee, to sit in the recess of congress, to be denominated "A Committee of the States," and to consist of one delegate from each state; and to appoint such other committees and civil officers as may be necessary for managing the general affairs of the united states under their direction—to appoint one of their number to preside, provided that no person be allowed to serve in the office of president more than one year in any term of three years; to ascertain the necessary sums of Money to be raised for the service of the united states, and to appropriate and apply the same for defraying the public expences—to borrow money, or emit bills on the credit of the united states, transmitting every half year to the respective states an account of the sums of money so borrowed or emitted—to build and equip a navy—to agree upon the number of land forces, and to

make requisitions from each state for its quota, in proportion to the number of white inhabitants in such state; which requisition shall be binding, and thereupon the legislature of each state shall appoint the regimental officers, raise the men and cloath, arm and equip them in a soldier like manner, at the expence of the united states, and the officers and men so cloathed, armed and equipped shall march to the place appointed, and within the time agreed on by the united states in congress assembled: But if the united states in congress assembled shall, on consideration of circumstances judge proper that any state should not raise men, or should raise a smaller number than its quota, and that any other state should raise a greater number of men than the quota thereof, such extra number shall be raised, officered, cloathed, armed and equipped in the same manner as the quota of such state, unless the legislature of such state shall judge that such extra number cannot be safely spared out of the same, in which case they shall raise, officer, cloath, arm and equip as many of such extra number as they judge can be safely spared. And the officers and men so cloathed, armed and equipped, shall march to the place appointed, and within the time agreed on by the united states in congress assembled.

The united states in congress assembled shall never engage in a war, nor grant letters of marque and reprisal in time of peace, nor enter into any treaties or alliances, nor coin money, nor regulate the value thereof, nor ascertain the sums and expences necessary for the defence and welfare of the united states, or any of them, nor emit bills, nor borrow money on the credit of the united states, nor appropriate money, nor agree upon the number of vessels of war, to be built or purchased, or the number of land or sea forces to be raised, nor appoint a commander in chief of the army or navy, unless nine states assent to the same: nor shall a question on any other point, except for adjourning from day to day be determined, unless by the votes of a majority of the united states in congress assembled.

The congress of the united states shall have power to adjourn to any time within the year, and to any place within the united states, so that no period of adjournment be for a longer duration than the space of six Months, and shall publish the Journal of their proceedings monthly, except such parts thereof relating to treaties, alliances or military operations as in their judgment require secresy; and the yeas and nays of the delegates of each state on any question shall be entered on the Journal, when it is desired by any delegate; and the delegates of a state, or any of them, at his or their request shall be furnished with a transcript of the said Journal, except such parts as are above excepted, to lay before the legislatures of the several states.

Article X

The committee of the states, or any nine of them, shall be authorised to execute, in the recess of congress, such of the powers of congress as the united states in congress assembled, by the consent of nine states, shall from time to time think expedient to vest them with; provided that no power be delegated to the said committee, for the exercise of which, by the articles of confederation, the voice of nine states in the congress of the united states assembled is requisite.

Article XI

Canada acceding to this confederation, and joining in the measures of the united states, shall be admitted into, and entitled to all the advantages of this union: but no other colony shall be admitted into the same, unless such admission be agreed to by nine states.

Article XII

All bills of credit emitted, monies borrowed and debts contracted by, or under the authority of congress, before the assembling of the united states, in pursuance of the present confederation, shall be deemed and considered as a charge against the united states, for payment and satisfaction whereof the said united states, and the public faith are hereby solemnly pledged.

Article XIII

Every state shall abide by the determinations of the united states in congress assembled, on all questions which by this confederation are submitted to them. And the Articles of this confederation shall be inviolably observed by every state, and the union shall be perpetual; nor shall any alteration at any time hereafter be made in any of them; unless such alteration be agreed to in a congress of the united states, and be afterwards confirmed by the legislatures of every state.

AND WHEREAS it hath pleased the Great Governor of the World to incline the hearts of the legislatures we respectively represent in congress, to approve of, and to authorize us to ratify the said articles of confederation and perpetual union. Know Ye that we the under-signed delegates, by virtue of the power and authority to us given for that purpose, do by these presents, in the name and in behalf of our respective constituents, fully and entirely ratify and confirm each and every of the said articles of confederation and perpetual union, and all and singular the matters and things therein contained: And we do further solemnly plight and engage the faith of our respective constituents, that they shall abide by the determinations of the united states in congress assembled, on all questions, which by the said confederation are submitted to them. And that the articles thereof shall be inviolably observed by the states we respectively represent, and that the union shall be perpetual. In Witness whereof we have hereunto set our hands in Congress. Done at Philadelphia in the state of Pennsylvania the ninth Day of July in the Year of our Lord one Thousand seven Hundred and Seventy-eight, and in the third year of the independence of America.

Constitution of the United States of America and Amendments*

Preamble

We the people of the United States, in order to form a more perfect union, establish justice, insure domestic tranquillity, provide for the common defense, promote the general welfare, and secure the blessings of liberty to ourselves and our posterity, do ordain and establish this Constitution for the United States of America.

Article I

Section 1 All legislative powers herein granted shall be vested in a Congress of the United States, which shall consist of a Senate and a House of Representatives.

Section 2 The House of Representatives shall be composed of members chosen every second year by the people of the several States, and the electors in each State shall have the qualifications requisite for electors of the most numerous branch of the State Legislature.

No person shall be a Representative who shall not have attained to the age of twenty-five years, and been seven years a citizen of the United States, and who shall not, when elected, be an inhabitant of that State in which he shall be chosen.

Representatives and direct taxes shall be apportioned among the several States which may be included within this Union, according to their respective numbers, *which shall be determined by adding to the whole number of free persons, including those bound to service for a term of years and excluding Indians not taxed, three-fifths of all other persons.*

---

*Passages no longer in effect are printed in italic type.

The actual enumeration shall be made within three years after the first meeting of the Congress of the United States, and within every subsequent term of ten years, in such manner as they shall by law direct. The number of Representatives shall not exceed one for every thirty thousand, but each State shall have at least one Representative; *and until such enumeration shall be made, the State of New Hampshire shall be entitled to choose three, Massachusetts eight, Rhode Island and Providence Plantations one, Connecticut five, New York six, New Jersey four, Pennsylvania eight, Delaware one, Maryland six, Virginia ten, North Carolina five, South Carolina five, and Georgia three.*

When vacancies happen in the representation from any State, the Executive authority thereof shall issue writs of election to fill such vacancies.

The House of Representatives shall choose their Speaker and other officers; and shall have the sole power of impeachment.

Section 3 The Senate of the United States shall be composed of two Senators from each State, chosen by the legislature thereof, for six years; and each Senator shall have one vote.

Immediately after they shall be assembled in consequence of the first election, they shall be divided as equally as may be into three classes. The seats of the Senators of the first class shall be vacated at the expiration of the second year, of the second class at the expiration of the fourth year, and of the third class at the expiration of the sixth year, so that one-third may be chosen every second year; and if vacancies happen by resignation or otherwise, during the recess of the legislature of any State, the Executive thereof may make temporary appointments until the next meeting of the legislature, which shall then fill such vacancies.

No person shall be a Senator who shall not have attained to the age of thirty years, and been nine years a citizen of the United States, and who shall not, when elected, be an inhabitant of that State for which he shall be chosen.

The Vice-President of the United States shall be President of the Senate, but shall have no vote, unless they be equally divided.

The Senate shall choose their other officers, and also a President *pro tempore,* in the absence of the Vice-President, or when he shall exercise the office of President of the United States.

The Senate shall have the sole power to try all impeachments. When sitting for that purpose, they shall be on oath or affirmation. When the President of the United States is tried, the Chief Justice shall preside: and no person shall be convicted without the concurrence of two-thirds of the members present.

Judgment in cases of impeachment shall not extend further than to removal from the office, and disqualification to hold and enjoy any office of honor, trust or profit under the United States: but the party convicted shall nevertheless be liable and subject to indictment, trial, judgment and punishment, according to law.

Section 4 The times, places and manner of holding elections for Senators and Representatives shall be prescribed in each State by the legislature thereof; but the Congress may at any time by law make or alter such regulations, except as to the places of choosing Senators.

The Congress shall assemble at least once in every year, and such meeting shall be on the first Monday in December, unless they shall by law appoint a different day.

Section 5 Each house shall be the judge of the elections, returns and qualifications of its own members, and a majority of each shall constitute a quorum to do business; but a smaller number may adjourn from day to day, and may be authorized to compel the attendance of absent members, in such manner, and under such penalties, as each house may provide.

Each house may determine the rules of its proceedings, punish its members for disorderly behavior, and with the concurrence of two-thirds, expel a member.

Each house shall keep a journal of its proceedings, and from time to time publish the same, excepting such parts as may in their judgment require secrecy; and the yeas and nays of the members of either house on any question shall, at the desire of one-fifth of those present, be entered on the journal.

Neither house, during the session of Congress, shall, without the consent of the other, adjourn for more than three days, nor to any other place than that in which the two houses shall be sitting.

Section 6 The Senators and Representatives shall receive a compensation for their services, to be ascertained by law and paid out of the treasury of the United States. They shall in all cases except treason, felony and breach of the peace, be privileged from arrest during their attendance at the session of their respective houses, and in going to and returning from the same; and for any speech or debate in either house, they shall not be questioned in any other place.

No Senator or Representative shall, during the time for which he was elected, be appointed to any civil office under the authority of the United States, which shall have been created, or the emoluments whereof shall have been increased, during such time; and no person holding any office under the United States shall be a member of either house during his continuance in office.

Section 7 All bills for raising revenue shall originate in the House of Representatives; but the Senate may propose or concur with amendments as on other bills.

Every bill which shall have passed the House of Representatives and the Senate, shall, before it become a law, be presented to the President of the United States;

if he approve he shall sign it, but if not he shall return it with objections to that house in which it originated, who shall enter the objections at large on their journal, and proceed to reconsider it. If after such reconsideration two-thirds of that house shall agree to pass the bill, it shall be sent, together with the objections, to the other house, by which it shall likewise be reconsidered, and, if approved by two-thirds of that house, it shall become a law. But in all such cases the votes of both houses shall be determined by yeas and nays, and the names of the persons voting for and against the bill shall be entered on the journal of each house respectively. If any bill shall not be returned by the President within ten days (Sundays excepted) after it shall have been presented to him, the same shall be a law, in like manner as if he had signed it, unless the Congress by their adjournment prevent its return, in which case it shall not be a law.

Every order, resolution, or vote to which the concurrence of the Senate and House of Representatives may be necessary (except on a question of adjournment) shall be presented to the President of the United States; and before the same shall take effect, shall be approved by him, or being disapproved by him, shall be repassed by two-thirds of the Senate and House of Representatives, according to the rules and limitations prescribed in the case of a bill.

Section 8   The Congress shall have power

To lay and collect taxes, duties, imposts, and excises, to pay the debts and provide for the common defense and general welfare of the United States; but all duties, imposts and excises shall be uniform throughout the United States;

To borrow money on the credit of the United States;

To regulate commerce with foreign nations, and among the several States, and with the Indian tribes;

To establish an uniform rule of naturalization, and uniform laws on the subject of bankruptcies throughout the United States;

To coin money, regulate the value thereof, and of foreign coin, and fix the standard of weights and measures;

To provide for the punishment of counterfeiting the securities and current coin of the United States;

To establish post offices and post roads;

To promote the progress of science and useful arts by securing for limited times to authors and inventors the exclusive right to their respective writings and discoveries;

To constitute tribunals inferior to the Supreme Court;

To define and punish piracies and felonies committed on the high seas and offenses against the law of nations;

To declare war, grant letters of marque and reprisal, and make rules concerning captures on land and water;

To raise and support armies, but no appropriation of money to that use shall be for a longer term than two years;

To provide and maintain a navy;

To make rules for the government and regulation of the land and naval forces;

To provide for calling forth the militia to execute the laws of the Union, suppress insurrections, and repel invasions;

To provide for organizing, arming, and disciplining the militia, and for governing such part of them as may be employed in the service of the United States, reserving to the States respectively the appointment of the officers, and the authority of training the militia according to the discipline prescribed by Congress;

To exercise exclusive legislation in all cases whatsoever, over such district (not exceeding ten miles square) as may, by cession of particular States, and the acceptance of Congress, become the seat of government of the United States, and to exercise like authority over all places purchased by the consent of the legislature of the State, in which the same shall be, for erection of forts, magazines, arsenals, dockyards, and other needful buildings;—and

To make all laws which shall be necessary and proper for carrying into execution the foregoing powers, and all other powers vested by this Constitution in the government of the United States, or in any department or officer thereof.

Section 9   *The migration or importation of such persons as any of the States now existing shall think proper to admit shall not be prohibited by the Congress prior to the year 1808; but a tax or duty may be imposed on such importation, not exceeding $10 for each person.*

The privilege of the writ of habeas corpus shall not be suspended, unless when in cases of rebellion or invasion the public safety may require it.

No bill of attainder or ex post facto law shall be passed.

No capitation, or other direct, tax shall be laid, unless in proportion to the census or enumeration herein before directed to be taken.

No tax or duty shall be laid on articles exported from any State.

No preference shall be given by any regulation of commerce or revenue to the ports of one State over those of another; nor shall vessels bound to, or from, one State, be obliged to enter, clear, or pay duties in another.

No money shall be drawn from the treasury, but in consequence of appropriations made by law; and a regular statement and account of the receipts and expenditures of all public money shall be published from time to time.

No title of nobility shall be granted by the United States: and no person holding any office of profit or trust under them, shall, without the consent of the Congress, accept of any present, emolument, office, or title, of any kind whatever, from any king, prince, or foreign state.

Section 10 No State shall enter into any treaty, alliance, or confederation; grant letters of marque and reprisal; coin money; emit bills of credit; make anything but gold and silver coin a tender in payment of debts; pass any bill of attainder, ex post facto law, or law impairing the obligation of contracts, or grant any title of nobility.

No State shall, without the consent of Congress, lay any imposts or duties on imports or exports, except what may be absolutely necessary for executing its inspection laws: and the net produce of all duties and imposts, laid by any State on imports or exports, shall be for the use of the treasury of the United States; and all such laws shall be subject to the revision and control of the Congress.

No State shall, without the consent of Congress, lay any duty of tonnage, keep troops or ships of war in time of peace, enter into any agreement or compact with another State, or with a foreign power, or engage in war, unless actually invaded, or in such imminent danger as will not admit of delay.

Article II

Section 1 The executive power shall be vested in a President of the United States of America. He shall hold his office during the term of four years, and, together with the Vice-President, chosen for the same term, be elected as follows:

Each State shall appoint, in such manner as the legislature thereof may direct, a number of electors, equal to the whole number of Senators and Representatives to which the State may be entitled in the Congress; but no Senator or Representative, or person holding an office of trust or profit under the United States, shall be appointed an elector.

The electors shall meet in their respective States, and vote by ballot for two persons, of whom one at least shall not be an inhabitant of the same State with themselves. And they shall make a list of all the persons voted for, and of the number of votes for each; which list they shall sign and certify, and transmit sealed to the seat of government of the United States, directed to the President of the Senate. The President of the Senate shall, in the presence of the Senate and House of Representatives, open all the certificates, and the votes shall then be counted. The person having the greatest number of votes shall be the President, if such number be a majority of the whole number of electors appointed; and if there be more than one who have such majority, and have an equal number of votes, then the House of Representatives shall immediately choose by ballot one of them for President; and if no person have a majority, then from the five highest on the list said house shall in like manner choose the President. But in choosing the President the votes shall be taken by States, the representation from each State having one vote; a quorum for this purpose shall consist of a member or members from two-thirds of the States, and a majority of all the States shall be necessary to a choice. In every case, after the choice of the President, the person having the greatest number of votes of the electors shall be the Vice-President. But if there should remain two or more who have equal votes, the Senate shall choose from them by ballot the Vice-President.

The Congress may determine the time of choosing the electors and the day on which they shall give their votes; which day shall be the same throughout the United States.

No person except a natural-born citizen, *or a citizen of the United States at the time of the adoption of this Constitution,* shall be eligible to the office of President; neither shall any person be eligible to that office who shall not have attained to the age of thirty-five years, and been fourteen years a resident within the United States.

In cases of the removal of the President from office or of his death, resignation, or inability to discharge the powers and duties of the said office, the same shall devolve on the Vice-President, and the Congress may by law provide for the case of removal, death, resignation, or inability, both of the President and Vice-President, declaring what officer shall then act as President, and such officer shall act accordingly, until the disability be removed, or a President shall be elected.

The President shall, at stated times, receive for his services a compensation, which shall neither be increased nor diminished during the period for which he shall have been elected, and he shall not receive within that period any other emolument from the United States, or any of them.

Before he enter on the execution of his office, he shall take the following oath or affirmation:—"I do solemnly swear (or affirm) that I will faithfully execute the office of the President of the United States, and will to the best of my ability preserve, protect and defend the Constitution of the United States."

Section 2 The President shall be commander in chief of the army and navy of the United States, and of the militia of the several States, when called into the actual service of the United States; he may require the opinion, in writing, of the principal officer in each of the executive departments, upon any subject relating to the duties of their respective offices, and he shall have power to grant reprieves and pardons for offenses against the United States, except in cases of impeachment.

He shall have power, by and with the advice and consent of the Senate, to make treaties, provided two-thirds of the Senators present concur; and he shall nominate, and by and with the advice and consent of the Senate, shall appoint ambassadors, other public ministers and consuls, judges of the Supreme Court, and all other officers of the United States, whose appointments are not herein otherwise provided for, and which shall be established by law: but Congress may by law vest the appointment of such inferior officers, as they think proper, in the President alone, in the courts of law, or in the heads of departments.

The President shall have power to fill up all vacancies that may happen during the recess of the Senate, by granting commissions which shall expire at the end of their next session.

Section 3 He shall from time to time give to the Congress information of the state of the Union, and recommend to their consideration such measures as he shall judge necessary and expedient; he may, on extraordinary occasions, convene both houses, or either of them, and in case of disagreement between them, with respect to the time of adjournment, he may adjourn them to such time as he shall think proper; he shall receive ambassadors and other public ministers; he shall take care that the laws be faithfully executed, and shall commission all the officers of the United States.

Section 4 The President, Vice-President and all civil officers of the United States shall be removed from office on impeachment for, and on conviction of, treason, bribery, or other high crimes and misdemeanors.

Article III

Section 1 The judicial power of the United States shall be vested in one Supreme Court, and in such inferior courts as the Congress may from time to time ordain and establish. The judges, both of the Supreme and inferior courts, shall hold their offices during good behavior, and shall, at stated times, receive for their services a compensation which shall not be diminished during their continuance in office.

Section 2 The judicial power shall extend to all cases, in law and equity, arising under this Constitution, the laws of the United States, and treaties made, or which shall be made, under their authority;—to all cases affecting ambassadors, other public ministers and consuls;—to all cases of admiralty and maritime jurisdiction;—to controversies to which the United States shall be a party;—to controversies between two or more States;—*between a State and citizens of another State;*—between citizens of different States;—between citizens of the same State claiming lands under grants of different States, and between a State, or the citizens thereof, and foreign states, citizens or subjects.

In all cases affecting ambassadors, other public ministers and consuls, and those in which a State shall be party, the Supreme Court shall have original jurisdiction. In all the other cases before mentioned, the Supreme Court shall have appellate jurisdiction, both as to law and fact, with such exceptions, and under such regulations, as the Congress shall make.

The trial of all crimes, except in cases of impeachment, shall be by jury; and such trial shall be held in the State where said crimes shall have been committed; but when not committed within any State, the trial shall be at such place or places as the Congress may by law have directed.

Section 3 Treason against the United States shall consist only in levying war against them, or in adhering to their enemies, giving them aid and comfort. No person shall be convicted of treason unless on the testimony of two witnesses to the same overt act, or on confession in open court.

The Congress shall have power to declare the punishment of treason, but no attainder of treason shall work corruption of blood, or forfeiture except during the life of the person attainted.

Article IV

Section 1 Full faith and credit shall be given in each State to the public acts, records, and judicial proceedings of every other State. And the Congress may by general laws prescribe the manner in which such acts, records, and proceedings shall be proved, and the effect thereof.

Section 2 The citizens of each State shall be entitled to all privileges and immunities of citizens in the several States.

A person charged in any State with treason, felony, or other crime, who shall flee from justice, and be found in another State, shall on demand of the executive authority of the State from which he fled, be delivered up, to be removed to the State having jurisdiction of the crime.

No person held to service or labor in one State, under the laws thereof, escaping into another, shall, in consequence of any law or regulation therein, be discharged from such service or labor, but shall be delivered up on claim of the party to whom such service or labor may be due.

Section 3 New States may be admitted by the Congress into this Union; but no new State shall be formed or erected within the jurisdiction of any other State; nor any State be formed by the junction of two or more States, or parts of States, without the consent of the legislatures of the States concerned as well as of the Congress.

The Congress shall have power to dispose of and make all needful rules and regulations respecting the territory or other property belonging to the United States; and nothing in this Constitution shall be so construed as to prejudice any claims of the United States, or of any particular State.

Section 4 The United States shall guarantee to every State in this Union a republican form of government, and shall protect each of them against invasion; and on application of the legislature, or of the executive (when the legislature cannot be convened), against domestic violence.

Article V

The Congress, whenever two-thirds of both houses shall deem it necessary, shall propose amendments to this Constitution, or, on the application of the legislatures of two-thirds of the several States, shall call a convention for proposing amendments, which, in either case, shall be valid to all intents and purposes, as part of this Constitution, when ratified by the legislatures of three-fourths of the several States, or by conventions in three-fourths thereof, as the one or the other mode of ratification may be proposed by the Congress; provided *that no amendments which may be made prior to the year one thousand eight hundred and eight shall in any manner affect the first and fourth clauses in the ninth section of the first article;* and that no State, without its consent, shall be deprived of its equal suffrage in the Senate.

Article VI

All debts contracted and engagements entered into, before the adoption of this Constitution, shall be as valid against the United States under this Constitution, as under the Confederation.

This Constitution, and the laws of the United States which shall be made in pursuance thereof; and all treaties made, or which shall be made, under the authority of the United States, shall be the supreme law of the land; and the judges in every State shall be bound thereby, anything in the Constitution or laws of any State to the contrary notwithstanding.

The Senators and Representatives before mentioned, and the members of the several State legislatures, and all executive and judicial officers, both of the United States and of the several States, shall be bound by oath or affirmation to support this Constitution; but no religious test shall ever be required as a qualification to any office or public trust under the United States.

Article VII

The ratification of the conventions of nine States shall be sufficient for the establishment of this Constitution between the States so ratifying the same.

Done in Convention by the unanimous consent of the States present, the seventeenth day of September in the year of our Lord one thousand seven hundred and eighty-seven and of the Independence of the United States of America the twelfth. In witness whereof we have hereunto subscribed our names.

Amendments to the Constitution*

Amendment I

Congress shall make no law respecting an establishment of religion, or prohibiting the free exercise thereof; or abridging the freedom of speech, or of the press; or the right of the people peaceably to assemble, and to petition the government for a redress of grievances.

Amendment II

A well-regulated militia being necessary to the security of a free State, the right of the people to keep and bear arms shall not be infringed.

Amendment III

No soldier shall, in time of peace, be quartered in any house without the consent of the owner, nor in time of war, but in a manner to be prescribed by law.

Amendment IV

The right of the people to be secure in their persons, houses, papers, and effects, against unreasonable searches and seizures, shall not be violated, and no warrants shall issue but upon probable cause, supported by oath or affirmation, and particularly describing the place to be searched, and the persons or things to be seized.

Amendment V

No person shall be held to answer for a capital, or otherwise infamous crime, unless on a presentment or indictment of a grand jury, except in cases arising in the land or naval forces, or in the militia, when in actual service in time of war or public danger; nor shall any person be subject for the same offense to be twice put in jeopardy of life or limb; nor shall be compelled in any criminal case to be a witness against himself, nor be deprived of life, liberty, or property, without due process of law; nor shall private property be taken for public use without just compensation.

Amendment VI

In all criminal prosecutions, the accused shall enjoy the right to a speedy and public trial, by an impartial jury of the State and district wherein the crime shall have been committed, which district shall have been previously ascertained by law, and to be informed of the nature and cause of the accusation; to be confronted with the witnesses against him; to have compulsory process for obtaining witnesses in his favor, and to have the assistance of counsel for his defense.

---

*The first ten Amendments (the Bill of Rights) were adopted in 1791.

Amendment VII

In suits at common law, where the value in controversy shall exceed twenty dollars, the right of trial by jury shall be preserved, and no fact tried by a jury shall be otherwise reexamined in any court of the United States, than according to the rules of the common law.

Amendment VIII

Excessive bail shall not be required, nor excessive fines imposed, nor cruel and unusual punishments inflicted.

Amendment IX

The enumeration in the Constitution, of certain rights, shall not be construed to deny or disparage others retained by the people.

Amendment X

The powers not delegated to the United States by the Constitution, nor prohibited by it to the States, are reserved to the States respectively, or to the people.

Amendment XI

[Adopted 1798]

The judicial power of the United States shall not be construed to extend to any suit in law or equity, commenced or prosecuted against one of the United States by citizens of another State, or by citizens or subjects of any foreign state.

Amendment XII

[Adopted 1804]

The electors shall meet in their respective States, and vote by ballot for President and Vice-President, one of whom, at least, shall not be an inhabitant of the same State with themselves; they shall name in their ballots the person voted for as President, and in distinct ballots the person voted for as Vice-President, and they shall make distinct lists of all persons voted for as President, and of all persons voted for as Vice-President, and of the number of votes for each, which lists they shall sign and certify, and transmit sealed to the seat of government of the United States, directed to the President of the Senate;—the President of the Senate shall, in the presence of the Senate and House of Representatives, open all the certificates and the votes shall then be counted;— the person having the greatest number of votes for President shall be the President, if such number be a majority of the whole number of electors appointed; and if no person have such majority, then from the persons having the highest numbers not exceeding three on the list of those voted for as President, the House of Representatives shall choose immediately, by ballot, the President. But in choosing the President, the votes shall be taken by States, the representation from each State having one vote; a quorum for this purpose shall consist of a member or members from two-thirds of the States,

and a majority of all the States shall be necessary to a choice. And if the House of Representatives shall not choose a President whenever the right of choice shall devolve upon them, before *the fourth day of March* next following, then the Vice-President shall act as President, as in the case of the death or other constitutional disability of the President.

The person having the greatest number of votes as Vice-President shall be the Vice-President, if such number be a majority of the whole number of electors appointed; and if no person have a majority, then from the two highest numbers on the list the Senate shall choose the Vice-President; a quorum for the purpose shall consist of two-thirds of the whole number of Senators, and a majority of the whole number shall be necessary to a choice. But no person constitutionally ineligible to the office of President shall be eligible to that of Vice-President of the United States.

Amendment XIII

[Adopted 1865]

Section 1 Neither slavery nor involuntary servitude, except as a punishment for crime whereof the party shall have been duly convicted, shall exist within the United States, or any place subject to their jurisdiction.

Section 2 Congress shall have power to enforce this article by appropriate legislation.

Amendment XIV

[Adopted 1868]

Section 1 All persons born or naturalized in the United States, and subject to the jurisdiction thereof, are citizens of the United States and of the State wherein they reside. No State shall make or enforce any law which shall abridge the privileges or immunities of citizens of the United States; nor shall any State deprive any person of life, liberty, or property, without due process of law; nor deny to any person within its jurisdiction the equal protection of the laws.

Section 2 Representatives shall be apportioned among the several States according to their respective numbers, counting the whole number of persons in each State, excluding Indians not taxed. But when the right to vote at any election for the choice of Electors for President and Vice-President of the United States, Representatives in Congress, the executive and judicial officers of a State, or the members of the legislature thereof, is denied to any of the male inhabitants of such State, being twenty-one years of age and citizens of the United States, or in any way abridged, except for participation in rebellion, or other crime, the basis of representation therein shall be reduced in the proportion which the number of such male citizens shall bear to the whole number of male citizens twenty-one years of age in such State.

Section 3 No person shall be a Senator or Representative in Congress, or Elector of President and Vice-President, or hold any office, civil or military, under the United States, or under any State, who, having previously taken an oath, as a member of Congress, or as an officer of the United States, or as a member of any State legislature, or as an executive or judicial officer of any State, to support the Constitution of the United States, shall have engaged in insurrection or rebellion against the same, or given aid or comfort to the enemies thereof. Congress may, by a vote of two-thirds of each house, remove such disability.

Section 4 The validity of the public debt of the United States, authorized by law, including debts incurred for payment of pensions and bounties for services in suppressing insurrection or rebellion, shall not be questioned. But neither the United States nor any State shall assume or pay any debt or obligation incurred in aid of insurrection or rebellion against the United States, or any claim for the loss of emancipation of any slave; but all such debts, obligations, and claims shall be held illegal and void.

Section 5 The Congress shall have power to enforce, by appropriate legislation, the provisions of this article.

Amendment XV

[Adopted 1870]

Section 1 The right of citizens of the United States to vote shall not be denied or abridged by the United States or by any State on account of race, color, or previous condition of servitude.

Section 2 The Congress shall have power to enforce this article by appropriate legislation.

Amendment XVI

[Adopted 1913]

The Congress shall have power to lay and collect taxes on incomes, from whatever source derived, without apportionment among the several States, and without regard to any census or enumeration.

Amendment XVII

[Adopted 1913]

Section 1 The Senate of the United States shall be composed of two Senators from each State, elected by the people thereof, for six years; and each Senator shall have one vote. The electors in each State shall have the qualifications requisite for electors of [voters for] the most numerous branch of the State legislatures.

Section 2 When vacancies happen in the representation of any State in the Senate, the executive authority of such State shall issue writs of election to fill such vacancies: Provided, that the Legislature of any State may empower the executive thereof to make temporary appointments until the people fill the vacancies by election as the Legislature may direct.

Section 3 This amendment shall not be so construed as to affect the election or term of any Senator chosen before it becomes valid as part of the Constitution.

Amendment XVIII

[Adopted 1919; Repealed 1933]

Section 1 After one year from the ratification of this article the manufacture, sale, or transportation of intoxicating liquors within, the importation thereof into, or the exportation thereof from the United States and all territory subject to the jurisdiction thereof, for beverage purposes, is hereby prohibited.

Section 2 The Congress and the several States shall have concurrent power to enforce this article by appropriate legislation.

Section 3 This article shall be inoperative unless it shall have been ratified as an amendment to the Constitution by the legislatures of the several States, as provided by the Constitution, within seven years from the date of the submission thereof to the States by the Congress.

Amendment XIX

[Adopted 1920]

Section 1 The right of citizens of the United States to vote shall not be denied or abridged by the United States or by any State on account of sex.

Section 2 The Congress shall have power to enforce this article by appropriate legislation.

Amendment XX

[Adopted 1933]

Section 1 The terms of the President and Vice-President shall end at noon on the 20th day of January, and the terms of Senators and Representatives at noon on the 3rd day of January, of the years in which such terms would have ended if this article had not been ratified; and the terms of their successors shall then begin.

Section 2 The Congress shall assemble at least once in every year, and such meeting shall begin at noon on the 3d day of January, unless they shall by law appoint a different day.

Section 3 If, at the time fixed for the beginning of the term of the President, the President-elect shall have died, the Vice-President–elect shall become President. If a President shall not have been chosen before the time fixed for the beginning of his term, or if the President-elect shall have failed to qualify, then the Vice-President–elect shall act as President until a President shall have qualified; and the Congress may by law provide for the case wherein neither a President-elect nor a Vice-President–elect shall have qualified, declaring who shall then act as President, or the manner in which one who is to act shall be selected, and such persons shall act accordingly until a President or Vice-President shall have qualified.

Section 4 The Congress may by law provide for the case of the death of any of the persons from whom the House of Representatives may choose a President whenever the right of choice shall have devolved upon them, and for the case of the death of any of the persons from whom the Senate may choose a Vice-President whenever the right of choice shall have devolved upon them.

Section 5 Sections 1 and 2 shall take effect on the 15th day of October following the ratification of this article.

Section 6 This article shall be inoperative unless it shall have been ratified as an amendment to the Constitution by the Legislatures of three-fourths of the several States within seven years from the date of its submission.

Amendment XXI

[Adopted 1933]

Section 1 The eighteenth article of amendment to the Constitution of the United States is hereby repealed.

Section 2 The transportation or importation into any State, Territory, or Possession of the United States for delivery or use therein of intoxicating liquors, in violation of the laws thereof, is hereby prohibited.

Section 3 This article shall be inoperative unless it shall have been ratified as an amendment to the Constitution by conventions in the several States, as provided in the Constitution, within seven years from the date of submission thereof to the States by the Congress.

Amendment XXII

[Adopted 1951]

Section 1 No person shall be elected to the office of President more than twice, and no person who has held the office of President, or acted as President, for more than two years of a term to which some other person was elected President shall be elected to the office of President more than once. But this article shall not apply to any person holding the office of President when this article was proposed by the Congress, and shall not prevent any person who may be holding the office of President, or acting as President, during the term within which this article becomes operative from holding the office of President or acting as President during the remainder of such term.

Section 2 This article shall be inoperative unless it shall have been ratified as an amendment to the Constitution by the legislatures of three-fourths of the several States within seven years from the date of its submission to the States by the Congress.

Amendment XXIII

[Adopted 1961]

Section 1 The District constituting the seat of Government of the United States shall appoint in such manner as the Congress may direct:

A number of electors of President and Vice-President equal to the whole number of Senators and Representatives in Congress to which the District would be entitled if it were a State, but in no event more than the least populous State; they shall be in addition to those appointed by the States, but they shall be considered for the purposes of the election of President and Vice-President, to be electors appointed by a State; and they shall meet in the District and perform such duties as provided by the twelfth article of amendment.

Section 2 The Congress shall have the power to enforce this article by appropriate legislation.

Amendment XXIV

[Adopted 1964]

Section 1 The right of citizens of the United States to vote in any primary or other election for President or Vice-President, for electors for President or Vice-President, or for Senator or Representative in Congress, shall not be denied or abridged by the United States or any State by reason of failure to pay any poll tax or other tax.

Section 2 The Congress shall have the power to enforce this article by appropriate legislation.

Amendment XXV

[Adopted 1967]

Section 1 In case of the removal of the President from office or of his death or resignation, the Vice-President shall become President.

Section 2 Whenever there is a vacancy in the office of the Vice-President, the President shall nominate a Vice-President who shall take office upon confirmation by a majority vote of both Houses of Congress.

Section 3 Whenever the President transmits to the President pro tempore of the Senate and the Speaker of the House of Representatives his written declaration that he is unable to discharge the powers and duties of his office, and until he transmits to them a written declaration to the contrary, such powers and duties shall be discharged by the Vice-President as Acting President.

Section 4 Whenever the Vice-President and a majority of either the principal officers of the executive departments or of such other body as Congress may by law provide, transmit to the President pro tempore of the Senate and the Speaker of the House of Representatives their written declaration that the President is unable to discharge the powers and duties of his office, the Vice-President shall immediately assume the powers and duties of the office as Acting President.

Thereafter, when the President transmits to the President pro tempore of the Senate and the Speaker of the House of Representatives his written declaration that no inability exists, he shall resume the powers and duties of his office unless the Vice-President and a majority of either the principal officers of the executive department[s] or of such other body as Congress may by law provide, transmit within four days to the President pro tempore of the Senate and the Speaker of the House of Representatives their written declaration that the President is unable to discharge the powers and duties of his office. Thereupon Congress shall decide the issue, assembling within forty-eight hours for that purpose if not in session. If the Congress, within twenty-one days after receipt of the latter written declaration, or, if Congress is not in session, within twenty-one days after Congress is required to assemble, determines by two-thirds vote of both Houses that the President is unable to discharge the powers and duties of his office, the Vice-President shall continue to discharge the same as Acting President; otherwise, the President shall resume the powers and duties of his office.

Amendment XXVI

[Adopted 1971]

Section 1 The right of citizens of the United States, who are eighteen years of age or older, to vote shall not be denied or abridged by the United States or by any State on account of age.

Section 2 The Congress shall have power to enforce this article by appropriate legislation.

Amendment XXVII

[Adopted 1992]

No law, varying the compensation for the services of the Senators and Representatives, shall take effect, until an election of Representatives shall have intervened.

Presidential Elections

Year	Number of States	Candidates	Parties	Popular Vote	% of Popular Vote	Electoral Vote	% Voter Participation[a]
1789	10	**George Washington**	No party			69	
		John Adams	designations			34	
		Other candidates				35	
1792	15	**George Washington**	No party			132	
		John Adams	designations			77	
		George Clinton				50	
		Other candidates				5	
1796	16	**John Adams**	Federalist			71	
		Thomas Jefferson	Democratic-Republican			68	
		Thomas Pinckney	Federalist			59	
		Aaron Burr	Democratic-Republican			30	
		Other candidates				48	
1800	16	**Thomas Jefferson**	Democratic-Republican			73	
		Aaron Burr	Democratic-Republican			73	
		John Adams	Federalist			65	
		Charles C. Pinckney	Federalist			64	
		John Jay	Federalist			1	
1804	17	**Thomas Jefferson**	Democratic-Republican			162	
		Charles C. Pinckney	Federalist			14	
1808	17	**James Madison**	Democratic-Republican			122	
		Charles C. Pinckney	Federalist			47	
		George Clinton	Democratic-Republican			6	
1812	18	**James Madison**	Democratic-Republican			128	
		DeWitt Clinton	Federalist			89	
1816	19	**James Monroe**	Democratic-Republican			183	
		Rufus King	Federalist			34	
1820	24	**James Monroe**	Democratic-Republican			231	
		John Quincy Adams	Independent Republican			1	
1824	24	**John Quincy Adams**	Democratic-Republican	108,740	30.5	84	26.9
		Andrew Jackson	Democratic-Republican	153,544	43.1	99	
		Henry Clay	Democratic-Republican	47,136	13.2	37	
		William H. Crawford	Democratic-Republican	46,618	13.1	41	
1828	24	**Andrew Jackson**	Democratic	647,286	56.0	178	57.6
		John Quincy Adams	National Republican	508,064	44.0	83	
1832	24	**Andrew Jackson**	Democratic	701,780	54.2	219	55.4
		Henry Clay	National Republican	484,205	37.4	49	
		Other candidates		107,988	8.0	18	

Presidential Elections (continued)

Year	Number of States	Candidates	Parties	Popular Vote	% of Popular Vote	Electoral Vote	% Voter Participation[a]
1836	26	**Martin Van Buren**	Democratic	764,176	50.8	170	57.8
		William H. Harrison	Whig	550,816	36.6	73	
		Hugh L. White	Whig	146,107	9.7	26	
1840	26	**William H. Harrison**	Whig	1,274,624	53.1	234	80.2
		Martin Van Buren	Democratic	1,127,781	46.9	60	
1844	26	**James K. Polk**	Democratic	1,338,464	49.6	170	78.9
		Henry Clay	Whig	1,300,097	48.1	105	
		James G. Birney	Liberty	62,300	2.3		
1848	30	**Zachary Taylor**	Whig	1,360,967	47.4	163	72.7
		Lewis Cass	Democratic	1,222,342	42.5	127	
		Martin Van Buren	Free Soil	291,263	10.1		
1852	31	**Franklin Pierce**	Democratic	1,601,117	50.9	254	69.6
		Winfield Scott	Whig	1,385,453	44.1	42	
		John P. Hale	Free Soil	155,825	5.0		
1856	31	**James Buchanan**	Democratic	1,832,955	45.3	174	78.9
		John C. Frémont	Republican	1,339,932	33.1	114	
		Millard Fillmore	American	871,731	21.6		
1860	33	**Abraham Lincoln**	Republican	1,865,593	39.8	180	81.2
		Stephen A. Douglas	Democratic	1,382,713	29.5	12	
		John C. Breckinridge	Democratic	848,356	18.1	72	
		John Bell	Constitutional Union	592,906	12.6	39	
1864	36	**Abraham Lincoln**	Republican	2,206,938	55.0	212	73.8
		George B. McClellan	Democratic	1,803,787	45.0	21	
1868	37	**Ulysses S. Grant**	Republican	3,013,421	52.7	214	78.1
		Horatio Seymour	Democratic	2,706,829	47.3	80	
1872	37	**Ulysses S. Grant**	Republican	3,596,745	55.6	286	71.3
		Horace Greeley	Democratic	2,843,446	43.9	b	
1876	38	**Rutherford B. Hayes**	Republican	4,036,572	48.0	185	81.8
		Samuel J. Tilden	Democratic	4,284,020	51.0	184	
1880	38	**James A. Garfield**	Republican	4,453,295	48.5	214	79.4
		Winfield S. Hancock	Democratic	4,414,082	48.1	155	
		James B. Weaver	Greenback-Labor	308,578	3.4		
1884	38	**Grover Cleveland**	Democratic	4,879,507	48.5	219	77.5
		James G. Blaine	Republican	4,850,293	48.2	182	
		Benjamin F. Butler	Greenback-Labor	175,370	1.8		
		John P. St. John	Prohibition	150,369	1.5		
1888	38	**Benjamin Harrison**	Republican	5,447,129	47.9	233	79.3
		Grover Cleveland	Democratic	5,537,857	48.6	168	
		Clinton B. Fisk	Prohibition	249,506	2.2		

Presidents and Vice Presidents (continued)

Year	Number of States	Candidates	Parties	Popular Vote	% of Popular Vote	Electoral Vote	% Voter Participation[a]
		Anson J. Streeter	Union Labor	146,935	1.3		
1892	44	**Grover Cleveland**	Democratic	5,555,426	46.1	277	74.7
		Benjamin Harrison	Republican	5,182,690	43.0	145	
		James B. Weaver	People's	1,029,846	8.5	22	
		John Bidwell	Prohibition	264,133	2.2		
1896	45	**William McKinley**	Republican	7,102,246	51.1	271	79.3
		William J. Bryan	Democratic	6,492,559	47.7	176	
1900	45	**William McKinley**	Republican	7,218,491	51.7	292	73.2
		William J. Bryan	Democratic; Populist	6,356,734	45.5	155	
		John C. Wooley	Prohibition	208,914	1.5		
1904	45	**Theodore Roosevelt**	Republican	7,628,461	57.4	336	65.2
		Alton B. Parker	Democratic	5,084,223	37.6	140	
		Eugene V. Debs	Socialist	402,283	3.0		
		Silas C. Swallow	Prohibition	258,536	1.9		
1908	46	**William H. Taft**	Republican	7,675,320	51.6	321	65.4
		William J. Bryan	Democratic	6,412,294	43.1	162	
		Eugene V. Debs	Socialist	420,793	2.8		
		Eugene W. Chafin	Prohibition	253,840	1.7		
1912	48	**Woodrow Wilson**	Democratic	6,296,547	41.9	435	58.8
		Theodore Roosevelt	Progressive	4,118,571	27.4	88	
		William H. Taft	Republican	3,486,720	23.2	8	
		Eugene V. Debs	Socialist	900,672	6.0		
		Eugene W. Chafin	Prohibition	206,275	1.4		
1916	48	**Woodrow Wilson**	Democratic	9,127,695	49.4	277	61.6
		Charles E. Hughes	Republican	8,533,507	46.2	254	
		A. L. Benson	Socialist	585,113	3.2		
		J. Frank Hanly	Prohibition	220,506	1.2		
1920	48	**Warren G. Harding**	Republican	16,143,407	60.4	404	49.2
		James M. Cox	Democratic	9,130,328	34.2	127	
		Eugene V. Debs	Socialist	919,799	3.4		
		P. P. Christensen	Farmer-Labor	265,411	1.0		
1924	48	**Calvin Coolidge**	Republican	15,718,211	54.0	382	48.9
		John W. Davis	Democratic	8,385,283	28.8	136	
		Robert M. La Follette	Progressive	4,831,289	16.6	13	
1928	48	**Herbert C. Hoover**	Republican	21,391,993	58.2	444	56.9
		Alfred E. Smith	Democratic	15,016,169	40.9	87	
1932	48	**Franklin D. Roosevelt**	Democratic	22,809,638	57.4	472	56.9
		Herbert C. Hoover	Republican	15,758,901	39.7	59	
		Norman Thomas	Socialist	881,951	2.2		

Presidential Elections (continued)

Year	Number of States	Candidates	Parties	Popular Vote	% of Popular Vote	Electoral Vote	% Voter Participation[a]
1936	48	**Franklin D. Roosevelt**	Democratic	27,752,869	60.8	523	61.0
		Alfred M. Landon	Republican	16,674,665	36.5	8	
		William Lemke	Union	882,479	1.9		
1940	48	**Franklin D. Roosevelt**	Democratic	27,307,819	54.8	449	62.5
		Wendell L. Willkie	Republican	22,321,018	44.8	82	
1944	48	**Franklin D. Roosevelt**	Democratic	25,606,585	53.5	432	55.9
		Thomas E. Dewey	Republican	22,014,745	46.0	99	
1948	48	**Harry S Truman**	Democratic	24,179,345	49.6	303	53.0
		Thomas E. Dewey	Republican	21,991,291	45.1	189	
		J. Strom Thurmond	States' Rights	1,176,125	2.4	39	
		Henry A. Wallace	Progressive	1,157,326	2.4		
1952	48	**Dwight D. Eisenhower**	Republican	33,936,234	55.1	442	63.3
		Adlai E. Stevenson	Democratic	27,314,992	44.4	89	
1956	48	**Dwight D. Eisenhower**	Republican	35,590,472	57.6	457	60.6
		Adlai E. Stevenson	Democratic	26,022,752	42.1	73	
1960	50	**John F. Kennedy**	Democratic	34,226,731	49.7	303	62.8
		Richard M. Nixon	Republican	34,108,157	49.5	219	
1964	50	**Lyndon B. Johnson**	Democratic	43,129,566	61.1	486	61.7
		Barry M. Goldwater	Republican	27,178,188	38.5	52	
1968	50	**Richard M. Nixon**	Republican	31,785,480	43.4	301	60.6
		Hubert H. Humphrey	Democratic	31,275,166	42.7	191	
		George C. Wallace	American Independent	9,906,473	13.5	46	
1972	50	**Richard M. Nixon**	Republican	47,169,911	60.7	520	55.2
		George S. McGovern	Democratic	29,170,383	37.5	17	
		John G. Schmitz	American	1,099,482	1.4		
1976	50	**James E. Carter**	Democratic	40,830,763	50.1	297	53.5
		Gerald R. Ford	Republican	39,147,793	48.0	240	
1980	50	**Ronald W. Reagan**	Republican	43,904,153	50.7	489	52.6
		James E. Carter	Democratic	35,483,883	41.0	49	
		John B. Anderson	Independent	5,720,060	6.6		
		Ed Clark	Libertarian	921,299	1.1		
1984	50	**Ronald W. Reagan**	Republican	54,455,075	58.8	525	53.3
		Walter F. Mondale	Democratic	37,577,185	40.6	13	
1988	50	**George H. W. Bush**	Republican	48,886,097	53.4	426	50.1
		Michael S. Dukakis	Democratic	41,809,074	45.6	111c	
1992	50	**William J. Clinton**	Democratic	44,909,326	43.0	370	55.2
		George H. W. Bush	Republican	39,103,882	37.4	168	
		H. Ross Perot	Independent	19,741,048	18.9		

Justices of the Supreme Court (continued)

Year	Number of States	Candidates	Parties	Popular Vote	% of Popular Vote	Electoral Vote	% Voter Participation[a]
1996	50	William J. Clinton	Democratic	47,402,357	49.2	379	49.1
		Robert J. Dole	Republican	39,196,755	40.7	159	
		H. Ross Perot	Reform	8,085,402	8.4		
		Ralph Nader	Green	684,902	0.7		
2000	50	George W. Bush	Republican	50,455,156	47.9	271	51.2
		Albert Gore	Democratic	50,992,335	48.4	266	
		Ralph Nader	Green	2,882,955	2.7		
2004	50	George W. Bush	Republican	62,039,073	50.7	286	55.3
		John F. Kerry	Democratic	59,027,478	48.2	251	
		Ralph Nader	Independent	240,896	0.2		
2008	50	Barack Obama	Democratic	69,498,459	53.0	365	61.7
		John McCain	Republican	59,948,283	46.0	173	
		Ralph Nader	Independent	739,165	0.55		

Candidates receiving less than 1 percent of the popular vote have been omitted. Thus the percentage of popular vote given for any election year may not total 100 percent.

Before the passage of the Twelfth Amendment in 1804, the electoral college voted for two presidential candidates; the runner-up became vice president.

Before 1824, most presidential electors were chosen by state legislatures, not by popular vote.

[a]Percent of voting-age population casting ballots.
[b]Greeley died shortly after the election; the electors supporting him then divided their votes among minor candidates.
[c]One elector from West Virginia cast her electoral college presidential ballot for Lloyd Bentsen, the Democratic Party's vice-presidential candidate.

Presidents and Vice Presidents

1. President	**George Washington**	1789–1797	18. President	**Ulysses S. Grant**	1869–1877
Vice President	John Adams	1789–1797	Vice President	Schuyler Colfax	1869–1873
2. President	**John Adams**	1797–1801	Vice President	Henry Wilson	1873–1877
Vice President	Thomas Jefferson	1797–1801	19. President	**Rutherford B. Hayes**	1877–1881
3. President	**Thomas Jefferson**	1801–1809	Vice President	William A. Wheeler	1877–1881
Vice President	Aaron Burr	1801–1805	20. President	**James A. Garfield**	1881
Vice President	George Clinton	1805–1809	Vice President	Chester A. Arthur	1881
4. President	**James Madison**	1809–1817	21. President	**Chester A. Arthur**	1881–1885
Vice President	George Clinton	1809–1813	Vice President	None	
Vice President	Elbridge Gerry	1813–1817	22. President	**Grover Cleveland**	1885–1889
5. President	**James Monroe**	1817–1825	Vice President	Thomas A. Hendricks	1885–1889
Vice President	Daniel Tompkins	1817–1825	23. President	**Benjamin Harrison**	1889–1893
6. President	**John Quincy Adams**	1825–1829	Vice President	Levi P. Morton	1889–1893
Vice President	John C. Calhoun	1825–1829	24. President	**Grover Cleveland**	1893–1897
7. President	**Andrew Jackson**	1829–1837	Vice President	Adlai E. Stevenson	1893–1897
Vice President	John C. Calhoun	1829–1833	25. President	**William McKinley**	1897–1901
Vice President	Martin Van Buren	1833–1837	Vice President	Garret A. Hobart	1897–1901
8. President	**Martin Van Buren**	1837–1841	Vice President	Theodore Roosevelt	1901
Vice President	Richard M. Johnson	1837–1841	26. President	**Theodore Roosevelt**	1901–1909
9. President	**William H. Harrison**	1841	Vice President	Charles Fairbanks	1905–1909
Vice President	John Tyler	1841	27. President	**William H. Taft**	1909–1913
10. President	**John Tyler**	1841–1845	Vice President	James S. Sherman	1909–1913
Vice President	None		28. President	**Woodrow Wilson**	1913–1921
11. President	**James K. Polk**	1845–1849	Vice President	Thomas R. Marshall	1913–1921
Vice President	George M. Dallas	1845–1849	29. President	**Warren G. Harding**	1921–1923
12. President	**Zachary Taylor**	1849–1850	Vice President	Calvin Coolidge	1921–1923
Vice President	Millard Fillmore	1849–1850	30. President	**Calvin Coolidge**	1923–1929
13. President	**Millard Fillmore**	1850–1853	Vice President	Charles G. Dawes	1925–1929
Vice President	None		31. President	**Herbert C. Hoover**	1929–1933
14. President	**Franklin Pierce**	1853–1857	Vice President	Charles Curtis	1929–1933
Vice President	William R. King	1853–1857	32. President	**Franklin D. Roosevelt**	1933–1945
15. President	**James Buchanan**	1857–1861	Vice President	John N. Garner	1933–1941
Vice President	John C. Breckinridge	1857–1861	Vice President	Henry A. Wallace	1941–1945
16. President	**Abraham Lincoln**	1861–1865	Vice President	Harry S Truman	1945
Vice President	Hannibal Hamlin	1861–1865	33. President	**Harry S Truman**	1945–1953
Vice President	Andrew Johnson	1865	Vice President	Alben W. Barkley	1949–1953
17. President	**Andrew Johnson**	1865–1869	34. President	**Dwight D. Eisenhower**	1953–1961
Vice President	None		Vice President	Richard M. Nixon	1953–1961

Presidents and Vice Presidents (continued)

35.	President	**John F. Kennedy**	1961–1963	40.	President	**Ronald W. Reagan**	1981–1989
	Vice President	Lyndon B. Johnson	1961–1963		Vice President	George H. W. Bush	1981–1989
36.	President	**Lyndon B. Johnson**	1963–1969	41.	President	**George H. W. Bush**	1989–1993
	Vice President	Hubert H. Humphrey	1965–1969		Vice President	J. Danforth Quayle	1989–1993
37.	President	**Richard M. Nixon**	1969–1974	42.	President	**William J. Clinton**	1993–2001
	Vice President	Spiro T. Agnew	1969–1973		Vice President	Albert Gore	1993–2001
	Vice President	Gerald R. Ford	1973–1974	43.	President	**George W. Bush**	2001–2009
38.	President	**Gerald R. Ford**	1974–1977		Vice President	Richard Cheney	2001–2009
	Vice President	Nelson A. Rockefeller	1974–1977	44.	President	**Barack Obama**	2009–
39.	President	**James E. Carter**	1977–1981		Vice President	Joseph Biden	2009–
	Vice President	Walter F. Mondale	1977–1981				

Justices of the Supreme Court

	Term of Service	Years of Service	Life Span		Term of Service	Years of Service	Life Span
John Jay	1789–1795	5	1745–1829	Stephen J. Field	1863–1897	34	1816–1899
John Rutledge	1789–1791	1	1739–1800	*Salmon P. Chase*	1864–1873	8	1808–1873
William Cushing	1789–1810	20	1732–1810	William Strong	1870–1880	10	1808–1895
James Wilson	1789–1798	8	1742–1798	Joseph P. Bradley	1870–1892	22	1813–1892
John Blair	1789–1796	6	1732–1800	Ward Hunt	1873–1882	9	1810–1886
Robert H. Harrison	1789–1790	—	1745–1790	*Morrison R. Waite*	1874–1888	14	1816–1888
James Iredell	1790–1799	9	1751–1799	John M. Harlan	1877–1911	34	1833–1911
Thomas Johnson	1791–1793	1	1732–1819	William B. Woods	1880–1887	7	1824–1887
William Paterson	1793–1806	13	1745–1806	Stanley Mathews	1881–1889	7	1824–1889
*John Rutledge**	1795	—	1739–1800	Horace Gray	1882–1902	20	1828–1902
Samuel Chase	1796–1811	15	1741–1811	Samuel Blatchford	1882–1893	11	1820–1893
Oliver Ellsworth	1796–1800	4	1745–1807	Lucius Q. C. Lamar	1888–1893	5	1825–1893
Bushrod Washington	1798–1829	31	1762–1829	*Melville W. Fuller*	1888–1910	21	1833–1910
Alfred Moore	1799–1804	4	1755–1810	David J. Brewer	1890–1910	20	1837–1910
John Marshall	1801–1835	34	1755–1835	Henry B. Brown	1890–1906	16	1836–1913
William Johnson	1804–1834	30	1771–1834	George Shiras Jr.	1892–1903	10	1832–1924
H. Brockholst Livingston	1806–1823	16	1757–1823	Howell E. Jackson	1893–1895	2	1832–1895
Thomas Todd	1807–1826	18	1765–1826	Edward D. White	1894–1910	16	1845–1921
Joseph Story	1811–1845	33	1779–1845	Rufus W. Peckham	1895–1909	14	1838–1909
Gabriel Duval	1811–1835	24	1752–1844	Joseph McKenna	1898–1925	26	1843–1926
Smith Thompson	1823–1843	20	1768–1843	Oliver W. Holmes	1902–1932	30	1841–1935
Robert Trimble	1826–1828	2	1777–1828	William D. Day	1903–1922	19	1849–1923
John McLean	1829–1861	32	1785–1861	William H. Moody	1906–1910	3	1853–1917
Henry Baldwin	1830–1844	14	1780–1844	Horace H. Lurton	1910–1914	4	1844–1914
James M. Wayne	1835–1867	32	1790–1867	Charles E. Hughes	1910–1916	5	1862–1948
Roger B. Taney	1836–1864	28	1777–1864	Willis Van Devanter	1911–1937	26	1859–1941
Philip P. Barbour	1836–1841	4	1783–1841	Joseph R. Lamar	1911–1916	5	1857–1916
John Catron	1837–1865	28	1786–1865	*Edward D. White*	1910–1921	11	1845–1921
John McKinley	1837–1852	15	1780–1852	Mahlon Pitney	1912–1922	10	1858–1924
Peter V. Daniel	1841–1860	19	1784–1860	James C. McReynolds	1914–1941	26	1862–1946
Samuel Nelson	1845–1872	27	1792–1873	Louis D. Brandeis	1916–1939	22	1856–1941
Levi Woodbury	1845–1851	5	1789–1851	John H. Clarke	1916–1922	6	1857–1945
Robert C. Grier	1846–1870	23	1794–1870	*William H. Taft*	1921–1930	8	1857–1930
Benjamin R. Curtis	1851–1857	6	1809–1874	George Sutherland	1922–1938	15	1862–1942
John A. Campbell	1853–1861	8	1811–1889	Pierce Butler	1922–1939	16	1866–1939
Nathan Clifford	1858–1881	23	1803–1881	Edward T. Sanford	1923–1930	7	1865–1930
Noah H. Swayne	1862–1881	18	1804–1884	Harlan F. Stone	1925–1941	16	1872–1946
Samuel F. Miller	1862–1890	28	1816–1890	*Charles E. Hughes*	1930–1941	11	1862–1948
David Davis	1862–1877	14	1815–1886	Owen J. Roberts	1930–1945	15	1875–1955
				Benjamin N. Cardozo	1932–1938	6	1870–1938

Justices of the Supreme Court (continued)

	Term of Service	Years of Service	Life Span		Term of Service	Years of Service	Life Span
Hugo L. Black	1937–1971	34	1886–1971	Arthur J. Goldberg	1962–1965	3	1908–1990
Stanley F. Reed	1938–1957	19	1884–1980	Abe Fortas	1965–1969	4	1910–1982
Felix Frankfurter	1939–1962	23	1882–1965	Thurgood Marshall	1967–1991	24	1908–1993
William O. Douglas	1939–1975	36	1898–1980	*Warren C. Burger*	1969–1986	17	1907–1995
Frank Murphy	1940–1949	9	1890–1949	Harry A. Blackmun	1970–1994	24	1908–1998
Harlan F. Stone	1941–1946	5	1872–1946	Lewis F. Powell Jr.	1972–1987	15	1907–1998
James F. Byrnes	1941–1942	1	1879–1972	*William H. Rehnquist*	1972–2005	33	1924–2005
Robert H. Jackson	1941–1954	13	1892–1954	John P. Stevens III	1975–	—	1920–
Wiley B. Rutledge	1943–1949	6	1894–1949	Sandra Day O'Connor	1981–	—	1930–
Harold H. Burton	1945–1958	13	1888–1964	Antonin Scalia	1986–	—	1936–
Fred M. Vinson	1946–1953	7	1890–1953	Anthony M. Kennedy	1988–	—	1936–
Tom C. Clark	1949–1967	18	1899–1977	David H. Souter	1990–	—	1939–
Sherman Minton	1949–1956	7	1890–1965	Clarence Thomas	1991–	—	1948–
Earl Warren	1953–1969	16	1891–1974	Ruth Bader Ginsburg	1993–	—	1933–
John Marshall Harlan	1955–1971	16	1899–1971	Stephen Breyer	1994–	—	1938–
William J. Brennan Jr.	1956–1990	34	1906–1997	John G. Roberts	2005–	—	1955–
Charles E. Whittaker	1957–1962	5	1901–1973	Samuel A. Alito, Jr.	2006–	—	1950–
Potter Stewart	1958–1981	23	1915–1985	Sonia Sotomayor	2009–	—	1954–
Byron R. White	1962–1993	31	1917–	Elena Kagan	2010–	—	1960–

Note: Chief justices are in italics.

*Appointed and served one term, but not confirmed by the Senate.

Index

Abbott, Edith, 546
Abenakis, 63
ABM Treaty (Anti-Ballistic Missile Systems), 827
Abolitionism, 296–300
  African American abolitionists, 299
  American Antislavery Society, 298
  colonization and, 296, 298
  immediatism, 298
  international antislavery movement, 297
  Lane Debates, 298
  moral suasion versus political action, 299–300
  opposition to, 299
  Quakers and, 352
  Wilmot Proviso and, 348
Aborigines, 447
Abortion, 275, 564
Accused persons, rights of, 184
Acheson, Dean, 742
Acoma Pueblo, 31
Act of Religious Toleration (1649), 40
Adams, Abigail, 149, **162**–163
Adams, Charles Francis, 396
Adams, Henry, 426
Adams, John, 106, 133, 142, 143, 149, 153, 202
  defense of British soldiers, 124
  election of 1796, 192–193
  election of 1800, 199
  presidency of, 193–194, 196
Adams, John Quincy
  Amistad case and, 236
  in election of 1824, 301–302
  as representative, 308
  as secretary of state, 222
Adams, Samuel, 125, 126, 133, 177
Adamson Act, 563
Adams-Onís Treaty, 222
Addams, Jane, **502**, 544, 555, 581, 582, 609
Adkins v. Children's Hospital (1923), 622
Advanced Research Projects Agency, 903
Advertising
  colonial, 94
  consumerism and, 627
  imperialism and, 572
  in late 19th century, 478
Affirmative Action, **820,** 831
  program, 839
Afghanistan
  covert assistance to, 857
  criticism of war in, 201
  Soviet invasion of, 816, 841
  U.S. war against, 887
Africa
  antiradicalism in, 830
  corn production, 21
  immigration from, 772

slaves and Anglo-American economy, 56
"Africa for the Africans," 426
African Americans, 76
  activism and, 524
  Black Power, 805
  civil rights, 782
  in Civil War, 386, 388, 389, 402
  in colonial revolution, 138, 140, 147, 151
  cultural nationalism, 817–818
  culture of, 817
  discrimination of, 552
  disfranchisement of, 522–523
  "Double V" campaign, 715
  education of, after emancipation, 409–410
  families in colonial times, 97
  free black communities, 245
  free black population, 164, 245
  freedpeople's lives, 164–165
  growth of black churches, 410
  Harlem Renaissance, 640–641
  jazz and, 641
  migration to cities, 491
  militancy among veterans, 613
  and the New Deal, 674
  political power of, 766–767
  proportion of total population (map), 165
  racial segregation and, 494–495, 523, 746, 748, 794
  Reconstruction and reunion of families, 409
  representation of, in mass culture, 510
  revolutionary ideology and, 163
  rioting, 787
  in Sierra Leone, 139
  in sports, 506, 554, 639, 670, 748
  urban migration, 609, 628
  in Vietnam War, 802
African Methodist Episcopal (AME) church, **165, 281,** 410
African societies, 9–11
  characteristics of, 25–26
  complementary gender roles, 10
  Portuguese trading posts, 13–14
  slavery in Guinea, 10–11
  West Africa (Guinea), 10
Agent Orange, 827
Agnew, Spiro, 831, 832
Agricultural Adjustment Act, **657,** 658
Agriculture. *See also* Farms and farming
  agriculture regions, 450
  in central Mexico, 3
  commercial, 273
  consumer and farm product prices, 527
  decline, during 1920s, 623

foreign trade and, 573
  hardship in Midwest and West, 526–527
  legislative and scientific aids, 452
  mechanization of, 451–452
  and rise of North American civilizations, 25
  sharecropping, 411–412
Aguinaldo, Emilio, **582**
AIDS epidemic, 862–863
Aid to Families with Dependent Children (AFDC), 663, 799
Airline deregulation, 854
Air traffic controller strike, 851
Alabama, 224
Alamo, 331
Alaska
  purchase of, 425
  statehood, 772
Albany Congress, 109, 111
Albany Regency, 308
Albee, Edward, 508
Alcatraz Island, 819
Alcohol abuse, 95
  temperance movement, 291, 293
Alcott, Louisa May, 382
Aldrich, Nelson W., 547, 560
Alexander II, czar of Russia, 530
Alfred P. Murrah Federal Building bombing, 882
Algerian oil embargo of 1973, 829
Algonquians, 7, 9, 39, 63
Alianza Federal de Mercedes (Federal Alliance of Grants), 819
Alien and Sedition Acts, **194,** 202, 207
Alien Registration Act, 713
Alito, Samuel, 892
Allende, Salvador, 830
Alliance for Progress, 790
All-volunteer force, **842**
Almshouses, 89
Almy, William, 225
Al Qaeda, **876,** 883, 900
  attack of 9/11/2001, 887
Altgeld, John P., 471, 544
Amalgamated Association of Iron and Steelworkers, 472
A.M.E. Zion Church, 410
America First Committee, 693
American and Foreign Anti-Slavery Society, 299
American Antislavery Society, 298
American Board of Customs Commissioners, 123
American Civil Liberties Union (ACLU), 616
American Colonization Society, 296, 426
American Dream, 756
American embassy bombings, 883
American Expeditionary Forces, **600**

American Federation of Labor, **471**–472, 665
American Friends Service Committee, 803
American ideals, 713–716
American Legion, 612, 693
American Peace Commission, 614
American Protestantism, 101
American Psychiatric Association, 823
American Renaissance, 295–296
American Revolution
  African Americans and, 138, 140
  alliance with France, 146–147, 154
  British evacuation of Boston, 142–143
  British strategy, 141–142
  campaign of 1777, 144–146
  choosing sides, 137–140, 154
  colonial government, 132–134
  Continental Army and Navy, 142, 147
  first year of war, 140–141
  formation of nations and, 139
  Greene and the Southern campaign, 151
  hardship and disease, 148–149
  Indian neutrality and hostility, 135–136
  Lexington and Concord, 140
  loyalists, 137–138
  neutrals, 138
  northern struggle, 144–147
  patriots, 137
  prisoners of war, 148
  surrender at Yorktown, 151–152
  symbolism, 152
  victory in the south, 149–153, 155
American societies, 2–6
  ancient America, 2–3
  Aztecs, 4, 6
  Cahokia, 5
  chronology, 3
  Mesoamerican civilizations, 4
  Pueblos and Mississippians, 4
American society
  culture wars, 861
  growth of religious right, 861
  homogenization of, 627
  new inequality, 862
  in 1980s, 860–865
  violence and anger in, 882
Americans with Disabilities Act, **871**
American System, 220–221, 229, 288, 302
American System of manufacturing, **269**
American Tobacco Company, 463
American Women Suffrage Association, 525
Amistad case, 236
Anaconda Copper Company, 442

Anaconda plan, **371**
Anarchists, 471
Ancient America, 2–3
"Ancient One," 24
Anderson, Marian, 674
Andros, Sir Edmund, 73
Angélique, Marie-Joseph, 79
Anglo-American rapprochement, 589
Anglo-Dutch wars, 65
Angola, 65, 830
Animals, 11, 808
Antagonisms, 88
Anthony, Susan B., 301, 407, 415, 525
Anticommunism. *See also* Communism
    in Congress, 765–766
    McCarthyism and "witch hunt," 765
    politics of, 764–765
Antietam, Battle of, **375**
Antifederalists, **177,** 181
Anti-imperialism, 576
Anti-Imperialist League, 582
Antimason Party, 305–306
Anti-Saloon League, **548**
Anti-Semitism, 689
Antislavery. *See* Abolitionism
Antitrust legislation, 482, 558
ANZUS Treaty, 742
Apaches, 63, 327, 437
Apartheid, 860, 866
Apollo 8, 812
Apollo program, 796
Apparel industry, 477–478
Appeasement, **688**
Appellate courts, 184
Appleton, Nathan, 225
Appomattox Court House, **399**
A&P stores, 478
Arab-Israeli conflict, 749–750, 859
Arab-Israeli Six-Day War, 830
Arafat, Yasir, 859
Architecture, 209
Arizona, 755
Arizona, 697
Arms, right to keep and bear, 184
Armstrong, Louis, 641
Armstrong, Neil, **838**
Army-McCarthy hearings, 766
Army of the Republic of Vietnam (ARVN), 800
Arnold, Benedict, 147, 151
Art. *See also* Jazz; Literature; Popular culture
    of the American West, 317–318, 329
Arthur, Chester A., 520
Article 10, 615
Articles of Confederation, **167**–169
    economic depression and, 172
    failure of, 157
    financial affairs, 169
    foreign affairs, 169–170
Artisans, preindustrial, 263
Arts Project, 663
Ashcroft, John, 888, 892
Asian Americans, 839
Asian immigrants, 772, 864, 896
Assembly, freedom of, 183

Assembly line production, 461, 463, 465
Assimilation, 438
Astronomy, 4
Aswan Dam, 750
Asylums, 291
Athletics. *See* Sports
Atlanta Compromise, 552
Atlanta University, 410
Atlantic Charter, **696**
Atlantic trading system
    African slavery and, 64–65
    exotic beverages, 67
    New England and the Caribbean, 68
    slaving voyages, 68
    trade routes (map), 66
Atomic bomb
    dropping of, on Japan, 722–723
    Manhattan Project, 708
    testing, 720
Atomic diplomacy, 733–734
Atomic Energy Commission (A.E.C.), 755
Attorney General, 184
Attucks, Crispus, 124
Audio cassette, 483
Austin, Moses, 330
Austin, Stephen, 330, 331
Australia, 139, 447, 742
Austria, 614
Autocratic rule, **73**
Automobile industry, 461, 463, 626–627
Avery, William Waightstill, 247
Axis powers, 696
Aztecs, 4, 6, 18

Ba'athist Party (Iraq), 843
Back to Africa movement, 426
Bacon, Nathaniel, 64, 77
Bacon's Rebellion, **64**
Bailey v. Drexel Furniture Company (1922), 622
Baker, Josephine, 640
Bakke, Allan, 839
Balboa, Vasco Núñez de, 17–18
Balch, Emily Greene, 610
Balfour Declaration, 614
Balkan Crisis, 882–883
Ball, George W., 802
Bank "holidays," 657
Banking system
    bank controversies, 305
    collapse of, and Panic of 1819
    crisis of Great Depression, 656–657
Banneker, Benjamin, 166
Bantu-speaking peoples, 9
Bao Dai, 751
Baptists, 205
Barbados, 68
Barbary Wars, 227
    First, 213
    Second, 219
Barbed wire, 453, 454
Barbie (doll), **777**
Barnum, P.T., 283
Barrios, 495, 629
Barrow, Bennet, 246
Bartering, 94
Barton, Clara, **382**

Bartram, John, 91
Bartram, William, 91
Baruch, Bernard, 606, 733
Baruch Plan, 733
Baseball, 282, 506, 639
    in Japan, 507
Batista, Fulgencio, 749
Battle at Yorktown, **151**
"Battle Hymn of the Republic" (Howe), 383
Battle of Antietam, **375**
Battle of Bud Dajo, 583
Battle of Bunker Hill, 140–141
Battle of Chancellorsville, 390
Battle of Concord, 140, 141, 150
Battle of Fallen Timbers, 196
Battle of Gettysburg, 391
Battle of Lexington, 140
Battle of New Orleans, 219
Battle of Put-in-Bay, 217
Battle of Shiloh, **374**
Battle of the Bulge, **718**
Battle of the Thames, 217
Battle of the Wilderness, 399
Baum, L. Frank, 537
Bay of Pigs, Cuba, 791
Beard, Charles, 546, 551, 610
"Bear Flag Rebellion," 337
Beat Generation, 778
The Beatles, 807, **808**
Beat (writers), **778**
Beaver Wars, **62**
Becknell, William, 324
Beecher, Catharine, 275, 276
Beecher, Lyman, 290, 298
Beecher, Mary, 276
Begin, Menachem, **840,** 841
Belgium, 693
Bell, Alexander Graham, 483, 552, 574
Bell, John, 362
Bellamy, Edward, 482
Bellamy, Francis, 782
Bemis, Edward, 482
Bennitt, James and Nancy, 244
Berbers, 9
Berenson, Senda, 506
Beringia, 2
Berkeley, John Lord, 59
Berkeley, William, 64
Berlin, Germany, 790
Berlin, Ira, 61
Berlin airlift, **737**
Berlin Wall, 790
Bernard, Francis, 120
Bernstein, Carl, 832
Berry, Chuck, 778, 808
Bessemer, Henry, 463
Bethlehem Steel Company, 465
Bethune, Mary McLeod, 662
Bibb, Henry, 299
Biblical creationism, 900
Bicameral legislature, 174
Bicycles, 506
Biddle, Nicholas, 305
Billboards, 478
Bill Haley and the Comets, 778
Bill of Rights, 176, 177, 183–184, **183**–184, 202
Biloxi Bay, 84
bin Laden, Osama, 883, **889**
Biogenetics, 898
Bird flu, 901

Birmingham, Alabama, 793
Birney, James G., 299, 309
Birth-control, 503, 555, 564, 632–633, 773
    decreasing family size and, 629
Birth of a Nation (film), 509, 563, 613
Birth rate, 759
Black codes, 413
Black Death epidemic, 11–12
Black Hawk War, 320–321
Black Kettle, 394, 437
"Black laws," 320
Blackmun, Harry, 831
Black Muslims, 805
Black Panthers, 805
Black Power, **805**
Blacks. *See* African Americans
"Black Sox scandal," 639
Black Thursday, 643
Blackwell, Henry, 300
Blaine, James G., 520
Blair, Ezell, 786
Blake, Eubie, 640
Bland-Allison Act, 519
Blatch, Harriot Stanton, 555, 556
"Bleeding Kansas," 358, 366
Blue-Gray fraternalism, 424
Blue laws, 51
Bly, Nellie, 509
Board of Trade and Plantations, 74
Boleyn, Anne, 36
Bolshevik Revolution, 602, 732
Bonaparte, Napoleon, 196
Bondsmen, 147
Bonnin, Gertrude, 438
Bonnin, Ray, 438
Bonsack, James, 463
Bonus Army, 655
Books, 510
Boone, Daniel, 131–132, 316–317
Boone, Pat, 778
Booth, John Wilkes, 399
Borden, Gail, 477
Border Ruffians, 358
Bork, Robert, 851
Bosque Redondo, 437
Bosses, **499**
Boston, British evacuation of, 142–143
Boston Associates, 225
Boston Manufacturing Company, 223, 225
Boston Massacre, 123, **124**
Boudinot, Elias, 239
Boulder (Hoover) Dam, 667
Bow, Clara, 634
Bowers v. Hardwick (1986), 851
Boxer Rebellion, **583**
Boycotts
    Continental Congress and, 133
    of Stamp Act, 122
Boylston, Zabdiel, 92
Bracero program, **708**
Bradley, Milton, 511
Bradwell, Myra, 427
Bradwell v. Illinois, 427
Brady, Matthew (photograph by), 375
Brandeis, Louis D., 550, 563
Brand name registry, 478
Brant, Mary and Joseph, **146**
Breckinridge, John C., 362

Breed's Hill, 140
Bremer, Paul, 890
Bretton Woods Conference, 732
A Briefe and True Report of the New Found Land of Virginia (Harriot), 23
British colonies
    colonial assemblies, 99, 105
    colonial cultures, 90–95, 104
    commerce and manufacturing in, 88, 104
    politics in, 99–100, 105
    regional economies, 89–90
    rioters and regulators, 100
    slave rebellions, 99–100
    wealth and poverty, 89
British Invasion (music), **808**
British Trans-Indian railroad, 569
British troops
    Boston Massacre, 124
    stationing of, in Boston, 124
Britton, Nan, 623
Brook Farm, 295
Brooks, Charles, 500
Brooks, Preston, 358
Brotherhood of Sleeping Car Porters, 674, 794
Brown, Albert G., 360
Brown, James, 807
Brown, James E., 392, 393
Brown, John, 343, 358, 361, 365, 366
Brown, Moses and Obadiah, 225
Brown, Noah, 217
Brown, Peter, 335
Brown, William Wells, 297
Brown Power, 817
Brown v. Board of Education, 523, 616, 756, **768,** 782
Bruce, Henry Clay, 314–315
Bryan, William Jennings, **535,** 537, 581, 593, 637
Bryant, William Cullen, 358
Brzezinski, Zbigniew, 840
Buchanan, James, 333, 358
Buchanan, Pat, 886
Bud Dajo, Battle of, 583
Buffalo Bill Cody, 432, 445
Buffalo hunting, 22, 26, 334–335
Buffalo slaughter, 435
Bulge, Battle of the, **718**
Bull Run, **371**
Bunch, Charlotte, 821
Bundy, McGeorge, 789
Bunker Hill, Battle of, 140–141
Buren, Martin Van, 304, 308–309, 348
Burger, Warren, 831
Burgoyne, John, 144–146
Burlend, Rebecca, 318
Burlingame Treaty, 575
Burma, 729
Burned-Over District, 290
Burnham, Daniel, 583
Burns, Anthony, 353
Burr, Aaron, 192–193, 199, 208
Burr Conspiracy, 208–209
Burroughs, George, 74
Burton, James, 388
Bus boycott, Montgomery, Alabama, 756, 782
Bush, George H. W., **865**
    Central American policy, 868

domestic issues, 871
election of, 866
end of Cold War and, 867–868
Middle East policy, 868–869
pardons, 859
Bush, George W., **886**
    contested election of, 886–887
    criticism of aggressive policies of, 892
    and Department of Homeland Security, 751
    economy and, 888–889, 894
    presidency of, 892–893
    war in Iraq, 889–890
    war on terrorism, 887
Bush, Neil, 855
Businesses and the war effort, 707
Business organizations, 622
Business reform, 562
Busing, 831
Butler, Andrew P., 358
Butler, William, 348
Byrd, James Jr., 882
Byrnes, James F., 733

Cabboto, Zuan. *See* Cabot, John
Cabeza de Vaca, Alvar Nuñez, 1
Cable News Network (CNN), 870
Cable television, 865
Cabot, John, **16**–17, 22, **39**
Cabot, Sebastian, 17
Cabral, Pedro Álvares, 17
Cahokia (City of the Sun), **4,** 5
Calendar, development of, 4
Calhoun, John C., 216, 221, 301, 304–305, 337, 348, 350
California
    admitted to the Union, 336, 349
    Gold Rush, 316, 322, 325, 335, 336
    population growth, 771
    tax revolt movement in, 835
    trails, 333–334
California Proposition 13, 835
Callender, James, 194
Calley, William, 824
Calumet (pipe), 6
Calvert, Cecilius, 40
Calvert, George (Lord Baltimore), 40
Calvin, John, **36**–37
Calvinists, 100
Cambodia, 824
Cameron, Evelyn, 451
Cameron, Paul, 366
Campaign of 1777, 144–146
Campbell, John A., 234, 392, 427
Camp David Accords, **840, 841,** 859
Camp Fire Girls, 744
Canada, 139
    border disputes, 309
    U.S.-Canadian boundary settlement, 222
    in War of 1812, 217, 219
Canals, 265, 267, 268
    and trade, 221
Canal Zone, 840
Caniba (Caribs), 16
Cannon, Joseph, 547
Capitalism, 424, 479
Capone, Al, 640

Cárdenas, Lázaro, 687
Cardozo, Francis, 410
Caribbean, 52, 137
    during American Revolution, 149, 151
    slavery in, 68–72
    trade and, 68
    warfare and hurricanes, 34–35
Carleton, James, 395
Carmichael, Stokely, 805
Carnegie, Andrew, 103, 463, **481,** 581
Carnegie Steel Company, 463, 472
Carolina colony, 60–61
Carpentier, Georges, 639
Carpetbaggers, **421**
Carretta, Vincent, 103
Carroll, Charles, 268
Carson, Kit, 395
Carson, Rachel, 779
Carter, Amy, 833
Carter, Jimmy, 816, 831, **840**
    Camp David accords and, 840, 841, 859
    divided administration of, 840
    election of, **833**
    human rights policy, 843
    Iranian hostage crisis and, 841–842
Carter, Rosalynn, 833
Carter Doctrine, 841
Carteret, George, 59
Cartier, Jacques, 17, 30
Carver, George Washington, 452
Cases of Conscience (Mather), 75
Cash registers, 464
Cass, Lewis, 348, 349
Cassatt, Alexander, 543
Castillo, Bernal Díaz del, 18
Castro, Fidel, 589, 743, 749
Catherine of Aragón, 36
Catholic Church
    conversion of "heathens" by, 12
    in European societies, 11
    Spanish colonization and, 18
Catholicism, 127
    anti-Catholicism, 280
    Jesuit missions in New France, 32, 34
Catlin, George, **318**
Catt, Carrie Chapman, **556**
Cattell, J. M., 610
Cattle industry, 668
Cattle ranching, 452–454
Caughlin, Charles, 661
Celebrity culture, 881
Censorship, 510
Census, 175
Central Intelligence Agency (CIA), 737, 743
    and Afghanistan, 841
    Castro and, 749, 791
    intervention in Guatemala, 749
    undercover in Angola, 830
    undercover in Chile, 830
A Century of Dishonor (Jackson), 438
Cermak, Anton, 654
Chaco Canyon, 4
Champlain, Samuel de, 30
Chancellorsville, Battle of, 390
Channing, William Ellery, 337
Chaplin, Charlie, 638

Chapman, Maria, 298
Charity Organization Societies, 498
Charles I, king of England, 56
Charles II, king of England, 56, 57
Charles River Bridge v. Warren Bridge (1837), 222
Charleston, South Carolina, 404
Charles Town, 86
Charles VII, king of France, 12
Chase, Salmon, 354, 395
Chase, Samuel, 207
Chávez, César, **818**
Checks and balances, **176**
Chemical industry, 463
Cheney, Dick, 889
Cheney, James, 794
Cherokee Nation v. Georgia (1831), 239
Cherokees, 113, 135–136, 330
Chesapeake, 214, 215
Chesapeake colony, 40–43, 61
    civic rituals, 93
    families, 42–43
    politics, 43
    slavery and, 69
    standard of living, 41–42
Cheshire Baptists, 204
Chesnut, James Jr., 399
Chesnut, Mary Boykin, 248, 392
Cheyennes, 394–395
Chiang Kai-shek, 691, 719, 738
Chicago, Illinois, 322, 768, 810
Chicano movement, 819
Chickasaws, 330
Child, Lydia Maria, 298
Childbearing, 248
Children
    in Chesapeake colonies, 43
    childhood obesity, 898
    child labor, 265, 467, 468, 551, 563, 622
    criminal prosecution of, 540
    declining birth rates, 503
    infant mortality, 42, 593, 625, 632
    mass-produced toys for, 511
    patterns of childhood, 504
    progressive education and, 549
    in temperance movement, 292
Children's Crusade, 793
Chile, 830
China
    challenges to communist rule, 866
    civil war, 738–739
    corn production, 21
    end to Sino-American hostility, 828
    in Korean War, 740
    Manchurian Crisis, 692
    Nixon and, 828
    Open Door policy, 583
    ouster of Mao Zedong, 691
    post-Vietnam War era, 827
    Sino-Soviet tensions, 827
    treaties with, 311
    U.S. relations and, 816
    and Vietnam War, 802
Chinese Exclusion Act, 442, 495, 719

Chinese immigrants, 268, 442, 493
  in California, 335
  discrimination against,
    494–495
  as railroad workers, 425
Chippewas, 113
Chisholm v. Georgia (1793), 185
Chivington, John, 394, 437
Chocolate trade, 67
Choctaws, 330
Christianity
  Christian fundamentalism, 636
  as motive for exploration, 12
Christmas bombing (Vietnam),
  825
Church attendance, 93
Churchill, Winston, **696**
  on Soviet iron curtain, 733
  WWII strategy, 705
Church of England, 36
CIA. *See* Central Intelligence
  Agency (CIA)
Cinque, Joseph, 236
Cities. *See also* City management;
  Urbanization; Urban
  neighborhoods
  colonial era, 97–98
  crime and violence, 498
  fire and, 98
  inner-city housing, 496
  living conditions in inner city,
    496–498
  poverty relief, 497–498
  social crises in, 862
City Beautiful movement, 502
City management, 498–502
  civic reform, 501–502
  law enforcement, 499
  political machines and, 499, 501
  social reform, 502
  urban engineers, 499
  water supply and sewage
    disposal, 498–499
City of the Sun (Cahokia), **4, 5**
"City upon a hill," **73**
Civic rituals, 93–94
Civilian Conservation Corps,
  658
Civil liberties, 713
  threats to, under Wilson,
    609–611
Civil rights, 766–770
  bus boycott, 768
  freedom rides and voter
    registration, 792–793
  growing black political power,
    766–767
  Kennedy and, 793
  marches, 792–794
  March on Washington, 794
  President's Committee on,
    767
  Project C, 795
  white resistance, 768
Civil Rights, U.S. Commission on
  (1957), 768
Civil Rights Act (1875), **425**
Civil Rights Act (1957), 769
Civil Rights Act (1964), **796**–797,
  812, 821, 861
  Affirmative Action, 820
Civil Rights Bill of 1866, 414
Civil service reform, 517

Civil War. *See also* Confederate Army;
  Confederate States of America;
  Union Army; specific battles
  African American recruits, 386,
    402
  antiwar sentiment, 393
  battlefield stalemate, 396
  Battle of Antietam, 375–376
  Bull Run, 371, 375
  causation, 365
  comparative resources, 373
  death toll and impact, 400–401
  disunity, 391–395
  fall of Atlanta, 396, 398
  in the far west, 373
  financial cost of, 399–400
  Fort Sumter and outbreak of,
    364–365
  hospitals and camp life,
    387–388
  Northern diplomatic strategy,
    395–396
  Peninsula Campaign, 373–375
  Sherman's March to the Sea,
    398–399
  soldiers in, 387–388
  strategies, 371–372
  surrender at Appomattox, 399
  Tennessee Campaign and
    Battle of Shiloh, 374
  Union naval campaign,
    372–373
  weapons, 388
Clanton family, 445
Clapp, Moses E., 440
Clapton, Eric, 808
Clark, Charles, 393
Clark, George Rogers, 146
Clark, Petula, 808
Clark, William A., 211, 455
Clarke, Edward, 635
Class inequities, 288
Clausewitz, Karl von, 396
Clay, Henry, 216, 220, 301, 305,
  337, 349
  and Missouri Compromise, 226
Clayton Anti-Trust Act, 562
Clayton-Bulwer Treaty, 587
Clean Air Act, 871
Clemenceau, Georges, 601, 614
Clermont, **264**
Cleveland, Grover, 520, 522, 534
  currency crisis and, 532
  Pullman strikes, 472, 522
Cleveland, OH, 322
  default on debt, 835
  pollution of Cuyahoga river,
    837
Clifford, Clark, 810
Clinton, Bill, **878**
  diplomacy of, 882
  healthcare goal, 880
  impeachment of, 418
  media scrutiny of, 881
  Middle East agreements, 882
  and "New Democrats,"
    879–880
  political partisanship and
    scandal, 881
Clinton, DeWitt, 216
Clinton, George, 208, 215
Clinton, Hillary Rodham, 127,
  879, 880

Clinton, Sir Henry, 149
Clothing, 477–478
Coacoochee, 241
Coal, 420
Coalition Governing Council, 890
Cobbett, William, 182
Code Duello, 247
Cody, Buffalo Bill, 432, 445
Coercive Acts, **126**–127
Coffee trade, 67
Cohan, George M., **508**
Cold Harbor, 399
Cold War
  American issue of, 792
  anticommunism and, 756,
    764–766
  in Asia, 738–739
  atomic diplomacy, 733–734
  beginning of, 732–733
  cost to Soviet Union, 827
  domestic politics in, 761–762
  end of, 867–868
  fears and policies, 756
  global balance of power, 757
  inevitability of, 734–735
  Kennedy and, 788–792
  massive retaliation and,
    742–743
  militarization of, 738
  new approach to, post-Vietnam
    War, 827
  nuclear weapons and, 738, 743,
    745
  People-to-People campaign,
    744
  renewal of, 839
  Soviet-American tensions,
    790–791
  U.S. as national security state,
    751
Cold Water Army, 292
Cole, 883
Cole, Nat King, 772
Colleges, 550. *see also* Education
College sports, 644
Collet, John (painting by), 102
Colombian immigration, 780
Colonial cultures, 90–95, 104
  Algonquian and English
    differences, 39
  the Enlightenment, 91, 93
  genteel culture, 90–91
  life in New England, 49–51
  "middle ground" rituals, 95
  oral cultures, 93
  religious and civic rituals,
    93–94
  rituals of consumption, 94–95
  tea and madeira, 95
Colonial families, 95–98, 104
  African American, 97
  city life and, 97–98
  European American, 96
  Indian and mixed-race, 96
  of New England, 49–50
Colonies and colonization. *See also*
  specific colonies
  Anglo-American, 56–62
  Carolina, 60–61
  Chesapeake, 40–43, 61
  chronology, 29, 57
  demand for laborers, 40–41
  Dutch, 34

  in early 18th century (map), 58
  English interest in, 36–38
  failures, 23, 27
  founding of (1565–1640), 32
  French, 30, 32, 34
  Jesuit missions in New France,
    32, 34
  lessons learned, 14
  mercantilism and, 72–74,
    76–77
  missionary activities, 48
  New England, 61–62
  New Jersey, 59–60
  New Mexico, 30
  New Netherland, 34
  New York, 57–59
  Pennsylvania, 60
  political autonomy challenged,
    73
  political structures, 62
  Quebec and Montreal, 30, 32
  settlements and Indian tribes
    (map), 33
  Spanish, 17, 30
  sugar cultivation, 35–36
Colored Farmers' National
  Alliance, 528
Colored Women's Federation, 555
Colson, Charles, 832
Columbian Exchange, **19**–22,
  26–27
  major items in (map), 20
  smallpox and other diseases,
    19–20
  sugar, horses, and tobacco,
    20, 22
Columbian Exposition, 502
Columbine High School, 882
Columbus, Christopher, **14**–16
Comanche Empire, 328, 330
Comanches, 63, 82, 327, 328
Comics, 509
Cominform, 737
Commerce
  in British colonies, 88
  regulation of, 175
  specialization of, 272–273
  writing materials, 161
Committee on Public
  Information, **610**
Committees of Correspondence,
  124, 127, 129
Committees of observation and
  inspection, 134
Committee to Defend America,
  693
Committee to Re-elect the
  President (CREEP), 832
Commodities markets, 322
Commons, John R., v
"Common school" movement,
  293
Common Sense (Paine), **143,** 154
Commonwealth period, 56
Commonwealth v. Hunt, **271**
Communal ideal, 47
Communications, international,
  576
Communism. *See also*
  Anticommunism
  in China, 738
  containment policy, 735–738,
    743

in Great Depression, 654
racial unrest, 612–613
Red Scare, 611
Communist Control Act (1954),
766
Community Action Programs,
798
Compact disc, 483
Compromise of 1850, 350–351,
353, 367
Compromise of 1877, 428–429
Computers, 865
Comstock, Anthony, **510**
Concord, Battle of, 140–141, 150
Confederate Army, 393–393. *See
also* Civil War
Confederate States of America,
362–364
centralization and, 376–377
changing roles of women, 378
disunity in, 391–392
food riots, 392
ideology of nationalism, 377
inequities of the draft, 379
transformation of the south,
376–379
Confederation Congress, 169,
173, 176, 180
Confiscation Acts, 384–385
Conglomerates, 479
Congo, 830
Congregationalists, 50, 101
Congressional Reconstruction,
418
Congress of Industrial
Organizations, **666**
Congress of Racial Equality
(CORE), 715, 792, 794
Conner, Howard, 702
Connor, Eugene "Bull," 793
Conquistadors, **18**
Conservation movement,
443–444, 559–560
Conservatism
neoconservatives, 848–849
Reagan and, 848–851
*Considerations on the Propriety of
Imposing Taxes on the British
Colonies* (Dulany), 117
Constantinople, 11
Constitution, U. S. *See also* Bill of
Rights
Article VI, 184–185
congressional and presidential
powers, 175–176
and the establishment of a
national bank, 187
Madison and, 173–174
opposition and ratification,
156, 176–178, 181
slavery and, 175, 181
Constitutional Convention, 173
Consumer culture, 773
Consumerism, 620
advertising and, 478
commonplace luxuries,
474–475
department and chain stores,
478
ready-made clothing, 477–478
of 1920s, 625–627
Consumption rituals, 94–95
Containment, **735**

Continental Army, 142
officer corps, 147–148
staffing of, 147, 155
Continental Association,
133–134
agreement, 134
Continental Congress, 127, **132**
committees of observation and
inspection, 134
First, 132–133, 154
Second, 138, 142, 169
Contra war in Nicaragua,
857–858
Convention of 1800, 201
Convention of 1818, 222
Cooke, Jay, 380
Coolidge, Calvin, 622, **624**
progressive reform, 624
prosperity under, 624
Cooney, Joseph, 458
Cooper, Peter, 266
Copland, Aaron, 642
Copley, John Singleton (painting
by), 91
Copperheads, **394**
Cordon sanitaire, 614
Corn, 3, 21
Cornwallis, Lord, **148,** 151
Coronado, Francisco Vásquez
de, 18
*Coronado Coal Company v. United
Mine Workers* (1922), 622
Corporate consolidation
movement, 478–481
Corporate debt, 644
Corporate downsizing, 855
Corporate growth, 222
Corporate income tax, 606
Corporations, 479
Corps of Discovery, 211–212, 227,
324
Corps of Topographical
Engineers, 324
Cortés, Hernán, 18
Cost of living, 475–476
Cotton, 209, 463, 526
cotton kingdom, **235**
demand for, after War of 1812,
220, 224
in a global economy, 247
mills, 214
Southern dependence on, 223
Cotton, John, 50
Cotton gin, 209
Council of Economic Advisors,
762
Coureurs de bois, 82
Courtship and dating, 633
Cousteau, Jacques, 574
Covenant Chain, 62
Covey, James, 236
Cowboys, 454
Cox, James M., 623
Coxey, Jacob, 533–534
Coxey's Army, 533–534
Craft unions, 471, 665
Crane, Timothy B., 287
Crawford, William H., 301
Crazy Horse, 437
Creeks, 71, 113, 171, 330
Creel, George, 610
Crime, 94, 95
mobs, 640

punishment of, 94
urban, 498, 862
"Crisis of masculinity," 776
The Crisis (Paine), 144
Crittenden, John J., 362
Crockett, Davy, 317
Cromwell, Oliver, 56
Cronkite, Walter, 796
Croquet, 506
Crosby, Alfred, 19
Cruel and unusual punishment,
184
Crummell, Alexander, 297
Crusades, 11
Cuba
battle for independence, 578
Bay of Pigs invasion, 791
exploration of, 15
immigration from, 780
independence from Spain, 581
Platt Amendment, 586
revolution in, 578–579, 749
sugar exports, 579
U.S. naval quarantine of, 791
Cuban Missile Crisis, 787, 791,
792
Cullen, Countee, 640
Cult of domesticity, 275
Cult of true womanhood, 275
Cultural adaptation, 495–496
Cultural imperialism, 569
Cultural transformation
diversity, 839
environmentalism, 837
sexuality and the family,
838–839
technology, 838
youth, 839
Culture. *See also* Popular culture
homogenization of, 886
nationalism and, 209
Culture areas, 6
Cumberland Road, 221
*Cummins v. County Board of
Education* (1899), 523
Currency Act, 115
Currency problems, 531–532
Custer, George A., 437
Custis, Martha, 142
Cycling, 506
Czechoslovakia, 614
German invasion of, 689
Soviet Union and, 733
Czolgosv, Leon, 557

da Gama, Vasco, 14
Daimler, Gottlieb, 461
Daley, Richard J, 810
Darrow, Clarence, 473, 637
Dating, 633
Daughters of Bilitis, 823
Daughters of Liberty, 122, 127
Dave Clark Five, 808
da Verrazzano, Giovanni, 17
Davis, Henry W., 407
Davis, Jefferson, 357, 363, **374,**
387, 390, 392, 396, 429
Davis, John W., 624
Dawes, William, 140
Dawes Act, 625
Dawes Severalty Act, **438,** 440
D-Day, 718

DDT (pesticide), 779
Deadwood, 445
Dean, James, 778
Dean, John, 832
Debs, Eugene V., **472,** 533, 545,
561, 611
Declaration of Independence, **144**
Declaration of Rights and
Grievances, 133
Declaratory Act, **119**
Decolonization, 729
British colonies, 729
in Third World, 746
U.S. colonies, 729
Decoration Day, 404
Deep Throat, **832**
Deere, John, 321
Defense of Marriage Act, 898
*Defense of the Constitutionality of the
Bank* (Hamilton), 187
Defense plant workers, 708
Deficit spending, 662
de Gaulle, Charles, 811
Deindustrialization, and U.S.
economy, 835
de Klerk, F. W., 866
De Lôme, Enrique Dupuy, 579
Demagogues, 661
DeMille, Cecil B., 620, 638
Democratic National Convention
(1964), 797
Democratic National Convention
(1968), 810–811
Democratic Party, 357–358
Democratic societies, 190
Democrats, 288, **302**–303
Dempsey, Jack, 639
Denison House, 544
Department of Education, 833
Department of Energy, 833
Department of Homeland
Security, 751, **888**
Department of the Interior, 326
Department stores, 478
Dependents' Pension Act, 520
Depression of 1890s, 531–534
consequences of, 532
protests, 532
Depression of 1930s. *See* Great
Depression
Deregulation, 854
de Soto, Hernán, 18
de Tocqueville, Alexis, 246, 261
Detroit, MI
bankruptcy, 835
as frontier, 136
settlement of, 322
urban unrest, 804
Detroit Unemployment Councils,
655
Dew, Thomas R., 234
Dewey, George, 581
Dewey, John, 549–550
Dewey, Thomas, 762
Dias, Bartholomew, 14
Díaz, Porfirio, 587
Dickinson, John, 120, 157
Diem. *See* Ngo Dinh Diem
Diem regime, 800
Dietary reform, 477
Digital revolution, 884–885
Dingley Tariff, 536
Disarmament treaties, 222

Discount brokerage houses, 837
Discount rate, 562
Discrimination
  against African Americans, 522, 552
  against European immigrants, 494
  racial, 494–495, 780
  women and, 556, 775
Diseases, 27
  in Civil War, 387–388
  Columbian Exchange, 19–20
  in Continental Army, 148–149
  germ theory of, 499
  global, 900
  health and life expectancy and, 632
  Indians and, 62, 436
  measles epidemic, 332
  in port cities, 98
  smallpox, 18, 92
  "swine flu," 901
  syphilis, 20
  urbanization and, 278
  in western territories, 334
Disfranchisement, 522–523
Disinformation projects, 743
Dissenters, 201
District courts, 184
Diversity, 839, 896–897
Division of labor, 6
Divorce, 300, 629
  in wartime, 712
Dix, Dorothea, **291**
Dixiecrats (States' Rights Democratic Party), 762
Dobson, James, 861
Dodd, Samuel, 479
Doegs, 64
Dole, Sanford B., 578
Dollar diplomacy, 588
Dominican Republic, 576
  immigration and, 780
Dominion of New England, 73
Domino theory, 734, **743**
Donnell, Ed, 449–450
Donnelly, Ignatius, 529
Donner Party, 333
"Don't ask, don't tell," 880
Double V campaign, 715
Douglas, Aaron, 642
Douglas, Stephen A., 349, 350
  in election of 1860, 361–362
  Kansas-Nebraska Act and, 353–354
  Lincoln-Douglas debates, 342–343
Douglass, Frederick, **250,** 297, 299, 301, 343, 366, 384, 429
Downsizing, 855
Draft, military, **842**
Drake, Sir Francis, 22
Dred Scott decision, 359-**360,** 366, 367, 427
Dresden bombing, 722
Drug legislation, 558
Dual-sex principle, 10
Du Bois, W. E. B., 546, 552, **553,** 613, 628
Duke, James B., 463
The Duke's Laws, 58
Dulany, Daniel, 117
Dulles, John Foster, **742**–743

Dunmore, Lord, **135,** 138, 148
Du Pont family, 463
Dust Bowl, 651
Dust storms, 661
Dutch colonization, 34
Dutch West India Company, 17, 34, 57
Dylan, Bob, 807
Dynamic Sociology (Ward), 481
Dysentery, 148

E. I. du Pont de Nemours and Company, 463
Earp brothers, 445
Earth Day, 837
East Germany, 790
East Indian Company, 125–126
East Jerusalem, 830
Eastman, Crystal, 556
Echohawk, Brummet (painting by), 241
Economic crisis
  credit and investment, 836–837
  currency problems, 531–532
  Depression of 1890s, 531–534
  Depression of 1930s, 643
  of late 1850s, 361
  Panic of 1907, 560
  of 1980s, 835
  stagflation, 834
  Van Buren and, 308–309
Economic expansion, 621
Economic Interpretation of the Constitution (Beard), 551
Economic stimulus program, 895
Economies, regional colonial
  bartering, 94
  Georgia, 89–90
  New England, 89
  South Carolina, 89
Economies of scale, 464
Economy
  cycles of boom and bust, 274
  government regulation of, 563
  of postwar America, 758–759
  Reaganomics, 851–856
  sectionalism and, 223–226
  of Sunbelt, 770–771
Ecuador, 780
Ederle, Gertrude, 639
Edgar Thompson steel plant, 463
Edison, Thomas, **459,** 460, 483, 509
Edison Electric Light Company, 460
Ed Sullivan Show, **808**
Education
  of blacks, 409–410
  compulsory school attendance laws, 467
  federal aid to, 171
  foreign universities and study abroad, 546
  growth of colleges and universities, 550
  progressive ideas, 549–550
  public schools, 293
  reform, 160, 162, 502
  of women, 157
  writing, 161
Educational Amendments Act of 1972, 644

Edwards, Haden, 331
Edwards, Jonathan, 101
Egalitarianism, 158–159
Egypt
  Camp David Accords, 841
  Six-Day War, 830
  Suez crisis, 745, 750
Eighteenth Amendment, **548**–549, 640
Eight-hour workday, 471
Eisenhower, Dwight D., 742, 763, 789
  and CIA, 743
  Cold War policies, 742
  conservatism of, 763
  on military-industrial complex, 751
  Pledge of Allegiance, 782
  Vietnam policy, 750
  as WWII general, 718
Eisenhower Doctrine, **750**–751
Election of 1786, **192**–193
Election of 1800, 199
Election of 1804, 208–209
Election of 1808, 215
Election of 1824, 301–302
Election of 1828, 302, 303
Election of 1844, 337
Election of 1848, 348
Election of 1852, 353
Election of 1864, 395
Election of 1868, 418
Election of 1876, 428–429
Election of 1896, 535–536
Election of 1908, 560
Election of 1912, 561
Election of 1928, 642
Election of 1940, 672
Election of 1948, 762
Election of 1960, 789
Election of 1964, 797
Election of 1980, 849
Election of 1988, 866
Election of 1992, 878
Election of 2000, 886–887
Election of 2004, 890
Election of 2008, 894–895
Elections
  colonial ritual and, 93
  fraud, 305
Electoral college, 176
Electrical industry, 460–461
Elgin National Watch Company, 465
Eliot, Charles W., 550
Eliot, John, 48
Eliot, T. S., 640
Elizabeth I, queen of England, 11, 23, 36
Ellsberg, Daniel, 815, 832
El Salvador, 857
Ely, Richard, 482
Emancipation, 180, 402
  advent of, 383–387
  Confederate plan for, 387
  Lincoln and, 384
  and manumission, 163–164
Emancipation Proclamation, **385**–386
Embargo Act of 1807, **214**
Emergency Banking Bill, 657
Emergency Relief Appropriation Act, 662

Emerson, Ralph Waldo, 295, 361
Emporium, 478
Empresarios, 330–331
Encomienda system, **18**
Enemy Alien Camps, 713
Enforcement Acts, **423**
England
  Canadian uprising, 309
  Civil War in, 56, 61
  imports from, 122
  social and economic change, 36
  Stuart monarchs, 37–38
English immigrants, 87
English monarchs
  Anne, 57
  Charles I, 37–38, 56
  Charles II, 56–57
  Elizabeth I, 36, 37
  Henry VIII, 36
  James I, 37–38, 40
  James II, 57, 73
  Mary, 57, 73
  William, 57, 73
English reformation, 36–37
Enlightenment, **91**
Entertainment, 638. *See also* Sports
  leisure time and, 505
  mass-market publications, 510
  movies, 509, 638
  show business, 508
  vaudeville, 486, 508
  WWII propaganda and, 710
Environmental concerns, 779–780, 837
Environmental law, 837
Environmental Protection Agency (EPA), 837
Epstein, Abraham, 632
Equal Employment Opportunity Commission (EEOC), 797
Equality League of Self Supporting Women, 556
Equal Opportunity Employment Commission (EEOC), 797, 820
Equal Rights Amendment, **821**
  Nixon support of, 831
  STOP-ERA movement, 823
Equiano, Olaudah, 103
Era of Good Feelings, **221,** 228
Ericsson, Leif, 16
Erie Canal, **221, 265,** 268
Espionage Act, **610**
Essay Concerning Human Understanding (Locke), 91
Estonia, 614, 689, 730, 867
Ethnic diversity
  geographic expansion and, 80–88, 104
  maintaining ethnic identities, 86, 88
Ethnic tension, 280–281
Eugenics, 551–552
Europe
  deportation of "undesirables" to new world, 84, 86
  Marshall Plan, 735, 737
  post Second World War division, 736
  post-Vietnam War, 827
  World War II battles, 718
European immigrants, 442, 493, 494

European-Indian warfare, 107–113
  Iroquois neutrality, 108–109
Europeans in North America
  contest between Spain and England, 22–23
  Roanoke, 23
  trade among Indians and Europeans, 22
European societies, 11–12
  effects of plague and warfare, 11–12
  gender, work, politics, and religion, 11
  male dominance of, 11
  motives for exploration, 12
  political and technological change, 12
Evangelists, **101,** 288
Evans, Hiram Wesley, 635
Evers, Medgar, 794
Evolution, 900
Excess profits tax, 606
Excise taxes, 606
Executive branch, 184
Executive privilege, 191
Exodusters, **442**
Expansionism, 570
Ex parte Milligan, 427
Experiments and Observations on Electricity (Franklin), 91
Exploration
  Christopher Columbus, 14–16
  early European, 13–14
  Hernán Cortés, 18
  John Cabot, 16–17
  map, 15
  in Mediterranean Atlantic, 13
  motives for, 12, 26
  Norse and other northern voyagers, 16
  Portuguese trading posts in Africa, 13–14
  Spanish conquests, 17–19

Factions, 188
Factories, 269–271, 285. *See also* Industrialization
  labor protests, 270–271
  wartime jobs for women, 608
Faith, Percy, 808
Fallen Timbers, Battle of, 196
Fallout shelters, 790
Fall River plan, 270
Falwell, Jerry, 849, 861, 863
Families. *See also* Colonial families
  birth control and, 629
  boarding and lodging, 504
  Chesapeake, 42–43
  contemporary changes in, 896, 898, 899
  declining birth rates, 503
  functions of kinship, 504–505
  gender roles, 775
  in Great Depression, 653
  holiday celebrations, 505
  household structures, 503
  "ideal," 274–275
  income distribution, 1929–1944, 664
  at midcentury, 773, 775
  of New England, 49–50

  sexuality and, 838–839
  slave families, 253–254
  smaller sizes of, 275, 284
  southern planters and, 248
  unmarried members of, 504
  urbanization and, 502–505
  in wartime, 712–713
"Fancy trade," 253
Farmers' Alliances, 528
Farmers' Holiday Association, 654
Farms and farming. *See also* Agriculture; Ranching
  agrarian unrest, 526
  commercial, 262, 273
  in Great Depression, 651
  in the Great Plains, 448–452
  labor-saving equipment, 273, 321–322, 357
  preemption policy, 326
  preindustrial farms, 262–263
  rural communities, 274
  sharecropping, 411–412, 526
  tenant farming, 526
Faubus, Orval, E., 769
Faulkner, William, 640
Fauset, Jessie, 640
Federal Farm Loan Act, 563
Federal Highway Act, 626
Federal Housing Administration (FHA), 760
Federalism, **176**
Federalists, **177,** 181
  decline of, 220
  Hamilton and, 188–189
The Federalist, 178
Federal public works projects, 654
Federal Reserve Act, 562
Federal Reserve Board, 562
Federal Theater Project, 663
Federal Trade Commission, 562, 622
Federal Writers' Project, 663
Fehrenbacher, Don, 400
Felt, W. Mark (Deep Throat), **832**
Femininity, 634
Feminism, 555
Ferdinand, Franz, 595
Ferdinand and Isabella of Spain, 12, 14
Ferraro, Geraldine, 854
Ferrero, Cyrus, 462, 576
Fidelity Investments, 837
Field, Cyrus, 462, 576
Field Order Number 15, 409
Fifteenth Amendment, **418**–419
"Fifty-four forty or fight," 337
Filene, E. A., 543
Filibustering, 356
Fillmore, Millard, 348
Film industry, 671. *See also* Movies
Finance
  Articles of Confederation and, 169
  depreciation of Continental currency, 170
Financial Panic of 1819, 224
Financial Panic of 1907, 560
Financiers, 480–481
Finland, 614
  Soviet invasion of, 693
Finlay, Carlos Juan, 586
Finney, Charles G., **290**
Fireside Chats, 657, 695
First Amendment, 183–184

First Bank of the United States, 187
First Congress, 183
First Continental Congress, 132–133, 154
First World War
  American production, 606
  Americans in battle, 602–603
  business-government cooperation, 605–606
  casualties, 603, 605
  chronology, 595
  decision for, 597–599
  declaration of, 598–599
  draft and soldiers of, 599–600
  in France, 601–602
  German declarations of war, 595
  labor shortage, 608–609
  mobilizing the home front, 605–609
  outbreak of, 595–596
  peace advocates, 597–598
  submarine warfare, 598
  taking sides, 596
  trench warfare, 600
  Wilson and domestic reforms, 563
  "Wilsonianism," 596
Fischer, Louis, 731
Fish, Hamilton, 427
Fish and fishing, 22, 213, 435
Fisk University, 410
Fitzgerald, F. Scott, 640
Fleming, Samuel, 247
Flintoff, John F., 242
Florida, Adams-Onis Treaty and, 222
Flynn, Elizabeth Gurley, 473
Folk culture, 242
Folk heroes, 445
Fongs, 493
Fong Yue Ting v. United States (1893), **493**
Food and drug legislation, 558
Food crops. *See* Agriculture
Food processing, 477
Food Stamp program, 799
Football, 506
Forbes, Charles, 623
Force Act, 304–305
Ford, Gerald, 816, 831, **832**
  and monetary theory, 835
  pardon of Nixon, 833
  as unelected president, 833
Ford, Henry, **461,** 463, 606
  WWII production and, 709
Ford Motor Company, 463, 466
  violence and labor disputes, 655
Fordney-McCumber Tariff Act, 622
Foreign affairs, 169–170, 184
Foreign policy
  CIA and, 743
  imperialism, 570–575
Foreign trade expansion, 573
Forest clearing (controlled burning), 3
Formosa Resolution, 745
Fort Detroit, 136
Fort Laramie Treaty, **334**
Fort Mims massacre, 219

Fort Orange, 34
Fort Stanwix, New York, 171
Fort Sumpter, **364**–365
Fort Ticonderoga, 141, 146
Fort Wagner, 389
"Forty-niners," 335
Fossett, Joseph, 230
Fourier, Charles, 295
Fourierists, 295
Fourteen Points, **602**
Fourteenth Amendment, **414**–415
Fourth Amendment, 184
Fox Indians, 320
France
  in First World War, 595
  North American colonies, 23
  posts along the Mississippi, 82–83
  Quasi-War, 193, 196
  territorial expansion, 81–82
Franklin, Aretha, 807
Franklin, Benjamin, 86, **91,** 103, 113, 119, 143, 146, 153, 173, 176, 185
"Fraternal cooperation" principle, 482
Fraternal societies, 474
Frazier, Garrison, 409
"Fredonia Republic," 331
Free blacks, 245
Freedmen's Bureau, **408,** 414, 430
Freedom of contract, 468
Freedom of speech, 616
Freedom of the seas, 213
Freedom Riders, 792
Freedom Schools, 794
Freeholders, 41
Freemasonry, 305
Free press, 99
Free silver, 534
Free Soil Party, 348–349
Free Speech Movement (FSM), **806**
Frémont, Jessie Benton, 324
Frémont, John C., **324,** 337, 347, 358, 384, 395
French and Indian War, 108
French Revolution, 189–190, 202
Frey, John, 458
Frick, Henry C., 472
Friedan, Betty, 820
Fries, John, 198
Fries's Rebellion, 198, 201, 203
Frontenac, Louise de Buade, 62
Frontier hostilities, 135–136, 154
Fuel Administration, 606
Fugitive Slave Act, **351**–352
Fugitive slave laws, 172, 175, 297
Fulbright, J. William, 698, 803
Fulkes, Minnie, 251
Full Employment Act, **761**
Fuller, Margaret, 295
Fulton, Robert, 222
Fundamentalism, **636**
Fundamental Orders of Connecticut, 47
Fur trade, 30, 59, 62, 77, 322–323
F.W. Woolworth (store), 786

Gabriel's Rebellion, 199, 200, 203
Gadsden Purchase, 569

Gag rule, 308
Gallatin, Albert, 207
Galloway, Joseph, 133
Galton, Francis, 551
Games (toys), 511
Gandhi, Mohandas, 617, 768
Gandy, Moses, 297
Garbage collection, 499
Garfield, James
    assassination of, 462, 520
    election of, 520
Garlic, Delia, 250
Garment industry, 271
Garrison, William Lloyd, 297,
    298, 299, 301
Garvey, Marcus, 613, **628**
Gaspée, 124
Gates, Bill, 885
Gates, Frederick, 575
Gates, Horatio, 151
Gay Pride movement, 823
Gays and lesbians, 504
    adoption of children by, 898
    culture of, 635
    domestic partner benefits, 898
    gay liberation, 823
Gaza Strip, 830, 841
The Gazette of the United States, 195
Geary Act, 495
Gender roles, 10, 25, 26. *See also*
    Women
General Electric Company, 460
General Land Office, 326
General Motors, 666, 758, 770
General Survey Act of 1824, 324
Genêt, Edmond, **190**
Geneva Accords, 751
Geneva Prisoners of War
    Convention, 741
Genizaros, 96
Genteel culture, 90–91
Gentilz, Theodore, 329
Geographic mobility, 492
Geography (Ptolemy), 12
George, David Lloyd, 614
George, Henry, 482
George III, king of England, 113
Georgia
    in American Revolution, 149,
        150
    settlement of, 89–90
Germain, Lord George, 141
German immigrants, 86, 280
Germany
    after First World War, 614
    aggression under Hitler,
        687–688
    attack of Soviet Union, 695
    in First World War, 597,
        602–603
    invasion of Czechoslovakia,
        689
    post WWII reconstruction, 732
    reparations, 645, 682, 684
    WWII invasions, 693
Gershwin, George, 642
Gettysburg, **390,** 391, 393
    Battle of, 391
Ghettos, 494
Ghost Dance, **440**
Gibbons v. Ogden (1824), 222
Gibbs, Jacob, 352
Gibbs, Josiah, 236

GI Bill of Rights, **757**–758, 782
Giddings, Joshua, 354
Gilded Age politics, 514, 521
Gilman, Charlotte Perkins, 555
Gilmore, William, 225
Gingrich, Newt, **880,** 881
Ginsberg, Allen, 778
Ginsburg, Ruth Bader, 776
Glaciers, 2
Gladden, Washington, 544
Glasnost, 860
Glenn, John, 796
Glidden, Joseph F., 453
Globalization, 884–887, **885,** 900
    of business, 885
    critics of, 885
    diseases and, 901
    McDonald's and, 886
Global marketplace, 532
Global telecommunications, 462
Global warming, **883**
Glorious Revolution, 73, **99**
Golan Heights, 830
Goldman, Emma, 612
Gold reserve, 532
Gold Rush, **322,** 325, 335, 340
Gold standard, 519, 534
    end of U.S. currency link to, 834
Gold Standard Act, 536
Goldwater, Barry, **797,** 800
Gompers, Samuel, **471,** 535, 582,
    609
Gonzales, Rudolfo "Corky," 819
Goodall, Jane, 574
Gooding, James Henry, 388
Goodman, Andrew, 794
Good Neighbor policy, **686**
Google, 903
Gorbachev, Mikhail S., 860, 866,
    867
Gore, Al, 878, **886**
"Gospel of Wealth," 481
Gould, Jay, **471**
Government
    Articles of Confederation, 169
    colonial assemblies, 99
    First Continental Congress,
        132–133
    reform, 547–548
    state constitutions, 143
Graft, 501
Graham, Billy, 773, 824
Grain Coast, 10
Grain exports, 89
Grand Coulee Dam, 668
Grange movement, 526, 527–528
Grant, Madison, 552
Grant, Ulysses S., **374**
    in Civil War, 390, 396
    election of, 418
    in Reconstruction, 417
Grants, 481
Grateful Dead, 807
Grattan Massacre, 334
Gray, Thomas R., 255
Great Atlantic Tea Company, 478
Great Awakening, **100**–101, 105
Great Britain. *See also* England
    Anglo-American relations,
        190–193
    Palestine and, 614
    and U.S. Civil War, 396, 397
    War of 1812, 216–220

Great Depression, 643
    Bonus Army, 655
    chronology, 652
    farmers and industrial workers,
        651
    labor rights and, 665–667
    marginal workers, 651–653
    marriage and birth rate, 759
    middle-class workers and, 653
    protest and social unrest,
        654–655
Great Lakes, 136
Great Plains
    farming and, 451–452
    hardships, 449
    horses and, 22
    settlement of, 449
    social isolation and, 449–450
"Great postal campaign," 298
Great Society, 787, **796,** 796–799,
    812
Great Wall of China, **828**
Greece, 734
Greeley, Horace, 357, 385, 424
Greenback Labor Party, **527**
Green Revolution, 748
Greenville, Indiana, 212
Grenada, 857
Grenville, George, 114–115
Grier, Robert, 360
Griffith, D. W., 509, 613
Grimké, Angelina and Sarah, **300**
Grosvenor, Gilbert H., 574
Guam, 581
Guanche people, 13
Guantánamo Bay, 586, 589
Guatemala, 749
Guinea. *See* West Africa (Guinea)
Guiteau, Charles, 520
Gulf of Tonkin Resolution, 800,
    824
Gulick, Luther H., 504
Gullah dialect, 70
Guzmán, Jacobo Arbenz, 749

Haight-Ashbury district of San
    Francisco, 809
Haiti, establishment of, 200
Haitian refugees, 200
Hakluyt, Richard, 23
Halberstam, David, 789
Hale, Stephen, 364
Hall, G. Stanley, 504
Hamer, Fanny Lou, 797
Hamilton, Alexander, **186,** 202,
    547
    death of, 208
    The Federalist and, 178
    financial plan of, 187
    First Bank of the United States
        and, 187
    on industrial development,
        187–188
    and *New York Evening Post,* 206
    Republicans and, 188–189
    as Treasury secretary, 186–188
    Washington's Farewell Address,
        192
Hammond, James Henry, 234,
    247
Hampton, Fred, 805
Hancock, John, 123

Handler, Ruth, 777
Handsome Lake, 198
Hanna, Marcus A., 534
Harding, Warren G., 622, **623**
    scandals in administration of,
        623–624
Harlem Renaissance, 640–641
Harlem unrest, 804
Harmar, Josiah, 196
Harney, William, 334
Harpers Ferry, 361, 365
Harriot, Thomas, 23, 46
Harris, Eric, 882
Harrison, Benjamin, 444, 520, 578
Harrison, William Henry, 308,
    520
    battle of Tippecanoe, 213
    death of, 310
    election of 1840, 309
    in War of 1812, 217, 218
Harte, Bret, 445
Hartford Convention of 1814,
    194, **220**
Hartford Female Seminary, 276
Harvard, 91
Hatch Act of 1887, 452
Haudenosaunee, 7
Hawai'i
    annexation of, 577–578
    attack on Pearl Harbor,
        696–699
    statehood, 578, 772
Hawkins, Benjamin, 197
Hawkins, John, 22
Hawley-Smoot Tariff, 654
Hawthorne, Nathaniel, 295
Hay, John, 583
Hayden, Lewis, 352
Hayes, Rutherford B., 521
    administration of, 519–520
    election of, 428
    labor unrest and, 470
Haymarket riot, 471, 532
Hayne, Robert Y., 304
Hay-Pauncefote Treaty, 589
Haywood, William "Big Bill," 473
Head Start program, 798
Health and nutrition, 632
Health reform, 502
Hearst, William Randolph, 509
Hefner, Hugh, 776
Hemings, Sally, 230
Hemingway, Ernest, 640
Henry, Guy V., 586
Henry, Joseph, 293
Henry, Patrick, 116–117, 133, 177
Henry, William, 419
Henry Street settlement, 544
Henry the Navigator, 13–14
Henry VII, king of England, 12, 16
Henry VIII, king of England, 36
Henson, Matthew, 574
Hepburn Act, 558
Herbert, Victor, 508
Herman's Hermits, 808
Hickok, Wild Bill, 445
Higher Education Act, Title IX,
    821
Highway Act (1956), 760
Highway system, 626
Hill, Anita, **872**
Hill, David, 534
Hill, Joe, 473

Hillsborough, Lord, 120
Hiraoka, Hiroshi, 507
Hiroshima, 722
Hispanic Americans, 491,
    864–865, 898
    Chicano movement, 819
    Mexican American activism,
        818
    visibility of, 839
Hispaniola, 15
Hiss, Alger, 766
Hitler, Adolf, 670, **682,** 687, 719
Ho Chi Minh, 617, 727, 739, 751,
    800, 804, 812
Ho Chi Minh city, 825
Hoffman, Elizabeth Cobbs, 790
Hohokam, 4
Holden, William W., 393
Holden v. Hardy (1896), 468, 551
Holding companies, 479–480
Hollies, 808
Holly, Buddy, 778, 808
Hollywood, CA, 778
Hollywood Ten, 764
Holmes, Oliver Wendell Jr., 550,
    611
Holocaust, **716**
Homelessness, 862
Homestead Act, **326,** 449
Homestead Steel Comapny, 463,
    532
Homestead Strike, **472**
Homosexuals, 504, 712, 776
    adoption of children by, 898
    domestic partner benefits, 898
    "don't ask, don't tell" military
        policy, 880
    gay and lesbian culture, 635
    gay liberation, 823
H1N1 bird flu, 901
Hood, John, 396
Hooker, Thomas, 47
Hoover, Herbert, 622, **653**
    administration of, 643
    election of, 642
    and Great Depression, 651–656
    as Secretary of Commerce, 623
Hoover, J. Edgar, 612, 628, 768,
    793
"Hooverville" shantytowns, 655
Hope, Bob, 824
Hope, John, 524
Horizontal integration, 479
Horses, 22
Hospital Sketches (Alcott), 382
Hostage crisis, Iranian, 841, 843
Houdini, Harry, 486
Household management, 632
House of Burgesses, **40,** 43
House of Delegates, 43
House Un-American Activities
    Committee (HUAC), 764
Housing
    boarding and lodging, 504
    codes and regulations, 496
    inner-city, 496
    new home technology, 496–497
    reform, 496, 502
Houston, Sam, 331, **336**
Howe, Elias Jr., 477
Howe, Julia Ward, 383
Howe, William, 142–145
Howlin' Wolf, 808

HUAC (House Un-American
    Activities Committee), 764
Hudson, Henry, 17, 34
Huerta, Dolores, 818
Huerta, Victoriano, 588
Hughes, Charles Evans, 563, 623
Hughes, Langston, 640
Huguenots, 30, **86,** 88
Huitzilopochtli, 4
Hull, William, 217
Hull House, 544
Human immunodeficiency virus
    (HIV), 863
Humphrey, Hubert, H., 766, 802,
    812
Hungary, 614, 745
    revolt, 745
    Soviet Union and, 733
Hunt, Jane, 300
Hunt, Thomas P., 292
Hurricanes
    in Caribbean, 35
    Hurricane Katrina, **893**–894
Hurston, Zora Neale, 640
Hussein, king of Jordan, 743
Hussein, Saddam, 843, 868, 870,
    889
Hutchinson, Anne, **50**–51
Hutchinson, Thomas, 118, 126
Huynh Cong "Nick" Ut, **826**
Hydrogen bomb, 738
Hylton v. U.S., 185

Ibn Saud, king of Saudi Arabia,
    750
Ickes, Harold, 662
Idaho, 444
Identity, politics of, 817–820
Illinois, 224, 318
Illiteracy, 93
Immediatism, 298
Immigrants/immigration
    African, 772
    "Americanization" of, 544
    Asian, 772, 864, 896
    Chinese, 268, 335, 442,
        493–495
    discrimination against,
        494–495
    European, 442, 493, 494
    fear of, 355
    Haitian, 200
    Japanese, 442, 493, 495, 575
    kinship obligations among,
        505
    Latin American, 626, 628–629,
        772, 780
    "new immigrants," 491
    quotas on, 636, **811**
    race thinking and, 575
    Scots-Irish, Scots, and
        Germans, 86, 87
    in show business, 508
    sources of, 637
    urbanization and, 279–280
    to U.S. cities, 491
Immigration Act of 1965, **798,
    811**
Immigration Reform and Control
    Act, **865**
Impeachment, **418**
Impeachment powers, 176

Imperial crises, 62–64
Imperialism, 570–575
    ambitions and strategies,
        576–577
    "civilizing" impulse, 575
    race thinking and the male
        ethos, 573, 575
    rise of U.S. economic power,
        573
    Spanish-American War,
        580–582
Incas, 18
Income tax, 561, 606, 711
Indentured servants, 29, **41,** 53,
    69
India, decolonization of, 729
Indiana, 224
Indian Citizenship Act, 625
Indian Removal Act, **238**
Indian Reorganization Act, 668,
    781
Indian Rights Association (IRA),
    438
Indians. *See also* Native cultures;
    specific tribes
    accommodation and, 237–238
    activism of, 819
    alcohol abuse by, 95
    of California, 336
    Cherokee Nation v. Georgia, 239
    confederacy of, 171
    containment policy, 425
    disease and, 436
    division of labor, 438
    divisions among, 212–213
    enslavement in the Carolinas,
        70–71
    European-Indian warfare,
        107–113
    expansion of European
        settlement and, 80, 110
    frontier hostilities, 135–136,
        154
    hostilities in Virginia, 39–40
    Indian families, 96
    and mixed-race families, 96
    negotiations with, 171
    New Deal and, 668
    Plains Indians, 434–435
    racial mixing, 327
    removal of, 238, 240, 320
    reservation system, 326
    Second Continental Congress
        and, 135
    Seminole wars, 241
    social services for, 625
    Society of American Indians,
        553
    trade with Europeans, 22
    Trail of Tears, 239–241
    treaties with, 237, 334
    war for eastern Colorado,
        394–395
    westward expansion and, 235,
        237–241, 323
Indian Self-Determination and
    Educatin Assistance Act, **819**
Indians of All Tribes, 819
Indian sovereignty, 196
Indian Trade and Intercourse Act
    of 1793, **197**–198
Indigo, slavery and, 70
Individualism, 296

Individual liberty, 206–207
Industrial development. *See also*
    specific industry
    federal support for, 188
    in the North, 223
    production in 1919, 461
    in the South, 377
Industrialization, 285
    accidents, 468
    early industry, 263–264
    factories and, 269–271
    garment industry
    in Reconstruction South,
        420–421
    technology and, 459–465
    urbanization and, 487–488
Industrial piracy, 225
Industrial revolution, 459
Industrial unions, 665
Industrial Workers of the World
    (IWW), 473, 609
Infant mortality, 42, 503, 625, 632
Inflation
    during American Revolution,
        149
    and Reaganomics, 852–853
Influenza pandemic of 1918, 603,
    604
*The Influence of Sea Power Upon
    History* (Mahan), 577
Information technology,
    884–885
Inner-city crises, 862
Insider trading, 855
Institite for Sex Research, 776
Insull, Samuel, 460, 631
Intel, 885
Intercultural rituals, 95
Interesting Narrative (Equiano), 103
Interior, Department of, 326
Interlocking directorates, 562
Intermediate-Range Nuclear
    Forces Treaty, **860**
Internal markets, 80
Internal Security (McCarran) Act
    (1950), 765
International communications,
    576–577
International Ladies' Garment
    Workers Union, 473
International Monetary Fund
    (IMF), 732, 885
Internet, 903
Internet Explorer, 903
Internment of Japanese
    Americans, 713
Interracial marriage, 76
Interstate commerce, 551
Interstate Commerce Act, **518**
Interstate Commerce
    Commission, 558, 622
Intifada, 859
Intolerable Acts, **126**–127
Investment bankers, 480
iPod, 483
Iran, 750
    hostage crisis, 816, 841, 843
    revolution, 842
Iran-Contra scandal, **859**
Iran-Iraq War, 868
Iraq, 729
    criticism of war in, 201
    fall of Baghdad, 890

government, 843
oil embargo of 1973, 829
Security Council resolutions and, 869
U.S. war against, 889–890, 892
Ireland, 280
Iron, 88, 420
Iroquois, 7
Fort Stanwix treaty and, 171
neutrality policy, 108–109, 135
New France and, 62
political structures, 9
Iroquois Confederacy, 62, 146, 198
Irrigation, 445–446
Islam
in 15th-Century Africa, 9
fundamentalism, 842, 883
influence on West Africa, 10
Isolationism, 688
Israel
Arab-Israeli conflict, 749–750
Camp David Accords, 841
and PLO, 859
Six-Day War, 830
Yom Kippur War, 829
Italian immigrants, 493
Italy, 688
Iwo Jima, 702, 721

Jackson, Andrew, 219, 220
elected president in 1828, 302, 303
in election of 1824, 301, 302
Indian removal and, 303
opponents, 303
on slavery, 336
on westward expansion and Indians, 237
Jackson, Helen Hunt, 438
Jackson, Michael, 865
Jackson, William Andrew 397
Jackson State University, 824
Jacobs, Harriet, 253
Jagger, Mick, 808
James, William, 481
James I, king of England, 22, 40
James II, king of England, 73
James the Duke of York, 57–59, 77
Jamestown, 38, 64
Japan
after First World War, 614
attack on Pearl Harbor, 696–697
expansionism in East Asia, 689, 692
in First World War, 595
post-Vietnam War, 827
reconstruction of, 732, 738
seizure of Manchuria, 692
U.S. demands on, 696
Japanese American internment, 713, 715
Japanese immigrants, 442, 493, 495, 575
Jarvis, Anna, 505
Jay, John, 133, 153, 190
The Federalist and, 178
Jay Treaty, 191, 193, 201, 213
Jazz, 641–642
The Jazz Singer (movie), 638

Jefferson, Martha, 230
Jefferson, Thomas, 157, 182, 547
on bill of rights, 177
on black race, 166
children of, 230
death of, 230
Declaration of Independence, 143–144
election as president (1800), 199, 228
election of 1796, 192–193
Hamilton and, 188–189
Indian relations, 212
Kentucky and Virginia Resolutions, 227
and Louisiana Purchase, 210, 211
political visions, 205–209
as Secretary of State, 185
slave trade and, 214–215
Virginia and Kentucky Resolutions and, 194
Jefferson Airplane, 807
Jeffries, James J., 554
Jerry, Ginney, 246
Jesuit missions, 32, 34, 52
Jesup, Thomas, 241
Jiang Jieshi (Chiang Kai-shek), 719, 738
Jim Crow, portrayal of, 282
Jim Crow laws, 523, 552, 715, 768, 792
Job Corps, 798
Jocelyn, Nathaniel (painting by), 236
Johnson, Andrew
and Fourteenth Amendment, 415–416
impeachment of, 418
pardon policy, 413
racial views of, 412–413, 416
Reconstruction plan, 412–413, 430
Johnson, Hiram, 547
Johnson, Jack, 554
Johnson, James Weldon, 613
Johnson, Lyndon Baines, 787, 796
Affirmative Action, 820
election of 1964
end of presidency, 810
foreign policy, 799–804
and the Great Society, 796
Immigration Act of 1965, 811
Vietnam and, 751, 799–804
War on Poverty, 798
Johnson, Richard M., 308
Johnson, Tom, 502
Johnson v. M'Intosh (1823), 324
Johnston, Joseph E., 390, 396
Joint-stock companies, 38
Jolliet, Louis, 62
Jones, Bobby, 639
Jones, Mary "Mother," 473
Jones, Samuel "Golden Rule," 502
Jones Act, 583
Joplin, Janis, 807
Jordan, 729
Jordan, Barbara, 861
Journalism, 509
Joy of Sex, 838
Judicial politics, 207
Judicial review, 208
Judiciary Act of 1789, 184

Judiciary Act of 1801, 199
Judiciary branch, 184–185
Julian, George, 414
The Jungle (Sinclair), 543
Junk bonds, 854
Justice Act, 126

Kaiser, William, 709
Kaiser Permanente Medical Care Program, 709
Kansas-Nebraska Act, 354, 358, 367
Kansas Territory, 343
Karenga, Maulana, 818
Kearney, Denis, 494
Kearny, Stephen, 345, 347
Keith, Benjamin, 508
Kelley, Florence, 502, 544, 551
Kelley, Oliver H., 527
Kellogg, John H., 477
Kellogg, William K., 477
Kellogg-Briand Pact, 681–682
Kelly, Abby, 299
Kennan, George F., 733, 738, 803
Kennedy, Anthony M., 851
Kennedy, Jacqueline, 789
Kennedy, John F., 787
assassination of, 787, 796, 800, 812
and Bay of Pigs, 791
and civil rights, 793
Cuba and, 743, 749
election of, 789
as president, 788
Kennedy, Joseph P., 788
Kennedy, Robert, 789, 790
assassination of, 787, 810
"Kennewick Man," 24
Ken societies, 493
Kent State University protest, 824
Kentucky, 135
Kentucky Resolution, 227
Kenya
bombing of American embassy, 883
U.S. ties to, 830
Kerensky, Aleksander, 602
Kern, Richard, 318
Kerner, Otto, 804
Kerner Commission, 862
Kerry, John, 890
Key, Francis Scott, 217
Khomeini, Ayatollah, 841
Khrushchev, Nikita, 745
Kickapoo, 330
Kim Il Sung, 740
King, Martin Luther, Jr., 768, 770, 793, 797
assassination of, 787, 810
J. Edgar Hoover and, 793
prophecy of, 794
King, Rodney, 877
King, Rufus, 208, 215, 221
King Cotton, 247
King George's War, 89, 108
King Philip's War, 55, 63–64
King William's War, 108
Kinks, 808
Kinsey, Alfred, 776
Kinship, 504–505
Kiowas, 327
Kipling, Rudyard, 582

Kissinger, Henry, 816, 825, 827
Kitchen Cabinet, 303
Kitchen debate, 745
Klebold, Dylan, 882
Knights of Columbus, 782
Knights of Labor, 470–471
Know-Nothings, 355
Knox, Frank, 693
Knox, Henry, 185, 197
Korean War, 739–742, 763
Chinese entry into, 740
consequences of, 742
peace agreement, 741
U.S. intervention, 740
Korematsu v. U.S. (1944), 715
Krushchev, Nikita, 787, 790
Ku Klux Klan, 405, 422–424, 612, 624, 635–636, 655, 767, 768
Kuwait, 868
oil embargo of 1973, 829
Kwanzaa, 818
Kyoto protocol, 887

Labor. See also Labor strikes; Labor unions; Labor violence; Work force
changing status of, 465–470
child labor laws, 563, 622
conditions of servitude, 41
court rulings on labor reform, 468, 470
demand for, in Chesapeake colonies, 40–41
division of, in families, 96
eight-hour workday bill, 424
occupational mobility, 492
organized, during WWII, 709
protests, 270–271, 532
reform, 548
women in workforce, 276, 466–467, 608, 633–634, 775–776
Labor strikes
during First World War, 611–612
sit-down strikes, 666, 667
Women's Emergency Brigade, 666
Labor unions, 271, 407–404, 609
Reagan and, 851
rivalries, 665–666
setbacks for, 623
Labor violence
Haymarket riot, 471
Homestead strike, 472
in the West, 473
Ladies Association, 151
Lafayette, Marquis de, 146
Laffer, Arthur, 852
Laffer curve, 852
La Follette, Robert M., 548, 561, 598, 609, 624
LaHayes, Beverly, 861
Lakotas, 334, 440
Lamar, Mirabeau, 331
Land claims (western claims and cessions), 168
Land Ordinance of 1785, 179
Land reclamation, 445
Land riots, 100
Land sales, 171
Lane Debates, 298

L'Anse aux Meadows, Newfoundland, 16
La Raza, 819
La Raza Unida (RUP), 819
La Salle, René-Robert Cavelier de, 62
las Casas, Bartolomé de, 18
Lasselle, Marie-Therese (self-portrait by), 136
Las Vegas, NV, 755
Latin America
  American air service in, 630
  anti-American sentiment, 791
  antiradicalism in, 830
  immigration from, 626, 628–629, 772, 780
  and the Monroe Doctrine, 223
  U.S. dominance in, 685–687
  U.S. hegemony in, 585
Latvia, 614, 689, 730, 867
Lavrov, Peter, 530
Law enforcement, 499
Leach, William R., 537
League of Nations, 594, 602, **614–616**
League of Women Voters, 693
Lean Bear, 394
Lear, Norman, 861
Lease, Mary, 529
Lebanon, 729
Lecompton Constitution, 360
Le Duc Tho, 825
Lee, Richard Henry, 133, 143, 177
Lee, Robert E., **374,** 390
Leflore, Greenwood, 246
Leisler, Jacob, 73
Leisure, 505
Le Moyne, Jacques (painting by), 8
Lend-Lease bill, **694**
L'Enfant, Pierre Charles, 209
Lenin, V. I., 602
Lennon, John, 808
Lesbians and gays. *See* Gays and lesbians
Levitt, William, 760, 774
Levittown, **774**
Lew, Barzillai, 148
Lewinsky, Monica, 881
Lewis, John L., 666
Lewis, Meriwether, 211
Lewis, Sinclair, 640
Lewis and Clark Expedition, **211–212,** 324
Lexington, Battle of, 140
Liberalism, 794–799
Liberia, 296, 426
Liberty Party, 309
Libyan Desert, 9
Libyan oil embargo, 829
Life expectancy, 476, 503, 632, 898
Life stages, 503–504
Lili'uokalani, princess of Hawaii, 578
Lincoln, Abraham
  assassination of, 399
  election of, 361–362
  Emancipation Proclamations, 385–386
  "House Divided" speech, 360
  on Kansas-Nebraska Act, 355
  Lincoln-Douglas debates, 342–343

reconstruction plan, 406–407
reelection of, 395
and republicanism, 357
second Inaugural Address, 400
Lincoln, Benjamin, 149
Lindbergh, Charles, 630, **639,** 671
Lindsey, Ben, 540
Lippmann, Walter, 735, 802
Literacy, 510
Literature
  of alienation, 640
  of American Renaissance, 295–296
  of the frontier, 316–317
Lithuania, 614, 689, 730, 867
Littlefield, Henry M., 537
Little Richard, 778
Little Rock, 748, 769
Little Rock Nine, 769
Little Turtle, 196
Livestock, 334
Living standards, in British colonies, 89
Livingston, Robert, 210, 222, 881
Lloyd, Harold, 638
Lobbyists, 424, 622
Lochner v. New York (1905), 468, 551
Locke, Alain, 640
Locke, John, 60, **91,** 93
Lodge, Henry Cabot, 570, 615
Logan, Deborah Norris, 182
Logan, George, 182
Log Cabin Bill, 326
Long, Huey, 661
Long, Stephen H., 318, 324
Long houses, 7
Looking Backward (Bellamy), 482
Lord Dunmore's War, **135**
Los Adaes, 82
Los Angeles, CA, 755
  racial turmoil, 877–878
"Lost Cause" tradition, 429
Lost Generation, 640
Louis, Joe, 671
Louisbourg (Nova Scotia), 89
Louisiana, 224
  function of, as French colony, 83
  map ca. 1720, 82
Louisiana Purchase, **210,** 211, 223, 227, 228
Louis XIV, king of France, 73
L'Ouverture, Toussaint, 200
Love Canal, NY, 837
Lovejoy, Elijah P., 299
Lowell, Francis Cabot, 223–225
Lowell, James Russell, 345
Lowell industrial village (Massachusetts), 223
Lowell plan of industrialization, **270**
Loyalists, **137**–138
Loyal Nine, 117–118
Luce, Henry, 699
Luis de Onís, Don, 222–223
Luján, Manuel, 339
Lumber industry, 322, 441–442
Lusitania, 593, 597
Luther, Martin, 36
Lynching, **522**
Lyon, Matthew, 194

MacArthur, Douglas, 738
  in Korea, 740–741
  in the Philippines, 721
Machine politics, 501
Machine-tool industry, 269
Macy's Department Store, 478
Madeira wine, 95
Madison, Dolley, 215, 217
Madison, James, **173–174,** 183
  on economic growth, 220
  election of, 215
  failed policies, 215–216
  The Federalist and, 178
  Hamilton and, 188–189
  Kentucky and Virginia Resolutions, 227
  on state debt, 187
  Virginia and Kentucky Resolutions and, 194
  War of 1812 and, 216
Madonna (singer), 865
Magazines, 510
Mahan, Alfred T., **577**
Mailer, Norman, 779
Mail-order companies, 450–451
Maine, 579
Maize, 3, 21, 29, 52
Malcolm X, 805
Malinche, 18
"Mammoth cheese," 204
Manchurian Crisis, 692
Mandela, Nelson, 866
Manhattan Project, **708**
Manifest destiny, **336, 345, 356**
Mann, Horace, **293**
Mann Act, 549, 551
Mann-Elkins Act, 560
Manufacturing. *See also* Industrial development; Industrialization
  in British colonies, 88, 104
  foreign trade expansion, 573
Manumission, 164
Manypenny, George, 438
Mao Zedong, 719, **738,** 828
Maple Floor Association v. U.S. (1929)
Marbury, William, 208
Marbury v. Madison, **208**
March on Washington, 794
Marco Polo, 12
Marin, John, 642
Marina, Doña, 18
Market economy, **271,** 284
Marquette, Jacques, 62
Marriage, 504
  among planters, 248
  at midcentury, 773, 775
Marryat, Frank (drawing by), 325
Marshall, George C., 715, 735
Marshall, James, 325
Marshall, John, 199, 208, 221, 222, 228, 335
Marshall, Thurgood, 716, 767
Marshall Field, 478
Marshall Plan, **735,** 737
Martha Washington Societies, 291
Martí, José, 578
Marx, Karl, 533
Mary, queen of England, 57, 73
Maryland, 40–43

colonial revolt in, 73
  House of Delegates, 43
Mason, James, 350, 396
Massachusetts, as royal colony, 73
Massachusetts Bay Company, 45
Massachusetts Government Act, 126
Massasoit, 45
Massive retaliation, 742–743
Mass media, 669, 671
Mass production, 269, 466, 487, 626
Mass transportation, 488
Masterson, William ("Bat"), 445
Mather, Cotton, 75, 92
Mather, Increase, 75
Mather, Stephen, 455
Matrilineal descent, 8
Mattachine Society, 823
Mattel toy company, 777
Mayas, 4
Mayflower, 44
Mayflower Compact, **45,** 47
Mayhew, Thomas, 48
McAdoo, William G., 624
McCain, Franklin, 786
McCain, John, 894
McCarran Act (1950), 765
McCarthy, Eugene, 810
McCarthy, Joseph R., 742, **765**
McCarthyism, 765
McClellan, George B., **371,** 374–375, 395
McClintock, Mary Ann, 300
McCormick, Cyrus, 321
McCormick's reaper, 321–322
McCulloch v. Maryland (1819), **221**
McDonald's, 886
McGovern, George, **831**
McKay, Claude, 613, 640
McKinley, William
  assassination of, 557
  China and Open Door policy, 583–584
  imperialism and, 579
  nomination and election, 534–535
  presidency of, 535
  Roosevelt and, 584
  Spanish-American War, 580–582
McKinley Tariff, 578
McNamara, Robert, 789, 791, 804
McNary-Haugen bills, 624
McNaughton, John, 815
McNeil, Joe, 786
McParland, James, 473
McVeigh, Timothy, 882
Meat Inspection Act, 551, 558
Meatpacking, 272
Meat-processing, 480
Medicaid program, **799**
Medical advances, 898
Medicare program, **799**
Medicine, legislation and, 558
Mehta, G. I., 746
Meigs, Montgomery, 380
Mellon, Andrew, 623, 624
Melville, Herman, 295, 345
Memorial Day, 404
Memorial Day Massacre, 667
Menendez, Francisco, 69
Menéndez, Pedro de Avilés, 30

Mental institutions, 291
Mercantilism, 72
Meredith, James, 793
Mergers, 480, 854–855
Merrick, Dwight, 458
Mesoamerican civilizations, 3, 4, 21
Mestizos, 18, 96, 442
Metacom (King Philip), 63
Metes and bounds, 179
Methodists, 205
Metis, 82
Mexican Americans, 817, 818
Mexican barrios, 495
Mexicas. *See* Aztecs
Mexico
  far north of (American Southwest), 328
  independence of, 330
  Mesoamerican civilizations, 4
  site of Tenochtitlán, 18
  U.S.-Mexican relations, 587–588, 686–687
  war with U.S., 332, 344–349, 366
Miami Confederacy, 196
Miami Indians, 320
Michigan lumber industry, 322
Microphones, 483
Microprocessor, 885
Middle class, 770–773
  ideal, 274–275
  limits of, 778–781
Middle East
  Eisenhower Doctrine, 750
  peace agreements, 883
  post-Vietnam War, 827
  Six-Day War, 830
  U.S. interests in, 859
  U.S. wars in, 891
"Middle ground" rituals, 95
Middle passage, **68**
Midway Islands, 427
Midwest settlement, 318–319, 340
Military
  "don't ask, don't tell" policy, 880
  draft of, 842
  morale problems in, 824
  westward expansion and, 324, 326
  women in, **842**
  in World War II, 715–718
Military-industrial complex, **763**
Milken, Michael, 854
Milligan, Lambdin P., 427
Milosevic, Slobodan, 883
Mind control drugs, 743
Miners, and labor violence, 532
Minie, Claude, 388
Minimum wage law, 622
Mining, 322, 441–442
Mining settlements, 335–336
Minkins, Shadrach, 351
Minkisi, 85
Minnesota lumber industry, 322
Minor, Rufus, 498
Minorities. *See also* African Americans; Asian Americans; Hispanic Americans
  rights of, 625
  in show business, 508–509
Minstrel shows, **508**

Missionaries, 48, 332, 568–569, 575
Missions, 82
Mississippi, 224, 794
Mississippians, 3, 4
Mississippi Freedom Democratic Party, 794, 797
Mississippi Plan, 523
Mississippi River exploration, 324
Missouri Compromise, 224, 226, **226,** 228, 229
Mixed-race families, 96
Model Cities program, 798
Mogollon, 4
Mohawks, 63
Molasses, 115
Mondale, Walter, 854
Monetary policy, 518–519
Money, colonial, 115
Monks Mound, 4
Monopolies, 481, 482
Monroe, James, 210
  election of, 221
  and "Era of Good Feelings," 221
  Non Importation Act and, 214
Monroe Doctrine, **223,** 578
Montana, 444
Montgomery bus boycott, 756, 768, 782
Montgomery Ward, 450
Montoya, Pablo, 347
Montreal, 30, 32
Moon, Lottie, 568, 583
Moral Majority, 849, 861
Moral reform, 290–291, 310, 502
Morgan, Daniel, 151
Morgan, J. P., 460, 463, 480, 558, 560, 562, 576, 630
Morgan, Lewis, 28
Morgan v. Virginia, 767
Mormon Cow Incident, 334
Mormons, **294,** 333, 444
Mormon Trails, 334
"Morning in America," 854
Morrill Land Grant Act, **381,** 452
Morse, Samuel F.B., 267
Mossadegh, Mohammed, 750
Motecuhzoma II, 6
Mother's Day, 505
Motley, Archibald (painting by), 641
Mott, Lucretia, 298, 300
Mountain Meadows Massacre, 333
Movable type, **12**
Movies, 509, 638, 671, 710, 865
  in Great Depression, 671
Muckrakers, **543**
Muguet, Peter, 67
Mugwumps, **516**
Muir, John, 455
Mujahidin, 841
Mulattos, 245
Muller v. Oregon (1908), 468, 550
Multinational corporations, 885
Multiracial Americans, 76
Murray, Elizabeth, 91
Murray, William Vans, 196
Murrow, Edward R., 695
Muskogeans, 7
Muslims. *See also* Islam
  African slaves as, 83
  Black, 805

Mutual aid societies, 493
Mutual Defense Assistance Act, 737
Mutual Security Treaty, 738
My Lai massacre, Vietnam War, **824**
Myrdal, Gunnar, 767

N. W. Ayer & Son, 478
NAACP, 509, 767, 794
Nader, Ralph, 798
Nagasaki, 723
Narragansetts, 45
Narrative of the Life of Frederick Douglass (Douglass), 250
Narváez, Pánfilo de, 18
Nasser, Gamal Abdul, 750
Natchez, 83
Natchitoches, 82
National Advisory Commission on Civil Disorders, 804
National Aeronautics and Space Administration (NASA), 743, 796
National Association for the Advancement of Colored People (NAACP), 509, **553,** 715
National Association of Colored Women, 555, 625
National Association of the Motion Picture Industry, 610
National Chicano Liberation Youth Conference, 819
National College Athletic Association (NCAA), 644
National Committee for Organizing Iron and Steel Workers, 611
National Congress of American Indians, 819
National Consumers League, 544, 551
National debt, 853
  after War for Independence, 186
National Defense Education Act (NDEA), 763
National Economic Council, 885
National Endowment for the Arts, 798, 831
National Endowment for the Humanities, 798, 831
National Geographic Magazine, 574
National Housing Act (1949), 780
National Industrial Recovery Act, **657**–658, 672
National Intelligencer, 206
Nationalism, 482
Nationalist program, 220–223, 229
  American System, 220–221
  boundary settlements, 222–223
  early internal improvements, 221
  Era of Good Feelings, 221–222
  market expansion, 222
  Monroe Doctrine, 223
National Labor Relations Board, 665
National Labor Relations (Wagner) Act, **665**

Mutual aid societies, 493
National Liberation Front (Vietcong), 752
National Mental Health Act (1946), 757
National Organization for Women (NOW), **797, 820–821**
National Origins Act of 1924, **636**
National parks, 455, 559
National Park Service, 455
National Progressive Republican League, 561
National Recovery Administration, **658**
National Research Council, 617
National Road, 221
National Security Act of July 1947, **737**
National Security Council (NSC), 737, 751
National Trade Union, 271
National Traffic and Motor Vehicle Safety Act (1966), 798
National War Labor Board, 609, 709
National Woman Suffrage Association, 525
Nation of Islam, 805
Native American activism, 819
Native American Graves Protection and Repatriation Act (NAGPRA), 24
Native American Rights Fund, 819
Native Americans. *See* Indians
Native cultures, 6–9, 817
  gendered division of labor, 6
  Ghost Dance, 440
  government "civilization" efforts, 439
  government policy and treaties, 436
  and loss of the West, 440
  map, 7
  reform of Indian policy, 437–438
  religion, 9
  reservation policy, 436–437
  resistance and, 437
  social organization, 7–8
  war and politics, 8–9
Naturalization Act, 194, 207
Natural resources, 433, 440–445
  conservation movement, 443–444
  Indian use of, 440
  mining and lumbering, 441–442
Navajo code talkers, 702
Navajos, 63, 327, 395, 437
Navalism, 577
Navigation Acts, 72
Nazi death camps, 716
Nazi Party, **687**
  eugenics and racial policy, 552
  persecution of Jews, 689
NDEA (National Defense Education Act), 763
Negro Business Men's Leagues, 524
Negro League, 639
"Negro rule" myth, 421

Neighborhoods. *See* Urban neighborhoods
Nelson, Isaac, 755
Nelson, Oleta, 755
Neoconservatives, **848**–849
Neolin, 113
Nestor, Agnes, 474
Netscape, 903
Neutrality acts, 356, **688**
    of 1935–1937, 688–689
Nevada, 755
Nevada, 697
New Age Movement, 838
New Amsterdam, **34**
Newark, NJ urban unrest, 804
Newburgh Conspiracy, **152**
New Deal, 657–659
    African Americans and, 674
    assessment of, 674–675
    business opposition to, 661
    economy before and after, 660
    left-wing critics, 662
    limits of, 671–675
    Native Americans and, 668
    political pressure and second New Deal, 661–665
    race and, 672–674
    in the South, 668–669
    in the West, 667–668
"New Democrats," 879–880
New England
    colonization of, 61–62
    contrasting religious patterns, 43–44
    founding of, 43–48, 53
    religious and civic rituals, 93
    towns, 47
    trade and, 68
Newfoundland, 16, 17
New France
    Iroquois and, 62
    Jesuit missions ins, 32, 34
    Quebec and Montreal, 30, 32
New Freedom, 561
New Harmony, **295**
New immigrants, **491**
New Jersey
    in American Revolution, 144
    colonization of, 59–60
New Jersey Plan, **174**
Newlands, Francis, 547
Newlands Reclamation Act, **446, 560**
"New Lights," 101
New Mexico, 30, **327**
    colonial population, 81
    early Latino settlers, 339
    Pueblo peoples and Spaniards in, 63
    settlement, 327
    in U.S.-Mexican war, 347
New Mexico Volunteers, 395
New morality, 620
New Nationalism, 561–562
New Netherland, **34**
New Orleans, 209–210
    Battle of, 219
    establishment of, 82
    and Hurricane Katrina, 893–894
    in War of 1812, 219
New Right, 861
Newspapers
    advertising and, 478

in colonial era, 98
of the early republic, 195
partisan press, 206
penny press, 282–283
yellow journalism, 509
New Sweden, 34
New York
    in American Revolution, 144
    colonial revolt in, 73
    colonization of, 57–59, 77
    slave rebellion, 99–100
New York City, 276
    draft riots, 394
    financial collapse, 835
    migrants to, 86
    slave uprising, 100
The New-York Journal, 195
New York Stock Exchange deregulation, 837
New Zealand, ANZUS Treaty and, 742
Nez Percé, 437
Ngo Dinh Diem, 800
Nguyen Van Thieu, 825
Nicaragua, 356, 857–858
Nicodemus, Kansas, 442
Nineteenth Amendment, 556, 608, **613**
Nine Years' War, 73–74
Nitze, Paul, 738
Nixon, Richard, 766, 789
    abuse of power, 843
    accusation of Alger Hiss, 766
    and Affirmative Action, 831
    China and, 828
    domestic agenda, 831
    domestic policy, 831
    election of, 812
    end of link to gold standard, 834
    enemies and Dirty Tricks, 831–832
    evidence to impeach, 832
    illegal acts of, 816
    impeachment and resignation, 832–833
    intentions on Vietnam War, 815
    military draft, **842**
    Oval office tapes, 832
    pardon by Ford, 833
    and Pentagon Papers, 815
    and press relations, 815
    resignation of, 832
    trip to China, **828**
    as Vice President, 742, 745
    Vietnam War, 823, 824, 827
    Watergate, 832
Nixon Doctrine, 827
NLRB v. Jones & Laughlin Steel Corp., 672
No Child Left Behind, **893**
Nomadic peoples
    of early North America, 6
    Paleo-Indians, 2–3
Non Importation Act, 214
Non-Intercourse Act (1809), 215
Noriega, Manuel, 868
Norris, George, 598
Norse, **16**
North
    business, industry, and agriculture, 379–380

draft riots in NYC, 394
economic nationalism, 381–382
industrial expansion and reconstruction, 424
and South compared, 231–233
wartime economy and society, 379–383
workers' militancy, 380–381
North, Lord, 122, 141
North, Oliver, **858**–859
North American Free Trade Agreement (NAFTA), **885**
North Atlantic Treaty Organization (NATO), **737**
North Carolina, 61
    Indian enslavement in, 70–71
North Dakota, 444
Northern Securities Company, 558
North Pole expeditions, 574
North Vietnam, 800
Northwest Ordinance, 171–172, 181
Northwest Passage, 17
Northwest Territory, 171, 196–197
Nova Scotia, 137, 139
Noyes, John Humphrey, 295
NSC-68, **738**
Nuclear accident (Three Mile Island), 837
Nuclear arms race, 733
    weapon stockpiling, 743
Nuclear proliferation, 723
Nullification, 227, 304, 305, 313
Nye, Gerald P., 688
Nye Committee hearings, 688–689

Oakley, Annie, 445
Obama, Barack, **894**
    election of, 894–895
    goals, 895–896
    healthcare reform, 895
Obama, Michelle, 895
Oberlin College, 298
Obesity, 865, 898
Occupational Safety and Health Administration (OSHA), 831
O'Connor, Sandra Day, 851, 892
Office of Indian Affairs, 326
Office of Price Administration, 710
Office of Strategic Services (OSS), 727
Office of War Information, 710
Oglethorpe, James, **89**
Ohio Company, 172
Oil embargo of 1973, 843
Oil industry, 442
Oil-refining industry, 626
Ojibwas, 440
OK Corral shootout, 445
O'Keeffe, Georgia, 642
Okinawa, 721
Oklahoma City bombing, 882
Old-age assistance, 632
"Old Lights," 101
Oliver, Andrew, 117–118
Olmecs, 4
Olney, Richard, 472, 578
Olympic Games of 1936

Oñate, Juan de, 30, 31
Oneida Colony, 295
O'Neill, Eugene, 640
Opechancanough, 39–40
Open Door policy, **583,** 588, 696
Open-range ranching, 453
Operation Desert Shield, 868
Operation Desert Storm, 869, 871
Operation Mongoose, 791
Operation Overlord, **718**
Operation Rolling Thunder, 800, 802
Oral cultures, 93
Oregon Trail, 324, 333–334
Oregon Treaty, 344–345
Organic Act, 578
Organization of Petroleum Exporting Countries (OPEC), 816, **829,** 830, 834
Organized labor. *See* Labor unions
Oriskany, New York, 146
Orlando, Vittorio, 614
Osages, 82
Osceola, 241
O'Sullivan, John L., 336
Oswald, Lee Harvey, 796
Otis, James Jr., 116
Ottawas, 113
Our Indian Wards (Manypenny), 438
Owen, Robert Dale, 295
Owenites, 295
Owens, Jesse, 670

Pago Pago, 577
Paine, Thomas, 143, 144, 158
Paiutes, 82
Pakistan, 729
Paleo-Indians, **2**
Palestine, 614, 749
Palestine Liberation Organization (PLO), 830, 859
Palestinians, 830, 841
Palin, Sarah, 894
Palmer, A. Mitchell, 612
Palmer Raids, 612
Palmerston, Lord, 309
Panama, 868
Panama Canal, 586–587, **587,** 840
Pan American Airways, 630
Pan-Americanism, 686
Panic of 1819, 224
Panic of 1837, **274**
Pan-Indian activism, 819
"Paper towns," 321
Paris Peace Accords, 810, 824–825
Paris Peace Conference, 614
Parker, George S., 511
Parker, Ralph, 731
Parker Brothers game company, 511
Parks, Rosa, 768
Parrington, Vernon L., 551
Partisan press, 206
Partisanship, 192, 202
Party politics, 301–303
    cultural-political alignments, 515–516
    nature of, 515–516
    party factions, 516
Passing of the Great Race (Grant), 552

Pastor, Tony, 508
Patch, Sam, 287
Patent laws, 222
Paternalism, 247–248
Paterson, William, 174
Patriotic Register, 195
Patriots, 137, 151
Patriots War, 218
Patti, Archimedes, 727
Paul, Alice, 556
Pawnees, 437
Paxton Boys, 114
Payne-Aldrich Tariff, 560
Peace Corps, 790
Peace Democrats, 393–394
Peace of Ryswick, 74
Peacetime sedition aacts, 612
Peale, Charles Wilson, 212
Peale, Titian Ramsay, 318
Pearl Harbor
    Japanese attack on, 696–697
    U.S. naval rights to, 578
Peary, Robert, 574
Pelosi, Nancy, 127
Peltry trade, 22
Pemberton, John, 390
Pendergast, Tom, 501
Pendleton Civil Service Act, 520
Penitentiaries and reform, 291
Penn, William, **60**
Pennington, J.W.C., 297
Pennsylvania
    colonization of, 60
    German immigrants to, 86
    settlement in west of, 135
Penny press, 282–283
Pentagon attack of 9/11, 887
Pentagon Papers, 815, **832**
People for the American Way, 861
People's Republic of China, 739
    in Cold War, 745–746
People-to-People campaign, 744
People v. Hall (1854), 335
Pequot War, **47**–48
Perestroika, 860
Perkins, Frances, **662**
Perkinson, Jack, 314
Perkinson, Pettis, 314
Perry, Matthew, 353
Perry, Oliver Hazard, 217
Perry, Rick, 227
Pershing, John J., 588, **600**
Persian Gulf, 841
Persian Gulf War, 869
Persico, Joseph, 695
Pesticides, 779
Petition, freedom of, 183
Pettigrew, James, 391
Phan Thi Kim Phuc, **826**
Philadelphia, Pennsylvania, 60, 276
The Philadelphia Plan, 820
Philippines
    cession of, 581
    independence, 729
    insurrection, 582–583
    U.S. and, 570
Pickering, John, 207
Pickett, George E., 391
Pickett's Charge, 391
Pierce, Franklin, 353
Pike, Zebulon, 324
Pilgrims, 44, 45

Pinchback, P.B.S., 410
Pinchot, Gifford, 560
Pinckney, Charles Cotesworth, 199, 208, 215
Pinckney, Thomas, 191, 192
Pinckney's Treaty, **191,** 196, 201, 210
Pingree, Hazen S., 501
Pinkerton Detective Agency, 472
Pinkney, William, 214
Pinochet, Augusto, 830
Pitt, William, 119
Pizarro, Francisco, 18
Plague, 11–12
Plains Indians, **434**–435
Planned obsolescence, 779
Planned Parenthood, 564
Planning commissions, 624
Plantation, **13, 231**
    model of plantation slavery, 14
    sugar and, 20, 22
Planters, in southern states/
    territories, 245–248
    cotton in a global economy, 247
    marriage and family among, 248
    newly rich, 246
    paternalism, 247–248
    social status and values of, 246–247
Platt Amendment, **586**
Playboy magazine, 776
Pledge of Allegiance, **782**
Plessy, Homer, 523
Plessy v. Ferguson (1896), **523,** 767, 768
The Plumbers, **832**
Plunkitt, George Washington, 501
Plymouth (Massachusetts), **44**
Pocahontas, 38
Poindexter, John M., 858
Pokanokets, 45, 46
Poland, 614
    German invasion of, 690
    revolt, 745
    Soviets and, 689, 732
Police forces, 499
Political extremism, 882
Political machines, **499,** 501
Political parties, 349
Politics. *See also* Party politics
    expanding participation in, 301
    party politics, 301–303
    pre-Columbian America, 9
    religion and, 307–308, 311
    women and, 215, 625
    and youth, 805–806
Polk, James K., 337, **344**–345, 366
    Oregon Treaty and, 344–345
    war with Mexico, 345–347
Polk, Leonidas, 529
Poll tax, 523
Polygamy, 333, 444
Ponce de León, Juan, 17
Pontiac, 113
Pools, 479
Popé, **63**
Pope Alexander VI, 16
Popular culture, 669, 671, 710. *See
    also* Entertainment; Film
    industry; Films
Popular Front, **662**

Population growth
    agricultural improvements
        and, 19
    in cities, 489
    declining birth rates and, 503
    free blacks and, 164
    geographic expansion and, 80–88
    Latinos and, 864–865
    in North American colonies, 80
    race and ethnic groups and, 896
Populism, 529–531, 535, 537, 661–662
Populist Party, **529**
Port Huron Statement, 805
Port Royal, 30
Portugal and Portuguese
    in the Azores, 13
    colonization in North
        America, 23
    slavery and, 14, 64
    trading posts in Africa, 13–14
    Treaty of Tordesillas, 16
"Positive good," **233**–234
Post, Charles W., 477
Post, Louis, 612
Postal service, Rural Free Delivery, 451
Postmaster General, 184
Post offices, 222
Postwar America, 757–761
    baby boom, 759–760
    economic growth, 758–759
    GI Bill, 757–758
    inequality of benefits, 760–761
    returning veterans, 757
    suburbanization, 760
Potato famine, 280
Potawatomis, 113
Potsdam Conference, 720
Potsdam Declaration, **722**
Pound, Ezra, 640
Pound, Roscoe, 550
Poverty, 780
    of Native Americans, 781
    by race, 1974–1990, 862
    relief, 497–498
Powderly, Terence V., 470
Powell, Colin, **889**
Powell, William Henry (painting
    by), 346
Powell Jr., Lewis, 831, 839
Powers, Francis Gary, 745
Powhatan, 38, 39
Prague Spring, 811
Prayer in public schools, 851
Preemption policy, 326
Prejudice. *See also* Discrimination
    against Jews, 494
    racial, 280
    religious, 280
Presbyterians, 37, 101
Prescott, Samuel, 140
Presidential deception, 698
Presidential powers
    commander-in-chief, 176
    in Constitution, 175, 176
    limitations on, 833
President's Committee on Civil
    Rights, 767
President's Organization on
    Unemployment Relief
    (POUR), 654

Presley, Elvis, **778**
Press, freedom of, 183
Price discrimination, 562
Prigg v. Pennsylvania (1842), 349
Primogeniture, 36
Printing press, **12**
Proclamation of 1763, **114,** 135
Professional Air Traffic
    Controllers Organization, 851
Professional organizations, 622
Progressive era, 540–547
    chronology, 542
    education, 549–550
    government and legislative
        reform, 547–549
    legal thought, 550–551
    national associations and
        foreign influences, 542–543
    new middle class and
        muckrakers, 543
    opponents of progressivism, 547
    settlement houses, 543–544
    Social Gospel, 544
    socialists, 544–545
    in South and West, 545, 547
    upper-class reformers, 543
    working-class reformers, 544
Progressive Party, 624, **762**
Prohibition, 548, 630, 640
Project C, 793, 795, **795**
Propaganda, 710
Prophetstown, Indiana, 212
Proposition 13, 835
Prostitution, 282, 549
Protective tariffs, 220
Protestant Reformation, **36**
Providence, Rhode Island, 50
Providence Island, 28
Provincial conventions, 134
Ptolemy, 12
Publications, mass-market, 510.
    See also Newspapers
Public heroes, 639
Publicity stunts, 283
Public schools, 293
Public welfare programs, 624
Public Works Administration, **659**
Public works projects, 667
Pueblo Revolt of 1680, **63**
Pueblos, 4, 7, 9, 327
Puerto Rico, 581, 586
    immigrants from, 629
Pulitzer, Joseph, 509
Pullman, George, 472
Pullman Strike, 472, 533
Pure Food and Drug Act, 551, 558
Puritans, 37
    covenant ideal, 47
    migration to New England, 45, 61
    Pequot War and aftermath, 47
Purity campaigns, 310
Put-in-Bay, Battle of, 217

Quakers, **60,** 138, 352
Quartering Act, 126
Quartermaster Department, 380
Quasi-War, 193, 196, 198, 201
Quebec, 30, 32
Quebec Act, 127

Queen Anne's War, 76, 108
Quetzalcoatl, temple of, 4
Quincy, Josiah Jr., 124
Quit-rents, 100
Quotas, immigration, 636, **811**

Race, 896
Race relations, 559
Race riots, 494
Race thinking, 575
Racial conflicts
  during First World War, 612
  in Los Angeles, 877–878
  during WWII, 712
Racial segregation, 494–495, 523,
  746, 748, 794
Racism, 163–166, 179, 180, 281.
  See also Discrimination
  manumission and, 163–164
  against Mexicans, 345
  racial segregation and violence,
    494–495
  racist theory, 165–166
  stereotyping, 282
  Third World relations and, 746
Radical Republicans, **384**
Radio, 627, 671
Radio news, 695
Railroad Administration, 606
Railroads, 266–268, 357, 420
  Adamson Act and, 563
  government grants to, 481
  regulation of, 517–518
  standard gauge and standard
    time, 448
  subsidies, 448
  westward development and,
    446
Railroad strikes, 470
Rain-in-the-Face, 437
Raleigh, Sir Walter, 23
Ranching, 452–454
Rand Corporation, 815
Randolph, A. Philip, **708**
Randolph, Edmund, 174
Rankin, Jeannette, 599, 698
Rationing, during WWII, 710
Rauschenbusch, Walter, 544
Ray, James Earl, 810
Reagan, Ronald, 764, 843, **848**.
  See also Reaganomics
  attacks on organized labor, 851
  attacks on social welfare
    programs, 850
  as California governor, 848
  conservative agenda, 848–849
  environmental policies, 850
  international relations and,
    856–860
  Iran-Contra scandal, 858–859
  and New Right, 851
  Nicaragua and, 857–858
  pro-business policies, 850–851
Reagan Doctrine, 857
Reaganomics, 851–856
  deregulation, 854
  inflation and, 852–853
  supply-side economics, 852
Real Whigs, 115
Reconstruction
  black codes, 413
  black voters and, 419–420

carpetbaggers and scalawags,
  421–422
Congressional plan for,
  414–419
Constitutional crisis, 417–418
failure of land redistribution,
  417
foreign expansion, 425, 427
general amnesty, 425
industrialization and mill
  towns, 420–421
Johnson's plan for, 412–413,
  417, 430
Liberal Republican revolt,
  424–425
Lincoln's 10 percent plan,
  406–407
military districts (map), 416
myth of "Negro rule," 421
in the North, 424
politics and, 419–423
Radicals and, 414, 417, 431
Republicans and racial equality,
  421
Republican state governments,
  420
retreat from, 423–429, 431
tax policy and corruption, 422
in the West, 425
white resistance, 419
Reconstruction Acts of 1867–
  1868, 416–417
Reconstruction Finance
  Corporation, **654**
Recorded sound, 483
Red Power, 817, 819
Red Scare, 611, 764
Red Stick Creeks, 219
Red Summer of 1919, 613
Reed, Walter, 586
Reform movements, 288.
  See also Abolitionism;
    Progressive era
  civic reform, 501–502
  civil service reform, 517
  controlling prostitution, 549
  engineering/science and, 293
  housing reform, 496
  labor reform, 548
  moral reform, 290–291,
    310, 502
  progressive reform, 624
  prohibition, 548
  public schools, 293
  social reform, 502
  women's rights, 300–301
Refrigeration, 464, 477
*Regents of the University of California
  v. Bakke,* 839
Regulator movements, 100
"Regulators," 419
Regulatory agencies, 622
Rehnquist, William, 831, 851, 892
Religion
  black churches, 410
  Catholicism, 11
  Christianity, 11
  Congregationalism, 50
  European societies, 11
  evangelical, 288
  freedom of, 40, 183
  fundamentalist Christians, 900
  Great Awakening, 100–102

maintaining religious
  identities, 86, 88
in Mesoamerica, 19
Native American culture, 9
in New England, 43–44, 53
and the New Right, 849
politics and, 307–308
postwar, 773
Quebec Act, 127
religious revivalism, 205,
  289–290, 311, 638
religious rituals, 93
Second Great Awakening, 289
slavery and, 11, 252
syncretism, 19
and therapeutic culture, 838
traditional African, 10
Religious right, 861
Relocation centers, 713
Reno, Janet, 871
Report on Manufactures (Hamilton),
  187–188
Report on Public Credit, **187**
Representation
  proposal for colonial
    represenation, 116
  virtual, 115, 128
Republicanism, 188–189
  defined, 156
  educational reform, 160, 162
  government design, 166–170
  varieties of, 158–159
Republican Party
  appeal of, 355, 357
  birth of, 354–355
  ideology of, 357
"Republican Revolution,"
  880–881
Republic Steel Plant strike, 667
Reserve Officers Training Corps
  (ROTC), 617
Resettlement Administration, 662
Resolution 687, 869
Resolution 688, 869
Resolution 1441, 890
Restoration colonies, 56
Retail, 478
Retirement, 632
Revenue Act, 115, 606
Revenue Act of 1789, 183
Revere, Paul, 120, 126, 140
Revivalism, 100–102, 289–290,
  311, 638
Revolution. *See* American
  Revolution
Revolution of 1800, 106
Reynolds, David, 732
Rhee, Syngman, 740
Rhode Island, 50
Rhode Island plan, 270
Rhodesia (Zimbabwe), 830
Rice, 70, 89
Rice, Thomas D., 282
Rice Coast, 10
Richmond, David, 786
Rickenbacker, Eddie, 601
Ridge, John, 239
Riesman, David, 779
Rights, statement of colonial,
  125
*Rights of the British Colonies Asserted
  and Proved* (Otis), 116
Riis, Jaco, 496

Ringgold, John (Johnny Ringo),
  445
Riolling Stones, 808
Riparian rights, 445
Ripley, George, 295
Riyadh, Saudi Arabia, 883
Roads, 264, 626
Roanoke Island, 23
Roberts, John, 892
Robertson, Pat, 861
Robinson, Jackie, 716, **767**
Rochester, NY, 276
Rockefeller, John D., 103, **479**
Rockingham, Lord, 119
Roebling, John A., 497
Roe v. Wade (1973), 564, **821,** 851
Rolfe, John, 38
Roman Catholic Legion of
  Decency, 671
Romania, 732
Romero, Tomas, 347
Roosevelt, Eleanor, **656,** 662, 674
Roosevelt, Franklin D., **656,** 761
  banking crisis and, 656–657
  death of, 719
  deception of, 698
  election of, 656
  evolving war views, 689
  Fireside Chats, 657, 695
  first hundred days, 657
  and National Park Service, 455
  New Deal achievements, 659
  populist strategies of, 664–665
  quarantine speech, 692–693
  recession of 1937–1939, 659
  relief programs, 658–659
  second New Deal, 661–665
  at Yalta Conference, 719
Roosevelt, Theodore, **557**–562
  athletics and, 506
  as civil service commissioner,
    520
  conservation and, 559–560
  Cuba and, 586
  food and drug legislation,
    558–559
  foreign policy, 584–589
  Latin America and, 585–586
  and Panama Canal, 586–587
  and Panic of 1907, 560
  peacemaking in East Asia, 588
  presidential authority, 585–586
  race relations and, 559, 575
  regulation of trusts, 557–558
  in Spanish American War, 557,
    581
Roosevelt Corollary, 587
Root-Takahira Agreement, 588
Rosenberg, Ethel, **766**
Rosenberg, Julius, **766**
Rosie the Riveter, **708**
Ross, Edward A., 551
Ross, John, 240
Rough Riders, 557, 581
Rowlandson, Joseph, 55
Rowlandson, Mary, 55, 63
Rowlandson, Thomas (sketch by),
  139
Royal African Company, 65
Rubinow, Isaac Max, 632
Ruby, Jack, 796
Rudyerd, William, 28, 36
Ruggles, David, 352

Rumsfeld, Donald, 889
Rum trade, 67, 68, 95, 115
Rural communities, 274
Rural Electrification
    Administration, 663
Rural Free Delivery, 451
Rush, Benjamin, 163
Rush-Bagot Treaty, 222
Rusk, Dean, 789
Russia, 867
    Bolshevik Revolution, 602
    civil war, 613
    in First World War, 595
Russian Revolution, 530
Russian Trans-Siberian Railway,
    569
Russo-Japanese War, 588
Ruth, George Herman "Babe,"
    639
Rwanda, 882

Sacagawea, **211**
Sacco, Nicola, 636
Sacco and Vanzetti, **636**
Sadat, Anwar al-, **840,** 841
Saharan Desert, 9
Saigon (Ho Chi Minh city), 825
"Sailing around the wind," 13, 26
Salazar, Kenneth, 339
Salem witchcraft trials, 74, 75
Salinger, J.D., 779
Salmon, 435
Samoa, 576, 581
San Antonio, 82
Sanchz, Oscar Arias, 858
San Diego, 82
Sandinistas, 857
Sandino, César Augusto, 857
San Francisco, 336
Sanger, Margaret, 552, 555, 564
Sanitary engineers, 499, 500
Santa Anna, General Antonio
    Lopez de, **331**
Santa Barbara, CA, 837
Santa Fe Trail, **324,** 334
São Tomé, 14
Saratoga, **146**
SARS, 901
Saudi Arabian oil embargo, 829
Sauks, 320–321
Savings and loan deregulation,
    854
Savio, Mario, 806
Scalawags, **422**
Scalia, Anton, 851
Schaw, Janet, 106, 122
Schenck v. U.S., 611
Schiff, Jacob, 480
Schlafly, Phyllis, 823
Schneiderman, Rose, 474
The School and Society (Dewey), 550
Schurz, Carl, 519
Schuyler, Elizabeth, 186
Schwartzkopf, Norman, 869
Schwerner, Michael, 794
Scientific management, 464–465
Scopes, John Thomas, 637
Scopes Trial, **636–638**
Scot immigrants, 86, 87
Scots-Irish immigrants, 86
Scott, Dred, 359
Scott, Edward and Clarence, 476

Scott, Harriet Robinson, 359
Scott, Thomas, 424
Scott, Winfield, 309, 353
Scottsboro Boys, 673
Scrymser, James A., 576
Scudder, Vida, 544
Sears Roebuck, 450
Secession, 362–364, 367
    states' rights and nullification,
    227
Secessionist churches, 290
Second Amendment, 184
Second Bank of the United States,
    220–221, 224, 305
Second Barbary War, 219
Second Bill of Rights, 761
Second Continental Congress,
    138, 142
Second Great Awakening, **289,** 312
Second World War. *See* World
    War II
Sectionalism, 223–226
Secular, **102**
Securities and Exchange
    Commission, 854
Sedition Act, 194, 201, 202, 610
Seditious libel, 99
Segregation
    of blacks, 494–495, 523, 715,
    747, 748, 794
    of sexes, 633
Selective Service Act, **599,** 717
Selective Training and Service Act,
    694
Self-Help, 552
Self-interest, 158–159
"Self-made men," 103
Seminoles, 330
Seminole wars, 241
Seneca Falls, **300**
Separate spheres, **275**
Separation of church and state,
    205
Separation of powers, **176,** 177
Separatists, 37, 44
September 11, 2001, **887**
Sequoia National Park, 455
Serra, Junipero, 82
Serres, Dominic the Elder
    (painting by), 112
Servicemen's Readjustment Act
    (GI Bill of Rights), **757–758**
Seventeenth Amendment, 561
Seven Years' War, 108, **111–**113,
    128, 136
Severe acute respiratory syndrome
    (SARS), 901
Sewage disposal, 498–499
Seward, William H., 362, 425, 576
Sewing machines, 464, 477, 572
Sex and culture, 809
Sex discrimination, 466
Sexual behavior, 776, 838
Sexual morality, 712
Sexual Revolution, 838
Seymour, Horatio, 418
Seymour, Samuel, 318
Shah of Iran, 841
Shakers, **294**
Sharecropping, **410–**412, 526
Shareholders, 222
Sharpless, James (painting by),
    186

Shaw, George Bernard, 510
Shaw, Robert Gould, 388
Shawnees, 131–132, 135, 136,
    212, 330
Shays, Daniel, 173
Shays's Rebellion, 173
Sheepherders, 453
Sheldon, Charles, 544
Shelley v. Kraemer, 767
Shell shock, 600–601
Shepherd, Matthew, 882
Sheppard-Towner Act, **625**
Sherman, William Tecumseh, 396
    Field Order Number 15, 409
    March to the Sea, 398–399
Sherman Anti-Trust Act, 482
Sherman Silver Purchase Act, **519,**
    531
Shi'ite Islamic Republic, 841
Shiloh, Battle of, **374**
Shipbuilding, 72
Ships, naval, 577
Show business, 508–509
Sierra Club, 444, 455
Sierra Leone, 139
Silk Road, 9
Silver, 534
Simmons, William J., 635
Simpson, James H., 318
Simpson, "Sockless Jerry," 529
Simpson-Rodino Act, 865
Sinai Peninsula, 830
Sinclair, Upton, 543
Sin fronteras, 629
Singer, Isaac M., 477
Singer Sewing Machine Company,
    572
Sino-Japanese War, 692
Sirhan, Sirhan, 810
Sit-down strikes, 666, 667
Sitting Bull, 437
Six-Day War, 830
Sixteenth Amendment, 561
Skokie, IL, 631
Slater, John, 225
Slater, Samuel, 223, 225, 264, **270**
Slaughter House cases, 427
Slave culture and resistance, 85,
    97, 251–255. *See also* Slaves
    and slavery
    African cultural survival,
    251–252
    black family and, 253–254
    Gabriel's Rebellion, 199
    Nat Turner's insurrection, 255
    rebellions in South Carolina
    and New York, 99–100
    religion and music, 252–253
    resistance strategies, 254–255
Slave Power Conspiracy, 347–348,
    353, 356, 359–360
Slaves and slavery. *See also* Slave
    culture and resistance
    Anglo-American economy and,
    56
    Atlantic trading system and,
    64–67
    in the Caribbean, 68–72
    and the Constitution, 175, 181
    constitutional provisions for,
    185
    Continental Association
    agreement, 133–134

domestic slave trade, 254
Dred Scott case, 359–360
    in 18th century, 83
    emancipation of, 384–387
    everyday conditions, 249
    families and, 97
    freedom of, 408–409
    fugitive slave laws, 172
    international slave trade,
    214–215
    involuntary migrants from
    Africa, 83–84
    in Latin America, 18
    middle passage, 68
    model of plantation slavery, 14
    in the North, 71
    Northwest Ordinance of 1787
    and, 171–172
    origins and destinations of
    slaves, 83
    proslavery arguments, 233–234
    rice and indigo and, 70
    sexual relations between
    masters and slaves, 248, 253
    slave life and labor, 249–251
    slave-master relationships, 251
    "slave power conspiracy,"
    347–348
    slave-trading practice, 83
    southern U.S. as slave society,
    234–235
    in southwest, 327
    violence/intimidation against,
    250
    West Africa and, 10–11, 65–66
    and westward expansion, 320
    work routines, 249–250
Slidell, John, 396
Sloan, John French (cartoon by),
    469
Small, Albion, 551
Smallpox, 19–20
    in Continental Army, 148
    inoculation, 92, 148
    New England epidemic in
    1630s, 48
Smith, Adam, 158
Smith, Alfred E., 624, 642–643
Smith, Bessie, 641
Smith, E. Kirby, 391
Smith, Jebediah, 324
Smith, John, **38**
Smith, Joseph, **294**
Smithson, James, 293
Smithsonian Institution, 293
Smith v. Allwright, 767
Smuggling, 72, 73
Snyder Act, 625
Social Darwinism, **481**
Social democracy, 546
Social Gospel, **544,** 551
Social housekeeping, 555
Socialists, 471, 533, 544–545
Social mobility, 492–493
Social science, 551
Social Security, 675, 759, 763, 898
Social Security Act, **663,** 672
Social unrest, 654–655
Social values, 632–633
Social welfare, 498
Society of American Indians, 553
Society of Friends (Quakers), 60
Society of Jesus (Jesuits), 32, 34

Solomon, Job Ben, 83
Somalia, 882
Sons of Liberty, **118**–120
Sony, 483
Sorenson, Theodore, 788
Sotomayor, Sonia, 127
South. *See also* Confederate States
of America
cities and industry, 377
New Deal in, 668–669
and North compared, 231–233
progressive reform in, 545, 547
proslavery arguments, 233–234
South Africa
apartheid, 860
U.S. relations, 830
South Carolina
African enslavement and,
69–70
in American Revolution,
149–151
claim of right of secession, 227
colonial economy, 89
Indian enslavement and, 70–71
rice cultivation and slavery, 83
secession and, 362–363
slave rebellion, 99–100, 140
slave trade, 214–215
South Dakota, 444
Southeast Asia and the Vietnam
War, **801**
Southern Christian Leadership
Conference (SCLC), 770,
793–794, 797
Southern industry, 463–464
Southern states and territories.
See also specific states
landless whites, 243–244
planters in, 245–248
as slave society, 234–235
social pyramid in, 241–245
South-North comparisons,
231–233
westward movement of, 235,
236
world-view and proslavery
argument, 233–234
yeoman farmers, 242–243
Southern Tenant Farmers' Union,
674
South Pass, 324
South Vietnam, 800
Southwest Ordinance, 197
Sovereignty, threats to, 213–214
The Sovereignty and Goodness of God
(Rowlandson), 55
Soviet Union
assistance to Cuban
government, 791
Cold War, 732–733
collapse of, 867–868
costs of Cold War, 827
German attack on, 695
Gorbachev and, 860
hostility of Korean War, 742
invasion of Afghanistan, 816,
841
invasion of Finland, 693
nuclear weapons and, 723, 738
perestroika and *glasnost*, 860
Reagan and, 856–857
reforms, 866
Sino-Soviet tensions, 827

Soviet-American tensions,
790–791
Sputnik launch, 763
U.S. recognition of, 684–685
U.S. relations with, 790
and Vietnam War, 802
Yalta Conference, 719
Space program, U.S., 796
Spain
conquest and colonization,
17–19, 23, 26
inflation and decline of, 19
Pinckney's Treaty, 196
territorial expansion, 81–82
Spalding, Eliza and Henry, 332
Spanish-American War, 536
anti-imperialist arguments,
581–582
Dewey in the Philippines, 581
motives for, 580–581
Treaty of Paris, 581
Spanish Armada, 22
Spanish Civil War, 688
Speakeasies, 629
Specie Circular, 308
Speech, freedom of, 183, 201
Spice Route, 9
Spices, 12
Spinning, symbolism of, 121, 122
Spinning mill, 223
Spirituals, **252**
Spock, Benjamin, **775**
Spoils system, **303**
Sports, 282, 639
African Americans in, 506, 554,
639, 670, 748
baseball, 506, 639
croquet and cycling, 506
football, 506
heroes of, 639
intercollegiate, 644
women and, 506, 644
Sputnik, **743**, 763
Squanto, 45
Sri Lanka, 729
St. Augustine, 30
St. Clair, Arthur, 196
St. Louis, 689
Stagflation, 834, 851
Stalin, Joseph, **705**, 730–732
Stamp Act, **116**–119, 129
demonstrations against,
117–119, 137
opposition and repeal, 119
Standardization, 464, 606
Standard Oil, 479, 480
Standards of living, 474–478
commonplace luxuries, 474–475
cost of living, 475–475
department and chain stores,
478
flush toilets and other
innovations, 476–477
food processing, 477
higher life expectancy, 476
ready-made clothing, 477–478
supplements to family income,
476
Stanton, Edwin M., 380, 417–418
Stanton, Elizabeth Cady, 300,
301, 407, 415, 525
Starr, Kenneth, 881
"The Star-Spangled Banner," 217

State debts, 186
State Department, 184, 185–186
State governments, 180
limiting, 167
Northwest Ordinance and, 172
state constitutions, 167
Statement of colonial rights, 125
States' rights
federal authority on, 768–770
Tenth Amendment, 227
States' Rights Democratic Party
(Dixiecrats), 762
Stationery supplies, 161
Steamboats, 264–265, 322
Steam power, 225
Stearns, Harold, 642
Steel, Ferdinand L., 243
Steel industry, 446, 463
Steel plow, 321–322
Steffens, Lincoln, 543, 546
Steinbeck, John, 663
Stem cell research, 898–899
Stephens, Alexander H., 348, 365,
393, 408, 413
Stephenson, David, 636
Stereotyping
of blacks, 282
of Japanese, 711
Steunenberg, Frank, 473
Stevens, John L., 578
Stevens, Thaddeus, 407, 414
Still, William, 352
Stimson, Henry L., 693, 733
Stockholders, 479
Stockman, David, 852
Stock market crash (1929), 643
Stock market speculation, 644
Stocks and investments, 837
Stone, Lucy, 300, 525
Stonewall Inn, 823
Stonewall riot, 823
Stono Rebellion, **100**
STOP-ERA movement, 823
Stowe, Harriet Beecher, 352
Strategic Defense Initiative, **857**
Strauss, Levi, 335
Streetcars, 488
Street cleaning, 500
Strouds, 95
Stuart monarchs of England, 57
Student activism, 806
Student Nonviolent Coordinating
Committee (SNCC), **792,**
794
Students for a Democratic Society
(SDS), 805
Submarine warfare, 598
Subsistence cultures, 434
Subtreasury, 528
Suburbs, 489, 629, 631, 760
Subways, 488
Suez Canal, 569
Suez crisis, 745, 750
Suffrage, 300–301, 415. *See also*
Women's rights
Nineteenth Amendment, 613
women's, 524–525, 555–556
Sugar, 13, 20, 22, 35–36, 72, 137
Sugar Act, **115**–116
Sugar Trust, 482
Sullivan, "Big Tim," 501, 544
Sully, Lawrence (painting by), 117
Summer, Donna, 838

Sumner, Charles, 354, 358, 407,
414
Sunbelt (U.S. South and
Southwest), **770**–771, 835,
836
Supreme Court. *See also* specific
justices
Supreme Court, U. S. *See also*
specific rulings
civil rights and, 767–768
establishment of, 184–185
under John Marshall, 208
Reagan and, 851
Roosevelt's court-packing plan,
672
Susquehannocks, 64
Sutter's Mill, 325, 335
Swahili language and culture, 9
Swann v. Charlotte-Mecklenburg, 831
Swanson, Gloria, 634
Swift, Gustavus, 480
Swine flu pandemic, 901
Switzerland, 86
Syncretism, 19
Syphilis, 20
Syria, 729, 830

Taft, William Howard, **560**–561
administration of, 560–561
as Chief Justice, 622
dollar diplomacy, 588
as governor of the Philippines,
575
Taft-Hartley Act, **762**
Taft-Katsura Agreement, 588
Taíno people, 15
"Talented Tenth," 553
Taliban, 887
Talleyrand, 193
Tallmadge, James Jr., 224
Tammany Hall, 501
Taney, Roger, 222, 359
Tanzania, bombing of American
embassy, 883
Taos Revolt, 347
Tappan, Arthur, 299
Tarbell, Ida M., 543
Tariff of Abominations, **303**
Tariffs
on foreign imports, 222
protective tariffs, 220
Tariff of 1816, 221
Tariff of 1833, 305
tariff policy, 518
tariff rates, 536
tariff reform, 563
Task system, **70, 249**
Tate, Allen, 231
Taxes and taxation
authority of national
government for, 175
excess profits tax, 606
excise taxes, 606
Fries's Rebellion, 198
income tax, 561, 606
issues leading to Constitution,
172–173
poll tax, 523
Real Whig ideology and, 115
Reconstruction policy and
corruption, 422
Social Security, 663

Tax reform, 563
Tax revolt movement, 835–836
Taylor, Frederick W., 464–465
Taylor, Major, 506
Taylor, Zachary, 217, 346, 348
Taylor Grazing Act, 668
Tea, 67, 95
Tea Act, **125**–126, 129
Teaching profession, 276
Teapot Dome scandal, 624
Tea tax, 119, 125
Technology
    and American life, 865, 900
    and cultural transformation,
        838
Tecumseh, **212**–213, 217, 220
Tejanos, **328,** 491
Telecommunications
    deregulation, 854
Telegraph, 267, 462
Telephone Operators'
    Department of the
    International Brotherhood
    of Electrical Workers, 473
Telephones, 464
Television, 772
Teller, Henry M., 534
Temperance, **291,** 293, 355
    Cold Water Army, 292
Tenant farming, 526
Tenement housing, 424
Tennessee Valley Authority (TVA),
    668–669
Tenochtitlán, 4, 6
Tenskwatawa, 212
Tenth Amendment, 227
Tenure of Office Act, 417, 418
Teotihuacán, 4
Territorial expansion. *See also*
    Imperialism
    Spanish and French, 81–82
Terrorism
    confronting, 900
    in 1980s, 859–860
    September 11 attack, 887
Tet offensive, 809–810
Texas
    annexation of, 332, 337–338
    colonial population, 81
    as Lone Star Republic, 331,
        336
    Mexican control of, 330–331
    politics of, 331
    settlement, 327–328, 340
    Spanish settlement in, 82
Texas Rangers, 331
Textile industry, 463–464
Thames, Battle of the, 217
Theaters, 282
Third Amendment, 184
Third World, 746–752
    decolonization, 746, 747
    development and
        modernization, 748
    interests in, 746
    nation building in, 790
    U.S. intervention in Guatemala,
        749
Thirteenth Amendment, **386,**
    407–408, 430
38th parallel, 741
Thomas, Allison, 727
Thomas, Clarence, **872**

Thomas, George H., 396
Thomas, Will, 24
Thoreau, Henry David, 295–296,
    361
Three-fifths clause, **175,** 415
Three Mile Island nuclear
    accident, 837
Thurmond, Strom, 762
Tiananmen Square, 866
Tijerina, Reies, 819
Tilden, Bill, 639
Tilden, Samuel J., 428
Till, Emmett, 768
Timber and Stone Act (1878), 442
Tippecanoe, Battle of, 213
Title IX, 644, 861
Tito, Josip Broz, 733
Tobacco, 22, 39, 64, 66, 78, 89,
    463, 526
Tocqueville, Alexis de, 246, 261
Toguri, Iva, 714
Toilets, 476
Tokyo Rose, 714
Tombstone, 445
Tompkins, Daniel, 221
Tom Thumb, 266
Townsend, Francis E., 661
Townshend, Charles, 119
Townshend Acts
    passage of, 119–120
    repeal of, 122
    resistance to, 120–125, 129
    tea tax, 119, 125
Township and range system, 179
Toys, 511
Trade, 77
    among Indians and
        Europeans, 22
    Atlantic system of, 64–68
    canals and, 221
    decline, following First World
        War, 684
    foreign trade expansion, 573
    with Indians, 95, 330
    network of, in British
        colonies, 88
    peltry, 22
    between states, 172–173
Trade associations, 622
Trademark law, 478
Trade unions. *See* Union
    movement
Trail of Tears, 239–241, **240**
Transatlantic cable, 576
Transcendentalism, **295**
Transcontinental Railroad, 324
Transportation, 285
    canals, 265, 267, 268
    funding of, 221
    government and, 266
    mass transportation, 488–489
    railroads, 266–268, 420, 446,
        448, 481, 517–518, 563
    regional connections, 266–267
    roads, 264, 267
    steamboats, 264–265
    urbanization and, 276
Transportation revolution, **273**
Travels (Marco Polo), 12
Treasury Department, 184, 186
Treasury notes, as national
    currency, 187
Treaty of Aix-la-Chapelle, 89

Treaty of Alliance, 146, 190
Treaty of Amity and Commerce,
    146
Treaty of Fort Jackson, 219
Treaty of Ghent, **219,** 228
Treaty of Greenville, 196, 203, 212
Treaty of Guadalupe and Hidalgo,
    347, 442, 819
Treaty of Kanagawa, 353
Treaty of Paris, **113, 153**
    Indian negotiations and, 171
    opposition ot provisions of,
        170
Treaty of Payne's Landing, 241
Treaty of Tordesillas, 16
Treaty of Versailles, 594, 616
Treaty on the Limitations of
    Anti-Ballistic Missile
    Systems, 827
Treaty on the Non-Proliferation
    of Nuclear Weapons, 723
Trenton, **144**
Tresca, Carlo, 473
Triangle Shirtwaist fire, 468, 469
Triangular trade, 65
Tripartite Pact, 696
Tripoli, 213
Trippe, Juan, 630
Troubled Asset Relief Program
    (TARP), 894
A True Picture of Emigration
    (Burlend), 318
Truman, Harry S, 761
    and atomic diplomacy, 733
    civil rights and, 767
    containment policy, 735
    election of 1948, 762
    "fair deal," 763
    firing of MacArthur,
        740–741
    non-recognition of People's
        Republic of China, 739
    postwar liberalism, 761–762
    presidency of, 719
    troops ordered to Korea, 763
    U.S. defense policy, 737
    world-view, 732
Truman Doctrine, **734,** 827
Trumbull, John, 209
Trumbull, Lyman, 414
Trusts, 479, 557–558
Truth, Sojourner, 299, 301
Tsenacommacah, 38
Tubman, Harriet, 299, 352
Tudor dynasty, 12
Turkey, 595, 734
Turkeys, 46
Turnage, Wallace, 369–370
Turner, Frederick Jackson, 315,
    432, 551, 577
Turner, Henry McNeal, 426
Turner, Nat, 234, **255**
Turner, Ted, 870
Tuscarora War, **71**
Tuskegee Institute, 552
Twain, Mark, 445, 581
Twelfth Amendment, 199, 203
Twenty-fifth Amendment, 310
Twenty-sixth Amendment, 839
Two Treatises of Government
    (Locke), 93
Tyler, Elizabeth, 635
Tyler, John, 309

    annexation of Texas and,
        337–338
    as president, 311
Typewriters, 464

U-2 incident, 745
Ukraine, 867
Uncle Tom's Cabin (Stowe), 351,
    352
Underground Railroad, 299, **352**
Underwood Tariff of 1913, 563
Undocumented workers, 864
Unemployed Councils, 654
Unemployment compensation,
    663
Uniforms, 477
Unilateralism, 192
Union Army. *See also* Civil War
    desertions, 393
    occupation zones, 391
    racism in, 388
Union movement, 470–474, 483.
    See also Labor unions
    excluded workers, 472
    women and, 472, 473–474
United Auto Workers (UAW), 667,
    770
United Daughters of the
    Confederacy, 429
United Farm Workers (UFW), 818
United Fruit Company, 749
United Mine Workers, 666
    strike, 709
United Nations, 733
United Provinces of Rio de la
    Plata, 223
United States. *See also* American
    society
    citizens suspicion of politicians
        and Vietnam War, 831
    corn production, 21
    deindustrialization, 835
    end of hostilities to China, 828
    isolationalism, 688
    postwar economic/strategic
        needs, 730, 732
    space program, 796
United States Information Agency
    (USIA), 744, 748
Universities, 550, 707
Unmarried status, 504
Unreasonable search and seizure,
    184
Unwed mothers, 712
Upward Bound program, 798
Urban engineers, 499
Urbanization, 276–284, 627–629.
    See also Cities; City
    management;
    Entertainment; Urban
    neighborhoods
    African American migration,
        628
    cities as symbols, 283–284, 286
    cultural adaptation, 495–496
    1880 and 1920, 490
    ethnic tensions, 280
    extremes of wealth, 278–279
    growth of modern city,
        487–493
    immigration and, 279–280
    major 19th c. cities (map), 277

market-related development, 278
mass transportation, 488
migration of poor blacks and whites, 420–421
population growth, 489
racism and, 281
urban boom, 276
urban culture, 281–282
urban in-migration, 489, 491
urban sprawl, 488–489
Urban League, 794
Urban neighborhoods, 493–496
  borderlands, 493–494
  cultural retention and change, 493
  Mexican barrios, 495
  racial segregation and violence, 494–495
Urban reform, 500
Urban unrest, 804
U.S. Commission on Civil Rights (1957), 768
U.S. Forest Service, 560
U.S. Military Academy at West Point, 216
U.S. Sanitary Commission, **382**
U.S. Steel Corporation, 463, 611
U.S. v. Cruikshank, 427
U.S. v. E. C. Knight Co., 482
U.S. v. Reese (1876), 523
USA PATRIOT Act, 201, **888**
U-2 spy plane, 791
Utah, 755
Utes, 63, 82, 327
Utopian communities, 288, 312
Utopian experiments, 294–296
  Mormons, 294
  Oneidans, Owenites, and Fourierists, 295
  Shakers, 294

Valentino, Rudolph, 639
Vallandigham, Clement L., 393
Van Buren, Martin, 236
  economic crisis and, 308–309
  on slavery, 336
Vance, Cyrus, 840
Vandenberg, Arthur, 734
Vanzetti, Bartolomeo, 636
Vaqueros, 452–453
Vare, "Duke," 501
Vassa, Gustavus, 103
Vaudeville, 486, 508
Veiller, Lawrence, 496
Venereal disease, 601
Venezuela, 578–579
Venona, 764
Vertical integration, **480**
Vespucci, Amerigo, 16, 17
Vetos, 303
Vice-admiralty courts, 72
Vicksburg, **390,** 393
Victory gardens, 606, 607, 710
Vietcong, 800
Vietnam War, 727–728, 790
  Agent Orange, 827
  American credibility, 804
  Americanization of, 802
  American soldiers in, 802–803
  cease fire agreement, 825
  Christmas bombing, 825

costs of, 825
debate over lessons of, 825
defeat, 843
difficulties of, 827
diplomatic recognition of, 885
as dividing issue in U.S. society, 823
Eisenhower and, 750–751
end of, 823–827
escalation of, 800, 802
Geneva Accords, 751–752
image of, **826**
invasion of Cambodia, 824
Johnson's policy, 799–804
Kennedy, John F. and, 787, 800
morale problems in military, 824
National Liberation Front (Vietcong), 752
Paris Peace Accords, 810, 824–825
protests against war, 803–804
protests and counter-demonstrations, 824
quest for indendence, 739
reunified under communist government, 825
Southeast Asia and, **801**
supply depots in Cambodia, 824
as television war, **826**
Tet offensive, 809–810
Tonkin Gulf Incident and resolution, 800
U.S. citizens faith in government, 830
Vietcong attacks, 800
Vietnam reunified under communist government, 825
youth and war in, 806
Villa, Pancho, 588
Villard, Henry, 460
Vingtoons, Johannes (painting by), 59
Vinland, **16**
Violence
  against slaves, 250, 253
  urban, 498
Virginia
  Algonquian and English cultural differences, 39
  Baptists in, 101–102
  founding of, 38–40, 53
  House of Burgesses, 43
  Indian assaults, 39–40
  Jamestown and Tsenacommacah, 38
  population, 1625, 42
  tobacco cultivation, 39
Virginia and Kentucky Resolutions, **194**
Virginia Company, 38–40
Virginia Plan, **174,** 175
Virginia Resolution, 227
Virginia Stamp Act Resolves, 116
Virgin Islands, 576
Virtual representation, 115, 128
Virtue
  artistic depiction of, 159, 160
  republicanism and, 156–166, 180
Volstead Act, 640
Voting

property restrictions for, 301
registration of black voters, 792
state regulation of, 206
voter intimidation, 305
Voting rights, 416, 418–419
Voting Rights Act, **797,** 812

Wade, Benjamin, 407
Wade-Davis bill, 407
Wagner Act, 665, 672
Waite, Davis "Bloody Bridles," 529
Wake Island, 581
Wald, Lillian, 502, 544
Waldseemüller, Martin, 16, 17
Walker, David, 296, 299
Walker, William, 356
Wallace, George C., 794, 812, 831
Wallace, Henry A., 623, 734, 762
Walmart, 865, 895
Waltham-Lowell Mills, 225
Waltham plan of industrialization, **270**
Wampanoags, 63
Wanamaker's, 478
War bonds, 711
Ward, Artemas, 140
Ward, Lester, 481, 551
War Department, 184, 185
Ware v. Hylton (1796), 185
Warfare. *See also* specific war
  in the Caribbean, 34–35
  Colonial wars (1689–1763), 108
  Europeans and Indians, 107–113
  frontier hostilities, 135–136, 154
  U.S. military personnel on active duty, 902
War Hawks, **216**
War Industries Board, 563, **606**
War of 1812, 216–220, 227–229
  American sovereignty reasserted, 219
  burning capitals, 217
  domestic consequences, 220, 229
  invasion of Canada, 217
  naval battles, 217
  recruitment, 216–218
  in the south, 218–219
  Treaty of Ghent, 219
War of Austrian Succession, 89, 108
War of the Spanish Succession, 76, 108
War on Poverty, 799
Great Society, **798**
War Powers Act of 1973, 825, 833
War Production Board, **707**
War psychosis, 600
Warren, Earl, 768, 796
Warren Commission, 796
War Revenue Act, 606
Warsaw Pact, 745, 867
Washington, Booker T., **552**–553, 559, 628
Washington, George, 133, **142,** 146, 173
  Farewell Address, 192
  France and, 190
  Jay Treaty debate, 191

presidency of, 185–188, 202
and Whiskey Rebellion, 188
Washington Naval Conference, **681**
Washington state, 444
Waste disposal, 498–499
Watergate scandal, 816, 831–833
Water rights, 445–446
Waters, Muddy, 808
Water supply, 498–499
Watertown Arsenal strike, 458
Watson, Tom, 529
Watt, James, 850
Watts riots, 804
Wayne, Anthony, 196
Wealth Tax Act, 664
Weapons of mass destruction (WMDs), 889, 890
Weaver, James B., 529, 531
Webster, Daniel, 304, 308, 311, 350
Webster, Noah, 209
Webster-Ashburton Treaty (1842), 309
Webster v. Reproductive Health Services (1989), 851
Weiss, Erich, 486
Weld, Theodore, 298, 299
Welfare, 498
Wells, Ida B., **522,** 525
West
  New Deal and, 667–668
  progressive reform in, 545, 547
West, Benjamin (engraving by), 114
West Africa (Guinea), 10
  Atlantic slave trade and, 65–66
  slavery in, 10–11
West Bank, 830, 841
West Berlin, 790
Western Federation of Miners, 473
Western Union Company, 609
Westinghouse, George, 460
Westinghouse Electric, 460
Westmoreland, William, 803
Westos, 70
West Point, 216
Westward development
  admission of new states, 444–445
  complex communities, 442–443
  folk heroes, 445
  irrigation and water rights, 445–446
  Newlands Reclamation Act, 446
  race and, 443
  railroad construction, 446
Westward expansion, 209–213, 318–322
  clearing land, 322
  cultural frontiers, 332–336
  federal government and, 322–326, 340
  Indians and, 235, 237–241, 320–321
  land speculation, 224, 321–322
  Lewis and Clark Expedition, 211–212
  Louisiana Purchase, 210, 211
  military and, 324, 326

Missouri Compromise, 224, 226
New Orleans, 209–210
politics of, 336–338, 341
public lands, 326
slavery debate, 349–350
southwestern borderlands, 327–332
transcontinental exploration, 324
Tyler and, 311
Westward settlement, 135, 196–198, 203
chronology, 316
considerations, 320
map, 319
myth of the west, 315–318, 340
Weyler, Valeriano, 579
Wharton, Edith, 640
Whey, 493
Whigs, 288, **305**
demise of, 355
and Democrat ideology compared, 307–311, 313
reform and, 307–308
Whiskey Rebellion, **188,** 190, 201
White, Hugh, 308
White, John (watercolor by), 23
White, Richard, 95
White Citizens Councils, 768
Whitefield, George, **101,** 102
White Hats, 528
White slavery, 549
White Slave Traffic Act, 549
Whitewater, 881
Whitman, Narcissa and Marcus, 332
Whitman, Walt, **383**
Whitney, Eli, **209**
Whyte, William H., 776, 779
Wilderness, Battle of the, 399
"The Wild West" show, 432
Wilkes, John, **120**
Wilkinson, James, 208
Willaerts, Adam (painting by), 44
Willard, Frances, 524, 525
William, king of England, 57, 73
William and Mary College, 91
Williams, Burt, 508
Williams, Roger, **50**
Wilmot, David, 348
Wilmot Proviso, **348,** 359
Wilson, Horace, 507
Wilson, William Dean, 702
Wilson, Woodrow, 505, **561**
administration of, 562–563
anti-Bolshevism of, 613
business regulation policy, 562
civil liberties record, 609–611
Mexico and, 588
racism of, 563
second term, 563
tariff and tax reform, 563

Wilson-Gorman Tariff, 579
Winnegagos, 320
Winthrop, John, **45,** 47, 53
Wisconsin
early settlement of, 320
lumber industry, 322
Witchcraft trials, 61–62, 74, 75
The Wizard of Oz (movie and book), 537
Wobblies, 473
"Woman Movement," 553, 555
Women. *See also* Gender roles; Women's rights
African American, 555
in agricultural societies, 9
birth-control and planned parenthood, 564
childbearing and, 248
in Civil War South, 378
division of labor and, 25
education of, 91, 157, 550
on farms, 273, 285
in First World War, 599
in "ideal" family, 274–275
in industrial jobs, 465
in labor protests, 270
minorities, employment of, 634
moral reform and, 290–291
political activism of, 127
political leadership in pre-Columbian America, 9
and politics, 215, 625
in postwar America, 761
and the republic, 162–163
in show business, 508–509
social mobility and, 493
in sports, 506, 644
unions and, 472
unmarried, 504
unwed mothers, 712
in U.S. military, 717
voters, 625
of the West, 443
in workforce, 276, 466–467, 608, 633–634, 775–776
WWII production and, 708–709
Women and Economics (Gilman), 555
Women's Christian Temperance Union, 524
Women's clubs, 555
Women's Committee of the Council of National Defense, 608
Women's Emergency Brigade, 666
Women's International League for Peace and Freedom, 803
Women's Loyal National League, 407

Women's Movement, 820–823
Women's National Indian Association, 438
Women's rights, 300–301, 312
legal rights, 300
political rights, 300–301
property and spousal rights, 300, 420
Seneca Falls Convention, 300
suffrage, 300–301, 415, 524–525, 555–556, 613
Women's Trade Union League, 473
The Wonders of the Invisible World (Mather), 75
Woods, Granville T., 460
Woodstock Festival, 807
Woodward, Bob, 832
Woolen mills, 214
Woolworth (store), 786
Worcester v. Georgia (1832), 239
Workday
eight-hour workday bill, 424
legislation, 550–551
Worker protests, 532
Workers' compensation, 624
Workforce
child labor, 467, 468
opportunities during WWII, 708
restructuring, 466–467
women in, 276, 466–467, 608, 633–634, 775–776
Workhouses, 89
Working conditions, 468
eight-hour workday, 471
wage work experience, 474
Works Progress Administration, **663**
World Bank, 732, 885
World Health Organization, 900
World Trade Center attack of 9/11, 887
World Trade Organization, **885**
World War I. *See* First World War
World War II, 703–706. *See also* Postwar America
allies on offensive in Europe, 706
bombing of Japan, 721–723
combat conditions, 717–718
in Europe, 718–719
"Europe First" strategy, 705–706
Holocaust, 716
home front, 707–713
Manhattan Project, 708
military in, 717–718
in the Pacific, 720–721
segregation of military in, 715–716

tension among allies, 718
U.S. entry into, 693–699
U.S. unpreparedness for, 704
war in the Pacific, 704–705
wartime prosperity, 710–711
women and, 708–709
Yalta Conference, 719
World Wide Web, 903
Wounded Knee, **440**
"The Wound Dresser" (Whitman), 383
Wright, Martha, 300
Wright, Richard, 663, 767
Writing supplies, 161
Writ of mandamus, 208
Wyoming, 444

XYZ Affair, **193**

Yale, 91
Yalta Conference, 719
Yamasees, 71
Yardbirds, 808
Yellow dog contracts, 623
Yellow journalism, 509
Yellowstone National Park, 444, 455
Yeoman farmers, **235,** 242
class tensions and, 244
folk culture of, 242
livelihoods of, 242–243
Yergin, Daniel, 829
Yom Kippur War, 829, 830
York (slave), 211–212
Yorktown, Battle at, **151**
Yosemite National Park, 455
Yosemite Valley, 444
Young, Brigham, 333
Young, Stella, 608
Young Americans for Freedom (YAF), 805
Young, Joseph, 437
Young Men's Christian Association (YMCA), 504
Young Women's Christian Association (YWCA), 504
Youth culture, 671, 776, 778, 806–807, 809, 839
Yucatan Peninsula, 4
Yugoslavia, 614, 733

Zenger, John Peter, **99**
Zhou Enlai, 828
Ziegfeld Follies, 508
Zimbabwe, 830
Zimmerman, Arthur, 598
Zitkala-Sa, 438
Zoning commissions, 624